GW00417582

PLANNING AND DEVELOPM
ACTS 2000–2007

PLANNING AND DEVELOPMENT ACTS
2000–2007
Annotated and Consolidated

STEPHEN DODD
B.C.L., LL.M., Barrister-at-Law.

ROUND HALL

THOMSON REUTERS

Published in 2008 by
Thomson Reuters (Professional) Ireland Limited
(Registered in Ireland, Company No. 80867.
Registered Office and address for service:
43 Fitzwilliam Place, Dublin 2, Ireland)
trading as Round Hall

Typeset by
Gough Typesetting Services
Dublin

Printed by
MPG Books, Bodmin, Cornwall

ISBN 978-1-85800-481-5

A catalogue record for this book
is available from the British Library

PREFACE

One of the purposes of the Planning and Development Act 2000 was to consolidate all the existing planning legislation which had been scattered over a plethora of statutes since the enactment of the Local Government (Planning and Development) Act 1963. However, less than eight years after coming into force, the 2000 Act has already been the subject of two substantive amending statutes (with another promised) as well as a myriad of more minor amendments. Whether this is indicative of lack of foresight on behalf of the legislature, poor draughtsmanship, the central nature of planning law as an instrument of evolving government policy or more broader social and economic change, it makes the task of producing a definitive and comprehensive code that more difficult. It also makes timing the publication of a consolidation and annotation precarious; with the label "consolidation" liable to be quickly undermined. Since its enactment, a considerable body of case law has fleshed out the not always pellucid provisions of the Act and commentary has been provided in the light of such. This book seeks to consolidate all of existing statutory provisions up to and including the Dublin Transport Authority Act 2008. The somewhat confusing title to the book as the Planning and Development Acts 2000 to 2007 has been dictated by the Water Services Act 2007, which provides that the Planning Acts are to be cited in such manner and read together as one. For this publication, I would like to thank the staff at Round Hall, in particular, Frieda Donohue and Martin McCann, for their restraint and patience. I would also like to thank my family, friends and colleagues for their assistance, in particular: my parents; Leonie Macauley B.L.; and Cian Carroll B.L.

Stephen Dodd
November 18, 2008

TABLE OF CONTENTS

TABLE OF CASES

IRELAND

EUROPEAN COURT OF JUSTICE

EUROPEAN COURT OF HUMAN RIGHTS

ENGLAND AND WALES

NORTHERN IRISH

NEW ZEALAND

TABLE OF LEGISLATION

Planning and Development Acts, 2000 to 2007—*contd.*

Planning and Development Acts, 2000 to 2007—*contd.*

Statutory Instruments

EUROPEAN DIRECTIVES

INTERNATIONAL TREATIES

PLANNING AND DEVELOPMENT ACTS 2000–2007

PART I

PRELIMINARY AND GENERAL

PART II

PLANS AND GUIDELINES

Chapter I — Development Plans

Chapter II — Local Area Plans

Chapter III — Regional Planning Guidelines

PART IV

ARCHITECTURAL HERITAGE

Chapter I — Protected Structures

Chapter II — Architectural Conservation Areas and Areas of Special Planning Control

PART V

HOUSING SUPPLY

PART VII

DISCLOSURE OF INTERESTS, ETC.

PART VIII

ENFORCEMENT

PART IX

STRATEGIC DEVELOPMENT ZONES

PART X

ENVIRONMENTAL IMPACT ASSESSMENT

PART XI

DEVELOPMENT BY LOCAL AND STATE AUTHORITIES, ETC.

PART XII

COMPENSATION

Chapter I — Compensation generally

Chapter II — Compensation in relation to decisions under Part III

Chapter III — Compensation in relation to sections 46, 85, 88, 182, 207 and 252

PART XIII

AMENITIES

PART XX

AMENDMENTS OF *ROADS ACT, 1993*

PLANNING AND DEVELOPMENT ACT 2000
(2000 No. 30)

An *Act* to revise and consolidate the law relating to planning and development by repealing and re-enacting with amendments the *Local Government (Planning and Development) Acts, 1963* to *1999*; to provide, in the interests of the common good, for proper planning and sustainable development including the provision of housing; to provide for the licensing of events and control of funfairs; to amend the *Environmental Protection Agency Act, 1992*, the *Roads Act, 1993*, the *Waste Management Act, 1996*, and certain other enactments; and to provide for matters connected therewith.   [*28th August, 2000*]

BE IT ENACTED BY THE OIREACHTAS AS FOLLOWS:

INTRODUCTORY NOTE

1–00   The Planning and Development Act 2000 (the "2000 Act") consolidates and modifies existing planning law into a single Act. The 2000 Act has since been amended on several occasions, most notably under the Planning and Development (Amendment) Act 2002 and the Planning and Development (Strategic Infrastructure) Act 2006 (the "2006 Act"). The Water Services Act 2007, in making some minor changes to the 2000 Act, states that the Planning Acts are to be cited as the Planning and Development Acts 2000 to 2007 and to be read together as whole (s.1(6)). The modern system of planning control entered into force on October 1, 1964 by virtue of the Local Government (Planning and Development) Act 1963 (the "1963 Act"), was amended on numerous occasions. The 2000 Act brings all of this together and introduces significant changes. The Minister for the Environment and Local Government, in introducing the Bill, stated (Seanad Second Stage, October 14, 1999):
> "At the moment, primary planning law is contained in 9 Acts dating from 1963 to 1999, and five sets of environmental impact assessment regulations from 1989 implementing EU directives. This Bill will consolidate all the Acts and much of the environmental impact assessment regulations in one Bill to the benefit of all users of the planning system. As well as consolidating existing provisions, the Bill contains many significant changes and new initiatives".

The 2000 Act, along with the Planning and Development Regulations 2001, as amended, is envisaged to constitute a complete code on planning law and so only isolated provisions of the previous Local Government (Planning and Development) Acts survive. The whole of the Local Government (Planning and Development) Acts of 1963, 1976, 1983, 1990, 1998 Nos 1 and 2 have been repealed. Only isolated sections of the 1982, 1991 and 1993 Acts remain in force. However, the 2000 Act only applies to development or works commenced after the commencement of the 2000 Act. The 2000 Act is supplemented by regulations, the principal regulations being the Planning and Development Regulations 2001 (S.I. No. 600 of 2001) (the "2001 Regulations"). The Bill was signed into law on August 28, 2000, though not before Pt V of the Bill, concerning social and affordable housing, was referred to the Supreme Court under Art.26 of the Constitution to consider its constitutionality. In *Re Article 26 and the Planning and Development Bill 1999* [2000] 2 I.R. 321, the Supreme Court upheld its constitutionality. During the course of his judgment, Keane C.J. made certain general remarks concerning planning law at 353, stating:
> "Planning legislation of the nature now under consideration is of general application and has been a feature of our law ever since the enactment of the Town and Regional Planning Act, 1934, although it did not take its modern, comprehensive form until the enactment of the 1963 Act. Every person who acquires or inherits land takes it subject to any restrictions which the general law of planning imposes on the use of

the property in the public interest. Inevitably, the fact that permission for a particular type of development may not be available for the land will, in certain circumstances, depreciate the value in the open market of that land. Conversely, where the person obtains a permission for a particular development the value of the land in the open market may be enhanced".

In *Lanigan & Benghazi v Barry*, unreported, High Court, Charleton J., February 15, 2008, Charleton J. commented that "[t]he legislation is an example of the application of democratic principle to the important question as to how the area in which a citizen lives, or carries on his or her business, may change". The Long Title to the Act refers to providing "in the interests of the common good" for proper planning and sustainable development. Insofar as the Planning Code represents restraints on the enjoyment of constitutionally protected private property rights it is justified in the interests of the common good.

The changes under the 2000 Act include the introduction of the concept of "proper planning and sustainable development", to replace "proper planning and development", as the general touchstone standard according to which the planning authority must make decisions. The concept of sustainable development reflects a greater environmental awareness, which is reflected in other provisions of the Act. Among the most striking features are the new social and affordable housing provisions (Pt V). These provisions mark the integration of housing within the planning system. A housing strategy must be prepared for inclusion in the development plan. Where a person applies for permission for residential development, a certain percentage of land may be required to be reserved for social and affordable housing. The provisions have subsequently been amended by the Planning and Development (Amendment) Act 2002, which allows for alternative means for a developer complying with the obligation. The 2000 Act makes changes to the provisions concerning development plans and other guidelines by introducing detailed procedures for the adoption, amendment or variation of the development plan. It also gives statutory recognition to regional development guidelines and local area plans. National plans also merit mention for the first time. However, the development plan still forms the centrepiece of the hierarchy of plans.

Significant changes have been made regarding the control of development. These include granting statutory recognition to outline planning permission and also to third-party submissions. It also allows the planning authority to reject a planning permission on the basis of failure to comply with a previous permission. On the restrictive side, a new system of fees has been introduced, most controversially regarding a fee for third party objectors. (the legality of which was upheld in the context of the EIA Directive by the European Court of Justice in *Commission v Ireland* (Case 216-05) November 9, 2006). A new qualifying requirement for a person appealing to An Bord Pleanála requires that they must have participated in the application before the planning authority. Each planning authority is now obliged to provide a list of approved newspapers in which applicants must publish notice of their intention to seek permission. Under the 2001 Regulations, planning authorities are also obliged to return any incomplete application as invalid. The 2000 Act also obliges planning authorities to introduce contribution schemes to provide transparency and certainty to the process of imposing, as a condition of planning permission, that the applicant pay a contribution towards certain infrastructural costs. The 2000 Act alters several time limits, by calculating them on the basis of weeks rather than months. Thus the appropriate time limit for an appeal from decision of a planning authority in relation to a planning application is four weeks from the day of the decision of the planning authority rather than one month, the former time limit; while the time limit for judicial review is eight weeks rather than two months.

Changes have also been made regarding an application for judicial review of a planning decision which were again revamped by the 2006 Act. The 2000 Act expands the scope of this restrictive form of review and introduces additional requirements. These include a stricter standing requirement, whereby an applicant must demonstrate a substantial interest, as opposed to a sufficient interest. The 2000 Act also provided that judicial review proceedings could only be taken by a person who participated in the decision-making process being challenged, although this requirement was removed by the 2006 Act. An extension to the strict time limit where the proceedings are not commenced within the eight weeks is allowed for "good and sufficient reasons" and where the delay was "outside the control" of the applicant (as introduced by the 2006 Act).

The Act introduces significant measures concerning the preservation of architectural heritage. These include detailed provisions on protected structures including the requirement that a record of protected structures must be contained in the development plan, and also the introduction of architectural conservations areas, which may include an area of special planning control.

Changes have been made in relation to enforcement. These include streamlining the procedure by providing one form of enforcement notice and planning injunction, abolishing warning notices, and introducing warning letters. The criminal provisions are also expanded and penalties increased. Also, the period for taking enforcement action has been extended from five to seven years. The scope of the planning injunction has also been expanded.

The concept of strategic development zones (SDZs) has also been introduced. This allows for the designation of certain sites as strategic development zones and the adoption of a planning scheme for the zone. Certain restrictive rules apply to development within such a zone. A number of additional powers have been granted to An Bord Pleanála. These include the transfer of the functions formerly performed by the Minister in relation to compulsory acquisition to An Bord Pleanála.

There have been some changes in relation to the rules for exempted development. With regard to determining whether a matter is or is not exempted development, the Act allows a person to seek a declaration from the planning authority before a referral can be made to An Bord Pleanála. There is a new category of exempted development under the 2001 Regulations for the exemption of telecommunications antennae (subject to defined size and emissions criteria) which are attached to the roofs of commercial structures (other than educational facilities or hospitals). This potentially has the effect of taking the issue of mobile telephone antennae out of the planning process. On the other hand, turbary no longer constitutes exempted development.

Changes have also been made in relation to development by a local authority. It is no longer necessary for a local authority to apply to itself and then to An Bord Pleanála. There is now a single application to An Bord Pleanála. Certain local authority development of land by itself or on its behalf require the publication of a notice in an approved newspaper and erection of a site notice. This creates greater transparency in the process. The construction costs threshold for the exemption of certain minor works by a local authority has been increased from IR£50,000 to €126,000. In relation to the compensation provisions, there is now a power for the court to extend the period for the making of a claim for compensation "in the interests of justice".

The Act extends planning control to developments on the foreshore and introduces a licensing system for events and funfairs. Events, within the meaning of the Act, are not deemed to constitute development, for which planning permission is required. Pre-planning consultations are given statutory recognition, while a registration system applies to quarries.

As can be seen from the above outline, the 2000 Act evinces a tentacular growth in the reach of planning law. The 2000 Act is not confined to questions of planning permission but enshrines a much broader concept of planning, embracing the concept of sustainable development as manifest in greater concern for the physical and natural environment and the integration of housing issues within the traditional planning process. The 2000 Act also indicates a more specialised approach to certain specific areas, e.g. by introducing a licensing system for events and funfairs and a registration system regarding quarries.

As noted the 2006 Act introduced significant changes most notably a special application process directly to An Bord Pleanála in the case of strategic infrastructure development. The 2006 Act was introduced in Dáil Éireann on February 16, 2006 and in Seanad Éireann on March 7, 2006 and was enacted on July 16, 2006. The Long Title to the Act states that it is:

> "an act to provide, in the interests of the common good, for the making directly to An Bord Pleanála of applications for planning permission in respect of certain proposed developments of strategic importance to the state; to make provision for the expeditious determination of such applications, applications for certain other types of consent or approval and applications for planning permissions generally; for those purposes and for the purpose of effecting certain other changes to the law

of planning and development to amend and extend the Planning and Development Acts 2000 to 2004; to amend the Transport (Railway Infrastructure) Act 2001 and the Acquisition of Land (Assessment of Compensation) Act 1919 and to provide for related matters."

Applications for strategic infrastructure development are made directly to An Bord Pleanála ("the Board") and the Act establishes a new Strategic Infrastructure Division within the Board to determine such applications. The main objective of the special procedure is to allow for the more expeditious determinations of such applications. An applicant for specific types of development relating to energy infrastructure, environmental infrastructure and transport infrastructure listed in the Seventh Schedule must enter into consultation with the Board. Where following such consultation, the Board serves a notice specifying either that the development would:

- be of strategic economic or social importance to the State or the region in which it would be situate;
- contribute substantially to the fulfilment of any of the objectives in the National Spatial Strategy or in any regional planning guidelines in force in respect of the area or areas in which it would be situate;or
- have a significant effect on the area of more than one planning authority,

then an application for such development must be lodged with the Board in accordance with the special application procedure.

Where the Board serves a notice stating that none of these conditions exist, then the application must be lodged to the planning authority under the ordinary procedure for planning applications.

The 2006 Act also includes a special planning consent procedure for major electricity transmission lines and strategic gas infrastructure development. It further makes some general amendments to the 2000 Act which include changes to the conditions of planning permissions which may be imposed; changes to the procedure for refusal of permission for past failures to comply with planning permission; allowing certain NGO's which promote environmental protection an automatic right of appeal to the Board or to institute judicial review proceedings in respect of development requiring an EIS; changes to the special judicial review procedure including expanding the scope of decisions to cover any "act done" by the planning authority or the Board under the 2000 Act; changes to the rules governing extension of time and certificates of appeal to the Supreme Court; to allow the amendment of planning permissions to correct clerical errors; to allow the alteration of a development where it would not constitute a material alteration of the permission; changes to the rules governing state authority development which require an EIS and alterations to the provisions concerning confirmation of compulsory acquisitions by the Board including that an oral hearing is now at the absolute discretion of the Board. The Act further makes amendments to the Railways (Infrastructure) Act 2001 concerning the approval of railway orders including the transfer of the function of approving railway orders from the Minister to the Board. The Planning and Development Regulations 2006 (S.I. No. 685 of 2006) (the "2006 Regulations") which amend the 2001 Regulations, have also been adopted to accompany many of the changes brought about by the 2006 Act.

Since the enactment of the 2000 Act it has been the subject considerable caselaw. The courts have at times been critical of some of the drafting and vagueness of the provisions. In *Harding v Cork County Council*, unreported, Supreme Court, May 2, 2008, Murray C.J. said with respect to the notion of substantial interest in s.50 that "the test laid down by the Oireachtas is vague and lacking in precision. It is left to the courts to interpret and apply the notion of "substantial interest" as best they can". In *Cork County Council v Shackleton/ Dun Laoghaire Rathdown County Council v Glenkerrin*, unreported, High Court, Clarke J., July 17, 2007, Clarke J. commenting on Pt V of the Act said:

"Courts are sometimes criticised for adopting interpretations of legislation which critics may regard as going against the 'spirit' of the legislation concerned. Whatever may, or may not, be the merits of any such criticism, it seems to me that the other side of that coin applies in this case. While the broad drift of the intention of the social and affordable housing provisions of Part V of the Act may be well clear (and has been identified by the Supreme Court), the reality is that it is very difficult to tell, with even a reasonable degree of certainty, as to how the Oireachtas intended that the legislation should work in practice. The devil is, indeed, in the detail. Without that detail there are no practical measures to benefit those who might need social or affordable housing. It has to be said that it is regrettable that the legislation does not appear to have received the level of detailed consideration in advance which it warranted. In such circumstances the courts are left with attempting to do their best with a legislative scheme that gives rise to very significant difficulties of interpretation at almost every turn."

In *CIE v An Bord Pleanala*, unreported, High Court, June 19, 2008, Clarke J. also said:

"I have to confess that this is by no means the first time when legislation in the planning and environmental field which I have had to consider has been drafted in a way which gives rise to very significant difficulties of interpretation. See, for example, *Maye v. Sligo Borough Council* [2007] IEHC 146, *Cork County Council v. Shackleton* [2007] IEHC 241 and *Glenkerrin Homes v. Dun Laoghaire Rathdown County Council* [2007] IEHC 241, which list only relates to cases which have happened to fall for decision by me. It is regrettable that often important provisions of legislation designed to protect the environment are produced in a way which gives rise to such a difficulty of interpretation that a significant risk of the legislation not achieving its end is created. Be that as it may courts, when faced with the product of such draughtsmanship, have to do the best they can".

Commencement

The Bill was signed into law on August 28, 2000. Section 270 of the Act provides that the Act shall come into operation on such day or days as the Minister may appoint by order or orders either generally or with reference to any particular purpose or provision. The Planning and Development Act 2000 (Commencement) Order 2000 (S.I. No. 349 of 2000) provided that ss.1, 2 (insofar as it relates to the sections commenced on that date), ss.13, 28, 29, 30, 93, 94, 95, 96, 97, 98, 99, 100, 101, 165, 166, 167, 168, 169, 170, 171, 262, 266, 269, and 270 of the Act came into operation on November 1, 2000. It also provided that ss.2 (insofar as it relates to the sections commenced on that date), ss.9, 10, 11, 12, 14, 15, 16, 17, 18, 19, 20, 21, 22, 23, 24, 25, 26, 27, 31 and the First Schedule to the Act, entered into force on January 1, 2001. The Planning and Development Act 2000 (Commencement) (No. 2) Order, 2000 (S.I. No. 449 of 2000) provided that s.2 (insofar as it relates to the sections commenced on that date), s.50 (insofar as it relates to decisions under subs.(2)(b)(iii) of that section), ss.71, 72, 73, 74, 75, 76, 77, 78, 182, 210, 211, 212, 213, 214, 215, 216, 217, 218, 219, 220, 221, 222, 223, 263, 264 (insofar as it relates to the repeal of s.55A of the Roads Act 1993, as inserted by s.6 of the Roads (Amendment) Act 1998), ss.265(3), 267, 268(1) (other than paras (a), (b), (c) and (d) of that subsection), ss.271, 272, 273, 274, 275, 276 and 277 of the Act, entered into force on January 1, 2001.

The Planning and Development Act 2000 (Commencement) (No. 2) Order 2001 (S.I. No. 335 of 2001) provided that: (a) s.2 insofar as it relates to the sections referred to in paras (b) and (c) of the article; (b) Chap.I of Pt VI; and (c) s.264 and the Sixth Schedule insofar as they relate to the repeals effected by art.3 of the Order, entered into force on July 20, 2001. Also s.3 of the Local Government (Planning and Development) Act 1976 (No. 20 of 1976) and ss.2, 3 (as inserted by s.1(a) of the Local Government (Planning and Development) Act 1998 (No. 9 of 1998)), ss.5, 7, 8 (as amended by s.1(b) of the Local Government (Planning and Development) Act 1998) and s.12 of the Local Government (Planning and Development) Act 1983 (No. 28 of 1983) were repealed.

The Planning and Development Act 2000 (Commencement) (No. 3) Order 2001 (S.I. No. 599 of 2001) provided that: (a) s.2; (b) ss.5 and 7; (c) Pt III; (d) Chap.III of Pt VI; (e) Pt VIII; (f) Pt X; (g) Pt XI; (h) Pt XII and the Second, Third, Fourth and Fifth Schedules; (i) Pt XV; (j) Pt XVII; (k) Pt XVIII, other than s.261; (l) s.264 and the Sixth Schedule, insofar as they relate to the repeals effected by art.5 of this Order; (m) s.265(1), (2) and (4); and (n) s.268(1)(d) and (3), commenced on March 11, 2002.

Also: (a) ss.3, 4, 6, 9, 42, 43, 44, 45, 46, 47, 48, 49 and 54 of the Local Government (Planning and Development) Act 1963 (No. 28 of 1963), as amended; (b) ss.7, 8, 9, 10, 11, 12, 13, 21(3), 32, 33 and 34 of the Local Government (Planning and Development) Act

1976 (No. 20 of 1976), as amended; (c) ss.4, 6, 9, 11, 13 and 14 of the Local Government (Planning and Development) Act 1983 (No. 28 of 1983), as amended; (d) the Local Government (Planning and Development) Act 1998 (No. 9 of 1998 insofar as not previously repealed; and (e) the Local Government (Planning and Development) Act 1999 (No. 17 of 1999) were repealed on January 21, 2002.

On March 11, 2002, insofar as not previously repealed—(a) the Local Government (Planning and Development) Act 1963; (b) the Local Government (Planning and Development) Act 1976; (c) the Local Government (Planning and Development) Act 1982 (No. 21 of 1982) (other than s.6); (d) the Local Government (Planning and Development) Act 1983; (e) the Local Government (Planning and Development) Act 1990 (No. 11 of 1990); (f) ss.44 and 45 of the Local Government Act 1991 (No. 11 of 1991); (g) the Local Government (Planning and Development) Act 1992 (No. 14 of 1992); and (h) the Local Government (Planning and Development) Act 1993 (No. 12 of 1992) (other than s.4) were repealed. On March 11, 2002, the Local Government (Planning and Development) Regulations 1994–2001 were revoked.

The Planning and Development Act 2000 (Commencement) Order 2001 (S.I. No. 153 of 2001) provided that on April 17, 2001, the following sections of the The 2000 Act would come into operation: (a) s.2 insofar as it relates to the sections referred to in paras (b)–(e) of the article; (b) ss.156, 157 and 158 insofar as they relate to prosecutions under ss.230, 233 or 235; (c) Pt XVI (other than s.239); (d) subss.(1) (other than paras (a), (b), (c) and (e) of that subsection) and (3)(a) of s.246; and (e) s.268(2).

By virtue of the Planning and Development (Strategic Infrastructure) Act 2006 (Commencement) Order 2006 (1) (S.I. No. 525 of 2006), sections 1, 2, 6(a), 7, 8, 9, 10, 11, 13, 21, 24, 26, 28, 31, 43, 44, 45, 46 and 48 of the 2006 Act, entered into force on October 17 2006. Under the Planning and Development (Strategic Infrastructure) Act 2006 (Commencement) (No. 2) (S.I. No. 553 of 2006) sections 14, 15 and 16 of the Act entered into force on November 14, 2006. Under the Planning and Development (Strategic Infrastructure) Act 2006 (Commencement) (No. 3) Order 2006 (S.I. No. No. 684 of 2006), ss.3, 4, 5, 6(b), (c) and (d), 12, 17, 18, 19, 20, 22, 23, 25, 27, 29, 30, 32, 33, 34, 35, 36, 37, 38, 39, 40, 41, 42, 47, 49, 50 and 51 of the Act came into force on January 31, 2007. These latter sections relate to the establishment of a strategic infrastructure division within An Bord Pleanála and the application procedure for certain types of strategic infrastructure development.

Parliamentary Debates

Planning and Development Act 2000
Seanad Second stage: October 14, October 20.
Seanad Committee: November 10, November 17, November 23.
Seanad Report: December 1, December 2.
Seanad Final stage: December 2.
Dáil Second stage: February 2, February 3, February 9, February 10, February 15, February 16, February 17, March 7, March 23, April 11.
Dáil Committee: April 11, April 12, April 13, April 18, April 19, April 20, May 2, May 10, May 11, May 16, May 17, May 18.
Dáil Report: June 13, June 14.
Dáil Final: stage June 14.
Back to Seanad: June 21.

Planning and Development (Strategic Infrastructure) Act 2006
Seanad Éireann First Stage Presented February 2, 2006; March 7, 2006 Order for Second Stage.
Second Stage: March 7, 2006: March 8, 2006; March 8, 2006.
Committee Stage : May 3, 2006, May 3, 2006, June 21, 2006.
Report and Final Stages : May 16, 2006.

Dáil Éireann
Second Stage: May 24, 2006: May 24, 2006: May 25, 2006: May 25, 2006: May 31,
    2006: June 1, 2006: June 13, 2006: June 14, 2006, June 15, 2006, June 15, 2006
Committee Stage: June 28, 2006
Report and Final Stages : July 4, 2006
Order for Report Stage: July 4, 2006
Returned to Seanad Éireann
July 6, 2006 [Seanad Bill amended by the Dáil] Report and Final stages
Enacted as Act Number 27 of 2006: Date of Signature: July 16, 2006

PART I

PRELIMINARY AND GENERAL

Short title

1–01   **1.**—This *Act* may be cited as the *Planning and Development Act, 2000 to
2007.*

NOTE

The title to the Act makes a stylistic change from the previous planning Acts which
were generally named as the Local Government (Planning and Development) Acts. The
omission of the title "Local Government" indicates the greater breadth and concern of the
2000 Act. While the local government, in its capacity as planning authority, has a central
role, the concept of planning implied by the concept of sustainable development reflects
as much a national issue as a local issue. The inflated horizon of planning law is further
evidenced in such matters as housing policy and preserving national heritage and greater
provision for co-operation between planning authorities. A local authority in performing
a function under the Planning Code is known as the "planning authority". However, it is
possible that the same development may be subject to other local authority legislation
such as the Waste Management Acts in which case the local authority will be known as
the sanitary authority.

Interpretation

1–02   **2.**—**(1)** In this *Act,* except where the context otherwise requires—
"acquisition of land" shall be construed in accordance with *section 213(2),*
and cognate words shall be construed accordingly;
"the Act of 1919" *means the Acquisition of Land (Assessment of Compensation)
Act, 1919;*
"the Act of 1934" *means the Town and Regional Planning Act, 1934;*
"the Act of 1963" *means the Local Government (Planning and Development)
Act, 1963;*
"the Act of 1976" *means the Local Government (Planning and Development)
Act, 1976;*
"the Act of 1982" *means the Local Government (Planning and Development)
Act, 1982;*
"the Act of 1983" *means the Local Government (Planning and Development)
Act, 1983;*
"the Act of 1990" *means the Local Government (Planning and Development)
Act, 1990;*
"the Act of 1992" *means the Local Government (Planning and Development)
Act, 1992;*

"the Act of 1993" *means the Local Government (Planning and Development) Act, 1993;*

"the Act of 1998" *means the Local Government (Planning and Development) Act, 1998;*

"the Act of 1999" *means the Local Government (Planning and Development) Act, 1999;*

"advertisement" *means any word, letter, model, balloon, inflatable structure, kite, poster, notice, device or representation employed for the purpose of advertisement, announcement or direction;*

"advertisement structure" *means any structure which is a hoarding, scaffold, framework, pole, standard, device or sign (whether illuminated or not) and which is used or intended for use for exhibiting advertisements or any attachment to a building or structure used for advertising purposes;*

"agriculture" *includes horticulture, fruit growing, seed growing, dairy farming, the breeding and keeping of livestock (including any creature kept for the production of food, wool, skins or fur, or for the purpose of its use in the farming of land), the training of horses and the rearing of bloodstock, the use of land as grazing land, meadow land, osier land, market gardens and nursery grounds*, and "agricultural" shall be construed accordingly;

"alteration" *includes—*

> *plastering or painting or the removal of plaster or stucco, or the replacement of a door, window or roof, that materially alters the external appearance of a structure so as to render the appearance inconsistent with the character of the structure or neighbouring structures;*

"appeal" *means an appeal to the Board;*

"architectural conservation area" shall be construed in accordance with *section 81(1);*

"area of special planning control" shall be construed in accordance with *section 85(8);*

"attendant grounds", *in relation to a structure, includes land lying outside the curtilage of the structure;*

"the Birds Directive" *means Council Directive No. 79/409/EEC of 2 April 1979* [*O.J. No. L 103/1, 25.4.1979*] *on the conservation of wild birds;*

"Board" *means An Bord Pleanála;*

"chairperson" *means the chairperson of the Board;*

"Commissioners" *means the Commissioners of Public Works in Ireland;*

"company", except in *section 149(5),* means a company within the meaning of *section 2 of the Companies Act, 1963,* or a company incorporated outside the State;

"Council Directive" *means Council Directive No. 85/337/EEC of 27 June 1985* [*O.J. No. L 175/40, 5.7.1985*] *on the assessment of the effects of certain public and private projects on the environment, as amended by Council Directive No. 97/11/EC of 3 March 1997* [*O.J. No. L 73/5, 14.3.1997*] *and any directive amending or replacing those directives;*

"dangerous substance" has the meaning assigned to it by the *Major Accidents Directive;*

"deputy chairperson" *means the deputy chairperson of the Board;*

"development" has the meaning assigned to it by *section 3,* and "develop" shall be construed accordingly;

"development plan" *means a development plan under section 9(1);*

"'DTA' means Dublin Transport Authority";

"endangered" *means exposed to harm, decay or damage, whether immediately or over a period of time, through neglect or through direct or indirect means*;

"enforcement notice" *means an enforcement notice under section 154;*

"environmental impact statement" *means a statement of the effects, if any, which proposed development, if carried out, would have on the environment*;

"European site" *means—*

> *a site—*
>
>> notified for the purposes of Regulation 4 of the European Communities *(Natural Habitats) Regulations, 1997 (S.I. No. 94 of 1997), subject to any amendments made to it by virtue of Regulation 5 of those regulations,*
>>
>> *or transmitted to the Commission in accordance with Regulation 5(4) of the said regulations,*
>>
>> *or added by virtue of Regulation 6 of the said regulations to the list transmitted to the Commission in accordance with Regulation 5(4) of the said Regulations,*
>>
>> *but only until the adoption in respect of the site of a decision by the Commission under Article 21 of the Habitats Directive for the purposes of the third paragraph of Article 4(2) of that Directive,*
>>
>> *a site adopted by the Commission as a site of Community importance for the purposes of Article 4(2) of the Habitats Directive in accordance with the procedure laid down in Article 21 of that Directive,*
>>
>> *a special area of conservation within the meaning of the European Communities (Natural Habitats) Regulations, 1997,*
>>
>> *an area classified pursuant to paragraph (1) or (2) of Article 4 of the Birds Directive;*

"exempted development" has the meaning specified in *section 4;*

"exhibit", *in relation to an advertisement, includes affix, inscribe, print, paint, illuminate and otherwise delineate*;

"existing establishment" has the meaning that it has in the *Major Accidents Directive;*

"fence" *includes a hoarding or similar structure but excludes any bank, wall or other similar structure composed wholly or mainly of earth or stone*;

"functional area" *means, in relation to a planning authority—*

> *in the case of the council of a county, its administrative county, excluding any borough or urban district, in the case of any other planning authority, its administrative area;*

"functions" *includes powers and duties*;

"Gaeltacht" *means the Gaeltacht within the meaning of the Ministers and Secretaries (Amendment) Act, 1956;*

" 'Greater Dublin Area' ('GDA') has the meaning assigned to it by section 3 of the Dublin Transport Authority Act 2008;",

"habitable house" *means a house which—*

is used as a dwelling,

is not in use but when last used was used, disregarding any unauthorised use, as a dwelling and is not derelict, or

was provided for use as a dwelling but has not been occupied;

"Habitats Directive" means Council Directive No. 92/43/EEC of 21 May 1992 [O.J. No. L 206/7, 22.7.1992] on the conservation of natural habitats and of wild fauna and flora;

"house" *means a building or part of a building which is being or has been occupied as a dwelling or was provided for use as a dwelling but has not been occupied, and where appropriate, includes a building which was designed for use as 2 or more dwellings or a flat, an apartment or other dwelling within such a building*;

"integrated pollution control licence" *means a licence under Part IV of the Environmental Protection Agency Act, 1992;*

"land" *includes any structure and any land covered with water (whether inland or coastal)*;

"local area plan" *means a local area plan under section 18;*

"local authority" *means a local authority for the purposes of the Local Government Act, 1941;*

"major accident" has the meaning assigned to it by the *Major Accidents Directive;*

"Major Accidents Directive" *means Council Directive 96/82/EC of 9 December 1996 [O.J. No. L 10 of 14.1.1997, p. 13] on the control of major accident hazards involving dangerous substances*;

"manager" *means—*

with respect to the corporation of a county borough, the manager for the purpose of the Acts relating to the management of the county borough, and

with respect to the council of a county, the corporation of a borough or an urban district council, the manager for the purposes of the County Management Acts, 1940 to 1994;

"Minister" *means the Minister for the Environment and Local Government*;

["National Spatial Strategy" *means the "National Spatial Strategy: 2002 – 2020" published by the Government on 28 November 2002, or any document published by the Government which amends or replaces that Strategy;*]

"new establishment" has the meaning that it has in the *Major Accidents Directive;*

"occupier", *in relation to a protected structure or a proposed protected structure, means—*

any person in or entitled to immediate use or enjoyment of the structure,

any person entitled to occupy the structure, and

any other person having, for the time being, control of the structure;

"ordinary member" *means a member of the Board other than the chairperson*;

"owner", *in relation to land, means a person, other than a mortgagee not in possession, who, whether in his or her own right or as trustee or agent for any other person, is entitled to receive the rack rent of the land or, where the land is not let at a rack rent, would be so entitled if it were so let*;

"party to an appeal or referral" *means the planning authority and any of the following persons, as appropriate—*

>   *the appellant,*

>   *the applicant for any permission in relation to which an appeal is made by another person (other than a person acting on behalf of the appellant),*

>   *in the case of a referral under section 5, the person making the referral, and any other person notified under subsection (2) of that section,*

>   *in the case of a referral under section 34(5), the applicant for the permission which was granted,*

>   *in the case of a referral under section 37(5), the person who made the application for permission which was returned by the planning authority,*

>   *any person served or issued by a planning authority with a notice or order, or copy thereof, under sections 44, 45, 46, 88 and 207,*

>   [*(ff) in the case of a referral under section 57(8), the person making the referral,*]

>   *in the case of a referral under section 96(5), a prospective party to an agreement under section 96(2),*

>   *in the case of an appeal under section 169, the development agency,*

>   *in the case of a referral under section 193, the person by whom the application for permission for erection of the new structure was made,*

>   *the applicant for a licence under section 254 in relation to which an appeal is made by another person (other than a person acting on behalf of the appellant),*

>   *and "party" shall be construed accordingly*

["permission" *means a permission granted under section 34 or 37G, as appropriate;*]

"permission regulations" *means regulations under section 33, 172(2) or 174;*

"planning application" *means an application to a planning authority in accordance with permission regulations for permission for the development of land required by those regulations*;

"planning authority" *means—*

>   *in the case of a county, exclusive of any borough or urban district therein, the council of the county,*

>   *in the case of a county or other borough, the corporation of the borough, and*

>   *in the case of an urban district, the council of the urban district*

>   *and references to the area of the planning authority shall be construed accordingly and shall include the functional area of the authority*

>   "prescribed" *means prescribed by regulations made by the Minister and "prescribe" shall be construed accordingly;*

"proposed protected structure" *means a structure in respect of which a notice is issued under section 12(3) or under section 55 proposing to add the structure, or a specified part of it, to a record of protected structures, and, where that notice so indicates, includes any specified feature which is within the attendant* grounds of the structure and which would not otherwise be included in this definition;

"protected structure" *means*—

> *a structure, or*
>
> *a specified part of a structure,*
>
> *which is included in a record of protected structures, and, where that record so indicates, includes any specified feature which is within the attendant grounds of the structure and which would not otherwise be included in this definition;*

"protection", *in relation to a structure or part of a structure, includes conservation, preservation and improvement compatible with maintaining the character and interest of the structure or part;*

"public place" *means any street, road, seashore or other place to which the public have access whether as of right or by permission and whether subject to or free of charge;*

"public road" has the same meaning as in the *Roads Act, 1993;*

"record of protected structures" *means the record included under section 51 in a development plan;*

[*"referral" means a referral to the Board under section 5, 34(5), 37(5), 96(5) or 193(2)*];

"regional authority" *means a body established in accordance with section 43 of the Local Government Act, 1991;*

"regional planning guidelines" *means regional planning guidelines made under Chapter III of Part II;*

"register" *means the register kept under section 7;*

" regional authorities within the GDA" means the Dublin Regional Authority and the Mid-East Regional Authority;

"registering authority" *means a registering authority within the meaning of the Registration of Title Act, 1964;*

"reserved function" *means*—

> *with respect to the council of a county or an elective body for the purposes of the County Management Acts, 1940 to 1994, a reserved function for the purposes of those Acts, and*
>
> *with respect to the corporation of a county borough, a reserved function for the purposes of the Acts relating to the management of the county borough;*

"risk" has the meaning assigned to it by the *Major Accidents Directive;*

"road" has the same meaning as in the *Roads Act, 1993;*

"seashore" has the same meaning as in the *Foreshore Act, 1933;*

"shares" *includes stock and "share capital" shall be construed accordingly;*

"special amenity area order" *means an order confirmed under section 203;*

"State authority" *means*—

> *a Minister of the Government, or*
>
> *the Commissioners;*

"statutory undertaker" *means a person, for the time being, authorised by or under any enactment or instrument under an enactment to*—

> *construct or operate a railway, canal, inland navigation, dock, harbour or airport,*

provide, or carry out works for the provision of, gas, electricity or telecommunications services, or

provide services connected with, or carry out works for the purposes of the carrying on of the activities of, any public undertaking;

["strategic downstream gas pipeline" *means any proposed gas pipeline, other than an upstream gas pipeline, which is designed to operate at 16 bar or greater, and is longer than 20 kilometres in length*;

"strategic gas infrastructure development" *means any proposed development comprising or for the purposes of a strategic downstream gas pipeline or a strategic upstream gas pipeline, and associated terminals, buildings and installations, whether above or below ground, including any associated discharge pipe*;

"strategic infrastructure development" *means—*

any proposed development in respect of which a notice has been served under section 37B(4)(a),

any proposed development by a local authority referred to in section 175(1) or 226(6),

any proposed development referred to in section 181A(1),

any proposed development referred to in section 182A(1),

any proposed strategic gas infrastructure development referred to in section 182C(1),

any scheme or proposed road development referred to in section 215,

any proposed railway works referred to in section 37(3) of the Transport (Railway Infrastructure) Act 2001 (as amended by the Planning and Development (Strategic Infrastructure) Act 2006), or

any compulsory acquisition of land referred to in section 214, 215A or 215B, being an acquisition related to development specified in any of the preceding paragraphs of this definition;

"Strategic Infrastructure Division" *means the division of the Board referred to in section 112A(1);*

"strategic upstream gas pipeline" *means so much of any gas pipeline proposed to be operated or constructed—*

as part of a gas production project, or

for the purpose of conveying unprocessed natural gas from one or more than one such project to a processing plant or terminal or final coastal landing terminal, as will be situate in the functional area or areas of a planning authority or planning authorities;]

"structure" *means any building, structure, excavation, or other thing constructed or made on, in or under any land, or any part of a structure so defined, and—*

where the context so admits, includes the land on, in or under which the structure is situate, and

in relation to a protected structure or proposed protected structure, includes—

the interior of the structure,

the land lying within the curtilage of the structure,

any other structures lying within that curtilage and their interiors, and

all fixtures and features which form part of the interior or exterior of any

> *structure or structures referred to in subparagraph (i) or (iii);*

"substratum of land" *means any subsoil or anything beneath the surface of land required—*

> *for the purposes of a tunnel or tunnelling or anything connected therewith, or*
>
> *for any other purpose connected with a scheme within the meaning of the Roads Act, 1993;*

"Transboundary Convention" *means the United Nations Economic Commission for Europe Convention on Environmental Impact Assessment in a Transboundary Context, done at Espoo (Finland), on 25 February, 1991;*

"transport strategy" has the meaning assigned to it by section 12 of the Dublin Transport Authority Act 2008;".

"traveller" *means a traveller within the meaning of section 2 of the Housing (Traveller Accommodation) Act, 1998;*

"unauthorised development" *means, in relation to land, the carrying out of any unauthorised works (including the construction, erection or making of any unauthorised structure) or the making of any unauthorised use;*

"unauthorised structure" *means a structure other than—*

> *a structure which was in existence on 1 October 1964, or*
>
> *a structure, the construction, erection or making of which was the subject of a permission for development granted under Part IV of the Act of 1963 or deemed to be such under section 92 of that Act [or under section 34 or 37G of this Act], being a permission which has not been revoked, or which exists as a result of the carrying out of exempted development (within the meaning of section 4 of the Act of 1963 or section 4 of this Act);*

"unauthorised use" *means, in relation to land, use commenced on or after 1 October 1964, being a use which is a material change in use of any structure or other land and being development other than—*

> *exempted development (within the meaning of section 4 of the Act of 1963 or section 4 of this Act), or*
>
> *development which is the subject of a permission granted under Part IV of the Act of 1963 [or under section 34 or 37G of this Act], being a permission which has not been revoked, and which is carried out in compliance with that permission or any condition to which that permission is subject;*

"unauthorised works" *means any works on, in, over or under land commenced on or after 1 October 1964, being development other than—*

> *exempted development (within the meaning of section 4 of the Act of 1963 or section 4 of this Act), or*
>
> *development which is the subject of a permission granted under Part IV of the Act of 1963 [or under section 34 or 37G of this Act], being a permission which has not been revoked, and which is carried out in compliance with that permission or any condition to which that permission is subject;*

"use", *in relation to land, does not include the use of the land by the carrying out of any works thereon;*

"warning letter" *means a notification in writing under section 152(1);*

"waste licence" *means a waste licence under Part V of the Waste Management Act, 1996;*

"works" *includes any act or operation of construction, excavation, demolition, extension, alteration, repair or renewal and, in relation to a protected structure or proposed protected structure, includes any act or operation involving the application or removal of plaster, paint, wallpaper, tiles or other material to or from the surfaces of the interior or exterior of a structure.*

(2) In this *Act* —

   (a) a reference to a section, Schedule, Chapter or Part is to a section, Schedule, Chapter or Part of this *Act,* unless it is indicated that reference to some other enactment is intended, and

   (b) a reference to a subsection, paragraph or subparagraph is to the subsection, paragraph or subparagraph of the provision in which the reference occurs, unless it is indicated that reference to some other provision is intended.

(3) In this *Act,* a reference to the carrying out of development on behalf of a State authority shall, where that authority is a Minister of the Government, be construed as including a reference to the carrying out of development by the Commissioners on behalf of the Minister.

(4) A reference in this *Act* to contravention of a provision includes, where appropriate, a reference to refusal or failure to comply with that provision.

(5) A reference in this *Act* to performance of functions includes a reference to the exercise of powers and the performance of duties.

(6) A reference in this *Act* to any other enactment shall, except where the context otherwise requires, be construed as a reference to that enactment as amended by or under any other enactment, including this *Act.*

(7) The doing of anything that is required under this *Act* to be done by resolution shall be a reserved function.

AMENDMENT HISTORY

Definition of "party to an appeal or referral" amended and definition of "referral" substituted by s.6 of the Planning and Development (Amendment) Act 2002 (No. 32 of 2002) which came into effect on December 24, 2002.

Definitions of "National Spatial Strategy" "permission", "strategic downstream gas pipeline", "strategic gas infrastructure development", "strategic infrastructure development", "Strategic Infrastructure Division", "strategic upstream gas pipeline" all inserted by s. 6 of the Planning and Development (Strategic Infrastructure) Act 2006 (No. 27 of 2006).

Definitions of "unauthorised structure", "unauthorised use" and "unauthorised works" amended by s.6 of the Planning and Development (Strategic Infrastructure) Act 2006 (No. 27 of 2006).

Definitions of "DTA", "Greater Dublin Area 'GDA'", "Regional Authorities within the GDA" and "Transport Strategy", were inserted by s.81 of the Dublin Transport Authority Act 2008, to commence on such date as the Minister may appoint.

NOTE

This section concerns general definitions under the Act. While many of these are clear, some require clarification:

"Advertisement": this definition is expanded from under the 1963 Act by adding "inflatable structure" to the definition. Section 3(2) provides that a material change of use takes place where any structure or other land or any tree or other object on land becomes used for the exhibition of advertisements. Part 2 of Sch.II to the 2001 Regulations sets out various classes of exempted development in relation to advertisements. Article 6(2) of the 2001 Regulations sets out the conditions for an advertisement to qualify as exempted development. The definition of advertisement is extremely wide-ranging. A change from one type of advertising to another within the definition may still constitute a material change of use. See *Dublin Corporation v Regan Advertising Limited* [1986] I.R. 171; [1989] I.R. 61: Blayney J. in the High Court (upheld by the Supreme Court) said at 177 "So an enormous number of things can constitute an advertisement. The difference between them can in my opinion be so great that a change from using a site for an advertisement of one kind to using it for an advertisement of a different kind can readily constitute a change of use"; see also *Dublin Corporation v Lowe and Signways Holdings Limited*, unreported, High Court, Morris P., February 4, 2000. Section 3(2)(a) of the Act expressly states that where any structure or other land or any tree or other object on land becomes used for the exhibition of advertisements, this constitutes a material change of use. However, while an advertisement may involve a change of use, it could also involve "works" such as in installing or altering a structure. See *Dublin Corporation v Lowe* [2004] 4 I.R. 259, where the Supreme Court treated advertisements as giving rise to works, albeit finding that the works were exempted development under s.4(1)(h). It has been held that certain changes to an established use of advertisement could give rise to abandonment. See *Fingal County Council v Crean*, unreported, High Court, Ó Caoimh J., October 19, 2001.

"Advertisement structure": this definition is also expanded from the 1963 Act with the additional phrase, "or any attachment to a building or structure used for advertising purposes". This additional phrase appears to have been introduced as a catch-all phrase.

"Agriculture": in this definition the category "the training of horses and the rearing of bloodstock" has been added, while the use of lands for turbary and for woodlands purposes ancillary to farmland, which was included under the 1963 Act, has been deleted. Under s.4(1)(a) the use of land for the purposes of agriculture is exempted development.

"Alteration": this definition has also been expanded with the inclusion of "or the removal of plaster or stucco" and a second category "(b) the replacement of a door, window or roof".

"Architectural conservation area": this definition differs from s.81(1) of the 1992 Act by the insertion of the words "a development plan shall include an objective to preserve the character of ...".

"Attendant grounds": this is a new definition and is broader than the term curtilage, in relation to which it is defined. Notwithstanding its importance, "curtilage" is not defined. However, as regards the meaning of "curtilage" see the general note on s.4. The distinction between curtilage and attendant ground has particular importance in the context of a protected structure in that while the curtilage of a protected structure forms part of the protected structure, the attendant grounds does not. Chapter 13 of the Architectural Heritage Guidelines 2004, states at para.13.2.1 that 'the attendant grounds of a structure are lands outside the curtilage of the structure but which are associated with the structure and are intrinsic to its function, setting and/or appreciation. In many cases, the attendant grounds will incorporate a designed landscape deliberately laid out to complement the design of the building or to assist in its function'. Paragraph 13.2.2 states:

"Where the curtilage of a protected structure has altered since the time of its construction, there may be important features of the original, or of a previous, curtilage which would not automatically be protected within the definition of the protected structure".

"Compulsory acquisition": s.213(2) enlists the performances of certain functions which are described as acquisitions of land, namely to:
• acquire land, permanently or temporarily, by agreement or compulsorily;
• acquire, permanently or temporarily, by agreement or compulsorily, any easement,

way-leave, water-right or other right over or in respect of any land or water or any substratum of land; and

- restrict or otherwise interfere with, permanently or temporarily, by agreement or compulsorily, any easement, way-leave, water-right or other right over or in respect of any land or water or any substratum of land.

"Exhibit": this definition has been slightly altered by the addition of the word "illuminate".

"Fence": this definition has been narrowed by the introduction of an exclusionary clause relating to a wall/bank of clay or stone. Classes 5 and 11 of Pt I of Sch.2 to the 2001 Regulations provide exemptions for certain fences in the context of dwellings.

"Greater Dublin Area 'GDA'": section 3 of the Dublin Transport Authority Act 2008 provides that The Greater Dublin Area comprises: (a) the city of Dublin, (b) the administrative counties of South Dublin, Fingal, Dun Laoghaire-Rathdown, Kildare, Wicklow and Meath, and (c) such other areas as may be declared by order, from time to time, by the Minister.

"Habitable house" and "house": these are new definitions and reflect the consolidation with the Housing Acts. This definition of house adopts the majority decision of the Supreme Court in *Smyth v Colgan* [1999] 1 I.R. 548, where in order for house to qualify as a dwelling it need not have already been dwelt in. Habitable house has been altered to exclude a derelict house. Class 50 of Pt I of Sch.2 to the 2001 Regulations excludes the demolition of a habitable house from constituting exempted development under that category which involves the demolition of structures. As to the meaning of "designed" mentioned in the definion of "house", see *McMahon v Dublin Corporation* [1996] 3 I.R. 509. An essential element of the notion of a "house" is that it must involve a "building".

"Local authority": much of the Local Government Act 1941 has been repealed by the Local Government Act 2001. Section 10 of the 2001 Act concerns local government areas, s.11 relates to the establishment and administrative areas of local authorities, while Pt VIII relates to local authority boundary alterations.

"Land": this definition has been altered so that it no longer includes the acquisition of land. The fact that land covers land covered with water whether inland or coastal does not in itself extend the jurisdictional scope of the Planning Code which is otherwise confined by the jurisdictional areas of local authorities as defined under the Local Government Act 2001. However, by virtue of Pt XV of the Act, the scope of the Planning Code is extended to cover development on the foreshore.

"National Spatial Strategy": this definition was introduced by the 2006 Act.

"Occupier": this was defined under the 1963 Act and differs from the definition under the Occupiers Liability Act 1995 where the emphasis is placed on the degree of control, which reflects the different objectives of the Acts. The fact of a separate definition of owner and occupier means that in certain instances either can be treated as the alternative for the other, such as for the service of a protection notice or enforcement action.

"Party to an appeal or referral": this constitutes a new definition, with considerable difference in language to the definition contained in s.1 of the 1992 Act. The term embraces the various applications which can be made.

"Planning Application": the definition of an application in accordance with the regulations means that an invalid application not in accordance with the regulations will not constitute a planning application within the meaning of this definition. In *Kelly v Roscommon County Council*, unreported, High Court, McGovern J., May 20, 2006, the Court rejected the claim that as the site notice had been erected within six months of the first application, it should have been on a yellow (rather than white) background as required under art.19(4) of the Planning and Development Regulations 2001. McGovern J. held that once the first application was deemed to be invalid (because the application description was incorrect), it ceased to be a "planning application" within the meaning of the Act.

"Proposed protected structure": s.12(3) relates to the service of notice of such proposal on an occupier or owner while s.55 concerns the procedure for addition to or deletion from the register of protected structures. The notion of proposed protected structure is important as by virtue of s.57(1), the special restrictions on exempted development apply not only to works to protected structures but also to works to a proposed protected structures. See *Córas Iompair Éireann v An Bord Pleanála*, unreported, High Court, Clarke J., June 19, 2008.

"Reserved functions": reserved functions are those taken by the elected members of the local authority as opposed to those undertaken by the permanent staff such as the County Manager. Most of the County Management Acts 1940–1994 were repealed under the Local Government Act 2001. Sections 131 and 132 of the 2001 Act concern reserved functions, while Sch.14 enlists certain reserved functions.

"Statutory undertaker": this definition has been altered to also include bodies carrying out telecommunications work.

"strategic infrastructure development": this definition is widely drawn and is not confined to the categories of development set out in the Seventh Schedule to which the special procedure of s.37 A and B are applicable. It also includes local authority development which requires an EIS under s.175(1), local authority development on the foreshore (s.226(6)); electricity or electricity transmission infrastructure (s.181A); strategic gas development infrastructure (s.181C); a road scheme or proposed road development under s.215 and the compulsory acquisition of land by the local authority which relate to any of the enlisted types of strategic infrastructure development.

"strategic upstream gas pipeline": relates to the approval procedure for strategic gas infrastructure under s.181C.

"Structure": in this definition the term "erections" has been removed, although it does not appear to be of any significance. A new part on protected structures has also been inserted.

"transport strategy"; s.12 of the Dublin Transport Authority Act 2008 provides that the DTA are to prepare a strategic transport plan. Section 12(3) states that the objective of the transport strategy shall be to provide a long-term strategic planning framework for the integrated development of transport infrastructure and services in the GDA. Section 12(4) states a transport strategy shall consider the future development of the transport system in the GDA for a period of not less than 12 years and not more than 20 years.

"Traveller": s.2 of Housing (Traveller Accommodation) Act 1998 simply states that "traveller means a person to whom s.13 of the Act of 1988 (as amended by this Act) applies". Section 13 of the Housing Act 1988, which relates to provision of halting sites for travellers, states at s.13(1) "this section applies to persons belonging to the class of persons who traditionally pursue or have pursued a nomadic way of life".

"Unauthorised development": this definition embraces "unauthorised works" and "unauthorised use" for which there are also separate definitions. This is in contrast to the 1963 Act where there was simply a definition of "unauthorised work". The central binary definition of works and use, whereby one is defined by reference to the other, is maintained. For a more detailed explanation of the terms see the note for s.3. A significant change in relation to the definitions of both "unauthorised use" and "unauthorised works", relates to para.(b) in both definitions under which development which is the subject of a permission granted is excluded from being unauthorised use or unauthorised works. The change concerns the insertion of a new clause which states "and which is carried out in compliance with that permission or any condition to which that permission is subject". This means that a development in non-compliance with conditions of a permission constitutes unauthorised development. This change is also evident under s.160 in relation to obtaining a planning injunction for unauthorised development. Under the previous legislation, s.27 of the 1976 Act distinguished between unauthorised development and development authorised by a permission in non-compliance with a condition. Section 160 abolishes this distinction by referring to a single category of unauthorised development. The definitions of unauthorised works, use and structure, all impliedly exclude pre-1963 Act uses from their scope. Section 39(4) provides there is no requirement to obtain permission for a purpose for which the land was used prior to October 1, 1964. That subsection also recognised that the established use may consist of more than one use; a normal use and also an occasional use or uses. The established use must not however have been abandoned or subject to manifest interruption. Equally, where an established use intensifies to such an extent as to amount to a material change of use, this will constitute development and may potentially fall within the scope of unauthorised use, unless permission is granted. It may also be noted that certain provisions of the Act, expressly deem certain development to be unauthorised even if they do not fall within the above definition. Thus in relation to the control of quarries, s.261(10) provides that:

> "(a) A quarry to which the section applies in respect of which the owner or operator fails to provide information in relation to the operations of the quarry in accordance with a requirements section 261(1) or in accordance with a requirement under 261(3) shall be unauthorised development.
>
> (b) Any quarry in respect of which a notification under section 261(7) applies shall, unless a planning application in respect of the quarry is submitted to the planning authority within the period referred to in that subsection, be unauthorised development."

"Use": the reason for the exclusion of works was explained by Keane J. in *Kildare County Council v Goode* [1999] 2 I.R. 495 as follows: "The reason for the latter provision can be made clear by an example. In ordinary parlance, putting up a building on farmland hitherto used for growing crops would be treated as changing the use of the land. Since, however, the construction of farm buildings is, to some extent, an exempted development, the draftsman found it necessary to provide that the carrying out of works on land, by itself and of itself, was not a use of land for the purposes of the Act of 1963". See also *Roadstone v An Bord Pleanála*, unreported, High Court, Finlay Geoghegan J., July 4, 2008.

"Warning letter": s.152(1) provides that where a representation is made that an unauthorised development is being carried out, the planning authority shall issue a warning letter unless such representation is frivolous or vexatious. Warning letters are fundamentally different from warning notices under the 1963 Act, in that warning letters are preliminary steps before considering whether to issue an enforcement notice. See also the note on Pt VIII.

"Works" has been expanded to include an extra clause in relation to protected structures or proposed protected structures.

Subsection (3) is a new section and provides that development on behalf of a State authority where that authority is a Minister of Government includes the carrying out of development by the Commissioner of Public works on behalf of such Minister.

Subsections (4)–(6) are of general application throughout the Act and relate to use of the words contravention, performance of functions and a reference to enactments.

Subsection (7) provides that any decision taken by resolution is a reserved function. Reserved functions are those performed by the elected members of the council rather than the permanent staff. The principal statement of reserved functions of local authorities is contained in the Local Government Act 2001 in relation to which see ss.131, 132 and Sch.14. Among the reserved functions under the 2000 Act are the making or varying of a development plan (ss.12 and 13); the making of a local area plan, (s.20(3)(d)(ii)); granting permission for an application in material contravention of the development plan (s.34(6)(a)(iv)); the making of a development contribution scheme (s.48(8)(a)); making a special planning control scheme (s.85(1)); making a code of conduct (s.150(1)); the making or varying of a planning scheme (s.169(4)(b) and s.171(1)); local authority development (s.179(4)(b)); declaring an area to be a special amenity area (s.202(1)); designating a landscape as a landscape conservation area (s.204(6)); making a tree preservation order (s.206); creating a public right of way over land (s.207); holding of an event by a local authority (s.238); making an agreement for sharing the cost for performing functions (s.244); and requesting the Minister to appoint a commissioner to carry out all or any of the functions of the authority (s.255(7)).

Development

1–03   **3.—(1)** In this *Act*, "development" *means, except where the context otherwise* *requires, the carrying out of any works on, in, over or under land or the making of any material change in the use of any structures or other land.*

(2) For the purposes of *subsection (1)* and without prejudice to the generality of that *subsection* —

(a) where any structure or other land or any tree or other object on land becomes used for the exhibition of advertisements, or

(b) where land becomes used for any of the following purposes—

   (i) the placing or keeping of any vans, tents or other objects, whether or not moveable and whether or not collapsible, for the purpose of caravanning or camping or habitation or the sale of goods,

   (ii) the storage of caravans or tents, or

   (iii) the deposit of vehicles whether or not usable for the purpose for which they were constructed or last used, old metal, mining or industrial waste, builders' waste, rubbish or debris,

the use of the land shall be taken as having materially changed.

(3) For the avoidance of doubt, it is hereby declared that, for the purposes of this *section,* the use as two or more dwellings of any house previously used as a single dwelling involves a material change in the use of the structure and of each part thereof which is so used.

NOTE

Certain slight modifications have been made to the language of the corresponding section in the 1963 Act. Thus under s.3(2)(b)(i) the word "habitation" has been inserted. Also under s.3(2)(b)(iii) the wording has been altered in relation to the deposit of vehicles with the additional clause "whether or not usable for the purpose for which they were constructed or last used".

Development is one of the key concepts in planning law. Where there is development, planning permission is required except where it is exempted development (s.32) or where the development commenced prior to October 1, 1964. The central concept embraces two possibilities; the carrying out of works or material change of use. Only material changes of use and not continued use or use per se can constitute development. Under s.2 the terms "use", "land", "works" and "structure" are all defined. The two concepts of "use" and "works" may overlap but in most instances are distinct concepts. See *Re Viscount Securities* [1978] 112 I.L.T.R. 17, per Finlay P.). The distinction may in certain circumstances seem artificial and is largely for the internal coherence of the Act. See *Dublin County Council v Sellwood Quarries* [1981] I.L.R.M. 23; *Kildare County Council v Goode* [1999] 2 I.R. 495; *Cairnduff v O'Connell* [1986] I.R. 73; *Esat Digifone v South Dublin County Council* [2002] 3 I.R. 585. In *Kildare County Council v Goode* [1999] 2 I.R. 495, Keane J. noted carrying out of works on land, by itself and of itself, was not a use of land for the purposes of the Act. However, in *Roadstone v An Bord Pleanála* unreported, High Court, Finlay Geoghegan J., July 3, 2008, noted that this does not preclude the works carried out on lands being taken into account in determining the use to which lands are being put, or whether there is a change in the use of the lands. However, the works are only indicative of the nature of the use as distinct from constituting of themselves the use of the lands. The fact that the definition of "use" expressly excludes works, means that the use entailed by the carrying of works under a exempted development provision would not be rendered ineffective by being restrained as a use. In general, the use of land will not be deemed a "change of use" by the erection of buildings or structures on it, but will be considered works, see *Paterson v Murphy* [1978] I.L.R.M. 85. Certain features of works include that it is generally a temporary activity and a means to an end, see *Kildare County Council v Goode* [1999] 2 I.R. 495, per Barron J. at 502. The determination as to whether a development constitutes works or change of use may be important, as certain provisions of the Act and Regulations apply exclusively to one or the other. This includes the compensation provisions whereby there is no entitlement to compensation for a refusal of permission where the development involves a material change of use and also certain exempted development categories which only apply to works or uses as the case may be. The placing of a new gravel base and the placing thereon of a new mobile home, has been held to constitute "works" and also a "structure". See *Sligo County Council v Martin*, unreported, High Court, O'Neill J., May 24, 2007. However, the placing of a telecommunication mast and equipment was more properly deemed to involve a material change of use rather than any works. See *Esat Digifone v South Dublin County Council* [2002] 3 I.R. 585.

Whether there has been a material change of use is largely a question of fact. See *Esat Digifone v South Dublin County Council* [2002] 3 I.R. 585, although the determination of a material change of use may sometimes involve making a finding of law; see *Butler v Dublin Corporation* [1999] 1 I.R. 565, per O'Flaherty J. at 585. In determining a material change of use, "material" means material for planning purposes, see *Westmeath County Council v Quirke*, unreported, High Court, Budd J., May 23, 1996. The assessment of materiality involves assessing not only the use itself but also its effects. In determining whether there has been a material change of use, factors such as the effect on the surrounding neighbourhood and the character of the use of the land are relevant. See *Carrickhall Holdings Limited v Dublin Corporation* [1983] I.L.R.M. 268. The court will however be reluctant to take into account different types of residential neighbourhoods in assessing material change of use, see *Dublin Corporation v Moore* [1984] I.L.R.M. 339. Visual effect may be taken into account. See *Westmeath County Council v Quirke*, unreported, High Court, Budd J., May 23, 1996. The difference in the nature of the activity being carried out may indicate a material change of use. See *Cusack & McKenna v Minister for Local Government*, unreported, High Court, McWilliam J., November 4, 1980. In assessing materiality, the court may take into consideration whether there has been any objection to the change of use, although this is not necessary, see *Monaghan County Council v Brogan* [1987] I.L.R.M. 564. A short term or transient use will not involve a material change of use. See *Butler v Dublin Corporation* [1999] 1 I.R. 565. A material change of use is the materiality for planning purposes of any change in use identified at the time it takes place. See *Roadstone v An Bord Pleanála* unreported, High Court, Finlay Geoghegan J., July 4, 2008.

Material change of use is determined by reference to the planning unit and so it may be important to determine what is the planning unit. The larger a planning unit is defined, the less significant or material may be the change of use. In *Esat Digifone v South Dublin County Council* [2002] 3 I.R. 585; [2002] 2 I.L.R.M. 547, Kearns J. said that the subdivision of the planning unit does not of itself give rise to a material change of use in the absence of some severance between the primary use and the new use. In assessing whether to treat a premises as a single planning unit, the court will look to see whether they were treated by the user as separate units, see *The Rehabilitation Institute v Dublin Corporation*, unreported, High Court, Barron J., January 14, 1988.

Examples of where there has been held to be a material change of use include *Carrick Hall Holdings v Dublin Corporation* [1983] I.L.R.M. 268, (change from a hotel licence without a public bar to an ordinary seven-day licence); *Monaghan County Council v Brogan* [1987] I.R. 333, (significant increase in slaughtering animals and change in purposes from food for animals to food for humans); *Dublin Corporation v O'Dwyer Bros*, unreported, High Court, Kelly J., May 2, 1997 (a sign over a pub); *McMahon v Dublin Corporation* [1997] 1 I.L.R.M. 227 (change of use of holiday homes for residential use); *Fusco v Aprile*, unreported, High Court, Morris J., June 6, 1997, (change of use from a convenience shop or neighbourhood shop to a food outlet); *Ampleforth T/A Fitzwilliam Hotel v Cherating Ltd* [2003] I.E.S.C. 27 (Supreme Court) April 11, 2003 (change from a restaurant with the limited serving of drink to an ordinary seven-day publican's trade use). A further factor indicating a material change, is the existence of a category of exempted development in relation to the subject matter; see *Esat Digifone v South Dublin County Council* [2002] 3 I.R. 585; [2002] 2 I.L.R.M. 547. There was not a material change of use in *Dublin County Council v Carty Builders* [1987] I.R. 355, where the doubling of caravans on a caravan site was held not to constitute a material change of use. However each case turns on its particular facts, so the value of cases as precedents is open to question, as noted by Kearns J. in *Esat Digifone v South Dublin County Council*.

Where there are two or more independent uses and one expands to absorb the whole site, such other use may be displaced so as to amount to a material change of use; see *Rehabilitation Institute v An Bord Pleanála*, unreported, High Court, Barron J., January 14, 1988. A material change of use can be deemed to occur in a portion of the premises, which is considered separate to the remainder, such as an advertisement on the façade of a building in *Dublin Corporation v Regan Advertising Limited* [1986] I.R. 171.

Where there is a material change of use without permission, it will not be possible to revert to the earlier use without permission. See *Grillo v Minister for Housing and Local Government* [1968] 208 E.G. 1201 and *Cusack and McKenna v Minister for Local Government and Dublin Corporation*, unreported, High Court, McWilliam J., November 4, 1980, although this may not apply where the permission is for a limited period only under s.39(3).

Certain changes of use come within classes of exempted development, set out in s.4 and also in the Planning Regulations, in particular see class 14 of Pt I, Sch.2.

Intensification

The notions of intensification and abandonment are applicable to both development involving material changes in use and works. See *Kildare County Council v Goode* [1999] 2 I.R. 495. Prior to this in *Patterson v Murphy* [1978] I.L.R.M. 85, it was suggested that an intensification of works, as distinct from use, may amount to a material change of use. In *Mason and McCarthy v KT Sand and Gravel* unreported, High Court, Smyth J., May 7, 2004, Smyth J. noted that "Previously, judicial authorities appear to have distinguished between intensification of use as opposed to works but this distinction appears to have been abandoned in the Supreme Court in *Kildare County Council v Goode* [1999] 2 I.R. 495".

As regards intensification of use involving a material change of use in *Butler v Dublin Corporation* [1999] 1 I.R. 565, Keane C.J. declared:

"Although the expression 'intensification of use' is not to be found in our planning code or its English equivalent, the legislatures in both jurisdictions must have envisaged that a particular use could be so altered in character by the volume of activities or operations being carried out that the original use must have been regarded as having been materially changed."

The intensification of the use of development which is already subject to planning permission can give rise to material change in use. See *Lanigan & Benghazi v Barry* unreported, High Court, Charleton J., February 15, 2008. The court will consider whether the intensification goes beyond the scope or terms of the planning permission. Some allowance will be made for normal business growth. See *Galway County Council v Lackagh Rock Company* [1985] I.R. 20. Where the plans and specifications of a planning permission indicate internal works, a developer cannot rely on s.4(1)(h) in implementing the permission to make alterations to such internal works. See *O'Connor v Dublin Corporation*, unreported, High Court, O'Neill J., October 4, 2000. In the case of an established pre-1964 use, the continuation to completion of the particular works will not be unauthorised. This involves ascertaining what was or might reasonably have been anticipated at the relevant date as having been involved in the works then taking place. See *Waterford County Council v John A. Wood Ltd* [1999] 1 I.R. 556. It may be noted however that the extension of development beyond the boundaries of the permitted development, may involves a material change of use of the land outside the site boundary as opposed to an intensification of use. The issue of intensification amounting to a material change of use involves, firstly a factual question as to whether there has been a change in use of the lands and secondly, the materiality of this change in use. See *Roadstone v An Bord Pleanála* unreported, High Court, Finlay Geoghegan J., July 4, 2008.

In *Royal Borough of Kensington and Chelsea v Secretary of State for the Environment* [1981] J.P.L. 50, Donaldson L.J. stated intensification meant a change to something different. Intensification has arisen in a series of quarrying cases where it was considered whether the quarrying works were materially different to those being carried out on or before October 1, 1964. See *The State (Stafford and Son) v Roadstone Ltd* [1980] I.L.R.M. 1, *Monaghan County Council v Brogan* [1987] I.R. 333; *Carrick Hall Holdings v Dublin Corporation* [1983] I.L.R.M. 268,; *Dublin County Council v Macken*, unreported, High Court, O'Hanlon

J., May 13, 1994; *Paul Lee and John Flynn v Michael O'Riordan*, unreported, High Court, O'Hanlon J., February 10, 1995; *McGrath Limestone Works v Galway County Council* [1989] I.L.R.M. 602; *Dublin County Council v Tallaght Block Co. Ltd* [1982] I.L.R.M. 469; *Cork County Council v Artfert Quarries Ltd*, unreported, High Court, Murphy J., December 2, 1982; *Galway County Council v Lackagh Rock Company* [1985] I.R. 20; *Paterson v Murphy* [1978] I.L.R.M. 85; *Stafford and Bates v Roadstone Ltd* [1980] I.L.R.M. 1. In *Dublin County Council v Sellwood Quarries* [1981] I.L.R.M. 23, the Court held the works were materially different to the works on October 1, 1964. Among the factors were the changes in the objects of the operations; the use of different production methods involving the increased use of machinery; intensification in scale from intermittent to substantial and increased area activity. In *Galway County Council v Lackagh Rock Company* [1985] I.R. 20, Barron J. held intensification in itself is not a material change of use but it must also be established that the intensification has affected the proper planning and development of the area. The test was to compare the matters which a planning authority would have considered had the application been made on October 1, 1964, and the present use. If such matters are materially different, then the nature of the use must equally be materially different. Relevant factors may include effects on the environment, the demands for local authority services, and on the amenities of residents. However, in *Monaghan County Council v Brogan* [1987] I.R. 333, Keane J. did not fully agree with this approach instead stressing the role of the Court in determining the matter, declaring:

> "It is for the Court to determine whether or not there has been a material change in the use of the land when an application is made under Section 27. No doubt, as Lord Parker C.J. pointed out in *East Barnet UDC v British Transport Commission* 'material' in this context means 'material for planning purposes'. Whether or not it is so material must be determined by the Court as a matter of fact and the absence of any evidence as to the views of the Planning Authority on the matter is not crucial".

In *Paterson v Murphy* [1978] I.L.R.M. 85 at 105, the Court found that the object of the operations was to produce a different product to that which had been produced prior to the coming into force of the Planning Acts. Four inch stone was being produced which was different to shale and it was used for a different purpose in the building industry and also fetched a different price. The Court also took account of the fact that the raw material in that case was being extracted by blasting on a regular basis and large crushing and screening was being used to produce stones of the correct dimensions which involved the use of ancillary equipment and a larger labour force.

In *Westmeath County Council v Quirke & Sons*, unreported, High Court, Budd J., May 23, 1996, it was said that massive intensification of a quiet, rural quarry is likely to have a considerable effect on the vicinity and so is likely to be a change in use which is material in the context of planning. In *Dublin County Council v Tallaght Block Co. Ltd* [1982] I.L.R.M. 469, the Supreme Court held the intensification of concrete block production to amount to a material change of use. This was evidenced by an increase in scale and area of operations, installation of plant, buildings and a wall. It is uncertain whether an intensification beyond permission post-1964 for which an application was granted could be restrained. The mere physical fact of intensification will not be sufficient in itself to amount to a material change of use, see *Dublin Corporation v O'Sullivan*, unreported, High Court, Finlay P., December 21, 1984. However, an increase in noise and traffic on a lane at an industrial estate was held to amount to a material change of use in *Molumby v Kearns*, unreported, High Court, O'Sullivan J., January 19, 1999. In *Mason and McCarthy v KT Sand and Gravel*, unreported, High Court, Smyth J., May 7, 2004, the extra works and volume of traffic in the operation of an essentially different type of business were considered conclusive.

In *Westmeath County Council v Quirke & Sons*, unreported, High Court, Budd J., May 23, 1996, the Court took account of the fact that there was a change of production from quarry run rock to crushed stone. And that there was an increase in the volume and size of trucks and machinery and traffic between the introduction of the Planning Acts and the date on which the matter came before the Court. In *Fingal County Council v H.E. Services Ltd*, unreported, High Court, Ó Caoimh J., January 25, 2002, the intensification of use of the storage of machinery which resulted in more and more vehicles being kept on the roadway in a situation where they represented a serious danger to other users of the roadway, was held to constitute a material change of use. In *Dublin Corporation v Aircold Refrigeration*

Ltd, unreported, High Court, March 8, 1995, O'Hanlon J. held there was a material change of use of a yard when used for the storage, manufacture or maintenance of freezer plant units which resulted in an appreciable rise in noise and fumes, present on a daily basis. In *Lanigan & Benghazi v Barry*, unreported, High Court, Charleton J., February 15 2008, where planning permission existed for three hours of racing on a Saturday or Sunday from April to October but the racing track was used all year round for up to 10 times the permitted number of hours per month, this amounted to a significant intensification of use by the nature and duration of the activity.

An ancillary use may intensify to such an extent that it ceases to be ancillary and becomes an independent use. In *Trio Thames Ltd v Secretary of State for the Environment and Reading Borough Council* [1984] J.P.L. 183, it was said:

"The Encyclopaedia of Planning, in paragraph 2-816, put it in these terms: 'The ancillary link may be lost also where the ancillary use grows to the point where it can no longer be said to be ancillary, but to have become a separate use in its own right. The consequence may be that the former ancillary use has supplanted the former primary use, or the land may now have a dual use, or it may have been split into two separate planning units'."

The ancillary use may therefore intensify so as to amount to a material change of use. See *Jillings v Secretary of State for the Environment* [1984] JPL 32; *Jones v Secretary of State for Environment* [1974] 28 P & CR 362 and *Burdle v Secretary of State for the Environment* [1972] 1 WLR 1207.

While the natural growth of a business may not in itself render a use unlawful, different considerations apply where the use or structure whose use has grown is itself unauthorised. See *Cork County Council v Slattery Pre-Cast Concrete Ltd*, unreported, High Court, Clarke J., September 19, 2008.

Abandonment

Where a use of land is abandoned any recommencement will amount to a material change of use. In *Sligo County Council v Martin,* unreported, High Court, O'Neill, May 24, 2007, where a mobile home in place since 1972 was replaced by new mobile home in 2000 and replaced again by a new mobile home in 2005 with the same dimension as the 1972 mobile home, it was held that the removal of the home in 2000 was a permanent change and the new mobile home in 2005 could not be regarded as the care or maintenance of the original mobile home with the intent that it would be replaced. A cessation of use will not in itself amount to abandonment, where there is an intention to resume the use, see *Dublin County Council v Tallaght Block Co. Ltd* [1982] I.L.R.M. 469, where the use of a site for block manufacturing resumed after eight years was held to be a material change of use. Whether there is such an intention to abandon is an objective test, to be inferred from the conduct of the user rather than his subjective state of mind, see *Kildare County Council v Goode* [1999] 2 I.R. 495.

Where a mill was destroyed by fire, the permission to use the premises also perished. See *Galway County Council v Connaught Proteins Limited*, unreported, High Court, March 28, 1980. In *Dublin Corporation v Lowe & Signways*, unreported, High Court, Morris P., February 4, 2000, the deliberate removal of an advertisement hoarding constituted an abandonment and it was irrelevant that it was subsequently replaced by a hoarding of the identical dimensions. See also *Fingal County Council v Crean*, unreported, High Court, Ó Caoimh J., October 19, 2001.

In *Cork County Council v Artfert Quarries Ltd*, unreported, High Court, Murphy J., December 2, 1982, where there was a lapse of four years in the use of an industrial building and an absence of a satisfactory explanation, the use was held to have been abandoned. In *Meath County Council v Daly* [1987] I.R. 391, the use of premises for car repairs and petrol sales was held to have been abandoned since 1964, when it had been used intermittently but from 1969 was used for some years by a double glazing company. In *McGrath Limestone Works v Galway County Council* [1989] I.L.R.M. 602, the Supreme Court rejected that use of a site for quarrying had been abandoned when planning permission had been granted for growing mushrooms in 1983 on 5 per cent of the site. It was held the permission for growing mushrooms had not been implemented and had ceased after only two years. A change of ownership of lands will not in itself mean there has been an abandonment of use. The nature of the owner, whether an individual, company or otherwise, is irrelevant, see *Furlong v AF & GW McConnell* [1990] I.L.R.M. 48. Although in *Dublin County Council v Tallaght Block Co.* [1982] I.L.R.M. 469, reference was made to cessation of use for a considerable period of time, it is clear that a short period of non-use can amount to an abandonment of use. See also *Dublin Corporation v Lowe & Signways*, unreported, High Court, Morris P., February 4, 2000. An existing user may be supplanted by a planning permission which is implemented. See *Westmeath County Council v Quirke & Sons*, unreported, High Court, Budd J., May 23, 1996.

The better view is that a valid planning permission itself cannot be abandoned (as opposed to the use under that permission) and will subsist for the life of the planning permission until it expires, see *Meath County Council v Daly* [1988] I.L.R.M. 274. In *Molloy v Minister for Equality and Law Reform* [2004] 2 I.R. 493, it was held that that a valid planning permission for a specific use of land could not be lost or abandoned where the original planning permission was capable of being implemented, notwithstanding that there had been a material unauthorised change of use in the meantime. Section 40(2)(b) provides that notwithstanding the life of a permission, the continuance of use will not be affected. However, this is in conflict with *Westmeath County Council v Quirke & Sons*, unreported, High Court, Budd J., May 23, 1996, where Budd J. suggested that a permission could be abandoned. However, see *Pioneer Aggregates (UK) v Secretary of State for the Environment* [1985] A.C. 132, where the House of Lords rejected the view that a valid planning permission could be abandoned.

Exempted development

1–04   **4.—(1)** The following shall be exempted developments for the purposes of this *Act* —

(a) development consisting of the use of any land for the purpose of agriculture and development consisting of the use for that purpose of any building occupied together with land so used;

(b) development by the council of a county in its functional area, exclusive of any borough or urban district;

(c) development by the corporation of a county or other borough in that borough;

(d) development by the council of an urban district in that district;

(e) development consisting of the carrying out by the corporation of a county or other borough or the council of a county or an urban district of any works required for the construction of a new road or the maintenance or improvement of a road;

(f) development carried out on behalf of, or jointly or in partnership with, a local authority that is a planning authority, pursuant to a contract entered into by the local authority concerned, whether in its capacity as a planning authority or in any other capacity;

(g) development consisting of the carrying out by any local authority or statutory undertaker of any works for the purpose of inspecting, repairing, renewing, altering or removing any sewers, mains, pipes, cables, overhead wires, or other apparatus, including the excavation of any street or other land for that purpose;

(h) development consisting of the carrying out of works for the maintenance, improvement or other alteration of any structure, being works which affect only the interior of the structure or which do not materially affect the external appearance of the structure so as to render the appearance inconsistent with the character of the structure or of neighbouring structures;

(i) development consisting of the thinning, felling and replanting of trees, forests and woodlands, the construction, maintenance and improvement of non-public roads serving forests and woodlands and works ancillary to that development, not including the replacement of broadleaf high forest by conifer species;

(j) development consisting of the use of any structure or other land within the curtilage of a house for any purpose incidental to the enjoyment of the house as such;

(k) development consisting of the use of land for the purposes of a casual trading area (within the meaning of the *Casual Trading Act, 1995*);

(l) development consisting of the carrying out of any of the works referred to in the *Land Reclamation Act, 1949,* not being works comprised in the fencing or enclosure of land which has been open to or used by the public within the ten years preceding the date on which the works are commenced.

(2)

(a) The Minister may by regulations provide for any class of development to be exempted development for the purposes of this *Act* where he or she is of the opinion that—

(i) by reason of the size, nature or limited effect on its surroundings, of development belonging to that class, the carrying out of such development would not offend against principles of proper planning and sustainable development, or

(ii) the development is authorised, or is required to be authorised, by or under any enactment (whether the authorisation takes the form of the grant of a licence, consent, approval or any other type of authorisation) where the enactment concerned requires there to be consultation (howsoever described) with members of the public in relation to the proposed development prior to the granting of the authorisation (howsoever described).

(b) *Regulations* under *paragraph (a)* may be subject to conditions and be of general application or apply to such area or place as may be specified in the regulations.

(c) *Regulations* under this *subsection* may, in particular and without prejudice to the generality of *paragraph (a),* provide, in the case of structures or other land used for a purpose of any specified class, for the use thereof for any other purpose being exempted development for the purposes of this Act.

(3) A reference in this Act to exempted development shall be construed as a reference to development which is—

(a) any of the developments specified in *subsection (1),* or

(b) development which, having regard to any regulations under *subsection (2),* is exempted development for the purposes of this Act.

(4) The Minister may, in connection with the Council Directive, prescribe

development or classes of development which, notwithstanding *subsection (1)(a),* shall not be exempted development.

(5) Before making regulations under this section, the Minister shall consult with any other State authority where he or she or that other State authority considers that any such regulation relates to the functions of that State authority.

NOTE

This section concerns exempted development. A development which would otherwise require planning permission will not require such permission where it falls within a category of exempted development: see s.32(a). Where development is exempted it is not necessary to obtain planning permission. Subsection (1) enlists 12 specific categories of exempted development. Under subs.(2) the Minister is also empowered to declare certain development to be exempted by way of regulation. In this respect arts 5–11 of the 2001 Regulations set out the additional categories of exempted development and various conditions attaching to such exempted development. An extensive list of categories and the conditions attaching to them are set out in Sch.2 to the 2001 Regulations. Under s.5, a declaration may be sought from a planning authority as to whether a development is exempted development, with an appeal to An Bord Pleanála. The fact that development is exempted development may also confer benefits under legislation. For example, the Building Control Regulations 1997 provides at s.7(2)(a)(i), that there is no requirement to obtain a valid commencement, prior to carrying out works on a building, where the works or the material change of use is exempted development.

In any enforcement proceedings it appears that the burden of proof is on a developer to prove that a development is within a category of exempted development. In *Dillon v Irish Cement Ltd*, unreported, Supreme Court, November 26, 1986, the Supreme Court held that regulations granting exemptions "should be strictly construed" and a developer must "clearly and unambiguously" come within the exemption. However, see the comments of Morris P. in *Westport UDC v Golden* [2002] 1 I.L.R.M. 439 where it was suggested the onus was on the applicant. See also *Dublin Corporation v Regan Advertising* [1989] I.R. 61 and *Carroll & Colley v Brushfields Ltd*, unreported, High Court, Lynch J., October 9, 1992. Reviewing the case law in *South Dublin County Council v Fallowvale Ltd*, unreported, High Court, McKechnie J., April 28, 2005, McKechnie J. considered the preponderance of authority was that where a development is sought to be excused as exempted development, "then the onus of establishing this point is upon he who asserts". While strictly speaking the onus being on the applicant to show a development is not exempted development would appear consistent with the onus being on the applicant to show a matter is unauthorised development, the matter is complicated by the fact that this would involve proving a negative, i.e. that a matter is not exempted development. Since an applicant could not be expected to make an argument for the developer that a matter may be exempted development, it will be the role of the developer to identify the relevant category or reason why a development is exempted.

The categories of development which are exempted under s.4 cover a multifarious range from ordinary activities to specialist activities or relating to identity of the body carrying out the particular development. Section 4(1)(a) refers to the use of land for agricultural purposes. This should be read as a change in use of land. The definition of land indicates that this includes the use of buildings on the land for agricultural purposes. The definition excludes turbary rights which would include peat extraction and bog drainage. An environmental impact statement ("EIS") may be required for certain large agricultural and afforestation activities, which means they will not constitute exempted development. See Pt II of Sch.10 to the 2001 Regulations. Much of the other categories of exempt development relate to activities carried out by the local authority including under subs.(b)–(d) whereby the planning authority need not seek permission to carry out development. However, a planning authority cannot carry out development which is in material contravention of the development plan. Under s.179 and Pt 8 of the Planning Regulations 2001, a separate consultation procedure is prescribed for certain local authority development. Other categories of exempted development carried out by the local authority include: subs.(e), the construction of a new road or the maintenance or improvement of a road (s.51 of the Roads Act 1993 provides that a proposed new road development shall not be carried out without the approval of the Minister, which approval is now required from An Bord Pleanála, under s.214); subs.(f), development carried out on behalf of, or jointly with, or in partnership with, a local authority relating to its functions; and subs.(g) development consisting of the carrying out of works by any local authority or statutory undertaker concerning any sewers, mains, pipes, cables, overhead wires, or other apparatus, including the excavation of any street. For the definition of statutory undertaker, see s.2.

As regards categories of exempted development open to all developers, one of the most important is category s.4(1)(h) concerning works for the maintenance, improvement or other alteration of any structure, being works which or which do not materially affect the external appearance of the structure so as to render the appearance inconsistent with the character of the structure or of neighbouring structures. This exemption is confined to "works" and does not apply to "uses". It is clear there are several elements to this category, which are:

*   it must concern works for the maintenance, improvement or other alteration of any structure (it does not cover a material change of use);
*   the works must only affect the interior of the structure or if they affect the exterior, it is not to such a material degree as to render the appearance inconsistent with the character of structure or of neighbouring structures.

This category is further qualified in relation to protected structures under s.57. The renewal or reconstruction of a part or of parts of a structure may be covered by the provisions of s.4(1)(h) of the Act of 2000 provided that the extent of that renewal or reconstruction is not such as to amount to the total or substantial replacement or rebuilding of the original structure. See *McCabe v Córas Iompair Éireann* [2007] 2 I.R. 392. The notion of intensification of use is to be distinguished from extensification of use in that intensification concerns an increase in the volume of the business, while extensification involves the incorporation of additional lands into the business even where they may not be an increase in overall volume of the business. See *Cork County Council v Slattery Pre-Cast Concrete Ltd*, unreported, High Court, Clarke J., September 19, 2008.

The mere fact that works materially affect the external appearance of a structure does not necessarily mean it is inconsistent with the character of the house itself or adjoining houses. In *Cairnduff v O'Connell* [1986] I.R. 73, Finlay C.J. said at 77 that "the test as to whether works materially affect the external appearance of the structure does not in any way depend on whether they affect that appearance for better or for worse". Finlay C.J. considered that the character of a terraced house would be much more dominantly affected by its street appearance than by its rear appearance. Furthermore, the character of the structure must relate to the shape, colour, design, ornamental feature and layout of the structure concerned.

In examining whether it is consistent with the character of the structure, the court will seek to compare the work with the type of building in which it takes place. In *Dublin Corporation v Bentham* [1993] 2 I.R. 58, Morris J. held the removal of Georgian windows and replacement with new aluminium windows not only affected the interior of the structure but also the exterior. The works will fall outside the category of exempted development where the works, even if not inconsistent with the character of the structure in which they take place, are inconsistent with the character of adjoining property; see *Dublin Corporation v O'Dwyer Bros*, unreported, High Court, Kelly J., May 2, 1997. The erection of two outside ducts was held not inconsistent with the character of structure or adjoining structures in *Westport UDC v Golden* [2002] 1 I.L.R.M. 439. In *McCabe v Córas Iompair Éireann* [2007] 2 I.R. 392, it was held that the replacement of a brick and stone arch bridge with a new flat rectangular pre-cast concrete deck structure was exempted development under s.4(1)(h). It was considered the character of a structure is assessed by looking objectively at the entity as a whole. All the features of the structure taken together and their interaction with each other, give a structure its character, although there may be exceptional cases in which a single feature is so outstandingly remarkable or so important from an aesthetic, architectural or engineering perspective, that it could properly and rationally be said to derive its entire character from that single feature.

Other categories of exempted development include: s.4(i), thinning, felling and replanting of trees, forests and woodlands (certain developments of this nature may require an EIS); and s.4(j), the use of any structure or other land within the curtilage of a house for any purpose incidental to the enjoyment of the house as such. Under this category, the structure or land must (a) be within the curtilage of a house and (b) be used for a purpose incidental enjoyment of the house. Grounds will be considered to be within the curtilage of a house where it is within the comfortable enjoyment of the house or serves the house or building in some necessary or useful way; see *Sinclair Lockhart's Trustees v Central Land Board* [1951] S.C. 358 and *Mathuen-Campbell v Walters* [1979] Q.B. 543. Smallness may be an aspect of curtilage; see *Dyer v Dorset County Council* [1988] 3 W.L.R. 213 and *McAlpine v Secretary of State for the Environment* [1995] J.P.L.B. 43. Buildings in different ownership may be deemed within the same curtilage; see *Attorney-General v Calderdale Borough Council* [1983] 46 P & C.R. 399. The question of what was within the curtilage, is a question of fact and degree. See *Skeritts of Nottingham Ltd v Secretary of State for the Environment* [2001] Q.B. 59. There must be sufficient connection between the use and the house. The parking of a car would appear to be sufficiently connected; see *Dublin Corporation v Moore* [1984] I.L.R.M. 339. Part I of the Second Schedule to the 2001 Regulations sets out several classes of exemptions for development within the curtilage of a house. For the definition of house, see s.2. Also s.4(k) concerns use of land for casual trading, while (l) refers to works under the Land Reclamation Act 1949. Under the 1949 Act, land reclamation is works carried out by the Minister either at the request of the occupier or at the Minister's initiative. See *Tralee UDC v Stack*, unreported, High Court, Barrington J., January 13, 1984. The primary object of the work must be to carry out land reclamation. See *Lennon v Kingdom Plant Hire Ltd*, unreported, High Court, Morris J., December 13, 1991, where the primary object was to gather boulders rather than improve the land. An exemption for land reclamation is also allowed under the 2001 Regulations under Class 11 of Pt III of the Second Schedule. See also *Dolan v Cooke*, unreported, Supreme Court, April 6, 2001.

Section 163 provides that development required by enforcement proceedings is exempted development, as are works required under a restoration or endangerment notice, under s.68.

Exempted Development under the Planning Regulations

As regards the categories under the 2001 Regulations, Pt I of the Second Schedule is entitled General and includes such matters as development within the curtilage of a house (classes 1–8) which includes house extensions where the floor area of any extension should not exceed 40 square metres; sundry works to a house, building or roadway (classes 9–13); change of use of a premises (class 14); temporary structures and uses (classes 15–20); development for industrial purposes (classes 21–22); development by statutory undertakers (defined under s.2) (classes 23–32); development for amenity or recreational purposes (classes 33–37); and miscellaneous (classes 38–55). Part II of the Second Schedule is solely devoted to advertisements. Part III is entitled Rural, while Pt IV of the Second Schedule concerns classes of use contained in classes 1–11, in which changes in use are considered exempted development. Article 10 of the Regulations also describes certain other development as exempted.

Article 9 of the Planning Regulations 2001 applies important restrictions to exempted development, whereby the status of certain development as exempted is lost where certain conditions apply. Twelve such conditions are enlisted which include if the development would contravene a condition attached to a permission under the Act or be inconsistent with any use specified in a permission under the Act. The condition need not be attached to a planning permission relating to the premises in which the development is to be carried out. See *Doolan v Murray*, unreported, High Court, Keane J., December 21, 1993. In *Dublin Corporation v Bord Telecom* [2002] 3 I.R. 327, Carroll J. held that an antennae structure did not come within the class of exemption of antennae support structures under the regulations, as it was erected on the area for some of the parking places to be provided under a condition of an earlier planning permission. Other conditions, inter alia, include the formation, laying out or material widening of a means of access to a public road the surfaced carriageway of which exceeds four metres in width; endangering public safety by reason of traffic hazard or obstruction of road users; interference with the character of a landscape, or a view or prospect of special amenity value or special interest, the preservation of which is an objective of a development plan; the extension, alteration, repair or renewal of an unauthorised structure; and obstructing any public right of way.

Exempted development under other statutes

Development may also be exempted development under certain other statutes. Under s.54(4)(a) of the Waste Management Act 1996 works consisting of or incidental to the carrying out of the development for the purpose of giving effect to a condition attached to a licence granted by the Environmental Protection Agency is exempted development. Under s.38 of the Transport (Railway Infrastructure) Act 2001 (No. 55 of 2001), works which are the subject of a railway order are exempted, more particularly:

> "(a) development consisting of the carrying out of railway works, including the use of the railway works or any part thereof for the purposes of the operation of a railway, authorised by the Minister and specified in a railway order or of any incidental or temporary works connected with such development; (b) development consisting of the carrying out of railway works for the maintenance, improvement or repair of a railway that has been built pursuant to a railway order."

See also s.19(6) of the Roads Act 1993; s.11(6) of the Derelict Sites Act 1990; and s.25 of the Dublin Docklands Development Authority Act 1997.

Declaration and referral on development and exempted development

5.—**(1)** If any question arises as to what, in any particular case, is or is not development or is or is not exempted development within the meaning of this Act, any person may, on payment of the prescribed fee, request in writing from the relevant planning authority a declaration on that question, and that person shall provide to the planning authority any information necessary to enable the authority to make its decision on the matter. **1–05**

(2)

    (a) Subject to *paragraph (b),* a planning authority shall issue the declaration on the question that has arisen and the main reasons and considerations on which its decision is based to the person who made the request under *subsection (1),* and, where appropriate, the owner and occupier of the land in question, within 4 weeks of the receipt of the request.

    (b) A planning authority may require any person who made a request under *subsection (1)* to submit further information with regard to the request in order to enable the authority to issue the declaration on the question and, where further information is received under this paragraph, the planning authority shall issue the declaration within 3 weeks of the date of the receipt of the further information.

    (c) A planning authority may also request persons in addition to those referred to in *paragraph (b)* to submit information in order to enable the authority to issue the declaration on the question.

(3)

    (a) Where a declaration is issued under this section, any person issued with a declaration under *subsection (2)(a)* may, on payment to the Board of such fee as may be prescribed, refer a declaration for review by the Board within 4 weeks of the date of the issuing of the declaration.

    (b) Without prejudice to *subsection (2),* in the event that no declaration is issued by the planning authority, any person who made a request under *subsection (1)* may, on payment to the Board of such fee as may be prescribed, refer the question for decision to the Board within

4 weeks of the date that a declaration was due to be issued under *subsection (2)*.

(4) Notwithstanding *subsection (1),* a planning authority may, on payment to the Board of such fee as may be prescribed, refer any question as to what, in any particular case, is or is not development or is or is not exempted development to be decided by the Board.

(5) The details of any declaration issued by a planning authority or of a decision by the Board on a referral under this section shall be entered in the register.

(6)

(a) The Board shall keep a record of any decision made by it on a referral under this section and the main reasons and considerations on which its decision is based and shall make it available for purchase and inspection.

(b) The Board may charge a specified fee, not exceeding the cost of making the copy, for the purchase of a copy of the record referred to in *paragraph (a)*.

(c) The Board shall, from time to time and at least once a year, forward to each planning authority a copy of the record referred to in *paragraph (a)*.

(d) A copy of the said record shall, at the request of a member of a planning authority, be given to that member by the manager of the planning authority concerned.

(7) A planning authority, before making a declaration under this section, shall consider the record forwarded to it in accordance with *subsection (6)(c)*.

NOTE

This section sets out a procedure to determine whether a matter constitutes development and/or whether it constitutes exempted development. The procedure assists in determining whether an application for planning permission is required to be made; if a matter is development and is not exempted development, planning permission, will be required. The procedure may also be invoked where enforcement action is threatened or even intiatied. While the determination of s.5 referral will not declare that a development is unauthorised development, this may be the direct implications of such determination. Where it is determined that a development is not authorised under a planning permission and is not exempted development, then ipso facto it is unauthorised development. The procedure allows the determination as to whether a development falls within the scope of an existing planning permission. See *Palmerlane Ltd v An Bord Pleanála* [1999] 1 I.L.R.M. 514 and *Grianán An Áileach v Donegal County Council* [2004] 2 I.R. 265. It does not however concern whether or not planning permission would ultimately be granted. See *Glancree Teoranta v Cafferkey*, unreported, High Court, Laffoy J., April 26, 2004. The determination under a section 5 reference involves a clarification of an existing situation by determining the precise planning status of a matter. The procedure is not confined to an existing development but can relate to a future development. Thus in advance of carrying out a development, a person can make a referral by submitting certain plans of a proposed development. The procedure under the section differs from s.5 of the previous legislation, which simply provided for a referral to An Bord Pleanála and an appeal on a point of law to the High Court. Instead, the procedure provides that a declaration must first be sought from the planning authority, with an appeal to be made to An Bord Pleanála. Under the previous s.5, the planning authority was precluded from determining whether a matter is development or exempted development; see *Dublin Corporation v McGrath*, unreported, High Court, McMahon J., November 17, 1978. The section also abolishes the procedure of an appeal to the High Court from the determination by An Bord Pleanála. Judicial review proceedings taken in respect of the appeal to An Bord Pleanála will be on the basis of the restricted judicial review procedure in s.50. The question for determination may involve both a legal and factual determination. Where the Board misinterprets a statutory provision in applying it to particular facts, the Court may quash the decision on the basis that it erred in law. See *Córas Iompair Éireann v An Bord Pleanála*, unreported, High Court, Clarke J., June 19, 2008. It would also appear that the interpretation of the nature or scope of a category of exempted development involves an issue of law and so where the planning authority or Board misinterprets such category, the court will not defer to its opinion. However, in dealing with a reference as to whether the intensification of a pre-1964 use, amounts to a material change of use, there must be first, a factual finding of a change of use and secondly, a finding of materiality of such change of use. See *Roadstone v An Bord Pleanála* unreported, High Court, Finlay Geogheghan J., July 4, 2008, where the court quashed the decision due to the absence of any factual finding.

However, in court proceedings, in an enforcement action such as under s.160, a court will not be precluded from determining whether a matter is development; see *State (Stafford and Son) v Roadstone Ltd* [1980] I.L.R.M. 1 and *Carrick Hall Holdings v Dublin Corporation* [1983] I.L.R.M. 268. In *Grianán An Áileach v Donegal County Council* [2004] 2 I.R. 265, the Supreme Court held that in the light of s.5, the High Court generally had no jurisdiction to make a declaration, in judicial review proceedings as to whether or not a matter was development or exempted development. To hold otherwise would lead to overlapping or unworkable jurisdictions. Two exceptions to this would be first, where enforcement proceedings were brought in the High Court, where it might determine whether there had been a material change of use or whether a development was sanctioned by an existing planning permission, as in *O'Connor v Kerry County Council* [1988] I.L.R.M. 660 (see also *State (Stafford and Son) v Roadstone Ltd* [1980] I.L.R.M. 1 and *Carrick Hall Holdings v Dublin Corporation* [1983] I.L.R.M. 268) and secondly, a court may be called upon to determine such question where a commercial or conveyancing document containing a particular term dealing with compliance with planning requirements, was the subject of litigation. See also the obiter comments of Geoghegan J. in the Supreme Court in *O'Mara v Van Morrison*, unreported, Supreme Court, Geoghegan J., October 13, 2003.

Subsection (1) provides that on the payment of a fee, a person may request in writing from the planning authority a declaration as to whether a matter is or is not development or is or is not exempted development. No specific procedure is prescribed as to the information to be contained in the request, simply providing that it must supply the information necessary. Section 127 specifies the general form in which any referral must take which would include a section 5 referral. In *O'Reilly v Wicklow County Council*, unreported, High Court, Quirke J., November 22, 2006, the Court rejected that a section 5 referral to An Bord Pleanála did not comply with s.127 insofar as it did not state in full the grounds of referral and the reasons, considerations and arguments on which they are based. While the documentation submitted to the Board was of poor quality, the Board was prepared to carry out a search of the documents to discover the "reasons, considerations and argument". It was held that while the requirements of s.127 were mandatory, the grounds did not have to be contained in a single document but could be within a series of documents and submitted in an informal manner. It appears that the request must be in the form of a question as to whether a matter is or is not development or exempted development. The planning authority and Board are not strictly confined to the question referred as in *Esat Digifone v South Dublin County Council* [2002] 3 I.R. 585, Kearns J. rejected that the Board could not alter the question asked in order to clarify the issue. Subsection (1) allows "any person" to seek a declaration and it would appear from this that persons other than the developer or the planning authority can seek such a declaration. Some doubt existed regarding the entitlement of a third party under the previous section: see *Fairyhouse v An Bord Pleanála & Meath County Council*, unreported, High Court, Finnegan J., July 18, 2001. In *Córas Iompair Éireann v An Bord Pleanála*, unreported, *ex tempore*, Murphy J., July 5, 2006, it was held that a third party such as An Taisce, could make a Section 5 reference in respect of development which occurred prior to March 11, 2002 (when the 2000 Act entered into force), as this was not giving retrospective effect to the 2000 Act. There is no public notice requirement nor is there provision for submissions by third parties. In a particular case, natural and constitutional justice may require that a third party has a right to make submissions in certain circumstances. This may most clearly arise where a party not carrying out a development makes a referral concerning the status of the development. In such case the developer should be informed of the referral and afforded an opportunity to make submissions. Failure to afford a developer such opportunity may result in a decision of the planning authority being quashed for absence of fair procedures as was the case in *Córas Iompair Éireann v Kildare County Council*, unreported, *ex tempore*, High Court, Murphy J., October 2005. Under s.134 the Board may at its absolute discretion permit an oral hearing to be held in a section 5 referral.

Subsection (2) provides that the planning authority must issue the declaration within four weeks of the request and the declaration must give the reasons and considerations upon which it is based. In arriving at its declaration, the planning authority must take into account the record of decisions on references given by An Bord Pleanála under s.5(7). Before issuing the declaration, the planning authority may request information from the appellant or from any other person. As with a request for further information concerning a planning application, the request should be a genuine request and not simply to delay time. See *State (Conlon Construction Limited) v Cork County Council*, unreported, High Court, Butler J., July 31, 1975 and *State (NCE Limited) v Dublin County Council* [1979] I.L.R.M. 249. Where the planning authority fails to issue the request within the prescribed time limits, there is no default mechanism or even sanction against the planning authority for its failure, except that under subs.(3)(b), a person can refer the matter to An Board Pleanála for a decision without waiting for the declaration of the planning authority. A default mechanism such as default planning permission is not appropriate due to the fact that it is essentially a question posed rather than an application.

Subsection (3) states that where a declaration is issued a person can within four weeks ask the Board to review the declaration. The language of the subsection used is that of a review rather than an appeal. As noted where the planning authority fails to make a declaration within the time limit, a person then has four weeks to refer the matter to An Bord Pleanála.

Subsection (4) concerns the fee for a declaration. Schedule 10 of the 2001 Regulations specifies the fee as being €80, while the fee for referral to the Board after December 10, 2007 is €220.

Subsection (5) provides that the details of the decision on the declaration or referral are to be issued in the planning register under s.8

Subsection (6) states that in making a decision on a reference, the Board must give its reasons and the considerations for the decision. It also provides that the Board must keep a record of its decisions, which can be valuable as precedents. These records can be made available to the public for inspection or a copy can be obtained for a fee. A copy of the records must also be forwarded to each planning authority annually and a copy of such must be given to a member of the planning authority, if he so requests, by the Manager of the planning authority. Subsection (6)(d) is not clearly drafted but it appears that a copy is to be given to a member deriving from the annual records sent to the planning authority rather than a copy coming from the An Bord Pleanála via the Manager. In making its decision, the Board need not give extensive reasons, though it must be sufficient to enable a person to formulate any claim for judicial review; see *Fairyhouse v An Bord Pleanála & Meath County Council*, unreported, High Court, Finnegan J., July 18, 2001.

Subsection (7), provides that in making a declaration the planning authority must have regard to the record of decisions on references issued by An Bord Pleanála.

It appears that both the Board and the planning authority have jurisdiction to decide on a declaration or reference even where the event has already taken place at the date of the decision; see *Fairyhouse v An Bord Pleanála & Meath County Council*, unreported, High Court, Finnegan J., July 18, 2001.

The Board has no jurisdiction on a reference under s.5(4) of the Act to determine what is or is not "unauthorised development. See *Roadstone v An Bord Pleanála*, unreported, High Court, Finlay Geoghegan J., July 4, 2008. However, where the planning authority and/or Board determines that an existing development is development and is not exempted development with the implication that it is unauthorised development and enforcement action is subsequently taken, it has yet to be determined whether a court is bound by such determination. It would appear the better view is that such determination is not legally binding on the court but will be of strong persuasive value. As a Section 5 referral is not strictly part of the enforcement function of a planning authority so there is no inconsistency in accepting that weight must be attached to determination even where enforcement action is taken by the same planning authority.

Power of examination, investigation and survey

6.—A planning authority and the Board shall each have all such powers of examination, investigation and survey as may be necessary for the performance of their functions in relation to this Act or to any other Act.   1–06

NOTE

This section is of general application, and affords to the planning authority and Board such powers of examination, investigation and survey necessary to perform its functions. The powers granted are not confined to the functions performed under the 2000 Act, but also extend to its functions under other legislation. The powers granted are wide ranging, with no definition of what is "necessary" provided. The section may best be understood as conferring a residual power on the planning authority and Board to carry out such examinations, investigations and surveys which are ancillary to the specific functions performed by the planning authority and the Board. Section 253 sets out the procedure for a person authorised by a planning authority to enter land. A similar power was in s.6(1) of the 1963 Act.

Planning register

7.—**(1)** A planning authority shall keep a register for the purposes of this Act in respect of all land within its functional area, and shall make all such entries and corrections therein as may be appropriate in accordance with *subsection (2),* and the other provisions of this Act and the regulations made under this Act.   1–07

(2) A planning authority shall enter in the register—
   (a) particulars of any application made to it under this Act for permission for development, for retention of development or for outline permission for development (including the name and address of the applicant, the date of receipt of the application and brief particulars of the development or retention forming the subject of the application),
   (b) where an environmental impact statement was submitted in respect of an application, an indication of this fact,
   (c) where a development, to which an application relates, comprises or is for the purposes of an activity in respect of which an integrated pollution control licence or a waste management licence is required, or a licence under the Local Government (Water Pollution) Act, 1977, is required in respect of discharges from the development, a statement as to that requirement,
   (d) where the development to which the application relates would materially affect a protected structure or is situated in an area declared to be an area of special amenity under section 202, an indication of this fact,
   (e) the complete decision of the planning authority in respect of any

such application, including any conditions imposed, and the date of the decision,

(f) the complete decision on appeal of the Board in respect of any such application, including any conditions imposed, and the date of the decision,

(g) where the requirements of *section 34 (6)* in regard to the material contravention of the development plan have been complied with, a statement of this fact,

(h) particulars of any declaration made by a planning authority under *section 5* or any decision made by the Board on a referral under that *section,*

(i) particulars of any application made under *section 42* to extend the appropriate period of a permission,

(j) particulars of any decision to revoke or modify a permission in accordance with *section 44,*

(k) particulars under *section 45* of any order, of any decision on appeal or of any acquisition notice for compulsory acquisition of land for open space,

(l) particulars of any notice under *section 46* requiring removal or alteration of any structure, or requiring discontinuance of any use or the imposition of conditions on the continuance thereof, including the fact of its withdrawal, if appropriate,

(m) particulars of any agreement made under *section 47* for the purpose of restricting or regulating the development or use of the land,

(n) particulars of any declaration issued by the planning authority under *section 57,* including the details of any review of the declaration,

(o) particulars of any declaration issued by the planning authority under *section 87,* including the details of any review of the declaration,

(p) particulars of any notice under *section 88* in respect of land in an area of special planning control, including, where such notice is withdrawn, the fact of its withdrawal,

(q) particulars of any certificate granted under *section 97,*

(r) particulars of any warning letter issued under *section 152,* including the date of issue of the letter and the fact of its withdrawal, if appropriate,

(s) the complete decision made under *section 153* on whether an enforcement notice should issue, including the date of the decision,

(t) particulars of any enforcement notice issued under *section 154,* including the date of the notice and the fact of its withdrawal or that it has been complied with, if appropriate,

[(tt)particulars of any development referred to in *section 179(4)(b),*]

(u) particulars of any statement prepared under *section 188* concerning a claim for compensation under this *Act,*

(v) particulars of any order under *section 205* requiring the preservation of any tree or trees, including the fact of any amendment or revocation of the order,

(w) particulars of any agreement under *section 206* for the creation of a public right of way over land,

(**x**) particulars of any public right of way created by order under *section 207,*

(**y**) particulars of any information relating to the operation of a quarry provided in accordance with *section 261,* and

(**z**) any other matters as may be prescribed by the Minister.

(**3**) The planning authority shall make the entries and corrections as soon as may be after the receipt of any application, the making of any decision or agreement or the issue of any letter, notice or statement, as appropriate.

(**4**) The register shall incorporate a map for enabling a person to trace any entry in the register.

(**5**) The planning authority may keep the information on the register, including the map incorporated under *subsection (4),* in a form in which it is capable of being used to make a legible copy or reproduction of any entry in the register.

(**6**)

(**a**) The register shall be kept at the offices of the planning authority and shall be available for inspection during office hours.

(**b**) The Minister may prescribe additional requirements in relation to the availability for inspection by members of the public of the register.

(**7**) Every document purporting to be a copy of an entry in a register maintained by a planning authority under this *section* and purporting to be certified by an officer of the planning authority to be a true copy of the entry shall, without proof of the signature of the person purporting so to certify or that he or she was such an officer, be received in evidence in any legal proceedings and shall, until the contrary is proved, be deemed to be a true copy of the entry and to be evidence of the terms of the entry.

(**8**) Evidence of an entry in a register under this *section* may be given by production of a copy thereof certified pursuant to this *section* and it shall not be necessary to produce the register itself.

(**9**) Where an application is made to a planning authority for a copy under this *section,* the copy shall be issued to the applicant on payment by him or her to the planning authority of the specified fee in respect of each entry.

AMENDMENT HISTORY

Subsection (2)(tt) inserted by s.7 of the Planning and Development (Strategic Infrastructure) Act 2006 (No. 27 of 2006).

NOTE

This section relates to the planning register which constitutes a record of various decisions and applications made or received by the planning authority. The planning register may be of importance to conveyancers in making enquires concerning the status of certain land. It is common practice for parties to carry out a planning search prior to the exchange of contracts. In this respect the Planning Register is not entirely comprehensive for the purposes of the planning search; other registers, such as the Building Control Act Register and the Derelict Sites Act Register, should be examined. It is also common for planning matters to be raised in pre-contract enquiries. Each planning authority is obliged to keep a planning register and make the changes where appropriate. A person is entitled to act on the basis of the correctness of the register. Also, the contents of the register must be construed objectively on the basis that it is a public document. See *Readymix (Éire) Ltd v Dublin County Council*, unreported, Supreme Court, July 30, 1974, where Henchy J. declared, "Since the permission notified to an applicant and entered in the register is a public document, it must be construed objectively as such, and not in the light of subjective considerations special to the applicant or those responsible for the grant of permission. Because the permission is an appendage to the title to the property, it may possibly not arise for interpretation until the property has passed into the hands of those who have no knowledge of any special circumstances in which it was granted."

The register also constitutes an important statutory record of pending planning application. See *Linehan v Cork County Council*, unreported, High Court, Finlay Geoghegan J., February 19, 2008, where it was distinguished from the weekly list kept under art.27 of the the the 2001 Regulations and also a voluntary internet planning enquiry system. The precise form in which the register must be kept is not specifically prescribed, although subs.(5) provides that the planning authority may keep the register in a form in which it is capable of being used to make a legible copy or reproduction of entry in the register. In practice many planning authorities do not maintain a separate written register, but maintain an enquiry system in electronic form and an archive of planning files. However, planning files are required to be maintained under s.38 and while the public may not be prejudiced by failing to maintain a separate written register, it is doubtful whether this practice is in strict compliance with the obligation to maintain a register under this section.

The inclusion of planning permissions in the register is important as, under s.39(1), planning permissions enures for the benefit of the land. The planning permission may incorporate other documents which may be considered in determining the scope of the permission; see *Readymix (Éire) Ltd v Dublin County Council*, unreported, Supreme Court, July 30, 1974; *Jack Barrett Builders Ltd v Dublin County Council*, unreported, Supreme Court, July 28, 1983; *Coffey v Hebron Homes Ltd*, unreported, High Court, O'Hanlon J., July 27, 1984 and *Glancree Teoranta v Cafferkey*, unreported, High Court, Laffoy J., April 26, 2004. In *XJS Investments Limited v Dun Laoghaire Corporation* [1987] I.L.R.M. 659, McCarthy J. said that planning documents (a) are not Acts of the Oireachtas or subordinate legislation emanating from skilled draftsmen and inviting the accepted canons of construction applicable to such material; and (b) are to be construed in their ordinary meaning as it would be understood by members of the public without legal training as well as by developers and their agents, unless such documents read as a whole necessarily indicates some other meaning. This definition was applied in *Kenny An Bord Pleanála* [2001] I I.R. 545 and *Westport v Golden* [2002] I I.L.R.M. 439; *Sweetman v Shell E & P Ireland Ltd* [2007] 3 I.R. 13. See also *Ampleforth v Cherating Ltd*, unreported, Supreme Court, April 11, 2003, where it was noted that legal definitions of words may be of some limited value in that within the planning community the legal meaning of a particular word or phrase may over long years of usage come to be the accepted meaning. Where an EIS is submitted with the planning application, must be considered as part of the documentation that must be looked at in determining the proper scope of the permission. See *Derrybrien v An Saorgus Energy Ltd*, unreported, High Court, Dunne J., June 3, 2005. The requirement for an application for planning permission to state the nature and extent of the intended development is to ensure that both the Planning Authority and any other person can evaluate or come to an appreciation of what is intended and that the true nature of the contemplated development can be understood and appraised. See *Mason and McCarthy v KT Sand and Gravel*, unreported, High Court, Smyth J., May 7, 2004. A planning permission must be read as a whole and so the interpretation of a planning condition must be read in the light of other conditions. See *Sweetman v Shell E & P Ireland Ltd* [2007] 3 I.R. 13. Planning permission is to be construed in a non-technical way and thus that planning permissions should be interpreted as an ordinary reader of the permission concerned would construe it. See *Cork County Council v Slattery Pre-Cast Concrete Ltd*, unreported, High Court, Clarke J, September 19, 2008, where it was noted that where the planning permission does not contain an express limitation on the scale of the business it may be necessary to infer the scale of the business for which permission has been granted from the underlying circumstances such as the scale of the physical facilities which are permitted to be constructed, or information included with the planning application itself.

Where there is uncertainty regarding the meaning of a planning permission, the procedure under s.5 should be invoked. In *Grianán an Áileach v Donegal County Council* [2004] 2 I.R. 265, the Supreme Court held that the existence of the Section 5 procedure meant the High Court did not have jurisdiction to grant declarations as to the correct interpretation of planning permissions.

Subsection (2) enlists the various entries of decisions and particulars which must be entered into the register. Unlike its predecessor in s.8 of the 1963 Act, it consolidates the list of matters in one subsection. The entries included are for: an application for planning permission, a submission of an EIS; a statement that a development requires an integrated pollution control licence or a waste management licence; applications which materially affect a protected structure or a special amenity area; a decision on an application for permission; the decision of An Bord Pleanála on an application for permission; and a statement that the procedure concerning the material contravention of the development plan under s.34(6) has been complied with. Apart from entries for planning permission applications, other matters to be included relate to: decisions on declaration or referrals under s.5; the extension, revocation or modification of a planning permission; for the acquisition notice for compulsory acquisition for open spaces, a notice requiring removal of a structure or discontinuance of use; an agreement regulating the use of land; a declaration as to whether a matter would materially affect a protected structure; a declaration as to whether a matter conflicts with a scheme for a special area of planning control; a certificate as to whether the social and affordable housing provisions apply to a development; the issue of a warning letter or enforcement notice; a claim for compensation; a tree preservation order; an agreement for the creation of a right of way and the particulars of such; and the operation of a quarry. The 2006 introduced para.t(a) which provides that particulars of local authority development approved under s.179(4)(b) must be entered in the Planning Register.

Subsection (3) provides that the planning authority must make the entries and corrections as soon as possible and subs.(4) states that the register should include a map to follow each entry. As regards the meaning of "as soon as possible" in *Harding v Cork County Council*, unreported, Supreme Court, May 2, 2008, in interpreting the phrase in the context of art.35 of the 2001 Regulations, Murray C.J. said it must be interpreted having regard to the ordinary burdens of administration in any organisation or body.

Subsection (5) provides the information must be in a form capable of being reproduced and subs.(6) states that it should be available for inspection by members of the public. Subsection (7) states that a certified copy of the register shall be accepted in legal proceedings as a true copy and the signature also accepted until the contrary is proved, which standard would be on the balance of probabilities. Subsection (8) provides that in legal proceedings a certified copy of an entry on the register will be accepted and it is not necessary to produce the whole register. Subsection (9) declares that a copy of each entry to the register can be made available to a member of the public on the payment of the appropriate fee.

Obligation to give information to local authority

8.—(1) A local authority may, for any purpose arising in relation to its **1–08** functions under this *Act* or any other enactment, by notice in writing require the occupier of any structure or other land or any person receiving, whether for himself or herself or for another, rent out of any structure or other land to state in writing to the authority, within a specified time not less than 2 weeks after being so required, particulars of the estate, interest, or right by virtue of which he or she occupies the structure or other land or receives the rent, as the case may be, and the name and address (so far as they are known to him or her) of every person who to his or her knowledge has any estate or interest in, or right over, or in respect of, the structure or other land.

(2) Every person who is required under this *section* to state in writing any matter or thing to a local authority and either fails so to state the matter or thing within the time appointed under this *section* or, when so stating any such matter or thing, makes any statement in writing which is to his or her knowledge false or misleading in a material respect, shall be guilty of an offence.

NOTE

This section grants a general power on the planning authority to request an occupier or person who received rent to state their estate or interest in the land or structure and to outline other persons who may have an estate or interest. The planning authority is given a wide discretion to issue a request to assist it in performing its functions either under the 2000 Act or under other legislation. This power may in particular be utilised by the planning authority in advance of taking enforcement action to ascertain the appropriate parties to be served.

Subsection (2) makes it a criminal offence for a person not to comply with a request to provide such information or to provide false or misleading material. The section is similar to s.9 of the 1963 Act.

PART II

PLANS AND GUIDELINES

CHAPTER 1

Development Plans

Obligation to make development plan

1–09   **9.**—**(1)** Every planning authority shall every 6 years make a development plan.

(2) Subject to *subsection (3),* a development plan shall relate to the whole functional area of the authority.

(3)

(a) A planning authority which is a county borough corporation, a borough corporation or an urban district council may, with the agreement of one or more planning authorities which are adjoining county councils, or on the direction of the Minister shall, make a single development plan for the area and the environs of the county borough, borough or urban district, as the case may be.

(b) Where it is proposed to make a development plan under *paragraph (a),* the planning authorities concerned shall make whatever arrangements they see fit to prepare the plan including the carrying out of the requirements of this *Chapter* as a joint function of the authorities concerned (and this *Chapter* shall be construed accordingly) except that where decisions are reserved to the members of the planning authorities concerned the decisions must be made by the members of each authority concerned subject to any agreement which those authorities may make for the resolution of differences between any such reserved decisions.

(4) In making a development plan in accordance with this *Chapter,* a planning authority shall have regard to the development plans of adjoining planning authorities and shall coordinate the objectives in the development plan with the objectives in the plans of those authorities except where the planning authority considers it to be inappropriate or not feasible to do so.

(5) In making a development plan in accordance with this *Chapter,* a planning authority shall take into account any significant likely effects the implementation of the plan may have on the area of any adjoining planning authority having regard in particular to any observations or submissions made by the adjoining authority.

(6) A development plan shall in so far as is practicable be consistent with such national plans, policies or strategies as the Minister determines relate to proper planning and sustainable development.

(6A) Each planning authority within the GDA shall ensure that its development plan is consistent with the transport strategy of the DTA.

(7)

   (a) The Minister may require 2 or more planning authorities to co-ordinate the development plans for their areas generally or in respect of specified matters and in a manner specified by the Minister.

   (b) Any dispute between the planning authorities in question arising out of the requirement under *paragraph (a)* shall be determined by the Minister.

AMENDMENT HISTORY

Section 6A inserted by s.82 of the Dublin Transport Authority Act 2008 is to be commenced on such date as the Minister shall appoint.

NOTE

This section concerns the obligation on planning authorities to make a development plan. The requirement to make a development plan is mandatory and not simply directory. See *Blessington Heritage Trust v Wicklow County Council* [1999] 4 I.R. 571, per McGuinness J. Under the scheme of the previous Acts, e.g. s.19 of the 1963 Act, there was an initial obligation to make a development plan within three years from the commencement of the Act, and an obligation to review the plan as occasion may require, being at least once every five years. Section 20 of the 1963 Act referred to a review of the plan and making any variations (whether by way of alteration, addition or deletion) which the planning authority considers necessary or the making of a new development plan. The 2000 Act removes the terminology of "review" of the plan or the means by which it may be reviewed, in favour of an obligation to "make" a plan. The import of the wording requiring a planning authority to make a development plan appears to imply that there is a requirement to replace the plan rather than simply to review it. A planning authority may of course include the same development objectives which were included in the previous plan where it deems this appropriate. Also omitted is reference to making the plan "as occasion may require". There is no reference to extension of the period for making the development plan as there was under s.43(1)(f) of the 1976 Act. It would appear, as under the previous legislation, it is not necessary for the six years to elapse before making the plan; see *Huntsgroves Development v Meath County Council* [1994] 2 I.L.R.M. 36, where it was reviewed after two years.

While there is a requirement to make a development plan every six years, subs.(1) provides that the planning authority must, not later than four years after the making of the development plan, give notice of its intention to review its existing development plan and prepare a new development plan. Section 12(14) provides that where there is a failure to make the development plan within the two years of the giving of notice under s.11(1), the obligation to make the plan shifts to the Manager of the planning authority.

Subsection (2) makes it a mandatory requirement that there is one development plan for the whole functional area. As such it will no longer be possible to make and review plans for one part of the area at a time. This was allowed under s.19(5) of the 1963 Act, which provided for the making of one or two or more developments plans. A planning authority may however make local area plans for specific areas under s.18, although such local area plans must be consistent with the development plan (s.19(2)) and in case of conflict, the development plan will take precedence (s.18(4)). Subsection (3) introduces a special provision in dealing, inter alia, with county boroughs or Urban District Councils making development plans in consultation with adjoining councils. Subsection (b) allows for co-operation between planning authorities. In general the level of co-operation and consultation is reflective of the special stress on the strategic nature of the plans. See also ss.85 and 86 of the Local Government Act 2001 concerning agreement between local authorities and joint discharge of functions, respectively.

The 2000 Act outlines a greater degree of co-operation between planning authorities. Subsection (4) makes it a mandatory requirement for a planning authority to have regard to the development plans of adjoining planning authorities and to co-ordinate objectives with such authorities except where it is inappropriate. Under subs.(5), the planning authority must take into account the effect of their plan on the adjoining authorities, where these effects are both significant and likely. Subsection (6) requires a development plan to be consistent with "national plans, policies or objectives" of the Minister as relate to proper planning and sustainable development. Where a plan or a draft plan is not consistent the Minister could issue a direction under s.31. Relevant national plans may include the National Development Plan 2000–2006 and the National Spatial Plan. The requirement of "consistency" does not require precisely adopting such plans or policies but implies that it must not conflict with the achievement of such plans, policies or strategies. See *Glencar Exploration Plc v Mayo County Council* [2002] 1 I.R. 84. In adopting the development plan the planning authority should take into account any ministerial guidelines and policy directives issued under ss.28 and 29 of this Act. A qualification to the requirement of consistency is reflected in the phrase "as far as practicable". This obligation only arises where the plans, policies or objectives are determined by the Minister to relate to proper planning and sustainable development. The requirement of "consistency" goes beyond merely a requirement "to take into account" or "have regard to". In the latter instances, a policy may be taken into account but still not followed for other reasons. The requirement of consistency relates to the end result as reflected in the development plan rather than the process of adopting the development plan. The use of the positive "consistent" rather than the negative of "not inconsistent" also implies a stronger obligation. Consistency requires that the plan must pursue the same objectives as the plans, policies or objectives of the Minister. Section 6A, inserted by the Dublin Transport Authority Act 2008, imposes an obligation on planning authorities in the Greater Dublin Area to ensure that the development plan is consistent with the strategic transport plan of the Dublin Transport Authority ("the DTA"). Subsection (7) allows a Minister to require two or more planning authorities to co-ordinate their development plans generally or in respect of a certain matter. The Minister is afforded a wide discretion in this respect and the subsection does not prescribe any specified circumstances to exist before he makes such a requirement. The Minister also has a wide discretion in the manner of the co-ordination. Any dispute between the planning authorities will be resolved by the Minister.

Content of development plans

1–10   **10.—(1)** A development plan shall set out an overall strategy for the proper planning and sustainable development of the area of the development plan and shall consist of a written statement and a plan or plans indicating the development objectives for the area in question.

(2) Without prejudice to the generality of *subsection (1),* a development plan shall include objectives for—

   (a) the zoning of land for the use solely or primarily of particular areas for particular purposes (whether residential, commercial, industrial, agricultural, recreational, as open space or otherwise, or a mixture of those uses), where and to such extent as the proper planning and sustainable development of the area, in the opinion of the planning authority, requires the uses to be indicated;

(b) the provision or facilitation of the provision of infrastructure including transport, energy and communication facilities, water supplies, waste recovery and disposal facilities (regard having been had to the waste management plan for the area made in accordance with the *Waste Management Act, 1996*), waste water services, and ancillary facilities;

(c) the conservation and protection of the environment including, in particular, the archaeological and natural heritage and the conservation and protection of European sites and any other sites which may be prescribed for the purposes of this *paragraph;*

(d) the integration of the planning and sustainable development of the area with the social, community and cultural requirements of the area and its population;

(e) the preservation of the character of the landscape where, and to the extent that, in the opinion of the planning authority, the proper planning and sustainable development of the area requires it, including the preservation of views and prospects and the amenities of places and features of natural beauty or interest;

(f) the protection of structures, or parts of structures, which are of special architectural, historical, archaeological, artistic, cultural, scientific, social or technical interest;

(g) the preservation of the character of architectural conservation areas;

(h) the development and renewal of areas in need of regeneration;

(i) the provision of accommodation for travellers, and the use of particular areas for that purpose;

(j) the preservation, improvement and extension of amenities and recreational amenities;

(k) the control, having regard to the provisions of the *Major Accidents Directive* and any regulations, under any enactment, giving effect to that *Directive,* of—

    (i) siting of new establishments,

    (ii) modification of existing establishments, and

    (iii) development in the vicinity of such establishments, for the purposes of reducing the risk, or limiting the consequences, of a major accident;

(l) the provision, or facilitation of the provision, of services for the community including, in particular, schools, crèches and other education and childcare facilities, and

(m) the protection of the linguistic and cultural heritage of the Gaeltacht including the promotion of Irish as the community language, where there is a Gaeltacht area in the area of the development plan.

(3) Without prejudice to *subsection (2),* a development plan may indicate objectives for any of the purposes referred to in the *First Schedule.*

(4) The Minister may prescribe additional objectives for the purposes of *subsection (2)* or for the purposes of the *First Schedule.*

[(5) The Minister may, for the purposes of giving effect to *Directive 2001/42/EC of the European Parliament and Council of 27 June 2001* on the assessment of the effects of certain plans and programmes on the environment (*No. 2001/42/EC, O.J. No. L 197, 21 July 2001 P. 0030–0037*), by regulations make provision in relation to consideration of the likely significant effects on the environment of implementing a development plan.]

(6) Where a planning authority proposes to include in a development plan any development objective the responsibility for the effecting of which would fall on another local authority, the planning authority shall not include that objective in the plan except after consultation with the other local authority.

(7) A development plan may indicate that specified development in a particular area will be subject to the making of a local area plan.

(8) There shall be no presumption in law that any land zoned in a particular development plan (including a development plan that has been varied) shall remain so zoned in any subsequent development plan.

AMENDMENT HISTORY

Subsection (5) substituted by r.4 of the European Communities (Environmental Assessment of Certain Plans and Programmes) Regulations 2004 (S.I. No. 435 of 2004), with effect from July 14, 2004.

NOTE

This section concerns the content of a development plan. It describes the general content of the plan as an overall strategy relating to "proper planning and sustainable development" and its physical form (written and containing a plan). The development plan must contain the matters in subs.(2) and may contain the matters set out in the First Schedule. No definition of sustainable development has been provided in the Act, though it has otherwise been defined as development that meets the needs of the present without compromising the ability of future generations to meet their own needs. The introduction of the phrase connotes a greater emphasis on the environmental planning aspect of development plans; see Dodd, "From National to Local Plans and the Concept of Sustainable Development under the Planning and Development Act 2000" [2003] 10 (4) I.P.E.L.J. 119. Other statutes have also supplemented the contents of the development plan. Section 19(10) of the Water Services Act 2007 provides that the development plan in relation to the functional area of a local authority shall be deemed to include the objectives for the time being contained in any water services strategic plan in force in relation to that area or any part of that area. In the event of conflict, the objectives of the water services strategy will override the development irrespective of whether or not the development plan is subsequent to the water services strategic plan. Also under s.169(9) of the present Act, a planning scheme for a strategic development forms part of the development plan and where there is conflict, the planning scheme will override the previous provisions.

Development plans are future oriented establishing a framework for development in the particular area. Although the content of development objectives in the plan may vary in their level of specificity, the plan itself is binding on the planning authority. See *McGarry v Sligo County Council* [1989] I.L.R.M. 768, where McCarthy J. described a development plan as "an environmental contract between the planning authority, the Council, and the community, embodying a promise by the Council that it will regulate private development in a manner consistent with the objectives stated in the plan and further, that the Council itself shall not effect any development which contravenes the plan materially". It has also been described as "to control and regulate the user and development of property by indicating, inter alia, the lines on which development permissions will be granted, and on which prohibitions on development and user will be imposed", per Butler J. in *Finn v Bray Urban District Council* [1969] I.R. 169. See also *Byrne v Fingal County Council* [2001] 4 I.R. 565: "a representation in solemn form, binding on all affected or touched by it". The binding nature of development plans is also reflected in the duty of the planning authority to secure its objectives under s.15. In *Central Dublin Development Association v Attorney-General* [1975] 109 I.L.T.R. 69, it was held development plans did not constitute an unjust attack on the property rights of the citizen. Section 178 prohibits a local authority from carrying out development in material contravention of the development plan, while under s.34(2) regard must be had to a development plan in determining a planning application where a permission would otherwise contravene the development plan, permission cannot be granted by the planning authority unless the special material contravention procedure under s.34(6) is followed. The contractual nature of the development plan, means that landowners should enjoy the same opportunity to obtain planning permission during the currency of the Development Plan for similar types of development. See *Cicol Ltd v An Bord Pleanála* unreported, High Court, Irvine J., May 8, 2008.

The notion of "development objectives" is not defined. In *Glencar Explorations Plc v Mayo County Council* [1992] 2 I.R. 237, Blayney J. opined in the High Court that objectives in the development plan must be positive in nature, although, on appeal, doubt was cast about this by the Supreme Court, though it was not expressly decided. See *Glencar Explorations Plc v Mayo County Council* [2002] 1 I.R. 84. Blayney J. also opined that the terms, policy and objective were not mutually exclusive, but declined to rule whether the planning authority had power to decide questions of policy and place them in the development plan. However, in the light of the increased emphasis on strategy and the concept of sustainable development under the 2000 Act, the adoption of policies would seem to be consistent with the spirit of the sections. An analogy could be made with waste management plans, where s.22(6) of the Waste Management Act 1996 as amended requires the local authority to set out its objectives in relation to, inter alia, preventing waste, encourage waste, etc, while s.22(7) states within prejudice to the generality of s.22(6), the plan should set out the "policies and objectives without" and priorities of the local authority.

Under s.15, there is a duty on a planning authority to take steps to secure the objectives of a development plan. It is well established that any member of the public can seek to restrain local authority development in material contravention of the development plan. See *Attorney-General (McGarry) v Sligo County Council* [1991] 1 I.R. 99. It appears that substantial local authority development must be included in the development plans. It is necessary for a local authority to include all its objectives in its plan, otherwise it would mean that the local authority could totally override its own plan; see *Keogh v Galway Corporation (No. 2)* [1995] 3 I.R. 457; *Roughan v Clare County Council*, unreported, High Court, Barron J., December 18, 1996 and *Wicklow Heritage Trust Ltd v Wicklow County Council*, unreported, High Court, McGuinness J., February 5, 1998. In certain cases a comparison was made with private sector development. In considering whether there was a material contravention, the court has considered whether a private developer would be granted planning permission for the same development; see *O'Leary v Dublin County Council* [1988] I.R. 150; *Wilkinson v Dublin County Council* [1991] I.L.R.M. 605 and *Ferris v Dublin County Council*, unreported, Supreme Court, November 7, 1990. This so-called private sector comparator is questionable, as the test for granting planning permission is more than whether there is a material contravention of the development, but it involves broader concerns of the proper planning and sustainable development of the area. In *Maye v Sligo County Council*, unreported, High Court, Clarke J., April 27, 2007, the court rejected that a default permission could be refused because a development was not in accordance with proper planning and sustainable development as opposed to being a material contravention of the development plan, thereby accepting that they constitute different standards.

Notion of Material Contravention

In order for a development to be a material contravention, there must be: (a) a contravention and (b) this contravention must be material. Material in this respect means material in planning terms. In order to amount to a contravention, the provision of the development plan must be of sufficient specificity so as to constitute contravention. Some provisions of a development plan may be of such a broad and general nature, that it is not strictly possible to describe any specific development as being a contravention. Also the plan must be read as a whole; the mere fact that a development is consistent with certain objectives does not mean that it cannot be in contravention of other objectives in the plan. Examples of material contravention have been where the development breached the zoning provisions of the plan; see *Grange Developments Ltd v Dublin County Council* [1986] I.R. 150 (industrial buildings on land zoned for agriculture); *O'Leary v Dublin County Council* [1988] I.R. 150 (a travellers halting site on an area zoned for high amenity). The fact that a particular development falls within a zoning where the type of development is permitted in principle or open for consideration, does not mean that the development may not be a material contravention of the development plan. See *Cicol Ltd v An Bord Pleanála* unreported, High Court, Irvine J., May 8, 2008, where it was said that uses of land described as being "permitted in principle" or "open for consideration" are merely guidelines in relation to the use of land and that there are a multitude of other factors including density, height, massing etc. to be considered by the Planning Authority when deciding whether or not any proposed development, whether "permitted in principle" or "open for consideration" is to be deemed to be one which does not materially contravene the Development Plan for the area. Apart from zoning, other examples of breaches of the development plan can be material contraventions, include restricting development along a road in the interests of visual amenity; see *Murray v Wicklow County Council* [1996] 2 I.R. 552; breaches of provisions on residential density; see *Tennyson v Dun Laoghaire Corporation* [1991] 2 I.R. 527; development of a rubbish dump adjacent to the area of a monument; see *McGarry v Sligo County Council* [1989] I.L.R.M. 768. See also *Dublin County Council v Marren* [1985] I.L.R.M. 593. Also development objectives prescribing general standards for development may be materially contravened by specific development. Examples include that no development should give rise to a fire hazard (*Calor Teoranta v Sligo County Council* [1991] 2 I.R. 267) and restrictions on development within certain distances from a road in the interests of visual amenity and tourism (*Murray v Wicklow County Council* [1996] 2 I.R. 552). The notion of material contravention has also arisen in the context of a claim for default planning permission. The courts have established that an applicant will not be entitled to default permission even where the planning authority fails to determine the application within the prescribed time limit, where the development would amount to a material contravention of the development plan. See *Maye v Sligo Borough Council*, unreported, High Court, Clarke J., April 27, 2007, where the proposed development contravened an objective to establish a linear park. A material contravention of the development plan is a higher test than merely showing that there are matters which might justify the refusal of the planning permission. See *Wicklow County Council v Forest Fencing t/a Abwood*, unreported, High Court, Charleton J., July 13, 2007, where it was said that if the extent of a deviation from what is specified in the development plan is such as might give rise to a reasonable expectation of opposition based on that deviation, then the deviation will be regarded as material. A material contravention of the development plan may be shown where the development in question is of a nature, or is on such a scale, that makes it likely that the planning authority would refuse permission for development for reasons that are based predominantly on the development plan.

A material contravention can also relate to a commitment to follow a certain procedure in the plan. In *Byrne v Fingal County Council* [2001] 4 I.R. 565, failure to abide by the consultation procedure regarding a halting site was in itself a material contravention of the development plan and should attract a similar sanction as if the classes of use had been contravened. In *Jeffers v Louth County Council*, unreported, High Court, Murphy J., April 5, 2001, in seeking to accommodate certain traveller families on the roadside, Murphy J. granted an injunction until the procedure set out in its Traveller Accommodation Programme had been complied with. Also in *Ní Chonghaile v Comhairle Chontae na Gaillimhe* [2004] 4 I.R. 138, where the development plan provided that a linguistic impact statement should be required in relation to every application for development in a Gaeltacht area and none was provided, this was a material contravention.

As mentioned above the failure to include certain proposed local authority development in the development, may mean that the local authority development may amount to a material contravention. See *Keogh v Galway Corporation (No. 2)* [1995] 3 I.R. 457; *Roughan v Clare County Council*, unreported, High Court, Barron J., December 18, 1996 and *Wicklow Heritage Trust Ltd v Wicklow County Council*, unreported, High Court, McGuinness J.,

February 5, 1998.

It should be noted that a challenge to local authority development on the basis that it is a material contravention of the development plan now falls within the special judicial review procedure under ss.50 and 50A of this Act as a result of the 2006 Act. This means a person challenging such decision must be able to establish, inter alia, a substantial interest. See *Harding v Cork County Council*, unreported, Supreme Court, May 2, 2008.

Interpretation of the Development Plan

It is now well established that the interpretation of the development plan involves a question of law: see *Tennyson v Dun Laoghaire Corporation* [1991] 2 I.R. 527; *Byrne v Fingal County Council* [2001] 4 I.R. 565; and *McGarry v Sligo County Council* [1989] I.L.R.M. 768, where the earlier decision of *An Taisce v Dublin Corporation*, unreported, High Court, O'Keefe P., January 31, 1973, was distinguished because there was a conflict of evidence. The importance of this lies in the fact that the court will not defer to the opinion of the planning authority as to whether there is a material contravention of the development plan. As was noted by McGuinness J. in *Wicklow Heritage Trust Ltd v Wicklow County Council*, unreported, High Court, McGuinness J., February 5, 1998, "the question is not whether the Senior Executive Planner or the County Manager were unreasonable in thinking that the Ballynagran site was not a material contravention; the question is whether they were correct in law in this opinion". This question is to be distinguished from assessing the merits of a particular development from a planning perspective; see *Ferris v Dublin County Council*, unreported, High Court, Finlay P., November 17, 1990 and *Duffy v Waterford Corporation*, unreported, High Court, McGuinness J., July 21, 1999. The interpretation of the development plan is to be distinguished from the assessment of a planning application. See *Dietacaron Ltd v An Bord Pleanála* [2005] 2 I.L.R.M. 32, which concerned whether revised plans constituted significant additional information. However, where a planning permission is challenged on the basis that it was a material contravention of the development plan and the special contravention procedure under s.34(6) was not followed, the interpretation of what is a material contravention would equally involve a question of law. See *Tennyson v Dun Laoghaire Corporation* [1991] 2 I.R. 527.

The development plan is to be interpreted according to its objective ordinary meaning. See *XJS Investments v Dun Laoghaire Corporation* [1987] I.L.R.M. 659, although there can be a degree of flexibility in the interpretation of zoning, see *Tom Chawke Caravans Ltd v Limerick County Council*, unreported, High Court, Flood J., February 1991. The proper interpretation is what a reasonably intelligent person, having no particular expertise in law or town planning would, make of the provision in the development plan; see *Tennyson v Dublin Corporation* [1991] 2 I.R. 527 and *Byrne v Fingal County Council* [2001] 4 I.R. 565; *Cicol Ltd v An Bord Pleanála*, unreported, High Court, Irvine J., May 8, 2008. It appears that the development plan ought to be interpreted as a stand alone document without reference to external documents unless expressly incorporated in the plan. It would also not appear appropriate to interpret the plan by reference to the process of adoption or its amendment history.

While the development plan applies to numerous functions under the Planning Acts, its most relevant application will be in determining planning applications and in controlling local authority development. Section 34(2)(a)(i) provides that, in determining whether to grant a planning permission, regard must be had to the development plan. If an authority is minded to grant permission which would materially contravene the development plan, it can only do so following the procedure set out in s.34(6)(a). This procedure requires notice to the public, consideration of submissions and a resolution of three quarters of the total members of the planning authority. A section 140 resolution under the Local Government Act 2001 (formerly s.4 of the County and County Managers Act 1955), directed to the County Manager, must also be passed. The existence of such procedure means that a planning authority is not absolutely bound by the terms of the development plan. An exception is also made with respect to the implementation of a waste management plan under s.22(10)B of the Waste Management 1996 as amended. The 2000 Act introduces some changes in relation to An Bord Pleanála and the development plan. Under s.14(8) of the 1976 Act, in relation to an appeal from an application for permission or retention, the Board could grant permission or approval even where the development materially contravened the development plan. Under s.37(2) of the Act, it can only grant permission where it has been refused by the planning authority because of a material contravention of the development plan, where certain specified conditions apply. In the case of strategic infrastructure developments, there are no restrictions on the Board. Even where a planning application is not in material contravention of the development plan, there is still an obligation on the planning authority and Board to have regard to the development plan. On the meaning of "have regard", see *McEvoy v Meath County Council* [2003] 1 I.L.R.M. 431. In determining whether a matter is a material contravention of the development plan, this must relate to the current development plan and not a draft plan. See *Ebonwood Limited v Meath County Council* [2004] 3 I.R. 34.

Other provisions of the Act in which the development plan is relevant include: regarding the record of protected structures and designation of architectural conservation areas under Pt IV; in designating the percentage of residential land reserved for social and affordable housing under Pt V; in relation to appeals against conditions under s.139, the Board is expressed to be restricted to considering, inter alia, the matters set out in s.34(2)(a) which includes the development plan. Section 47 provides a sterilisation agreement which cannot restrict the exercise of powers, unless such powers would materially contravene the development plan. Under s.150(2)(i), the planning authority or Board must set out a Code of Conduct dealing with the development plan. Under s.169(8), in considering a draft planning scheme, the Board shall take account of the development plan. Under s.169(9), a planning scheme adopted under the section is deemed to form part of the development plan in force in the area of the scheme. In relation to development within a class affecting the environment under s.176, the Board in determining whether to grant permission will take into account the development plan under s.176(12). Under art.9 of the 2001 Regulations certain matters otherwise within the definition of exempted developments will be excluded if in breach of development plans, and exempted development status may also be lost in relation to protected structures under s.57. Also under the Fourth Schedule, many of the reasons for refusal of planning which exclude compensation relate to terms of the development plan

In relation to subs.(2), there is a mandatory requirement on authorities to include the above enlisted objective in development plans, while there is a discretion to include matters listed in the First Schedule. The 2000 Act introduced a much longer list of objectives which must be included in the development plan. It also abolishes any distinction between objectives for county boroughs, urban districts and other areas. Entirely new objectives include: (c) the conservation of the environment; (d) the integration of planning and sustainable development into the social and cultural area; (g) the preservation of architectural conservation areas (see under s.81, which may include an area of special planning control designated under s.84); (e) the preservation of the character of the landscape (see landscape conservation areas under s.204); (l) the preservation of services such as schools; (k) the control under the Major Accidents Directive; and (m) the protection of the Gaeltacht. A record of protected structures must be included in the development plan under s.51. A planning scheme for a strategic development zone forms part of, and supersedes any conflict with, a development plan under s.169(9). Also a housing strategy proposed under s.94 forms part of the development plan. Section 95 gives some guidances as to the contents of the housing strategy.

Subsection (2)(i) concerning the provision of accommodation for travellers, and the use of particular areas for that purpose was introduced by the Housing (Traveller Accommodation) Act 1998. This obligation to include this objective is mandatory. See *O'Reilly v Limerick County Council*, unreported, High Court, McMenamin J., March 29, 2006, where there was also held to be a breach of s.13(2) of the Housing Act, 1988.

Section 10(2)(a) somewhat alters the old zoning provision, making it clear that zoning must be integrated within the concept of "proper planning and sustainable development". Zoning was defined in *O'Connor v Clare County Council*, unreported, High Court, Murphy J., February 11, 1994, as "a wider area where activities or developments having some measure of uniformity may be undertaken by a considerable number of owners or occupiers". However, he went on to say that that there would be "nothing to prevent a planning authority from indicating a specific development objective in relation to a limited area with a view to or as a consequence of formulating a development objective in relation to an adjoining larger area". Zoning is similar, though distinguishable from being reserved for a "particular purpose" under para.2(b)(iv) of the Second Sched., which is relevant in claims for compensation, see *Attorney-General v Shortt* [1983] I.L.R.M. 377 and *Monastra Development v Dublin County Council* [1992] 1 I.R. 468 and *Malahide Community Council v Dublin County Council* [1997] 3 I.R. 383. It appears that the notion of zoning and reservation are sometimes confused. See *Ebonwood v Meath County Council* [2004] 3 I.R. 34, where it was suggested that retaining a railway route selection corridor was a zoning objective. Under s.191(2) compensation shall not be payable in respect of the refusal of permission for any development based on any change of the zoning of land as a result of the making of a new development plan. Subsection (8) provides there is no presumption that an area zoned in a particular manner will remain so zoned. Paragraph 20 of the Fourth Schedule also excludes compensation for development which would materially contravene certain zoning objectives. This removes any claim of legitimate expectation that an area will remain zoned in a particular way. The planning authority has a discretion in zoning an area as indicated by the expression "in the opinion" of the planning authority that the proper planning and development of the area requires the uses indicated. This means that, while the development plan must include zoning provision, the precise type of zoning (whether residential, commercial, industrial, etc.) is a matter of discretion and the development plan need not include zoning for all of these types. However, one express qualification to this is that under s.95(1) the planning authority must ensure that sufficient and suitable land is zoned for residential use or a mixture of residential and other uses, to meet the requirements of the housing strategy and to ensure that scarcity of land does not occur at any time during the period of the development plan. The reference in s.10(2)(a) to "or otherwise, or a mixture of those uses" refers to the preceding specified types of development (i.e. residential, commercial, industrial, etc.) and does not open entirely different categories of development. See *Abbeydrive v Kildare County Council*, unreported, Macken J., June 17, 2005, where it was rejected that the special amenity character and quality of a village, constituted a land use objective. Although not required by the 2000 Act, the format often used by planning authorities is to zone areas according to categories based on the likelihood of development being allowed such as "normally permissible", "open for consideration", or "not permissible". Notwithstanding these categories, a development may be a material contravention of the zoning objective, even where most of the development was permitted in principle or open for consideration. See *Cicol Ltd v An Bord Pleanála*, unreported, High Court, Irvine J., May 8, 2008, where the zoning was "to preserve and provide for open space and recreational amenities", even though the development was permitted in principle or open for consideration, it was held the development was primarily of residential and mixed commercial use and the nature and scale of the proposed development was such that it would contravene in a material way the zoning objective. The same area may be zoned for several purposes. Section 94 provides that a housing strategy must be prepared which will form part of the development plan. A specified percentage, not more than 20 per cent of the land zoned for residential or mixed residential and other use, must be reserved for the purposes of social and affordable housing. Section 95 provides "sufficient and suitable" land must be so zoned, to ensure a scarcity of such land does not occur during the period of the development plan. The Department of Local Government and the Environment has published *Guidelines for Planning Authorities—Part V of the Planning and Development Act 2000*, which state at para.8.2 that, in deciding on the amount of land to be zoned for the six-year period of the plan, the authority should select an area greater than that calculated to accommodate the required number of houses so as to ensure that there is no undue shortage of zoned and serviced land at any stage during the plan period. In respect of each area zoned for residential use or a mixture of residential and other use, different percentages or objectives may be specified. It is not entirely clear whether the 20 per cent limit is an overall limit for the whole of the development plan or whether every particular area zoned for residential purpose cannot have more than 20 per cent allocated for social and affordable housing. It appears that the latter is the better view. The planning authority may fix a low percentage or none at all in certain areas, in order to counteract social segregation.

In relation to the sites prescribed under subs.(3)(c), art.12 of the 2001 Regulations, prescribes any area designated as a natural heritage area under s.18 of the Wildlife (Amendment) Act 2000 (No. 38 of 2000), and any area the subject of a notice under s.16(2)(b) of the Wildlife (Amendment) Act 2000.

Subsection (3) concerns matters which the planning authority may at its discretion include in the development plan. This is in contradistinction to the matters contained in subs.(2), which are mandatory. It seems to follow from this that the planning authority is confined to including the matters which are contained in subs.(2) and the First Schedule. If the development plan included matters not falling within either of these categories, it would be ultra vires. However, the matters are of such a broad nature, this would rarely, if ever, arise. The 1963 Act as amended, set out objectives in its Third Schedule. The First Schedule to the present Act is far more detailed than the Schedule to the 1963 Act. It includes a new section described as Location and Pattern of Development. Other sections are Control of Areas and Structures; Community Facilities; Environment and Amenities; and Infrastructure and Transport. Section 10 must be read in conjunction with Chap.IV relating to Ministerial Guidelines and Directives. Under subs.(4), the Minister may expand the objectives to be included in a development plan by regulation. No such regulations have yet to be made.

Under subs.(5), the development plan must contain a separate section concerning the likely significant effects on the environment. This is a mandatory requirement. This was inserted to comply with the European Directive on Strategic Environmental Assessment (Directive 2001/42/EC), where an environmental assessment is required to be carried out on development plans before they are adopted. However, in addition to subs.(5), the obligations under the Directives are are now set out in arts. 13A to 13J of the Planning and Development Regulations 2004 (as inserted by the Planning and Development (Strategic Environmental Assessment) Regulations 2004 (S.I. No. 436 of 2004)). Where the development plan is: (a) for an area whose population is more than 10,000 persons or (b) if less than 10,000 but where the planning authority has determined its implemention would be likely to have significant effects on the environment, then an environmental assessment must be carried out on any new development plan: see Article 13B of the 2001 Regulations. This involves the preparation of an environmental report, the content of which is set out in Sched.2B to the Regulations and art.13E. Under art.13J the planning authority is also obliged to monitor the significant environmental effects of the implementation of the development plans in order to identify at an early stage unforeseen adverse effects and to be able to undertake appropriate remedial action.

Subsection (6) provides that a planning authority cannot include an objective in a development plan, the implementation of which requires action by another planning authority, except where it has consulted the other authority. This subsection should be read in conjunction with ss.9(4) and 9(5), under which a planning authority must co-operate with adjoining planning authorities and also must take into account the significant likely effect on the area of an adjoining authority in the preparation of their development plan; see ss.85 and 86 of the Local Government Act 2001.

Under subs.(7), the development plan may prescribe that a specified area is subject to a local area plan. Local area plans are described in Chap.II of Pt 2, ss.18–20, which was amended under the 2002 Act. Section 22 of the Roads Act 1993 provides that the Road Authority may make representations to the planning authority with regard to the content of its development plan.

Preparation of draft development plan

1–11   **11.—(1)** Not later than 4 years after the making of a development plan, a planning authority shall give notice of its intention to review its existing development plan and to prepare a new development plan for its area.

(2) A notice under *subsection (1)* shall be given to the Minister, any prescribed authorities, any adjoining planning authorities, the Board, any relevant regional authority and any town commissioners and city and county development boards within the functional area of the authority and shall be published in one or more newspapers circulating in the area to which the development plan relates and shall—

    (a) state that the planning authority intends to review the existing development plan and to prepare a new development plan,

    (b) indicate that submissions or observations regarding the review of the existing plan and the preparation of a new development plan may be made in writing to the planning authority within a specified period (which shall not be less than 8 weeks),

    (c) indicate the time during which and the place or places where any background papers or draft proposals (if any) regarding the review of the existing plan and the preparation of the new development plan may be inspected.

(3)

    (a) As soon as may be after giving notice under this *section* of its intention to review a development plan and to prepare a new development plan, a planning authority shall take whatever additional measures it considers necessary to consult with the general public and other interested bodies.

    (b) Without prejudice to the generality of *paragraph (a)*, a planning authority shall hold public meetings and seek written submissions regarding all or any aspect of the proposed development plan and may invite oral submissions to be made to the planning authority regarding the plan.

    (c) In addition to *paragraphs (a) and (b)*, a planning authority shall take whatever measures it considers necessary to consult with the providers of energy, telecommunications, transport and any other relevant infrastructure and of education, health, policing and other services in order to ascertain any long-term plans for the provision of the infrastructure and services in the area of the planning authority and the providers shall furnish the necessary information to the planning authority.

(4)

    (a) Not later than 16 weeks after giving notice under *subsection (1)*, the manager of a planning authority shall prepare a report on any submissions or observations received under *subsection (2) or (3)* and the matters arising out of any consultations under *subsection (3)*.

    (b) A report under *paragraph (a)* shall—

        (i) list the persons or bodies who made submissions or observations under this *section* as well as any persons or bodies consulted by the authority,

        (ii) summarise the issues raised in the submissions and during the consultations, where appropriate,

        (iii) give the opinion of the manager to the issues raised, taking account of the proper planning and sustainable development of the area, the statutory obligations of any local authority in the area, and any relevant policies or objectives for the time being of the Government or of any Minister of the Government, and

        (iv) state the manager's recommendations on the policies to be included in the draft development plan.

(bb) In the case of each planning authority within the GDA, a report under paragraph (a) shall summarise the issues raised and the recommendations made by the DTA in a report prepared in accordance with section 31B and outline the recommendations of the manager in relation to the manner in which those issues and recommendations should be addressed in the draft development plan.

(c) A report under *paragraph (a)* shall be submitted to the members of the planning authority, or to a committee of the planning authority, as may be decided by the members of the authority, for their consideration.

(d) Following the consideration of a report under *paragraph (c)*, the members of the planning authority or of the committee, as the case may be, may issue directions to the manager regarding the preparation of the draft development plan, and any such directions must take account of the statutory obligations of any local authority in the area and any relevant policies or objectives for the time being of the Government or of any Minister of the Government, and the manager shall comply with any such directions.

(e) Directions under *paragraph (d)* shall be issued not later than 10 weeks after the submission of a report in accordance with *paragraph (c)*.

(f) In issuing directions under *paragraph (d)*, the members shall be restricted to considering the proper planning and sustainable development of the area to which the development plan relates.

(5)

(a) The manager shall, not later than 12 weeks following the receipt of any directions under *subsection (4)(d)*, prepare a draft development plan and submit it to the members of the planning authority for their consideration.

(b) The members of a planning authority shall, as soon as may be, consider the draft development plan submitted by the manager in accordance with *paragraph (a)*.

(c) Where the draft development plan has been considered in accordance with *paragraph (b)*, it shall be deemed to be the draft development plan, unless, within 8 weeks of the submission of the draft development plan under *paragraph (a)*, the planning authority, by resolution, amends that draft development plan.

AMENDMENT HISTORY

Section 11(4)(bb) was inserted by s.83 of the Dublin Transport Authority Act 2008, to be commenced on such date as the Minister shall appoint.

NOTE

This section concerns the initiation of the procedure for the making of a new development plan. Subsection (1) sets out that notice of intention to review the development plan and to prepare a new plan must be made within four years after the making of the plan, which must be set against the mandatory requirement in s.9 that the planning authority must have completed the new plan within the six years. There is, therefore, two years within which the planning authority must have completed the adoption of a new development plan: see also s.12(14). However, prior to giving notice under subs.(1) the provisions relating to an environmental assessment under arts 13A and 13B of the the 2001 Regulations (as inserted by the Planning and Development (Strategic Environment Assessment) Regulations 2004, (S.I. No. 436 of 2004), must be carried out. Article 13A provides that where a planning authority proposes to prepare a development plan for an area which has less than 10,000 persons, the planning authority must decide whether or not the implementation of a new development plan would be likely to have significant effects on the environment, taking account of the relevant factors set out in Sch.2A of the Regulations. Where the planning authority decides it would not have such significant effects, it must send notice to the EPA, the Minister for the Environment where it may have significant effects in relation to architectural or archaeological heritage or to nature conservation or to the Minister for Communications and Marine, where it might have significant effects on fisheries or the marine environment. The notice must, inter alia, allow such body to make submissions or observations within a specified period being not less than four weeks. Following the end of such period, the planning authority will again re-consider whether the plan would be likely to have significant effects on the environment taking into account the criteria in Sch.2A and any submissions or observations received. Having made such determination, the planning authority must as soon as practicable, make a copy of the decision (including, if applicable, any reasons for not requiring an environmental assessment) available for public inspection and notify any body to whom the notice was sent. Where the planning authority proposes: (a) to make a development plan for an area with 10,000 persons or more; or (b) if the area is less than 10,000 persons and it has determined that the implementation of the development plan would be likely to have significant effects on the environment, then the notice given under s.11(1) must also state that the planning authority proposes to carry out an environmental assessment as part of the review of the existing development plan and the preparation of the new plan and that for these purposes the planning authority will prepare an environmental report of the likely significant effects on the environment of implementing the new plan.

The Act introduces on a statutory basis a more extensive public consultation process than existed under the previous Acts. The public participation now commences with the preparation of the draft development plan, i.e. the public can have an input into what is contained in the draft plan. Under the previous legislation public consultation only commenced after the draft development plan had been prepared, with the public then have an opportunity to comment on the draft plan. Under s.12, the public also have an opportunity to comment on the draft development plan. The previous legislation required the planning authority to put the draft plan on "public display", while the present legislation is expressed in terms of "notice" to the public. In this respect one or more newspaper notices must be published in newspapers circulating in the area to which the development plan realtes. In addition to this newspaper, notice subs.(2) refers to certain bodies which must be given specific notice of the initiation of the review process and the contents of such notice, which are mandatory. Article 13 of the 2001 Regulations sets out 27 prescribed authorities for the purposes of this section (the EPA were added as a prescribed authority under the 2006 Planning Regulations). There are no limitation on the nature of the submissions or observations which may be made by members of the public nor is any such person required to demonstrate any particular interest before making a submission. However, such submissions should relate to the potential content of the new development plan. Subsection (2)(c) envisages that there already be in existence background papers or draft papers relating the review and these must be available for inspection by the public. There is however no obligation to prepare such background papers or draft proposals.

It appears that the housing strategy which forms part of the development plan under s.94, should be one of first matters to be prepared. The *Guidelines for Planning Authorities—Part V of the Planning and Development Act 2000* state at para.2.6 that "[a]s the housing strategy will inform the whole development plan, work on the collection of data to input into the strategy should be one of the first tasks undertaken in preparing the draft development plan as a whole".

Having given notice to the public of its intention to review the plan, subs.(3) requires the planning authority to take any "additional measure" it considers necessary in order to consult the public and other interested bodies. Although this section is expressed in mandatory terms with the use of the word "shall", this is qualified by the fact that the planning authority is required to take measures "it considers necessary". If the planning authority considers it is not necessary to take additional measures, then it would appear that it cannot be compelled to do so. Subsection (3)(b) states that the planning authority "shall" hold public meeting and invite submissions and "may" invite oral submissions. The unqualified use of the word "shall" in relation to public meetings and inviting submissions in contrast to the use of the word "may" invite oral submissions, prima facie, implies that there is a mandatory obligation on the planning authority to hold public meetings and invite submissions. However, this subsection is expressed to be without prejudice to the generality of subs.(3)(a) where the planning authority is obliged to take such additional measures where "it considers necessary". Furthermore, subs.(3)(b) refers to public meetings and seeking submissions regarding "all or any aspect" of the proposed development plan, which also implies an element of discretion. Viewed in this light, it is submitted that the better view is that there is no mandatory obligation on the planning authority to hold public meeting or invite further submissions (except in the newspaper notice under subs.(2) where it does not deem it necessary. The planning authority also has a discretion whether to consult with relevant providers infrastructure and services specified in subs.(3)(c).

Aricle 13D of the the the 2001 Regulations provides that as soon as practicable after giving notice under s.11(1), notice must be sent to the EPA and also the Minister for the Environment and Minister for Communications, Marine and Natural Resources, where appropriate, stating that;

1. as part of the review and the preparation of a new development plan, the planning authority will prepare an environmental report of the likely significant effects on the environment of implementing the plan;
2. the environmental report is required to include the information that may reasonably be required, taking into account:
    (a) current knowledge and methods of assessment;
    (b) the contents and level of detail in the plan;
    (c) the stage of the plan in the decision making process; and
    (d) the extent to which certain matters are more appropriately assessed at different levels in the decision making process in order to avoid duplication of environemtnal assessment; and
3. indicate that a submission or observation in relation to the scope and level of detail of the information to be included in the environmental report may be made to the planning authority within a specified period which shall be not less than 4 weeks from the date of the notice.

The content of the environmental report should contain the matters set out in Sch.2B and art.13E.

The preparatory stage of the draft development plan itself involves a sequence of steps which may be summarised as follows; notice and invitation to the public/other bodies to make submissions and public participation; further consultation with the public and infrastructure providers; preparation of the report by the Manager of the planning authority; consideration of the report by the planning authority and issuing of any directions; preparation of the draft plan by the Manager; and the submission and consideration of the draft development plan. A specific time frame is delineated in relation to the procedure. However, s.12(16) states that a person shall not question the validity of a development plan where the steps were not completed within the time allowed, which means that such time limits are not absolute requirements. There must be a minimum of eight weeks allowed for the making of submissions, while the manager of the planning authority must prepare a report on the submissions within 16 weeks at the latest, from the date of the notice inviting submissions. The report must be completed at the end of this 16-week period. The obligation is to "summarise" the issues raised and the submissions received. There is no obligation to circulate to each member of the planning authority the entirety of the objections and submissions received, prior to their consideration of the proposal. See *Sandyford Environmental Planning v Dun Laoghaire Rathdown County Council*, unreported, High Court, McKechnie J., June 30, 2004, where the Court rejected a claim that that the Manager was so influenced by institutional bias that he was incapable of compiling an objective report. In summarising the submissions the Manager is not bound to use any formula or follow any specified method. This obligation applies even if a longer period than eight weeks is allowed for the making of submissions. Subsection (4)(bb) which was inserted by the Dublin Transporation Act 2008 provides that in respect of planning authorities within the Greater Dublin Area, the report must summarise the issues raised and the recommendations made by the DTA, which report must be prepared in accordance with s.31B and outline the recommendations of the manager in relation to the manner in which those issues and recommendations should be addressed in the draft development plan.

There is no time specified between the preparation and submission of the report to the planning authority, though it would appear to be immediate or as so soon as may be. The planning authority has 10 weeks from the submission of the report to issue any directions. If the planning authority does not issue a direction within the 10 weeks, the matter will revert back to the Manager who must prepare the draft development plan. The Manager has a maximum of 12 weeks from receipt of any directions to prepare the draft development plan. It appears that if the planning authority has not issued directions, there is still an obligation on the Manager to prepare the draft within a 12-week period which will commence from the end of the 10 weeks allowed for the planning authority to make directions. The Manager must prepare and submit the report to the planning authority within the 12-week period (in contrast to the earlier report on the submissions where there is an obligation to prepare, with no mention of submission, within the 16-week period). Following this, the planning authority "as soon as may be", must consider the plan. There is therefore a requirement of promptness on the planning authority without an exact period being specified. Once the plan is considered by the planning authority, it is deemed to constitute the draft development plan, subject to allowing the authority to amend the draft plan by resolution within eight weeks from the submission of the plan. It appears that the draft submitted by the Manager will not automatically become the draft development plan after eight weeks as the plan can only be deemed to be the draft development plan where it has been "considered" by the planning authority. The above procedure has also been supplemented by art.13C of the the 2001 Regulations, which provides that a draft plan prepared by the manager under s.11(5) shall be accompanied by or include an environmental report.

Making of development plan

12.—(1) Where the draft development plan has been prepared in accordance **1–12** with *section 11,* the planning authority shall within 2 weeks of the period referred to in *section 11(5)(c)* —

    (a) send notice and a copy of the draft development plan to the Minister, the Board, the prescribed authorities, [...], any town commissioners and city and county development boards within the area, and

    (b) publish notice of the preparation of the draft in one or more newspapers circulating in its area.

(2) A notice under *subsection (1)* shall state that—

    (a) a copy of the draft may be inspected at a stated place or places and at stated times during a stated period of not less than 10 weeks (and the copy shall be kept available for inspection accordingly), and

    (b) written submissions or observations with respect to the draft made to the planning authority within the stated period will be taken into consideration before the making of the plan.

(3)

    (a) Where the draft includes any provision relating to any addition to or deletion from the record of protected structures, the planning authority shall serve on each person who is the owner or occupier of the proposed protected structure or the protected structure, as the case may be, a notice of the proposed addition or deletion, including the particulars.

(b) A notice under *paragraph (a)* shall state—

    (i) that a copy of the proposed addition or deletion may be inspected at a stated place or places and at stated times during a stated period of not less than 10 weeks (and the copy shall be kept available for inspection accordingly),

    (ii) that written submissions or observations with respect to the proposed addition or deletion made to the planning authority within the stated period will be taken into consideration before the making of the addition or deletion,

    (iii) whether or not the proposed addition or deletion was recommended by the Minister for Arts, Heritage, Gaeltacht and the Islands, and

    (iv) that, if the proposed addition or deletion was recommended by the Minister for Arts, Heritage, Gaeltacht and the Islands, the planning authority shall forward to that Minister for his or her observations a copy of any submission or observation made under *subparagraph (ii)* (and any such observations shall be taken into consideration accordingly).

(4)

(a) Not later than 22 weeks after giving notice under *subsection (1)* and, if appropriate, *subsection (3),* the manager of a planning authority shall prepare a report on any submissions or observations received under *subsection (2) or (3)* and submit the report to the members of the authority for their consideration.

(b) A report under *paragraph (a)* shall—

    (i) list the persons or bodies who made submissions or observations under this *section,*

    (ii) summarise the issues raised by the persons or bodies in the submissions or observations, and

    (iii) give the response of the manager to the issues raised, taking account of any directions of the members of the authority or the committee under *section 11(4),* the proper planning and sustainable development of the area, the statutory obligations of any local authority in the area and any relevant policies or objectives of the Government or of any Minister of the Government and, if appropriate, any observations made by the Minister for Arts, Heritage, Gaeltacht and the Islands under *subsection (3)(b)(iv).*

(bb) In the case of each planning authority within the GDA, a report under paragraph (a) shall summarise the issues raised and the recommendations made by the DTA in its written submission prepared in accordance with section 31C and outline the recommendations of the manager in relation to the manner in which those issues and recommendations should be addressed in the development plan.

(5)

(a) The members of a planning authority shall consider the draft plan and the report of the manager under *subsection (4)*.

   (b) The consideration of a draft plan and the manager's report under *paragraph (a)* shall be completed within 12 weeks of the submission of the manager's report to the members of the authority.

(6) Where, following the consideration of the draft development plan and the manager's report, it appears to the members of the authority that the draft should be accepted or amended, subject to *subsection (7)*, they may, by resolution, accept or amend the draft and make the development plan accordingly.

(7)

   (a) In case the proposed amendment would, if made, be a material alteration of the draft concerned, the planning authority shall, not later than 3 weeks after the passing of a resolution under *subsection (6)*, publish notice of the proposed amendment in at least one newspaper circulating in its area.

   (b) A notice under *paragraph (a)* shall state that—

      (i) a copy of the proposed amendment of the draft development plan may be inspected at a stated place and at stated times during a stated period of not less than 4 weeks (and the copy shall be kept available for inspection accordingly), and

      (ii) written submissions or observations with respect to the proposed amendment of the draft made to the planning authority within the stated period shall be taken into consideration before the making of any amendment.

(8)

   (a) Not later than 8 weeks after giving notice under *subsection (7)*, the manager of a planning authority shall prepare a report on any submissions or observations received under that *subsection* and submit the report to the members of the authority for their consideration.

   (b) A report under *paragraph (a)* shall—

      (i) list the persons or bodies who made submissions or observations under this *section,*

      (ii) summarise the issues raised by the persons or bodies in the submissions,

      (iii) give the response of the manager to the issues raised, taking account of the directions of the members of the authority or the committee under *section 11(4)*, the proper planning and sustainable development of the area, the statutory obligations of any local authority in the area and any relevant policies or objectives for the time being of the Government or of any Minister of the Government.

(9)

   (a) The members of a planning authority shall consider the amendment and the report of the manager under *subsection (8)*.

   (b) The consideration of the amendment and the manager's report under *paragraph (a)* shall be completed not later than 6 weeks after the submission of the manager's report to the members of the authority.

(10)

    (a) The members of the authority shall, by resolution, having considered the amendment and the manager's report, make the plan with or without the proposed amendment, except that where they decide to accept the amendment they may do so subject to any modifications to the amendment as they consider appropriate.

    (b) The requirements of *subsections (7) to (9)* shall not apply in relation to modifications made in accordance with *paragraph (a)*.

(11) In making the development plan under *subsection (6) or (10)*, the members shall be restricted to considering the proper planning and sustainable development of the area to which the development plan relates, the statutory obligations of any local authority in the area and any relevant policies or objectives for the time being of the Government or any Minister of the Government.

(12)

    (a) Where a planning authority makes a development plan, it shall publish a notice of the making of the plan in at least one newspaper circulating in its area.

    (b) A notice under this *subsection* shall state that a copy of the plan is available for inspection at a stated place or places (and the copy shall be kept available for inspection accordingly).

    (c) In addition to the requirements of *paragraphs (a) and (b)*, a planning authority shall send a copy of the development plan to the Minister, the prescribed authorities, any adjoining planning authorities, the Board, any town commissioners and city and county development boards within its area.

(13) As soon as may be after making an addition to or a deletion from the record of protected structures under this *section,* a planning authority shall serve on the owner and on the occupier of the structure concerned a notice of the addition or deletion, including the particulars.

(14) Where a planning authority fails to make a development plan within 2 years of the giving of notice under *section 11(1)*, notwithstanding any other provision of this *Part*, the manager shall make the plan subject to the proviso that so much of the plan that has been agreed by the members of the planning authority shall be included as part of the plan as made by the manager.

(15) When considering the draft development plan, or amendments thereto, a planning authority may invite such persons as it considers appropriate to make oral submissions regarding such plan or amendment.

(16) A person shall not question the validity of the development plan by reason only that the procedures as set out under *subsections (3) to (5) of section 11 and subsections (1), (4), (5), (6), (8) and (9) of this section* were not completed within the time required under the relevant *subsection*.

(17) A development plan made under this *section* shall have effect 4 weeks from the day that it is made.

Subsection (1)(a) was amended by s.247 of the Local Government Act 2001 (2001 No. 37), which, by the Local Government Act 2001 (Commencement) Order 2001 (S.I. No. 458 of 2001), came into effect on October 9, 2001 and deleted the words "any town commissioners and city and county development boards within the area".

Subsection (4)(bb) was inserted by s.84 of the Dublin Transport Authority Act 2008 to be commenced on such dates as the Minister shall appoint.

Subsection (6) amended by s.7 of the Planning and Development (Amendment) Act 2002 (2002 No. 32), which came into effect on December 24, 2002, by substituting "subsections (1), (4), (5), (6), (7), (8) and (9)" for "subsections (1), (4), (5), (6), (8) and (9)".

NOTE

This section concerns the procedure for the adoption of the draft development plan. Subsequent to the preparation of the draft development plan, a similar procedure of notice and public consultation must be followed in relation to the draft development plan. Where an environmental impact assessment ("EIA") is required, the draft plan must be accompanied by or include an environmental report. See art.13C of the 2001 Regulations as amended. There are however some differences in the parties and in the time frames involved. Under subs.(1), within two weeks of the draft development plan being prepared, the planning authority must give notice of such to the Minister for the Environment, An Bord Pleanála, certain prescribed bodies, any town commissioners in the area and any city or county development boards in the area. Article 13 of the Regulations 2001 sets out 27 prescribed authorities for the purposes of this section (the EPA were added as a prescribed authority under the 2006 Planning Regulations). Notice must also be given to the public by way of newspaper notice. Subsection (2) sets out the contents of the notice, providing a period for inspection of the draft plan and also inviting submissions. Where an EIA is required, the draft plan must be accompanied by or include an environmental report. See art.13C of the 2001 Regulations as amended. Article 13F of the 2001 Regulations as amended, provides that a copy of the draft development plan and the environmental reports must be sent to another Member State of the European Communities where either (a) the planning authority considers that the environment of such Member State is likely to be significantly affected by the implementation of the plan or (b) where such other Member State, likely to be significantly affected, makes such requests. This is in addition to the requirement to send a copy of the draft development plan to the bodies set out in s.12(1) and to publish a newspaper notice. Article 3 (as inserted by art.5 of the 2004 Regulations) defines Member State as "any State, other than Ireland, which is a Member State of the European Communities". Prior to sending notice, the Minister must be consulted. The Department of the Environment, Heritage and Local Government *Guidelines for Regional Authorities and Planning Authorities on the Assessment of the Effects of Certain Plans and Programmes on the Environment Guidelines* note at para. 5.12, that such consultation should be done in the form of a written communication to the Spatial Policy Section, Department of the Environment, Heritage and Local Government, Custom House, Dublin 1. A copy of the draft plan and associated environmental report should accompany the written communication. The primary purpose of this consultation is to provide information to the Department on activity levels in transboundary consultations. If the Member State so requests, consultations must be entered into by the planning authority, for which a reasonable timeframe must be agreed. The Guidelines provide at para.5.13 that the consultations with the other Member State must be carried out and completed within the statutory timeframes set out in the 2000 Planning Act. At para.5.11, the *Guidelines* state that with regard to the timing of transboundary consultations, the formal requirement in the Directive and Regulations is that such consultations should take place following preparation of the draft plan and associated environmental report. However, as a matter of best practice, it is recommended that transboundary consultations should begin as early as possible in the process of plan preparation. The report prepared by the Manager under s.12(4) regarding submissions or observations in relation to the draft plan and also any report under s.12(8) concerning submissions or observation regarding any material alteration of the draft plan, should take account of such transboundary consultations.

Subsection (3) provides that where the development plan concerns the addition or deletion of a protected structure, notice of such must be sent to the owner/occupier, allowing a period for inspection, and for the making of submissions. Such notice must also inform the owner/occupier whether the change was recommended by the Minister for Arts, etc. (who must be forwarded any submissions received).

A longer minimum period of 10 weeks is allowed for invitations of submissions from the public in relation to the draft plan. Equally, a longer period of a maximum of 22 weeks (as opposed to 16 weeks under s.11) is allowed to the Manager of the planning authority to prepare a report on the submissions and also to submit the report to the planning authority (also in contrast to s.11). The report of the Manager must "summarise" the issues raised and the submissions received. There is no obligation to circulate to each member of the planning authority the entirety of the objections and submissions received, prior to their consideration of the proposal. See *Sandyford Environmental Planning v Dun Laoghaire Rathdown County Council*, unreported, High Court, McKechnie J., June 30, 2004, in the context of a report on a variation, where the Court rejected a claim that that the Manager was so influenced by institutional bias that he was incapable of compiling an objective report. In summarising the submissions the Manager is not bound to use any formula or follow any specified method. Subsection (4)(1)(bb) provides in the case of planning authorities in the Greater Dublin Area, the report shall include a summary of the issues raised and the recommendations made by the DTA in its written submission prepared in accordance with s.31C and outline the recommendations of the manager in relation to the manner in which those issues and recommendations should be addressed in the development plan.

Where an EIA is required, the draft plan must be accompanied by or include an environmental report. See art.13C of the 2001 Regulations as amended. There is a 12-week period for the planning authority to consider the draft plan and Manager's report, at the end of which the planning authority should accept or seek to amend the draft plan. The planning authority can decide to accept or amend the draft plan earlier than the allowed 12 weeks. The planning authority has a discretion under s.12(15) to invite oral submissions. This differs from the former s.21(2)(c) where a ratepayer could make a request to state his case before a person appointed by the planning authority. Once the planning authority passes a resolution accepting or amending the draft development plan, the development plan will be adopted. Article 13H of the 2001 Regulations provides that the planning authority is obliged to take into account the environmental report, submissions or observations and any consultations with other Members States regarding transboundary environmental effects, during the preparation of the plan and prior to its formal adoption. However if an amendment to the draft plan is a material alteration of the draft plan, a further process of notice and public consultation is required, similar to the preparatory and draft stage, though with a shorter time period. It would appear that the assessment of whether an amendment is a material alteration of the draft development plan is reviewable by the court on a similar basis as to whether a permission is a material contravention of the development plan. An equivalent provision was introduced under s.37 of the 1976 Act (inserted as s.21A of the 1963 Act), following *Finn v Bray UDC* [1969] I.R. 169, where Butler J. held that a notice of a "material alteration" of an earlier draft must be displayed for the public to make submissions on. More than one amendment may be made to a draft development plan or draft variation. See *Raggett v Athy Urban District Council* [2000] 1 I.R. 469.

Not less than three weeks after the resolution making the material alteration, notice must be given to the public of such material alteration by means of a newspaper circulating in the area. A minimum of four weeks notice must be allowed for inspection or for the making of submissions. Article 13G of the 2001 Regulations provides that where appropriate, the notice must also state that information on the likely significant effects on the environment of implementing the proposed amendment will also be available for inspection and that a submission or observation in relation to that information within the stated period will also be taken into consideration. Within eight weeks, at the latest, of the notice the Manager must prepare and submit a report on the submissions to the planning authority. The planning authority is allowed a maximum of six weeks to consider the report. The planning authority

must pass a resolution accepting the plan with or without the amendment. The courts will be slow to interfere with the democratic decision to pass such a resolution. In *Malahide Community Council v Fingal County Council*, unreported, Supereme Court, December 19, 1994, the Supreme Court reversed the decision of Kinlen J., who had held that the planning authority, in amending its plan, did not consider in detail planning considerations and relied almost exclusively on an agreement. Lynch J. considered the trial judge had wrongly applied the conditions necessary before a planning permission for a specific development can be granted to the altogether different task of making and reviewing a development plan for the whole area of the planning authority. The authority may accept the amendment plan subject to "modifications", in which case the whole procedure need not be carried out again. There is no obligation to re-advertise the plan which otherwise would lead to an endless circular process; see *Construction Industry Federation v Dublin City Council*, unreported, High Court, Gilligan J., March 4, 2004 approving *Duffy v Waterford Corporation*, unreported, High Court, McGuinness J., July 21, 1999. However it seems clear that such modification should amount to minor alteration and ought not constitute a material contravention of the draft development plan, which precipitated the original procedure. See *White v Dublin Corporation*, unreported, Ó Caoimh J., June 21, 2002, where Ó Caoimh J. said, in the context of modifying an application for permission, that the term "modifying" suggests changes of a limited nature such that any changes will be slight or partial. It appears that, unlike under the previous legislation, the material alteration procedure cannot be commenced again; see *Raggett v Athy UDC* [2000] 1 I.R. 469. The development plan would appear to be "made" on the date of the resolution of the authority accepting it. The plan will come into force four weeks after this resolution. The last stage following the making of the plan involves notification to the public and other bodies and persons prescribed for the making of the development plan. Under subs.(12), a newspaper notice of the adoption of the plan must be published and copy must be sent to the prescribed authorities. Article 13I of the 2001 Regulations provides that the notice must also state that a statement is also available, summarising:
1. how environmental considerations have been integrated into the plan:
2. how:
    (a) the environmental report prepared pursuant to article 13C;
    (b) submissions and observations made to the planning authority in response to a notice under s.12(1) or 12(7) of the Act; and
    (c) any consultations under art.13F, have been taken into account during the preparation of the plan;
3. the reasons for choosing the plan, as adopted, in the light of the other reasonable alternatives dealt with; and
4. the measures decided upon to monitor, in accordance with art.13J, the significant environmental effects of implementation of the plan.

A copy of the statement must also be sent to the prescribed bodies and to any Member State consulted in relation to transboundary effects.

Subsection (13) provides after deletion or addition of a protected structure in the development plan, a notice of such must be sent to the owner or occupier. Under subs.(14) where the planning authority fails to make the development plan within two years of giving their notice of intention, the Manager must make the plan, albeit including such parts which have already been decided by the planning authority. Subsection (15) provides that in making the draft development plan or amendment to such, the planning authority may invite persons to make oral submissions. Subsection (16) provides that the validity of a development plan cannot be impugned because the various time limits for completion of each stages were not complied with. This provision was inserted to deal with *Blessington Heritage Trust Ltd v Wicklow County Council* [1999] 4 I.R. 571, where a review of a plan was quashed for being reviewed outside the time limit. This means that a development plan, once completed, cannot be called into question because certain time limits were not adopted. This does not detract from the positive obligation on the Manager and planning authority to satisfy the time limits. There is nothing to prevent a person from seeking to compel the planning authority or the Manager to carry out their functions, if they are breached, by seeking an order of mandamus, where the process of the making of the plan has not been completed. This section does not exclude challenging a plan where the prescribed time for submissions from the public or for notice were not allowed.

Subsection (17) states that the development plan will take effect four weeks after it has been made.

In relation to the various times prescribed for the stages involved in the acceptance of the draft development plan and material amendments to the draft, s.12(16) states the failure to complete within the time required will not be a reason for challenging the validity of the development plan. While the plan could not be quashed on such basis, while the process is ongoing there would appear no reason why the planning authority could not be compelled to carry out a step in the process where it has failed to do within the time required.

Where a planning application is lodged, the applicable development plan will be the plan in force at that time. In *Ebonwood v Meath County Council* [2003] 3 I.R. 34, the Court rejected the suggestion that a planning authority could have regard to a draft development plan. That decision concerned a claim for compensation and it may perhaps be too strict to interpret the decision as meaning that a planning authority cannot have some regard to pending plans. It appears that a planning permission can be refused as premature pending the making of certain statutory plans. Thus para.3 of the Fourth Schedule excludes compensation where the reason for refusal is that "[d]evelopment of the kind proposed would be premature by reference to the order of priority, if any, for the development indicated in the development plan or pending the adoption of a local area plan in accordance with the development plan". This appears to implicitly accept that the planning authority can have regard to local area plans which are pending and refuse permission on the basis that the application is premature. While the above refers to local area plans, there would appear to be no reason why the same principle would not apply to development plans for the purposes of having regard to such pending plans. The fact that such plan is merely pending and so there is no guarantee that any proposal contained in the plan would be adopted, would mean that the planning authority would not be entitled to exclusively rely upon the pending plan and ignore the existing plan. However, if a development was incompatible with the future proper planning and development of the area in such a manner as to frustrate future development set out in the plan, this could be a proper planning consideration

As discussed in relation to the note on s.10, examples of where there has been held to be a material contravention of the development plan include *McGarry v Sligo County Council* [1989] I.L.R.M. 768; *Wilkinson v Dublin County Council* [1991] I.L.R.M. 605; *Ferris v Dublin County Council*, unreported, Supreme Court, November 7, 1990; *Keogh v Galway County Borough Corporation (No. 1)* [1995] 1 I.L.R.M. 141; *Keogh v Galway Corporation (No. 2)* [1995] 2 I.L.R.M. 312.

Variation of development plan

1–13   **13.—(1)** A planning authority may at any time, for stated reasons, decide to make a variation of a development plan which for the time being is in force.

(2) Where a planning authority proposes to make a variation in a development plan, it shall—

  (a) send notice and copies of the proposed variation of the development plan to the Minister, the Board and, where appropriate, to any adjoining planning authority, the prescribed authorities, any town commissioners and city and county development boards within the area of the development plan,

  (b) publish notice of the proposed variation of the development plan in one or more newspapers circulating in that area.

(3) A notice under *subsection (2)* shall state—

  (a) the reason or reasons for the proposed variation,

  (b) that a copy of the proposed variation may be inspected at a stated place or places and at stated times during a stated period of not less than 4 weeks (and the copy of the draft variation shall be kept available for inspection accordingly), and

(c) that written submissions or observations with respect to the proposed variation made to the planning authority within the said period will be taken into consideration before the making of the variation.

(4)

(a) Not later than 8 weeks after giving notice under *subsection (2)(b),* the manager of a planning authority shall prepare a report on any submissions or observations received under that *subsection* and shall submit the report to the members of the authority for their consideration.

(b) A report under *paragraph (a)* shall—

    (i) list the persons or bodies who made submissions or observations under this *section,*

    (ii) summarise the issues raised by the persons or bodies in the submissions,

    (iii) give the response of the manager to the issues raised, taking account of the proper planning and sustainable development of the area, the statutory obligations of any local authority in the area and any relevant policies or objectives for the time being of the Government or of any Minister of the Government.

(bb) In the case of each planning authority within the GDA, a report under paragraph (a) shall summarise the issues raised and the recommendations made by the DTA in its written submission prepared in accordance with section 31D and outline the recommendations of the manager in relation to the manner in which those issues and recommendations should be addressed in the proposed variation.

(5)

(a) The members of a planning authority shall consider the proposed variation and the report of the manager under *subsection (4).*

(b) The consideration of the variation and the manager's report under *paragraph (a)* shall be completed not later than 6 weeks after the submission of the manager's report to the members of the authority.

(6)

(a) The members of a planning authority, having considered the proposed variation and manager's report, may, by resolution as they consider appropriate, make the variation, with or without modifications, or they may refuse to make it.

(b) The requirements of *subsections (2) to (5)* shall not apply in relation to modifications made in accordance with *paragraph (a).*

(7) In making a variation under this *section,* the members of the authority shall be restricted to considering the proper planning and sustainable development of the area to which the development plan relates, the statutory obligations of any local authority in the area and any relevant policies or objectives for the time being of the Government or any Minister of the Government.

(8)

(a) Where a planning authority makes a variation in a development plan, it shall publish a notice of the making of the variation in at least one newspaper circulating in its area.

(b) A notice under this *subsection* shall state that a copy of the development plan as varied is available for inspection at a stated place or places (and the copy shall be kept available for inspection accordingly).

(c) In addition to the requirements of *paragraphs (a) and (b),* a planning authority shall send a copy of the variation to the Minister, the Board and, where appropriate, to the prescribed authorities, any adjoining planning authorities, any town commissioners and city and county development boards within its area.

(9) When considering a variation of a development plan in accordance with this *section,* a planning authority may invite such persons as it considers appropriate to make oral submissions regarding the variation.

(10) A person shall not question the validity of a variation in a development plan by reason only that the procedures as set out in this *section* were not completed within the time required.

(11) A variation made to a development plan shall have effect from the day that the variation is made.

[(12) The Minister may, for the purposes of giving effect to *Directive 2001 /42/EC of the European Parliament and Council of 27 June 2001* on the assessment of the effects of certain plans and programmes on the environment *(No. 2001/42/EC, O.J. No. L 197, 21 July 2001 P. 0030–0037)*, by regulations make provision in relation to consideration of the likely significant effects on the environment of implementing a variation of a development plan.]

AMENDMENT HISTORY

Subs.(12) inserted by *r.5 of the European Communities (Environmental Assessment of Certain Plans and Programmes) Regulations 2004* (S.I. No. 435 of 2004) with effect from July 14, 2004.

Subs.(4)(bb) was inserted by s.85 of the Dublin Transport Authority Act 2008 to be commenced on such date as the Minister may appoint.

NOTE

This section concerns the variation of the development plan and allows a wide discretion to the planning authority to vary the development plan. Subsection (1) provides that the planning authority can at "any time" vary the development plan, though it must give express reasons for doing so. It appears that the local authority can enter into agreements under s.47 in connection with a variation to re-zone land. See *McHugh v Kildare County Council* [2006] 1 I.R. 100, where an agreement was upheld whereby the applicant agreed to transfer 20 per cent of his land to the Council, if the planning authority re-zoned the remainder of his land. Where the planning authority proposes to make a variation, a similar procedure for the preparation or adoption of the development plan involving notice and public consultation is required. Under the previous legislation, the procedure for variation of a development plan was strictly construed; see *Ferris v Dublin County Council,* unreported, Supreme Court, November 7, 1990; *Keogh v Galway Corporation (No.1)* [1995] 3 I.R. 457; *Keogh v Galway Corporation (No.2)* [1995] 3 I.R. 457. By way of summary of the timeframe, a minimum period of four weeks for public inspection and submissions is required. The Manager must prepare and submit the report within eight weeks of the notice, while consideration of the report by the planning authority must be completed within six weeks. Once the variation is accepted a similar process of public display must be followed.

Subsection (2) provides where a planning authority proposes to make a variation to the development plan, it must send a notice of such to certain bodies and prescribed authorities and also publish a notice in the newspaper. Article 13 of the 2001 Regulations sets out 27 prescribed authorities for the purposes of this section (the EPA were added as a prescribed authority under the 2006 Planning Regulations). Subsection (3) sets out the content of the notice, stating the reason for the variation, that the variation can be inspected, and inviting submissions. The reason or reasons must then be incorporated in the notice required to be published under s.13(3)(a). See *Sandyford Environmental Planning v Dun Laoghaire Rathdown County Council*, unreported, High Court, McKechnie J., June 30, 2004, where McKechnie J. said the objective is to put the public on notice of matters likely to interest those concerned and to do so in such a way that any member, who informatively considers the notice, will recognise the essentials of the proposal, and depending on detail or complexity, will be alerted sufficiently to further evaluate the underlying reasons for that proposal. As the reasons are to be stated through the medium of a newspaper notice, it is not practical or feasible to give extensive reasons. A local authority should not adopt a minimalist standard to the contents of such a notice and, if anything, should err on the side of an expansive approach. Article 13K of the 2001 Regulations as amended, provides that before giving notice of its intention to make a variation, the planning authority must consider whether or not the proposed variation would be likely to have significant effects on the environment, taking into account relevant criteria set out in Sch.2A. The procedure for giving such consideration involves a screening process similar to art.13A. The SEA is therefore is not mandatory, but is required to be carried out if the screening process concludes that the proposed variation would be likely to have significant effects on the environment. This process applies to the variation of any development plans, irrespective of whether the population of the area exceeds 10,000 persons. Where the planning authority decides it would not have such significant effects, it must send notice to the EPA, the Minister for the Environment where it may have significant effects in relation to architectural or archaeological heritage or to nature conservation or to the Minister for Communications and Marine, where it might have significant effects on fisheries or the marine environment. The notice must, inter alia, allow such body to make submissions or observations within a specified period being not less than 4 weeks. Following the end of such period, the planning authority will again re-consider whether the plan would be likely to have significant effects on the environment taking into account the criteria in Sch.2A and any submissions or observations received. Having made such determination, the planning authority must as soon as practicable, make a copy of the decision (including, if applicable, any reasons for not requiring an environmental assessment) available for public inspection and notify any body to whom the notice was sent. Article 13L of the 2001 Regulations provides that a proposed variation of the development plan must be accompanied by or include an environmental report. Article 13M provides that before giving notice under subs.(2), a notice must be sent to the environmental authorities regarding the carrying out of an environmental assessment with a view to obtaining their feedback on the content of an environmental report. Article 13N sets out the content of the environmental report, while art.13O requires forwarding a copy of the environmental report and proposed variation to a Member State, where it is considered to have transboundary environmental effects.

Under subs.(4), not later than four weeks after the notice, the Manager must prepare a report which, listing the persons, the issues raised, the Manager's opinion and his recommendation. The obligation is to "summarise" the issues raised and the submissions received. There is no obligation to circulate to each member of the planning authority the entirety of the objections and submissions received, prior to their consideration of the proposal. See *Sandyford Environmental Planning v Dun Laoghaire Rathdown County Council*, unreported, High Court, McKechnie J., June 30, 2004, where the Court rejected a claim that that the Manager was so influenced by institutional bias that he was incapable of compiling an objective report. In summarising the submissions the Manager is not bound to use any formula or follow any specified method. Subsection (4)(1)(bb) provides that where the planning authorities are situated within the Greater Dublin Area, the report of the Manager shall include a summary of the issues raised and the recommendations made by the DTA in its written submission prepared in accordance with s.31D and outline the recommendations of the manager in relation to the manner in which those issues and recommendations should be addressed in the proposed variation.

Subsection (5) declares that the planning authority must consider the variation and report, which must be completed not later than six weeks after receipt of the report.

Under subs.(6), the planning authority may by resolution, make the variation with or without modification or refuse the variation. The variation is limited to modifications; as to the meaning of which see *White v Dublin Corporation*, unreported, High Court, Ó Caoimh J., June 21, 2002. Article 13P of the 2001 Regulations provides that the planning authority shall take account of the environmental report, any submissions or observations made and any consultations with a Member State in the event of a transboundary effect, during the making of the variation and before its adoption. There is no requirement to re-advertise the making of any modifications. See subs.(6)(b) and also *Construction Industry Federation v Dublin City Council*, unreported, High Court, Gilligan J., March 4, 2004 approving *Duffy v Waterford Corporation*, unreported, High Court, McGuinness J., July 21, 1999. Under subs.(7) in making the decision to make the variation, the planning authority is limited to considering the proper planning and sustainable development of the area, the statutory obligations of the local authority, and the policies or objectives of the Government or Minister. Subsection (8) provides that after making a variation, the planning authority must publish a notice of the variation in the newspaper, stating a copy is available for inspection. The planning authority must also send a copy to the prescribed bodies. Article 13Q of the 2001 Regulations provides in the event of strategic environmental assessment being required, the notice must state that a statement is also available, summarising:

1. how environmental considerations have been integrated into the variation;
2. how:
   (a) the environmental report prepared pursuant to art.13I;
   (b) submissions and observations made to the planning authority in response to a notice under s.13(2) of the Act; and
   (c) any consultations under art.13O have been taken into account during the preparation of the plan;
3. the reasons for choosing the plan, as adopted, in the light of the other reasonable alternatives dealt with; and
4. the measures decided upon to monitor, in accordance with art.13R, the significant environmental effects of implementation of the plan.

A copy of the statement must also be sent to the prescribed bodies and to any Member State consulted in relation to transboundary effects.

Under subs.(9), in considering a variation, the planning authority may invite oral submissions. Subsection (10) is similar to s.12(16) in prohibiting a person from questioning the validity of the variation after it has been adopted. This provision was inserted to deal with *Blessington Heritage Trust Ltd v Wicklow County Council* [1999] 4 I.R. 571, where a review of a plan was quashed for being reviewed outside the time limit. However, before the variation is adopted a person can seek to compel compliance with the time limits. Under subs.(11), a variation will take effect immediately on being made which is in contrast to the development plan itself, which has effect only four weeks after being made.

Public rights of way in development plans

1–14   **14.—(1)** Where a planning authority proposes to include, for the first time, a provision in a development plan relating to the preservation of a specific public right of way, it shall serve notice (which shall include particulars of the provision and a map indicating the right of way) of its intention to do so on any owner and occupier of the land over which the right of way exists.

(2) A notice served under *subsection (1)* shall state that—

(a) the planning authority proposes to include a provision in the development plan relating to the preservation of the public right of way,

(b) written submissions or observations regarding the proposal may be made to the planning authority within a stated period of not less than 6 weeks and that the submissions or observations will be taken into consideration by the planning authority, and

(c) where, following consideration of any submissions or observations received under *paragraph (b),* the planning authority considers that the provision should be adopted, or adopted subject to modifications, a right of appeal to the Circuit Court exists in relation to such provision.

(3) The members of a planning authority, having considered the proposal and any submissions or observations made in respect of it, may, by resolution as they consider appropriate, recommend the inclusion of the provision in the development plan, with or without modifications, or may recommend against its inclusion and any person on whom notice has been served under *subsection (1)* shall be notified of the recommendation accordingly and a copy of such notice shall be published in at least one newspaper circulating in the area.

(4) Any person who has been notified of the recommendation of the planning authority under *subsection (3)* may, before the expiration of the 21 days next following the notification, appeal to the Circuit Court against the inclusion in the development plan of the proposed provision, and the Court, if satisfied that no public right of way exists, shall so declare and the provision shall accordingly not be included.

(5)

(a) The taking of an appeal under *subsection (4)* shall not prejudice the making of a development plan under *section 12* except in regard to the inclusion of the proposed provision which is before the Court.

(b) Where a development plan has been made under *section 12* and the Court, having considered an appeal under *subsection (4),* decides that the public right of way exists, the proposed provision under this *section* shall be deemed to be part of the development plan.

(6) Where any existing development plan contains any provision relating to the preservation of a public right of way, the provision may be included in any subsequent development plan without the necessity to comply with this *section.*

(7)

(a) Nothing in this *section* shall affect the existence or validity of any public right of way which is not included in the development plan.

(b) The inclusion of a public right of way in a development plan shall be evidence of the existence of such a right unless the contrary is shown.

NOTE

This section concerns the procedure for including the preservation of a right of way in the development plan for the first time. The section introduces some minor changes to the previous law contained in s.21 of the 1963 Act in relation to preservation of a public right of way, by stipulating that the procedure only applies where the inclusion of the preservation of a public right of way is included "for the first time". The obligations do not arise where the public right of way was included in an existing development plan. The situation is unclear where the right of way was included in an earlier plan though not in the existing development plan. It would appear not to apply in such instance.

Subsection (1) provides that the planning authority must serve a notice, including particulars and a map, on the owner or occupier of the land. Subsection (2) sets out the content of the notice, which must include a statement of the proposal, an invitation to make submissions or observations and the fact that an appeal lies to the Circuit Court from a decision of the planning authority. A shorter period is prescribed for notice and submissions, being a minimum of six weeks as opposed to three months under the previous Act. Subsection (3) provides that the planning authority may, by resolution, recommend the inclusion of the provision, with or without modification, or recommend its exclusion. The owner and occupier will be given notice of such recommendation and a notice of the decision shall be published in the newspaper. Under subs.(4), a person served with the notice has 21 days to appeal the decision to the Circuit Court. There is no provision to extend such time. The right of appeal is not open to the general public but is strictly confined to the persons served, which will be the owner and occupier. Subsection (5) provides that where an appeal has been made in relation to the inclusion of the public right of way, this will not affect the making of the development plan. The time for the entry into force of the whole development plan will not therefore be delayed until the resolution of such appeal, with the exception of the actual provision itself. Once the court has adjudicated on the matter, such provision will thereafter form part of the development plan if it finds in favour of the planning authority. Subsection (6) makes it clear that the procedure only applies to a public right of way introduced in a development plan for the first time. If it already has been included, there is no necessity to go through the procedure. Subsection (7) provides that the fact that a public right of way has not been included in the development plan, does not mean it does not exist or has been rendered defunct. The inclusion of the public right of way in the plan will amount to evidence of its existence unless the contrary is shown. The inclusion raises a presumption in favour of its existence, although it will not be conclusive. It implicitly accepts that a public right of way could have been wrongly asserted in the development plan. To reverse such presumption, a person would have to present evidence on the balance of probabilities to the effect that such a public right of way does not exist.

General duty of planning authority to secure objectives of development plan

1–15   **15.—(1)** It shall be the duty of a planning authority to take such steps within its powers as may be necessary for securing the objectives of the development plan.

(2) The manager of a planning authority shall, not more than 2 years after the making of a development plan, give a report to the members of the authority on the progress achieved in securing the objectives referred to in *subsection (1)*.

NOTE

This section prescribes a general positive duty on the planning authority to secure the objectives of the development plan. The planning authority is required not simply to adhere to the development plan but also to give effect to its objectives. Steps which they may take include the powers granted to it in the rest of the Act such as in relation to housing, compulsory purchase, etc. A similar duty was contained in s.22(1) of the 1963 Act. From the environmental contract analogy of McCarthy J. in *McGarry v Sligo County Council* [1989] I.L.R.M. 768, it may be argued that like any contract, a member of the community should be able to enforce compliance analogous to specific performance in contract. The contents of the development plan, however, are framed in terms of "objectives", which by nature are aspirational. Also the phrase "within its power" can be read as a limitation on the duty, insofar as it reflects practical limitations to achieving its goals. The planning authority clearly has a discretion in the overall functioning of the local authority. While private law-type duty requiring strict compliance is not appropriate, the duty is not empty.

The duty can be used to support a challenge to restrain local authority development in material contravention of the development plan. See also s.178. It could also be used in certain individual circumstances, such as in *Hynes v An Bord Pleanála*, unreported, High Court, Laffoy J., December 10, 1997, where it was claimed the planning authority could not consent to a planning application over some of its land where the development would be a material contravention of the plan. The planning authority should also arguably take enforcement action to secure the objectives of the development plan, in appropriate instances. See also *Browne v Cashel UDC*, unreported, High Court, Geoghegan J., March 26, 1993. Subsection (2) provides that the Manager must draw up a report on the progress in attaining the objectives of the development plan, not later than two years after the making of the development plan. In *O'Mahony v An Bord Pleanála* unreported, O'Neill J. February 18, 2005, a challenge to the confirmation of a CPO for proposed road improvements was rejected where it was alleged the planning authority had failed to have regard to the fact land was zoned residential in breach of s.15, by ensuring there was adequate access to lands. The Department of the Environment *Guidelines for Planning Authorities—Part V of the Planning and Development Act 2000* provide that the County Manager must address his mind to achievement of the housing strategy, and where there has been changes in the housing market since the creation of the housing strategy, report the matter to the elected members and where appropriate, make recommendations. Also relevant in this respect is the Article 13J of the the 2001 Regulations which incorporates Directive 2001/42/EC on Strategic Environmental Assessment. Under this provision the planning authority is required to monitor the significant environmental effects of the implementation of the development plan in order, inter alia, to identify at an early stage unforeseen adverse effects and to be able to undertake appropriate remedial action. Article 13J(2) provides that the report of the Manager under s.15(2) must include information in relation to the progress on and the results of, monitoring the significant effects of implementation of the development plan.

Copies of development plans

16.—(1) A planning authority shall make available for inspection and purchase by members of the public copies of a development plan and of variations of a development plan and extracts therefrom.   **1–16**

(2) A planning authority shall make available for inspection and purchase by members of the public copies of a report of a manager of a planning authority prepared under *sections 11(4), 12(4) and (8) and 13(4)* and extracts therefrom.

(3) Copies of the development plan and of variations of a development plan and reports of the manager referred to in *subsection (2)* and extracts therefrom shall be made available for purchase on payment of a specified fee not exceeding the reasonable cost of making a copy.

NOTE

This section concerns the making available of the development plan and other reports for inspection to members of the public. Subsection (2) relates to making available for inspection or purchase copies of the report of the Manager relating to: submissions; on the notice of intention to make a development plan (s.11(4)); submissions on the prepared draft development plan (s.12(4)); submissions on a proposed amendment to the draft development plan (s.12(8)); and submissions on a proposed variation to the development plan (s.13(4)). Subsection (3) provides that the fee for the purchase of the plan and reports shall not exceed the reasonable cost of making a copy. Development plans are accessible to the public on the websites of most planning authorities although there is no obligation to include such plans.

Evidence of development plans

1–17   **17.—(1)** A document purporting to be a copy of a part or all of a development
plan and to be certified by an officer of a planning authority as a correct copy
shall be evidence of the plan or part, unless the contrary is shown, and it shall
not be necessary to prove the signature of the officer or that he or she was in
fact such an officer.

    (2) Evidence of all or part of a development plan may be given by production
of a copy thereof certified in accordance with this *subsection* and it shall not
be necessary to produce the plan itself.

NOTE

    This section allows for proof of the development plan in court proceedings. Certification
by a planning officer that the development plan or part thereof is a correct copy will
be presumed to be evidence of such unless the contrary is shown. It appears that this
presumption can be rebutted on the balance of probabilities. It further provides it is not
necessary to prove the certification by proving the signature or that the person had the
capacity of officer. This is however a presumption which can be rebutted on the balance
of probabilities. Subsection (2) provides that a copy of the plan as certified will amount to
evidence of the plan. See similar provision concerning a Manager's Order under s.151(6)
and (7) of the Local Government Act 2001.
    This provision coincides with s.21(6) of the 1963 Act, though it differs slightly by
omitting the phrase "prima facie evidence" in favour of evidence unless the contrary is
shown, which is a similar standard.

CHAPTER II

Local Area Plans

Local area plans

1–18   **18.—(1)** A planning authority may at any time, and for any particular area
within its functional area, prepare a local area plan in respect of that area.

    (2) Two or more planning authorities may co-operate in preparing a local
area plan in respect of any area which lies within the combined functional area
of the authorities concerned.

    (3)

        (a) When considering an application for permission under *section 34,* a
planning authority, or the Board on appeal, shall have regard to the
provisions of any local area plan prepared for the area to which the
application relates, and the authority or the Board may also consider
any relevant draft local plan which has been prepared but not yet
made in accordance with *section 20.*

        (b) When considering an application for permission, a planning authority,
or the Board on appeal, shall also have regard to any integrated area
plan (within the meaning of the *Urban Renewal Act, 1998*) for the
area to which the application relates.

    (4)

        (a) A local area plan prepared under this *section* shall indicate the period
for which the plan is to remain in force.

        (b) A local area plan may remain in force in accordance with *paragraph* *(a)* notwithstanding the variation of a development plan or the making of a new development plan affecting the area to which the local area plan relates except that, where any provision of a local area plan conflicts with the provisions of the development plan as varied or the new development plan, the provision of the local area plan shall cease to have any effect.

(5) A planning authority may at any time amend or revoke a local area plan.

(6) A planning authority may enter into an arrangement with any suitably qualified person or local community group for the preparation, or the carrying out of any aspect of the preparation, of a local area plan.

NOTE

The 2000 Act gives statutory recognition for the first time to local area plans, though they existed prior to the Act. The concept of local area plans is to provide a more detailed template for development over a smaller area than contained in a development plan. In contrast to the situation in England, local area plans are not integrated within the development plans (which may be either a unitary development plan or a structure plan with local area plans). The planning authority has a discretion in defining the boundaries which a local area plan covers. Local area plans are designed to cover narrower areas within the area of competence of the authority, as opposed to the whole area under a development plan. Local area plans are a reflection of the fact there may be particular issues or interests affecting a local area. In contrast to development plans, the planning authority has a greater flexibility in the creation and revocation of local area plans. The planning authority can choose the time and the scope of the area for the creation of the local area plan, although local area plans are mandatory in the circumstances specified in s.19(1)(b). Under subs.(2), two or more planning authorities can co-operate in the creation of any local area plan for joint areas.

Although local area plans have independent status, they are subordinate in status to development plans and must be consistent with the development plan. See Dodd, "From National to Local Plans and the Concept of Sustainable Development" [2003] 10 (4) I.P.E.L.J. 119. Section 10(7) provides that a development plan may indicate that specified development in a particular area will be subject to the making of a local area plan. Subsection (3)(a) provides that a planning authority or Board on appeal, must have regard to the local area plan in determining a planning application. Where a draft plan has been prepared but not yet adopted, the planning authority or Board has a discretion whether to have regard to it. Under subs.(4), local area plans will remain in force even where the development plan has been subject to variation or where a new development plan has been made. Under subs.(3)(b), the planning authority must also have regard to integrated area plans, which effectively have the status of local area plans. Section 7(4) of the Urban Renewal Act 1998 declares:

"An integrated area plan shall consist of a written statement and a plan indicating the objectives for (a) the social and economic renewal, on a sustainable basis, of the area to which the plan relates, and (b) improvements in the physical environment of that area".

Under subs.(4), the local area plan will indicate the period for which it is in force. There is, therefore, no prescribed life for a local area plan, although the local area plan should specify its duration. In practice many local area plans have a specified life of six years (in order to be consistent with development plans), although it is clear that a local area plan can specify a life of greater or less than six years. Under subs.(5), the planning authority may amend or revoke the plan at any time. The planning authority has freedom to amend or revoke the local area plan though it must do so in accordance with the procedure of public consultation set out in s.20. Subsection (6) allows the planning authority to obtain assistance from suitably qualified persons or community groups in the preparation of the plan. This would enable the planning authority to employ certain consultants in the preparation. Local area plans also have implications for compensation. Under para.15 of the Fourth Schedule, compensation is excluded where permission is refused, by reason that development would materially contravene an objective in a local area plan. Also, under para.3, a reason for refusal which would exclude compensation is that development would be premature, inter alia, pending the adoption of a local area plan in accordance with the development plan.

Application and content of local area plans

1–19   **19.—(1)**

(a) A local area plan may be prepared in respect of any area, including a Gaeltacht area, or an existing suburb of an urban area, which the planning authority considers suitable and, in particular, for those areas which require economic, physical and social renewal and for areas likely to be subject to large scale development within the lifetime of the plan.

(b) A local area plan shall be made in respect of an area which—

(i) is designated as a town in the most recent census of population, other than a town designated as a suburb or environs in that census,

(ii) has a population in excess of 2,000, and

(iii) is situated within the functional area of a planning authority which is a county council.

(c) *Section 20(3)(a)* shall be complied with—

(i) in the case of the first local area plan, not later than 2 years after the making of a development plan under this *Part,* and

(ii) notwithstanding *section 18(5),* at least every 6 years after the making of the previous local area plan.

[(2) A local area plan shall be consistent with the objectives of the development plan and shall consist of a written statement and a plan or plans which may include—

(a) objectives for the zoning of land for the use solely or primarily of particular areas for particular purposes, or

(b) such other objectives in such detail as may be determined by the planning authority for the proper planning and sustainable development of the area to which it applies, including detail on community facilities and amenities and on standards for the design of developments and structures.]

[(2A) Each planning authority within the GDA shall ensure that its local area plans are consistent with the transport strategy of the DTA.]

(3) The Minister may provide in regulations that local area plans shall be prepared in respect of certain classes of areas or in certain circumstances and a planning authority shall comply with any such regulations.

[(4) The Minister may, for the purposes of giving effect to *Directive 2001 /42/EC of the European Parliament and Council of 27 June 2001* on the assessment of the effects of certain plans and programmes on the environment (*No. 2001/42/EC, O.J. No. L 197, 21 July 2001 P. 0030–0037*), by regulations make provision in relation to consideration of the likely significant effects on the environment of implementing a local area plan.]

AMENDMENT HISTORY

Subsection (2) substituted by s.8 of the Planning and Development (Amendment) Act 2002 (No. 32 of 2002) which came into effect on December 24, 2002.

Subsection (4) substituted by r.6 of the European Communities (Environmental Assessment of Certain Plans and Programmes) Regulations 2004 (S.I. No. 435 of 2004), with effect from July 14, 2004.

Subsection (2A) inserted by s.86 of the Dublin Transport Authority Act 2008, to be commenced on such date as the Minister shall appoint.

NOTE

This section concerns when a local area plan is mandatory and the contents of local area plans. A planning authority has a discretion in the making of a local area plan in the circumstances set out in subs.(1)(a), while local area plans are mandatory in relation to areas designated as towns within subs.(1)(b). Under the 1963 Act there was a requirement to make development plans for scheduled towns. A local area plan may now be prepared for such scheduled towns.

A new subs.(2) was inserted under s.8 of the Planning and Development (Amendment) Act 2002. This subsection provides that the local area plan must comprise a written statement and be consistent with the objectives of the development plan. The objectives may be determined by the planning authority which must relate to the proper planning and sustainable development of the area. Subsection (2)(b) enlists matters such as details on community facilities and amenities and on standards for the design of developments and structures which may be included, though this is clearly not exhaustive. The difference between the new subs.(2) and that under the 2000 Act is the insertion of subs.(2)(a) which provides that the plan may include objectives in relation to the zoning of particular areas of land for particular purposes. The inclusion of this objective is nevertheless at the discretion of the planning authority. The planning authority therefore has a wide discretion as regards the content of local area plans. As the local area plan is lower in the hierarachy of plans than a development plan, the local area plan will typically be made after the making of a development plan. Subsection (2A) provides in the case of planning authorities within the Greater Dublin Area, they shall ensure that their local area plans are consistent with the transport strategy of the Dublin Tranport Authority

The only subsection which expressly deals with timeframes to make a new plan is s.19(1)(c)(ii) which states s.20(3)(a) shall be complied with at least every six years since the making of the plan. Section 20(3)(a) mentioned concerns sending a notice of a proposal to make, amend or revoke a local area plan to the Board and to prescribed authorities and also publish a public newspaper notice. Section 18(5) also mentioned in s.19(1)(c) provides that a planning authority may at any time amend or revoke a local area plan. Section 19(1)(c) therefore only refers to s.20(3)(a) and not to the entire s.20(3) which sets out the process following notification including the actual making, amending or revoking of the plan which is instead taken under s.20(3)(d)(ii). However, a complication arises from the fact that certain local area plans are mandatory. The requirement to make a local area plan for certain towns or area implies that that there must always be in force a local area plan for that town or area. If the life of the previous mandatory local area plan for that area is merely six years, then merely following the outer time limits under s.19(1)(c) of giving notice after six years, means that there would be a lapse between the life of the previous local area plan and the new local area plan – this is not permitted. There is no prescribed time limit for the life of a local area plan although s.18(4)(a) states that a local area plan prepared under the section shall specify the period for which the plan is to remain in force. There is no requirement that a local area plan is of six years duration. Thus, while a local area plan must specify the period, this period may be greater or less than six years' duration. Thus, arising from the mandatory obligation to have local area plans, there is an obligation to ensure that a new local area plan is in force prior to the expiration of the previous plans. This means that where the life of the previous mandatory plan is six years, a new or reviewed plan must be made prior to the expiration of the six-year period. In respect of non-mandatory local area plans under s.19(1)(a), there is no obligation to even amend or make an additional local area plan. The pre-existing plan will simply lapse.

Subsection (3) allows the Minister to prescribe local area plans to be prepared for certain classes of area or in particular circumstances. Under subs.(4), the local area plan must contain information on the likely significant effects on the environment in the implementation of the plan, and the Minister may make regulations for these purposes.

Regulations have been made pursuant to subs.(4) to provide for strategic environmental assessments of local area plans. In this respect art.14A of the the 2001 Regulations sets out a procedure for determining whether such assessment is required. An environmental assessment is mandatory for making a local area plan or an amendment to a local area plan, for an area the population of which is more than 10,000 persons. With respect to a local area plan for an area with a population less than 10,000 persons, an environmental assessment is only mandatory, where the plan would be likely to have significant effects on the environment. In respect of plans for an area with a population less than 10,000, art.14A(2) provides that a screening process must be carried out prior to sending notice of an intention to review the plan under s.20(3). Under this screening process the planning authority will consider whether or not the implementation of a new development plan would be likely to have significant effects on the environment. Schedule 2A sets out the criteria for determining whether a plan is likely to have a significant effect on the environment. Where the planning authority determines that it would have such likely effects, sub-art.6 applies, whereby the planning authority must make a copy of the decision available for inspection. However, where the planning authority does arrive at a determination as to whether there would be likely significant effects, under sub-art.4, the planning authority must notify the prescribed authorities and indicate that submissions or observations must be made within a specified period, which will not be less than four weeks. Notification of the Environmental Protection Agency is mandatory in all circumstances, while notification of the Minister for the Environment, Heritage and Local Government and the Minister for Communications, Marine and Natural Resources, is conditional on certain circumstances applying. Under sub-art.5, the planning authority will then determine whether there is such a likely effect taking into account the submissions and also the criteria in Sch.2A. As soon as practicable after making a determination, the planning authority shall:

1. make a copy of its decision, including, as appropriate, the reasons for not requiring an environmental assessment, available for public inspection at the offices of the planning authority during office hours; and
2. notify its decision to any environmental authority which was notified.

Where an environmental assessment is to be carried out then under art.14B, the planning authority is obliged to prepare an environmental report of the likely significant effects on the environment of implementing the local area plan or amended plan, prior to giving notice of the intention to make a local area plan under s.20(3). The Guidelines provide at para.4.4 that in terms of the practical presentation of the environmental report, it is entirely a matter for the plan making authority as to whether it is included in the actual plan or presented as a separate document. Where it is included in the plan, it should be clearly identifiable as the "environmental report". However, if the report is too long to be included in the plan, a summary chapter should be included in the plan—with the full report included as an appendix or as a separate document. Also at para.4.5, the Guidelines provide that work on the draft plan and the Environmental Report should proceed in tandem. It notes that if the SEA process is to add value to plan-making, the preparation of the report must influence the choice of the preferred plan strategy, and of any mitigation measures needed to offset potential adverse effects of implementing that strategy. Article 14C provides that notice must be sent to the environmental authorities regarding the carrying out of an environmental assessment with a view to obtaining their feedback on the content of an environmental report. Article 14D sets out the content of the environmental report

Consultation and adoption of local area plans

1–20   **20.—(1)** A planning authority shall take whatever steps it considers necessary to consult the public before preparing, amending or revoking a local area plan including consultations with any local residents, public sector agencies, non-governmental agencies, local community groups and commercial and business interests within the area.

(2) A planning authority shall consult Údarás na Gaeltachta before making, amending or revoking a local area plan under *subsection (3)* for an area which includes a Gaeltacht area.

(3)

(a) The planning authority shall, as soon as may be after consideration of any matters arising out of consultations under *subsections (1) or (2)* but before making, amending or revoking a local area plan—

    (i) send notice of the proposal to make, amend or revoke a local area plan to the Board and to the prescribed authorities (and, where applicable, it shall enclose a copy of the proposed plan or amended plan),

    (ii) publish a notice of the proposal in one or more newspapers circulating in its area.

(b) A notice under *paragraph (a)* shall state—

    (i) that the planning authority proposes to make, amend or revoke a local area plan,

    (ii) that a copy of the proposal to make, amend or revoke the local area plan and (where appropriate) the proposed local area plan, or proposed amended plan, may be inspected at such place or places as are specified in the notice during such period as may be so stated (being a period of not less than 6 weeks),

    (iii) that submissions or observations in respect of the proposal made to the planning authority during such period will be taken into consideration in deciding upon the proposal.

(c)

    (i) Not later than 12 weeks after giving notice under *paragraph (b),* the manager of a planning authority shall prepare a report on any submissions or observations received pursuant to a notice under that *paragraph* and shall submit the report to the members of the planning authority for their consideration.

    (ii) A report under *subparagraph (i)* shall—

        (I) list the persons who made submissions or observations,

        (II) summarise the issues raised by the persons in the submissions or observations,

        (III) contain the opinion of the manager in relation to the issues raised, and his or her recommendations in relation to the proposed local area plan, amendment to a local area plan or revocation of a local area plan, as the case may be, taking account of the proper planning and sustainable development of the area, the statutory obligations of any local authority in the area and any relevant policies or objectives for the time being of the Government or of any Minister of the Government.

[(cc) In the case of each planning authority within the GDA, a report under subparagraph (c)(i) shall summarise the issues raised and the recommendations made by the DTA in a report prepared in accordance with section 31E and outline the recommendations of the manager in relation to the manner in which those issues and recommendations should be addressed in the proposed local area plan.]

[(d)

    (i) The members of a planning authority shall consider the proposal to make, amend or revoke a local area plan and the report of the manager under *paragraph (c)*.

    (ii) Following consideration of the manager's report under *subparagraph (i)*, the local area plan shall be deemed to be made, amended or revoked, as appropriate, in accordance with the recommendations of the manager as set out in his or her report, 6 weeks after the furnishing of the report to all the members of the authority, unless the planning authority, by resolution—

        (I) subject to *paragraphs (e), (f), (g) and (h)*, decides to make or amend the plan otherwise than as recommended in the manager s report, or

        (II) decides not to make, amend or revoke, as the case may be, the plan.

(e)

    (i) Where, following the consideration of the manager's report, it appears to the members of the authority that the proposal (being a proposal to make or amend a local area plan) should be varied or modified, and the proposed variation or modification would, if made, be a material alteration of the proposal concerned, the planning authority shall, not later than 3 weeks after the passing of a resolution under *paragraph (d)(ii)*, publish notice of the proposed variation or modification in one or more newspapers circulating in its area.

    (ii) A notice under *subparagraph (i)* shall state that—

        (I) a copy of the proposed variation or modification of the proposal may be inspected at a stated place and at stated times during a stated period of not less than 4 weeks (and the copy shall be kept available for inspection accordingly), and

        (II) written submissions or observations with respect to the proposed variation or modification of the proposal made to the planning authority within the stated period shall be taken into consideration before the making of any variation or modification.

(f)

    (i) Not later than 8 weeks after giving notice under *paragraph (e)*, the manager of a planning authority shall prepare a report on any submissions or observations received pursuant to a notice under that *paragraph* and submit the report to the members of the authority for their consideration.

     (ii) A report under *subparagraph (i)* shall—

       (I) list the persons who made submissions or observations under *paragraph (e),*

       (II) summarise the issues raised by the persons in the submissions or observations,

       (III) contain the opinion of the manager in relation to the issues raised, and his or her recommendations in relation to the proposed variation or modification to the proposal, including any amendment to that proposed variation or modification he or she considers appropriate, taking account of the proper planning and sustainable development of the area, the statutory obligations of any local authority in the area and any relevant policies or objectives for the time being of the Government or of any Minister of the Government.

(g)

     (i) The members of a planning authority shall consider the proposed variation or modification of the proposal and the report of the manager under *paragraph (f).*

     (ii) Following consideration of the manager's report under *subparagraph (i),* the local area plan shall be deemed to be made or amended, as appropriate, with the variation or modification proposed by the members of the planning authority or, if different from that variation or modification, the variation or modification as recommended in the manager s report under *subparagraph (i),* 6 weeks after the furnishing of the report to all the members of the authority, unless, where such a recommendation for a different variation or modification is so made, the planning authority, by resolution, decides to make or amend the plan otherwise than in accordance with that recommendation (and the variation or modification the members of the authority so decide upon shall be the original variation or modification proposed by them, subject to such amendment of it as they consider appropriate).

  (h) The requirements of *paragraphs (e) to (g)* shall not apply in relation to an amendment made in accordance with *paragraph (g)(ii).*

  (i) When performing their functions under this *subsection,* the members of the authority shall be restricted to considering the proper planning and sustainable development of the area, the statutory obligations of any local authority in the area and any relevant policies or objectives for the time being of the Government or of any Minister of the Government.]

(4) The Minister may make regulations or issue guidelines in relation to the preparation of local area plans.

(5) A planning authority shall send a copy of any local area plan made under this *Chapter* to any bodies consulted under *subsection (1), (2) or (3),* the Board and, where appropriate, any prescribed body.

AMENDMENT HISTORY

Paragraph (d) of subs.(3) substituted, and paras (e)–(i) of subs.(3) inserted by s.9 of the Planning and Development (Amendment) Act 2002 (No. 32 of 2002) which came into effect on December 24, 2002.

Subsection (3)(cc) inserted by s.87 of the Dublin Transport Authority Act 2008 to be commenced on such date as the Minister shall appoint.

NOTE

This section concerns the procedure for the making and amending of local area plans. The procedure is similar to the making and amending of a development plan.

Subsection (1) provides that the planning authority "shall take whatever steps it considers necessary" to consult the public before the making, amending or revoking of a local area plan. While the use of the word "shall" implies a mandatory obligation, this is tempered by the discretionary element, allowing for the opinion of the planning authority as to what it considers necessary. While the subsection goes on to include consultation with any local residents, public sector agencies and other bodies stated, it would appear that there is no obligation to consult such bodies in every circumstance. The planning authority may not consider it necessary to consult such bodies in a particular instance. The use of the word "shall" nevertheless means that the planning authority does not have *carte blanche* as to whether it consults the public. There is an obligation to consult the public, though the extent and manner of such consultation will be guided by what it considers necessary. Under subs.(2), where the local area plan covers an area of the Gaeltacht, the planning authority must consult with Údarás na Gaeltachta.

Subsection (3) provides that following the consultation, the planning authority must send a notice of the proposal in relation to the plan to An Bord Pleanála and also to certain prescribed authorities. Article 14 of the 2001 Regulations as amended designates the prescribed authorities, for the purposes of the section, as the Minister, any local authority, including town commissioners, in the area to which the local area plan, proposed local area plan or proposed amended plan, as appropriate, relates, and any relevant city and county development board, and any planning authority whose area is contiguous to the area to which the local area plan, proposed local area plan or proposed amended plan, as appropriate, relates. In addition to this, the planning authority must also publish a notice of the proposal in one or more local newspapers circulating in the area. As regards the content of such notice in both cases, the notice must state the nature of the proposal, indicate that the proposal may be inspected at a specified place and period and also that submissions may be made in relation to the proposal within the specified period (not less than six weeks).

However, prior to the notice being given, art.14A of the the 2001 Regulations provides that the planning authority must determine the need for a strategic environmental assessment. Such assessment is mandatory where the population of the area for the local plan is more than 10,000 or if less than 10,000, where the planning authority has determined that the plan would be likely to have significant effects on the environment under the procedure set out in art.14A. Where the assessment is required, the planning authority must prepare an environemental report following scoping from certain prescribed bodies. Article 14E provides that the notice of the proposal to make or amend the local area plan must state that the planning authority has prepared an environmental report of the likely significant effects on the environment of implementing the local area plan or amended plan and that submissions or observations may be made in respect thereof. The notice must also be sent to the authorities set out in art.13A(4) These authorities set out in art.13A(4), concern the Environmental Protection Agency; the Minister for the Environment, Heritage and Local Government, where it appears to the planning authority that the plan might have significant effects in relation to the architectural or archaeological heritage or to nature conservation and the Minister for Communications, Marine and Natural Resources, where it appears to the planning authority that the plan might have significant effects on fisheries or the marine environment. Article 14E provides that a copy of the proposal to make or amend the local area plan and the environmental reports must be sent to another Member State of the European Communities where either, the planning authority considers that the environment of such Member State is likely to be significantly affected by the implementation of the plan or where such other Member State, likely to be significantly affected, makes such request. Article 3 (as inserted by art.5 of the 2004 Regulations) defines Member State as "any State, other than Ireland, which is a Member State of the European Communities". Prior to sending notice, the Minister must be consulted. The Guidelines at para.5.12 note that such consultation should be done in the form of a written communication to the Spatial Policy Section, Department of the Environment not less than 12 weeks after the giving of the notice, the Manager must prepare a report on the submissions, and send it to the members of the planning authority. As with the development plan, the report of the Manager is merely required to "summarise" the issues raised and the submissions received. There is no obligation to circulate to each member of the planning authority the entirety of the objections and submissions received prior to their consideration of the proposal. See *Sandyford Environmental Planning v Dun Laoghaire Rathdown County Council*, unreported, High Court, McKechnie J., June 30, 2004. Subsection (3)(cc) provides that in the case of planning authories situated within the Greater Dublin Area, the report shall include a summary of the issues raised and the recommendations made by the Dublin Tranport Authority in a report prepared in accordance with s.31E and outline the recommendations of the manager in relation to the manner in which those issues and recommendations should be addressed in the proposed local area plan.

The amendments under the 2002 Act provides a more elaborate procedure than was the case under the 2000 Act, and is more in line with the procedure concerning a development plan. The members of the planning authority must consider the report and the proposal comprising the recommendation in the report will be adopted unless the planning authority, by resolution, decides to refuse the proposal or decides to vary or modify the proposal. Where an environmental assessment is required, art.14H of the 2001 Regulations provides that the planning authority shall take account of:

1. the environmental report;
2. any submission or observation made to the planning authority in response to a notice under s.20(3) of the Act; and
3. any consultations under art.14F, during the preparation or amendment of the plan, and before its adoption.

Where the planning authority decides to vary or modify the proposal and where such variation is a material alteration of the original proposal, the planning authority must publish a notice of the proposed variation in one or more newspapers in the area. Where an environmental assessment is necessary art.14G of the the 2001 Regulations provides that information on the likely significant effects on the environment of implementing the proposed variation or modification will also be available for inspection and that a submission or observation in relation to such information made to the planning authority within the period stated in the notice will also be taken into consideration before the making of any variation or modification.

The notice must state the nature of the proposed variation, indicate that the proposal may be inspected at a specified place and period (not less than four weeks), and also provide that submissions may be made in respect of the proposal within the specified period. Not less than eight weeks after the giving of the notice, the Manager of the planning authority must prepare a report on any submissions and send it to the members of the planning authority. The report must enlist the persons who made such submissions, the contents of such, the opinion of the Manager on such submissions and the recommendation of the Manager on the proposal, having regard to the matters stated in the subsection. The members of the planning authority must then consider the report. The proposed variation will be deemed adopted within six weeks of submission of the report, unless where the Manager's recommendation in his report was for a different variation to that originally proposed and the planning authority pass a resolution refusing to accept the different variation. Where the planning authority makes such a resolution, the proposed variation adopted will be the original proposed variation. Any different variation in the recommendation will not itself be subject to the elaborate procedure for variation of the proposal already outlined. In general, the planning authority in performing its functions is restricted to considering the proper planning and sustainable development of the area, the statutory obligations of any local authority in the area, and any relevant policies or objectives for the time being of the

Government or of any Minister of the Government.

Under subs.(4), the Minister may make regulations in relation to the preparation of local area plans, while under subs.(5), the planning authority must send a copy of the new or amended local area plan to An Bord Pleanála, prescribed bodies, or any other bodies consulted during the process. Where an environmental assessment of the plan was carried out, art.14I(1) of the 2001 Regulations provides that as soon as may be following the making or amending of a local area plan, the planning authority shall prepare a statement summarising:

1. how environmental considerations have been integrated into the plan;
2. how:
    a. the environmental report prepared pursuant to article 14B;
    b. submissions and observations made to the planning authority in response to a notice under s.20(3) of the Act; and
    c. any consultations under art.14F, have been taken into account during the preparation or amendment of the plan;
3. the reasons for choosing the plan or amendment, as adopted, in the light of the other reasonable alternatives dealt with; and
4. the measures decided upon to monitor, in accordance with article 14J, the significant environmental effects of implementation of the plan or amended plan.

Article 14I (2) also states a planning authority shall, as soon as may be following the making or amending of a local area plan:

1. publish notice, in accordance with sub-art.(3), of the making or amending of a local area plan in at least one newspaper with a sufficiently large circulation in the area covered by the local area plan;
2. in addition to the requirements of s.20(5) of the Act, send a copy of the statement referred to in sub-art.(1) to the bodies referred to in s.20(5) of the Act; and
3. send a copy of the plan and the statement referred to in sub-art.(1) to the authorities referred to in art.13A(4), as appropriate, and to any Member State consulted under art.14F, as appropriate.

Article 14I (3) also states that a notice under sub-art.(2)(i) shall state that a copy of the local area plan and the statement referred to in sub-art.(1) are available for inspection at a stated place or places (and a copy shall be kept available for inspection accordingly).

CHAPTER III

Regional Planning Guidelines

Power to make regional planning guidelines

1–21   21.—[(1) A regional authority—
    (*a*) may—
        (i) after consultation with the planning authorities within its region, or
        (ii) in the case of the regional authorities within the GDA, after consultation with the planning authorities within their regions and the DTA, or
    (*b*) shall, at the direction of the Minister, make regional planning guidelines.]

[(2) Regional planning guidelines may be made for a whole region or for one or more parts of a region, but shall, in the case of the GDA, be made jointly by the regional authorities within the GDA.]

    (3)
        (a) The Minister may direct one or more regional authorities to make

regional planning guidelines in respect of the combined area of the regional authorities involved or in respect of any particular part or parts of the area which lie within the area of those regional authorities.

(b) Where it is proposed to make regional planning guidelines, the regional authorities concerned shall make whatever arrangements they see fit to prepare the guidelines,

including the carrying out of the functions of this *Chapter* as a joint function of the authorities concerned, and this *Chapter* shall be construed accordingly.

(4) Notwithstanding any other provision of this *Act,* the strategic planning guidelines for the greater Dublin area prepared for Dublin Corporation, Dún Laoghaire-Rathdown County Council, Fingal County Council, Kildare County Council, Meath County Council, South Dublin County Council, Wicklow County Council and the Department of the Environment and Local Government in conjunction with the Dublin Regional Authority and the Mid-East Regional Authority published on 25 March, 1999, shall have effect as if made under this *Part.*

(5) The Minister may make regulations concerning the making of regional planning guidelines and related matters.

AMENDMENT HISTORY

Subsections (1) and (2) were substituted under s.88 of the Dublin Transport Authority Act 2008 to be commenced on such date as the Minister shall appoint.

NOTE

This section gives statutory recognition to regional guidelines for the first time. Subsection (1) provides that the guidelines are made at the direction of the Minister. Subsections (1) and (2) were substituted under the Dublin Transport Authority Act 2008, to provide that in the case of planning authorities in the Greater Dublin Region, the regional authority must consult with the planning authorities in the area and also with the DTA. Planning authorities must have regard to regional planning guidelines in drawing up development plans. In terms of hierarchy of plans, regional plans have less importance than development plans. Section 2 defines regional authorities as a body established in accordance with s.43 of the Local Government Act 1991. Regional planning guidelines are more long term than development or local area plans, being for a period of 12–20 years. The Regional Authorities have a discretion whether to make guidelines, though they are obliged to do so when the Minister directs. Subsection (1) provides that the regional planning authority in make the guidelines must consult with the planning authorities in its area as set out in s.22. The precise nature of the consultation process is not specified. Subsection (2) provides that the regional planning guidelines may be made for the whole region or a part thereof. In the case of the Greater Dublin Area, they must be made jointly by the regional authorities in that area. However, in the case of planning, subs.(3) provides that the Minister may direct a regional planning authority to make guidelines in respect of the combined area of certain regional authorities. The regional authority will itself make the arrangements for the carrying out of its function. Subsection (4) provides that the Strategic Planning Guidelines for the Greater Dublin Area of March 25, 1999, are deemed to be made under the section. Subsection (5) allows for the Minister to make regulations concerning the making of the guidelines.

Co-operation of planning authorities with regional authority

22.—(1) Where a regional authority intends to make regional planning 1–22 guidelines in accordance with *section 24,* or to review existing guidelines under *section 26,* it shall, as soon as may be, consult with all the planning authorities within the region (or part thereof, as the case may be) in order to make the necessary arrangements for making the guidelines.

(2)

   (a) A planning authority shall assist and co-operate with a regional authority in making arrangements for the preparation of regional planning guidelines and in carrying out the preparation of the guidelines.

   (b) The provision of assistance under *paragraph (a)* shall include the provision of financial assistance, the services of staff and the provision of accommodation, where necessary, and the regional authorities and planning authorities shall agree on such matters based on the proportion of the population of the area for which the regional planning guidelines are prepared resident in the functional areas of the planning authorities concerned.

   (c) In the absence of agreement under *paragraph (b),* a regional authority may request the relevant planning authorities to provide assistance under this *section,* and the request shall be based on the proportion of the population of the area for which the regional planning guidelines are prepared resident in the functional areas of the planning authorities concerned, and a planning authority shall not refuse a reasonable request for assistance.

NOTE

This section sets out the procedure for making regional planning guidelines. Subsection (1) provides that where a regional planning authority intends to make or review guidelines, it must consult with the planning authorities within the region.

Subsection (2) provides that there is a duty of co-operation and assistance on the planning authority with the regional planning authority in making preparations for the guidelines. It further sets out certain examples of assistance and that agreement is to be reached between them based on proportion of the population of the area. In the absence of agreement, the regional authority can request assistance. The request must be based on the proportion of the population of the area for which guidelines are prepared. In addition, the request must be reasonable. The planning authority must comply with any reasonable request.

By virtue of s.25, the planning authorities and regional development authorities should also agree the procedure for making the guidelines.

Content and objectives of regional planning guidelines

1–23　　**23.—(1)**

   (a) The objective of regional planning guidelines shall be to provide a long-term strategic planning framework for the development of the region for which the guidelines are prepared.

   (b) The planning framework referred to in *paragraph (a)* shall consider the future development of the region for which the guidelines are prepared for a period of not less than 12 years and not more than 20 years.

(2) The guidelines shall address, for the whole of the region to which the guidelines relate, in accordance with the principles of proper planning and sustainable development, the following matters—

(a) projected population trends and settlement and housing strategies;

(b) economic and employment trends;

(c) the location of industrial and commercial development;

(d) transportation, including public transportation;

(e) water supply and waste water facilities;

(f) waste disposal;

(g) energy and communications networks;

(h) the provision of educational, health care, retail and other community facilities;

(i) the preservation and protection of the environment and its amenities, including the archaeological, architectural and natural heritage;

(j) such other matters as may be prescribed.

[(3) The Minister may, for the purposes of giving effect to *Directive 200 1/42/EC of the European Parliament and Council of 27 June 2001* on the assessment of the effects of certain plans and programmes on the environment (*No. 2001/42/EC, O.J. No. L 197, 21 July 2001 P. 0030–0037*), by regulations make provision in relation to consideration of the likely significant effects on the environment of implementing regional planning guidelines.]

(4)

(a) When making regional planning guidelines the regional authority shall take account of the proper planning and sustainable development of the whole of the region to which the guidelines relate, the statutory obligations of any local authority in the region and any relevant policies or objectives for the time being of the Government or of any Minister of the Government, including any national plans, policies or strategies specified by the Minister to be of relevance to the determination of strategic planning policies.

(b) When making regional planning guidelines which affect the Gaeltacht, the regional authority shall have regard to the need to protect the linguistic and cultural heritage of the Gaeltacht.

[(c) When making regional planning guidelines the regional authorities within the GDA shall ensure that the guidelines are consistent with the transport strategy of the DTA.]

(5) Without prejudice to the generality of *subsections (2) and (3),* the Minister may issue guidelines on the content of regional planning guidelines and regional authorities shall have regard to those guidelines.

AMENDMENT HISTORY

Subsection (3) substituted by r.7 of the European Communities (Environmental Assessment of Certain Plans and Programmes) Regulations 2004 (S.I. No. 435 of 2004) with effect from July 14, 2004.

Subsection (4)(c) inserted by s.89 of the Dublin Transport Authority Act 2008, to be commenced on such date as the Minister shall appoint.

NOTE

This section sets out the purpose and content of the guidelines. Subsection (1) provides that the objectives of the guidelines are in the long term and relate to future development for a period of between 12 and 20 years. Subsection (2) sets out the matters which the guidelines must contain. All of these matters must be addressed in the guidelines. Subsection (3) provides that the guidelines should refer to the likely significant effects on the environment. A similar provision applies under s.10(5) in relation to development plans. Subsection (4) refers to the standards according to which the decision to make the guidelines must be made. These are: the proper planning and sustainable development of the area; the statutory obligations on the planning authority; and the national plans and policies specified by the Minister to be relevant. National plans and policies would include the national development plan and the national spatial plan. Subsection (4)(b) provides that in relation to guidelines affecting the Gaeltacht, regard must be had to its linguistic and cultural heritage. Also, subs.(4)(c) provides in the case of the Greater Dublin Area, regional authorities are obliged to ensure that the guidelines are consistent with the transport strategy of the DTA. Subsection (5) allows the minister to make regulations in relation to the content of the guidelines.

Consultation regarding regional planning guidelines

1–24   **24.—(1)** As soon as may be after agreeing any necessary arrangements under *section 21,* a regional authority shall give notice of its intention to make the regional planning guidelines.

(2) A notice under *subsection (1)* shall be given to the Minister, the Board, the prescribed authorities and any town commissioners in the area and shall be published in one or more newspapers circulating in the region for which the regional planning guidelines are prepared and shall—

(a) state that the regional authority intends to make regional planning guidelines,

(b) indicate the matters to be considered in the guidelines, having regard to *section 23,*

(c) indicate that submissions regarding the making of the regional planning guidelines may be made in writing to the regional authority within a specified period (which shall not be less than 8 weeks).

(3) A regional authority shall consider any submissions received under *subsection (2)* before preparing the draft regional planning guidelines.

(4) When a regional authority prepares the draft of the regional planning guidelines it shall, as soon as may be—

(a) send notice and copies of the draft guidelines to the Minister, the Board, the prescribed authorities and any town commissioners in its area, and

(b) publish notice of the preparation of the draft in one or more newspapers circulating in its area.

(5) A notice under *subsection (4)* shall state—

(a) that a copy of the draft guidelines may be inspected at a stated place or places and at stated times during a stated period of not less than 10 weeks (and the copy shall be kept available for inspection accordingly), and

(b) that written submissions or observations with respect to the draft made to the regional authority within the stated period will be taken into consideration before the guidelines are adopted.

[**(5A)** When the regional authorities within the GDA prepare the draft of the regional planning guidelines they shall include a statement in that draft on the actions being taken or proposed to ensure effective integration of transport and land use planning, including in particular—

(a) a statement explaining how the regional authorities propose to address the matters identified in the report of the DTA prepared in accordance with section 31F, and

(b) where the regional authorities do not propose to address, or propose to only partially address, any matter identified in the report of the DTA prepared in accordance with section 31F, a statement of the reasons for that course of action.]

(6) Following the consideration of submissions or observations under *subsection (5),* and subject to *section 25,* the regional authority shall make the regional planning guidelines subject to any modification considered necessary.

(7)

(a) Where a regional authority makes regional planning guidelines, it shall publish a notice of the making of the guidelines in at least one newspaper circulating in the functional area of each planning authority in the region for which the guidelines are prepared.

(b) A notice under this *subsection* shall state that a copy of the guidelines is available for inspection at a stated place or places (and the copy shall be kept available for inspection accordingly).

AMENDMENT HISTORY

Section 24(5A) inserted by s.90 of the Dublin Transport Authority Act 2008, to be commenced on such date as the Minister may appoint.

NOTE

This section sets out the full procedure for making the regional guidelines. Subsection (1) provides that, having entered into arrangement with the planning authorities in relation to provision of assistance, the regional planning authority must issue a notice of its intention to make the guidelines. Subsection (2) sets out that the notice must be given to certain bodies and prescribed authorities and sets out the content of the notice, which should include the statement of intent to make the guidelines, the matters to be included, and an invitation to make submissions. Article 15 of the 2001 Regulations as amended sets out 26 prescribed authorities for the purposes of this section. These include the Minister for the Environment, An Bord Pleanála, other government Ministers and other state bodies. A strategic environmental assessment must be carried out in preparing the guidelines. Article 15A of the 2001 Regulations provides that notice under s.24(1) of the Act shall, in addition to the requirements of s.24(2) of the Act, state that:

1. the regional authority proposes to carry out an environmental assessment as part of the making of regional planning guidelines; and
2. for this purpose, the regional authority will prepare an environmental report of the likely significant effects on the environment of implementing the regional planning guidelines.

Article 15C provides that as soon as practicable after the giving of notice under s.24(1) of the Act, the regional authority shall give notice to certain environmental authorities which are the Environmental Protection Agency; the Minister for the Environment, Heritage and Local Government, where it appears to the regional authority that the plan might have significant effects in relation to the architectural or archaeological heritage or to nature conservation and the Minister for Communications, Marine and Natural Resources, where it appears to the regional authority that the plan might have significant effects on fisheries or the marine environment. Notification of the Environmental Protection Agency is mandatory in all circumstances, while notification of the Minister for the Environment, Heritage and Local Government and the Minister for Communications, Marine and Natural Resources, is conditional, depending on the stated circumstances applying. The Guidelines provide at para.3.15 that some informal scoping can take place towards the end of the six-year life of the guidelines, but formal scoping should begin as soon as practicable after the giving of notice by the regional authority under s.24(1) of the 2000 Act of its intention to make new guidelines. The publication of a regional Issues Paper will also facilitate both scoping and public consultation. Also at para.3.16, the Guidelines provide that it is recommended that at the end of the scoping procedure, the plan-making authority should prepare a brief scoping report of its conclusions as to what information is to be included in the environmental report, taking account of any recommendations from the environmental authorities. Article 15D sets out the content of the environmental report which is to accompany or be included with the regional planning guidelines. More specifically, the report must identify, describe and evaluate the likely significant effects on the environment of implementing the proposed variation and reasonable alternatives taking account of the objectives and the geographical scope of the proposed variation. The content set out are similar to Arts 13D, 13F, 14D concerning the content of an environmental report in connection with the making of a development plan. Under sub-art.2, the requirement is only to include the information which may "reasonably" be required, with the regional authority having a discretion in assessing what is reasonable. There is an obligation "to take account" of the matters enlisted in sub-art.2. The Guidelines provide at para.4.8 that in practice this means firstly that SEA involves collating currently available, relevant environmental data; it does not require major new research. Where data deficiencies or gaps exist, this should be acknowledged in the report. Secondly, it notes that certain strategic planning issues may already have been determined at national or regional level, whereas other more detailed issues will more appropriately be left for consideration at local area plan level. The report must include the information specified in Sch.2B and the other matters listed in sub-art.1. These matters are mandatory, although trivial or de minimus matters may be overlooked. Article 15E states that that a copy of the regional planning guidelines and the environmental reports must be sent to another Member State of the European Communities where either the planning authority considers that the environment of such Member State is likely to be significantly affected by the implementation of the plan or where such other Member State likely to be significantly affected makes such request.

Subsection (3) states that the regional planning authority must consider any submissions received and prepare draft guidelines. Article 15F of the 2001 Regulations provides that the regional authority shall take account of:

1. the environmental report;
2. any submission or observation made to the regional authority in response to a notice under s.24(4) of the Act; and
3. any consultations under art.15E, during the preparation of the guidelines, and before their adoption.

Article 5 of the Planning and Development (Regional Planning Guidelines) Regulations 2003 (S.I. No.175 of 2003) provides that not later than 16 weeks after the giving of notice under s.24(1), the Director (or an officer or officers nominated to do so on his or her behalf) shall prepare a report on any submissions received under s.24(2)(c) of the Act. In the case of the Dublin and Mid-East Regional Authorities, as referred to at para.(2), not later than 16 weeks after the giving of notice under s.24(1) of the 2000 Act, the Directors (or officers nominated to do so on their behalf) shall jointly prepare a report on any submissions received under s.24(2)(c) of the Act.

Article 5(3) states that the report shall:

1. list the persons or bodies who made submissions under s.24 of the Act as well as any persons or bodies consulted by the regional authority;
2. summarise the issues raised in the submissions and during the consultations, where appropriate;
3. give the opinion of the Director, or, in the case of a report prepared under sub-art.(2), the opinion of the Directors, on the issues raised, taking account of the proper planning and sustainable development of the whole of the region to which the guidelines relate, the statutory obligations of any local authority in the region and any relevant policies or objectives for the time being of the Government or of any Minister of the Government, including the National Spatial Strategy; and
4. state the Director's recommendations on the policies to be included in the draft

regional planning guidelines, in the case of a report prepared under sub-art.(1); or
5. state the Directors' joint recommendations on the policies to be included in the draft regional planning guidelines, in the case of a report prepared under sub-art.(2).

Article 5(4) to (9) set out further steps including that the authorities shall consider the report and the regional authority or authorities, or the committee of the regional authority or authorities, as the case may be, may issue directions to the Director or Directors (in the case of the Dublin and Mid-East Regional Authorities), which must not be issued later than 10 weeks after the report. Article 5(7) provides that directions must take account of the proper planning and sustainable development of the whole of the region to which the guidelines relate, the statutory obligations of any local authority in the region and any relevant policies or objectives for the time being of the Government or of any Minister of the Government, including the National Spatial Strategy and the Director or Directors, as the case may be, shall comply with such directions

Under subs.(4), having prepared the draft guidelines, a copy must be sent to certain bodies and a notice of the publication of the draft must be published in a newspaper. Article 15B of the 2001 Regulations provides that the guidelines shall be accompanied by or include an environmental report. Article 7(1) of the 2003 Regulations provides that not later than 22 weeks after the giving of notice under s.24(4) of the Act, the Director (or an officer or officers nominated to do so on his or her behalf) shall prepare a report on any submissions or observations received under s.24(5) of the Act and submit the report to the members of the regional authority for their consideration. In the case of the Dublin and Mid-East Regional Authorities, not later than 22 weeks after the giving of notice under s.24(4) of the Act, the Directors (or officers nominated to do so on their behalf) shall jointly prepare a report on any submissions or observations received under s.24(5) of the Act and submit the report to the members of the regional authorities for their consideration. Article 7(3) states that the report should:
1. list the persons or bodies who made submissions or observations under s.24(5) of the Act;
2. summarise the issues raised by the persons or bodies in the submissions or observations; and
3. give the response of the Director (or Directors in the case of the Dublin and Mid-East Regional Authorities) to the issues raised, taking account of any directions of the members under art.6(6), the proper planning and sustainable development of the region, the statutory obligations of any local authority in the region and any relevant policies or objectives for the time being of the Government or of any Minister of the Government, including the National Spatial Strategy.

Article 8 of the 2003 Regulations provide as follows. Subsection (5) provides that the notice must state that a copy of the draft is available for inspection and that written submissions may be sent in. Subsection (6) provides that having considered the submissions, the regional development authority can make the guidelines, though subject to certain modification. Subsection (7) provides that having made the regional planning guidelines, a notice to such effect must be inserted in a newspaper, which should indicate that a copy is available for inspection. Article 15G(1) of the 2001 Regulations provides that a notice under s.24(7)(a) of the Act shall specify that a statement is also available summarising:
1. how environmental considerations have been integrated into the guidelines;
2. how:
   a. the environmental report prepared pursuant to art.15B;
   b. submissions and observations made to the regional authority in response to a notice under s.24(4) of the Act: and
   c. any consultations under art.15E,
   have been taken into account during the preparation of the guidelines;
3. the reasons for choosing the guidelines, as adopted, in the light of the other reasonable alternatives dealt with; and
4. the measures decided upon to monitor, in accordance with art.15H, the significant environmental effects of implementation of the guidelines.

Furthermore, art.15H(2) provides that the regional authority shall send a copy of the regional planning guidelines and the statement referred to in sub-art.(1) to:
1. the authorities specified in art.13A(4), as appropriate, and

2. any Member State consulted under art.15E.

Article 15J of the 2001 Regulations provides that the regional authority shall monitor the significant environmental effects of implementation of the regional planning guidelines in order, inter alia, to identify at an early stage unforeseen adverse effects and to be able to undertake appropriate remedial action and, for this purpose, existing monitoring arrangements may be used, if appropriate, with a view to avoiding duplication of monitoring. Article 7(4) of the 2003 Regulations provides that the report shall be considered by the members of the regional authority or authorities, as appropriate, as part of its consideration of submissions or observations in accordance with s.24(6) of the Act.

Subsection (5A) provides that in the case of the Greater Dublin Area, the regional authorities in preparing draft guidelines shall include a statement in the draft on the actions being taken or proposed to ensure effective integration of transport and land use planning, including a statement explaining how the regional authorities propose to address the matters identified in the report of the DTA prepared in accordance with s.31F and where the regional authorities do not propose to address, or propose to only partially address, any matter identified in the report of the DTA prepared in accordance with s.31F, a statement of the reasons for that course of action. Thus, the draft guidelines must fully address all matters in the report of the DTA and where they only partially address such matters, there should be a statement of reasons explaining why this is the case.

Procedure for making regional planning guidelines

1–25　　**25.—(1)** As part of the consultation between a regional authority and the relevant planning authorities under *section 22,* the authorities concerned shall agree on a procedure for preparing and making the regional planning guidelines under *section 24.*

(2) Matters to be considered under *subsection (1)* shall include the establishment of committees to oversee and consider preparation of the guidelines.

(3) The authorities concerned shall agree on the membership of the committees under *subsection (2)* and shall also agree on the roles of those committees in preparing the draft guidelines, considering submissions or observations under *section 24,* and drawing up reports in respect of the guidelines.

(3A) When the regional authorities in the GDA make regional planning guidelines they shall include in the guidelines a statement on the actions being taken or proposed to ensure effective integration of transport and land use planning, including in particular—

(a) a statement explaining how the regional authorities propose to address the matters identified in the report of the DTA prepared in accordance with section 31G, and

(b) where the regional authorities do not propose to address, or propose only to partially address, any matter identified in the report of the DTA prepared in accordance with section 31G, a statement of the reasons for that course of action.

(4) The making of regional planning guidelines under *section 24(6)* shall be a matter for the members of the regional authority concerned, following the consideration of any report or reports from the committees referred to in *subsection (2).*

(5) The Minister may make regulations, or issue guidelines, with regard to the procedures to be adopted under this *section,* including the number, functions and membership of any committees set up in accordance with *subsection (2)*.

AMENDMENT HISTORY

Section 25(3A) was inserted by s.91 of the Dublin Transport Authority Act 2008, to be commenced on such date as the Minister may appoint.

NOTE

This section concerns the framework for co-operation between the regional development authority and the planning authorities in the making of the guidelines. Subsection (1) provides that the procedure for the making and co-operation of the guidelines should be agreed with the planning authorities after the notice of intention of making the guidelines under s.22. Subsection (3) concerns the establishment of the committee to prepare the guidelines and subs.(4) relates to the membership and role of the committee members. Subsection (4) provides that the making of the guidelines is a matter for the committee members having considered submissions. Subsection (5) provides that the Minister may make regulations in relation to the procedure.

Subsection (3A) states that in the case of the Greater Dublin Area, the guidelines shall include a statement on the actions being taken or proposed to ensure effective integration of transport and land use planning, including a statement explaining how the regional authorities propose to address the matters identified in the report of the DTA prepared in accordance with s.31F and where the regional authorities do not propose to address, or propose to only partially address, any matter identified in the report of the DTA prepared in accordance with s.31F, a statement of the reasons for that course of action. It is clear therefore that the guidelines must fully address all matters in the report of the DTA and where they do not or only partially address such matters, there should be a statement of reasons explaining why this is the case.

Review of regional planning guidelines

26.—(1) Where a regional authority has made regional planning guidelines, it shall, not later than 6 years after the making of such guidelines and not less than once in every period of 6 years thereafter, review such guidelines and when so reviewing, it may revoke the guidelines or make new regional planning guidelines. 1–26

(2) Before a regional authority revokes guidelines referred to in *subsection (1)* (other than for the purpose of making new regional planning guidelines), it shall consult with the planning authorities within its region.

(3) Where the regional authority makes new guidelines, it shall follow the procedures laid down in *sections 22, 24 and 25*.

(4) Where new guidelines are made under *subsection (1)*, they shall supersede any previous regional planning guidelines for the relevant area.

NOTE

This section concerns review of the guidelines and provides that the regional authority must review the guidelines not later than six years after making them and not less than once every six years. The review is of considerable importance as under s.27(5) the planning authority will not be obliged to have regard to the guidelines in making its development plan, if the guidelines have not been made within the previous six years. Subsection (2) provides that before a regional authority revokes the guidelines, it must consult with the planning authorities for the region. Subsection (3) affirms that in renewing the guidelines, the procedure set out in ss.22–24, concerning the initial making of them, must be followed.

Subsection (4) provides that where new guidelines are made, they will replace the previous guidelines for the area. Article 15J of the 2001 Regulations provides that the regional authority shall monitor the significant environmental effects of implementation of the regional planning guidelines in order, inter alia, to identify at an early stage unforeseen adverse effects and to be able to undertake appropriate remedial action and, for this purpose, existing monitoring arrangements may be used, if appropriate, with a view to avoiding duplication of monitoring.

Regional planning guidelines and development plans

1–27   **27.—(1)** A planning authority shall have regard to any regional planning guidelines in force for its area when making and adopting a development plan.

(2) The Minister may, by order, determine that planning authorities shall comply with any regional planning guidelines in force for their area, or any part thereof, when preparing and making a development plan, or may require in accordance with *section 31* that an existing development plan comply with any regional planning guidelines in force for the area.

(3) An order under *subsection (2)* may relate to regional planning guidelines generally, or one or more specified guidelines, or may relate to specific elements of those guidelines.

(4) Following the making of regional planning guidelines for their area, planning authorities shall review the existing development plan and consider whether any variation of the development plan is necessary in order to achieve the objectives of the regional planning guidelines.

(5) For the purposes of this *section,* a planning authority may have, but shall not be obliged to have, regard to any regional planning guidelines after 6 years from the making of such guidelines.

NOTE

This section concerns the relationship between the regional planning guidelines and the development plan. Subsection (1) provides that the planning authority must have regard to the plans when making the development plan. The obligation "to have regard" to such guidelines does not require them to rigidly or "slavishly" comply with the guidelines' recommendations or even necessarily to fully adopt the strategy and policies outlined therein. They are however obliged to inform themselves fully of and give reasonable consideration to the guidelines. See *McEvoy v Meath County Council* [2003] 1 I.R. 208. Subsection (2) allows the Minister to direct the planning authority to take account of the guidelines in its development plan. Subsection (3) declares that an order by the Minister may relate to the regional planning guidelines in general, one or more specific guidelines, or specific elements of the guidelines. Subsection (4) provides that following the making of the guidelines, the planning authority must review the existing development plan and consider whether a variation is necessary. Subsection (5) provides that where the guidelines are in existence for more than six years, the planning authority is no longer obliged to have regard to the guidelines but can do so at its discretion. The regional planning guidelines are made for a period of 12–20 years, although they are required to be reviewed at least every six years. Notwithstanding the unclear phrase "in existence", it would appear that subs.(5) means that the planning authority is not obliged to have regard to the guidelines where they have not been subject to review within the previous six years.

CHAPTER IV

Guidelines and Directives

Ministerial guidelines

28.—**(1)** The Minister may, at any time, issue guidelines to planning   **1–28**
authorities regarding any of their functions under this *Act* and planning
authorities shall have regard to those guidelines in the performance of their
functions.

(2) Where applicable, the Board shall have regard to any guidelines
issued to planning authorities under *subsection (1)* in the performance of its
functions.

(3) Any planning guidelines made by the Minister and any general policy
directives issued under *section 7 of the Act of 1982* prior to the commencement
of this *Part* and still in force immediately before such commencement shall
be deemed to be guidelines under this *section*.

(4) The Minister may revoke or amend guidelines issued under this
section.

(5) The Minister shall cause a copy of any guidelines issued under this
section and of any amendment or revocation of those guidelines to be laid
before each House of the Oireachtas.

(6) A planning authority shall make available for inspection by members
of the public any guidelines issued to it under this *section*.

(7) The Minister shall publish or cause to be published, in such manner as
he or she considers appropriate, guidelines issued under this *section*.

NOTE

This section allows the Minister to issue guidelines to the planning authority and Board
in performing their functions. The planning authority and Board are obliged to "have regard"
to such guidelines. To have regard to such guidelines does not require them to rigidly or
"slavishly" comply with the guidelines' recommendations or even necessarily to fully adopt
the strategy and policies outlined therein. They are however obliged to inform themselves
fully of and give reasonable consideration to the guidelines. See *McEvoy v Meath County
Council* [2003] 1 I.R. 208 and *Glenkerrin v Dun Laoghaire Rathdown County Council*,
unreported, High Court, April 26, 2007. In *Glencar Explorations plc v Mayo County Council*
[2002] 1 I.R. 84, Keane C.J. said:

"The fact that they are obliged to have regard to policies and objectives of the
government or a particular Minister does not mean that, in every case, they are
obliged to implement the policies and objectives in question. If the Oireachtas had
intended such an obligation to rest on the planning authority in a case such as the
present, it would have said so."

Guidelines issued may take a certain view of the law and where they do so, they can
have no binding effect. In fact guidelines should be approached with caution where they
purport to take a particular interpretation of the law. Although the Guidelines issued
under this section are published and available for inspection, the concerns expressed by
Streatfield J. *Patchett v Leathem* [1948] 65 TLR 69, in relation to circulars are apposite,
where he declared:

"Whereas ordinary legislation, by passing through both Houses of Parliament or at least
lying on the table of both House is this twice blessed, this type of so-called legislation
is at least four times cursed. First, it has seen neither House of Parliament; secondly,
it is unpublished and is inaccessible even to those whose valuable rights of property
may be affected; thirdly, it is a jumble of provisions, legislative, administrative, or

directive in character and sometimes difficult to disentangle one from the other; and fourthly, it is expressed not in the precise language of an Act of Parliament or an Order in Council but in the more colloquial language of correspondence, which is not always susceptible of the ordinary canons of construction".

In fact, the courts are free to disagree with any view of the law expressed in a guideline. Where the planning authority or Board follow guidelines which are erroneous, this will not justify its decision. See *Sherwin v An Bord Pleanála*, unreported, High Court, Edwards J., July 3, 2007. Guidelines are to be distinguished from directives under s.29, where the planning authority has no discretion whether to follow the content of a directive. Under s.255(4) the Minister has power to appoint a commissioner to take over the functions or particular function of a planning authority, for stated reasons, where, inter alia, the planning authority has not complied with guidelines under s.28.

Pre-existing guidelines issued under s.7 of the Local Government (Planning and Development) Act 1982 ("the 1982 Act"), which also allowed the Minister to issue policy directives, are to remain in force. Among the guidelines issued under the 2000 Act are the Architectural Heritage Protection for Places of Worship; Best Practice Urban Design Manual (February 2008); Childcare Facilities Guidelines; Design Standards for New Apartments; Development Contribution Scheme for Planning Authorities; Development Management Guidelines (June 2007); Development Plans Guidelines (June 2007); Funfair Guidance; Implementing Regional Planning Guidelines- Best Practice Guidance; Landscape and Landscape Assessment and Appendices; Quarries and Ancillary Activities; Redevelopment of Certain Lands in the Dublin Area, primarily for Affordable Housing; Residential Density Guidelines 1999; Retail Planning Guidelines; Strategic Environmental Assessment (SEA); Sustainable Rural Housing and Map; Taking in Charge of Residential Developments Circular Letter PD 1/08; Telecommunications Antennae and Support Structures; Wind Energy Development. Also published are Draft Planning Guidelines on Sustainable Residential Development in Urban Areas (February 2008).

After the guidelines are issued, revoked or amended, they must be placed before both Houses of the Oireachtas. The wording in the past tense, indicates that the process of issuing does not require them to be placed before each House prior to having been deemed to be issued. This is in contrast to the process of issuing of directives under s.29(5), which provides that where the Minister proposes to issue, amend or revoke a policy directive, the Minister must place them before both Houses. Also in contrast to s.(29)(5), this section is silent on the need for resolution, simply requiring the matter to be placed before both Houses. The Minister must publish the guidelines and the planning authority must make the guidelines available for inspection by the public. It appears there is no obligation to make draft guidelines available until they are adopted. As to the status of draft guidelines, without precisely deciding their status, in *Irish Hardware v South Dublin County Council*, unreported, High Court, Butler J., July 19, 2000, Butler J. refused leave based on a challenge that the planning authority had not taken into account Draft Retail Planning Guidelines. He held that the planning authority had taken into account the substance of government policy underlining the provisions.

Ministerial policy directives

1–29   **29.—(1)** The Minister may, from time to time, issue policy directives to planning authorities regarding any of their functions under this *Act* and planning authorities shall comply with any such directives in the performance of their functions.

(2) Where applicable, the Board shall also comply with any policy directives issued to planning authorities under *subsection (1)* in the performance of its functions.

(3) The Minister may revoke or amend a policy directive issued under this *section*.

(4) Where the Minister proposes to issue, amend or revoke a policy directive under this *section,* a draft of the directive, amendment or revocation shall be laid before both Houses of the Oireachtas and the policy directive shall not be issued, amended or revoked, as the case may be, until a resolution approving the issuing, amending or revocation of the policy directive has been passed by each House.

(5) The Minister shall cause a copy of any policy directive issued under this *section* to be laid before each House of the Oireachtas.

(6) A planning authority shall make available for inspection by members of the public any policy directive issued to it under this *section.*

(7) The Minister shall publish or cause to be published, in such manner as he or she considers appropriate, policy directives issued under this *section.*

NOTE

This section allows the Minister to issue policy directives to planning authorities and to An Bord Pleanála, relevant to their functions. Directives differ from guidelines under s.28, as the planning body and Board have no discretion whether to comply with a policy directive. This is in contrast to guidelines. See *McEvoy v Meath County Council* [2003] 1 I.R. 208. The process of issuing, amending or revoking a directive is more complicated than in the case of guidelines. Before any of these steps may be taken, a resolution of both Houses of the Oireachtas must be made. In addition to this, having passed a resolution, the newly issued, amended or revoked directive must subsequently be placed before both Houses. The Minister must publish the guidelines and the planning authority must make the guidelines available for inspection by the public.

Under s.255(4) the Minister has power to appoint a commissioner to take over the functions or particular function of a planning authority, for stated reasons, where, inter alia, the planning authority has not complied with a directive under s.29.

[Limitation on Ministerial power

30.—(1) Notwithstanding *section 28 or 29* and subject to *subsection (2),* the **1–30** Minister shall not exercise any power or control in relation to any particular case with which a planning authority or the Board is or may be concerned.

(2) *Subsection (1)* shall not affect the performance by the Minister of functions transferred (whether before or after the passing of the Minister for the *Environment and Local Government (Performance of Certain Functions) Act, 2002*) to him or her from the Minister for Community, Rural and Gaeltacht Affairs by an order under *section 6(1) of the Ministers and Secretaries (Amendment) Act, 1939.* Notwithstanding *section 28 or 29,* the Minister shall not exercise any power or control in relation to any particular case with which a planning authority or the Board is or may be concerned.]

AMENDMENT HISTORY

Section 30 was substituted by s.1 of the Minister for the Environment and Local Government (Performance of Certain Functions) Act 2002 (No. 24 of 2002), which came into effect on July 3, 2002.

NOTE

This section provides that the Minister may not issue guidelines or directives in relation to a particular planning application. In *Weston v An Bord Pleanála,* unreported, High Court, McMenamin J. March 14, 2008, it was noted that under this section the primacy of a planning authority in dealing with each individual case (as opposed to a class) is statutorily enshrined. Thus guidelines and directives must be of a general nature and cannot concern a particular case. They also should not be disguised as a means of controlling a particular case by being framed in general terms.

Ministerial directions regarding development plans

1–31   **31.—(1)** Where the Minister considers that any draft development plan fails to set out an overall strategy for the proper planning and sustainable development of the area of a planning authority or otherwise significantly fails to comply with this *Act,* the Minister may, for stated reasons, direct the authority to take such specified measures as he or she may require to ensure that the development plan, when made, is in compliance with this *Act* and, notwithstanding the requirements of *Chapter I,* the authority shall comply with any such direction.

[**(1A)**(a) Where a submission received by the Minister prepared in accordance with section 31C(1) or section 31D(1) contains a statement of the type referred to, respectively, in section 31C(1)(b) or section 31D(1)(b) the Minister may, for stated reasons, direct a planning authority to take such specified measures, as he or she may require, to review or vary the draft development plan or proposed variation to ensure consistency between the draft development plan or proposed variation and the transport strategy of the DTA and the authority shall comply with any such direction.

(b) Where the Minister decides not to issue a direction under this subsection, he or she shall inform the DTA in writing of the reasons for such decision.

(c) Nothing in this subsection shall preclude the Minister from issuing a direction in circumstances other than those referred to in paragraph (a).]

(2) Where the Minister considers that any development plan fails to set out an overall strategy for the proper planning and sustainable development of the area of the authority or otherwise significantly fails to comply with this *Act,* the Minister may, for stated reasons, direct the authority to take such specified measures, as he or she may require to review or vary the development plan to ensure compliance with this *Act* and the authority shall comply with any such direction.

(3) Where the Minister directs a planning authority to take specified measures under *subsection (2),* he or she may specify any of those provisions of *Chapter I* which are to apply in respect of such specified measures and any other provisions of that *Chapter* shall be disregarded.

[**(4)** In exercising any power conferred on them by the Act, neither the manager nor the elected members of any planning authority shall exercise the power in conflict with any direction which the Minister may give under subsections (1), (1A) or (2).]

(5) The Minister shall cause a copy of any direction issued under this *section* to be laid before each House of the Oireachtas.

(6) A planning authority shall make available for inspection by members of the public any direction issued to it under this *section.*

AMENDMENT HISTORY

Section 31(1A) was inserted by s.92 of the Dublin Transport Authority Act 2008.

Section 31(4) was substituted under s.92 of the Dublin Transport Authority Act 2008.

NOTE

This section allows the Minister to issue directions to a planning authority regarding the content of its draft development plan and existing development plans in certain circumstances. The Minister is empowered to issue such a direction where the development plan fails to set out an overall strategy for the proper planning and sustainable development of the area or otherwise significantly fails to comply with this Act. Subsection (1) concerns directions regarding draft development plans, while subs.(2) relates to existing development plans. The direction relates to a specified measure, which means that the direction must set out the content of the measure. However, the purpose of the direction must be to ensure that the development "is in compliance with this Act", which means the draft development plan or existing development plan must be deficient in some manner. A direction under this section cannot be used by the Minister for mere policy making; the draft or existing development plan must not be in compliance with some provisions with the 2000 Act. There is no guidance provided as to what may constitute such a significant failure. An example might be where a planning authority fails to adopt a housing strategy under s.94, or adopted a strategy which failed to take into account certain mandatory matters or where there was a breach of Ministerial policy directive. It is clear that the power under this section will only be used in exceptional circumstances. Where the Minister finds that there has been such a failure, the Minister must give reasons for such a finding and specify the measures required. Where the direction requires variation or amendment of a plan already adopted, the Minister may specify what procedural steps must be taken to make the amendment or variation, in which case the normal process for a variation under s.13, will not apply. Section 31(3) provides that the direction may specify certain provisions in Chapter 1 and in such case, other provisions are to be disregarded. The nature of "specified measures" is not entirely clear. However, on balance it would appear to encompass both the content of any variation and also the procedural steps to be taken to bring the variation about. It is not necessary for the Minister to specify such procedural steps but he may do so at his discretion. The obligation to comply with the directive applies to both the Manager and elected member of the planning authority. The rationale for s.31(4) would appear to be to prevent the exercise of any power which could compromise or frustrate the subject of the direction in the period pending the determination as to whether to formally adopt it as a variation to the plan. This does not mean that the content of the direction immediately forms part of the development plan. The terms of s.31(4) are that the Manager and elected must not exercise any power "in conflict" with the direction. the effect of s.31(4) is that it creates an exception to the general position that a pending plan, whether a draft plan or proposed variation, cannot be taken into account by the planning authority. See *Ebonwood v Meath County Council* [2004] 3 I.R. 34, in the context of a compensation claim. Once a direction is issued under s.31, the planning authority must follow the procedure under s.13 and initiate the procedure for a variation of the development plan with the context of the direction being put forward as the proposed variation. As the variation involves a democratic procedure whereby members of the public have the opportunity to make submissions on the proposed variation, it would appear to follow that there can be no absolute requirement that the content of direction must be adopted as a variation in all cases. It may be noted that where direction relates to government policy, s.9(6) provides that the development plan must be consistent with government policy, which means there is very limited discretion to refuse to adopt the contents of the direction notwithstanding submissions from the public. The direction does not require a resolution of both Houses of the Oireachtas as required in the case of general directives under s.29.

Subsection (1A) relates to the Greater Dublin Area in respect of statements prepared by the DTA.

[**Ministerial directions regarding regional planning guidelines**

1–32   **31A.**—(1) Where the Minister considers that any draft regional planning guidelines fail to set out an overall strategy for the proper planning and sustainable development of the area of a regional authority or otherwise significantly fail to comply with this Act, the Minister may, within 4 weeks of receipt of a notice under section 24(4), for stated reasons, direct the authority, or authorities, to take such specified measures as he or she may require to ensure that the regional planning guidelines, when made, are in compliance with this Act and, notwithstanding the requirements of Chapter III, the authority shall comply with any such direction.

(2)(a)   Where a submission received by the Minister prepared in accordance with section 31G(1) contains a statement of the type referred to in section 31G(1)(b), the Minister may, for stated reasons, direct the authorities to take such specified measures, as he or she may require, to review the draft regional planning guidelines to ensure consistency between the draft regional planning guidelines and the transport strategy of the DTA and the authorities shall comply with any such direction.

(b)   Where the Minister decides not to issue a direction under this subsection, he or she shall inform the DTA in writing of the reasons for such decision.

(c)   Nothing in this subsection shall preclude the Minister from issuing a direction in circumstances other than those referred to in paragraph (a).

(3) Where the Minister considers that any regional planning guidelines fail to set out an overall strategy for the proper planning and sustainable development of the area of the authority or otherwise significantly fail to comply with this Act, the Minister may, within 4 weeks of the making of guidelines under section 24(6), for stated reasons, direct the regional authority, or authorities, to take such specified measures, as he or she may require to review the regional planning guidelines to ensure compliance with this Act and the authority shall comply with any such direction.

(4) Where the Minister directs a regional authority to take specified measures under subsection (3), he or she may specify any of those provisions of Chapter III which are to apply in respect of such specified measures and any other provisions of that Chapter shall be disregarded.

(5) In exercising any power conferred on it by this Act, a regional authority shall not exercise the power in conflict with any direction which the Minister may give under subsections (1) to (3).

(6) The Minister shall cause a copy of any direction issued under this section to be laid before each House of the Oireachtas.

(7) A regional authority shall make available for inspection by members of the public any direction issued to it under this section.]

AMENDMENT HISTORY

This section was inserted by s.93 of the Dublin Transport Authority Act 2008, to be commenced on such date as the Minister may appoint.

NOTE

This section allows the Minister to give directions to regional planning authorities where the guidelines or draft guidelines fail to set out an overall strategy for the proper planning and sustainable development of the area of a regional authority or otherwise significantly fail to comply with this Act. Subsection (1) concerns draft guidelines, whereby the Minister may issue such direction within four weeks of receiving notice of the draft guidelines. The Minister may for stated reasons direct the authority to take specified measures. Subsection (3) allows the Minister to issue such directions after such guidelines have been made. The Minister may within four weeks of the making of the guidelines issue a direction. The regional planning authorities is obliged to comply with any direction given by the Minister under this section. Furthermore, under subs.(4), the authority must not exercise any powers in conflict with a direction.

PART IIA

DTA and LAND USE PROVISION

DTA role in preparation of draft development plan

31B.—(1) Where a notice is received by the DTA under section 11(2) it   **1–33** shall prepare and submit to the relevant planning authority a report on the issues which, in its opinion, should be considered by the planning authority in the review of its existing development plan and the preparation of a new development plan.

(2) The report under subsection (1) shall address, but shall not be limited to—

  (a) the transport investment priorities for the period of the development plan,

  (b) the scope, if any, to maximise the performance of the transport system by effective land use planning,

  (c) recommendations regarding the optimal use, location, pattern and density of new development taking account of its transport strategy, and

  (d) recommendations on the matters to be addressed in the development plan to ensure the effective integration oftransport and land use planning.

NOTE

This section applies to the preparation of development plans by planning authorities in the greater Dublin area. Having received notice of the intention of the planning authority to review its existing development plan, the DTA must prepare a report to be submitted to the planning authority regarding the transporation matters specified in subs.(2). The period of the development plan will be six years so the report should reflect this period.

DTA role in making of development plan

31C.—(1) Where a notice is received by the DTA under section 12(1) it   **1–34** shall, as part of any written submission on the draft development plan, state whether, in its view, the draft development plan is—

  (a) consistent with its transport strategy, or

  (b) not consistent with its transport strategy and in such case what amendments to the draft plan it considers necessary to achieve such consistency.

(2) The DTA shall send copies of a submission prepared under this section to the Minister and the Minister for Transport.

NOTE

This section provides that where the DTA receives notice of the preparation of the draft development plan from a planning authority within the greater Dublin area, it is obliged to make a submission dealing with whether the draft plan is consistent or not consistent with the transport strategy. The submission which can be made is not confined to such matters.

DTA role in variation of development plan

1–35   **31D.**—(1) Where a notice is received by the DTA under section 13(2) it shall, as part of any written submission on the proposed variation, state whether, in its view, the proposed variation is—

   (a) consistent with its transport strategy, or

   (b) not consistent with its transport strategy and in such case what amendments to the proposed variation it considers necessary to achieve such consistency.

(2) The DTA shall send copies of a submission prepared under this section to the Minister and Minister for Transport.

NOTE

Where notice of a proposed variation of the development plan is received, the DTA must state in any submission whether the proposed variation is consistent with the transport strategy and if not, the Amendments which would achieve consistency.

DTA role in the making, amending or revoking of local area plans by planning authorities

1–36   **31E.**—(1) Where a notice is received by the DTA under section 20(3)(a)(i), it shall prepare and submit to the relevant planning authority a report on the issues which, in its opinion, should be considered by the planning authority in making, amending or revoking a local area plan.

(2) The report under subsection (1) shall address, but shall not be limited to—

   (a) the transport investment priorities for the period of the local area plan,

   (b) the scope, if any, to maximise the performance of the transport system by effective land use planning,

   (c) recommendations regarding the optimal use, location, pattern and density of new development taking account of its transport strategy, and

   (d) recommendations on the matters to be addressed in the local area plan to ensure the effective integration of transport and land use planning.

NOTE

Where the DTA receives notice of a proposal to make, amend or revoke a local area plan of a planning authority within the greater Dublin area, it must prepare a report which must include the matters set out in subs.(2). Unlike a development plan, there is no specific life for a local area plan, although the local area plan should specify its duration. The submissions of the DTA are not limited to the matters in subs.(2).

Co-operation of DTA with regional authorities

31F.—(1) Where the regional authorities within the GDA intend to make   **1–37** regional planning guidelines in accordance with section 24, or to review existing guidelines under section 26, they shall, as soon as may be, consult with the DTA in order to make the necessary arrangements for making the guidelines.

(2) The DTA shall assist and co-operate with the regional authorities in the GDA in making arrangements for the preparation of regional planning guidelines and in carrying out the preparation of the guidelines.

(3)(a) In carrying out its function under subsection (2), the DTA shall prepare and submit to the regional authorities, within 6 weeks of the commencement of consultation under subsection (1), a report on the issues which, in its opinion, should be considered by the regional authorities in making regional planning guidelines.

   (b) The report prepared under paragraph (a) shall address, but shall not be limited to—

   (i) the transport investment priorities for the period of the regional planning guidelines,

   (ii) the scope, if any, to maximise the performance of the transport system by effective land use planning,

   (iii) recommendations regarding the optimal use, location, pattern and density of new development taking account of its transport strategy, and

   (iv) recommendations on the matters to be addressed in the regional planning guidelines to ensure effective integration of transport and land use planning.

NOTE

This section requires regional authorities within the greater Dublin area to consult with the DTA, where they intend to make regional planning guidelines or to review existing guidelines. Under subs.(2), the DTA is obliged to assist and co-operate in making arrangements for the preparation of the guidelines and in carrying out the preparations. The DTA must prepare and submit a report to the regional authorities within six weeks of the commencement of consultations on the matters to be considered in making the guidelines. This obligation to submit the report after six weeks applies irrespective of the state of the consultations. The report should include the matters in subs.(3), although these matters are not exhaustive.

DTA role in preparation of draft regional planning guidelines

31G.—(1) Where a notice is received by the DTA under section 24(4) it shall,   **1–38** as part of any written submission on the draft regional planning guidelines, state whether, in its view, the draft regional planning guidelines are—

(a) consistent with its transport strategy, or

(b) not consistent with its transport strategy and in such case what amendments to the draft guidelines it considers necessary to achieve such consistency.

(2) The DTA shall send copies of a submission prepared under this section to the Minister and Minister for Transport.

NOTE

This section provides that where the DTA receives notice of the preparation of draft guidelines, the DTA must state as part of any submission whether the draft guidelines are consistent or not consistent with its transport strategy and suggest amendments to achieve consistency.

Request by DTA for Minister to issue guidelines or policy directives

1–39   **31H.**—The DTA may, in relation to its functions, request the Minister to issue guidelines under section 28 or a policy directive under section 29 to a planning authority within the GDA.

NOTE

This section allows the DTA to request the Minister to issue guidelines or directives to a planning authority within the Greater Dublin Area.

Requirement for transport impact assessment for certain classes of development

1–40   **31I.**—(1) The Minister may, in respect of the GDA and following consultation with the DTA, make regulations specifying—

(a) classes of development, including strategic infrastructure development, requiring the submission of a transport impact assessment in respect of applications for development, and

(b) the format and content of a transport impact assessment.

(2) Regulations under subsection (1) may require that a transport impact assessment demonstrate that the proposed development in respect of which the assessment has been prepared would be consistent with the transport strategy of the DTA.

(3) Before granting permission for a development which requires a transport impact assessment under regulations made under subsection (1), a planning authority shall satisfy itself that the applicant has demonstrated that the proposed development would be consistent with the transport strategy of the DTA.

(4) In this section 'transport impact assessment' means a report outlining what additional transport impacts a particular proposed development will generate and how it will integrate into existing transport patterns.

NOTE

This section allows the Minister to make regulations regarding development requiring the submission of a transport impact assessment and format and content for such assessment. Subsection (3) provides that where a transport impact assessment is required for certain development, the planning authority must be satisfied that it is consistent with the transport strategy of the DTA. This implies that where it is inconsistent, the planning authority must refuse permission.

Transport strategy and planning process

31J.—In any case in the GDA where—   **1–41**
    (a) a planning or local authority, a regional or State authority or An Bord Pleanála is carrying out any relevant function under or transferred by Part II, X, XI or XIV, or
    (b) a planning authority or An Bord Pleanála is carrying out any relevant function under any other Act,
the transport strategy of the DTA shall be a consideration material to the proper planning and sustainable development of the area or areas in question.

NOTE

This section provides that the transport strategy of the DTA constitutes a material planning consideration, for the purposes of the planning or local authority, a regional or State authority or where An Bord Pleanála is carrying out any relevant function under or transferred by Part II (plans and guidelines), X (Environmental Impact Assessment), XI (Development by Local and State Authority) or XIV (Acquisition of Land). However, under (b) it is more broadly stated to be deemed to be a material planning consideration in performing any relevant function under the Act.

PART III

CONTROL OF DEVELOPMENT

General obligation to obtain permission

32.—**(1)** Subject to the other provisions of this *Act,* permission shall be   **1–42**
required under this Part—
    (a) in respect of any development of land, not being exempted development, and
    (b) in the case of development which is unauthorised, for the retention of that unauthorised development.
(2) A person shall not carry out any development in respect of which permission is required by *subsection (1),* except under and in accordance with a permission granted under this Part.

NOTE

This is the essential provision regarding planning permission which triggers the planning code. The section is a restatement of s.24 of the 1963 Act, subject to certain modifications. Planning permission is required where there is development. Development and exempted development are defined in ss.3 and 4 of the Act, respectively. Full permission or outline permission under s.36 may be sought. The section omits the reference in the 1963 Act to exclusion of the requirement to seek permission where the "development commenced before the appointed day", which was October 1, 1964. This is now dealt with under s.39(4). Its omission does not mean retention permission needs to be sought in respect of such development. Subsection (2) makes clear that the development must be carried out strictly in accordance with the planning permission granted.

The determination of a planning application is an administrative rather than judicial procedure. See *McKone Estates v Dublin County Council* [1995] 2 I.L.R.M. 283. However, the planning authority in making the determination must act in a judicial manner. See *P & F Sharpe v County Manager* [1989] I.L.R.M. 565. The duty imposed under subs.(2) is not expressed as imposing duty under criminal law; s.2 defines unauthorised use and unauthorised works as, inter alia, development other than development which is the subject of a permission and which is carried out in accordance with that permission. The 2000 Act transfers the section dealing with the criminal offence of carrying out unauthorised development to s.151, Pt VIII which deals with Enforcement. While no time limit was specified for prosecutions under s.24 of the 1963 Act, a time limit of seven years is specified for such prosecutions under s.157. Section 100 of the Waste Management Act 2001, as inserted by s.26(2)(d) of the Protection of the Environment Act 2003, provides that in performing their functions under the Planning and Development Acts 2000 to 2002, and in particular their functions under Pt III, planning authorities and An Bord Pleanála shall ensure that such measures as are reasonably necessary are taken to serve appropriate provision for the management of waste (and in particular recyclable materials) within developments, including the provision of facilities for the storage, separation and collection of such waste (and in particular, such materials) and the preparation by the appropriate persons of suitable plans for the operation of such facilities.

Where a structure or use is unauthorised development, there is no entitlement to carry out exempted development in respect thereof. This is specifically provided in arts 9(1)(a)(viii) and 10(1)(d) of the the 2001 Regulations, but it is also implied by subs.(1), with the absence of a reference to exempted development in (b) in contrast with (a).

Retention application relates to development which has already commenced or even is completed. In *Weston v An Bord Pleanála*, unreported, High Court, McMenamin J., March 14, 2008, it was said that the Act provides for a heightened level of scrutiny by the planning authority in the case of an unauthorised development which is the subject matter of a retention application. It was further noted that the primary supervisory role of the authorities in individual cases is enhanced in retention applications. It was concluded that in the case of a retention permission, conditions may be imposed even in the circumstances of an exempted development. However, in *Commission v Ireland* (Case C-215/06), the European Court of Justice held that in allowing for the grant of retention permission for development for which an EIA is required even where no exceptional circumstances are proved, Ireland had failed to comply with its obligations under Directive 85/337. While this judgment only applies to development which requires an EIA or EIS, it means that amending legislation is required to abolish the entitlement to obtain retention permission for development requiring an EIA, subject to exceptional circumstances existing.

An application for retention permission is not an implied acceptance that the development is unauthorised development. A developer is not estopped from claiming that a development, which he has carried out without the benefit of planning permission, is in fact and in law exempted development, by reason only of having made an application for planning permission for the retention of that development. See *Fingal County Council v William P. Keeling & Sons* [2005] 2 I.R. 108. Equally an application for retention permission, will not mean that the time for taking enforcement action will be suspended or start again at the end of the determination of the retention application.

Regulations regarding applications for permission

1–43   **33.—(1)** The Minister shall by regulations provide for such matters of procedure and administration as appear to the Minister to be necessary or expedient in respect of applications for permission for the development of land.

(2) Without prejudice to the generality of *subsection (1)*, regulations under this *section* may make provision for the following—

   (a) requiring the submission of information in respect of applications for permission for the development of land;
   (b) requiring any applicants to publish any specified notices with respect

to their applications;

(c) enabling persons to make submissions or observations on payment of the prescribed fee and within a prescribed period;

(d) requiring planning authorities to acknowledge in writing the receipt of submissions or observations;

(e) requiring any applicants to furnish to any specified persons any specified information with respect to their applications;

(f) requiring planning authorities to—

   (i)

      (I) notify prescribed authorities of such proposed development or classes of development as may be prescribed, or

      (II) consult with them in respect thereof,
    and

   (ii) give to them such documents, particulars, plans or other information in respect thereof as may be prescribed;

(g) requiring any applicants to submit any further information with respect to their applications (including any information as to any estate or interest in or right over land) or information regarding any effect on the environment which the development may have;

(h) enabling planning authorities to invite an applicant to submit to them revised plans or other drawings modifying, or other particulars providing for the modification of, the development to which the application relates and, in case the plans, drawings or particulars are submitted to a planning authority in response to such an invitation, enabling the authority in deciding the application to grant a permission for the relevant development as modified by all or any of the plans, drawings or particulars;

(i) requiring the production of any evidence to verify any particulars of information given by any applicants;

(j) requiring planning authorities to furnish to the Minister and to any other specified persons any specified information with respect to applications and the manner in which they have been dealt with;

(k) requiring planning authorities to publish or give notice of their decisions in respect of applications for permission, including the giving of notice thereof to prescribed bodies and to persons who made submissions or observations in respect of such applications;

(l) requiring an applicant to submit specified information to the planning authority with respect to development, or any class of development, carried out by a person to whom *section 35(7)* applies pursuant to a permission granted to the applicant or to any other person under this Part or under Part IV of the Act of 1963.

(3)

   (a) Regulations under this section may, for the purposes of securing the attainment of an objective included in a development plan pursuant to *section 10(2)(m)*, require any applicant for permission to provide the planning authority with such information, in respect of development (including development of a particular class) that the applicant proposes to carry out in a Gaeltacht area, as it may specify.

(b) A requirement to which *paragraph (a)* applies may relate to development belonging to a particular class.

(c) Before making regulations containing a requirement to which *paragraph (a)* applies the Minister shall consult with the Minister for Arts, Heritage, Gaeltacht and the Islands.

(4) Regulations under this section may make additional or separate provisions in regard to applications for outline permission within the meaning of section 36.

NOTE

This section allows for the making of regulations in relation to planning applications. In this respect the principal regulations are the 2001 Regulations which have been subject to amendments, most notably by the 2006 Regulations (S.I. No. 265 of 2006). The Regulations concerning planning applications are contained in Chs 1 and 2 of Pt IV of the Regulations, which entered into force on March 11, 2002. These Regulations supersede Pt IV of the Local Government (Planning and Developmment) Regulations 1994 (S.I. No. 84 of 1994).

The Regulations largely restate the old Regulations, though with certain modifications. The articles of the Regulations dealing with the matters specified in this section include the following: art.22 (contents of planning applications generally); art.17 (requirement to publish notice, including a newspaper notice under art.18 and a site notice under art.19); art.29 (submissions/observations in relation to planning permission); art.26 (acknowledgement of receipt of application and submissions/observations); art.33 (requirement to furnish further information); art.28 (notice to certain bodies); art.34 (revised plans); art.33(1)(b) (verification of particulars) and art.39 (provision of certain information to the Minister). Section 35(7) refers to persons who have failed to comply with a previous planning permission, which can be a ground for refusal. As regards newspaper notices under art.18, a new provision requires each planning authority to approve a list of newspapers that have a sufficiently large circulation. As regards a site notice under art.19, a specific form is now set out in the Schedule to the Regulations. The purpose of the public notices is to notify the public of a planning application, who may then wish to make submissions: see *Crodaun Homes v Kildare County Council* [1983] I.L.R.M. 1; *Monaghan UDC v Alf-a-Bet Promotions Ltd* [1980] I.L.R.M. 64; *Cunningham v An Bord Pleanála*, unreported, High Court, Lavan J., May 3, 1990 and more generally see Dodd, "Public Notices and Planning Applications" [2004] 11(2) I.P.E.L.J. 58. The 2006 Regulations introduced a standard form for planning applications.

However, in *White v Dublin City Council* [2004] 1 I.R. 545, Fennelly J. described the argument that the statutory notices are for the benefit of the public and are not directed to any individuals, as an unduly narrow interpretation. He pointed out that the members of the public likely to be most closely affected by a planning application are the nearest neighbours. Under art.34 of the 2001 Regulations where a planning authority is disposed to grant permission subject to modifications, it may invite the submission of revised plans. Under art.35, where a planning authority receives significant additional information it will send copies of such matters to the prescribed bodies and persons who made submissions. It must also require the publication of a new newspaper notice marked "Further Information" or "Revised Plans". The courts will review the decision of a planning authority as to whether such extra steps are required under the standard of irrationality. See *White v Dublin City Council* [2004] 1 I.R. 545.

A wide range of people can make a planning application. Even a person without a legal interest in the land can make an application for planning permission. It is not entirely clear whether it is necessary for such a person to have the consent or approval of the person having the legal interest. This was suggested in *Frescati Estates Limited v Walker* [1975] I.R. 177, though these comments were classified as obiter by Keane J., in *Keane v An Bord Pleanála* [1998] 2 I.L.R.M. 241.

The contents of the planning application are set out under art.22, while a standard planning application form was introduced under the 2006 Regulations, which is at Form No. 2 of Sch.3 to the Regulations. The payment of a fee is an essential element of a valid application; see *Calor Teo v Sligo County Council* [1991] 2 I.R. 267. The planning application must include full and accurate information and be in accordance with the planning Regulations. Minor or trivial misstatements will not invalidate the application where there has been substantial compliance: see also *Cork County Council v Readymix & Cronin*, unreported, High Court, McGuinness J., June 15, 1999; *McCabe v Harding Investment* [1984] I.L.R.M. 105; *Molloy v Dublin County Council* [1990] 1 I.R. 90. A misdescription of the applicant will not normally mean the application is invalid. A simple typographical mistake in the name of applicant will not usually invalidate the application; see *The State (Toft) v Galway Corporation* [1981] I.L.R.M. 439; *Schwestermann v An Bord Pleanála* [1994] 3 I.R. 437. Among the factors to be considered will be whether the error was intentional and whether the public were misled; see *McDonagh v Galway Corporation* [1995] 1 I.R. 191. In *State (Finglas Industrial Estates Ltd) v Dublin County Council*, unreported, Supreme Court, February 17, 1983, an application was invalid because the company had not been incorporated. A distinction must be drawn between the adequacy of the application and the adequacy of the notification to the public: see *Browne v An Bord Pleanála* [1991] 2 I.R. 209. In *Dooley v Galway County Council* [1992] 2 I.R. 136, the use of a townland to describe the location when eighteen townlands were of the same name, was not adequate.

Regulations introduced on a statutory basis for the first time include art.29 of the Regulations, enabling persons to make observations. Persons are not defined but it is clear that it goes beyond a person with a direct interest in the property and embraces third parties. A fee however is required in respect of the making of such submissions or observations which is set at €20 under Sch.10 to the 2001 Regulations. The legality of charging a fee for submissions or observations in the context of applications requiring an EIA was upheld by the European Court of Justice in *Commission v Ireland* (Case C-216/05). Also introduced are: (d) art.26 acknowledging submissions; (e) art.33 requiring applicant to furnish information to specified persons; (f)(ii)art.28 requiring planning authorities to give bodies specified documents, plans etc.; (k) an expansion of the requirement to give notice to bodies and persons who made submissions; (l) the requirement to submit information in relation to previous permissions.

Permission for development

34.—(1) Where— 1–44

    (a) an application is made to a planning authority in accordance with permission regulations for permission for the development of land, and

    (b) all requirements of the regulations are complied with,

the authority may decide to grant the permission subject to or without conditions, or to refuse it.

    (2)

    (a) When making its decision in relation to an application under this section, the planning authority shall be restricted to considering the proper planning and sustainable development of the area, regard being had to—

        (i) the provisions of the development plan,

        (ii) the provisions of any special amenity area order relating to the area,

        (iii) any European site or other area prescribed for the purposes of *section 10(2)(c),*

        (iv) where relevant, the policy of the Government, the Minister or any other Minister of the Government,

    (v) the matters referred to in *subsection (4),* and

    (vi) any other relevant provision or requirement of this Act, and any regulations made thereunder.

(b) In considering its decision in accordance with *paragraph (a),* a planning authority shall consult with any other planning authority where it considers that a particular decision by it may have a significant effect on the area of that authority, and the authority shall have regard to the views of that other authority and, without prejudice to the foregoing, it shall have regard to the effect a particular decision by it may have on any area outside its area (including areas outside the State).

(c) [Subject to section 99F of the Environmental Protection Agency Act 1992,] and section 54 (as amended by section 257 of this Act) of the Waste Management Act, 1996, where an application under this section relates to development which comprises or is for the purposes of an activity for which an integrated pollution control licence or a waste licence is required, a planning authority shall take into consideration that the control of emissions arising from the activity is a function of the Environmental Protection Agency.

(3) A planning authority shall, when considering an application for permission under this section, have regard to—

    (a) in addition to the application itself, any information relating to the application furnished to it by the applicant in accordance with the permission regulations,

    (b) any written submissions or observations concerning the proposed development made to it in accordance with the permission regulations by persons or bodies other than the applicant.

(4) Conditions under *subsection (1)* may, without prejudice to the generality of that subsection, include all or any of the following—

    [**(a)** conditions for regulating the development or use of any land which adjoins, abuts or is adjacent to the land to be developed and which is under the control of the applicant if the imposition of such conditions appears to the planning authority—

        (i) to be expedient for the purposes of or in connection with the development authorised by the permission, or

        (ii) to be appropriate, where any aspect or feature of that adjoining, abutting or adjacent land constitutes an amenity for the public or a section of the public, for the purposes of conserving that amenity for the public or that section of the public (and the effect of the imposition of conditions for that purpose would not be to burden unduly the person in whose favour the permission operates);]

    (b) conditions for requiring the carrying out of works (including the provision of facilities) which the planning authority considers are required for the purposes of the development authorised by the permission;

    (c) conditions for requiring the taking of measures to reduce or prevent—

(i) the emission of any noise or vibration from any structure or site comprised in the development authorised by the permission which might give reasonable cause for annoyance either to persons in any premises in the neighbourhood of the development or to persons lawfully using any public place in that neighbourhood, or

(ii) the intrusion of any noise or vibration which might give reasonable cause for annoyance to any person lawfully occupying any such structure or site;

(d) conditions for requiring provision of open spaces;

(e) conditions for requiring the planting, maintenance and replacement of trees, shrubs or other plants or the landscaping of structures or other land;

(f) conditions for requiring the satisfactory completion within a specified period, not being less than 2 years from the commencement of any works, of the proposed development (including any roads, open spaces, car parks, sewers, watermains or drains or other public facilities), where the development includes the construction of 2 or more houses;

(g) conditions for requiring the giving of adequate security for satisfactory completion of the proposed development;

(h) conditions for determining the sequence and timing in which and the time at which works shall be carried out;

(i) conditions for the maintenance or management of the proposed development (including the establishment of a company or the appointment of a person or body of persons to carry out such maintenance or management);

(j) conditions for the maintenance, until taken in charge by the local authority concerned, of roads, open spaces, car parks, sewers, watermains or drains and other public facilities or, where there is an agreement with the local authority in relation to such maintenance, conditions for maintenance in accordance with the agreement;

(k) conditions for requiring the provision of such facilities for the collection or storage of recyclable materials for the purposes of the proposed development;

(l) conditions for requiring construction and demolition waste to be recovered or disposed of in such a manner and to such extent as may be specified by the planning authority;

(m) conditions for requiring the provision of roads, including traffic calming measures, open spaces, car parks, sewers, watermains or drains, facilities for the collection or storage of recyclable materials and other public facilities in excess of the immediate needs of the proposed development, subject to the local authority paying for the cost of the additional works and taking them in charge or otherwise entering into an agreement with the applicant with respect to the provision of those public facilities;

(n) conditions for requiring the removal of any structures authorised by the permission, or the discontinuance of any use of the land so authorised, at the expiration of a specified period, and the carrying out of any works required for the re-instatement of land at the expiration of that period;

(o) conditions in relation to appropriate naming and numbering of, and the provision of appropriate signage for, the proposed development;

(p) conditions for requiring, in any case in which the development authorised by the permission would remove or alter any protected structure or any element of a protected structure which contributes to its special architectural, historical, archaeological, artistic, cultural, scientific, social or technical interest—

  (i) the preservation by a written and visual record (either measured architectural drawings or colour photographs and/or audio-visual aids as considered appropriate) of that structure or element before the development authorised by the permission takes place, and

  (ii) where appropriate, the architectural salvaging of any element, or the re-instatement of any element in a manner specified by the authority;

(q) conditions for regulating the hours and days during which a business premises may operate.

(5) The conditions under *subsection (1)* may provide that points of detail relating to a grant of permission may be agreed between the planning authority and [the person carrying out the development; if the planning authority and that person cannot agree on the matter the matter may be referred to the Board for determination].

(6)

(a) In a case in which the development concerned would contravene materially the development plan, a planning authority may, notwithstanding any other provision of this *Act,* decide to grant permission under this *section,* provided that the following requirements are complied with before the decision is made, namely—

  (i) notice in the prescribed form of the intention of the planning authority to consider deciding to grant the permission shall be published in at least one daily newspaper circulating in its area and the notice shall specifically state which objective of the development plan would be materially contravened by granting this permission,

  (ii) copies of the notice shall be given to the applicant and to any person who has submitted a submission or observation in writing in relation to the development to which the application relates,

  (iii) any submission or observation as regards the making of a decision to grant permission and which is received by the planning authority not later than 4 weeks after the first publication of the notice shall be duly considered by the authority, and

      (iv) a resolution shall be passed by the authority requiring that a decision to grant permission be made.

  (b) It shall be necessary for the passing of a resolution referred to in *paragraph (a)* that the number of the members of the planning authority voting in favour of the resolution is not less than three-quarters of the total number of the members of the planning authority or where the number so obtained is not a whole number, the whole number next below the number so obtained shall be sufficient, and the requirement of this *paragraph* is in addition to and not in substitution for any other requirement applying in relation to such a resolution.

  (c) Where—

      (i) notice is given pursuant to [*section 140 of the Local Government Act, 2001*], of intention to propose a resolution which, if passed, would require the manager to decide to grant permission under this *section,* and

     (ii) the manager is of the opinion that the development concerned would contravene materially the development plan,

  he or she shall, within one week of receiving the notice, make, by order, a declaration stating his or her opinion (a copy of which shall be furnished by him or her to each of the signatories of the notice) and thereupon the provisions of *subparagraphs (i), (ii) and (iii) of paragraph (a)* shall apply and have effect and shall operate to cause the notice to be of no further effect.

  (d) If a resolution referred to in *subparagraph (iv) of paragraph (a)* is duly passed, the manager shall decide to grant the relevant permission.

(7) Notwithstanding [*section 140 of the Local Government Act, 2001*]—

  (a) the notice specified in [*subsection (3)*] of that *section* shall, in the case of a resolution under that *section* relating to a decision of a planning authority under this *section or section 42,* be signed—

      (i) if the land concerned is situated in a single local electoral area, by not less than three-quarters of the total number of the members who stand elected to the authority for that area, or where the number so obtained is not a whole number, the whole number next below the number so obtained shall be sufficient, and

     (ii) if the land concerned is situated in more than one local electoral area, by not less than three-quarters, as respects each such area, of the total number of the members of the authority who stand elected for that area, or where the number so obtained is not a whole number, the whole number next below the number so obtained shall be sufficient,

  and

  (b) it shall be necessary for the passing of a resolution under that *section* relating to a decision referred to in *paragraph (a)* that the number of the members voting in favour of the resolution is not less than three-quarters of the total number of members of the authority, or where the number so obtained is not a whole number, the whole number next below the number so obtained shall be sufficient.

(8)

    (a) Subject to *paragraphs (b), (c), (d) and (e),* where—

        (i) an application is made to a planning authority in accordance with the permission regulations for permission under this *section,* and

        (ii) any requirements of those regulations relating to the application are complied with,

    a planning authority shall make its decision on the application within the period of 8 weeks beginning on the date of receipt by the planning authority of the application.

    (b) Where a planning authority, within 8 weeks of the receipt of a planning application, serves notice in accordance with the permission regulations requiring the applicant to give to the authority further information or to produce evidence in respect of the application, the authority shall make its decision on the application within 4 weeks of the notice being complied with, provided that the total period is not less than 8 weeks.

    (c) Where, in the case of an application accompanied by an environmental impact statement, a planning authority serves a notice referred to in *paragraph (b),* the authority shall make its decision within 8 weeks of the notice being complied with.

    (d) Where a notice referred to in *subsection (6)* is published in relation to the application, the authority shall make its decision within the period of 8 weeks beginning on the day on which the notice is first published.

    (e) Where, in the case of an application for permission for development that—

        (i) would be likely to increase the risk of a major accident, or

        (ii) is of such a nature as to be likely, if a major accident were to occur, and, having regard to all the circumstances, to cause there to be serious consequences,

    a planning authority consults, in accordance with the permission regulations, with a prescribed authority for the purpose of obtaining technical advice regarding such risk or consequences, the authority shall make a decision in relation to the application within 4 weeks beginning on the day on which the technical advice is received.

    (f) Where a planning authority fails to make a decision within the period specified in *paragraph (a), (b), (c), (d) or (e),* a decision by the planning authority to grant the permission shall be regarded as having been given on the last day of that period.

(9) Where, within the period of 8 weeks beginning on the date of receipt by the planning authority of the application, the applicant for a permission under this *section* gives to the planning authority in writing his or her consent to the extension of the period for making a decision under *subsection (8),* the period for making the decision shall be extended for the period consented to by the applicant.

(10)

    (a) A decision given under this *section or section 37* and the notification of the decision shall state the main reasons and considerations on which the decision is based, and where conditions are imposed in relation to the grant of any permission the decision shall state the main reasons for the imposition of any such conditions, provided that where a condition imposed is a condition described in *subsection (4),* a reference to the *paragraph of subsection (4)* in which the condition is described shall be sufficient to meet the requirements of this *subsection.*

    (b) Where a decision by a planning authority under this *section* or by the Board under *section 37* to grant or to refuse permission is different, in relation to the granting or refusal of permission, from the recommendation in—

        (i) the reports on a planning application to the manager (or such other person delegated to make the decision) in the case of a planning authority, or

        (ii) a report of a person assigned to report on an appeal on behalf of the Board,

    a statement under *paragraph (a)* shall indicate the main reasons for not accepting the recommendation in the report or reports to grant or refuse permission.

(11)

    (a) Where the planning authority decides under this *section* to grant a permission—

        (i) in case no appeal is taken against the decision, it shall make the grant as soon as may be after the expiration of the period for the taking of an appeal,

        (ii) in case an appeal or appeals is or are taken against the decision, it shall not make the grant unless, as regards the appeal or, as may be appropriate, each of the appeals—

            (I) it is withdrawn, or

            (II) it is dismissed by the Board pursuant to *section 133 or 138,* or

            (III) in relation to it a direction is given to the authority by the Board pursuant to *section 139,* and, in the case of the withdrawal or dismissal of an appeal or of all such appeals, as may be appropriate, it shall make the grant as soon as may be after such withdrawal or dismissal and, in the case of such a direction, it shall make the grant, in accordance with the direction, as soon as may be after the giving by the Board of the direction.

    (b) Where the Board decides on appeal under section 37 to grant a permission, it shall make the grant as soon as may be after the decision.

(12) An application for development of land in accordance with the permission regulations may be made for the retention of unauthorised development and this section shall apply to such an application, subject to any necessary modifications.

(13) A person shall not be entitled solely by reason of a permission under this section to carry out any development.

AMENDMENT HISTORY

Subsection (2) substituted by reg.3 of the European Communities (Energy Performance of Buildings) Regulations 2005 (S.I. No.872 of 2005), which came into effect on December 21, 2005.

Subsection (4)(a) substituted by s.8(1) of the Planning and Development (Strategic Infrastructure) Act 2006 (No. 27 of 2006).

Subsection (5) amended by s.8(2) of the Planning and Development (Strategic Infrastructure) Act 2006 (No. 27 of 2006).

Subsection (6)(c)(i) was amended by s.5 of the Local Government Act 2001 (No. 37 of 2001), which, by the Local Government Act, 2001 (Commencement) (No. 3) Order 2001 (S.I. No. 588 of 2001), came into effect on January 1, 2002.

Subsection (7) was amended by s.5 of the Local Government Act 2001 (No. 37 of 2001), which, by the Local Government Act, 2001 (Commencement) (No. 3) Order 2001 (S.I. No. 588 of 2001), came into effect on January 1, 2002.

NOTE

This section concerns the decision on an application for planning permission. Subsection (1) provides that where there is a valid planning application, the planning authority may decide to grant or refuse permission. The subsection refers to two types of decision, i.e. granting or refusing and so does not explicitly state whether a local authority can issue a split decision, i.e. both granting and refusing part of an application. However, it is submitted that the power to issue a split decision is reasonably incidental to the power to grant or refuse permission. Such power to issue a split decision should however be exercised in accordance with certain principles. The split decision ought not result in permitting development which is materially different from the permission applied for. In *Kent County Council v Secretary of State for the Environment* [1976] 33 P&CR 70, Sir Douglas Frank QC, sitting as a deputy High Court judge, held that the test was one of severability: could the part of the development being permitted be severed from the rest of the application which was being refused? However, in *Bernard Wheatcroft Ltd v Secretary of State for the Environment* [1982] 42 P&CR 233, Forbes J. rejected the severability test but held that the question was whether the permission granted was in substance that for which permission had been sought. This involved considering whether the development had been so changed that the grant deprived those who would have been consulted on the changed development of the opportunity of consultation. The planning authority must ensure that fair procedures are satisfied. See *Johnson v Secretary of the State for the Environment*, unreported, High Court, June 8, 2007.

Application in accordance with Regulations

It would appear to follow from subs.(1) that where a valid planning application has not been made in accordance with the Regulations, the planning authority cannot waive non-compliance as it has no power to grant permission in such circumstances.

However, in assessing Regulations, the courts have developed the concepts of mandatory or directory requirements. If mandatory, non-compliance will render any application invalid; if merely directory, the non-compliance will not affect the application's validity. For the distinction, see *State (Elm Developments Ltd) v An Bord Pleanála* [1981] I.L.R.M. 108. The 2001 Regulations apply a stricter approach to non-compliance with certain Regulations, by declaring the application invalid. Article 26(3)(a) of the 2001 Regulations provides that where any of the requirements of arts 18 (newspaper notice); 19(1)(a) (prescribed form of the site notice); or 22 (planning application) and, as may be appropriate, of arts 24 (plans and particulars for outline permission); or 25 (planning application for electricity undertaking) has not been complied with, the application is invalid. Article 26(3) appears to leave no discretion to the planning authority, while under the previous Regulations they had a certain discretion or at least were obliged to direct other steps such as, in the case of an inadequate or misleading notice, a requirement to erect another notice. The application will also be invalid where the notice in the newspaper or the site notice, because of its content or for any other reason, is misleading or inadequate for the information of the public. Even where the application has been acknowledged, the planning authority can revisit the validity of the application following a site inspection. See art.26(4) of the 2001 Regulations.

It should be noted, however, that even if the above are mandatory requirements, a court in any judicial review proceedings still has discretion to refuse relief, due to the discretionary nature of judicial review. In *Dunne v An Bord Pleanála*, unreported, High Court, McGovern J., December 14, 2006, the Court exercised discretion to refuse relief regarding technical objections to the erection of a site notice, i.e. where there was a failure to indicate that habitable houses were being demolished and on the maps submitted. However, there may not be a suitable party to challenge an application grounded upon an invalid notice, especially where they failed to participate at the hearing; see *Harding v Cork County Council*, unreported, Supreme Court, May 2, 2008, where Kearns J. said notwithstanding any illegality in the planning process, this will not enable a person to bring proceedings where they do not otherwise have a substantial interest. Murray C.J. suggested that where the illegality in the process is personal or peculiar to the applicant such as the failure to adequately notify under art.35 of the 2001 Regulations a person who had submissions, then this could give rise to a substantial interest. However, it is clear that general complaints that the planning authority had failed to observe the law during the planning process could not give rise to a substantial interest. Thus a failure of the developer to provide all the further information which was demanded by the planning authority, to send an appropriate fee with the revised plan, to erect a site notice in respect of that plan or the failure of the planning authority to give a statement indicating the main reasons for not accepting the planner's recommendation, could not involve an interest which is peculiar or personal to an applicant. See *Shea v Kerry County Council* [2003] 4 I.R. 143.

Apart from this, under the previous case law, the courts had developed a *de minimis* type rule whereby trivial or insubstantial non-compliance could be overlooked; see *Monaghan UDC v Alf-a-Bet Promotions Ltd* [1980] I.L.R.M. 64. The *de minimis* rule arguably survives on the basis that it could not have been the intention of the legislature that very minor defects would mean the application should be invalid.

As regards site notices, there is a requirement to include a "brief description of the nature and extent of the development", with the words "brief description" being added by the 2006 Regulations. Examples of inadequate descriptions of the development include *Monaghan v Alf-a-Bet Promotions Ltd* [1980] I.L.R.M. 64 (failure to state that a drapery shop was being changed to a betting and amusement arcade); *Keleghan v Corby* [1977] 111 I.L.T.R. 144 (failure to state that a new access was being made from a cul de sac to a school) and *Cunningham v An Bord Pleanála* unreported High Court, Lavan J., May 3, 1990. In *Marshall v Arklow Town Council* [2004] 4 I.R. 92, where there was a conflict of evidence as to whether a site was erected which the Court could not resolve, it was held there was an obligation on the planning authority to inspect a site notice and if no inspection is carried out within that five-week period then the decision is not in compliance with the provisions of s.34(1) of the 2000 Act. In *Kelly v Roscommon County Council*, unreported, High Court, McGovern J., May 20, 2006, the Court rejected a claim that as the site notice had been erected within six months of the first application, it should have been on a yellow (rather than white) background as required under art.19(4) of the 2001 Regulations. McGovern J. held that once the first application was deemed to be invalid (because the application description was incorrect), it ceased to be a "planning application" within the meaning of the Act. Article 19(4) of the Regulations as amended by the 2006 Regulations, makes clear that the requirement of the yellow background is only required where the earlier application was valid.

In relation to maps, in *Dublin County Council v Marren* [1985] I.L.R.M. 593, an application was declared invalid as it did not comply with the form of maps and plans required. In *Irish Hardware Association v South Dublin County Council*, unreported, High Court, Butler J., July 19, 2000, Butler J. said, obiter, that the failure to furnish elevation drawings would be fatal, though on the facts he found that the same were, in fact, furnished.

The adequacy of maps was also raised in *White v Dublin Corporation*, unreported, High Court, Ó Caoimh J., June 21, 2002, where the drawings submitted omitted to show a conservatory. Ó Caoimh J., however, held there was substantial compliance with the Regulations. In *Seery v An Bord Pleanála*, unreported, High Court, Quirke J., November 26, 2006, the Court set aside the grant of permission where certain layout plans significantly misrepresented the size and location of the adjoining landowners dwelling. Relief may be refused where an error in maps were de minimis See *Ní Chonghaile and Others v Galway County Council* [2004] 4 I.R. 138, where Ó Caoimh J. declined to grant certiorari against the council in the making of its decision, where it had before it, a site map which was not accurate but where the error was minor, and where another map was available to the County Council.

As regards a request for further information, in the case law under the previous legislation, the request for further information must be a valid request, otherwise it will not have the effect of extending the time; see *The State (Conlon Construction Limited) v Cork County Council*, unreported, High Court, Butler J., July 31, 1975; *The State (N.C.E Limited) v Dublin County Council*, unreported, Supreme Court, December 4, 1979; *O'Connor Downtown Properties Ltd v Nenagh UDC* [1993] 1 I.R. 1. In contrast, see *Murphy v Navan Urban District Council*, unreported, High Court, Ó Caoimh J., July 31, 2001. The court may hold there was a want of fair procedures, where the applicant was not given the opportunity to supply such information as in *McGoldrick v An Bord Pleanála* [1997] 1 I.R. 497.

Proper Planning and Sustainable Development

Subsection (2) provides, that when determining whether to grant permission, the planning authority is "restricted" to considering the proper planning and sustainable development of the area. This means considerations to be taken into account must serve a planning purpose, which means it must relate to the character of use of the land; see *Vasiliou v The Secretary of State for Transport* [1991] 2 All E.R. 77. In *Great Portland Estates Plc v Westminster City Council* [1984] 3 All E.R. 744, in the House of Lords, Lord Scarman said a planning purpose is one which relates to the character of the use of the land. He noted that only in exceptional circumstances would the personal circumstances of the applicant be taken into account. This approach was approved in *Griffin v Galway County Manager*, unreported, High Court, Blayney J., October 31, 1990, where a section 4 resolution was invalid, as a planning authority member had taken into account personal matters of the applicant; see also *Flanagan v Galway County Manager*, unreported, High Court, Blayney J., May 25, 1989 and *Malahide Community Council v Fingal County Council* [1997] 3 I.R. 383. Note also that s.39(1) provides that planning permission enures for the benefit of the land. See *Mason and McCarthy v KT Sand and Gravel*, unreported, High Court, Smyth J., May 7, 2004. The proper planning and development of the area at the time of the decision must be taken into account, rather than proper planning and development which obtained at an earlier stage; see *Langrath v Bray Urban District Council*, unreported, High Court, Morris P., June 25, 2001. The fear or apprehensions of a community in relation to a development will not in itself amount to a proper planning consideration. See *Eircell v Leitrim County Council* [2000] 1 I.R. 479, in the context of the revocation of a planning permission. Proper planning and development will however include consideration of the impact on the community. See *Keane v An Bord Pleanála* [1998] 2 I.L.R.M. 241, where Keane J. said the planning authority is not confined to consideration of the consequences of the development on the physical environment, but is also entitled to take into account its impact on people, under the common good. Economic considerations may amount to planning considerations to be borne in mind when granting or refusing planning permission. See *Northumberland County Council v Secretary of State for the Environment* [1989] 59 P. & C.R. 468. The notion of "proper planning and sustainable development" is the overall touchstone standard according to which the planning application is determined.

As to the matters enlisted in subs.(2), to which regard must be had, these include: the development plan which is dealt with under Pt II of the Act; Special Amenity Area Orders under Pt XIII, ss.202 and 203 of the Act, the contents of which may be reflected in the development plan under s.10(2)(c). In relation to the meaning of "have regard", see *McEvoy v Meath County Council* [2003] 1 I.L.R.M. 431, where the obligation "to have regard" to guidelines, was held not to require the planning authority to rigidly or "slavishly" comply with the guidelines' recommendations or even necessarily to fully adopt the strategy and policies outlined therein. They were held however obliged to inform themselves fully of and give reasonable consideration to the guidelines. The planning authority or Board may have regard to matters in the development plan without necessarily referring to same as being part of the development plan and stating it within the main reasons and considerations under subs.(10). See *Ryanair v An Bord Pleanála* [2004] 2 I.R. 334. While there is an obligation to have regard to the development plan, the planning authority has no power to grant permission where the development would be a material contravention of the development plan except where the special procedure under s.34(6) has been satisfied.

Section 36(20) of the Water Services Act 2007 provides that:

> "An application for permission under Part III of the Planning and Development Act 2000 shall not be refused by a planning authority or the Board solely on the ground that the development to which the application relates is not specifically referred to in the water services strategic plan in force in relation to the functional area of the planning authority if the planning authority or the Board, as the case may be, considers the development will facilitate the achievement of the objectives of that water services strategic plan".

Section 8(4) of the Roads Act 2007 provides that neither a planning authority or An Bord Pleanála shall decide to grant or grant planning permission nor shall a decision by such be regarded as having been given under s.34(8) of the 2000 Act in respect of the developments referred to in s.46 of the Roads Act 1993 in respect of a national road or a proposed road development for the construction of a national road declared to be a motorway.

Subsection (2) explicitly incorporates consideration of any European site or area prescribed as well as relevant Ministerial or Governmental policy, which was not specified under the previous Acts. Section 10(2)(c) refers to the conservation and protection of the environment including the architectural and natural heritage and the conservation and protection of European sites and other sites prescribed for the purpose of the section. The European Communities (Natural Habitats) Regulations 1997 require an assessment of a planning application likely to have a significant effect on a European site. Permission must be refused where it adversely affects the integrity of the European site, except where required by imperative reasons of overriding public interest. As regards other relevant provisions under the Act to which the planning authority must have regard, these could include: that a protected structure may be affected (s.57); that the land is within an architectural conservation area (s.82); or an area of special planning control (s.87); the social and affordable housing provisions under Pt V, an EIA, that the land is within a strategic development zone (s.170); any local area plan in force (s.18(3)); and any Ministerial guidelines and directives (ss.28 and 29). As regards an integrated pollution licence or a waste management licence, see ss.256 and 257.

The decision to grant permission is an executive decision as opposed to a reserved decision. The elected members only have a role in the material contravention of the development plan procedure, under subs.(6) or in invoking s.140 of the Local Government Act 2001, to direct the Manager to make a decision to grant.

The 2000 Act imports a new mandatory obligation on the planning authority to consult with another authority but only where the decision may have "significant effect" on that other area, though there is no procedure set out for such consultation. However, even where it is of the view that the decision may not have a "significant effect", there is still in all cases an obligation on the authority to have regard to the effect the decision may have outside its area. This new provision concerning the areas adopts the position stated in *Keane v An Bord Pleanála* [1998] 2 I.L.R.M. 241, where the area was held not to be co-extensive with the area of the relevant planning authority. Section 256 of the 2000 Act provides that where a licence or revised licence is granted under the Environmental Protection Agency Act 1992, the planning authority, in considering any development comprising the activity, cannot impose conditions in relation to the control of emissions. Also under the section, the planning authority may refuse permission for the development where it is unacceptable on environmental grounds regarding the proper "planning and sustainable development". In considering the development, the planning authority may request the Environmental Agency to make observations. Section 257 applies similar terms in relation to a waste licence.

The rule of *res judicata* can apply to decisions on planning applications. Where a planning authority has refused a permission upon an application, they may refuse to accept a subsequent identical application in the absence of a change of circumstances; see *Athlone Woollen Mills Limited v Athlone Urban District Council* [1950] I.R. 1 and *State (Kenny and Hussey) v An Bord Pleanála*, unreported, Supreme Court, December 20, 1984. A planning authority cannot however subsequently plead *res judicata* where it has already accepted and processed the application; see *Littondale v Wicklow County Council* [1996] 2 I.L.R.M. 519. Where a subsequent planning permission imposes the same conditions as an earlier permission, the failure to challenge the earlier conditions will not in itself give rise to a successful plea of *res judicata*; see *Ashbourne Holdings v An Bord Pleanála* [2003] 2 I.R. 114; see also *State (Kenny) v An Bord Pleanála*, unreported, Supreme Court, December 20, 1984. However, if a planning authority sees fit to confine its ground for refusal of an application to a single ground, it does not preclude itself from relying on other grounds if a similar application is made in relation to the same lands, after that first ground of objection has been successfully disposed of. See *Aprile v Naas Urban District Council* [1985] I.L.R.M. 510. While a planning application should be considered de novo it should also take into account the planning history of the site. See *Fitzgerald v An Bord Pleanála*, unreported, High Court, Murphy J., November 11, 2005. In *Grealish v An Bord Pleanála*, unreported, High Court, Laffoy J., February 2, 2005, res judicata was considered not to apply to a 2003 decision refusing permission based on a 1997 decision permitting development as the latter was a temporary permission to retain a structure for five years and so was adjudicating on a different issue.

A planning authority is entitled to arrive at a decision contrary to that recommended by its planning officials. The planning authority will be afforded a wide discretion in reaching such decision; see *P and F Sharpe Limited v Dublin City and County Manager* [1989] I.R. 701; *Child v Wicklow County Council* [1995] 2 I.R. 447 and *Carty and Carty Construction v Fingal County Council* [1999] 3 I.R. 577. The planning authority must however act in accordance with fair procedures in determining the planning application. See *Jerry Beades Construction Ltd v Dublin Corporation*, unreported, High Court, McKechnie J., September 7, 2005, where it was held the decision by the planning authority was arrived at contrary to fair procedures and in breach of natural and constitutional justice and that this had also tainted the decision of the Board.

Submissions or Observations

Subsection (3) imposes an obligation on the planning authority to consider any submissions furnished by the applicant. This gives statutory recognition to the right of members of the public to make submissions (so called third-party objectors), although these were matters which were in practice considered under the 1994 Regulations. In *State (Haverty) v An Bord Pleanála* [1987] I.R. 485, Murphy J. recognised that the right of members of the public to object was not based upon any proprietary interest. See also *State (Stanford) v Dun Laoghaire*, unreported, Supreme Court, February 20, 1981, where the right of third parties to make objections within a reasonable time was recognised, and also *The State (Córas Iompair Éireann) v An Bord Pleanála*, unreported, Supreme Court, December 12, 1984. The procedure is set out under art.29 of the 2001 Regulations, which provides that a person may make a submission or observation in writing in relation to a planning application within five weeks from the date of receipt of the application. It seems to follow from art.30 of the Regulations, whereby a planning authority cannot determine an application until five weeks since its receipt, that a minimum of five weeks are allowed for submissions. Article 29(3) provides that where submission is received after the five-week period, it must be returned and the person notified that it cannot be considered by the planning authority. Article 29(4) (as inserted under the 2006 Regulations) provides that where the planning authority so consents, a submission or observation under sub-art.(1) may be made in electronic form. It appears that this may be a general consent in the manner set out in s.248. Article 29A (as inserted by the 2006 Regulations) provides that where submissions, observations or a request to be made, or documents, particulars or other information to be submitted to the planning authority within a specified period and the last day of that period is a public holiday (within the meaning of the Organisation of Working Time Act 1997) or any other day on which the offices of the planning authority are closed, the submissions, observations or request or documents, particulars or other information (as the case may be) shall be regarded as having been received before the expiration of that period if received by the authority on the next following day on which the offices of the authority are open. An acknowledgement of receipt of the submission or observations under art.31 may be important, as apart from the parties, only a person who makes a submission or observation can appeal the matter to An Bord Pleanála. A standard form acknowledgement is contained at Form No. 3 of Sch.3 to the 2001 Regulations, as amended. In *Lynch v Dublin City Council*, unreported, High Court, Ó Caoimh J., July 25, 2003, the failure to issue an acknowledgement to allow a third party appeal did not render the decision of the planning authority invalid. Where significant additional data is received by the planning authority following a request for further information or revised plans for which the planning authority requires re-advertisement under art.35 of the 2001 Regulations, there will be a further opportunity to make submissions or observations. A further opportunity to make submissions may also arise where the material contravention procedure is invoked under s.34(6). The 2001 Regulations introduced a fee for making submissions or observations, which was set at €20. The legality of charging a fee for submissions or observations in the context of application requiring an EIA was upheld by the European Court of Justice in *Commission v Ireland* (Case C-216/05). Section 246(3) provides that a submission or observation shall not be considered by the planning authority unless the fee has been received by the planning authority. The neutral phase of submissions or observations rather than objections is used to reflect the fact the submission or observation need not be against the particular development. It appears that a person may bind themselves not to make future objections to planning applications. See *Connolly v An Bord Pleanála*, unreported, High Court, Irvine J., July 8, 2008.

The erection of a valid site notice and the publication of a valid newspaper notice, is inextricably linked with the right of third parties to make objections. In *Marshall v Arklow County Council (2)* [2004] 4 I.R. 92, Peart J. said:

"It follows that the requirement of having a site notice in place and in conformity with the Regulations is a very important requirement. The purpose which it serves is a vital one, if the intention of the legislature that each person likely to be affected by a planning decision shall have the right to lodge an objection and have their views heard before a planning decision is made, is to be achieved".

There are no specific rules regarding service of the planning authority in either the 2000 Act, as amended, or the 2001 Regulations. This is in contrast to service of an appeal or referral on An Bord Pleanála, where s.127(5) applies. In *Fahy v Dublin City Council*, unreported, High Court, *ex tempore*, Quirke J., April 11, 2005, Quirke J. rejected that submissions or observations had to have been received at the offices of the planning department of the respondent within five weeks; it was sufficient where they had been delivered at the mayor's residence in the Mansion House within the period and sent by internal post to the planning department, albeit received outside the five weeks.

The right to object may be deemed to constitute the vindication of a civil right within the meaning of art.6 of the European Convention on Human Rights, which may be asserted in Ireland using the European Convention on Human Rights Act 2003. In *Ortenberg v Austria* [1994] E.C.H.R. 42, the European Court of Human Rights held that the rights of an adjacent landowner to object to a planning permission involved the vindication of a civil right within art.6, which would necessitate a right of access to a tribunal. See also the English case of *R (Friends Provident) v Environment Secretary* [2002] W.L.R. 1450, where Forbes J. declared at 1475 that:

"I am of the view that there is no reason in principle, in an appropriate case, why the scope of article 6 should not extend to the administrative decision-making process relating to a third party's objection to the grant of planning permission, provided it directly affects that third party's civil rights".

However, the entitlements afforded to third parties under the Irish Planning Code would appear to exceed any entitlements which may be asserted under the European Convention.

A person who made submissions must receive a notice of the decision under art.31, within three working days of the date of the decision. The notice must contain the matter specified in that article which now also includes at (g) (inserted by the 2006 Regulations) that in deciding a planning application the planning authority, in accordance with s.34(3) of the Act, has regard to submissions or observations received in accordance with these Regulations.

Planning Conditions

Subsection (4) concerns the conditions which can be imposed in granting a planning permission. Conditions form an essential part of the planning permission. See *Pyx Granite Co. Ltd v Ministry of Housing and Local Government & Anor* [1958] I QB 554, where Hodgson noted that "[t]he permission given has been given subject to those conditions, and non constat but that no permission would have been given at all if the condition had not been attached." See also *Mason and McCarthy v KT Sand and Gravel,* unreported, High Court, Smyth J., May 7, 2004. A development not carried out in accordance with the conditions of a planning permission will constitute unauthorised development within the meaning of s.2. Where the condition relates to the "ongoing use" of the land, there are no time limitations on the taking of enforcement action. See s.160(6)(a)(b), although if the condition does not relate to ongoing use, the normal seven year limitation period applies.

The list of conditions is not exhaustive, as the planning authority has a general power to impose conditions under s.34(1). However, conditions granted under the general power must be of the same nature to those set out in subs.(4): see *State (Abenglen Properties) v Dublin Corporation* [1984] I.R. 381. Nevertheless in *Ashbourne Holdings v An Bord Pleanála* [2003] 2 I.R. 114, Hardiman J. noted there is a general power to impose conditions even if it is outside the scope of any of the specified conditions. Provided that the condition lies outside the scope of any specified conditions in subs.(4), the planning authority may impose such condition where such condition is in accordance with the objectives of the Act and has a rational justification. See *Weston v An Bord Pleanála*, unreported, High Court, McMenamin J., March 14, 2008. Unless the power exercised comes within the scope of any one of the seventeen specified circumstances (when it will require to be strictly construed), the power otherwise, and the jurisdiction vested, is a "general" one. However, where a condition is imposed under the general power to impose conditions as opposed to one of the specific conditions under s.34(4), there may be enhanced obligation to state the "main reasons" for the decision which derives from the necessity to ensure that the condition is within the four walls of the Act as a whole. See *Weston v An Bord Pleanála*, unreported, High Court, McMenamin J., March 14, 2008. In relation to the specified conditions, it must be imposed for the purpose for which the power is specified. See *Brady v Environmental Protection Agency* [2007] 3 I.R. 232.

Much of the specified conditions enlisted are the same as under s.26(2) of the 1963 Act. Subsection (4)(a) provides that adjoining controlled land may be sought to be regulated to act as a counterbalance to the development, such as by allowing open space. The 2006 Act amended s.34(4)(a) by adding a new subpara.(ii). This means that a condition can be imposed regulating the use of adjoining land under the control of the applicant, either where it is expedient in connection with the development or for the purposes of conserving a public amenity for the public. In order for (ii) to apply:

1. an aspect or feature of the adjoining land must constitute an amenity for the public;
2. the condition must conserve the amenity for the public; and
3. the condition must not impose an undue burden on the applicant.

There is no definition of what constitutes a "public amenity" in this context. The amended condition therefore now allows a condition which was held to be ultra vires under the former section in *Ashbourne Holding v An Bord Pleanála* [2003] 2 I.R. 114. In that case the condition required that public access was to be allowed to a golf course adjoining a clubhouse. The Supreme Court held that "expedient" meant advantageous to the development and the condition was ultra vires as it could not be advantageous to the development, which was the construction of a clubhouse, to allow the public to traverse the golf course. This condition would therefore now be permissible under (ii). There is no requirement in 4(a)(ii) that the condition is relevant to the development. However, the harshness of this potential condition is mitigated by the fact that it must satisfy a proportionality condition, whereby the condition must not impose an undue burden on the person in whose favour permission operates.

The requirement that a condition is expedient for the development requires that it be of benefit or advantage to the permitted development and not to a wider area; see *Ashbourne Holding Ashbourne Holding v An Bord Pleanála* [2003] 2 I.R. 114 (public access to a golf course not expedient for a clubhouse) and *State (FPH Properties SA) v An Bord Pleanála* [1987] I.R. 698 (restoration of historic building on nearby lands not expedient to development). Subsection (4)(b) slightly expands the provision in parenthesis from "provision of car parks" to "provision of facilities". This is to ensure that ancillary matters connected with the development are taken care of. The facilities will depend on the nature of the development. In relation to any public or commercial building, access for disabled persons, (c) is similar to s.39(c) of the 1976 Act, with the addition of the word "or site" after structure in (c)(ii). The equivalent provision in the 1976 Act was expressly inserted, after such conditions were held invalid in *Dunne v Dublin County Council* [1974] I.R. 45; (d) open space reflects the general protection of the environment in the community; s.45 allows for enforcement of such a condition; (e) a tree preservation order may also be made under s.205; (f) constitutes a new provision requiring the satisfactory completion in not less than two years where the development includes the construction of two or more houses. See also s.180 concerning the taking in charge of estates. This condition appears to be designed to ensure that housing estates are built on a regular rather than sporadic basis: (g) the requirement to give security is now also buttressed by s.35, where a permission may be refused altogether due to failure to carry out a previous permission; see also contributions required under a contribution scheme under ss.48 and 49. Several provisions have been newly introduced to ensure that development is carried out in proper fashion. These are temporary insofar as they relate to the construction of the development rather than the completed development and include: (h) the sequence and timing of works; (i) maintenance/management of the proposed development; (j) maintenance of public facilities; (k) facilities for collection/storage of recyclable materials; and (l) construction/demolition of waste to be recovered. In relation to (m), although a similar provision was contained in s.26(2)(f), a number of additional clauses have been added which include the reference to "traffic calming measures", "facilities for collection or storage of recyclable materials and public facilities" and also the final clause: "subject to the local authority paying for the costs of additional works and taking them in charge etc." This provision essentially enables the authority to link the development to the surrounding area and so to matters which are not directly relevant to the development. This is subject to the requirement of the planning authority to pay the costs of additional works, which caters for the situation in *McDonagh v Galway Corporation* [1996] 1 I.R. 191. It allows the planning authority to take into account other possible future development. This is written in very broad terms but should be subject to a requirement of reasonableness. A condition requiring a contribution may be imposed in accordance with a general, special or supplementary contribution scheme adopted under ss.48 and 49. It may be noted in relation to water supply, s.55(4) of the Water Servives Act 2007 provides that where a water services authority is also the relevant planning authority, the grant of a permission under Part III of the 2000 Act in relation to a structure, if it is indicated in the permission, will include the agreement of the water services authority to the connection of that structure to its waterworks for the purposes of the section, subject to such conditions as the water services authority may require, consistent with its functions. Section 55(5) provides that;

> "as a condition to the agreement of a water services authority to the connection of a premises to water supplies which are provided, or to be provided, by the water services authority or any person providing water services jointly with it or on its behalf, the water services authority may, in its absolute discretion and for the purposes of this section, require—
>
> > (i) that the length or overall capacity of the service connection, or such related pipes or accessories as it considers necessary, be increased to such extent beyond technical requirements as it may specify so as to enable adjoining or other premises to be connected to a waterworks, but subject to the water services authority—
> >
> > > (I) paying for any consequential increase in the cost of providing and installing the service connection or related pipes or accessories; and

(II)taking the service connection or related pipes or accessories into its charge or otherwise entering into an agreement in relation to their future use with the person seeking its agreement to connect the premises to the said water services, as if the requirement was a requirement under section 34(4)(m) of the Act of 2000; or

(ii) that the service connection, or such related pipes or accessories as it considers necessary, be opened for inspection or testing, or otherwise inspected or tested, by an authorised person.

(b) For the purposes of the application of section 34(4)(m) of the Act of 2000 to this subsection, a reference to a planning authority shall be deemed to include a reference to a water services authority".

A similar provision also applies in relation to waste water works under s.61(5) to (12).

Subsection (4)(n) concerns temporary permissions; (o) is a new provision dealing with appropriate naming and numbering and signage for the proposed development. Also new are: (p) in relation to protected structures; and (q) regulating hours and days when a business may operate. A further important condition may be imposed under s.96, requiring the applicant or other interested person to enter into an agreement for the transfer of land to the local authority. Section 190 provides that compensation may be payable for reduction in value of interest in land as a result of a condition, although there is no subsection like s.26(7) of the 1963 Act which provided for compensation where unduly onerous conditions are imposed. The Fifth Schedule sets out conditions which may be imposed on the granting of planning permission without the planning authority being liable to pay compensation.

The Irish courts have yet to fully address the issue of negative conditions or Grampian-type conditions, which may provide that no development may commence until certain mattera is on adjoining land have been satisfied. In *Grampian Regional Council v City of Aberdeen District Council* [1984] 47 P & CR 633, the House of Lords upheld such conditions, although it held that a positive condition requiring a developer to take steps to secure the stopping up of a highway would have been invalid as a positive obligation which was outside his powers to guarantee. In *British Railway Board v Secretary of State for the Environment* [1994] JPL 32, the House of Lords rejected that the mere fact that a desirable condition appeared to have no reasonable prospect of fulfilment did not mean that planning permission must necessarily be refused. See also *Merritt v Secretary of State for the Environment and Transport and the Regions* [2000] JPL 371 and *R(Shina) v Secretary of State for the Environment, Transport and the Environment* [2002] JPL 1132. However, even such negatively phrased Grampian conditions have yet to be approved in Ireland. See *Parolen v Drogheda Corporation*, unreported, High Court, Finnegan P., May 14, 2003.

The conditions which may be imposed are subject to the general restraint that they must be pursuant to the proper planning and sustainable development of the area. In *State (Abenglen Properties) v Dublin Corporation* [1984] I.R. 381, Walsh J. declared of the equivalent provision of s.26 of the 1963 Act that the planning authority was restricted by statute to considering:

"[T]he proper planning and development of the area of the authority (including the preservation and improvement of the amenities thereof), regard having been had to the provisions of the development plan, the provisions of any special amenity area order relating to the said area"

and to the matters referred to in subs.(2) of s.26. Any conditions which go outside those objectives are ultra vires. If a condition concerns a subject matter dealt with in a specified condition but fails to meet the full requirements of the condition, it cannot be sought to be justified under the general power. A condition must fulfil all of the requirements of the subparagraph to be valid. See *Ashbourne Holdings v An Bord Pleanála* [2003] 2 I.R. 114, where it was said that the restrictions on the vires to impose conditions require to be strictly construed. In relation to the general power to impose conditions. It was held that the conditions must be of the same nature as those indicated in the particulars set out in the former s.26(2). Furthermore, even where the developer agrees to a condition, this cannot expand the power of the planning authority to impose the condition where it would otherwise be outside their power under s.26. In assessing the condition, the reason for the decision must also be assessed as to whether the condition supports the reasons; see *Killiney and*

Ballybrack Development Association v The Minister for Local Government and Templefinn Estates, unreported, Supreme Court, April 24, 1978.

A former restriction on the nature of the conditions was that the conditions must relate to the permitted development, see *Pyx Granite Company Ltd v Minister for Housing and Local Government* [1958] 1 Q.B. 554, per Lord Denning; see also *Newbury District Council v Secretary of State for the Environment* [1981] AC 578; *Fawcett Properties v Buckingham County Council* [1961] A.C. 636. In *Brady v Environmental Protection Agency* [2007] 3 I.R. 232, in the context of conditions imposed under a EPA licence, it was noted for such condition to be valid:

"[I]t must be within the powers of the issuing authority; that such condition must be imposed for the purpose for which the power to grant conditions was specified (here it is for environmental protection purposes); and it must be reasonably related to the activity that is to be permitted in the avoidance of the harm for which licensing of an activity is required by legislation".

However, this is now expressly permitted where the conditions falls within the circumstances specified in subs.(4)(a)(ii) as amended. The condition must be imposed for a planning purpose and not some other ulterior purpose. In *Dunne Ltd v Dublin County Council* [1974] I.R. 45, Pringle J. held that a condition requiring houses to be constructed to provide sound insulation against aircraft noise was ultra vires and should have been dealt with by the building regulations (though s.26(bb) of the 1976 Act was inserted to allow imposition of conditions to deal with the effect of noise, now under s.34(4)(c)). A condition requiring a developer to notify purchasers and tenants of the opinion of the Minister of Transport about aircraft noises, was held to be unreasonable and ultra vires. In *British Airports Authority v Secretary of State for Scotland* [1979] S.L.T. 197, the Scottish Court of Sessions held that a condition requiring the British Airports Authority to control the direction of takeoff and landing of aircraft at an airport was ultra vires, as the matter was in the control of the Civil Aviation Authority; see also *R. v Hillingdon London Borough Council, Ex p Royco Homes Ltd* [1974] Q.B. 720. Conditions must also relate to the planning application and ought not seek to interfere with existing use rights. See *State (O'Hara and McGuinness Ltd) v An Bord Pleanála*, unreported, High Court, Barron J., May 8, 1986.

Conditions must also be certain and unambiguous. Conditions may be held void for vagueness; see *Ashbourne Holdings v An Bord Pleanála* [2003] 2 I.R. 114; *Irish Asphalt Ltd v An Bord Pleanála*, unreported, High Court, Costello J., July 28, 1995; *Houlihan v An Bord Pleanála*, unreported, High Court, October 4, 1993; *Dun Laoghaire Corporation v Frescati Estates Ltd* [1982] I.L.R.M. 469 and *Mixnam's Properties Ltd v Chertsey UDC* [1965] A.C. 735. However, there may be some onus on a developer to attempt to understand the condition. See *O'Donnell v Donegal County Council*, unreported, High Court, O'Hanlon J., July 25, 1982. Where enforcement action is based on a planning condition which is unclear, the court may decline to grant relief. See *Liffey Beat v Dublin City Council* [2005] 2 I.R. 478, where it was said that reasonable care should be taken by planning authorities and An Bord Pleanála to make the terms and conditions which applied to planning permissions comprehensible to the parties who had an interest in the property to be developed and to the members of the public who had an interest in the proper planning and development of the area in which they resided. However, a condition may be construed in a manner which may allow it to be given an intelligible meaning. See *Fawcett Properties Ltd v Buckingham County Council* [1961] A.C. 636.

Planning conditions may be challenged in judicial review proceedings on the basis that they are irrational. In *Associated Provincial House v Wednesbury Corporation* [1947] 2 All E.R. 680, Lord Greene M.R. declared:

"In planning matters it is clear that the condition must be fair and reasonable and must relate to the proposed development. If the court is to interfere, a condition must be wholly unreasonable, that is, such as could find no justification in the minds of reasonable men".

The irrationality principles are also applicable to conditions in Ireland, although a high standard must be satisfied; see *O'Keeffe v An Bord Pleanála* [1993] 1 I.R. 39; *Coonagh v An Bord Pleanála*, unreported, High Court, Budd J., February 26, 1998; *O'Connor v Dublin Corporation and Bog Developments*, unreported, High Court, O'Neill J., October 3, 2000. The practice of a developer volunteering a planning gain, such as offering the public access to lands, was disapproved of by the Supreme Court in *Ashbourne Holdings Ltd v An Bord Pleanála* [2003] 2 I.R. 114. Though note in the context of strategic infrastructure applications, such conditions are expressly permitted provided certain circumstances exist. See s.37G(7) and (8).

The court will be reluctant to hold that a developer no longer has an obligation to comply with a condition due to a change in circumstances. See *Dublin County Council v Brennan and McGowan*, unreported, High Court, O'Hanlon J., June 28, 1985. A planning authority is not, however, required to engage in dialogue with the applicant before imposing a condition. See *Drogheda v Louth County Council*, unreported, High Court, Morris P., April 11, 1997.

Points of Detail

Subsection (5) provides that points of detail may be concluded between the developer and the planning authority with an appeal to An Bord Pleanála. The 2006 Act amended s.34(5) by providing that points of detail relating to a grant of permission may be agreed between the planning authority and the person carrying out the development (as opposed to the person who was granted the permission as stated in the 2000 Act). Such conditions may be imposed in accordance with the principles set out by the Supreme Court in *Boland v An Bord Pléanala* [1996] 3 I.R. 435. Hamilton C.J. said:

"In imposing a condition, that a matter be left to be agreed between the developer and the planning authority, the Board is entitled to have regard to:
(a) the desirability of leaving to a developer who is hoping to engage in a complex enterprise a certain limited degree of flexibility having regard to the nature of the enterprise;
(b) the desirability of leaving technical matters or matters of detail to be agreed between the developer and the planning authority, particularly when such matters or such details are within the responsibility of the planning authority and may require redesign in the light of the practical experience;
(c) the impracticability of imposing detailed conditions having regard to the nature of the development;
(d) the functions and responsibilities of the planning authority;
(e) whether the matters essentially are concerned with off-site problems and do not affect the subject lands;
(f) whether the enforcement of such conditions require monitoring or supervision".

Blayney J. accepted these criteria and added a further one, which was:

"Could any member of the public have reasonable grounds for objecting to the work to be carried out pursuant to the condition, having regard to the precise nature of the instructions in regard to it laid down by the board, and having regard to the fact that the details of the work have to be agreed by the planning authority".

Boland was applied in *McNamara v An Bord Pleanála* [1996] 2 I.L.R.M. 339, and by O'Neill J. in *O'Connor v Dublin Corporation & Borg Developments*, unreported, High Court, O'Neill J., October 3, 2000. The principles were also applied in *Ryanair v An Bord Pleanála*, unreported, High Court, Ó Caoimh J., February 27, 2004, where Ó Caoimh J. upheld conditions requiring agreement of details of the material, colours and textures of external finishes and in relation to the final design of the west end of the proposed pier, regarding its length and arrangement. A third party may seek to make submissions regarding matters left over for agreement. See *McNamara v An Bord Pleanála* [1996] 2 I.L.R.M. 339. In entering into such agreement the planning authority and person carrying out the development, must ensure that the agreement is within the scope of the true or correct meaning of the condition. See *O'Connor v Dublin Corporation*, unreported, High Court, O'Neill J., October 3, 2002. Where the agreement goes beyond the scope of such condition, the agreement will be ultra vires. In assessing whether such agreement is beyond the scope of the condition, a Court will not defer to the opinion of parties and so the applicable standard of review is not *O'Keeffe* irrationality or unreasonableness. The court will not therefore afford the planning authority a discretion in its interpretation of the condition, but will examine the condition itself to assess whether the planning authority interpreted the condition correctly; see *Gregory v Dun Laoghaire Rathdown County Council*, unreported, High Court, Geoghegan J., July 16, 1996. In *Dooner v Longford County Council*, unreported, High Court, McGovern J., October 25, 2007, an agreement between a developer and planning authority whereby the main building would be moved 14.5 metres to the north-east was held to involve a substantial movement having regard to the nature of the site and did not come within the limited flexibility permitted to developers by *Boland v An Bord Pleanála*. However, in *Kenny v Dublin City Council*, unreported, High Court, Murphy J., September 8, 2004, it was noted that the faithful implementation of a decision depends on the degree of specificity of the conditions. The more specific, the less discretion there is regarding their implementation.

In *Ryanair v An Bord Pleanála*, unreported, High Court, Ó Caoimh J., February 27, 2004, Ó Caoimh J., in holding that An Bord Pleanála (as well as the planning authority) has power to impose these types of conditions, noted that s.34(5) recognised an existing power to impose such conditions. A distinction may be made between conditions in a planning permission which, for their implementation require the "approval" of the planning authority and conditions which require the "agreement" of the planning authority; see *Kenny v An Bord Pleanála (No.1)* [2001] 1 I.R. 565. In imposing a condition under s.34(5) it is not mandatory to include terms allowing for a reference to the respondent in default of agreement and so the absence of a "default of agreement" wording could not make the permission invalid on that account alone. See *Mulholland v An Bord Pleanála (No. 2)* [2006] 1 I.R. 453.

The public have no right to have any input in terms of the compliance with the agreement or approval. Although note the comments of Barr J. in *McNamara v An Bord Pleanála (2)* [1996] 2 I.L.R.M. 339, who suggested that third parties would be entitled to make representations. Third parties can however institute judicial review proceedings. See *Arklow Holidays v An Bord Pleanála*, unreported, High Court, Clarke J., January 18, 2006. In any challenge to a compliance decision, an issue may arise on the facts as to when the applicant learned of the decision. See *Kenny v Dublin City Council*, unreported, High Court, September 8, 2000, where relief was refused because of delay. However, in *Cosgrave v Dublin City Council*, unreported, High Court, Smyth J., January 18, 2005 where a delay was held justifiable on the facts, it was noted that the compliance must not be ambiguous as what is approved.

Material Contravention Procedure

Subsection (6) concerns the procedure to be followed to permit development which would materially contravene the development plan. A grant of permission in material contravention of the development plan which has not been authorised under this procedure will be invalid. See *Tennyson v Dun Laoghaire Corporation* [1991] 2 I.R. 527. This largely restates, with certain modifications, s.26(3) of the 1963 Act. This does not apply to certain development within s.22(10)(B) of the Waste Management Act 1996, as inserted by the Waste Management (Amendment) Act 2001. See also s.26 of the Protection of the Environment Act 2003. The adoption of a development plan is a reserved function, i.e. exercised by the elected members of the planning authority as opposed to an executive function exercised by the Manager of the planning authority. The proposal to grant permission in material contravention of the development plan therefore requires a resolution of the elected planning authority. By comparison with s.26(3), this former provision referred to developments which "contravene materially the development plan *or special amenity order*", this latter clause being omitted from the new provision. Under s.140 of the Local Government Act 2001 (the former s.4 of the City and County Management (Amendment) Act 1955) the elected members may direct the Manager to grant planning permission for a particular development. See *Sharpe v Dublin County Council* [1989] I.L.R.M. 565, where the Supreme Court held a s.4 resolution could apply to a grant or refusal of planning permission and that a County Manager must comply with any such direction. The elected members must act in a judicial manner. Once the elected members have acted in a judicial manner, the County Manager has no discretion as whether to obey the direction. However, if the manager is of the opinion that the development would materially contravene the development plan, he must within one week of the notice, make by order a declaration stating his opinion. Where the Manager states this opinion, the material contravention procedure must be complied with.

The notice of intention to consider deciding to grant the permission must be published in a newpaper circulating in the area and must specifically identify the objective of the development plan which would be materially contravened. Article 36 of the 2001 Regulations as amended prescribes the notice set out in Form No. 5 of Sch.3 or a form substantially to like effect. The provision expands from 21 days to four weeks the period for submissions/observations. Article 36(2) of the Regulations provides that any person or body may make a submission or observation in writing to a planning authority as regards the making of a decision to grant planning permission in accordance with s.34(6) of the Act not later than four weeks after the first publication of the notice. Article 36(3) states that a submission or observation must:

1. state the name and address, and telephone number and e-mail address, if any, of the person or body making the submission or observation; and
2. indicate the address to which any correspondence relating to the application should be sent.

The planning authority is therefore required to acknowledge receipt of the submissions/ observations. This is confirmed by art.36(4) of the Regulations, which requires an acknowledgement to be issued as soon as may be. Article 36(5) declares where a submission is received outside the four week period, the planning authority shall return to the person or body concerned the submission or observation received and notify the person or body that their submission or observation cannot be considered by the planning authority.

A resolution requires three-quarters of the total elected members of the planning authority (as under ss.44 and 45 of the 1991 Act) in favour of the proposal. In *Kerry County Council v Lovett*, unreported, Supreme Court, June 4, 2003, Keane C.J. noted the effect of a resolution is not to vest in the elected members of the council the function of deciding to grant or withhold permission but to direct the Manager to make a decision to grant a planning permission. Time for the purposes of an appeal to the Board only runs from the Manager's decision. A resolution may be challenged on the grounds of being unreasonable. The resolution must also be valid and lawful. In *Wicklow County Council v Wicklow County Manager*, unreported, High Court, Ó Caoimh J., February 26, 2003, it was said that the Manager may decline to comply with the terms of the resolution where he considers the resolution invalid. In *Browne v Dundalk Urban District Council* [1993] I.L.R.M. 328, where a resolution would have procured a breach of contract, it was held to be unlawful. In *Flanagan v Galway County Council* [1990] 2 I.R. 66, a section 4 resolution was held invalid as personal circumstances of the applicant had been taken into account, i.e. that the applicant would be forced to emigrate. In *Griffin v Galway County Manager*, unreported, High Court, Blayney J., October 31, 1990, where a resolution was passed for permission for a house which would materially contravene the development plan, and the County Manager refused to obey this, the motion was held to be invalid having not been adopted in a judicial manner as irrelevant "personal circumstances" had been taken into account. In *Kenny Homes Ltd v Galway City and County Manager* [1995] 1 I.R. 178, Blayney J. held a s.4 resolution invalid as it was framed so that the council could not have considered all the matters under s.26 of the 1963 Act and had failed to have regard to a particular objection. In *Child v Wicklow County Council* [1995] 2 I.R. 447, Costello P. held a section 4 resolution passed invalid, as being ultra vires. There was no explanation for ignoring expert advice and failing to take into account that previous planning applications in respect of the site had been refused. Subsection (7)(a)(ii) concerns land, the subject of the permission, which is located in more than one local electoral area. In such circumstances, not less than three quarters of the elected members of all the relevant areas must vote in favour of the resolution. By virtue of subsection (6)(d), once the resolution is passed directing the Manager to grant permission, the Manager is obliged to do so.

Time for making the determination

Subsections (8) and (9) introduce certain changes to the time limits. The general obligation is for the planning authority to decide on the application within eight weeks of the receipt of the application (as opposed to two months under s.26(4)(b)(iii)). Article 30 of the Planning Regulations 2001 imposes a minimum period of five weeks for the determination from date of receipt of the application. In calculating the time for determination, the first day of receipt is included in the calculation of 8 weeks: see the Interpretation Act 2005. Section 251(1) provides that when calculating the time limit the period between December 24 and January 1, inclusive, shall be disregarded. Where the planning authority seeks further information, the period for determination is extended whereby the decision on the application must be made within four weeks of the request being complied with. The 2000 Act introduces a shorter period of four weeks as opposed to two months under the 1963 Act. However, where the application is accompanied by an EIS, the decision must be made within eight weeks of the request being complied with. Article 33 of the 2001 Regulations concerns requests for further information. Once a request for further information is made, it cannot request an applicant to submit further information or evidence, except as may be reasonably necessary to clarify the matters dealt with in the response or where the request is made in relation to an EIA (under art.108(2)) or in relation to transboundary pollution (art.128(1)). Where a request for further information is not complied with after six months, the planning application will be declared to be withdrawn (although the planning authority may agree to extend the period for up to three additional months, as provided in art.33(3) inserted under the 2006 Regulations). For a request for further information to be valid, the information must be necessary or the evidence must be reasonably required. Such request cannot be used for an improper purpose or to defer the decision. See *State (NCE Ltd) v Dublin City Council* [1979] I.L.R.M. 249 and *Illium Properties Ltd v Dublin City Council*, unreported, High Court, O'Leary J., October 15, 2004, where O'Leary J said:

"The power of the planning authority to request further information under this Article is limited to matters which fall within Article 33. Article 33 requests should not (indeed cannot) be used to vary a planning application. Variation can only be done by agreement or by condition (and in these circumstances to a limited extent only in view of the public interest in planning applications) or by re-application. If a planning authority cannot get agreement or cannot apply suitable conditions to its decision it must accept or refuse the application as submitted. The authority is not the developer and should stay within its remit".

Thus the request should be confined to planning matters and the subject matter of the application. It should also not seek to rectify planning breaches. A request for additional information to be included in a planning application under art.22A of the 2001 Regulations does not have the effect of extending the time for making a decision.

Also, where the planning authority publish a notice of intention to grant permission which materially contravenes the development plan, the decision must be made within eight weeks from when the notice is published. Section 34(8)(e) covers situations where a permission is likely to increase the risk of major accident or if an accident were to occur, though its risk may not be increased, it would be likely to have serious consequences. Part II of the 2001 Regulations concerns the Major Accidents Directive. In such circumstances, a planning authority must make a decision within four weeks of receiving technical advice in relation to such risks or consequences. A further exception is where an application is made to court under s.35(4) within eight weeks, to refuse permission due to past failures to comply with a permission, then the eight-week period will not apply. Under subs.(9), time can be extended by the applicant consenting in writing within the eight-week period. Where an EIA development is likely to have significant effects on a transboundary state, art.130 of the 2001 Regulations provides that the planning authority shall not make its decision until after the view, if any, of the transboundary state has been received in response to consultations or the consultations are otherwise complete.

Subsection (8)(f) concerns default planning permission where the authority has failed to make the decision within the mandatory period, i.e. within eight weeks or such other modified period. Under the former s.26(4)(a)(iii), default permission applied where the applicant failed to receive notice within the period. See *Flynn v Dublin Corporation*, unreported, High Court, Kelly J., December 19, 1996. Now, it appears, default permission will not apply where the applicant was notified outside the period, so long as the decision was actually made within the period. Under art.31 of the 2001 Regulations, notification of the decision must be given to the applicant and any other person who made submissions within three working days of the decision. Default permission may be granted where the planning authority served a notice seeking further information, which was deemed not to be a proper notice and so did not extend the time for the decision; see *Illium Properties*

Ltd v Dublin City Council, unreported, High Court, O'Leary J., October 15, 2004, and
O'Connor's Downtown Properties v Nenagh UDC [1993] 1 I.R. 1.

Default planning permission will not be granted if the application does not substantially
comply with the permission regulations. Deviations from the requirements will only
be overlooked where shown to be trivial or technical; see *Monaghan UDC v Alf-a-Bet
Promotions Ltd* [1980] I.L.R.M. 64, per Henchy J. and *Molloy & Walsh v Dublin County
Council* [1990] I.L.R.M. 633, where the *de minimis* rule was applied where the application
wrongly stated that property was vested in a person and also where the site plan did not
include the name and addresses of the persons who prepared it. On the other hand, in
Crodaun Homes v Kildare County Council [1983] I.L.R.M. 1, an error in description of land
meant default permission could not operate. In *Dublin County Council v Marren* [1985]
I.L.R.M. 593, Barrington J. held default permission could not apply where there was a
failure to include any drawings of floor plans, elevation or sections, and by the failure to
indicate the north point on all maps. Where a planning authority refuses to grant a planning
permission, judicial review proceedings may be necessary, where the section 50 judicial
review procedure will apply.

Until the adoption of the 2006 Planning and Development Regulations, an invitation to
submit revised plans did not have the effect of extending time to make a decision. Article
34 of the Regulations provides that the planning authority may invite an applicant to submit
revised plans or drawings modifying or other particulars providing for the modification, of
the development. The planning authority must invite the applicant to submit revised plans
within the eight-week period and the applicant must indicate in writing that he intends to
submit such revised drawings within the period specified by the planning authority, which
must not be later than the eight weeks from the receipt of the planning application. Article
34(3) of the 2001 Regulations, as amended, now also provides that where a person accepts in
writing an invitation to submit revised plans, he must also consent to the extension of time in
accordance with s.34(8). The question of whether a revised plan amounts to a modification
within the meaning of art.34, is an issue of planning expertise, reviewable under the standard
of irrationality. See *Dietacaron v An Bord Pleanála* [2005] 2 I.L.R.M. 32.

Also prior to the adoption of the 2006 Regulations, where a request for further
information is raised which contains significant additional data such that a re-advertisement
is necessary under art.35 of the 2001 Regulations, the four week period specified in
s.34(8)(b) was deemed to run from when the information is provided and not from when
the developer re-advertises the information in a newspaper. See *Maye v Sligo Borough
Council,* unreported, High Court, Clarke J., April 27, 2007. This has been changed as a
result of art.35(4) of the 2001 Regulations as amended by the 2006 Regulations, which
now provides that the four-week period referred to in s.34(8)(b) of the Act shall not, in a
case where the planning authority considers that the further information, evidence, revised
plans, drawings or particulars received contain significant additional data, commence until
the planning authority has received both a copy of the newspapers notice advertising the
new information/revised plans and of the site notice erected.

The assessment of whether information constitutes significant additional information
so as to require re-advertisement under art.35, is an exercise of planning judgment and
expertise and the court will not interfere with such assessment except where it is considered
irrational. See *Kinsella v Dundalk Town Council,* unreported, High Court, December 3,
2004 and *Klohn v An Bord Pleanála,* unreported, High Court, McMahon J., April 23, 2008.
However, in *White v Dublin City Council* [2004] 1 I.R. 545, the Supreme Court decided that
the decision not to require a further public notice was irrational, where the planning official
asked the wrong question in deciding whether to require further public notices.

Default permission cannot apply where the planning authority did not have the statutory
power to grant the application; see *State (Pine Valley Developments) v Dublin County
Council* [1982] I.L.R.M. 169. It is not possible to obtain a default planning permission where
the development constitutes a material contravention of a development plan: see *Walsh v
Kildare County Council* [2001] 1 I.R. 483; *Calor Teo v Sligo County Council* [1991] 2 I.R.
267; *Abbeydrive v Kildare County Council,* unreported, High Court, Murphy J., November
29, 2005. Material contravention of a development plan involves a two-part test; first, the
development must be in contravention of the development plan and, secondly the manner
of the contravention must be material. The rationale for default planning permission not

applying where it is material contravention of the development plan relates to the vires of the planning officials concerned. See *Maye v Sligo Borough Council*, unreported, High Court, Clarke. J, April 27, 2007. In *McGovern v Dublin Corporation* [1999] 2 I.L.R.M. 314, Barr J. refused default permission on the basis that the development plan stated the type of development was only "open for consideration". However, in *Maye v Sligo Borough Council*, unreported, High Court, Clarke. J, April 27, 2007, it was said that the Court will not refuse default permission merely because the development was contrary to proper planning and sustainable development. It was further stated that the scale of the development is not an appropriate factor to be taken into account in the exercise of the court's discretion in refusing a default position. However, the comparison with a normal planning application returned in *Wicklow County Council v Forest Fencing t/a Abwood*, unreported, High Court, Charleton J., July 13, 2007, where it was said that if the extent of a deviation from what is specified in the development plan is such as might give rise to a reasonable expectation of opposition based on that deviation, then the deviation will be regarded as material. A material contravention of the development plan may be shown where the development in question is of a nature, or is on such a scale, that makes it likely that the planning authority would refuse permission for development for reasons that are based predominantly on the development plan. It is submitted the analogy with anticipated opposition to a planning application is unhelpful and the appropriate approach is to decide as a matter of law whether the development is a material contravention of the development plan. It is clear that a material contravention of the development plan is a higher test than merely showing that there are matters which are might justify the refusal of the planning permission. In *Flaherty & Flynn Properties v Dublin Corporation*, unreported, High Court, December 19, 1996, Kelly J. held the court did not have a discretion to hold default permission was not granted where it was argued that the appeal procedure was open to the applicant. See also, Blayney J. in *Molloy*, who held that there was no decision to appeal against. See also, *State (Pine Valley Developments) v Dublin County Council* [1982] I.L.R.M. 169; *Wicklow County Council v Child*, unreported, Supreme Court, December 3, 1997; *Colgan v Dublin Corporation*, unreported, High Court, Costello J., March 19, 1991. In *Maye v Sligo Borough Council*, unreported, High Court, Clarke. J, April 27, 2007, it was suggested that the court might refuse relief as a matter of discretion. In that case it was because the applicant had given no indication to the planning authority that it was contesting its views as to the operation of the statutory time limit. It would appear that a default planning permission is not possible where the development requires an EIA, which follows from the fact that a planning authority is obliged to carry out the assessment prior to making its decision. The potential impact of the European Convention on Human Rights upon the default planning permission regime has yet to be considered. This could arise in the context of neighbouring landowners whose interests are affected by the grant of a default permission, especially where they made submissions or observations on the planning application.

The language of s.34(8)(f) differs from s.26(4) which referred to failure "to make a decision" within the time period as opposed to the planning authority which "[does] not give notice of their decision" to the applicant. This change appears to connote that if a decision is made within the time period but is notified outside the period, default permission will not be activated, while under the 1963 Act, default permission would apply. This appears to deal with the situation in *Flaherty & Flynn Properties v Dublin Corporation*, unreported, High Court, Kelly J., December 19, 1996, where the planning authority had made the decision on the second-last day of the period but served the notice of the decision after the period, default permission was held to have applied. Thus, the provision appears to render defunct the caselaw such as *State (Murphy) v Dublin County Council* [1970] I.R. 253 and *Freeney v Bray UDC* [1982] I.L.R.M. 29; see also *O'Neill v Clare County Council* [1983] I.L.R.M. 141. So long as the decision made within the time limit determines the planning application, the possibility of default permission will not arise. Thus, even an invalid decision will prevent a default planning permission arising. See *State (Abenglen) v Dublin Corporation* [1984] I.R. 381. Where there is an entitlement to default permission, there is a deemed decision to grant permission. An applicant will require to seek declaratory and mandatory relief in order to obtain the actual grant of permission. The better view is that such application is covered by the special judicial review procedure under s.50.

Section 8(4) of the Roads Act 2007 provides that default permission cannot arise in in respect of the developments referred to in s.46 of the Roads Act 1993 in respect of a national road or a proposed road development for the construction of a national road declared to be a motorway.

Subsection (9) restates s.39(f) of the 1976 Act, though it allows only eight weeks for the receipt of written consent as opposed to the appropriate period under the 1976 Act, so the written consent will have to be given within the eight weeks as opposed to within an extended period sought by a request.

Reasons and Considerations

Subsection (10) imposes a more onerous obligation concerning the provision of reasons for a decision, referring to the "main consideration and reasons". This has brought about an expansion of the obligations which existed under the earlier legislation. This expansion involves:

1. an obligation on both the planning authority and the Board to give reasons irrespective of whether the decision is to grant or refuse permission;
2. an obligation to state the main reasons and considerations on which a decision is based; and
3. an obligation to state the main reasons for not accepting the recommendation of the respondent's inspector.

See *Mulholland v An Bord Pleanála (2)* [2006] 1 I.R. 453, where however it was noted that the pre-existing case law on adequacy of reasons continues to apply. It was further noted that in order for the statement of considerations to pass muster at law, it must satisfy a similar test to that applicable to the giving of reasons. The statement of considerations must therefore be sufficient to:

1. give to an applicant such information as may be necessary and appropriate for him to consider whether he has a reasonable chance of succeeding in appealing or judicially reviewing the decision;
2. arm himself for such hearing or review;
3. know if the decision maker has directed its mind adequately to the issues which it has considered or is obliged to consider; and
4. enable the courts to review the decision.

There was an obligation to give reasons under s.26(8) of the 1963 Act (as inserted by s.39(g) of the 1976 Act). The extent of reasons required was not stringent under the previous legislation: see *State (Sweeney) v Minister for the Environment* [1979] I.L.R.M. 35; *State (Aprile) v Naas UDC*, unreported, High Court, O'Hanlon J., November 22, 1983; *Aer Rianta v An Bord Pleanála*, unreported, High Court, Kelly J., June 25, 2002. The requirement to give reasons does not involve a requirement to give a discursive judgment. See *O'Donoghue v An Bord Pleanála* [1991] I.L.R.M. 750. In *Ni Eili v Environmental Protection Agency*, unreported, Supreme Court, July 13, 1999, Murphy J. approved of the statement of Evans L J. in *MJT Securities Ltd v Secretary of State for the Environment* [1989] J.P.L. 138 who said:

> "The Inspector's statutory obligation was to give reasons for his decision, and the courts can do no more than say that the reasons must be 'proper, intelligible and adequate' as has been held. What degree of particularity is required must depend on the circumstances of each case. In the instant set of proceedings there were two such circumstances of relevance. The first was the medium by which such reasons must be stated namely in a newspaper notice and secondly the nature of the underlying event which gives rise to the requirement to give reasons. In this case that was simply a proposal not an ultimate decision."

In terms of satisfying the requirement to state the main reasons and considerations, reliance can also be placed on the reason given for the imposition of planning conditions. See *O'Keeffe v An Board Pleanála* [1993] 1 I.R. 39.

There is a distinction between reasons and considerations. In *Cicol Ltd v An Bord Pleanála*, unreported, High Court, Irvine J., May 8, 2008, it was said that the word "considerations" refers to all of the matters which are in being and are brought to the attention of the planning authority or the Board prior to the point at which they make their decision. By way of contrast, the word "reasons" must relate to the post-decision analysis of the basis for the decision and those "reasons" may or may not encompass all of the "considerations" which lead up to that decision. In that case it was held that the Board had cross-referenced its decision to the Inspector's report in terms of the matters which it considered prior to reaching its decision and that it thereby complied with its statutory obligations under s.34(10)(a) of the 2000 Act. In *Ryanair v An Bord Pleanála*, unreported, High Court, Ó Caoimh J., February 27, 2004, Ó Caoimh J. said that "the word 'consideration' may not necessarily be the same as the term 'reasons' but the reasons for a decision may undoubtedly include the considerations of the Board and in this way indicate the matters contemplated in reaching its decision". He pointed out the requirement was only for the "main" reasons and considerations, which indicate there may be subsidiary reasons and considerations. In *Grealish v An Bord Pleanála*, unreported, High Court, O'Neill J., October 24, 2006, O'Neill J. quashed a refusal of permission in 2003, where there were no reasons given for departing from previous grants in 1990 and 1997 in respect of the same development and there was no change in the physical environment. It was held that while the Board was entitled to reach a different decision on a later application in respect of the same development, the reasons and considerations upon which a change of stance has been adopted must be clear, so the appellant can see the appeal has been determined in a fair and rational manner and that the public interest in the integrity of the Board is upheld.

Also under the 1976 Act, the obligation on the planning authority only arose where the permission was refused or granted subject to conditions, while under the 2000 Act, the obligation applies to all decisions including the grant of permission. The obligation to give reasons concerning all decisions on appeal equally applied under the 1976 Act. A new clause is added in relation to conditions described in s.34(4). However, s.34(10)(b) also introduces a significant new requirement to give reasons for not accepting the recommendations in the reports. In *Ryanair v An Bord Pleanála*, unreported, High Court, Ó Caoimh J., February 27, 2004, it was noted that it can be inferred that the Board accepted the report of its inspector to the extent that it did not depart from his recommendation. See also *Fairyhouse Club Ltd v An Bord Pleanála*, unreported, High Court, Finnegan J., July 18, 2001. In certain cases it has been held that where a local authority or Board does not depart from its planners or inspectors report, it can be assumed that the reasons contained in such reports were accepted, even if not expressly stated. See *Mulholland v An Bord Pleanála (2)* [2006] 1 I.R. 453 and *R.(Hereford Waste Watchers Limited) v Hereford Council* [2005] EWHC 191 (Admin), February 18, 2005. The reasons when seen in the light of the inspector's report and Board's direction may be adequate. See *Aer Rianta cpt v An Bord Pleanála*, unreported, High Court, Kelly J., June 25, 2002. However, a more stringent approach adopted in *Deerland Construction Ltd v The Aquaculture Licences Appeals Board*, unreported, High Court, Kelly J., September 9, 2008, which may signal a departure from this case law. This case concerned an equivalent requirement of ALAB to give the "main reasons and considerations" for its decision. Where the decision said it had decided to issue a licence as recommended in the technical adviser's report, Kelly J. held regard could not be had to the advisors report to supplement the lack of reasons stated on the face of the decision. He considered the earlier decisions in *Fairyhouse* and *Mulholland* had not taken into account a whole body of case law in England touching on the topic. See *Nash v Chelsea College of Art and Design* [2001] E.W.H.C. Admin. 538. Kelly J. held that the adequacy of the reasons was made a condition of the legality of the decision and that a failure to state reasons at the time of the decision invalidated the decision. The duty to give reasons for not following the recommendation of the inspector, only relates to the decision to grant or refuse permission and does not extend to not accepting a condition recommended by the inspector. See *Dunne v An Bord Pleanála*, unreported, High Court, McGovern J., December 14, 2006.

Several reason for refusing permission can be given. Where one of several grounds for refusal are found to be invalid, a court is not entitled to exercise its discretion to decline to grant relief on the basis that the other reasons were valid and the applicant would have gained nothing of benefit from any successful outcome of the judicial review proceedings. See *Talbot v An Bord Pleanála*, unreported, Supreme Court, July 23, 2008, where the Supreme Court reversed Peart J.'s judgment in which he had refused leave, with the Supreme Court holding that a judge is not entitled to presume in advance what the outcome of an application will be. Where the Court finds that the reasons given were inadequate, the appropriate remedy may be to remit the matter back to the decision-maker rather than quashing the decision.

See *R(On the application of Richardson) v North Yorkshire County Council* [2004] 2 P & CR 15. On the other hand the express statutory duty to give reasons is bound up with the decision and it is arguably not possible to separate this duty (by subsequently remedying it) from the decision. It may therefore follow that the decision should be quashed.

In respect of conditions of planning permission, there is a requirement to state simply the main reasons but not considerations. See *Weston v An Bord Pleanála*, unreported, High Court, McMenamin J., March 14, 2008. However, in that case it was noted that where condition is based on the general power to impose conditions as opposed to one of the specific conditions under s.34(4), there is an enhanced obligation to state the "main reasons" for the decision which derives from the necessity to ensure that the condition imposed is within the four walls of the Act as a whole. While the court may have regard to particular context in construing a reason, this does not mean that any extrinsic information can be offered to justify a condition. See *Killiney and Ballybrack Development Association Limited v The Minister for Local Government & Anor.* [1987] I.L.R.M. 878, where the Minister had sought to justify conditions on the basis of instructions received from his client but which had not been contained in the condition itself, Henchy J. noted the condition in question must stand or fall by its written terms and conditions. The reasons given must fairly and reasonably justify the conditions, otherwise the condition may be invalid. Where the application relates to a development for which an EIA was carried out, there may be an enhanced obligation in giving reasons and considerations in respect of the EIA element. This follows in particular from art.9(1) of Directive 2003/35, (which was required to be in force by June 25, 2005), which requires the competent authorities to make available to the public, the content of the decision and any conditions attached thereto; the main reasons and considerations on which the decision is based including information about the public participation process and a description, where necessary, of the main measures to avoid, reduce and if possible, offset the major adverse effects.

Following a decision to grant permission, a notification of the decision to grant permission will be sent to the applicant and this will be followed by the formal grant of permission which is a further step. Subsection (11) largely restates s.26(9)(a) and (b) of the 1963 Act. It retains the requirement to make the grant "as soon as may be", without including a specific period. On the meaning of "as soon as may be", see *Harding v Cork County Council*, unreported, Supreme Court, May 2, 2008. Article 31 of the Planning Regulations 2001 prescribes the form of notification. In the event of no appeal, the grant of permission will follow not earlier than three working days after the expiry of the period for appeal.

Subsection (12) dealing with retention permission was contained in s.27 of the 1963 Act. The 2000 Act makes it clear that the exact same rules apply in relation to an application for retention as applies for permission. In determining a retention application, neither the planning authority nor Board should have regard to the fact the development is in place and that refusal may necessitate the removal of a structure: see *State (Fitzgerald) v An Bord Pleanála* [1985] I.L.R.M. 117; *Village Residents Association Ltd v An Bord Pleanála (No. 1)* [2000] 1 I.R. 65. Under s.162(3), enforcement action cannot be stayed or withdrawn by reason of an application for retention permission. Also under s.191(4), compensation is not payable where permission is refused for retention of an unauthorised structure. However, in *Commission v Ireland* (Case C-215/06), the European Court of Justice held that in allowing for the grant of retention permission for development for which an EIA is required even where no exceptional circumstances are proved, Ireland had failed to comply with its obligations under Directive 85/337. While this judgment only applies to development which requires an EIA or EIS, it means that amending legislation is required to abolish the entitlement to obtain retention permission for development requiring an EIA, subject to exceptional circumstances existing.

Distinct Statutory Code

Subsection (13) repeats s.26(11) of the 1963 Act. This reflects the fact that planning permission is permissive in nature rather than granting rights to carry out the development assertable against all persons. Other permissions or rights may need to be obtained before the development can occur. Compliance with one statutory regime does not absolve the effected party from compliance with a different regime unless such is expressly provided for. The fact that a party has complied some other statutory code, does not mean they are compliance with the Planning Code. See *Curley v Galway Corporation*, unreported, High Court, Kelly J., December 11, 1998, where Kelly J. said:

"I cannot conceive of a situation where the court can, in order to enable Galway Corporation to comply with its statutory obligations under one piece of legislation, permitted to breach obligations imposed upon it by another piece of legislation. In particular the court cannot permit the fulfilment of a statutory obligation, for example, under the Waste Management Act by the commission of offences under the planning legislation".

See also *South Dublin County Council v Fallowvale*, unreported, High Court, McKechnie J., April 28, 2005, where compliance with the Aviation Code did not mean there was compliance with the Planning Code.

Equally, permission under the Planning Code does not absolve an applicant from any obligation to obtain permission under some other legal code or regime. In *Convery v Dublin City Council* [1996] 3 I.R. 161, Keane J. said the planning authority:

"[C]annot be said to have authorised the developer by the grant of a permission to commit an act which would be otherwise unlawful, whether because it interfered, for example, with the right to light of other property owners or created an unacceptable hazard for such persons such as the plaintiff in *Weir v Dun Laoghaire Corporation* [1983] I.R 242". (In *Weir* a lay-by constructed was two inches lower than the surface of a road).

See also *Houlihan v An Bord Pleanála*, unreported, High Court, Murphy J., October 4, 1993, where Murphy J. said planning permission does not "grant or confer on the applicant ... any property rights or dispense him from the necessity of obtaining whatever way-leaves, permissions or licences as may be required under other legislation to enable the development to be completed". In *William Bennett Construction v Greene* [2004] 2 I.L.R.M. 96, where land was sold on with outline permission showing a drain for disposal of seweage running over adjoining land retained by the vendor, it was held there was no easement in existence at the time of the grant for the benefit of the property granted over the property retained and so there was no room for the application of the doctrine that the grantor cannot derogate from his grant. In *Nolan v Minister for Environment* [1991] 2 I.R. 548, it was held that the Local Government (Roads and Motorways) Act 1974 (the "1974 Act") was to be regarded as a self-contained and separate statutory code which was not subject to the provisions of the Planning Acts and that the Minister had power, by virtue of s.10 of the 1974 Act, to consent to the relocation of the power line regardless as to whether such a relocation would be classed as an exempt development for the purposes of the Planning Acts. However, while persons retain rights to bring an action for nuisance even where there is planning permission, the lawful redevelopment of an area can affect the standard by which an action in nuisance is judged. See *Lanigan & Benghazi v Barry*, unreported, High Court, Charleton J., February 15, 2008.

In *Re Tivoli Cinema Ltd in the matter of Licensing Acts*, unreported, High Court, Lynch J., January 24, 1994, Lynch J. said " the planning code and licensing code are separate and distinct." See also *Keane v An Bord Pleanála* [1998] 2 I.L.R.M. 241, in which a licence was required for a radio mast. In *Pioneer Aggregates v Secretary of State* [1984] 2 All E.R. 358, Scarman L.J. said a planning permission is "a permission that certain rights of ownership be exercised": see also *Howard v Commissioner of Public Works* [1994] 3 I.R. 394; *Cablelink v An Bord Pleanála* [1999] 1 I.R. 596 ("a condition providing that no development should take place until a licence had been acquired would have added nothing to the planning permission", per Carroll J.); *Carty v Dublin County Council*, unreported, High Court, Barrington J., March 6, 1984; and *Re Commonage at Glennamaddoo* [1992] 1 I.R. 297. However, in *State (Boyd) v Cork County Council*, unreported, High Court, Murphy J., February 18, 1983, Murphy J. suggested that damages in tort to a neighbour may be a planning consideration.

This is not to say there can be no interaction between the Planning Code and other statutory regimes. Objections can be made to the renewal of the intoxicating liquor licence based on an allegation of habitual user in contravention of the Planning Acts. See *Re Comhaltas Ceoltóirí Éireann*, unreported, High Court, Finlay P., December 14, 1977. Although in *Re Tivoli Cinema Limited* [1992] 1 I.R. 412, Lynch J. distinguished between the planning and licensing code, he also noted that a use of any part of the premises other than the bar for supplying and/or consuming intoxicating liquor will involve an unauthorised use of such other part of the premises which could be restrained under the planning code and might then be used as a ground of objection to renewal of the licence if such wrongful use were to be allowed. Where premises are not constructed in accordance with a planning permission, this could be a ground for objection to a licence on the basis of the unfitness of the premises. In *Application by Thomas Kitterick* [1973] I.L.T. 105, Walsh J. noted that where premises are "erected in violation of other statutory provisions or whose then conditions does not comply with the requirements of other statutory provisions it appears to me to be quite contrary to the policy of the courts that the licence should be granted notwithstanding the illegalities".

Refusal of planning permission for past failures to comply

1–45   **35.**—**(1)** Where, having regard to—

    (a) any information furnished pursuant to regulations made under *section 33(2)(1)*, or

    (b) any information available to the planning authority concerning development carried out by a person to whom this section applies, pursuant to a permission (in this subsection and *subsection (2)* referred to as a "previous permission") granted to the applicant or to any other person under this Part or Part IV of the Act of 1963,

the planning authority is satisfied that a person or company to whom this section applies is not in compliance with the previous permission, or with a condition to which the previous permission is subject, the authority may form the opinion—

    (i) that there is a real and substantial risk that the development in respect of which permission is sought would not be completed in accordance with such permission if granted or with a condition to which such permission if granted would be subject, and

    (ii) that planning permission should not be granted to the applicant concerned in respect of that development.

(2) In forming its opinion under *subsection (1)*, the planning authority shall only consider those failures to comply with any previous permission, or with any condition to which that permission is subject, that are of a substantial nature.

(3) An opinion under this subsection shall not be a decision on an application for permission for the purposes of this Part.

[(4) If the planning authority considers that there are good grounds for its being able to form the opinion under *subsection (1)* in relation to an application for permission in respect of the development concerned and, accordingly, to exercise the power under *subsection (5)* to refuse that permission, it shall serve a notice in writing on the applicant to that effect and that notice shall—

    (a) specify the failures to comply that the authority intends to take into consideration with regard to the proposed exercise of that power, and

    (b) invite the applicant to make submissions to the authority, within a period specified in the notice, as to why the applicant considers that the authority should not exercise that power (whether because the applicant contends the views of the authority in relation to compliance by the applicant or any other person with any previous permission, or any condition to which it is subject, are incorrect or that there are not good grounds for forming the opinion under *subsection (1)*).]

[(5) If the planning authority, having considered any submissions made to it in accordance with a notice under *subsection (4),* proceeds to form the opinion under *subsection (1)* in relation to the application concerned it shall decide to refuse to grant the permission concerned and notify the applicant accordingly.]

[(6) The applicant may, within 8 weeks from the receipt of that notification, notwithstanding *sections 50 and 50A,* apply, by motion on notice to the planning authority, to the High Court for an order annulling the planning authority's decision and, on the hearing of such application, the High Court may, as it considers appropriate, confirm the decision of the authority, annul the decision and direct the authority to consider the applicant's application for planning permission without reference to the provisions of this section or make such other order as it thinks fit.]

[(6A) If, in pursuance of *subsection (6),* the High Court directs the planning authority to consider the applicant's application for planning permission without reference to the provisions of this section, the planning authority shall make its decision on the application within the period of 8 weeks from the date the order of the High Court in the matter is perfected but this subsection is subject to the provisions of *section 34(8)* as applied to the foregoing case by *subsection (6B).*]

[(6B) For the purposes of the foregoing case the provisions of *section 34(8)* shall apply with the following modifications:

    (a) in *paragraph (a) of section 34(8),* after "*paragraphs (b), (c), (d) and (e)* ", there shall be inserted "and section 35(6A)";

    (b) for the reference in *paragraph (b) of section 34(8)* to "8 weeks of the receipt of a planning application" there shall be substituted "8 weeks of the date the order of the High Court in the matter is perfected";

    (c) in *paragraph (f) of section 34(8),* after "*paragraph (a), (b), (c), (d) or (e)* ", there shall be inserted ", the period specified in *section 35(6A)* or, as the case may be, the period specified in *paragraph (b), (c), (d) or (e)* as that paragraph is applied by virtue of *section 35(6B)* "; and

    (d) any other necessary modifications.]

[(6C) No appeal shall lie to the Board from a decision of a planning authority to refuse to grant planning permission under *subsection (5).*]

(7) In this section, "a person to whom this section applies" means—

    (a) the applicant for the permission concerned,

    (b) a partnership of which the applicant is or was a member and which, during the membership of that applicant, carried out a development referred to in *subsection (1)(b),*

    (c) in the case where the applicant for permission is a company—

        (i) the company concerned is related to a company (within the meaning of *section 140(5)* of the Companies Act, 1990) which carried out a development referred to in *subsection (1)(b),* or

    (ii) the company concerned is under the same control as a company which carried out a development referred to in *subsection (1)(b),* where "control" has the same meaning as in *section 26(3)* of the Companies Act, 1990,

or

  (d) a company which carried out a development referred to in *subsection (1)(b),* which company is controlled by the applicant—

    (i) where "control" has the same meaning as in *section 26(3)* of the Companies Act, 1990, or

    (ii) as a shadow director within the meaning of *section 27(1)* of the Companies Act, 1990.

AMENDMENT HISTORY

Subsection (4), (5) and (6) substituted by s.9 of the Planning and Development (Strategic Infrastructure) Act 2006 (No. 27 of 2006).

Subsection (6A), (6B) and (6C) inserted by s.9 of the Planning and Development (Strategic Infrastructure) Act 2006 (No. 27 of 2006).

NOTE

This section introduced a new procedure for refusing permission based on failure to comply with a previous permission and was modified under the 2006 Act. It is unique in that the refusal is not based on planning considerations relating to the development itself, but rather on the person who is seeking to carry out the development. The refusal is not based simply on the planning history of specific lands but the history of the applicant himself. Under the previous legislation, such a reason would appear not to amount to a consideration based on proper planning and development and so would be ultra vires. The 2006 Act introduced a new procedure for a refusal on such basis. The changes reflect the fact that planning authorities have been very reluctant to invoke this power. The previous procedure under the 2000 Act was that the planning authority was required to apply to the High Court for authorisation to refuse planning permission on such basis where it had formed the opinion that there would be a real and substantial risk of non-compliance. The 2006 Act removes the requirement for the planning authority to receive authorization from the High Court. Instead, under the new procedure, if the planning authority considers that there are "good grounds" for forming an opinion that there is a real and substantial risk of non-compliance, it must serve a notice on the applicant specifying the past failures which it intends to take into consideration and invite the applicant to make submissions on the alleged past failures and/or why they would not constitute good grounds for forming the opinion. The submission may be that the views of the authority in relation to compliance by the applicant or any other person with any previous permission, or any condition to which it is subject, are incorrect or that there are not good grounds for forming the opinion. For the purposes of subs.(1), it appears that the previous non-compliance with a permission or conditions thereof must still persist at the time the planning authority forms its opinion. However, the fact that the past failure is immune from enforcement action because the limitation period is expired, will not exclude consideration of such past failure. Unauthorised development which is immune from enforcement action remains illegal. See *Dublin Corp v Mulligan,* unreported, High Court, May 6, 1980. While it is an essential precondition for invoking this procedure, that the person is not in compliance with the previous permission, or with a condition to which the previous permission is subject, it not entirely clear to what extent the planning authority can also take into account other factors in forming the view that there is a real and substantial risk that the development would not be completed. However, it is clear that by virtue of subs.(1)(a) that the planning authority can have regard to the information supplied in the planning application to whch the proposed development, in forming its opinion. The particular features of the proposed development and indeed any information supplied in the planning application can be taken into account.

The provision is not punitive in the sense that the refusal is punishment for failure to carry out the previous permission. It should not therefore be considered as a form of enforcement mechanism which are contained in Pt VIII. Instead it is directed towards the new permission sought and the relevance of the previous failure is to constitute evidence for a "real and substantial risk" that the new development will not be completed in accordance with the permission. It is clear that a high burden must be satisfied before such determination is made. There must be a "real and substantial risk" that the development would not be completed in accordance with the permission, and the past failure must be of a "substantial nature". Subsection (2) makes clear that the planning authority is strictly confined to considering past failures of a substantial nature. Thus, de minimis or technical breaches would not be sufficient. The complicated procedure reflects the serious nature of the application which essentially constitutes an abridgement of the constitutional property rights of an individual. Subsection (3) makes clear the forming of the opinion of such a real and substantial risk of non-compliance is not itself a decision on an application for permission.

The planning authority must consider any submissions before deciding to refuse permission. There is no appeal from such decision to An Bord Pleanála. The only means of challenging such decision is for the applicant to bring an application to the High Court within eight weeks seeking to annul the decision. If the Court annuls the decision, the Court will direct the planning authority to consider the application without any further regard to s.35. In such event, the planning authority must make its decision within eight weeks of the perfection of the High Court order, otherwise the applicant may be entitled to default planning permissions in accordance with the normal rules under s.34(8). The eight weeks run from the date of the perfection of the order rather than the date of delivery of the judgment.

Subsection (7) sets out the persons to whom the section applies. In deciding to refuse an applicant, the planning authority is not confined to considering previous planning applications which involved precisely the same applicant; it can also cover previous applications by a partnership of which the applicant was a member; also where the applicant is a company, it can cover previous applications by a company related to the applicant or which controls or is controlled by the applicant.

Outline permission

36.—(1) An application under section 34 may be made to a planning authority in accordance with the permission regulations for outline permission for the development of land.   1–46

(2) Where outline permission is granted under section 34, that permission shall not operate to authorise the carrying out of any development to which the outline permission relates until a subsequent permission has been granted under that section.

(3)

(a) Where outline permission has been granted by a planning authority, any subsequent application for permission must be made not later than 3 years beginning on the date of the grant of outline permission, or such longer period, not exceeding 5 years, as may be specified by the planning authority.

(b) The outline permission shall cease to have effect at the end of the period referred to in *paragraph (a)* unless the subsequent application for permission is made within that period.

(c) Sections 40, 41 and 42 shall not apply to the grant of an outline permission.

(4) Where an application for permission is made to a planning authority consequent on the grant of outline permission, the planning authority shall not refuse to grant permission on the basis of any matter which had been decided in the grant of outline permission, provided that the authority is satisfied that the proposed development is within the terms of the outline permission.

(5) No appeal may be brought to the Board under section 37 against a decision of a planning authority to grant permission consequent on the grant of outline permission in respect of any aspect of the proposed development which was decided in the grant of outline permission.

(6) In this section, "outline permission" *means permission granted in principle under section 34 for the development of land subject to a subsequent detailed application for permission under that section.*

NOTE

This section places outline planning permission on a statutory footing, when previously it was based under the Local Government (Planning and Development) Regulation 1994 (S.I. No. 86 of 1994). Subsection (6) defines outline planning permission as amounting to a permission in principle. There is no attempt to define the meaning of "in principle". In *State (Pine Valley) v Dublin County Council* [1984] I.R. 40, Barrington J. explained outline permissions as "when the developer applies subsequently for an approval the planning authority is only concerned with the details of the means whereby the developer proposes to complete the development that has been approved in principle by the planning authority". A developer still requires planning approval before he can proceed with the development, which will be an application for permission consequent on the grant of outline permission. Articles 20 and 21 of the 1994 Regulations formerly dealt with outline permissions, now provided for under art.21 of the 2001 Regulations. Section 36 introduces a new, more restricted, time frame for a subsequent application for permission. Subsection (3) provides that the normal length is for three years, though the planning authority can alter this and grant a longer period, though not more than five years. Subsection (4) is a new provision which provides that matters decided in the outline permission cannot be raised again in the full application for permission as a ground for refusal. This effectively enshrines a form of issue estoppel. This is further supported by subs.(5), which provides that, in respect of matters dealt with in the outline permission, there can be no appeal to An Bord Pleanála against a decision by the planning authority to grant permission consequent upon the outline permission in respect of grounds dealt with in the outline permission. Although subs.(4) prohibits refusing permission based on matters already decided in the outline permission, it does not expressly exclude imposing conditions in relation to such matters. Under the previous Regulations where outline permission has been granted, the planning authority could still impose conditions which could have been imposed in the outline permission; see *State (Tern Houses) v An Bord Pleanála* [1985] I.R. 725. The extent of conditions which may be imposed in the subsequent grant may depend upon the terms of the outline permission and the conditions imposed therein. In certain circumstances, it appears that additional conditions may be imposed if there was a change in the circumstances between the grant of outline permission and the consideration of the full permission: see *State (Kenny) v An Bord Pleanála*, unreported, High Court, Carroll J., February 23, 1984 and *Irish Asphalt Ltd v An Bord Pleanála*, unreported, High Court, Costello P., July 28, 1995.

An appeal can of course be taken in respect of matters not dealt with in the outline permission. An appeal can also be taken against the actual grant of outline planning permission. The effect of these two subsections is to afford greater weight and security to outline permissions. Article 21 of the 2001 Regulations provides that outline planning permission cannot be granted for:
- retention of development;
- development which would consist of or comprise the carrying out of works to a protected structure or a proposed protected structure; or
- development which comprises or is for the purposes of an activity requiring an integrated pollution licence or a waste licence.

Also under art.96 of the Regulations, an outline application may not be made with respect to development prescribed for the purposes of an EIA. Also under art.134, an application cannot be made regarding the provision or modification to an establishment which is subject to the Major Accidents Regulations.

Appeal to Board

37.—(1)   1–47

    (a) An applicant for permission and any person who made submissions or observations in writing in relation to the planning application to the planning authority in accordance with the permission regulations and on payment of the appropriate fee, may, at any time before the expiration of the appropriate period, appeal to the Board against a decision of a planning authority under *section 34.*

    (b) Subject to *paragraphs (c) and (d),* where an appeal is brought against a decision of a planning authority and is not withdrawn, the Board shall determine the application as if it had been made to the Board in the first instance and the decision of the Board shall operate to annul the decision of the planning authority as from the time when it was given; and *subsections (1), (2), (3) and (4) of section 34* shall apply, subject to any necessary modifications, in relation to the determination of an application by the Board on appeal under this *subsection* as they apply in relation to the determination under that *section* of an application by a planning authority.

    (c) *Paragraph (b)* shall be construed and have effect subject to *sections 133, 138 and 139.*

    (d) In *paragraph (a) and subsection (6),* "the appropriate period" *means the period of four weeks beginning on the day of the decision of the planning authority.*

(2)

    (a) Subject to *paragraph (b),* the Board may in determining an appeal under this *section* decide to grant a permission even if the proposed development contravenes materially the development plan relating to the area of the planning authority to whose decision the appeal relates.

    (b) Where a planning authority has decided to refuse permission on the grounds that a proposed development materially contravenes the development plan, the Board may only grant permission in accordance with *paragraph (a)* where it considers that—

        (i) the proposed development is of strategic or national importance,

        (ii) there are conflicting objectives in the development plan or the objectives are not clearly stated, insofar as the proposed development is concerned, or

        (iii) permission for the proposed development should be granted having regard to regional planning guidelines for the area, guidelines under *section 28,* policy directives under *section 29,* the statutory obligations of any local authority in the area, and any relevant policy of the Government, the Minister or any Minister of the Government, or

> (iv) permission for the proposed development should be granted having regard to the pattern of development, and permissions granted, in the area since the making of the development plan.
>
> **(c)** Where the Board grants a permission in accordance with *paragraph (b),* the Board shall, in addition to the requirements of *section 34 (10),* indicate in its decision the main reasons and considerations for contravening materially the development plan.

(3) Subject to *section 141 (2),* the provisions of *subsection (1)* authorising appeals to be made before the expiration of the appropriate period within the meaning of that *subsection* shall be construed as including a provision that an appeal received by the Board after the expiration of the appropriate period shall be invalid as not having been made in time.

(4)

> **(a)** Notwithstanding *subsection (1),* where in accordance with the permission regulations any prescribed body is entitled to be given notice of any planning application, that body shall be entitled to appeal to the Board before the expiration of the appropriate period within the meaning of that *subsection* where the body had not been sent notice in accordance with the regulations.
>
> **(b)** The Board may dismiss any appeal made under *paragraph (a)* where it considers the body concerned was not entitled to be sent notice of the planning application in accordance with the permission regulations.
>
> **[(c)** Notwithstanding *subsection (1),* a body or organization referred to in *paragraph (d)* shall be entitled to appeal to the Board against a decision by a planning authority on an application for development (being development in respect of which an environmental impact statement was required to be submitted to the planning authority in accordance with *section 172*) before the expiration of the appropriate period within the meaning of that subsection.
>
> **(d)** The body or organisation mentioned in *paragraph (c)* is a body or organisation (not being a State authority, a public authority or a governmental body or agency)—
>> **(i)** the aims or objectives of which relate to the promotion of environmental protection,
>> **(ii)** which has, during the period of 12 months preceding the making of the appeal, pursued those aims or objectives, and
>> **(iii)** which satisfies such additional requirements (if any) as are prescribed under *paragraph (e).*
>
> **(e)** The Minister may prescribe additional requirements which a body or organisation of the foregoing kind must satisfy in order to make an appeal under *paragraph (c),* being requirements of a general nature and for the purposes of promoting transparency and accountability in the operation of such organisations, including requirements—
>> **(i)** in relation to its membership,
>> **(ii)** that the pursuit of its aims or objectives be otherwise than for profit,

        (iii) in relation to the possession of a specified legal personality and the possession of a constitution or rules,

        (iv) that the area of environmental protection to which its aims or objectives relate is relevant to the class of matter into which the decision, the subject of the appeal, falls.

  (f) The Board may dismiss any appeal made under *paragraph (c)* where it considers that the body or organization concerned does not satisfy the requirements of *paragraph (d)(i), (ii) or (iii)*.]

(5)

  (a) No application for permission for the same development or for development of the same description as an application for permission for development which is the subject of an appeal to the Board under this *section* shall be made before—

        (i) the Board has made its decision on the appeal,

        (ii) the appeal is withdrawn, or

        (iii) the appeal is dismissed by the Board pursuant to *section 133 or 138*.

  (b) Where an application for permission referred to in *paragraph (a)* is made to a planning authority, the planning authority shall notify the applicant that the application cannot be considered by the planning authority and return the application and any other information submitted with the application in accordance with the permission regulations, and any fee paid.

  (c) A dispute as to whether an application for permission is for the same development or is for development of the same description as an application for permission which is the subject of an appeal to the Board may be referred to the Board for determination.

(6)

  (a) Notwithstanding *subsection (1)(a),* a person who has an interest in land adjoining land [in respect of which a decision to grant permission has been made] may, within the appropriate period and on payment of the appropriate fee, apply to the Board for leave to appeal against a decision of the planning authority under *section 34.*

  (b) An application under *paragraph (a)* shall state the name and address of the person making the application, the grounds upon which the application is made, and a description of the person's interest in the land.

  (c) The Board shall, within one week from the receipt of an application under *paragraph (a),* require, by notice in writing, the planning authority concerned to submit to the Board copies of the materials referred to in *subparagraph (i) of section 128(a),* the report referred to in *subparagraph (ii) of that section,* and the decision and notification referred to in *subparagraph (iii) of that section* and the planning authority shall comply with such requirement within one week from the date of receiving the notice.

  (d) The Board, or any member or employee of the Board duly authorised by the Board in that behalf, shall, where an applicant under this *subsection* shows that—

      (i) the development [in respect of which a decision to grant permission has been made] will differ materially from the development as set out in the application for permission by reason of conditions imposed by the planning authority to which the grant is subject, and

      (ii) that the imposition of such conditions will materially affect the applicant's enjoyment of the land or reduce the value of the land,

    within 4 weeks from the receipt of the application grant the applicant leave to appeal against the decision of the planning authority under *subsection (1)*.

  (e) The Board shall notify in writing the applicant and the planning authority of a decision to grant or refuse an application under this *subsection* within 3 days from its making.

  (f) A person to whom leave to appeal has been granted under this *subsection* shall bring the appeal within 2 weeks from the receipt of the notification under *paragraph (e)*.

  (g) Notwithstanding *section 34(11)(a)(i)*, where an application is made under this *subsection* a planning authority shall not make a grant of permission unless the application is refused.

  (h) Where leave to appeal is granted under this *subsection, subsection (2) of section 126* shall apply subject to the modification that the reference therein to 18 weeks shall be construed as a reference to 14 weeks.

  (i) Where leave to appeal is granted under this *section,* a planning authority that has complied with *paragraph (c)* shall, in respect of the appeal, be deemed to have complied with the requirements of *section 128.*

AMENDMENT HISTORY

Subsection (4)(c) to (f) inserted by s.10 of the Planning and Development (Strategic Infrastructure) Act 2006 (No. 27 of 2006).

Subsection (6) amended by s.10 of the Planning and Development (Amendment) Act 2002 (No. 32 of 2002) which came into effect on December 24, 2002.

Subsection (6)(a) amended by s.10(a) of the Planning and Development (Amendment) Act 2002, by substituting "in respect of which a decision to grant permission has been made" for "in respect of which permission has been granted".

Subsection (6)(d)(i) amended by s.10(b) of the Planning and Development (Amendment) Act 2002, by substituting "in respect of which a decision to grant permission has been made" for "in respect of which permission has been granted".

NOTE

This section concerns the procedure for an appeal to An Bord Pleanála. Subsection (1)(d) provides that the time limit within which to appeal is four weeks (formerly one month), the calculation of which is set out in s.141. The four weeks run from the date of the decision of the planning authority rather than from the date of notification of the decision of the planning authority or the date when such notification was received. There is no provision for extension of time, so any appeal outside the time limit will be invalid. These time limits must be strictly complied with. See *McCann v An Bord Pleanála* [1997]

1 I.R. 264, where a court upheld the rejection of an appeal because it was one day out of time, and also *Graves v An Bord Pleanála* [1997] 2 I.R. 205, where there was not proper service within the time limits. When the last date for receipt of an appeal or other material falls on a weekend, public holiday or other day when the offices of the Board are closed, the latest date for receipt will be the next day on which the offices of the Board are open. Where the elected members pass a resolution under s.140 of the Local Government 2001 directing the Manager to grant permission, time runs from the Manager's decision rather than from the date of the resolution. See *Kerry County Council v Lovett*, unreported, Supreme Court, June 4, 2003. The period from December 24 to January 1 inclusive (i.e. 9 days) is excluded for the purposes of calculation of all periods of time in relation to planning appeals. The 2000 Act narrows the category of persons entitled to appeal by introducing a standing requirement, as compared to under s.3 of the 1992 Act (as amending s.26(5) of the 1963 Act), where any person was entitled to appeal. The appeal must also be made in the correct form as set out in s.127, where the requirements are mandatory. Subsection (1) provides that apart from an applicant for permission, only persons who had participated in the application to the planning authority, by making a submission or observations in writing, can appeal. There are three general exceptions to this. First, under subs.(4), prescribed bodies which were entitled to be given notice of the planning application, but who were not sent a notice in accordance with the Regulations, are entitled to appeal. The Board may dismiss the appeal where it considers that the body was not in fact entitled to have been given notice. Secondly, under subs.(6), a person who has an interest in land which adjoins land for which permission has been granted may appeal for leave to appeal to the Board. This is not an entitlement to appeal, per se. It is only after leave is granted can such person bring an appeal. Leave can only be granted where the two specific conditions in subs.(6)(d) are fulfilled. These conditions are that the development will differ materially from the development in the application for permission by reason of the imposed conditions and the conditions will materially affect the enjoyment of the land or reduce its value. The rationale for this is that where there is a material alteration from the application due to the imposition of the conditions, the earliest opportunity for a person to object would only arise at an appeal stage. To apply for leave to appeal, a person must state their name, the grounds for appeal and their interest in the land. While interest in land is not defined, it is not necessary for the applicant to be the owner, so long as they have some interest in the land. Subsection (6) sets out a different time frame in the case of leave to appeal. The Board must grant leave within four weeks where the conditions exist and the applicant then has two weeks to bring their appeal. The general rule of 18 weeks does not apply; instead, 14 weeks as the general rule for the Board to determine the application.

The third exception to the general requirement that only persons who made valid submissions or observations to the planning authority, may appeal, was introduced by the 2006 Act, which allows a body or organisation (not being a State authority, a public authority or a governmental body or agency) which has sought to promote certain environmental objectives over the last 12 months, an entitlement to appeal to An Bord Pleanála notwithstanding that it did not make submissions or observations to the planning authority. This amendment appears to have been made in order to satisfy Ireland's requirements under the Directive 2003/35/EC. The Minister may also prescribe certain specified matters which the body or organization must satisfy. The Minister has yet to make any such regulations. The Minister may limit the entitlement of a body or organization in the area of environmental protection to appeal to bodies which specifically relate to the class of matter to which the decision relates. The Board itself may assess whether the body satisfies the relevant criteria to entitle it to appeal. There is no guidance as to what is the meaning or scope of the objective of "environmental protection".

The fees for appealing to An Bord Pleanála after the December 10, 2007 are as follows:

- Appeal against a decision of a planning authority on a planning application relating to commercial development, made by the person by whom the planning application was made, where the application relates to unauthorised development: €4,500 or €9,000 if EIS involved.
- Appeal against a decision of a planning authority on a planning application relating to commercial development, made by the person by whom the planning application

was made, other than the above appeal: €1,500 or €3,000 if EIS involved.
- Appeal against a decision of a planning authority on a planning application made by the person by whom the planning application was made, where the application relates to unauthorised development, other than an aforementioned appeal: €660.
- Appeal other than an aforementioned appeal: €220.
- Application for leave to appeal: €110.
- Appeal following a grant of leave to appeal: €110. The fee of €220 therefore applies to:
  — All third party appeals except where the appeal follows a grant of leave to appeal;
  — First party normal planning appeals (s.37) not involving commercial or unauthorised development, or an EIS.

Commercial development includes two or more dwellings.

The same time limits apply to appeals by the applicant (first-party appeals) and appeals by persons who made submissions (third-party appeals). It appears in the case of an applicant it is not open to him to radically alter the nature of the proposed development by adapting the proposals in the light of the reasons for refusal by the planning authority. The more appropriate course would be to lodge a retention application. A particular difficulty arises in terms of the time limits where the planning authority fails to notify or inadequately notifies a person who made submissions which results in them not lodging an appeal within time. There is no provision for an extension of time. Where judicial review proceedings have been taken the pragmatic course (if questionable), has been adopted for all parties to agree to an extension of time with the court making a consent order extending time. In *Lynch v Dublin City Council*, unreported, High Court, Ó Caoimh J., July 25, 2003, the Court declined to quash the decision of the planning authority on discretionary grounds. However, it must be said that as the error in notification is entirely subsequent to the decision to grant permission (and could not have effected the same), it would appear entirely inappropriate to quash the decision of the planning authority. While this means the third party may be left with no remedy under the Planning Code, the status of an objector as being low on the spectrum of interests must be stressed. See *State (Haverty) v An Bord Pleanála* [1987] I.R. 485 and also the comments of Kearns J. in *Harding v Cork County Council*, unreported, Supreme Court, May 2, 2008.

Subsection (1)(b) provides that the Board determines the appeal *de novo*. Where a decision of the Board annuls the decision of the planning authority, its decision will be deemed void ab initio. However, the mere taking of an appeal will not annul the decision of the planning authority, as it is only when the decision of the Board is "given" that it will have this effect. Thus if an appeal is taken but is withdrawn prior to the Board making its determination, the decision of the planning authority will still subsist. In *O'Keeffe v An Bord Pleanála* [1993] 1 I.R. 39, per Costello J. at 52, in the High Court, said:

> "This means that it is determining the matter *de novo* and without regard to anything that had transpired before the planning authority ... It would follow that I should construe this statute as meaning that no defect in the proceedings before the planning authority should have any bearing or impose legal constraints on the proceedings before the Board".

However, it appears that in certain instances what transpired before the planning authority can taint the decision of the Board on appeal. See *Jerry Beades Construction Ltd v Dublin Corporation*, unreported, High Court, McKechnie J., September 7, 2005, where it was held the decision by the planning authority was arrived at contrary to fair procedures and in breach of natural and constitutional justice and that this had also tainted the decision of the Board. See also the comments of Clarke J. in *Harding v Cork County Council*, unreported, High Court, Clarke J., October 12, 2006. In *Hynes v An Bord Pleanála*, unreported, High Court, McGuiness J., July 30, 1998, it was suggested that An Bord Pleanála cannot simply ignore a situation where the original planning application was clearly invalid. See also *Secry v An Bord Pleanála*, unreported, High Court, Quirke J., November 26, 2003. On the other hand, the fact that s.50A and s.50 requires judicial review proceedings to be brought within eight weeks in respect of any decision made or act done by the planning authority may mean that a challenge to a decision of the Board based on matters which transpired before the planning authority, would be out of time. In *Harding v Cork County Council*, unreported, Supreme Court, May 2, 2008, it was noted that an applicant ought not always just sit back and leave the process proceed at length until it reaches its final conclusion and then seek to impugn the final decision where it would have been properly open to such a person to seek a remedy at an earlier stage. Section 138 allows an appeal againt a condition or conditions only, in which case its decision could not annul the decision of the planning authority except in respect of the relevant condition or conditions. Section 48(10)(a) also allows a limited right of appeal against a condition requiring payment of a contribution.

Under s.126 there is an obligation on the Board to deal with appeals expeditiously. The general rule is that the Board must make a determination within 18 weeks from the receipt of the application, unless varied by the Minister or unless the Board serves a reasoned notice that it would not be possible to determine within the time. However, there is no entitlement to default permission where the Board fails to make a decision within a specific timeframe. Under s.34(10), in giving its decision, the Board must state the main reasons and considerations on which the decision is based and the main reasons for any conditions imposed. Also, the Board must indicate the main reasons for not accepting the recommendation in the report of its inspector, to grant or refuse permission. Under s.34(11) where the Board decides to grant permission, it shall take the grant as soon as may be after the decision. Although in the context of art.35 of the 2001 Regulations, in *Harding v Cork County Council*, unreported Supreme Court, May 2, 2008, Murray C.J. said in considering "as soon as may be" it may be borne in mind that it is an administrative procedure and requirements as to time must be interpreted having regard to the ordinary burdens of administration in any organisation or body.

Subsection (2) allows the Board to make a grant of planning permission even where the planning authority had rejected the application on grounds that it materially contravened the development plan. The Board, unlike the planning authority, can grant a permission which materially contravenes the development plan, without the necessity of going through the elaborate machinery required under s.34(6) before a planning authority can do so. The Board must have regard to the development plan. In *Kildare County Council v An Bord Pleanála*, unreported, High Court, McMenamin J., March 10, 2006, in the context of a road scheme it was noted: "The weight which ought to be attached to the objectives in the context of the Board's assessment of the proposed road development plan is a matter for the Board. Thus while relevance is a matter of law for the court weight is a matter of discretion for the decision maker". Subsection (2), however, considerably circumscribes the power of the Board to grant a permission where the planning authority has refused permission because the development materially breaches the development plan. Under the previous legislation, the Board could grant such permission for any reason within its discretion. Subsection (2)(b) limits the Board's discretion to do so, based on four specified reasons. In addition to this, subs.(2)(c) introduces a requirement for the Board to give the main reasons and considerations for granting such a permission. However, this restriction does not apply where the planning authority allowed a material contravention of the development plan by mistake or having followed the material contravention procedure in s.34(6). Apart from any constraints, the Board is obliged to have regard to the development plan. Thus, on appeal, the Board is entitled to refuse permission on the basis of a material contravention of the development plan, even where the planning authority granted permission. See *Cicol Ltd v An Bord Pleanála*, unreported, High Court, Irvine J., May 8, 2008, where it was held that there was no requirement that the Board, on hearing an appeal, should attach any special weight to the planning authority's own interpretation of its plan. It was further held that having found that the development was a material contravention of the development plan, there was no obligation on the Board to go on to consider of its own motion whether it should grant planning permission on the basis of other considerations which were not ventilated by the applicant in the course of the appeal. The Board is also constrained by other plans. See *Cosgrove v An Bord Pleanála*, unreported, High Court, Kelly J., May 27, 2004, where it was held that the Board in departing from the county waste management plan was not constrained by, the Land Fill Directive 1999/31/EC, which did not apply to it.

Under subs.(5), a person is prohibited from making a planning application for the same development or for a development of the same description, as an appeal which has yet to be determined before the Board. The planning authority has no discretion to admit an application in such circumstances where the matter is still pending before the Board. In

Swords Cloghran Properties v Fingal County Council, unreported, High Court, Herbert J, June 29, 2006 it was held that in order for a second application to be considered the "same" (and so returned without consideration under s.37(5)(a)) as an appeal pending before the Board, it must, in every material respect, be an exact repetition of a previous application for permission. It is not necessary that the appeal to the Board pre-dated the lodging of the second application. Thus where the developer lodged the second application the day before the appeal, this could not circumvent the application of subs.(5). Also it was held that default permission did not arise as returning the application constituted a "decision" being made within the eight-week period.

Where the matter ceases to be pending before the Board in the three circumstances outlined in subs.(5)(a), an applicant may also be restrained from making an application for the same development or for development of the same description under the doctrine of *res judicata* in planning matters which has been developed by the courts. Under this doctrine, where a planning authority has refused a permission upon an application, they may refuse to accept a subsequent identical application in the absence of a change of circumstances; see *Athlone Woollen Mills Limited v Athlone Urban District Council* [1950] I.R. 1 and *Littondale v Wicklow County Council* [1996] 2 I.L.R.M. 519. Under subs.(5)(2), where the same application is made, the planning authority will return the application. Any dispute as to whether the matter concerns the same application can be resolved by determination of An Bord Pleanála.

Article 74 of the 2001 Regulations provides that as soon as may be having made a decision, the Board must notify any party to the appeal and person who made submissions under s.130. Article 74(2) as amended provides that the notice must specify:

1. the reference number of the appeal;
2. the reference number of the planning application concerned in the register of the planning authority;
3. the date of the order of the Board in relation to the appeal;
4. the development to which the decision relates;
5. the nature of the decision and the main reasons and considerations on which the decision is based;
6. in the case of a decision to grant a permission subject to conditions—any conditions to which the permission is subject and the main reasons for the imposition of any such conditions, provided that where a condition imposed is a condition described in s.34(4) of the Act, a reference to the paragraph of the said subs.(4) in which the condition is described shall be sufficient;
7. in the case of a decision to grant a permission for a structure—any purpose for which the structure may or may not be used;
8. in the case of a decision to grant a permission—any condition specifying points of detail relating to a grant of permission to be agreed by the planning authority and the person to whom the permission is granted;
9. in the case of a decision to grant a permission—any period specified by the Board pursuant to s.41 of the Act as the period during which the permission is to have effect;
10. that in making a decision on an appeal the Board, in accordance with s.34(3) of the Act, has regard to submissions or observations received in accordance with these Regulations;
11. in the case of a decision to grant or refuse a permission where the decision by the Board is different, in relation to the granting or refusal of permission, from the recommendation of the report of a person assigned to report on an appeal on behalf of the Board—the main reasons for not accepting such recommendation; and
12. in the case of a decision to grant a permission for a development which materially contravenes the development plan where the planning authority had refused a permission on that ground—the main reasons and considerations for materially contravening the development plan.

[Board's jurisdiction in relation to certain planning applications

37A.—(1) An application for permission for any development specified in **1–48** the Seventh Schedule (inserted by the *Planning and Development (Strategic Infrastructure) Act 2006*) shall, if the following condition is satisfied, be made to the Board under *section 37E* and not to a planning authority.

(2) That condition is that, following consultations under *section 37B,* the Board serves on the prospective applicant a notice in writing under that section stating that, in the opinion of the Board, the proposed development would, if carried out, fall within one or more of the following paragraphs, namely—

(a) the development would be of strategic economic or social importance to the State or the region in which it would be situate,

(b) the development would contribute substantially to the fulfilment of any of the objectives in the National Spatial Strategy or in any regional planning guidelines in force in respect of the area or areas in which it would be situate,

(c) the development would have a significant effect on the area of more than one planning authority.

(3) In *subsection (2)* "prospective applicant" means the person referred to in *section 37B(1).*]

AMENDMENT HISTORY

Section 37A inserted by s.3 of the Planning and Development (Strategic Infrastructure) Act 2006 (No. 27 of 2006).

NOTE

This section introduces a special planning application procedure where a development:

1. falls within one of the categories of development specified in the Seventh Schedule; and

2. the Board serves a notice, after mandatory consultations, specifying that the development comes within one or more of the three circumstances specified in subs.(2).

If these conditions do not apply, then the normal planning procedure of application to the planning authority under s.34 and appeal to An Bord Pleanála under s.37, applies.

The Seventh Schedule is inserted in the 2000 Act under s.5 of the 2006 Act. The Seventh Schedule specifies three categories of infrastructure development which are; Energy; Transport and Environmental infrastructure. There are 13 categories of energy infrastructure; four categories of transport infrastructure and 11 categories of environmental infrastructure. A person wishing to apply for development which falls within any of the categories in the Seventh Schedule must enter into consultation with the Board under s.37B. The special planning application will apply, if the Board then serves a notice stating that:

• the development would be of strategic economic or social importance to the State or the region in which it would be situated; or

• the development would contribute substantially to the fulfilment of any of the objectives in the National Spatial Strategy or in any regional planning guidelines in force in respect of the area or areas in which it would be situated; or

• the development would have a significant effect on the area of more than one planning authority.

The Board can specify more than one circumstance, however if it specifies any of one of such three circumstances, the special planning application procedure will apply. It is not necessary that the Board considers the development comes within all three circumstances.

While the nature and scale of some the developments specified in the Seventh Schedule means that it may be likely to satisfy one of the three circumstances, the notification by the Board is an entirely independent criterion. The assessment of whether any of the three circumstances apply, does not involve an assessment of the planning application but solely whether any or the three circumstances exist. This is not to say that the matters raised in the three circumstances will not be relevant to the assessment of the planning merits of any application. The Board is obliged to take into account the "policies and objectives" of the Government. See *Keane v An Bord Pleanála* [1998] 2 I.L.R.M. 241. The fact that the Board specifies that one or more of the conditions apply does not provide any assurance that the planning application will be granted and does not involve examining the development by reference to the standard of proper planning and sustainable development.

[Discussions with Board before making of application

1–49   **37B.**—**(1)** A person who proposes to apply for permission for any development specified in the Seventh Schedule shall, before making the application, enter into consultations with the Board in relation to the proposed development.

(2) Such a person is referred to subsequently in this section and in *sections 37C and 37D* as a "prospective applicant".

(3) In any consultations under *subsection (1),* the Board may give advice to the prospective applicant regarding the proposed application and, in particular, regarding—

   (a) whether the proposed development would, if carried out, fall within one or more of *paragraphs (a) to (c) of section 37A(2),*

   (b) the procedures involved in making a planning application and in considering such an application, and

   (c) what considerations, related to proper planning and sustainable development or the environment, may, in the opinion of the Board, have a bearing on its decision in relation to the application.

(4) Where, following consultations under this section, the Board is of the opinion that the proposed development would, if carried out—

   (a) fall within one or more of *paragraphs (a) to (c) of section 37A(2),* it shall serve a notice in writing on the prospective applicant stating that it is of that opinion, or

   (b) not fall within any of those paragraphs, it shall serve a notice in writing on the prospective applicant stating that it is of that opinion.

(5) A notice under *subsection (4)(b)* shall include a statement that the prospective applicant's application for permission, if it is proceeded with, must be made to the appropriate planning authority (and such an application, if it is proceeded with, shall be made to that planning authority accordingly).

(6) The Board shall serve a copy of a notice under *subsection (4)(a) or (b),* as the case may be, on the appropriate planning authority.

(7) No application for permission in respect of a development referred to in *subsection (1)* shall be made to a planning authority unless or until a notice is served under *subsection (4)(b)* in relation to the development.

(8) In this section "appropriate planning authority" means whichever planning authority would, but for the enactment of *section 3 of the Planning and Development (Strategic Infrastructure) Act 2006,* be the appropriate planning authority to deal with the application referred to in *subsection (1).*]

AMENDMENT HISTORY

Section 37B inserted by s.3 of the Planning and Development (Strategic Infrastructure) Act 2006 (No. 27 of 2006).

NOTE

This section sets on the procedure providing for consultations between a prospective applicant and the Board, where the applicant proposes to carry out any one of the developments specified in the Seventh Schedule. This is a form of pre-planning consultation. It is nevertheless different from the pre-planning consultations with a planning authority envisaged under s.247 of the 2000 Act, as there is a mandatory obligation on the prospective applicant to enter into such consultation with the Board. Subsection (3) provides that in such consultations, the Board may give such advice in advance as to whether the development would come within one of the three circumstances specified in subs.(37)(A)(2). Although this subsection is couched in terms of "advice", such advice will not amount to a binding representation by the Board that it would not eventually serve a notice under subs.(37)(A)(2). This follows from s.37C(3) which provides that the consultation cannot be relied upon in the planning process or in any legal proceedings. The Board may also offer advice on the procedure for making and deciding the planning application and matters of proper planning and sustainable development which the Board may consider relevant in determining the application. Although the three enlisted matters of advice are not exhaustive and so advice can certainly be given on other relevant matters.

Article 210(1) of the 2001 Regulations (as inserted by the 2006 Regulations) provides that on receipt of a request to enter into pre-application consultations, the Board shall notify the relevant planning authority of the request. Article 210(2) states that the Board shall, during the course of a pre-application consultation, indicate to a prospective applicant:

1. the plans, particulars or other information which the Board will require for the purposes of consideration of an application;
2. the time frames and sequencing to be applied to the application process; and
3. any other matters in relation to the application process as the Board considers appropriate.

Article 210(3) prescribes steps where the Board is of the opinion that the proposed development would be likely to have significant effects on the environment in a transboundary State. Article 210(4) provides that the Board may, during the course of a pre-application consultation, require a prospective applicant to give notice to the public or to carry out consultations with the public in advance of an application being submitted, including:

- the erection or fixing of notice or notices on the site in a form to be specified by the Board;
- the provision of a specific place or a specific website to make available the application, EIS and any other relevant documentation for inspection or purchase at a fee not exceeding the reasonable cost of making a copy;
- the use of local or national media; or
- the holding of meetings, with any person or body or for the public.

These requirements are at the discretion of the Board.

Article 210(5) provides during the course of a pre-application consultation, the Board may indicate which of the bodies prescribed under art.213 should, in its opinion, be notified by the prospective applicant of the making of an application and the prospective applicant shall notify those bodies. Also art.210(6) provides that nothing shall prevent the Board from requiring a prospective applicant for permission to submit further information or from giving further notice to the public or to any person or body.

Following the consultation, the Board must serve a notice specifying that it is of the opinion that:

- development falls within one of the three criteria specified in subs.(37)(A)(2) and so the special planning application procedure applies; or
- that the development does not fall within such criteria and so the normal planning application procedure will apply.

In the event that the notice states that the development does not fall within any of the three criteria, it must specify the planning authority to which the application should be made. Such planning authority must also be served with the notice. The notice must specifically state that if the development is to proceed, the application must be made to the relevant planning authority. An applicant cannot make an application to the planning authority until the notice issues, even if the applicant expects (due to advice given in the consultations) that the Board will state that the three criteria do not apply. However, it is the fact that the matter falls within the seventh schedule as opposed to the holding of a consultation, which means that application cannot be made until the Board issue a notice.

[Section 37B: supplemental provisions

1–50   **37C.—(1)** A prospective applicant shall, for the purposes of consultations under *section 37B,* supply to the Board sufficient information in relation to the proposed development so as to enable the Board to assess the proposed development.

(2) The holding of consultations under *section 37B* shall not prejudice the performance by the Board of any other of its functions under this Act or regulations under this Act and cannot be relied upon in the formal planning process or in legal proceedings.

(3) The Board shall keep a record in writing of any consultations under *section 37B* in relation to a proposed development, including the names of those who participated in the consultations, and a copy of such record shall be placed and kept with the documents to which any planning application in respect of the proposed development relates.

(4) The Board may consult with any person who may, in the opinion of the Board, have information which is relevant for the purposes of consultations under *section 37B* in relation to a proposed development.

AMENDMENT HISTORY

Section 37C inserted by s.3 of the Planning and Development (Strategic Infrastructure) Act 2006 (No. 27 of 2006).

NOTE

This section concerns the information to be submitted to the Board for the purposes of a consultation under s.37B and states that the matters discussed at a consultation are without prejudice to the formal planning process or legal proceeding. The section does not prescribe information to be submitted; merely providing that "sufficient information" must be furnished. It would appear that the assessment of what is "sufficient information" is a matter for the Board to determine in its discretion. Subsections (2) and (3) are similar to s.247(2) and (5) respectively of the 2000 Act in relation to pre-planning consultations before the planning authority. It appears to follows from subs.(2) that not only the fact of holding such consultation but the matters discussed or statements made at such consultations cannot subsequently be relied upon by an applicant. Any statements made cannot create an estoppel type argument restraining the Board from adopting an incompatible position in the planning process. The stark language of subs.(2) would make it difficult for an applicant to assert a claim of legitimate expectation based upon the matters discussed at the consultation. While the subsection is not framed as an immunity from suit type provision, it prohibits reliance on the consultation in support of a claim in legal proceedings. Irrespective of subs.(2), it is doubtful whether at common law an official owes a duty of care to an applicant in such consultations. Certainly, in England it has consistently been held that advice or guidance sought from a local authority on planning matters, will not generally give rise to a duty of care by such officials. See *Tidman v Reading Borough Council* [1994] 3 P.L.R. 72; *Fashion*

Brokers Ltd v Clarke Hayes and Cannock Chase Council [2000] P.N.L.R. 473; *Hewings v Teignbridge District Council*, unreported, November 15, 1995; *Welton v North Cornwall District Council* [1997] 1 W.L.R. 570; *Haddow v Secretary of State for the Environment* [2000] Env. Lr. 212. Officials are nevertheless under a duty to act in good faith in the conduct of duties; where an official acts with male fides, this may give rise to a claim for damages based upon the tort of misfeasance in public office.

Under subs.(3) the Board has an obligation to retain a record of the consultations which should be kept with the planning application. The subsection is silent as to the precise content of such record (apart from stating it should include the names of persons who participated) and also for how long such record is to be retained. It would appear that such record need not be an exhaustive account of everything discussed at the consultation but it should give a broad outline of matters discussed at the consultation. As regards the time for retaining such record, the subsection does not state that the record must be retained after the planning application is determined. Under s.146, as amended by the 2006 Act, documents relating to any appeal or referral or to a decision of the Board, must be available to members of the public for at least five years. Under subs.(4), the Board is afforded a wide discretion to consult with any person who may have information relevant to the proposed planning application. The reference to "any person" does not include the proposed applicant, who has an obligation to hold a consultation. It will depend on the nature of the proposed application, as to who the Board might deem appropriate to consult in respect of the application. It is for the Board to determine in the exercise of its judgment whether to consult any such person and so there is no entitlement of any such person to be consulted. The subsection is to facilitate the Board in its consultation and not to confer a right on any person to be consulted.

[Opinion by Board on information to be contained in environmental impact statement

37D.—**(1)** Where a notice has been served under *section 37B(4)(a)* in   **1–51** relation to proposed development, a prospective applicant may request the Board to give to him or her an opinion in writing prepared by the Board on what information will be required to be contained in an environmental impact statement in relation to the development.

(2) On receipt of such a request the Board shall—

    (a) consult with the requester and such bodies as may be specified by the Minister for the purpose, and

    (b) comply with the request as soon as is practicable.

(3) A prospective applicant shall, for the purposes of the Board's complying with a request under this section, supply to the Board sufficient information in relation to the proposed development so as to enable the Board to assess the proposed development.

(4) The provision of an opinion under this section shall not prejudice the performance by the Board of any other of its functions under this Act or regulations under this Act and cannot be relied upon in the formal planning process or in legal proceedings.]

AMENDMENT HISTORY

Section 37D inserted by s.3 of the Planning and Development (Strategic Infrastructure) Act 2006 (No. 27 of 2006).

NOTE

This section provides that where the Board has served a notice stating that the planning application must be made to the Board under the strategic infrastructure procedure, an applicant may request the opinion of the Board as to what must be contained in any EIS to accompany such application. There is a similar mechanism in relation to an ordinary planning application under s.173(5) of the 2000 Act. It is at the discretion of an applicant whether to make such a request; there is no obligation to do so, although it may be prudent where the applicant is uncertain about the matters to be contained in the EIS. Upon receipt of the request, the Board has an obligation to consult with the requester and any prescribed bodies. Article 211(1) of the 2001 Regulations (inserted by the 2006 Regulations) prescribes the specified bodies as the Minister for the Environment, Heritage and Local Government, the Environmental Protection Agency, the Minister for Communications, Marine and Natural Resources, and the relevant planning authority. Also art.211(2) provides that the Board may invite submissions or observations in relation to the information to be contained in the EIS from the bodies referred to in art.213.

Again as with consultation under s.37C, subs.(4) provides that the opinion given by the Board cannot prejudice its formal consideration of the planning application. The subsection also effectively affords the Board an immunity from reliance on such opinion by the applicant or any other person in any legal proceedings. Once submitted, the Board can subsequently decide that the EIS is inadequate.

[Application to Board

1–52 **37E.**—**(1)** An application for permission for development in respect of which a notice has been served under *section 37B(4)(a)* shall be made to the Board and shall be accompanied by an environmental impact statement in respect of the proposed development.

(2) The Board may refuse to deal with any application made to it under this section where it considers that the application for permission or the environmental impact statement is inadequate or incomplete, having regard in particular to the permission regulations and any regulations made under *section 177* or to any consultations held under *section 37B*.

(3) Before a person applies for permission to the Board under this section, he or she shall—

  (a) publish in one or more newspapers circulating in the area or areas in which it is proposed to carry out the development a notice indicating the nature and location of the proposed development and—

   (i) stating that—

    (I) the person proposes to make an application to the Board for permission for the proposed development,

    (II) an environmental impact statement has been prepared in respect of the proposed development, and

    (III) where relevant, the proposed development is likely to have significant effects on the environment of a Member State of the European Communities or other party to the Transboundary Convention,

   (ii) specifying the times and places at which, and the period (not being less than 6 weeks) during which, a copy of the application and the environmental impact statement may be inspected free of charge or purchased on payment of a specified fee (which fee shall not exceed the reasonable cost of making such copy),

   (iii) inviting the making, during such period, of submissions and observations to the Board relating to—

     (I) the implications of the proposed development for proper planning and sustainable development, and

     (II) the likely effects on the environment of the proposed development, if carried out, and

   (iv) specifying the types of decision the Board may make, under *section 37G,* in relation to the application,

  (b) send a prescribed number of copies of the application and the environmental impact statement to the planning authority or authorities in whose area or areas the proposed development would be situated,

  (c) send a prescribed number of copies of the application and the environmental impact statement to any prescribed authorities together with a notice stating that submissions or observations may, during the period referred to in *paragraph (a)(ii),* be made in writing to the Board in relation to—

   (i) the implications of the proposed development for proper planning and sustainable development, and

   (ii) the likely effects on the environment of the proposed development, if carried out, and

  (d) where the proposed development is likely to have significant effects on the environment of a Member State of the European Communities or a state which is a party to the Transboundary Convention, send a prescribed number of copies of the application and the environmental impact statement to the prescribed authority of the relevant state or states together with a notice stating that submissions or observations may, during the period referred to in *paragraph (a)(ii),* be made in writing to the Board.

 (4) The planning authority for the area (or, as the case may be, each planning authority for the areas) in which the proposed development would be situated shall, within 10 weeks from the making of the application to the Board under this section (or such longer period as may be specified by the Board), prepare and submit to the Board a report setting out the views of the authority on the effects of the proposed development on the environment and the proper planning and sustainable development of the area of the authority, having regard in particular to the matters specified in *section 34(2).*

 (5) The manager of a planning authority shall, before submitting any report in relation to a proposed development to the Board under *subsection (4),* submit the report to the members of the authority and seek the views of the members on the proposed development.

 (6) The members of the planning authority may, by resolution, decide to attach recommendations specified in the resolution to the report of the authority; where the members so decide those recommendations (together with the meetings administrator's record) shall be attached to the report submitted to the Board under *subsection (4).*

 (7) In *subsection (6)* "the meetings administrator's record" means a record prepared by the meetings administrator (within the meaning of *section 46 of the Local Government Act 2001*) of the views expressed by the members on the proposed development.

(8) In addition to the report referred to in *subsection (4),* the Board may, where it considers it necessary to do so, require the planning authority or authorities referred to in that subsection or any planning authority or authorities on whose area or areas it would have a significant effect to furnish to the Board such information in relation to the effects of the proposed development on the proper planning and sustainable development of the area concerned and on the environment as the Board may specify.]

AMENDMENT HISTORY

Section 37E inserted by s.3 of the Planning and Development (Strategic Infrastructure) Act 2006 (No. 27 of 2006).

NOTE

This section concerns the procedure for lodging a planning application to the Board including the publication of notice and the procedure for obtaining the view of the planning authority on the planning application. Subsection (1) makes clear that all strategic infrastructure planning applications must be accompanied by an EIS which must be lodged at the same time. Under subs.(2) the Board may refuse to accept the planning application as valid where it is inadequate or incomplete, having regard in particular to the permission regulations and the consultations under s.37B. Although the expression "refuse to deal" is not entirely clear, it appears the Board is entitled to return the application rather than accept the application and submit a request for further information. The Board may at its discretion request further information. Article 210(2) of the 2001 Regulations (as inserted by the 2006 Regulations) provides that the Board shall, during the course of a pre-application consultation, indicate to a prospective applicant, inter alia, the plans, particulars or other information which the Board will require for the purposes of consideration of an application. Article 214 of the 2001 Regulations (as inserted by the 2006 Regulations) provides that when making an application for strategic infrastructure development, the applicant shall send to the Board:
1. 10 copies of the plans and particulars of the proposed development (including any plans, particulars or other information indicated by the Board under art.210(2)) and of the EIS;
2. a copy of the published newspaper notice in accordance as may be appropriate;
3. a list of the bodies notified of the application, as may be appropriate, and an indication of the date on which notice was sent; and
4. a list of any other public notice given or other public consultations conducted by the applicant, including any notice or consultations done on foot of a requirement by the Board under art.210, and an indication of the date or dates of such additional notice or consultations.

Article 214(2) states that where the Board so consents or specifies, any or all of the copies or other information specified in sub-art.(1) shall be given in electronic form.

Prior to lodging the planning application, the applicant must publish a newspaper notice referring to the proposed application and EIS, specifying the times and place where it can be inspected and also inviting submissions. As regards the making of submissions, art.217(1) (a) provides that any submission or observation to the Board in relation to an application shall be made within the period specified in the notice and shall be accompanied by such fee (if any) as may be payable and shall state:
1. the name and address and the telephone number or email address, if any, of the person making the submission or observation and the name and address and the telephone number or email address, if any, of any person acting on his or her behalf;
2. the subject matter of the submission or observation; and
3. the reasons, considerations and arguments on which the submission or observation is based in full.

Article 217(1)(b) states that where the Board so consents, a submission or observation may be made in electronic form. Article 217(2) provides that the Board shall acknowledge in writing the receipt of any submission or observation referred to in sub-art.(1) as soon as may be following receipt of the submission or observation. The acknowledgement and any further correspondence from the Board in relation to the matter shall be issued in the format in which the submission or observation was received unless otherwise agreed. Article 217(3) declares that any submissions or observations that do not comply with sub-art.(1) shall not be considered by the Board, while in art.217(4) a person who makes submissions or observations to the Board in accordance with this article shall not be entitled to elaborate upon the submissions or observations or make further submissions or observations in relation to the application and any such elaboration, submissions or observations that is or are received by the Board shall not be considered by it. One qualification to this is that the Board may, at any time before making its decision ask any person to make submissions or observations or elaborate upon submissions or observations in relation to an application. However in a particular case fair procedures may require that a party be given an opportunity to respond to submissions. This is however subject to the need for finality. See *Klohn v An Bord Pleanála*, unreported, High Court, McMahon J., April 23, 2008.

Unlike in the case of an ordinary planning application, there is no mandatory requirement to erect a site notice in all cases. However, by virtue of art.210(4), the Board may require the publication of a site notice during the holding of the pre-application consultation. The period for inspection and making submissions must not be less than six weeks. Article 212 of the 2001 Regulations, as amended, provides that any notice which an applicant is required to give to the public shall indicate the types of decision the Board can make in relation to the application. Copies of the application and EIS must also be sent to the relevant planning authority and to any other prescribed authorities with a notice inviting submissions. Where the proposed development is likely to have significant effects on the environment of a Member State or of a state which is a party to the Transboundary Convention, copies must also be sent to prescribed authorities of those states. Subsection (4) provides that the planning authority where the proposed development is situated must prepare and submit a report to the Board within 10 weeks of the application being made. The report must set out the views of the planning authority on the effects of the proposed development on the environment and proper planning and sustainable development of the area. Prior to submitting the report, the local authority manager must submit the report to the elected members of the local authority to obtain their views. The elected members may decide by resolution to attach recommendations to the report. While subs.(6) does not clarify the nature of the recommendation, it would appear that the recommendation is open-ended and so could involve a recommendation to grant or refuse the application or to attach conditions to deal with some aspect of the development. There is however, no obligation on the elected members to make any recommendation. Elected members therefore have a direct input into the planning process which they do not enjoy in respect of ordinary planning applications except where they pass a resolution directing permission to be granted which is in material contravention of the development plan. The recommendation of the elected members is to be appended to the report which is submitted rather than contained within the report. The meeting's administrator record must also be submitted to the Board which involves the minutes of any meeting of the elected members where the report was considered and views expressed. Under subs.(8), the Board also has a general power to require the relevant planning authorities to submit further information.

[Section 37E: supplemental provisions

37F.—(1) Before determining any application for permission under *section 37E* the Board may, at its absolute discretion and at any time—   **1–53**

    (a) require the applicant for permission to submit further information, including a revised environmental impact statement,

    (b) indicate that it is considering granting permission, subject to the applicant for permission submitting revised particulars, plans or drawings in relation to the development,

    (c) request further submissions or observations from the applicant for permission, any person who made submissions or observations, or any other person who may, in the opinion of the Board, have information which is relevant to the determination of the application,

(d) without prejudice to *subsections (2) and (3),* make any information relating to the application available for inspection, notify any person or the public that the information is so available and, if it considers appropriate, invite further submissions or observations to be made to it within such period as it may specify, or

(e) hold meetings with the applicant for permission or any other person—

    (i) where it appears to the Board to be expedient for the purpose of determining the application, or

    (ii) where it appears to the Board to be necessary or expedient for the purpose of resolving any issue with the applicant for permission or any disagreement between the applicant and any other party, including resolving any issue or disagreement in advance of an oral hearing.

(2) Where an applicant submits a revised environmental impact statement to the Board in accordance with *subsection (1)(a)* or otherwise submits further information or revised particulars, plans or drawings in accordance with *subsection (1),* which, in the opinion of the Board, contain significant additional information on the effect of the proposed development on the environment to that already submitted, the Board shall—

(a) make the information, particulars, plans or drawings, as appropriate, available for inspection,

(b) give notice that the information, particulars, plans or drawings are so available, and

(c) invite further submissions or observations to be made to it within such period as it may specify.

(3) Where the Board holds a meeting in accordance with *subsection (1)(e),* it shall keep a written record of the meeting and make that record available for inspection.

(4) The Board, or an employee of the Board duly authorised by the Board, may appoint any person to hold a meeting referred to in *subsection (1)(e).*

(5) Before making a decision under *section 37G* in respect of proposed development comprising or for the purposes of an activity for which an integrated pollution control licence or a waste licence is required, the Board may request the Environmental Protection Agency to make observations within such period (which period shall not in any case be less than 3 weeks from the date of the request) as may be specified by the Board in relation to the proposed development.

(6) When making its decision under *section 37G* on the application the Board shall have regard to the observations, if any, received from the Environmental Protection Agency within the period specified under *subsection (5).*

(7) The Board may, at any time after the expiration of the period specified in a notice under *section 37E(3)(a)* for making submissions or observations, make its decision under *section 37G* on the application.

(8) The making of observations by the Environmental Protection Agency under this section shall not prejudice any other function of the Agency.]

AMENDMENT HISTORY

Section 37F inserted by s.3 of the Planning and Development (Strategic Infrastructure) Act 2006 (No. 27 of 2006).

NOTE

This section concerns certain powers or measures which the Board may apply prior to determining an application for strategic infrastructure development. Subsection (1) sets out certain steps which the Board may take at its discretion including:

1. requesting an applicant to submit further information including a revised EIS;
2. requesting an applicant to submit revised plans or drawings;
3. requesting further submissions/observations from the applicant or other person;
4. a general power to make information available or notify any person; and
5. a power to hold meetings.

All these powers are discretionary rather than obligatory. Thus the power to make information available and to invite submissions is supplemental to the mandatory obligation on an applicant to make information available and invite submissions under s.37E of the Act. The Board has a broad power to hold meetings where it considers it expedient or for the specific purpose of resolving a dispute between the applicant or other party. Under subs.(4), the Board may appoint a person to hold the meeting and by virtue of subs.(3), a record must be kept of the conduct of the meeting, which must also be available for inspection. This provision therefore gives statutory authority to post-planning meeting, the legality of which had been questioned on the grounds of excluding the public and absence of fair procedures. See *Ballintubber Heights Ltd v Cork County Council*, unreported, High Court, Ó Caoimh J., June 21, 2002. The holding of meetings is distinct from an oral hearing, which is governed by s.134.

Although the Board is said to have an absolute discretion in the exercise of its powers, these powers must be exercised in accordance with fair procedures. Under subs.(2), the Board is obliged to make available for inspection and invite submissions on any revised EIS and must also make available and invite submissions on any information which contains significant additional information on the effect of the proposed development on the environment. Thus, where a revised EIS is submitted the Board is obliged in all cases to make this available for inspection and to invite submissions. This does not require any expert assessment of the revised EIS. However, in assessing whether information submitted contains significant additional information on the effects of the development on the environment, the Board will be exercising planning judgment and expertise. This decision will only be reviewable by the courts under the high standard of irrationality and so the courts will not generally substitute their own view on the matter. See *Dietacaron Ltd v An Bord Pleanála* [2005] 2 I.L.R.M. 32 and *Kinsella v Dundalk Town Council*, unreported, High Court, Kelly J., December 3, 2004. The only circumstance in which the court may intervene is where it considers the Board's decision was irrational under the *O'Keeffe* standard (*O'Keeffe v An Bord Pleanála* [1993] 1 I.R. 39). See *White v Dublin City Council* [2004] 1 I.R. 545.

Subsections (5) and (6), provides that where the application involves a proposed development for which an integrated pollution control licence or a waste licence is required, it must notify the EPA and allow the EPA a period of not less than three weeks to make submissions thereon. The references in subs.(5) to the proposed development "comprising" or "for the purposes of an activity" which requires a license, encompass development that may be for a particular use which necessitates a licence or works or structures which concern an activity for which a licence is required. Any submissions received by the Board from the EPA within the specified period must be taken into account by the Board. Subsection (7) states the earliest time after which the Board may makes its determination on the application for strategic development. This must, of course, be read subject to any other requirements of the Act, such as where the Board has invited the making of further submissions under subs.(2). In such case, the Board must await the end of the period for the making of such submission before the making its determination.

[Decision by Board on application under section 37E

1–54   **37G.**—**(1)** When making a decision in respect of a proposed development for which an application is made under *section 37E,* the Board may consider any relevant information before it or any other matter to which, by virtue of this Act, it can have regard.

(2) Without prejudice to the generality of *subsection (1),* the Board shall consider—

    (a) the environmental impact statement submitted under *section 37E(1),* any submissions or observations made, in response to the invitation referred to in *section 37E(3),* within the period referred to in that provision, the report (and the recommendations and record, if any, attached to it) submitted by a planning authority in accordance with *section 37E(4),* any information furnished in accordance with *section 37F(1)* and any other relevant information before it relating to—

        (i) the likely consequences of the proposed development for proper planning and sustainable development in the area in which it is proposed to situate the development, and

        (ii) the likely effects on the environment of the proposed development,

    (b) any report or recommendation prepared in relation to the application in accordance with *section 146,* including the report of the person conducting any oral hearing of the proposed development and the written record of any meeting referred to in *section 37F(3),*

    (c) the provisions of the development plan or plans for the area,

    (d) the provisions of any special amenity area order relating to the area,

    (e) if the area or part of the area is a European site or an area prescribed for the purposes of *section 10(2)(c),* that fact,

    (f) if the proposed development would have an effect on a European site or an area prescribed for the purposes of *section 10(2)(c),* that fact,

    (g) the matters referred to in *section 143,*

    (h) any relevant provisions of this Act and of any regulations made under this Act.

(3) The Board may, in respect of an application under *section 37E* for permission—

    (a) decide—

        (i) to grant the permission, or

        (ii) to make such modifications to the proposed development as it specifies in its decision and grant permission in respect of the proposed development as so modified, or

        (iii) to grant permission in respect of part of the proposed development (with or without specified modifications of it of the foregoing kind),

    or

    (b) decide to refuse to grant the permission, and a decision to grant permission under *paragraph (a)(i), (ii) or (iii)* may be subject to or without conditions.

(4) Where an application under *section 37E* relates to proposed development which comprises or is for the purposes of an activity for which an integrated pollution control licence or a waste licence is required, the Board shall not, where it decides to grant permission, subject that permission to conditions which are for the purposes of—

   (a) controlling emissions from the operation of the activity, including the prevention, limitation, elimination, abatement or reduction of those emissions,
      or
   (b) controlling emissions related to or following the cessation of the operation or the activity.

(5) Where an application under *section 37E* relates to proposed development which comprises or is for the purposes of an activity for which an integrated pollution control licence or a waste licence is required, the Board may, in respect of that development, decide to refuse a grant of permission under this section, where the Board considers that the development, notwithstanding the licensing of the activity, is unacceptable on environmental grounds, having regard to the proper planning and sustainable development of the area in which the development will be situated.

(6) The Board may decide to grant a permission for development, or any part of a development, under this section even if the proposed development, or part thereof, contravenes materially the development plan relating to any area in which it is proposed to situate the development.

(7) Without prejudice to the generality of the Board's powers to attach conditions under *subsection (3)* the Board may attach to a permission for development under this section—

   (a) a condition with regard to any of the matters specified in *section 34(4),*
   (b) a condition requiring the payment of a contribution or contributions of the same kind as the appropriate planning authority could require to be paid under *section 48 or 49* (or both) were that authority to grant the permission (and the scheme or schemes referred to in *section 48 or 49,* as appropriate, made by that authority shall apply to the determination of such contribution or contributions),
   (c) a condition requiring the applicant to submit further information to it or any other local or state authority, as the Board may specify before commencing development, or
   (d) a condition requiring—
      (i) the construction or the financing, in whole or in part, of the construction of a facility, or
      (ii) the provision or the financing, in whole or in part, of the provision of a service,
   in the area in which the proposed development would be situated, being a facility or service that, in the opinion of the Board, would constitute a substantial gain to the community.

(8) A condition attached pursuant to *subsection (7)(d)* shall not require such an amount of financial resources to be committed for the purposes of the condition being complied with as would substantially deprive the person in whose favour the permission operates of the benefits likely to accrue from the grant of the permission.

(9) In *subsection (7)(b)* "appropriate planning authority" means whichever planning authority would, but for the enactment of *section 3 of the Planning and Development (Strategic Infrastructure) Act 2006,* be the appropriate planning authority to grant the permission referred to in this section.

(10) The conditions attached under this section to a permission may provide that points of detail relating to the grant of the permission may be agreed between the planning authority or authorities in whose functional area or areas the development will be situate and the person carrying out the development; if that authority or those authorities and that person cannot agree on the matter the matter may be referred to the Board for determination.

(11) Without prejudice to the generality of *section 18(a) of the Interpretation Act 2005,* a reference, however expressed, in this section or *sections 37H to 37J* to the area in which the proposed development would be situated includes, if the context admits, a reference to the 2 or more areas in which the proposed development would be situated and cognate references shall be construed accordingly.]

AMENDMENT HISTORY

Section 37G inserted by s.3 of the Planning and Development (Strategic Infrastructure) Act 2006 (No. 27 of 2006).

NOTE

This section concerns the actual determination by the Board of the application for strategic infrastructure development. Subsection (1) states in general terms that the Board may consider any relevant information before it and other matters it can take into account under the Act. The subsection offers no guidance as to what is "relevant information" for these purposes. While the assessment of how "relevant" a matter is would appear to involve an exercise of planning judgment, this will not entitle the Board to take into account matters outside the concept of proper planning and sustainable development. Equally, the subsection offers no guidance on meaning of "other matter" which the Board can take into account under the Act. Where the Board takes into account irrelevant considerations or matters which it is not entitled to do so under the Act, it will be deemed to have acted ultra vires. Subsection (2) sets out specified matters which the Board is obligated to take into account when making its determination. The use of the phrase "without prejudice to the generality of subsection (1)" means that the specified matters in subs.(2) are not exhaustive. The specified matters in subs.(2) include the EIS and all associated submissions and information and also the likely effects of the proposed development on the environment. This requirement involves the Board carrying out an EIA. One of the main vehicles for carrying out the EIA is a consideration of the EIS, though it is not confined to considering the EIS and associated information. See *Klohn v An Bord Pleanála*, unreported, High Court, McMahon J., April 23, 2008. Other specified matters which must be taken into account include the development plan or plans, where the development is to be located, any special amenity order or affected European site or area (where applicable) including those prescribed under s.10(2)(c), matters specified in s.143 (including policies and objective of the Government, Minister, etc.; national interests and the national spatial plan, etc.) and any other relevant provisions of the 2000 Act or the Regulations.

Subsection (3) sets out the type of decisions which the Board may make in determining the application. The determination may involve granting the permission, granting the permission subject to modifications, granting part of the development or refusing the application. The subsection explicitly allows the making of a split decision, i.e. both granting and refusing part of the development. There is no explicit provision for a split decision under s.34(1) in relation to an ordinary planning application, although this may be reasonably incidental to its powers. However, the power to issue a split decision should be exercised in accordance with certain principles. The split decision ought not result in permitting development which is materially different from the permission applied for. In *Kent County Council v Secretary of State for the Environment* [1976] 33 P&CR 70, Sir Douglas Frank QC, sitting as a deputy High Court judge, held that the test was one of severability: could the part of the development being permitted be severed from the rest of the application which was being refused? However, in *Bernard Wheatcroft Ltd v Secretary of State for the Environment* [1982] 42 P & CR 233 Forbes J rejected the severability test but held that the question was whether the permission granted was in substance that for which permission had been sought. This involved considering whether the development had been so changed that the grant deprived those who would have been consulted on the changed development of the opportunity of consultation. The planning authority must ensure that fair procedures are satisfied. See *Johnson v Secretary of the State for the Environment*, unreported, High Court, June 8, 2007. In respect of these positive decisions, to grant all or part of the development or to grant subject to modification, the Board may impose conditions. Article 219 of the 2001 Regulations as amended provides that the notice of the decision made by the Board shall state that, in making a decision, the Board has had regard to any submissions or observations received in accordance with the 2000 Act or the Regulations. Subsection (4) provides that where the proposed development comprises or is for the purposes of an activity for which an integrated pollution control licence or a waste licence is required, the Board cannot impose conditions controlling emissions. Subsection (5) provides that the Board may refuse an application which is unacceptable on environmental grounds even where it concerns an activity for which an integrated pollution control licence or a waste licence is required. Thus, notwithstanding that the EPA would have power to refuse the licence on environmental grounds, the Board may also refuse permission on this basis. However, the fact that it cannot impose the conditions specified in subs.(4) means that it cannot impose these types of mitigation measures. Subsection (6) provides that the Board may grant permission even where the development materially contravenes the development plan. This is similar to s.37(2)(a) in respect of ordinary planning applications, although the constraints on the Board under s.37(2)(b) where the planning authority had refused permission on grounds of material contravention, clearly cannot apply to strategic infrastructure application. It may be noted that one of the reasons in s.37(2)(b) for which the Board can depart from the planning authorities view, is where the proposed development is of strategic or national importance. Nonetheless, while the power of the Board to grant permission is not constrained by provisions of the development plan, the Board must take into account the provisions of the development plan under subs.(2)(c).

Subsection (7) sets out a non-exhaustive list of certain conditions which the Board may impose, which is without prejudice to the general power to impose conditions. The Board may impose any of the types of conditions which may be imposed by the planning authority or Board in an ordinary application for planning permission under s.34(4) which would include the amendments to this subsection under the 2006 Act. The Board may also impose a condition requiring a development contribution in accordance with the general or special contribution schemes adopted by the local authority under ss.48 and 49, in whose jurisdiction the development is located. Subsection (9) provides that the appropriate planning authority for these purposes is the planning authority which would have formerly had jurisdiction to grant permission for the development. It would appear that where the development is located within the area of several local authorities, then the Board may impose contributions under local authority schemes proportionate to the extent to which development is located within the area of such local authorities. A condition may be imposed requiring further information to be submitted to the Board, local authority or state authority. No guidance is given as to the nature of this further information. There would appear to be limits to what further information may be required by way of condition. It would appear that such information ought not to contain significant additional information relating to the development as the public would have had no opportunity to consider or to make submissions on such information. Subsection (7)(d) allows for the imposition of a condition requiring a "planning gain" to the community. This is a radical and novel condition which could not be imposed in respect of the development granted under ss. 34 or 37 of the Act. Any such condition would be ultra vires for not being relevant to the development. The concept of a developer granting a planning gain to the community outside the normal planning process was expressly disapproved of by the Supreme Court in *Ashbourne Holdings v An Bord Pleanála* [2003] 2 I.R. 114. Considerable flexibility is afforded as to the nature of the planning gain, which may be either a facility or a service. The only criterion is that the facility or service must be of "substantial gain" to the community. The applicant may be required either to construct the facility or may finance the construction of such facility. Similarly, the applicant may provide or finance the service. Subsection (8) provides that the financial commitment must not be so onerous as to deprive the applicant of the substantial benefit of the grant of approval. There must be a degree of proportionality between the financial burden of the condition and the benefit of the approval. This may prove difficult to assess, particularly the exact benefit likely to accrue from the approval. Although the criteria are vague and difficult to apply, the inbuilt proportionality requirement may mean that it would escape a challenge on the basis of constitutional invalidity. The condition may be sought to be justified on the basis that it is in the interests of the common good and it is proportionate to its objective in accordance with the principle set out in *Article 26 and the Planning and Development Bill* [2002] 2 I.R. 292, in respect of Pt V of the 2000 Act. Subsection (10) allows the Board to impose conditions allowing for points of detail to be determined between the planning authority and the person carrying out the development. Such a condition is permitted in respect of planning applications under s.34(5). Such conditions may be imposed in accordance with the principles set out by the Supreme Court in *Boland v An Bord Pleanála* [1996] 3 I.R. 435. In entering into such agreement the planning authority and person carrying out the development, must ensure that the agreement is within the scope of the true or correct meaning of the condition. See *O'Connor v Dublin Corporation*, unreported, High Court, O'Neill J., October 3, 2002. Where the agreement goes beyond the scope of such condition, the agreement will be ultra vires. In assessing whether such agreement is beyond the scope of the condition, a court will not defer to the opinion of parties and so the applicable standard of review is not *O'Keeffe* irrationality or unreasonableness. Where the planning authority and person carrying out the development cannot reach agreement, the matter may be referred to the Board for resolution. For a more detailed discussion of this type of condition see the note on s.34(5). Subsection (11) applies to a situation where the development is situated in the area of more than one planning authority. The reference to s.18(a) of the Interpretation Act 2005 relates to the rule that a word importing the singular shall be read as also importing the plural and vice versa.

[Section 37G: supplemental provisions

1–55   **37H.—(1)** The Board shall send a copy of a decision under *section 37G* to the applicant, to any planning authority in whose area the development would be situated and to any person who made submissions or observations on the application for permission.

(2) A decision given under *section 37G* and the notification of the decision shall state—

  (a) the main reasons and considerations on which the decision is based,

  (b) where conditions are imposed in relation to the grant of any permission, the main reasons for the imposition of any such conditions, and

  (c) the sum due to be paid to the Board towards the costs to the Board of determining the application under *section 37E,* and, in such amount as the Board considers to be reasonable, to any planning authority that incurred costs during the course of consideration of that application and to any other person as a contribution to the costs incurred by that person during the course of consideration of that application (each of which sums the Board may, by virtue of this subsection, require to be paid).

(3) A reference to costs in *subsection (2)(c)* shall be construed as a reference to such costs as the Board in its absolute discretion considers to be reasonable costs, but does not include a reference to so much of the costs there referred to as have been recovered by the Board by way of a fee charged under *section 144*.

(4) A grant of permission under *section 37G* shall be made as soon as may be after the making of the relevant decision but shall not become operative until any requirement made under *subsection (2)(c)* in relation to the payment by the applicant of a sum in respect of costs has been complied with.

(5) Where an applicant for permission fails to pay a sum in respect of costs in accordance with a requirement made under *subsection (2)(c)* the Board, the authority or any other person concerned (as may be appropriate) may recover the sum as a simple contract debt in any court of competent jurisdiction.

(6) A person shall not be entitled solely by reason of a permission under *section 37G* to carry out any development.]

AMENDMENT HISTORY

Section 37H inserted by s.3 of the Planning and Development (Strategic Infrastructure) Act 2006 (No. 27 of 2006).

NOTE

This subsection concerns the procedure following the determination of the application by the Board. The Board must send a copy of the decision to the applicant, to the planning authority and to any person who made submissions. The specified matters to be included in the notification have been expanded under arts 219 and 220 of the Regulations. Article 219 provides that any notice of a decision made by the Board in respect of an application for permission shall state that in making a decision, the Board has had regard to any submissions or observations received in accordance with the Act or Regulations. Also art.220 provides that the notice shall include:
1. the reference number of the application;
2. the development to which the decision relates;
3. the nature of the decision;
4. the date of the decision;
5. the main reasons and considerations on which the decision is based; and
6. any conditions attached to a decision, including conditions relating to community gain and the main reasons for the imposition of any such conditions.

Unlike in the case of a general appeal or referral to the Board, there is specific requirement under subs.(2)(c) to indicate the costs to be payable by the applicant. This is a novel provision and will apply irrespective of the outcome of the application, whether it is granted with or without modification or refused. The section does not state any standard according to which the Board should exercise its discretion in relation to costs. However, it is clear that the Board should act in a judicial and reasonable manner in the exercise of this power. It appears that in an appropriate case, the Board could consider that no sum is to be paid to the Board or to other parties. Nevertheless the policy underlying the provision appears to envisage that in most cases the reasonable costs of the Board will be paid. The Board would appear to retain a discretion in terms of awarding costs to the planning authority and a contribution to the costs of other parties. The express reference to a "contribution" to the costs of other persons, appears to envisage that the full costs of such other persons may not be required to be paid. Other person can potentially include third parties such as members of the public who participated in the process. In the case of both the Board itself and the planning authority, the costs should be "reasonable" costs, although it is for the Board itself to assess what is reasonable in this context. Insofar as the Board assesses it own cost this offends the general principle that no person should be judge of its own cause. The costs to the Board do not include the fees payable to the Board for lodging the application, which is a fee set out under s.144. This costs provision differs from the general power of the Board to award costs and expenses under s.145, under which the planning authority may be directed to pay costs or the appellant may be directed to pay costs where certain specified circumstances exist, such as where the appeal is not successful in substance or was taken for the purposes of delay, etc. There is a distinction between the notification of the decision to grant permission and the actual grant of permission, which must follow "as soon as may be" after the decision to grant. There is no guidance as to what is meant by this phrase, although it would appear to be analogous to "as soon as practicable". Subsection (3) makes the actual grant of permission conditional upon the applicant paying the costs as specified in the notice of the decision. The permission therefore cannot be implemented until the costs are paid. If a party attempts to implement such permission prior to paying the costs, the development would constitute unauthorised development. Where the costs are not paid, all parties to whom such costs are owed can sue for recovery of the sum as a contract debt.

Subsection (6) makes clear that the mere grant of permission does not absolve the applicant from complying with any other legal requirements such as property rights or licensing requirements, etc. in order to carry out the development. This is also similarly reflected in s.34(13). Planning permission is permissive in nature; it does not grant an absolute right to carry out the development. Other permissions or rights may need to be obtained before the development can be implemented. In *Convery v Dublin City Council* [1996] 3 I.R. 161, Keane J. said the planning authority "cannot be said to have authorised the developer by the grant of a permission to commit an act which would be otherwise unlawful, whether because it interfered, for example, with the right to light of other property owners or created an unacceptable hazard for such persons such as the plaintiff in *Weir v Dun Laoghaire Corporation* [1983] I.R. 242" (in *Weir* a lay-by constructed was two inches lower than the surface of a road). See also *Houlihan v An Bord Pleanála*, unreported, High Court, Murphy J., October 4, 1993, where Murphy J. said planning permission does not "…grant or confer on the applicant … any property rights or dispense him from the necessity of obtaining whatever way-leaves, permissions or licences as may be required under other legislation to enable the development to be completed". In *Re Tivoli Cinema Ltd in the matter of Licensing Acts*, unreported, High Court, Lynch J., January 24, 1994, Lynch J. said "the planning code and licensing code are separate and distinct"; see also *Keane v An Bord Pleanála* [1998] 2 I.L.R.M. 241, where a licence was required for a radio mast. In *Pioneer Aggregates v Secretary of State* [1984] 2 All E.R. 358, Scarman L.J. said a planning permission is "a permission that certain rights of ownership be exercised"; see also *Howard v Commissioner of Public Works* [1994] 3 I.R. 394; *Cablelink v An Bord Pleanála* [1999] 1 I.R. 596 ("a condition providing that no development should take place until a licence had been acquired would have added nothing to the planning permission", per Carroll J.); *Carty v Dublin County Council*, unreported, High Court, Barrington J., March 6, 1984; and *Re Commonage at Glennamaddoo* [1992] 1 I.R. 297. However, in *State (Boyd) v Cork County Council*, unreported, High Court, Murphy J., February 18, 1983, Murphy J. suggested that damages in tort to a neighbour may be a planning consideration.

[Regulations

1–56   **37I.—(1)** The Minister may make regulations to provide for such matters of procedure and administration as appear to the Minister to be necessary or expedient in respect of—

    (a) consultations under *section 37B,*

    (b) the giving of an opinion under *section 37D,*

(c) applications for permission under *section 37E,* and

(d) decisions under *section 37G.*

(2) Without prejudice to the generality of *subsection (1),* regulations under this section may—

(a) make provision for matters of procedure in relation to the making of an application under *section 37E,* including the giving of public notice and the making of applications in electronic form, and

(b) make provision for matters of procedure relating to the making of observations by the Environmental Protection Agency under *section 37F(5)* and matters connected therewith.]

AMENDMENT HISTORY

Section 37I inserted by s.3 of the Planning and Development (Strategic Infrastructure) Act 2006 (No. 27 of 2006).

NOTE

This section is an enabling provision, which allows the Minister to make regulations in relation to "matters of procedure and administration" in respect of certain specified matters. In this respect the Minister has issued the 2006 Regulations, with Pt 18 dealing with strategic infrastructure applications. The regulations must relate to matters of procedure and administration, otherwise they will be ultra vires. The specified matters relate to the pre-application consultations with the Board under s.37B, the opinion of the Board on matters to be included in an EIS under s.37D and decisions on the application under s.37G. Subsection (3) relates to more specific matters, which include lodging the application electronically. Article 214(2) provides that where the Board so consents or specifies, any or all of the copies or other information to be specified in an application shall be given in electronic form.

[Objective of the Board in relation to applications under section 37E

37J.—**(1)** It shall be the duty of the Board, having regard to the special **1–57** importance of applications relating to development that may fall within *section 37A(2),* to ensure that—

(a) consultations held on foot of a request under *section 37B* are completed, and

(b) a decision under *section 37G* on an application made under *section 37E* is made, as expeditiously as is consistent with proper planning and sustainable development and, for that purpose, to take all such steps as are open to it to ensure that, in so far as is practicable, there are no avoidable delays at any stage in the holding of those consultations or the making of that decision.

(2) Without prejudice to the generality of *subsection (1)* and subject to *subsections (3) to (6),* it shall be the objective of the Board to ensure that a decision under *section 37G* on an application made under *section 37E* is made—

(a) within a period of 18 weeks beginning on the last day for making submissions or observations in accordance with the notice referred to in *section 37E(3)(a),* or

(b) within such other period as the Minister may prescribe either generally or in respect of a particular class or classes of matter.

(3) Where it appears to the Board that it would not be possible or appropriate, because of the particular circumstances of the matter with which the Board is concerned, to determine the matter within the period referred to in *paragraph (a) or (b) of subsection (2)* as the case may be, the Board shall, by notice in writing served on the applicant for permission, any planning authority involved and any other person who submitted submissions or observations in relation to the matter before the expiration of that period, inform the authority and those persons of the reasons why it would not be possible or appropriate to determine the matter within that period and shall specify the date before which the Board intends that the matter shall be determined.

(4) Where a notice has been served under *subsection (3),* the Board shall take all such steps as are open to it to ensure that the matter is determined before the date specified in the notice.

(5) The Minister may by regulations vary the period referred to in *subsection (2)(a)* either generally or in respect of a particular class or classes of applications referred to in *section 37E,* where it appears to him or her to be necessary, by virtue of exceptional circumstances, to do so and, for so long as the regulations are in force, this section shall be construed and have effect in accordance therewith.

(6) Where the Minister considers it to be necessary or expedient that a certain class or classes of application under *section 37E* that are of special strategic, economic or social importance to the State be determined as expeditiously as is consistent with proper planning and sustainable development, he or she may give a direction to the Board that priority be given to the determination of applications of the class or classes concerned, and the Board shall comply with such a direction.

(7) The Board shall include in each report made under *section 118* a statement of the number of matters which the Board has determined within a period referred to in *paragraph (a) or (b) of subsection (2)* and such other information as to the time taken to determine such matters as the Minister may direct.]

Amendment history

Section 37J inserted by s.3 of the Planning and Development (Strategic Infrastructure) Act 2006 (No. 27 of 2006).

Note

This section imposes a general duty on the Board to deal with the application as expeditiously as possible. The section is however aspirational as there are no strict consequences for the Board such as a default approval being granted for failing to meet the time limits. The general duty is also heavily qualified by the phrases "as is consistent with proper planning and sustainable development" and "to ensure that, in so far as is practicable". Clearly, the Board is in best position to decide what is consistent with proper planning and sustainable development and what is practicable. Equally, the specified period of 18 weeks to decide the application is expressed to be an "objective" and is thus not a strict requirement. Thus while the Board may be criticized for failing to discharge its duty, this will not give rise to any rights in the applicant except where the delay was exceptional. Nevertheless, where the Board is unable to meet the 18-week objective it must serve a notice on the applicant specifying a date before which it intends to make its decision. This general duty of the Board to act expeditiously is also contained in s.126 in respect of appeals and referrals and is expressed in similar terms. The Minister may make regulations varying the 18-week period in respect of certain classes of development due to exceptional circumstances. The period may potentially be longer or shorter than the 18-week period. The Minister may also direct that the Board give priority to certain classes of development, although the power to make directions requires the decision to be made within a specified period. As under s.126(6), the Board must include in its Annual Report the time taken to determine such applications.

[Nuclear installations: no development in respect of them authorised

37K.—Nothing in this Act shall be construed as enabling the authorisation 1–58 of development consisting of an installation for the generation of electricity by nuclear fission.]

AMENDMENT HISTORY

Section 37K inserted by s.3 of the Planning and Development (Strategic Infrastructure) Act 2006 (No. 27 of 2006).

NOTE

This section provides that the Act cannot be implied to potentially authorise a development for generating electricity by nuclear fission.

Availability of documents relating to planning applications

38.—**(1)** Where a planning authority gives its decision in respect of a 1–59 planning application the following documents shall be made available within 3 working days for inspection and purchase by members of the public during office hours at the offices of the authority:

    (a) a copy of the planning application and of any particulars, evidence, environmental impact statement, other written study or further information received or obtained by the authority from the applicant in accordance with regulations under this *Act*;

    (b) a copy of any submissions or observations in relation to the planning application which have been received by the authority;

    (c) a copy of any report prepared by or for the authority in relation to the planning application;

    (d) a copy of the decision of the authority in respect of the planning application and a copy of the notification of the decision given to the applicant; and

    (e) a copy of any documents relating to a contribution or other matter referred to in *section 34(5)*.

(2) Without prejudice to the *Freedom of Information Act, 1997,* and the *European Communities Act, 1972 (Access to Information on the Environment) Regulations, 1998* (S.I. No. 125 of 1998), and any regulations amending those regulations [and the *Data Protection Acts 1988 and 2003*], the documents referred to under *subsection (1)* shall be available for inspection for a period of not less than 7 years after the making of the decision by the authority.

(3) Any document referred to in *paragraphs (a) and (b) of subsection (1)* which is received or obtained by a planning authority shall be made available for inspection and purchase by members of the public at the office hours of the authority from as soon as may be after receipt of the document until a decision is made on the application.

(4) Copies of documents under this *section* shall be available for purchase on payment of a specified fee not exceeding the reasonable cost of making such a copy.

(5) At the end of the period for the availability of documents referred to in *subsection (2)*, a planning authority shall retain at least one original copy of each of those documents in a local archive in accordance with *section 65 of the Local Government Act, 1994.*

(6) The Minister may prescribe additional requirements in relation to the availability for inspection by members of the public of documents relating to planning applications.

(7) This *section* shall apply in respect of any application made to a planning authority after the commencement of this *section.*

AMENDMENT HISTORY

Subsection (2) amended by s.11 of the Planning and Development (Strategic Infrastructure) Act 2006 (No. 27 of 2006).

NOTE

This section allows for a more extensive category of documents to be made available and for a longer period than under ss.5 and 6 of the 1992 Act. There is no obligation on the planning authority to police, superintend or supervise the planning file so as to ensure that all the documents remain intact at all times. See *Cosgrove v An Bord Pleanála*, unreported, High Court, Kelly J., May 27, 2004. The requirement under subs.(1) to make the documents available within three working days is a new addition. The specified list of documents is not entirely comprehensive of all documents relating to the planning application. Thus, an acknowledgement of the planning application issued by the planning authority under art.26 of the 2001 Regulations, which means that the application was not returned as invalid, is not specifically required to be placed on the planning file. Section 247(5) provides that records of pre-planning consultations shall be placed and kept with the documents to which any planning application in respect of the proposed development relates. While it is not expressly stated that such records should be available for inspection by the public, it would appear appropriate that such records are available for inspection. Subsection (2) considerably extends the period for inspection from one month or where an appeal is taken, until the appeal is dealt with, to a general period of not less than seven years after the making of the decision. Section 38(2) was amended by the 2006 Act to provide that the requirement to make planning documents available for inspection is without prejudice to the Data Protection Acts 1988 and 2003. This subsection is also without prejudice to any rights under the Freedom of Information Act 1997 and the European Communities Act 1972 (Access to Information on the Environment) Regulations 1998. The entitlements to documents under a Freedom of Information request may be used to obtain documents not included in the planning file. These laws are in parallel to any rights under subs.(2) and which are not subject to the same seven-year time period. Subsection (5) provides that at the end of the seven-year period, the planning authority is now required to archive the documents. Subsection (1) expands the list of documents which are to be made available including: subs.(1)(b) a copy of the submissions/observations received in relation to the planning application; and subs.(1)(e) documents in relation to contributions or points of detail to be agreed between the applicant and planning authority under s.34(5). Subsection (3) provides that the requirement to make the documents available extends to applications which have yet to be determined. These documents must be available "as soon as possible". Also new is subs.(4), which provides the fee for making available copies should not exceed reasonable costs and provision for the Minister to make prescriptions.

Supplemental provisions as to grant of permission

39.—**(1)** Where permission to develop land or for the retention of **1–60** development is granted under this *Part,* then, except as may be otherwise provided by the permission, the grant of permission shall enure for the benefit of the land and of all persons for the time being interested therein.

(2) Where permission is granted under this *Part* for a structure, the grant of permission may specify the purposes for which the structure may or may not be used, and in case the grant specifies use as a dwelling as a purpose for which the structure may be used, the permission may also be granted subject to a condition specifying that the use as a dwelling shall be restricted to use by persons of a particular class or description and that provision to that effect shall be embodied in an agreement under *section 47.*

(3)

(**a**) Where permission to develop land is granted under this *Part* for a limited period only, nothing in this *Part* shall be construed as requiring permission to be obtained thereunder for the resumption, at the expiration of that period, of the use of the land for the purpose for which it was normally used before the permission was granted.

(**b**) In determining for the purposes of this *subsection* the purposes for which land was normally used before the grant of permission, no account shall be taken of any use of the land begun in contravention of this *Part.*

(4) Notwithstanding anything in this *Part,* permission shall not be required under this *Part,* in the case of land which, on 1 October, 1964, was normally used for one purpose and was also used on occasions, whether at regular intervals or not, for any other purpose, for the use of the land for that other purpose on similar occasions after 1 October, 1964.

NOTE

This section contains miscellaneous provisions relating to planning permission. Subsection (1) provides that planning permission attaches and passes with the land itself rather than with the person who applied for permission. This means that where there is a transfer of ownership of the land, the planning permission attached to the land also transfers to the new owner. In *Mason and McCarthy v KT Sand and Gravel,* unreported, High Court, Smyth J., May 7, 2004, Smyth J. explained this stating that it:

"[M]eans no more or no less than that the planning permission, with all its terms and conditions advantages and disadvantages and limitations, is available to the land and is not personal grant, and unlike a pre 1963 Act user cannot be abandoned. It, in a colloquial sense, becomes 'part of the title' hence the necessity of its objective construction".

See also *Readymix (Éire) Ltd v Dublin County Council,* unreported, Supreme Court, July 30, 1974, where Henchy J. declared:

"Since the permission notified to an applicant and entered in the register is a public document, it must be construed objectively as such, and not in the light of subjective considerations special to the applicant or those responsible for the grant of permission. Because the permission is an appendage to the title to the property, it may possibly not arise for interpretation until the property has passed into the hands of those who have no knowledge of any special circumstances in which it was granted."

This is a key provision from a conveyancing perspective. A successor in title will inherit any planning permissions with the title of the land. The normal life of a planning permission is five years, as set out in s.40. The obligation to comply with conditions of a planning permission may be subsequently passed to another party where the land to which the planning permission attached, is sold: see *Dublin County Council v Brennan and McGowan*, unreported, High Court, O'Hanlon J., June 28, 1985. Letters of compliance with financial contribution conditions of a planning permission have achieved a status of quasi documents of title. See *Glenkerrin v Dun Laoghaire Rathdown County Council*, unreported, High Court, Clarke J., April 26, 2007, where it was held that the issuance of certificates of compliance had become a universal practice such that certificates of compliance have come to be regarded by conveyancers as an essential document to be passed over on the closing of a transaction involving a property to which the regime applies. It was held however that a planning authority could discontinue such practice by giving reasonable notice.

The planning permission may incorporate other documents which may be considered in determining the scope of the permission; see *Readymix (Éire) Ltd v Dublin County Council*, unreported, Supreme Court, July 30, 1974; *Jack Barrett Builders Ltd v Dublin County Council*, unreported, Supreme Court, July 28, 1983 and *Coffey v Hebron Homes Ltd*, unreported, High Court, O'Hanlon J., July 27, 1984. In *XJS Investments Limited v Dun Laoghaire Corporation* [1987] I.L.R.M. 659, McCarthy J. said that planning documents (a) are not Acts of the Oireachtas or subordinate legislation emanating from skilled draftsmen and inviting the accepted canons of construction applicable to such material; and (b) are to be construed in their ordinary meaning as it would be understood by members of the public, without legal training as well as by developers and their agents, unless such documents read as a whole necessarily indicates some other meaning; see also *Ampleforth v Cherating Ltd*, unreported, Supreme Court, April 11, 2003. Where there is some doubt about the meaning of a planning permission, the appropriate procedure is to make a referral under s.5 rather than seeking a declaration from the High Court as to the meaning of a planning permission. See *Grianán An Áileach v Donegal County Council* [2004] 2 I.R. 265.

Two or more planning permissions may be granted in relation to the same land; see *Schwestermann v An Bord Pleanála* [1994] 3 I.R. 437. A planning permission must generally be completed in its entirety except where any particular development is severable from the rest. See *Horne v Freeney*, unreported, High Court, Murphy J., July 7, 1982. Where two or more planning permissions are granted over the same land the developer cannot partially develop the land under each permission, where the permissions are inconsistent. See *Dwyer Nolan Developments v Dublin County Council* [1986] I.R. 130, where Carroll J. noted a developer cannot operate two mutually inconsistent planning permissions at the same time but must opt for one or the other. However, partial development may be authorised development provided it can be regarded as severable. See also *Blainroe Estate Management v Blainroe Limited*, unreported, High Court, Geoghegan J., March 18, 1994. Where parts of land are subject to different planning permission, it will not be appropriate to interpret conditions of one permission as applying to all the land. See *Ryan v Roadstone Dublin Ltd*, unreported, High Court, O'Donovan J., March 6, 2006, where in relation to a quarry it was held that the principal permission and the Western Quarry permission must be construed separately; each being interpreted according to its individual terms.

Subsection (2) allows a condition to specify a purpose for which a structure may or may not be used. There is no requirement for a planning permission to specify a purpose. However, where it does specify such purpose, this purpose will form part of the scope of the permission. The previous legislation provided under s.28(6) of the 1963 Act that where no use is specified "the permission shall be construed as including permission to use the structure for the purpose for which it is designed". In *Readymix (Éire) Ltd v Dublin County Council*, unreported, Supreme Court, July 30, 1974, it was held that "design" was regarded as "intended" and that to determine whether or not a use was indicated it was necessary to look to the relevant documentation which included the planning application, the documents and plans submitted with it, and to the permission itself. In *McMahon v Dublin Corporation* [1996] 3 I.R. 509, it was noted that the approach was to look to the documentation and determine objectively a particular use. Otherwise the permitted use would be any use to which the premises might be capable of being put. On the facts it was held that the purpose for which the plaintiffs' homes had been designed was private residential, whereas the use to which they were currently being put was commercial. As this provision was not re-enacted in the 2000 Act, it is questionable whether the existing case law is of any assistance in determining the permitted use of a structure.

Subsection (2) also provides that where the grant specifies as a dwelling the purpose for which the structure may be used, the condition may limit the persons who are permitted to use the dwelling. An agreement must be entered into, under s.47, between the planning authority and the interested person in relation to such conditions, and entered in the register. The use of a dwelling may be restricted to persons of a "particular class or description". It is not uncommon for permission to impose a condition limiting use or occupancy to a particular class of persons. This may reflect provisions of a development plan, whereby permission for a dwelling may only be granted to persons who fulfil certain criteria such as having lived in the area for a certain number of years, were born in the area, work in the area—whether in agriculture or otherwise—in a Gaeltacht area, or who have the ability to speak Irish. The restrictive condition may therefore be imposed to reflect the requirements of the development plan. The validity of such conditions (and indeed provisions of the development plan) are open to question both in terms of the Irish Constitution, European Union law and the European Convention on Human Rights. Where such conditions are imposed in a rigid manner, the condition may be deemed disprorportionate to the aim sought to be achieved. It may be noted that the Department of the Environment Sustainable Rural Housing guidelines refers to an occupancy condition requiring the dwelling to be first occupied as the place or residence of the applicant, members of the applicant's immediate family or their heirs for a period of seven years, unless consent is granted by the planning authority for occupation by persons who belong to the same category of housing need.

Subsection (3) provides that permission for a limited period will not by itself amount to abandonment of the previous use. The previous use may therefore be resumed at the expiration of the limited planning permission, without the need for another planning application. There will need to be proof, that the land was "normally used" for the previous use. Although there is no definition of "normally used" it would appear that a previous occasional use will not be sufficient. However, where the previous use was an unauthorised use, a person will not however be entitled to resume such use.

Subsection (4) provides there is no requirement to obtain permission for a purpose for which the land was used prior to October 1, 1964. Subsection (4) also recognised that the established use may consist of more than one use; a normal use and also an occasional use or uses. This section recognises a pre-1963 Act use, the 1963 Act having commenced on October 1, 1964. The definitions of unauthorised works, use and structure in s.2, also impliedly exclude pre-1963 Act uses from their scope. Such use must nevertheless not have been abandoned: see *J. Wood & Company v Wicklow County Council* [1995] I.L.R.M. 51. In relation to abandonment see note on s.4. There may be a factual dispute as to the extent of the pre-1964 use. In *Waterford County Council v John A. Wood Ltd* [1999] 1 I.R. 556, in the context of a quarry it was held that exclusion for pre-1964 use does not confer on the particular developer a licence to carry on generally the trade or occupation in which he was engaged but merely permits the continuation to completion of the particular works commenced before the appointed day at an identified location. This involves establishing the facts to ascertain what was or might reasonably have been anticipated at the relevant date as having been involved in the works then taking place. Among the factors Murphy J. mentioned as relevant on the facts included; whether at the appointed day, the operator owned the adjoining land; the position of roadways alongside; and whether limestone deposits were substantial and run onto other lands. In *Kildare County Council v Goode* [1999] 2 I.R. 495 Barron J. said at 505:

> "The activity so found by the learned trial judge to have been subsisting on the appointed day would not have constituted an uncompleted development in the sense contemplated by s. 24(1) of the Act. In order to constitute such an uncompleted development involving an extractive industry, it would have been necessary to have in existence an open pit or quarry of a reasonably defined body of material to be excavated continuously until exhaustion".

Even where there was pre-1963 use, the use may subsequently have intensified so as to amount to a material change of use, which therefore requires planning permission. Intensification has arisen in a series of quarrying cases where it was considered whether the quarrying works were materially different to those being carried out on or before October 1, 1964. See *The State (Stafford and Son) v Roadstone Ltd* [1980] I.L.R.M. 1; *Monaghan County Council v Brogan* [1987] I.R. 333; *Carrick Hall Holdings v Dublin Corporation*

[1983] I.L.R.M. 268; *Dublin County Council v Macken*, unreported, High Court, O'Hanlon J., May 13, 1994; *Paul Lee and John Flynn v Michael O'Riordan*, unreported, High Court, O'Hanlon J., February 10, 1995; *McGrath Limestone Works v Galway County Council* [1989] I.L.R.M. 602; *Dublin County Council v Tallaght Block Co. Ltd* [1982] I.L.R.M. 469; *Cork County Council v Artfert Quarries Ltd*, unreported, High Court, Murphy J., December 2, 1982; *Galway County Council v Lackagh Rock Company* [1985] I.R. 20. In *Paterson v Murphy* [1978] I.L.R.M. 85; *Stafford and Bates v Roadstone Ltd* [1980] I.L.R.M. 1. In *Dublin County Council v Sellwood Quarries* [1981] I.L.R.M. 23, the Court held the works were materially different to the works on October 1, 1964. Among the factors were the changes in the objects of the operations; the use of different production methods involving the increased use of machinery; intensification in scale from intermittent to substantial and increased area activity. See for more detail the note on s.4.

Limit of duration of permission

1–61   **40.**—**(1)** Subject to *subsection (2),* a permission granted under this *Part,* shall on the expiration of the appropriate period (but without prejudice to the validity of anything done pursuant thereto prior to the expiration of that period) cease to have effect as regards—

    (a) in case the development to which the permission relates is not commenced during that period, the entire development, and

    (b) in case the development is commenced during that period, so much of the development as is not completed within that period.

(2)

    (a) *Subsection (1)* shall not apply—

        (i) to any permission for the retention on land of any structure,

        (ii) to any permission granted either for a limited period only or subject to a condition which is of a kind described in *section 34(4)(n),*

        (iii) in the case of a house, shop, office or other building which itself has been completed, in relation to the provision of any structure or works included in the relevant permission and which are either necessary for or ancillary or incidental to the use of the building in accordance with that permission, or

        (iv) in the case of a development comprising a number of buildings of which only some have been completed, in relation to the provision of roads, services and open spaces included in the relevant permission and which are necessary for or ancillary or incidental to the completed buildings.

    (b) *Subsection (1)* shall not affect—

        (i) the continuance of any use, in accordance with a permission, of land,

        (ii) where a development has been completed (whether to an extent described in *paragraph (a)* or otherwise), the obligation of any person to comply with any condition attached to the relevant permission whereby something is required either to be done or not to be done.

(3) In this section and in *section 42*, "the appropriate period" means—

    (a) in case in relation to the permission a period is specified pursuant to *section 41*, that period, and

(b) in any other case, the period of five years beginning on the date of the grant of permission.

NOTE

This section concerns the duration of a planning permission and largely corresponds to s.2 of the 1982 Act. Subsection (3) provides that the basic time limit for permission is five years unless a longer period is specified in s.41. Where a longer period is specified, art.31(h) of the 2001 Regulations requires this to be stated in the notification of the decision to grant planning permission. Subsection (1) provides where the period of planning permission expires, the permission will cease to have effect for all of the development, where none of the development has been commenced or where it has partly been completed, for so much of the uncompleted development. This implies that the completed part of the incomplete development will remain valid. The better view is that a valid planning permission itself cannot be abandoned (as opposed to the use under that permission) and will subsist for the life of the planning permission until it expires, see *Meath County Council v Daly* [1988] I.L.R.M. 274. In *Molloy v Minister for Equality and Law Reform* [2004] 2 I.R. 493, it was held that that a valid planning permission for a specific use of land could not be lost or abandoned where the original planning permission was capable of being implemented, notwithstanding that there had been a material unauthorised change of use in the meantime. Subsection (2)(a) provides that the section does not apply to retention permission, as clearly the development is already completed and its retention is all that is sought. It also does not apply to a temporary permission nor to a permission to which a condition under s.34(4)(n) applies, which concerns conditions for requiring the removal of any structures authorised by the permission, or the discontinuance of any use of the land so authorised, at the expiration of a specified period, and the carrying out of any works required for the re-instatement of land at the expiration of that period. An unlimited period applies under subs.(2)(a)(iii) in relation to any structure or "works" encompassed by the permission and which are necessary, ancillary or incidental to the "use" of any house, shop, office or other building which itself has been completed—the key word being "use" in this context. Similarly, under subs.(2)(a)(iv), an unlimited period applies with respect to "the provision of roads, services or open spaces", though it omits any reference to the use of the building, simply referring to "necessary for or ancillary or incidental to" the completed buildings. The rationale for this exception is not to absolve a developer from the duty to complete infrastructural development or certain commons areas; otherwise such a developer could ignore such developments and thereby profit from his failure to complete the entire the development. Subsection (2)(b) provides that the section does not concern the continuance of use of land nor an obligation of a person to comply with a condition whereby something is required either to be done or not to be done. Certain conditions may require ongoing action and so the time limitations do not apply to compliance with such condition.

Power to vary appropriate period

41.—Without prejudice to the powers conferred on them by this *Part* to grant a permission to develop land for a limited period only, in deciding to grant a permission under [*section 34, 37 or 37G*], a planning authority [or the Board] or the Board, as may be appropriate, may, having regard to the nature and extent of the relevant development and any other material consideration, specify the period, being a period of more than 5 years, during which the permission is to have effect, and in case the planning authority [or the Board] exercises, or refuses to exercise, the power conferred on it by this *section,* the exercise or refusal shall be regarded as forming part of the relevant decision of the authority or the Board under [*section 34, 37 or 37G*].   **1–62**

Amended by s.12 of the Planning and Development (Strategic Infrastructure) Act 2006 (No. 27 of 2006).

Note

This section empowers the planning authority or Board to grant a planning permission for longer than the normal five-year period set out in s.40. In deciding whether to grant such a longer period, the planning authority or Board may have regard to the nature and extent of the relevant development and any other relevant material consideration. The decision as to the length of the permission forms part of the decision whether to grant the permission and is not a separate matter. In considering whether to vary the length of the permission, the planning authority may have "regard to the nature and extent of the relevant development and any other material consideration". In practice, a longer period than five years may be granted in the case of large developments or where subsequent approvals are required. There is no definition of "other material considerations" and it would appear to allow a wide discretion to the planning authority or Board, so long as the consideration is material in planning terms. The section was amended by the 2006 Act to provide that the section also applies to strategic infrastructure permissions granted under s.37G.

Power to extend appropriate period

1–63   **42.—(1)** On application a planning authority shall, as regards a particular permission, extend the appropriate period, by such additional period as the authority considers requisite to enable the development to which the permission relates to be completed, if each of the following requirements is complied with—

(a) the application is in accordance with such regulations under this *Act* as apply to it;

(b) any requirements of, or made under, those regulations are complied with as regards the application;

(c) the authority is satisfied in relation to the permission that—

(i) the development to which the permission relates commenced before the expiration of the appropriate period sought to be extended,

(ii) substantial works were carried out pursuant to the permission during that period, and

(iii) the development will be completed within a reasonable time;

(d) the application is made prior to the end of the appropriate period.

(2) Where—

(a) an application is duly made under this *section* to a planning authority,

(b) any requirements of, or made under, regulations under *section 43* are complied with as regards the application, and

(c) the planning authority does not give notice to the applicant of its decision as regards the application within the period of 8 weeks beginning on—

(i) in case all of the requirements referred to in *paragraph (b)* are complied with on or before the day of receipt by the planning authority of the application, that day, and

(ii) in any other case, the day on which all of those requirements stand complied with, subject to *section 246(3),* a decision by the planning authority to extend, or to further extend, as may be appropriate, the period, which in relation to the relevant permission is the appropriate period, by such additional period as is specified in the application, shall be deemed to have been given by the planning authority on the last day of the 8 week period.

(3)

(a) Where a decision to extend an appropriate period is given under *subsection (1),* or, pursuant to *subsection (2),* such a decision is deemed to have been given, the planning authority shall not further extend the appropriate period, unless each of the following requirements is complied with—

(i) an application in that behalf is made to it in accordance with the regulations under *section 43;*

(ii) any requirements of, or made under, the regulations are complied with as regards the application;

(iii) the authority is satisfied that the relevant development has not been completed due to circumstances beyond the control of the person carrying out the development.

(b) An appropriate period shall be further extended under this *subsection* only for such period as the planning authority considers requisite to enable the relevant development to be completed.

(4) Particulars of any application made to a planning authority under this *section* and of the decision of the planning authority in respect of the application shall be recorded on the relevant entry in the register.

(5) Where a decision to extend, or further to extend, is given under this *section,* or, pursuant to *subsection (2),* such a decision is deemed to have been given, *section 40* shall, in relation to the permission to which the decision relates, be construed and have effect subject to and in accordance with the terms of the decision.

NOTE

This section allows a planning authority to extend the period for permission by whatever period it deems fit to enable the development to be completed. This repeats s.4 of the 1982 Act. Subsection (1) specifies four conditions which must be met. Where all such four conditions are met, the planning authority is obliged to grant an extension of time. It does not have a discretion whether to extend the time, although it does have a discretion in assessing whether the conditions are met (in particular condition (c)) and also as to the appropriate period by which time should be extended. The decision is to be made without any public consultation process or input from the public. See *Coll v Donegal County Council*, unreported, July 5, 2005. However, the onus of proof is on the applicant to prove that the facts come within the conditions for the grant of an extension. In *State (McCoy) v Dun Laoghaire Corporation* [1985] I.L.R.M. 533, Gannon J. said the previous s.4(1) is "expressed in mandatory terms bearing both positive and negative aspects. It confers on the planning authority not merely the power but rather the obligation to extend the duration of a planning permission in relation to uncompleted development upon which a developer has embarked". Consideration of any matters other than the specified conditions is precluded; see *Littondale v Wicklow County Council* [1996] 2 I.L.R.M. The meaning of substantial works may vary with the particular development. See *Frenchurch Properties Limited v*

Wexford County Council [1992] 2 I.R. 268, where Lynch J. said:

"It is not a valid objection that the planning authority holds a view that, in a general sense, 'substantial work' would connote a substantial proportion of the authorised development and perhaps as much as 40% to 50% of that development provided that the planning authority decide each case on its own merits ... It is a matter for the planning authority, *bona fide*, using its own expertise and judgment to decide whether or not substantial works were carried out pursuant to the permission".

The courts have declined to give a rigid meaning to substantial works. See *Garden Village Construction Company Limited v Wicklow County Council* [1994] 1 I.L.R.M. 354, where Geoghegan J. declined to apply some mathematical formula and stated that substantial should be given its ordinary meaning, i.e. the opposite of "insubstantial". It would appear that the appropriate approach is to compare the extent of the works carried out with the entire development for which permission was granted. Thus whether works are "substantial" is to be considered not in vacuo but having regard to the nature and extent of the works permitted under the particular permission which it is sought to extend. See *Littondale v Wicklow County Council* [1996] 2 I.L.R.M. 519. However, in respect of larger developments, this comparative approach will have less relevance. Thus in *Frenchurch Properties Limited v Wexford County Council* [1992] 2 I.R. 268, Lynch J. noted that; "…in very large development 'substantial works' might have been carried out even though a much lesser proportion than 40% to 50% of the development might have been completed before the expiration of the planning permission". While the assessment of whether substantial works have been carried out is a planning judgment within the discretion of the planning authority, if the planning autohority misinterprets the concept of "substantial works" such as by excluding considerations of matters which ought to have been included, then this would amount to an error of law reviewable by the courts under a more exacting standard of review. The applicant must demonstrate substantial "works" have been carried out. It is not therefore sufficient for the applicant to state how much money he has expended in relation to the development, without particularising the precise works which have been carried out. Expenditure is only relevant insofar as it reflects works (as defined in s.2) which have been carried out.

The substantial works must also be "pursuant to the permission". See *State (McCoy) v Dun Laoghaire Corporation* [1985] I.L.R.M. 533. Thus, in *Garden Village Construction Company Limited v Wicklow County Council* [1994] 1 I.L.R.M. 354, the Supreme Court rejected that infrastructure works on adjacent sites which benefited the site under the permission could be considered to be pursuant to the permission. It was said that development which took place other than on the relevant plot, the subject of the permission, could not be said to have been carried out "pursuant to" it and whether such development benefited the relevant plot is immaterial. However, this is distinguishable from floor slabs and steel works specifically designed for the development. The mere fact the material was manufactured off-site did not exclude the works as being pursuant to the permission. The planning authority cannot take into account the fact that the development is not being carried out in compliance with the planning permission. See *McDowell v Roscommon County Council*, unreported, High Court, Finnegan P., December 21, 2004, where it was stated that the planning authority must consider whether the development relates to the permission and not whether it is in full compliance with the same. It was held that it was not appropriate to use the determination of an application for extension as a quasi-enforcement measure to ensure compliance with the Planning Code. However, the test stated being that the development "relates" to the permission would appear to be more liberal than the existing case law and not strictly in accordance with the requirement that work must be "pursuant" to the permission. However, it may be a question of degree depending on the extent of the unauthorised development as to whether the works could be deemed to be "pursuant" to the permission.

Exempted development works carried out under Class 16 or 17 of Pt 11 of Sch.2 to the 2001 Regulations, would appear to be made "pursuant to the permission". Both these classes exempt structures, works, plant or machinery needed temporarily in connection with that development. However, while such works may be deemed to made be "pursuant to the permission", the status of the works as being exempted would appear to be relevant to the "substantiality" of such works. It would also appear that where works such as land remediation is carried out pursuant to a waste licence even in preparation for the development, then this could not be deemed to be made pursuant to the permission.

There is no precise guidance as to the requirement that the development must be completed within a reasonable time. In making an application, the applicant is required under art.42(k) of the 2001 Regulations to state the date on which the development is expected to be completed. This will therefore offer some guidance to the planning authority in assessing whether the development can be completed within a reasonable time. The scale, nature and conduct of the applicant would appear to be relevant in assessing this factor. In *Coll v Donegal County Council*, unreported, High Court, Peart J., July 7, 2005, where a condition required road realignment which would involve extinguishment of a public right of way before development commenced but a motion had refused to extinguish such right of way, Peart J. considered the council could revisit a motion to extinguish the right of way and that in those circumstances it could reasonably have formed the view that the development would be completed in a reasonable of time.

A planning authority is not generally obliged to enter into dialogue with the applicant before deciding on the application for an extension of the life of the planning permission. However, where a specific matter upon which the applicants relied on to a significant extent is specifically disallowed by the planning authority, fair procedures may require communication of this in advance of the determination. See *Frenchurch Properties v Wexford County Council* [1992] 2 I.R. 268. However, it appears this will only arise in exceptional circumstances. In *Littondale v Wicklow County Council* [1996] 2 I.L.R.M. 519 a claim that fair procedures required advanced dialogue on an issue was rejected where it was held that it was patently obvious to the applicant, having regard to the decision of the planning authority on foot of an earlier application for an extension, that the issue had to be addressed in its submissions to the planning authority.

Article 41 of the 2001 Regulations provides that the application for extension must be made not earlier than one year prior to the expiry of the period. Under subs.(2), where there is an application to extend, and the planning authority fails to respond within eight weeks, a default extension will be granted. As with default planning permission under s.34(8)(f), the application must have been validly made and the Regulations complied with. There must not have been a change in the development plan so that the development would be a material contravention of the development plan. Strict compliance is not necessary so long as there is substantial compliance. Unlike default permission where the decision must be made within the period, default extension of time applies where the applicant was not notified within the period, even if the decision was made within the period. Where the planning authority notifies the applicant by registered post, the applicant will not be notified until he actually receives such notice in the post; see *Flynn v Dublin Corporation*, unreported, High Court, Kelly J., December 19, 1996; *Flynn v Wicklow County Council*, unreported, High Court, Flood J., December 1, 1995 and *Freeney v Bray UDC* [1982] I.L.R.M. 29.

Subsection (3) provides that a second extension period can only be granted where three conditions are met, which include that the development has not been completed "due to circumstances beyond the control" of the developer, in contrast to the previous provisions; see *Flynn v Dublin Corporation*, unreported, High Court, Kelly J., December 19, 1996, where there were four extensions of time. In applying for an subsequent extension it would not appear necessary to satisfy the initial conditions for an extension again as these were already satisfied when the first extension was granted. There is no definition of "circumstances beyond the control" but it appear to depend on the particular facts of any application. The planning authority must only grant the extension for such period which is necessary for its completion. Subsection (4) provides that when an extension is granted, the details must be entered onto the Planning Register. Subsection (5) provides that where an extension is given, s.40 concerning the cessation of the permission and duration of permission will be modified accordingly. No provision is made for third-party participation nor for an appeal to An Bord Pleanála. Fair procedures may require a planning authority to alert an applicant to its views that a significant matter upon which the applicant relies is invalid to allow the applicant to persuade the planning authority otherwise.

Regulations regarding sections 40, 41 and 42

1–64   **43.**—**(1)** The Minister may make regulations providing for any matter of procedure in relation to applications under *section 42* and making such incidental, consequential or supplementary provision as may appear to him or her to be necessary or proper to give full effect to any of the provisions of *section 40, 41 or 42*.

(2) Without prejudice to the generality of *subsection (1)*, regulations under this *section* may—

> **(a)** specify the time at which applications under *section 42* may be made, the manner in which those applications shall be made and the particulars they shall contain,
>
> **(b)** require applicants to furnish to the planning authority any specified information with respect to their applications (including any information regarding any estate or interest in or right over land),
>
> **(c)** require applicants to submit to a planning authority any further information relevant to their applications (including any information as to any such estate, interest or right),
>
> **(d)** require the production of any evidence to verify any particulars or information given by any applicant, and
>
> **(e)** require the notification (in a prescribed manner) by planning authorities of decisions on applications.

NOTE

This section allows for the making of Regulations in relation to the revocation of a planning permission. This is contained in Ch.3 of the 2001 Regulations. Article 41 provides that the application for extension of time shall not be made earlier than one year before the expiration of the period sought to be extended. Article 42 sets out the content of the application to extend, while art.43 sets out the content of an application to further extend the appropriate period. An application to extend the life of the permission shall be accompanied by the prescribed fee as prescribed by art.170 and include:

> the name and address, and telephone number and e-mail address, if any, of the applicant and of the person, if any, acting on behalf of the applicant;
> 1. the address to which any correspondence relating to the application should be sent;
> 2. the location, townland or postal address of the land or structure concerned, as may be appropriate;
> 3. the legal interest in the land or structure held by the applicant;
> 4. the development to which the permission relates;
> 5. the date of the permission and its reference number in the register;
> 6. the date on which the permission will cease to have effect;
> 7. the date of commencement of the development to which the permission relates;
> 8. particulars of the substantial works carried out or which will be carried out pursuant to the permission before the expiration of the appropriate period;
> 9. the additional period by which the permission is sought to be extended; and
> 10. the date on which the development is expected to be completed.

Article 43 provides that an application under s.42 of the 2000 Act to extend further the appropriate period as regards a particular permission shall be made in writing and shall contain the particulars referred to at paragraphs (a) to (h) inclusive of art.42 and the following additional particulars:

> 1. particulars of the works (if any) carried out pursuant to the permission since the permission was extended or further extended;

2. the period by which the permission is sought to be extended further,;
3. the date on which the development is expected to be completed; and
4. the circumstances beyond the control of the person carrying out the development due to which the development has not been completed.

Article 44 provides that upon receipt of the application, the planning authority must stamp the documents and consider whether the application complies with the content requirements. Where it does comply, the planning authority will send an acknowledgment, or where it considers it does not comply, the planning authority will by notice in writing require the applicant to furnish further particulars. Article 45 states that the planning authority may request the applicant to furnish further information or produce evidence to verify the particulars. The determination of whether it is appropriate for the Council to seek further information is a matter for discretion of the planning authority and is a matter of planning judgment. See *Kinsella v Dundalk UDC*, unreported, High Court, Kelly J., December 3, 2004. Article 46 sets out the content of a decision on an application to extend, while art.47 provides that the weekly list shall include applications to extend or to extend further.

Revocation or modification of permission

44.—(1) If the planning authority considers that it is expedient that any permission to develop land granted under this *Part* should be revoked or modified, it may serve a notice in accordance with *subsection (3)* on the applicant and on any other person who, in its opinion, will be materially affected by the revocation or modification.   **1–65**

(2) A planning authority shall neither revoke nor modify a permission under this *section* unless the development to which the permission relates no longer conforms with the provisions of the development plan.

(3) The notice referred to in *subsection (1)* shall—

    (a) refer to the permission concerned,

    (b) specify the provisions of the development plan to which the permission no longer conforms, and

    (c) invite the person or persons served with the notice to make written submissions or observations to the planning authority within the period specified in the notice (being not less than 4 weeks from the service of the notice) concerning the proposed revocation or modification.

(4) A planning authority may decide to revoke or modify a permission and, when making its decision, shall have regard to any submissions or observations made under *subsection (3)(c)*.

(5) Where a planning authority decides to revoke or modify a permission under *subsection (4),* it shall specify in the decision the provisions of the development plan to which the permission no longer conforms, and the main reasons and considerations on which the decision is based.

(6) A person served with a notice under *subsection (1)* may, at any time within 4 weeks of the date of the decision, appeal to the Board against the decision.

(7) Where an appeal is brought under this *section* against a decision, the Board may confirm the decision with or without modifications, or annul the decision, and it shall specify the main reasons and considerations for its decision.

(8) The power conferred by this *section* to revoke or modify permission to develop land may be exercised—

(a) where the permission relates to the carrying out of works, at any time before those works have been commenced or, in the case of works which have been commenced and which, consequent on the making of a variation in the development plan, will contravene the plan, at any time before those works have been completed,

(b) where the permission relates to a change of the use of any land, at any time before the change has taken place,

but the revocation or modification of permission for the carrying out of works shall not affect so much of the works as have been previously carried out.

(9) A planning authority may at any time, for stated reasons, by notice in writing withdraw a notice served under this *section.*

(10) Particulars of a decision made under this *section* shall be entered in the register.

(11) The revocation or modification under this *section* of a permission shall be a reserved function.

NOTE

This section affords the planning authority a discretion to revoke or modify a planning permission where it no longer conforms with the provisions of a development plan. It deals with a situation where a development which was in accordance with the development plan when permission was granted is no longer in accordance with the plan due to changes in the development plan. The planning authority can only revoke or modify a permission where it no longer conforms with the development plan. Although "no longer conforms" is not defined, it would appear to be analogous to a material contravention of the new development plan. However, where there is a change in the development plan there is no obligation on the planning authority to revoke a planning permission. Equally, it would appear the mere fact that there has been a relevant change in the development plan does not automatically mean that there is a good reason to modify or revoke the permission. See *Hughes v An Bord Pleanála*, unreported, High Court, Geoghegan J., July 30, 1999, where it was said that the mere fact that a condition precedent to the exercise of the power to revoke exists does not necessarily mean that there are in fact good reasons for revoking. This provision is more restrictive than under the previous provision, in s.30 of the 1963 Act, whereby a planning authority could not revoke or modify a permission unless there had been a change of circumstances relating to the proper planning and development of the area concerned. The decision to revoke solely operates on the permission granted and will not affect existing development already carried out pursuant to such permission so as to require the demolishing or undoing of work done. This is clear from subs.(8), which confines the exercise of the power of revocation to the two circumstances set out in that subsection. With respect to the carrying out of works, the power to revoke a permission exists before works under such permissions have commenced or where such works have commenced, the decision to revoke must take place before the works are completed. However, this subsection must be read subject to the presumption against restrospective interference with vested rights. In *Coras Iompair Éireann v An Bord Pleanála*, unreported, High Court, Clarke J., June 19, 2008, it was held that revoking the exempted development character of works (by means of a proposal to add a structure to the register of protected structure) could not prevent the completion of works, where such works were inextricably connected with the works already carried out. While the presumption against retrospective effect whereby laws are presumed not to interfere with or impair vested rights can be rebutted, it is submitted that the language of s.8(a) could not be interpreted as revoking permission to finish works under a permission where such works are inextricably connected with works already carried out pursuant to the permission. Where such works are severable from the works already carried out, then the revocation may have such effect. See also *Dublin County Council v Grealy* [1990] 1 I.R. 77. In the case of a change of use of land, the decision to revoke, must take place before the change of use is complete. It will be a question of fact whether works (or uses) have been carried out which relate to the development. In *Electricity Supply Board v Cork County Council*, unreported, High Court, Finnegan J., June 28, 2000, it was held that steel as ordered and manufactured was site specific in relation to this development in so far as the base sections of masts required for the development was concerned.

Under the previous legislation (s.30(6) of the 1963 Act, as amended), the power to revoke was a reserved function. In *Hughes v An Bord Pleanála*, unreported, High Court, Geoghegan J., July 30, 1999, Geoghegan J. noted that a revocation required two essential steps; a decision to be taken on a vote by the councillors that it is expedient that the particular permission should be revoked, and the service of a notice of revocation on the owner and occupier of the land affected and on any other person, who in the opinion of the Council would be affected by the revocation. The power to revoke is no longer a reserved function but a more elaborate procedure of notice and inviting submissions must be followed. Before taking a decision to revoke the planning authority must serve a notice set out in subs.(3) on the applicant to whom permission for the development was granted and also on any other person materially affected. The content of the notice is set out in subs.(3) and the notice must state that submissions can made by the applicant or other relevant person within a period of four weeks from the service of the notice. This change was inserted as a result of the decision in *Eircell v Leitrim County Council* [2000] 1 I.R. 479, where it was held that in revoking the permission, the council was obliged to act judicially, by giving prior notification of an intention to revoke. As the revocation or modification affects vested rights, a person affected by the proposed decision, may have further entitlements under fair procedures such as having sight of background documents. In *Electricity Supply Board v Cork County Council*, unreported, High Court, Finnegan J., June 28, 2000, it was held the applicant was entitled to have either sight of the material circulated at the councillers meeting where the revocation was considered or at the very least a sufficiently detailed statement of the contents thereof to enable it to make submissions in relation thereto and which submissions ought to have been considered by the planning authority.

Subsection (4) provides that in making a decision whether to revoke or modify the permission, the planning authority must consider such submissions. Also under subs.(5), its decision must specify the provision of the development plan which the development no longer complies with and also the reasons and considerations upon which the decision is based. These are two separate requirements and so it would not be sufficient reasons and considerations to merely state that the development no longer complies with a provision of the development plan. See *Hughes v An Bord Pleanála*, unreported, High Court, Geoghegan J., July 30, 1999. Subsection (6) only enables a person who was served with the notice to appeal the decision to revoke to An Bord Pleanála. This appeal must be taken within four weeks of the date of when the actual decision was made. Subsection (9) allows for the withdrawal of the revocation notice. It does not allow the withdrawal of the decision to revoke, which would revive the planning permission. Subsection (10) requires the decision to revoke to be entered into the register. Subsection (11) states that the decision to revoke is a reserved function and so must be performed by the elected members of the council rather than the permanent executive council.

Acquisition of land for open spaces

45.—(1) Where—   1–66
    (a) development is being or has been carried out pursuant to a permission under *section 34,*
    (b)
        (i) a condition requiring the provision or maintenance of land as open space, being open space to which this *section* applies, was attached to the permission, or
        (ii) it was either explicit or implicit in the application for the permission that land would be provided or maintained as such open space,

(c) the planning authority has served on the owner of the land a written request that, within a period specified in the request (being a period of not less than 8 weeks commencing on the date of the request), he or she will provide, level, plant or otherwise adapt or maintain the land in a manner so specified, being a manner which in its opinion would make it suitable for the purpose for which the open space was to be provided, and

(d) the owner fails to comply or to secure compliance with the request within the period so specified,

the planning authority may, if it thinks fit, publish in a newspaper circulating in the district a notice (an "acquisition notice") of its intention to acquire the land by order under this *section* and the acquisition notice shall specify a period (being a period of not less than 4 weeks commencing on the date on which the notice is published) within which an appeal may be made under this *section*.

(2) Where a planning authority publishes an acquisition notice, it shall serve a copy of the notice on the owner of the land to which the notice relates not later than 10 days after the date of the publication.

(3) Any person having an interest in the land to which an acquisition notice relates may within the period specified in the notice appeal to the Board.

(4) Where an appeal is brought under this *section* the Board may—

(a) annul the acquisition notice to which the appeal relates, or

(b) confirm the acquisition notice, with or without modification, in respect of all or such part of the relevant land as the Board considers reasonable.

(5) If a planning authority publishes an acquisition notice and either—

(a) the period for appealing against the notice has expired and no appeal has been taken, or

(b) an appeal has been taken against the notice and the appeal has been withdrawn or the notice has been confirmed whether unconditionally or subject to modifications,

the planning authority may make an order in the prescribed form which order shall be expressed and shall operate to vest the land to which the acquisition notice, or, where appropriate, the acquisition notice as confirmed, relates in the planning authority on a specified date for all the estate, term or interest for which immediately before the date of the order the land was held by the owner together with all rights and liabilities which, immediately before that date, were enjoyed or incurred in connection therewith by the owner together with an obligation to comply with the request made under *subsection (1)(c)*.

(6) Where a planning authority has acquired by an order under this *section* land which is subject, either alone or in conjunction with other land, to a purchase annuity, payment in lieu of rent, or other annual sum (not being merely a rent under a contract of tenancy) payable to the Minister for Agriculture, Food and Rural Development or to the Commissioners, the authority shall become and be liable, as from the date on which the land is vested in them by the vesting order, for the payment to the Minister or to the Commissioners, as the case may be, of the annual sum or such portion thereof as shall be apportioned by that Minister or by the Commissioners, on the land as if the land had been transferred to the authority by the owner thereof on that date.

(7) When a planning authority makes an order under this *section* in relation to any land, it shall send the order to the registering authority under the *Registration of Title Act, 1964,* and thereupon the registering authority shall cause the planning authority to be registered as owner of the land in accordance with the order.

(8) Where a claim is made for compensation in respect of land to which an order under this *section* relates, the claim shall, in default of agreement, be determined by arbitration under the *Acquisition of Land (Assessment of Compensation) Act, 1919,* in the like manner in all respects as if such claim arose in relation to the compulsory acquisition of land, but subject to the proviso that the arbitrator shall have jurisdiction to make a nil award and to the following provisions:

    (a) the arbitrator shall make a nil award, unless it is shown by or on behalf of the owner that an amount equal to the value of the land to which the relevant permission under *section 34* relates, being that value at the time when the application for the permission was made, as a result of the development has not been recovered and as a further such result will not in the future be recoverable by disposing of the land which is land to which the permission relates and which is not land to which the order relates, and

    (b) in the assessment of the value of the land to which the order relates, no regard shall be had to its value for use other than as open space and a deduction shall be made in respect of the cost of carrying out such works as may be necessary to comply with the request made pursuant to *subsection (1)(c).*

(9) A planning authority shall enter in the register—

    (a) particulars of any acquisition notice published by it,

    (b) the date and effect of any decision on appeal in relation to any such notice, and

    (c) particulars of any order made under this *section,*

and every entry shall be made within the period of 7 days commencing on the day of publication, receipt of notification of the decision or the making of the order, as may be appropriate.

(10) This *section* applies to any form of open space (whether referred to as open space or by any other description in the relevant application for a permission or in a condition attached to the relevant permission), being land which is not described in the application or condition either as private open space or in terms indicating that it is not intended that members of the public are to have resort thereto without restriction.

NOTE

This section allows a planning authority to acquire land where a developer failed to provide open space as required under a planning permission. Open spaces may be required under permission by virtue of an express condition or where the planning application expressly or impliedly indicates land is to be maintained as open space. This could arise by implication where areas on maps furnished with the planning application were marked open space. While there is no strict definition of "open space", subs.(10) provides that it is not necessary that the description open space is used in the condition or planning application, so long as it is not described as private open space or indicated that it is not intended that the public have free access. It would therefore appear that an essential element of open space is that it is not private and members of the public have unrestricted access. Difficulties in interpretation of the meaning of open space can sometimes arise where a residential development is enclosed with restricted access through gates. In such case it is unclear whether open space means areas where all residents have free access or where the general public can have access. Planning authorities should therefore ensure that conditions clearly define what is meant by open space as to whether it is open to any member of the public or simply other residents. In some cases, it may be advisable for a condition to require the developer to enter an agreement with the planning authority under s.47 ensuring access for members of the public or making a dedication of the open space areas for public use. It may be noted that s.20 of the Open Spaces Act 1906 defines open space as "any land, whether inclosed or not, on which there are no buildings or of which not more than one-twentieth part is covered with buildings, and the whole or the remainder of which is laid out as a garden or is used for purposes of recreation, or lies waste and unoccupied". The development plans of planning authorities often require that a certain percentage of estates or large residential developments is allocated to open space. The plans for such development will therefore typically include an area marked as open space. It may be noted that this provision was first introduced under s.25 of the 1976 Act, and cannot apply to development carried out prior to the entry into force of that Act. See *Dublin County Council v Grealy* [1990] 1 I.R. 77.

Where the provision of open space is a condition of or required by the planning permission, the planning authority can take enforcement action under Pt VIII to ensure compliance. However, this section allows an alternative means of enforcing compliance by allowing the planning authority to acquire the land. The planning authority may serve an acquisition notice and follow the procedure set out in the section. The land which the planning authority may seek to acquire is not the entire development but the land which is necessary to fulfil the requirement to provide or maintain open space. The planning authority cannot exceed the amount of land which is necessary for these purposes. Subsection (10) states that open space constitutes land which is open to the public without restriction and applies to all forms of open space, whether or not so described in the permission, so long as it is not described as private open space or in a manner indicating members of the public do not have unrestricted access.

Before serving an acquisition notice the planning authority must have served on the owner a written request requiring the owner within a period of not less than eight weeks to provide, level, plant or otherwise adapt or maintain the land in a manner suitable for open space. Where the owner has failed to comply with such request, the planning authority may publish the acquisition notice in a local newspaper stating its intention to acquire the land under this section and specifying a period of not less than four weeks within which it may be appealed to An Bord Pleanála. Subsection (2) provides that the planning authority must serve a copy of the notice on the owner within 10 days of its publication. Subsection (3) provides that any person who has an interest in the land may appeal to An Bord Pleanála within the specified period. The right to appeal is therefore not confined to the owner of the land nor to persons on whom the written request or notice was served. Under subs.(4), the Board may annul or confirm the notice, with or without modification. It would seem to be a matter for the Board to decide how to conduct the appeal. Subsection (5) declares the planning authority can make an order vesting the land in the planning authority after either the notice has been confirmed, the appeal has been withdrawn, or where no appeal was made within the specified period. Once the planning authority makes the vesting order, it will acquire the interest of the previous owner. The time-scale of steps therefore involved may be summarised as follows:

• written request to owner—not less than eight weeks;
• publication of acquisition notice—not less than four weeks to appeal;
• service of acquisition notice on owner—within 10 days of publication;
• where no appeal, order by planning authority acquiring land;
• where appeal and notice confirmed by the Board—followed by order by planning authority (or after where appeal withdrawn).

Under subs.(7), the planning authority must register its interest under the Registration of Title Act 1964 and under subs.(9), also enter particulars for the acquisition in the planning register.

Under subs.(8), the owner of the land can claim compensation for the acquisition, which in the absence of agreement will be assessed by an arbitrator under the general rules. The arbitrator will make a nil award in circumstances where the owner has recovered land equal in value to the land acquired or will be recoverable in the future by disposal of the land. This means that no compensation will be payable where the value of the lands (other than the open space lands) has increased in value as a result of implementing the planning permission. Thus, there will be a nil award where there is a planning gain as a result of the planning permission. Furthermore, the value of the land will be assessed solely on the basis of its use for open space and a deduction shall be made in respect of the cost of rendering the land suitable as open space.

Requiring removal or alteration of structure or discontinuance of use

46.—**(1)** If a planning authority decides that, in exceptional **1–67** circumstances-

    (a) any structure should be demolished, removed, altered or replaced,

    (b) any use should be discontinued, or

    (c) any conditions should be imposed on the continuance of a use,

the planning authority may serve a notice on the owner and on the occupier of the structure or land concerned and on any other person who, in its opinion, will be affected by the notice.

(2) *Subsection (1)* shall not apply to any unauthorised development unless the notice under this *section* is served after seven years from the commencement of the unauthorised development.

(3) A notice referred to in *subsection (1)* shall—

    (a) specify the location of the structure or land concerned,

    (b) specify the steps that will be required to be taken within a specified period, including, where appropriate—

        (i) the demolition, removal, alteration or replacement of any structure, or

        (ii) the discontinuance of any use or the continuance of any use subject to conditions,

    and

    (c) invite any person served with the notice to make written submissions or observations to the planning authority in respect of the matters referred to in the notice within a specified period (being not less than 4 weeks from the date of service of the notice).

(4) A planning authority may, having regard to any submissions or observations made in accordance with *subsection (3)(c),* decide to confirm the notice, with or without modifications, or not to confirm the notice.

(5) A planning authority, in deciding whether to confirm a notice pursuant to this *section,* shall consider—

    (a) the proper planning and sustainable development of the area,

    (b) the provisions of the development plan,

    (c) the provisions of any special amenity area order, any European site or other area designated for the purposes of *section 10(2)(c)* relating to the area, and

    (d) any other relevant provision of this *Act* and any regulations made thereunder.

(6) Where a notice is confirmed by a planning authority under *subsection (4),* any person served with the notice may, within 8 weeks of the date of service of the notice, appeal to the Board against the notice.

(7) Where an appeal is brought under this *section* against a notice, the Board may confirm the notice with or without modifications or annul the notice, and the provisions of *subsection (5)* shall apply, subject to any necessary modifications, to the deciding of an appeal under this *subsection* by the Board, as they apply to the making of a decision by the planning authority.

(8) A notice under this *section* (other than a notice which is annulled) shall take effect—

  (a) in case no appeal against it is taken, on the expiration of the period for taking an appeal, or

  (b) in case an appeal or appeals are taken against it and not withdrawn, when the appeal or appeals have been either withdrawn or decided.

(9) If, within the period specified in a notice under this *section,* or within such extended period as the planning authority may allow, any demolition, removal, alteration or replacement required by the notice has not been effected, the planning authority may enter the structure and may effect such demolition, removal, alteration or replacement as is specified in the notice.

(10) Where a notice under this *section* is complied with, the planning authority shall pay to the person complying with the notice the expenses reasonably incurred by the person in carrying out the demolition, removal, alteration or replacement specified in the notice, less the value of any salvageable materials.

(11) Where any person served with a notice under this *section* fails to comply with the requirements of the notice, or causes or permits the failure to comply with the requirements, he or she shall be guilty of an offence.

(12) Particulars of a notice served or confirmed under this *section* shall be entered in the register.

(13)

  (a) A planning authority may, for stated reasons, by notice in writing withdraw a notice served under this *section.*

  (b) Where a notice is withdrawn pursuant to this *subsection* by a planning authority, the fact that the notice was withdrawn shall be recorded by the authority in the register.

NOTE

This section enables a planning authority to serve a notice:
- to demolish or alter a structure;
- to discontinue a use; or
- to impose conditions on use.

While the planning authority has a discretion whether to serve such a notice, it may only be exercised in exceptional circumstances. Considering the draconian nature of the power proof of exceptional circumstances would appear to be a matter going to jurisdiction. As the notice may interfere with vested rights and the exercise of property rights this requirement should be strictly construed. While exceptional circumstances are not defined, it would appear that the circumstances must be planning matters. It appears it may not be appropriate to use this power for certain emergency situations such as dealing with derelict or dangerous buildings, which are more appropriately dealt with under other local government legislation. The notice may be served on the owner or occupier or any person affected by the notice. The notice imposes an obligation on such person to carry out the terms of the notice. Subsection (2) provides that a notice can only be served in relation to unauthorised development, seven years after the commencement of the unauthorised development. This is to safeguard the enforcement provisions contained in Pt VIII of the 2000 Act, which is the more appropriate means of handling unauthorised use so long as the time limit of seven years for enforcement action has not expired. However, there is no requirement the structure or land is unauthorised development for the purposes of serving a notice. The notice can also be used with respect to authorised structures or uses of lands. Subsection (3) concerns the content of the notice, which must specify certain matters such as the location of the structure or land, the steps required to be taken, such as demolition or discontinuance of use, the time within which the steps must be taken. The notice must also invite submissions, allowing a period not less than four weeks. Under subs.(4), after the period for submissions, the planning authority may decide to confirm or not to confirm the notice. No minimum period is specified for the steps to be taken set out in the notice. Under subs.(5), in making such decision the planning authority must consider the proper planning and sustainable development of the area, the development plan, any special amenity order and any regulations made. Under subs.(6), where the notice is confirmed, a person served with the notice can appeal such confirmation to An Bord Pleanála within eight weeks. Under subs.(7), where there is an appeal, the Board can annul or confirm the notice, with or without modifications. If the Board confirms it, the notice takes effect at such time. Where there is no appeal within the time allowed or the appeal is withdrawn, the notice will thereupon take effect at that time. The timeframe of steps involved may be summarised as follows:

- service of notice—invitation to make submissions for period not less than 4 weeks;
- confirmation by planning authority—eight weeks to appeal to the Board;
- notice takes effect if confirmed by the Board or time for appeal expires.

Under subs.(9), if the owner/occupier has not taken the steps required in the notice within the specified period, the planning authority may enter the structure and carry out the steps themselves. Under subs.(10), the owner/occupier will be compensated for reasonable expenses incurred for carrying out the steps required by the notice. Under subs.(11), a person who fails to comply with a notice, or causes or permits a failure to comply, commits a criminal offence.Particulars of the notice must be entered in the planning register. Under subs.(13), the planning authority may withdraw the notice for stated reasons, and such withdrawal must also be entered in the register.

Agreements regulating development or use of land

47.—(1) A planning authority may enter into an agreement with any person **1–68** interested in land in their area, for the purpose of restricting or regulating the development or use of the land, either permanently or during such period as may be specified by the agreement, and any such agreement may contain such incidental and consequential provisions (including provisions of a financial character) as appear to the planning authority to be necessary or expedient for the purposes of the agreement.

(2) A planning authority in entering into an agreement under this *section* may join with any body which is a prescribed authority for the purposes of *section 11*.

(3) An agreement made under this *section* with any person interested in land may be enforced by the planning authority, or any body joined with it, against persons deriving title under that person in respect of that land as if the planning authority or body, as may be appropriate, were possessed of adjacent land, and as if the agreement had been expressed to be made for the benefit of that land.

(4) Nothing in this *section,* or in any agreement made thereunder, shall be construed as restricting the exercise, in relation to land which is the subject of any such agreement, of any powers exercisable by the Minister, the Board or the planning authority under this *Act,* so long as those powers are not exercised so as to contravene materially the provisions of the development plan, or as requiring the exercise of any such powers so as to contravene materially those provisions.

(5) Particulars of an agreement made under this *section* shall be entered in the register.

NOTE

This section allows the planning authority to enter into agreement with persons having an interest in land for the purposes of restricting its use or development. This would include so-called sterilisation agreements whereby land is restricted from being developed either permanently or for a specified period. It could also include agreements to be entered into pursuant to a condition of planning prior to commencing development. Whether such agreement would be valid may depend upon the condition upon which the agreement is based. However, the agreement must relate to the "development or use of the land". It is not necessary that agreement is related to a planning permission or even proposed future development. In *JA Pye (Oxford) Limited v South Gloucestershire DC and Others* [2001] E.W.C.A. Civ. 450, Lord Latham commenting on an equivalent provision in England, stated:

"It is therefore clear that it is not a pre-condition for the validity of a s.52 agreement that it should relate to any proposed development. The vires of any such agreement depends simply and solely upon whether or not it was entered into 'for the purpose of restricting or regulating the development or the use of the land'. The October 1979 agreement was clearly entered into for the relevant purpose. Indeed there is, in effect, no dispute about Avon's powers to enter into it. The question is whether or not in doing so it acted unreasonably in a Wednesbury sense".

This was approved in *McHugh v Kildare County Council* [2006] 1 I.R. 100, where an agreement was upheld whereby the applicant agreed to transfer 20 per cent of his land to the Council, if the Council re-zoned the remainder of his land. Gilligan J. noted that purpose of the agreement was to accept the offer of 20 per cent of the plaintiff's lands so that they would be developed for small industry independently of the adjoining private industrial development and this purpose came within the ambit of restricting or regulating the development or use of the land. See also *R. v South North Hamptonshire District Council ex. P. Crest Homes* [1995] JPL 200, where an agreement to transfer land for community purposes, was considered to involve restricting or regulating the use of land. However, in *Wimpey Homes Holding Ltd v Secretary of State for the Environment* [1993] 2 PLR 54, the transfer of land per se, did not involve restricting or regulating the use of land.

Section 39(2) provides that permission may be granted subject to a condition specifying that the use as a dwelling shall be restricted to use by persons of a particular class or description and that provision to that effect shall be embodied in an agreement under section 47. This provision covers occupancy conditions, i.e. restricting the type of persons who are occupying the land such as an agreement restricting the occupancy of land in a Gaeltacht area to persons proficient in the Irish language. The condition may restrict occupancy to persons who have lived in the area for a certain number of years, were born in the area, work in the area whether in agriculture or otherwise or in a Gaeltacht area, or have the ability to speak Irish. The restrictive condition may be imposed to reflect the requirements of the development plan in the area. The validity of such conditions (and indeed provisions of the development plan) are open to question both in terms of the Irish constitution, European Union law and the European Convention on Human Rights. Where such conditions are imposed in a rigid manner, the condition may be deemed disproportionate to the aim sought to be achieved. Where the condition is deemed invalid, it would to appear to follow that the agreement will also be unenforceable. However, in *JA Pye (Oxford) Limited v South*

Gloucestershire DC and Others [2001] E.W.C.A. Civ. 450, it was suggested the mere fact that a planning authority may have taken into account an irrelevant consideration (i.e. the agreement) in deciding the planning application, did not necessarily mean that the agreement itself was invalid.

Therefore while an agreement need not be related to a planning permission, there is nothing to prevent a planning authority from imposing other conditions requiring the developer to enter into an agreement so long as the subject matter of the planning condition is a proper planning consideration. Where the condition is merely to extract a planning gain which has no connection with the development, this condition may be void. See *Ashbourne Holdings Ltd v An Bord Pleanála* [2003] 2 I.R. 114. Where a planning condition requires the entry into an agreement, the use of the term "agreement" is questionable. However, the notion of agreement is also used under s.96, under which a condition may require a developer to enter into an agreement for the transfer of land or other alternative transaction, for the purposes of social and affordable housing. Moreover, there is no requirement for a developer to implement a planning permission and so the issue of an agreement will only arise where the developer chooses to implement the planning permission.

Under subs.(2), the planning authority may enter into agreement jointly with a prescribed body for the purposes of s.11. Article 13 of the Planning Regulations sets out 27 prescribed bodies for these purposes. The agreement entered into will bind successors in title to the landowner or other claiming through him. This constitutes a statutory exception to the concept of privity of contract. Similar to s.39(1), therefore in relation to planning permission, the agreement attaches to the land rather than to the parties. Subsection (4) provides that agreement will bind the planning authority to a limited extent insofar as the agreement cannot be construed as restricting the powers of the planning authority (or the Minister or the Board) under the Act, so long as such exercise does not materially contravene the development plan or require the exercise of powers to breach such provisions.

It appears that a sterilisation agreement restricting the further development of land cannot prevent the planning authority from considering the proper planning and development of the area when determining a planning application. Thus, in *Langarth Properties v Bray Urban District Council,* unreported, High Court, Morris P., June 25, 2001, planning permission was refused by the planning authority because of a sterilisation agreement but was granted on appeal to An Bord Pleanála. Morris P. held that it was not open for the planning authority to rely upon the statutory agreement because to prevent or inhibit the development of lands other than by reason of the proper planning and sustainable development of the area would be an unconstitutional interference with the rights of private ownership. However, it is submitted that this decision should not be interpreted as meaning that a planning permission can effectively negate a pre-existing agreement. The existence of such agreement which attaches to the land ought to be a proper planning consideration. Even if taking everything into account, the proper planning and sustainable development of the area justifies the grant of planning permission, this does not mean that the sterilisation agreement is set aside. Section 34(13) provides that a person shall not be entitled solely by reason of a permission to carry out any development. Thus, notwithstanding the grant of permission, it does not follow that the implementation of the permission can be restrained under the terms of the agreement. Subsection (5) provides that particulars of the agreement must be entered in the planning register.

Development contributions

48.—(1) A planning authority may, when granting a permission under **1–69** *section 34,* include conditions for requiring the payment of a contribution in respect of public infrastructure and facilities benefiting development in the area of the planning authority and that is provided, or that is intended will be provided, by or on behalf of a local authority (regardless of other sources of funding for the infrastructure and facilities).

(2)

    (a) Subject to *paragraph (c),* the basis for the determination of a contribution under *subsection (1)* shall be set out in a development contribution scheme made under this *section,* and a planning authority may make one or more schemes in respect of different parts of its functional area.

(b) A scheme may make provision for payment of different contributions in respect of different classes or descriptions of development.

(c) A planning authority may, in addition to the terms of a scheme, require the payment of a special contribution in respect of a particular development where specific exceptional costs not covered by a scheme are incurred by any local authority in respect of public infrastructure and facilities which benefit the proposed development.

(3)

(a) A scheme shall state the basis for determining the contributions to be paid in respect of public infrastructure and facilities, in accordance with the terms of the scheme.

(b) In stating the basis for determining the contributions in accordance with *paragraph (a),* the scheme shall indicate the contribution to be paid in respect of the different classes of public infrastructure and facilities which are provided or to be provided by any local authority and the planning authority shall have regard to the actual estimated cost of providing the classes of public infrastructure and facilities, except that any benefit which accrues in respect of existing development may not be included in any such determination.

(c) A scheme may allow for the payment of a reduced contribution or no contribution in certain circumstances, in accordance with the provisions of the scheme.

(4) Where a planning authority proposes to make a scheme under this *section,* it shall publish in one or more newspapers circulating in the area to which the scheme relates, a notice—

(a) stating that a draft scheme has been prepared,

(b) giving details of the proposed contributions under the draft scheme,

(c) indicating the times at which, the period (which shall be not less than 6 weeks) during which, and the place where, a copy of the draft scheme may be inspected, and

(d) stating that submissions or observations may be made in writing to the planning authority in relation to the draft scheme, before the end of the period for inspection.

(5)

(a) In addition to the requirements of *subsection (4),* a planning authority shall send a copy of the draft scheme to the Minister.

(b) The Minister may make recommendations to the planning authority regarding the terms of the draft scheme, within 6 weeks of being sent the scheme.

(6)

(a) Not later than 4 weeks after the expiration of the period for making submissions or observations under *subsection (4),* the manager of a planning authority shall prepare a report on any submissions or observations received under that *subsection,* and submit the report to the members of the authority for their consideration.

(b) A report under *paragraph (a)* shall—

    (i) list the persons or bodies who made submissions or observations under this *section,*

    (ii) summarise the issues raised by the persons or bodies in the submissions or observations, and

    (iii) give the response of the manager to the issues raised, taking account of the proper planning and sustainable development of the area.

(7) The members of the planning authority shall consider the draft scheme and the report of the manager under *subsection (6),* and shall have regard to any recommendations made by the Minister under *subsection (5).*

(8)

(a) Following the consideration of the manager's report, and having had regard to any recommendations made by the Minister, the planning authority shall make the scheme, unless it decides, by resolution, to vary or modify the scheme, otherwise than as recommended in the manager's report, or otherwise decides not to make the scheme.

(b) A resolution under *paragraph (a)* must be passed not later than 6 weeks after receipt of the manager's report.

(9)

(a) Where a planning authority makes a scheme in accordance with *subsection (8),* the authority shall publish notice of the making, or approving, of the scheme, as the case may be, in at least one newspaper circulating in its area.

(b) A notice under *paragraph (a)* shall—

    (i) give the date of the decision of the planning authority in respect of the draft scheme,

    (ii) state the nature of the decision, and

    (iii) contain such other information as may be prescribed.

(10)

(a) Subject to *paragraph (b),* no appeal shall lie to the Board in relation to a condition requiring a contribution to be paid in accordance with a scheme made under this *section.*

(b) An appeal may be brought to the Board where an applicant for permission under *section 34* considers that the terms of the scheme have not been properly applied in respect of any condition laid down by the planning authority.

(c) Notwithstanding *section 34(11),* where an appeal is brought in accordance with *paragraph (b),* and no other appeal of the decision of a planning authority is brought by any other person under *section 37,* the authority shall make the grant of permission as soon as may be after the expiration of the period for the taking of an appeal, provided that the person who takes the appeal in accordance with *paragraph (b)* furnishes to the planning authority security for payment of the full amount of the contribution as specified in the condition.

(11) Where an appeal is brought to the Board in respect of a refusal to grant permission under this *Part,* and where the Board decides to grant permission, it shall, where appropriate, apply as a condition to the permission the provisions of the contribution scheme for the time being in force in the area of the proposed development.

(12) Where payment of a special contribution is required in accordance with *subsection (2)(c),* the following provisions shall apply—

> **(a)** the condition shall specify the particular works carried out, or proposed to be carried out, by any local authority to which the contribution relates,
>
> **(b)** where the works in question—
>
> > **(i)** are not commenced within 5 years of the date of payment to the authority of the contribution,
> >
> > **(ii)** have commenced, but have not been completed, within 7 years of the date of payment to the authority of the contribution, or
> >
> > **(iii)** where the local authority decides not to proceed with the proposed works or part thereof,
>
> the contribution shall, subject to *paragraph (c),* be refunded to the applicant together with any interest that may have accrued over the period while held by the local authority,
>
> **(c)** where under *subparagraph (ii) or (iii) of paragraph (b),* any local authority has incurred expenditure within the required period in respect of a proportion of the works proposed to be carried out, any refund shall be in proportion to those proposed works which have not been carried out.

(13)

> **(a)** Notwithstanding *sections 37 and 139,* where an appeal received by the Board after the commencement of this *section* relates solely to a condition dealing with a special contribution, and no appeal is brought by any other person under *section 37* of the decision of the planning authority under that *section,* the Board shall not determine the relevant application as if it had been made to it in the first instance, but shall determine only the matters under appeal.
>
> **(b)** Notwithstanding *section 34(11),* where an appeal referred to in *paragraph (a)* is received by the Board, and no appeal is brought by any other person under *section 37,* the authority shall make the grant of permission as soon as may be after the expiration of the period for the taking of an appeal, provided that the person who takes the appeal furnishes to the planning authority, pending the decision of the Board, security for payment of the full amount of the special contribution as specified in the condition referred to in *paragraph (a).*

(14)

> **(a)** Money accruing to a local authority under this *section* shall be accounted for in a separate account, and shall only be applied as capital for public infrastructure and facilities.
>
> **(b)** A report of a local authority under *section 50 of the Local Government*

Act, 1991, shall contain details of monies paid or owing to it under this *section* and shall indicate how such monies paid to it have been expended by any local authority.

(15)

(a) A planning authority may facilitate the phased payment of contributions under this *section,* and may require the giving of security to ensure payment of contributions.

(b) Where a contribution is not paid in accordance with the terms of the condition laid down by the planning authority, any outstanding amounts due to the planning authority shall be paid together with interest that may have accrued over the period while withheld by the person required to pay the contribution.

(c) A planning authority may recover, as a simple contract debt in a court of competent jurisdiction, any contribution or interest due to the planning authority under this *section.*

(16)

(a) A planning authority shall make a scheme or schemes under this *section* within 2 years of the commencement of this *section.*

(b) Notwithstanding the repeal of any enactment by this *Act,* the provisions of *section 26 of the Act of 1963,* in relation to requiring contributions in respect of expenditure by local authorities on works which facilitate development, shall continue to apply pending the making of a scheme under this *section,* but shall not apply after two years from the commencement of this *section.*

(17) In this *section —*

"public infrastructure and facilities" *means—*

(a) *the acquisition of land,*

(b) *the provision of open spaces, recreational and community facilities and amenities and landscaping works,*

(c) *the provision of roads, car parks, car parking places, sewers, waste water and water treatment facilities, drains and watermains,*

(d) *the provision of bus corridors and lanes, bus interchange facilities (including car parks for those facilities), infrastructure to facilitate public transport, cycle and pedestrian facilities, and traffic calming measures,*

(e) *the refurbishment, upgrading, enlargement or replacement of roads, car parks, car parking places, sewers, waste water and water treatment facilities, drains or watermains, and*

(f) *any matters ancillary to paragraphs (a) to (e);*

"scheme" *means a development contribution scheme made under this section;*

"special contribution" *means a special contribution referred to in subsection (2)(c).*

NOTE

This section concerns the making of a contribution scheme which is to apply to a condition of a planning permission requiring the payment of a development contribution. The scheme imposes a new means of calculating contributions compared to the previous legislation whereby contributions were determined in each individual planning application without reference to any scheme. Ministerial Circular on *Development Contributions*, Circular Letter PD 4/2003, June 27, 2003, states that the change to the contribution system was to increase its flexibility and the range of infrastructure that can be funded. Every planning authority was obliged to adopt a scheme within two years of the section commencing, which was on March 11, 2002. Under the transitional provisions, the planning authority could continue to impose conditions on an individual basis under the former s.26 of the 1963 Act. On appeal from a refusal of permission, An Bord Pleanála can impose a condition based on the contribution scheme for the time being in force in the area of the proposed development. See subs.(11). Also in respect of strategic planning infrastructure developments, s.37G(7) provides that the Board can attach a condition requiring the payment of a contribution or contributions of the same kind as the appropriate planning authority could require to be paid under s.48 or 49 (or both) were that authority to grant the permission (and the scheme or schemes referred to in s.48 or 49, as appropriate, made by that authority shall apply to the determination of such contribution or contributions).

Under the previous legislation, failure to fulfil a condition requiring contributions imposed under s.26(2)(g) or 26(2)(h) of the 1963 Act meant exceptionally, by virtue of s.26(10)(a) of the 1963 Act, that the permission was of no effect until the condition had been complied with. This meant that such permission was considered unauthorised development for the purposes of taking a planning injunction under s.27 of the 1976 Act. This was in contrast to failure to fulfil other conditions of the permission. Breach of any other conditions would not render the development unauthorised for the purposes of s.27 of the 1976 Act, but development authorised by a permission in non-compliance with a condition. Due to the consequences of non-compliance with a financial contribution condition, the practice was adopted of planning authorities issuing compliance certificates in respect of such conditions. Due to this practice, the issuance of compliance certificates came to be regarded as quasi-title documents. See *Glenkerrin v Dun Laoghaire Rathdown County Council*, unreported, High Court, Clarke J., April 26, 2007, where it was held that the issuance of certificates of compliance had become a universal practice such that certificates of compliance had come to be regarded by conveyancers as an essential document to be passed over on the closing of a transaction involving a property to which the regime applies. It was held however that a planning authority could discontinue such practice by giving reasonable notice. It may be noted however that under the 2000 Act, the definition of unauthorised work and unauthorised use has been altered so that breach of any planning condition will mean the development is deemed to be unauthorised. Financial contribution conditions or non-compliance therewith no longer have any special effect or status. The effect of this change in the law means that there is no reason to afford unique status to financial contribution conditions nor is there arguably any special need for certicates of compliance in respect of such conditions. Conditions requiring financial contribution payment are typically framed as pre-commencement conditions, i.e. no development may commence until the payment is made. Where there is non-compliance, planning authorities can use the enforcement provisions in Pt VIII of the Act to ensure payment of contributions. The fact that under subs.(15)(c) a planning authority can also seek to recover the contribution or interest due thereon as a simple contract debt, does not exclude taking enforcement action to ensure compliance with the condition.

While under subs.(1), there is no absolute obligation on the planning authority to impose a condition requiring a contribution, the particular contribution scheme adopted may oblige the planning authority to impose such condition. However, the introduction of the contribution scheme cannot effect planning conditions requiring a contribution under a permission granted under the previous legislation. Once the contribution scheme has been adopted, the planning authority has no residual power to impose such conditions other than in accordance with the scheme.

The contribution may be imposed for the purposes of public infrastructure and facilities benefiting development in the area. Subsection (17) sets out a definition of public infrastructure and facilities. The public infrastructure and facilities project need not be carried out by the local authority itself but may be carried out on its behalf. There need not be a direct connection between the development contribution paid and works done which facilitate that development. See *Construction Industry Federation v Dublin City Council*, unreported, High Court, Gilligan J., March 4, 2004. However, this is contrast to public infrastructure projects or services in a supplementary scheme adopted under s.49, where such projects or services must provide some benefit to the development to which the permission relates.

Subsection (2) provides that a development contribution scheme may provide for different payments in respect of different classes of development. In addition to the general contribution scheme, a special contribution payment may be required in the case of specific exceptional costs not covered by a scheme. In the event of a dispute in respect of a special contribution, the onus is on the planning authority to demonstrate that the condition is appropriate. See *Construction Industry Federation v Dublin City Council*, unreported, High Court, Gilligan J., March 4, 2004. Subsection (12) provides that in case of a special contribution, the condition must specify the particular works. There is also provision for return of the payment, in whole or in part, where the works are not completed within the life of the permission.

Subsection (3) provides that the scheme must state the basis for determining the contribution for each class infrastructure and facilities. In setting the contribution, the planning authority must have regard to the actual cost of providing the public infrastructure and facilities. The costs to be taken into account includes infrastructure or services which are currently being provided and those which may be provided in the future. Provision may also be made for no contribution or a reduced contribution. In *Construction Industry Federation v Dublin City Council*, unreported, High Court, Gilligan J., March 4, 2004, Gilligan J. declared none of the provisions require a draft general scheme to specify the individual projects which the planning authority intends to fund wholly or partly from money raised under that scheme, nor is the scheme required to set out the level of detail as to costs or timing. The underlying data and analysis need not be included in the scheme. In setting out how the scheme was determined, it is permissible to refer to consultant reports and to have incorporated them within the scheme, although the report need not contain all the information. The court rejected as hypothethical the claim that in the absence of identifying projects under the general scheme, an applicant could be required to make a double contribution under both a general and special contribution scheme.

The Circular provides that in determining the infrastructure and facilities for which contributions will be levied, regard should be had to the development plan and any specific strategies under the plan. Other possible sources are local area plans, the Annual Report of programme of capital projects, the County Development Board Strategy, village and urban renewal projects, the Annual Roads Programme, etc. However, the basis for determining the contribution levels must be adequately justified and supported. The Circular noted that there is no requirement that the contribution solely benefits the area of the development. Planning authorities can include contributions towards the cost of infrastructure and facilities which have already been recently provided and which continue to benefit new development in the authority's area. The Circular notes that authorities should bear in mind that development contributions are not intended to cover the full annual capital cost of all infrastructure within the authority's area and should not be set at an excessively high level. Planning authorities should also determine the proportion of the capacity of the infrastructure and facilities provided that will benefit existing development and reduce the estimate of contributions to be paid accordingly. In relation to water and wastewater infrastructure, local authorities should exclude costs recoverable from developers in accordance with the Government water-pricing framework; see Circular L 16/02.

The contribution scheme is made by the elected members while under the previous legislation the imposition of conditions requiring contribution was an executive decision. Subsection (4) sets out the procedure for adopting a scheme and provides that a newspaper notice must be published including the matters set out in the subsection which are mandatory. The notice must invite submissions or observations to be made. The Minister can also make recommendations within six weeks of being sent notice of the scheme. As in the case of preparation of a draft development plan, the Manager must prepare a report in respect of the submissions, summarising the issues and giving a response. The requirement to summarise, means there is no requirement to circulate the entire submissions. See *Sandyford Environmental Planning v Dun Laoghaire Rathdown County Council*, unreported, High

Court, McKechnie J., June 30, 2004. This report, along with any recommendation from the Minister, must be considered by the elected members. While subs.(6)(b) does not refer to any recommendation by the Manager, merely his response to the issues raised, subs.(8)(a) refers to the scheme as recommended in the Manager's report. The scheme will be adopted as recommended in the report, unless the planning authority pass a resolution within six weeks after receipt of the report to vary or modify the scheme. If the planning authority decides to vary or amend the scheme, there is no requirement to re-advertise the scheme or to allow further submissions or observations from the public; see *Construction Industry Federation v Dublin City Council*, unreported, High Court, Gilligan J., March 4, 2004, approving *Duffy v Waterford Corporation*, unreported, High Court, McGuinness J., July 21, 1999. This is in contrast to material alterations of a draft development plan under s.12(7) and it is possible that in a particular case fair procedures may require re-advertisement where a material alteration is made. Having made the scheme, the planning authority must publish a newspaper notice.

Once adopted, the scheme cannot be challenged in imposing a condition for contribution in respect of a planning application. The condition may only be challenged on the basis that the scheme was applied incorrectly. In the case of such appeal against the condition, the planning authority may still grant the planning permission where the applicant furnishes the planning authority with security for payment of the full amount. Security for payment would appear to cover any security which would guarantee future payment of the money. Where an applicant has provided such security for payment and the contribution in the condition is altered, the planning authority will not be entitled to take up the security for the full amount. Where an appeal is made regarding the condition for special contribution only, the Board will only consider the point of appeal, while the planning authority can also grant the permission where security is made regarding the payment. The jurisdiction of the Board to hear an appeal under subs.(10)(b) is limited to whether the scheme has been properly applied. The Board cannot review or consider the merits of the scheme. See *Cork City Council v An Bord Pleanála* [2007] 1 I.R. 761, where the Board had decided that the term "gross floor area" used in a General Development Contribution Scheme ought to be the same as "gross floor scheme" under art.3 of the 2001 Regulations and indicated it was inconsistent with land use efficiency. Kelly J. held the Board had no power to rewrite the scheme and quashed the decision

Monies acquired by the planning authority from the contributions must be put into a separate account for public infrastructure and facilities, to ensure that the monies are not spent on other matters. The Circular provides that development contributions can only be levied as capital funding for public infrastructure and facilities and as such cannot be used to pay current costs. For example, refurbishment, upgrading, enlargement or replacement referred to in (e) above should all involve adding value to a network, rather than simply the maintenance of a network that already exists. The planning authority may also request for payment of the contribution by way of stages or phased payments. Interest is payable where there is a breach of the terms of payment.

The Act does not specify the lifetime of a development contribution scheme. The scheme should however be adopted for a specific period. When deciding on the lifetime of the scheme, the Circular states that the planning authority should consider the period within which the provision of capital projects may be reasonably projected. A planning authority may decide to relate the lifetime of the scheme to that of the development plan, though the circular provides that it would be advisable to review the scheme at 2–3 year intervals at least, where the scheme is adopted for a longer period.

In respect of special contribution schemes, the refund should be in proportion to the work not carried out and include any interest accrued over the period while held by the local authority. Unlike contributions levied under a general scheme, these contributions may be appealed.

Planning authorities can use the enforcement provisions in Pt VIII of the Act to ensure payment of contributions.

Supplementary development contribution schemes

49.—**(1)** A planning authority may, when granting a permission under   **1–70**
section 34, include conditions requiring the payment of a contribution in
respect of any public infrastructure service or project—

    (a) specified in a scheme made by the planning authority (hereafter in
this section referred to as a "supplementary development contribution
scheme"),

    (b) provided or carried out, as may be appropriate, by a planning
authority or, pursuant to an agreement entered into by a local
authority, any other person, and

    (c) that will benefit the development to which the permission relates
when carried out.

(2)

    (a) The amount, and manner of payment, of a contribution under
subsection (1) shall be determined in accordance with a supplementary
development contribution scheme.

    (b) A supplementary development contribution scheme shall
specify—

        (i) the area or areas within the functional area of the planning
authority, and

        (ii) the public infrastructure project or service,

    to which it relates, and more than one such scheme may be made in
respect of a particular area.

    (c) A supplementary development contribution scheme may make
provision for the payment of different contributions in respect of
different classes or descriptions of development.

(3) Subsections (3), (4), (5), (6), (7), (8), (9), (10), (11) and (15) of section
48 shall apply to a scheme subject to—

    (a) the modification that references in those subsections to a scheme
shall be construed as references to a supplementary development
contribution scheme,

    (b) any other necessary modifications, and

    (c) the provisions of this section.

(4)

    (a) A planning authority may enter into an agreement with any person in
relation to the carrying out, or the provision, as may be appropriate,
of a public infrastructure project or service.

    (b) Without prejudice to the generality of *paragraph (a),* an agreement
may make provision for—

        (i) the manner in which the service or project is to be provided or
carried out, as the case may be, including provision relating to
construction or maintenance of any infrastructure or operation
of any service or facility,

        (ii) arrangements regarding the financing of the project or service
and the manner in which contributions paid or owed to a
planning authority pursuant to a condition under *subsection
(1)* may be applied in respect of that project or service,

(iii) the entry into such further agreements as may be necessary with any other person regarding the financing and provision of such service or carrying out of such project,

(iv) the entry into force, duration and monitoring of the agreement (including the resolution of disputes).

(5) A planning authority shall not, pursuant to a condition under *subsection (1)*, require the payment of a contribution in respect of a public infrastructure project or service where the person concerned has made a contribution under section 48 in respect of public infrastructure and facilities of which the said public infrastructure project or service constituted a part.

(6) A planning authority may, at any time, by resolution, amend a supplementary development contribution scheme for the purpose of modifying the manner of determining a contribution pursuant to a condition under *subsection (1)* where the cost of carrying out or providing, as the case may be, the public infrastructure project or service is less than the cost that was estimated when the planning authority first determined the amount of the contribution.

(7) In this section, "public infrastructure project or service" means—

(a) the provision of particular rail, light rail or other public transport infrastructure, including car parks and other ancillary development,

(b) the provision of particular new roads,

(c) the provision of particular new sewers, [waste water] and water treatment facilities, drains or watermains and ancillary infrastructure.

AMENDMENT HISTORY

Subsection (7) amended by s.11 of the Planning and Development (Amendment) Act 2002 (No. 32 of 2002) which came into effect on December 24, 2002.

NOTE

This scheme allows the planning authority to make a supplementary contribution scheme. It differs from the general contribution scheme under s.48, in so far as it will not cover the whole area of the planning authority. Also several schemes can be made even in respect of a particular area, and the scheme relates to a "public infrastructure project or service" as opposed to "public infrastructure and facilities". A "public infrastructure project or service" is defined under subs.(7), which was amended under the 2002 Act and relates to a specific project or service as opposed to public infrastructure in general. It appears also that it is a matter of discretion for the planning authority as to whether they wish to make a supplemental contribution scheme. Subsection (1) provides that a planning authority may impose a condition requiring a contribution in accordance with the supplemental scheme, where the project or service would benefit the development. In the case of a general contribution scheme, there is no requirement that the development specifically benefit from the public infrastructure or facility which could be anywhere in the area of the planning authority. The Ministerial Circular on *Development Contributions*, Circular Letter PD 4/2003, June 27, 2003 notes with regard to the requirement that supplementary contribution schemes must benefit the development in the case of a rail or light rail project, for example, provision of the infrastructure will facilitate increased residential densities surrounding the infrastructure. However, the planning authority cannot impose a condition under the supplemental scheme in respect of the development, where a condition under the general contribution scheme has also been imposed where the public infrastructure project or service forms part of the public infrastructure or facilities. Subsection (3) provides that the same procedure for adoption of the general contribution scheme applies in relation to the supplemental contribution scheme, in terms of newspaper notice, submissions, Manager report, making of the scheme etc.

Subsection (4) provides that the planning authority may enter into an agreement with a person in relation to the provision of a public infrastructure project or service, which includes the financing of the project. This subsection envisages such arrangement as a public-private partnership, in respect of which see the State Authorities (Public Private Partnership Arrangements) Act 2002.

Subsection (6) allows a simple procedure for amending the supplemental contribution development scheme in modifying the manner of determining the amount of the contribution, where the planning authority overestimated the cost of carrying out the project. There is no provision for amending the scheme to increase the amount where the planning authority underestimated the amount of the scheme. It appears in such instance a new scheme would have to be made following the procedure imported under subs.(3). As with any planning conditions, planning authorities can use the enforcement provisions in Pt VIII of the Act to ensure payment of contributions.

[Judicial review of applications, appeals, referrals and other matters

50.—**(1)** Where a question of law arises on any matter with which the   **1–71** Board is concerned, the Board may refer the question to the High Court for decision.

(2) A person shall not question the validity of any decision made or other act done by—

    (a) a planning authority, a local authority or the Board in the performance or purported performance of a function under this Act,

    (b) the Board in the performance or purported performance of a function transferred under *Part XIV,* or

    (c) a local authority in the performance or purported performance of a function conferred by an enactment specified in *section 214* relating to the compulsory acquisition of land, otherwise than by way of an application for judicial review under Order 84 of the Rules of the Superior Courts (S.I. No. 15 of 1986) (the "Order").

(3) *Subsection (2)(a)* does not apply to an approval or consent referred to in *Chapter I or II of Part VI.*

(4) A planning authority, a local authority or the Board may, at any time after the bringing of an application for leave to apply for judicial review of any decision or other act to which *subsection (2)* applies and which relates to a matter for the time being before the authority or the Board, as the case may be, apply to the High Court to stay the proceedings pending the making of a decision by the authority or the Board in relation to the matter concerned.

(5) On the making of such an application, the High Court may, where it considers that the matter before the authority or the Board is within the jurisdiction of the authority or the Board, make an order staying the proceedings concerned on such terms as it thinks fit.

(6) Subject to *subsection (8),* an application for leave to apply for judicial review under the Order in respect of a decision or other act to which *subsection (2)(a)* applies shall be made within the period of 8 weeks beginning on the date of the decision or, as the case may be, the date of the doing of the act by the planning authority, the local authority or the Board, as appropriate.

(7) Subject to *subsection (8),* an application for leave to apply for judicial review under the Order in respect of a decision or other act to which *subsection (2)(b) or (c)* applies shall be made within the period of 8 weeks beginning on the date on which notice of the decision or act was first sent (or as may be the requirement under the relevant enactment, functions under which are transferred under *Part XIV* or which is specified in *section 214,* was first published).

(8) The High Court may extend the period provided for in *subsection (6) or (7)* within which an application for leave referred to in that subsection may be made but shall only do so if it is satisfied that—

(a) there is good and sufficient reason for doing so, and

(b) the circumstances that resulted in the failure to make the application for leave within the period so provided were outside the control of the applicant for the extension.

(9) References in this section to the Order shall be construed as including references to the Order as amended or replaced (with or without modification) by rules of court.]

AMENDMENT HISTORY

Subsection (2) substituted, and all three amendments to subs.(4), by s.12 of the Planning and Development (Amendment) Act 2002 (No. 32 of 2002) which came into effect on December 24, 2002.

Section 50 substituted by s.13 of the Planning and Development (Strategic Infrastructure) Act 2006 (No. 27 of 2006).

NOTE

The 2006 Act introduced an entirely new s.50 and s.50A in relation to judicial review of planning decisions. The Act restructures the former s.50, with the new substituted s.50 containing general provisions regarding judicial review and s.50A dealing with leave to bring judicial review.

Section 50 generally deals with judicial review with the exception of subs.(1) which allows the Board to refer a question of law to the High Court in respect of any matter which the Board is concerned. The former subs.(1) referred to any question of law arising on any appeal or referral. This change gives a broader scope to the subsection and would allow the Board to state a question in the context of a strategic infrastructure application. The Board has rarely exercised this power and has a discretion whether to choose to do so. The mechanism would appear similar to the power of an arbitrator to state a case on a question of law. In certain very limited and exceptional circumstances, an arbitrator can be compelled to state a case and it is possible the Board could be compelled to do so. See *Hogan v St. Kevin's company and Purcell* [1986] I.R. 80.

Scope of Section 50

Subsection (2) makes clear that all acts or decisions of An Bord Pleanála and the planning authority made under the 2000 Act as amended must be challenged under the special judicial review procedure under s.50. Among the differences between section 50 judicial review and the ordinary judicial review procedure in Ord.84 of the RSC are: shorter time limits to bring the application (eight weeks rather than three or six months depending on the relief); the leave stage is on notice; the threshold for leave is substantial grounds rather than an arguable case; an applicant must have a substantial interest rather than sufficient interest and a certificate for leave to appeal must be obtained for an appeal to the Supreme Court. A restricted procedure was first introduced under the 1976 Act, by inserting s.82(3A) in the 1963 Act. Commenting on the equivalent provision under the previous planning legislation,

Finlay C.J. said in *KSK Enterprises Limited v An Bord Pleanála* [1994] 2 I.R. 128:

"From these provisions, it is clear that the intention of the legislature was greatly to confine the opportunity of persons to impugn by way of judicial review decisions made by the planning authorities and in particular one must assume that it was intended that a person who has obtained a planning permission should, at a very short interval after the date of such decision, in the absence of a judicial review, be entirely legally protected against subsequent challenge to the decision that was made and therefore presumably left in a position to act with safety upon the basis of that decision".

Similarly, in respect of the 2000 Act, in *Harding v Cork County Council*, unreported, Supreme Court, May 2, 2008, Kearns J. commented:

"It is impossible to conceive of these legislative provisions as being intended for any purpose other than to restrict the entitlement to bring court proceedings to challenge decisions of planning authorities. There is an obvious public policy consideration driving this restrictive statutory code. Where court proceedings are permitted to be brought, they may have amongst their outcomes not merely the quashing or upholding of decisions of planning authorities but also the undesirable consequences of expense and delay for all concerned in the development project as the court process works its way to resolution. The Act of 2000 may thus be seen as expressly underscoring the public and community interest in having duly authorised development projects completed as expeditiously as possible".

See also *Harrington v An Bord Pleanála* [2006] 1 I.R. 388.

The new section significantly expands the scope of decisions which are subject to the special judicial review procedure. In addition to "decisions", the new section inserts the words "or act done" by the Board, planning authority, local authority. This means that not only formal decisions but also acts of the Board and local authority are subject to judicial review. The notion of an "act" in this context is not defined but it would appear to encompass acts of the local authority or Board within the decision making process. This has implications for the time limits for instituting judicial review proceedings, as noted in *Linehan v Cork County Council*, unreported, High Court, Finlay Geoghegan J., February 19, 2008, where it was noted that the change in the Act may mean that acts or decision may have to be challenged as they occur rather than waiting until the final decision at the end of a process. Thus any act, albeit not a formal decision within the context of planning application is subject to judicial review under s.50. There may be some difficulty in identifying an act for these purposes. An act may be part of a series of acts and so it would appear that it is only acts which have an element of finality which may be appropriate to judicially review. Where the planning authority or Board "act" in a manner which may give rise to grounds for judicial review, it may not be appropriate to bring proceedings if the Board or planning authority can rescue the situation by some action later in the process. See for example *Huntstown v An Bord Pleanála* [1999] 1 I.L.R.M. 281, the judicial review application (for failure to order production of a document) prior to completing the oral hearing was deemed premature, where the Board could have ordered production of the document at any time prior to the determination. It is unclear whether the absence of an act or inaction of the local authority or the Board, where an applicant alleges they ought to have acted, may be covered. The better view is that they would not unless some particular point in time can be identified with certainty. Acts or decisions of the planning authority and local authority are covered. Thus where the local authority is deemed to be acting in a capacity other than as planning authority under the Act, its acts or decision will be covered by s.50. The phrase "purported performance" of a function means that even where the planning authority or Board acts or makes a decision which is ultra vires its function under the Act, where it purports to perform such function under the Act, this will still fall within s.50.

The section vastly expands the scope of decisions of the local authority or planning authority which are covered by s.50. Under the former s.50, as amended by the 2002 Act, the only decisions of local authorities or planning authorities which were covered by s.50 were decisions:

- on an application for a permission;
- under s.179 (local authority development); or
- in accordance with s.216.

Among the acts or decision now covered which did not fall within the scope of the former s.50 include, inter alia, decisions of the planning authority in relation to the making and varying of the development plans or local area plans under Pt II of the Act; decisions under Pt III other than on applications for permission such as, inter alia, on points of detail in relation to planning conditions under s.34(5), extension of the life of a permission under s.42, revocation of a permission under s.44, development contribution schemes under ss.48 and 49; also decisions on the making of a CPO under Pt XIV and decisions in the context of Pt IV (architectural heritage) such as a proposal to add protected structure or issuing endangerment or restoration notices, Pt VIII (enforcement) including the service of enforcement notices; Pt IX (strategic development zones); Pt XII (compensation); Pt XIII (amenities) such as making tree preservations orders; Pt XIV (events and funfairs) including the granting of licences thereunder. Subsection (3) provides that the restricted form of judicial review does not apply to an approval or consent under Ch.1 or 2 of Pt VI, which relates to the establishment and constitution of An Bord Pleanála (Ch.1) and the organisation and staffing, etc. of An Bord Pleanála (Ch.2). Subsection (50)(2)(c) provides for judicial review of the making of a CPO by a local authority under any of the enactments enlisted in s.214. Prior to this being introduced under the 2006 Act, the only decision of a planning authority in context of a CPO process which fell within s.50, was the confirmation of its own CPO in the limited circumstances under s.216. It may be noted that s.78(4) of the Housing Act 1966, provides that "(4) Subject to the provisions of subsection (2) of this section, a person shall not question a compulsory purchase order by prohibition or certiorari or in any legal proceedings whatsoever". Section 78(2) allowed a person aggrieved to challenge the confirmation of a CPO by the Minister (the function is now transferred to the Board) by making an application to the court within three weeks on specified grounds. Although not explicitly repealed, s.78(2) appears to be superseded by s.50 as amended, insofar as it provides that a person may not question the validity of the enlisted acts or decision otherwise than by way application for judicial review under Ord.84.

Where any of the reliefs sought come within s.50, an applicant must proceed under s.50, even if other reliefs do not come within the section. See *Goonery v Meath County Council*, unreported, High Court, Kelly J., July 25, 1999. The court may consider whether the thrust of the proceedings is to quash a decision falling within s.50. See *Kinsella v Dundalk Town Council*, unreported, High Court, Kelly J., December 3, 2004. However, there are certain decisions taken under the 2000 Act as amended, for which the ordinary judicial review procedure still applies such as a decision of a statutory arbitrator, whether under Pt V regarding social and affordable housing provisions or the compensation provisions. See *Cork County Council v Shackleton*, unreported, High Court, Clarke J., June 19, 2007. Also decisions of the Minister such as under ss.28, 29 and 31 are not covered by s.50.

A constitutional challenge can be included in a Section 50 judicial review. See *Hynes v An Bord Pleanála*, unreported, High Court, Laffoy J., December 10, 1997. The constitutional challenge must be within the factual matrix of challenging a decision of the planning authority, local authority or Board. Much of the existing case law suggests that a planning decision otherwise within s.50, will not be treated differently simply because it raises an issue of European law. See *McNamara v An Bord Pleanála* [1998] 3 I.R. 453, where it was held the existence of time limits to bring proceedings was not incompatible with EC law. See also *Derrybrien Co-operative Society Ltd v Saorgus Energy Ltd*, unreported, High Court, Dunne J., June 3, 2005. Thus in *Lancefort Ltd v An Bord Pleanála* [1997] 2 I.L.R.M. 508, Morris P. refused leave for the ground that the State had not properly implemented the EIS Directive 85/337/EC, as this did not concern the particular decision of the Board. It may, however, be possible to test their implementation by means of plenary proceedings. *Lancefort* was applied and confirmed in *Cosgrave v An Bord Pleanála*, unreported, High Court, Kelly J., April 21, 2004. Thus a court will consider whether there has been a failure to implement a Directive where it is necessary for the purposes of resolving the litigation. See *Arklow Holdings Ltd v An Bord Pleanála (No. 2)* [2007] 4 I.R. 124, where it was suggested leave will only be granted where there were substantial grounds for believing that no interpretation could be placed on the national legislation which was consistent with the European provision. However, in respect of the "substantial interest" and "substantial grounds", there has been some suggestion of a difference in approach in relation to decisions or proposed development requiring an EIS. See the notes in relation to the same under s.50A.

The clause at the end of subs.(2) that a person shall not question the matters set out therein, otherwise than by way of judicial review under Ord.84 was first introduced under the Local Government (Planning and Development) 1992 Act and means that procedural exclusivity applies to challenging the decisions by means of judicial review under Ord.84; the proceedings cannot be taken by means of a plenary summons. In general, in Ireland ordinary judicial review proceedings can also be taken by means of plenary summons rather than by notice of motion and affidavit under Ord.84; see *O'Donnell v Dun Laoghaire Corporation* [1991] I.L.R.M. 301; *Murphy v Wicklow County Council*, unreported, High Court, O'Sullivan J., December 19, 1999. The phrase "shall not question the validity of", means that the collateral challenging or questioning of such acts or decisions in other types of proceedings will not be permitted. This also supported by the long standing principle that there is a presumption that the acts of planning authority and Board are valid. See *Re Comhaltas Ceoltóirí Éireann*, unreported, High Court, Finlay P., December 14, 1977, where Finlay P. said in the context of a case stated on a licensing objection that "it is a rebuttable presumption that its acts are valid. A challenge to the validity of the acts of a planning authority can only be made by review on certiorari or by a substantive action seeking a declaration of invalidity" (though note a substantive action is now no longer possible). This principle of presumption of validity has also been applied to decisions of the Board. See *Lancefort v An Bord Pleanála*, unreported, McGuinness J., March 12, 1998 and *Evans v An Bord Pleanála*, unreported, High Court, Kearns J., November 7, 2003.

The fact that a formal order of certiorari is not sought does not necessarily mean that the valditiy of the decision is not being questioned. See *Goonery v Meath County Council*, unreported, High Court, Kelly J., July 25, 1999. The validity of a planning permission cannot be challenged in a Section 160 proceedings and a planning permission will be assumed valid unless revoked. See *Cantwell v McCarthy*, unreported, High Court, Murphy J., November 1, 2006. See also *Derrybrien v Saorgas Energy*, unreported, High Court, Dunne J., June 3, 2005, where a claim that development was unauthorised because an EIS was invalid was deemed to be a retrospective attempt to object to the planning permission or to challenge the validity of the permission. Where a planning application was deemed invalid by the planning authority, proceedings cannot be instituted by way of special summons seeking a declaration that a planning application was valid. See *Lennon v Limerick County Council*, unreported, High Court, Laffoy J., April 3, 2006, where such proceedings were struck out as being frivolous and vexatious and an abuse of the process of the courts. A person can bind themselves not to bring judicial review proceedings, in which case an application can be made to dismiss an application brought. See *Ryanair v An Bord Pleanála*, unreported, High Court, Clarke J., January 11, 2008. See also *Connolly v An Bord Pleanála*, unreported, High Court, Irvine J., July 8, 2008, where a vendor agreed not to object directly and/or indirectly to any planning application to be made by the purchaser, this was held to include a challenge to a planning application by way of judicial review.

Where an act or decision covered by s.50 requires a subsequent act or decision, the court will examine whether a challenge to the subsequent act or decision seeks to call into the question the validity of the original act or decision. For example, a challenge to a compliance agreement in the context of planning condition under imposed s.34(5), must relate to whether the agreement falls within the condition rather than a challenge to the condition itself. Where a planning condition requires the extinguishment of a road, a challenge to the process of extinguishment under s.73 of the Roads Act 1993 will not be covered by s.50. See *Coll v Donegal County Council*, unreported, July 5, 2005. However, in *Salafia v An Bord Pleanála*, unreported, High Court, Smyth J., March 1, 2006, which involved a challenge under ordinary judicial review proceedings to a Ministerial direction under the national monuments legislation in the context of a motorway, it was held that the proceedings involved a collateral challenge to the route selection of the motorway which was decided by the Board some three years earlier. Section 50 must be deemed to apply to legal proceedings and so the prohibition on questioning the validity of the decisions other than under Ord.84, ought not exclude questioning the validity of the decision of the planning authority by raising jurisdictional issues in an appeal to An Bord Pleanála. It would also appear not to exclude a defendant calling into question the validity of a planning condition in seeking to resist enforcement proceedings. In such case, the court may consider the applicant to have failed to discharge the burden of proof or alternatively may decline relief as a matter of discretion. See *Liffey Beat v Dublin City Council* [2005] 2 I.R. 478. See more generally *Blanchfield v Harnett* [2002] 2 I.L.R.M. 435.

The fact that s.50 imports Ord.84 means that unless otherwise varied the rules applicable to Ord.84 also apply to Section 50 judicial review proceedings. Discovery, interrogatories and applications to cross examine are all applicable in judicial review proceedings by virtue of Ord.84, r.25. Discovery will rarely be granted in judicial review proceedings; see *Re Rooneys Application* [1995] N.I. 398; *Re Glor na nGael Application* [1991] N.I. 117. This is supported in several recent Irish decisions; see *Sheehy v Ireland*, unreported, High Court, Kelly J., July 30, 2002; *Shortt v Dublin City Council*, unreported, High Court, Ó Caoimh J., February 21, 2003. See Dodd, "Judicial Review and Discovery: Part I and II" [2004] 4, 5 I.L.T. 64, 80. An order to cross examine should be served under RSC Ord.40, r.1. Oral evidence may be given in such circumstances.

An application for an interlocutory injunction may be made in the context of a judicial review which will be based on the test set out in *Campus Oil Ltd v Minister for Industry and Commerce* [1983] I.R. 88; see *Ryanair Ltd v Aer Rianta*, unreported, High Court, Kelly J., January 25, 2001; *Martin v An Bord Pleanála* [2002] 2 I.R. 655 where the Court declined to place a stay on an appeal before the Board pending the outcome of proceedings claiming that Directive 85/337/EEC, had not been correctly transposed into Irish domestic law. In the context of planning, the fact that leave has already been granted indicates that an applicant should satisfy the fair question to be tried part of the test. It would appear that interlocutory relief is not available where leave has yet to be granted, as r.20(7) appears to be based on the premise that leave has been granted. The adequacy of damages will not normally be relevant to the applicant, as damages are rarely awarded in judicial review. Also, the adequacy of damages to the decision-maker is also not wholly appropriate. The adequacy of damages to any restrained developer will however be relevant, although this should form part of the balance of convenience test. Preserving the status quo may be relevant to the balance of convenience, whereby implementing the permission the proceeding would be rendered moot. See *Birmingham v Birr Urban District Council* [1998] 2 I.L.R.M. 136 and *Dunne v Dun Laoghaire Rathdown County Council* [2003] 2 I.R. 567, where an injunction was granted restraining the defendant from injuring or interfering with a national monument. Where interlocutory relief is granted, the court may require an applicant to grant an undertaking as to damages: see *Martin v An Bord Pleanála* [2002] 2 I.R. 655; *O'Brien v Tipperary South Riding County Council*, unreported, High Court, Ó Caoimh J., October 22, 2002, and *Broadnet Ireland Ltd v Office of the Director of Telecommunications Regulation* [2000] 3 I.R. 281. The court must be in a position to assess whether the undertaking is supported by adequate means. The court may also require a fortified undertaking as to damages: see *O'Connell v Environmental Protection Agency* [2001] 4 I.R. 494. In *Harding v Cork County Council* [2006] 1 I.R. 294, it was held the court had jurisdiction to make an order prior to the hearing of a leave application, restraining the processing of an appeal to An Bord Pleanála pending the outcome of the leave application. Such jurisdiction derives from Ord.84, r.25 or, in any event, from the inherent jurisdiction of the court. Also in *Harding v An Bord Pleanála*, unreported, High Court, Clarke J., January 31, 2007, the court affirmed that it had jurisdiction to grant a stay on the appeal to the Board pending the outcome of an appeal to the Supreme Court of the refusal of an application for judicial review. The granting of a stay of the appeal to the Board is not comparable to an injunction restraining the operation of an Act of the Oireachtas but is simply to enable the issues raised in the judicial review proceedings to be addressed. See *O'Brien v Tipperary County Council*, unreported, High Court, Ó Caoimh J., October 22, 2002.

Judicial review of planning matters may potentially be entered into the Commercial Court under RSC Ord.63A, r.1(g) which involves appeals from or judicial review of decisions given by a person or body authorised by statute to make such decisions where the judge in charge of the commercial list considers it appropriate for entry in the list having regard to the commercial or any other aspect thereof. See *Mulholland v An Bord Pleanála* [2005] 3 I.R. 1, where it was said such a case should be capable of admission to the list if it could be demonstrated that a commercial development or process or substantial sums of money whether by way of profit, investment, loan or interest were likely to be jeopardised if the case was not given a speedy hearing or was denied the case management procedures available in the Commercial Court. This is so where one or more of the parties to the suit are involved in commerce, giving a broad meaning to that term. Such parties would include entities involved in commercial activities whether they be individuals, corporate bodies, semi-state bodies, state bodies or, indeed, the State itself in an appropriate case. However, there are no hard and fast rules and so the court will retain a discretion whether to admit such a case.

Stay on Judicial Review Proceedings

Section 4 concerns an application to stay the judicial proceedings where it relates to matters before the local authority or Board. This subsection along with subs.(5), makes some changes to the former corresponding s.50(3), which only concerned appeals or referral pending before the Board. The new subsection expands this to matters pending before the local authority or the Board. However, the new subsection limits the party which make such application to the "planning authority, a local authority or the Board", when the former subsection allowed "any party to an appeal" before the Board to make the application. The notion of "party to appeal" would have included the applicant developer, who no longer comes within the scope of the subsection. The purpose of this subsection, is to enable the planning authority or Board to rule on some matter which is related to the act or decision challenged and where it is appropriate that the planning authority or Board shall do so. In *Harding v An Bord Pleanála* [2006] 1 I.R. 294, Kelly J. noted that the former s.50(3) was a discretionary power and that if all of the matters raised were capable of determination by An Bord Pleanála, he would have considered making such order. It is clear under subs.(4) that it must be established that the matter is "within the jurisdiction" of the planning authority or Board. The import of this notion is unclear. The determination of the judicial review proceedings themselves may have an impact on whether the matter is within the jurisdiction of the planning authority or the Board. The judicial review proceedings may seek a stay on the matter before the planning authority or Board, on the basis that the grounds of challenge will render the remaining process invalid. The determination of the meaning of "within the jursidiction" bears some analogy to the issue as to whether an appeal is an adequate remedy, although the latter may involve broader considerations, as was noted in *Kinsella v Dundalk Town Council*, unreported, High Court, Kelly J., December 3, 2004, where Kelly J., in dealing with exhaustion of local remedies, referred to the former s.50(3). See *Harding v Cork County Council*, unreported, High Court, Clarke J., October 12, 2006, where it was held that an appeal will be regarded as an adequate remedy in a two stage statutory or administrative process unless either:

- the matters complained of in respect of the first stage of the process are such that they can taint the second stage of the process or effect the overall jurisdiction; or
- the process at the first stage is so flawed that it can reasonably be said that the person concerned had not been afforded their entitlement to a proper first stage of the process in any meaningful sense.

However, insofar as the continuation of the judicial proceedings or of the process before the planning authority/Board may render the other moot, it is submitted that where the legality of the process before the planning authority/Board may be determined by the judicial review proceedings, the court should be slow to grant a stay. See *P & F Sharpe Ltd v Dublin City and County Manager* [1989] I.R. 701; *Ardoyne House Management Ltd v Dublin Corporation* [1998] 2 I.R. 147.

The application for a stay may be brought "at any time" after the bringing of the application for leave. While the "bringing" of the leave application is not defined, the better view is that does not mean the "grant" or moving of the application for judicial review but merely that proceedings have been properly instituted. It follows that an application for a stay can be made at any time from the commencement of proceeding until their determination. It also follows that it is possible to apply to have the stay on the judicial review proceeding lifted. In order for an application for a stay to be made, the matter must already be before the planning authority or Board and it is not enough for a person to assert that they intend bringing the matter before the planning authority or Board or that they could bring the matter before the planning authority or Board.

Time Limits

Section 6 sets the time limit for taking proceedings at eight weeks (prior to the 2000 Act it was two months). Subsection (6) introduced under the 2006 Act amends the previous wording (s.50(4)(a)(i)) by inserting the words "or, as the case may be, the date of the doing of the act", which reflects the expanded scope of s.50 to cover any decisions "or act done" under the 2000 Act. The 2006 Act simplifies the calculation of time by providing in respect of a decision or act of a planning authority or An Bord Pleanála, the time limit runs from the date of the decision as opposed to the date of notification to the applicant for planning permission as was the case prior to the 2000 Act under the previous planning Acts. See *Keelgrove Properties v An Bord Pleanála* [2000] 1 I.R. 47 and in *Henry v Cavan County Council* [2001] 4 I.R. 1. The date of the decision of the Board is the date when the formal decision of the Board issues. See *Friends of the Curragh Environment Ltd v An Bord Pleanála (No. 1)*, unreported, High Court, Kelly J., July 14, 2006. The only exception to this relates to decisions or acts of the Board relating to compulsory acquisition functions under Pt XIV or by a local authority in respect of transferred functions under s.214. In these cases, the period only commences when the notice of the decision is sent (as opposed to received) or published, as the case may. The new subs.(50) adds that time will run from when notice "was first sent" and then adds in parenthesis from when the notice was first published as may be the requirement under the relevant enactment. Under the former s.50 (which did not include decisions of local authorities making a CPO), with respect to challenges to the confirmation of a CPO by the Board, time ran from when notice of the decision was first published. However, where there is no statutory obligation to send a notice to a person, time will run from the date of publication even where the determination of the Board was sent to the applicant in advance of the formal publication of the decision. See *Sweetman v An Bord Pleanála* [2007] 2 I.L.R.M. 328.

The previous rules regarding the calculation of time still apply. Thus the first day of the eight-week period should be included with the last day excluded; see *McCann v An Bord Pleanála* [1997] 1 I.L.R.M. 314. The time limit expires on midnight of the last day. See *Lancefort Ltd v An Bord Pleanála*, unreported, High Court, Morris J., May 13, 1997. Proceedings are commenced when the necessary parties set out in s.50A(2) have been served with the grounding documentation. For the proceeding to have commenced within the eight-week period, it is not sufficient to merely file the notice of motion, the notice of motion must also be served on all of the necessary parties; see *KSK Enterprises Ltd v An Bord Pleanála* [1994] 2 I.L.R.M. 1 and *Goonery v Meath County Council*, unreported, High Court, Kelly J., July 25, 1999. However, it is not necessary for leave to have been granted or the application moved within the eight weeks, if the parties are served and the application properly grounded within the eight-week period; see *Tennyson v Dun Laoghaire Corporation* [1991] 2 I.R. 527. There are no special rules of court dealing with services, in which case the normal rules of service apply. While s.250 concerns service of notices or orders, it unlikely that this could be deemed to apply to judicial review proceedings. This follows from the fact that a motion on notice is not strictly a notice per se and that s.250 merely relates to notices within the context of the planning code and not legal proceedings. Furthermore, s.50 also requires service of a statement of grounds and a grounding affidavit, which clearly do not constitute notices or orders and so it would appear anomalous if the notice of motion could be served but the statement of grounds and affidavit could not.

Even if proceedings are commenced within the eight-week period, it has been suggested that there is also an independent "promptness" requirement as imported from RSC Ord.84, r.21(1), on the basis of which leave may be refused. See *State (Cussen) v Brennan* [1981] I.R. 181, in the context of ordinary judicial review. In *Harrington v An Bord Pleanála* [2006] 1 I.R. 388, Macken J. said had it been necessary to do so, she would have found that the applicant had not complied with the requirement to move promptly, having filed his papers in the matter on the last day of the statutory period permitted. See also *O'Connell v Environmental Protection Agency* [2001] 4 I.R. 494. However, in contrast in *Marshall v Arklow Town Council* [2004] 4 I.R. 92, Peart J. said it cannot be said that even though an application is brought within that period of eight weeks, the Court could nevertheless refuse leave because it regarded the applicant as not having moved promptly within the eight-week period. In *Dekra Éireann Teoranta v Minister for the Environment* [2003] 2 I.L.R.M. 210, in respect of Ord.84A which concerns judicial review of public service contracts, Fennelly J. noted that an application within time cannot normally be defeated in absence of some special factor. However in England it has been recognised the promptness requirement applies with particular force in challenging a grant of permission. See *R. v North West Lecicestershire District Council ex parte Moses* [2000] Env. L.R. 443 and *Bristol City Council ex parte Anderson*, unreported, March 9, 1998.

The requirement to bring proceedings within eight weeks from when the decision is made or act done may mean that the court will carefully scrutinise as to whether proceedings could have been brought to challenge an earlier act. See *Linehan v Cork County Council*, unreported, High Court, Finlay Geoghegan J., February 19, 2008, where it was noted that the change in the Act may mean that acts or decision may have to be challenged as they occur rather than waiting until the final decision at the end of a process. Even prior to the change, the courts had refused leave where a decision was based on an earlier decision which was not challenged. See *Salafia v Minister for the Environment*, unreported, High Court, Smyth J., March 1, 2006. Prior to the change, there was also some suggestion that an applicant would be required to bring proceedings in advance of the formal decision when the grounds are known by seeking an order of prohibition. See *Openneer v Donegal County Council* [2006] 1 I.L.R.M. 150. See *O'Connor v Cork County Council*, unreported, High Court, Murphy J., November 1, 2005, as an example where an applicant sought an order of prohibition and a stay on the process. In *Harding v Cork County Council*, unreported, Supreme Court, May 2, 2008, Murray C.J. noted an applicant who was denied a right under law:

> "[S]hould not always just sit back and leave the process proceed at length until it reaches its final conclusion and then seek to impugn the final decision where it would have been properly open to such a person to seek a remedy at an earlier stage, such as by way of mandamus, requiring the authority to observe the statutory right in question. That is something which a Court would fully take into account when deciding whether or not to grant leave to bring judicial review. It may be otherwise where for example the decision was taken before the breach of the legal right could reasonably have been known or before there was an opportunity to seek any other properly available remedy".

Thus in certain cases the facts may not fully emerge until well after the "acts" done and indeed after the formal decision. See *Jerry Beades Construction Ltd v Dublin Corporation*, unreported, High Court, McKechnie J., September 7, 2005. This may particularly be the case where the public do have full rights of public participation in the relevant process. The full facts and nature of the "acts done" may not be immediately known or apparent and this may only emerge at a later date.

Where not commenced within the time limit, the court has a discretion to extend time under subs.(8) where the applicant can show both "good and sufficient reason" and also an additional requirement introduced under the 2006 Act that the failure to bring the application within the period was outside the control of the applicant. The two matters may clearly overlap; if the failure to bring the application within time was not outside the control of the applicant, an applicant may not have good and sufficient reason to extend the time. However, it is at least possible that a court may consider that an applicant has a good an sufficient reason but may still be unable to show that the failure to institute proceedings was beyond their control. The absence of a saver to extend time under the 1976 Act was held to be unconstitutional by the Supreme Court in *White v Dublin City Council* [2004] 1 I.R. 545; see also Ó Caoimh J. in the High Court, *White v Dublin City Council*, unreported, High Court, Ó Caoimh J., June 21, 2002; see also *Brady v Donegal County Council* [1989] 1 I.L.R.M. 282 (the Supreme Court declined to determine the matter); *Blessington Community & District Council Ltd v Wicklow County Council* [1997] 1 I.R. 273 and *Tuohy v Courtney* [1994] 3 I.R. 1.

An applicant must demonstate that there is good and sufficient reason for extending time, rather than merely good and sufficient reason for the delay. As regards the approach for seeking an extension of time, in *Kelly v Leitrim County Council* [2005] 2 I.R. 404, it was said that the legislative intent for speedy resolution of planning matters was best met by the following procedure:

1. an applicant who wished to move for leave outside the eight-week period would seek, in his notice of motion, both the relevant extension of time and leave itself;

2. the application would necessarily be accompanied by a statement required to ground the application for leave and evidence sought to be relied upon for the extension of time; and

3. it would then be within the election of the respondent whether it wished the court to consider the merits of the applicant's case when adjudicating on the issue of the extension of time or to leave the issue over to the hearing of the substantive leave application.

In *Marshall v Arklow Town Council* [2004] 4 I.R. 92, it was said that the question of delay in commencing proceedings and an application to extend time must be disposed of by the court before any consideration as to whether the applicants had made out a significant case to be granted leave to apply for judicial review. However, the court has considered the merits of grounds as part of the analysis of whether there are grounds to extend time. See *O'Shea v Kerry County Council* [2003] 4 I.R. 143 and *GK v Minister for Justice* [2002] 2 I.R. 418. An example of a successful claim of good and sufficient reason was where the delay arose from a defect in a public notice. See *Marshall v Arklow Town Council* [2004] 4 I.R. 92, where it was alleged a site notice was not erected, Peart J. held if the sign was in situ the applicant did not see it and therefore were not aware in fact that time was running against them and that when they realised the position, they acted as speedily as could be expected in the circumstances. However a mere complaint that the applicant did not see a notice due to its location was not sufficient in *O'Shea v Kerry County Council*.

In ordinary judicial review, time can be extended where there is "good reason" for doing so under Ord.84, r.21. In such context the case law has established as among relevant factors whether to extend time may include the length of the delay, prejudice and the merits of the case. For an examination of the factors see *De Róiste v Minister for Defence* [2001] 1 I.R. 190. Leave can be set aside where the extension of time was erroneously granted; see *MCD v Commission to Inquire into Child Abuse* [2003] 2 I.R. 348. In *Dekra Éireann Teoranta v Minister for the Environment and Local Government* [2003] 2 I.L.R.M. 210, it was noted that,

> "An applicant, who is unable to furnish good reason for his own failure to issue proceedings for judicial review at the earliest opportunity and in any event within three months from the date when grounds for the application first arose will not normally be able to show good reason for an extension of time".

In *Hogan v Waterford County Manager*, unreported, High Court, Herbert J., April 30, 2003, Herbert J. said an applicant must show some positive reason why a failure to allow an extension of the stipulated time would be unjust and unreasonable. As regards the meaning of "good and sufficient reason", in the context of asylum law see *GK v Minister for Justice, Equality and Law Reform* [2002] 2 I.R. 418 and *Sallim v Minister for Justice Equality and Law Reform* [2002] 2 I.R. 163; see also *B v The Governor of the Training Unit Glengariff Parade*, unreported, Supreme Court, January 30, 2002.

In the context of s.50 in *Kelly v Leitrim County Council* [2005] 2 I.R. 404, Clarke J. summarised as relevant factors:

(a) the length of time specified in the relevant statute within which the application must be made;

(b) the question of whether third party rights may be affected;

(c) notwithstanding (b) above, there is nonetheless a clear legislative policy involved in all such measures which requires that, irrespective of the involvement of the rights of third parties, determinations of particular types should be rendered certain within a short period of time as part of an overall process of conferring certainty on certain categories of administrative or quasi-judicial decisions. Therefore, while it may well be legitimate to take into account the fact that no third party rights are involved, that should not be regarded as conferring a wide or extensive jurisdiction to extend time in cases where no such rights may be affected. The overall integrity of the processes concerned is, in itself, a factor to be taken into account;

(d) blameworthiness;

(e) the nature of the issues involved;

(f) the merits of the case.

In determining whether the circumstances for failure to make an application for leave within the period was outside the control of the applicant, the court may consider when the grounds of challenge came to the knowledge of the applicant or ought to have come to his knowledge if he made reasonable and appropriate inquiries. Prior to this additional requirement being inserted under the 2006 Act, the court had considered when the grounds of challenge came to the knowledge of the applicant. In *Jerry Beades Construction Ltd v Dublin Corporation*, unreported, High Court, McKechnie J., September 7, 2005, considered the applicant was justified in not issuing proceedings until he had a comprehensive account from a planning official as to how a planning application had been dealt with internally. However, in *Openneer v Donegal County Council* [2006] 1 I.L.R.M. 150, in refusing an extension, the court did not accept that the position was only established upon receipt of a letter prior to proceedings commencing. In *Kenny v Dublin City Council*, unreported, High Court, Murphy J., September 8, 2004, in refusing relief on grounds of delay, it was said that any delay of the planning authority in dealing with the applicant's correspondence had to be seen within the context of previous applications.

Where there is a delay on the part of the applicant's (technical or legal) agent then that delay is attributable to the applicant as the principal. See *S v Minister for Justice, Equality and Law Reform and Others* [2002] 2 I.R. 167 and *Casey v An Bord Pleanála*, unreported, High Court, Murphy J., October 14, 2003, where it was further noted that the court is entitled to have regard to the overall conduct of the applicant. As regards the length of delay, in *Kelly v Leitrim County Council* [2005] 2 I.R. 404, a delay of 19 days was considered significant in the context of s.50 and where the applicant had expert planning advice. In the *Openneer v Donegal County Council* [2006] 1 I.L.R.M. 150 where there was delay of some five months, an extension was refused.

As regards prejudice, it is well established that absence of prejudice cannot per se present a good and sufficient reason for extending time. See *Kelly v Leitrim County Council* [2005] 2 I.R. 404. In *Hogan v Waterford County Manager*, unreported, High Court, Herbert J., April 30, 2003, Herbert J., in the context of waste management, said lack of prejudice to the respondent and to third parties is an essential precondition of the applicant obtaining an extension of time. The applicant must show also some good reason besides why in the interest of justice the time for bringing a judicial review application should be extended. Prejudice to a third party developer may be a significant factor in refusing relief. See *Kenny v Dublin City Council*, unreported, High Court, Murphy J., September 8, 2004 and *Lynch v Dublin City Council*, unreported, High Court, Ó Caoimh J., July 25, 2003. It therefore follows that prejudice, if present, may be a significant factor in declining to grant an extension of time.

[Section 50: supplemental provisions

50A.—(1) In this section—   1–72
"Court", where used without qualification, means the High Court (but this definition shall not be construed as meaning that subsections (2) to (6) and (9) do not extend to and govern the exercise by the Supreme Court of jurisdiction on any appeal that may be made);
"Order" shall be construed in accordance with section 50;
"section 50 leave" means leave to apply for judicial review under the Order in respect of a decision or other act to which section 50(2) applies.

(2) An application for *section 50* leave shall be made by motion on notice (grounded in the manner specified in the Order in respect of an ex parte motion for leave)—

    (a) if the application relates to a decision made or other act done by a planning authority or local authority in the performance or purported performance of a function under this Act, to the authority concerned and, in the case of a decision made or other act done by a planning authority on an application for permission, to the applicant for the permission where he or she is not the applicant for leave,

(b) if the application relates to a decision made or other act done by the Board on an appeal or referral, to the Board and each party or each other party, as the case may be, to the appeal or referral,

(c) if the application relates to a decision made or other act done by the Board on an application for permission or approval, to the Board and to the applicant for the permission or approval where he or she is not the applicant for leave,

(d) if the application relates to a decision made or other act done by the Board or a local authority in the performance or purported performance of a function referred to in *section 50(2)(b) or (c),* to the Board or the local authority concerned, and

(e) to any other person specified for that purpose by order of the High Court.

(3) The Court shall not grant *section 50* leave unless it is satisfied that—

(a) there are substantial grounds for contending that the decision or act concerned is invalid or ought to be quashed, and

(b)

    (i) the applicant has a substantial interest in the matter which is the subject of the application, or

    (ii) where the decision or act concerned relates to a development identified in or under regulations made under *section 176,* for the time being in force, as being development which may have significant effects on the environment, the applicant—

        (I) is a body or organisation (other than a State authority, a public authority or governmental body or agency) the aims or objectives of which relate to the promotion of environmental protection,

        (II) has, during the period of 12 months preceding the date of the application, pursued those aims or objectives, and

        (III) satisfies such requirements (if any) as a body or organisation, if it were to make an appeal under *section 37(4)(c),* would have to satisfy by virtue of *section 37(4)(d)(iii)* (and, for this purpose, any requirement prescribed under *section 37(4)(e)(iv)* shall apply as if the reference in it to the class of matter into which the decision, the subject of the appeal, falls were a reference to the class of matter into which the decision or act, the subject of the application for *section 50* leave, falls).

(4) A substantial interest for the purposes of *subsection (3)(b)* (i) is not limited to an interest in land or other financial interest.

(5) If the court grants *section 50* leave, no grounds shall be relied upon in the application for judicial review under the Order other than those determined by the Court to be substantial under *subsection (3)(a).*

(6) The Court may, as a condition for granting *section 50* leave, require the applicant for such leave to give an undertaking as to damages.

(7) The determination of the Court of an application for *section 50* leave or

of an application for judicial review on foot of such leave shall be final and no appeal shall lie from the decision of the Court to the Supreme Court in either case save with leave of the Court which leave shall only be granted where the Court certifies that its decision involves a point of law of exceptional public importance and that it is desirable in the public interest that an appeal should be taken to the Supreme Court.

(8) *Subsection (7)* shall not apply to a determination of the Court in so far as it involves a question as to the validity of any law having regard to the provisions of the Constitution.

(9) If an application is made for judicial review under the Order in respect of part only of a decision or other act to which *section 50(2)* applies, the Court may, if it thinks fit, declare to be invalid or quash the part concerned or any provision thereof without declaring invalid or quashing the remainder of the decision or other act or part of the decision or other act, and if the Court does so, it may make any consequential amendments to the remainder of the decision or other act or the part thereof that it considers appropriate.

(10) The Court shall, in determining an application for *section 50* leave or an application for judicial review on foot of such leave, act as expeditiously as possible consistent with the administration of justice.

(11) On an appeal from a determination of the Court in respect of an application referred to in *subsection (10)*, the Supreme Court shall—

    (a) have jurisdiction to determine only the point of law certified by the Court under *subsection (7)* (and to make only such order in the proceedings as follows from such determination), and

    (b) in determining the appeal, act as expeditiously as possible consistent with the administration of justice.

(12) Rules of court may make provision for the expeditious hearing of applications for *section 50* leave and applications for judicial review on foot of such leave.]

AMENDMENT HISTORY

Section 50A inserted by s.13 of the Planning and Development (Strategic Infrastructure) Act 2006 (No. 27 of 2006).

NOTE

This section specifically concerns the application for leave to seek judicial review. Judicial review proceedings are commenced in the High Court as reflected in the definition of "Court" in subs.(1). With respect judicial review proceedings entered into the Commercial Court (see *Mulholland v An Bord Pleanála* [2005] 3 I.R. 1), the practice has been adopted of having combined hearings whereby the leave and substantive hearing are held at the same time in the interests of saving time and costs. While it is clear that the parties can consent to the grant of leave, such a combined hearing where leave has not been granted can pose some procedural confusion. Where a statement of opposition is filed on a without prejudice basis, it is not justified to confine the respondents to the points raised in opposition. This arises from the fact that there is no obligation for a respondent to file any papers including a replying affidavit at leave stage and that some matters such as substantial interest, extension of time and adequacy of an appeal, are more appropriately dealt with at leave stage. It follows that any statement of opposition cannot have the function of narrowing the issues raised which would be the case if leave had already been granted.

Subsection (2) provides that the procedure for taking the proceedings is by notice of motion, statement of grounds and grounding affidavit, as set out in Ord.84. Such documents are not deemed "pleadings" within the meaning of RSC Ord.125; see *Ahern v Minister for Industry and Commerce* [1990] 1 I.R. 55. The subsection sets out the parties which must be served with the proceedings which depends upon the decision or act challenged and is in similar terms to the former subs.(4)(b). All of the parties mentioned therein must be served with all of the necessary papers (notice of motion, statement required to ground application for judicial review and grounding affidavit) before the proceedings may be deemed to have been properly instituted. Section 2 provides a detailed definition of "party to an appeal or referral" which is relevant to (b). In the context of a planning appeal to the Board, the parties will include the planning authority, the person making the appeal and the applicant for permission. See *Murray v An Bord Pleanála* [2000] 1 I.R. 42. A strategic infrastructure development application would appear to be covered under (c). It follows that in respect of a strategic infrastructure application in which a notice has been served under s.37B(4)(a) that it is necessary to apply to the Board rather than to the planning authority under the permission procedure, the planning authority in whose area the proposed development is proposed to take place, is not a mandatory party for the purposes of service under subs.(2)(e) requires service on any other person specified for that purpose by order of the High Court. See *O'Keeffe v An Bord Pleanála* [1993] 1 I.R. 39. It may be noted that Ord.84, r.22(2) of the Rules of the Superior Courts provides that "[t]he notice of motion or summons must be served on all persons directly affected". Whether a person should be joined will depend upon whether it is "necessary in order to enable the court effectually and completely to adjudicate upon and settle all questions involved in the cause or matter". See *BUPA (IRL) Ltd v Health Insurance Authority* [2006] 1 I.L.R.M. 308. However, persons who might have a vital interest in the outcome of a particular application for judicial review, but who are only indirectly affected may not come within the terms of RSC Ord.84, r.22. See *Monopower v Monaghan County Council*, unreported, High Court, Herbert J., July 10, 2006, where Herbert J. refused an order to join local residents on the basis that they were merely indirectly effected. Similarly, the court declined to join the Minister for the Environment, notwithstanding that an article of the Planning Regulations was being challenged. RSC Ord.84 r.26 states that a person who desires to be heard in opposition on the motion or summons and appears to the court to be a proper person to be heard shall be heard notwithstanding that he has not been served with notice of the motion or the summons. Thus a person who may have a significant contribution to make to the proceedings, but who may not come within the definition of a person "directly affected" might still be heard under r.26, if the trial judge considers this to be necessary in the interests of justice. See *Monopower v Monaghan County Council*, unreported, High Court, Herbert J., July 10, 2006.

Subsection (3) states that the two main threshold requirements for leave are that the applicant must demonstrate both substantial grounds and substantial interest. These are two separate and independent requirements. See *Harding v Cork County Council*, unreported, Supreme Court, May 2, 2008, in which it was said that the existence of substantial grounds cannot make good a lack of "substantial interest". The court will first examine whether an applicant has substantial interest before it considers the issue of substantial grounds. In *Sweetman v An Bord Pleanála* [2007] 2 I.L.R.M. 328, Clarke J. rejected the contention that the requirement for leave and limitations on the scope of inquiry in judicial review, amounted to a barrier to an entitlement to judicial review under the European Directive 2003/35/EC for public participation in respect of the drawing up of certain plans and programmes. Even if there are substantial grounds to the effect that a greater level of scrutiny is mandated by the Directive in relation to environmental judicial review applications (such as under art.10a), such greater level of scrutiny (as with fundamental human rights) can be accommodated within the existing judicial review regime.

Substantial Grounds

Substantial grounds is a higher standard than prima facie grounds, which is required for leave in ordinary judicial review. As regards ordinary judicial review; see *G v DPP* [1994] 1 I.R. 374. As regards the meaning of substantial grounds, in *McNamara v An Bord Pleanála* [1995] 2 I.L.R.M. 125, Carroll J. said:

"[I]n order for a ground to be substantial it must be reasonable, it must be arguable, it must be weighty. It must not be trivial or tenuous. However, I am not concerned in trying to ascertain what the eventual result would be … [a] ground that does not stand any chance of being sustained (for example where the point has already been decided in another case) could not be said to be substantial. I draw a distinction between the grounds and the various arguments put forward in support of those grounds. I do not think I should evaluate each argument and say whether it is sound or not. If I consider a ground as such to be substantial I do not also have to say that the Applicant is confined in this argument at the next stage to those which I believe may have some merit".

Carroll J.'s definition has been approved in numerous cases; see *Keane v An Bord Pleanála*, unreported, High Court, Murphy J., June 20, 1995; *Mulhall v An Bord Pleanála*, unreported, High Court, McCracken J., June 10, 1996; *Blessington Community & District Council v Wicklow County Council*, unreported, High Court, Kelly J., July 19, 1996; *Maire de Faoite v An Bord Pleanála*, unreported, High Court, Laffoy J., May 2, 2000, and also *RGDATA v An Bord Pleanála*, unreported, High Court, Barron J., April 30, 1996 and *Mulholland v An Bord Pleanála (2)* [2006] 1 I.R. 453. The Supreme Court endorsed the *McNamara* test in *Illegal Immigrants (Trafficking) Bill 1999* [2000] 2 I.R. 360. This is despite some difficulties in terms of the language, see comments of Geoghegan J. in *Jackson Way Properties v Minister for the Environment*, unreported, High Court, Geoghegan J., May 20, 1995. See also *Scott v An Bord Pleanála* [1995] 1 I.L.R.M. 424 and *Irish Cement Ltd v An Bord Pleanála*, unreported, High Court, McCracken J., February 24, 1998. The definition may be criticised as it uses language such as arguable or trivial which fails to distinguish substantial grounds from the test in ordinary judicial review. See *G v DPP* [1994] 1 I.R. 374. However, the passage may perhaps best be understood not as defining the cut-off threshold which must be met (such as arguable or trivial) but a list of qualities all of which qualities substantial grounds will possess. The difficulties in providing a satisfactory definition of substantial grounds was noted by McKechnie J. in *Kenny v An Bord Pleanála (No. 1)* [2001] 1 I.R. 565 who stated:

"Indeed in a consideration of these words, one can think of grounds which could be both reasonable and arguable and yet still fall significantly short of meeting the threshold of being substantial. The words 'trivial or tenuous' are undoubtedly helpful but more so as words of elimination rather than words of qualification. The description of being 'weighty' and of 'real substance' are in my view of considerable importance in the interpretation of this threshold phrase. However, it must also be remembered that, from a base of say opposite substantial, namely, insubstantial, an applicant must navigate the considerable distance in between, and in addition must arrive at and meet the threshold while still afloat and on course. In truth I feel, while many attempts have been made to explain or convey 'the equivalent of its meaning' I am not certain that one can better the original phrase itself."

In *Harrington v An Bord Pleanála* [2006] 1 I.R. 388, Macken J. said:

"It can only be on the basis of the particular and peculiar facts of each individual case that a court can determine whether or not one has reached the area of 'weighty' which is constituted by an accumulation of argument on the law and/or the establishment of facts which taken together make it abundantly clear that the matter is sufficiently strong to be considered weighty".

A similar criteria of substantial grounds applies under other enactments such as the Illegal Immigrants (Trafficking) Act 2000, s.5. amending the Immigration Act 1999; the Transport (Railway Infrastructure) Act 2001, s.47(2)(b); the Electricity Regulation Act 1999, s.32(2); the Roads (Amendment) Act 1998, s.6(2); the Irish Takeover Panel Act 1997, s.13(3); the Fisheries (Amendment) Act 1997, s.73(2); the Waste Management Act 1996, s.43(5)(b) and the Transport (Dublin Light Rail) Act 1996, s.12(2)(b).

While it is clear from the judgment in *Harding v Cork County Council*, unreported, Supreme Court, May 2, 2008, that substantial interest and substantial grounds are separate requirements, where an applicant is relying upon grounds or defects by which he was not personally prejudiced, this may be relevant to the exercise of the courts discretion whether to grant relief. See *Dunne v An Bord Pleanála*, unreported, High Court, McGovern J., December 14, 2006. Where the dispute concerns factual matters, see *Murphy v Greene* [1990] 2 I.R. 566 and *O'Dowd v North Western Health Board* [1983] I.L.R.M. 186. It has been suggested that factual issues should not generally be sought to be resolved at leave stage (see *Village Residents Association Ltd v An Bord Pleanála (No. 1)* [2001] 1 I.R. 65) though considering the nature of judicial review, controversies of fact may only arise to a limited extent (see *Byrne v Wicklow County Council*, unreported, High Court, Keane J., November 3, 1994). In *Kenny v An Bord Pleanála (No. 1)* [2001] 1 I.R. 565, it was noted that while the court ought not to resolve conflicts of fact on an application for leave, nonetheless within the existing limitations an evaluation of the factual matrix should be made. This was endorsed in *Mulholland v An Bord Pleanála (No. 2)* [2006] 1 I.R. 453, where Kelly J. noted that having found there were substantial grounds he ought not to give detailed reasons for such finding as this would be a waste of time and contrary to the approach of the High Court (Carroll J.) in *McNamara v An Bord Pleanála* [1995] 2 I.L.R.M. 125. See *Arklow Holidays Limited v An Bord Pleanála and Wicklow County Council*, unreported, High Court, Clarke J., January 18, 2006, where it was held that where leave is granted following opposing arguments as to whether there are substantial grounds, the court should not express any view on the relevant strengths of those arguments.

Where on the affidavits sworn in the proceedings there is a direct dispute between the averments of the deponents as to relevant facts, for the purposes of the leave application the court should make an assumption in favour of the applicants. See *Linehan v Cork County Council*, unreported, High Court, Finlay Geogheghan J., February 19, 2008, where Finlay Geoghegan J. said she would not exclude the possibility of a court considering it appropriate, in a particular case, to determine a disputed fact as part of a leave application. It is possible that there could be facts in dispute which are so central to the existence or absence of substantial grounds that it would be considered appropriate even at the leave stage to determine by cross-examination or otherwise disputed facts. A respondent might adduce independent documentary evidence in conflict with averments of an applicant's deponent. This would however be an exception to the general rule.

It appears that the grounds for judicial review must be formulated with some precision. See *McNamara v An Bord Pleanála (2)* [1996] 2 I.L.R.M. 339, in the context of an application to amend a statement of grounds outside the time limit, Barr J. said the time limits "clearly means not only that he must initiate proceedings and specify the relief claimed within the two month time limit, but when so doing, he must also specify the grounds on which relief is sought". See also *State (Glover) v District Judge McCarty* [1981] I.L.R.M. 47. In ordinary judicial review RSC Ord.84, r.23(2) allows an amendments of grounds. See *McCormick v Garda Síochána Complaints Board* [1997] 2 I.R. 489, where Costello P. stated that an amendment may be allowed where facts come to light which could not be known at the time leave was obtained and when the amendment would not prejudice the respondent; see also *Ní Éili v Environmental Protection Agency* [1997] 2 I.L.R.M. 458. It would appear to follow from the fact that an extension of time can be granted in instituting proceedings under s.50 that grounds can be amended outside the time limits based on similar principles.

Judicial review is concerned with the decision-making process rather than the decision itself. The grounds must therefore generally relate to errors of law or illegalities. A decision on whether to grant or refuse planning permission will only be overturned on grounds of irrationality; see *O'Keeffe v An Bord Pleanála* [1993] 1 I.R. 39. The court cannot interfere with a decision merely because it is satisfied on the facts that it would have raised different inferences and conclusions or is satisfied that the case against the decision is stronger than the case for it; see also *State (Keegan) v Stardust Victim's Compensation Tribunal* [1986] I.R. 642; *Bailey v Mr Justice Flood*, unreported, High Court, Morris P., March 6, 2000; *Camara v Refugee Appeals Tribunal*, unreported, High Court, Kelly J., July 26, 2000; *Aer Rianta v Commissioner for Aviation Regulation*, unreported, High Court, O'Sullivan J., January 16, 2003. The courts will not intervene by way of judicial review to quash decisions of administrative tribunals (such as the Board) in the absence of evidence of illegality. The function of the court in an application for judicial review is limited to determining whether or not an impugned decision was legal, not whether or not it was correct. See *Power v An Bord Pleanála*, unreported, High Court, Quirke J., January 17, 2006. In *Kildare County Council v An Bord Pleanála*, unreported, High Court, McMenamin J., March 10, 2006 it was said, "the road was to be approved was vested in the respondent and in determining that question the evaluation of evidence, and the application of the appropriate legal criteria was also a matter for the respondent". In deciding whether a decision is irrational the court will consider whether there were any materials, facts and information properly before the Board from which it could arrive at its decision; the volume of material is immaterial. See *M A Ryan v An Bord Pleanála*, unreported, High Court, Peart J., February 6, 2003.

Where rights under European law or constitutional rights are involved there has been some suggestions that a higher level of scrutiny may be applied. This may include a more exacting standard of review of merits than under *O'Keeffe* irrationality. See *Sweetman v An Bord Pleanála* [2007] 2 I.L.R.M. 328, in the context of considering art.10a of Directive 2003/35/EC which required a review of substantive legality, Clarke J. considered that Irish judicial review goes a long way towards and may well meet this requirement. It was noted that there is the potential for flexibility in the approach to be taken in respect of judicial review in appropriate cases such as in England where there has evolved the doctrine of "anxious scrutiny" whereby a higher level of scrutiny is applied to cases involving fundamental human rights. Clarke J. noted that:

"It seems to me that a similar approach can be adopted in planning cases. To the extent that it may be argued successfully that there are substantial grounds to the effect that a greater level of scrutiny is mandated by the Directive in relation to environmental judicial review applications, then such greater level of scrutiny can, by analogy with the position adopted in respect of fundamental human rights cases, be accommodated within the existing judicial review regime. To the extent that substantial grounds needs to be established in order that leave be obtained then leave should be granted where it can be demonstrated that there are substantial grounds for the applicant challenged applying a level of scrutiny which the court is, in turn, satisfied meets a substantial grounds test".

See *Klohn v An Bord Pleanála*, unreported, High Court, McMahon J., April 23, 2008. where it was noted that where the decision under review is based on national legislation inspired by an EU Directive, the standard of review adopted by the EU itself might be more appropriate, the reason being "first, the *O'Keeffe* standard is too low; second, the adoption of the EU standard will go someway to ensuring uniformity throughout the Community in these matters". See also *Siac Construction Ltd v Mayo County Council* [2002] 3 I.R. 148, in the context of European public procurement law, where Fennelly J. noted that the test of manifest error was not to be equated with the test that a decision must plainly and unambiguously fly in the face of reason and common sense. As regards constitutional rights in *O'Callaghan v Members of the Tribunal of Inquiry into Planning Matters*, unreported, July 7, 2004, O'Neill J. stated:

"Whether the encroachment into the constitutional right is justified depends upon the validity of the factors relied upon to justify it and given, that what is thought to be justified is a breach of, or encroachment into a constitutional right, the factors put forward to justify them are properly to be assessed with the kind of caution or circumspection which may be aptly described as anxious scrutiny".

See also *Clinton v An Bord Pleanála*, unreported, Supreme Court, May 2, 2007, in which Geoghegan J. said:

"The power conferred on an administrative body such as a local authority or An Bord Pleanála to compulsorily acquire land must be exercised in accordance with the requirements of the Constitution, including respecting the property rights of the affected landowner (East Donegal Co-Operative v. The Attorney General [1970] I.R. 317). Any decisions of such bodies are subject to judicial review. It would insufficiently protect constitutional rights if the court, hearing the judicial review application, merely had to be satisfied that the decision was not irrational or was not contrary to fundamental reason and common sense".

Substantial Interest

The notion of substantial interest, which is the locus standi criterion under s.50 was introduced by the 2000 Act. Prior to this under the previous Planning Act, there was simply the requirement under ordinary judicial review to demonstrate a "sufficient interest". The change was clearly intended to raise the threshold or heighten the bar which applicants for leave to bring judicial review proceedings must cross. See *Harding v Cork County Council*, unreported, Supreme Court, May 2, 2008. A rigorous approach to standing is justified by the underlying scheme of the statutory judicial review procedure. See *Harrington v An*

Bord Pleanála [2006] 1 I.R. 388. The preponderance of authority suggests that the issue of locus standi should be resolved at the leave stage. See *Harding v Cork County Council*, unreported, Supreme Court, May 2, 2008, where the Supreme Court approved the approach of Clarke J. in the High Court, who said that substantial interest should determined at leave stage and also generally before considering whether they were substantial grounds. See also *Lancefort v An Bord Pleanála* [1999] 2 I.R. 270. In *Murphy v Cobh Town Council*, unreported, High Court, McMenamin J., October 26, 2006, it was said that standing should be determined at leave stage and should not, absent exceptional circumstances, be revisited at the full hearing. However, in *Moriarty v South Dublin County Council*, unreported, High Court, Moriarty J., November 24, 2005, it was said that even where the court grants leave, the court at full hearing can re-examine whether the applicant has the necessary substantial interest. Where the court finds that the applicant does not have substantial interest, it is not appropriate for the court to go any further to consider whether there was substantial grounds as this will be redundant. See *Harding v Cork County Council*, unreported, High Court, Clarke J., October 12, 2006 which was approved in the Supreme Court. As noted above it is clear that substantial interest and substantial grounds are separate requirements. As noted by Kearns J. in *Harding*, the "'substantial grounds' and 'substantial interest' requirements of s.50 create two fences, not one and that an applicant who fails to establish the latter has no entitlement to obtain leave merely because he has grounds which are substantial". The suggestion in *Friends of the Curragh Environment Ltd v An Bord Pleanála (No. 2)* [2007] 1 I.L.R.M. 386 that the court will have regard to the grounds of challenge would appear incorrect in the light of the judgment in *Harding*.

Subsection (3)(b) states that the substantial interest is "in the matter which is the subject of the application" and in this regard the word "application" means the application for leave to apply for judicial review, while the word "matter" means the development project itself and the outcome of the planning process in relation to it (and does not mean the legal proceedings). See *Harding v Cork County Council*, unreported, Supreme Court, May 2, 2008.

The only guidance in the Act regarding the meaning of substantial interest is provided in s.50A(4) which provides that "substantial interest" is not limited to an interest in land or other financial interest. By only providing a limited negative definition, substantial interest is left open, leaving the courts to elucidate the concept on a case by case basis. The case law prior to *Harding* provides some guidance as to circumstances in which an applicant could have a substantial interest. In *O'Shea v Kerry County Council* [2003] 4 I.R. 143, Ó Caoimh J. considered that subs.(4)(d) indicated that the term was not to be narrowly construed and that a general interest that the law be followed is not a substantial interest. Equally an interest in planning matters is not enough. See *O'Brien v Dun Laoghaire-Rathdown County Council*, unreported, High Court, O'Neill J., June 1, 2006. In contrast, under the ordinary judicial review procedure, public interest that statutory bodies act in accordance with law may still be sufficient interest; see *Mulcreevy v Minister For Environment*, unreported, Supreme Court, January 27, 2004. In *O'Shea*, despite being a nearby land owner, the applicant had failed to show how she was affected.

The Supreme Court addressed the meaning of substantial interest in *Harding v Cork County Council*, unreported, Supreme Court, May 2, 2008, where it was held that to have a substantial interest within the meaning of s.50 of the Act of 2000, it is necessary for an applicant to establish:

- that he has an interest in the development the subject of the proceedings which is "peculiar and personal" to him.;
- that the nature and level of his interest is significant or weighty;
- that his interest is affected by or connected with the proposed development.

The Supreme Court also approved of the formulation by Clarke J. in the High Court who said:

"It seems to me, therefore that, having identified the interest which an applicant has either expressed (or might be taken to have been prevented from having expressed) the court should, by reference to that interest, identify the importance of the interest by reference to criteria such as: (a) The scale of the project and the extent to which the project might be said to give rise to a significant alteration in the amenity of the area concerned. The greater the scale and the more significant the alteration in the area than the wider range of persons who may legitimately be able to establish a substantial interest (b) the extent of the connection of the applicant concerned to the effects of the project by particular reference to the basis of the challenge which he puts forward to the planning permission and the planning process (c) such other factors as may arise on the facts of an individual case".

The Supreme Court noted whether the interests of a particular applicant fulfil those requirements depends upon all of the circumstances of a particular case. There was an obvious public policy consideration driving this restrictive statutory code. It does not necessarily follow that, because an applicant has an interest in land or financial interest which is affected by the development, such applicant will have a substantial interest, although this may often be the case in a particular set of facts. Equally, it does not necessarily mean that a person without an interest in land or financial interest must always fall outside the category of those who have a substantial interest, but simply that other types of interest can count towards whether a person has a substantial interest. The interest must be weighty and personal to the applicant in the sense that he has a demonstrable stake in the project, perhaps shared with others, deriving from the proximity and connectedness of his interest to the proposed development and its likely or probable effects. While all three members of the Supreme Court were in agreement on the general principles, there was one difference regarding whether a substantial interest could arise during the planning process. Murray C.J. noted that "[w]hile certain delineations can be made in defining what "substantial interest" may or may not amount to, the phrase is not susceptible to a general or all embracing definition or formula covering all cases".

The judgments were divided upon whether an applicant could have "substantial interest" in the decision-making process. Kearns J. said that a person must always have a substantial interest in the development project itself and the Act does not itself provide an exception from the scope of its provisions where some want of process has occurred in the case of an objector who lacks substantial interest. However, Murray C.J. said even if an applicant does not have a "substantial interest" related to the development, a person who has exercised a statutory right to participate in the planning process may, in limited circumstances, potentially have a "substantial interest" related to the exercise of that right. This specifically related to a person who had previously made submissions who was required to be "personally" notified under art.35(1) of the 2001 Regulations that significant further information was received and so this right was "personal or peculiar" to him. Murray C.J. stressed that general complaints that the planning authority had failed to observe the law during the planning process could not give rise to a substantial interest. Thus a failure of the developer to provide all the further information which was demanded by the planning authority; to send an appropriate fee with the revised plan; to erect a site notice in respect of that plan or the failure of the planning authority to give a statement indicating the main reasons for not accepting the planner's recommendation, could not involve an interest which is peculiar or personal to an applicant. Finnegan J. said he would leave over to another case whether a breach of art.35 could give rise to a substantial interest.

While the judgment in *Harding* related to law prior to the scope of s.50 being extended to "acts done", the criteria in *Harding* relating to substantial interest are equally applicable to a challenge to "acts done" as in the context of the decision making process. Subject to the one possible exception discussed above, the substantial interest must relate to the development project itself so where the "act done" is in the context of an application for a proposed development, the substantial interest must relate to the proposed development. An applicant for judicial review should therefore clearly address the nature of his substantial interest in the papers grounding his application for judicial review. It is not enough that an applicant merely asserts that they are a nearby resident or owner of land, they should also seek to explain how their interest may be affected by the proposed development. In the previous case law nearby residency was relevant in finding an applicant to have locus standi: see *Law v The Minister for Local Government and Traditional Homes Ltd*, unreported, High Court, Deele J., May 30, 1974 and *Seery v An Bord Pleanála*, unreported, High Court, Finnegan J., June 2, 2000. However, in *O'Shea v An Bord Pleanála* [2003] 4 I.R. 143 the applicant was held not to have a substantial interest even though they were an adjoining landowner. Also in *O'Brien v Dun Laoghaire-Rathdown County Council*, unreported, High Court, O'Neill J., June 1, 2006, a person who lived some 77 metres away from the proposed development was held not to have a substantial interest. The court took into account, inter alia, that the nature of the project was that it would not affect her visual amenties.

The requirement that an interest must be peculiar or personal to an applicant does not mean that if some other party has the same or similar interest in the subject matter of the application that both are thereby excluded from having a "substantial interest". The proposed development the subject matter of the application is one which affects the applicant personally or individually in a substantial way as distinct from any interest which the wider community, not so personally and individually affected might have in the proposed development. See *Cumann Tomás Daibhis v South Dublin County Council,* unreported, High Court, O'Neill J., March 30, 2007 approved in *Harding v Cork County Council,* unreported, Supreme Court, May 2, 2008. A company director cannot rely upon lands owned by the company in order to assert an interest. See *Moriarty v South Dublin County Council,* unreported, High Court, Hanna J., November 24, 2005. Similarly, an agent or a member of consulting engineers who had been retained by an applicant for planning permission, could not attribute to himself the interests of the applicant for permission. See *Lennon v Limerick County Council,* unreported, High Court, Laffoy J., April 3, 2006. See also by analogy *O'Brien v Dun Laoghaire-Rathdown County Council,* unreported, High Court, O'Neill J., June 1, 2006, where in respect of the now abolished independent requirement to have made submissions, submissions made by An Taisce could not be attributed to the applicant, although she was an active member of the same and assisted with such submissions.

The scale of the project and extent to which it significantly alters amenities was a factor in the case law prior to *Harding.* See *Murphy v Wicklow County Council,* unreported, High Court, Kearns J., March 19, 1999, where Kearns J. found there was sufficient interest for environmental protesters to challenge a development at the Glen of the Downs, holding that the case was exceptional and should not be interpreted as giving a "green light" for similar protests at other locations lacking the unique environmental and statutory mantle which pertains to the Glen of the Downs. See also *Sweetman v An Bord Pleanála* [2007] 2 I.L.R.M. 328. However, in *Salafia v An Bord Pleanála,* unreported, High Court, Smyth J., March 1, 2006, in a challenge to a road scheme near the Hill of Tara, where the applicant had not participated in the planning process and was not resident in the area or in County Meath, he was held not able to meet even the lower "sufficient interest" standard.

The clear separation between substantial interest and substantial grounds which are two fences rather than one, calls into question the line of case law which suggests that an applicant would not have a substantial interest if it relates to a matter which could have been addressed in the appeal to An Bord Pleanála. This was so held in *Ryanair v An Bord Pleanála,* unreported, High Court, Ó Caoimh J., February 27, 2004, Ó Caoimh J. who applied the dicta of Keane J. at p.315 in *Lancefort Ltd v An Bord Pleanála (No.2)* [1999] 2 I.R. 270. See also *Harrington v An Bord Pleanála* [2006] 1 I.R. 388 where the point was raised by another party. The better view is that this can no longer represent the law in the light of the judgment of the Supreme Court in *Harding.* It must follow from the fact that a person cannot gain a substantial interest by participating in the decision-making process as stated in *Harding,* that such person equally cannot lose a substantial interest by either not participating or failing to raise a ground which was asserted in the judicial review proceedings. This further follows from the fact that substantial interest must be in the development project itself. Although somewhat confusingly, Clarke J. in the High Court had referred to assessing the extent of connection by reference to the grounds put forward in the planning process, it appears that he was using the word "grounds" to mean the interest put forward in the planning process or application. Until the enactment of the 2006 Act, there was an independent requirement to have participated in the planning process, as was noted by the Supreme Court. There is no basis for suggesting that Clarke J. considered this requirement as being necessary for the purposes of substantial interest. The Supreme Court in *Harding* made no finding to the effect that prior participation or raising a particular ground, was in any way relevant to substantial interest. It therefore follows from the above that any suggestion of a type of issue-specific locus standi has no statutory basis whatsoever and the decisions in *Ryanair* and *Harrington* no longer accurarely represent the law. While failure to raise a ground in an appeal or oral hearing may be relevant to the exercise of the courts discretion in judicial review proceedings, it can have no relevance to the concept of substantial interest. Furtheremore as noted that 2006 Act abolished the additional requirement which was contained in s.50(4)(c) of the 2000 Act that the applicant must also have participated in the planning process which is being challenged by making observations or submissions or showing good and sufficient reasons for not so participating. Any suggestion that this prior participation could re-emerge as a necessary element of substantial interest would completely undermine the legislative intent in abolishing this requirement.

It is also clear from the judgment in *Harding* that there is no room for any exception to the requirement to demonstrate a substantial interest on the basis of a serious abuse process. This was suggested in *Harrington v An Bord Pleanála* [2006] 1 I.R. 388, where it was said the fact that an applicant does not have a substantial interest does not mean that the court should be precluded from scrutinising a serious failure to properly apply the law. See also *O'Brien v Dun Laoghaire-Rathdown County Council*, unreported, High Court, O'Neill J., June 1, 2006. Again, any suggestion of an exception is not justified in the light of the judgment in *Harding*.

Where a development, the subject of proceedings, requires an EIS, the substantial interest requirement may be interpreted with some flexibility or limited adjustment in individual cases. However, the clear judicial indications are that any modification, if any, would be minor. This stems from art.10a of the Directive 2003/35/EC for public participation in respect of the drawing up of certain plans and programmes relating to the environment which amends to EIA Directive 85/337/ECC, which provides, inter alia, that:

> "Member States shall ensure that, in accordance with the relevant national legal system, members of the public concerned (a) having a sufficient interest, or alternatively, (b) maintaining the impairment of a right, where administrative procedural law of a Member State requires this as a precondition, have access to a review procedure before a court of law or another independent and impartial body established by law to challenge the substantive or procedural legality of decisions, acts or omissions subject to the public participation provisions of this Directive".

In *Harding v Cork County Council*, unreported, Supreme Court, May 2, 2008, with respect to Directive 2003/35/EC, Kearns J. said it was probably correct that what constitutes a sufficient interest and impairment of a right are expressly reserved by art.10a of the relevant Directive to the individual Member States, although it was not necessary to decide this point. Also, while the Act falls to be interpreted in the light of the terms and objectives of the Directive in question it is an established principle that such an interpretative approach does not mean that the Act be interpreted contra legem. This is in line with *Sweetman v An Bord Pleanála* [2007] 2 I.L.R.M. 328, where, in the context of a road scheme it was held the requirement to meet a higher "substantial interest" rather than the former "sufficient interest" does not breach the "sufficient interest" test set out in art.10a. It was noted that art.10a provides that "what constitutes a sufficient interest and impairment of a right shall be determined by the member state". It was held that the terms "substantial interest" and "sufficient interest" have a particular meaning in Irish judicial review law. Clarke J. rejected that the requirement for leave and limitations on the scope of inquiry in judicial review, amounted to a barrier to an entitlement to judicial review under the Directive noting:

> "If it should prove to be necessary, on the facts of any individual case, to give a more generous interpretation of the requirement of 'substantial interest' so as to meet the 'wide access to justice' criteria set out in Article 10a then there would be no difficulty in construing the term 'substantial interest' in an appropriate manner. It seems to me that it follows, therefore, that the term 'substantial interest' needs to be construed having regard to the requirement that Article 10a, (in the cases to which it applies, such as this) and having regard to the requirement that there be wide access to justice".

In *Friends of the Curragh Environment Ltd v An Bord Pleanála (No. 1)*, unreported, High Court. Kelly J., July 14, 2006, it was held that art.10a was not sufficiently clear, precise and unconditional as to have direct effect. It was also held that the requirements of review could be met by the Board and it was doubtful whether art.10a would apply to judicial review proceedings in court. It may be noted however, that in respect of strategic planning infrastructure applications the application is made directly to the Board.

The rule in *Henderson v Henderson* (1843) 3 Hare 100, to the effect that a party to previous litigation is bound not only by matters actually raised but by matters which ought properly have been raised but were not, is applicable to the planning process. See *Arklow Holidays v An Bord Pleanála*, unreported, High Court, Clarke J., October 5, 2007, where relief was refused as each of the grounds of challenge to the Board's decision raised issues which were equally capable of having been raised in an earlier challenge to the original decision by the planning authority. The court left open whether the rule may apply where no challenge is, in fact, brought to the original planning decision by the local authority but where the grounds sought to be relied on to challenge a decision of the Board could have been raised had such a challenge been brought. This decision has been certified for appeal to the Supreme Court.

The motive for challenging a decision will not deprive an applicant of locus standi if he otherwise has a right to challenge. See *The State (Tern Houses) v An Bord Pleanála* [1985] I.R. 725 and *State (Abenglen) v Dublin Corporation* [1984] I.R. 381. The fact that the applicant is a public representative is a factor to be taken into account in determining his locus standi; see *O'Connell v Cork Corporation* [2001] 3 I.R. 602, in the context of the Waste Management Acts.

Even where an applicant has locus standi, the degree to which such person is affected may be taken into account in the exercise of the court's discretion whether to grant relief, see *Cunningham v An Bord Pleanála*, unreported, High Court, Lavan J., May 3, 1990. Where an issue of the constitutionality of a planning provision is raised, the applicant must have already established some factual circumstances to ground the application; see *Blessington Community and District Council v Wicklow County Council* [1997] 1 I.R. 273 and *Brady v Donegal County Council* [1989] I.L.R.M. 282. Constitutional challenges can be included in a judicial review application under s.50; see *Lancefort Ltd v An Bord Pleanála* [1997] 2 I.L.R.M. 508 and *Hynes v An Bord Pleanála*, unreported, High Court, Laffoy J., December 10, 1997.

A company can have locus standi to bring a judicial review proceedings. The same criteria of substantial interest will apply to the standing of a company as to an individual, subject to the fact that the type of interests may vary due its corporate nature. However, in *Moriarty v South Dublin County Council*, unreported, High Court, Hanna J., November 24, 2005, it was suggested that a rival business may not have standing in the absence of evidence of an impact on the company's business. Nonetheless, it is clear that a company's property or financial interest may be affected which will be relevant to whether it has a substantial interest. The property must however be held by the company rather than its members. See *Springview v Cavan Development Ltd* [2000] 1 I.L.R.M. 437. This interest must not be remote. See *Ballintubber Heights Ltd v Cork Corporation*, unreported, High Court, Ó Caoimh J., June 21, 2002, where the only relevant interest was an option to purchase neighbouring lands. An issue may arise, however, where the company was simply incorporated for the purpose of the judicial review application as to whether it has locus standi. In *Lancefort v An Bord Pleanála (No.2)* [1999] 2 I.R. 270, Keane J. recognised that a company formed after the decision could, in certain particular circumstances, potentially have locus standi. In her dissenting judgment in *Lancefort*, Denham J. noted at 293 that the financial circumstances of the company will be relevant and an award of security of costs may be necessary. The court may have regard to the memorandum of agreement and articles of association of the company, see *Springview v Cavan Development Ltd* [2000] 1 I.L.R.M. 437. The court may look behind the interest of the company and the extent of its interest; see *Ballintubber Heights Ltd v Cork Corporation*, unreported, High Court, Ó Caoimh J., June 21, 2002. The extent to which the interest of its members may be taken into account may depend on the nature of the company. Sufficient interest was held to exist in *Blessington Heritage Trust Ltd v Wicklow County Council* [1999] 4 I.R. 571, where McGuinness J. held that the applicant company largely comprised local people who had demonstrated concern for the environment over a period of years. The above cases must however be read subject to the more exacting standard of substantial interest, as delineated in *Harding* and it is unlikely that such facts would meet the standard. An unincorporated trade association or representative association whose members have an interest in the matter may have locus standi. However, where its members could have brought the challenge itself, this may mean the body does not have locus standi. In *Construction Industry Federation of Ireland v Dublin City Council* [2005] 2 I.R. 496, the CFI was held not to have "sufficient interest" to challenge a planning contribution scheme adopted by the local authority. McCracken J. noted:

"This is a challenge which could be brought by any of the members of the applicant who are affected and would then be related to the particular circumstances of that member. The members themselves are, in many cases, very large and financially substantial companies, which are unlikely to be deterred by the financial consequences of mounting a challenge such as this. Unlike many of the cases in which parties with no personal or direct interest have been granted locus standi, there is no evidence before the court that, in the absence of the purported challenge by the applicant, there would have been no other challenge".

However, it appears the nature and purpose of the representative body may be relevant. In *Chambers v An Bord Pleanála* [1992] 1 I.R. 134, where there were 19 appellants, it was noted that it was understandable that applicants left it to a representative body to deal with an appeal to the Board.

Even where an applicant has locus standi to challenge, an order for security for costs may be made where the applicant has chosen to take proceedings because his financial position meant costs could not be successfully pursued against him, see *Fallon v An Bord Pleanála* [1991] 2 I.R. 380. Security for costs may be awarded against a company under s.390 of the Companies Act 1963 and in relation to an individual in the Supreme Court under RSC Ord.58. Security for costs need not be sought prior to the application for leave; see *Village Residents Association Ltd v An Bord Pleanála (No. 2)* [2000] 4 I.R. 321. Security for costs will not normally be granted where proceedings concern a question of law of exceptional public importance; see *Lanceforth v An Bord Pleanála* [1998] 2 I.R. 511 and *Lismore Homes Ltd v Bank of Ireland Finance Ltd (No. 2)* [1999] 1 I.R. 501.

Section 50A(3)(b)(ii) introduced an exception to the requirement to demonstrate a substantial interest where the decision or act relates to a development which requires an EIS. It provides that a body or organisation (not being a State authority, a public authority or a governmental body or agency) which has sought to promote certain environmental objectives over the last 12 months will be entitled to take judicial review proceedings of such decision or act. It will not have to demonstrate that it has a substantial interest. The amendment was made in order to satisfy Ireland's requirements under the Aahaus Directive. Such bodies also have an automatic right of appeal to An Bord Pleanála with respect to planning application which requires an EIS under s.37(4)(c). The minister may also prescribe certain specified matters which the body or organisation must satisfy. The minister has yet to make any such regulations. The minister may limit the entitlement of a body or organisation in the area of environmental protection to appeal to bodies which specifically relate to the class of matter to which the decision relates. Although not expressly stated, the introduction of this exception is an attempt to implement art.1(2) of Directive 2003/35/EC for public participation in respect of the drawing up of certain plans and programmes relating to the environment, which provides that NGO's promoting environmental protection and meeting any requirements of national law are deemed to have an interest for the purposes of "the public concerned". NGO's are also mentioned in art.10a.

Subsection (5) was introduced by the 2006 Act and makes clear that a party can only rely upon grounds for which leave was granted. This was the pre-existing position, although there was no express provision stating this to be the case. Subsection (6) was also introduced by the 2006 Act and provides that the court may require the applicant to give an undertaking as to damages as a condition of the grant of leave. This means that a party granted leave must undertake to reimburse the respondent or other parties for damages incurred as a result of leave being granted. While the former section did not contain such provision, the courts had recognised that they had power to do so under RSC Ord.84 r.20(6) which allows the court to impose conditions on the grant of leave and may require an undertaking as to damages. See *Seery v An Bord Pleanála* [2001] 2 I.L.R.M. 151. In *Coll v Donegal County Council (No.2)*, unreported, High Court, Dunne J., March 29, 2007, the court refused to order the applicant to provide an undertaking as to damages where the proceedings raised a public law issue involving the extinguishment of a right of way. See also *O'Connell v Environmental Protection Agency* [2001] 4 I.R. 494.

Certificate for Leave to Appeal

Subsection (7) includes a further restriction in the special judicial review procedure whereby following a decision of the High Court on the judicial review application, an appeal can only be taken to the Supreme Court, where the High Court judge grants specific leave on the basis that the appeal would involve a point of law of exceptional public importance, etc. In ordinary judicial review proceedings there is no requirement to grant leave to appeal. This restriction also applied under the previous planning legislation. Subsection (11)(a) introduced under the 2006 Act means that where a certificate for leave to appeal to the Supreme Court is granted, the Supreme Court will only have jurisdiction to determine the exact point certified by the High Court. This reverses the position in *Clinton v An Bord Pleanála* [2007] 1 I.R. 272, which reaffirmed *Scott v An Bord Pleanála*, which held that the Supreme Court was not confined to the exact point certified but could consider all the grounds.

To amount to a point of law of exceptional public importance, the point must be of such gravity to transcend the interests and considerations of the parties before the court; see *Lanceforth Ltd v An Bord Pleanála*, unreported, High Court, Morris J., July 23, 1997; *Kenny v An Bord Pleanála (No. 2)* [2001] 1 I.R. 704; *Neville v An Bord Pleanála*, unreported, High Court, O'Caoimh J., October 12, 2001; *Begley v An Bord Pleanála*, unreported, High Court, Ó Caoimh J., May 23, 2003. In *Harding v Cork County Council*, unreported, High Court, Clarke J., November 30, 2006, said in order for a question of law arising to be properly regarded as one of exceptional public importance it should have the capability of affecting a significant number of cases. In *Gritto v Minister for Justice, Equality and Law Reform*, unreported, High Court, March 16, 2005, Laffoy J. noted at p.2 that the requirement that the decision involve "a point of law of exceptional public importance" imposes a higher threshold than if the requirement merely related to a "point of law of public importance. The jurisdiction to certify such a case must be exercised sparingly. See *Glancre Teoranta v Mayo County Council*, unreported, High Court, McMenamin J. July 13, 2006. Leave may be refused on the ground that the principles raised in the High Court decision are already well established law and any additional arguments could not justify the appeal. In *Glancre Teoranta v Mayo County Council*, unreported, High Court, McMenamin J., July 13, 2006, it was said that "'uncertainty' cannot be 'imputed' to the law by an applicant simply by raising a question as to the point of law. Rather the authorities appear to indicate that the uncertainty must arise over and above this, for example in the daily operation of the law in question". In *Harding v Cork County Council*, unreported, High Court, Clarke J., November 30, 2006, the court in certifying a point referred to the public interest to have definitive clarification of the legal principles involved from the Supreme Court.

The notion of "point of law" means that purely factual matters cannot be certified. See *Neville v An Bord Pleanála*, unreported, High Court, Ó Caoimh J., October 12, 2001. In *Harrington v An Bord Pleanála (No. 2)*, unreported, High Court, Macken J., March 16, 2006, it was noted that it was difficult to see how a point of exceptional public importance could arise in the absence of a finding of general application. However, in *Harding v Cork County Council*, unreported, High Court, Clarke J., November 30, 2006 it was noted that:

> "It seems likely, therefore, that in many cases, there will be a broad and a narrow question. The broad question will concern general principles. The narrow, the application of those principles to the facts of the case. Where the principles by reference to which a court should approach an important aspect of planning law have not been the subject of an authoritive ruling of the Supreme Court and where exceptionally important questions are raised by the issue concerned, it may well be appropriate to express the issue arising in general terms even though the court, will, necessarily, concentrate on the application of those principles to the facts of an individual case".

Regard must be had to the decision itself rather than the merits of the arguments; see *Lancefort Ltd v An Bord Pleanála*, unreported, High Court, Morris J., July 23, 1997. The point of law must arise from the decision itself, rather than a matter which could have been part of the decision or even that it was mooted; see *Lancefort Ltd v An Bord Pleanála*, unreported, High Court, McGuinness J., March 31, 1998; *Ashbourne Holding Ltd v An Bord Pleanála (No. 3)*, unreported, High Court, Kearns J., June 19, 2001. However, in *Harding v Cork County Council*, unreported, High Court, Clarke J., November 30, 2006, this was said not to be an absolute rule as there are many circumstances in which an issue which may arise in the course of argument may not be dealt with in the course of the court's judgment.

While the court may come to the view that it is unnecessary to deal with some issues that arose in the course of argument, it may be possible that the court, due to inadvertence, fails to deal with a point which arose in the course of argument and which, if it be a good point, could have affected the result of the case notwithstanding the other findings made by the court and set out in the court's judgment. The point of law must arise from the judgment determining proceedings whether this is the leave or substantive hearing but cannot arise from the decision on the whether to certify for an appeal. See *Arklow Holidays Ltd v An Bord Pleanála (No. 3)*, unreported, High Court, Clarke J., September 8, 2006. It would appear leave is not required to appeal a refusal to extend time: see *B & S v Governor of Training Unit Glengarrif Parade* [2002] 2 I.L.R.M. 161.

The requirement that the point of law is of "exceptional public importance" and that "it is desirable in the public interest that an appeal should be taken to the Supreme Court" are cumulative requirements. See *Raiu v Refugee Appeals Tribunal* unreported, February 26, 2003 and *Begley v An Bord Pleanála*, unreported, High Court, Ó Caoimh J., May 23, 2003. Even where a matter involves a point of law of exceptional public importance, the court may still refuse to certify where it considers that it not in public interest to do so. See *Arklow Holdings v An Bord Pleanála* [2007] 4 I.R. 112, where Clarke J., having found that there was a point of law of exceptional public importance, nevertheless refused to certify a ground on the basis that to certify it would not be in the public interest. In this respect, Clarke J. took into account the importance of the project and consequences of delay. See also *Glanacre Teoranta v Mayo County Council*, unreported, High Court, McMenamin J., July 13, 2006, where it was considered that there was no public interest in further expression of the applicant's concerns. The technical nature of the point may also be a factor against granting a certificate: see *Arklow Holdings v An Bord Pleanála* [2007] 4 I.R. 112. The term "technical" describes a point which could have had no possible bearing on the merits of the process under review other than formal compliance such as where there was no evidence of prejudice as a result of the non-compliance or evidence that it could have affected anything substantive in the planning process See *Arklow Holdings v An Bord Pleanála*, unreported, High Court, Clarke J., January 11, 2008, in a subsequent certificate judgment.

Where the trial judge refuses to certify leave, no appeal lies from such a decision to refuse a certificate of appeal, see *Irish Hardware Association v South Dublin County Council* [2001] 2 I.L.R.M. 291. Also in *Irish Asphalt v An Bord Pleanála* [1996] 2 I.R. 179, the Supreme Court rejected the argument that the issue of whether the point of law involved one of exceptional public importance was a separate issue. It was therefore prohibited to appeal such a refusal.

Leave to appeal is required both to appeal a decision after a full hearing of judicial review and also a decision refusing to grant leave to take judicial review proceedings. In the latter instance, it would seem logically difficult to obtain leave to appeal. Note the comments of McKechnie J., obiter, in *Kenny v An Bord Pleanála (No. 2)*, unreported, High Court, McKechnie J., March 2, 2001. However, it is clear that a point of law can arise from the decision, which does not specifically relate to the actual grounds of challenge. In *Harding v Cork County Council*, unreported, Supreme Court, May 2, 2008, the point of law related to the nature of substantial interest. While in *Talbot v An Bord Pleanala*, unreported, High Court, Peart J., June 21, 2005, the point certified related to whether a court can exercise its discretion to refuse relief where quashing a decision to grant permission would not assist the applicant where there are other valid reasons for the permission. Nonetheless in *Hodgers v Cork County Council*, unreported, High Court, Murphy J., May 25, 2006, it was said that the standard required to establish a point of law of exceptional public importance must necessarily be greater than that required to establish substantial grounds. There is no time limit prescribed for making an application for leave to appeal, though in practice the matter is usually indicated at the time of judgment. In *Ní Ghruagáin v An Bord Pleanála*, unreported, High Court, Murphy J., June 19, 2003, an application for leave three months after judgment was refused on grounds of delay. The normal 21 days to lodge an appeal will not run until the court delivers its judgment certifying the point of law and so will not run from the date of the substantive judgment.

Subsection (8) provides the one exception to the requirement to obtain leave, where the question of law concerns the alleged unconstitutionality of a legal provision. See *Scott v An Bord Pleanála* [1995] 1 I.L.R.M. 424. However, see *Jackson Way Properties Ltd v*

Minister for the Environment and Local Government [1994] 4 I.R. 608.

Subsection (9) allows for severance of a decision which is challenged. Where part of the decision is challenged, the court may declare that part of the decision only invalid. It may not be possible to sever one part of a decision from the whole decision and it will depend on the facts of the case whether this is the case. Where the court declares part only of the decision invalid, it may make certain directions as regards the remainder of the decision.

Subsection (10) imposes an additional obligation on the High Court to act as swiftly as is consistent with administering justice in dealing with certain decisions, this obligation also extends to the Supreme Court in deciding a certified point of law under subs.(11)(b).

Based on the law prior to the changes in the 2006 Act, it was held in *Talbot v An Bord Pleanála*, unreported, Supreme Court, July 23, 2008, that having answered the questions, the Supreme Court can either grant leave itself in appropriate cases or make an order remitting the entire matter to the High Court. However, the change in subs.(11) which provides the Supreme Court have jurisdiction to determine only the point of law certified by the court and to make such orders which follow from the determination, means that in most cases, it will not be appropriate for the Supreme Court to grant leave unless the point answered directly relates to the grant of leave and so therefore the matter should remit the matter to the High Court.

Discretion and Exhaustion of Local Remedies

Apart from the above matters it should be noted that judicial review is a discretionary remedy. In *Talbot v An Bord Pleanála*, unreported, Supreme Court, July 23, 2008, it was conceded that it could not be maintained that a judge at the hearing of an application for leave to apply for judicial review is precluded as a matter of law, in a proper case, from exercising a judicial discretion to refuse leave. However, the Supreme Court answered a certified question by holding that a court cannot refuse leave by drawing an inference from the material put before the court on the application for leave that any future application for planning permission would be refused in any event on a ground or grounds which was/were not sought to be impugned in the proceedings for judicial review. The Supreme Court reversed a finding in the High Court that in a challenge to a reason for refusal of permission, it would be futile to grant relief as there were other reasons for refusal not challenged in the proceedings. It has been suggested that where there is a breach of the EIA Directive, the exercise of discretion may be more limited. See *Berkeley v Secretary of State for the Environment* [2001] 2 A.C. 603, although this has not applied in other cases. See *R. (Jones) v Mansfield District Council* [2004] 2 P & CR 14 and *Younger Homes (Northern) Ltd v First Secretary of State* [2005] 1 P & CR 14.

It is well recognised that leave can be refused where there is an alternative remedy open to the applicant: see *G v DPP* [1994] 1 I.R. 374; *State (Glover) v McCarthy* [1981] I.L.R.M. 47; *Nova Colour Graphic Supplies Ltd v Employment Appeals Tribunal* [1987] I.R. 426; *Mythen v Employment Appeals Tribunal* [1990] 1 I.R. 98; *Memorex v Employment Appeals Tribunal* [1992] I.R. 184; *McGoldrick v An Bord Pleanála* [1997] 1 I.R. 497; and *Stefan v Minster for Justice* [2001] 4 I.R. 203. In *Kinsella v Dundalk Town Council*, unreported, December 3, 2004, it was said compared to ordinary judicial review, the requirement that an applicant demonstrate that judicial review is the only or a more appropriate remedy than another one available applies with at least equal if not more force to a s.50 application. An issue as to the adequacy of appeal should generally be dealt with prior to considering whether there are substantial grounds for challenge. See *Harding v Cork County Council*, unreported, High Court, October 12, 2006, that subject to one exception, where the parties persuade the court that an appeal to the Board would be an adequate remedy, then it is unnecessary to consider whether there are substantial grounds. An exception to this approach may be made where a multiplicity of grounds are raised where the cumulative effect of all of the issues complained of might render the process before the planning authority so flawed that it would justify reaching a conclusion that an appeal would not be an adequate remedy. In such instance it may be necessary for the court to consider each of the grounds put forward to assess whether they are substantial. It may then be necessary to revisit the question of the adequacy or otherwise of an appeal to the Board based upon a review of those grounds in respect of which it has been successfully established that the applicant has substantial grounds for challenge. This approach was approved by Murray C.J. on appeal before the Supreme Court. See *Harding v Cork County Council*, unreported, Supreme Court, May 2, 2008.

The existence of an alternative remedy is not a bar to relief, merely a matter which the court can consider in the exercise of its discretion: see *Buckley v Kirby* [2000] 3 I.R. 431; *Stefan v Minister for Justice* [2001] 4 I.R. 203. In *Tomlinson v Criminal Injuries Compensation Tribunal* [2006] 4 I.R. 321, the Supreme Court held that where the core issue is the jurisdiction of the respondent to make the decision, the right of an alternative remedy is not so weighty a factor as to exclude the applicant from the court. In seeking to challenge a decision of a planning authority, an appeal to An Bord Pleanála will be the appropriate remedy where the matter concerns a question of fact. In *State (Abenglen) v An Bord Pleanála* [1984] I.R. 381, Henchy J. said at 405:

> "where Parliament has provided a self-contained administrative and quasi-judicial scheme, postulating only a limited use of the courts, *certiorari* should not issue when, as in the instant case, use of the statutory procedure for the correction of error was adequate (and, indeed, more suitable) to meet the complaints on which the application for *certiorari* is grounded".

He refused relief because the alleged errors of law were not made in excess of jurisdiction and did not appear on the face of the record of the respondents' decision. He further declared:

> "Because of the technicality of the objections raised by *Abenglen*, because the resolution of these objections require oral evidence, and because the resulting decision would probably govern cases, past, present or future, I would in the exercise of my discretion, refuse *certiorari* on the ground that *Abenglen* should have pursued the appellate procedure that was open to them under the Acts".

However, in *Kinsella v Dundalk Town Council*, unreported, High Court, December 3, 2004, Kelly J. rejected as artificial the proposition that issues of law should be decided by the courts and issues of fact are decided by the Board; the real test was whether the applicant would suffer any injustice if left to his remedy before An Bord Pleanála. In *McGoldrick v An Bord Pleanála* [1997] 1 I.R. 497, Barron J. said:

> "It is not just a question whether an alternative remedy exists or whether the applicant has taken steps to pursue such remedies. The true question is which is the more appropriate remedy considered in the context of common sense, the ability to deal with the question raised on principles of fairness."

In *Harding v Cork County Council*, unreported, High Court, October 12, 2006, it was noted that the planning process as relates to objectors creates a significantly different process at the separate stage of the initial application before the planning authority on the one hand and an appeal (if one be brought) to the Board, of the other hand. The mere fact that an issue in respect of which complaint is made relating to the first stage of a two-stage process will not be dealt with by an appellant body dealing with the second stage, does not necessarily mean that an appeal would not be an adequate remedy. Clarke J. said that an appeal will be regarded as an adequate remedy in a two stage statutory or administrative process unless either:

- the matters complained of in respect of the first stage of the process are such that they can taint the second stage of the process or effect the overall jurisdiction; or
- the process at the first stage is so flawed that it can reasonably be said that the person concerned had not been afforded their entitlement to a proper first stage of the process in any meaningful sense.

See *Jerry Beades Construction Ltd v Dublin Corporation*, unreported, High Court, McKechnie J., September 7, 2005 as an example where the Board was under a misapprehension as to material matters by virtue of the process engaged in while the matter was being dealt with by the planning authority.

In *P. & F. Sharpe Ltd v Dublin City and County Manager* [1989] I.R. 701, Finlay C.J. said at 721 that:

> "The powers of An Bord Pleanála on the making of an appeal to it would be entirely confined to the consideration of the matters before it on the basis of proper planning and development of the area and it would have no jurisdiction to consider the question of the validity, from a legal point of view, of the purported decision by the County Manager. It would not, therefore, be just for the developers who are respondents

in this appeal to be deprived of their right to have that decision quashed for want of validity."

See also *Ardoyne Houses Management Ltd v Dublin Corporation* [1998] 2 I.R. 147. In *Eircell v Leitrim County Council* [2000] 1 I.R. 479, O'Donovan J. exercised his discretion in favour of an applicant in the interests of justice, stating, "if for no other reason than that the public at large are entitled to know that the planning authority cannot ride rough shod over principles of constitutional justice and fair procedures". Whether an EC Directive has been properly implemented in Ireland is more appropriately dealt with in judicial review proceedings and a remedy by way of the appeal to An Bord Pleanála does not represent an alternative. See *O'Brien v Tipperary County Council*, unreported, High Court, O'Caoimh J., October 22, 2002.

The court will consider whether the alternative remedy is more appropriate. See *McGoldrick v An Bord Pleanála* [1997] 1 I.R. 497 where Barron J. said:

"The true question is which is the more appropriate remedy in the context of common sense, the ability to deal with the questions raised and the principles of fairness; provided, of course, that the applicant has not gone too far down one road to be estopped from changing his or her mind".

An example of where relief was refused in favour of an appeal to An Bord Pleanála is *Delgany Area Residents Association v Wicklow County Council*, unreported, High Court, Barr J., May 28, 1998, where the grounds of challenge were that a development was similar to an earlier planning decision, so as to be covered by such decision. See also *Byrne v Wicklow County Council*, unreported, High Court, Keane J., November 3, 1994.

Costs

The general rule is that costs follow the event. In the absence of special or unusual circumstances, the normal default position should remain that costs should follow the event. See *Veolia Water UK v Fingal County Council (No. 2)* [2007] 2 I.R. 81. In *Dunne v Dun Laoghaire Rathdown County Council*, unreported, Supreme Court, December 6, 2007, the Supreme Court said the rule of law that costs normally follow the event, that the successful party to proceedings should not have to pay the costs of those proceedings which should be borne by the unsuccessful party has an obvious equitable basis. As a counterpoint to that general rule of law the court has a discretionary jurisdiction to vary or depart from that rule of law if, in the special circumstances of a case, the interests of justice require that it should do so. In *Usk and District Residents Association v Environmental Protection Agency*, unreported, High Court, Clarke J., February 15, 2007, it was noted that costs should normally follow the event and:

"[W]here that successful party is a defendant, respondent, or, indeed, a notice party who opposes an application, then that position should be departed from only where the court is satisfied that there are good grounds for taking the view that the costs of the proceedings as a whole (including any appropriate interlocutory applications) have been clearly increased by reason of an unreasonable position adopted by that successful party in respect of some issue which has not already been the subject of a costs order reflecting the relevant unreasonableness".

It may be appropriate to award the applicant their costs of the leave application independently of the outcome of the judicial review proceedings. See *Usk and District Residents Association v Environmental Protection Agency* [2007] 4 I.R. 157, where costs were reserved on the basis that it was not unreasonable to oppose leave. A court may exercise its discretion to depart from the general rule of costs following the event where:

- the plaintiff was acting in the public interest in a matter which involved no private personal advantage and
- the issues raised by the proceedings are of sufficient general public importance to warrant an order for costs being made in his favour.

Both elements must be satisfied. See *Harrington v An Bord Pleanála*, unreported, High Court, Macken J., July 11, 2006; *McEvoy v Meath County Council* [2003] 1 I.R. 208 and *Sinnott v Martin* [2004] 1 I.R. 121. However, even when these two general factors are present they are not the determining factors in favour of an award of costs to a plaintiff pursing public interest litigation. See *Dunne v Dun Laoghaire Rathdown County Council*, unreported, Supreme Court, December 6, 2007, where it was said any departure from the general rule is one which must be decided by a court in the circumstances of each case. Also where a court considers that it should exercise a discretion to depart from the normal rule as to costs it is not completely at large but must do so on a reasoned basis indicating the factors which in the circumstances of the case warrant such a departure. While the fact that a person has a sufficient interest would not debar them from costs on the basis of a public interest challenge, a party may not qualify where they sought to protect their own direct commercial interest. See *Cork County Council v Shackleton*, unreported, High Court, Clarke J., October 12, 2007. In *Sweetman v An Bord Pleanala*, unreported, High Court, Clarke J., October 25, 2007, it was held that the implementation of the Directive could effect the interests and entitlements of those whose decision are challenged, the authorities giving decisions and the rights of challengers and the judgment had led to potential evolution of jurisprudence in the area and so the applicant, although unsuccessful, was entitled to half of his costs against the State.

A notice party may be entitled to an award of costs. See *O'Connor v Nenagh Urban District Council*, unreported, Supreme Court, May 16, 2002, where among the factors for upholding an award of costs were:

- whereas there was an element of public interest, the application as originally drafted sought specific remedies potentially detrimental to the notice party;
- the notice party was a necessary party;
- the notice party participated fully in the trial;
- the notice party was an entirely innocent party and acted in good faith at all times;
- the notice party was successful in the proceedings;
- no compelling reasons have been established as to why costs should not follow the event; and
- the learned trial judge exercised his discretion in accordance with law.

However, in England it has been held that a notice party developer will not normally be entitled to costs unless he can show there was likely to be separate issue in respect of which he was entitled to be heard or unless he has an interest which requires separate representation. See *Bolton Metropolitan District Council v Secretary of State for the Environment* [1995] 3 P.L.R. 37. However, the fact proceedings are intimately concerned with the rights and entitlements of a notice may mean a notice party is entitled to costs. See *Usk and District Residents Association v Environmental Protection Agency*, unreported, High Court, Clarke J., February 15, 2007.

It is also clear that an award of costs may be made against a notice party. Thus, where a notice party takes on the role of the sole or main defendant, then ordinarily the position of notice party in respect of costs is the same as a defendant. See *Cork County Council v Shackleton*, unreported, High Court, Clarke J., October 12, 2007. Where test cases involve private parties there is no basis from departing from the ordinary rules of costs. See *Cork County Council v Shackleton*, unreported, High Court, Clarke J., October 12, 2007, though different considerations apply where one of the parties is a public authority. The court may consider that the litigation may have been necessitated by the complexity or difficulty of the legislation for which the Minister or Ireland were responsible.

Article 10a of Directive 2003/35/EC for public participation in respect of the drawing up of certain plans and programmes relating to the environment, provides that the review procedure must not be prohibitively preventive. In *Sweetman v An Bord Pleanála* [2007] 2 I.L.R.M. 328 it was held this was not intended to cover the exposure of a party to reasonable legal costs in judicial review proceedings. RSC Ord.99, r.4 may permit a pre-emptive or protective costs order. See *Village Residents Association Ltd v An Bord Pleanála (No. 2)* [2000] 4 I.R. 321. In *Friends of the Curragh Environment Ltd v An Bord Pleanála*, unreported, High Court, Kelly J., July 14, 2006, Kelly J. refused to make a pre-emptive costs order on the basis that the proceedings did not involve one of general public importance where there was established jurisprudence on the issues. He considered an order would only be made in the most exceptional circumstances and where the interests of justice require such. Kelly J. held Directive 2003/35/EC did not have direct effect and it is doubtful whether it could apply to costs in court proceedings.

PART IV

ARCHITECTURAL HERITAGE

CHAPTER I

Protected Structures

Record of protected structures

1–73   **51.—(1)** For the purpose of protecting structures, or parts of structures, which form part of the architectural heritage and which are of special architectural, historical, archaeological, artistic, cultural, scientific, social or technical interest, every development plan shall include a record of protected structures, and shall include in that record every structure which is, in the opinion of the planning authority, of such interest within its functional area.

(2) After consulting with the Minister for Arts, Heritage, Gaeltacht and the Islands, the Minister shall prescribe the form of a record of protected structures.

(3) Subject to any additions or deletions made to the record, either under this *Part* or in the course of a review of the development plan under *Part II,* a record of protected structures shall continue to be part of that plan or any variation or replacement of the plan.

NOTE

This section provides that a planning authority must include within their development plan a Record of Protected Structures (RPS) which forms part of the development plan. Section 10(2)(f) provides that a development plan shall include objectives for the protection of structures, or parts of structures, which are of special interest under one or more of the following headings:

- architectural;
- historical;
- archaeological;
- artistic;
- cultural;
- scientific;
- technical;
- social.

Where a structure is designated a protected structure this will have significant impacts on the planning control of such structure. Section 2 defines "protected structure" as meaning:

"(a) a structure, or (b) a specified part of a structure, which is included in a record of protected structures, and, where that record so indicates, includes any specified feature which is within the attendant grounds of the structure and which would not otherwise be included in this definition".

Meanwhile "structure" is defined as meaning:

"any building, structure, excavation, or other thing constructed or made on, in or under any land, or any part of a structure so defined, and—(a) where the context so admits, includes the land on, in or under which the structure is situate, and (b) in relation to a protected structure or proposed protected structure, includes (i) the interior of the structure, (ii) the land lying within the curtilage of the structure, (iii) any other structures lying within that curtilage and their interiors, and (iv) all fixtures and features which form part of the interior or exterior of any structure or structures referred to in *subparagraph (i)* or *(iii)*".

The record of a protected structures has been prescribed under art.51 of the Planning Regulations 2001, which provides that a record of protected structures shall contain in respect of each protected structure: an identifying number and an address; one or more maps showing the location of each protected structure to the scale that enables clear identification of such structures (which map may contain additional information); and any other information that the planning authority considers necessary.

Where a structure is designated a protected structure, the protected status extends to land within the curtilage of the protected structure. However, where the protected structure is merely a "specified part" of a structure, this will not include the curtilage of such structure. See *Begley v An Bord Pleanála*, unreported, High Court, Ó Caoimh J., January 14, 2003. The record may of course refer to special features within the attendant grounds, which will then form part of the protected structure. The precise extent of the curtilage of a protected structure may be subject to dispute and so the planning authority in adding a protected structure should ensure that the map included in the record of protected structure should clearly outline the curtilage of the structure. The notion of curtilage is not defined under the Act. Curtilage is however to be distinguished from attendant grounds of the structures, which is defined in s.2 as "in relation to a structure, includes land lying outside the curtilage of the structure". The Architectural Heritage Guidelines 2004 define curtilage as "a parcel of land immediately associated with the protected structure and which was or is in use for the purposes of the structure". The Guidelines also define attendant grounds at para.13.2.1 as lands outside the curtilage of the structure but which are associated with the structure and are intrinsic to its function, setting and/or appreciation. The concept of curtilage has however, been considered in certain English case law. In *Sinclair Lockhart's Trustees v Central Land Board* [1950] 1 P & CR 195 defined curtilage as:

> "grounds which is used for the comfortable enjoyment of a house... and thereby as an integral part of the same, although it has not been marked off or enclosed in any way. It is enough that it serves the purposes of the house... in some necessary or reasonably useful way".

The notion of "curtilage" was also defined in *Dyer v Dorset County Council* [1989] Q.B. 346, in the context of a dwellinghouse as "a small court, yard, garth or piece of ground attached to a dwellinghouse and forming one enclosure with it, or so regarded by the law; the area attached to and containing a dwellinghouse and its outbuildings." In *McAlpine v Secretary of State for the Environment* [1995] 1 PLR 16, it was said that: "curtilage is constrained to a small area about a building, it is not necessary for there to be physical enclosure but the land needs to be regarded in law as part of one enclosure with the house and overall the term has a restrictive meaning". However, it not the case that the curtilage of a building must always be small, or that the notion of smallness is inherent in the expression. See *Skeritts of Nottingham Ltd v Secretary of State for the Environment* [2001] Q.B. 59. In *James v Secretary of State for the Environment* [1990] 61 P & CR 234, the court stated three criteria for determining whether land is within the curtilage of a building namely: physical layout; ownership past and present; use or function, past and present. In *Skeritts of Nottingham Ltd v Secretary of State for the Environment* [2001] Q.B. 59, it was said the term curtilage is not a term of art but is a question of fact and degree. The decision of the planning authority or the Board as to whether a matter falls within the curtilage of a protected structure would appear to be mixed question of fact and law. Any factual determination may only be challenged on grounds of irrationality. See *Coras Iompair Eireann v An Bord Pleanála*, unreported, High Court, Clarke J., June 19, 2008. However, it is submitted where the Board or planning authority misconstrues the concept of protected structure in applying it to particular facts, this should be reviewable by the courts under a more exacting standard on the basis that they erred in law.

Section 2 also includes a definition of "proposed protected structure" which is defined as:

> "[A] structure in respect of which a notice is issued under s.12(3) or under s.55 proposing to add the structure, or a specified part of it, to a record of protected structures, and, where that notice so indicates, includes any specified feature which is within the attendant grounds of the structure and which would not otherwise be included in this definition".

Furthermore s.2 defines that "protection" as in relation to a structure or part of a structure, to include conservation, preservation and improvement compatible with maintaining the character and interest of the structure or part.

Part IV, concerning protected structures and architectural conservation areas, is consistent with the concept of "sustainable" development which permeates the Act. Protected structures are an aspect of national heritage. Therefore, relevant matters also include the National Heritage Plan and the Heritage Council established as a statutory body under the Heritage Act 1995. Its role is to propose policies and priorities for the identification, protection, preservation and enhancement of the national heritage. Dúchas, the Heritage Service, was abolished in 2003, with responsibility for its function directly passing to the newly named Department of the Environment, Heritage and Local Government. The National Monuments Acts 1930 to 1994 gives responsibility to the Department of the Environment to protect archaeological sites and monuments that have been identified under the Archaeological Survey of Ireland. See *Mulcreevy v Minister for the Environment* [2004] 1 I.L.R.M. 419 and *Dunne & Lucas v Dun Laoghaire-Rathdown County Council* [2003] 1 I.R. 567, in relation to a road development at Carrickmines. Also of note is the Architectural Heritage (National Inventory) and Historic Monuments (Miscellaneous Provisions) Act 1999, which implements art.2 of the Council of Europe Convention for the Protection of the Architectural Heritage of Europe (Granada Convention). It states that for the purpose of precise identification of monuments, groups of structures and sites to be protected, each member state will undertake to maintain inventories of that architectural heritage.

The decision to designate a protected structure is within the discretion of the planning authority, although it must take into account representations by the Minister for Arts, Heritage, Gaeltacht and the Islands under s.53. Planning authorities will generally employ a conservation officer with special expertise in the area. In interpreting the matters listed in subs.(1) as to what may constitute a protected structure, the *Architectural Heritage Protection, Guidelines for Planning Authorities* were adopted in November 2004. The Department of Environment has also published *Guidelines for Planning Authorities on Architectural Heritage Protection for Places of Public Worship* (Nov. 2003). As can be seen from the list of considerations in subs.(1), protected structures can include a broad spectrum of interests to be protected.

Subsection (3) provides that the record of protected structures may be altered by addition or deletion under the procedure set out in s.55 or by way of review of the development plan under the procedure under ss.11 and 12. The record of protected structures will continue to be part of the plan until either of these procedures are followed.

Guidelines by Minister for Arts, Heritage, Gaeltacht and the Islands

1–74   **52.—(1)** The Minister for Arts, Heritage, Gaeltacht and the Islands shall, after consulting with the Minister, issue guidelines to planning authorities concerning development objectives—

> **(a)** for protecting structures, or parts of structures, which are of special architectural, historical, archaeological, artistic, cultural, scientific, social or technical interest, and
>
> **(b)** for preserving the character of architectural conservation areas,

and any such guidelines shall include the criteria to be applied when selecting proposed protected structures for inclusion in the record of protected structures.

(2) The Minister for Arts, Heritage, Gaeltacht and the Islands may, after consulting with the authorities of any religious denominations which he or she considers necessary, issue guidelines to planning authorities concerning—

> **(a)** the issue of declarations under *section 57* in respect of protected structures which are regularly used as places of public worship, and
>
> **(b)** the consideration by planning authorities of applications for

development affecting the interior of such protected structures.

(3) In considering development objectives, a planning authority shall have regard to any guidelines issued under this *section.*

(4) In this *section,* "development objective" *means an objective which, under section 10, a planning authority proposes to include in its development plan.*

<small>NOTE</small>

This section allows the Minister to issue guidelines to the planning authority concerning protected structures. In this respect, *Architectural Heritage Protection, Guidelines for Planning Authorities* were adopted in 2004. Subsection (1) refers to guidelines concerning the "development objectives" of the planning authority, enlisted in s.10, which can include criteria for the selection of matters to be included in the record of protected structures. Chapter 2 of the Guidelines set out criteria for determining whether the structure has a special interest under the following headings:

- architectural;
- historical;
- archaeological;
- artistic;
- cultural;
- scientific;
- technical;
- social.

In order to be protected, a structure need only have a special interest under one of the heading, although each category may overlap. Subsection (2) provides more specific guidelines can be issued in respect of the issue of declarations under s.57, in relation to places of public worship as to what type of works would or would not materially affect the character of a protected structure or that of the element of the structure protected, and also guidelines in respect of planning applications concerning the interior of a protected structure. In this respect, the Department of Environment has published *Guidelines for Planning Authorities on Architectural Heritage Protection for Places of Public Worship* (Nov. 2003). Although subs.(1) uses the word "criteria" which are to be set out in the guidelines, such criteria still constitute guidelines and will not be binding on the planning authority.

Subsection (3) provides that the planning authority must have regard to such guidelines. The planning authority is clearly not bound by guidelines but must give consideration to such guidelines. As to the meaning of "have regard" see *McEvoy v Meath County Council* [2003] 1 I.R. 208.

Recommendations to planning authorities concerning specific structures

53.—(1) The Minister for Arts, Heritage, Gaeltacht and the Islands may, in   **1–75** writing, make recommendations to a planning authority concerning the inclusion in its record of protected structures of any or all of the following—

    (a) particular structures;

    (b) specific parts of particular structures;

    (c) specific features within the attendant grounds of particular structures.

(2) A planning authority shall have regard to any recommendations made to it under this *section.*

(3) A planning authority which, after considering a recommendation made to it under this *section,* decides not to comply with the recommendation, shall inform the Minister for Arts, Heritage, Gaeltacht and the Islands in writing of the reason for its decision.

NOTE

This section allows the Minister to make recommendations to the planning authority in relation to individual protected structures for their inclusion in the record of protected structures. The recommendation may relate to:
- particular structures;
- specific parts of particular structures; or
- specific features within the attendant grounds of particular structures.

The recommendation therefore may cover all or part of a particular structure or may include features within the attendant grounds of a structure. Although "features" is not defined, it clearly is not confined to structures. As noted in the note on s.51, the notion of attendant grounds is an area outside the curtilage of a structure. Thus where a structure is designated as a protected structure which therefore include the lands within the curtilage of a protected structures, it appears that the Minister can recommend that the protected status be extended to matters within the attendant grounds of the structure. The planning authority is not bound to follow such recommendations but it must have regard to them in deciding whether to include the protected structure within the record. In relation to the meaning of "have regard to" in a planning context, see *McEvoy v Meath County Council* [2003] I.L.R.M. 208. If the planning authority rejects such recommendation, it must inform the Minister in writing of the reason for the rejection.

Additions to and deletions from record of protected structures

1–76   **54.—(1)** A planning authority may add to or delete from its record of protected structures a structure, a specified part of a structure or a specified feature of the attendant grounds of a structure, where—
  (a) the authority considers that—
      (i) in the case of an addition, the addition is necessary or desirable in order to protect a structure, or part of a structure, of special architectural, historical, archaeological, artistic, cultural, scientific, social or technical interest, whether or not a recommendation has been made under *section 53,* or
      (ii) in the case of a deletion, the protection of the structure or part is no longer warranted,
      and
  (b) the addition or deletion is made when making a development plan under *Part II* or in accordance with *section 55.*

  (2) The making of an addition to, or a deletion from, a record of protected structures shall be a reserved function.

NOTE

This section empowers the planning authority to add or a delete a particular structure or part thereof from the record of protected structures, irrespective of whether the Minister has made a recommendation. The planning authority may add a structure where it deems it "necessary or desirable", while it may delete a structure from the record where it considers protection "is no longer warranted". The addition or deletion may be made by following the procedure set out in s.55 or through the process of review of the development plan set out in ss.11 and 12. The decision to add or delete a structure from the record of protected structures is to be made by the elected members of the council, i.e. a reserved function rather than by the executive members of the council.

Procedure for making additions or deletions

1–77   **55.—(1)** A planning authority which proposes, at any time other than in the course of making its development plan under *Part II,* to make an addition to or a deletion from its record of protected structures shall—

    (a) serve on each person who is the owner or occupier of the proposed protected structure or the protected structure, as the case may be, a notice of the proposed addition or deletion, including the particulars,

    (b) send particulars of the proposed addition or deletion to the Minister for Arts, Heritage, Gaeltacht and the Islands and to any other prescribed bodies, and

    (c) cause notice of the proposed addition or deletion to be published in at least one newspaper circulating in its functional area.

    (2) A notice under *paragraph (a) or (c) of subsection (1)* shall state the following—

    (a) that particulars of the proposed addition or deletion may be inspected at a specified place, during a specified period of not less than 6 weeks;

    (b) that, during such period, any person may make written submissions or observations, with respect to the proposed addition or deletion, to the planning authority, and that any such submissions or observations will be taken into consideration before the making of the addition or deletion concerned;

    (c) whether or not the proposed addition or deletion was recommended by the Minister for Arts, Heritage, Gaeltacht and the Islands;

    (d) that, if the proposed addition or deletion was recommended by the Minister for Arts, Heritage, Gaeltacht and the Islands, the planning authority shall forward to that Minister for his or her observations a copy of any submission or observation made under *paragraph (b).*

    (3) Before making the proposed addition or deletion, the planning authority shall—

    (a) consider any written submissions or observations received under *subsection (2)(b),* and

    (b) have regard to any observations received from the Minister for Arts, Heritage, Gaeltacht and the Islands, concerning those submissions or observations, within 4 weeks after the receipt by that Minister of a copy of the submissions or observations.

    (4) Within 12 weeks after the end of the period allowed under *subsection (2)(a)* for inspection, the planning authority shall decide whether or not the proposed addition or deletion should be made.

    (5) Within 2 weeks after making an addition to or a deletion from the record of protected structures, a planning authority shall serve on the owner and on the occupier of the structure concerned a notice of the addition or deletion, including the particulars.

NOTE

    This section sets out the procedure to be followed by the planning authority in adding to or deleting from the record of protected structures. The procedure is an alternative to adding or deleting through the process of review of the development plan. When proposing to add or delete to the record, the planning authority must give notice of the proposal to the owner/occupier of the structure, send notice of the particulars of the proposal to the Minister and prescribed bodies, and cause a notice to be published of the proposal in a newspaper circulating in the area. Article 52 of the Planning Regulations 2001 as amended designates the prescribed bodies as the Heritage Council, An Taisce, An Chomhairle Ealaíon and Fáilte Ireland. The newspaper notice must include the matters set out in subs.(2) allowing for inspection of the proposal, affording the opportunity to make submissions or observations, stating whether the matter was recommended by the Minister and if so, that the submissions or observations may be forwarded to the Minister.

Under subs.(4), the planning authority, in making its decision on the proposal, must have regard to observations or submissions received including from the Minister on such submissions or observations (if received within four weeks from when the Minister received the proposal). On the meaning of "have regard", see *McEvoy v Meath County Council* [2003] 1 I.R. 208. The planning authority is obliged to come to a decision not later than 12 weeks after the end of the period allowed for inspection. The period allowed for inspection is within the discretion of the planning authority, but must not be less than six weeks. Under subs.(5), where the planning authority decides to add or delete from the record, it must give notice to the owner/occupier within two weeks of the decision. A literal reading of subs.(5) appears to be that where the planning authority decides not to confirm the proposal to add to or delete from the record, there is no requirement to notify the owner/occupier. However, this must be read subject to the notion fair procedures and it is submitted that the owner and occupier of structure must be notified of the determination, irrespective of whether the decision is to add or delete from the record of protected structures.

Registration under Registration of Title Act, 1964

1–78   **56.**—Where a structure, a specified part of a structure or a specified feature within the attendant grounds of a structure is included in the record of protected structures, its inclusion may be registered under the *Registration of Title Act, 1964,* in the appropriate register maintained under that *Act,* as a burden affecting registered land (within the meaning of that *Act*).

NOTE

This section allows for the registration of the fact that a structure or part thereof is included in the record of protected structures as a burden on the land in the relevant Land Registry folio. This allows notice to prospective purchasers of land that the land includes a protected structure.

Works affecting character of protected structures or proposed protected structures

1–79   **57.**—**(1)** Notwithstanding *section 4(1)(h),* the carrying out of works to a protected structure, or a proposed protected structure, shall be exempted development only if those works would not materially affect the character of—

  (a) the structure, or
  (b) any element of the structure which contributes to its special architectural, historical, archaeological, artistic, cultural, scientific, social or technical interest.

(2) An owner or occupier of a protected structure may make a written request to the planning authority, within whose functional area that structure is situated, to issue a declaration as to the type of works which it considers would or would not materially affect the character of the structure or of any element, referred to in *subsection (1)(b),* of that structure.

(3) Within 12 weeks after receiving a request under *subsection (2),* or within such other period as may be prescribed, a planning authority shall issue a declaration under this *section* to the person who made the request.

(4) Before issuing a declaration under this *section,* a planning authority [or the Board] shall have regard to—

    (a) any guidelines issued under *section 52,* and

    (b) any recommendations made to the authority under *section 53.*

(5) If the declaration relates to a protected structure that is regularly used as a place of public worship, the planning authority [or the Board]—

    (a) in addition to having regard to the guidelines and recommendations referred to in *subsection (4),* shall respect liturgical requirements, and

    (b) for the purpose of ascertaining those requirements shall—

        (i) comply with any guidelines concerning consultation which may be issued by the Minister for Arts, Heritage, Gaeltacht and the Islands, or

        (ii) if no such guidelines are issued, consult with such person or body as the planning authority considers appropriate.

(6) When considering an application for permission for the development of land under *section 34* which—

    (a) relates to the interior of a protected structure, and

    (b) is regularly used as a place of public worship,

the planning authority, and the Board on appeal, shall, in addition to any other requirements of the *Act,* respect liturgical requirements.

(7) A planning authority may at any time review a declaration issued under this *section* but the review shall not affect any works carried out in reliance on the declaration prior to the review.

[(8) Any person to whom a declaration under *subsection (3),* or a declaration reviewed under *subsection (7)* has been issued, may, on payment to the Board of such fee as may be prescribed, refer the declaration for review by the Board within 4 weeks from the date of the issuing of the declaration, or the declaration as reviewed, as the case may be.]

[(9) A planning authority shall cause—

    (a) the details of any declaration issued by that authority, or of a decision by the Board on a referral, to be entered on the register kept by the authority under *section 7,* and

    (b) a copy of the declaration or decision, as appropriate, to be made available for inspection by members of the public, during office hours, at the office of the authority, following the issue of the declaration or decision.]

(10)

    (a) For the avoidance of doubt, it is hereby declared that a planning authority or the Board on appeal—

        (i) in considering any application for permission in relation to a protected structure, shall have regard to the protected status of the structure, or

        (ii) in considering any application for permission in relation to a proposed protected structure, shall have regard to the fact that it is proposed to add the structure to a record of protected structures.

(b) A planning authority, or the Board on appeal, shall not grant permission for the demolition of a protected structure or proposed protected structure, save in exceptional circumstances.

AMENDMENT HISTORY

Subsections (4) and (5) amended, and subss.(8) and (9) substituted by s.13 of the Planning and Development (Amendment) Act 2002 (No. 32 of 2002) which came into effect on December 24, 2002.

NOTE

This section provides that works which would otherwise be exempted development will not be exempted, unless the works do not materially affect the character of the structure or any element of the structure which contributes to the special interest of the structure. Works will not be exempted where the structure is designated a protected structure except where the restricted criteria in subs.(1) are satisfied. It should be noted that an expanded definition of works is provided in relation to a protected structure, with s.2 defining "works" as:

"any act or operation of construction, excavation, demolition, extension, alteration, repair or renewal and, in relation to a protected structure or proposed protected structure, includes any act or operation involving the application or removal of plaster, paint, wallpaper, tiles or other material to or from the surfaces of the interior or exterior of a structure".

As the definition of protected structure includes land within the curtilage of the protected structure, this restrictive criteria in subs.(1) will also apply to works within the curtilage of the protected structure. The precise scope of this de-exempting of works is not entirely clear from the language used in subs.(1). Subsection (1) commences with the phrase "Notwithstanding s.4(1)(h)", which appears to suggest that the modification to the availability of exempted development is confined merely to the category of exempted development under s.4(1)(h). Section 4(1)(h) exempts:

"development consisting of the carrying out of works for the maintenance, improvement or other alteration of any structure, being works which affect only the interior of the structure or which do not materially affect the external appearance of the structure so as to render the appearance inconsistent with the character of the structure or of neighbouring structures".

This is supported by considering that in respect of a similar de-exempting provision in respect of area of special planning control, s.87(1) states "notwithstanding section 4 and any regulations made thereunder". The difference is language would appear to imply a difference in treatment. Also while art.9(1)(a)(xii) of the 2001 Regulations disapplies any exemption of development where a structure is located within an architectural conservation area, there is no similar provision in relation protected structures. The alternative interpretation of subs.(1) is that applies to works carried out under all categories of exempted development whether specified in s.4 or set out in Sch.2 to the 2001 Regulations. In *Coras Iompair Éireann v An Bord Pleanála*, unreported, High Court, Clarke J., June 19, 2008, it was held that while on a literal interpretation, subs.(1) only restricted works carried out under the exempted development category of s.4(1)(h), this would lead to an absurd result. The court adopted a purposive interpretation in holding that subs.(1) restricted works under all categories of exempted development including exempted development categories under the 2001 Regulations and not merely under s.4(1)(h).

The effect of subs.(1) is of course not to prohibit works, which would otherwise be exempted development, from being carried out but requires that an application for planning permission be made. It should further be noted that the restriction on claiming exempted development in respect of a protected structure under subs.(1) only applies to works and does not apply to "uses" of the protected structure. Thus, a person can still claim exempted development status in respect of changes of use of the protected structure. Finally, works which would otherwise be exempted development in respect of a non-protected structure, are not per se prohibited from being carried out with respect to a protected structure. Instead in order to be exempted, the works must fulfil more stringent criteria set out in subs.(1) which is that the works must not materially affect the character of the structure, or any element of the structure which contributes to its special architectural, historical, archaeological, artistic, cultural, scientific, social or technical interest. As to the meaning of the "character" of the structure, in *McCabe v Coras Iompair Éireann* [2007] 2 I.R. 392, it was said the character of a structure is assessed by looking objectively at the entity as a whole. All the features of the structure taken together and their interaction with each other, give a structure its character, although there may be exceptional cases in which a single feature is so outstandingly remarkable or so important from an aesthetic, architectural or engineering perspective, that it could properly and rationally be said to derive its entire character from that single feature.

The restriction on works which would otherwise be exempted development applies not only to works to a protected structures but also to works to a proposed protected structure. The rationale for this appears to be that as the process between proposing to add a structure to the register of protected structure and its actual designation as a protected structure may take some time, a person could attempt to carry out the works prior to its formal designation and render nugatory its protected status. However, a proposal to add a structure to the record of protected structure cannot prevent the carrying out of exempted development works to completion, where such works had already commenced at the time of the proposal. This was so held in *Coras Iompair Éireann v An Bord Pleanála*, unreported, High Court, Clarke J., June 19, 2008, where the base to a radio mast, fencing and a control room were in place at the time of making the proposal, although the radio mast itself was not erected. The Board held that any continuing works to erect the actual mast would not be exempted development by virtue of the proposal made by the Council. Clarke J. quashed the decision of the Board, holding that the proposal to add a structure to the list of protected could not have retrospective effect so as to interfere with vested rights. While the applicant had not yet erected the mast, the works carried out were inextricably bound up with the erection of the mast and so the erection of the mast was exempted development.

Subsection (2) allows the occupier/owner of a protected structure to apply to the planning authority for a declaration as to what works may not materially affect the character of the structure or element thereof. A request for a declaration must be made in writing and the planning authority must give such declaration within 12 weeks.

Before issuing the declaration, the planning authority must have regard to any Ministerial guidelines issued under s.52 or Ministerial recommendation under s.53. In this respect the *Architectural Heritage Protection, Guidelines for Planning Authorities* were adopted in 2004. Subsection (5) provides that where the protected structure relates to a public place of worship, there is an additional requirement to take into account liturgical requirements. In making the decision as to whether the works materially affect the character of the structure, the correct approach is to consider the liturgical requirement and Ministerial Guidelines as part of that assessment under subs.(1). See *Sherwin v An Bord Pleanála*, unreported, High Court, Edwards J., July 3, 2007, where it was held that the Board was wrong in determining first whether the works materially effected the character under s.57(1) and then separately considering whether the works respected liturgical requirements (taking into account of Ministerial guidelines) under ss.57(4) and (5). The Department of Environment has also published *Guidelines for Planning Authorities on Architectural Heritage Protection for Places of Public Worship* (November 2003), which states at para.3:

"Respecting liturgical requirements includes recognising that churches may wish to adapt places of public worship in the light of contemporary revisions of their worship and mission. Thus church authorities may, in their places of public worship, require flexibility in the provision and arrangement of seating, in the openness of space, for example, for a baptismal font area; for the enlargement of an existing sanctuary or chancel, or for the relocation of the altar-table and lectern. A church authority may also seek flexibility in the associated use of buildings and spaces within the curtilage, such as for access to another space or building for processions, children's liturgy and Sunday school".

The requirement to take into account liturgical requirement also extends to an application of planning permission concerning the interior of protected structures relating to a public place of worship. In considering whether to issue a declaration, para.6 of the *Guidelines for Planning Authorities on Architectural Heritage Protection for Places of Public Worship* provides that:

> "Planning authorities should consider whether any substantial structural changes or alterations to the existing plan form are required for the proposed alterations, for example, the subdivision of important existing spaces, as well as any consequential effects in other parts of the building. Any proposed removal or alteration/destruction of important fixtures and fittings, for example galleries, box pews or fixed seating, will require careful consideration. The age, rarity and craftsmanship of the internal fixtures and fittings can contribute to the architectural coherence of the whole building and, even where not original to the building, the internal fixtures and fittings can be an important part of a later remodelling of the interior. Impact on decoration, for example any interesting decorative schemes such as stencilled decoration, tiling or panelling, should be taken into account. It would also be appropriate to consider any proposals to minimise the impact of proposed changes. Any proposals to store or salvage fixtures and fittings proposed for removal should also be assessed carefully".

The Guidelines also state that early consultation between the planning authority and the relevant church authority is necessary.

The planning authority can review a declaration issued, although it will have no effect on work already carried out in reliance on such declaration. The precise legal status of a declaration is not entirely clear. It would appear to estop the planning authority from taking enforcement action in respect of work carried out in conformity with the declaration. If enforcement action was taken by a member of the public, the declaration would present weighty evidence against the grant of an injunction.

The procedure for review of a declaration was amended under the 2002 Amendment Act which deleted the provision under the 2000 Act, which stated that a declaration shall not prejudice the application of the general reference procedure as to whether a matter is exempted development under s.5. It would appear therefore that a s.5 reference may not be appropriate where the declaration procedure may be invoked. The 2002 Act amended this subsection by providing that a person to whom a declaration was issued may refer such declaration for review by An Bord Pleanála within four weeks of the issue of the declaration. As the declaration may only be requested by an owner or occupier, it means that only the owner or occupier who requested the declaration has the right to refer the matter to An Bord Pleanála for review. Although the issue of a declaration is susceptible to judicial review, which come within ss.50A and 50, a person may be advised to exhaust local remedies by referring the matter to An Bord Pleanála. However, where there was an absence of fair procedures before the planning authority or some matter which would taint the review by the Board it may not be necessary to exhaust such remedy. See *Harding v Cork County Council*, unreported, High Court, Clarke J., October 12, 2006. The decision of An Bord Pleanála in reviewing the declaration may itself be subject to judicial review within ss.50A and 50.

Subsection (10) provides that the planning authority and the Board shall have regard to the protected status or proposed status of the protected structure in determining an application for planning permission. Because of the status of protected structures in the development plan, a planning application affecting a protected structure may amount to a material contravention of the development plan, in which case the special procedure under s.34 for grant of such permission must be followed. Subsection (10)(b) provides that permission for demolition of the protected structure can only be granted in exceptional circumstances. In *O'Brien v Dun Laoghaire-Rathdown County Council*, unreported, High Court, O'Neill J., June 1, 2006, it was said that the provisions of s.57(10)(b) are clear and they are expressed in mandatory terms and are to the effect that where a planning authority is considering the demolition of a protected structure it can only do so if it considers that there are exceptional circumstances which justify demolition. It appears that there must be evidence that the planning authority specifically consider whether exceptional circumstances exist before granting permission for demolition of a protected structure.

Duty of owners and occupiers to protect structures from endangerment

58.—**(1)** Each owner and each occupier shall, to the extent consistent **1–80** with the rights and obligations arising out of their respective interests in a protected structure or a proposed protected structure, ensure that the structure, or any element of it which contributes to its special architectural, historical, archaeological, artistic, cultural, scientific, social or technical interest, is not endangered.

(2) The duty imposed by *subsection (1)* in relation to a proposed protected structure arises at the time the owner or occupier is notified, under *section 55* or under *Part II,* of the proposal to add the structure to the record of protected structures.

(3) Neither of the following shall be considered to be a breach of the duty imposed on each owner and each occupier under this *section* —

  (a) development in respect of which permission under *section 34* has been granted;

  (b) development consisting only of works of a type which, in a declaration issued under *section 57(3)* to that owner or occupier, a planning authority has declared would not materially affect the character of the protected structure or any element, referred to in *subsection (1) of this section,* of that structure.

(4) Any person who, without lawful authority, causes damage to a protected structure or a proposed protected structure shall be guilty of an offence.

(5) Without prejudice to any other defence that may be available, it shall be a good defence in any proceedings for an offence under *subsection (4)* to prove that the damage to the structure resulted from works which were—

  (a) urgently required in order to secure the preservation of the structure or any part of it,

  (b) undertaken in good faith solely for the purpose of temporarily safeguarding the structure, and

  (c) unlikely to permanently alter the structure or any element of it referred to in *subsection (1).*

NOTE

    This section imposes a duty on any owner/occupier to ensure that a protected structure or proposed protected structure is not endangered. This duty arises from the notice of a proposal to add the structure to the record of protected structures. There is no breach of duty where work is carried out in accordance with a planning permission granted or work is of a type covered under a s.57 declaration. It appears that the duty of the occupier/owner is not confined to refraining from acting (or omitting to act) so as to endanger the protected structure, but also extends to affording protection against the action of third parties. In the light of the definition of endangerment in s.2, it appears that an owner can fail in their duty to ensure a protected structure is not endangered by omitting to take steps or measures to prevent endangerment. The precise extent of the duty of an owner or occupier, will be proportionate to their rights and obligations with respect to the structure. The criminal offence of causing damage to the protected structure applies only to the person who caused the damage. The penalties for such offence are set out in Pt VIII of the Act. Subsection (5) sets out a defence to such an offence, although other defences may be available. Subsection (5) sets out three conditions which must all be satisfied for the purposes of this defence. Where a person causes damage to a protected structure, it will be a good defence to show that this resulted from works which were urgently required to preserve the structure, were taken in good faith solely to temporarily safeguard the structure and were unlikely to permanently alter the structure or any part of it. This defence involves several elements, all of which must be satisfied. Thus if the works had some purpose other than to temporaily safeguard the structure, the defence will not be available. Equally, if the works were of a permanent nature, it may not qualify under (b) or (c). Proof of urgency must also be demonstrated. This may involve proof that the preservation of the structure or any part of its would be at risk unless urgent action was required. The defence may be open even if the situation of urgency arose through the severe neglect of an owner and the owner, so long as such person acted in good faith and the other elements of the defence are present.

Notice to require works to be carried out in relation to endangerment of protected structures

1–81   **59.—(1)** Where, in the opinion of the planning authority, it is necessary to do so in order to prevent a protected structure situated within its functional area from becoming or continuing to be endangered, the authority shall serve on each person who is the owner or occupier of the protected structure a notice—

   (a) specifying the works which the planning authority considers necessary in order to prevent the protected structure from becoming or continuing to be endangered, and

   (b) requiring the person on whom the notice is being served to carry out those works within a specified period of not less than 8 weeks from the date the notice comes into effect under *section 62.*

(2) After serving notice under *subsection (1)* on a person, a planning authority may—

   (a) at its discretion, assist the person in carrying out the works required under the notice, and

   (b) provide such assistance in any form it considers appropriate, including advice, financial aid, materials, equipment and the services of the authority's staff.

(3) Any person on whom a notice under *subsection (1)* has been served may, within 4 weeks from the date of service of the notice, make written representations to the planning authority concerning—

   (a) the terms of the notice,

   (b) the provision of assistance under *subsection (2),* and

   (c) any other material considerations.

(4) After considering any representations made under *subsection (3),* the planning authority may confirm, amend or revoke the notice, and shall notify the person who made the representations of its decision.

(5) Particulars of a notice served under this *section* shall be entered in the register.

NOTE

   This section allows the planning authority to serve an endangerment notice on an owner/occupier of the protected structure, requiring works to be carried out to prevent the endangerment within a specified period of not less than eight weeks from when the notice takes effect. Section 2 defines endangerment as "exposed to harm, decay or damage, whether immediately or over a period of time, through neglect or through direct or indirect means". On one view, the above definition is very wide and is not confined to situations of urgency or emergencies but can extend to risks which are not immediate. This is also supported by the fact that subs.(1) refers to a notice to prevent a protected structure "from becoming or continuing to be endangered", which means that the endangerment may happen in the future. However the reference in the definition of endangerment to "over a period of time", may be deemed to refer to the process or the cause of the harm, decay or damages to which the structure is currently exposed and does not mean that the exposure to decay, harm or damage may appear at some future date. However, the better view is while the structure need not be presently endangered, the risk of the structure "becoming" endangered must not too remote and so there should be some objective evidence the demonstrate such risk. As regards the works which may be required in the notice, it appears these must be limited to preventing the structure from being endangered within the notion of "endangerment" under s.2. Thus it would not be appropriate for an endangerment notice to require restoration of a structure as this ought more properly be the subject of a restoration notice under s.60.

The notice itself must "specify" the works with sufficient particularity so as to comply with s.59(1)(a). A notice which is vague may fail to meet this requirement. This is particularly the case considering that failure to comply with an endangerment notice is a criminal offence under s.63. See by analogy with enforcement notices, *Dundalk UDC v Lawlor* [2005] 2 I.L.R.M. 106. In deciding what works are required, the planning authority must give due weight to the status of the structure as a protected structure. This would also appear implicit in the fact that s.79 provides that the local authority, in its capacity as sanitary authority, must before issuing a notice under s.3(1) of the Local Government (Sanitary Services) Act 1964 (a notice to the owner to carry out such works (including the demolition of the structure) to prevent the structure from being a dangerous structure) consider whether instead to issue an endangerment notice under s.59 or a notice under s.11 of the Derelict Sites Act 1990, specifying measures necessary in order to prevent land from becoming or continuing to be a derelict site.

The planning authority may at its discretion assist the person in carrying out the works in any form it deems appropriate. A person on whom the notice is served may, within four weeks of service, make representations to the planning authority in respect of the terms of the notice or in relation to assistance, which must be considered by the planning authority when deciding whether to amend, confirm or revoke the notice. Under s.61(1)(c) of the 2000 Act, a person who made representations can appeal to the District Court against a s.59 notice on certain specified grounds. By virtue of s.62, the appeal will operate as stay on the notice until the court makes its determination.

Notice to require restoration of character of protected structures and other places

60.—(1) In this section, "works", in relation to a structure or any element of **1–82** a structure, includes the removal, alteration or replacement of any specified part of the structure or element, and the removal or alteration of any advertisement structure.

(2) A planning authority may serve a notice that complies with *subsection (3)* on each person who is the owner or occupier of a structure situated within its functional area, if—

(a) the structure is a protected structure and, in the opinion of the planning authority, the character of the structure or of any of its elements ought to be restored, or

(b) the structure is in an architectural conservation area and, in the opinion of the planning authority, it is necessary, in order to preserve the character of the area, that the structure be restored.

(3) A notice under *subsection (2)* shall—

(a) specify the works required to be carried out for the purposes of restoring the structure or element referred to in the notice,

(b) state that the person on whom the notice is served may, within a specified period of not less than 8 weeks from the date of the service of the notice, make written representations to the planning authority concerning the notice,

    (c) invite that person to enter into discussions with the planning authority, within a specified period of not less than 8 weeks from the date of the service of the notice, concerning the notice and in particular concerning—

        (i) the provision by the planning authority of advice, materials, equipment, the services of the authority's staff or other assistance in carrying out the works specified in the notice, and

        (ii) the period within which the works are to be carried out,

    (d) specify the period within which, unless otherwise agreed in the discussions under *paragraph (c),* the works shall be carried out, being a period of not less than 8 weeks from the end of the period allowed for entering into discussions, and

    (e) state that the planning authority shall pay any expenses that are reasonably incurred by that person in carrying out the works in accordance with the notice, other than works that relate to an unauthorised structure which has been constructed, erected or made 7 years or less prior to the service of the notice.

(4) In deciding whether to serve a notice under this *section,* a planning authority shall have regard to any guidelines issued under *section 52* and any recommendations made under *section 53.*

(5) If the invitation under *subsection (3)(c)* to enter into discussions is accepted, the planning authority shall facilitate the holding of those discussions.

(6) After considering any representations made under *subsection (3)(b)* and any discussions held under *subsection (5),* the planning authority may confirm, amend or revoke the notice and shall notify the person who made the representations of its decision.

(7) Particulars of a notice served under this *section* shall be entered in the register.

NOTE

    This section empowers the planning authority to serve a restoration notice on the owner/ occupier of a structure requiring certain restoration works to be carried out. There is no definition of "restoration" in the Act, although it is related to the notion of "conservation". The Department of the Environment Conservation Guidelines state that "[c]onservation of historic buildings can generally be considered as the action taken to prevent decay and to prolong the life of our national heritage". Also at para.7.21 of the *Architectural Heritage Protection, Guidelines for Planning Authorities,* conservation is described as "the process of caring for buildings and places and of managing change to them in such a way as to retain their character and special interest". Restoration is distinguished from reconstruction, with the former being referred to as "returning a heritage object to a known earlier state, without the introduction of new material". These Guidelines prescribe restoration rather than replacement and recommend the use of processes which are reversible or substantially reversible. The conservation principles prescribed include retention or restoration, conservation based on research, minimum physical intervention and maintenance of visual setting.

    Subsection (1) gives an expanded definition of "works", which supplements the expanded definition of works in relation to a protected structure under s.2 which defines works as:

"[A]ny act or operation of construction, excavation, demolition, extension, alteration, repair or renewal and, in relation to a protected structure or proposed protected structure, includes any act or operation involving the application or removal of plaster, paint, wallpaper, tiles or other material to or from the surfaces of the interior or exterior of a structure".

The service of a notice is not confined to protected structures but also extends to structures situated in an architectural conservation area. The works which may be required are broadly stated to include the removal, alteration or replacement of any specified part of the structure or element, and the removal or alteration of any advertisement structure. The contents of the notice set out in subs.(3) are mandatory and must specify the works required; allow the owner/occupier to make written submissions or observations; invite the owner/occupier to enter discussions with the planning authority concerning assistance by the planning authority or concerning the time frame for completion; specify the period for which the works are to be performed (if not agreed); and also specify that the planning authority will pay certain expenses reasonably incurred. The restoration notice differs from the endangerment notice under s.59 in inviting owners/occupiers to enter into discussions and also in specifying the planning authority will pay certain expenses reasonably incurred. In issuing the notice, the planning authority must have regard to any ministerial guidelines issued under s.52 or ministerial recommendation issued under s.53. The planning authority must consider any representations or discussions entered into in deciding whether to confirm, amend or revoke the notice.

Appeals against notices

61.—(1) Within 2 weeks after being notified under *section 59(4) or* **1–83** *60(6)* of the confirmation or amendment of a notice, any person who made representations in relation to the notice may appeal against the notice to the District Court, on any one or more of the following grounds:

- **(a)** that the person is not the owner or occupier of the structure in respect of which the notice has been served;
- **(b)** that, in the case of a notice under *section 59(1),* compliance with the requirements of the notice would involve unreasonable expense, and that the person had stated in representations made to the planning authority under *section 59(3)* that he or she did not have the means to pay;
- **(c)** that the person has already taken all reasonable steps to—
  - **(i)** in the case of a notice under *section 59(1),* prevent the structure from becoming or continuing to be endangered,
  - **(ii)** in the case of a notice under *section 60(2)* in relation to a protected structure, restore the character of the structure or the element, or
  - **(iii)** in the case of a notice under *section 60(2)* in relation to a structure that forms part of a place, area, group of structures or townscape referred to in *paragraph (b) of that subsection,* assist in restoring the character of that place, area, group of structures or townscape, as the case may be;
- **(d)** that the time for complying with the notice is unreasonably short.

(2) Notice of an appeal under *subsection (1)* shall be given to the planning authority, and it shall be entitled to appear, be heard and adduce evidence on the hearing of the appeal.

(3) On the hearing of the appeal, the District Court may, as it thinks proper—

(a) confirm the notice unconditionally,

(b) confirm the notice subject to such modifications or additions as the Court thinks reasonable, or

(c) annul the notice.

(4) Where the notice is confirmed under *subsection (3)(b)* subject to modifications or additions, the notice shall have effect subject to those modifications or additions.

NOTE

This section allows a person to appeal the confirmation or amendment of an endangerment or restoration notice to the District Court within two weeks of the date of confirmation or amendment of the notice. A standing requirement applies to taking an appeal in that the appellant must have made representations or observations in relation to the notice when it was served. Subsection (2) sets out four potential grounds of appeal, which depend on whether the challenged notice is an endangerment or restoration notice. The appeal to the District Court is therefore not an unrestricted right of appeal but is restricted to four specified grounds: (a) to (d) set out above. A person may appeal on the basis of one or more of such grounds. In order to avail of the ground of unreasonable expense under (b), the appellant must have made a representation to the planning authority that they did not have the means to pay. The grounds under (c) involves the appellant demonstrating that he has already taken all reasonable steps. This means that at the time of appeal, these steps must already have been taken and it not sufficient for an appellant to claim that he will carry out such steps. The question of what are reasonable steps will depend upon the particular facts of the case. As regards ground (d) that the time for compliance was unreasonably short, this will depend upon the extent and nature of the measures required. Where the local authority confirms a notice, a party could also seek to challenge the notice in judicial review proceedings. Where the grounds of challenge do not fall within the four specified grounds above, judicial review would be the appropriate remedy.

There is no prescribed notice of appeal, though such notice must be served on the planning authority. It appears that the form of the notice of appeal is that specified in DCR Ord.100, with the notice of appeal being in the form of Form 100.1 contained in DCR Sch.D. The structure of review is similar to review of other local authority notices such as a fire safety notice under the Fire Services Act 1981. The court has a discretion at the hearing whether to confirm, modify or annul the notice. The court has discretion in making any order.

Effective date of notices

1–84   **62.**—A notice under *section 59(1) or 60(2)* shall not have effect until the expiry of 4 weeks from the date of service of the notice, subject to the following exceptions—

(a) if any representations have been made under *section 59 or 60* in relation to the notice, and no appeal is taken within the period allowed under *section 61(1),* the notice has effect on the expiry of the appeal period;

(b) if an appeal is taken under *section 61(1)* and the notice is confirmed, the notice has effect on the date on which the decision of the District Court is pronounced, or the date on which that order is expressed to take effect, whichever is later;

(c) if an application is made to the District Court under *section 65(1)* and an order is made under *section 65(2)(a),* the notice has effect on the date on which the decision of the Court is pronounced, or the date on which that order is expressed to take effect, whichever is later.

NOTE

This section concerns the date on which an endangerment or restoration notice takes effect. The notice will usually have effect four weeks from the date of service, subject to three exceptions. Where representations are made but no appeal taken, the notice will take effect two weeks from the confirmation or amendment of the notice. If an appeal is taken, the notice will have effect from the date of decision of the court or such other date as the court directs. If an application is made to the District Court under s.65 where a person cannot carry out the works without the consent of another person, the notice takes effect from the date of the court's decision or such other date the court directs. The taking of an appeal therefore effectively acts as a stay on the order until the matter is determined by the court.

Offence relating to endangerment of protected structures

63.—A person who fails to comply with a notice served on him or her under *section 59(1)* shall be guilty of an offence.   **1–85**

NOTE

This section creates the criminal offence of failing to comply with an endangerment notice served. The penalties for such are set out in Pt VIII.

Owners' powers in relation to notices concerning endangerment or restoration of structures

64.—Any person who is the owner of the land or structure in respect of   **1–86**
which a notice under *section 59(1) or 60(2)* has been served, and his or her servants or agents, may enter that land or structure and carry out the works required under the notice.

NOTE

This section empowers an owner served with an endangerment or restoration notice to enter the land or structure to carry out the works. This section may be relevant where the owner has leased the land or structure which restricts his ability to enter the land or structure.

Application to District Court for necessary consent

65.—**(1)** A person served with a notice under *section 59(1) or 60(2)* may   **1–87**
apply to the District Court for an order under *subsection (2) of this section* if—
   (a) that person is unable, without the consent of another person, to carry out the works required under the notice, and
   (b) the other person withholds consent to the carrying out of those works.
   (2) If, on hearing an application under *subsection (1)*, the District Court determines that the other person's consent has been unreasonably withheld—
   (a) the Court may, at its discretion, deem that consent to have been given, and
   (b) in that case, the person making the application shall be entitled to carry out the works required under the notice.

NOTE

This section allows a person served with an endangerment or restoration notice to make an application to the District Court where they have been unable to obtain the consent of another person whose consent is necessary to carry out the works. Section 64 only confers on owners the right to enter the land and carry out the works and so any other person served with a notice who is not an owner may require the consent of other persons to enter the land and carry out the works. In this application where the court decides that the consent of the other person was unreasonably withheld, it has the power to deem such consent given, entitling the person to carry out the works. A court order made pursuant to an application would be a defence to an action for trespass by the other persons, so long as the applicant does not exceed what is necessary for the carrying out of the works.

Jurisdiction of District Court

1–88   **66.**—The jurisdiction conferred on the District Court—

(a) by *section 61* in relation to an appeal against a notice, or

(b) by *section 65* in relation to an application for an order deeming consent to have been given,

shall be exercised by a judge of that Court having jurisdiction in the district in which the structure that is the subject of the appeal or application is situated.

NOTE

This section provides that the appropriate District Court for hearing an appeal under ss.61 or 65 is a court in the district in which the structure is situated.

Application to court for contribution to cost of carrying out works on endangered structures

1–89   **67.**—**(1)** A person who has been served with a notice under *section 59(1)*, and who has carried out the works required under the notice, may apply to a court of competent jurisdiction for an order directing that all, or such part as may be specified in the order, of the cost of those works be borne by some other person who has an interest in the structure concerned.

(2) On the hearing of an application under *subsection (1)*, the court shall make such order as it considers just, having regard to all the circumstances of the case.

NOTE

This section allows a person who carried out the works required under an endangerment notice served upon him to apply to court to direct that the costs of the works be paid by some other person who has an interest in the structure. The appropriate court to which to make the application will depend on the amount claimed, and so will depend on the jurisdictional limits of the courts. Such an application can only be made against the local authority where it has a proprietary interest in the structure in its capacity as landowner. The court has complete discretion in making an order in respect of all or part of the costs. The court may take into account the extent of the interest of the respective parties and all the circumstances of the case.

Carrying out of certain works to be exempted development

1–90   **68.**—The carrying out of any works specified in a notice under *section 59(1) or 60(2)* shall be exempted development.

NOTE

This section provides that works carried out required under an endangerment or restoration notice is exempted development and does not require planning permission.

Planning authority's power to carry out works to protected structures and other places

69.—Where a person on whom a planning authority has served a notice under *section 59(1) or 60(2)* fails to comply with the notice, the planning authority may take such steps as it considers reasonable and necessary to give effect to the terms of the notice including—

1–91

   (a) entry on land by authorised persons in accordance with *section 252,* and

   (b) the carrying out, or arranging the carrying out, of the works specified in the notice.

NOTE

This section provides that where a person fails to carry out the works required under an endangerment or restoration notice, the planning authority has a discretion to take steps to give effect to the notice. In this respect, the planning authority may enter on the land under s.252 and carry out the works required. Section 252 sets out the procedure and limits to authorised person entering lands. These include, inter alia, that consent of the owner must be sought, or failing such, a minimum of 14 days notice of intention to enter is given; that entry may only take place at all reasonable times between the hours of 9am and 6pm, or during business hours; and that an authorised person may take all steps reasonably necessary for the purpose of entry and so may survey, carry out inspections, make plans, take photographs, take levels, make excavations, etc. The planning authority may carry out the works itself or may engage others to carry out the works on its behalf.

Recovery by planning authority of expenses for carrying out works on endangered structures

70.—A planning authority which serves a notice under *section 59(1)* in respect of a protected structure may—

1–92

   (a) recover (whether as a simple contract debt in a court of competent jurisdiction or otherwise), from the owner or occupier, any expenses reasonably incurred by the authority under *section 69,* including any assistance provided under *section 59(2),* and

   (b) secure those expenses by—

   (i) charging the protected structure under the *Registration of Title Act, 1964,* or

   (ii) an instrument vesting any interest in the protected structure in the authority subject to a right of redemption by the owner or occupier.

NOTE

This section allows the planning authority to recover expenses it incurred in entering the land to carry out the works after the person served failed to do so. The planning authority can sue for such expenses in court on the basis of a contract debt and/or may seek to secure the expenses by registering a burden on the protected structure in the Land Registry or by vesting an interest in the planning authority subject to redemption by the owner/occupier.

Power to acquire protected structure

1–93   **71.—(1)** A planning authority may acquire, by agreement or compulsorily, any protected structure situated within its functional area if—

    (a) it appears to the planning authority that it is necessary to do so for the protection of the structure, and

    (b) in the case of a compulsory acquisition, the structure is not lawfully occupied as a dwelling house by any person other than a person employed as a caretaker.

(2) In this *section and sections 72 to 77,* a reference to a protected structure shall be construed to include a reference to any land which—

    (a) forms part of the attendant ground of that structure, and

    (b) is, in the planning authority's opinion, necessary to secure the protection of that structure,

whether or not the land lies within the curtilage of the structure or is specified as a feature in the record of protected structures.

NOTE

This section allows a planning authority to compulsorily acquire or by agreement acquire a protected structure. This section can only be invoked where two conditions are satisfied; that the planning authority considers that it is necessary to protect the structure and, where sought to be compulsorily acquired, the structure is not occupied as a dwelling other than by a caretaker. The power of the local authority to compulsorily acquire is set out in s.214 and is also contained in other Acts such as under s.10 (as amended by s.86 of the Housing Act 1966) of the Local Government (No. 2) Act 1960. Attendant grounds are defined in s.2 as land outside the curtilage of the protected structure and so outside the definition of a protected structure. However, for the purposes of compulsory acquisition, subs.(2) provides that it will extend to land which forms part of the attendant grounds of the structure.

Notice of intention to acquire protected structure compulsorily

1–94   **72.—(1)** A planning authority intending to acquire any protected structure compulsorily under this *Part* shall—

    (a) publish in one or more newspapers circulating in its functional area a notice—

        (i) stating its intention to acquire the protected structure compulsorily under this *Part,*

        (ii) describing the structure to which the notice relates,

        (iii) naming the place where a map showing the location of the protected structure is deposited and the times during which it may be inspected, and

        (iv) specifying the time within which (not being less than 4 weeks), and the manner in which, objections to the acquisition of the structure may be made to the planning authority,

    and

    (b) serve on every owner, lessee and occupier (except tenants for one month or a period less than one month) of the structure a notice which complies with paragraph (a).

(2) In this section, "owner", in relation to a protected structure, means—

    (a) a person, other than a mortgagee not in possession, who is for the time being entitled to dispose (whether in possession or reversion) of the fee simple of the protected structure, and

(b) a person who, under a lease or agreement the unexpired term of which exceeds 5 years, holds or is entitled to the rents or profits of the protected structure.

NOTE

This section sets out the procedure to be followed by a planning authority in seeking to compulsorily acquire a protected structure. This involves publishing a newspaper notice which must contain the four matters set out in subs.(1). This notice must also be served on every owner, lessee and occupier of the structure, with a particular definition of owner being provided in subs.(2)(b). Occupiers who are tenants for one month or less, need not be served.

A protected structure may involve a part of a specific structure, so it is open to question whether the power to compulsorily acquire extends to the full structure of which the protected structure forms part. In certain instances it may not be feasible to compulsorily acquire a protected structure forming part of another structure without acquiring the entire structure.

Objection to compulsory acquisition of protected structure

73.—(1) Any person, on whom a notice of the proposed compulsory   **1–95** acquisition of a protected structure has been served under *section 72(1)(b),* may, within the time and in the manner specified in the notice, submit to the planning authority concerned an objection to the proposed compulsory acquisition referred to in the notice.

(2) A person who has submitted an objection under *subsection (1)* may withdraw the objection by notice in writing sent to the planning authority concerned.

(3) Where an objection submitted to a planning authority under *subsection (1)* is not withdrawn, the planning authority shall not acquire the protected structure compulsorily without the consent of the Board.

(4) An application for the Board's consent to the compulsory acquisition of a protected structure shall be made within 4 weeks after the expiry of the time allowed, under *subsection (1),* for submitting an objection to that acquisition, and shall be accompanied by the following—

(a) the relevant map,
(b) a copy of the objection made under *subsection (1)* to the planning authority,
(c) the planning authority's comments (if any) on the objection, and
(d) such other documents and particulars as may be prescribed.

(5) On receipt of the planning authority's comments (if any) on the objection, the Board shall, by notice served on the person who made the objection, send a copy of the comments to that person who may, within 3 weeks from the date of the service of the notice, make observations to the Board in relation to the comments.

(6) On application under *subsection (4),* the Board may, as it thinks fit, grant or refuse to grant consent to the compulsory acquisition of all or part of a protected structure referred to in a notice published under *section 72.*

NOTE

This section allows a person who has been served with a compulsory acquisition notice of the protected structure to raise objections. Where an objection is raised within the time allowed in the notice, the planning authority must obtain the consent of An Bord Pleanála in order to acquire the structure. The planning authority must seek the consent of the Board within four weeks from the expiry of the time for making objections and also furnish the Board with a map, the objections, and the planning authorities' comments thereon, as well as other prescribed documents. Article 53 of the Planning Regulations 2001 prescribes the documents for these purposes as a copy of the relevant notice published in accordance with s.72(1)(a) of the Act, and a copy of the relevant notice served in accordance with s.72(1)(b) of the 2000 Act. These requirements are mandatory, so if the planning authority fails to take these steps within four weeks, a new notice will be required to be served. The furnishing of the Board with the documents is also mandatory, see by analogy with *McAnenley v An Bord Pleanála* [2002] 2 I.R. 763. The objectors must be furnished with the comments of the planning authority and then have another three weeks to make further observations in relation to the comments to the Board. Such observations must be only in response to the comments and cannot raise new unrelated objections. The Board then has a discretion to grant or refuse the compulsory acquisition. It also has a discretion to grant the acquisition for part only of the protected structure which is sought to be acquired. It is not entirely clear whether this procedure could be said to amount to an appeal or referral. It does not come within the definition of a referral, so the only remaining classification is that of an appeal. No express provision is made for an oral hearing. The general provisions regarding conducting of appeals before the Board will apply including s.135 whereby the Board has an absolute discretion as to whether to hold an oral hearing.

Vesting order for protected structures

1–96　　**74.—(1)** After complying with *section 73,* a planning authority may, by vesting order, acquire a protected structure if—

    (a) no objection is submitted to the planning authority under *section 73,*

    (b) any objection submitted under *section 73* is subsequently withdrawn, or

    (c) the Board consents to the compulsory acquisition of the structure by the planning authority.

(2) Where a planning authority becomes aware, before making a vesting order in respect of a protected structure, that the structure is subject (whether alone or in conjunction with other land) to—

    (a) any annuity or other payment to the Minister for Agriculture, Food and Rural Development or to the Commissioners, or

    (b) any charge payable to the Revenue Commissioners on the death of any person, the planning authority shall forthwith inform the Minister for Agriculture, Food and Rural Development, the Commissioners or the Revenue Commissioners, as the case may be, of its intention to make the vesting order.

(3) Within 2 weeks after making a vesting order, a planning authority shall—

    (a) publish, in one or more newspapers circulating within its functional area, a notice—

        (i) stating that the order has been made,

        (ii) describing the protected structure to which it relates, and

        (iii) naming a place where a copy of the order and the attached map may be seen during office hours at the offices of the authority,

and

(b) serve on every person appearing to the authority to have an interest in the protected structure to which the order relates, a notice stating that the order has been made and the effect of the order.

NOTE

This section allows the planning authority to formally acquire the protected structure by way of vesting order. The planning authority can issue a vesting order where there is no objection to its notice, where any objection is withdrawn, or where the Board consents to the acquisition. Under subs.(2), a notice must be sent by the planning authority to the Minister for Agriculture and Revenue Commissioners in respect of an annuity or charge if the planning authority is aware of such matters before making the vesting order. It is unlikely that the vesting order would be deemed invalid where there is a failure to inform these parties before making the vesting order. The requirement to publish a notice in the newspaper and also to serve any person with an interest in the structure, within two weeks, is mandatory. The requirement to serve a notice on persons with an "interest" is not therefore confined to persons who were served with the original notice of intention to compulsorily acquire, which comprised the owner, lessee and occupier under s.72(1)(b).

Form and effect of vesting order

75.—**(1)** A vesting order by which a planning authority acquires a protected structure under this *Part* shall be in the prescribed form, and shall have attached to it a map showing the location of the protected structure.   **1–97**

(2) A vesting order shall be expressed and shall operate to vest the protected structure to which it relates in the planning authority in fee simple, free from encumbrances and all estates, rights, titles and interests of whatsoever kind on a specified date (in this *section* referred to as the vesting date) not earlier than 3 weeks after the making of the order.

(3) Notwithstanding *subsection (2),* where a planning authority has acquired by a vesting order a protected structure which is subject, either alone or in conjunction with other land, to an annual sum payable to the Minister for Agriculture, Food and Rural Development or the Commissioners, the planning authority shall become and be liable, as from the vesting date, for the payment to that Minister or those Commissioners, as the case may be, of—

(a) that annual sum, or

(b) such portion of it as shall be apportioned by the Minister or the Commissioners, as the case may be,

as if the protected structure had been transferred to the authority by the owner on that date.

(4) For the purposes of *subsection (3),* an "annual sum" *means a purchase annuity, a payment in lieu of rent, or any other annual sum that is not merely a rent under a contract of tenancy.*

NOTE

This section concerns the form and effect of a vesting order to acquire the protected structure. The effect of a vesting order will be to vest the fee simple of the protected structure in the planning authority, free from any other interests. The only exception to this is where the protected structure is subject to an annual charge to the Minister for Agriculture, Food and Rural Development or to the Revenue Commissioners. The order will have effect not earlier than three weeks after the making of the order. Article 54(1) of the Planning Regulations prescribes Form No.1 of Sch.4 of the Regulations, or a form of substantially like effect, as the form for the purpose of the vesting order.

Registration of acquired title and amendment of vesting order

1–98   **76.—(1)** On making a vesting order in relation to a protected structure, a planning authority shall send the order to the registering authority which, on receipt of the order, shall immediately cause the planning authority to be registered as owner of the land in accordance with the order.

(2) On the application of any person, a planning authority may amend a vesting order made by the authority if—

(a) the authority is satisfied that the vesting order contains an error, whether occasioned by it or otherwise, and

(b) the error may be rectified without injustice to any person.

(3) Where a copy of an order under *subsection (2),* amending a vesting order, is lodged with the registering authority, that authority shall rectify its register in such manner as may be necessary to make the register conform with the amending order.

NOTE

This section provides for the registration of the vesting order with the registration authority. In the case of registered land, this will be the Land Registry and in the case of unregistered land, it will be the Registry of Deeds. The section allows a person to apply to the planning authority to correct an error in the vesting order, which may be performed where it does not lead to injustice to other parties.

Compensation for interest in protected structure

1–99   **77.—(1)** Any person who, immediately before a vesting order is made, has any estate or interest in, or any right in respect of, the protected structure acquired by the order, may apply to the planning authority within one year (or such other period as the High Court, on application to it, may allow) after the making of the order for compensation in respect of the estate, interest or right.

(2) On application under *subsection (1),* the planning authority shall, subject to *subsection (4),* pay to the applicant by way of compensation an amount equal to the value (if any) of the estate, interest or right.

(3) The compensation to be paid by the planning authority under this *section* in relation to any estate, interest or right in respect of the protected structure shall, in default of agreement, be determined by arbitration under and in accordance with the *Acquisition of land (Assessment of Compensation) Act, 1919.*

(4) Where, after a planning authority makes a vesting order in relation to a protected structure, any sum (including a sum for costs) remains due to the authority by any person under an order of a court for payment of an amount due (whether under this *Act* or any other *Act,* or whether remaining due after deducting expenses reasonably incurred by the authority under this *Act* in relation to the structure), the amount of any compensation payable to that person under this *section* shall be reduced by the amount of that sum.

(5) *Sections 69 to 79 of the Lands Clauses Consolidation Act, 1845,* as amended or adapted by or under the *Second Schedule to the Housing of the Working Classes Act, 1890,* or any other *Act,* shall apply in relation to compensation to be paid by a planning authority under this *section* as if such compensation were a price or compensation under that *Act* as so amended.

(6) Where money is paid into court by the planning authority under *section 69 of the Lands Clauses Consolidation Act, 1845,* as applied by this *section,* no costs shall be payable by that authority to any person in respect of any proceedings for the investment, payment of income, or payment of capital of such money.

NOTE

This section concerns the right to compensation of a person who had an interest in the protected structure compulsorily acquired. The application to the planning authority for compensation must be made within one year of the vesting order, although it appears that the High Court may extend the period. The amount of compensation payable is an amount equal to the value of the estate or interest. Where the planning authority and the person cannot agree the amount of compensation, it may be referred to arbitration. The amount of compensation payable may be reduced by any amount which the person owes to the planning authority. This allows the planning authority to set off against the compensation any amount owed to it by such person whether arising under this statute or any other statute. The set off can also include costs, which could include an order for costs in legal proceedings made in favour of the local authority.

Use of protected structure acquired by planning authority

78.—A planning authority may—   1–100
   (a) use a protected structure acquired by it under this *Act* or any other enactment for any purpose connected with its functions, or
   (b) sell, let, transfer or exchange all or any part of that protected structure,
and in so doing shall have regard to its protected status.

NOTE

This section affords a discretion to the planning authority in deciding how to use the protected structure after having acquired it, so long as it is connected with its functions. The planning authority can also sell, let, transfer or exchange all or part of the protected structure. Although the provision states that the planning authority shall have regard to its protected status, if the planning authority were to use or allow the structure to be used in a manner which was incompatible with its protected status, this would be a material contravention of the development plan.

Obligations of sanitary authorities in respect of protected structures

79.—**(1)** Before issuing a notice under *section 3(1) of the Local Government*   1–101
(Sanitary Services) Act, 1964, in respect of a protected structure or a proposed protected structure, a sanitary authority shall consider—
   (a) the protected status of the structure, and
   (b) whether, instead of a notice under *section 3(1) of that Act,* a notice

should be issued under *section 59(1) or section 11 of the Derelict Sites Act, 1990.*

(2) As soon as practicable after serving or proposing to serve a notice in accordance with *section 3(1) of the Local Government (Sanitary Services) Act, 1964,* in respect of a protected structure or a proposed protected structure, a sanitary authority shall inform the Minister for Arts, Heritage, Gaeltacht and the Islands of the particulars of the notice if he or she recommended that the structure be protected.

(3) A sanitary authority which carries out works on a protected structure, or a proposed protected structure, under *section 3(2) of the Local Government (Sanitary Services) Act, 1964,* shall as far as possible preserve that structure (or elements of that structure which may be of special architectural, historical, archaeological, artistic, cultural, scientific, social or technical interest), in as much as the preservation of that structure is not likely to cause a danger to any person or property.

(4) When carrying out works in accordance with *section 3(2) of the Local Government (Sanitary Services) Act, 1964,* on a protected structure or a proposed protected structure, a sanitary authority shall, as soon as practicable, inform the Minister for Arts, Heritage, Gaeltacht and the Islands of the works if he or she recommended that the structure be protected.

NOTE

This section concerns service by the local authority, in its capacity as sanitary authority, of a dangerous buildings notice, where the building in question is a protected structure. Under s.3(1) of the Local Government (Sanitary Services) Act 1964 (the "1964 Act"), a sanitary authority may, if they so think fit, give a notice to the owner of a dangerous structure, inter alia, to carry out such works (including the demolition of the structure) as will, in the opinion of the authority, prevent the structure from being a dangerous structure. Subsection (1) provides that before issuing such a notice, the sanitary authority must take into account the protected status of the structure and consider whether instead to issue an endangerment notice under s.59 or a notice under s.11 of the Derelict Sites Act 1990 (the "1990 Act"), specifying measures necessary in order to prevent land from becoming or continuing to be a derelict site. In order to be a "derelict site" within the meaning the Act, the land must be likely to detract to a material degree from "the amenity character and appearance of land in the neighbourhood". See *Hussey v Dublin City Council,* unreported, High Court, O'Higgins J., December 14, 2007. The rationale for this section is that the local authority in its capacity as sanitary authority is also obliged to give due weight to the status of a structure as a protected structure before requiring drastic steps such as the demolition of the structure under s.3(1) of the 1990 Act. The sanitary authority is not prohibited from serving a notice under s.3(1) of the 1964 Act, and where it does so (and where it performs the works), it must inform the Minister for Arts, Heritage, Gaeltacht and the Islands of the particulars of the notice if he or she recommended that the structure be protected. Where the sanitary authority enters the land under s.3(2) of the 1964 Act to carry out the works, it must as far as possible preserve the structure insofar as it is not likely to cause a danger.

Grants to planning authorities in respect of functions under this Part

1–102   **80.**—With the consent of the Minister for Finance, the Minister may, out of moneys provided by the Oireachtas, make grants to planning authorities in respect of any or all of their functions under this *Part,* including grants for the purpose of defraying all or part of the expenditure incurred by them in—

(a) assisting persons on whom notice is served under *section 59(1) or 60(2)* in carrying out works in accordance with the notice, and

(b) assisting any other person in carrying out works to protected structures in accordance with such conditions as may be specified by a planning authority for the receipt of such assistance.

NOTE

This section allows the Minister for Finance to grant money to planning authorities for expenditure incurred in assisting persons carrying out works required under an endangerment or restoration notice and assisting persons carrying out other works to protected structures on the basis of conditions specified by the planning authority.

CHAPTER II

Architectural Conservation Areas and Areas of Special Planning Control

Architectural conservation areas

81.—(1) A development plan shall include an objective to preserve the   **1–103** character of a place, area, group of structures or townscape, taking account of building lines and heights, that—

(a) is of special architectural, historical, archaeological, artistic, cultural, scientific, social or technical interest or value, or

(b) contributes to the appreciation of protected structures,

if the planning authority is of the opinion that its inclusion is necessary for the preservation of the character of the place, area, group of structures or townscape concerned and any such place, area, group of structures or townscape shall be known as and is in this *Act* referred to as an "architectural conservation area".

(2) Where a development plan includes an objective referred to in *subsection (1),* any development plan that replaces the first-mentioned development plan shall, subject to any variation thereof under *section 13,* also include that objective.

NOTE

This section provides for the objective of the preservation of an "architectural conservation area" to be inserted as an objective of the development plan. Such an objective relates to the architecture of an area as opposed to areas of scenic areas which may be designated an area of special amenity under s.202 or be declared a landscape conservation area under s.204. Although described as an "area", subs.(1) provides that the objective may be to preserve the character of a place, area, group of structures or townscape. The interests protected by an architectural conservation area may be similar to a protected structure (in particular where the area concerns a "group of structures), although the former seeks to preserve the "character" of a place, area, group of structures or townscape, as opposed to an individual structure or part of a structure. Subsection (1) provides that the development plan may seek to preserve an area due its is special architectural, historical, archaeological, artistic, cultural, scientific, social or technical interest or value or because it contributes to the "appreciation" of protected structures. This means that where there are existing protected structures, an area may be designated not to further protect the protected structures, but to assist in their appreciation. However, an architectural conservation area need not contain protected structures. It is a matter for the discretion of the planning authority as to whether it is necessary to designate an area as an architectural conservation area. However, a matter of relevance is "building lines and heights" mentioned in subs.(1), which must be taken into account.

The objective of preservation of an architectural conservation area will remain in any replacement development plan, unless specifically removed.

Development in architectural conservation areas

1–104   **82.—(1)** Notwithstanding *section 4(1)(h),* the carrying out of works to the exterior of a structure located in an architectural conservation area shall be exempted development only if those works would not materially affect the character of the area.

(2) In considering an application for permission for development in relation to land situated in an architectural conservation area, a planning authority, or the Board on appeal, shall take into account the material effect (if any) that the proposed development would be likely to have on the character of the architectural conservation area.

NOTE

This section provides that works on a structure located in an architectural conservation area which would otherwise be exempted development will lose such status unless the works would not materially affect the character of the area. The section is similar to s.57(1) in relation to protected structures. In *Coras Iompair Éireann v An Bord Pleanála*, unreported, High Court, Clarke J., June 19, 2008, it was held that while on a literal interpretation of the equivalent provision s.57(1) only restricted works carried out under the exempted development category of s.4(1)(h), this would lead to an absurd result. The court adopted a purposive interpretation in holding that subs.(1) restricted works under all categories of exempted development under s.4 including exempted development categories under the 2001 Regulations and not merely under s.4(1)(h).

It may be noted that in any case art.9(1)(a)(xii) expressly provides that development will not be exempted development where the works to the exterior of a structure within an architectural conservation area would materially affect the character of the architectural preservation area.

Subsection (2) provides that in an application for planning permission under s.34 concerning land within an architectural conservation area, the planning authority and Board must take into account its material effect on the character of the architectural conservation area. Depending on the objective in the development plan, it is possible that the development may also be in material contravention of objectives of the development plan concerning the preservation of the architectural conservation area (though this will not necessarily be the case), in which case, the special procedure for material contravention subs.(34)(6) must be followed before the planning authority can grant permission. It may further be noted that under para.13 of Sch.4 compensation is excluded where a reason for refusal of permission is that the proposed development would adversely affect an architectural conservation area.

Power to acquire structure or other land in architectural conservation area

1–105   **83.—(1)** A planning authority may acquire, by agreement or compulsorily, any land situated within an architectural conservation area if the planning authority is of the opinion—

   (a) that it is necessary to so do in order to preserve the character of the architectural conservation area, and

   (b)

      (i) the condition of the land, or the use to which the land or any structure on the land is being put, detracts, or is likely to detract, to a material degree from the character or appearance of the architectural conservation area, or

(ii) the acquisition of the land is necessary for the development or renewal of the architectural conservation area or for the provision of amenities in the area.

(2) A planning authority shall not compulsorily acquire any land under *subsection (1)* that is lawfully occupied as a dwelling house by any person other than a person employed therein as a caretaker.

(3) *Sections 71(2) to 78 of this Act* shall, subject to any necessary modifications, apply to acquisitions under *subsection (1)* and references in those provisions to a protected structure shall, for the purposes of this *section,* be construed as references to a structure or other land situated within an architectural conservation area.

NOTE

This section empowers the planning authority to acquire any land within an architectural conservation area in certain circumstances, whether by agreement or by means of compulsory acquisition. Subsection (1) provides that the planning authority may seek to acquire the land where: (a) it is necessary to preserve its character and (b) where the condition of the land or use of the land or any structure on the land, detracts or is likely to detract to a material degree from its character or where the land is necessary for renewal of the area or alternatively where acquisition of the land is necessary for development or renewal of the area or for provision of amenities in the area. Both conditions (a) and (b) must be present, although (b) presents two possible alternatives, where the state or use of the land is detracting (or is likely to detract) to a material degree or alternatively for the purposes of development or renewal of the land. The provision is couched in discretionary terms with such words as "may acquire", where the planning is "of the opinion", that it is "necessary".

Subsection (2) is similar to s.71(1)(b) concerning protected structures, whereby the planning authority cannot acquire land occupied as a dwelling except where used by a caretaker. The provisions concerning the acquisition of protected structures in ss.71(2)–78 relating to notice, objections, vesting order, registration, compensation and use, equally apply in relation to acquisition of land within an architectural conservation area. It may be noted that under s.71(2) there is an extended definition of a protected structure for the purposes of compulsory acquisition, which provides that a reference to a protected structure shall be construed to include a reference to any land which forms part of the attendant ground of that structure, and is, in the planning authority's opinion, necessary to secure the protection of that structure, whether or not the land lies within the curtilage of the structure or is specified as a feature in the record of protected structures. However, it appears that insofar as the terms in the definition may be not relevant to an architectural conservations area, (except perhaps where it contains a group of protected structures), this does not operate to extend the notion of architectural conservation area for the purposes of compulsory acquisition.

Area of special planning control

84.—(1) A planning authority may, if it considers that all or part of an   **1–106** architectural conservation area is of special importance to, or as respects, the civic life or the architectural, historical, cultural or social character of a city or town in which it is situated, prepare a scheme setting out development objectives for the preservation and enhancement of that area, or part of that area, and providing for matters connected therewith.

(2) Without prejudice to the generality of *subsection (1),* a scheme prepared under that *subsection* may include objectives (and provisions for the furtherance or attainment of those objectives) for—

    (a) the promotion of a high standard of civic amenity and civic design;

    (b) the preservation and protection of the environment, including the architectural, archaeological and natural heritage;

    (c) the renewal, preservation, conservation, restoration, development or redevelopment of the streetscape, layout and building pattern, including the co-ordination and upgrading of shop frontages;

    (d) the control of the layout of areas, density, building lines and height of structures and the treatment of spaces around and between structures;

    (e) the control of the design, colour and materials of structures, in particular the type or quality of building materials used in structures;

    (f) the promotion of the maintenance, repair or cleaning of structures;

    (g) the promotion of an appropriate mix of uses of structures or other land;

    (h) the control of any new or existing uses of structures or other land;

    (i) the promotion of the development or redevelopment of derelict sites or vacant sites; or

    (j) the regulation, restriction or control of the erection of advertisement structures and the exhibition of advertisements.

(3) A scheme prepared under *subsection (1)* shall be in writing and shall be consistent with the objectives of the relevant development plan and any local area plan or integrated area plan (within the meaning of the *Urban Renewal Act, 1998*) in force relating to the area to which the scheme relates.

(4)

    (a) A scheme prepared under *subsection (1)* shall indicate the period for which the scheme is to remain in force.

    (b) A scheme may indicate the order in which it is proposed that the objectives of the scheme or provisions for their furtherance or attainment will be implemented.

(5) A scheme shall contain information, including information of such class or classes as may be prescribed by the Minister, on the likely significant effects on the environment of implementing the scheme.

(6) In this *section, and sections 85 and 86 —*

    "city" *means a county borough*;

    "town" *means a borough (other than a county borough), an urban district or a town having town commissioners that has a population in excess of 2,000.*

NOTE

This section allows the planning authority to prepare a special planning control scheme setting out development objectives for the preservation and enhancement of an architectural conservation area. The area must first be designated an architectural conservation area in the development plan before a scheme can be prepared. The scheme can be for all or part of such area. An architectural conservation area for which a scheme is made is named an area of special planning control under s.85(8). The planning authority need not prepare a scheme in respect of every architectural conservation area but may do so at its discretion where the area is of special importance to, or as respects, either the civic life or the architectural, historical, cultural or social character, of a city or town. The scheme may be not only for the purposes of preservation but also for the "enhancement" of the area. Subsection (2) sets out matters which may be included in the scheme, although the scheme is not confined to these. The scheme may deal with matters of design, layout, building lines, repairs, renewal, etc. The matters set out in this subsection indicate that the scheme can be very specific by including such matters under (e) as the design, colour and materials of the structures and type and quality of building material used. It can deal with both new and existing structures. Subsection (3) provides that the scheme must be consistent with the objectives of the development plan and any local area plan. These objectives are not confined to the objectives relating to architectural conservations areas but includes all the objectives of the plan. There is no specific time-limit for which the scheme may be in force and it may indicate the order in which its objectives are sought to be implemented. The scheme must also contain information on the likely significant effects on the environment of implementing the scheme.

Special planning control scheme

85.—**(1)** *Subsections (2), (3), (4), (5) and (6)* shall, upon the passing of a   **1–107** resolution by the planning authority concerned, be complied with in relation to the scheme specified in the resolution.

(2) The planning authority shall, as soon as may be after the passing of a resolution under *subsection (1)* —

  (a) notify in writing the Minister, the Board and such other persons as may be prescribed, of the preparation of the scheme,

  (b) send copies of the scheme to each of the persons referred to in *paragraph (a),* and

  (c) publish a notice of the preparation of the scheme in one or more newspapers circulating in the city or town concerned.

(3) A notice under *subsection (2)* shall—

  (a) indicate the place or places at which, and the period (being not less than 8 weeks) during and times at which, a copy of the scheme may be inspected (and a copy of the scheme shall be kept available for inspection accordingly), and

  (b) invite submissions or observations in relation to the scheme within such period (being not less than 8 weeks) as is specified in the notice.

(4)

  (a) Where the scheme prepared under *subsection (1)* includes an objective or provision relating to—

    (i) the co-ordination, upgrading or changing of specified shop frontages,

    (ii) the control of the layout of specified areas, the density, building lines and height of specified structures and the treatment of spaces around and between specified structures,

    (iii) the control of the design, colour and materials of specified structures.

    (iv) the promotion of the maintenance, repair or cleaning of specified structures,

    (v) the control of the use or uses of any specified structure or other land in the area,

(vi) the discontinuance of the existing use of any specified structure or other land,

(vii) the development or redevelopment of specified derelict or vacant sites, or

(viii) the control of specified advertisement structures or of the exhibition of specified advertisements,

the planning authority shall, as soon as may be after the making of a resolution under *subsection (1),* notify in writing each person who is the owner or occupier of land thereby affected, of the objective or provision concerned.

(b) A notice under *paragraph (a)* shall refer to the land concerned and shall—

(i) specify the measures that are required to be undertaken in respect of the structure or other land to ensure compliance with the proposed objective or objectives,

(ii) indicate the place or places at which, and the period (being not less than 8 weeks) during and times at which, a copy of the scheme may be inspected (and the copy shall be kept available for inspection accordingly), and

(iii) invite submissions or observations in relation to the proposed objective or provision within such period (being not less than 8 weeks) as is specified in the notice.

(5)

(a) Not later than 12 weeks after giving notice under *subsection (2)* and, where appropriate, a notification under *subsection (4),* whichever occurs later, the manager of a planning authority shall prepare a report on any submissions or observations received in relation to a scheme prepared under *subsection (1)* and shall submit the report to the members of the authority for their consideration.

(b) A report under *paragraph (a)* shall—

(i) list the persons who made submissions or observations in relation to the scheme,

(ii) give a summary of the matters raised in those submissions or observations, and

(iii) include the response of the manager to the submissions or observations.

(6) In responding to submissions or observations made in relation to a scheme prepared under *subsection (1),* the manager of a planning authority shall take account of the proper planning and sustainable development of the area, the statutory obligations of any local authority in the area and any relevant policies or objectives of the Government or of any Minister of the Government.

(7) A planning authority may, after considering a scheme prepared under *subsection (1)* and the report of the manager under *subsection (5),* by resolution, approve the scheme with or without modifications, or refuse to so approve, and a scheme so approved shall be known as and is referred to in this *Part* as an "approved scheme".

(8) An architectural conservation area, or that part of an architectural

conservation area, to which a scheme approved by a planning authority under *subsection (7)* applies shall be known as and is referred to in this *Act* as an "area of special planning control".

(9)

   (a) Where a planning authority approves a scheme under *subsection (7)*, it shall publish a notice thereof in one or more newspapers circulating in the city or town concerned.

   (b) A notice under *paragraph (a)* shall indicate the place or places at which, and times during which, an approved scheme may be inspected (and a copy thereof shall be kept available for inspection accordingly).

   (c) A planning authority shall send a copy of the scheme to the Minister, the Board and such other persons as may be prescribed.

NOTE

This section concerns the procedure for adopting a special planning control scheme in relation to an architectural conservation area. The procedure bears certain similarities to the procedure for adopting a development plan under s.12. The planning authority must first pass a resolution concerning the proposal of such scheme. Notice in writing and copies of the scheme must be sent to the Minister, the Board and other prescribed bodies. Article 55 of the Planning Regulations describes these prescribed bodies as the Minister for Arts, Heritage, Gaeltacht and the Islands, the Heritage Council, An Taisce, An Chomhairle Ealaíon, Bord Fáilte Éireann, and the appropriate chamber of commerce. A newspaper notice must be published stating inspections of the scheme can be made and inviting submissions on the scheme within not less than eight weeks. Where the scheme includes an objective concerning any specific land or structure, a notice must be sent to the owner or occupier specifying the measures required, also indicating where the scheme can be inspected and inviting submissions within a period of not less than eight weeks. The terms of subs.(4), implies that the structure or land must be specifically named in the objective of the scheme rather than merely affected by general objectives relating to land or structures.

Within 12 weeks after the last notice was sent, the County Manager must prepare a report in relation to the issues and submissions, having regard to the proper planning and sustainable development of the area, the statutory obligations of any local authority in the area, and the relevant policies or objectives of the Government or any Minister. By analogy with a report prepared by the Manager for variation of a development plan, there is no obligation to circulate to each member of the planning authority the entirety of the objections and submissions received prior to their consideration of the proposal. See *Sandyford Environmental Planning v Dun Laoghaire Rathdown County Council*, unreported, High Court, McKechnie J., June 30, 2004, where it was noted that in summarising the submissions, the Manager is not bound to use any formula or follow any specified method. Under subs.(6) the Manager must take into account the proper planning and sustainable development of the area, statutory obligations of any local authority in the area and any relevant policies or objectives of the Government or of any Minister.

The planning authority, having considered the Manager's report, may by resolution approve the scheme with or without modifications (in which case it will be known as an "approved scheme"), or refuse to approve the scheme. There is no similar provision to the procedure for preparation of a draft development plan, whereby if the planning authority makes an amendment, which is a material alteration of the plan, there is a requirement to give further notice and invite submissions. In fact, subs.(7) uses the word modification rather than amendment or variation which suggests that only minor alterations (and not material alterations) are permitted. See *White v Dublin Corporation*, unreported, High Court, Ó Caoimh J., June 21, 2002, on the meaning of "modification" in the context of revised applications for planning permission. This restriction to modifications as if radical changes could be made, the public would have been excluded from commenting upon the same. Following approval, the planning authority must publish a newspaper notice stating where the scheme can be inspected and also send a notice to the Minister, the Board and other prescribed bodies.

Variation and review of scheme

1–108   **86.**—**(1)** A planning authority shall, from time to time as circumstances require and in any case not later than 6 years after—

(a) its approval under *section 85(7),* or

(b) it has most recently been reviewed,

review an approved scheme and may by resolution, amend or revoke the scheme.

(2) Where a planning authority proposes to amend an approved scheme under this *section, section 85* shall, subject to any necessary modifications, apply as respects any such amendment.

(3) Notice of the revocation of an approved scheme under this *section* shall be given in one or more newspapers circulating in the city or town concerned.

(4) The amendment or revocation of an approved scheme shall be without prejudice to the validity of anything previously done thereunder.

NOTE

This section allows for the review of a special planning control scheme. The planning authority has an obligation to review the scheme within six years from approval or since its last review, although it may, at its discretion, review the scheme more regularly "from time to time" as circumstances require. The planning authority may amend or revoke the scheme. The same procedure for the making of the scheme under s.85, concerning notice, submissions, Manager's report, etc. must be followed. Notice of the revocation must be published in one or more newspapers circulating in the city or town concerned.

Development in special planning control area

1–109   **87.**—**(1)** Notwithstanding *section 4* and any regulations made thereunder, any development within an area of special planning control shall not be exempted development where it contravenes an approved scheme applying to that area.

(2) When considering an application for permission in relation to land situated in an area of special planning control, a planning authority, or the Board on appeal, shall, in addition to the matters set out in *section 34,* have regard to the provisions of an approved scheme.

(3) An owner or occupier of land situated in an area of special planning control may make a written request to the planning authority, within whose functional area the area of special planning control is situated, for a declaration as to—

(a) those developments or classes of development that it considers would be contrary or would not be contrary, as the case may be, to the approved scheme concerned,

(b) the objectives or provisions of the approved scheme that apply to the land, or

(c) the measures that will be required to be undertaken in respect of the land to ensure compliance with such objectives or provisions.

(4) Within 12 weeks of receipt by a planning authority of a request under *subsection (3)*, or within such other period as may be prescribed by regulations of the Minister, a planning authority shall issue a declaration under this *section* to the person who made the request.

(5) A planning authority may at any time rescind or vary a declaration under this *section.*

(6) The rescission or variation of a declaration under *subsection (5)* shall not affect any development commenced prior thereto in reliance on the declaration concerned and that the planning authority has indicated, in accordance with *paragraph (a) of subsection (3),* would not be contrary to an approved scheme.

(7) A declaration under this *section* is without prejudice to the application of *section 5.*

(8) A planning authority shall cause—

    (a) the particulars of any declaration issued by that authority under this *section* to be entered on the register kept by the authority under *section 7,* and

    (b) a copy of the declaration to be made available for inspection by members of the public during office hours, at the principal office of the authority, following the issue of the declaration.

NOTE

This section describes the effect of an area of special planning control on planning applications and also concerns declarations issued by the planning authority on works which can be carried out in the area. Subsection (1) development, which would otherwise be exempted, will no longer be available where it contravenes the scheme. This subsection is stricter than similar de-exemptions for being in an architectural conservations area (s.82(1)) or in relation to a protected structure (s.57(1)), insofar as it does not allow any qualifications. However, unlike those similar provisions, subs.(1) makes explicitly clear that development may not qualify under any categories of exempted development whether under s.4 or under the 2001 Regulations. See *Coras Iompair Éireann v An Bord Pleanála*, unreported, High Court, Clarke J., June 19, 2008.

In an application for planning permission within the area, the planning authority must have regard to the provisions of the scheme, as well as the matters set out in s.34(2). A mechanism is provided to allow the owner or occupier of land within the scheme to seek a written declaration from the planning authority to clarify certain matters, any one of which can be the subject of the request. These are: what developments on the land are or are not contrary to the scheme; the objectives of the scheme in relation to the land; and the nature of the measures required to ensure compliance with the scheme. The planning authority must issue a declaration within 12 weeks and may rescind or vary the declaration at any time. The precise legal status of a declaration is not entirely clear. A declaration may be subject to the ordinary judicial review procedure. It appears the planning authority would be estopped from taking any action which is contrary to their declaration. However, it appears that the declaration relates specifically to the requester's land and cannot be relied upon by other landowners. However, any recision or variation to a declaration cannot prevent development from being completed which has already been commenced at the time of the recission or variation where declaration had indicated that such development would not be contrary to an approved scheme. Where appropriate, a person can also make a section 5 declaration as to whether a matter is or is not development or exempted development. Any declaration must be entered in the planning register under s.7 and must be made available for inspection.

Service of notice relating to structures or other land in an area of special planning control

1–110   **88.**—**(1)** A planning authority may serve a notice that complies with *subsection (2)* on each person who is the owner or occupier of land to which an objective or provision of an approved scheme applies.

(2) A notice under *subsection (1)* shall—

(a) refer to the structure or land concerned,

(b) specify the date on which the notice shall come into force,

(c) specify the measures required to be undertaken on the coming into force of the notice including, as appropriate, measures for—

    (i) the restoration, demolition, removal, alteration, replacement, maintenance, repair or cleaning of any structure, or

    (ii) the discontinuance of any use or the continuance of any use subject to conditions,

(d) invite the person on whom the notice is served, within such period as is specified in the notice (being not less than 8 weeks from the date of service of the notice) to make written representations to the planning authority concerning the notice,

(e) invite the person to enter into discussions with the planning authority, within such period as is specified in the notice (being not less than 8 weeks from the date of service of the notice) concerning the matters to which the notice refers and in particular concerning—

    (i) the period within which the measures specified in the notice are to be carried out, and

    (ii) the provision by the planning authority of advice, materials, equipment, the services of the authority's staff or other assistance required to carry out the measures specified in the notice,

(f) specify the period within which, unless otherwise agreed in the discussions entered into pursuant to an invitation in the notice in accordance with *paragraph (e),* the measures specified in the notice shall be carried out, being a period of not less than 8 weeks from the date of the coming into force of the notice,

(g) state that the planning authority shall pay any expenses that are reasonably incurred by that person in carrying out the steps specified in the notice, other than expenses that relate to unauthorised development carried out not more than 7 years prior to the service of the notice, and

(h) state that the planning authority shall, by way of compensation, pay, to any person who shows that as a result of complying with the notice—

    (i) the value of an interest he or she has in the land or part thereof existing at the time of the notice has been reduced, or

    (ii) he or she, having an interest in the land at that time, has suffered damage by being disturbed in his or her enjoyment of the structure or other land,

a sum equal to the amount of such reduction in value or a sum in respect of the damage suffered.

(3) If the invitation in a notice in accordance with *subsection (2)(d)* to enter into discussions is accepted, the planning authority shall take all such measures as may be necessary to enable the discussions concerned to take place.

(4) After considering any representations made and any discussions held pursuant to invitations in a notice under *subsection (2),* the planning authority may confirm, amend or revoke the notice and shall notify in writing the person to whom the notice is addressed.

(5) Any person served with a notice under *subsection (1)* may, within 8 weeks from the date of notification of the confirmation or amendment of the notice under *subsection (4),* appeal to the Board against the notice.

(6) Where an appeal is brought under *subsection (5)* against a notice, the Board may, after taking into account—

    (a) the proper planning and sustainable development of the area,

    (b) the provisions of the development plan for the area,

    (c) any local area plan or integrated area plan (within the meaning of the *Urban Renewal Act, 1998*) in force relating to the area to which the scheme relates, and

    (d) the provisions of the approved scheme concerned,

confirm with or without modification, or annul, the notice.

(7) A notice served by a planning authority under *subsection (1)* may, for stated reasons, by notice in writing, be withdrawn.

(8) A notice under this *section* (other than a notice that has been withdrawn) shall not come into force—

    (a) until the expiry of any period within which an appeal against the notice may be brought, or

    (b) where an appeal is taken against the notice, when the appeal has been withdrawn or decided, as may be appropriate.

NOTE

This section allows the service of a notice requiring certain works or changes in use relating to structures or land, in an area of special planning control. The nature and procedure of the notice bears certain similarities to a restoration notice under s.60 regarding protected structures. The notice served on the owner or occupier can require a broad spectrum of measures including the restoration, demolition, removal, alteration, replacement, maintenance, repair or cleaning of any structure, or the discontinuance of any use or the continuance of any use, subject to conditions. The notice must invite the owner/occupier to make submissions or observations and also to enter into discussions with the planning authority, allowing not less than eight weeks to do so. Subsection (3) provides that if the invitation to enter discussions is accepted, the planning authority must take all such measures as may be necessary to enable the discussions to take place. The discussions will relate to the matters to which the notice refers and also the period to carry out the measure specified in the notice and also regarding assistance to be provided by the planning authority. Like a restoration notice, the notice must provide that the planning authority will pay any expenses reasonably incurred by that person in carrying out the steps in the notice, other than expenses relating to unauthorised development within the last seven years. However, an additional requirement not mentioned in the restoration notice is that the planning authority must pay compensation to the person where there was reduction in value of their interest or damage to enjoyment of their land as a result of complying with the notice. Section 198 provides that compensation will be a sum equal to the amount of the reduction in value or a sum in respect of the damage suffered

The planning authority must consider any representations or discussions in deciding whether to confirm, amend or revoke the notice. The owners/occupiers must be notified of such decision, and have eight weeks to appeal the notice to An Bord Pleanála. The appeal must be in the general form of s.127. The Board in making its decision must consider the proper planning and sustainable development of the area, the development plan, any local area plan or integrated area plan and the terms of the scheme. The Board has a discretion whether to confirm the notice with or without modification, or annul the notice. The planning authority may withdraw the notice for stated reasons. The notice will have effect, if no appeal is taken, at the end of the eight-week period allowed from the decision or where there is an appeal, from the date of the Board's decision or date of withdrawal, where withdrawn.

Implementation of the notice under section 88

1–111   **89.**—If, within 8 weeks from the date of the coming into force of the notice or such longer period as may be agreed by the planning authority and the person to whom the notice is addressed, the restoration, demolition, removal, alteration, replacement, maintenance, repair or cleaning required by the notice has not been effected, the planning authority may, subject to *section 252,* enter the structure or land and may effect such restoration, demolition, removal, alteration, replacement, maintenance, repair or cleaning as is specified in the notice.

NOTE

This section enables the planning authority to enter the land under the procedure of s.252 in order to carry out the measures required under the notice, where the owners/occupiers has failed to take such measures within eight weeks of the notice coming into force. The extent of powers of entry are set out in s.252.

Court may compel compliance with notice under section 88

1–112   **90.**—(1) Where a person served with a notice under *section 88* fails to comply with a requirement of the notice, or causes or permits a person to fail to comply with such a requirement, the High Court or the Circuit Court may, on the application of the planning authority, order any person to comply with the notice or to do, or refrain from doing or continuing to do, anything that the Court considers necessary or expedient to ensure compliance with the terms of the said notice.

(2) An order under *subsection (1)* may, without prejudice to that *subsection,* require such person as is specified in the order to carry out any works, including the restoration, demolition, removal, alteration, replacement, maintenance, repair or cleaning of any structure or other feature, or the discontinuance of any use, or continuance thereof subject to such conditions as are specified in the order.

(3)

(a) An application to the High Court or the Circuit Court for an order under *subsection (1)* shall be by motion and the Court when considering the matter may make such interim or interlocutory order, if any, as it considers appropriate.

(b) The order by which an application under this *section* is determined may contain such terms and conditions (if any) as to the payment of costs as the Court considers appropriate.

(4) *Rules of Court* made in respect of *section 27 of the Act of 1976* (inserted

by *section 19 of the Act of 1992*) shall apply with any necessary modifications to an application under this *section*.

(5)

    (a) An application under *subsection (1)* to the Circuit Court shall be made to the judge of the Circuit Court for the circuit in which the land the subject of the application is situated.

    (b) The Circuit Court shall have jurisdiction to hear and determine an application under this *section* where the rateable valuation of the land the subject of the application does not exceed €253.95 [£200].

    (c) Where the rateable valuation of any land the subject of the application under this *section* exceeds €253.95 [£200], the Circuit Court shall, if an application is made to it in that behalf by any person having an interest in the proceedings, transfer the proceedings to the High Court, but any order made or act done in the course of such proceedings before the transfer shall be valid unless discharged or varied by order of the High Court.

AMENDMENT HISTORY

Provision is made to amend this *section* by the substitution of "market value" for "rateable valuation", and the substitution of " €3,000,000" for "£200" by s.53 of the Civil Liability and Courts Act 2004 (No. 31 of 2004).

However, at the date of publication of this volume, s.53 of the 2004 Act has not yet been brought into effect.

NOTE

This section enables the planning authority to obtain a court order compelling the owners/occupiers to carry out the requirement of a notice. The planning authority can also make such application in respect of a person who causes or permits a person to fail to comply with a notice. Thus the application under this section is not confined to persons on whom the notice was served. There is no time limit specified which must elapse after the entry into force of the notice before a court order may be sought. It would appear that the planning authority could apply any time after the period allowed for compliance set out in the notice. The court procedure bears certain similarities to an injunction in relation to unauthorised development under s.160. As under s.160, the court has a discretion whether to make an order. The court order is discretionary and the court also has a discretion in terms of the measures required to comply with the notice. The court may order a person to comply with the notice or to do or to refrain from doing or continuing to do, anything the court considers necessary or expedient to comply with the notice. Subsection (2) sets out a range of measures which can be ordered by the court. The court may also set out the terms of the order including the payment of costs. In the light of the fact that s.88(2)(g) provides that the planning authority shall pay any expenses that are reasonably incurred by that person in carrying out the steps specified in the notice, it may be appropriate for the court to include this as a term of the court order.

As with s.160, the application may be made by notice of motion grounded upon affidavit. The rules of court application are the same as are applicable in s.160 applications. In relation to the High Court, the applicable rules are contained in RSC Ord.103, while in relation to the Circuit Court, the relevant rules are contained in CCR Ord.56. There are similar jurisdictional rules for each court as regards s.160. It appears that where the rateable valuation of the land is less than €253, the Circuit Court has jurisdiction. However, this does not mean it has exclusive jurisdiction and that the matter cannot be entered into the High Court. However, costs penalties may be incurred if it is entered in the High Court where the rateable valuation is less than €253 under s.17 of the Courts Act 1981. The application must be made to a Circuit Court in the circuit in which the land is situated. However, it is clear that if the rateable valuation exceeds €253, the High Court has exclusive jurisdiction. Where an application is made in the Circuit Court, where the rateable valuation exceeds €253, the party may apply for proceedings to be transferred to the High Court. Unlike a planning injunction under s.160, the application can only be made by the planning authority and cannot be made by members of the public.

Offence to fail to comply with notice under section 88

1–113   **91.**—Where a person served with a notice under *section 88* fails to comply with a requirement of the notice, or causes or permits a person to fail to comply with such a requirement, he or she shall be guilty of an offence.

NOTE

This section creates a criminal offence of failing to comply with the s.88 notice or causing or permitting a person to fail to comply. The offence will be committed where the steps have not been completed within the time limit allowed in the notice. The penalties regarding the offence are set out in Pt VIII.

Permission not required for any development required under this Chapter

1–114   **92.**—Notwithstanding *Part III,* permission shall not be required in respect of a development required by a notice under *section 88* or an order under *section 90.*

NOTE

This section provides that it is not necessary to apply for planning permission in order to carry out the measures required under a notice under s.88 or with a court order under s.90. The development required by the measures will therefore be exempted development.

PART V

HOUSING SUPPLY

Interpretation

1–115   **93.**—**(1)** In this *Part* —
"accommodation needs" *means the size of the accommodation required by an eligible person determined in accordance with the regulations made by the Minister under section 100(1)(a);*
"affordable housing" *means houses or land made available, in accordance with section 96(9) or (10), for eligible persons;*
"eligible person" *means, subject to subsection (3) and to the regulations, if any, made by the Minister under section 100(1)(b), a person who is in need of accommodation and whose income would not be adequate to meet the payments on a mortgage for the purchase of a house to meet his or her accommodation needs because the payments calculated over the course of a year would exceed 35 per cent of that person's annual income net of income tax and pay related social insurance;*
"housing strategy" *means a strategy included in a development plan in accordance with section 94(1);*
"market value", *in relation to a house, means the price which the*

> unencumbered fee simple of the house would fetch if sold on the open market;
>
> "mortgage" *means a loan for the purchase of a house secured by mortgage in an amount not exceeding 90 per cent of the price of the house.*

(2) For the purposes of this *Part,* the accommodation needs of an eligible person includes the accommodation needs of any other person who might reasonably be expected to reside with the eligible person.

(3) In determining the eligibility of a person for the purposes of this *Part,* the planning authority shall take into account—

(a) half the annual income, net of income tax and pay related social insurance, of any other person who might reasonably be expected to reside with the eligible person and contribute to the mortgage payments, and

(b) any other financial circumstances of the eligible person and any other person who might reasonably be expected to reside with the eligible person and contribute to the mortgage payments.

(4) For the avoidance of doubt, it is hereby declared that, in respect of any planning application or appeal, compliance with the housing strategy and any related objective in the development plan shall be a consideration material to the proper planning and sustainable development of the area.

NOTE

Part V of 2000 Act concerns the housing strategy of the local authority. The objective of Pt V is to integrate housing within the planning system, which were previously treated as largely distinct codes. This is principally to be achieved by the incorporation of the housing strategy in the development plan and imposition of a condition on a grant of certain planning permissions to develop houses that a specified perecentage is be reserved for social and affordable housing. As to the distinction between social housing and affordable housing, in *Cork County Council v Shackleton/Dun Laoghaire Rathdown County Council v Glenkerrin,* unreported, High Court, Clarke J., July 17, 2007, it was noted that:

"[S]ocial housing stems from the obligation of the local authority to provide rented accommodation to persons in need of housing in accordance with its statutory obligations. On the other hand affordable housing is a mechanism whereby qualifying persons may become entitled to purchase property at a reduced price".

It may be noted that in addition to affordable housing under Pt V, other affordable housing schemes include the Shared Ownership Scheme (introduced in 1991); 1999 Affordable Housing Scheme (introduced in 1999), Affordable Housing Initiative – AHI (introduced in 2003).

One difficulty with Pt V relates to the nature of any planning permission which is merely permissive; there is no obligation on a person to implement a planning permission granted to them. The mechanism for implementing a condition to reserve part of the land for social and affordable housing is arrived at by means of agreement within the framework of the condition. The agreement does not appear to have life outside the planning permission and so is not subject to independent enforcement. The linking of the housing strategy to the implementation of planning permission thereby poses some difficulties in terms of projection and delivery of the housing strategy of the local authority. If a developer changes his mind and decides not to implement the planning permission, a planning authority cannot compel such person to implement the permission along with the social and affordable housing agreement.

The constitutionality of Pt V, more particularly the planning condition requiring a developer to transfer lands for social and affordable housing was upheld by the Supreme Court in *The Planning and Development Bill 1999* [2000] 2 I.R. 321, where Keane C.J. said:

"In the present case, as a condition of obtaining a planning permission for the development of lands for residential purposes, the owner may be required to cede some part of the enhanced value of the land deriving both from its zoning for residential purposes and the grant of permission in order to meet what is considered by the Oireachtas to be a desirable social objective, namely the provision of affordable housing and housing for persons in the special categories and of integrated housing. Applying the tests proposed by Costello J. in *Heaney v Ireland* and subsequently endorsed by this court, the court in the case of the present Bill is satisfied that the scheme passes those tests. They are rationally connected to an objective of sufficient importance to warrant interference with a constitutionally protected right and, given the serious social problems which they are designed to meet, they undoubtedly relate to concerns which, in a free and democratic society, should be regarded as pressing and substantial. At the same time, the court is satisfied that they impair those rights as little as possible and their effects on those rights are proportionate to the objectives sought to be attained".

This section generally concerns the definitions and elaborates the criteria for persons to be eligible for affordable housing under the Act. The essential scheme is that lower-priced housing, called affordable housing, is made available to persons falling below an income threshold defined by reference to mortgage payments. Accommodation needs means the size of the accommodation required by an eligible person. For these purposes, subs.(2) provides that the accommodation needs includes any other person who might reasonably be expected to reside with the eligible person. An eligible person for affordable housing is defined as a person whose annual income is insufficient to make the mortgage payment for a house to meet his accommodation needs, which applies where the annual payments would exceed 35 per cent of that person's annual income, net of income tax and pay related social insurance. In determining eligibility, subs.(3) provides that the planning authority will take into account:

- half the annual income, net of income tax and pay related social insurance, of any other person who might reasonably be expected to reside with the eligible person and contribute to the mortgage payments; and
- any other financial circumstances of the eligible person and any other person who might reasonably be expected to reside with the eligible person and contribute to the mortgage payments.

There are no express provisions in Part V dealing with what makes the houses "affordable". This is in contrast to the definition of "affordable housing" in s.5(1) of the Housing (Miscellaneous Provisions) Act 2002 (which will be discussed below), which defines "affordable housing" as a house made available "at a price less than the market value". It would appear that affordable housing scheme must at the very least mean that an "eligible persons" in purchasing an affordable housing should have mortgage payments which ought not to exceed 35 per cent of that person's annual income net of income tax and pay related social insurance.

The Act gives no guidance as to the meaning of persons "who might reasonably be expected to reside" with the eligible person. Clearly this would include immediate family: wife, husband, children, etc. Beyond this it is not entirely clear, but certainly may apply to close relatives such as father, mother, brother, sister, etc.

Subsection (4) provides that for the avoidance of doubt, in respect of any planning application or appeal, compliance with the housing strategy and any related objective in the development plan shall be a consideration material to the proper planning and sustainable development. Section 34(2)(a) provides that in making a decision on a planning application, the planning authority shall have regard to the provisions of the development plan. As the housing strategy forms part of the development plan, a planning authority must have regard to the housing strategy under that subsection.

As already noted, the effect of Pt V is to incorporate housing within the framework of planning law. The concept of social and affordable housing is consistent with the theme of sustainable development contained in the 2000 Act. In respect of Pt V, the Department of Local Government and the Environment has published numerous guidelines including *Guidelines for Planning Authorities—Part V of the Planning and Development Act, 2000* as well as a *Model Housing Strategy and Step-by-Step Guide to Part V of the Planning* and Development Act, 2000.

Housing was included in the *National Development Plan 2000–2006* (NDP) for the first time, with €6 billion earmarked in the NDP for social and affordable housing, designed to meet the housing needs of over 90,000 households. The Department has published housing design guidelines: *Quality Housing for Sustainable Communities*, which revised the 1999 *Social Housing Design Guidelines*. The Government also issued a housing policy statement: *Delivering Homes, Sustaining Communities*. The National Action Plan for Social Inclusion (NAP inclusion) was published in February 2007 and has a 10-year timescale up to 2016. The Plan is closely linked to the new National Development Plan 2007-2013.

Housing strategies

94.—(1)   1–116

(a) Each planning authority shall include in any development plan it makes in accordance with *section 12* a strategy for the purpose of ensuring that the proper planning and sustainable development of the area of the development plan provides for the housing of the existing and future population of the area in the manner set out in the strategy.

(b) (i) Subject to *subparagraph (ii)*, any development plan made by a planning authority after the commencement of this *section* shall include a housing strategy in respect of the area of the development plan.

(ii) Where before the commencement of this *section* a planning authority has given notice under *section 21A(2)* (inserted by the *Act of 1976*) of the *Act of 1963* of a proposed amendment of a draft development plan, it may proceed in accordance with *section 266* without complying with *subparagraph (i)*, but where a development plan is so made, the planning authority shall take such actions as are necessary to ensure that, as soon as possible and in any event within a period of 9 months from the commencement of this *section,* a housing strategy is prepared in respect of the area of the development plan and the procedures under *section 13* are commenced to vary the development plan in order to insert the strategy in the plan and to make such other changes as are necessary arising from the insertion of the strategy in the plan pursuant to this *Part.*

(c) A planning authority shall take such actions as are necessary to ensure that, as soon as possible and in any event within a period of 9 months from the commencement of this *section,* a housing strategy is prepared in respect of the area of the development plan and the procedures under *section 13* are commenced to vary the development plan in order to insert the strategy in the plan and to make such other changes as are necessary arising from the insertion of the strategy in the plan pursuant to this *Part.*

(d) A housing strategy shall relate to the period of the development plan or, in the case of a strategy prepared under *paragraph (b)(ii) or paragraph (c),* to the remaining period of the existing development plan.

(e) A housing strategy under this *section* may, or pursuant to the direction of the Minister shall, be prepared jointly by 2 or more planning authorities in respect of the combined area of their development plans and such a joint strategy shall be included in any development plan that relates to the whole or any part of the area covered by the strategy and the provisions of this *Part* shall apply accordingly.

(2) In preparing a housing strategy, a planning authority shall have regard to the most recent housing assessment or assessments made under *section 9 of the Housing Act, 1988,* that relate to the area of the development plan.

(3) A housing strategy shall take into account—

  (a) the existing need and the likely future need for housing to which *subsection (4)(a)* applies,

  (b) the need to ensure that housing is available for persons who have different levels of income,

  (c) the need to ensure that a mixture of house types and sizes is developed to reasonably match the requirements of the different categories of households, as may be determined by the planning authority, and including the special requirements of elderly persons and persons with disabilities, and

  (d) the need to counteract undue segregation in housing between persons of different social backgrounds.

(4)

  (a) A housing strategy shall include an estimate of the amount of—

    (i) housing for persons referred to in *section 9(2) of the Housing Act, 1988,* and

    (ii) affordable housing, required in the area of the development plan during the period of the development plan and the estimate may state the different requirements for different areas within the area of the development plan.

  (b) For the purpose of making an estimate under *paragraph (a)(ii),* a planning authority may exclude eligible persons who own or have previously owned a house.

  (c) Subject to *paragraph (d),* a housing strategy shall provide that as a general policy a specified percentage, not being more than 20 per cent, of the land zoned for residential use, or for a mixture of residential and other uses, shall be reserved under this *Part* for the provision of housing for the purposes of either or both *subparagraphs (i) and (ii) of paragraph (a).*

  (d) *Paragraph (c)* shall not operate to prevent any person (including a local authority) from using more than 20 per cent. of land zoned for residential use, or for a mixture of residential and other uses, for the provision of housing to which *paragraph (a)* applies.

(5)

  (a) When making an estimate under *subsection (4)(a)(ii),* the planning authority shall have regard to the following:

    (i) the supply of and demand for houses generally, or houses of a particular class or classes, in the whole or part of the area of the development plan;

    (ii) the price of houses generally, or houses of a particular class or classes, in the whole or part of the area of the development plan;

(iii) the income of persons generally or of a particular class or classes of person who require houses in the area of the development plan;

(iv) the rates of interest on mortgages for house purchase;

(v) the relationship between the price of housing under *subparagraph (ii),* incomes under *subparagraph (iii)* and rates of interest under *subparagraph (iv)* for the purpose of establishing the affordability of houses in the area of the development plan;

(vi) such other matters as the planning authority considers appropriate or as may be prescribed for the purposes of this *subsection.*

(b) *Regulations* made for the purposes of this *subsection* shall not affect any housing strategy or the objectives of any development plan made before those regulations come into operation.

NOTE

This section concerns the making of a housing strategy which is to form part of the development plan. The planning authority was obliged to create a housing strategy within nine months of the commencement of s.94 of the Act (i.e. by August 1, 2001). Subsection (1) provides that the housing strategy ensures that the proper planning and sustainable development of the area should provide for the existing and future population of the area. This subsection therefore clearly links housing strategy under the general touchstone standard of the Planning Code of the proper planning and sustainable development of the area. *The Guidelines for Planning Authorities—Part V of the Planning and Development Act 2000* ("the Guidelines") provide at para.2.2 that by integrating the housing strategy into the development plan process, planning authorities can aim to ensure that sufficient land is zoned and serviced to meet the housing needs of all sectors of the population. Subsection (1) envisaged following the procedure for varying the development plan under s.13 in order to adopt the housing strategy. This provision is only of historical value now, as local authorities will have adopted housing strategies. A local authority, in reviewing its development, must review the housing strategy as part of the development plan. The housing strategy must have the same life of the development, i.e. six years. Subsection (2)(e) allows two or more planning authorities to jointly prepare the housing strategy in respect of the combined area of their development plan. The Minister may also issue a direction requiring the strategy to be prepared jointly. As with any element of the development plan, the local authority has a duty to secure the objectives of the housing strategy under s.15. Under s.34, the planning authority cannot grant any permission which is a material contravention of the housing strategy except where it follows the material contravention procedure set out in s.34(6). Furthermore, under s.178(3), the planning authority is prohibited from effecting any development which is a material contravention of the housing strategy.

The Guidelines state at para.2.6 that "as the housing strategy will inform the whole development plan, work on the collection of data to input into the strategy should be one of the first tasks undertaken in preparing the draft development plan as a whole". Paragraph 2.7 provides that the Manager's report required under s.11(4)(a) of the Act must, therefore, provide a separate summary of the issues raised in relation to the housing strategy, the Manager's response to the issues, and the policies the Manager proposes to pursue in preparing the draft housing strategy. As regards the content of the housing strategy, the Guidelines state that, regard should be had in the housing strategy to the *Residential Density Guidelines for Planning Authorities* issued by the Department of the Environment in September 1999, which should reflect on the amount and location of land zoned for residential purposes.

Subsection (3) sets out matters which the strategy is required to take into account. While the planning authority is obligated to take these matters into account, the manner in which it does so is a matter for the discretion of the planning authority. One of the matters is a general requirement to avoid undue social segregation. This consideration has the objective to ensure that areas have a mix of persons of different social, educational, cultural and even ethnic background and to avoid the partitioning of areas devoted to persons of similar background.

Subsection (4) states that the housing strategy should include an estimate of persons included within s.9(2) of the Housing Act 1988 which includes (persons who are:

*   homeless;
*   travellers;
*   living in accommodation that is unfit for human habitation or is materially unsuitable for their adequate housing;
*   living in overcrowded accommodation;
*   sharing accommodation with another person or persons and who, in the opinion of the housing authority, have a reasonable requirement for separate accommodation;
*   young persons leaving institutional care or without family accommodation;
*   in need of accommodation for medical or compassionate reasons;
*   elderly;
*   disabled or handicapped; or
*   in the opinion of the housing authority, not reasonably able to meet the cost of the accommodation which they are occupying or to obtain suitable alternative accommodation.

Each category set out is to be read disjunctively. See *O'Reilly v Limerick County Council*, unreported, High Court, March 29, 2006. It should also include an estimate for affordable housing within the area of the development plan. For the purposes of this estimate the strategy may exclude eligible persons who own or have previously owned a house.

Subsection (4)(c) provide that the housing strategy must provide as a general policy that a specified percentage of land zoned for residential use or mixture of residential and other uses, must be reserved for social and affordable housing. This requirement is also repeated in s.95(1)(b). The precise import of the phrase "as a general policy" is not entirely clear, as it appears to implicitly acknowledge that the local authority may have exceptions to the general policy in the strategy. This exceptions could include that in certain areas a greater (up to 20 per cent) or lesser percentage or even no percentage will be reserved for social and affordable housing. Section 95(1)(c) also allows for the making of specific objectives in respect of each area zoned residential use or mixed residential and other uses. While the requirement to have a general policy is a mandatory requirement, the local authority has some discretion in the contents of such policy. The precise percentage reserved is a matter for the discretion of the planning authority, though this is subject to a maximum of 20 per cent. Equally, it is a matter for the discretion of the local authority whether the specified percentage relates to land zoned as residential or whether it relates to land zoned as mixture of residential and other uses or possibly both. By virtue of s.10(2)(a) the zoning of land is a matter within the discretion of the planning authority in making the development plan. However, it is doubtful whether it is correct for a housing strategy to allow a housing authority discretion to determine the ratio between social and affordable in respect of a particular development on a case by case basis. Subsection (4)(d) provides that the requirement that a maximum of 20 per cent of such land is reserved for social and affordable housing, does not prevent a person (including the local authority) from using more than 20 per cent of any land for social and affordable housing purposes. Subsection (5) sets out matters to which the local authority will have regard in estimating the requirement for affordable housing for the area. On the meaning of "have regard", see *McEvoy v Meath County Council* [2003] 1 I.R. 208. The matters enlisted in subs.(5) require the local authority to consider the current market conditions in the area including the general level of supply and prices of particular classes of houses. It must also consider the income of particular classes of persons, the rates of interest on mortgages and the relationship between price, income and rates of interest. In assessing these factors, the local authority will need to take into account the fact that the housing strategy is for six years.

Housing strategies and development plans

95.—(1) 1–117

    (a) In conjunction with the inclusion of the housing strategy in its development plan, a planning authority shall ensure that sufficient and suitable land is zoned for residential use, or for a mixture of residential and other uses, to meet the requirements of the housing strategy and to ensure that a scarcity of such land does not occur at any time during the period of the development plan.

    (b) A planning authority shall include objectives in the development plan in order to secure the implementation of the housing strategy, in particular, any of the matters referred to in *section 94(3),* including objectives requiring that a specified percentage of land zoned solely for residential use, or for a mixture of residential and other uses, be made available for the provision of housing referred to in *section 94(4)(a).*

    (c) Specific objectives as referred to in *paragraph (b)* may be indicated in respect of each area zoned for residential use, or for a mixture of residential and other uses, and, where required by local circumstances relating to the amount of housing required as estimated in the housing strategy under *section 94(4)(a),* different specific objectives may be indicated in respect of different areas, subject to the specified percentage referred to in *section 94(4)(c)* not being exceeded.

    (d) In order to counteract undue segregation in housing between ersons of different social backgrounds, the planning authority may indicate in respect of any particular area referred to in *paragraph (c)* that there is no requirement for housing referred to in *section 94(4)(a)* in respect of that area, or that a lower percentage than that specified in the housing strategy may instead be required.

  (2) Nothing in *subsection (1)* shall prevent any land being developed exclusively for housing referred to in *section 94(4)(a)(i) or (ii).*

  (3)

    (a) The report of the manager under *section 15(2)* shall include a review of the progress achieved in implementing the housing strategy and, where the report indicates that new or revised housing needs have been identified, the manager may recommend that the housing strategy be adjusted and the development plan be varied accordingly.

    (b) The manager of a planning authority shall, where he or she considers that there has been a change in the housing market, or in the regulations made by the Minister under *section 100,* that significantly affects the housing strategy, give a report on the matter to the members of the authority and, where he or she considers it necessary, the manager may recommend that the housing strategy be adjusted and the development plan be varied accordingly.

NOTE

    This section concerns the content of the housing strategy as contained within the context of the development plan. Under subs.(1)(1) there is an obligation on local authorities to include "sufficient and suitable land" to be zoned for residential use in a development plan in order to meet the requirements of the housing strategy. The words "in conjunction with" the housing strategy means that the planning authority must take into account the general requirements of the housing strategy in deciding how much and what land is to be zoned for residential use or for mixed residential and other uses.

While the planning authority generally has a discretion in zoning an area, as indicated by the expression "in the opinion" of the planning authority in s.10(2)(a), this is qualified by the mandatory terms of subs.(1)(1). The question of what is suitable and also sufficient must be interpreted in the light of the housing strategy. The extent of zoning for residential or mixed residential and other uses must ensure that a scarcity of land does not occur at any time during period of the development plan. The period of the development is six years. If a scarcity of land zoned residential did arise during the life of plan, the planning authority could seek to vary the plan under s.13 to provide for additional land to be zoned residential. However, the terms of subs.(1) provide that such scarcity should not occur "at any time" during the period of the plan, so the level of zoning should be sufficient and suitable for the entire six-year period. The Guidelines state at para.8.2 that in deciding on the amount of land to be zoned for the six-year period of the plan, the authority should select an area greater than that calculated to accommodate the required number of houses so as to ensure that there is no undue shortage of zoned and serviced land at any stage during the plan period.

Subsection (1)(b) requires the planning authority to include objectives to secure the "implementation" of the housing strategy. Objectives relating to implementation therefore concern the manner in which the housing strategy is to be achieved. These objectives may include to secure any of the matters enlisted in s.94(3) which are:

- the existing need and the likely future need for housing to which subs.(4)(a) applies;
- the need to ensure that housing is available for persons who have different levels of income;
- the need to ensure that a mixture of house types and sizes is developed to reasonably match the requirements of the different categories of households, as may be determined by the planning authority, and including the special requirements of elderly persons and persons with disabilities;
- the need to counteract undue segregation in housing between persons of different social backgrounds.

Use of the phrase "in particular" means that these objectives are not confined to the objective requiring a specified percentage of the land zoned residential to be made available for social and affordable housing.

Subsection (1)(b) further provides that the development plan shall include objectives relating for the implementation of the objective that a specified percentage of land zoned for residential use or for a mixture of residential and other uses, is made available for social and affordable housing. This therefore relates to the objective in the housing strategy referred to in s.94(4)(c). Subsection (1)(c) further provides that the planning authority can include specific objectives in respect of each area zoned for residential use or mixed residential and other uses. This may include specifying different percentages of the land to be reserved for social and affordable housing for different areas, so long as the maximum of 20 per cent is not exceeded. It appears that this provision would also appear to allow the planning authority to specify a different percentage for social (e.g. 15 per cent) and affordable housing (5 per cent) or any specified percentage so long as the total does not exceed 20 per cent. In order to counteract undue segregation in housing between persons of different social backgrounds, the Guidelines provide at para.9.4 that a planning authority may indicate that there is no requirement for social and affordable housing in a particular area or that a lower percentage than that provided for in the housing strategy is required.

Subsection (2) provides that the previous section is not to be interpreted as preventing the entire area of any land from being developed for social and affordable housing.

Subsection (3) provides that the County Manager in drawing up a progress report on the development plan under s.15(2) must address his mind to the achievement of the housing strategy. Also, where the Manager considers there has been changes in the housing market since the creation of the housing strategy, he must report the matter to the elected members and, where appropriate, make recommendations such as that the housing strategy be adjusted and the development plan varied accordingly.

[Provision of social and affordable housing, etc.

96.—[(1) Subject to *subsection (13) and section 97,* where a development 1–118
plan objective requires that a specified percentage of any land zoned solely for
residential use, or for a mixture of residential and other uses, be made available
for housing referred to in *section 94(4)(a),* the provisions of this *section* shall
apply to an application for permission for the development of houses on land to
which such an objective applies, or where an application relates to a mixture of
developments, to that part of the application which relates to the development
of houses on such land, in addition to the provisions of *section 34.*

(2) A planning authority, or the Board on appeal, shall require as a condition
of a grant of permission that the applicant, or any other person with an interest
in the land to which the application relates, enter into an agreement under this
section with the planning authority, providing, in accordance with this *section,*
for the matters referred to in *paragraph (a) or (b) of subsection (3).*

(3)

    (a) Subject to *paragraph (b),* an agreement under this *section* shall
provide for the transfer to the planning authority of the ownership
of such part or parts of the land which is subject to the application
for permission as is or are specified by the agreement as being part
or parts required to be reserved for the provision of housing referred
to in *section 94(4)(a).*

    (b) Instead of the transfer of land referred to in *paragraph (a)* and
subject to *paragraph (c)* and the other provisions of this *section,* an
agreement under this *section* may provide for—

        (i) the building and transfer, on completion, to the ownership
of the planning authority, or to the ownership of persons
nominated by the authority in accordance with this *Part,* of
houses on the land which is subject to the application for
permission of such number and description as may be specified
in the agreement,

        (ii) the transfer of such number of fully or partially serviced sites
on the land which is subject to the application for permission
as the agreement may specify to the ownership of the planning
authority, or to the ownership of persons nominated by the
authority in accordance with this *Part,*

        (iii) the transfer to the planning authority of the ownership of
any other land within the functional area of the planning
authority,

        (iv) the building and transfer, on completion, to the ownership of the
planning authority, or to the ownership of persons nominated
by the authority in accordance with this *Part,* of houses on
land to which *subparagraph (iii)* applies of such number and
description as may be specified in the agreement,

        (v) the transfer of such number of fully or partially serviced sites
on land to which *subparagraph (iii)* applies as the agreement

may specify to the ownership of the planning authority, or to the ownership of persons nominated by the authority in accordance with this *Part,*

(vi) a payment of such an amount as specified in the agreement to the planning authority,

(vii) a combination of a transfer of land referred to in *paragraph (a)* (but involving a lesser amount of such land than if the agreement solely provided for a transfer under that *paragraph*) and the doing of one or more of the things referred to in the preceding subparagraphs,

(viii) a combination of the doing of 2 or more of the things referred to in *subparagraphs (i) to (vi),*

but, subject, in every case, to the provision that is made under this *paragraph* resulting in the aggregate monetary value of the property or amounts or both, as the case may be, transferred or paid by virtue of the agreement being equivalent to the monetary value of the land that the planning authority would receive if the agreement solely provided for a transfer of land under *paragraph (a).*

(c) In considering whether to enter into an agreement under *paragraph (b),* the planning authority shall consider each of the following:

(i) whether such an agreement will contribute effectively and efficiently to the achievement of the objectives of the housing strategy;

(ii) whether such an agreement will constitute the best use of the resources available to it to ensure an adequate supply of housing and any financial implications of the agreement for its functions as a housing authority;

(iii) the need to counteract undue segregation in housing between persons of different social background in the area of the authority;

(iv) whether such an agreement is in accordance with the provisions of the development plan;

(v) the time within which housing referred to in *section 94(4)(a)* is likely to be provided as a consequence of the agreement.

(d) Where houses or sites are to be transferred to the planning authority in accordance with an agreement under *paragraph (b),* the price of such houses or sites shall be determined on the basis of—

(i) the site cost of the houses or the cost of the sites (calculated in accordance with *subsection (6)*), and

(ii) the building and attributable development costs as agreed between the authority and the developer, including profit on the costs.

(e) Where an agreement under this *section* provides for the transfer of land, houses or sites, the houses or sites or the land, whether in one or more parts, shall be identified in the agreement.

(f) In so far as it is known at the time of the agreement, the planning authority shall indicate to the applicant its intention in relation to the provision of housing, including a description of the proposed houses, on the land or sites to be transferred in accordance with *paragraph (a) or (b)*.

(g) Nothing in this *subsection* shall be construed as requiring the applicant or any other person (other than the planning authority) to enter into an agreement under *paragraph (b)* instead of an agreement under *paragraph (a)*.

(h) For the purposes of an agreement under this *subsection,* the planning authority shall consider—

    (i) the proper planning and sustainable development of the area to which the application relates,

    (ii) the housing strategy and the specific objectives of the development plan which relate to the implementation of the strategy,

    (iii) the need to ensure the overall coherence of the development to which the application relates, where appropriate, and

    (iv) the views of the applicant in relation to the impact of the agreement on the development.

    (v) Government guidelines on public procurement shall not apply to an agreement made under *paragraph (a) or (b)* except in the case of an agreement which is subject to the requirements of *Council Directive No. 93/37/EEC* on the co-ordination of procedures relating to the award of Public Works Contracts and any directive amending or replacing that directive.

(4) An applicant for permission shall, when making an application to which this *section* applies, specify the manner in which he or she would propose to comply with a condition to which *subsection (2)* relates, were the planning authority to attach such a condition to any permission granted on foot of such application, and where the planning authority grants permission to the applicant subject to any such condition it shall have regard to any proposals so specified.

(5) In the case of a dispute in relation to any matter which may be the subject of an agreement under this *section,* other than a dispute relating to a matter that falls within *subsection (7),* the matter may be referred by the planning authority or any other prospective party to the agreement to the Board for determination.

(6) Where ownership of land is transferred to a planning authority pursuant to *subsection (3),* the planning authority shall, by way of compensation, pay to the owner of the land a sum equal to—

    (a)

        (i) in the case of—

            (I) land purchased by the applicant before 25 August 1999, or

            (II) land purchased by the applicant pursuant to a legally enforceable agreement entered into before that date or in exercise of an option in writing to purchase the land granted or acquired before that date,

        the price paid for the land, or the price agreed to be paid for the land pursuant to the agreement or option, together with such sum in respect of interest thereon (including, in circumstances where there is a mortgage on the land, interest paid in respect of the mortgage) as may be determined by the property arbitrator,

    (ii) in the case of land the ownership of which was acquired by the applicant by way of a gift or inheritance taken (within the meaning of the *Capital Acquisitions Tax Act, 1976*) before 25 August 1999, a sum equal to the market value of the land on the valuation date (within the meaning of that *Act*) estimated in accordance with *section 15 of that Act,*

    (iii) in the case of—

        (I) land purchased before 25 August 1999, or

        (II) land purchased pursuant to a legally enforceable agreement to purchase the land entered into before that date, or in exercise of an option, in writing, to purchase the land granted or acquired before that date,

(where the applicant for permission is a mortgagee in possession of the land) the price paid for the land, or the price agreed to be paid for the land pursuant to the agreement or option, together with such sum in respect of interest thereon calculated from that date (including any interest accruing and not paid in respect of the mortgage) as may be determined by the property arbitrator, or

  (b) the value of the land calculated by reference to its existing use on the date of the transfer of ownership of the land to the planning authority concerned on the basis that on that date it would have been, and would thereafter have continued to be, unlawful to carry out any development in relation to that land other than exempted development, whichever is the greater.

(7)

  (a) Subject to *paragraph (b),* a property arbitrator appointed under *section 2 of the Property Values (Arbitration and Appeals) Act, 1960,* shall (in accordance with the *Acquisition of Land (Assessment of Compensation) Act, 1919*), in default of agreement, fix the following where appropriate:

    (i) the number and price of houses to be transferred under *subsection (3)(b)(i), (iv), (vii) or (viii);*

    (ii) the number and price of sites to be transferred under *subsection (3)(b)(ii), (v), (vii) or (viii);*

    (iii) the compensation payable under *subsection (6)* by a planning authority to the owner of land;

    (iv) the payment of an amount to the planning authority under *subsection (3)(b)(vi), (vii) or (viii);* and

    (v) the allowance to be made under *section 99(3)(d)(i).*

  (b) For the purposes of *paragraph (a), section 2(2) of the Acquisition of Land (Assessment of Compensation) Act, 1919,* shall not apply and the value of the land shall be calculated on the assumption that it was at that time and would remain unlawful to carry out any development in relation to the land other than exempted development.

(c) *Section 187* shall apply to compensation payable under *subsection (6).*

(8) Where it is a condition of the grant of permission that an agreement be entered into in accordance with *subsection (2)* and, because of a dispute in respect of any matter relating to the terms of such an agreement, the agreement is not entered into before the expiration of 8 weeks from the date of the grant of permission, the applicant or any other person with an interest in the land to which the application relates may—

    (a) if the dispute relates to a matter falling within *subsection (5),* refer the dispute under that *subsection* to the Board, or

    (b) if the dispute relates to a matter falling within *subsection (7),* refer the dispute under that *subsection* to the property arbitrator,

and the Board or the property arbitrator, as may be appropriate, shall determine the matter as soon as practicable.

(9)

    (a) Where ownership of land or sites is transferred to a planning authority in accordance with *subsection (3),* the authority may—

      (i) provide, or arrange for the provision of, houses on the land or sites for persons referred to in *section 94(4)(a),*

      (ii) make land or sites available to those persons for the development of houses by them for their own occupation, or

      (iii) make land or sites available to a body approved for the purposes of *section 6 of the Housing (Miscellaneous Provisions) Act, 1992,* for the provision of houses on the land for persons referred to in *section 94(4)(a).*

    (b) Pending the provision of houses or sites in accordance with *paragraph (a)(i),* or the making available of land or sites in accordance with *paragraph (a)(ii) or (iii),* the planning authority shall maintain the land or sites in a manner which does not detract, and is not likely to detract, to a material degree from the amenity, character or appearance of land or houses in the neighbourhood of the land or sites.

(10)

    (a) Where a house is transferred to a planning authority or its nominees under *subsection (3)(b),* it shall be used for the housing of persons to whom *section 94(4)(a)* applies.

    (b) A nominee of a planning authority may be a person referred to in *section 94(4)(a)* or a body approved for the purposes of *section 6 of the Housing (Miscellaneous Provisions) Act, 1992,* for the provision of housing for persons referred to in *section 94(4)(a).*

(11) Notwithstanding any provision of this or any other enactment, if a planning authority becomes satisfied that land, a site or a house transferred to it under *subsection (3)* is no longer required for the purposes specified in *subsection (9) or (10),* it may use the land, site or house for another purpose connected with its functions or sell it for the best price reasonably obtainable and, in either case, it shall pay an amount equal to the market value of the land, site or house or the proceeds of the sale, as the case may be, into the separate account referred to in *subsection (12).*

(12) Any amount referred to in *subsection (11)* and any amount paid to a planning authority in accordance with *subsection (3)(b)(vi), (vii) or (viii)* shall be accounted for in a separate account and shall only be applied as capital for its functions under this *Part* or by a housing authority for its functions in relation to the provision of housing under the *Housing Acts, 1966* to *2002.*

(13) This *section* shall not apply to applications for permission for—

    (a) development consisting of the provision of houses by a body standing approved for the purposes of *section 6 of the Housing (Miscellaneous Provisions) Act, 1992,* for the provision of housing for persons referred to in *section 9(2) of the Housing Act, 1988,* where such houses are to be made available for letting or sale,

    (b) the conversion of an existing building or the reconstruction of a building to create one or more dwellings, provided that 50 percent or more of the existing external fabric of the building is retained,

    (c) the carrying out of works to an existing house, or

    (d) development of houses pursuant to an agreement under this *section.*

(14) A planning authority may, for the purposes of an agreement under this section, agree to sell, lease or exchange any land within its ownership to the applicant for permission, in accordance with section 211.

(15) In this section, "owner means—

    (a) a person, other than a mortgagee not in possession, who is for the time being entitled to dispose (whether in possession or reversion) of the fee simple of the land, and

    (b) a person who, under a lease or agreement the unexpired term of which exceeds 5 years, holds or is entitled to the rents or profits of the land.]

AMENDMENT HISTORY

Section 96 substituted for the above by s.3 of the Planning and Development (Amendment) Act 2002 (No. 32 of 2002) which came into effect on December 24, 2002.

NOTE

This section imposes a requirement on applicants for planning permission to develop houses on land, to enter into an agreement with the planning authority to transfer part of the land or enter some other arrangement in order to satisfy the social and affordable housing requirement specified in the housing strategy. Section 3 of the Planning and Development (Amendment) Act 2002 inserted a new s.96 to replace the original s.96 in the 2000 Act. The principal change under the new s.96 was to provide a greater range of options to the type of agreement which may be entered into. The requirement applies to a person applying for permission for the development of houses on land, which is specified in the development plan as being land zoned for residential use or for a mixture of residential and other uses and for which the development plan provides that a specified percentage of such land is to be reserved for social and affordable housing. Thus for subs.(1) to apply, a number of elements must exist, namely, there must be:

    • an application for permission for development of houses;

    • the application must relate to land which is zoned residential or mixed residential and other use; and

    • the development plan for the area must require that a specified percentage of such land is to be reserved for social and affordable housing.

Section 94(4)(c) provides that a housing strategy must provide that as a general policy a specified percentage not being more than 20 per cent of the land zoned for residential use or for mixed residential and other uses, must be reserved for social and affordable housing. However, s.95(1)(c) provides that specific objectives may be indicated in respect of each such area which may include that different percentages being reserved for social and affordable housing, so long as the maximum of 20 per cent is not exceeded. It therefore follows that an applicant for permission to development houses should check the development plan for the area, to see what percentage of the land which he wishes to develop is reserved for social and affordable housing. In practice, many planning authorities specifiy the maximum of 20 per cent for all areas zoned residential or mixed residential and other uses, though it is open to a planning authority to specify a nil percentage for certain specific areas. The notion of "mixed residential and other uses" is not entirely clear. Within a zoning category a development plan may often include a matrix of types of development which are "normally permissible", "open for consideration" or "not permissible". However, the mere fact that residential development is open for consideration or is allowed in exceptional circumstances, does not necessarily mean that the area is zoned for "mixed residential and other uses". It appears that this requirement means that the residential use must be one of the primary uses.

The planning application must be for "houses", which is defined very broadly in s.2 to include any dwelling and includes flat and apartments. Insofar as a holiday home constitutes a dwelling it would appear to also fall within this section. Where a planning application contains both residential and non-residential development, the social and affordable housing requirements of s.96 will only apply to that part of the application which relates to the development of houses. Subsection (1) states that it is subject to subs.(13) and s.97. Under subs.(13), the requirements in s.96 will not apply to any of the four specified developments which comprise:

- social housing developments by approved bodies;
- the conversion of an existing building or the reconstruction of a building to create one or more dwellings, provided that at least 50 per cent of the existing external fabric of the building is retained;
- the carrying out of works to an existing house; or
- developments pursuant to a social and affordable housing agreement under the section.

An exemption may also exist with respect to certain specified developments in s.97 which include "stand alone" developments consisting of four houses or less or "stand alone" developments for housing on land of 0.1 hectares or less. However, unlike under subs.(13) where the exemption is automatic, for the exemption to apply under s.97 it is necessary for an applicant to apply for a certificate of exemption prior to lodging the planning permission. Thus even if a development falls within a category of development specified in s.97, if a certificate of exemption was not sought and obtained prior to the lodging the planning application, the obligation under s.96 will still apply to the development.

Nature of Planning Condition

Subsection (2) provides that the means by which the social and affordable housing requirements are to be met is by the imposition of a planning condition which requires the applicant (or any other person with an interest in the land to which the application relates) to enter into an agreement with the planning authority for the transfer of lands or other alternatives. If an applicant is of course refused permission, the imposition of a condition cannot arise. The new subs.(2) alters the original subs.(2) by providing that the planning authority "shall" as opposed to "may" require as a condition of a grant of permission that the applicant enter into an agreement. This means that there is a mandatory obligation on the planning authority to include a planning condition for social and affordable housing in respect of relevant residential applications. If the planning authority fails to impose such a condition, it would appear that such planning permission would be invalid. The constitutionality of such condition was upheld by the Supreme Court in the art.26 reference, *Planning and Development Bill* [2002] 2 I.R. 292 on the basis that it was a measure designed to achieve an objective of sufficient importance to warrant interference with a constitutionally-protected right and the measure impaired that right as little as possible so as to be proportionate to the objective. Though it is described as a "condition", it is clearly of a radically different nature to the conditions imposed under s.34(4) or more generally s.34(1). First, the condition is mandatory, unlike any conditions imposed under s.34(1) or (4), which are discretionary. Secondly, the contents of the conditions are arrived at as a result of an agreement, as opposed to being unilaterally imposed under s.34. Thirdly, the section describes its own special referral mechanism of a referral to An Bord Pleanála or an arbitrator where the terms cannot be agreed. Having made a proposal or even entered into an agreement as regards the condition, if may be difficult for a person to appeal such condition under s.139 to An Bord Pleanála. Such an appellant would inevitably be faced with an estoppel type defence. However, where there is no agreement and a general condition is imposed, a developer may wish to appeal against the form of wording of a condition. Equally where an inappropriate condition is imposed in the light of a proposal, a developer may wish to appeal or institute judicial review proceedings.

Agreement

The transfer of land or other alternatives is to be secured by means of the agreement required by the condition. This somewhat complicated arrangement was commented upon in *Cork County Council v Shackleton/Dun Laoghaire Rathdown County Council v Glenkerrin*, unreported, High Court, Clarke J., July 17, 2007, where Clarke J. said that:

> "[T]he section does not, therefore, say (as one might have suspected that it might say) that in the event that a person avails of a relevant planning permission, that person has an obligation to meet certain specified social and affordable housing obligations. Rather the obligation is imposed through the mechanism of an agreement which is required to be entered into by virtue of a planning permission condition".

The agreement does not appear to have life outside the planning permission and so is not subject to independent enforcement in the absence of the planning permission being implemented. There is no obligation to carry out a planning permission after it is granted and so despite having entered into an agreement to reserve part for social and affordable housing, there is nothing the planning authority can do if the developer changes his mind and decides not to implement the planning permission. Equally, the section gives no guidance as to when such agreement legally takes effect.

Paragraph 10.3 of the Guidelines provides that the planning authority should seek to negotiate agreement on the transfer at the earliest possible stage in any pre-planning discussions. The intention to make an agreement should be written into the planning permission as a condition in general terms and both the authority and the developer should have a common understanding of the nature of the agreement when the decision to grant permission is made. In *Glenkerrin v Dun Laoghaire Rathdown County Council*, unreported, High Court, Clarke J., April 26, 2007, Clarke J. commented that:

> "[T]here is very considerable merit in the suggestion made by the Minister in those guidelines that as many as possible of the issues which arise in relation to compliance with Part V should be resolved at or prior to the original grant of planning permission with only matters of detail or valuation left over"

Clarke J., however, acknowledged that it may or may not have been the intention that the Act would work in this way.

Article 22(2)(e) of the 2001 Regulations as amended by the 2006 Regulations, provides that a planning application must be accompanied by:

> "[I]n the case of an application for permission for the development of houses or of houses and other development, to which section 96 of the Act applies, proposals as to how the applicant proposes to comply with a condition referred to in sub-section (2) of that section to which the permission, if granted, would be subject".

Form no 2. of Sch.3 to the 2006 Regulations contains a standard planning application form. Question 16 of the form requires the applicant to specify the manner in which it is proposed to comply with Pt V. Article 33(2) of the original 2001 Regulations did not allow a request for further information to be made with respect to such proposal. Under the new art.33(1) of the amended 2001 Regulations a request can be made with respect to any aspect of the planning application (which would include the Pt V proposal) which the authority considers necessary to enable it to deal with the application. The meaning of "proposals" is not defined and so the level of detail required for such proposal is not specified. At a very minimum, it would appear that the proposal must indicate the type of Pt V agreement which the applicant would prefer to enter. The proposal may also contain the details of any such agreement, relating to the identity or location, etc. of the land or units. The issue of the adequacy of a proposal must be assessed under art.26 upon receipt of the planning application. The requirement to specify a proposal for a Pt V condition to comply with the regulations is merely a formal requirement; it does not mean that the proposal must be acceptable to the Council based on its housing strategy. It may would not be correct for a planning authority to invalidate a planning application because it was not favourable to a proposal. On the other hand, where a developer makes a proposal in his planning application, he may potentially be prevented from resiling from that proposal after permission has been granted by making a different type of proposal. See *An Bord Pleanála Referral Reference 4.RH2003*, January 2005. However, of relevance in this respect may be the precise nature of the condition imposed in the grant of permission by the planning authority, in particular whether there is reference made to the terms of the proposal. Where it is merely a general condition, the developer may subsequently be allowed to insist on the default transfer of land. The planning authority cannot uses its powers under art.33 (further informations) or art.34 (to invite revised plans) of the 2001 Regulations, to compel a developer to change his proposals such as to submit a proposal for one of the alternative types of arrangements. However, a planning authority could use art.34 in certain circumstances such as where it is seeking to impose the default position of the transfer of land, by requiring the developer to submit revised plan which would identify the lands to be transferred.

While the mode of agreement should ideally be specified in the condition, the precise form of such planning condition is not defined. Where the mode of agreement is not resolved at the time of granting permission, the form typically imposed by An Bord Pleanála is as a pre-commencement condition stating "[p]rior to the commencement of development, the developer shall enter into an agreement with the planning authority". However, there is no obligation that the planning condition should be in such form and some planning authorities do not frame the condition as a pre-commencement condition but merely state "[t]he developer shall enter into agreement with the planning authority" within eight weeks of the grant of permission.

There is no provision for participation of the public in the agreement to be entered into between the applicant and planning authority. If the planning authority acquires land under the default position, the Pt XI procedure for local authority development will apply to development of land irrespective of whether the planning authority is to develop the land itself or the other options are invoked such as development by an approved body under s.96(9). Where the Pt XI procedure has been invoked, the developer will simply be in the position of neighbouring landowner. At this stage, the ownership of the land will already have been transferred to the planning authority. The developer is entitled as any other member of the public to make submissions on the housing development pursuant to art.81 of the 2001 Regulations. The Pt XI procedure to develop the land for housing following its transfer pursuant to Pt V is no different to any other Pt XI procedure. The submissions by the public will be summarised and assessed in a report by the manager and the elected members may vary, amend or reject the scheme in the light of the report.

Enforcement Action

As with any planning condition, enforcement action can be taken where the development is being carried out without any agreement being entered into in accordance with the Pt V planning condition. The developer can refer any dispute to the arbitrator or An Bord Pleanála. Somewhat peculiarly, the planning authority can only refer the dispute to An Bord Pleanála. Therefore where the dispute relates to a matter specified in subs.(7) as within the jurisdiction of the arbitrator, the planning authority has no power to make a referral. However, the existence of a referral mechanism to the Board or an arbitrator does not oust the ability of the planning authority to take enforcement action under Pt VIII, although the existence of such referral mechanism may be a matter which the court can take into account in the exercise of its discretion. Enforcement action will relate to the commencement of development rather than the fact that an agreement was not entered into. Irrespective of whose fault it is that an agreement was not entered into, this does not entitle a developer to commence development. While a planning authority is entitled to take enforcement action under Pt VIII of the Act, a court could potentially exercise its discretion to refuse relief where it considered the conduct of the planning authority meant it was as much to blame for an agreement not being entered. It would nevertheless depend on the particular circumstances of the case. Where the planning condition is framed as a pre-commencement condition, the commencement of development without an agreement having been entered means that such development is unauthorised development. In the case of a pre-commencement condition, where development is commenced and an agreement is subsequently entered into, this will not constitute strict compliance. However, in the context of s.160 planning injunction proceedings, a court will not generally grant relief where such conditions have been satisfied notwithstanding that they were not satisfied prior to commencement of development. See *Mountbrook Homes Limited v Oldcourt Developments Limited*, unreported, High Court, April 22, 2005 and *Eircell v Bernstoff*, unreported, High Court, Barr J., February 18, 2000.

In *Glenkerrin Homes v Dun Laoghaire Rathdown County Council*, unreported, High Court, Clarke J., April 26, 2007, the court rejected the claim that a refusal to give a certificate of compliance in respect of a financial contribution payments as a means of enforcing obligations under the social and affordable housing terms of a planning permission, amounted to an impermissible form of collateral enforcement. The court however held that based on existing practice the planning authority was obliged to provide certificates of compliance in relation to financial contributions, unless there was, in respect of a certificate sought in relation to any particular unit, reasonable grounds for believing that there was a risk that the grant of such certificate (and the closure of a sale arising from its grant) would leave the planning authority in a position where, at the high water mark of its case, it would not be in a position to secure the units to which it is entitled. While the planning authority was not entitled to adopt a blanket policy of not supplying any certificates of compliance in the absence of an agreement under Pt V, it could refuse a certificate in respect of particular apartments where it has reasonable grounds for believing that the grant of such a certificate would facilitate a sale which would deprive it of the opportunity to obtain the benefit of achieving the transfer of units in the development, under Part V, of a type and value consistent with the maximum case that it makes. Also, while there was a legitimate expectation for the issue of certificates based on existing practice, it was further held that the planning authority was entitled to discontinue such practice after having given reasonable notice as would reasonably allow those who have conducted their affairs in accordance with the practice to consider and implement an alternative means for dealing with the issues arising.

Agreement to Transfer Land or Alternative

Subsection (3) concerns the type or nature of the agreement to be entered into. The transfer of land is the default requirement, with the other options being matters for negotiation. A planning authority cannot require a developer to enter into one of the alternative arrangements. See *Cork County Council v Shackleton*, unreported, High Court, Clarke J., July 19, 2007. Subsection (3)(g) specifically provides that a developer cannot be compelled to enter an alternative arrangement rather than the transfer of land. Where the developer/applicant proposes to comply with Pt V by the transfer of 20 per cent of the land of the site the local authority is obliged to accept this as the method of compliance. The section does not however state whether the developer can compel the planning authority to enter into an arrangement other than the transfer of land. The better view is that as a general rule the planning authority can insist on the default transfer of land and cannot be compelled to enter an alternative arrangement. However, where the development has reached a significant stage of completion prior to such agreement being reached, it will not be possible for the planning authority to require the transfer of land under the default option and so an alternative arrangement will be necessary. See *Glenkerrin Homes v Dun Laoghaire Rathdown County Council*, unreported, High Court, Clarke J., April 26, 2007. It follows that in certain circumstances (such as where the default position is no longer possible because development has commenced) the local authority can have an alternative agreement imposed. See *Cork County Council v Shackleton/Dun Laoghaire Rathdown*

County Council v Glenkerrin, unreported, High Court, Clarke J., July 17, 2007, where it was said that the Board can impose such an alternative on a planning authority although the Board would require to be satisfied that on a proper consideration of the matters set out in subs.(3)(c) and (h) that it was appropriate to enter into any agreement which it proposed to impose. Equally, in *Glenkerrin Homes v Dun Laoghaire Rathdown County Council*, unreported, High Court, Clarke J., April 26, 2007, it was noted at para.9.8, that where, without having reached an agreement as to how to meet the social and affordable housing obligations in respect of the planning permission concerned, the developer proceeds to complete the development, the developer, therefore, places itself in a position where the only means of complying with its obligations is to provide either such units or cash. While the developer concerned could not, therefore, have had an agreement in respect of units or cash imposed upon it at the beginning, it has exposed itself to that possibility by rendering any other means of meeting its obligations impossible.

The default position refers to the transfer of land per se, rather than with the houses built on it. The reference to "part or parts of the land" in s.96(3)(a) connotes that the 20 per cent of the land need not be all together; several plots of the land may be identified, with the total area amounting to 20 per cent of the land. It is open to a planning authority to impose a condition requiring the transfer land under the default obligation which identified the precise 20 per cent or otherwise of the land to be transferred. The identification of the land could be made during the process of considering the planning application by the planning authority writing to the developer under art.34 stating that it is disposed to grant permission subject to a condition requiring the transfer of 20 per cent of the land under s.96(3)(a) and invite the developer to submit revised plans or drawings identifying the 20 per cent of the land and altering the development accordingly. In the alternative, the planning authority could identify the precise 20 per cent of land and then could invite the submission of revised plans pursuant to art.34 of the 2006 Regulations to take account of the land so identified.

Subsection (3) altered the original subs.(3) by providing that the arrangement can concern land other than the subject matter of the planning application. It also introduced as an option the payment of a sum of money and also a combination of the various options. This constitutes an exception to the general principle that a condition of planning permission must be related to the land, the subject matter of the application. There are other alterations in respect of the language of subs.(3). Subsection (3)(c) introduces new matters for the guidance of the planning authority in deciding whether to enter into an agreement. In *Glenkerrin Homes v Dun Laoghaire Rathdown County Council*, unreported, High Court, Clarke J., April 26, 2007, Clarke J. described this as the criteria to be met by the local authority in reaching agreement by it in relation to any alternative agreement that it might enter into. Paragraph 14.1 of the Guidelines states that provision of houses, with the agreement of the developer, as part of a development is the preferred route from the point of view of achieving social integration and protecting the integrity of the development. Certainly this would be the simpler than entering into another separate agreement with the developer to build the houses on the local authority's behalf. The Guidelines continue that, in general, the development of the areas subject to the agreement should be integrated with the rest of the development, such that a plan of the proposed development in its entirety should be drawn up by the developer in cooperation with the planning authority. Such a plan would show the land/sites subject to the agreement and how its development would fit in with the overall proposed development. It appears that a housing strategy can specify the preference of the planning authority for a certain type of agreement. In *Glenkerrin Homes v Dun Laoghaire Rathdown County Council*, unreported, High Court, Clarke J., April 26, 2007, at para.10.2, Clarke J. commented on the housing strategy, noting:

> "That policy appears to have been in favour of obtaining units rather than land or money. The stated reason for that policy, which appears to me to be entirely reasonable, was that having regard to the needs of Dun Laoghaire Rathdown in respect of both social and affordable housing and having regard to the limited developable land available, those needs and obligations were more readily met by purchasing (at the beneficial price provided for in the legislation) units in each development".

If the calculation of the price for the transfer of land under the default position is not value for money to the planning authority, then this may be a reason why it may wish to negotiate an alternative arrangement, if possible. Entering into an alternative arrangement in such circumstances would be consistent with the criteria set out in s.96(3)(c). If the agreement for an alternative arrangement is not forthcoming from the developer, the local authority would have no choice but to acquire the land under the default position with the price to be calculated in accordance with s.96(6).

Section 96(3)(c) concerns the criteria which the planning authority must apply in deciding whether to enter into one of the alternative arrangements. A precondition for this is of course that the developer has proposed one of these alternative. If the developer has not, the planning authority cannot compel him to do so subject to the default position still being possible. As regards the criteria:

    i.   Effectiveness and efficiency may depend on the precise objectives of the housing strategy of a planning authority. The housing strategy may identify certain particular needs or requirements or even a preference for one of the alternative types of agreements.

    ii. In relation to best use of resources and financial implications, if the planning authority does not have the money to pay for the transfer of completed houses or they consider the price for such is not value for money, an alternative arrangement such as the payment of money or even the default position may be appropriate.

    iii. To counteract undue segregation, this may in particular depend on the location of the development.

    iv. "Provisions of the development plan" is not confined to the housing strategy, thus matters of infrastructure or other development or indeed any other objective identified in the plan may be relevant.

    v. Timing includes how quickly the social and affordable houses can be delivered.

Commenting on these criteria, in *Cork County Council v Shackleton/Dun Laoghaire Rathdown County Council v Glenkerrin*, unreported, High Court, July 17, 2007, Clarke J., said:

> "It would be fair to say that the criteria which the local authority are required, as planning authority, to take into account, are concerned with ensuring that any such alternative agreement meets the planning and housing obligations of that authority under both the legislation as a whole, and its development plan incorporating its housing strategy in particular".

It appears that on appeal the Board must also consider the same criteria.

Calculation of Number of Units/Alternatives

Where the default position applies, there is no difficulty in calculating the amount of land to be transferred, i.e. the percentage reserved for social and affordable housing in the development, most likely 20 per cent of the land. However, greater difficulties arise where one the alternative arrangements are entered into. The final paragraph of subs.(3)(b) sets out a formula for calculating what is to be transferred under one of the alternative arrangement. This paragraph means that the calculation of the number of units to be transferred must be read against the benchmark of the default position which is the transfer of 20 per cent of the land. Therefore for the purposes of this calculation, the alternative arrangement is converted to monetary terms. Under this formula the "aggregate monetary value of the property or amounts or both" to be transferred must be "equivalent to the monetary value" of the default position. The term "aggregate monetary value of the property or amounts of both" represents the net benefit, converted where appropriate into money, to the local authority concerned. The net benefit of any alternative agreement must be the same, in money or money terms, as the planning gain. See *Cork County Council v Shackleton/ Dun Laoghaire Rathdown County Council v Glenkerrin*, unreported, High Court, Clarke J., July 17, 2007. The correct method to calculate the number of units is to divide the total planning gain (i.e. 20 per cent of the total market/development value less 20 per cent of the existing use value of the land) by the planning gain per site (i.e. the development value of the site per dwelling less the existing site use value per dwelling). The Court in *Shackleton* rejected the method put forward by the respondents which was to calculate the planning gain (i.e. market/development value of 20 per cent of the land less existing use value) on the land and divide this by the sum of the average planning gain per site plus the site costs and construction costs. This would involve the planning authority not paying any price for the unit. Clarke J. said:

> "[T]he only means by which the local authority can obtain an equivalent monetary benefit (as required by the proviso) is if the total value of the sites attributable to the built housing units transferred, represents 20% of the planning gain. The reason why this is so stems from the fact that the payment of what I have described as the building costs is neutral. The price at which built housing units must be transferred is required, by subs. (3)(d), to be as defined in that subsection".

Also where the housing strategy of one of the local authorities said that as a guide 20 per cent of the total floor area of the development should be transferred, Clarke J. did not accept this as a correct method for calculating the number of units to be transferred. Clarke J. goes on to say that floor area may be relevant for the purpose of calculating the site area in the case of apartments. However, this merely means that floor area is only relevant in attributing a site to a particular apartment; it does not mean that it is relevant calculating the overall area or space to be transferred.

Even where units are to be provided, it may be necessary for the developer also to pay a small financial contribution because the total amount of the economic benefit which the local authority is entitled to obtain under the provisions of s.96 may not correlate to an exact number of units. See See *Glenkerrin Homes v Dun Laoghaire Rathdown County Council*, unreported, High Court, Clarke J., April 26, 2007.

Compensation

Subsection (6) refers to "compensation" to be paid. The default option whereby up to 20 per cent of the land must be transferred is in effect a form of taking or compulsory acquisition albeit not under the traditional methods of compulsory acquisition powers. Section 213(2) distinguishes between acquisition by agreement or compulsorily. The transfer of land under the default position is a hybrid between agreement and acquisition. By virtue of s.3(a) the planning authority can compel the developer to enter into an agreement to transfer the land. The element of compulsion means that it is of the nature of a "taking" or compulsory acquisition. While in general a public interest must be demonstated in order to compulsorily acquire land, the public interest is mandated in the legislation. See *Article 26 and the Planning and Development Bill 1999* [2000] 2 I.R. 321. On the other hand, the transfer mechanism is by means of the developer and planning authority entering into an "agreement". The main benefit for the planning authority is not that it allows them to acquire the land (it could use its powers of compulsory acquisition to do this) but that it gains the land or other alternative at a discount. This discount means that it does not pay any of the value which was enhanced as a result of the planning permission. As was noted by the Supreme Court in *Article 26 and the Planning and Development Bill 1999* [2000] 2 I.R. 321, the developer is "to cede some part of the enhanced value of the land deriving both from its zoning for residential purposes and the grant of permission in order to meet what is considered by the Oireachtas to be a desirable social objective." The Court further stated:

> "Inevitably, the fact that permission for a particular type of development may not be available for the land will, in certain circumstances, depreciate the value in the open market of that land. Conversely, where the person obtains a permission for a particular development the value of the land in the open market may be enhanced".

Compensation is to be calculated in accordance with s.96(6). Commenting on this subsection in *Cork County Council v Shackleton/Dun Laoghaire Rathdown County Council v Glenkerrin*, unreported, High Court, Clarke J., July 17, 2007, Clarke J. said "[It] is, reasonably accurately, described as a section which is designed to prevent there being included in the value of any such land, any 'hope value'. It is, of course, the case that land in respect of which it might be anticipated that more beneficial zoning or planning permission might be obtained (but where such zoning or permission has not yet been obtained) can have anything from a marginal to a quite significant enhancement to its value by reference to the expectation of the marketplace that the land may be capable of more beneficial development in the future. It is clear that the intention of subs.(6) was to exclude any such enhanced value in the relevant calculation".

Price and Site Value

Subsection (3)(d), relating to the price to be paid by the planning authority to the developer for entering the arrangement for the transfer of sites or built units on site. This subsection subsumes other subsections under the original s.96, with minor changes in language. In the case of the transfer of built units on site, there are two elements to the "price", which are

1. the "site cost" of the house which is to be "calculated in accordance with the subs. (6)"; and
2. the building and development costs including profit on those costs.

The "price" is therefore the amount to be paid by the local authority for the transfer of houses or sites. Somewhat confusingly, subs.(6) however, refers to the amount to be paid for site as "compensation". In all but very exceptional circumstances, the valuation will be calculated in accordance with subs.(6)(b) rather than (6)(a), as being the greater amount. In *Cork County Council v Shackleton/Dun Laoghaire Rathdown County Council v Glenkerrin*, unreported, High Court, Clarke J., July 17, 2007, the court rejected that the price can be included in the calculation of the number of units to be transferred so the planning authority would pay no price. It was noted that if this were the case a whole range of intermediate positions as to the amount of units to be transferred could be adopted which would leave the number of units to be transferred in a state of complete uncertainty.

In calculating site cost no account can be taken of any potential planning permission including the planning permission giving rise to the condition for social and affordable housing. In *Cork County Council v Shackleton/Dun Laoghaire Rathdown County Council v Glenkerrin*, unreported, High Court, Clarke J., July 17, 2007, it was noted that the intention of subs.(3)(d) was to ensure that the site cost element of the price of any house which was to be transferred was to be calculated on the existing use with no hope value basis. However, it was noted that subs.(3)(d) provided that "site cost" was to be calculated in accordance with subs.(6) which refers to the existing use "on the date of the transfer of ownership of the land to the planning authority concerned". In the case of the default position there is no difficulty as the land is transferred before any building takes place, however, a problem arises in the case of the transfer of units where building has already taken place on the land and so by the time any built housing unit is transferred, the use of the land will have changed. Notwithstanding these difficulties the court concluded that the site cost was to be calculated on the basis of the existing use which existed prior to the construction of houses on the land. It was noted that the use of the term "site" in s.(3)(d) allows for the possibility of a construction which concentrates on the site value prior to development rather than the value of land on which on housing unit has been built. This also allows for a more harmonious interpretation of s.96 as otherwise the price that would have to be paid for a built housing unit would be greater than the combined price that would have to have been paid had the default provision been availed of. The fact that a developer agrees to build on the remaining 20 per cent of the site does not entitle him to anything more than the statutory price for carrying out that work. At para.7.17, Clarke J. said that in calculating the site value of an apartment, the arbitrator should have regard to areas which do not formally form part of the "site" of a built housing unit itself such as roads and open areas of a housing estate and more complex questions arise in relation to the built common areas frequently found within individual apartment blocks. As regards calculating the site value of an apartment, he stated at para.7.15, that the appropriate approach is to divide the entirety of a site occupied by a block of apartments, by the number of apartments in that block, weighted for the size of such apartments.

As regards attributable and construction costs, in *Cork County Council v Shackleton/ Dun Laoghaire Rathdown County Council v Glenkerrin*, unreported, High Court, Clarke J., July 17, 2007, Clarke J. referred to "construction and attributable costs" as the price at which the local authority could have arranged for the construction of the housing unit concerned by a separate builder in the marketplace, including any appropriate share of common development works and the profit which such a builder would be likely to command in the marketplace generally. It may be noted that the Guidelines state that regard should be had to labour, materials and plant in carrying out the physical work; design team fees (architects, engineers, planners, quantity surveyors, etc.); planning application and possible planning appeal fees; fire certificate fees; any development contributions required by the planning authority or An Bord Pleanála or any connection charges required by the planning authority; other utility connection charges (electricity, gas, telephone, etc.); overheads; and financing costs associated with the above. These costs should be determined as an average per unit over the entire development, adjusted to reflect the varying sizes of dwelling units being provided. Also in relation to profit, profit is to be taken as meaning a reasonable profit, determined by reference to prices for work pertaining to competitive tenders for similar work current in the locality. However, in *Cork County Council v Shackleton/Dun Laoghaire Rathdown County Council v Glenkerrin*, unreported, High Court, Clarke J., July 17, 2007, Clarke J. at para.10.2 commented on the Guidelines stating that while it is proper to have regard to such guidelines, building and development costs and profit should be determined by the arbitrator, by reference to what he is satisfied would be the open market rate for those matters at the relevant time and in the relevant locality. It should be noted that the only explicit provision for "attributable development costs" in s.96 is contained in s.96(3)(d) which only arises in the context of agreements for the transfer of houses or sites under s.96(3)(b) and so does not cover agreements for the transfer of land which is under s.96(3)(a).

The date of valuation may be specified in the agreement. However, where this is not agreed and the matter is referred to arbitrator, in respect of units already built the date of valuation should be at the date of the arbitration. In *Cork County Council v Shackleton/ Dun Laoghaire Rathdown County Council v Glenkerrin*, unreported, High Court, Clarke J., July 17, 2007, Clarke J. noted at paras 10.4 and 10.5 of his judgment that as the valuation of the existing use value of the property concerned is to be conducted as of the date of transfer, the open market value of the property to be used for the purposes of calculating the planning gain should be as of the same date. The arbitrator should do the best he can to estimate what the open market value would be as of the likely date of transfer on the basis of whatever evidence may be available to assist him in determining when that date might be. For all practical purposes, therefore, the valuation of the land should be as of the date of the arbitration. If, however, there are special circumstances from which it can properly be inferred that the relevant default transfer (hypothetically), and the relevant alternative agreement to transfer (in practice) would be at some significantly removed period of time from the arbitration, then that is factor which the arbitrator can properly take into account in his calculations.

In the circumstances that the calculation of compensation is greater under subs.(6)(a) rather than subs.(6)(b), subs.(6)(a) provides that where the land was purchased or a legally enforceable agreement or option was entered into prior to August 25, 1999, the compensation payable is the price paid for the land together with interest thereon. The price paid must have been for the purchase of the land rather than for some arrangement to develop the land. The reference to land purchased pursuant to a "legally enforceable agreement" means that the requirements under the Statute of Frauds (Ireland) Act 1695 or otherwise to render the agreement enforceable must be satisfied. Compensation is similarly calculated with respect to a mortgagee in possession purchasing the land prior to August 25, 1999. In the case of land acquired by gift or inheritance before August 25, 1999, compensation is payable based upon the market value of the land on the valuation date.

Terms of the Agreement

Subsection (3)(h) although similar to subs.(3)(c) concerns the terms of the agreement entered into as opposed to the criteria for determining whether to enter into an alternative agreement which is dealt within subs.(3)(c). The subsection indicates that the planning authority must not only take into account its own interest and goals in relation to sustainable development and the housing strategy, but also the interests and views of the developer. The considerations set out in subs.(3)(h) applies to both agreements for the transfer of land under (a) and the other alternatives set out in (b). This is in contrast to s.96(3(c) which only applies to the alternative type agreement under (b). Once it has been decided to invoke the default position, the identification of the land to be transferred is a matter which would come within the considerations set out in s.96(3)(h) of the Planning and Development Act 2000, as amended. A consideration of the criteria set out in s.96(3)(h) reveals that it involves a balancing of the planning and housing considerations (as in (a) "proper planning" and (b) "housing strategy") with the considerations particular to the development (as in (c) "overall coherence of the development" and (d) "the views of the applicant").

Apart from these general standards s.96 gives no clear guidance on the terms of the agreement, which is a matter for negotiation or determination by the Board or arbitrator in the event of a dispute. There is no legal requirement, for example, for the planning authority to pay the developer the money for the transfer prior to commencing development, and this would seem to follow from the fact that the agreement is only activated once the permission is sought to be implemented. Nor is there any prescription as to when such payment is due, such as requiring development to have been completed. It appears that these are matters for negotiation between the parties, as they can agree. It is not possible to exhaustively or prescriptively list the nature and extent of terms of any agreement, as this will depend on the development and the parties concerned. However, subs.(3)(e) provides that where an agreement provides for the transfer of land, houses or sites, the houses or sites or the land, whether in one or more parts, shall be identified in the agreement. Meanwhile, under subs.(3)(f) the obligation on the planning authority to indicate its intention in relation to the provision of house on the land arises at the time of the agreement rather than at the time of the grant of permission. The obligation is conditional insofar as the requirement to notify extends only insofar as the planning authorities' intention is known at the time; there is no strict obligation to have already finalised its intentions at that stage.

Referral to the Board or Arbitrator

Subsection (5) removed certain restrictions under the original s.96, in providing that any dispute in relation to a matter which may be the subject of an agreement may be referred to An Bord Pleanála for determination except in respect of the matters under subs.(7), where the arbitrator has power to determine such matters as the price of the house, compensation, etc. These are available after the expiration of eight weeks from the date of grant of permission. Under subs.(5) the planning authority may refer an appropriate matter to the Board, but it has no power to refer the matters listed in subs.(7) to the arbitrator. Subsection (8) allows the applicant or any person with an interest in the land to refer the matter to the Board or property arbitrator where appropriate. This power does not extend to the local authority. Subsection (5) makes it clear that "any matter" which may be the subject of an agreement can either be referred to the Board or the property arbitrator. In *Glenkerrin Homes v Dun Laoghaire Rathdown County Council*, unreported, High Court, April 26, 2007, Clarke J. rejected the suggestion that in the absence of some form of agreement in principle between the parties as to the manner in which the social and affordable housing requirement is to be met, the dispute resolution mechanisms could not be operated. The term "agreement", must, therefore, be taken in the context of subs.(5) and thus must be taken to include an arrangement determined by the appropriate dispute resolution mechanism.

The Board determines a dispute concerning the type of agreement to be entered into. The property arbitrator has no jurisdiction to impose upon a local authority an obligation to accept a type of arrangement in principle which that local authority does not wish to accept. The arbitrator will only have jurisdiction to determine a dispute, once the it has been resolved which type of agreement is applicable. The type of agreement applicable may as a result of:
- an agreement in principle between the parties;
- a determination by the Board; or
- the fact that other options are no longer, in practice, available.

See *Glenkerrin Homes v Dun Laoghaire Rathdown County Council*, unreported, High Court, April 26, 2007.

While it is clear that a dispute concerning the type of agreement is to be entered into is a matter for referral to the Board, the subsections are silent on who determination the identity and location of units in a development which are to be transferred. One means of determining the allocation of responsibility between the Board and arbitrator is that all other matter not specified in sub.(7) must be referred to the Board. Another possible means of distinction is that disputes concerning issue of housing needs or planning requirements should be referred to the Board while issues concerning valuation or calculation should be referred to the arbitrator. However, in *Glenkerrin Homes v Dun Laoghaire Rathdown County Council*, unreported, High Court, April 26, 2007, Clarke J. held that the type of disputes which can be referred to the Board are, at the level of principle as to the precise manner in which the obligations are to be met on the facts of any individual case, i.e. the provision of cash, other land, serviced sites, a combination of those, or the like. Disputes concerning the precise means of implementing the obligation in principle which relate to the identification of types of units to be transferred, the price and number of such units and the like can then be determined by the property arbitrator. It was further held that the property arbitrator has jurisdiction to identify, in case of dispute, which units should, in fact, be transferred. He considered that where the units in a development are of different types, then the question of the identification of the units to be transferred on foot of an agreement is so inextricably linked to the question of the number and price of the units to be so transferred, that it seems to that a jurisdiction to determine those matters must necessarily be implied. He further noted at para.94 that it is not possible to fix a price until the type of unit is identified by reference to any factor that might be material in identifying the price. It may not, on the other hand, be possible to identify, with any precision, the precise types of units, or mix of units, to be transferred until such time as the relativity between the prices to be attributable to such units has itself been determined. It appears that this will involve the arbitrator making certain planning judgments. In the later judgment of *Cork County Council v Shackleton/ Dun Laoghaire Rathdown County Council v Glenkerrin*, unreported, High Court, Clarke J., July 17, 2007, it was further said that where the sites are not homogenous the property arbitrator must do the best that he can (in the absence of agreement) to identify a set of housing units for transfer where the aggregate of the planning gain attributable to the site on which each of those units has been built approximates to 20 per cent of the total planning gain on the development as a whole, subject only to a balancing payment. In selecting which types of sites and units require to be included in such an arrangement, the property arbitrator should give all due weight to the reasonable requirements of the planning authority involved as to the type of accommodation which they need to supply for the purposes of social or affordable housing or both.

Under subs.(7) a property arbitrator will be appointed under the Acquisition of Land (Assessment of Compensation) Act 1919. Somewhat anomalously as the developer can only refer the matter to the arbitrator, the developer will be technically classified as the claimant, even though the dispute may involve the amount to be paid or number of houses to be transferred by the developer to the planning authority. As regards the reference in subs.(7)(2) to s.2(2) of the Acquisition of Land (Assessment of Compensation) Act 1919, this provides:

> "The value of the land shall, subject as hereinafter provided, be taken to be the amount which the land, in its condition at the time of acquisition, if sold in the open market by a willing seller, might have been expected to have realised at the date of the second publication in the Gazette of the declaration under s.3. Provided that this rule shall not affect the assessment of compensation of any damage sustained by the person interested by reason of severance or by reason of acquisition injuriously affecting his other property or his earnings or for disturbance or any other matter not directly based on the value of the land".

The purpose of excluding this rule is to exclude the hope value which is inherent in open marker value.

A party may request the arbitrator to state a case for the High Court. The jurisdiction to state a case is set out in s.6 of the Acquisition of Land (Assessment of Compensation) 1919 which provides:

> "(1) The decision of a property arbitrator upon any question of fact, shall be final and binding on the parties, and the persons claiming under them respectively, but the property arbitrator may, and shall, if the High Court so directs, state at any stage of the proceedings, in the form of a special case for the opinion of the High Court, any question of law arising in the course of the proceedings, and may state his award as to the whole or part thereof in the form of a special case for the opinion of the High Court."

There is also jurisdiction to state a case under s.35 of the Arbitration Act 1954, which provides that:

"(1) An arbitrator or umpire may, and shall if so directed by the Court, state; (a) any question of law arising in the course of the reference, or (b) any award or any part of an award, in the form of a special case for the decision of the Court. (2) A special case with respect to an interim award or with respect to a question of law arising in the course of a reference may be, stated, or may be ordered by the Court to be stated, notwithstanding that proceedings under the reference are still pending".

Where an arbitrator declines to state a case, the court may direct an arbitrator to state a case. In *Hogan v St. Kevin's company and Purcell* [1986] I.R. 80, Murphy J. cited the principles set out by the Court of Appeal decision in *Halfdan Grieg and Co. v Sterling Coal* [1973] Q.B. 843 and noted:

"[I]f the issues were matters of fact and not of law the arbitrator should refuse to state a case. If, on the other hand, the issue raised points of law, it would depend on the point of law whether or not the arbitrator should exercise his discretion in favour of the application to state the case. Lord Denning then went on to lay down the following three conditions, namely, (1) that the point of law should be real and substantial; (2) that the point of law should be clear-cut and capable of being accurately stated as a point of law; (3) that the point of law should be of such importance that the resolution of it was necessary for the proper determination of the case. The distinguished Master of the Rolls then went on to say that if those three requisites were satisfied then the arbitrator or umpire should state a case."

It may be noted that where the courts have refused to compel an arbitrator to state a case such as the above, the rationale for such reluctance is because the parties had voluntarily submitted the dispute to arbitration and so courts are slow to usurp the function of the chosen tribunal. However, this does not apply where the arbitrator is a statutory arbitrator and the Council did not agree to the matter being referred to arbitration. In *Dublin Corporation v MacGinley and Shackleton*, unreported, High Court, June 22, 1986, Murphy J. stated:

"Whilst I recognise that ordinarily an arbitrator should state a case and the High Court will direct a case to be stated where a point of law arises in the course of an arbitration which is real and substantial and one which is appropriate in its substance and in its form for the decision by the High Court (see the decision in Hogan & Ors, in St. Kevins Company & Anor. delivered on the 22nd day of January 1986) on the other hard both the arbitrator and the Court in the exercise of their respective discretions would properly refuse to state a case or direct the statement of a case on a point of law which was either without substance or adequately covered by authority".

The determination of an arbitrator is subject to judicial review which is not within the scope of s.50. Thus ordinary principles of judicial review will apply. See *Cork County Council v Shackleton*, unreported, High Court, Clarke J., July 17, 2007, where the court quashed the determination of the arbitrator. The court also declined to refuse relief on the basis that the planning authority had failed to request the arbitrator to state a case on the matter. It was noted that it would not necessarily have been a more expeditious or, indeed, more appropriate means of dealing with the issue concerned. It was, therefore, a reasonable judgment to take to allow the arbitration to take its course and to permit the property arbitrator to reach his conclusion.

The arbitrator is not expressly required to give reasons for his award. However, in *Manning v Shackleton* [1996] 3 I.R. 85, it was said, while there is no obligation to give reasons, an arbitrator may be compelled to give a breakdown of the calculation of his award. Keane J. noted in relation to a breakdown of calculation:

"To require the arbitrator so to do would not in any sense be to subvert the finality of his award or to encourage litigation: on the contrary, the legislation expressly envisages that he should do so on request and it seems immaterial, in this context, whether the request is made during the course of the hearing or after the publication of the award".

However, it is possible that the requirement to give reasons may have to re-assessed in the light of art.6 of the European Convention on Human Rights.

Under subs.(7)(d), s.187 allows for the recovery of compensation as a simple contract debt from the planning authority. Under subs.(9), where the ownership of land or sites are transferred to the planning authority, it can provide social housing, allow such persons to provide such a house, or allow a body approved under the Housing Act 1992 to provide such houses. Paragraph 13.1 of the Guidelines provides that the Government is committed to developing the role of the voluntary and cooperative housing sector and to expanding the contribution of the sector to social housing. It further notes that voluntary and co-operative housing bodies currently provide social rented family-type accommodation using capital funding under the voluntary housing schemes. They also contribute to the provision of special needs housing such as sheltered housing to meet the accommodation needs of elderly persons, persons with disabilities, and other persons who require supportive housing responses to meet their needs. The Guidelines state that planning authorities should take a proactive role in facilitating the involvement of the voluntary and co-operative housing sector (even when there is none approved in the area) in the provision of housing on land or sites earmarked for transfer by developers under Pt V.

Under subs.(11), the planning authority may dispose of a house no longer required for its purposes and pay the sum into a separate bank account to be used for housing purposes.

The original s.96(15) provided that a planning permission made after August 25, 1999, but before a housing strategy was in place, thus avoiding the social and affordable housing requirements, only had a duration of two years. This was omitted from the new s.96 under the 2002 Act and is dealt with under s.96A. Subsection (13)(a) states planning permission is not required for development consisting of the provision of social housing by an approved housing body for letting only (i.e. under the Rental Subsidy Scheme or the Capital Assistance Scheme).

[Restoration of normal limit of duration for certain permissions

96A.—[*Sections 40 to 42* shall apply to permissions granted under *Part*   1–119
IV of the Act of 1963 or under *Part III of this Act* pursuant to an application made after 25 August 1999 and to which this *Part* would have applied if the application for permission had been made after the inclusion of a housing strategy in the development plan under *section 94(1)*.]

AMENDMENT HISTORY

Section 96A inserted by s.4 of the Planning and Development (Amendment) Act 2002 (No. 32 of 2002) which came into effect on December 24, 2002.

NOTE

This section relates to planning permission granted for housing developments prior to a housing strategy having been adopted. Under the original 2000 Act, these permissions would only have effect for two years, described as withering provisions. This was designed to target permissions in relation to which a social and affordable housing condition was not imposed because the strategy was not in place when the application was made. The effect of this section is to extend the life of such permission by applying ss.40–42, concerning the duration of planning permission, which is normally five years, though this can be varied or extended. However, in exchange for extending the life of these permission a levy system is imposed under s.96B.

[Levy to be paid in consideration of restoration effected by section 96A

96B.—[(1) In this *section* —   1–120
"house" *means—*
    (a) *a building or part of a building which has been built for use as a dwelling, and*
    (b) *in the case of a block of apartments or other building or part of a building comprising 2 or more dwellings, each of those dwellings;*

"market value", *in relation to a house, means the price which the house might reasonably be expected to fetch on a sale in the open market*;

"relevant house means a house, permission for which would have ceased to have effect or expired but for *section 4 of the Planning and Development (Amendment) Act 2002.*

(2) There shall be deemed to be attached to a permission referred to in *section 96A* a condition providing that there shall, in accordance with *subsections (3) to (5)*, be paid to the planning authority an amount in respect of—

    (a) unless *paragraph (b)* applies as respects the particular house, the first disposal of each relevant house built on foot of that permission,

    (b)

        (i) it is built on foot of that permission by a person for his or her own occupation, or

        (ii) it is built on foot of that permission for a person (the first-mentioned person) by another for the first-mentioned person s occupation and that other person is not the person from whom the first-mentioned person acquires his or her interest in the land on which the house is built,

the completion of the building of that relevant house on foot of that permission.

(3) In subsection (2) "first disposal", in relation to a relevant house, means whichever of the following first occurs after the house is built—

    (a) the sale, at arm s length, of the house (whether the agreement for that sale is entered into before or after the building of the house is completed),

    (b) the granting of a tenancy or lease in respect of the house for the purpose of the grantee of the tenancy or lease occupying the house, or

    (c) the sale, otherwise than at arm s length, of the house (whether the agreement for that sale is entered into before or after the building of the house is completed) or the transfer of the beneficial interest in the house.

(4) The amount of the payment referred to in subsection (2) shall be—

    (a) where the disposal of the house concerned falls within *subsection (3)(a)* —

        (i) if the consideration paid to the vendor by the purchaser equals or exceeds €270,000, an amount equal to 1 per cent of the consideration so paid,

        (ii) if the consideration paid to the vendor by the purchaser is less than €270,000, an amount equal to 0.5 per cent of the consideration so paid,

    (b) where either—

        (i) the disposal of the house concerned falls within *subsection (3)(b) or (c)*, or

        (ii) *subsection (2)(b)* applies as respects the house concerned, an amount equal to—

            (I) if the market value of the house at the time of the disposal or upon the completion of its building, equals or exceeds €270,000, 1 per cent of the market value of the house at the time of that disposal or upon that completion,

(II) if the market value of the house at the time of the disposal or upon such completion is less than €270,000, 0.5 per cent of the market value of the house at the time of that disposal or upon such completion.

(5) The payment referred to in *subsection (2)* shall be made at such time as the planning authority specifies (and the time that is so specified may be before the date on which the disposal concerned of the relevant house is effected).

(6) Any amount paid to a planning authority in accordance with this *section* shall be accounted for in a separate account and shall only be applied as capital for its functions under this *Part* or by a housing authority for its functions in relation to the provision of housing under the *Housing Acts, 1966* to *2002*.

(7)

(a) The planning authority shall issue, in respect of the payment to it of an amount (being the amount required to be paid under this *section* in a particular case), a receipt, in the prescribed form, to the payer stating that the liability for payment of that amount in the case concerned has been discharged.

(b) A document purporting to be a receipt issued under this *subsection* by the planning authority shall be prima facie evidence that the liability for the payment of the amount to which it relates has been discharged.

(8) Any of the following—

(a) a provision of a contract of sale of a house,

(b) a provision of a contract for the building for a person of a house for his or her occupation,

(c) a covenant or other provision of a conveyance of an interest in a house,

(d) a covenant or other provision of a lease or tenancy agreement in respect of a house,

(e) a provision of any other agreement (whether oral or in writing),

which purports to require the purchaser, the person referred to in *paragraph (b)*, the grantee of the interest or the grantee of the lease or tenancy, as the case may be, to pay the amount referred to in *subsection (2)* or to indemnify another in respect of that other s paying or liability to pay that amount shall be void.

(9) Any amount paid by the purchaser, person referred to in *subsection (8)(b)* or grantee of an interest or a lease or tenancy, pursuant to a provision or covenant referred to in *subsection (8)*, may be recovered by him or her from the person to whom it is paid as a simple contract debt in any court of competent jurisdiction.

(10) This *section* shall not apply to permissions for development consisting of the provision of 4 or less houses, or for housing on land of 0.1 hectares or less.

(11) For the avoidance of doubt, in this *section* "sale", *in relation to a house, includes any transaction or series of transactions whereby the vesting by the builder in another person of the interest in the land on which the house is built by the builder is effected separately from the conclusion of the arrangements under which the house is built for that other person by the builder.*]

AMENDMENT HISTORY

Section 96B inserted by s.4 of the Planning and Development (Amendment) Act 2002 (No. 32 of 2002) which came into effect on December 24, 2002.

NOTE

This section was introduced under the Planning and Development (Amendment) Act 2002 in respect of permission which would have ceased to have effect or expired but for s.96A extending the life of such permission. The section provides for the payment of a levy to the planning authority on the sale or disposal of a house. Under the original s.96(15), a planning permission made after August 25, 1999, but before a housing strategy was in place, thus avoiding the social and affordable housing requirements, only had a duration of two years. It is therefore this type of permission to which the levy applies. The levy applies to the permission whose life has been extended under under s.96A. Despite the overbroad wording under s.96A, the section is clearly intended to apply to planning permissions in relation to which a social and affordable housing condition was not imposed because the strategy was not in place when the application was made. Subsection (10) provides that the section does not apply to permissions for development consisting of the provision of four or less houses, or for housing on land of 0.1 hectares or less. The requirement of payment of a levy is imposed by way of condition attached to the planning permission and applies where the house is disposed of for the first time. Subsection (4) sets out the rate of the levy to be calculated. In the case of arm's length transactions, the levy is based on the actual consideration paid, otherwise it is based on the market value. If the market value or consideration exceeds €270,000, the levy is 1 per cent, while if it is below this amount, the levy is 0.5 per cent. Under subs.(5), the planning authority has a discretion to specify when the payment is to be made. This would mean the planning authority can require the payment to be made before the date of disposal or sale. The amount is paid into a separate account under subs.(6), with a receipt for payment issuing under subs.(7). Under subs.(8), any agreement seeking to pass on costs to the purchaser or grantee (rather than the vendor or grantor) of the payment of the levy, is void. Subsection (11) provides that the section will apply to sales where the vesting of interest in land is by means of a separate contract to any contract or arrangement concerning the building of the land.

Development to which section 96 shall not apply

1–121   **97.—(1)** In this *section* —

"applicant" *includes a person on whose behalf a person applies for a certificate*;

"the court" other than in *subsections (19) and (21),* means the Circuit Court for the circuit in which all or part of the development, to which the application under *subsection (3)* relates, is situated.

(2) For the purposes of this *section* —

    (a) 2 or more persons shall be deemed to be acting in concert if, pursuant to an agreement, arrangement or understanding, one of them makes an application under *subsection (3)* or causes such an application to be made, and

    (b) land in the immediate vicinity of other land shall be deemed in any particular case not to include land that is more than 400 metres from the land second-mentioned in this *subsection.*

(3) A person may, before applying for permission in respect of a development—

    (a) consisting of the provision of 4 or fewer houses, or

    (b) for housing on land of [0.1] hectares or less,

apply to the planning authority concerned for a certificate stating that *section 96* shall not apply to a grant of permission in respect of the development concerned (in this *section* referred to as a "certificate"), and accordingly, where the planning authority grants a certificate, *section 96* shall not apply to a grant of permission in respect of the development concerned.

(4) Subject to—

    (a) *subsections (6) and (12),* and

    (b) compliance by the applicant for a certificate with *subsection (8),*

a planning authority to which an application has been made under and in accordance with this *section* may grant a certificate to the applicant.

(5) An application for a certificate shall be accompanied by a statutory declaration made by the applicant—

    (a) giving, in respect of the period of 5 years preceding the application, such particulars of the legal and beneficial ownership of the land, on which it is proposed to carry out the development to which the application relates, as are within the applicant's knowledge or procurement,

    (b) identifying any persons with whom the applicant is acting in concert,

    (c) giving particulars of—

        (i) any interest that the applicant has, or had at any time during the said period, in any land in the immediate vicinity of the land on which it is proposed to carry out such development, and

        (ii) any interest that any person with whom the applicant is acting in concert has, or had at any time during the said period, in any land in the said immediate vicinity, of which the applicant has knowledge,

    (d) stating that the applicant is not aware of any facts or circumstances that would constitute grounds under *subsection (12)* for the refusal by the planning authority to grant a certificate,

    (e) giving such other information as may be prescribed.

  (6)

    (a) A planning authority may require an applicant for a certificate to provide it with such further information or documentation as is reasonably necessary to enable it to perform its functions under this *section.*

    (b) Where an applicant refuses to comply with a requirement under *paragraph (a),* or fails, within a period of 8 weeks from the date of the making of the requirement, to so comply, the planning authority concerned shall refuse to grant the applicant a certificate.

(7) A planning authority may, for the purpose of performing its functions under this *section,* make such further inquiries as it considers appropriate.

(8) It shall be the duty of the applicant for a certificate, at all times, to provide the planning authority concerned with such information as it may reasonably require to enable it to perform its functions under this *section.*

(9) The Minister may make regulations in relation to the making of an application under this *section.*

(10) Where a planning authority fails within the period of 4 weeks from—

  (a) the making of an application to it under this *section,* or

  (b) (in the case of a requirement under *subsection (6)*) the date of receipt by it of any information or documentation to which the requirement relates,

to grant, or refuse to grant a certificate, the planning authority shall on the expiry of that period be deemed to have granted a certificate to the applicant concerned.

(11) Particulars of a certificate granted under this *section* shall be entered on the register.

(12) A planning authority shall not grant a certificate in relation to a development if the applicant for such certificate, or any person with whom the applicant is acting in concert—

  (a) has been granted, not earlier than 5 years before the date of the application, a certificate in respect of a development, and the certificate at the time of the application remains in force, or

  (b) has carried out, or has been granted permission to carry out, a development referred to in *subsection (3),* not earlier than—

    (i) 5 years before the date of the application, and

    (ii) one year after the coming into operation of this *section,*
    in respect of the land on which it is proposed to carry out the first-mentioned development, or land in its immediate vicinity, unless—

      (I) the aggregate of any development to which *paragraph (a) or (b)* relates and the first-mentioned development would not, if carried out, exceed 4 houses, or

      (II) (in circumstances where the said aggregate would exceed 4 houses) the aggregate of the land on which any development to which *paragraph (a) or (b)* relates, and the land on which it is proposed to carry out the first-mentioned development, does not exceed [0.1] hectares.

(13) Where a planning authority refuses to grant a certificate, it shall by notice in writing inform the applicant of the reasons for its so refusing.

(14)

  (a) Where a planning authority to which an application has been made under *subsection (3)* refuses to grant a certificate to the applicant, he or she may, not later than 3 weeks from the date on which the applicant receives notification of the refusal by the planning authority to grant the certificate, or such later date as may be permitted by the court, appeal to the court for an order directing the planning authority to grant to the applicant a certificate in respect of the development.

  (b) The court may at the hearing of an appeal under *paragraph (a)* —

    (i) dismiss the appeal and affirm the refusal of the planning authority to grant the certificate, or

    (ii) allow the appeal and direct the planning authority to grant the applicant a certificate in respect of the development concerned.

(15) A planning authority shall comply with a direction of the court under this *section*.

(16)

    (a) Subject to *paragraph (b)*, a planning authority shall revoke a certificate, upon application in that behalf being made to it by the owner of land to which the certificate related, or by any other person acting with the permission of such owner.

    (b) A planning authority shall not revoke a certificate under this *subsection* where permission has been granted in respect of the development to which the certificate relates.

(17) A person who, knowingly or recklessly—

    (a) makes a statutory declaration under *subsection (5)*, or

    (b) in purported compliance with a requirement under *subsection (6)*, provides a planning authority with information or documentation, that is false or misleading in a material respect, or who believes any such statutory declaration made, or information or documentation provided in purported compliance with such requirement, by him or her not to be true, shall be guilty of an offence and shall be liable—

        (i) on summary conviction to a fine not exceeding €1,904.61 [£1,500] or to imprisonment for a term not exceeding 6 months, or to both, or

        (ii) on conviction on indictment to a fine not exceeding €634,869.04 [£500,000] or to imprisonment for a term not exceeding 5 years, or to both.

(18) A person who—

    (a) forges, or utters, knowing it to be forged, a certificate purporting to have been granted under this *section* (hereafter in this *subsection* referred to as a "forged certificate"),

    (b) alters with intent to deceive or defraud, or utters, knowing it to be so altered, a certificate (hereafter in this *subsection* referred to as an "altered certificate"), or

    (c) without lawful authority or other reasonable excuse, has in his or her possession a forged certificate or an altered certificate, shall be guilty of an offence and shall be liable—

        (i) on summary conviction to a fine not exceeding €1,904.61 [£1,500] or imprisonment for a term not exceeding 6 months, or to both, or

        (ii) on conviction on indictment to a fine not exceeding €634,869.04 [£500,000] or imprisonment for a term not exceeding 5 years, or to both.

(19) Where a person is convicted on indictment of an offence under *subsection (17) or (18)*, the court may in addition to any fine or term of imprisonment imposed by the court under that *subsection* order the payment into court by the person of an amount that in the opinion of the court is equal to the amount of any gain accruing to that person by reason of the grant of a certificate on foot of the statutory declaration, information or documentation, as the case may be, to which the offence relates, and such sum shall, when paid in accordance with such order, stand forfeited.

(20) All sums that stand forfeited under *subsection (19)* shall be paid to the planning authority that granted the certificate concerned and shall be accounted for in the account referred to in *section 96(13)* and be applied only for the purposes specified in that *section.*

(21) Where a person is convicted of an offence under *subsection (17),* the court may revoke a certificate granted on foot of a statutory declaration, information or documentation to which the offence relates, upon application being made to it in that behalf by the planning authority that granted the certificate.

(22) A person shall not, solely by reason of having been granted a certificate, be entitled to a grant of permission in respect of the development to which the certificate relates.

AMENDMENT HISTORY

Subsection (3) amended by s.5 of the Planning and Development (Amendment) Act 2002 (No. 32 of 2002) which came into effect on December 24, 2002.

Subsection (12) amended by s.5 of the Local Government (No.2) Act 2003 (No. 17 of 2003) which came into effect on June 2, 2003.

NOTE

This section allows certain applicants for permission to apply to the planning authority for a certificate to the effect that the social and affordable housing requirements in s.96 are not applicable. The only applicants eligible are where the application for permission concerns "stand alone" developments consisting of four houses or less or "stand alone" developments for housing on land of 0.1 hectares or less. Section 96(1) states that "subject to subsection (13) and section 97", where a development plan objective requires that a specified percentage of any land zoned solely for residential use, be made available for social and affordable housing referred, s.96 shall apply to an application for permission for the development of houses on land to which such an objective applies. Under subs.(96)(13), the requirements in s.96 will not apply to any of the four specified developments which comprise:
- social housing developments by approved bodies;
- the conversion of an existing building or the reconstruction of a building to create one or more dwellings, provided that at least 50 per cent of the existing external fabric of the building is retained;
- the carrying out of works to an existing house; or
- developments pursuant to a social and affordable housing agreement under the section.

However, in contrast to s.96(13) where the exemption is automatic, for the exemption to apply under s.97 it is necessary to apply for a certificate of exemption prior to lodging the planning permission. Thus, even if a development falls within a category of development specified in s.97, if a certificate of exemption was not sought and obtained prior to the lodging the planning application, the obligation under s.96 will still apply to the development.

It is not entirely clear that where the conditions for an application apply that a person will be automatically be granted a certificate on proof of such conditions. It appears that the planning authority retains a discretion in making such decision. The Guidelines state at para.12.3 that the planning authority can refuse to grant a person a certificate if, based on the information provided by the person and any other knowledge, it believes that a person is trying to avoid the application of a social and affordable housing condition. Subsection (5) provides that the application for a certificate must be accompanied by a statutory declaration setting out details of the particulars and interest in the property. The statutory declaration should include such matters as particulars of any interest the applicant has or has had in land in the immediate vicinity and any interest that any person with whom he is acting in concert has or has had in the immediate vicinity. The purpose of this appears to be guard against an applicant attempting to avoid his obligations by submitting a number of sub-threshold developments. Under subs.(6), the planning authority may seek further information, while it is a criminal offence under subs.(17) to knowingly or recklessly provide a false or misleading declaration or information. Substantial penalties are imposed. In addition to the normal penalties, the court can revoke the certificate and make the person pay to the planning authority the equivalent of any gain they made by reason of the grant of a certificate. Under subs.(8), an applicant must provide the planning authority with all such information as it may reasonably require, while under subs.(6), if an applicant refuses to provide further information or fails to provide the information within eight weeks, the planning authority may refuse the certificate. Subsection (10) allows for the grant of a certificate by default, whereby a certificate will be deemed to have been granted if a decision is not made within four weeks of lodging the application or of providing the further information. Subsection (12) excludes the grant of a certificate where a certificate has already been granted in certain circumstances.

Under subs.(13), the planning authority must inform the applicant in writing of the decision, who then has three weeks within which to appeal the decision to the Circuit Court. Subsection (14) allows the Circuit Court to extend time to appeal a refusal of a certificate where the applicant fails to lodge his appeal within the three-week period. The Circuit Court Rules 2007 (S.I. No. 312 of 2007) amends CCR Ord.56 by the introduction of a new Order 56, which provides at r.2 that that all applications by way of an appeal against the refusal by a planning authority to grant a certificate under s.97, shall be brought by way of a Civil Bill, being a Planning Civil Bill in accordance with Form 2L in the Schedule of Forms. It appears that the court will consider the matter *de novo*. Where the court allows the appeal and directs the planning authority to grant the applicant a certificate, the planning authority is obliged to comply with the direction under subs.(15). Under subs.(16), the planning authority must revoke a certificate upon application by the owner of the land to which the certificate relates or by any other person acting with the permission of such owner. However, the planning authority cannot revoke such certificate where permission has been granted in respect of the permission to which the certificate relates.

Allocation of affordable housing

98.—**(1)** Affordable housing may be sold or leased only to eligible persons who qualify in accordance with a scheme established by a planning authority under *subsection (2)*. **1–122**

(2) For the purposes of *subsection (1)*, each planning authority shall establish a scheme which determines the order of priority to be accorded to eligible persons.

(3) Without prejudice to the generality of *subsection (2)*, when establishing a scheme referred to in that *subsection,* the planning authority shall have regard to the following:

(a) the accommodation needs of eligible persons, in particular eligible persons who have not previously purchased or built a house for their occupation or for any other purpose;

(b) the current housing circumstances of eligible persons;

(c) the incomes or other financial circumstances of eligible persons (and priority may be accorded to eligible persons whose income level is lower than that of other eligible persons);

(d) the period for which eligible persons have resided in the area of the development plan;

(e) whether eligible persons own houses or lands in the area of the development plan or elsewhere;

(f) distance of affordable housing from places of employment of eligible persons;

(g) such other matters as the planning authority considers appropriate or as may be prescribed for the purposes of this *section.*

(4) A planning authority—

(a) shall, when making or reviewing a development plan under *Part II,* and

(b) may, at any other time, review a scheme made under this *section* and, as it sees fit, make amendments to the scheme or make a new scheme.

(5) The making of a scheme under this *section* and the making of an amendment to any such scheme shall be reserved functions.

(6) For the purposes of allocation under this *section,* a planning authority may, from time to time, set aside such specified number or proportion of affordable houses, for such eligible persons or classes of eligible persons, as it considers appropriate.

(7) In this *section* and *section 99,* "lease" *means a shared ownership lease within the meaning of section 2 of the Housing (Miscellaneous Provisions) Act, 1992.*

Note

This section provides for the establishment of a scheme by planning authorities to determine the allocation of affordable housing. Affordable housing is only available to eligible persons under s.93. Some guidance for the making of the scheme are set out in subs.(3). None of provisions of Pt V specifies the financial terms or price according to which the affordable housing is to be made available. The phrases "provide for or arrange" (s.96(9)(a)(i)); "shall be used" (s.96(10)) and "may be sold or lease" (s.98(1)), give no indication or guidance of the price or other financial terms by which affordability is achieved. However, the clawback provision in s.99(3) implicitly envisages that the price paid by such person (which includes a person purchasing affordable housing) is less than the market value, although it does set out any means of calculating the discounted price or price paid. The discounted price may be related to the "planning gain" by which the planning authority acquires the land from the developer at a discount. In the case of direct sales, this is most clearly the case, as the purchaser nominated by the local authority may pay the developer a price which incorporates the discount on the land. The Guidelines state at para.18.3 that the allocation of social housing will be done in accordance with the Scheme of Letting Priorities prepared by the planning authority under s.11 of the Housing Act 1988 and taking account of the assessment of needs carried out under s.9 of that Act. Also, while individuals may be eligible for both social and affordable housing, completely separate lists must be operated for the allocation of such housing. The scheme of priorities may be reviewed, and if necessary amended, by the members of the planning authority at any time. The actual allocation of housing is a function of the Manager. The scheme can only apply to eligible persons defined under s.93. The scheme may establish priorities between different eligible persons. The planning authority may alter the scheme when varying or making a development plan or can do so independently at any time. The scheme can specify exact percentages of houses for certain types of elegible persons. The making or varying of the scheme is a matter for the elected members. The courts will be very reluctant to intervene in terms of the allocation of houses by the local authority. In *McDonagh v Cork County Council,* unreported, High Court, Kinlen J., January 12, 1998, Kinlen J. said: "[t]his court cannot order the local authority how to exercise its respective powers and direct for a certain person to be allocated a certain house in the absence of a specific contract". Also in *McDonagh v Clare County Council,* unreported, High Court,

Smyth J., May 20, 2004, Smyth J. declared the rights conferred by the Housing Acts, "are real and to be honoured and give effect—but this does not confer absolute and unqualified rights—they are resource dependent". Also while an applicant may express a preference for a type of accommodation:

> "[T]here is no obligation on the Housing Authority to provide immediately such specified accommodation—it must not only assess needs and priorities but have regard to all other persons who have needs and to its availability of accommodation".

In *Doherty v South Dublin County Council (2)* [2007] 2 I.R. 696, albeit in the context of traveller accommodation, it was noted that any proposed intervention by the court should take into account that it was the responsibility of the legislature and executive to decide the allocation of resources and the priorities applied by them.

Controls on resale of certain houses

99.—**(1)** Where houses are provided or sites made available in accordance　**1–123** with *section 96(9) or (10),* the sale or lease of those houses or sites shall be subject to such conditions (if any) as may be specified by the planning authority.

(2) Without prejudice to the generality of *subsection (1),* terms and conditions under those subsections may provide for—

  (a) the notification of the planning authority of the resale of any house or land, and

  (b) the basis on which any house sold or leased under this *Part* may be occupied.

(3)

  (a) Terms and conditions under this *section* shall require, subject to *paragraphs (b) and (c),* that where any house or land sold to any person in accordance with *subsection (1)* is first resold before the expiration of 20 years from the date of purchase, the person selling the house or land shall pay to the planning authority out of the proceeds of the sale an amount equal to a percentage of the proceeds, which percentage is calculated in accordance with the following formula—

  $Y \times 100\ Z \times 100$

  where—

> Y is the difference between the market value of the house or land at the time of sale to the person and the price actually paid, and Z is the market value of the house at the time of sale to the person.

  (b) The amount payable under *paragraph (a)* shall be reduced by 10 per cent in respect of each complete year after the 10th year during which the person to whom the house or land was sold has been in occupation of the house or land as his or her normal place of residence.

  (c) Where the amount payable under *paragraph (a)* would reduce the proceeds of the sale (disregarding solicitor and estate agent's fees and costs) below the price actually paid, the amount payable shall be reduced to the extent necessary to avoid that result.

  (d)

      (i) In calculating the amount payable under *paragraph (a),* due allowance shall be made for any material improvements made by the person to whom the house or land was sold.

(ii) For the purpose of this *paragraph,* "material improvements" *means improvements made to the house (whether for the purpose of extending, enlarging, repairing or converting the house), but does not include decoration, or any improvements carried out on the land including the construction of a house.*

[(3A)

(a) As soon as practicable after a house or land is sold in accordance with *subsection (1),* the planning authority shall make an order charging the house or land with an amount that shall be expressed in the order in the following terms.

(b) Those terms are that the amount charged is an amount equal to the amount (if any) that may subsequently become payable under *subsection (3)(a)* in respect of the house or land.

(c) An order under *paragraph (a)* shall be deemed to be a mortgage made by deed within the meaning of the *Conveyancing Acts 1881* to *1911* and to have been executed, at the time of the sale of the house or land in accordance with *subsection (1),* in favour of the planning authority for a charge of the amount referred to in *paragraph (b).*

(d) Accordingly, the planning authority shall, as on and from the making of such an order in respect of a house or land—

(i) be deemed to be a mortgagee of the house or land for the purposes of the *Conveyancing Acts 1881* to *1911,* and

(ii) have in relation to the charge referred to in *paragraph (c)* all the powers conferred by those Acts on mortgagees under mortgages made by deed.

(e) Where a planning authority makes an order under *paragraph (a)* it shall, as soon as practicable thereafter, cause the order to be registered in the Registry of Deeds or the Land Registry, as appropriate, and it shall be a sufficient description of the amount in respect of which the charge to which the order relates is being registered to state that amount to be the amount referred to in *section 99(3A)(b) of the Planning and Development Act 2000.*

(f) An order under *paragraph (a)* affecting a house or land which is registered land within the meaning of the *Registration of Title Act 1964* shall be registrable as a burden affecting such land whether the person named in such order as the owner of the land is or is not registered under the said *Act* as the owner of such land.

(g) A charge created by virtue of an order under *paragraph (a)* shall not be regarded as a prior mortgage for the purposes of *section 22(4) of the Building Societies Act 1989.*

(h) A planning authority may, subject to *paragraph (i),* enter into an agreement with a holder of a licence under the *Central Bank Act 1971,* a building society or other financial institution that a charge proposed to be created by it by an order under *paragraph (a)* shall have a priority, as against a mortgage or charge proposed to be created in favour of that holder, society or institution, that is different from the priority the charge would otherwise have if this *paragraph* had not been enacted.

(i) A planning authority may only enter into such an agreement if it considers that the agreement will enable the person to whom the house or land concerned is proposed to be sold in accordance with *subsection (1)* to obtain an advance of moneys from the holder, society or institution referred to in *paragraph (h)* for the purposes of purchasing the house or land.

(j) Any amount that becomes payable to a planning authority under *subsection (3)(a)* may, without prejudice to any other power in that behalf, be recovered by the authority from the person concerned as a simple contract debt in any court of competent jurisdiction.

(k) For the avoidance of doubt, neither an order under *paragraph (a)* nor a charge that arises under it shall be regarded as a conveyance for the purposes of *section 3 of the Family Home Protection Act 1976.*]

(4) Any moneys accruing to a planning authority arising out of the resale of any house or land, subject to terms and conditions in accordance with *subsection (1),* shall be paid into the separate account referred to in *section 96(13)* and shall be subject to the other requirements of that *subsection.*

AMENDMENT HISTORY

Subsection (3A) inserted by s.2 of the Housing (Miscellaneous Provisions) Act 2004 (No. 43 of 2004) with effect from December 21, 2004.

NOTE

This section provides that where houses or sites are made available under the social and affordable housing provision in s.96, terms and conditions may be attached in relation to the sale or lease of such houses. This will include a mandatory "clawback" condition. The houses or site made available may be subject to such terms and conditions as the planning authority may specify. It appears that this must be specified at the time such site was made available. Subsection (2) provides that the terms and conditions may provide for the notification of the planning authority for resale or the basis on which house could be occupied. Subsection (2) does not purport to be an exhaustive list of conditions and the two conditions stated in subs.(2) are not mandatory. However, under subs.(3), the terms and conditions must require that where a person sells or leases the house within 20 years of purchase, there is an obligation to pay the planning authority certain of the proceeds calculated on the basis of the formula set out in the subsection. This condition is therefore mandatory and is known as the "clawback" clause. The amount payable will be reduced by a tenth for every year of occupation beyond the tenth year. Material improvements may also be taken into account to reduce the amount payable. The Guidelines provide at para.20.1 that this approach will ensure that there is no profiteering while at the same time allowing purchasers to retain the full benefits of ownership after a reasonable time. The planning authority should reduce the amount payable so that the proceeds of the sale (excluding solicitors' and auctioneers' fees and costs) are not reduced below the price actually paid. Section 3A was inserted under the Housing Act 2004 and provides that as soon as practicable after a house is sold, the planning authority must make an order charging the house or land in the amount equal to amount which may become payable under subs.(3)(a). Once the charging order is made, the planning authority is deemed to be a mortgagee and it must also cause the order to be registered in Registry of Deeds or Land Registry as appropriate.

The clawback provision in s.99(3) implicitly envisages that the price paid by such person (which includes a person purchasing affordable housing) is less than the market value, although it does not set out any means of calculating the discounted price or price paid. The precise means by which local authorities set the discounted price is vague.

Regulations under this Part

1–124　　**100.—(1)** The Minister may make regulations-

(a) specifying the criteria for determining the size of the accommodation required by eligible persons, including minimum and maximum size requirements, having regard to any guidelines specified by the Minister in respect of the provision of housing under the *Housing Acts, 1966* to *1998,*

(b) governing the determination of income for the purposes of *section 93,*

(c) specifying matters for the purposes of *section 94(5) or 98(3),* and

(d) setting out requirements related to terms and conditions referred to in *section 99(1).*

(2) *Regulations* made under *subsection (1)* may apply either generally or by reference to a specified class or classes of eligible persons or to any other matter as may be considered by the Minister to be appropriate.

NOTE

This section allows the Minister to make regulations concerning various matters such as the type of accommodation, the calculation of income, estimating the affordable housing needs (s.94(5)) or making the scheme for affordable housing (s.98(3)). There is no express residual power conferred on the Minister and so the Minister may only make regulations on the specified matters.

Housing and planning authority functions

1–125　　**101.—(1)** Where a planning authority performing any function under this *Part* is not the housing authority for the area of the function, the planning authority shall consult with the housing authority for the area with respect to the performance of that function.

(2) In this *section,* a reference to a "housing authority" *means a housing authority as defined pursuant to section 23(2) of the Housing (Miscellaneous Provisions) Act, 1992.*

NOTE

This section provides for consultation between the planning authority and the housing authority where they do not concern the same local authority. In most cases, the same local authority will be acting in its capacity as planning authority and as housing authority.

PART VI

AN BORD PLEANÁLA

CHAPTER 1

Establishment and Constitution

Continuation of Bord Pleanála

102.—(1) An Bord Pleanála shall continue in being notwithstanding the repeal of any enactment effected by this *Act.*   **1–126**

(2) The Board shall perform the functions assigned to it by this *Act.*

(3) The chairman, deputy chairman and any other member of the Board in office immediately prior to the coming into force of this *section* under an enactment repealed by this *Act* shall continue in office as chairperson, deputy chairperson and other member, respectively, for a term ending on the day on which his or her appointment would have expired under the repealed enactment.

NOTE

This section concerns the continuity in being of An Bord Pleanála. An Bord Pleanála was established on January 1, 1977 by S.I. No. 307 of 1976 under the Local Government (Planning and Development) Act 1976 (this was continued under S.I. No. 45 of 1984). The constitution and organisation of An Bord Pleanála were largely dealt with under the 1976 Act, the Local Government (Planning and Development) Act 1983, and Pt XI of the Local Government (Planning and Development) Regulations 1994. All of these enactments have been repealed in totality. The 2000 Act provides for the continuity of An Bord Pleanála as it existed prior to the repeal of these measures. An Bord Pleanála is now located at 64 Marlborough Street, Dublin 1.

Board to be body corporate, etc.

103.—(1) The Board shall be a body corporate with perpetual succession and a seal and power to sue and be sued in its corporate name and to acquire, hold and dispose of land.   **1–127**

(2) The seal of the Board shall be authenticated by the signature of the chairperson or of some other member, or of an employee of the Board or of a person whose services are availed of by the Board by virtue of *section 122,* who is authorised by the Board to act in that behalf.

(3) Judicial notice shall be taken of the seal of the Board and every document purporting to be an instrument made by the Board and to be sealed with the seal (purporting to be authenticated in accordance with *subsection (2)*) of the Board shall be received in evidence and be deemed to be such an instrument without proof unless the contrary is shown.

NOTE

This section concerns the legal status of An Bord Pleanála. The section is almost identical to s.2 of the Local Government (Planning and Development) Act 1983, which Act repealed certain provisions of the 1976 Act and allowed for the continuation of An Bord Pleanála. Under s.122(1) the Minister may provide services (including services of staff) to the Board on such terms and conditions (including payment for such services) as may be agreed and the Board may avail of such services. This is similar to s.21(3) of the 1976 Act, though it was expressed as an interim measure, pending sufficient appointments being made. Under s.122(2), the Board may provide services to the Minister in similar circumstances.

Board to consist of chairperson and 9 other members

1–128   **104.—(1)** Subject to *subsections (2) and (3) of this section,* the Board shall consist of a chairperson and [9 ordinary members].

(2) The Minister may by order increase the number of ordinary members where he or she is of the opinion that the number of appeals, referrals or other matters with which the Board is concerned is at such a level so as to necessitate the appointment of one or more additional Board members to enable the Board fulfil its duty and objective under *section 126.*

(3) Where an order is proposed to be made under *subsection (2),* a draft of the order shall be laid before each House of the Oireachtas and the order shall not be made until a resolution approving of the draft has been passed by each such House.

(4)

    (a) Notwithstanding *subsection (2) of this section or subsection (3) of section 106,* where the Minister is of the opinion that one or more than one additional ordinary member should be appointed as a matter of urgency due to the number of appeals, referrals or other matters with which the Board is concerned, the Minister may, pending the making and approval of an order under *subsections (2) and (3) of this section,* appoint one or more than one person from among the officers of the Minister who are established civil servants for the purposes of the *Civil Service Regulation Act, 1956,* or from among the employees of the Board, on a temporary basis.

    (b) A person shall not be appointed to be an ordinary member under this *subsection* for a term in excess of 9 months. (5) An order made under *subsection (2)* shall have effect for such a period not exceeding 5 years as shall be specified therein.

AMENDMENT HISTORY

Subsection (1) amended by s. 14 of the Planning and Development (Strategic Infrastructure) Act 2006 (No. 27 of 2006).

NOTE

This section concerns the membership of the Board. Subsection (1) is a new provision which prescribes the Board as consisting of a Chairperson and nine ordinary members. The 2006 Act amended s.104(1) by increasing the number of ordinary members of the Board from seven to nine members. The remainder of this section repeats s.1 of the Local Government (Planning and Development) Act 1998, which itself was substituted for s.3 of the 1983 Act. Section 126 imposes a duty on the Board to dispose of appeals or referrals expeditiously to ensure there are no avoidable delays, prescribing a maximum of 18 weeks to reach a determination. Under s.106(3), the Minister may appoint an ordinary member to replace an existing member who indicates an inability or unwillingness to take part or is incapacitated for any period, until an appointment is made by the committee.

Appointment of chairperson

105.—(1) The chairperson shall be appointed by the Government.   **1–129**

(2) There shall be a committee ("the committee") consisting of—

(a) the President of the High Court,

(b) the Cathaoirleach of the General Council of County Councils,

(c) the Secretary-General of the Department of the Environment and Local Government,

(d) the Chairperson of the Council of An Taisce - the National Trust for Ireland,

(e) the President of the Construction Industry Federation,

(f) the President of the Executive Council of the Irish Congress of Trade Unions, and

(g) the Chairperson of the National Women's Council of Ireland.

(3) Where—

(a) any of the persons referred to in *subsection (2)* signifies at any time his or her unwillingness or inability to act for any period as a member of the committee, or

(b) any of the persons referred to in *subsection (2)* is through ill-health or otherwise unable so to act for any period,

the Minister may, when making a request under *subsection (7)*, appoint another person to be a member of the committee in his or her place and that person shall remain a member of the committee until such time as the selection by the committee pursuant to the request is made.

(4) Where the Minister makes a request under *subsection (7)* and at the time of making the request any of the offices referred to in *subsection (2)* is vacant, the Minister may appoint a person to be a member of the committee and that person shall remain a member of the committee until such time as the selection of the committee pursuant to the request is made.

(5) Where, pursuant to *subsection (3) or (4)*, the Minister appoints a person to be a member of the committee, he or she shall, as soon as may be, cause a notice of the appointment to be published in *Iris Oifigiúil*.

(6)

(a) The Minister may by order amend *subsection (2)*.

(b) The Minister may by order amend or revoke an order under this *subsection* (including an order under this *paragraph*).

(c) Where an order under this *subsection* is proposed to be made, the Minister shall cause a draft thereof to be laid before both Houses of the Oireachtas and the order shall not be made until a resolution approving of the draft has been passed by each such House.

(d) Where an order under this *subsection* is in force, *subsection (2)* shall be construed and have effect subject to the terms of the order.

(7)

(a) The committee shall, whenever so requested by the Minister, select 3 candidates, or if in the opinion of the committee there is not a sufficient number of suitable applicants, such lesser number of candidates as the committee shall determine, for appointment to be the chairperson and shall inform the Minister of the names of the candidates, or, as may be appropriate, the name of the candidate, selected and of the reasons why, in the opinion of the committee, they are or he or she is suitable for the appointment.

(b) In selecting candidates the committee shall have regard to the special knowledge and experience and other qualifications or personal qualities which the committee considers appropriate to enable a person effectively to perform the functions of the chairperson.

(8) Except in the case of a re-appointment under *subsection (12)*, the Government shall not appoint a person to be the chairperson unless the person was selected by the committee under *subsection (7)* in relation to that appointment but—

(a) if the committee is unable to select any suitable candidate pursuant to a particular request under *subsection (7)*, or

(b) if the Government decides not to appoint to be the chairperson any of the candidates selected by the committee pursuant to a particular request,

then either—

(i) the Government shall appoint a person to be the chairperson who was a candidate selected by the committee pursuant to a previous request (if any) in relation to that appointment, or

(ii) the Minister shall make a further request to the committee and the Government shall appoint to be the chairperson a person who is selected by the committee pursuant to the request or pursuant to a previous request.

(9) The Minister may make regulations as regards—

(a) the publication of the notice that a request has been received by the committee under *subsection (7)*,

(b) applications for selection by the committee, and

(c) any other matter which the Minister considers expedient for the purposes of this *section.*

(10) A person who is, for the time being—

(a) entitled under the Standing Orders of either House of the Oireachtas to sit therein,

(b) a member of the European Parliament, or

(c) a member of a local authority, shall be disqualified from being appointed as the chairperson.

(11) The chairperson shall be appointed in a wholetime capacity and shall not at any time during his or her term of office hold any other office or employment in respect of which emoluments are payable.

(12) Subject to the other provisions of this *section,* the chairperson shall hold office for a term of 7 years and may be re-appointed by the Government for a second or subsequent term of office, provided that a person shall not be re-appointed under this *subsection* unless, at the time of his or her re-appointment, he or she is or was the outgoing chairperson.

(13)

(a) The chairperson may resign his or her office as chairperson by letter addressed to the Minister and the resignation shall take effect on and from the date of the receipt of the letter by the Minister.

(b) The chairperson shall vacate the office of chairperson on attaining the age of 65 years [: but where the chairperson is a new entrant (within the meaning of the *Public Service Superannuation (Miscellaneous Provisions) Act 2004*) appointed on or after 1 April 2004, then the requirement to vacate office on grounds of age shall not apply].

(c) A person shall cease to be the chairperson if he or she—

    (i) is nominated either as a member of Seanad Éireann or for election to either House of the Oireachtas or to the European Parliament,

    (ii) is regarded pursuant to *Part XIII of the Second Schedule to the European Parliament Elections Act, 1997,* as having been elected to that Parliament to fill a vacancy, or

    (iii) becomes a member of a local authority.

(d) A person shall cease to be the chairperson if he or she—

    (i) is adjudicated bankrupt,

    (ii) makes a composition or arrangement with creditors,

    (iii) is convicted of any indictable offence in relation to a company,

    (iv) is convicted of an offence involving fraud or dishonesty, whether in connection with a company or not,

    (v) is sentenced by a court of competent jurisdiction to a term of imprisonment,

    (vi) is the subject of an order under *section 160 of the Companies Act, 1990,* or

    (vii) ceases to be resident in the State.

(14)

(a) There shall be paid by the Board to the chairperson the same salary as is paid to a judge of the High Court.

(b) Subject to the provisions of this *section,* the chairperson shall hold office on such terms and conditions (including terms relating to allowances for expenses) as the Minister, with the consent of the Minister for Finance, determines.

(15) The chairperson may be removed from office by the Government if he or she has become incapable through ill-health of effectively performing his or her functions, or if he or she has committed stated misbehaviour, or if his or her removal appears to the Government to be necessary for the effective performance by the Board of its functions, and in case the chairperson is removed from office under this *subsection,* the Government shall cause to be laid before each House of the Oireachtas a statement of the reasons for the removal.

AMENDMENT HISTORY

Subsection (13) amended by s.3 of the Public Service Superannuation (Miscellaneous Provisions) Act 2004, (No.7 of 2004), which came into effect on March 25, 2004.

NOTE

This section governs the process of selection of the Chairperson of the Board. It almost entirely re-enacts s.5 of the 1983 Act, with only some slight modifications. The section describes a seven member committee whose task it is, in co-operation with the Minister, to select the Chairperson of the Board. One of the minor changes to the previous provision in s.5 of the 1983 Act is the addition of s.105(13)(d), prescribing certain other factors which would disqualify a person from acting as Chairperson. Article 57 of the Planning Regulations 2001 describes the procedure upon request being made to the committee for the candidates of chairperson. Before meeting, the committee must cause an advertisement to be published inviting applications for appointment (specifying a period for application not less than three weeks). Article 58 refers to the content of any application. Under art.59, the committee may require an applicant to submit further particulars, or under art.60, to attend for an interview. Under art.61, a person may cease to be entitled to further consideration by the committee where they do not submit the further particulars or attend for the interview.

Appointment of ordinary members

1–130   106.—[(1) The Minister shall appoint the 9 ordinary members of the Board as follows:

> (a) 2 members shall be appointed from amongst persons nominated for such appointment by such organisations that, in the Minister's opinion, are representative of persons whose professions or occupations relate to physical planning, engineering and architecture as may be prescribed;
>
> (b) 2 members shall be appointed from amongst persons nominated for such appointment by such organisations that, in the Minister's opinion, are concerned with economic development, the promotion of and carrying out of development, the provision of infrastructure or the development of land or otherwise connected with the construction industry as may be prescribed;
>
> (c) 2 members shall be appointed from among persons nominated for such appointment by such—
>> (i) organisations that, in the Minister's opinion, are representative of the interests of local government,
>> (ii) bodies representing farming, and (iii) trade unions, as may be prescribed;
>
> (d) 2 members shall be appointed from among persons nominated for such appointment by such—
>> (i) organisations that, in the Minister's opinion, are representative of persons concerned with the protection and preservation of the environment and of amenities,
>> (ii) voluntary bodies and bodies having charitable objects,
>> (iii) bodies that, in the Minister's opinion, have a special interest or expertise in matters relating to rural and local community development, the promotion of the Irish language or the promotion of heritage, the arts and culture,
>> (iv) bodies that are representative of people with disabilities, and
>> (v) bodies that are representative of young people, as may be prescribed;
>
> (e) one member shall be appointed from among the officers of the Minister who are established civil servants for the purposes of the *Civil Service Regulation Act 1956.*

[(2) The Minister shall prescribe at least 2 organisations for the purposes of each of *paragraphs (a) to (d) of subsection (1).*]

(3) Where the Minister decides to appoint one or more members to the Board pursuant to an order under *section 104(2)* —

    (a) where not more than [6 additional members] are appointed, not more than one shall be appointed from among persons selected by organisations which are prescribed for the purposes of a particular *paragraph of subsection (1);*

    (b) where [more than 6 but not more than 12 additional members] are appointed, not more than 2 shall be appointed from among persons selected by organisations which are prescribed for the purposes of a particular *paragraph of subsection (1).*

(4) An organisation prescribed for the purposes of [*paragraph (a), (b), (c) or (d)*], shall, whenever so requested by the Minister, nominate such number of candidates (not being less than two) as the Minister may specify for appointment as an ordinary member and shall inform the Minister of the names of the candidates nominated and of the reasons why, in the opinion of the organisation, they are suitable for appointment.

(5) Except in the case of an appointment pursuant to [*subsection (1)(e)*] or a re-appointment under *subsection (12)* and subject to *subsection (6) and section 108(4),* the Minister shall not appoint a person to be an ordinary member unless the person was nominated pursuant to a request under *subsection (4)* in relation to that appointment.

(6) Where—

    (a) pursuant to a particular request under *subsection (4),* an organisation refuses or fails to nominate any candidate, or

    (b) the Minister decides not to appoint as an ordinary member any candidate nominated by the organisations pursuant to a particular request under that *subsection,*

    then—

        (i) the Minister shall appoint as an ordinary member a person who was among those nominated by such an organisation pursuant to a previous request (if any) under that *subsection* in relation to that appointment,

        (ii) the Minister shall make a further request and shall appoint as an ordinary member a person who was among those nominated pursuant to that request or pursuant to another request made in relation to that appointment, or

        (iii) the Minister shall appoint as an ordinary member a person selected by a committee established under *subsection (7).*

(7)

    (a) There shall be a committee ("the committee") consisting of—

        (i) the chairperson,

        (ii) the Assistant-Secretary of the Department of the Environment and Local Government with responsibility for planning and sustainable development, and

        (iii) the Chairperson of the Heritage Council.

    (b) The committee shall, whenever so requested by the Minister—

        (i) by notice in one or more national newspapers, invite applications for appointment as an ordinary member by suitably qualified persons,

(ii) select 3 candidates, or if in the opinion of the committee there is not such a sufficient number of suitable applicants, such lesser number of candidates as the committee shall determine, for appointment as an ordinary member, having regard to the knowledge and experience and other qualifications or personal qualities which the committee considers appropriate to enable a person effectively to perform the functions of an ordinary member, and

(iii) inform the Minister of the names of the candidates or, as may be appropriate, the name of the candidate, selected and of the reasons why, in the opinion of the committee, they are or he or she is suitable for the appointment.

(8) Where a request is made under *subsection (4),* failure or refusal by the organisation of whom the request is made to nominate the number of candidates specified in the request shall not preclude the appointment as an ordinary member of a person who was nominated in relation to that appointment either by the organisation or by any other organisation.

(9) The Minister may make regulations as regards—

(a) the period within which the Minister is to be informed in accordance with *subsection (4),* and

(b) any other matter which the Minister considers expedient for the purposes of this *section.*

(10) A person who is for the time being—

(a) entitled under the Standing Orders of either House of the Oireachtas to sit therein,

(b) a member of the European Parliament, or

(c) a member of a local authority,

shall be disqualified from being appointed as an ordinary member.

(11) Each of the ordinary members shall be appointed in a whole-time capacity and shall not at any time during his or her term of office hold any other office or employment in respect of which emoluments are payable.

(12) Subject to *section 108(4)(b),* an ordinary member shall hold office for such term (not exceeding 5 years) as shall be specified by the Minister when appointing him or her to office and may be re-appointed by the Minister for a second or subsequent term of office provided that a person shall not be re-appointed under this *subsection* unless, at the time of his or her re-appointment, he or she is or was an outgoing member of the Board.

(13)

(a) An ordinary member may resign his or her membership by letter addressed to the Minister and the resignation shall take effect on and from the date of the receipt of the letter by the Minister.

(b) A person shall vacate the office of ordinary member on attaining the age of 65 years [: but where the ordinary member is a new entrant within the meaning of the *Public Service Superannuation (Miscellaneous Provisions) Act 2004)* appointed on or after 1 April 2004, then the requirement to vacate office on grounds of age shall not apply].

(c) A person shall cease to be an ordinary member if he or she—

    (i) is nominated either as a member of Seanad Éireann or for election to either House of the Oireachtas or to the European Parliament,

    (ii) is regarded pursuant to *Part XIII of the Second Schedule to the European Parliament Elections Act, 1997,* as having been elected to that Parliament to fill a vacancy, or

    (iii) becomes a member of a local authority.

(d) A person shall cease to be an ordinary member of the Board if he or she—

    (i) is adjudicated bankrupt,

    (ii) makes a composition or arrangement with creditors,

    (iii) is convicted of any indictable offence in relation to a company,

    (iv) is convicted of an offence involving fraud or dishonesty, whether in connection with a company or not,

    (v) is sentenced by a court of competent jurisdiction to a term of imprisonment,

    (vi) is the subject of an order under *section 160 of the Companies Act, 1990,* or

    (vii) ceases to be resident in the State.

(14)

(a) There shall be paid by the Board to each ordinary member such remuneration and allowances for expenses as the Minister, with the consent of the Minister for Finance, determines.

(b) Subject to the other provisions of this *section,* an ordinary member shall hold office on such terms and conditions as the Minister, with the consent of the Minister for Finance, determines.

(15) An ordinary member may be removed from office by the Minister if he or she has become incapable through ill-health of effectively performing his or her functions, or if he or she has committed stated misbehaviour, or if his or her removal appears to the Minister to be necessary for the effective performance by the Board of its functions, and in case an ordinary member is removed from office under this *subsection,* the Minister shall cause to be laid before each House of the Oireachtas a statement in writing of the reasons for the removal.

AMENDMENT HISTORY

Subsection (1) substituted by s.15(a) of the Planning and Development (Strategic Infrastructure) Act 2006 (No. 27 of 2006).

Subsection (2) substituted by s.15(a) of the Planning and Development (Strategic Infrastructure) Act 2006 (No. 27 of 2006).

Subsection (3) was amended by s.247 of the Local Government Act 2001 (No. 37 of 2001), which, by the Local Government Act 2001 (Commencement) Order 2001 (S.I. No. 458 of 2001), came into effect on October 9, 2002.

Subsection (4) amended by s.15(b) of the Planning and Development (Strategic Infrastructure) Act 2006 (No. 27 of 2006).

Subsection (5) amended by s.15(c) of the Planning and Development (Strategic

Infrastructure) Act 2006 (No. 27 of 2006).

Subsection (13) amended by s.3 of the Public Service Superannuation (Miscellaneous Provisions) Act 2004 (No. 7 of 2004), which came into effect on March 25, 2004.

Section 247(b) of the Local Government Act 2001, amended the 2000 Act in s.106(3)(i) by the substitution in para.(a) of "6 additional members" for "5 additional members", and (ii) by the substitution in para.(b) of "more than 6 but not more than 12 additional members" for "more than 5 but not more than 10 additional members".

NOTE

This section introduces some changes concerning the appointment of ordinary members of the Board (s.7 of the 1983 Act). It specifically provides that there is to be seven ordinary members, while no specific number was described under the previous legislation. Each of these seven members are appointed following nomination from seven separate types of organisations, persons or bodies. Section 7 of the previous Act referred to only five such groups. The 2006 Act substituted new subs.(106)(1) and (2). The subsections alter the range of interested bodies from which members are appointed. The 2006 Act increased from one to two members, the number of members appointed from professions relating to physical planning, engineering and architecture and also two members from persons concerned with economic development, the promotion of and carrying out of development, etc. Under (c) two persons are appointed from bodies that represent local government and farming and also trade unions. Under the former section one person was appointed from both bodies representing local government and also from bodies representing rural and local community development. Under (d) two persons are appointed from bodies representing five different interests with three of these being new which are: the Irish language and arts and heritage; disabilities; and young people.

The groups are defined somewhat differently under the 2000 Act compared to the previous Planning Acts. Article 64 of the Planning Regulations 2001 as amended by thte 2006 Regulations sets out the prescribed organisations. Thus in relation to s.106(1)(a), the organisations are defined as relating to "physical planning, engineering and architecture" rather than simply "physical planning and development" under the previous provision. Also, in (c) the organisations are described as "concerned with economic development, the promotion of and carrying out of development, the provision of infrastructure or the development of land or otherwise connected with the construction industry". The repealed provision referred to those "concerned with the promotion of economic development or are representatives of either or both of the following, namely, persons carrying on the business of developing land or persons employed or engaged in or otherwise with the construction industry". Also, (d) describes "organisations which in the Minister's opinion are representative of the interests of local government", while the previous provision referred to "organisations which in his opinion are in relation to the community, concerned with the promotion of social, economic or general interests". The two new categories of bodies concern rural and local community development; and the promotion of the Irish language, the promotion of the arts and culture, or bodies which are representative of people with disability. A new provision provides that the Minister must prescribe at least two organisations for the purposes of each of the seven categories. Where the Minister invokes the additional members provision under s.104(2), the prescribed organisations have a limited role in the appointment (the provision somewhat differs from s.2A introduced under the 1998 Act which referred to not more than four (as opposed to five) additional members and between four and eight (as opposed to five to ten) concerning the input of the prescribed bodies).

The nomination process is the same as under the previous legislation, whereby when requested by the Minister, the organisation will nominate at least two candidates. The Minister must make the appointment from among such candidates, although this is subject to the qualification set out in subs.(6), where there is a failure to make nomination or the Minister does not accept those nominated. It is clear that the Minister therefore retains a discretion to refuse to make an appointment from among the nominees. In addition to the Minister making a further request to the organisation, the section introduces a new procedure whereby the Minister can request a specific committee established under subs.(7) to make a nomination following notification process.

Again, s.13(d) introduces a new disqualification criteria for ordinary members which applies also to the Chairperson.

The regulations for the procedure of committee requested to select candidates for ordinary member under subs.(7) is the same as for the committee for the chairperson under s.105(7). Articles 57–61 of the Planning Regulations therefore are equally applicable to the committee, while arts 62 and 63 concern its conduct. Article 65 of the Regulations also provides where a request is made to a prescribed organisation under subs.(4), the organisation must within eight weeks, select the number of candidates, inform the Minister of the names and reasons for each selected candidate, and send to the Minster their curriculum vitae and written consent of each candidate.

Appointment of deputy chairperson

107.—(1) The Minister shall appoint from among the ordinary members   1–131 a person to be the deputy chairperson and the appointment shall be for such period as shall be specified in the appointment.

(2) If at any time the deputy chairperson ceases to be an ordinary member of the Board, he or she shall thereupon cease to be the deputy chairperson.

(3) The deputy chairperson shall, in addition to his or her remuneration as an ordinary member, be paid by the Board such additional remuneration (if any) as the Minister, with the consent of the Minister for Finance, determines.

(4) The deputy chairperson may resign his or her office as deputy chairperson by letter addressed to the Minister and the resignation shall take effect on and from the date of the receipt of the letter by the Minister.

NOTE

This section concerns the appointment and functions of the deputy chairperson. This repeats verbatim the previous provision under s.8 of the 1983 Act.

Board's quorum, vacancies, etc.

108.—(1) The quorum for a meeting of the Board shall be 3.   1–132

(2) Subject to *subsection (1),* the Board may act notwithstanding a vacancy in the office of chairperson or deputy chairperson or among the ordinary members.

(3) Where a vacancy occurs or is due to occur in the office of chairperson or deputy chairperson or among the ordinary members, the Minister shall, as soon as may be, take steps to fill the vacancy.

(4)
- **(a)** Where, owing to the illness of the chairperson or of an ordinary member, or for any other reason, a sufficient number of members of the Board is not available to enable the Board effectively to perform its functions, the Minister may, as an interim measure, appoint from among the officers referred to in [*section 106(1)(e)*] or the employees of the Board, one or more persons to be an ordinary member.
- **(b)** A person shall not be appointed to be an ordinary member under this *subsection* for a term in excess of one year.

AMENDMENT HISTORY
Subsection (4)(a) amended by s.16 of the Planning and Development (Strategic Infrastructure) Act 2006 (No. 27 of 2006).

NOTE

This section concerns the quorum and vacancies for the Board. The section contains no change from s.12 of the 1983 Act. The quorum is set at three of the members of the Board (except where the additional members' power has been activated). The 2006 Act amended s.108(4) to provide that where the Board is not able to effectively performs its functions due to the unavailability of members, the Minister may make interim appointments to the Board. Such persons were formerly appointed from among civil servants under s.106(1)(g) but by virtue of this substitution, are appointed from among bodies relating to rural and local community development under s.106(1)(e).

CHAPTER II

Organisation, Staffing, etc.

Performance of Board

1–133   **109.—(1)** The Board shall supply the Minister with such information relating to the performance of its functions as he or she may from time to time request.

(2)
   (a) The Board shall conduct, at such intervals as it thinks fit or the Minister directs, reviews of its organisation and of the systems and procedures used by it in relation to appeals and referrals.
   (b) Where the Minister gives a direction under this *section,* the Board shall report to the Minister the results of the review conducted pursuant to the direction and shall comply with any directive which the Minister may, after consultation with the Board as regards those results, give in relation to all or any of the matters which were the subject of the review.

(3) The Board may make submissions to the Minister as regards any matter pertaining to its functions.

(4) The Minister may consult with the Board as regards any matter pertaining to the performance of—
   (a) the functions of the Board, or
   (b) the functions assigned to the Minister by or under this *Act* or by any other enactment or by any order, regulation or other instrument thereunder.

NOTE

This section concerns the co-ordination between An Bord Pleanála and the Minister. It reflects the greater accountability of the Board to the Minister concerning performance of its functions, which stem from the transfer of various functions under s.214 to the Board which were formerly performed by the Minister. While subs.(1) corresponds to the previous s.9(2) of the 1976 Act, the other provisions are newly introduced. The section reflects a two-way relationship whereby the Board may make submissions to the Minister regarding its functions. The section concerns the supply of information, review, directions and consultation with the Minister.

Chairperson to ensure efficient discharge of business of Board, etc.

110.—**[(1)** The chairperson and, subject to the overall direction of the   **1–134**
chairperson or where *subsection (1A)* applies, the deputy chairperson shall
each have the function of—

 (a) ensuring the efficient discharge of the business of the Board, and

 (b) arranging the distribution of the business of the Board among its
 members.]

(1A) The functions referred to in *subsection (1)* shall also fall to be
performed by the deputy chairperson where the chairperson is not available
or where the office of chairperson is vacant.]

[(1B) The chairperson may assign to any ordinary member any function
necessary to ensure the best or most efficient discharge of the business of the
Board.]

[(1C) The chairperson, or the deputy chairperson where the chairperson is
not available or where the office of chairperson is vacant, shall take all practical
steps to ensure that the organisation and disposition of the staff and resources
of the Board are such as to enable the Strategic Infrastructure Division to
discharge its business expeditiously.]

(2) Where the chairperson is of the opinion that the conduct of an ordinary
member has been such as to bring the Board into disrepute or has been
prejudicial to the effective performance by the Board of all or any one or more
of its functions, he or she may in his or her absolute discretion—

 (a) require the member of the Board to attend for interview and there
 interview the member privately and inform him or her of such
 opinion, or

 (b) where he or she considers it appropriate to do so, otherwise
 investigate the matter,

and, if he or she considers it appropriate to do so, report to the Minister the
result of the interview or investigation.

Amendment history

 Subsection (1) substituted by s.17 of the Planning and Development (Strategic
Infrastructure) Act 2006 (No. 27 of 2006).
 Subsection (1A) inserted by s.17 of the Planning and Development (Strategic
Infrastructure) Act 2006 (No. 27 of 2006).
 Subsection (1B) inserted by s.17 of the Planning and Development (Strategic
Infrastructure) Act 2006 (No. 27 of 2006).
 Subsection (1C) inserted by s.17 of the Planning and Development (Strategic
Infrastructure) Act 2006 (No. 27 of 2006).

NOTE

 This section sets out the function of the Chairperson who has the role of allocating the
business of the Board among its members, which may involve a determination under s.112
that the Board should act in divisions in a particular case. The Chairperson has control
regarding the internal working of the Board. This section repeats s.6 of the 1983 Act. The
2006 Act substituted a new s.110(1), the changes include eliminating the former statement
that the functions under subs.(1) would be performed by the deputy chairperson where the
chairperson was not available or vacant. The new subs.(1) states that the task of ensuring the
efficient discharge of business and arranging allocation of business lies with the chairperson.
It also adds the words "subject to the overall direction of the chairperson". Subsections (1A)

to (1C) are new and relate to the performance of such functions where the chairperson is unavailable and the assigning of functions to ordinary members.

Meetings and procedure of Board

1–135   **111.—(1)** The Board shall hold such and so many meetings as may be necessary for the performance of its functions.

(2) The chairperson and each ordinary member at a meeting of the Board shall have a vote.

(3) At a meeting of the Board—

    (a) the chairperson shall, if present, be chairperson of the meeting,

    (b) if the chairperson is not present the deputy chairperson shall, if present, be chairperson of the meeting, and

    (c) if neither the chairperson nor the deputy chairperson is present, the ordinary members who are present shall choose one of their number to be chairperson of the meeting.

(4) Every question at a meeting of the Board relating to the performance of its functions shall be determined by a majority of votes of the members present and, in the event that voting is equally divided, the person who is chairperson of the meeting shall have a casting vote.

(5)

    (a) Subject to this *Act,* and to any regulations made thereunder, and subject also to any other enactment or order, regulation or other instrument thereunder, which regulates or otherwise affects the procedure of the Board, the Board shall regulate its own procedure and business.

    (b) The Minister may require the Board to keep him or her informed of the arrangements made under this *subsection* for the regulation of its procedure and business.

(6)

    (a) Subject to *paragraphs (b) and (c),* the Board may perform any of its functions through or by any member of the Board or other person who has been duly authorised by the Board in that behalf.

    (b) *Paragraph (a)* shall be construed as enabling a member of the Board finally to determine points of detail relating to a decision on a particular case if the case to which an authorisation under that *paragraph* relates has been considered at a meeting of the Board prior to the giving of the authorisation and that determination shall conform to the terms of that authorisation.

    (c) *Paragraph (a)* shall not be construed as enabling the Board to authorise a person who is not a member of the Board finally to determine any particular case with which the Board is concerned.

(7) The Board shall arrange to keep a written record of all its decisions including the names of those present at a meeting of the Board and the number of those persons who vote for or against those decisions.

NOTE

This section concerns the conduct of meeting of the Board and its procedure. The Board possesses control over how it conducts its internal procedure, though subject to existing regulations and keeping the Minister informed. Voting is by a majority of members present, with the Chairperson having a casting vote where there is a tie. This section corresponds to s.11 of the 1983 Act, with the addition of subs.(7), which requires the Board to keep a written record of its meetings. This is in line with a general policy of increased transparency. The Freedom of Information Act applies to An Bord Pleanála.

Divisions of Board

112.—**(1)** Whenever the Minister or the chairperson considers that, for the   **1–136** speedy dispatch of the business of the Board, it is expedient that the Board should act by divisions, he or she may direct accordingly, and until that direction is revoked—

> **(a)** the chairperson shall assign to each division the business to be transacted by it, and
>
> **(b)** for the purpose of the business so assigned to it, each division shall have all the functions of the Board.

(2) A division of the Board shall consist of not less than 3 members of the Board.

(3) The chairperson, or in his or her absence, a person acting as chairperson of a meeting of a division of the Board, may at any stage before a decision is made, transfer the consideration of any appeal or referral from the division to a meeting of all available members of the Board, where the chairperson considers the appeal or referral to be of particular complexity or significance.

[(4) This section is without prejudice to *section 112A*.**]**

AMENDMENT HISTORY

Subsection (4) inserted by s.18 of the Planning and Development (Strategic Infrastructure) Act 2006 (No. 27 of 2006).

NOTE

This constitutes a new provision and makes explicit the power of the Board to act in division with the business being allocated by the Chairperson. This means that in relation to a particular appeal or referral, certain issues involved can be divided up between members of the Board. Even where the division has only three members., the quorum requirement under s.108 of three applies, so all members of the division would need to be present. Both the Minister or the Chairperson may at their discretion direct that the Board should act by division, though only in the interest of the speedy dispatch of business. The 2006 Act amended that such section is without prejudice to the new s.112A concerning the strategic infrastructure division.

[Strategic Infrastructure Division

112A.—**(1)** A division of the Board which shall be known as the Strategic   **1–137** Infrastructure Division is established on the commencement of *section 19 of the Planning and Development (Strategic Infrastructure) Act 2006.*

(2) That division is in addition to any division for the time being constituted under *section 112.*

(3) The Strategic Infrastructure Division—

> **(a)** shall, subject to *subsections (8) and (9),* determine any matter falling to be determined by the Board under this Act in relation to strategic infrastructure development, and

(b) shall determine any other matter falling to be determined by the Board under this or any other enactment, including any class of appeals or referrals, that the chairperson or the deputy chairperson may from time to time assign to it.

(4) For the purpose of business of either of the foregoing kinds, the Strategic Infrastructure Division shall have all the functions of the Board.

(5) The Strategic Infrastructure Division shall consist of the chairperson and the deputy chairperson and 3 other ordinary members nominated by the chairperson to be, for the time being, members of the Division.

(6) The chairperson may authorise any other ordinary member to act in place of any member of the Strategic Infrastructure Division referred to in *subsection (5)* where the latter member is absent.

(7) The quorum for a meeting of the Strategic Infrastructure Division shall be 3.

(8) Either—

(a) the chairperson or, in his or her absence, the deputy chairperson, or

(b) a person acting as chairperson of a meeting of the Division, may, at any stage before a decision is made by the Division, transfer the consideration of any matter from the Strategic Infrastructure Division to a meeting of all available members of the Board where he or she considers the matter to be of particular complexity or significance.

(9) The chairperson may, if he or she considers that the issues arising in respect of any particular case of strategic infrastructure development, or any particular class or classes of such case, are not of sufficient complexity or significance as to warrant that case, or that class or those classes of case, being dealt with by the Strategic Infrastructure Division, transfer the consideration of that case, or that class or those classes of case, to another division or part of the Board.]

AMENDMENT HISTORY

Subsection (4) inserted by s.19 of the Planning and Development (Strategic Infrastructure) Act 2006 (No. 27 of 2006).

NOTE

This section concerns the establishment and composition of the strategic infrastructure division of the Board which came into being on January 31, 2007, when the section was commenced. It deals with all matters falling within the definition of strategic infrastructure development under s.2 of the 2000 Act, as inserted by s.6 of the 2006 Act. The infrastructure division is a permanent division which is in addition to divisions of the Board which may be established under s.112. The division deals with all strategic infrastructure applications and any other appeals or referrals which the chairperson may from time to time assign. The division is to comprise five members: the chairperson, deputy chairperson and three nominated ordinary members. The quorum is three and where ordinary members are absent, other ordinary members can be authorised to act instead. Subsection (8) allows the chairperson or other authorised person to transfer consideration of any matter to a meeting of all available members of the Board, where it is of particular complexity or significance. There is no guidance as to when a matter may be considered of such particular significance or complexity and so it is a matter for the discretion of the chairperson. There are no limits as to when the transfer can take place or the scope of the matter to be transferred. A matter can therefore be transferred at any time prior to the determination of the application. It appears that the matter for consideration may be a particular aspect of the application or could relate to the entire application. Subsection (9) is the reverse of subs.(8) insofar as it allows the chairperson to transfer a case being dealt with by the strategic infrastructure division to another division on the basis that it is not of sufficient complexity or significance. Again there is no guidance as to the meaning of "sufficient complexity or significance" and so the assessment of such is for the discretion of the chairperson. The circumstances where a strategic infrastructure application is not considered of "sufficient complexity or significance" is unlikely to apply to Seventh Schedule development as the Board would have already served a notice under s.37A(2) stating its opinion that the development would be of strategic economic or social importance to the State/region etc., would contribute substantially to the fulfilment of any of the objectives in the National Spatial Strategy or the development would have a significant effect on the area of more than one planning authority. One circumstance in which such transfer could occur is where there was a change in circumstances subsequent to the service of notice by the Board under s.37A. The wording refers to "sufficient complexity" or "significance" which means that an application could be significant though not of such sufficient complexity to be dealt with by such division. The wording of subs.(9) differs from subs.(8) in that it refers to the transfer of consideration of "that case" (rather than transfer of "any matter" under subs.(8)) which implies that the entire application/referral is to be transferred. Notwithstanding that there is no reference in subs.(9) as to when the transfer may take place (subs.(8) says "at any stage"), the absence of any restriction appears to mean that the transfer can take place at any time.

Prohibition on disclosure of information relating to functions of Board

113.—(1) No person shall, without the consent of the Board (which may be given to the person, subject to or without conditions, as regards any information, as regards particular information or as regards information of a particular class or description), disclose—   **1–138**

    (a) any information obtained by him or her while serving as a member or employee of, or consultant or adviser to, the Board or as a person whose services are availed of by the Board by virtue of *section 120(2) or 122,* or

    (b) any information so obtained relative to the business of the Board or to the performance of its functions.

(2) A person who contravenes *subsection (1)* shall be guilty of an offence.

(3) Nothing in *subsection (1)* shall prevent—

    (a) disclosure of information in a report made to the Board or in a report made by or on behalf of the Board to the Minister,

    (b) disclosure of information by any person in the course of and in accordance with the functions of his or her office,

    (c) disclosure of information in accordance with the *Freedom of Information Act, 1997,* or

    (d) disclosure of information in accordance with the *European Communities Act, 1972 (Access to Information on the Environment) Regulations, 1998,* and any regulations amending or replacing those regulations.

NOTE

This section imposes a duty of confidentiality upon Board members in relation to information acquired during the course of their functions. A similar prohibition on disclosure of information was contained in s.13 of the 1983 Act. Breach amounts to a criminal offence. This would appear to import the general provisions for criminal offences under the Act under ss.156–158. Curiously however, these sections make no mention of an offence under s.113(2), although reference is made to other offences under the Act. The offence was described as a summary offence (with a fine not exceeding £1000) under the previous s.13(2), as amended, but no such mention is made in the present provision. The section also adds that it should not be construed as affecting disclosure under freedom of information measures. An Bord Pleanála has produced a specific freedom of information request application form. Each person has a right to access to records held by the Board; correction of personal information relating to oneself held by the Board where it is inaccurate, incomplete or misleading; and access to reasons for decisions made by the Board directly affecting oneself. Also within the scope of the Acts are all records relating to personal information held by the Board irrespective of when created; all other records created from the date on which the Freedom of Information Act comes into effect (April 21, 1998); and any other records necessary to the understanding of a current record. The right of access does not apply to "exempt records" which are specified in detail in the Acts. The Acts do not apply to records already publicly available. For example, an appeal determined by the Board is available for purchase/inspection under the Board's public access system. The Board has produced a *Code of Conduct for Board Members Certain Employees and Certain Other Persons* on January 20, 2003, para.6 of which concerns disclosure of information. Paragraph 6.3 provides information should not be given by any Board member or employee to any party, observer or other member of the public, concerning the names of the Board member or the Inspector dealing with particular cases; specific information in relation to Board meetings; attendance at future Board meetings; future leave arrangements of Board members; the contents of an Inspector's recommendation/report; or the terms of a Board direction, during the currency of an appeal or referral, until they are generally available in accordance with proper procedures.

Prohibition of certain communications in relation to appeals, etc.

1–139   **114.—(1)** Any person who communicates with the chairperson, an ordinary member, an employee of, or consultant or adviser to, the Board or a person whose services are availed of by the Board by virtue of *section 120(2) or 122* for the purpose of influencing improperly the consideration of an appeal or referral or a decision of the Board as regards any matter shall be guilty of an offence.

(2) If the chairperson or an ordinary member or an employee of, or consultant or adviser to, the Board or a person whose services are availed of by the Board by virtue of *section 120(2) or 122,* becomes of the opinion that a communication is in contravention of *subsection (1),* it shall be his or her duty not to entertain the communication further and shall disclose the communication to the Board.

NOTE

This section creates a new offence of communicating with the Board in order to improperly influence its considerations. A similar prohibition was contained in s.14 of the 1983 Act although it did not amount to a offence. The section also broadens the nature of the prohibition to go beyond actual Board members to also include communications to employees, consultants, advisors or person who have provided services to the Board. Such person who receives the communication, in addition to not entertaining it, must also positively disclose the communication to the Board.

Indemnification of members and employees of Board and other persons

115.—Where the Board is satisfied that a member of the Board, an employee   1–140
of the Board or a person whose services are provided to the Board under
section 120(2), 122 or 124(1) has discharged his or her duties in relation to the
functions of the Board in a bona fide manner, it shall indemnify the member,
employee or person against all actions or claims howsoever arising in respect
of the discharge by him or her of his or her duties.

NOTE

This is a new section which involves a statutory duty to indemnify certain claims
against persons who have acted in a bona fide manner on behalf of the Board. The Board
nevertheless may at its own discretion determine whether the duties were performed in a
bona fide manner. The Board may still be held vicariously liable for actions of such persons
under tort law.

Grants to Board

116.—There may, subject to such conditions, if any, as the Minister thinks   1–141
proper, be paid to the Board in each financial year out of moneys provided by
the Oireachtas a grant or grants of such amount or amounts as the Minister,
with the consent of the Minister for Finance and after consultation with the
Board in relation to its programme of expenditure for that year, may fix.

NOTE

This section concerns the financing of An Bord Pleanála and corresponds to s.7 of the
1976 Act.

Accounts and audits of Board

117.—**(1)** The Board shall keep in such form as may be approved by the   1–142
Minister, after consultation with the Minister for Finance, all proper and usual
accounts of all moneys received or expended by it.

(2) Accounts kept under this *section* shall be submitted by the Board to the
Comptroller and Auditor General for audit at such times as the Minister shall
direct and, when audited shall, together with the report of the Comptroller and
Auditor General, be presented to the Minister who shall cause copies to be
laid before each House of the Oireachtas.

NOTE

This section concerns the keeping of account by An Bord Pleanála. The section reflects
the financial accountability of the Board to the Minister and corresponds to the former
provision of s.8 of the 1976 Act.

Annual report and information to Minister

118.—The Board shall, not later than the 30th day of June in each year,   1–143
make a report to the Minister of its proceedings during the preceding year and
the Minister shall cause copies of the report to be laid before each House of
the Oireachtas.

NOTE

This section concerns the making of an Annual Report by An Bord Pleanála.

The date before which the report must be made has been brought forward from September 30 (as under s.9(1) of the 1976 Act) to June 30. Among the matters which must be included in the report are, under s.124(2), a statement of the names of the persons engaged as consultants or advisors by the Board during the year to which the report relates; s.126(6), a statement of the number of appeals and referrals that it has determined within the 18-week period or other period prescribed by the Minister, and such information as to the time taken to determine appeals and referrals as the Minister may direct. Its Annual Report for 2002 is dated June 23, 2003.

Superannuation of members of Board

1–144   **119.—(1)** The Minister may, with the consent of the Minister for Finance, make a scheme or schemes for the granting of pensions, gratuities or other allowances to or in respect of the chairperson and ordinary members ceasing to hold office.

(2) A scheme under this *section* may provide that the termination of the appointment of the chairperson or of an ordinary member during that person's term of office shall not preclude the award to him or her under the scheme of a pension, gratuity or other allowance.

(3) The Minister may, with the consent of the Minister for Finance, amend a scheme made by him or her under this *section*.

(4) If any dispute arises as to the claim of any person to, or the amount of, any pension, gratuity, or allowance payable in pursuance of a scheme under this *section,* the dispute shall be submitted to the Minister who shall refer it to the Minister for Finance, whose decision shall be final.

(5) A scheme under this *section* shall be carried out by the Board in accordance with its terms.

(6) No pension, gratuity or other allowance shall be granted by the Board to or in respect of any person referred to in *subsection (1)* ceasing to hold office otherwise than in accordance with a scheme under this *section.*

(7) Every scheme made under this *section* shall be laid before each House of the Oireachtas as soon as may be after it is made and if either such House, within the next 21 days on which that House has sat after the scheme is laid before it, passes a resolution annulling the scheme, the scheme shall be annulled accordingly, but without prejudice to the validity of anything previously done thereunder.

NOTE

This section concerns the superannuation and pension schemes for former Board members and re-enacts s.9 of the 1983 Act.

Employees of Board

1–145   **120.—(1)** The Board shall appoint such and so many persons to be employees of the Board as the Board, subject to the approval of the Minister, given with the consent of the Minister for Finance, as to the number and kind of those employees, from time to time considers appropriate, having regard to the need to ensure that an adequate number of staff are competent in the Irish language so as to be able to provide service through Irish as well as English.

(2) The Board may employ a person in a part-time capacity to be remunerated by the payment of fees in such amounts as the Board may, with the approval of the Minister, given with the consent of the Minister for Finance, from time to time determine.

(3) An employee of the Board shall hold his or her employment on such terms and conditions as the Board, subject to the approval of the Minister, from time to time determines.

(4) There shall be paid by the Board to its employees out of moneys at its disposal such remuneration and allowances as the Board, subject to the approval of the Minister, with the consent of the Minister for Finance, from time to time determines.

NOTE

This section concerns appointment of employees of the Board. It re-enacts with minor changes s.10 of the 1976 Act. The only change is in the first subsection with the addition of the last clause, "having regard to the need to ensure that an adequate number of staff are competent in the Irish language so as to be able to provide service through Irish as well as English". This new clause simply reflects that the need to ensure adequate service in the Irish language was one factor which the legislator deemed it appropriate to emphasise.

Superannuation of employees of Board

121.—(1) The Board shall prepare and submit to the Minister for his or   **1–146** her approval, a scheme or schemes for the granting of pensions, gratuities and other allowances on retirement or death to or in respect of such whole-time employees of the Board as it considers appropriate.

(2) The Board may, at any time, prepare and submit to the Minister a scheme amending a scheme under this *section.*

(3) Where a scheme is submitted to the Minister pursuant to this *section,* the Minister may, with the consent of the Minister for Finance, approve the scheme without modification or with such modification (whether by way of addition, omission or variation) as the Minister shall, with such consent, think proper.

(4) A scheme submitted to the Minister under this *section* shall, if approved of by the Minister, with the consent of the Minister for Finance, be carried out by the Board in accordance with its terms.

(5) A scheme approved of under this *section* shall fix the time and conditions of retirement for all persons to or in respect of whom pensions, gratuities or other allowances are payable under the scheme, and different times and conditions may be fixed in respect of different classes of persons.

(6) If any dispute arises as to the claim of any person to, or the amount of, any pension, gratuity or other allowance payable in pursuance of a scheme under this *section,* the dispute shall be submitted to the Minister who shall refer it to the Minister for Finance, whose decision shall be final.

(7) Every scheme approved of under this *section* shall be laid before each House of the Oireachtas as soon as may be after it is approved of and if either House within the next 21 days on which that House has sat after the scheme is laid before it, passes a resolution annulling the scheme, the scheme shall be annulled accordingly, but without prejudice to the validity of anything previously done thereunder.

NOTE

This section concerns the drawing up of a scheme for superannuation of employees of the Board, which is submitted to the Minister, and also providing for dispute resolution in case of disputes. It re-enacts s.11 of the 1976 Act.

Provision of services by Minister to Board

1–147   **122.—(1)** For the purposes of enabling the Board to perform its functions, the Minister may provide services (including services of staff) to the Board on such terms and conditions (including payment for such services) as may be agreed and the Board may avail of such services.

(2) The Board may provide services (including services of staff) to the Minister on such terms and conditions (including payment for such services) as may be agreed and the Minister may avail of such services.

NOTE

This section allows both the Board and the Minister to provide services to each other in the performance of their functions. It would appear to be for a temporary measure to be given effect to if a contingency arises. Where the Minister provides services to the Board which includes the supply of staff, then by virtue of s.102(2), the seal of the Board can be authenticated by the signature of such person. Section 21(3) of the 1976 Act envisaged, as an interim measure, the Minister making available services to the Board, pending the Board making sufficient appointments. This former provision reflected the fact that the Board had only just been established and the provision of such services would be made until the Board had fully established itself. It therefore differs from s.122, which concerns an ongoing relationship between the Minister and the Board. This is further reflected by the fact that the Board itself may provide such services to the Minister.

Membership of either House of the Oireachtas, etc.

1–148   **123.—(1)** Where a person who is an employee of the Board is nominated as a member of Seanad Éireann or for election to either House of the Oireachtas or the European Parliament, or is regarded pursuant to *Part XIII of the Second Schedule to the European Parliament Elections Act, 1997,* as having been elected to that Parliament to fill a vacancy, or becomes a member of a local authority, he or she shall stand seconded from employment by the Board and shall not be paid by, or be entitled to receive from, the Board any remuneration or allowances—

   (a) in case he or she is nominated as a member of Seanad Éireann in respect of the period commencing on his or her acceptance of the nomination and ending when he or she ceases to be a member of that House,

   (b) in case he or she is nominated for election to either such House or to the European Parliament, or is regarded as having been elected to the European Parliament, in respect of the period commencing on his or her nomination or appointment and ending when he or she ceases to be a member of that House or Parliament or fails to be elected or withdraws his or her candidature, as may be appropriate, or

(c) in case he or she becomes a member of a local authority, in respect of the period commencing on his or her becoming a member of the local authority and ending when he or she ceases to be a member of that authority.

(2) A person who is for the time being entitled under the Standing Orders of either House of the Oireachtas to sit therein or is a member of the European Parliament shall, while he or she is so entitled or is such a member, be disqualified from becoming an employee of the Board.

(3) A person who is for the time being a member of a local authority shall, while holding office as such member, be disqualified from becoming an employee of the Board.

NOTE

This section is to ensure that Board employees cannot hold certain political positions, in the interests of independence and confidentiality. It largely re-enacts s.12 of the 1976 Act. Section 147 requires Board employees to make a declaration of disclosure of interests in business, land, etc.

Consultants and advisers to Board

124.—(1) The Board may from time to time engage such consultants or   **1–149**
advisers as it considers necessary for the performance of its functions and any fees due to a consultant or adviser engaged pursuant to this *section* shall be paid by the Board out of moneys at its disposal.

(2) The Board shall include in each report made under *section 118* a statement of the names of the persons (if any) engaged pursuant to this *section* during the year to which the report relates.

NOTE

This section allows the Board to engage consultants or advisors in performing its functions. It appears that such consultants or advisors can be engaged in conducting a particular appeal or referral or more generally. This section is a truncated version of s.13 of the 1976 Act, which required, inter alia, that the Board maintain a list of persons willing to act as consultants or advisors. This has not been re-enacted under the 2000 Act. The s.118 report refers to the Annual Report of the Board in relation its proceedings, which must be placed before the Minister not later than June 30 each year.

CHAPTER III

Appeal Procedures, etc.

[Appeals, referrals and applications with which the Board is concerned

125.—This Chapter shall apply—   **1–150**
   (a) to appeals and referrals to the Board, and
   (b) to the extent provided, to applications made to the Board under *section 37E* and any other matter with which the Board may be concerned, but shall not apply to appeals under *section 182(4)(b)*.]

AMENDMENT HISTORY

Substituted by s.20 of the Planning and Development (Strategic Infrastructure) Act 2006 (No. 27 of 2006).

NOTE

This section provides that the provisions in Ch.III generally apply to appeals and referrals before An Bord Pleanála. The 2006 Act amended the section to provide that the provisions of Ch.III, also apply, to the extent provided, to strategic infrastructure applications under s.37E and other matters. The provisions of Ch.III do not apply to appeals under s.182(4)(b), where an owner of land refuses to give consent to a local authority to lay cables, wires or pipelines and any ancillary apparatus over or under his the land, and whereby the local authority can appeal this refusal to An Bord Pleanála.

Other appeals under the Act which An Bord Pleanála can hear include: s.44(6), appeals against the revocation or modification of a planning permission; s.45(3), appeals against the acquisition of land for open space; s.46(6), appeals against the removal or alteration of a structure or the discontinuance of a use; s.88(5), appeals against a notice requiring measures to be taken relating to a structure or other land in an area of Special Planning Control; s.169(6), appeals against the making of a planning scheme in a strategic development zone (SDZ); s.171(2), appeals against the revocation of a planning scheme in a strategic development zone (SDZ); s.182(4), appeals by a local authority against the refusal of consent by an owner/occupier to lay cables, wires and pipelines on his/her property; s.207(5), appeals against the creation of a public right of way; s.254(6), appeals in relation to licensing of an appliance, apparatus, structure, cable or other matter on a public road; and s.261(9), appeals in relation to the imposition, restating, addition, or modification of conditions of certain quarries.

Meanwhile, referrals under the 2000 Planning Act include: s.5(3)(b) referral where a planning authority fails to issue a declaration within four weeks of the due date of a question as to what is or is not development or exempted development; s.5(4), referral by a planning authority of a question as to what is or is not development or exempted development; s.34(5), referral for points of detail relating to a grant of permission in default of agreement between the planning authority and the developer; s.37(5), referral of a dispute as to whether an application for permission is for the same development/description as one on appeal; s.57(8), referral for review by the Board by a person to whom a declaration under subs.(57)(3) or a declaration reviewed under subs.(57)(7) has been issued by a planning authority relating to a protected or proposed protected structure; s.96(5), referral of a dispute relating to an agreement concerning compliance with the social and affordable housing requirements; and s.193(2), referral of a dispute or question as to whether a new structure replaces a demolished or destroyed structure.

Other applications under the 2000 Planning Act include: s.37(6), concerning an application by an adjoining owner for leave to appeal a decision of a planning authority on a planning application; s.73(3), for application by a planning authority for consent to acquire a protected structure; s.83(3), an application by a planning authority for consent to acquire a structure or other land in an architectural conservation area; s.172(3), a request by an applicant/intending applicant for planning permission for exemption from a requirement to prepare an EIS in relation to a planning application; s.173(3), a request by a person to scope an EIS where the person is required to submit an EIS to the Board; s.175(3), for approval of a development by or on behalf of a local authority requiring EIA; and s.175(8), an application by a local authority for exemption from a requirement to prepare an EIS. Under art.117 of the 2001 Regulations, a request may be made by a local authority to scope an EIS where the authority is required to submit an EIS to the Board in relation to proposed development by or on behalf of the authority. Also under art.120(3), application to determine whether sub-threshold development proposed to be carried out by a local authority would be likely to have significant effects on the environment; s.203(2), for submission by a planning authority for confirmation of a special amenity order; s.214, concerning an application by a local authority for authorisation of compulsory acquisition of lands under various enactments (including an application by a sanitary authority for a provisional order under the Water Supplies Act 1942); s.215, concerning an application by a roads authority for approval of a proposed road development/road scheme (includes EIS scoping and sub-threshold directions as in arts 117 and 120(3) above); and s.226(1), in relation to an application by a local authority for approval of proposed development wholly or partly on the foreshore which requires environmental impact development.

Duty and objective of Board in relation to appeals and referrals

126.—**(1)** It shall be the duty of the Board to ensure that appeals and referrals **1–151** are disposed of as expeditiously as may be and, for that purpose, to take all such steps as are open to it to ensure that, in so far as is practicable, there are no avoidable delays at any stage in the determination of appeals and referrals.

(2) Without prejudice to the generality of *subsection (1)* and subject to *subsections (3), (4) and (5)*, it shall be the objective of the Board to ensure that every appeal or referral is determined within—

  (a) a period of 18 weeks beginning on the date of receipt by the Board of the appeal or referral, or

  (b) such other period as the Minister may prescribe in accordance with *subsection (4)*, either generally or in respect of a particular class or classes of appeals or referrals.

(3)

  (a) Where it appears to the Board that it would not be possible or appropriate, because of the particular circumstances of an appeal or referral or because of the number of appeals and referrals which have been submitted to the Board, to determine the appeal or referral within the period referred to in *paragraph (a)* or (b) of *subsection (2)*, as the case may be, the Board shall, by notice in writing served on the parties to the appeal or referral before the expiration of that period, inform those parties of the reasons why it would not be possible or appropriate to determine the appeal or referral within that period and shall specify the date before which the Board intends that the appeal or referral shall be determined, and shall also serve such notice on each person who has made submissions or observations to the Board in relation to the appeal or referral.

  (b) Where a notice has been served under *paragraph (a)*, the Board shall take all such steps as are open to it to ensure that the appeal or referral is determined before the date specified in the notice.

(4) The Minister may by regulations vary the period referred to in *subsection (2)(a)* either generally or in respect of a particular class or classes of appeals or referrals where it appears to him or her to be necessary, by virtue of exceptional circumstances, to do so and for so long as such regulations are in force this section shall be construed and have effect in accordance therewith.

(5) Where the Minister considers it to be necessary or expedient that—

  (a) appeals from decisions (of a specified class or classes) of planning authorities under section 34, or

  (b) referrals of a specified class or classes,

relating to development of a class or classes of special strategic, economic or social importance to the State, be determined as expeditiously as is consistent with proper planning and sustainable development, the Minister may give a direction to the Board to give priority to the class or classes of appeals or referrals concerned, and the Board shall comply with such direction.

(6) The Board shall include in each report made under section 118 a statement of the number of appeals and referrals that it has determined within a period referred to in *paragraph (a)* or (b) of *subsection (2)* and such other information as to the time taken to determine appeals and referrals as the Minister may direct.

NOTE

This section imposes a general duty on the Board to act expeditiously in disposing of an appeal or referral. This section re-enacts, with certain changes, s.2 of the 1992 Act. In addition to the general duty of expedition, it is an objective of the Board that a determination is reached within 18 weeks from the receipt of the appeal or referral (although this time limit may be varied by the Minister). The use of the word "objective" indicates that it is not a mandatory requirement that the matter be determined within 18 weeks. There is no procedure for a default decision for failure to make the decision within the period. The previous time limit prescribed under s.2 of the 1992 Act was four months. One qualification to this time limit is under s.37(6) of the 2000 Act, in relation to appeals to the Board by persons who have an interest in the land adjoining the land for which permission has been granted. In such instance the matter must be determined within 14 weeks. For the Board to depart from the general time constraint, it must have formed the view that it was not possible or appropriate to determine the matter in such time, and must give notice to the parties involved of its view, also specifying the date by which it will make the determination.

There is further provision for Ministerial intervention in the case of appeals from a decision of a planning authority under s.34 or in relation to certain classes of development of special importance to the State, whereby the Minister may direct the Board to give priority to such matters. The s.118 report refers to the Annual Report of the Board to the Minister. Appeals under other Acts include s.7(1)(a) of the Building Control Act 1990 concerning an applicant who is dissatisfied with the decision of a building control authority relating to a dispensation from, or relaxation of, any requirement of building Regulations. Also, s.7(1)(b) concerns an applicant who is dissatisfied with the decision of a building control authority relating to an application for a fire safety certificate. Under s.8 of the Water Pollution Acts 1977 and 1990, there is an appeal by a person in relation to a grant, refusal, modification or revocation of a licence to discharge effluent to waters. Under s.20, there is an appeal in relation to a licence to discharge to a sewer by an occupier of the premises concerning the revocation or modification of, or attachment of conditions to, the licence, or a person whose application for the licence is refused. Section 34 of the Air Pollution Act 1987 provides for an appeal by a person in relation to a grant or refusal of a licence under s.32 or a revised licence under s.33 of the Act to discharge emissions to the atmosphere.

Provisions as to making of appeals and referrals

1–152   **127.—(1)** An appeal or referral shall—

    (a) be made in writing,

    (b) state the name and address of the appellant or person making the referral and of the person, if any, acting on his or her behalf,

    (c) state the subject matter of the appeal or referral,

    (d) state in full the grounds of appeal or referral and the reasons, considerations and arguments on which they are based,

    (e) in the case of an appeal under s.37 by a person who made submissions or observations in accordance with the permission regulations, be accompanied by the acknowledgement by the planning authority of receipt of the submissions or observations,

    (f) be accompanied by such fee (if any) as may be payable in respect of such appeal or referral in accordance with section 144, and

    (g) be made within the period specified for making the appeal or referral.

(2)

    (a) An appeal or referral which does not comply with the requirements of *subsection (1)* shall be invalid.

    (b) The requirement of *subsection (1)(d)* shall apply whether or not the appellant or person making the referral requests, or proposes to request, in accordance with section 134, an oral hearing of the appeal or referral.

(3) Without prejudice to section 131 or 134, an appellant or person making the referral shall not be entitled to elaborate in writing upon, or make further submissions in writing in relation to, the grounds of appeal or referral stated in the appeal or referral or to submit further grounds of appeal or referral and any such elaboration, submissions or further grounds of appeal or referral that is or are received by the Board shall not be considered by it.

(4)

    (a) An appeal or referral shall be accompanied by such documents, particulars or other information relating to the appeal or referral as the appellant or person making the referral considers necessary or appropriate.

    (b) Without prejudice to section 132, the Board shall not consider any documents, particulars or other information submitted by an appellant or person making the referral other than the documents, particulars or other information which accompanied the appeal or referral.

(5) An appeal or referral shall be made—

    (a) by sending the appeal or referral by prepaid post to the Board,

    (b) by leaving the appeal or referral with an employee of the Board at the offices of the Board during office hours (as determined by the Board), or

    (c) by such other means as may be prescribed.

NOTE

This section concerns the correct form in which appeals or referrals must be made to the Board. This must be strictly complied with. The seven matters enlisted in subs.(1) are mandatory, so failure to include any of them will render the application invalid. See *O'Reilly v Wicklow County Council*, unreported, High Court, Quirke J., November 22, 2006. Substantial compliance may however be sufficient. See *Murphy v Cobh Town Council*, unreported, High Court, McMenamin J., October 26, 2006. This mandatory obligation follows from the unqualified statement in subs.(2) that an appeal or referral which does not comply with the specified requirement "shall" be invalid. All of the requirements must be satisfied within the relevant period for making the appeal or referral.

While under subs.(1)(a) the appeal must be in writing, there is no requirement that appeal be contained in one document. See *O'Connor v An Bord Pleanála*, unreported, High Court, Finlay Geoghegan J., January 24, 2008. The information can be contained within a series of documents and submitted in an informal manner. See *O'Reilly v Wicklow County Council*, unreported, High Court, Quirke J., November 22, 2006.

Under subs.(1)(b) as regards the name of the appellant or person making the referral, it appears that the person named must be the person entitled to make the appeal or referral and not the name of an agent. While an agent can clearly lodge or prepare the appeal on behalf of such person, the actual name of the appellant cannot be the agent. See by analogy with application for judicial review where an agent or a member of consulting engineers who had been retained by an applicant for planning permission, could not attribute to himself the interests of the applicant for permission. See *Lennon v Limerick County Council*, unreported, High Court, Laffoy J., April 3, 2006. With respect to accuracy of the name, in *Kenney Construction v An Bord Pleanála*, unreported, High Court, O'Neill J., February 10, 2005, the misdescription of a third party appellant by the omission of the word Limited was held not to render the appeal invalid. As regards, the requirement to state the address, in *O'Connor v An Bord Pleanála*, unreported, High Court, Finlay Geoghegan J., January 24, 2008, it was held this requirement was mandatory and not merely directory. However, while the letter of appeal did not state the address it expressly referred to and enclosed the acknowledgement from the planning authority of receipt of submissions/observations. This acknowledgment referred to the address of the appellant and so this constituted compliance with s.127(1)(b).

Under subs.(1)(c) the subject matter of the appeal or referral, in the case of an appeal of a decision of the planning authority in an application for planning permission, this would appear to be the decision of the planning authority or the application for permission which was the subject of such decision.

Under subs.(1)(d) the requirement to state the grounds of appeal in full must be read in the light of subs.(3) which prohibits an appellant or person making the referral in elaborating in writing or making further submissions or submitting further grounds of appeal or referral. However, under s.4(a) a person can submit other documents, particulars or other information which may accompany the appeal or referral. In *O'Reilly v Wicklow County Council*, unreported, High Court, Quirke J., November 22, 2006, Quirke J. rejected that a section 5 referral did not comply with s.127 insofar as it did not state in full the grounds of referral and the reasons, considerations and arguments on which it was based. He considered while the documentation submitted to the Board was poor quality, the Board was prepared to carry out a search of the documents to discover the "reasons, considerations and argument". While the requirements of s.127 were mandatory, the grounds did not have to be contained in a single document but could be within a series of documents and submitted in an informal manner.

Under subs.(1)(e) only a person who made submissions or observations has an entitlement to appeal. Therefore such a person must also submit the acknowledgement by the planning authority of receipt of submissions or observations. Under art.29(2) of the 2001 Regulations, the planning authority must acknowledge in writing the receipt of submissions or observations as soon as may be. The acknowledgment therefore refers to that issued under art.29 and not a letter informing a person of a third party appeal under art.69. See *Murphy v Cobh Town Council*, unreported, High Court, McMenamin J., October 26, 2006, where the subsequent letter giving notice of the appeal which was submitted with the appeal referred to previous communications from which it could readily be inferred that submissions or observations had been made. Where the planning authority had issued letters of similar layout and the appellant had mistakenly lodged the letter, it was held there was substantial compliance as no prejudice had occurred save of a technical or trivial way. It may be noted that by virtue of the 2001 Regulations, as amended by the 2006 Regulations, there is now a prescribed form for acknowledgement of receipt of a submission or observation at Form 3 contained in Sch.3. As regards the statement that an appeal or referral be "accompanied by" the acknowledgement, in *O'Connor v An Bord Pleanála*, unreported, High Court, Finlay Geoghegan J., January 24, 2008, it was held that these the words did not necessarily indicate that an acknowledgement would be excluded from constituting part of the appeal for the purposes of compliance with the requirements of s.127(1).

Under subs.(1)(f) the fee must be paid within the relevant period, otherwise the appeal or referral will be invalid. See *Calor Teo v Sligo County Council* [1991] 2 I.R. 267 by analogy with the fee for applications. Under s.144, the Board, with the approval of the Minister, determines fees for appeals or referrals. The fees payable to An Bord Pleanála after the December 10, 2007 are as follows:

- application for strategic infrastructure development or a request to alter the terms of such development already permitted or approved: €100,000;

- appeal against a decision of a planning authority on a planning application relating to commercial development, made by the person by whom the planning application was made, where the application relates to unauthorised development: €4,500 or €9,000 if EIS involved;
- appeal against a decision of a planning authority on a planning application relating to commercial development, made by the person by whom the planning application was made, other than the above appeal: €1,500 or €3,000 if EIS involved;
- appeal against a decision of a planning authority on a planning application made by the person by whom the planning application was made, where the application relates to unauthorised development, other than an aforementioned appeal: €660;
- appeal other than an aforementioned appeal: €220;
- application for leave to appeal: €110;
- appeal following a grant of leave to appeal: €110;
- referral: €220;
- reduced fee payable by specified bodies: €110;
- request from a party for an oral hearing of an appeal or referral: €50.

In *Finnegan v An Bord Pleanála* [1979] I.L.R.M. 134, the former requirement to pay a deposit to appeal to An Bord Pleanála was held not unconstitutional.

With respect to subs.(1)(g) the requirement to make the appeal or referral within the relevant period, tends to be strictly construed. Under s.37, there are four weeks to lodge an appeal (s.37(1)(d)), though under s.37(6)(f), where leave to appeal is granted, the applicant must lodge his appeal within two weeks. The appropriate period for making the appeal or referral will depend on the nature of the appeal or referral. The appeal will be deemed to have been "made" within the time limits when the service requirements of subs.(5) have been satisfied. In relation to sending the appeal by prepaid post, it appears that the appeal must be received by the Board within the appropriate time limit and it is not simply enough to have posted it within the time limit. The appeal or referral documents may be left at the Board during office hours, but must be left with an employee of the Board personally. As stated in *Graves v An Bord Pleanála* [1997] 2 I.R. 205, it is not sufficient that an employee may subsequently come into possession of the documents. In addition to the above it appears that where an appellant or person making the referral wishes to request an oral hearing, he must do so within the relevant period for appeal or referral.

Under subs.(4)(a), the appellant or person making the referral can submit other documents, particulars or information (which must accompany the appeal or referral) which they consider necessary or appropriate. This therefore affords a discretion to the appellant or person making the referral as regards what they wish to accompany the appeal or referral relevant to the appeal, to accompany the appeal notice. The appellant must include all documents upon which reliance will be placed at the appeal as an appellant cannot subsequently seek to furnish further documentation after the time limit for the appeal, nor can they seek to make further submissions or grounds of appeal. If such submissions are made, the Board is prohibited from considering them. An exception to this is under ss.131 and 132, whereby the Board may, in the interest of justice, request further submissions from a party or the submission of a particular document or information. Also, where, under s.134, the Board decides at its discretion to hold an oral hearing, submissions may be made at such hearing. Under the previous legislation, the corresponding provision was contained in s.4 of the 1992 Act.

[Submission of documents, etc. to Board by planning authorities

128.—(1) Where an appeal or referral is made to the Board the planning authority concerned shall, within a period of 2 weeks beginning on the day on which a copy of the appeal or referral is sent to it by the Board, submit to the Board— **1–153**

    (a) in the case of an appeal under *section 37* —

        (i) a copy of the planning application concerned and of any drawings, maps, particulars, evidence, environmental impact statement, other written study or further information received or obtained by it from the applicant in accordance with regulations under this Act,

(ii) a copy of any submission or observation made in accordance with regulations under this Act in respect of the planning application,

(iii) a copy of any report prepared by or for the planning authority in relation to the planning application, and

(iv) a copy of the decision of the planning authority in respect of the planning application and a copy of the notification of the decision given to the applicant,

(b) in the case of any other appeal or referral, any information or documents in its possession which is or are relevant to that matter.

(2) The Board, in determining an appeal or referral, may take into account any fact, submission or observation mentioned, made or comprised in any document or other information submitted under *subsection (1)*.]

AMENDMENT HISTORY

Substituted by s. 21 of the Planning and Development (Strategic Infrastructure) Act 2006 (No. 27 of 2006).

NOTE

This section concerns documents which must be sent by the planning authority to the Board in the event of an appeal. The 2006 Act substituted a new section with the main change to insert subs.(128)(1)(a)(iii) providing that the planning authority must send to the Board a copy of submissions or observations received and also under subs.(2) that the Board may take into account any fact, submission or observations contained in any document or information submitted. Subsection (2) is therefore open-ended and relates to all documents/information transferred to the Board. The specified documents (or relevant documents where it does not concern an appeal in relation to planning permission under s.37) must be sent to the Board within two weeks from when a copy of the appeal or referral is sent to the planning authority by the Board. This is a mandatory requirement and failure to complete it will render the decision of the Board invalid. All of the enlisted documents must be transmitted. See *McAnenley v An Bord Pleanála* [2002] 2 I.R. 763, where Kelly J. held there to have been substantial non-compliance where the decision of the planning authority to grant permission was not forwarded to the Board, even though a copy of the notification to grant permission had been forwarded. This section re-enacts s.6 of the 1992 Act. Also under art.127 of the 2001 Regulations, the planning authority must also notify the Board where the development is subject to a transboundary consultation under Pt 10 of the 2001 Regulations.

Where an appeal or referral has been sent to the planning authority, then under art.68 of the Planning Regulations 2001, as amended by the 2006 Regulations, it must, as soon as may be, make available for inspection or purchase during office hours the documents relating to the appeal/referral until the appeal/referral is withdrawn, dismissed, determined or subject to a direction under s.139 as the case may be. Although in the context of art.35 of the 2001 Regulations, in *Harding v Cork County Council*, unreported, Supreme Court, May 2, 2008, Murray C.J. said that in considering "as soon as may be", it may be borne in mind that it is an administrative procedure and requirements as to time must be interpreted having regard to the ordinary burdens of administration in any organisation or body.

Also under art.69, the planning authority must notify in writing any person who made a submission or observation in relation to the planning application in respect of which the appeal has been made. By virtue of art.70, the weekly list of the planning authority under art.32 must indicate planning applications in respect of which an appeal has been made. Under art.72, the Board must also maintain a weekly list of appeals and referrals received. Under art.71, in the case of an application for leave to appeal, where the Board has notified the planning authority of such, the planning authority must, as soon as shall be, notify the applicant for permission of the application for leave.

Submissions or observations by other parties

129.—**(1)** The Board shall, as soon as may be after receipt of an appeal or referral, give a copy thereof to each other party. **1–154**

(2)

    (a) Each other party may make submissions or observations in writing to the Board in relation to the appeal or referral within a period of 4 weeks beginning on the day on which a copy of the appeal or referral is sent to that party by the Board.

    (b) Any submissions or observations received by the Board after the expiration of the period referred to in *paragraph (a)* shall not be considered by the Board.

(3) Where no submissions or observations have been received from a party within the period referred to in *subsection (2),* the Board may without further notice to that party determine the appeal or referral.

(4) Without prejudice to *section 131 or 134,* a party shall not be entitled to elaborate in writing upon any submissions or observations made in accordance with *subsection (2)* or make any further submissions or observations in writing in relation to the appeal or referral and any such elaboration, submissions or observations that is or are received by the Board shall not be considered by it.

NOTE

This section concerns the making of submissions or observations by parties to the appeal. The other parties to the appeal are allowed an opportunity to respond to the appeal documents by making submissions. In many cases, the other party will simply be the planning authority who made the determination. Section 2(1) defines "party to an appeal or referral" as:

"[T]he planning authority and any of the following persons, as appropriate—

    (a) the appellant,

    (b) the applicant for any permission in relation to which an appeal is made by another person (other than a person acting on behalf of the appellant),

    (c) in the case of a referral under section 5, the person making the referral, and any other person notified under subsection (2) of that section,

    (d) in the case of a referral under section 34(5), the applicant for the permission which was granted,

    (e) in the case of a referral under section 37(5), the person who made the application for permission which was returned by the planning authority,

    (f) any person served or issued by a planning authority with a notice or order, or copy thereof, under sections 44, 45, 46, 88 and 207,

    (ff) in the case of a referral under section 57(8), the person making the referral,

    (g) in the case of a referral under section 96(5), a prospective party to an agreement under section 96(2),

    (h) in the case of an appeal under section 169, the development agency,

    (i) in the case of a referral under section 193, the person by whom the application for permission for erection of the new structure was made,

(j) the applicant for a licence under section 254 in relation to which an appeal is made by another person (other than a person acting on behalf of the appellant). In the case of a third party appeal under s.37, the other parties will include the applicant for permission as well as the planning authority."

As with the case of the appellant or person making a referral under s.127, strict time limits apply in relation to making submissions. All submissions must be made within four weeks of a copy of the appeal/referral being sent to such party. The four weeks run from when submissions are sent by the Board rather than when they are received. Apart from the statutory requirements, fair procedures require that every party should be aware of submissions and have a reasonable opportunity to respond; see *State (Genport Ltd) v An Bord Pleanála* [1983] I.L.R.M. 12 and *State (Stanford) v Dun Laoghaire*, unreported, Supreme Court, February 20, 1981. Subsection (2)(b) makes clear that submissions received after the four weeks cannot be considered and is mandatory terms. Equally, the Board cannot consider any elaborations in writing of the submissions. Again, the exception to making submissions outside the time limit may arise where the Board invokes s.131 to request further submissions, or s.132 to request documents/information, or where an oral hearing is to be held under s.134. This section re-enacts s.7 of the 1992 Act, where the period to make submissions was one month.

Submissions or observations by persons other than parties

1–155   **130.—(1)**

(a) Any person other than a party may make submissions or observations in writing to the Board in relation to an appeal or referral, other than a referral under *section 96(5)*.

(b) Without prejudice to *subsection (4)*, submissions or observations may be made within the period specified in *subsection (3)* and any submissions or observations received by the Board after the expiration of that period shall not be considered by the Board.

(c) A submission or observation shall—

(i) be made in writing,

(ii) state the name and address of the person making the submission or observation and the name and address of any person acting on his or her behalf,

(iii) state the subject matter of the submission or observation,

(iv) state in full the reasons, considerations and arguments on which the submission or observation is based, and

(v) be accompanied by such fee (if any) as may be payable in accordance with *section 144*.

(2) Submissions or observations which do not comply with *subsection (1)* shall be invalid.

(3) The period referred to in *subsection (1)(b)* is—

(a) where notice of receipt of an environmental impact statement is published in accordance with regulations under *section 172(5)*, the period of 4 weeks beginning on the day of publication of any notice required under those regulations,

(b) where notice is required by the Board to be given under *section 142(4)*, the period of 4 weeks beginning on the day of publication of the required notice,

(c) in any other appeal under this *Act*, the period of 4 weeks beginning on the day of receipt of the appeal by the Board or, where there is more than one appeal against the decision of the planning authority, on the day on which the Board last receives an appeal, or

(d) in the case of a referral, the period of 4 weeks beginning on the day of receipt by the Board of the referral.

(4) Without prejudice to *section 131 or 134,* a person who makes submissions or observations to the Board in accordance with this *section* shall not be entitled to elaborate in writing upon the submissions or observations or make further submissions or observations in writing in relation to the appeal or other matter and any such elaboration, submissions or observations that is or are received by the Board shall not be considered by it.

(5) *Subsections (1)(b) and (4)* shall not apply to submissions or observations made by a Member State of the European Communities (within the meaning of the *European Communities Act, 1972*) or another state which is a party to the *Transboundary Convention,* arising from consultation in accordance with the *Council Directive* or the *Transboundary Convention,* as the case may be, in relation to the effects on the environment of the development to which the appeal under *section 37* relates.

NOTE

This section concerns submissions or observations by an observer, i.e. persons other than the parties to the appeal. Any member of the public may make submissions in relation to the appeal or referral to the Board. In an appeal from a decision of the planning authority on an application for planning permission, the right of a person to make submissions does not depend on having made submissions before the planning authority. The only type of referral to which this section does not apply is a s.96(5) referral concerning a dispute which relates to a social and affordable housing agreement. As with an appeal under s.127, a non-party who seeks to make a submission under this section must be in strict compliance with the five matters stated in subs.(1)(c) which are all mandatory. However, by analogy with the requirements of s.127, it would appear that there is no requirement that the specified matter be contained in one document. See *O'Connor v An Bord Pleanála*, unreported, High Court, Finlay Geoghegan J., January 24, 2008. The information can be contained within a series of documents and submitted in an informal manner. See *O'Reilly v Wicklow County Council*, unreported, High Court, Quirke J., November 22, 2006. The case law with respect to requirements of s.127, would appear equally applicable to this section. In this regard, therefore see the note on s.127. After December 10, 2007, the fee for submissions or observations (by "observer") on strategic infrastructure development applications, appeals and referrals, is €50.

Failure to comply with any of these matters will render the submissions invalid. The time limit within which to make submissions must also be strictly satisfied. In general the time limit is set at four weeks from the day of the receipt of the appeal or referral by the Board (or the day of receipt of the last appeal, where there is more than one), subject to certain variations to this. Thus where there is an EIS in connection with the appeal, the four weeks will run from the date of publication of the notice of receipt of the EIS by the Board. Also, where the Board invokes its power under s.142(4) to require any party to an appeal or referral to give public notice (such as requiring notice to be given at the site or by publication in a newspaper circulating in the district in which the land or structure to which the appeal relates is located), the four weeks run from the date of publication of such notice. Again, no submissions can be made outside this time limit, subject to the Board requesting further submissions (s.131), requesting a document or information (s.132), or where an oral hearing is held (s.134). The strict time limits for submissions do not apply in the special case of observations made by a Member State in relation to effects on the environment of a development where covered by the relevant European law.

Under art.74 of the Planning Regulations 2001 as amended, the Board, must as soon as may be, following its decision, notify any person who made submissions or observations. Article 74(2) specifies the content of such notice. The notice must specify:

1. the reference number of the appeal,
2. the reference number of the planning application concerned in the register of the planning authority,
3. the date of the order of the Board in relation to the appeal,
4. the development to which the decision relates,
5. the nature of the decision and the main reasons and considerations on which the decision is based,
6. in the case of a decision to grant a permission subject to conditions — any conditions to which the permission is subject and the main reasons for the imposition of any such conditions, provided that where a condition imposed is a condition described in section 34(4) of the Act, a reference to the paragraph of the said subsection (4) in which the condition is described shall be sufficient,
7. in the case of a decision to grant a permission for a structure — any purpose for which the structure may or may not be used,
8. in the case of a decision to grant a permission — any condition specifying points of detail relating to a grant of permission to be agreed by the planning authority and the person to whom the permission is granted,
9. in the case of a decision to grant a permission — any period specified by the Board pursuant to section 41 of the Act as the period during which the permission is to have effect,
10. that in making a decision on an appeal the Board, in accordance with section 34(3) of the Act, has regard to submissions or observations received in accordance with these Regulations,
11. in the case of a decision to grant or refuse a permission where the decision by the Board is different, in relation to the granting or refusal of permission, from the recommendation of the report of a person assigned to report on an appeal on behalf of the Board — the main reasons for not accepting such recommendation, and
12. in the case of a decision to grant a permission for a development which materially contravenes the development plan where the planning authority had refused a permission on that ground — the main reasons and considerations for materially contravening the development plan.

This section re-enacts s.8 of the 1992 Act, although the time limit for making submissions was one month.

Power of Board to request submissions or observations

1–156   **131.**—Where the Board is of opinion that, in the particular circumstances of an appeal or referral, it is appropriate in the interests of justice to request—

   (a) any party to the appeal or referral,
   (b) any person who has made submissions or observations to the Board in relation to the appeal or referral, or
   (c) any other person or body,
        to make submissions or observations in relation to any matter which has arisen in relation to the appeal or referral, the Board may, in its discretion, notwithstanding *section 127(3), 129(4), 130(4) or 137(4)(b),* serve on any such person a notice under this *section* —
        (i) requesting that person, within a period specified in the notice (not being less than 2 weeks or more than 4 weeks beginning on the date of service of the notice) to submit to the Board submissions or observations in relation to the matter in question, and
        (ii) stating that, if submissions or observations are not received

before the expiration of the period specified in the notice, the Board will, after the expiration of that period and without further notice to the person, pursuant to *section 133,* determine the appeal or referral.

NOTE

This section allows the Board discretion to seek further submissions in relation to any matter which has arisen in relation to an appeal or referral. This section allows the Board to request general submissions or observations, while under s.132 it can request a specific document or information. The Board may invoke the section in circumstances where it is of the view that a person or body should be entitled to make submissions due to matters arising in the appeal or to clarify certain issues (although this latter objective could be more appropriately achieved under s.132). The power under this section constitutes a qualification to the strict time limits for the appellant, other parties or non-parties to make submissions under ss.127, 129 and 130 respectively.

The submissions can be sought from a party to the appeal, a non-party who has already made submissions, or simply from any person or body, irrespective of whether they have made submissions. The section is therefore broader than the corresponding former s.10 of the 1992 Act, where the request for submissions was confined to parties to the appeal or parties who had made submissions. While the Board may at its discretion seek such submissions, it must do so "in the interests of justice". It is possible that fair procedure may require the Board to exercise its discretion in a particular manner: see by analogy, *State (Stanford) v Dun Laoghaire,* unreported, Supreme Court, February 20, 1981 and *State (Genport) v An Bord Pleanála* [1983] I.L.R.M. 12. In *State (Havarty) v An Bord Pleanála* [1987] I.R. 485, Murphy J. noted they could be exceptional circumstances where "further communications from the developer extended the original submission so radically as to constitute a different or additional case and in that event natural justice might well require An Bord Pleanála to postpone its decision until it had afforded interested parties an opportunity of commenting upon the revised submission". However, Murphy J. stated the general position as follows:

"The essence of natural justice is that it requires the application of broad principles of commonsense and fair play to a given set of circumstances in which a person is acting judicially. What will be required must vary with circumstances of the case. What will be required must vary with circumstances of the case. At one end of the spectrum it will be sufficient to afford a party the right to make informal observations and at the other constitutional justice may dictate that a party concerned should have the right to be provided with legal aid and to cross-examine witnesses supporting the case against him. I have no doubt that on an appeal to the planning board the rights of an objector - as distinct from a developer exercising property rights - the requirements of natural justice fall within the former rather than the latter range of the spectrum. This flows from the nature of the interest which is being protected, the number of possible objectors, the nature of the function exercised by the planning board and the limited criteria by which appeals are required to be judged and the practical fact that in any proceedings whether oral or otherwise there must be finality. Some party must have the last word. The substantive reality of the present case is that the prosecutrix and the Sefton Residents' Association put forward a detailed professional argument before the planning authority in the first instance and the planning board in relation to the appeal. I can appreciate their concern that they might have wished to expand upon their argument or to raise counter-arguments to those made in reply by the developers but I have no doubt that the real substance of their case was before An Bord Pleanála and duly considered by it. If there was in fact a material conflict of evidence that could not have been resolved by additional submissions or observations. Disputes of that nature could only be adequately dealt with in an oral hearing"

The consultation process is not interminable and the Board is entitled to call a halt to inviting further submissions. See *Finnegan v An Bord Pleanála* [1979] I.L.R.M. 134, where it was said there must be some limitation to the indefinite extension of an appeal or inquiry. The court may also take into account the nature and extent of submissions already made. See *Klohn v An Bord Pleanála*, unreported, High Court, McMahon J., April 23, 2008, where the court rejected a claim that the Board should have afforded the applicant another opportunity to respond to submissions by the developer. The court took into account the level of participation and the level of information available to the applicant. Also there was no such a radical change between what the developer originally proposed and what was to be found in his appeal to bring it within the exception contemplated in *Haverty*.

Where the Board requests a document under s.132, it may decide that fair procedures require it to serve a notice under s.131, allowing such other parties to make submissions or observations on the document. See *Huntstown v An Bord Pleanála* [1999] 1 I.L.R.M. 281. This section cannot be used by the Board to allow a person out of time to make a submission. See *Rowan v An Bord Pleanála*, unreported, High Court, Feeney J., May 26, 2006, where a notice sent to a person who made submissions in purported compliance with art.69 of the 2001 Planning Regulations failed to specify when the appeal was actually received by the Board, this was held to be a mandatory requirement.

Where the Board invokes the power under this section, it serves a notice of request on such relevant person or body specifying a period of between two and four weeks from the date of service of the notice, within which such submissions should be made. There is no provision for extension of this time. Even where a person is given less than two weeks, this will not necessarily breach this requirement. In *Ryanair v An Bord Pleanála* [2004] 2 I.R. 334, where the applicant was requested to make submissions by a deadline some 11 days after receipt of the notice. Ó Caoimh J. refused leave as this non-compliance did not preclude them from making submissions, as they did in fact make the submissions within the period. This was applied in *Hickey v An Bord Pleanála*, unreported, High Court, Smyth J., June 10, 2004, where Smyth J. refused leave, although the applicants were only given 13 days rather than the required 14 days, under the previous legislation, to make the submissions. He considered that there had been substantial compliance.

Power of Board to require submission of documents, etc.

1–157   132.—(1) Where the Board is of opinion that any document, particulars or other information may be necessary for the purpose of enabling it to determine an appeal or referral, the Board may, in its absolute discretion, serve on any party, or on any person who has made submissions or observations to the Board in relation to the appeal or referral, as appropriate, a notice under this *section* —

   (a) requiring that person, within a period specified in the notice (being a period of not less than two weeks beginning on the date of service of the notice) to submit to the Board such document, particulars or other information as is specified in the notice, and

   (b) stating that, in default of compliance with the requirements of the notice, the Board will, after the expiration of the period so specified and without further notice to the person, pursuant to *section 133,* dismiss or otherwise determine the appeal or referral.

(2) Nothing in this *section* shall be construed as affecting any other power conferred on the Board under this *Act* to require the submission of further or additional information or documents.

NOTE

This section allows the Board a discretion to request particular documents or information which it considers necessary to determine the appeal/referral. Unlike s.131 concerning a request for submissions, the request is confined to parties to the appeal or persons who have already made submissions. The section states emphatically that the request is at the "absolute discretion" of the Board; this was not stated in the former provision in the 1992 Act. The request is made by serving notice on the relevant person, specifying a period of between two and four weeks within which such documents or information must be furnished to the Board. This time limit must be strictly complied with (under the previous legislation the time limit was for a period of not less than 14 days). In *Huntstown v An Bord Pleanála* [1999] 1 I.L.R.M. 281, Geoghegan J. noted that, under the previous provision, the requirement that the documents are necessary for the purposes of determining the appeal is not synonymous with "relevant". A document may only become necessary where the Board cannot properly determine the appeal without them. Also, where the Board requests a document, it may decide that fair procedures require it to serve a notice under s.131, allowing such other parties to make submissions or observations. He noted that the Board can make such request at any time prior to its final determination. By way of sanction, for failure to comply with the request, the Board has a discretion to dismiss the case or otherwise dispose of it. The Board has broader powers to require production of documents in the context of an oral hearing under s.135(5).

Powers of Board where notice served under section 131 or 132

133.—Where a notice has been served under *section 131 or 132,* the Board, at any time after the expiration of the period specified in the notice, may, having considered any submissions or observations or document, particulars or other information submitted by the person on whom the notice has been served, without further notice to that person determine or, in the case of a notice served under *section 132,* dismiss the appeal or referral.   1–158

NOTE

This section allows the Board to dismiss the appeal or referral having considered the submissions or information supplied following a request under ss.131 or 132. The Board can only make such determination after the time given for a response to the request has expired. There is no requirement for the Board to give notice to the parties of an intention to make such determination. This section re-enacts s.11 of the 1992 Act.

[Oral hearings of appeals, referrals and applications

134.—**(1)** The Board may in its absolute discretion, hold an oral hearing of an appeal, a referral under *section 5* or an application under *section 37E.*   1–159

(2)

  (a) A party to an appeal or a referral under *section 5* or an applicant under *section 37E* or any person who makes a submission or observation under *section 37E* may request an oral hearing of the appeal, referral or application, as appropriate.

  (b)

   (i) A request for an oral hearing of an appeal, referral or application shall be made in writing to the Board and shall be accompanied by such fee (if any) as may be payable in respect of the request in accordance with *section 144.*

   (ii) A request for an oral hearing of an appeal, referral or application which is not accompanied by such fee (if any) as may be payable in respect of the request shall not be considered by the Board.

  (c)

(i)   A request by an appellant for an oral hearing of an appeal under *section 37* shall be made within the appropriate period referred to in that section and any request received by the Board after the expiration of that period shall not be considered by the Board.

(ii) Where a provision of this Act, other than *sections 37 and 254(6),* authorizing an appeal to the Board enables the appeal only to be made within, or before the expiration of, a specified period or before a specified day, a request by an appellant for an oral hearing of an appeal may only be made within, or before the expiration of, the specified period or before the specified day and any request for an oral hearing not so received by the Board shall not be considered by the Board.

(iii) A request by a person making a referral, by an applicant under *section 37E* or by an appellant under *section 254(6)* for an oral hearing of the referral, application or appeal, as the case may be, shall accompany the referral, application or appeal, and any request for an oral hearing received by the Board, other than a request which accompanies the referral, application or appeal, shall not be considered by the Board.

(d) A request by a party to an appeal or referral other than the appellant, or by a person who makes a submission or observation in relation to an application under *section 37E,* for an oral hearing shall be made—

(i)   in respect of an appeal or referral, within the period referred to in *section 129(2)(a)* within which the party may make submissions or observations to the Board in relation to the appeal or referral,

(ii) in respect of an application under *section 37E,* within the period specified in a notice under that section within which the person may make submissions or observations to the Board in relation to the application, and any such request received by the Board after the expiration of that period shall not be considered by the Board.

(3) Where the Board is requested to hold an oral hearing of an appeal, referral or application and decides to determine the appeal, referral or application without an oral hearing, the Board shall serve notice of its decision on—

(a) the person who requested the hearing and on each other party to the appeal or referral or, as appropriate, (unless he or she was the requester) the applicant under *section 37E,* and

(b) each person who has made submissions or observations to the Board in relation to the appeal, referral or application (not being the person who was the requester).

(4)(a) A request for an oral hearing may be withdrawn at any time.

(b) Where, following a withdrawal of a request for an oral hearing under *paragraph (a),* the appeal, referral or application falls to be determined without an oral hearing, the Board shall give notice that it falls to be so determined—

    (i) to each other party to the appeal or referral or, as appropriate, (unless he or she was the person who withdrew the request) the applicant under *section 37E,* and

    (ii) to each person who has made submissions or observations to the Board in relation to the appeal, referral or application (not being the person who withdrew the request).]

AMENDMENT HISTORY

Subsection (5) was inserted by s.247 of the Local Government Act 2001 (No. 37 of 2001), which, by the Local Government Act 2001 (Commencement) Order 2001 (S.I. No. 458 of 2001), came into effect on October 9, 2001.

Substituted by s.22 of the Planning and Development (Strategic Infrastructure) Act 2006 (No. 27 of 2006).

NOTE

This section allows the Board an absolute discretion in determining whether there is to be an oral hearing of the appeal or referral. The use of the phrase "absolute discretion" indicates that no party or person has a right to an oral hearing. This was also provided for under the former s.16 of the Local Government (Planning and Development) 1976 Act which had amended the 1963 Act, which had provided a person bringing a planning appeal had a right to an oral hearing. In *Finnegan v An Bord Pleanála* [1979] I.L.R.M. 134, this change in the law was held constitutionally permissible. A party to an appeal (defined under s.2(1) or a referral under s.5 (as to whether a matter is development or exempted development), may however request the Board to hold an oral hearing in relation to the appeal or referral. The 2006 Act substituted a new section with the main change being to incorporate references to a strategic infrastructure application and some changes in the layout of the subsections by breaking the section into further parts. Subsection (1) is amended by adding the words "or an application under section 37E", which makes clear that the Board has an absolute discretion in deciding whether to hold an oral hearing in respect of a strategic infrastructure application. Subsection (2) adds that an applicant or person who makes submissions regarding a strategic infrastructure application may request an oral hearing. In the context of a strategic infrastructure application, which is made directly to the Board, the particular circumstances of the case may mean that fair procedures may necessitate an oral hearing. In this regard support may be placed on art.6(1) of the European Convention on Human Rights to support an entitlement to an oral hearing. See *Adlard v Secretary of State* [2002] P & CR 202.

The decision to refuse an oral hearing may be challenged on grounds of unreasonableness, although it would be difficult to succeed; see *Hynes v An Bord Pleanála,* unreported, High Court, Laffoy J., December 10, 1997. The entitlement to make such request is confined to a party to the appeal and so cannot generally be made by a person who simply has made submissions with the exception of a person who made a submission or observation in respect of an application for a strategic planning infrastructure development. Subsection (2)(b) provides that the request must be made in writing, along with payment of the prescribed fee; otherwise the request cannot be considered by the Board. After December 10, 2007, the fee for a request for an oral hearing of an appeal or referral is €50.

As regards the time for making a request, in general, the request for an oral hearing by the appellant must be made within the time allowed for making an appeal or referral. In case of an appeal under s.37 in relation to a planning permission, such request for an oral hearing must be made within four weeks from the day of the decision of the planning authority. A request for oral hearing by a party to an appeal, other than the appellant, must be made within the four-week period from when the Board sent a copy of the appeal or referral to those allowed to make submissions under s.129(2)(a). It appears that the request for an oral hearing need not accompany the appeal itself but both must be made within the four-week period.

Subsection (3) provides that where the Board refuses a request to hold an oral hearing, it must serve a notice of its decision on the person making the request, each party to the appeal or applicant as appropriate, as well as any person who has made submissions. Subsection (4) provides that a request may be withdrawn at any time. In such case, the Board must serve a notice on each party to the appeal or applicant as appropriate, as well as any person who has made submissions, stating that the matter is to be determined without an oral hearing. The previous corresponding provision was contained in s.12 of the 1992 Act.

[Further power to hold oral hearings

1–160   **134A.—(1)** Where the Board considers it necessary or expedient for the purposes of making a determination in respect of any of its functions under this Act or any other enactment, it may, in its absolute discretion, hold an oral hearing and shall, in addition to any other requirements under this Act or other enactment, as appropriate, consider the report and any recommendations of the person holding the oral hearing before making such determination.

(2) *Section 135* shall apply to any oral hearing held in accordance with *subsection (1)* and that section shall be construed accordingly.

(3) This section is in addition to *section 134.*]

AMENDMENT HISTORY

Inserted by s.22 of the Planning and Development (Strategic Infrastructure) Act 2006 (No. 27 of 2006).

NOTE

This section was inserted by the 2006 Act and applies where the Board has decided that it is necessary or expedient to hold an oral hearing. The section implies that the Board may decide to have an oral hearing even in the absence of a request for an oral hearing. Subsection (1) states that there is an obligation on the Board to consider the report and recommendations of the person holding the oral hearing before making its determination. Subsection (2) provides that s.135 regarding the conduct of an oral hearing, also applies to an oral hearing which the Board requires to take place under this section

Supplemental provisions relating to oral hearings

1–161   **135.—[(1)** The Board or an employee of the Board duly authorised by the Board may assign a person to conduct an oral hearing of an appeal, referral or application on behalf of the Board.]

[(2)′ The person conducting an oral hearing of an appeal, referral or application shall have discretion as to the conduct of the hearing and shall conduct the hearing expeditiously and without undue formality (but subject to any direction given by the Board under *subsection (2A)*).]

[(2A) The Board may give a direction to the person conducting an oral hearing that he or she shall require persons intending to appear at the hearing to submit to him or her, in writing and in advance of the hearing, the points or a summary of the arguments they propose to make at the hearing; where such a direction is given that person shall comply with it (and, accordingly, is enabled to make such a requirement).]

[(2B) Subject to the foregoing provisions, the person conducting the oral hearing—

    (a) shall decide the order of appearance of persons at the hearing,

    (b) shall permit any person to appear in person or to be represented by another person,

(c) may limit the time within which each person may make points or arguments (including arguments in refutation of arguments made by others at the hearing), or question the evidence of others, at the hearing,

(d) may refuse to allow the making of a point or an argument if—

   (i) the point or a summary of the argument has not been submitted in advance to the person in accordance with a requirement made pursuant to a direction given under *subsection (2A),*

   (ii) the point or argument is not relevant to the subject matter of the hearing, or

   (iii) it is considered necessary so as to avoid undue repetition of the same point or argument,

(e) may hear a person other than a person who has made submissions or observations to the Board in relation to the subject matter of the hearing if it is considered appropriate in the interests of justice to allow the person to be heard.]

[**(3)** A person conducting an oral hearing of any appeal, application or referral may require any officer of a planning authority or a local authority to give to him or her any information in relation to the appeal, application or referral which he or she reasonably requires for the purposes of the appeal, application or referral, and it shall be the duty of the officer to comply with the requirement.]

(4) A person conducting an oral hearing of any [appeal, referral or application] may take evidence on oath or affirmation and for that purpose may administer oaths or affirmations, and a person giving evidence at any such hearing shall be entitled to the same immunities and privileges as if he or she were a witness before the High Court.

(5)

(a) Subject to *paragraph (b),* the Board in relation to an oral hearing of any [appeal, referral or application] may, by giving notice in that behalf in writing to any person, require that person to do either or both of the following:

   (i) to attend at such time and place as is specified in the notice to give evidence in relation to any matter in question at the hearing;

   (ii) to produce any books, deeds, contracts, accounts, vouchers, maps, plans, documents or other information in his or her possession, custody or control which relate to any such matter.

(b) Where a person is given a notice under *paragraph (a)* :

   (i) the Board shall pay or tender to any person whose attendance is required such reasonable subsistence and travelling expenses to be determined by the Board in accordance with the rates for the time being applicable to senior planning authority officials;

   (ii) any person who in compliance with a notice has attended at any place shall, save in so far as the reasonable and necessary expenses of the attendance have already been paid to him or her, be paid those expenses by the Board, and those expenses shall, in default of being so paid, be recoverable as a simple contract debt in any court of competent jurisdiction.

(6) Every person to whom a notice under *subsection (5)* has been given who refuses or wilfully neglects to attend in accordance with the notice or who wilfully alters, suppresses, conceals or destroys any document or other information to which the notice relates or who, having so attended, refuses to give evidence or refuses or wilfully fails to produce any document or other information to which the notice relates shall be guilty of an offence.

(7) Where any person—

(a) wilfully gives evidence which is material to the oral hearing and which he or she knows to be false or does not believe to be true,

(b) by act or omission, obstructs or hinders the person conducting the oral hearing in the performance of his or her functions,

(c) refuses to take an oath or to make an affirmation when legally required to do so by a person holding the oral hearing,

(d) refuses to answer any question to which the person conducting an oral hearing may legally require an answer, or

(e) does or omits to do any other thing which, if the inquiry had been by the High Court, would have been contempt of that court,

the person shall be guilty of an offence.

(8)

(a) An oral hearing may be conducted through the medium of the Irish or the English language.

(b) Where an oral hearing relates to development within the Gaeltacht, the hearing shall be conducted through the medium of the Irish language, unless the parties to the [appeal, referral or application] to which the hearing relates agree that the hearing should be conducted in English.

(c) Where an oral hearing relates to development outside the Gaeltacht, the hearing shall be conducted through the medium of the English language, unless the parties to the [appeal, referral or application] to which the hearing relates agree that the hearing should be conducted in the Irish language.

Amendment history

Substituted by s.23 of the Planning and Development (Strategic Infrastructure) Act 2006 (No. 27 of 2006).

Note

This section allows the Board to appoint a person to conduct an oral hearing of an appeal or referral. Such a person need not be a Board member or employee of the Board. The 2006 Act made several modifications to this section including under subs.(1) which adds the word "application" which means it applies to a strategic infrastructure application. Subsection (2) restructures the previous subs.(2) and adds subss.(2A) and (2B). Article 76 of the 2001 Regulations provides that where the Board decides to hold an oral hearing it:

1. must inform relevant persons and any other person or body which it considers appropriate and give such persons and bodies not less than five working days notice of the time and place of the opening of the oral hearing or such shorter notice as may

be accepted by all such persons or bodies;
2. shall make available for inspection at its offices and at the offices of the local authority or planning authority, as appropriate, a copy of any correspondence, documents, particulars or other information received from any relevant persons in accordance with the provisions of the Act or these Regulations for a period commencing not later than seven days before the commencement of the oral hearing and ending on the last day of the oral hearing; and
3. shall make available for inspection at the place the oral hearing is held a copy of any correspondence and other information referred to in paragraph (b) for the duration of the oral hearing.

Article 76(2) provides that art.76(1) shall not require the Board to make available models or such other information or particulars as may be determined by the Board at the offices of the local authority or planning authority or at the place of the holding of the oral hearing where the making available of models or other information or particulars would lead to undue administrative or technical difficulties. Article 76(3) states that the Board may, where it considers appropriate, give any person or body informed of the holding of an oral hearing under sub-art.(1)(a) a copy of any correspondence, documents, particulars or other information received from relevant persons in accordance with the provisions of the Act or these Regulations. Also art.76(4) states that the Board may, at any time before the opening of an oral hearing, alter the time or place of the opening of the hearing and, in the event of such alteration, the Board shall give relevant persons and any other person or body informed of the holding of an oral hearing under sub-art.(1) notice of not less than three working days of the new time and place or such shorter notice as may be accepted by all such persons or bodies.

Subsection (2) provides that the person conducting the oral shall have a general discretion as to the conduct of the hearing. The amendment under 2006 Act provides that the person is required to conduct the hearing "expeditiously" as well as without undue formality. This may be subject to directions issued by the Board under subs.(2A). Under subs.(2A), the Board may direct the person conducting the oral hearing to require persons appearing at the oral hearing to submit in advance written points or a summary of the arguments to be made at the oral hearing. A direction issued is mandatory and must be complied with by the person conducting the oral hearing. There is no prescribed standard as to when the Board may issue a direction and so the Board has a general discretion. Under subs.(2B), the person conducting the oral hearing will decide the order of appearance. Depending on the nature of the oral hearing there may be numerous participants. He shall also permit a person to be appear in person or to be represented. The person conducting the oral hearing has no discretion in this respect. Under subs.(2B), new elements include limiting the time within which persons may make points or arguments (subs.(2B)(c)) and refusing to allow certain points or arguments if the matter was not submitted in advance according to a direction or the matter is not relevant and would involve undue repetition(subs.(2B)(d)). These particular provisions limiting time to make arguments or refusing to allow certain arguments, must be read subject to the requirements of fair procedures and/or natural and constitutional justice. Notwithstanding the explicit power of the person conducting the oral hearing to act in such manner, such provisions cannot authorise him to act contrary to fair procedures. These new statutory provisions gives explicit recognition to the power of a person holding the oral hearing to limit arguments subject to the requirements of fair procedures. In *Keane v An Bord Pleanála*, unreported, High Court, Murphy J., June 20, 1995, it was recognised that a person conducting an oral hearing has a general discretion in limiting excessive legal argument or submissions. The person conducting the hearing may at their discretion allow a person who has not made written submissions to be heard in the interests of justice.

The main change in subs.(3) is to provide that the section also applies to strategic infrastructure applications.

There is nothing to preclude a person appearing at an oral hearing from elaborating on their submissions at the oral hearing. It appears that where a legal issue arises at the oral hearing, an objection should be made, as failure to do so could prejudice a subsequent judicial review application on such ground. This is now particularly relevant as a result of the changes in s.50 dealing with judicial review which now provides that any decision or "act done" by the Board falls within s.50. See *Linehan v Cork County* Council, unreported, High Court, Finlay Geoghegan J., February 19, 2008, where it was suggested that such changes may mean an applicant cannot now await the outcome of the decision. See also the comments of Murray C.J. in *Harding v Cork County Council*, unreported, Supreme Court, May 2, 2008. Even under the former legislation there was a suggestion that an applicant could prejudice his position by failing to act—see *Lancefort v An Bord Pleanála* [1998] 2 I.L.R.M. 401—although this ought not to have effect on the requirement to have a substantial interest. See *Harding v Cork County Council*, unreported, Supreme Court, May 2, 2008 and the note on s.50. Notwithstanding these changes the court may still have to decide whether it may be appropriate to bring a judicial review application prior to the determination by the Board. Thus in *Max Developments v An Bord Pleanála* [1994] 2 I.R. 121, where an issue arose as to whether a development required an EIS, the inspector said he would adjourn the oral hearing to allow an application to the High Court. Where no application was made, and the applicant challenged the decision after determination, leave was refused due to the failure to challenge the decision at the time; see also *Healy v Dublin County Council*, unreported, High Court, Barron J., April 29, 1993, and *Sloan v An Bord Pleanála* [2003] 2 I.L.R.M. 61. In contrast, in *Huntstown v An Bord Pleanála* [1999] 1 I.L.R.M. 281, the judicial review application (for failure to order production of a document) prior to completing the oral hearing was deemed premature, where the Board could have ordered production of the document at any time prior to the determination. Where judicial review proceedings are taken, an applicant may seek to stay the oral hearing before the Board. The principles applicable are those applicable in an interlocutory injunction under the test in *Campus Oil Ltd v Minister for Industry and Commerce* [1983] I.R. 82; see *Martin v An Bord Pleanála* [2002] 2 I.R. 655, where the application was declined.

Article 77 of the 2001 Regulations provides that the Board or person conducting the oral hearing may adjourn or reopen the hearing, or proceed with the hearing, notwithstanding that a relevant person has failed to attend. Notice of the re-opening of the oral hearing must be given to each relevant person and other person informed, not less than one week before the said time unless all such persons accept shorter notice. An oral hearing under s.218 or on which a report has been submitted to the Board shall not be re-opened unless the Board considers it expedient to so direct. Article 78 allows the Board to appoint another person to conduct the oral hearing, if the person appointed is unable or fails to conduct the oral hearing. Also, where a person appointed fails to complete the oral hearing or fails to submit a report, the Board may appoint another person to conduct a new oral hearing.

Under subs.(3) the person conducting the hearing has the power to require an officer of a planning authority to furnish relevant information and under subs.(4) the power to take evidence or oath or affirmation.Subsection (5) provides that the Board (as opposed to the person conducting the oral hearing) may serve a written notice on a person requiring them to attend the oral hearing or to produce certain documentation for the purposes of the hearing (for which any expenses incurred, the Board will make recompense). A person who refuses or wilfully neglects to comply with such notice is deemed to have committed an offence. It appears from this that there must be some element of intentional wrongdoing or recklessness for an offence to be committed. A person who fails to comply due to a mistake or even negligence will not have committed an offence. The mistake would have to be a bona fide mistake. The power of the person conducting the hearing is strengthened by the creation of five new specific offences for persons who appear before the hearing. These reflect a certain degree of wrongdoing and non-cooperation. These include a general offence of obstructing the oral hearing, and more broadly, any conduct which would amount to contempt of court before the High Court.

Subsection (8) provides that the language in which the appeal or referral is conducted is English where the development is outside a Gaeltacht area and Irish where within a Gaeltacht area, unless all of the parties agree otherwise. The provision dealing with a person conducting an oral hearing were largely set out in the former ss.82(4)–(7) of the 1963 Act.

Convening of meetings on referrals

1–162   **136.—(1)** Where it appears to the Board to be expedient or convenient for the purposes of determining a referral under *section 34(5), 96(5) or 193(2),* the Board may, in its absolute discretion, convene a meeting of the parties.

(2) The Board shall keep a record in writing of a meeting convened in accordance with this *section* and a copy of the record shall be placed and kept with the documents to which the referral concerned relates and, where the referral is connected with an appeal, with the documents to which the appeal concerned relates.

NOTE

This section allows the Board a discretion to convene a meeting between the parties in relation to certain referrals made to the Board. Such a convened meeting is not the same as an oral hearing, and the Board has a discretion as to matters which would arise at such meetings, although a record must be kept of what occurred. The referrals to which this applies are: s.34(5), concerning a disagreement between a planning authority and the applicant as regard points of detail of a planning permission; s.96(5), a dispute concerning an agreement in respect of social and affordable housing requirements; and s.193(2), in the context of compensation for a refusal of planning permission, a dispute as to whether a new structure would or does substantially replace a structure demolished or destroyed.

Matters other than those raised by parties

137.—(1) The Board in determining an appeal or referral may take into account matters other than those raised by the parties or by any person who has made submissions or observations to the Board in relation to the appeal or referral if the matters are matters to which, by virtue of this *Act,* the Board may have regard.   **1–163**

(2) The Board shall give notice in writing to each of the parties and to each of the persons who have made submissions or observations in relation to the appeal or referral of the matters that it proposes to take into account under *subsection (1)* and shall indicate in that notice—

    (a) in a case where the Board proposes to hold an oral hearing of the appeal or referral, or where an oral hearing of the appeal or referral has been concluded and the Board considers it expedient to re-open the hearing, that submissions in relation to the matters may be made to the person conducting the hearing, or

    (b) in a case where the Board does not propose to hold an oral hearing of the appeal or referral, or where an oral hearing of the appeal or referral has been concluded and the Board does not consider it expedient to re-open the hearing, that submissions or observations in relation to the matters may be made to the Board in writing within a period specified in the notice (being a period of not less than 2 weeks or more than 4 weeks beginning on the date of service of the notice).

(3) Where the Board has given notice, in accordance with *subsection (2)(a),* the parties and any other person who is given notice shall be permitted, if present at the oral hearing, to make submissions to the Board in relation to the matters which were the subject of the notice or which, in the opinion of the person conducting the hearing, are of relevance to the appeal or referral.

    (4)

        (a) Submissions or observations that are received by the Board after the expiration of the period referred to in *subsection (2)(b)* shall not be considered by the Board.

(b) Subject to *section 131,* where a party or a person referred to in *subsection (1)* makes submissions or observations to the Board in accordance with *subsection (2)(b),* that party or person shall not be entitled to elaborate in writing upon those submissions or observations or make further submissions or observations in writing in relation to the matters referred to in *subsection (1)* and any such elaboration, submissions or observations that is or are received by the Board shall not be considered by it.

NOTE

This section allows the Board to consider matters not raised in the submissions by the parties. This is reflective of the role of the Board which is performing a public function in the public interest and so has a general interest going beyond the interests of the parties involved. In *Stack v An Bord Pleanála*, unreported, High Court, Ó Caoimh J., March 7, 2003, it was held that an earlier decision of the Board was not in reality a new matter that required the application of the former s.13(2) of the Act of 1992 or any specific notification to the applicants insofar as the same was taken into consideration by the Board. It was noted that an earlier decision is a matter of public record and was a matter of which knowledge must at least be imputed to the applicants as the decision in question was made before the appeal. The matters which the Board may raise must be within the parameters set out in the Act and so must relate to the proper planning and sustainable development of the area. See also *Fairyhouse Club v An Bord Pleanála*, unreported, High Court, Finnegan J., July 18, 2001. However, in *McGoldrick v An Bord Pleanála* [1997] 1 I.R. 497, fair procedure was held to have been breached where an applicant was not given warning that his application was not being treated on the basis upon which it was being put forward, both on fact and in law.

Where the Board proposes to take into account matters not raised by the parties, it must notify the parties and persons who made submissions or observation of these matters, inviting them to make submissions. If an oral hearing is proposed to be held or has been held, the notice may indicate that it is expedient to re-open such hearing and the parties may make the submissions at such hearing. Where there has been no oral hearing proposed or the oral hearing has concluded, the notice may invite the parties to make submissions within 2–4 weeks of receipt of the notice. No submissions may be made outside this period (except where the Board has requested further submissions under s.131).

As with s.131, this section also cannot be used by the Board to allow a person out of time to make a submission. See *Rowan v An Bord Pleanála*, unreported, High Court, Feeney J., May 26, 2006, where a notice sent to a person who made submissions in purported compliance with art.69 of the 2001 Planning Regulations failed to specify when the appeal was actually received by the Board was held to breach a mandatory requirement. This section re-enacts s.13 of the 1992 Act.

Board may dismiss appeals or referrals if vexatious, etc.

1–164   **138.—(1)** The Board shall have an absolute discretion to dismiss an appeal or referral—

[(a) where, having considered the grounds of appeal or referral or any other matter to which, by virtue of this Act, the Board may have regard in dealing with or determining the appeal or referral, the Board is of the opinion that the appeal or referral—

(i) is vexatious, frivolous or without substance or foundation, or

> **(ii)** is made with the sole intention of delaying the development or the intention of securing the payment of money, gifts, consideration or other inducement by any person,]
> **(b)** where, the Board is satisfied that, in the particular circumstances, the appeal or referral should not be further considered by it having regard to—
>> **(i)** the nature of the appeal (including any question which in the Board's opinion is raised by the appeal or referral), or
>> **(ii)** any previous permission which in its opinion is relevant.

(2) A decision made under this *section* shall state the main reasons and considerations on which the decision is based.

(3) The Board may, in its absolute discretion, hold an oral hearing under *section 134* to determine whether an appeal or referral is made with an intention referred to in *subsection (1)(a)(ii)*.

AMENDMENT HISTORY

Amended by s. 24 of the Planning and Development (Strategic Infrastructure) Act 2006 (No. 27 of 2006).

NOTE

This section enables the Board to dismiss an application in certain circumstances. Section 18 of the 1976 Act allowed the Board to serve a notice where a reference or appeal was vexatious or being unnecessarily delayed, stating the Board will, after a period specified in the notice, determine the matter without further notice. In *Finnegan v An Bord Pleanála* [1979] I.L.R.M. 134, it was said the purpose of the section is to prevent appeals or references which are without reality or substance.

The 2006 Act altered subs.(138)(1)(a) with the main change being the addition of the words "or any other matter to which, by virtue of this Act, the Board may have regard in dealing with or determining the appeal or referral". This means that in assessing whether to dismiss the appeal for the stated reasons, the Board is not confined to considering the grounds of appeal or referral. The extent of other matters which the Board may take into account under the added words are not precisely set out, other than stating it must be a matter which the Board may have regard in dealing with or determining the appeal. The matters to which the Board may have regard in determining an appeal are embraced by the general standard of proper planning and sustainable development. Subsection (2) provides that where the Board dismisses an appeal or referral it must give the main reasons and considerations.

The Board may dismiss the appeal where the appeal or referral is frivolous or vexatious or without substance or foundation. As to the meaning of this phrase some guidance may be gleaned from the case law striking out court proceedings for being frivolous and vexatious or disclosing no cause of action; see *Sun Fat Chan v Osseous Ltd* [1992] 1 I.R. 425, where it was emphasised the jurisdiction should be used sparingly and only in clear cases; see also *Supermac's Ireland Ltd v Katesan (Naas) Ltd*, unreported, High Court, Macken J., March 15, 1999. In *Doe v Armour Pharmaceutical Inc*, unreported, High Court, Morris P., July 31, 1997, it was said a claim will not be struck out where there is a serious dispute of fact. In *McSorley v O'Mahony*, unreported, High Court, Costello J., November 6, 1996, it was held to be an abuse of process where proceedings would be of no benefit to the plaintiff and would cause harm to the defendant. Similar principles can arguably be applied in respect of an appeal or referral before the Board.

An appeal or referral can be dismissed where the sole intention is to delay the development or for the intention of securing the payment, etc. It is not enough simply to prove that a motivation for the appeal/referral was to delay the development or to secure certain payment; such must be the sole intention of making the application. This would therefore appear to be a high standard to satisfy. There is provision for an oral hearing to determine whether such sole intention exists in a particular case. The Board is afforded a wide discretion in each instance, in particular the third-mentioned ground, where the application should not be considered further because of the "nature of the appeal". This will therefore depend upon the precise facts of any appeal.

The Board can also dismiss an appeal where it decides that the appeal should not be considered further because of previous permissions which are relevant. Previous planning permissions may be relevant under the rule of res judicata or as a precedent; see *Delgany Area Residents Association v Wicklow County Council*, unreported, High Court, Barr J., May 28, 1998.

A dismissal by the Board has a specific meaning, distinct from a refusal of the appeal. The Board may also dismiss an appeal under s.133 after having invoked its power to request documents under s.132. Also under s.37(4)(b), the Board may dismiss any appeal taken by a prescribed body where it considers the body concerned was not entitled to be sent notice of the planning application in accordance with the permission regulations; see *McCabe v Harding Investments* [1984] I.L.R.M. 105, and *Finnegan v An Bord Pleanála* [1979] I.L.R.M. 134. The previous power to dismiss appeal or referrals was under s.14 of the 1992 Act. Section 18(3) of the 1976 Act which enabled the Board, where it considered that an appeal was vexatious, to direct that the deposit lodged in relation to an appeal be forfeited, has not been re-enacted.

Appeals against conditions

1–165   **139.—(1)** Where—

    (a) an appeal is brought against a decision of a planning authority to grant a permission,

    (b) the appeal relates only to a condition or conditions that the decision provides that the permission shall be subject to, and

    (c) the Board is satisfied, having regard to the nature of the condition or conditions, that the determination by the Board of the relevant application as if it had been made to it in the first instance would not be warranted,

then, subject to compliance by the Board with *subsection (2),* the Board may, in its absolute discretion, give to the relevant planning authority such directions as it considers appropriate relating to the attachment, amendment or removal by that authority either of the conditions or conditions to which the appeal relates or of other conditions.

(2) In exercising the power conferred on it by *subsection (1),* apart from considering the condition or conditions to which the relevant appeal relates, the Board shall be restricted to considering—

    (a) the matters set out in *section 34(2)(a),* and

    (b) the terms of any previous permission considered by the Board to be relevant.

NOTE

This section allows the Board to issue directions to a planning authority in respect of an appeal against conditions only. Where the Board considers that considering the nature of the conditions, the determination should be as if it had been made at first instance, it may direct the planning authority to remove or amend such conditions. Where the Board forms such view, this then constitutes an exception to the general provision of s.37(1)(b) where the decision operates to annul the decision of the planning authority as from the time it was given. The Board has a discretion as to whether to make such a direction, but in so doing it is restricted to considering the proper planning and sustainable development of the area and other matters set out in s.34(2)(a), as well as any relevant previous planning permissions. Previous planning permissions may be relevant under the rule of res judicata or as a precedent; see *Delgany Area Residents Association v Wicklow County Council*, unreported, High Court, Barr J., May 28, 1998, and *MCD Management Services Ltd v Kildare County Council* [1995] 2 I.L.R.M. 532. Under art.72 of the Planning Regulations 2001, the Board must make available a weekly list which includes, inter alia, appeals or referrals determined, dismissed or withdrawn. This section re-enacts s.15 of the 1992 Act. The 2006 Act modified the section to incorporate references to strategic infrastructure applications.

Withdrawal of appeals, applications and referrals

140.—[(1)   1–166
    (a) A person who has made—
        (i) an appeal,
        (ii) a planning application to which an appeal relates,
        (iii) a referral,
        (iv) an application for permission or approval (as may be appropriate) in respect of a strategic infrastructure development,
        may withdraw, in writing, the appeal, application or referral at any time before that appeal, application, or referral is determined by the Board.
    (b) As soon as maybe after receipt of a withdrawal, the Board shall notify each other party or person who has made submissions or observations on the appeal, application or referral of the withdrawal.]
  (2)
    (a) Without prejudice to *subsection (1),* where the Board is of the opinion that an appeal or [an application for permission or approval (as may be appropriate) in respect of a strategic infrastructure development,] or a referral has been abandoned, the Board may serve on the person who made the appeal, application or referral, as appropriate, a notice stating that opinion and requiring that person, within a period specified in the notice (being a period of not less than two weeks or more than four weeks beginning on the date of service of the notice) to make to the Board a submission in writing as to why the appeal, application or referral should not be regarded as having been withdrawn.
    (b) Where a notice has been served under *paragraph (a),* the Board may, at any time after the expiration of the period specified in the notice, and after considering the submission (if any) made to the Board pursuant to the notice, declare that the appeal, application or referral, as appropriate, shall be regarded as having been withdrawn.
  (3) Where, pursuant to this *section,* a person withdraws a planning application to which an appeal relates, or the Board declares that an application is to be regarded as having been withdrawn, the following provisions shall apply as regards the application:
    (a) any appeal in relation to the application shall be regarded as having been withdrawn and accordingly shall not be determined by the Board, and
    (b) notwithstanding any previous decision under *section 34* by a planning

authority as regards the application, no permission shall be granted under that *section* by the authority on foot of the application.

AMENDMENT HISTORY

Substituted by s.25 of the Planning and Development (Strategic Infrastructure) Act 2006 (No. 27 of 2006).

NOTE

This section concerns the withdrawal of an appeal or referral before An Bord Pleanála, including the power of the Board to declare an appeal withdrawn. Subsection (1)(a) is new with the main change being a change in layout and the reference to strategic infrastructure development. It provides that a person who made an appeal, referral or planning application to which the appeal relates or application for strategic infrastructure development, may withdraw such matter before the Board determines the matter. The section not only covers withdrawals of appeals or referral but also allows the applicant for permission to withdraw the planning application to which the appeal relates. The applicant for permission will not be the appellant where there is only a third party appeal against the grant of permission. Once the matter is received by the Board, it will notify the other parties or persons who made submissions as soon as may be. The significance of such withdrawal means under subs.(3) that not only will the appeal not be determined but also any previous grant of permission by the planning authority at first instance will no longer exist. Where judicial review proceedings are taken by a party against the grant of permission which has also been appealed, the developer who was granted permission can render the judicial review proceedings moot by giving written notice of the withdrawal of the planning application to the Board. This may sometimes be done in order to facilitate a settlement of the judicial review proceedings.

Subsection (2) provides that where the Board deems an appeal, planning application to which an appeal relates, or referral to have been abandoned, the Board must notify the applicant of their view, giving them an opportunity to respond by submissions within two to four weeks. At the end of such period, irrespective of whether submissions in response were made, the Board may declare that the appeal, planning application or referral has been abandoned. This section restates s.16 of the 1992 Act.

Time for decisions and appeals, etc.

1–167   **141.—(1)** Where a requirement of or under this *Act* requires a planning authority or the Board to give a decision within a specified period and the last day of that period is a public holiday (within the meaning of the [*Organisation of Working Time Act, 1997*]) or any other day on which the offices of the planning authority or the Board are closed, the decision shall be valid if given on the next following day on which the offices of the planning authority or Board, as the case may be, are open.

(2) Where the last day of the period specified for making an appeal or referral is a Saturday, a Sunday, a public holiday (within the meaning of the [*Organisation of Working Time Act, 1997*]) or any other day on which the offices of the Board are closed, an appeal or referral shall (notwithstanding any other provision of this *Act*) be valid as having been made in time if received by the Board on the next following day on which the offices of the Board are open.

(3) Where a requirement of or under this *Act* requires submissions, observations or a request to be made, or documents, particulars or other information to be submitted, to the Board within a specified period and the last day of that period is a public holiday (within the meaning of the [*Organisation* *of Working Time Act, 1997*]) or any other day on which the offices of the Board are closed, the submissions, observations or request of documents, particulars or other information (as the case may be) shall be regarded as having been received before the expiration of that period if received by the Board on the next following day on which the offices of the Board are open.

AMENDMENT HISTORY

Section 141 was amended by s.247 of the Local Government Act 2001 (No. 37 of 2001), which, by the Local Government Act 2001 (Commencement) Order 2001 (S.I. No. 458 of 2001), came into effect on October 9, 2001.

Section 247(d) of the Local Government Act 2001 amended the 2000 Act by the substitution in s.141 of "Organisation of Working Time Act, 1997" for "Holidays (Employees) Act, 1973" in each place where it occurred.

NOTE

This section has general application to the reckoning of time deadlines, where the last day falls on a public holiday, Sunday or outside office hours where appropriate. Subsection (1) provides that where a decision of a planning authority or Board is to be given within a specified period and the last day is a public holiday or a day when the offices of the planning authority or Board is closed, the decision may be given on the next following day on which the offices of the Board or authority are open. This subsection applies to both the planning authority and the Board, unlike s.17 of the 1992 Act, which applied only to the Board. Similarly, under subs.(2) in relation to an appeal or referral where the end of the relevant period falls on a Sunday, holidays or outside office hours, where appropriate, such appeal or referral will be valid if received by the Board on the next following day on which the offices of the Board are open. Under subs.(3) a similar rules applies in relation to the submission of observations, documents, particulars or other information to the Board.

Regulations regarding appeals and referrals

142.—(1) The Minister may by regulations-   **1–168**
  (a) provide for such additional, incidental, consequential or supplemental matters as regards procedure in respect of appeals as appear to the Minister to be necessary or expedient, and
  (b) make such provision as regards procedure in respect of referrals as appear to the Minister to be necessary or expedient.

(2) Without prejudice to the generality of *subsection (1),* regulations under this *section* may enable the Board where it is determining an appeal under *section 37* to invite an applicant and enable an applicant so invited to submit to the Board revised plans or other drawings modifying, or other particulars providing for the modification of, the development to which the appeal relates.

(3) Where plans, drawings or particulars referred to in *subsection (2)* are submitted to the Board in accordance with regulations under this *section,* the Board may, in determining the appeal, grant a permission for the relevant development as modified by all or any of the plans, drawings or particulars.

(4) Without prejudice to the generality of *subsection (1),* the Board may require any party to an appeal or referral to give such public notice in relation thereto as the Board may specify and, in particular, may require notice to be given at the site or by publication in a newspaper circulating in the district in which the land or structure to which the appeal or referral relates is situate.

NOTE

    This section enables the Minister to make regulations regarding the procedure for appeals or referrals. Chapter 11 of Pt 7 of the 2001 Regulations sets out regulations in respect of appeals and referrals and other functions of the Board. Subsection (2) allows the making of regulations whereby the Board can invite revised plans. In this respect art.73 of the 2001 Regulations provides that the Board, in considering an appeal, may invite the applicant for permission to submit to the Board revised plans or drawings modifying, or other particulars providing for the modification of, the development to which the appeal relates, and the applicant so invited may submit such number of plans, drawings or particulars as the Board may require. The Board may grant a permission for the development as modified. The planning authority has a similar power to invite revised plans under art.34. The Board may merely "invite" such plans; which does not amount to a request. The invitation for revised plans can only amount to "modification" of the development, as the word "revised" plans suggest. In *White v Dublin Corporation*, unreported, High Court, Ó Caoimh J., June 21, 2002, Ó Caoimh J. said, in the context of a planning authority modifying an application for permission, that the term "modifying" suggests changes of a limited nature such that any changes will be slight or partial. The nature of term modification, was not addressed by the Supreme Court in *White v Dublin Corporation*. However, from *Dietacaron Ltd v An Bord Pleanála* [2005] 2 I.L.R.M. 32 it would appear the Board has a general discretion to invite modifications, which the court will only interfere with on grounds of irrationality. This was so held in *Dietacaron* where Quirke J. rejected the claim that the request for revised plans went beyond a modification and so was ultra vires. Quirke J. contrasted this issue with the interpretation of a development plan stating:

    "The assessment of the nature and extent of such 'modifications' and the conduct of a comparison in order to establish whether the changes invited so radically alter the nature of the development as to comprise a new planning application is not a matter which could safely or reasonably be undertaken by the court placing itself in the position occupied by a reasonably intelligent member of the public".

    Where a person submits revised plans or drawings, under s.143(2) the Board may grant permission in accordance with the revised plans or drawings. Subsection (4) concerns a general power of the Board to require a party to an appeal or referral to give public notice, which may be a site notice or a local newspaper notice. The Board may specify the nature of such notice.

[Board to have regard to certain policies and objectives

1–169   **143.—(1)** The Board shall, in performing its functions, have regard to—

    (a) the policies and objectives for the time being of the Government, a State authority, the Minister, planning authorities and any other body which is a public authority whose functions have, or may have, a bearing on the proper planning and sustainable development of cities, towns or other areas, whether urban or rural,

    (b) the national interest and any effect the performance of the Board's functions may have on issues of strategic economic or social importance to the State, and

    (c) the National Spatial Strategy and any regional planning guidelines for the time being in force.

    (2) In this section "public authority" means any body established by or under statute which is for the time being declared, by regulations made by the Minister, to be a public authority for the purposes of this section.]

AMENDMENT HISTORY

    Substituted by s.26 of the Planning and Development (Strategic Infrastructure) Act 2006 (No. 27 of 2006).

This section imposes a general obligation on the Board to have regard to certain policies and objectives. The obligations under the section applies to the Board in performing any of its functions. Subsection (1) provides that it is to have regard to the policies and objectives of the Government, other public bodies, state authorities, Minister, planning authorities, and public authorities prescribed by the Minister as having a function bearing on the proper planning and sustainable development. Under ss.28(2) and 29(2), the Board may be required to have regard to guidelines or policies issued by the Minister. Also under s.34(2)(a), in a planning application, the planning authority must have regard to any relevant policy of the Government, the Minister or any other Minister of the Government. In requiring the Board to "have regard" to these matters, s.143 is expressed in stronger terms than the former s.5 of the 1976 Act, which required the Board to "keep itself informed of these matters". The requirement to "have regard" does not mean, in every case, that there is an obligation to implement the policies and objectives in question; see *Glencar Exploration Plc v Mayo County Council* [2002] 1 I.R. 84. There is no requirement to rigidly or slavishly comply with the policies or objectives, although the Board cannot ignore them and proceed as if they did not exist; see *McEvoy v Meath County Council* [2003] 1 I.R. 208. The requirement "to have regard" is less onerous than a requirement "to take into account"; see *R v CD* [1976] 1 N.Z.L.R. 436. The 2006 substituted a new section with the main changes being to add ss.143(1)(b) and (c). In this respect, s.143(1)(b) requires the Board to have regard to national interests and the effect of the Board's functions on issues of strategic economic or social importance to the state. This section may be criticised on grounds that it undermines the independence of the Board. However, the Board does not have a policy-making role. The current National Development Plan 2007 to 2013 is not mentioned. However, it is questionable whether the NDP can be of such nature as to be relevant to the functions of the Board in the context of determining an appeal or referral. In *Kavanagh v Ireland*, unreported, High Court, Smyth J., July 31, 2007, Smyth J. described the NDP as a

> "[F]inancial plan or framework setting out what the Government sees as the investment priorities for the next seven years, and how resources can be invested amongst different investment priorities. It is not designed or intended to set any kind of framework for the granting or refusing of permissions for the carrying out of projects or to have any influence on the physical planning process (even if planning authorities or An Bord Pleanála may note it or do have regard to it i.e. the NDP) in their decisions".

Smyth J. said it was essentially a financial or budgetary plan and even if a project of national significance was mentioned in the NDP this would be for administrative purposes as indicative of the type of project that would be financed out of a particular financial envelope.

The general requirements under this section are not confined to strategic infrastructure applications (although it may have more relevance to such applications) but relate to any function performed by the Board. The section gives no guidance as to how the national interest or issues of strategic, economic or social importance are to be ascertained. Government guidelines or policy documents issued by the government may be of some assistance in this respect. Subsection (143)(1)(c) requires the Board to have regard to the National Spatial Strategy and any regional planning guidelines in force. The National Spatial Strategy 2002–2020 (published on November 28, 2002) is a 20-year national planning framework for Ireland which aims to achieve a better balance of social, economic and physical development across Ireland, supported by more effective and integrated planning. The NSS requires that areas of sufficient scale and critical mass be built up through a network of gateways and hubs. While the National Development Plan 2000–2006 identified Dublin, Cork, Limerick/Shannon, Galway and Waterford as existing gateways, the NSS designated four new national level gateways—the towns of Dundalk and Sligo and the linked gateways of Letterkenny/(Derry) and the Midland towns of Athlone/Tullamore/Mullingar. The NSS also identified nine, strategically located, medium-sized "hubs" with the objective that these will support, and be supported by, the gateways and will link out to wider rural areas. The hubs are Cavan, Ennis, Kilkenny, Mallow, Monaghan, Tuam and Wexford, along with the linked hubs of Ballina/Castlebar and Tralee/Killarney. NSS is sought to be implemented through the incorporation of its strategic policies into regional and local planning by regional and local authorities and other national plans. As regards regional guidelines, the Planning and Development (Regional Planning Guidelines) Direction 2003, formally directs each regional authority to make Regional Planning Guidelines for the whole of its region, while the Planning and Development (Regional Planning Guidelines) Regulations 2003 (S.I. No. 175 of 2003) sets out a number of requirements in relation to the preparation of Regional Planning Guidelines.

Fees payable to Board

1–170   **144.—(1)** Subject to the approval of the Minister, the Board may determine fees in relation to appeals, referrals, the making of an application under *section 37(5)* [or in respect of a strategic infrastructure development (including an application under *section 146B* or the submission of an environmental impact statement under 146C)], the making of submissions or observations to the Board under *section 130,* and requests for oral hearings under *section 134,* and may provide for the payment of different fees in relation to different classes or descriptions of [appeals, referrals and applications], for exemption from the payment of fees in specified circumstances and for the waiver, remission or refund in whole or in part of fees in specified circumstances.

(2) The Board shall review the fees determined under subsection (1) from time to time, but at least every three years, having regard to any change in the consumer price index since the determination of the fees for the time being in force, and may amend the fees to reflect the results of that review, without the necessity of the Minister's approval under subsection (1).

(3) For the purposes of this section, "change in the consumer price index" means the difference between the All Items Consumer Price Index Number last published by the Central Statistics Office before the date of the determination under this section and the said number last published before the date of the review under subsection (2), expressed as a percentage of the last-mentioned number.

(4) Where the Board determines or amends fees in accordance with this section, it shall give notice of the fees in at least one newspaper circulating in the State, not less than 8 weeks before the fees come into effect.

(5) Fees determined in accordance with regulations under section 10(1)(b) of the Act of 1982 shall continue to be payable to the Board in accordance with those regulations until such time as the Board determines fees in accordance with this *section.*

(6) The Board shall specify fees for the making of copies under *section 5(6)(a),* not exceeding the cost of making the copies.

AMENDMENT HISTORY

Subsection (1) amended by s. 27 of the Planning and Development (Strategic Infrastructure) Act 2006 (No. 27 of 2006).

NOTE

This section allows the Board, with the approval of the Minister, to set the fees for various matters before it relating to appeals or referrals. The current guide to fees payable by the Board provides that the fees payable to An Bord Pleanála after the December 10, 2007 are as follows:

- application for strategic infrastructure development or a request to alter the terms of such development already permitted or approved: €100,000;
- appeal against a decision of a planning authority on a planning application relating to commercial development, made by the person by whom the planning application was made, where the application relates to unauthorised development: €4,500 or €9,000 if EIS involved;
- appeal against a decision of a planning authority on a planning application relating to commercial development, made by the person by whom the planning application was made, other than the above appeal: €1,500 or €3,000 if EIS involved;
- appeal against a decision of a planning authority on a planning application made by the person by whom the planning application was made, where the application relates to unauthorised development, other than an aforementioned appeal: €660;
- appeal other than an aforementioned appeal: €220;
- application for leave to appeal: €110;
- appeal following a grant of leave to appeal: €110;
- referral: €220;
- reduced fee payable by specified bodies: €110;
- request from a party for an oral hearing of an appeal or referral: €50.

The Board can amend the fees, without Ministerial approval, to reflect changes in inflation in accordance with the consumer price index. All other amendments would require the approval of the Minister. Where fees have been newly determined, public notice must be given in at least one national newspaper at least eight weeks before the changes are due to become effective. The 2006 Act amended this section with the main change being to incorporate references to strategic infrastructure applications.

Expenses of appeal or referral

145.—**(1)** Where an appeal or referral is made to the Board—   **1–171**
    (a) the Board, if it so thinks proper and irrespective of the result of the appeal or referral, may direct the planning authority to pay—
        (i) to the appellant or person making the referral, such sum as the Board, in its absolute discretion, specifies as compensation for the expense occasioned to him or her in relation to the appeal or referral, and
        (ii) to the Board, such sum as the Board, in its absolute discretion, specifies as compensation to the Board towards the expense incurred by the Board in relation to the appeal or referral,

    and

    [(b) in case—
        (i) the decision of the planning authority in relation to an appeal or referral is confirmed or varied and the Board, in determining the appeal or referral, does not accede in substance to the grounds of appeal or referral, or
        (ii) the appeal or referral is decided, dismissed under *section 138* or withdrawn under *section 140* and the Board, in any of those cases, considers that the appeal or referral was made with the intention of delaying the development or securing a monetary gain by a party to the appeal or referral or any other person, the Board may, if it so thinks proper, direct the appellant or person making the referral to pay—
            (I) to the planning authority, such sum as the Board, in its absolute discretion, specifies as compensation to the

planning authority for the expense occasioned to it in relation to the appeal or referral,

(II) to any of the other parties to the appeal or referral, such sum as the Board, in its absolute discretion, specifies as compensation to the party for the expense occasioned to him or her in relation to the appeal or referral, and

(III) to the Board, such sum as the Board, in its absolute discretion, specifies as compensation to the Board towards the expense incurred by the Board in relation to the appeal or referral.]

(2) Any sum directed under this *section* to be paid shall, in default of being paid, be recoverable as a simple contract debt in any court of competent jurisdiction.

AMENDMENT HISTORY

Substituted by s.28 of the Planning and Development (Strategic Infrastructure) Act 2006 (No. 27 of 2006).

NOTE

This section allows the Board to make an award approximating to an order for costs. It differs somewhat from costs insofar as the award is expressed as compensation for expenses rather than the costs or expenses incurred. The Board has complete discretion in making such an award. While in court proceedings costs normally follow the event, i.e. the successful party, subs.(1)(a) states that "irrespective of the result of the appeal or referral", the Board may direct a sum to be paid. The section envisages the Board taking account of a broad set of circumstances. Even though an appeal may have been unsuccessful, the Board may consider that a public interest was served by the taking of the appeal and some recompense should be made to the appellant. The Board can direct that a sum be paid by the planning authority to an appellant or the Board. Under subs.(1)(b) an appellant may be directed to make a payment where the appeal or referral was not acceded to in substance by the Board (and applies even where the Board acceded to some technical insubstantial matter) or even where acceded to, the Board considers the appeal or referral was made with the intention of delaying the development or securing a monetary gain by a third party. Such a direction to pay may be made in favour of the planning authority, the Board or a party to the appeal (though not a non-party who has made submissions). The 2006 amends s.145(1)(b) with the main changes being in subs.(b)(ii) with the addition of the words "the appeal or referral is decided, dismissed under s.138 or withdrawn under s.140 and the Board, in any of those cases". These additional words make it clear that the Board can issue such direction where the appeal/referral is decided, dismissed or withdrawn. It appears that where an application is made to the Board for costs, it should expressly make a decision on such application and should not ignore the provision. See *Clinton v An Bord Pleanála*, unreported, High Court, Finnegan P., March 15, 2005.

Reports and documents of the Board

1–172   **146.—(1)** The Board or an employee of the Board duly authorised by the Board may, in connection with the performance of any of the Board's functions under this *Act,* assign a person to report on any matter on behalf of the Board.

(2) A person assigned in accordance with *subsection (1)* shall make a written report on the matter to the Board, which shall include a recommendation, and the Board shall consider the report and recommendation before determining the matter.

[**(3)** Where, during the consideration by it of any matter falling to be decided by it in performance of a function under or transferred by this Act or any other enactment, the Board either—

    (a) is required by or under this Act or that other enactment to supply to any person documents, maps, particulars or other information in relation to the matter, or

    (b) considers it appropriate, in the exercise of its discretion, to supply to any person such documents, maps, particulars or information ("relevant material or information"), *subsection (4)* applies as regards compliance with that requirement or such supply in the exercise of that discretion.]

[**(4)** It shall be sufficient compliance with the requirement referred to in *subsection (3)* for the Board to do both of the following (or, as appropriate, the Board, in the exercise of the discretion referred to in that subsection, may do both of the following), namely:

    (a) make the relevant material or information available for inspection—

        (i) at the offices of the Board or any other place, or

        (ii) by electronic means;

    and

    (b) notify the person concerned that the relevant material or information is so available for inspection.]

[**(5)** Within 3 days following the making of a decision on any matter falling to be decided by it in performance of a function under or transferred by this Act or under any other enactment, the documents relating to the matter—

    (a) shall be made available by the Board for inspection at the offices of the Board by members of the public, and

    (b) may be made available by the Board for such inspection—

        (i) at any other place, or

        (ii) by electronic means,

    as the Board considers appropriate.]

[**(6)** Copies of the documents referred to in *subsection (5)* and of extracts from such documents shall be made available for purchase at the offices of the Board, or such other places as the Board may determine, for a fee not exceeding the reasonable cost of making the copy.]

[**(7)** The documents referred to in *subsection (5)* shall be made available by the means referred to in *paragraph (a)* of that subsection for a period of at least 5 years beginning on the third day following the making by the Board of the decision on the matter concerned.]

<small>AMENDMENT HISTORY</small>

Subsections (3), (4), (5), (6) and (7) substituted by s.29 of the Planning and Development (Strategic Infrastructure) Act 2006 (No. 27 of 2006).

<small>NOTE</small>

This section concerns the Board assigning a person to report on a matter and the making of certain documents available to the public. Subsection (1) provides that the Board may assign a person to report on any matter to the Board. Subsection (2) states that the report of a person assigned to report on any matter will include a recommendation which must be considered by the Board before determining the matter. A person so assigned could include an inspector charged with inspecting a site. Article 75 of the 2001 Regulations provides that the Board may arrange for the carrying out of inspections in relation to an appeal by a person appointed for that purpose by the Board. If evidence not disclosed at a public hearing is sent to the Board as part a report of the inspector, this may be a ground for quashing the decision. See *Killiney and Ballybrack Development Association Ltd. v Minister for Local Government and Templefinn Estates Ltd (No. 1) (1978)* 112 I.L.T.R. 69, where the inclusion of an account of a visual inspection of the area adjoining the land to be developed had not been disclosed, this rendered the decision invalid. The inspectors recommendation is not binding on the Board. However, s.34(10)(b) provides in the context of a planning appeal that where the decision of the Board is different from the recommendation of a person assigned to report on the appeal, then the statement of the main reasons and consideration of its decision must indicate the main reasons for not accepting the recommendation in the report. Where the Board does not depart from its planner's or inspector's report, it can be assumed that the reasons contained in such reports were accepted, even if not expressly stated. See *Mulholland v An Bord Pleanála (2)* [2006] 1 I.R. 453. As an inspector's report merely contains recommendations, with the ultimate decision being taken by the Board, it appears that the inspector's report is not open to judicial review. See *Lord Ballyedmond v The Commission for Energy Regulation*, unreported, High Court, Clarke J., June 22, 2006.

The 2006 Act inserted a new subs.(3) and relates to where maps, particulars or other information are required to be supplied to any person or where the Board in the exercise of its discretion, considers it appropriate to supply any persons with such matters. Subsection (4) sets out the means of compliance by which maps, particulars or other information are to be supplied and provides that it is sufficient if the matters are available for inspection at the offices of the Board or are made available by electronic means. The subsection does not explain the meaning of "electronic means" but it could include posting on the Internet or emailing the matters to the appropriate persons. However, whether the matters are made available at the offices or by electronic means, the Board must also notify the person that such matters are available for inspection in such manner. The Board is not obliged to notify by such electronic means, however, if it chooses to do so in discharge of its obligation to notify, it must ensure the accuracy of the information. See *O'Connor v Cork County Council*, unreported, High Court, Murphy J., November 1, 2005. However, where the Board is not required to supply certain information but decides to do so in the exercise of its discretion and does so by electronic means, the Board may not have the same obligation to ensure the accuracy of such information. See *Linehan v Cork County Council*, unreported, High Court, Finlay Geoghegan J., February 19, 2008. Subsection (5) is new and provides that the Board must make available the documents relating to any decision at the offices of the Board within three days of the decision. In referring to "the performance of any function" it is expressed in broader terms than the former subs.(3)(a) which it replaced under the orginal 2000 Act, which applied to documents relating to an appeal or referral; a decision of the Board under s.175 concerning development requiring an EIS; or under Pt XIV relating to the acquisition of land. The new subs.(5) provides that the obligation to make available is within three days rather than three working days as stated in the former subsection. In the context of a planning appeal, the extent of documents to be made available is not defined but would appear to cover the entire file which would include the decision itself, the application/appeal, any submissions received and reports, etc. The obligation to make available only arises after the decision has been made and so does not require them to be made available pending the outcome of the decision. An application for discovery of documents in possession of the Board may be refused where they are available for public inspection. See *Arklow Holdings v An Bord Pleanála*, unreported, High Court, Clarke J., August 3, 2005. In addition to making the documents available at its offices, the Board may also at its discretion make the documents available at any other place or by electronic means. The latter would therefore include posting the matter on the Internet. This is not however a mandatory requirement. Subsection (6) requires copies of documents to be available for purchase. Subsection (7) requires the documents relating to the decision to be made available for a period of at least five years.

Additional powers of Board in relation to permissions, decisions, approvals, etc.

Amendments of permissions, etc. of clerical or technical nature

146A.—**(1)** Subject to *subsection (2)* — 1–173
  (a) a planning authority or the Board, as may be appropriate, may amend a planning permission granted by it, or
  (b) the Board may amend any decision made by it in performance of a function under or transferred by this Act or under any other enactment, for the purposes of—
    (i) correcting any clerical error therein,
    (ii) facilitating the doing of any thing pursuant to the permission or decision where the doing of that thing may reasonably be regarded as having been contemplated by a particular provision of the permission or decision or the terms of the permission or decision taken as a whole but which was not expressly provided for in the permission or decision, or
    (iii) otherwise facilitating the operation of the permission or decision.

(2) A planning authority or the Board shall not exercise the powers under *subsection (1)* if to do so would, in its opinion, result in a material alteration of the terms of the development, the subject of the permission or decision concerned.

(3) A planning authority or the Board, before it decides whether to exercise the powers under *subsection (1)* in a particular case, may invite submissions in relation to the matter to be made to it by any person who made submissions or observations to the planning authority or the Board in relation to the permission or other matter concerned, and shall have regard to any submissions made to it on foot of that invitation.

(4) In this section "term" includes a condition.]

AMENDMENT HISTORY

Inserted by s.30 of the Planning and Development (Strategic Infrastructure) Act 2006 (No. 27 of 2006).

NOTE

This section allows a planning authority or the Board to amend a planning permission (including a planning condition) or other decision of the Board on certain specified grounds. There are no time limits as to when the planning authority or Board may exercise its power to amend the permission/decision. It also appears that an amendment can be made at any stage whether before, during or after the implementation of the permission. The section does not set out who may request such alteration (unlike s.146B) and so there are no restrictions in this regard. Subsection (1) sets out three circumstances when the planning authority or Board may exercise this power, namely:
  (i) to correct clerical errors;
  (ii) facilitate doing anything contemplated, though not expressly stated, by the permission or decision; or
  (iii) otherwise facilitating the operation of the permission or decision.
  Clerical errors refer to administrative errors in the drafting of the decision rather than

matters of a substantive nature. It is therefore analogous to the "slip rule" which allows correcting errors of a clerical nature of judges or arbitrators. The second heading (ii) which relates to "facilitating the doing of anything" pursuant to the permission or decision, is expressed in broad terms. Such amendment may only be allowed where the matter can reasonably be regarded as having been contemplated by either a provision of a permission/ decision or the permission/decision, taken as whole. Under general rules of construction, a permission may be deemed as having authorised matters which are clearly implied from the permission. However, making this rule of construction an express provision reduces uncertainty. The use of the word "reasonably" implies that the standard is objective, while the word "contemplated" implies that it must have been considered by the planning authority/ Board when viewed objectively. Although, it refers to the provisions of a permission/ decision or the permission/decision taken as a whole, it appears that regard may be had to documentation other than the permission/decision in interpreting whether the matter can reasonably be regarded as having been contemplated. This is consistent with the fact that in interpreting a planning permission, regard may be had to the planning application and other accompanying documentation. See *Readymix (Éire) Ltd v Dublin County Council*, unreported, Supreme Court, July 30, 1974. In *Mason and McCarthy v KT Sand and Gravel*, unreported, High Court, Smyth J., May 7, 2004, Smyth J noted that although a condition in a planning permission requiring works to be carried out may impliedly include permission for those works, the scope of the permission was a matter of construction, subject to the principle that the permission could not go beyond the scope of the application or matters reasonably incidental thereto.

The third heading (iii) of otherwise facilitating the operation of the permission/decision, is also expressed in broad terms and must be deemed to cover matters which could not reasonably be regarded as having been contemplated under (ii). This third category could cover matters of design or technical difficulties which become apparent when implementing the permission. This does not represent a significant departure as a planning permission covers immaterial variations of planning permission which were unforeseen at the time of permission but emerge when the developer proceeds with the work. See *O'Connell v Dungarvan Energy Ltd*, unreported, High Court, Finnegan J., February 27, 2001. However, one general limitation to amending under any of the three headings, is stated in subs.(2) which is that it must not result in a material alteration of the terms of the development. However, the words "in its opinion" implies that the assessment of what is a material alteration is a matter for the planning judgment of the planning authority or Board. In this respect an analogy could be made with the assessment of the materially of modifications in revised plans under art.34 of the Planning Regulations 2001. See *Dietacaron Ltd v An Bord Pleanála* [2005] 2 I.L.R.M. 32, where Quirke J. noted:

> "The assessment of the nature and extent of such "modifications" and the conduct of a comparison in order to establish whether the changes invited so radically alter the nature of the development as to comprise a new planning application is not a matter which could safely or reasonably be undertaken by the court placing itself in the position occupied by a reasonably intelligent member of the public".

Under subs.(3), the planning authority or Board may invite submissions from any person who made submissions in relation to the permission/other matter. There is no mandatory obligation on the planning authority/Board to invite such submissions and so it is a matter of discretion. However, this provision must be read subject to general principles of fair procedures. However, the fact that the amendment cannot constitute a material alteration of the permission/decision, means that it may be difficult for such party to subsequently claim that the matter was of such significance so as to require an opportunity to make submissions. However, the planning authority/Board may make such invitation in order to assist its assessment of whether the amendment would constitute a material alteration. It should also be noted that the general obligations arising from the requirement of fair procedures in the planning process will not be as extensive where the party concerned is an objector. See *State (Haverty) v An Bord Pleanála* [1987] I.R. 485 and *Klohn v An Bord Pleanála*, unreported, High Court, McMahon J., April 23, 2008.

[Alteration by Board of Strategic infrastructure development on request made of it

146B.—**(1)** Subject to *subsections (2) to (8)* and *section 146C*, the Board   **1–174** may, on the request of any person who is carrying out or intending to carry out a strategic infrastructure development, alter the terms of the development the subject of a planning permission, approval or other consent granted under this Act.

(2)

(a) As soon as practicable after the making of such a request, the Board shall make a decision as to whether the making of the alteration to which the request relates would constitute the making of a material alteration of the terms of the development concerned.

(b) Before making a decision under this subsection, the Board may invite submissions in relation to the matter to be made to it by such person or class of person as the Board considers appropriate (which class may comprise the public if, in the particular case, the Board determines that it shall do so); the Board shall have regard to any submissions made to it on foot of that invitation.

(3) If the Board decides that the making of the alteration—

(a) would not constitute the making of a material alteration of the terms of the development concerned, it shall alter the planning permission, approval or other consent accordingly and notify the person who made the request under this section, and the planning authority or each planning authority for the area or areas concerned, of the alteration,

(b) would constitute the making of such a material alteration, it shall determine whether to—

(i) make the alteration,

(ii) make an alteration of the terms of the development concerned, being an alteration that would be different from that to which the request relates (but which would not, in the opinion of the Board, represent, overall, a more significant change to the terms of the development than that which would be represented by the latter alteration), or

(iii) refuse to make the alteration.

(4) Before making a determination under *subsection (3)(b),* the Board shall determine whether the extent and character of—

(a) the alteration requested under *subsection (1),* and

(b) any alternative alteration it is considering under *subsection (3)(b)(ii),* are such that the alteration, were it to be made, would be likely to have significant effects on the environment (and, for this purpose, the Board shall have reached a final decision as to what is the extent and character of any alternative alteration the making of which it is so considering).

(5) If the Board determines that the making of either kind of alteration referred to in *subsection (3)(b)* —

(a) is not likely to have significant effects on the environment, it shall proceed to make a determination under *subsection (3)(b),* or

(b) is likely to have such effects, the provisions of *section 146C* shall apply.

(6) If, in a case to which *subsection (5)(a)* applies, the Board makes a determination to make an alteration of either kind referred to in *subsection (3)(b),* it shall alter the planning permission, approval or other consent accordingly and notify the person who made the request under this section, and the planning authority or each planning authority for the area or areas concerned, of the alteration.

(7) In making a determination under *subsection (4),* the Board shall have regard to the criteria for the purposes of determining which classes of development are likely to have significant effects on the environment set out in any regulations made under *section 176.*

(8)

(a) Before making a determination under *subsection (3)(b) or (4),* the Board shall—

(i) make, or require the person who made the request concerned under *subsection (1)* to make, such information relating to that request available for inspection for such period,

(ii) notify, or require that person to notify, such person, such class of person or the public (as the Board considers appropriate) that the information is so available, and

(iii) invite, or require that person to invite, submissions or observations (from any foregoing person or, as appropriate, members of the public) to be made to it in relation to that request within such period, as the Board determines and, in the case of a requirement under any of the preceding subparagraphs, specifies in the requirement; such a requirement may specify the means by which the thing to which it relates is to be done.

(b) The Board shall have regard to any submissions or observations made to it in accordance with an invitation referred to in *paragraph (a).*

(c) The Board shall notify any person who made a submission or observation to it in accordance with that invitation of its determination under *subsection (3)(b) or (4).*

(9) In this section "term" has the same meaning as it has in *section 146A.*]

AMENDMENT HISTORY

Inserted by s.30 of the Planning and Development (Strategic Infrastructure) Act 2006 (No. 27 of 2006).

NOTE

This section allows the Board to alter the terms of a strategic infrastructure development which has already been subject to permission, approval or consent. The section only concerns strategic infrastructure development and is expressed in different terms from s.146A insofar as it allows altering the "development" rather than the permission, approval or consent to which such development is subject. However, the approval of alterations to the development inevitably involves alteration to the underlying permission or approval. The request for alteration can only be made by the person carrying out the development or by the person who intends to carry out the development. Thus, the person making the request need not be the original applicant for the permission. The request can be made prior to the commencement of development or during the implementation of the development; but it appears that such request cannot be made where the development is complete. This is consistent with the fact that the request for alteration is of the development rather than the permission. Under subs.(2), the Board must decide as soon as practicable whether the alteration is a material alteration. Before making this assessment, the Board has a discretion whether to invite submissions. Invitations may be sought from the public in general or from a more limited class of person, such as persons who made submissions on the original permission, approval or consent. However, under subs.(8), the Board must require the person making the request to make available information relating to the request for inspection by the public. The Board must also require such person to notify certain classes of persons (which could include the entire public where it considers appropriate) that such information is to be available for inspection and that submissions may be made. It is for the Board to determine the period for inspection/submissions and the place where the information is available for inspection. The Board must have regard to any submissions received before making its determination. Under subs.(3), where the Board considers that the alteration is not a material alteration, it must make such alteration and has no discretion to refuse. However, where it considers that the alteration is a material alteration, it has a discretion either to make the alteration, make a different alteration so long as it is not more significant than the requested alteration or to refuse to make such alteration.

Prior to making a determination as to whether to make the alteration or to make a different alteration, the Board must assess whether the extent and character of such alteration would be likely to have significant effects on the environment. By virtue of subs.(7), the Board must apply the general criteria for assessing significant effects on the environment under s.176 (concerning the requirement to carry out an EIS), more particularly set out in Sch.7 of the 2001 Regulations. It would appear that the assessment of whether the matter has significant effects on the environment is a matter within the discretion of the Board exercising their expertise and planning judgment. An analogy could be made with *Kinsella v Dundalk Town Council*, unreported, High Court, Kelly J., December 3, 2004, where Kelly J. noted that:

"The task of assessing whether 'significant additional data' is contained in a response involves the exercise of planning expertise and judgment which this Court does not have and is precisely the kind of question which falls within the competence of an expert decision maker. This Court can only interfere with such decision within the strict limitations of its judicial review function which I have already outlined".

If the Board decides that the alteration has significant effects on the environment, then notice must be published under s.146C; otherwise the Board can make its determination. Under subs.(6), if the Board determines to make the alteration it must then notify the person who made the request for the alteration, the planning authority for the area concerned and by virtue of subs.(8)(c), any person who made submissions. The steps involved in the above process therefore involve the following:

1. Request for alteration received by the Board.
2. The Board must require person making request to make information available for inspection and notify certain classes of persons and to invite submissions from such persons.
3. The Board considers whether to invite submissions from certain classes of persons.
4. The Board determines whether the alteration or alternative alteration would be likely to have significant effects on the environment.
5. If it has significant effects on the environment, the procedures set out in s.146C must be followed.
6. The Board has regard to submissions received.
7. The Board makes its determination which may be:
   (a) to make the alteration
   (b) to make a different alternation or

(c) to refuse to make the alteration.

8. The Board notifies its determination to the person making the request, to the planning authority for the area concerned and to any person who made submissions on the proposed alteration.

[Preparation of environmental impact statement for purposes of section 146B

1–175   **146C.—(1)** This section applies to a case where the determination of the Board under *section 146B(4)* is that the making of either kind of alteration referred to in *section 146B(3)(b)* is likely to have significant effects on the environment.

(2) In a case to which this section applies, the Board shall require the person who made the request under *section 146B* ("the requester") to prepare an environmental impact statement in relation to the proposed alteration of the terms of the development concerned and, in this subsection and the following subsections of this section, "proposed alteration of the terms of the development concerned" means—

    (a) the alteration referred to in *subsection (3)(b)(i)*, and

    (b) any alternative alteration under *subsection (3)(b)(ii)* the making of which the Board is considering (and particulars of any such alternative alteration the making of which is being so considered shall be furnished, for the purposes of this subsection, by the Board to the requester).

(3) An environmental impact statement under this section shall contain—

    (a) any information that any regulations made under *section 177* require to be contained in environmental impact statements generally under this Act, and

    (b) any other information prescribed in any regulations made under *section 177* to the extent that—

        (i) such information is relevant to—

            (I) the given stage of the consent procedure and to the specific characteristics of the development or type of development concerned, and

            (II) the environmental features likely to be affected, and

        (ii) the person or persons preparing the statement may reasonably be required to compile it having regard to current knowledge and methods of assessment,

    and

    (c) a summary, in non-technical language, of the information referred to in *paragraphs (a) and (b)*.

(4) When an environmental impact statement under this section is prepared, the requester shall as soon as may be—

    (a) submit a copy of the statement to the Board, together with either—

        (i) a copy of the published notice referred to in *paragraph (c)*, or

        (ii) a copy of the notice proposed to be published in accordance with *paragraph (c)* together with details of its proposed publication and date,

(b) publish a notice, in the prescribed form, in one or more newspapers circulating in the area in which the development concerned is proposed to be, or is being, carried out—

(i) stating that an environmental impact statement has been submitted to the Board in relation to the proposed alteration of the terms of the development concerned,

(ii) indicating the times at which, the period (which shall not be less than 4 weeks) during which and the place or places where a copy of the environmental impact statement may be inspected,

(iii) stating that a copy of the environmental impact statement may be purchased on payment of a specified fee (which fee shall not exceed the reasonable cost of making such copy), and

(iv) stating that submissions or observations may be made in writing to the Board before a specified date (which date shall not be less than 4 weeks after the notice was first published) in relation to the likely effects on the environment of the proposed alteration of the foregoing terms,

(c) send a copy of the environmental impact statement together with a notice in the prescribed form to the local authority or each local authority in whose functional area the proposed development would be situate and to any prescribed body or person stating that—

(i) the statement has been submitted to the Board in relation to the proposed alteration of the terms of the development concerned,

(ii) before a specified date (which date shall be the same as provided or proposed to be provided for by the notice under *paragraph (b)*) submissions or observations may be made in writing to the Board in relation to the likely effects on the environment of the proposed alteration of the foregoing terms,

(d) send a copy of the environmental impact statement, together with a notice in the prescribed form, to a Member State of the European Communities or a state which is a party to the Transboundary Convention where, in the Board's opinion, the proposed alteration of the terms of the development concerned is likely to have significant effects on the environment in that state, together with a notice (in the prescribed form, if any) stating that—

(i) the statement has been submitted to the Board in relation to the likely effects on the environment of the proposed alteration of the foregoing terms,

(ii) before a specified date (which date shall be the same as provided or proposed to be provided for by the notice under *paragraph (b)*) submissions or observations may be made in writing to the Board in relation to the likely effects on the environment in that state of the proposed alteration of those terms, and the Board may, at its discretion and from time to time, extend any time limits provided for by this subsection.

(5) On the preceding subsections having been complied with, the Board shall, subject to *subsections (6) and (7),* proceed to make a determination under *section 146B(3)(b)* in relation to the matter.

(6) In making that determination, the Board shall, to the extent that they appear to the Board to be relevant, have regard to the following:

    (a) the environmental impact statement submitted pursuant to *subsection (4)(a),* any submissions or observations made in response to the invitation referred to in *subsection (4)(b) or (c)* before the date specified in the notice concerned for that purpose and any other relevant information before it relating to the likely effects on the environment of the proposed alteration of the terms of the development concerned;

    (b) where such alteration is likely to have significant effects on the environment in another Member State of the European Communities, or a state which is a party to the Transboundary Convention, the views of such Member State or party;

    (c) the development plan or plans for the area in which the development concerned is proposed to be, or is being, carried out (referred to subsequently in this subsection as "the area");

    (d) the provisions of any special amenity area order relating to the area;

    (e) if the area or part of the area is a European site or an area prescribed for the purposes of *section 10(2)(c),* that fact;

    (f) if the development concerned (were it to be carried out in the terms as they are proposed to be altered) would have an effect on a European site or an area prescribed for the purposes of *section 10(2)(c),* that fact;

    (g) the matters referred to in *section 143;*

    (h) any social or economic benefit that would accrue to the State, a region of the State or the area were the development concerned to be carried out in the terms as they are proposed to be altered;

    (i) commitments entered into and the stage at which the development concerned has progressed under the permission, approval or other consent in the terms as originally granted; and

    (j) any relevant provisions of this Act and of any regulations made under this Act.

(7) The Board shall not make a determination under *section 146B(3)(b)* in a case to which this section applies at any time prior to the date specified, pursuant to *subparagraph (iv) of subsection (4)(b),* in the notice under *subsection (4)(b).*

(8) Where the Board makes a determination under *section 146B(3)(b)* in a case to which this section applies—

    (a) it shall give public notice of the determination (including notice in the area in which the development concerned is proposed to be, or is being, carried out) and inform any state to which an environmental impact statement has been sent under *subsection (4)(d)* of the determination, including, if the determination is of the kind referred to in *paragraph (b),* particulars of the determination, and

(b) if the determination is a determination to make an alteration of either kind referred to in *section 146B(3)(b),* it shall alter the planning permission, approval or other consent accordingly and notify the requester of the alteration.

(9) Without prejudice to the generality of *section 18(a) of the Interpretation Act 2005,* a reference, however expressed, in this section to the area in which the proposed development would be situated includes, if the context admits, a reference to the 2 or more areas in which the proposed development would be situated and cognate references shall be construed accordingly.]

AMENDMENT HISTORY

Inserted by s.30 of the Planning and Development (Strategic Infrastructure) Act 2006 (No. 27 of 2006).

Note

This section applies where the Board considers that an alteration has a significant effect on the environment such that an EIS is necessary. It applies where the alteration was requested by the applicant or where it is an alteration suggested by the Board. The EIS must contain the information set out in para.1 of Sch.6 to the 2001 Regulations. It must also contain the information set out in para.2 of Sch.6 to the extent that it is relevant to the consent procedure, to the type of development involved and the environmental features likely to be affected. These considerations are the same as those set out at art.94 of the 2001 Regulations. Under subs.(4), the requester must submit a copy of the EIS to the Board along with a proposed or published newspaper notice. The newspaper notice must be published stating that an EIS has been submitted; that it is available for inspection for a specified period not less than four weeks; that it is available for purchase and that submissions may be made within a period not less than four weeks. Article 217 of the 2001 Regulations as amended prescribes a specific form in which the submissions must be made. The Board shall acknowledge in writing the receipt of any submission or observation as soon as may be following receipt of the submission or observation. Any submissions or observations that do not comply with the prescribed form shall not be considered by the Board. A person who makes submissions or observations to the Board shall not be entitled to elaborate upon the submissions or observations or make further submissions or observations except where the Board before making its decision asks such person to make submissions or observations or elaborate upon submissions or observations in relation to an application.

A copy of the EIS and prescribed notice must also be sent to the relevant local authority which should state that submissions may be made to the Board. A copy of the EIS and the prescribed notice must also be sent to a Member State of the European Communities or a state which is a party to the Transboundary Convention where the Board considers that the proposed alteration of the terms of the development is likely to have significant effects on the environment in that state. Article 221 of the 2001 Regulations states that where the requester is required to send a copy of the EIS, together with a notice, to a Member State of the European Communities or a State which is a party to the Transboundary Convention, the Board shall indicate the bodies in the States to be notified following consultation with the Minister for the Environment, Heritage and Local Government, the Environmental Protection Agency, the Minister for Communications, Marine and Natural Resources or the relevant planning authority as appropriate. The notice must include:

- a description of the development, including location;
- the reference number of the initial approval or permission;
- the nature and extent of the proposed alteration;
- the name and address of the requestor; and
- the types of the decision the Board may make in relation to the application.

The Board has a discretion whether to extend any time limit. Subsection (6) sets out the matters which the Board is to have regard in making its determination on whether to permit the alteration. These are all mandatory considerations. However, the requirement "to have regard" does not mean that the Board is required to slavishly adhere to such matters. See *McEvoy v Meath County Council* [2003] 1 I.R. 208. Under subs.(6)(a) the Board must carry out an EIA taking into account the enlisted matters. Among other matters to take into account include under (c) is the plan for the area, although the Board may permit the alteration even if the alteration would constitute a material contravention of the development plan. Also, under (h), the Board must consider any social or economic benefit that would accrue to the State or area. This potentially imports a broader range of considerations than would be covered under the notion of proper planning and sustainable development. Under (i) the Board must have regard to commitments entered into and the stage at which the development concerned has progressed. Thus where the requester has entered into commitments, which would be assisted by permitting the alteration, then this will be a relevant consideration. Equally, the extent of advancement of the development will be a relevant consideration in assessing whether to permit the alteration. Subsection (7) provides that the Board may not make its determination until the period allowed for making submissions has expired. Under subs.(8), when the Board makes its determination it must publish a public notice and inform any State to which the EIS was submitted. If the Board determines to make the alteration, it must make the alterations to the relevant permission, consent, or approval and notify the requester. Subsection (9) refers to s.18(a) of the Interpretation Act 2005, which provides that a word importing the singular shall be read as also importing the plural, and a word importing the plural shall be read as also importing the singular. Subsection (9) merely means that a reference to the singular "area" when used in the section will be deemed to refer to two or more areas, where applicable to the particular development.

[Application of sections 146A to 146C to railway orders

1–176   **146D.**—Sections 146A to 146C shall apply to a railway order under the *Transport (Railway Infrastructure) Act 2001* (whether made before or after the amendment of that Act by the *Planning and Development (Strategic Infrastructure) Act 2006*) as they apply to a permission, decision or approval referred to in them with the following modifications:

1.   a reference in those sections to the terms of the development shall be construed as a reference to the terms of the railway works, the subject of the railway order;

2.   a reference in those sections to altering the terms of the development shall be construed as a reference to amending, by order, the railway order with respect to the terms of the railway works, the subject of the railway order; and

3.   a reference in *section 146A* to submissions or observations made to the Board in relation to the permission or other matter concerned shall be construed as a reference to submissions made to the Minister for Transport or the Board, as the case may be, under the *Transport (Railway Infrastructure) Act 2001* in relation to the railway order.]

AMENDMENT HISTORY

Inserted by s.30 of the Planning and Development (Strategic Infrastructure) Act 2006 (No. 27 of 2006).

NOTE

This section provides that s.146A to 146C concerning amendments and alterations are applicable, subject to certain modifications, to amendments/alterations of a railway order. Under s.43(2) of the Transport (Railway Infrastructure) Act 2001, the Minister for Transport may make an order:

> "[A]uthorising the applicant to construct, maintain, improve and, subject to *section 11 (7)* in the case of the Agency, operate the railway or the railway works specified in the order or any part thereof, in such manner and subject to such conditions, restrictions and requirements (and on such other terms) as the Minister thinks proper and specifies in the order".

The main difference is that the amendments/alterations concern a railway order under which railway works are undertaken.

PART VII

Disclosure of Interests, etc.

Declaration by members, etc. of certain interests

147.—**(1)** It shall be the duty of a person to whom this *section* applies to give to the relevant body a declaration in the prescribed form, signed by him or her and containing particulars of every interest of his or hers which is an interest to which this *section* applies and for so long as he or she continues to be a person to whom this *section* applies it shall be his or her duty where there is a change regarding an interest particulars of which are contained in the declaration or where he or she acquires any other interest to which this *section* applies, to give to the relevant body a fresh declaration.   1–177

(2) A declaration under this *section* shall be given at least once a year.

(3)

    (a) This *section* applies to the following persons:

        (i) a member of the Board;

        (ii) a member of a planning authority;

        (iii) an employee of the Board or any other person—

            (I) whose services are availed of by the Board, and

            (II) who is of a class, description or grade prescribed for the purposes of this *section;*

        (iv) an officer of a planning authority who is the holder of an office which is of a class, description or grade so prescribed.

    (b) This *section* applies to the following interests:

        (i) any estate or interest which a person to whom this *section* applies has in any land, but excluding any interest in land consisting of any private home within the meaning of *paragraph 1 (4) of the Second Schedule to the Ethics in Public Office Act, 1995;*

        (ii) any business of dealing in or developing land in which such a person is engaged or employed and any such business carried on by a company or other body of which he or she, or any nominee of his or hers, is a member;

        (iii) any profession, business or occupation in which such a person is engaged, whether on his or her own behalf or otherwise, and which relates to dealing in or developing land.

(4) A person to whom this *section* applies and who has an interest to which this *section* applies shall be regarded as complying with the requirements of *subsection (1)* if he or she gives to the relevant body a declaration referred to in that *subsection* :

    (a) within the period of twenty-eight days beginning on the day on which he or she becomes such a person,

    (b) in case there is a change regarding an interest particulars of which are contained in a declaration already given by the person or where the person acquires any other interest to which this *section* applies, on the day on which the change occurs or the other such interest is acquired.

(5) For the purposes of this *section,* a person to whom this *section* applies shall be regarded as having an estate or interest in land if he or she, or any nominee of his or hers, is a member of a company or other body which has an estate or interest in the land.

(6) For the purposes of this *section,* a person shall not be regarded as having an interest to which this *section* applies, if the interest is so remote or insignificant that it cannot reasonably be regarded as likely to influence a person in considering or discussing, or in voting on, any question with respect to any matter arising or coming before the Board or authority, as may be appropriate, or in performing any function in relation to any such matter.

(7) Where a person to whom this *section* applies has an interest to which this *section* applies by reason only of the beneficial ownership of shares in a company or other body by him or her or by his or her nominee and the total value of those shares does not exceed the lesser of—

    (a) [€13,000], or

    (b) one-hundredth part of the total nominal value of either the issued share capital of the company or body or, where that capital is issued in shares of more than one class, the issued share capital of the class or classes of shares in which he or she has an interest,

subsection (1) shall not have effect in relation to that interest.

(8) The Board and each planning authority shall for the purposes of this *section* keep a register ("the register of interests") and shall enter therein the particulars contained in declarations given to the Board or the authority, as the case may be, pursuant to this *section.*

(9) The register of interests shall be kept at the offices of the Board or the planning authority, as the case may be, and shall be available for public inspection during office hours.

(10) Where a person ceases to be a person to whom this *section* applies, any particulars entered in the register of interests as a result of a declaration being given by the person to the relevant body pursuant to this *section* shall be removed, as soon as may be after the expiration of the period of five years beginning on the day on which the person ceases to be such a person, from the register of interests by that body.

(11) Subject to *subsection (12),* a person who fails to comply with *subsections (1) and (2)* or who, when purporting to comply with the requirements of *subsection (1),* gives particulars which are false or which to his or her knowledge are misleading in a material respect, shall be guilty of an offence.

(12) In any proceedings for an offence under this *section* it shall be a defence for the defendant to prove that at the relevant time he or she believed, in good faith and upon reasonable grounds, that—

(a) the relevant particulars were true,

(b) there was no matter as regards which he or she was then required to make a declaration under *subsection (1),* or

(c) that the matter in relation to which the offence is alleged was not one as regards which he or she was so required to make such a declaration.

(13)

(a) For the purposes of this *section and sections 148 and 149* —

(i) a manager shall be deemed to be an officer of every planning authority for which he or she is manager,

(ii) an assistant county manager for a county shall be deemed to be an officer of every planning authority in the county, and

(iii) an officer of a planning authority who, by virtue of an arrangement or agreement entered into under any enactment, is performing functions under another planning authority, shall be deemed to be also an officer of the other authority.

(b) In this *section* "relevant body" *means—*

(i) in case a person to whom this section applies is either a member or employee of the Board, or other person whose services are availed of by the Board, the Board, and

(ii) in case such a person is either a member or officer of a planning authority, the authority.

AMENDMENT HISTORY

Subsection (7) amended by s.1 and Schedule to the Euro Changeover (Amounts) Act 2001 (No. 16 of 2001) with effect from January 1, 2002.

NOTE

This section provides that persons connected with the Board and planning authority (including members, officers and employees) must a make declaration disclosing their interest in land. This provision is designed to ensure that the independent functioning of the Board or the planning authority in performance is not vitiated by any personal interest. The various classes of persons enlisted in subs.(3) are obliged to make a declaration in the prescribed form of their interest (including being a member of a company which has such interest, though subject to threshold qualification in subs.(7), in any business of dealing in or developing, and any profession or occupation involving the developing of land. The obligation will not arise where the interest is so remote and insignificant that it cannot reasonably be regarded as likely to influence a person in considering any matter before the Board or planning authority, where appropriate. The declaration must be provided within two days of a person becoming a person required to make a declaration, and where there is a change in the particulars of the declaration, particulars of such change must be given on the day of the change or acquisition of interest. A person who fails to make the declaration or who gives a false declaration will be guilty of an offence. Certain defences to the offence are set out, which are based on a bona fide and reasonable belief. The contents of the declaration are set out in a register of interests, which are available to inspection by the public.

The particulars of any person's interest will continue to be held on the register for five years after they have ceased to hold their relevant position. The section reflects certain of the standards reflected in the Ethics in Public Office Act 1995, as well as in such legislation as Public Bodies Corrupt Practices Act 1899 and the Prevention of Corruption Act 1916. This section re-enacts s.32 of the 1976 Act. Article 180 of the 2001 Regulations sets out the class, description or grade prescribed for the purposes of the section. These are:

- every employee of the Board, except those in an employment for which the qualifications are not wholly or in part professional or technical, and the maximum remuneration is less than the maximum remuneration for the office of Executive Officer in the Civil Service;
- every officer of the Minister, pursuant to arrangement made under s.122(1); and
- every person employed in a part-time capacity by the Board in accordance with s.120(2) of the Act, who is engaged in duties relating to appeals, referrals or other matters which fall to be determined by the Board under the Act or other enactment.

Also, every person engaged as a consultant or adviser to the Board under s.124 of the Act is prescribed for the purposes of s.150. Paragraph 2.3.1 of the Board's Code of Conduct referred to in s.150 provides that where a person has a pecuniary or other beneficial interest referred to in subss.(3), (4) or (5) of s.147, by reason only of the beneficial ownership of shares in a company or other body by him/her or by his/her nominee and the total value of those shares does not exceed the lesser of—€13,000 or one-hundredth part of the total nominal value of either the issued share capital of the company or body or, where that capital is issued in shares of more than one class, the issued share capital of the class or classes of shares in which he or she has an interest the statutory requirements concerning declarations and disclosures do not apply in relation to that interest.

Requirements affecting members, etc. who have certain beneficial interests

1–178   **148.—(1)** Where a member of the Board has a pecuniary or other beneficial interest in, or which is material to, any appeal, contribution, question, determination or dispute which falls to be decided or determined by the Board under any enactment, he or she shall comply with the following requirements:

(a) he or she shall disclose to the Board the nature of his or her interest;

(b) he or she shall take no part in the discussion or consideration of the matter;

(c) he or she shall not vote or otherwise act as a member of the Board in relation to the matter;

(d) he or she shall neither influence nor seek to influence a decision of the Board as regards the matter.

(2) Where, at a meeting of a planning authority or of any committee of a planning authority, a resolution, motion, question or other matter is proposed or otherwise arises either pursuant to, or as regards the performance by the authority of a function under this *Act* or in relation to the acquisition or disposal by the authority of land under or for the purposes of this *Act* or any other enactment, a member of the authority or committee present at the meeting shall, if he or she has a pecuniary or other beneficial interest in, or which is material to, the matter—

(a) at the meeting, and before discussion or consideration of the matter commences, disclose the nature of his or her interest, and

(b) withdraw from the meeting for so long as the matter is being discussed or considered,

and accordingly, he or she shall take no part in the discussion or consideration of the matter and shall refrain from voting in relation to it.

(3) A member of a planning authority or of any committee of a planning authority who has a pecuniary or other beneficial interest in, or which is material to, a matter arising either pursuant to, or as regards the performance by the authority of a function under this *Act,* or in relation to the acquisition or disposal by the authority of land under or for the purposes of this *Act* or any other enactment, shall neither influence nor seek to influence a decision of the authority as regards the matter.

(4) Where the manager of a planning authority has a pecuniary or other beneficial interest in, or which is material to, any matter which arises or comes before the authority either pursuant to, or as regards the performance by the authority of a function under this *Act,* or in relation to the acquisition or disposal by the authority of land under or for the purposes of this *Act* or any other enactment, he or she shall, as soon as may be, disclose to the members of the planning authority the nature of his or her interest.

(5)

    (a) Where an employee of the Board, a consultant or adviser engaged by the Board, or any other person whose services are availed of by the Board has a pecuniary or other beneficial interest in, or which is material to, any appeal, contribution, question or dispute which falls to be decided or determined by the Board, he or she shall comply with the following requirements:

        (i) he or she shall neither influence nor seek to influence a decision of the Board as regards the matter;

        (ii) in case, as such employee, consultant, adviser or other person, he or she is concerned with the matter, he or she shall disclose to the Board the nature of his or her interest and comply with any directions the Board may give him or her in relation to the matter.

    (b) Where an officer of a planning authority, not being the manager, has a pecuniary or other beneficial interest in, or which is material to, any matter which arises or comes before the authority, either pursuant to, or as regards the performance by the authority of a function under this *Act,* or in relation to the acquisition or disposal of land by the authority under or for the purposes of this *Act* or any other enactment, he or she shall comply with the following requirements:

        (i) he or she shall neither influence nor seek to influence a decision of the authority as regards the matter; and

        (ii) in case, as such officer, he or she is concerned with the matter, he or she shall disclose to the manager of the authority the nature of his or her interest and comply with any directions the manager may give him or her in relation to the matter.

(6) For the purposes of this *section* but without prejudice to the generality of *subsections (1) to (5),* a person shall be regarded as having a beneficial interest if—

    (a) he or she or his or her spouse, or any nominee of his or her or of his or her spouse, is a member of a company or any other body which has a beneficial interest in, or which is material to, a resolution, motion, question or other matter referred to in *subsections (1) to (5),*

(b) he or she or his or her spouse is in partnership with or is in the employment of a person who has a beneficial interest in, or which is material to, such a resolution, motion, question or other matter,

(c) he or she or his or her spouse is a party to any arrangement or agreement (whether or not enforceable) concerning land to which such a resolution, motion, question or other matter relates, or

(d) his or her spouse has a beneficial interest in, or which is material to, such a resolution, motion, question or other matter.

(7) For the purposes of this *section,* a person shall not be regarded as having a beneficial interest in, or which is material to, any resolution, motion, question or other matter by reason only of an interest of his or her or of any company or of any other body or person referred to in *subsection (6)* which is so remote or insignificant that it cannot reasonably be regarded as likely to influence a person in considering or discussing, or in voting on, any question with respect to the matter, or in performing any function in relation to that matter.

(8) Where a person has a beneficial interest referred to in *subsection (1), (2), (3), (4) or (5)* by reason only of the beneficial ownership of shares in a company or other body by him or her or by his or her spouse and the total value of those shares does not exceed the lesser of—

(a) [€13,000], or

(b) one-hundredth part of the total nominal value of either the issued share capital of the company or body or, where that capital is issued in shares of more than one class, the issued share capital of the class of shares in which he or she has an interest,

none of those subsections shall have effect in relation to that beneficial interest.

(9) Where at a meeting referred to in *subsection (2)* a disclosure is made under that *subsection,* particulars of the disclosure and of any subsequent withdrawal from the meeting pursuant to that *subsection* shall be recorded in the minutes of the meeting.

(10) Subject to *subsection (11),* a person who contravenes or fails to comply with a requirement of this *section* shall be guilty of an offence.

(11) In any proceedings for an offence under this *section* it shall be a defence for the defendant to prove that at the time of the alleged offence he or she did not know and had no reason to believe that a matter in which, or in relation to which, he or she had a beneficial interest had arisen or had come before, or was being considered by, the Board or the relevant planning authority or committee, as may be appropriate, or that the beneficial interest to which the alleged offence relates was one in relation to which a requirement of this *section* applied.

AMENDMENT HISTORY

Subsection (8) amended by s.1 and Schedule of the Euro Changeover (Amounts) Act 2001 (No. 16 of 2001) with effect from January 1, 2002.

NOTE

This section concerns matters arising during the functioning of the Board or planning authority, whereby every member, employee, or officer concerned is obliged to disclose any pecuniary or beneficial interest they have in the matter. In addition to declaring their interest, a Board member or member of a planning authority, who has an interest in a matter to be determined by such body, must take no part in the consideration, nor may they vote or seek to influence the decision. Also, where a member of a planning authority or authority manager has a pecuniary or beneficial interest in any function to be performed by the authority, they must not seek to influence the performance of such. There are similar obligations of disclosure and non-influence in the case of employees of the Board and officers of the planning authority. The section requiring disclosure of interest in land applies "to any other enactment", as well as to the 2000 Act. A beneficial interest is defined as including where the spouse of the person is a member of a company having an interest in the matter, is in partnership or employment with a person having an interest, is a party to an agreement concerning the land, or simply has a beneficial interest in the matter in question. The obligation to disclose does not apply where the beneficial interest is very remote or insignificant. Failure to comply with the obligations in this section can amount to an offence although there are certain defences open where the person acted bona fide and reasonably. This section re-enacts s.33 of the 1976 Act.

Supplemental provisions relating to sections 147 and 148

149.—(1) Proceedings for an offence under *section 147 or 148* shall **1–179** not be instituted except by or with the consent of the Director of Public Prosecutions.

(2) Where a person is convicted of an offence under *section 147 or 148*—

    (a) the person shall be disqualified from being a member of the Board,

    (b) in case the person is a member of the Board, he or she shall on conviction accordingly cease to be a member of the Board,

    (c) in case the person is a member of a planning authority or a member of any committee of a planning authority, he or she shall on conviction cease to be a member of the authority or the committee, as may be appropriate,

    (d) in case the person is a member of both a planning authority and any one or more such committees, he or she shall on conviction cease to be a member of both the authority and every such committee, and

    (e) in case the person by virtue of this *subsection* ceases to be a member of a planning authority or any such committee, he or she shall be disqualified for being a member of the authority or committee during the period which, but for the cessation of his or her membership of the authority or committee under this *section,* would be the remainder of his or her term.

(3) A disqualification under this *section* shall take effect on the expiry of the ordinary time for appeal from the conviction concerned or if an appeal is brought within that time, upon the final disposal of that appeal.

(4) In case a person contravenes or fails to comply with a requirement of *section 147, 148 or 150,* or acts as a member of the Board, a planning authority or committee of a planning authority while disqualified for membership by virtue of this *section,* the fact of the contravention or failure or of his or her so acting, as the case may be, shall not invalidate any act or proceeding of the Board, authority or committee.

(5) Where any body which is a company within the meaning of *section 155 of the Companies Act, 1963,* is deemed under that *section* to be a subsidiary of another or to be another such company's holding company, a person who is a member of the first-mentioned such company shall, for the purposes of *sections 147 and 148* be deemed also to be a member of the other company.

NOTE

This section concerns prosecution of persons who failed to comply with their declaration or disclosure obligations under ss.147 and 148. Proceedings can only be taken with the consent of the DPP, and so cannot be subject to private prosecution in court. Where a person is found guilty of such offence, they will be disqualified or cease to be a member of the Board or planning authority, as appropriate. The disqualification takes effect from the time any appeal is disposed of or where the time for an appeal has expired. The section provides that where a person has been guilty of an offence under ss.147, 148 or 150 in relation to the code of conduct, this will not render void any act taken by the relevant Board, authority or committee on which such person may have acted. This section re-enacts s.34 of the 1976 Act.

Codes of conduct

1–180   **150.—(1)**
   (a) Every planning authority, by resolution, and the Board shall adopt a code of conduct for dealing with conflicts of interest and promoting public confidence in the integrity of the conduct of its business which must be followed by those persons referred to in *subsection (3)*.
   (b) A code of conduct under this *section* shall be adopted within one year of the commencement of this *section*.
(2) A code of conduct shall consist of a written statement setting out the planning authority's or the Board's policy on at least the following matters:
   (a) disclosure of interests and relationships where the interests and relationships are of relevance to the work of the authority or the Board, as appropriate;
   (b) membership of other organisations, associations and bodies, professional or otherwise;
   (c) membership of, or other financial interests in, companies, partnerships or other bodies;
   (d) undertaking work, not being work on behalf of the authority or the Board, as the case may be, both during and after any period of employment with the authority or the Board, whether as a consultant, adviser or otherwise;
   (e) acceptance of gifts, sponsorship, considerations or favours;
   (f) disclosure of information concerning matters pertaining to the work of the authority or the Board, as appropriate;
   (g) following of proper procedure in relation to the functions of the authority and the Board including the procedures for—
      (i)
         (I) the review, making and variation of development plans,
         (II) the review, making and amendment of local area plans,

  (III) the processing of planning applications and appeals, and

  (IV) the granting of permission which would materially contravene the development plan, including the use of resolutions referred to in *section 34(6)(c),*

 and

 (ii) the disclosure by members and employees of the authority or of the Board of any representations made to such members or employees whether in writing or otherwise in relation to those matters.

(3) This *section* shall apply to—

 (a) a member of the Board,

 (b) a member of a planning authority,

 (c) an employee of the Board or any other person—

  (i) whose services are availed of by the Board, and

  (ii) who is of a class, description or grade prescribed for the purposes of this *section,*

 and

 (d) an officer of a planning authority who is the holder of an office which is of a class, description or grade so prescribed.

(4)

 (a) It shall be a condition of appointment of persons listed at *subsection (3)(a)* that they shall comply with the code of conduct.

 (b) It shall be a condition of taking up and holding office by persons listed at *subsection (3)(b)* that they shall comply with the code of conduct.

 (c) It shall be a condition of employment of persons listed at *subsection (3)(c) and (d)* that they shall comply with the code of conduct.

(5) A planning authority or the Board may at any time review a code of conduct adopted under this *section* and may—

 (a) amend the code of conduct, or

 (b) adopt a new code of conduct.

NOTE

 This section obliges every planning authority and also An Bord Pleanála to adopt a code of conduct in relation to conflicts of interest and promotion of public confidence in the integrity of its business within one year of the commencement of the section.

 The code of conduct must deal with such matters as disclosure of interests, membership of organisations, membership of companies, work outside the authority, acceptance of gifts, disclosure of information regarding work for the authority or Board, the following of proper procedure in relation to certain specified functions, etc. The Board and each planning authority has a discretion as regards the standards in such codes of conduct. A code of conduct may also include additional matters to those enlisted in the present section. The code of conduct must apply to members of the Board and planning authority, to certain employees of the Board, and also to certain officers of the planning authority. It is a condition of employment and taking up of office for such persons to comply with the code of conduct. The code may be amended or replaced by the Board and planning authority at any time.

 An Bord Pleanála adopted a *Code of Conduct for Board Members, Certain Employees and Certain Other Persons* on January 20, 2003. This Code of Conduct deals with such matters as membership of organisations, associations and other bodies membership or financial interest in companies, partnerships or other bodies undertaking of work during and after membership or employment, acceptance of gifts, disclosure of information, public procurement, accuracy of information, work or external environment, consideration of appeals, improper communications, procedures at Board meetings, procedures for employees of other dealings with cases and assignment of files or other works.

PART VIII

ENFORCEMENT

Offence

1–181   **151.**—Any person who has carried out or is carrying out unauthorised development shall be guilty of an offence.

NOTE

This section creates the general offence of carrying out unauthorised development. A similar offence to s.151 was contained in s.24(3) of the 1963 Act. The offence can relate to unauthorised development carried out in the past or being carried on in the present and so still ongoing. Development is defined in s.3 as comprising works and material changes of use, while unauthorised works and unauthorised use, are defined in s.2 as development which was commenced on or after October 1, 1964 and which is not; (a) exempted development; (b) granted under a planning permission and carried out in accordance with the permission and conditions contained therein. In *Westmeath County Council v Quirke*, unreported, High Court, Budd J., May 23, 1996, Budd J. said with reference to a material change of use under the previous legislation:
"It seems to follow that every use is an unauthorised use unless:
  1. It was commenced before the appointed day; or (pre-1st October 1964).
  2. It is an immaterial change from an authorised use.
  3. Being a development, it is the subject matter of a permission granted under section 26 of the 1963 Act;
  4. Being a development, that it constitutes an exempted development."
One change under the 2000 Act is to incorporate within the definition of unauthorised use and unauthorised work, that development which is not carried out in accordance with conditions of a permission is classified as unauthorised development.
The criminal offence of carrying out unauthorised development is consistent with the general obligation in s.32 not to carry out unauthorised development. The offence under s.151 is limited to persons carrying out unauthorised development. It is therefore not enough to prove that a person was the owner of land on which the unauthorised development took place, although the court may draw inferences from this fact. It must however, be proved that owner carried out the development or directed some other person to carry out the unauthorised development on their behalf. An essential element of the prosecution is to prove that unauthorised development took place. However, in proving this the prosecution is assisted by certain presumptions. Under s.156(6) it is assumed, until the contrary is shown by the defendant, that the subject matter of the prosecution was development and was not exempted development. While the offence under this section is separate from the offence of non-compliance with an enforcement notice under s.154(8), s.156(7) provides that where an enforcement notice has been served under s.154, it shall be a defence to a prosecution under s.151 or s.154 if the defendant proves that he or she took all reasonable steps to secure compliance with the enforcement notice. The penalties for an offence under this section are set out in s.156(1). A planning authority cannot be compelled to prosecute a person under s.151 as it is a matter within their discretion. In practice, planning authorities bring more prosecutions for non-compliance with an enforcement notice under s.154(8) than prosecutions under this section. One limitation to a prosecution under this section is that the court has no jurisdiction to order a person to reverse the unauthorised

development. However, this is in contrast to a prosecution for non-compliance with an enforcement notice, where the court has a discretion to order the terms of the enforcement to be complied with. However, where a person has been convicted for an offence under this section, the planning authority could choose to institute injunction proceedings under s.160 to reverse the unauthorised development and seek to rely on fact of the conviction in support of its application.

Warning letter

152.—(1) Where—   1–182
  (a) a representation in writing is made to a planning authority by any person that unauthorised development may have been, is being or may be carried out, and it appears to the planning authority that the representation is not vexatious, frivolous or without substance or foundation, or
  (b) it otherwise appears to the authority that unauthorised development may have been, is being or may be carried out,
the authority shall issue a warning letter to the owner, the occupier or any other person carrying out the development and may give a copy, at that time or thereafter, to any other person who in its opinion may be concerned with the matters to which the letter relates.

(2) Notwithstanding *subsection (1),* where the development in question is of a trivial or minor nature the planning authority may decide not to issue a warning letter.

(3) A planning authority shall issue the warning letter under *subsection (1)* as soon as may be but not later than 6 weeks after receipt of the representation under *subsection (1).*

(4) A warning letter shall refer to the land concerned and shall—
  (a) state that it has come to the attention of the authority that unauthorised development may have been, is being or may be carried out,
  (b) state that any person served with the letter may make submissions or observations in writing to the planning authority regarding the purported offence not later than four weeks from the date of the service of the warning letter,
  (c) state that when a planning authority considers that unauthorised development has been, is being or may be carried out, an enforcement notice may be issued,
  (d) state that officials of the planning authority may at all reasonable times enter on the land for the purposes of inspection,
  (e) explain the possible penalties involved where there is an offence, and
  (f) explain that any costs reasonably incurred by the planning authority in relation to enforcement proceedings may be recovered from a person on whom an enforcement notice is served or where court action is taken.

NOTE

This section concerns the issue of a warning letter in respect of potential unauthorised development. This is a new mechanism introduced by the 2000 Act and is not to be confused with the warning notices under s.26(1) of the 1963 Act. Where a representation in writing is received from a member of the public (which representation is not frivolous or without substance), or if it appears to the planning authority itself that an unauthorised development may have been, is being or may be carried out, the planning authority must issue a warning letter to the occupier, owner, developer or any other person concerned with the matter. Where such circumstances exist, the planning authority has no discretion to refuse to issue a warning letter and so could be compelled to do so by an order of mandamus.

There is therefore an express obligation on the planning authority to take such steps with respect to an unauthorised development which did not exist under the previous legislation. The reference in subs.(1) to unauthorised development which "may have been, is being or may be carried out", means that a warning letter may potentially be issued with respect to unauthorised development in the past, present or future. Where a representation in writing is received, the warning letter must be issued as soon as may be and not later than six weeks after receipt of the representation. By virtue of s.157(4) there is a seven-year time limit to issue a warning letter which runs from the date of the commencement of the unauthorised development or from the beginning of the expiration of the life of the planning permission. There is a broad range of persons on whom a warning letter may be served, which includes the owner, occupier or any other person carrying out the development. In practice, the planning authority may issue several warning letters, where the owner, occupier or person carrying out the development is not the same person or where there are several owners or occupiers. In the case of a company, the planning authority may choose to issue a warning letter to both the company and its controlling directors. The final paragraph in subs.(1) also allows the planning authority to give a copy to any person who may be concerned with the matter. The giving of a copy therefore relates to persons who have not been issued with a warning letter.

A warning letter issued under this section has has a distinct statutory character and is not merely a formal letter warning of the institution of enforcement proceedings. This is underlined by the fact that s.7(2)(r) provides that a planning authority must enter on the planning register particulars of any warning letter issued under s.152, including the date of issue of the letter and the fact of its withdrawal, if appropriate. The issuing of a warning letter is something which should be requested and indeed disclosed in any requisitions on sale of any land. The existence of an outstanding warning letter may cause difficulties for a vendor who wishes to provide a certificate that the lands are in accordance with planning. Notwithstanding this, there are no specific consequences or sanction which directly flow from the issue of a warning letter except that it is in the nature of a preliminary step which may result in the issue of an enforcement notice. The contents of a warning letter are set out in subs.(4), the failure to contain any of which will render the warning letter liable to being quashed in a judicial review application. The letter must invite submissions from the recipients of the warning letter concerning the claim that unauthorised development may have been, is being or may be carried out. It appears that the warning letter should clearly identify the nature of the unauthorised development and it is not enough for the letter to vaguely state that unauthorised development may have been, is being or may be carried out.

Decision on enforcement

1–183   **153.—(1)** As soon as may be after the issue of a warning letter under *section 152,* the planning authority shall make such investigation as it considers necessary to enable it to make a decision on whether to issue an enforcement notice.

    (2)

      (a) It shall be the duty of the planning authority to ensure that decisions on whether to issue an enforcement notice are taken as expeditiously as possible.

      (b) Without prejudice to the generality of *paragraph (a),* it shall be the objective of the planning authority to ensure that the decision on whether to issue an enforcement notice shall be taken within 12 weeks of the issue of a warning letter.

(3) A planning authority, in deciding whether to issue an enforcement notice shall consider any representations made to it under *section 152(1)(a)* or submissions or observations made under *section 152(4)(b)* and any other material considerations.

(4) The decision made by the planning authority under *subsection (1)* including the reasons for it shall be entered by the authority in the register.

(5) Failure to issue a warning letter under *section 152* shall not prejudice the issue of an enforcement notice or any other proceedings that may be initiated by the planning authority.

NOTE

This section sets out the procedure following the issue of the warning letter leading to a determination by the planning authority as to whether to issue an enforcement notice. Following the issue of the warning letter, this section sets out a number of mandatory procedural steps which the planning authority must take. These are:

- the planning authority must make such investigation as it considers necessary to enable it to make a decision on whether to issue an enforcement notice (s.153(1));
- the planning authority must ensure that decisions on whether to issue an enforcement notice are taken as expeditiously as possible (s.153(2));
- in determining whether to issue an enforcement notice, the planning authority must consider any submissions received and any "other material considerations" (s.153(3));
- the decision made by the planning authority as to whether to take enforcement action including the reasons for it must be entered by the authority in the register (s.153(5)).

The investigations will typically involve a planning officer carrying out an inspection. Where a complaint and warning letter has been issued, the officer may be said to have "reasonable grounds" for believing that unauthorised development was/is taking place within the meaning of s.253(1) and so there is no requirement for the officer to give notice to the owner/occupier before entering the land. The statement that it is an objective of the planning authority to ensure the decision on whether to issue an enforcement is taken within 12 weeks of the issue of the warning letters does not amount to a mandatory cut-off point of 12 weeks but merely an obligation on the authority to endeavour to aspire to such timeframe. However, many planning authorities adopt a practice of issuing warning letters and failing to make any formal decision on whether to issue an enforcement notice. In the absence of a formal decision there is no scope for assuming that the planning authority has declined to serve an enforcement notice. As a warning letter is a matter which must be entered on the Planning Register, this can potentially cause difficulties in the sale of land. It is submitted therefore that in certain circumstances, the planning authority can be compelled to make a formal decision on the issuing of an enforcement notice and that this should be entered on the register. The entry on the register should also include the reasons for the decision.

However, while the planning authority has a mandatory obligation to follow the above procedural steps it has a discretion whether to issue an enforcement notice. A challenge to the decision of the planning authority not to issue an enforcement notice in judicial review proceedings would be assessed on the high standard of irrationality under *O'Keeffe v An Bord Pleanála* [1993] 1 I.R. 39. Any attempt to compel the planning authority to take enforcement action by seeking an order of mandamus in judicial review proceedings, would most likely fail. Apart, from this, the fact that any member of the public can institute planning injunction proceedings under s.160, would mean that there is alternative remedy to the relief sought.

However, in determining whether to issue an enforcement notice, the planning authority must consider any representation regarding the issue of a warning, any submissions received in response to the warning letter and any "other material considerations". There is no definition of what constitutes "other material considerations". The previous legislation, s.31 of the 1963 Act, provided that the planning authority was obliged to consider the development plan before serving an enforcement notice. The development plan could in certain circumstances be deemed such a material consideration. The extent and nature of the unauthorised development and a history of non-compliance may potentially be material considerations, although it is not possible to exhaustively delimit the same. Planning authorities do not generally have any explicit policy regarding enforcement action and there is no requirement to specify its enforcement policy in the development plan. Where the unauthorised development requires an EIS, this may clearly be a material consideration in deciding whether to issue an enforcement notice. Under the EIA Directive, Member States are required to take all the general or particular measures necessary to ensure that projects which are likely to have significant effects on the environment are subject to assent. See *Aannemersbedrijf P.K. v Gedeputeerde Staten van Zuid-Holland* C-72/95 [1996] ECR I-5403. In *Commission v Ireland Case C-215/06* July 3, 2008, it was held that in allowing a retention application in respect of certain developments requiring an EIS and in not taking enforcement action, Ireland had breached the EIA Directive. Thus the fact that an unauthorised development requires an EIA, may be a factor in deciding to issue an enforcement action. It may be a reason to issue an enforcement notice or a reason to take injunction proceedings under s.160 instead of issuing an enforcement notice, on the basis that an injunction may be more appropriate in order to more expeditiously restrain the unauthorised development.

If in the course of an investigation, a planning inspector expresses an opinion that a matter is exempted development or that the planning authority will not issue an enforcement notice, this will not be binding on the planning authority. The decision on whether to issue an enforcement notice is taken by the Manager and so any statement from a planning inspector would be ultra vires. See *Dublin Corporation v McGrath*, unreported, High Court, McMahon J., November 17, 1978, where a representation by an official of a planning authority to a developer that a building amounted to exempted development, was held not to bind a planning authority. See also *Greendale Building Company v Dublin County Council* [1977] 1 I.R. 256.

Subsection (5) states that failure to issue a warning letter will not prejudice the issue of an enforcement notice or other proceedings which may be issued by the planning authority. Under s.155, in the case of urgency, the planning authority can issue an enforcement notice without a warning letter having been sent. In considering whether such urgent action is required, the planning authority will consider the nature of the unauthorised development and any other material considerations (s.155). The better view is that subs.(5) does not reflect a general power to issue an enforcement letter without a warning letter having been issued but merely means that where the planning authority is otherwise empowered to take other proceedings, the absence of a warning letter will not prejudice the issue of the same. As noted under s.155, the planning authority can issue an enforcement notice without a warning letter where urgent action is required, while the issue of a warning letter is not necessary for the planning authority to institute injunction proceedings under s.160. Section 160(7) provides that seeking an injunction will not prejudice the taking of any other enforcement action.

Enforcement notice

1–184   **154.—(1)**

    (a) Where a decision to enforce is made under *section 153* or where urgent action is required under *section 155,* the planning authority shall, as soon as may be, serve an enforcement notice under this *section.*

    (b) Where an enforcement notice is served under this *section,* the planning authority shall notify any person who made representations under *section 152(1)(a)* and any other person, who in the opinion of the planning authority may be concerned with the matter to which the notice concerned relates, not being a person on whom the enforcement notice was served, of the service of the enforcement notice.

(2) Where the planning authority decides not to issue an enforcement notice, it shall notify any person to whom the warning letter was copied under *section 152* and any other person who made a representation under that *section* of the decision in writing within 2 weeks of the making of that decision.

(3)

    (a) An enforcement notice under *subsection (1)* shall be served on the person carrying out the development and, where the planning authority considers it necessary, the owner or the occupier of the land or any other person who, in the opinion of the planning authority, may be concerned with the matters to which the notice relates.

    (b) If, subsequent to the service of the enforcement notice, the planning authority becomes aware that any other person may be carrying out development or is an owner or occupier of the land or may be affected by the notice, the notice may be served on that person and the period specified for compliance with the notice shall be extended as necessary to a maximum of 6 months, and the other person or persons on whom the notice had previously been served under *paragraph (a)* shall be informed in writing.

(4) An enforcement notice shall take effect on the date of the service thereof.

(5) An enforcement notice shall refer to the land concerned and shall—

    (a)

        (i) in respect of a development where no permission has been granted, require that development to cease or not to commence, as appropriate, or

        (ii) in respect of a development for which permission has been granted under *Part III,* require that the development will proceed in conformity with the permission, or with any condition to which the permission is subject,

    (b) require such steps as may be specified in the notice to be taken within a specified period, including, where appropriate, the removal, demolition or alteration of any structure and the discontinuance of any use and, in so far as is practicable, the restoration of the land to its condition prior to the commencement of the development,

    (c) warn the person or persons served with the enforcement notice that, if within the period specified under *paragraph (b)* or within such extended period (not being more than 6 months) as the planning authority may allow, the steps specified in the notice to be taken are not taken, the planning authority may enter on the land and take such steps, including the removal, demolition or alteration of any structure, and may recover any expenses reasonably incurred by them in that behalf,

    (d) require the person or persons served with the notice to refund to the planning authority the costs and expenses reasonably incurred by the authority in relation to the investigation, detection and issue of the enforcement notice concerned and any warning letter under section 152, including costs incurred in respect of the remuneration and other expenses of employees, consultants and advisers, and the planning authority may recover these costs and expenses incurred by it in that behalf, and

   (e) warn the person or persons served with the enforcement notice that if within the period specified by the notice or such extended period, not being more than 6 months, as the planning authority may allow, the steps specified in the notice to be taken are not taken, the person or persons may be guilty of an offence.

(6) If, within the period specified under *subsection (5)(b)* or within such extended period, not being more than 6 months, as the planning authority may allow, the steps specified in the notice to be taken are not taken, the planning authority may enter on the land and take such steps, including the demolition of any structure and the restoration of land, and may recover any expenses reasonably incurred by it in that behalf.

(7) Any expenses reasonably incurred by a planning authority under paragraphs (c) and (d) of *subsection (5)* and *subsection (6)* may be recovered—

   (a) as a simple contract debt in any court of competent jurisdiction from the person or persons on whom the notice was served, or

   (b) secured by—

   (i) charging the land under the Registration of Title Act, 1964, or

   (ii) where the person on whom the enforcement notice was served is the owner of the land, an instrument vesting the ownership of the land in the authority subject to a right of redemption by the owner within five years.

(8) Any person on whom an enforcement notice is served under *subsection (1)* who fails to comply with the requirements of the notice (other than a notice which has been withdrawn under *subsection (11)(a)* or which has ceased to have effect) within the specified period or within such extended period as the planning authority may allow, not exceeding 6 months, shall be guilty of an offence.

(9) Any person who knowingly assists or permits the failure by another to comply with an enforcement notice shall be guilty of an offence.

(10) Particulars of an enforcement notice shall be entered in the register.

   (11)

   (a) A planning authority may for stated reasons by notice in writing to any person served with the notice, and, where appropriate, any person who made a representation under *section 152(1)(a)*, withdraw an enforcement notice served under this section.

   (b) Where an enforcement notice is withdrawn pursuant to this subsection by a planning authority or where a planning authority finds that an enforcement notice has been complied with, the fact that the enforcement notice was withdrawn and the reason for the withdrawal or that it was complied with, as appropriate, shall be recorded by the authority in the register.

(12) An enforcement notice shall cease to have effect 10 years from the date of service of the notice under *subsection (1)* or, if a notice is served under *subsection (3)(b)*, 10 years from the date of service of the notice under that subsection.

(13) A person shall not question the validity of an enforcement notice by reason only that the person or any other person, not being the person on whom the enforcement notice was served, was not notified of the service of the enforcement notice.

(14) A report of a local authority under section 50 of the Local Government Act, 1991, shall contain details of the number of enforcement notices issued under this section, warning notices issued under section 153, prosecutions brought under section 157 and injunctions sought under section 160 by that authority.

NOTE

This section concerns the procedure which follows a decision whether to serve an enforcement notice. Where the planning authority decides to issue an enforcement notice, it must serve it as soon as may be. As to the meaning of "as soon as may", see *Harding v Cork County Council*, unreported, Supreme Court, May 2, 2008, where Murray C.J. suggested that in interpreting such a phrase (albeit in a different context), that allowance should be made for the administrative burden on planning authorities. The enforcement notice will take effect on the date of service (subs.(4)) and will have effect for 10 years from such date (subs.(12). The planning authority is not required to warn a person (other than through a section 152 warning letter) that an enforcement notice is to be served. See *O'Connor v Kerry County Council* [1988] I.L.R.M. 660. Where the planning authority decides to issue an enforcement notice, it must notify any person who made representations that an unauthorised development may have been, is being or may be carried out. It must also notify any other concerned person, other than a person served with the enforcement notice. Where it decides not to issue an enforcement notice, the planning authority must notify any person to whom the warning was copied and any person who made a representation in writing within two weeks.

The enforcement notice may be served on the person carrying out the development, and where necessary, on the owner or the occupier of the land, and on other concerned persons. The making of an enforcement notice involves both a decision to make an enforcement notice and also the preparation and service of the notice. The two steps cannot be merged into one; see *Dublin Corporation v O'Callaghan*, unreported, High Court, Herbert J., February 13, 2001, where Herbert J. said:

"[T]he making of a decision by a planning authority that it was expedient to serve an Enforcement Notice must be attended by some formality, by some recording of the fact that a decision to serve such a Notice has been taken and of the basis upon which it has been determined that it was expedient to do so".

This section prescribes a single type of enforcement notice to which the seven year limitation period applies. The previous legislation prescribed different types of enforcement notices including under s.35 of the 1963 Act, an enforcement notice where development was not being carried out in accordance with a permission and enforcement notices under s.31 of the Act 1963, where development was being carried out without permission or where development was in non-compliance with a condition of a permission. Difficulties under the previous legislation concerning the type of enforcement notice where some different rules apply, will not arise; see *Dublin County Council v Hill* [1994] 1 I.R. 86. However, notwithstanding these changes, it appears that it is still necessary to identify which type of breach is involved in the enforcement notice.

By virtue of s.157(4) there is a seven-year time limit to serve an enforcement notice from the commencement of the unauthorised development. The time will therefore run from the commencement of the works or the material change of use. In the case of a material change of use, time will only run from when such use amounts to a "material" change of use. Under the previous legislation, the limitation period was generally five years except under s.35 of the 1963 Act, where no time limit was imposed for service of an enforcement notice where development was not being carried out in accordance with a permission.

The range of persons who may be served with an enforcement is widely drawn under subs.(3). In addition to the person carrying out the development, the enforcement notice may also be served on the owner or occupier of the land (even if not the person carrying out the development) and also on any person, who in the opinion of the planning authority, may be concerned with the matters in the notice. Having served an enforcement notice, a planning authority may subsequently serve the notice on other persons, in which case the specified period for compliance will be extended (to a maximum of six months) and any person previously served will be informed. The main consequences of failure to comply with an enforcement notice is that it is a criminal offence under subs.(8). It is also a criminal offence to knowingly assist or permit the failure to comply with an enforcement notice. The penalties for such an offence are set out in s.156(1). Also under s.156(8) a person may also be ordered to take the steps specified in the enforcement notice. It appears that the court has a discretion whether to make such order. Furtheremore if the steps required in the enforcement notice have not been taken within the period allowed, subs.(6) provides that the planning authority can enter on the land and take such steps, including the demolition of any structure and the restoration of land, and may recover any expenses reasonably incurred. Furthermore, under s.161, a person convicted will be required to pay the costs and expenses of the action unless the court considers there are special and substantial reasons for not doing so. These costs are not confined to legal costs but also include costs relating to the investigation and detection of the offence.

The contents of the notice set out in subs.(5) are mandatory and so failure to follow the prescribed contents will render the notice invalid. Subs.(5)(a) deals with two forms of unauthorised development (the notice should identify which category of breach is being alleged); (i) where no permission has been granted at all and (ii) where permission has been granted but the development has not been carried out in accordance with the permission and conditions thereof. In the case of the former, the notice requires the development to cease or not to commence (where it relates to an anticipated breach), while in the case of the latter, the notice must require the development to proceed in conformity with the permission and any condition of the permission. However, these categories may overlap. Where a development is not proceeding in conformity with a permission, this may involve requiring the person served to cease some type of development and instead proceed with some other development which is in accordance with the permission. It is not entirely clear whether an enforcement notice can simply require a person to cease some unauthorised development under subs.(5)(a) without requiring any further steps to be taken under subs.(5)(b). The layout of subs.(5) envisages that an enforcement notice in addition to requiring a person to cease the development should also specify steps (in accordance with subs.(5)(b)) by which a person can regularise their position, otherwise their position would be entirely frozen. While English planning law allows the service of stop notices, requiring a person to cease some development, no such mechanism exists under Irish law. An enforcement notice which merely requires a person to cease an unauthorised development reduces an enforcement notice to a form of stop notice and may potentially lead to uncertainty insofar as the requirement to specify steps gives clear directions to allow a person to regularize their position. The better view is therefore that an enforcement notice which simply requires a person to cease the unauthorised development is not a valid enforcement notice.

The requirements in subs.(5)(b) mean that the notice must specify both the steps required and also the time in which such steps must be taken. This requirement to "specify" will be strictly construed. As the failure to comply with an enforcement notice is a criminal offence, the enforcement notice must be defined with clarity and precision. The enforcement notice will be construed strictly and in accordance with the natural and ordinary meaning of the words used and there is no scope for any kind of purposive of or teleological approach. See *Dundalk Town Council v Lawlor* [2005] 2 I.L.R.M. 106, where it was held that the requirement in subs.(5)(b) which states the notice must specify the steps to be taken "within a specified period", meant that the "specified" period must be capable of having its beginning and end clearly ascertained. Thus an enforcement notice which required the steps to be taken immediately failed to specify a period within which the steps were to be accomplished and also failed to specify with sufficient precision the time permitted for the required steps to be taken. Furthermore, the requirement to specify the steps which must be taken means that the enforcement notice should set out such steps with clarity and precision. The steps can include the matters as set out, such as the removal, demolition or alteration of any structure or the restoration of land to its condition prior to the commencement of the development. However, in *Dundalk Town Council v Lawlor* [2005] 2 I.L.R.M. 106, it was held that it was not sufficient merely to recite the phrases used in subs.(5)(b), such as demolition or alteration of any structure or to "return site to its previous condition" where this fails to clearly and precisely indicate to the person served with the notice what exactly has to be done in order to comply with the notice.

In some cases, it will not be practicable to return the development to its condition prior to the unauthorised development being carried out. Thus if a structure or premises was in a state of dereliction or disrepair, it would not be reasonable to require a person to return it to this state. Thus subs.(5)(b) uses the phrase "in so far as practicable" a person may be required to return the land to its condition prior to the commencement of the development. While ideally an enforcement notice should use such phrase, the failure of an enforcement notice to so state, will not render the enforcement notice invalid. See *Dundalk Town Council v Lawlor* [2005] 2 I.L.R.M. 106, where it was said that the phrase "in so far as practicable" would be imported into every notice even though not expressly stated.

Subsection (8) makes it an offence for a person to fail to comply with the requirements of the enforcement notice within the specified period. It is somewhat unclear as to what are the precise element of this offence. In *Davoren v Galway County Council*, unreported, High Court, Quirke J., 2005, it was said that proof of unauthorised development was not an element of the offence of non-compliance with an enforcement notice. This arose in the context of a case stated where it was claimed that an enforcement notice could be issued with respect to development which was unauthorised by reason of not being completed within the life of a planning permission. In answering the questions, the court said the offence of non-compliance merely involved proof of failure to carry out the steps specified within the notice within the specified period; where the developer considered the development was not unauthorised then the appropriate remedy was to institute judicial review proceedings. It is submitted that it is questionable whether this determination is correct. It may be noted that in *Clare County Council v Floyd* [2007] 2 I.R. 671, it appeared to be suggested, obiter, that evidence of unauthorised development was an element of the offence. However, to find that a person must either comply with an enforcement notice on pain of committing a criminal offence or institute judicial review seeking to quash the notice would lead to considerable injustice. If a person does not institute judicial review proceedings to quash the notice, then this would mean that a person is guilty of a criminal offence in failing to take the steps in the enforcement notice, is if the planning authority was entirely erroneous in its view that the development was unauthorised development. This injustice is further underlined by the fact that while a person may make submissions in response to a warning letter there is no provision for making submissions with respect to the issue of an enforcement notice. The issuing of an enforcement notice is therefore quite different from the issuing of an endangerment notice under s.59 or a restoration notice under s.60, where the planning authority issues a notice and allows the person served to make submissions on the notice. The planning authority must then take into account such submissions before deciding whether or not to confirm such notices. There is then a right of appeal against such notices to the District Court. No such safeguards exist with respect to an enforcement notice; a person served is faced with a fait accompli when served with the notice. It is suggested that the courts should lean against an interpretation which could render an offence under s.154(6) unconstitutional or in breach of the European Convention on Human Rights (in particular art.6 and possibly art.1 of the First Protocol or art.8, where the development concerns a dwelling). It is further submitted that to exclude a defence that the development is not authorised on the basis that judicial review proceedings could be taken is not consistent with prosecutions in other contexts. See *Listowel Urban District Council v McDonagh* [1968] I.R. 312, which concerned a conviction for breach of a local authority prohibition on the erection of temporary dwellings. Where the defendant wished to challenge the validity of the orders at the hearing in the Circuit Court, the Supreme Court held that this was open to the defendant and he was not obliged to take proceedings seeking an order of certiorari. See also *Blanchfield v Hartnett* [2002] 2 I.L.R.M. 435, which concerned a challenge to the validity of certain orders in the context of a forgery trial, the Supreme Court rejected the argument that the invalidity of such orders could only be raised in judicial review proceedings. It may be noted that although the holding in *Davoren* could not classified as obiter, the case stated did not specifically request the High Court to determine whether proof of an unauthorised development is a necessary element of a prosecution under s.154(8) and it was only in answering certain other questions that the court made such pronouncement. Aside from whether proof of unauthorised development is an element of the offence, the procedure itself whereby the planning authority concludes that a matter is unauthorised development and serves an enforcement notice which can have very significant consequences, may itself be vulnerable to challenge under the European Convention on Human Rights, in particular art.6. There is no right of appeal nor ability to make submissions after the notice has been served.

Where a person is served with an enforcement notice and the person disputes whether the development is unauthorised, such a person can seek a declaration under s.5. However, considering that the declaration must be sought from the same planning authority which has issued the enforcement notice, there may be little benefit in doing so. While the person may then refer the matter to An Bord Pleanála, the time for compliance in the enforcement notice may have long past before the Board issues its determination.

As regards other elements of a prosecution for the offence of non-compliance with an enforcement notice under subs.(8), it is not necessary to prove either the existence of a complaint, an investigation leading to a warning letter or the warning letter itself. See *Clare County Council v Floyd* [2007] 2 I.R. 671, where it was said the proofs required are the service of the enforcement notice and evidence of an unauthorised development. The mental element may be inferred from evidence establishing the control of the accused over the development in question. The mental element required in a prosecution is an intentional or reckless failure to comply with an enforcement notice which must coincide with the fault of carrying on an unauthorised development; this can happen at any stage while the unauthorised development exists. Failure to comply with an enforcement notice is a continuing offence. Where an accused is acquitted of such offence, the Council can issue a new enforcement notice in respect of the development as once the dates in the enforcement notices are different, two separate offences are alleged. It may further be noted that under the Local Government Act 2001, the taking of court proceedings by a planning authority requires a manager's order. The court may allow the planning authority to prove it in court; see *Kildare County Council v Goode*, unreported, High Court, Morris P., June 13, 1997, and *O'Connor v Kerry County Council* [1988] I.L.R.M. 660. Therefore in a prosecution under s.154(8), a further necessary proof is a manager's order authorising the proceedings and/or any delegation order where the decision was taken by a person other than the manager.

As with any summary prosecution, a defendant may seek disclosure of documents from the planning authority in accordance with the principles set out in *DPP v Gary Doyle* [1994] 2 I.R. 286. In that case the Supreme Court noted that while there was no general obligation on the prosecution to furnish, on request, the statements of the proposed witnesses, in a particular case fair procedures may require that an accused be given advance notice of the material evidence against him. See also *O'Driscoll v Judge Wallace* [1995] 1 I.R. 237 and *David Whelan v DPP*, unreported, Supreme Court, March 3, 2004. In the context of a planning prosecution for non-compliance with an enforcement notice, there would appear to be no absolute entitlement of the defendant to disclosure of documents. The making of a *Gary Doyle* order will be within the discretion of the trial judge taking into account the nature of the unauthorised development and other particular circumstances of the case. While not specifically required by the Rules, it would appear to be good practice for a defendant to make a written request for disclosure in advance of the first return date. Ideally such request should itemise the categories of documents requested. In the context of a planning prosecution under s.154, a defendant may seek disclosure of inspector's reports including any photographs taken, as well the enforcement notice and the manager's order (and any delegation order) authorising both the issue of the enforcement notice and the issue of the summons. Although not strictly within the *Gary Doyle* case law, a defendant may also seek a list of witnesses which the planning authority proposes to call in support of the prosecution case.

Apart from issues regarding the elements of a prosecution under s.154(8), s.156(7) provides that it is a defence that a person took all reasonable steps to secure compliance with the enforcement notice. There is no definition of reasonable steps and it will depend upon the nature of the unauthorised development and the precise steps taken, whether such steps were reasonable. It appears that such steps must have been taken within the period specified in the enforcement notice. In a prosecution under s.154(8) it will be assumed until the contrary is shown by the defendant that the subject matter of the prosecution is development and is not exempted development; see s.156(6). Also by virtue of s.162(1) the onus of proofing the existence of a planning permission is on the defendant.

Section 162(2) provides that it shall not be a defence to a prosecution that a defendant applied for or has been granted retention planning permission, if this occurred after the initiation of proceedings; the sending of a warning letter; or the service of any enforcement notice in case of urgency. While s.162(3) provides that no enforcement action shall be stayed or withdrawn by reason of an application for or grant of retention permission. However, there is nothing to prevent a planning authority consenting to adjourn a prosecution pending the outcome of a retention application. The grant of a retention application may be relevant in particular to whether a court may order the terms of enforcement notice to be complied with under s.156(8).

Under subs.(11), the planning authority has a general discretion whether to withdraw an enforcement notice. Where the planning authority withdraws the notice it must notify the person upon whom it was served and also any person who initially made respresentations regarding the unauthorised development. Such notice must also state the reason for withdrawal. Furthermore, the fact of withdrawal and the reasons for withdrawal must be stated on the register kept under s.7. Equally, where the planning authority finds the notice was complied with, the fact of compliance and the reason for a finding of compliance must be stated on the register. The distinction made between withdrawal and compliance means that it would not appear to be appropriate for the planning authority to withdraw a notice on the basis that it was complied with. In such instance, it is appropriate to record compliance on the register.

Subsection (12) provides that the enforcement shall cease to have effect after ten years. In respect of a summary prosecution for non-compliance with an enforcement notice, s.157(2) provides that proceedings may be commenced within six months from when the offence was committed or at any time within six months from the date when sufficient evidence to justify the prosecutions comes to the prosecutors knowledge. However, this does not mean that a summary prosecution for failure to comply with an enforcement notice must be brought within six months from the end of the period for compliance specified in the enforcement notice. The fact that an enforcement notice only ceases to have effect ten years from the date of service, means that there is a continuing obligation on the person served to comply with the steps required in the notice. This obligation does not cease merely because the specified period for compliance has expired. Where a person has not complied with the notice they will be guilty of a continuing offence. See *Clare County Council v Floyd* [2007] 2 I.R. 671. Where an inspector from the planning authority visits the land at some date after the expiry of the time limit for compliance, evidence of non-compliance at the date of inspection may form the basis for a prosecution for an offence of non-compliance with the enforcement notice on the date of inspection. There will be a six months period to bring a summary prosecution in respect of the offence on such date. However, if a person continues to breach the terms of the enforcement notice, a subsequent inspection which establishes non-compliance at such inspection may form the basis of another prosecution.

Issue of enforcement notice in cases of urgency

155.—(1) Where, in the opinion of the planning authority, due to the nature   **1–185** of an unauthorised development and to any other material considerations, it is necessary to take urgent action with regard to the unauthorised development, notwithstanding *sections 152* and *153,* it may serve an enforcement notice under section 154.

(2) Where an enforcement notice is issued in accordance with *subsection (1),* any person who made a representation under *section 152(1)(a)* shall be notified in writing within two weeks of the service of the notice.

NOTE

This section allows the planning authority to serve an enforcement notice in cases of urgency without having completed the procedure set out in ss.152 and 153, which involves the issue of a warning letter inviting submission from the persons served and other consequential procedurals steps. This constitutes a general exception to the normal procedure of issuing a warning notice and/or completion of the subsequent steps set out in s.153. This section must be read in the light of s.153(5) which recognises that failure to issue a warning letter will not prejudice the issue of an enforcement notice. The notion of "urgent action" is not defined, however, it would appear to entail a situation where the normal procedure for serving a warning letter and allowing a period for submissions could result in significant prejudice or risk in planning terms. The phrase "in the opinion of the planning authority" implies that deference should be shown to the views of the planning authority in their assessment that urgent action is necessary. In making such an assessment, the planning authority may consider the nature of the unauthorised and any other material considerations. While "materials considerations" is not defined, such considerations must be matters which are material in planning terms and so within the scope of the Act as matters relating to the proper planning and sustainable development of the area. However, in order for an enforcement notice issued under this section to be valid, the planning authority must demonstrate that it expressly considered that urgent action was required. While a court may only review its opinion that urgent action was required on grounds of irrationality, the court will require proof that the planning authority specifically considered and came to the view that urgent action was required. Evidence may be presented of an inspector's report where the urgency of such action was considered. However, in the absence of any such proof, the issuing of the enforcement notice under this section will be ultra vires. Furthermore, in order for the enforcement notice to be valid, the manager's order authorising the issue of the enforcement notice should specifically refer to s.155 and expressly state the view that urgent action is necessary. An enforcement notice issued under the authority of this section must in all other respects comply with the content and procedure for an enforcement notice issued under s.154.

Where an enforcement notice is issued under this section, any person who made a representation concerning the unauthorised development under s.152(1), must be informed within two weeks of the issue of the notice.

Penalties for offences

1–186　　　**156.—(1)** A person who is guilty of an offence under [section] 58(4), 63, [135(7),] 151, 154, 205, 230(3), [239 or 247] shall be liable—
> (a) on conviction on indictment, to a fine not exceeding €12,697,380.78 [£10,000,000], or to imprisonment for a term not exceeding 2 years, or to both, or
> (b) on summary conviction, to a fine not exceeding €1,904.61 [£1,500], or to imprisonment for a term not exceeding 6 months, or to both.

(2) Where a person is convicted of an offence referred to in *subsection (1)* and there is a continuation by him or her of the offence after his or her conviction, he or she shall be guilty of a further offence on every day on which the contravention continues and for each such offence shall be liable—
> (a) on conviction on indictment, to a fine not exceeding €12,697.38 [£10,000] for each day on which the offence is so continued, or to

imprisonment for a term not exceeding 2 years, or to both, provided that if a person is convicted in the same proceedings of 2 or more such further offences the aggregate term of imprisonment to which he or she shall be liable shall not exceed 2 years, or

(b) on summary conviction, to a fine not exceeding €507.89 [£400] for each day on which the offence is so continued or to imprisonment for a term not exceeding 6 months, or to both, provided that if a person is convicted in the same proceedings of 2 or more such further offences the aggregate term of imprisonment to which he or she shall be liable shall not exceed 6 months.

(3) Where a person is convicted of an offence referred to in *subsection (1)* involving the construction of an unauthorised structure, the minimum fine shall be—

(a) on conviction on indictment, the estimated cost of the construction of the structure or €12,697.38 [£10,000], whichever is less, or

(b) on summary conviction, the estimated cost of the construction of the structure or €634.87 [£500], whichever is less, except where the person convicted can show to the court's satisfaction that he or she does not have the necessary financial means to pay the minimum fine.

(4) Any person who is guilty of an offence under this Act other than an offence referred to in *subsection (1)* (or a further offence under *subsection (2)*) shall be liable, on summary conviction, to a fine not exceeding €1,904.61 [£1,500] or, at the discretion of the court, to imprisonment for a term not exceeding 6 months or to both.

(5) If the contravention in respect of which a person is convicted under *section 46(11)*, 208(2)(b) or 252(9) is continued after the conviction, that person shall be guilty of a further offence on every day on which the contravention continues and for each such offence he or she shall be liable on summary conviction to a fine not exceeding €507.89 [£400].

(6) In a prosecution for an offence under *sections 151* and *154* it shall not be necessary for the prosecution to show, and it shall be assumed until the contrary is shown by the defendant, that the subject matter of the prosecution was development and was not exempted development.

(7) Where an enforcement notice has been served under section 154, it shall be a defence to a prosecution under section 151 or 154 if the defendant proves that he or she took all reasonable steps to secure compliance with the enforcement notice.

(8) On conviction of an offence under section 154, the court may, in addition to imposing the penalties specified in *subsection (1)* and *(2)*, order the person convicted to take the steps specified in the enforcement order to be taken.

[(9) Where a person is convicted, on indictment, of an offence under *section 135(7)*, the court may, where it finds that the act or omission constituting the offence delayed the conduct of the oral hearing concerned referred to in *section 135(7)*, order—

(a) the person convicted, or

(b) any body with whose consent, connivance or approval the court is satisfied the offence was committed, to pay to the Board or to any

party or person who appeared at the oral hearing such an amount
as is equal to the amount of any additional costs that it is shown
to the court to have been incurred by the Board, party or person in
appearing or being represented at the oral hearing by reason of the
commission of the offence.]

AMENDMENT HISTORY

Subsection (1) was amended by s.247 of the Local Government Act 2001 (No. 37 of
2001), which, by the Local Government Act 2001 (Commencement) Order 2001 (S.I. No.
458 of 2001), came into effect on October 9, 2001. This amendment involved the substitution
of "section" for "sections", and the substitution of "239 or 247" for "239 and 247".

Subsection (1) was amended by s.31 of the Planning and Development (Strategic
Infrastructure) Act 2006 (No. 27 of 2006).

NOTE

This section concerns the penalties for certain offences under the Act. The offences
listed in subs.(1) are:
*   causing damage to a protected structure (s.58(4));
*   failing to comply with a notice for works on the structure (s.63(1));
*   giving false evidence, obstructing, etc. an oral hearing before the Board (s.135(7)
    which was added by the 2006 Act);
*   carrying out unauthorised development (s.151) and failing to comply with an
    enforcement notice (s.154(8));
*   knowingly assisting in the breach of an enforcement notice (s.154(9));
*   breaching a tree protection order (s.205);
*   organising an event other than in accordance with a licence (s.230(3));
*   failure to comply with a notice requiring compliance with the rules regarding funfairs
    (s.239); and
*   seeking a favour or benefit in connection with a pre-planning consultation (s.247).

The fines for conviction on indictment or summarily are €12,697,380.78 and €1,904.61,
respectively. Subsection (2) provides that it is a further offence on every day on which
the contravention continues after conviction. In relation to any offence set out in subs.(1),
subs.(3) sets out a minimum offence where the offence involves the construction of an
unauthorised structure. Subsection (5) creates a further offence on every day on which the
contravention continues, after conviction for offences concerning failure to comply with
a notice requiring removal or alteration of structure or discontinuance of use (s.46(11));
damaging or obstructing a public right of way (s.208(2)(b)); and obstructing an authorised
person from entering land (s.252(9). As in any criminal trial, the burden of proof is on the
prosecution which must prove the offence beyond all reasonable doubt rather than on the
balance of probabilities. The prosecution may however be assisted by three presumptions
of facts which need not be proved unless such presumption is rebutted. These are: that
proceedings were commenced within the appropriate period (s.157(4)(c)), that the subject
matter is development and not exempted development (s.156(6)), and also there is no
requirement to prove the non-existence of a permission (s.162(1)). The presumptions may
however be rebutted and where this is the case, the planning authority must prove the
matters. For the presumption to be rebutted it is not entirely clear what standard of evidence
the defendant must adduce.

The phrase it shall be presumed "until the contrary is proved" in a criminal context
normally places a burden on the accused to prove on the balance of probabilities.
Therefore, to simply raise a reasonable doubt or to discharge an evidential burden of
"sufficient evidence", would appear insufficient to amount to a rebuttal. Subsection (6) is
a new presumption. Any questions concerning its constitutionality would be dispelled by
consideration of the Supreme Court judgments in *Hardy v Ireland* [1994] 2 I.R. 550, and
in particular, *O'Leary v Attorney-General* [1995] 1 I.R. 254.

Subsection (7) provides that where an enforcement notice is issued, then in a prosecution for carrying out unauthorised development under s.151 or non-compliance with an enforcement notice under s.154, it is a defence that a person took all reasonable steps to secure compliance with the enforcement notice. There is no definition of reasonable steps and it will depend upon the nature of the unauthorised development and the precise steps taken, whether such steps were reasonable. It appears that such steps must have been taken within the period specified in the enforcement notice.

Subsection (8) provides upon conviction for an offence under s.154, the court may order the person convicted to take the steps specified in the enforcement order to be taken. This would appear to be at the discretion of the court. If a court is minded to do so, a court could place a stay on the order to allow the defendant to take the steps required in the notice. If a person fails to comply with the notice after such order is made, they will be guilty of a continuing offence for every day of non-compliance and liable for further conviction under subs.(2). The defendant will also be guilty of contempt of court and liable for attachment and committal. Section 162(2) provides that it shall not be a defence to a prosecution that a defendant applied for or has been granted retention planning permission, if this occurred after (i) the initiation of proceedings; (ii) the sending of a warning letter; or (iii) the service of any enforcement notice in case of urgency. While s.162(3) provides that no enforcement action shall be stayed or withdrawn by reason of an application for or grant of retention permission. Notwithstanding these provisions, the grant of a retention application may be relevant in particular to whether a court may order the terms of an enforcement notice to be complied with under s.156(8). In such circumstances a planning authority may consent to adjourn a prosecution pending the outcome of a retention application.

The 2006 Act amended subs.(1) to provide that the offence under s.135(7) concerning giving false evidence to, obstructing, etc an oral hearing before the Board, is added to the list of offences to which the specified penalties are applicable. A new subs.(9) also provides that where a person is convicted on indictment of an offence concerning an oral hearing under s.135(7), the court may order that the convicted person or other body who consented, connived in the offence, pay the Board or persons who appeared at the hearing, an amount equal to additional costs incurred as a result of the offence. This only applies to offences on indictment and not to summary convictions. Furthermore, the court must be satisfied that the offence delayed the conduct of the oral hearing.

Prosecution of offences

157.—(1) Subject to section 149, summary proceedings for an offence under this Act may be brought and prosecuted by a planning authority whether or not the offence is committed in the authority's functional area.   **1–187**

(2) Notwithstanding *section 10(4)* of the Petty Sessions (Ireland) Act, 1851, and subject to *subsection (3)* of this section, summary proceedings may be commenced—

    (a) at any time within 6 months from the date on which the offence was committed, or

    (b) at any time within 6 months from the date on which evidence sufficient, in the opinion of the person by whom the proceedings are initiated, to justify proceedings comes to that person's knowledge, whichever is the later.

(3) For the purposes of this section, a certificate signed by or on behalf of the person initiating the proceedings as to the date or dates on which evidence described in *subsection (2)(b)* came to his or her knowledge shall be evidence of the date or dates and in any legal proceedings a document purporting to be a certificate under this section and to be so signed shall be deemed to be so signed and shall be admitted as evidence without proof of the signature of the person purporting to sign the certificate, unless the contrary is shown.

(4)

   (a) No warning letter or enforcement notice shall issue and no proceedings for an offence under this Part shall commence—

      (i) in respect of a development where no permission has been granted, after seven years from the date of the commencement of the development;

      (ii) in respect of a development for which permission has been granted under Part III, after seven years beginning on the expiration, as respects the permission authorising the development, of the appropriate period within the meaning of section 40 or, as the case may be, of the period as extended under section 42.

   (b) Notwithstanding *paragraph (a),* proceedings may be commenced at any time in respect of any condition concerning the use of land to which the permission is subject.

   (c) It shall be presumed until the contrary is proved that proceedings were commenced within the appropriate period.

(5) Proceedings for other offences under this Act shall not be initiated later than 7 years from the date on which the offence concerned was alleged to have been committed.

NOTE

This section concerns matters relating to the prosecution of offences and taking enforcement proceedings. Under subs.(1), the planning authority can bring a prosecution even where the offence was outside its functional area, which reverses s.80(1) of the 1963 Act, whereby the offence must have been committed in its area. The planning authority can only institute proceedings in respect of summary offences. While the 2000 Act creates both summary and indictable offences, the planning authority cannot institute proceedings in relation to a charge on indictment. Under the previous legislation in respect of indictable offences, the planning authority could prosecute such offences summarily up to the stage the District Court declined jurisdiction. See *TDI Metro Ltd v Delap (2)* [2000] 4 I.R. 520. Section 80 of the 1963 Act, as amended, referred to "prosecuted summarily"; however, subs.(1) uses the phrase "summary proceedings", which would appear to rule out indictable offences prosecuted summarily.

Subsection (2) modifies the Petty Sessions Act 1851, whereby summary offences must be commenced within six months, by allowing proceedings to be commenced within six months of the date on which evidence sufficient, in the opinion of the person by whom the proceedings are initiated, to justify proceedings comes to that person's knowledge. By way of proof of when sufficient evidence came to the planning authority's knowledge, subs.(3) allows a certificate signed by the person initiating proceedings to state when the evidence came to their knowledge. The content of this certificate may be rebutted on the balance of probabilities. In the case of a summary prosecution for failure to comply with an enforcement notice, the six-month time limitation does not run from the end of the period for compliance specified in the enforcement notice. The fact that an enforcement notice only ceases to have effect ten years from the date of service means that there is a continuing obligation on the person served to comply with the steps required in the notice. This obligation does not cease merely because the specified period for compliance has expired. Where a person has not complied with the notice, they will be guilty of a continuing offence. See *Clare County Council v Floyd* [2007] 2 I.R. 671. Where an inspector from the planning authority visits the land at some date after the expiry of the time limit for compliance, evidence of non-compliance at the date of inspection may form the basis for a prosecution for an offence of non-compliance with the enforcement notice on that date. There will be a six-month period to bring a summary prosecution in respect of the offence on such date. However, if a person continues to breach the terms of the enforcement notice, a subsequent inspection which gathers evidence of such non-compliance at such subsequent inspection may form the basis of another prosecution.

Subsection (4) states that the issuing of a warning letter, an enforcement notice, or the commencement of proceedings for a criminal offence under Pt VIII (offences under ss.151 and 154) must be made within seven years from the date of the commencement of the unauthorised development. A similar time limit applies with respect to a planning injunction under s.160(6). The seven years run from the commencement of the unauthorised development; or where permission has been granted for the development, the seven years run, from the expiration of the planning permission (the normal life of which is five years under s.40 unless extended under s.42). Where a use commerces but is interrupted or abandoned, a new limitation period will run from the date of recommencement of such use. See *South Dublin County Council v Balfe*, unreported, High Court, Costello P., November 3, 1995. Equally, where there is an intensification of use amounting to material change of use, time will run from the date of such intensification. See *Cork County Council v Slattery Pre-cast Concrete Ltd*, unreported, High Court, Clarke J., September 19, 2008. However, the fact that a person applies for retention permission of an unauthorised use, will have no effect on the limitation period. A retention application will not have the effect of suspending the limitation period nor will a new limitation commence in the event of a refusal of retention permission. It may also be noted the mere fact that a person applies for retention permission will not estop a defendant from subsequently claiming, in the event of a refusal, that development was not unauthorised development. See *Fingal County Council v William Keeling & Sons* [2005] 2 I.R. 108. In the case of an offence, the seven-year time limitation relates to the commencement of the unauthorised development rather than the date of any particular offence. Under subs.(4)(b) there is no time limitation for commencing proceedings in respect of a planning condition concerning the use of the land. This however only applies to commencing proceedings rather than the issuing of a warning letter or enforcement notice. Thus it may be possible to bring a prosecution under s.151 in respect of such condition outside the seven-year limitation period, but it will not be possible to issue a warning letter or enforcement notice. Under the previous legislation, the limitation period was five years and so this was extended to seven years under the 2000 Act, which entered into force on March 11, 2002. Where an unauthorised development was commenced prior to March 11, 2002, the seven year limitation period will apply. See *Cork County Council v Slattery Pre-cast Concrete Ltd.*, unreported, High Court, Clarke J., September 19, 2008, where it was held that such amendment could not be characterised as a retrospective interference with the rights or entitlements of an individual whose wrongful actions remained capable of being subject to enforcement proceedings as of the date of the statutory amendment, where the effect of the amendment is simply to prolong the period during which enforcement proceedings could be taken. Clarke J. noted, however, that where a limitation period expires there may be an argument as to whether the re-opening of such a limitation period might amount to a retrospective measure.

In relation to any proceedings there is a presumption that they were commenced within the time limit. This presumption may be rebutted on the balance of probabilities. As noted, no time limit applies to proceedings in respect of a condition concerning the use of land to which the permission is subject. This does not apply to unauthorised use per se, merely a condition in respect of use. Unauthorised development which is immune from enforcement action because the time has expired, still retains its status as unauthorised development, even though no enforcement action can be taken. See *Dublin Corp v Mulligan*, unreported, High Court, May 6, 1980. In respect of such development certain disadvantages still apply, such as the loss of exempted development status; see the note on s.160(6). Subsection (5) provides that in respect of all offences under the Act other than in Pt VIII, proceedings must be commenced within seven years from when the offence concerned was alleged to have been committed. A person convicted may also be required to pay costs under s.161.

Offences by bodies corporate

158.—(1) Where an offence under this Act is committed by a body corporate or by a person acting on behalf of a body corporate and is proved to have been   **1–188**

so committed with the consent, connivance or approval of, or to have been facilitated by any neglect on the part of a person being a director, manager, secretary or other officer of the body or a person who was purporting to act in any such capacity, that person shall also be guilty of an offence and shall be liable to be proceeded against and punished as if he or she were guilty of the first-mentioned offence.

(2) Where the affairs of a body corporate are managed by its members, *subsection (1)* shall apply in relation to the acts and defaults of a member in connection with his or her functions of management as if he or she were a director of the body corporate.

NOTE

This section concerns an offence committed by a company. A person who is a director, manager, secretary or other officer of the body or a person who was purporting to act in any such capacity may be guilty of an offence, where:
- the actual offence was committed by the body corporate or a person on behalf of the company; and
- it is proved to have been committed with the consent, connivance or approval of, or facilitated by the neglect of such director, manager, secretary or other officer, etc.

Both elements must be satisfied in order for an offence to be commited by such persons.

The list of persons is very broadly drafted to include persons purporting to act in the capacity of such director, manager, secretary or other officer, etc. Some mental element is necessary to hold a company officer liable, though the reference to neglect indicates that it is not necessary to prove actual intention on the part of such person.

The body corporate itself may be prosecuted and found guilty of an offence under Pt VIII including under ss.151 or 154. The common law has developed the concepts of vicarious liability and the doctrine of "identification" to allow for criminal liability of companies. See *Tesco Supermarkets v Nattrass* [1971] 1 Q.B. 133.

Payment of fines to planning authorities

1–189 **159.**—Where a court imposes a fine or affirms or varies a fine imposed by another court for an offence under this Act, it shall provide by order for the payment of the amount of the fine to the planning authority and the payment may be enforced by the authority as if it were due to it on foot of a decree or order made by the court in civil proceedings.

NOTE

This section provides that where a fine is imposed for an offence under the Act, the court may direct that the fine be paid to the relevant planning authority. It appears that this applies not only where the prosecution is taken by the planning authority but also where the prosecution is taken by the DPP.

Injunctions in relation to unauthorised development

1–190 **160.**—**(1)** Where an unauthorised development has been, is being or is likely to be carried out or continued, the High Court or the Circuit Court may, on the application of a planning authority or any other person, whether or not the person has an interest in the land, by order require any person to do or not to do, or to cease to do, as the case may be, anything that the Court considers necessary and specifies in the order to ensure, as appropriate, the following:

    (a) that the unauthorised development is not carried out or continued;

    (b) in so far as is practicable, that any land is restored to its condition prior to the commencement of any unauthorised development;

    (c) that any development is carried out in conformity with the permission pertaining to that development or any condition to which the permission is subject.

(2) In making an order under *subsection (1)*, where appropriate, the Court may order the carrying out of any works, including the restoration, reconstruction, removal, demolition or alteration of any structure or other feature.

(3)

    (a) An application to the High Court or the Circuit Court for an order under this section shall be by motion and the Court when considering the matter may make such interim or interlocutory order (if any) as it considers appropriate.

    (b) Subject to section 161, the order by which an application under this section is determined may contain such terms and conditions (if any) as to the payment of costs as the Court considers appropriate.

(4)

    (a) Rules of court may provide for an order under this section to be made against a person whose identity is unknown.

    (b) Any relevant rules of Court made in respect of section 27 (inserted by section 19 of the Act of 1992) of the Act of 1976 shall apply to this section and shall be construed to that effect.

(5)

    (a) An application under this section to the Circuit Court shall be made to the judge of the Circuit Court for the circuit in which the land which is the subject of the application is situated.

    (b) The Circuit Court shall have jurisdiction to hear and determine an application under this section where the rateable valuation of the land which is the subject of the application does not exceed €253.95 [£200].

    (c) The Circuit Court may, for the purposes of *paragraph (b)*, in relation to land that has not been given a rateable valuation or is the subject with other land of a rateable valuation, determine that its rateable valuation would exceed, or would not exceed, €253.95 [£200].

    (d) Where the rateable valuation of any land which is the subject of an application under this section exceeds €253.95 [£200], the Circuit Court shall, if an application is made to it in that behalf by any person having an interest in the proceedings, transfer the proceedings to the High Court, but any order made or act done in the course of such proceedings before the transfer shall be valid unless discharged or varied by the High Court by order.

(6)

    (a) An application to the High Court or Circuit Court for an order under this section shall not be made—

        (i) in respect of a development where no permission has been granted, after the expiration of a period of 7 years from the date of the commencement of the development, or

(ii) in respect of a development for which permission has been granted under Part III, after the expiration of a period of 7 years beginning on the expiration, as respects the permission authorising the development, of the appropriate period (within the meaning of section 40) or, as the case may be, of the appropriate period as extended under section 42.

(b) Notwithstanding *paragraph (a),* an application for an order under this section may be made at any time in respect of any condition to which the development is subject concerning the ongoing use of the land.

(7) Where an order has been sought under this section, any other enforcement action under this Part may be commenced or continued.

AMENDMENT

Provision is made to amend this section, by the substitution of "market value" for "rateable valuation", and the substitution of " €3,000,000" for "£200" by s.53 of the Civil Liability and Courts Act 2004 (No. 31 of 2004). However, at the date of publication, s.53 of the 2004 Act has not yet been brought into effect.

NOTE

This section concerns a planning injunction in connection with unauthorised development. The section contains some significant changes compared to the previous legislation contained in s.27 of the 1976 Act. A planning injunction can be granted in relation to unauthorised development which "has been, is being or is likely to be carried out or continued" and so can cover future development which can be restrained by *quia timet* relief which was not allowed under the former s.27. See *Mahon v Butler* [1997] 3 I.R. 369. Quia timet relief will only be granted where there is a proven substantial risk of danger; see *Szabo v Esat Digifone Limited* [1998] 2 I.L.R.M. 102. Subsections (1) and (2) concern the scope of the order which the court can make. The court has a wide-ranging discretion to fashion orders which it deems appropriate with subs.(1) referring to "anything that the Court considers necessary". The court is not restricted to the form of orders sought by an applicant in their notice of motion.

Subsection (2) specifies certain types of works which the court may order. The power of the court to a make mandatory order is now beyond doubt, with the subs.(2) providing that "the Court may order the carrying out of any works, including the restoration, reconstruction, removal, demolition or alteration of any structure or other feature". This was subject to some doubt under s.27, where in some cases the courts refused to grant orders where the development was already complete; see *Loughnane v Hogan* [1987] I.R. 322, *Dublin Corporation v Bentham* [1993] 2 I.R. 58. It was considered that the summary nature of the proceedings meant it was inappropriate to make mandatory orders where the matter related to development without the benefit of any permission, although such orders could be granted where the matter related to development not in conformity with a permission. See *Dublin County Council v Kirby* [1985] I.L.R.M. 325. Court orders were also refused to order partial compliance with a planning permission after the development has been completed; see *Dublin County Council v Browne*, unreported, High Court, Gannon J., October 6, 1987 and *Dublin Corporation v McGowan* [1993] 1 I.R. 405. Although mandatory order, were made in other circumstances; see *Meath County Council v Thornton*, unreported, High Court, O'Hanlon J., February 25, 1994 and *Fitzpatrick v O'Connor*, unreported, High Court, March 11, 1988. These restrictions have now been removed. In *Cantwell v McCarthy*, unreported, Murphy J., November 1, 2006, it was noted that subs.(2) only concerns works. However, it is clear the court is not restricted in these terms and can also order the cessation of any type of unauthorised use under subs.(1). The power to restore land prior to the commencement of development is qualified by the expression "as far as is practicable". The order for restoration may relate to "any land".

Subsection (1)(c), in relation to ordering conformity with a permission, differs from the previous s.27(2) by expressly stating that an order can be made requiring compliance with any condition rather than taking steps to conform with the permission. It is also expressed to relate to a permission "pertaining to that development". It may not be possible to comply with a condition where it was required to be carried out prior to the commencement of development; see *Eircell Ltd v Bernstoff*, unreported, High Court, Barr J., February 18, 2000. Nonetheless it is open to the court to merely make an order providing that a specific condition is complied with.

The section creates one category of unauthorised development, while under the former s.27 there was a distinction between development in breach of planning permission and unauthorised development. This is consistent with the changes in relation to the definitions of "unauthorised use" and "unauthorised works"under s.2, where in relation to both definitions development which is the subject of a permission granted is excluded from being unauthorised use or unauthorised work, where it is "carried out in compliance with the permission or any condition to which that permission is subject".

The persons against whom an order can be made is drafted broadly, with subs.(1) providing that an order may be made with respect to "any person". Typically the appropriate defendants will be the owner and occupier of the relevant lands, though the court is not confined to making order against such persons. It was recognised under the previous legislation that orders could be made against the directors of a company. In *Dublin County Council v Elton Homes Ltd* [1984] I.L.R.M. 297, Barrington J. said the most effective way of ensuring compliance by a company would be to make an order against the company directors as well. Although non-compliance with the requirement of the Companies Acts will not be sufficient reason; see *Dublin County Council v O'Riordan* [1985] I.R. 159. Personal liability might attach to the directors where there was wilful default on their part; see *Sligo County Council v Cartron Bay Construction Ltd*, unreported, High Court, Ó Caoimh J., May 25, 2001.

Public Watchdog Application

The entitlement to take an injunction is afforded to the planning authority and members of the public, reflecting its community "watchdog role"; see *Morris v Garvey* [1982] I.L.R.M. 177. There is therefore no locus standi requirement. The ability to bring an application is not based on any property right but to procure the performance of a public duty or to prevent its breach; see *State (Haverty) v An Bord Pleanála* [1988] I.L.R.M. 545. This does not involve the court deciding issues akin to good planning; see *Furlong v A.F. & G.W. McConnell* [1990] I.L.R.M. 48. There is no requirement for an applicant to demonstrate prejudice. See *Cantwell v McCarthy*, unreported, High Court, Murphy J., November 1, 2006. The existence of this public watchdog application, where there is no locus standi requirement, is not unique in Irish environmental law. Other examples include s.28 of the Air Pollution Act 1977 prohibiting or restricting an emission the continuance of which would give rise to a serious risk of air pollution or contravenes the terms of a licence; under the Local Government (Water Pollution) Act 1977 any person may apply to the High Court for an order prohibiting the entry of polluting matter to waters, etc.; s.57 of the Waste Management Act 1996 provides that an application can be made by any person for an order requiring a person holding, recovering or disposing of waste to carry out specified steps or to prevent or limit pollution or to require a person to refrain from or cease doing any specified act; under ss.5 and 6 of the Foreshore Act 1992 an injunction may be granted to prohibit the removal of beach material. Also although not strictly an injunction, under s.108 of the Environmental Protection Act 1992 any person can apply to the District Court for an order to prevent or limit noise which has become a nuisance. See *Southern Hotel Sligo v Iarnrod Eireann*, unreported, High Court, Hedigan J., July 13, 2007.

The planning authority has a discretion whether to seek an injunction under s.160. A challenge to the decision of the planning authority not to bring injunction proceedings in judicial review proceedings would be assessed on the high standard of irrationality under *O'Keeffe v An Bord Pleanála* [1993] 1 I.R. 39. Any attempt to compel the planning authority to take enforcement action by seeking an order of mandamus in judicial review proceedings, would most likely fail. Apart from this, the fact that any member of the public can institute planning injunction proceedings under s.160, would mean that there is alternative remedy to the relief sought. A further consideration is the limited resources of local authorities. In context of housing policy, in *Doherty v South Dublin County Council*, unreported, High Court, Charleton J., January 22, 2007, Charleton J. commented that the council had obligations only in accordance with its resources and its scheme of priorities. One exception to this may be under the EIA Directive, under which Member States are required to take all general or particular measures necessary to ensure that projects which are likely to have significant effects on the environment are subject to assent. See *Aannemersbedrijf P.K. v Gedeputeerde Staten van Zuid-Holland* C-72/95 [1996] ECR I-5403. In *Commission v Ireland* C-215/06 July 3, 2008, the ECJ held that in allowing for retention applications in respect of certain developments requiring an EIS and in not taking enforcement action, Ireland had breached the EIA Directive. The European Convention on Human Rights could be a source of an obligation to take enforcement action albeit in extreme cases. In *Antonetto v Italy* [2000] ECHR 378, the European Court of Human Rights held that the plaintiff's right to peaceful enjoyment of her possessions under art.1 of the First Protocol had been infringed by the refusal of the Italian authorities to enforce a court order to demolish an illegally built building which obstructed her right to light and devalued her property. See also *Guerra v Italy* [1998] ECHR 7; *Lopez Ostra v Spain* [1994] ECHR 46; *Surugiu v Romania*, ECHR, April 20, 2004.

Procedure

Section 160 is still a summary procedure; it is commenced by notice of motion and affidavit and it is not appropriate to resolve complex issues of facts, which are more properly resolved under plenary summons. See *Dublin County Council v Kirby* [1985] I.L.R.M. 325, where it was described as a "fire brigade section", and *Waterford County Council v John A Woods* [1999] 1 I.R. 556; *Mahon v Butler* [1997] 3 I.R. 389; *Dublin County Council v O'Riordan* [1985] I.R. 159; *Fingal County Council v RFS Ltd*, unreported, High Court, Morris P., February 6, 2000, and *Dublin Corporation v Garland* [1982] I.L.R.M. 104, although it could be argued that the scope of the injunction has been so expanded that it is anomalous to continue to view it as a summary type procedure. If it appears that a defence put forward by the respondent is one where oral evidence, and even pleadings and discovery are necessary or desirable, the court can order such directions as to pleadings and mode of trial as may be appropriate. See *Limerick County Council v Tobin t/a Harry Tobin Sand and Gravel*, unreported, High Court, Peart J., August 15, 2007. The procedure is initiated by notice of motion grounded upon affidavit. A respondent will generally be confined at the hearing to points of defence raised in the affidavit; see *South Dublin County Council v Balfe*, unreported, High Court, Costello J., November 3, 1995. An application to have the matter heard on oral evidence should be made at interlocutory stage; see *White v McInerney Construction Ltd* [1995] I.L.R.M. 374. A party can serve notice to cross examine a deponent on the content of their affidavits. Any assertion in an affidavit which is not contradicted shall be deemed to have been established on the balance of probability and that where an assertion is contradicted, the onus of proof in respect thereof shall be deemed not to have been satisfied. See *Ryan v Roadstone Ltd*, unreported, High Court, O'Donovan J., March 6, 2006.

Subsection (4)(b) of the 2000 Act provides that any relevant Rules of Court made in respect of s.27 of the 1976 Act applies to the section. The practice and procedure of a Section 27 application to the High Court was set out in RSC Ord.103, while an application in the Circuit Court is set out in CCR Ord.56. The injunction is a permanent injunction and hearsay evidence is not allowed; see *Dublin Corporation v O'Sullivan*, unreported, High Court, Finlay P., December 21, 1984. However, the normal exception to the hearsay rules such as the admissibility of declarations against interest, will apply. See *South Dublin Council v Balfe*, unreported, High Court, Costello J., November 3, 1995. There is no provision for the payment of damages; see *Ellis v Nolan*, unreported, High Court, McWilliam J., May 6, 1983. In *Leen v Aer Rianta*, unreported, High Court, McKechnie J., August 1, 2003, McKechnie J. declined to decide whether the court has power to issue a declaration of non-compliance under s.160. There is nothing to prevent a private applicant from seeking both a general injunction and a planning injunction in the same proceedings; see *MMDS Television v South Eastern Community Deflector Association*, unreported, High Court, Carroll J., April 8, 1997. The court may decline to grant a planning injunction where it has already granted a general injunction; see *Vitalograph v Ennis District Council*, unreported, High Court, Kelly J., April 23, 1997. A private applicant can also combine a nuisance claim and a planning injunction in the same proceedings. See *Molumby v Kearns*, unreported, High Court, O'Sullivan J., January 19, 1999 and *Lanigan & Benghazi v Barry*, unreported, High Court, Charleton J., February 15, 2008.

There is no express requirement for an applicant to give an undertaking as to damages. It was suggested by Herbert J., obiter, in *Grimes v Punchestown Development* [2002] 1 I.L.R.M. 409, that an undertaking as to the damages may be required in certain circumstances. The better view is that there is no such requirement. This follows from the fact that the main rationale for giving an undertaking as to damages is to allow the court to make an order pending the final determination of the case. However, s.160 proceedings constitute a permanent injunction and so the rationale does not apply. See *Limerick County Council v Tobin*, unreported, High Court, Peart J., August 15, 2005. However, it appears that in respect of interim or interlocutory relief under subs.(3), an undertaking as to damages may be appropriate.

Under the Local Government Act 2001, the taking of court proceedings by a planning authority requires a manager's order to have been made. In the case of a planning injunction, the order should be exhibited in the grounding affidavit. However, even where not exhibited, the court may allow the planning authority to prove it in court. In *Kildare County Council v Goode*, unreported, High Court, Morris P., June 13, 1997, where the applicant raised the absence of the Manager's Order, Morris P. held that there is vested in the court a discretion to permit the applicant to prove this order by producing it in court.

Subsection (3) expressly allows the making of interim or interlocutory orders. However, the summary nature of the injunction would appear to mean it is superfluous to seek interlocutory relief. Interlocutory relief can be obtained applying the normal *Campus Oil* [1983] I.R. 88 principles for interlocutory injunctions. See *Limerick County Council v Tobin t/a Harry Tobin Sand and Gravel*, unreported, High Court, Peart J., August 15, 2007, where Peart J. considered damages would not be an adequate remedy for the planning authority which is acting in the public interest. The court will then examine whether damages would be an adequate remedy to the defendant and where the balance of convenience lies. The fact that the court may order a restoration of the land did not mean that the balance of convenience favoured refusal, where the prospect of restoration would be remote as a result of continuing works on the land. In cases of urgency, an ex parte injunction can be sought in a s.160 proceedings.

Subsection (5) provides that where the rateable valuation of the property is below €253.94, the Circuit Court will have jurisdiction to hear and determine an application. The Circuit Courts jurisdiction is confined to cases where the rateable valuation does not exceed €253.94. The better view is that this does not oust the jurisdiction of the High Court where the rateable valuation is less than €253.94. Both the High Court and Circuit have co-extensive jurisdiction in such case. This is supported by the fact that while under subs.(5)(d) the Circuit Court is obligated to transfer a matter to the High Court where the rateable value exceeds €253.94 once an application is made, there is no analogous provision stating that there is an obligation on the High Court to remit where the rateable valuation is less than €253.94. Nonetheless, where the proceedings are commenced in the High Court in respect of land which is less than €254, a party could bring a motion to seek to remit the matter to the Circuit Court. However, the court has a discretion whether to do so. See *O'Shea v Mallow UDC* [1994] 2 I.R. 117, where under general principles the court may refuse to remit where it is reasonable and proper to retain the action in the High Court. However, where proceedings are taken in the High Court where the rateable valuation is less than €253.94, costs penalties may be incurred under s.17 of the Courts Act 1981, as a result of which a successful applicant may be restricted to obtaining Circuit Court costs. However, again this would be a matter for the discretion of the trial judge. Under the 1976 Act, there was simply an option to take such proceedings in the Circuit or High Court as the jurisdiction of both courts was co-extensive. Provision is made to amend this subsection,

by the substitution of "market value" for "rateable valuation", and the substitution of "
€3,000,000" for "€253.94" by s.53 of the Civil Liability and Courts Act 2004 (No. 31 of
2004). However, at the date of publication, s.53 of the 2004 Act has not yet been brought
into effect. It may be said that the use of rateable valuation is largely inappropriate to
determine jurisdiction in the context of unauthorised development. This is especially the
case where the unauthorised development concerns an unauthorised use of land where
there may be limited number of buildings on the land. The rateable valuation of such land
may be low due to the small amount of buildings even though the unauthorised use may
be very extensive and significant.

Onus of Proof

Unlike certain criminal prosecutions, there is no express provision establishing or
applying any evidential presumption in proceedings taken under s.160. Section 160
proceedings are civil and the presumptions under s.162 and 157(4)(c), are inapplicable.
See *South Dublin County Council v Fallowvale*, unreported, High Court, McKechnie J.,
April 28, 2005. Nevertheless it is generally accepted that the applicant bears the onus of
proof; see *Dublin Corporation v O'Sullivan*, unreported, High Court, Finlay P., December
21, 1984 in which Finlay P. stated:
> "I am satisfied, since the Applicants come seeking relief which would affect the
> ordinary property rights of the Defendant and which potentially could cause him
> loss that in the absence of some express provision to the contrary that does not exist
> either in Section 27 of the 1976 Act or otherwise in the planning code that the general
> position must be that it is upon the Applicants there rests the onus of proving the
> case which they are making."

See also *Dublin Corporation v Regan Advertising* [1989] I.R. 61; *Molumby v Kearns*,
unreported, High Court, O'Sullivan J., January 19, 1999; and *Fingal County Council v RFS
Ltd*, unreported, High Court, Morris P., February 6, 2000; *Sweetman v Shell E & P Ireland
Ltd* [2007] 3 I.R. 13. See also *Ryan v Roadstone*, unreported, High Court, March 6, 2006,
where it was noted that the applicant must establish facts from which the court can raise the
probable inference that what the applicant asserts is true. However, where the respondent
seeks to raise a defence based on a claim that the development is exempted development,
the respondent will bear the onus of proof to establish this. See *Dillon v Irish Cement*,
unreported, Supreme Court, November 26, 1986, where Walsh J. said: "To that extent I
am satisfied that these Regulations should by a court be strictly construed in the sense that
for a developer to put himself within them he must be clearly and unambiguously within
them in regard to what he proposes to do". This was however distinguished in *Westport
UDC v Golden* [2002] 1 I.L.R.M. 439, where Morris P. rejected that it was authority for
the proposition that the onus lay on the respondent. However, in *South Dublin County
Council v Fallowvale*, unreported, High Court, McKechnie J., April 28, 2005. McKechnie
J. found that:
> "[T]here is clear preponderance of authority in favour of the proposition that when
> the development complained of is sought to be excused under cover of either s. 4 of
> the Act of 2000 or under the exempted developments provisions in the Regulations
> then the onus of establishing this point is upon he who asserts".

Also in *Mason and McCarthy v KT Sand and Gravel,* unreported, High Court, Smyth J.,
May 7, 2004, Smyth J. noted that "[i]n the case of exempted development - the burden of
proof of entitlement rests on the Respondent". In *Callan v Boyle*, unreported, High Court,
Murphy J., March 20, 2007, it was noted that while the onus of proof is on the applicant to
advance satisfactory evidence before the court regarding his complaints and so there may
be no obligation on the respondent to disprove the applicant's contentions, nonetheless
where objective, credible evidence is adduced, the court may have regard to the absence
of available evidence either from the respondent, the operator, or by the licensor (in that
case relating to extraction). As regards proof of a material change of use amounting to
unauthorised development, photographic evidence may be adduced in support of the same.
See *Callan v Boyle,* unreported, High Court, Murphy J., March 20, 2007, where two sets
of photographs taken before 2004 and in 2006 were adduced which showed a significant
topographical change to the quarry site. Aerial photographs and ordinance surveys were

also adduced in support of the application in *South Dublin County Council v Fallowvale*, unreported, High Court, McKechnie J., April 28, 2005.

Where enforcement action is based on non-compliance with a planning condition, the planning condition must be of sufficient clarity to justify granting relief. See *Liffey Beat v Dublin City Council* [2005] 2 I.R. 478, where relief was declined to enforce a planning permission which prohibited the use of the premises as a "nightclub or similar function type of premises". Where the permitted use of property is restricted or confined by a condition or a number of conditions, then the terms of those conditions should be clearly comprehensible and capable of definition and explanation. It was further noted that as the planning process was intended to be substantially consultative in nature, reasonable care should be taken by a planning authority or An Bord Pleanála to provide any clarification sought by a party having an interest in the property as to the nature and extent of restrictions imposed by a condition within a planning permission. Where the applicant is a planning authority relying on a planning condition which it drafted it may be construed against the applicant. See *Cork County Council v Cliftonhall Limited and Others*, unreported, High Court, Finnegan J., April 6, 2001, where Finnegan J. said, "[i]n any event insofar as the planning permission is ambiguous it should be construed contra proferentem i.e. against the applicant". However, this cannot alter the general principles of construction that a planning permission including planning conditions, must be construed objectively. However there is no principle of law which proposes that the proper interpretation of a planning condition is the one which is the least onerous to the developer by reference to a principle of contra proferentem or any extension thereof. See *Altara Developments v Ventola Ltd*, unreported, High Court, O'Sullivan J., October 6, 2005. In *Mason and McCarthy v KT Sand and Gravel*, unreported, High Court, Smyth J., May 7, 2004, Smyth J. noted that although a condition in a planning permission requiring works to be carried out may impliedly include permission for those works, the scope of the permission was a matter of construction, subject to the principle that the permission could not go beyond the scope of the application or matters reasonably incidental thereto.

It will not be a defence for a respondent to claim that it has obtained a permission/licence under some other statutory code (and is in compliance thereof) which also governs the development. Compliance with one statutory regime does not absolve the party from compliance with a different regime unless such is expressly provided for. See *Curley v Galway Corporation*, unreported, High Court, Kelly J., December 11, 1998, where Kelly J. said:

> "I cannot conceive of a situation where the court can, in order to enable Galway Corporation to comply with its statutory obligations under one piece of legislation, permitted to breach obligations imposed upon it by another piece of legislation. In particular the court cannot permit the fulfilment of a statutory obligation, for example, under the Waste Management Act by the commission of offences under the planning legislation".

See also *South Dublin County Council v Fallowvale*, unreported, High Court, McKechnie J., April 28, 2005, where compliance with the Aviation Code did not mean there was compliance with the Planning Code. See also *Keane v An Bord Pleanála and Others* [1998] 1 I.L.R.M. 241; *Cablelink v An Bord Pleanála* [1999] 1 I.R. 596 and *Carthy v Fingal County Council* [1999] 3 I.R. 577.

Discretionary Refusal of Relief

The granting of a planning injunction is still a discretionary remedy, and so the case law under s.27 is equally applicable. This was confirmed in *Leen v Aer Rianta*, unreported, High Court, McKechnie J., August 1, 2003. In *Morris v Garvey* [1982] I.L.R.M. 177, Henchy J. said where a case of unauthorised development has been made out, it would require exceptional circumstances (such as genuine mistake, acquiescence over a long period, the triviality or mere technicality of the infraction, gross or disproportionate hardship or such like extenuating or excusing factors) before the court should refrain from making whatever order (including an order for attachment for contempt in default of compliance) as is "necessary to ensure that the development is carried out in conformity with the permission". The discretionary nature of remedy has been more stressed in later cases; see *Leen v Aer*

Rianta, unreported, High Court, McKechnie J., August 1, 2003. The court is not bound to exercise its discretion in one way; see *Avenue Properties Ltd v Farrell Homes Ltd* [1982] I.L.R.M. 21 in which Barrington J. noted:

> "[I]t would appear that applicants under Section 27 could range from a crank or busybody with no interest in the matter at one of the scale to, on the other end of the scale, persons who have suffered real damage through the unauthorised development or who though, they have suffered no damage peculiar to themselves, bring to the attention of the Court outrageous breaches of the Planning Act which ought to be restrained in the public interest. In these circumstances it appears to me all the more important that the Court should have a wide discretion as to when it should and when it should not intervene."

See also *White v McInerney Construction Ltd* [1995] 1 I.L.R.M. 374 and *Dublin County Council v Matra Investments Ltd* [1980 114 I.L.T.R. 306. However, see *Wicklow County Council v Forest Fencing t/a Abwood,* unreported, High Court, Charleton J., July 13, 2007, where it was said that the balancing of discretion must start with the duty of the court to uphold the principle of proper planning for developments under clear statutory rules. It is submitted that it should be emphasised that the onus is on the respondent to prove that relief should be refused. The listing of discretionary factors which have been taken into account in past cases, can create the misleading impression that the court must undertake some general balance of convenience type exercise in deciding whether to grant relief. Such a test which applies in an interlocutory injunction is not appropriate to a statutory injunction under this section. As each case turns on its particular facts, previous case law where the court has declined relief is of limited precedential value except to offer general guidance on the type of factors which may be considered. Notwithstanding the above, among the matters which have been considered in the existing case law in the exercise of discretion include:

- The reasonableness of the conduct of both parties will be relevant to the exercise of discretion. With respect to the applicant, a party must come to court with clean hands. See *O'Connor v Hetherington Ltd,* unreported, High Court, Barr J., May 28, 1987 (relief was refused where the applicant did not disclose that proceedings were financed by a competitor of the respondent); *Leech v Reilly,* unreported, High Court, O'Hanlon J., April 26, 1983 (where the applicant had not facilitated the genuine attempts of the respondent to comply with the conditions). An applicant should disclose relevant facts before the court; see *Fusco v Aprile,* unreported, High Court, Morris P., June 6, 1997. The fact that an applicant is seeking to protect his personal interests, such as his dwelling, will not preclude relief; see *Cairnduff v O'Connell* [1986] I.R. 73. In *Conroy v Craddock,* unreported, High Court, Dunne J., July 31, 2007, where there was evidence that the applicant had sought the agreement of other members of a joint venture to his plans for developing his part of the site and that in default of agreement had then commenced litigation, this was considered a questionable motivation for bringing proceedings. See also *Altara Developments Ltd v Ventola Ltd,* unreported, High Court, O'Sullivan J., October 6, 2005, the court took into account that the application was presented on the basis that the second applicant was a local resident who lived in the immediate vicinity of the site and this turned out to be incorrect.

- With respect to the respondent in *Dublin Corporation v McGowan* [1993] 1 I.R. 405, Keane J., in refusing relief, considered it would be manifestly unjust to have the draconian machinery brought against a person who behaved in good faith throughout. In *Leen v Aer Rianta,* unreported, High Court, McKechnie J., August 1, 2003, McKechnie J. had regard to the bona fides of the respondent in its dealings with the planning authority. In *Altara Developments v Ventola Ltd,* unreported, High Court, O'Sullivan J., October 6, 2005, O'Sullivan J. refused to make an order where the respondent had received professional advice that what he was doing was in compliance with planning permission before proceeding with a particular phase of the development in question. He noted:

> "This is not a case of a developer pushing ahead regardless. On the contrary it has proceeded since November 2004 with the active support and blessing of the planning authority and in the reasonably held opinion that it was not in breach of the planning permission. In the circumstances I decline to make any order

curtailing the respondent's construction works as requested by the applicant". In *Sweetman v Shell E & P Ireland Ltd.* [2007] 3 I.R. 13, it was noted that there had not been any deliberate disregard by Shell of the requirements or any attempt to avoid the obligations imposed by same. It had also expended very considerable monies and it bona fide believed that the planning authority agreed that it had complied with the conditions of the planning permission. On the other hand, the court will consider whether the respondent was conscious of the need for permission or acted with reckless disregard of the need for such; see *Dublin Corporation v Maiden Poster Sites Ltd* [1983] I.L.R.M. 48; *Curley v Galway Corporation*, unreported, High Court, Kelly J., December 11, 1998 (a deliberate and conscious violation of terms of a planning permission); and *Cavan County Council v Eircell Ltd*, unreported, High Court, Geoghegan J., March 10, 1999. In *Dublin Corporation v O'Dwyer Bros*, unreported, High Court, Kelly J., May 2, 1997, Kelly J. refused to put a stay on a injunction to allow an application for retention that would allow the respondents to continue to profit from its wrongdoing. The level of co-operation demonstrated by the respondent both before and after the institution of proceedings is relevant. In *Westport UDC v Golden* [2002] 1 I.L.R.M. 439, it was said that the court would not refuse an injunction where it would lend support for uncooperative conduct. Of relevance may be that the unauthorised use continued to the date of the hearing and the respondents planning history. See *Galway County Council v Connacht Proteins Ltd*, unreported, High Court, Barrington J., March 28, 1980. The fact that the respondent fully contests proceedings may also be a factor; see *Dublin Corporation v O'Dwyer*, unreported, High Court, Kelly J., May 2, 1997. In *Cork County Council v Slattery Pre-cast Concrete Ltd.*, unreported, High Court, September 19, 2008, Clarke J. granted relief taking into account the reckless and very significant breach of the Planning Acts, that An Bord Pleanála had rejected the respondent's retention application, the discreditable conduct of the respondents in expanding development after having lodged a retention application, and that the respondents had already gained substantial profits as a result of the unauthorised development.

- Public convenience or interest may be a factor. This could be reflected in certain economic reasons such as loss of employment to the community; see *Stafford v Roadstone Ltd* [1980] I.L.R.M. 1; *Glenroe Estates Management Company Ltd v IGR*, unreported, High Court, March 18, 1994; and *Dublin County Council v Sellwood Quarries Ltd* [1981] I.L.R.M. 23. In *Grimes v Punchestown Development* [2002] 1 I.L.R.M. 409, Herbert J. in refusing an injunction to restrain a pop concert, took into account the disappointment to the very large number of members of the public and enormous waste of public time and expense for bodies such as An Garda Síochána, the health inspectorate, road authorities, fire authorities, etc. In *Leen v Aer Rianta*, unreported, High Court, McKechnie J., August 1, 2003, which concerned a passenger terminal at Shannon airport, McKechnie J. took into account the public interest in ensuring that the airport was not closed down, which would affect a multiplicity of bodies and entities as well as the interests of the wider community. McKechnie J. said that in general any element or feature of public interest which arises from the particular circumstances can be taken into account. On the other hand, the fact of a health hazard or nuisance to local residence may favour granting relief; see *Galway County Council v Connacht Proteins Ltd*, unreported, High Court, Barrington J., March 28, 1980. However, the public interest in restraining unauthorised development may outweigh any loss of employment or contribution to the community of the business. See *Callan v Boyle*, unreported, High Court, Murphy J., March 20, 2007 where an order was granted restraining a quarry notwithstanding the fact that the business supplied materials in demand, employed 20 persons and contributed indirectly to the livelihood of some 100 suppliers and subcontractors operating in a radius of 10 to 15 miles of the quarry. See also *Wicklow County Council v Forest Fencing t/a Abwood*, unreported, High Court, Charleton J., July 13, 2007, where an order was granted notwithstanding claims of effect on livelihood and employment.

- Even though an application is made within the statutory time period, delay, or laches, may be a factor in refusing relief. In *Leen v Aer Rianta*, unreported, High Court,

McKechnie J., August 1, 2003, McKechnie J. opined, *obiter*, that it was unclear whether delay could be a ground for refusing relief where the application was within the time limit under the section, although it certainly plays a part in whether to place a stay on the order. In *Dublin Corporation v Lowe*, unreported, High Court, Morris P., February 4, 2000, Morris P. noted unreasonable delay could amount to acquiescence, though not on the facts of the case; see also *Dublin Corporation v Mulligan*, unreported, High Court, Finlay P., May 6, 1980. Whether there is delay will depend on the particular facts of each case; see *Dublin Corporation v Kevans*, unreported, High Court, Finlay P., July 14, 1980 (where a lengthy stay was placed on the order as the enforcement action had not been pursued with urgency); and *Fingal County Council v H.E. Services*, unreported, High Court, Ó Caoimh J., January 25, 2002. In *Grimes v Punchestown Developments Company Ltd* [2002] 1 I.L.R.M. 409, Herbert J. took into account that the applicant had not sought to institute proceedings until shortly before the concert was to take place, despite the fact it had been widely publicised. Where the delay would result in great hardship to the respondent this will be a factor against granting relief. See *Conroy v Craddock*, unreported, High Court, Dunne J., July 31, 2007. In *Sweetman v Shell E & P Ireland Ltd.* [2007] 3 I.R. 13, the court took into account the fact that the applicant had carried out on his behalf an inspection of the site but failed to institute proceedings some months later by which time Shell had carried out substantial realignment roadworks at considerable expense.

- The court may refuse an order where the violation is merely technical or minor; see *Avenue Properties v Farrell Homes* [1982] I.L.R.M. 21; *Marry v Connaughten*, unreported, High Court, O'Hanlon J., January 25, 1984; *White v McInerney Construction Ltd* [1995] 1 I.L.R.M. 374; and *Morris v Garvey* [1982] I.R. 319. Where there is substantial compliance, the court may decline relief. See *Conroy v Craddock*, unreported, High Court, Dunne J., July 31, 2007. Immaterial variations from a planning permission are allowed where the developer acted in good faith; see *O'Connell v Dungarvan Energy Ltd*, unreported, High Court, Finnegan J., February 27, 2001; and *Cork County Council v Cliftonhall*, unreported, High Court, Finnegan J., April 6, 2001. Planning permissions should be interpreted with some degree of flexibility so as to allow for the practical reality that buildings can sometimes not be built precisely as the plans indicate. See *Wicklow County Council v Forest Fencing t/a Abwood*, unreported, High Court, Charleton J., July 13, 2007.
- Where an injunction would impose undue hardship on a respondent, this may be a factor against granting the injunction; see *Avenue Properties Ltd v Farrell Homes Ltd* [1982] I.L.R.M. 21, and *Westport UDC v Golden* [2002] 1 I.L.R.M. 439, where Morris P. took into account the extent to which the respondent contributed to the situation. In *Curley v Galway Corporation*, unreported, High Court, Kelly J., December 11, 1998, which concerned an unlawful landfill, the difficulty of the corporation in complying with its statutory obligations under the Waste Management Acts was offset by the deliberate and conscious nature of the violation and the fact that the court could not allow a breach of planning legislation to fulfil duties under other legislation.
- The purpose of the parties in carrying out the unauthorised development such as for commercial benefit may be taken into account; see *Dublin Corporation v Maiden Poster Sites* [1983] I.L.R.M. 48; and *Dublin Corporation v O'Dwyer Bros*, unreported, High Court, Kelly J., May 2, 1997, where the court took into account the fact that respondent had persisted in the unauthorised use for commercial profit. See also *Cork County Council v Slattery Pre-cast Concrete Ltd*, unreported, High Court, Clarke J., September 19, 2008.
- A court may not grant the injunction where it is superfluous; see *Dublin Corporation v O'Dwyer Bros* above; *Eircell v Bernstoff*, unreported, High Court, Barr J., February 18, 2000. Nor will an injunction be granted where it would predetermine some other matter; see *Scariff v Commissioners of Public Works*, unreported, High Court, Flood J., March 15, 1995. In the case of pre-commencement planning conditions, the court will not generally grant relief where such conditions have been satisfied notwithstanding that they were not satisfied prior to commencement of development. See *Mountbrook Homes Limited v Oldcourt Developments Limited*, unreported, High Court, April 22, 2005 and *Eircell v Bernstoff*, unreported, High Court, Barr J.,

February 18, 2000.
- A court may decline relief where it could cause a nuisance. See *Cantwell v McCarthy*, unreported, High Court, Murphy J., November 1, 2006, where the court refused to make an order which would block an outfall pipe which would result in accumulation of water and cause a nuisance. However, there will be no grounds to refuse relief where the premises constitute a health hazard and nuisance to local residents. See *Galway County Council v Connacht Proteins*, unreported, High Court, Barrington J., March 28, 1980.
- In certain cases the court has taken into account the absence of harm including to the applicant. Although there is no locus standi requirement under s.27, the absence of any connection may be a factor to be considered in exercising discretion; see *Grimes v Punchestown Development* [2002]1 I.L.R.M. 409 and *Stafford v Roadstone Ltd* [1980] 1 I.L.R.M. 1. In *Sweetman v Shell E & P Ireland Ltd*. [2007] 3 I.R. 13. Smyth J. accepted that while it was not necessary for an applicant to prove that any planning harm resulted from a non-compliance and that mere compliance is all that need be proved, where a person has not proved that he/she has suffered any detriment as a result of the alleged non-compliance, to seek to move the court to grant injunctive relief in permanent form in their absence "lacks the urgency of reality".
- Opinion of the planning authority. Where proceedings are instituted by a member of the public, the views of the planning authority will be a relevant factor. See *Grimes v Punchestown Developments Company Ltd* [2002] 1 I.L.R.M. 409. In *Sweetman v Shell E & P Ireland Ltd* [2007] 3 I.R. 13, the court took into account the fact that the planning authority had refrained from not only enforcement proceedings but confirmed that it was satisfied that Shell has complied with the conditions. In *Altara Developments v Ventola Ltd*, unreported, High Court, O'Sullivan J., October 6, 2005, the fact that the respondent had acted with the support of the planning authority in carrying out the development was a factor in refusing relief. On the other hand, a court is not obliged to grant an injunction simply because the planning authority considers it necessary or expedient. *South Bucks District Council v Porter (No. 1)* [2003] A.C. 558.

The Irish courts have yet to address whether the entitlements under the European Convention on Human Rights may modify the principles for granting s.160 injunctions. Where the unauthorised development relates to a dwelling, the rights under art.8 (right to respect for private and family life, home and correspondence) may be engaged. See *South Bucks District Council v Porter (No. 1)* [2003] A.C. 558, which concerned an injunction sought against certain gypsies, the House of Lords considered it must weigh the personal circumstances of the respondents against the grant of an injunction. Article 1 of the First Protocol (entitlement to peaceful enjoyment of possessions) may also be engaged by a s.160 injunction. However, it submitted that the existing Irish principles can accommodate consideration of the European Convention on Human Rights factors. The notion of hardship is wide enough to embrace the type of personal factors as were recognised in *South Bucks District Council v Porter (No. 1)* [2003] A.C. 558 in respect of art.8. Furthermore, the Irish courts already apply a form of proportionality as reflected in the discretionary factors it may take into account in refusing relief.

It is not a defence to a planning injunction for a developer to say that obtaining planning permission would be a matter of formality; see *Monaghan County Council v Brogan* [1987] I.L.R.M. 564. It should be noted that a developer is not estopped from claiming that a development, which he has carried out without the benefit of planning permission, is in fact and in law exempted development, by reason only of having made an application for planning permission for the retention of that development. See *Fingal County Council v William P. Keeling & Sons* [2005] 2 I.R. 108, where the Supreme Court reversed the previously understood position stated in *Dublin County Council v Tallaght Block Company Limited*, unreported, Supreme Court, May 17, 1983, that where a person lodged a retention application they were estopped from later claiming that the development was exempted development.

The referral of questions, as to whether development is or is not exempted under the procedure of s.5, to the planning authority for a declaration, with review by An Bord Pleanála, will not oust the court's jurisdiction under s.160; see *Cork Corporation v O'Connell* [1982]

I.L.R.M. 505; *Dublin Corporation v Tallaght Block Company Ltd*, unreported, Supreme Court, May 17, 1983. In *Grianán An Áileach v Donegal County Council* [2004] 2 I.R. 265, the Supreme Court recognises the while the s.5 procedure ousted the courts jurisdiction to make declaration concerning the status of whether a matter is or is not unauthorised development, a s.160 application, was one of the exceptional circumstances in which the court could make a determination concerning unauthorised development.

Where the court grants an injunction under s.160, and the respondent fails to comply with the order, this will constitute contempt of court. The matter can be brought back before the court seeking such measures as sequestration of assets or an application for attachment and committal; see *Curley v Galway County Council*, unreported, High Court, Kelly J., March 21, 2001; *Sligo County Council v Cartron Bay Construction*, unreported, High Court, Ó Caoimh J., May 25, 2001; and *Leech v Reilly*, unreported, High Court, O'Hanlon J., April 26, 1983. In *South Bucks District Council v Porter* [2003] 2 A.C. 558, the House of Lords noted that in the context of a planning injunction that "[w]hen making an order, the court should ordinarily be willing to enforce it if necessary. The rule of law is not well served if orders are made and disobeyed with impunity."

Section 163 now expressly provides that planning permission is not required in respect of development required by an order under s.160.

Time Limitations

Subsection (6) provides that the time for making an application for an injunction has been extended from five years under 1992 Act to seven years. It appears that an application will be deemed to have been "made" when it has been issued and served on the appropriate parties. Where no permission has been granted for the development, the seven years will run from the date of commencement of the development. Where permission has been granted but the development has not been properly implemented according to its terms, the seven years run from the end of the life of the permission, which is normally five years, unless varied. Typically, there will be 12 years from the date of the grant of planning permission to take such action. There is a no time limit prescribed with respect to a condition concerning the ongoing use of land. This only applies to a condition concerning "ongoing use"; the normal seven-year rule will apply to other conditions. Where a use commerces but is interrupted or abandoned, a new limitation period will run from the date of recommencement of such use. See *South Dublin County Council v Balfe*, unreported, High Court, Costello P., November 3, 1995. In *Lanigan & Benghazi v Barry*, unreported, High Court, Charleton J., February 15, 2008, it was noted that:

> "There is nothing in the Planning and Development Act, 2000, or its predecessor, which authorises a court to ignore, by virtue of the passage of time, a completely new user of a site, or an intensification of a use in respect of which some form of planning permission has been granted and which has been entirely altered by the illegal user thereof".

Equally, where there is an intensification of use amounting to material change of use, time will run from the date of such intensification. However, the fact that a person applies for retention permission of an unauthorised use, will have no effect on the limitation period. It will not have the effect of suspending the limitation period nor will a new limitation commence in the event of a refusal of retention permission. It may also be noted that the mere fact that a person applies for retention permission will not estop a defendant from subsequently claiming, in the event of a refusal, that development was not unauthorised development. See *Fingal County Council v William Keeling & Sons* [2005] 2 I.R. 108. The existence of an ancillary use does not amount to "development" or a material change of use. It is only where such ancillary use intensifies to such a degree as to become an independent or dual use that "development" for the purposes of enforcement action may be deemed to have commenced. On the nature of intensification of an ancillary use, see *Jones v Secretary of State for Environment* [1974] 28 P & CR 362.

Unauthorised development which is immune from enforcement action because the time has expired still retains its status as unauthorised development, even though no enforcement action can be taken against it. See *Dublin Corp v Mulligan*, unreported, High Court, May 6, 1980. In respect of such development certain disadvantages still apply. These include that certain exempted development provisions are excluded in relation to further development regarding the unauthorised development. Under art.9(1)(a)(viii) of the 2001 Regulations, works to an unauthorised structure cannot enjoy exempted development status, while under art.10(1)(d), the exempted development category of change of use within the classes specified in Pt 4 of Sch.2 does not apply where the existing use is an unauthorised use. In *O'Connor v Nenagh UDC*, unreported, High Court, July 16, 1996, Geoghegan J. suggested that the illegal but immune status of an unauthorised development could mean that an owner would not be able to claim compensation if the matter was compulsarily acquired by the State. See also Sch.2, para.2(b)(v). It could also be taken into account in the context of s.35, which allows refusal of permission for past failures to comply.

A difficult question is whether an unauthorised development which was immune from enforcement because the five years had passed under the previous legislation would lose such immunity because of the extension of the period to seven years. See *Cork County Council v Slattery Pre-cast Concrete Ltd*, unreported, High Court, Clarke J., September 19, 2008. The better view is that such immunity is not lost as there is no express statement that the provision has retrospective effect; see *Hamilton v Hamilton* [1982] I.R. 466. This rule was applied in the context of planning law in *Kenny v An Bord Pleanála (No. 1)* [2001] 1 I.R. 565. However, the problem is largely theoretical now as two years have passed since Pt VIII commenced on March 11, 2002. Where an unauthorised development was commenced prior to March 11, 2002 but was not immune from enforcement, the seven year limitation period will apply. See *Cork County Council v Slattery Pre-cast Concrete Ltd.*, unreported, High Court, Clarke J., September 19, 2008, where it was held that such amendment could not be characterised as a retrospective interference with the rights or entitlements of an individual whose wrongful actions remained capable of being subject to enforcement proceedings as of the date of the statutory amendment, where the effect of the amendment is simply to prolong the period during which enforcement proceedings could be taken.

Subsection (7) makes it clear that there is no bar to issuing criminal proceedings, an enforcement notice and a planning injunction at the same time in respect of the same unauthorised development.

Costs of prosecutions and applications for injunctions

161.—(1) The court shall, unless it is satisfied that there are special and substantial reasons for not so doing, order the person to pay—   **1–191**

  (a) where a person is convicted of an offence under this Part, to the planning authority, or

  (b) where the person is the subject of an order under section 160, to the planning authority or to any other person as appropriate,

the costs and expenses of the action, measured by the court.

(2) Where costs or expenses are to be paid to the authority, they shall include any such costs or expenses reasonably incurred by the authority in relation to the investigation, detection and prosecution of the offence or order, as appropriate, including costs incurred in respect of the remuneration and other expenses of employees, consultants and advisers.

NOTE

This section provides that a person convicted of an offence or against whom a s.160 order is made will be required to pay the applicant's cost and expenses unless there are special and substantial reasons for not doing so. While there is no definition of "special and substantial reason", it would appear to involve a two part test, i.e. there must be special and also substantial reasons. The word "special" implies that it is different from the normal, while "substantial" implies that this difference is weighty. This provision may be deemed to modify the general discretion of the court in awarding costs and places a higher onus on a respondent to demonstrate why costs should not follow the event. In the context of case law for planning injunctions under the former s.27, it was noted in *Grimes v Punchestown Developments Company Ltd*, unreported, Supreme Court, December 20, 2002, that the public watchdog nature of s.160 is relevant to the issue of costs. The conduct of the applicant may deprive them of costs such as *Donegal County Council v O'Donnell*, unreported, High Court, O'Hanlon J., June 25, 1982, where the planning authority had dealt with the planning application in an unsatisfactory manner. In *Dublin Corporation v Bentham* [1993] 2 I.R. 58, costs were awarded to a respondent, despite certain orders being granted against him, where he had defeated a point raised as a test case. In respect of a successful respondent defending proceedings, the normal rules that costs follow the event means that a respondent normally will be entitled to their costs, although again this will not apply in exceptional circumstances; see *Cork County Council v Cliftonhall Ltd*, unreported, High Court, Finnegan J., April 6, 2001, and *Fingal County Council v RFS Ltd*, unreported, High Court, Morris P., February 6, 2000.

It is clear from the section that costs are not confined to legal costs but also include costs and expenses relating to the investigation and detection of the offence or order in the manner described in subs.(2). In the context of criminal prosecution, it is the practice of planning authority to submit a bill of costs and expenses to the court for the purposes of measuring costs. However, a court can also simply make an order for costs to be taxed in default of agreement.

Evidence of permission

1–192   **162.—(1)** In any proceedings for an offence under this Act, the onus of proving the existence of any permission granted under Part III shall be on the defendant.

(2) Notwithstanding *subsection (1)* of this section, it shall not be a defence to a prosecution under this Part if the defendant proves that he or she has applied for or has been granted permission under *section 34(12)* —

    (a) since the initiation of proceedings under this Part,

    (b) since the date of the sending of a warning letter under section 152, or

    (c) since the date of service of an enforcement notice in a case of urgency in accordance with section 155.

(3) No enforcement action under this Part (including an application under section 160) shall be stayed or withdrawn by reason of an [application for permission for retention of unauthorised development] under *section 34(12)* or the grant of that permission.

AMENDMENT HISTORY

Subsection (3) was inserted by s.247 of the Local Government Act 2001 (No. 37 of 2001), which, by the Local Government Act 2001 (Commencement) Order 2001 (S.I. No. 458 of 2001), came into effect on October 9, 2001.

NOTE

Subsection (1) provides that in the case of a prosecution for an offence under the Act, the onus of proving the existence of a permission is on the defendant. This presumption only applies to criminal offence and does not therefore apply to planning injunction proceedings taken under s.160.

Subsection (2) provides that it shall not be a defence to a prosecution that a defendant applied for or has been granted retention planning permission, if this occurred after the initiation of proceedings; the sending of a warning letter; or the service of any enforcement notice in case of urgency. Again, this only applies to prosecutions for criminal offences and so does not apply to section 160 proceedings. Subsection (3) provides that no enforcement action shall be stayed or withdrawn by reason of an application for or grant of retention permission. This subsection applies to all types of enforcement action and expressly includes section 160 proceedings.

This is a new provision and excludes the practice of raising a grant of retention permission as a defence. The application for retention permission is made under s.34(12). Under the previous practice, it was not uncommon to adjourn or place a stay on an order in enforcement proceedings, pending the determination of an application for retention permission. Subsection (2) appears to respond to concerns expressed by Geoghegan J. in *Cavan County Council v Eircell Ltd*, unreported, High Court, Geoghegan J., March 10, 1999, where in refusing an adjournment of a section 27 application, Geoghegan J. said that:

> "There is a widespread belief (the truth or falsity of which is irrelevant) that a retention permission is easier to obtain than an original permission for development. It is important that there would not be a public perception that the Respondent might be abusing the system in this way in order to achieve its ends even if that is not in fact the case".

Subsection (3) removes any discretion to place a stay for such reason. However, there is nothing to prevent a planning authority from consenting to adjourn a prosecution or planning injunction proceedings pending the outcome of a retention application. The determination of a retention application may clearly have an impact on the nature of any order the court may make. Thus, in the case of prosecution for non-compliance with an enforcement notice, it will clearly be relevant to the exercise of the court's discretion under s.156(8) as to whether to order a person convicted to take the steps specified in the enforcement notice. It will also be relevant to the nature of an order which the court may make in a section 160 application. It should be noted that a developer is not estopped from claiming that a development, which he has carried out without the benefit of planning permission, is in fact and in law exempted development, by reason only of having made an application for planning permission for the retention of that development. See *Fingal County Council v Keeling Bros* [2005] 2 I.R. 108, in which the Supreme Court reversed the previously understood position stated (albeit obiter) in *Dublin County Council v Tallaght Block Company Limited*, unreported, Supreme Court, May 17, 1983, that where a person lodged a retention application they are estopped from later claiming that the development is exempted development. However, in *Commission v Ireland Case C-215/06*, European Court of Justice, July 3, 2008, the court held that in allowing for the grant of retention permission for development for which an EIA is required even where no exceptional circumstances are proved, Ireland had failed to comply with its obligations under Directive 85/337. While this judgment only applies to development which requires an EIA or EIS, it means that amending legislation is required to abolish the entitlement to obtain retention permission for development requiring an EIA, subject to exceptional circumstances existing.

While subs.(3) means that court may not stay the enforcement action pending the making or outcome of a retention application, there is nothing to prevent a court at its discretion placing a stay on any order granting an injunction under s.160, to allow a respondent to apply for retention permission in respect of the unauthorised development. The court may allow a specified time for the respondent to make the application with the caveat that where such application is not made within the specified period, the order will have immediate effect. Equally, where a retention application is lodged, the order would have effect in the event of a refusal of the retention permission. The court may decline to place a stay where the respondent would continue to profit from an unauthorised development; see *Dublin Corporation v Maiden Site Posters Ltd* [1983] I.L.R.M. 48. In *Dublin Corporation v Kevans*, unreported, High Court, Finlay P., July 14, 1980, a lengthy stay placed on the order was allowed as the enforcement action had not been pursued with urgency. Where a retention application has already been refused, the court will be very reluctant to allow a stay to enable another application to be lodged. In *Cork County Council v Slattery Pre-cast Concrete Ltd.*, Unreported, High Court, Clarke J., September 19, 2008, Clarke J. said it would require very considerable extenuating circumstances for a court to have sympathy for a party who has already failed on a retention application and, who wishes to continue on with an unauthorised development in the hope that a second and more modest retention application might succeed. The approach of the respondent to proceedings, such as fully contesting the issues, may militate against the grant of a stay. See *Dublin Corporation v*

O'Dwyer Bros, unreported, High Court, Kelly J., May 2, 1997, where Kelly J. refused to put a stay on a injunction to allow an application for retention; see also *Furlong v A.F. & G.W. McConnell* [1990] I.L.R.M. 48. The public interest may be a factor; see *Galway Corporation v Curley*, unreported, High Court, Kelly J., December 11, 1998, where a stay was reluctantly placed in relation to receiving refuse, as local residents could have difficulties over the Christmas period in disposing of waste. A history of breaching orders may be a factor against granting a stay. See *Coates v South Buckinghshire District Council* [2005] JPL 668 and *Mid-Bedfordshire DC v Brown* [2005] JPL 1060.

Permission not required for any works required under this Part

1–193   **163.**—Notwithstanding Part III, permission shall not be required in respect of development required by a notice under section 154 or an order under section 160 (disregarding development for which there is in fact permission under Part III).

NOTE

This section provides that planning permission is not required to carry out the development required under the terms of an enforcement notice or a planning injunction, which means that such development is exempted development. In the context of section 160 proceedings which are settled between the planning authority and the defendant, it may be advisable to require the court to make a consent order in terms of any settlement to ensure that the development required will be exempted development.

Transitional arrangements for offences

1–194   **164.**—Notwithstanding any repeal of any enactment ("repealed enactment") by this Act, where proceedings have been initiated in respect of any offence under the repealed enactment, or an enforcement notice or a warning notice (within the meaning of the relevant provisions) has issued under any provision of the repealed enactment, or an application to a Court has been made under section 27 of the Act of 1976, the relevant provision which applied before the repeal shall continue to so apply until the proceedings have been finalised, the notices complied with or withdrawn or the application determined, as the case may be.

NOTE

This section provides that where proceedings have been initiated or notices have been issued under the previous repealed legislation, those provisions will continue to apply until the proceedings have been finalised. Notwithstanding the passage of time since the entry into force of Pt VIII on the March 11, 2002, this transitional provision could still potentially have relevance where proceedings under the repealed legislation were adjourned generally with liberty to re-entry. Where the proceedings are re-entered, the provisions of the repealed legislation will be applicable.

PART IX

STRATEGIC DEVELOPMENT ZONES

Interpretation

1–195   **165.**—In this Part—

"development agency" *means the Industrial Development Agency (Ireland), Enterprise Ireland, the Shannon Free Airport Development Company Limited, Údarás na Gaeltachta, the National Building Agency Limited,* [*the Grangegorman Development Agency, a local authority or such other person as may be prescribed by the Minister for the purposes of this Part;*]

"strategic development zone" *means a site or sites to which a planning scheme made under section 169 applies.*

AMENDMENT HISTORY

Definition of "development agency" amended by s.42 of the Grangegorman Development Agency Act 2005 (No. 21 of 2005) with effect from July 11, 2005.

NOTE

The 2000 Act introduces the concept of strategic development zones in Irish planning law. The principal effect of a designation of a strategic development zone (SDZ) is that special planning permission rules apply, which are described in s.170. Once a strategic development zone has been designated, the special planning rules allow for greater certainty and speed with respect to individual planning applications within the zone. SDZ's therefore constitute a form of accelerated planning schemes, such as the Docklands Development Authority set up under the Docklands Development Authority Act 1997. This section simply defines the meaning of development agency, which must be consulted at various stages in the formation of a strategic development zone. The definition of development agencies includes local authorities and certain specified national agencies.

Designation of sites for strategic development zones

166.—**(1)** Where, in the opinion of the Government, specified development **1–196** is of economic or social importance to the State, the Government may by order, when so proposed by the Minister, designate one or more sites for the establishment, in accordance with the provisions of this Part, of a strategic development zone to facilitate such development.

(2) The Minister shall, before proposing the designation of a site or sites to the Government under *subsection (1),* consult with any relevant development agency or planning authority on the proposed designation.

(3) An order under *subsection (1)* shall—

(a) specify the development agency or development agencies for the purposes of section 168,4

(b) specify the type or types of development that may be established in the strategic development zone, and

(c) state the reasons for specifying the development and for designating the site or sites.

(4) The Minister shall send a copy of any order made under this section to any relevant development agency, planning authority and regional authority and to the Board.

(5) Development that is specified in an order under *subsection (3)* shall be deemed to include development that is ancillary to, or required for, the purposes of development so specified, and may include any necessary infrastructural and community facilities and services.

(6) The Government may revoke or amend an order made under this section.

NOTE

This section enables the Government to designate certain sites as strategic development zones. One or more sites may be designated to facilitate specified development which is of economic or social importance to the State. Thus more than one site may be designated, the development must be specified and such development must be of economic or social importance to the State. While the order is made by the Government, it is proposed by the Minister following consultation with the development agencies set out in s.165 or planning authority.

Subsection (3) provides that the order must specify the development agency or agencies for the purpose of preparing a scheme under s.168, the type of development in question, and also state the reasons for both specifying the development and designating the site. Under s.168(1), the scheme must be prepared within two years of the order, which means the order will have a life of two years. Under subs.(4) development in this respect may include development which is ancillary to or required for the purposes of the development. This development must therefore be subsidiary to the development specified in the order and this can include infrastructural and community facilties or services. This could therefore include roads and other supporting services. A copy of the order when made must be sent to the relevant planning authorities, regional authorities, development authorities and the Board.

Acquisition of site for strategic development zone

1–197　　**167.—(1)** A planning authority may use any powers to acquire land that are available to it under any enactment, including any powers in relation to the compulsory acquisition of land, for the purposes of providing, securing or facilitating the provision of, a site referred to in *section 166(1)*.

(2) Where a person, other than the relevant development agency, has an interest in land, or any part of land, on which a site or sites referred to in an order under *section 166(1)* is or are situated, the relevant development agency may enter into an agreement with that person for the purpose of facilitating the development of the land.

(3) An agreement made under *subsection (2)* with any person having an interest in land may be enforced by the relevant development agency against persons deriving title under that person in respect of that land.

NOTE

This section enables a planning authority to exercise any of its powers to facilitate or secure the provision of a designated site. The powers would include any powers of the local authority under the Local Government Act 2001 or its powers to compulsorily acquire land. It appears the planning authority can use its powers to facilitate it at any time, such as before or after the making of a planning scheme. Rather than compulsorily acquiring the land, subs.(2) enables a development agency to enter into a agreement with a property holder in order to facilitate the relevant development of the land. Under subs.(3), if there is any breach in the agreement, the development agency may bring proceedings against any successor in title of the other party to the agreement. This indicates that the agreement will bind successors in title and not just the two parties under privity of contract.

Planning scheme for strategic development zones

1–198　　**168.—(1)** Where a site is designated under section 166, the relevant development agency or, where an agreement referred to in section 167 has been made, the relevant development agency and any person who is a party to the agreement, may, as soon as may be and in any case not later than 2 years after the making of an order under section 166, prepare a draft planning scheme in respect of all or any part of the site and submit it to the relevant planning authority.

(2) A draft planning scheme under this section shall consist of a written statement and a plan indicating the manner in which it is intended that the site is to be developed and in particular—

> **(a)** the type or types of development which may be permitted to establish on the site (subject to the order of the Government under section 166),
>
> **(b)** the extent of any such proposed development,
>
> **(c)** proposals in relation to the overall design of the proposed development, including the maximum heights, the external finishes of structures and the general appearance and design,
>
> **(d)** proposals relating to transportation, including public transportation, the roads layout, the provision of parking spaces and traffic management,
>
> **(e)** proposals relating to the provision of services on the site, including the provision of waste and sewerage facilities and water, electricity and telecommunications services, oil and gas pipelines, including storage facilities for oil or gas,
>
> **(f)** proposals relating to minimising any adverse effects on the environment, including the natural and built environment, and on the amenities of the area, and
>
> **(g)** where the scheme provides for residential development, proposals relating to the provision of amenities, facilities and services for the community, including schools, crèches and other education and childcare services.

[**(3)** The Minister may, for the purposes of giving effect to Directive 200 1/42/EC of the European Parliament and Council of 27 June 2001 on the assessment of the effects of certain plans and programmes on the environment (No. 200 1/42/EC, O.J. No. L 197, 21 July 2001 P. 0030 - 0037); by regulations make provision in relation to consideration of the likely significant effects on the environment of implementing a planning scheme.]

(4)

> **(a)** A draft planning scheme for residential development shall be consistent with the housing strategy prepared by the planning authority in accordance with Part V.
>
> **(b)** Where land in a strategic development zone is to be used for residential development, an objective to secure the implementation of the housing strategy shall be included in the draft planning scheme as if it were a specific objective under *section 95(1)(b)*.

(5) Where an area designated under section 166 is situated within the functional area of two or more planning authorities the functions conferred on a planning authority under this Part shall be exercised—

> **(a)** jointly by the planning authorities concerned, or
>
> **(b)** by one of the authorities, provided that the consent of the other authority or authorities, as appropriate, is obtained prior to the making of the scheme under section 169,

and the words "planning authority" shall be construed accordingly.

AMENDMENT HISTORY

Subsection (3) substituted by r.8 of the European Communities (Environmental Assessment of Certain Plans and Programmes) Regulations 2004 (S.I. No. 435 of 2004) with effect from July 14, 2004.

NOTE

This section provides for the making of a planning scheme in respect of a strategic development zone. Not later than two years after the order designating the scheme, the development agency (together with any party it entered into an agreement with under s.167) may prepare a draft scheme and submit it to the planning authority. The draft can be in respect of all or part of the site. The scheme will be in written form, setting out the manner in which the site is intended to be developed. Subsection (2) sets out some of the matters to be included such as the type and extent of any development, its overall design, provision of infrastructure such as transportation roads, site services (such as water, electricity, sewage, telecommunications, etc.), and proposals for minimising the effect on the environment. Where the site concerns residential development, the proposal should also concern amenities, facilities and community services such as for education and crèches. Article 179A of the 2001 Regulations provides that a draft planning scheme shall be accompanied by or include an environmental report. Article 179B states that prior to the preparation of an environmental report under art.179A, the relevant development agency shall give notice to the environmental authorities specified in art.13A(4), as appropriate. The notice must:

- state that, as part of the preparation of a draft planning scheme, an environmental report will be prepared of the likely significant effects on the environment of implementing the scheme;
- state that the environmental report is required to include the information that may reasonably be required, taking into account:
  — current knowledge and methods of assessment;
  — the contents and level of detail in the planning scheme;
  — the stage of the planning scheme in the decision-making process; and
  — the extent to which certain matters are more appropriately assessed at different levels in the decision-making process in order to avoid duplication of environmental assessment; and
- indicate that a submission or observation in relation to the scope and level of detail of the information to be included in the environmental report may be made to the relevant development agency within a specified period which shall be not less than four weeks from the date of the notice.

Article 179C provides that an environmental report shall identify, describe and evaluate the likely significant effects on the environment of implementing the planning scheme and any reasonable alternatives taking account of the objectives and the geographical scope of the scheme and, for this purpose, the report shall;

- contain the information specified in Sch.2B,
- take account of any submission or observation received in response to a notice under art.179B(1); and
- be of sufficient quality to meet the requirements of these Regulations.

Also art.179C(2) provides that an environmental report shall include the information that may reasonably be required taking into account:

- current knowledge and methods of assessment;
- the contents and level of detail in the planning scheme;
- the stage of the planning scheme in the decision-making process; and
- the extent to which certain matters are more appropriately assessed at different levels in the decision-making process in order to avoid duplication of environmental assessment.

Subsection (3) provides that the Minister may make regulations for the purposes of

Directive 2001/42/EC in relation to consideration of the likely significant effects on the environement of implementing the plan. In this respect the 2004 Planning Regulations inserted arts 179A to 179J into the 2001 Regulations. Subsection (4) provides that a draft planning scheme for residential development should be prepared with regard to the housing strategy contained in the development plan for the relevant area. An objective to secure the implementation of the housing strategy in the planning scheme is treated as if it were an objective to secure its implementation in the development plan under s.95(1)(b). A strategic development zone and the scheme thereunder can touch on the jurisdictional area of more than one planning authority, so in such case, the scheme should be prepared in consultation with the other planning authorities or with the consent of the other planning authorities; see Local Government Act 2001, ss.85 and 86, relating to agreements concerning functions and the joint discharge of functions.

Making of planning scheme

169.—**(1)** Where a draft planning scheme has been prepared and submitted **1–199** to the planning authority in accordance with section 168, the planning authority shall, as soon as may be—

    (a) send notice and copies of the draft scheme to the Minister, the Board and the prescribed authorities,

    (b) publish notice of the preparation of the draft scheme in one or more newspapers circulating in its area.

(2) A notice under *subsection (1)* shall state—

    (a) that a copy of the draft may be inspected at a stated place or places and at stated times during a stated period of not less than 6 weeks (and the copy shall be kept available for inspection accordingly), and

    (b) that written submissions or observations with respect to the draft scheme made to the planning authority within the stated period will be taken into consideration in deciding upon the scheme.

(3)

    (a) Not longer than 12 weeks after giving notice under *subsection (2)* the manager of a planning authority shall prepare a report on any submissions or observations received under that *subsection* and submit the report to the members of the authority for their consideration.

    (b) A report under *paragraph (a)* shall—

        (i) list the persons or bodies who made submissions or observations under this *section,*

        (ii) summarise the issues raised by the persons or bodies in the submissions or observations,

        (iii) give the response of the manager to the issues raised, taking account of the proper planning and sustainable development of the area, the statutory obligations of any local authority in the area and any relevant policies or objectives for the time being of the Government or of any Minister of the Government.

(4)

    (a) The members of a planning authority shall consider the draft planning scheme and the report of the manager prepared and submitted in accordance with *subsection (3).*

(b) The draft planning scheme shall be deemed to be made 6 weeks after the submission of that draft planning scheme and report to the members of the planning authority in accordance with *subsection (3)* unless the planning authority decides, by resolution, to—

    (i) make, subject to variations and modifications, the draft planning scheme, or

    (ii) decides not to make the draft planning scheme.

(c) Where a draft planning scheme is—

    (i) deemed, in accordance with *paragraph (b),* to have been made, or

    (ii) made in accordance with *paragraph (b)(i),* it shall have effect 4 weeks from the date of such making unless an appeal is brought to the Board under *subsection (6).*

(5)

(a) Following the decision of the planning authority under *subsection (4)* the authority shall, as soon as may be, and in any case not later than 6 working days following the making of the decision—

    (i) give notice of the decision of the planning authority to the Minister, the Board, the prescribed authorities and any person who made written submissions or observations on the draft scheme, and

    (ii) publish notice of the decision in one or more newspapers circulating in its area.

(b) A notice under *paragraph (a)* shall—

    (i) give the date of the decision of the planning authority in respect of the draft planning scheme,

    (ii) state the nature of the decision,

    (iii) state that a copy of the planning scheme is available for inspection at a stated place or places (and the copy shall be kept available for inspection accordingly),

    (iv) state that any person who made submissions or observations regarding the draft scheme may appeal the decision of the planning authority to the Board within 4 weeks of the date of the planning authority's decision, and

    (v) contain such other information as may be prescribed.

(6) The development agency or any person who made submissions or observations in respect of the draft planning scheme may, for stated reasons, within 4 weeks of the date of the decision of the planning authority appeal the decision of the planning authority to the Board.

(7)

(a) The Board may, following the consideration of an appeal made under this *section,* approve the making of the planning scheme, with or without modifications or it may refuse to approve it.

(b) Where the Board approves the making of a planning scheme in accordance with *paragraph (a),* the planning authority shall, as soon as practicable, publish notice of the approval of the scheme in at least one newspaper circulating in its area, and shall state that a copy of the planning scheme is available for inspection at a stated place or places (and a copy shall be kept available for inspection accordingly).

(8) In considering a draft planning scheme under this *section* a planning authority or the Board, as the case may be, shall consider the proper planning and sustainable development of the area and consider the provisions of the development plan, the provisions of the housing strategy, the provisions of any special amenity area order or the conservation and preservation of any European Site and, where appropriate—

(a) the effect the scheme would have on any neighbouring land to the land concerned,

(b) the effect the scheme would have on any place which is outside the area of the planning authority, and

(c) any other consideration relating to development outside the area of the planning authority, including any area outside the State.

(9) A planning scheme made under this *section* shall be deemed to form part of any development plan in force in the area of the scheme until the scheme is revoked, and any contrary provisions of the development plan shall be superseded.

NOTE

This section sets out the procedure by which a draft planning scheme is adopted. The procedure has some similarities to the adoption or making of a development plan under s.12. The planning authority must ensure notice of the preparation of the draft planning scheme is published in a newspaper and a further notice and copies of the scheme must be sent to the Minister, the Board and the prescribed authorities. The environmental report prepared under art.179C must also be sent to such authorities. Article 179(1) of the 2001 Regulations states that the prescribed authorities for these purposes are the relevant regional authorities and any planning authority within or contiguous to the site. Article 179(2), as amended by the 2006 Regulations, also sets out 21 different types of development for each of which additional prescribed bodies must be sent a copy. In practice, the planning authority may also make the draft planning scheme available on its website. The notice must also be sent to prescribed authorities under art.13A(4) which are:

* the Environmental Protection Agency;
* where it appears to the planning authority that the plan might have significant effects in relation to the architectural or archaeological heritage or to nature conservation, the Minister for the Environment, Heritage and Local Government; and
* where it appears to the planning authority that the plan might have significant effects on fisheries or the marine environment, the Minister for Communications, Marine and Natural Resources.

Article 179E of the 2001 Regulations provides that in addition to the notification requirements under s.169(1) of the Act, a planning authority shall, following consultation with the Minister, forward a copy of the draft planning scheme and associated environmental report to a Member State: (a) where the planning authority considers that implementation of the planning scheme is likely to have significant effects on the environment of such Member State, or (b) where a Member State, likely to be significantly affected, so requests. Article 179E(2) provides that where a Member State is sent a copy of a draft planning scheme and environmental report under sub-art.(1) and it indicates that it wishes to enter into consultations before the adoption of the scheme, the planning authority shall:

* enter into consultations with the State concerned in relation to the likely transboundary environmental effects of implementing the scheme and the measures envisaged to reduce or eliminate such effects; and
* agree with the State concerned:
  — a reasonable timeframe for the completion of the consultations, having regard

to the timeframes for the making of a planning scheme under s.169 of the Act; and

— detailed arrangements to ensure that the authorities referred to in art.6(3) of the SEA Directive and the public referred to in art.6(4) of the SEA Directive in the Member State concerned are informed and given an opportunity to forward their opinion within a reasonable timeframe.

The notice must state that the draft plan and environemtnal report (by virtue of art.179A) can be inspected at stated places and times and that written observations can be made in respect of it for a period of not less than six weeks. Not later than 12 weeks after the notice, the Manager must prepare a report setting out the issues and submissions and send it to the planning authority. By analogy with a report prepared by the Manager for variation of a development plan, there is no obligation to circulate to each member of the planning authority the entirety of the objections and submissions received, prior to their consideration of the proposal. See *Sandyford Environmental Planning v Dun Laoghaire Rathdown County Council*, unreported, High Court, McKechnie J., June 30, 2004, where it was noted that in summarising the submissions the Manager is not bound to use any formula or follow any specified method. Article 179E(3) of the 2001 Regulations provides that the report shall take account of any transboundary consultations under art.179E.

The draft planning scheme will be deemed to be made six weeks after the submission of the draft scheme and report, unless the planning authority decides to make the scheme subject to variations or not to make the scheme.

Subsection (8) provides that in considering the scheme, the planning authority (and on appeal, the Board), must consider the proper planning and sustainable development, the development plan, the housing strategy, any special amenity order or conservation/ preservation order of a European site. Also where appropriate, the planning authority or the Board must consider the effect of the scheme on neighbouring lands, its effect on any place outside the area of the planning authority and any other consideration relating to, any place outside the area of the planning authority, including outside the State. Article 179F of the 2001 Regulations provides that the planning authority shall take account of:

- the environmental report;
- any submission or observation made to the planning authority in response to a notice under s.169(1) of the Act; and
- any consultations under art.179E, during the authority's consideration of the draft planning scheme, and before its adoption.

Where the planning authority varies the scheme, there is no similar provision to the procedure for a development plan requiring re-advertisement where the variation is a material alteration of the development plan.

Once made, the scheme will have effect four weeks from that date. A notice then must be sent to various bodies concerning the decision and a notice must also be advertised in a newspaper circulating in the area. The notice requirements apply whether or not the draft scheme was adopted. Subsection (5)(b) provides that the notice must, inter alia, state the date and nature of the decision, when and where the scheme is available for inspection, and provide that any person who made submissions can appeal the matter to the Board within four weeks of the date of the decision of the planning authority. Article 179G provides that the notice shall state that a statement is also available summarising:

- how environmental considerations have been integrated into the scheme;
- how:
  — the environmental report prepared pursuant to art.179A;
  — submissions and observations made to the planning authority in response to a notice under s.169(1) of the Act; and
  — any consultations under art.179E,
  have been taken into account during the planning authority's consideration of the draft scheme;
- the reasons for choosing the scheme, as adopted, in the light of the other reasonable alternatives dealt with; and
- the measures decided upon to monitor, in accordance with art.179J, the significant environmental effects of implementation of the scheme.

Subsection (6) provides that the development body or any person who made submissions can appeal the decision to An Bord Pleanála within four weeks and state the reasons for appeal. There is therefore no general right of appeal open to the public and in this respect the participation requirements are similar as in judicial review under s.50. There is also no express right of appeal granted to the prescribed bodies. The Board may then approve the scheme with or without modification or may refuse it. Article 179H of the 2001 Regulations provides that the Board shall also take account of:

- the environmental report prepared pursuant to art.179A;
- any submission or observation made to the planning authority in response to a notice under s.169(1) of the Act; and
- any consultations under art.179E, during the Board's consideration of the scheme.

Article 179I(1) provides that where the Board, under s.169(7)(a) of the Act, approves the making of a planning scheme without modification:

- the notice required under s.169(7)(b) of the Act shall indicate that the statement referred to in art.179G(1) is also available for inspection; and
- the planning authority shall give notice of the approval of the scheme, and the availability for inspection of the statement referred to in art.179G(1), to the authorities specified in art.13A(4), as appropriate, and to any Member State consulted under art.179E.

Article 179I(2) states that where the Board, under s.169(7)(a) of the Act, approves the making of a planning scheme with modifications, it shall indicate in its decision any amendments required to the statement referred to in art.179G(1) arising from its modification of the scheme, and shall direct the planning authority to amend the statement accordingly. Article 179I(3) provides that where this applies:

- the notice required under s.169(7)(b) of the Act shall indicate that the statement referred to in art.179G(1), as amended on foot of any direction under sub-art.(2), where appropriate, is also available for inspection; and
- the planning authority shall give notice of the approval of the scheme, and the availability for inspection of the statement referred to in art.179G(1), as amended on foot of any direction under sub-art.(2), where appropriate, to the authorities specified in art.13A(4), as appropriate, and to any Member State consulted under art.179E.

The Board has discretion regarding its own procedure; it will however be subject to the rules concerning appeals set out in Ch.III of Pt VI. Under subs.(9), the planning scheme, once made, forms part of the development plan and where there is conflict, the planning scheme will override the previous provisions.

Article 179J provides that where the relevant development agency or, where an agreement referred to in s.167 of the Act has been made, the relevant development agency and any person who is a party to the agreement, shall monitor the significant environmental effects of implementation of the planning scheme in order, inter alia, to identify at an early stage unforeseen adverse effects and to be able to undertake appropriate remedial action and, for this purpose, existing monitoring arrangements may be used, if appropriate, with a view to avoiding duplication of monitoring.

Application for development in strategic development zone

170.—(1) Where an application is made to a planning authority under **1–200** *section 34* for a development in a strategic development zone, that *section* and any permission regulations shall apply, subject to the other provisions of this *section*.

(2) A planning authority shall grant permission in respect of an application for a development in a strategic development zone where it is satisfied that the development, where carried out in accordance with the application or subject to any conditions which the planning authority may attach to a permission, would be consistent with any planning scheme in force for the land in question, and no permission shall be granted for any development which would not be consistent with such a planning scheme.

(3) Notwithstanding *section 37,* no appeal shall lie to the Board against a decision of a planning authority on an application for permission in respect of a development in a strategic development zone.

(4) Where the planning authority decides to grant permission for a development in a strategic development zone, the grant shall be deemed to be given on the date of the decision.

NOTE

This section provides that some of the normal planning permission provisions are modified with respect to applications for development within a strategic development. In general the provisions of s.34 and the permission regulations apply, subject to the special rules set out in the section. Subsection (2) provides that the planning authority will grant planning permission for any development consistent with the planning scheme in force for the land but will not grant permission for a development inconsistent with the planning scheme. This limits the normal discretion of the planning authority in considering an application, depending on whether the application is consistent or inconsistent with the scheme. Nevertheless, it is still left to the planning authority to decide whether a matter is consistent or inconsistent with the scheme. The concept of "consistent" is not very exacting, although this will depend on how detailed the planning scheme is. The procedure for applying for permission within the zone is the normal planning procedure. Subsection (3) also removes the right of appeal to An Bord Pleanála against a decision on an application for permission within the strategic development zone. The justification for these qualifications of the normal rules are that the public and all other persons already had an input into the making of the earlier scheme, in respect of which the individual application is determined. Unlike a normal decision on a planning permission under s.34, where the grant of permission is four weeks after the decision to grant permission, subs.(4) provides that where the planning authority decides to grant permission, the grant is deemed to be given on the date of the decision.

Revocation of planning scheme

1–201   **171.—(1)** A planning authority may by resolution, with the consent of the relevant development agency, amend or revoke a planning scheme made under this *Part.*

(2) Where a planning authority proposes to amend a planning scheme under this *section* it shall comply with the procedure laid down in *section 169 and that section* shall be construed accordingly.

(3) Notice of the revocation of a planning scheme under this *section* shall be given in at least one newspaper circulating in the area of the planning authority.

(4) The amendment or revocation of a planning scheme shall not prejudice the validity of any planning permission granted or anything done in accordance with the terms of the scheme before it was amended or revoked except in accordance with the terms of this *Act.*

(5) Without prejudice to the generality of *subsection (4), sections 40 and 42* shall apply to any permission granted under this *Part.*

NOTE

This section allows the planning authority to amend or revoke a planning scheme with the consent of the relevant development agency. As the amendment is made by resolution, the decision is reserved for the elected members of the authority. In amending the scheme, the same procedure for the making of the scheme set out in s.169 must be followed. Where there is an amendment or revocation of the scheme, any planning permission or thing done in accordance with scheme will not be prejudiced. Subsection (4) provides that the general rules concerning the five-year life of a permission under s.40, and the extension of the life under s.42, apply under Pt IX.

PART X

ENVIRONMENTAL IMPACT ASSESSMENT

Requirement for environmental impact statement

172.—(1) Where a planning application is made in respect of a development **1–202** or class of development referred to in regulations under *section 176,* that application shall, in addition to meeting the requirements of the permission regulations, be accompanied by an environmental impact statement.

(2) In addition to the matters set out in *section 33(2),* the Minister may make permission regulations in relation to the submission of planning applications which are to be accompanied by environmental impact statements.

(3)

(**a**) At the request of an applicant or of a person intending to apply for permission, the Board may, having afforded the planning authority concerned an opportunity to furnish observations on the request, and where the Board is satisfied that exceptional circumstances so warrant, grant in respect of a proposed development an exemption from a requirement of or under regulations under this *section* to prepare an environmental impact statement, except that no exemption may be granted in respect of a proposed development if another Member State of the European Communities or other state party to the *Transboundary Convention,* having been informed about the proposed development and its likely effects on the environment in that State, has indicated that it intends to furnish views on those effects.

[(**b**) The Board shall, in granting an exemption under *paragraph (a),—*

(**i**) consider whether the effects, if any, of the proposed development on the environment should be assessed in some other form, and

(**ii**) make available to members of the public the information relating to the exemption decision referred to under *paragraph (a),* the reasons for granting such exemption and the information obtained under any other form of assessment referred to in *subparagraph (i),* and the Board may apply such requirements regarding these matters in relation to the application for permission as it considers necessary or appropriate.]

(**c**) The Board shall, as soon as may be, notify the planning authority concerned of the Board's decision on any request made under *paragraph (a),* and of any requirements applied under *paragraph (b).*

(**d**) Notice of any exemption granted under *paragraph (a),* of the reasons for granting the exemption, and of any requirements applied under *paragraph (b)* shall, as soon as may be—

(i) be published in *Iris Oifigiúil* and in at least one daily newspaper published in the State,

(ii) be given, together with a copy of the information, if any, made available to the members of the public in accordance with *paragraph (b),* to the Commission of the European Communities.

(4)

(a) A person who makes a request to the Board for an exemption under *subsection (3)* shall, as soon as may be, inform the planning authority concerned of the making of the request and the date on which it was made.

(b) Notwithstanding *subsection (8) of section 34,* the period for making a decision referred to in that *subsection* shall not, in a case in which a request is made to the Board under *subsection (3) of this section,* include the period beginning on the day of the making of the request and ending on the day of receipt by the planning authority concerned of notice of the Board's decision on the request.

(5) In addition to the matters provided for under *Part VI, Chapter III,* the Minister may prescribe additional requirements in relation to the submission of appeals to the Board which are to be accompanied by environmental impact statements.

AMENDMENT HISTORY

Paragraph 3(b) substituted by reg.4 of the European Communities (Environmental Impact Assessment)(Amendment) Regulations 2006 (S.I. No. 659 of 2006).

NOTE

This section concerns applications for planning permission which require an EIS. Article 16 of the 2001 Regulations provides that an application under this section must also comply with the general requirement of a planning application under Pt 4 of the 2001 Regulations as amended. The requirement of submitting an EIS arises under certain European Directives, principally the Directive 85/337/EEC (as amended by Directive 97/11/EC) on the assessment of the effects of certain public and private projects on the environment. The deadline for implementation of the Directive was July 3, 1998. This was further amended by Directive 2003/35/EEC of May 26, 2003, relating to public participation in respect of the drawing up of certain plans and programmes relating to the environment and amending the earlier Directives with respect to public participation and access to justice. This latter Directive increases the extent of public participation in the EIA process and was required to be in force by June 25, 2005. Directive 85/337/EEC was implemented in Ireland through the planning legislation, in conjunction with the Environmental Protection Act 1992. The Directive itself has been held to have direct effect in *Berkeley v Secretary for the Environment* [2001] 2 A.C. 603 and *World Wildlife Fund v Autonome Provinz Bozen* C-435/97 [1999] E.C.R. I-5613, which means it can be relied on before the national courts and before the planning authority and Board. It appears it can be relied upon even if this may have consequential effects for a private developer. See *R v Durham County Council ex p. Huddlestone* [2000] 1 W.L.R. 1484 and *Wells v Secretary of State for Transport, Local Government and the Regions* C-201/02 [2004] E.C.R. I-723. Irish measures must be interpreted in the light of the Directive. The Irish courts will adopt a purposive approach in interpreting national law in the light of the Directive. See *Klohn v An Bord Pleanála,* unreported, High Court,

McMahon J., April 23, 2008, *O'Connell v Environmental Protection Agency* [2003] 1 I.R. 530 and *Maher v An Bord Pleanála* [1999] 2 I.L.R.M. 198.

While Pt X is headed Environmental Impact Assessment, it goes on to deal with an EIS. The EIS is a document submitted by the developer, while the EIA is a process which is an ongoing exercise carried out by the decision maker. See *Klohn v An Bord Pleanála*, unreported, High Court, McMahon J., April 23, 2008, where it was noted that while the EIS is intended to comprehensive it is rarely definitive but is a seminal document which will set the agenda for subsequent discussion and deliberation which will provide a body of information which will enable a decision maker to make its assessment in full possession of the environmental factors. See also *Berkeley v Secretary for the Environment* [2001] 2 A.C. 603, where the House of Lords referred to the EIS as a single and accessible compilation produced by the applicant at the very start of the application process.

Part 10 of the 2001 Regulations (S.I. No. 600 of 2001), sets out the rules governing EIAs. The prescribed classes of development which require an EIS are set out in Sch.5 of the Regulations. The content of an EIS is stated at art.94 of the Regulations as requiring the information set out in para.1 of Sch.6, and the information set out in para.2 of Sch.6 where certain conditions apply. It must also contain a summary in non-technical language of the information required to be specified. The content of Sch.6 is similar to Annex III of the Directive.

An EIA will be required in respect of development which falls into any of three categories namely, where it involves:

• an Annex I project set out in the Directive and contained in Pt 1 of Sch.5 of the 2001 Regulation;
• an Annex II project, where the thresholds set out in Sch.5 of the 2001 Regulations are exceeded; and
• where the project is of type under Sch.5 but is sub-threshold the conditions set out therein, but nevertheless has been determined by the planning authority or An Bord Pleanála to be a development likely to have significant effects on the environment based on the criteria set out in Sch.7 of the Regulations.

The content of Sch.7 is similar to Annex IV of the Directive. Under arts 103 and 109 of the Planning Regulations 2001, the planning authority and the Board respectively may require an EIS in sub-threshold cases. Under Art.103, the planning authority and the Board have an obligation to "consider" whether an EIS is required rather than to make a formal decision. One exception to this is in Art.103, where the planning authority must decide whether a sub-threshold development would be likely to have significant effects on the environment in the case of European sites and land subject to specified designations under the Wildlife (Amendment) Act 2000. Potential mitigation measures ought not to be taken into account in deciding whether significant effects are likely. See *British Telecommunications plc. v Gloucester City Council* [2002] 2 P & CR 33. Under art.112, the Board is required to publish a newspaper notice of any appeal in which it requested and received an EIS.

In the case of sub-threshold development, in certain cases it has been suggested the decision of the planning authority as to whether an EIS is required as having a significant effect on the environment will only be reviewed on grounds of irrationality; see *Waddington v An Bord Pleanála*, unreported, High Court, Butler J., December 21, 2000. However, the obligations of Members States under the Directive to ensure that the objectives of the Directive are not undermined, may require a more exacting review. See *World Wildlife Fund v Autonome Provinz Bozen* C 435/97 [1999] ECR I 5613. In considering whether the project has a significant effect on the environment, such effects are not limited to adverse effects; see *O'Nualláin v Dublin Corporation* [1999] 4 I.R. 137. A project may not be split up in order to avoid the requirements of the Directive. However, in *O'Connell v O'Connell*, unreported, High Court, Finnegan J, March 29, 2001, it was suggested that an inspector in an oral hearing was confined to inquire into the scheme which was the subject matter of the application. Nonetheless in *Arklow Holdings v An Bord Pleanála (No.2)* [2007] 4 I.R. 124, leave was granted to challenge the decision of the inspector and the Board who considered it was not necessary to assess the impact of aspects of a development which was outside the waste water treatment plant itself.

Planning Permission as a development consent

The EIA Directive will require an EIS where there is a "development consent". The 1985 Directive does not require a succession of EIA's each time new material is uncovered in the course of a project which had already been the subject of an EIA. See *Dunne v Minister for the Environment (2)* [2007] 1 I.R. 194. However, the notion of development consent is a matter of Community and not national law. See *R (on the application of Wells) v Secretary of State for Transport* C 201/02 [2004] ECR I 723, where it was held that a decision which replaced not only the terms but the very substance of a prior consent constituted a new development consent. For the purposes of this section the application for planning permission is the development consent which requires an EIS. A compliance agreement between a planning authority and developer pursuant to a condition of planning agreement will not constitute a development consent requiring an EIS. See *O'Connor v Dublin Corporation & Borg Developments*, unreported, High Court, O'Neill J., October 3, 2000. However, the condition requiring such agreement may be invalid, if the prescribed criteria were impermissibly wide so as to exclude the public from appropriate consultation. See *Arklow Holidays Ltd v An Bord Pleanála* [2007] 1 I.L.R.M. 125. In relation to planning conditions see also *Sweetman v An Bord Pleanála*, [2007] 2 I.L.R.M. 328 and *R (Hereford Waste Watchers Ltd.) v Hereford Council* [2005] Env. L.R. 29.

The requirement to prepare an EIS applies to all applications for planning permission in respect of the specific development/projects including where the relevant development/project is being carried out by a state authority. However, in respect of exempted state authority development which requires an EIS, the procedure is carried out under ss.181A to 181C. The notion of development under s.3 appears to be broader than the notion of project as used under the Directive, where a project is defined as "the execution of construction works or of other installations or schemes and other interventions in the natural surroundings and landscape including those involving the extracting of mineral resources". See art.1(2) of the Directive. Where a development would otherwise constitute exempted development, art.9(1)(c) of the Regulations 2001 provides that the benefit of exempted development will not apply where the development is subject to a requirement to obtain an EIA. In such instances an application for planning permission will have to be made. Article 96 provides that an outline planning permission application cannot be made in respect of a prescribed class of development requiring an EIS. Article 97 provides that where an EIS is required, the applicant for permission must submit 10 copies. Article 98 of the Regulations provide that a newspaper notice of a planning application (required under art.18) which is accompanied by an EIS must state that an EIS will be submitted to the planning authority with the application and that an EIS will be available for inspection or purchase during office hours of the planning authority. Under art.105, in a sub-threshold case, where the planning authority requires an EIS, the applicant must publish a newspaper notice of an intention to submit the EIS not more than two weeks before submission. The requirement of public notice appears to be mandatory, the failure to comply with which will render any decision on the application invalid. See *O'Nualláin v Dublin Corporation* [1999] 4 I.R. 137. Under art.107, where a planning application is accompanied by an EIS, the planning authority must send a copy of the EIS to the prescribed bodies. Under arts 114 and 115, an EIS received by the Board must be available for inspection or purchase at the offices of the Board and planning authority, respectively.

Under the former 1963 Act as inserted by the Environmental Protection Act 1992, s.98(1), where an integrated pollution licence or waste management licence had been granted, the planning authority and Board were prohibited from considering the risk that the development would cause environmental pollution in deciding whether to grant a planning application. In *O'Connell v Environmental Protection Agency* [2003] 1 I.R. 530, the Supreme Court rejected that Ireland had failed to properly implement the EIS Directives, holding that s.98(1) prohibited the planning authorities and the Board from considering the risk of environmental pollution at substantive planning decision stage and not at the earlier stage when deciding whether to seek an EIS. In *Cosgrave v An Bord Pleanála*, unreported, High Court, Kelly J., April 21, 2004, it was claimed that s.98(1) of the 1992 Act and s.54 of the Waste Management Act 1996, which precludes An Bord Pleanála from consideration of matters relating to the risk of environmental pollution, did not properly implement Directive 85/337/EEC. Kelly J. held that this claim could not be made in judicial review proceedings. Again under the former legislation, in *Martin v An Bord Pleanála (No. 2)*, unreported, the Supreme Court, May 10, 2007, the Supreme Court held the division of responsibility between the EPA and the Board in carrying out an EIA was in compliance with Directive 85/337/EEC. The Board, in carrying out an EIA for the planning application, was precluded from considering any matters relating to "the risk of environmental pollution from the activity", which would be considered by the EPA in granting a waste licence. An EIA in relation to a project may be carried out by more than one competent authority, whose decisions will comprise the "development consent". The Directive does not require that one competent body must carry out a "global assessment" or a "single assessment" of the relevant environmental factors. Planning permission on its own (without the waste licence) does not constitute "development consent". Once the competent authorities have carried out an EIA before development consent is given, there is compliance with the Directive. See also *Ringaskiddy and District Residents Association v Environmental Protection Agency*, unreported, Supreme Court, July 31, 2008.

Section 98(1) of the 1992 Act has been amended by s.256 of the 2000 Act, which provides that a planning permission may be refused where a planning authority or An Bord Pleanála considers the development, notwithstanding that a licence has been granted under the Environmental Protection Agency Act 1992 or the Waste Management Acts. Section 54 of the Waste Management Act 1996 has also been amended by s.257 in similar manner. The section merely prohibits the imposition of planning conditions controlling emissions relating to the activity requiring the licence.

The EIA process is however, purely procedural and the EIA legislation does not require an authority to refuse approval for a development solely on the basis that it would have adverse effects on the environment. See *Kildare County Council v An Bord Pleanála*, unreported, High Court, McMenamin J., March 10, 2006

Article 31 concerns the publication of notice of the decision by a planning authority on an application for permission, while s.34(10) requires the decision to state the main reasons and considerations. These requirements should reflect the fact that an EIA was carried out with the application. This follows in particular from art.9(1) of Directive 2003/35, (which was required to be in force by June 25, 2005), which imposes a requirement to make available to the public, the content of the decision and any conditions attached thereto; the main reasons and considerations on which the decision is based include information about the public participation process and a description, where necessary, of the main measures to avoid, reduce and if possible, offset the major adverse effects.

Adequacy of the EIS

Under arts 108 and 111, the planning authority and the Board respectively, must consider the adequacy of the EIS submitted. Article 108(2) provides that where the planning authority decides that the EIS does not comply with art.94 or any relevant written opinion given by the authority under art.95(4), as appropriate, it is obligated to require the applicant to submit further information. The mere fact that Board does not refer explicitly in any note or memorandum to considering adequacy of the EIS does not mean the court should conclude that the Board did not consider the adequacy of the EIS or whether it complied with art.94 of the 2001 Regulations and Sch.6. See *Klohn v An Bord Pleanála*, unreported, High Court, McMahon J., April 23, 2008, however, it was said because of the greater emphasis in Directive 2003/35/EC, (which was not in force at the time) on public participation, especially art.10a, in future, it might be prudent for the Board to confirm positively that it has made such a determination whenever it arises.

However, where an EIS has been carried out, the court will not enter an investigation as to the quality of the EIS undertaken. The court will only review the adequacy of the EIS as determined by the Board or planning authority under the high standard of irrationality. See *Kenny v An Bord Pleanála (No. 1)* [2001] 1 I.R. 565, where McKechnie J. said:

> "[O]nce the statutory requirements have been satisfied I should not concern myself with the qualitative nature of the EIS or the debate on it had before the Inspector. These are not matters of concern to this Court".

In *Kildare County Council v An Bord Pleanála*, unreported, High Court, McMenamin J., March 10, 2006, it was noted that: "[W]hereas the interpretation of statutory provisions which trigger the requirement for EIS is a question of statutory construction for the courts (*Maher v An Bord Pleanála* [1999] 2 I.L.R.M. 198); the consideration of the quality or adequacy of the information on the likely environmental impact of a proposed development involves the exercise of a statutory discretion for the discretion".

See also *Murphy v Wicklow County Council*, unreported, High Court, Kearns J., March 19, 1999. It appears that where an EIS entirely omitted to deal with an express requirement, then the statutory requirements would not have been satisfied. In *O'Mahony v An Bord Pleanála*, unreported, High Court, O'Neill J., February 18, 2005, it was suggested that an EIS of a road scheme which failed to deal with future development and the likelihood of zoned development would be a significant deficiency and a failure to comply with the relevant Directive.

On the other hand, certain qualitative deficiencies in the EIS may be remedied as part of the overall EIA process. In *Klohn v An Bord Pleanála*, unreported, High Court, McMahon J., April 23, 2008, it was noted that a flaw or deficiency in the EIS will not invariably inflict a fatal wound in the assessment process, which is carried out at a later phase with the benefit of additional submissions or observations and informed by its own expertise. An over-formalistic approach to the requirements is inappropriate. The question is whether the EIS is so deficient so as to prevent a subsequent proper assessment or to deprive the relevant parties (or the public) of a real opportunity to participate. In *Power v An Bord Pleanála*, unreported, High Court, Quirke J., January 17, 2005, where the European Commission had made a submission to the Board considering an EIS, this was not in itself a ground to challenge the Board's subsequent approval of the development. In *Kildare County Council v An Bord Pleanála*, unreported, High Court, McMenamin J., March 10, 2006, it was noted that a distinction must be drawn between the level of deficiency in an EIS sufficient to justify rejection of the application at the outset and the level of deficiency in an EIS leading to a refusal of permission on the merits. See also *R. (Blewett) v Derbyshire County Council* [2004] JPL 751.

Exemptions

Subsection (3) allows a person seeking permission to apply to An Bord Pleanála for an exemption from the requirement to submit an EIS. The Board will only grant such exemption in exceptional circumstances, and only after having afforded the planning authority an opportunity to make submissions. No exemption may be granted where a Member State or State party has indicated that it intends to furnish views on the effects on the environment. Article 104 of the 2001 Regulations provides that a notice requiring an EIS will cease to have effect where an exemption is granted. Also under art.110, where an EIS is granted, the Board may not request an EIS. Article 100 provides that where the Board, in granting an exemption, imposed other requirements, the development must comply with these requirements. Under art.101, on receipt of the Board's decision, the planning notice must stamp the notice with date of receipt. Subsection (3)(b) provides that in granting an exemption, the Board must consider whether the effects, if any, of the proposed on the environment should be assessed in some other form. The Board must make available to the public information relating to the exemption decision, the reasons for granting the exemption and information obtained under any other form of assessment.

Permission for development requiring environmental impact assessment

1–203   **173.—(1)** In addition to the requirements of *section 34(3),* where an application in respect of which an environmental impact statement was submitted to the planning authority in accordance with *section 172,* the planning authority, and the Board on appeal, shall have regard to the statement, any supplementary information furnished relating to the statement and any submissions or observations furnished concerning the effects on the environment of the proposed development.

[(2)

(a) If an applicant or a person intending to apply for permission so requests, the planning authority concerned shall give a written opinion on the information to be contained in an environmental impact statement, subject to–

    (i) consultation with the Board, and

    (ii) any prescribed consultations, to be carried out by the planning authority in relation to such an opinion, and the written opinion shall be given before the submission by that person of an application for the grant of planning permission.

(b) The giving of a written opinion in accordance with *paragraph (a)* shall not prejudice the exercise by the planning authority concerned or the Board of its powers under this Act, or any regulations made thereunder, to require the person who made the request to submit further information regarding the application concerned or, as the case may be, any appeal.

(c) The Minister may, by regulations, provide for additional, incidental, consequential or supplementary matters as regards procedures in respect of the provision of a written opinion under *paragraph (a)*.]

(3)

(a) Where a person is required by or under this *Act* to submit an environmental impact statement to the Board, he or she may, before submitting the statement, request the Board to provide him or her with its opinion as to the information that should be contained in such statement, and the Board shall on receipt of such a request provide such opinion in writing.

(b) The giving of a written opinion in accordance with *paragraph (a)* shall not prejudice the exercise by the Board of its powers pursuant to this *Act* or any regulations under this *Act,* to require the applicant to submit specified information in relation to any appeal to which the environmental impact statement relates.

(c) The Minister may make regulations in relation to the making of a request or providing an opinion to which this *subsection* relates.

AMENDMENT HISTORY

Subsection (2) substituted by s.32 of the Planning and Development (Strategic Infrastructure) Act 2006 (No. 27 of 2006).

NOTE

Subsection (1) provides that where a planning application requires an EIS, the planning authority and the Board on appeal, in determining a planning application, will have regard to the statement, any additional information required and any submissions regarding the effect of the development on the environment. This ongoing process of consideration constitutes the EIA required by Directive which is distinct from the EIS which is merely the document produced by the developer. For this distinction between the EIA and EIS see *Klohn v An Bord Pleanála*, unreported, High Court, McMahon J., April 23, 2008, where it was noted that while the EIS is a seminal document produced by the developer, the EIA is an ongoing dynamic process undertaken by the decision maker. In the interval between the EIS and

EIA, the decision maker will have gathered information from many other sources.

Subsections (2) and (3) provides a mechanism (known as "scoping") where an applicant or person intending to apply for permission who is under some doubt as to what should be included in an EIS, can seek a written opinion from the planning authority or the Board on appeal, in advance of submitting the EIS. Subsection (2) concerns a request to the planning authority while subs.(3) concerns a request to the Board. The 2006 Act amended subs.(2) with main changes being in (a)(i) which provides that the planning authority must consult with the Board before giving its written opinion. Also in (b) the words "or the Board" and "or as the case may be, any appeal" are inserted to make clear that the written opinion will also not prejudice the Board in requiring a person to submit further information. Article 95 of the 2001 Regulations as amended, sets out the procedure following a request for a written opinion. The Article specifies the information which must be contained in a request for a written opinion and that the planning authority or Board, having received the request, must notify certain bodies of the request, who then have four weeks to make a submission as to the content of the EIS. These bodies are specified in art.95(2) as amended as:

- the Minister for the Environment, Heritage and Local Government;
- the Environmental Protection Agency;
- the Minister for Communications, Marine and Natural Resources;
- in the case of the Board, the relevant planning authority;
- in the case of a planning authority, the Board; and
- any other body referred to in art.28, as appropriate.

The information which must contained in the request is:

- the name and address, and telephone number and e-mail address if any, of the person making the request and of the person, if any, acting on behalf of the person making the request, or, in the case of development proposed by a local authority, the name and address, and telephone number and e-mail address, if any, of the authority;
- the location, townland or postal address of the land or structure to which the request relates (as may be appropriate), and shall include a location map marked so as to clearly identify:
  — the land or structure to which the application relates and the boundaries thereof in red;
  — any land which adjoins, abuts or is adjacent to the land to be developed and which is under the control of the applicant or the person who owns the land which is the subject of the application in blue; and
  — any wayleaves in yellow;
- a brief description of the nature of the proposed development and of its possible effects on the environment;
- if the proposed development comprises or is for the purposes of an activity requiring an integrated pollution control licence or a waste licence, an indication of that fact;
- if the proposed development relates to the provision of, or modifications to, an establishment, an indication of that fact.

The planning authority or Board must give the written opinion within three weeks of the expiry of the period for making submissions, or the end of the period where the planning authority or Board sought further information to enable it to give the written opinion (art.95(3)). The issuing of a written opinion is without prejudice to the right of the planning authority or Board to request further information. Under art.33 of the Planning Regulations 2001, the planning authority may, within six weeks of the receipt of the planning application, by notice in writing require an applicant to submit further information to enable them to deal with the application or to produce evidence reasonably required to verify certain information given or in relation to the application. Also under art.128, in relation to a development likely to have significant effect on the environment of a transboundary state, a planning authority may request information.

In the case of an appeal to the Board, art.112 of the 2001 Regulations provides that the Board shall publish, in at least one approved newspaper, notice of any appeal in respect of which it has requested and received an EIS under art.109. Article 112(2) states the content of such notice as:

- the name of the planning authority;

- the reference number of the planning application;
- the reference number of the appeal;
- the name of the appellant;
- the name of the applicant;
- the location, townland or postal address of the land or structure to which the application relates (as may be appropriate);
- a brief description of the nature and extent of the proposed development;
- that an EIS has been received by the Board in respect of the appeal;
- where, and the period during which, the EIS will be available for inspection or purchase, and
- that a submission or observation on the appeal may be made to the Board, on payment of the appropriate fee, within four weeks beginning on the date of publication of the notice.

Transboundary environmental impacts

174.—(1)   1–204

    (a) The Minister may make regulations in respect of applications for development which require the submission of an environmental impact statement, where the planning authority[, or the Board in dealing with any application or appeal,] is aware that the development is likely to have significant effects on the environment in another Member State of the European Communities or a state which is a party to the *Transboundary Convention* or where the other State concerned considers that the development would be likely to have such effects.

    (b) Without prejudice to the generality of *paragraph (a)*, regulations under this *subsection* may make provision for the following:

       (i) the notification of the Minister regarding the application;

      (ii) the submission of information to the Minister regarding the application;

   (iii) the notification of the other State involved and the provision of information to that State;

    (iv) the making of observations and submissions regarding the application from the other State involved and the entering into consultations with that State;

    (v) the extension of time limits for the making of decisions under this *Act.*

  (2) In addition to the requirements of [*sections 34(3), 37G(2), 146C(6), 173(1), 181B(1), 182B(1) and 182D(1)*], the planning authority or the Board, as the case may be, shall have regard, where appropriate, to the views of any Member State of the European Communities or other party to the *Transboundary Convention* in relation to the effects on the environment of the proposed development.

  (3) Notwithstanding any other provisions of this *Act,* a planning authority or the Board, as the case may be, may, following the consideration of any submissions or observations received or any consultations entered into by a planning authority or the Board, impose conditions on a [grant of permission or approval] in order to reduce or eliminate potential transboundary effects of any proposed development.

  [**(4)** In any case where–

(a) notification has been received from another Member State of the European Communities or other party to the Transboundary Convention, in respect of any development, or

(b) a planning authority or a State authority requests, or in any other case where the Minister otherwise decides,

the Minister may request another Member State of the European Communities or other party to the Transboundary Convention to forward information in respect of any development which is subject to the Council Directive or Transboundary Convention and which is likely to have significant environmental effects in Ireland.]

(5)

(a) The Minister or a State authority or planning authority having consulted with the Minister, may decide to forward submissions or observations to, or enter into discussions with, the other state involved in respect of the development referred to in *subsection (4)* regarding the potential transboundary effects of that development and the measures envisaged to reduce or eliminate those effects.

(b) The Minister may make regulations regarding the provision of public notification of any environmental impact statement or other information received by the Minister, State authority or planning authority under *subsection (4),* and the making of submissions or observations regarding the information.

(6) The Minister may enter into an agreement with any other Member State of the European Communities or other party to the *Transboundary Convention* regarding the detailed procedures to be followed in respect of consultations regarding proposed developments which are likely to have significant transboundary effects.

AMENDMENT HISTORY

Subsections (1), (2) and (3) amended by s.33 of the Planning and Development (Strategic Infrastructure) Act 2006 (No. 27 of 2006).

Subsection (4) substituted by reg.5 of the European Communities (Environmental Impact Assessment)(Amendment) Regulations 2006 (S.I. No. 659 of 2006).

NOTE

This section concerns developments requiring an EIS, which are likely to have significant effects on the environment in another State of the European Union or in a State party to the Transboundary Convention. The 2006 Act amended the section to incorporate references to strategic infrastructure applications dealt with by the Board. The Transboundary Convention means the United Nations Economic Commission for European Convention on Environmental Impact Assessment in a Transboundary Context, at Espoo (Finland), on February 25, 1991. Regulations in relation to this section are set out in Ch.5 of Pt 10 of the Planning Regulations 2001 as amended by the 2006 Regulations under arts 124–132. Article 124 provides that where a development is likely to have such significant effects, the planning authority or Board must notify the Minister "as soon as may be after receipt of the application". Under art.125, where the minister forms the view that a development would be likely to have such effect or where a transboundary state considers such would be the case, the Minister may require the planning authority or Board to furnish specified details. Under art.126, the Minister, having consulted with the planning authority or Board, must provide information on the development including the EIS to the State concerned and enter into consultation with such State. Under art.128, the planning authority or Board may require an applicant to submit further information in relation to the application. Where the response includes significant additional information, various parties including the Minister must be notified of the response and a notice must be published in an approved newspaper of the further information. At the end of the process, subs.(3) provides that following consideration of any submissions or observations received or consultations entered into, the planning authority or Board may decide to impose conditions on the proposed development to reduce or eliminate the potential transboundary effect on the environment.

Subsection (4) concerns the reverse situation where a development abroad is likely to have effect on the environment in Ireland (and which development is covered by the relevant international or European law). Where notification is received from another Member State that this is the case or where a planning authority, state authority or the Minister otherwise decides, the Minster may request the relevant European Union State or transboundary State to forward details of the development. The Minister, State authority or relevant planning authority may make submissions to such other State regarding the effect on the Irish environment, which may include measures to reduce such effects. Under art.132 of the Regulations, having received information from such transboundary state, the Minister must notify any planning authority likely to be affected by such proposed development. The planning authority must as soon as may be publish notice in an approved newspaper stating that information has been received in relation to such development and inviting submissions to be made within a specified period. After consultation with the Minister, the relevant planning authority may enter into consultation with the State concerned regarding the potential transboundary effects.

Environmental impact assessment of certain development carried out by or on behalf of local authorities

175.—**(1)** Where development belonging to a class of development,   **1–205** identified for the purposes of *section 176,* is proposed to be carried out—

- **(a)** by a local authority that is a planning authority, whether in its capacity as a planning authority or in any other capacity, or
- **(b)** by some other person on behalf of, or jointly or in partnership with, such a local authority, pursuant to a contract entered into by that local authority whether in its capacity as a planning authority or in any other capacity,

within the functional area of the local authority concerned (hereafter in this *section* referred to as "proposed development"), the local authority shall prepare, or cause to be prepared, an environmental impact statement in respect thereof.

(2) Proposed development in respect of which an environmental impact statement has been prepared in accordance with *subsection (1)* shall not be carried out unless the Board has approved it with or without modifications.

(3) Where an environmental impact statement has been prepared pursuant to *subsection (1),* the local authority shall apply to the Board for approval.

(4) Before a local authority makes an application for approval under *subsection (3),* it shall—

- **(a)** publish in one or more newspapers circulating in the area in which it is proposed to carry out the development a notice indicating the nature and location of the proposed development and—
    - **(i)** stating that—
        - **(I)** it proposes to seek the approval of the Board for the proposed development,
        - **(II)** an environmental impact statement has been prepared

in respect of the proposed development,

[(III) it is notifying a Member State of the European Communities or any other party to the Transboundary Convention of its opinion that the proposed development to which the application for approval to An Bord Pleanála relates would be likely to have significant effects on the environment in that State,

(IV) the Board may give approval to the application for development with or without conditions or may refuse the application for development,]

(ii) specifying the times and places at which, and the period (not being less than 6 weeks) during which, a copy of the environmental impact statement may be inspected free of charge or purchased, and

(iii) inviting the making, during such period, of submissions and observations to the Board relating to—

(I) the implications of the proposed development for proper planning and sustainable development in the area concerned, and

(II) the likely effects on the environment of the proposed development,

if carried out,

and

(b) send a copy of the application and the environmental impact statement to the prescribed authorities together with a notice stating that submissions or observations may, during the period referred to in *paragraph (a)(ii)*, be made in writing to the Board in relation to—

(i) the likely effects on the environment of the proposed development, and

(ii) the implications of the proposed development for proper planning and sustainable development in the area concerned, if carried out.

[(5)

(a) The Board may–

(i) if it considers it necessary to do so, require a local authority that has applied for approval for a proposed development to furnish to the Board such further information in relation to—

(I) the effects on the environment of the proposed development, or

(II) the consequences for proper planning and sustainable development in the area in which it is proposed to situate the said development of such development, as the Board may specify, or

(ii) if it is provisionally of the view that it would be appropriate to approve the proposed development were certain alterations (specified in the notification referred to in this subparagraph) to be made to the terms of it, notify the local authority that it is of that view and invite the authority to make to the terms of the proposed development alterations specified in the notification and, if the authority makes those alterations, to furnish to it such information (if any) as it may specify in relation to the development, in the terms as so altered, or, where necessary, a revised environmental impact statement in respect of it.

(b) If a local authority makes the alterations to the terms of the proposed development specified in a notification given to it under *paragraph (a),* the terms of the development as so altered shall be deemed to be the proposed development for the purposes of this section.

(c) The Board shall—

    (i) where it considers that any further information received pursuant to a requirement made under *paragraph (a)(i)* contains significant additional data relating to—

        (I) the likely effects on the environment of the proposed development, and

        (II) the likely consequences for the proper planning and sustainable development in the area in which it is proposed to situate the said development of such development,

    or

    (ii) where the local authority has made the alterations to the terms of the proposed development specified in a notification given to it under *paragraph (a)(ii),* require the local authority to do the things referred to in *paragraph (d).*

(d) The things which a local authority shall be required to do as aforesaid are—

    (i) to publish in one or more newspapers circulating in the area in which the proposed development would be situate a notice stating that, as appropriate—

        (I) further information in relation to the proposed development has been furnished to the Board, or

        (II) the local authority has, pursuant to an invitation of the Board, made alterations to the terms of the proposed development (and the nature of those alterations shall be indicated) and, if it be the case, that information in relation to the terms of the development as so altered or a revised environmental impact statement in respect of the development has been furnished to the Board, indicating the times at which, the period (which shall not be less than 3 weeks) during which and the place, or places, where a copy of the information or the environmental impact statement referred to in clause (I) or (II) may be inspected free of charge or purchased and that submissions or observations in relation to that information or statement may be made to the Board before the expiration of the indicated period, and

    (ii) to send to each prescribed authority to which notice was given pursuant to *subsection (4)(b)* —

> **(I)** a notice of the furnishing to the Board of, as appropriate, the further information referred to in *subparagraph (i)(I);* or the information or statement referred to in *subparagraph (i)(II),* and
>
> **(II)** a copy of that further information, information or statement, and to indicate to the authority that submissions or observations in relation to that further information, information or statement may be made to the Board before the expiration of a period (which shall not be less than 3 weeks) beginning on the day on which the notice is sent to the prescribed authority by the local authority.]

(6) Before making a decision in respect of a proposed development under this *section,* the Board shall consider—

> **(a)** [the environmental impact statement submitted pursuant to *subsection (1) or (5)(a)(ii),* any submission or observations made in accordance with *subsection (4) or (5)*] and any other information furnished in accordance with *subsection (5)* relating to—
>
> > **(i)** the likely effects on the environment of the proposed development, and
> >
> > **(ii)** the likely consequences for proper planning and sustainable development in the area in which it is proposed to situate the said development of such development,
>
> **(b)** the views of any other Member State of the European Communities or a state which is a party to the *Transboundary Convention* to which a copy of the environmental impact statement was sent, and
>
> **(c)** the report and any recommendations of the person conducting a hearing referred to in *subsection (7)* where evidence is heard at such a hearing relating to—
>
> > **(i)** the likely effects on the environment of the proposed development, and
> >
> > **(ii)** the likely consequences for proper planning and sustainable development in the area in which it is proposed to situate the said development of such development.

(7) The person conducting an oral hearing in relation to the compulsory purchase of land which relates wholly or partly to a proposed development under this *section* in respect of which a local authority has applied for approval shall be entitled to hear evidence relating to—

> **(a)** the likely effects on the environment of the proposed development, and
>
> **(b)** the likely consequences for proper planning and sustainable development in the area in which it is proposed to situate the said development of such development.

(8)

> **(a)** The Board may where it is satisfied that exceptional circumstances so warrant, grant an exemption in respect of proposed development from a requirement under *subsection (1)* to prepare an environmental

impact statement except that no exemption may be granted in respect of proposed development where another Member State of the European Communities or a State party to the *Transboundary Convention* has indicated that it wishes to furnish views on the effects on the environment in that State of the proposed development.

[**(b)** The Board shall, in granting an exemption under *paragraph (a),*–
  (i) consider whether the effects, if any, of the proposed development on the environment should be assessed in some other form, and
  (ii) make available to members of the public the information relating to the exemption decision referred to under *paragraph (a)*, the reasons for granting such exemption and the information obtained under any other form of assessment referred to in *subparagraph (i)*,

and the Board may apply such requirements regarding these matters in relation to the application for approval as it considers necessary or appropriate.]

(c) Notice of any exemption granted under *paragraph (a)* of the reasons for granting the exemption, and of any requirements applied under *paragraph (b)* shall, as soon as may be—
  (i) be published in *Iris Oifigiúil* and in at least one daily newspaper published in the State, and
  (ii) be given, together with a copy of the information, if any, made available to the members of the public in accordance with *paragraph (b)*, to the Commission of the European Communities.

[**(9)**
  (a) The Board may, in respect of an application for approval under this section of proposed development—
    (i) approve the proposed development,
    (ii) make such modifications to the proposed development as it specifies in the approval and approve the proposed development as so modified,
    (iii) approve, in part only, the proposed development (with or without specified modifications of it of the foregoing kind), or
    (iv) refuse to approve the proposed development, and may attach to an approval under *subparagraph (i), (ii) or (iii)* such conditions as it considers appropriate.
  (b) Without prejudice to the generality of the foregoing power to attach conditions, the Board may attach to an approval under *paragraph (a)(i), (ii) or (iii)* a condition requiring—
    (i) the construction or the financing, in whole or in part, of the construction of a facility, or
    (ii) the provision or the financing, in whole or in part, of the provision of a service, in the area in which the proposed development would be situated, being a facility or service that, in the opinion of the Board, would constitute a substantial gain

to the community.

(c) A condition attached pursuant to *paragraph (b)* shall not require such an amount of financial resources to be committed for the purposes of the condition being complied with as would substantially deprive the person in whose favour the approval operates of the benefits likely to accrue from the grant of the approval.]

[(9A)

(a) The Board shall direct the payment of such sum as it considers reasonable by the local authority concerned to the Board towards the costs and expenses incurred by the Board in determining an application under this section for approval of a proposed development, including—

  (i) the costs of holding any oral hearing in relation to the application,

  (ii) the fees of any consultants or advisers engaged in the matter, and

  (iii) an amount equal to such portion of the remuneration and any allowances for expenses paid to the members and employees of the Board as the Board determines to be attributable to the performance of duties by the members and employees in relation to the application, and the local authority shall pay the sum.

(b) If a local authority fails to pay a sum directed to be paid under *paragraph (a),* the Board may recover the sum from the authority as a simple contract debt in any court of competent jurisdiction.]

(10)

(a) Where an application under this *section* relates to proposed development which comprises or is for the purposes of an activity for which an integrated pollution control licence or a waste licence is required, the Board shall not, where it decides to approve the proposed development, subject that approval to conditions which are for the purposes of—

  (i) controlling emissions from the operation of the activity, including the prevention, limitation, elimination, abatement or reduction of those emissions, or

  (ii) controlling emissions related to or following the cessation of the operation of the activity.

(b) Where an application under this *section* relates to proposed development which comprises or is for the purposes of an activity for which an integrated pollution control licence or a waste licence is required, the Board may, in respect of any proposed development comprising or for the purposes of the activity, decide to refuse the proposed development, where the Board considers that the development, notwithstanding the licensing of the activity, is unacceptable on environmental grounds, having regard to the proper planning and sustainable development of the area in which the development is or will be situate.

(c)

(i) Before making a decision in respect of proposed development comprising or for the purposes of an activity, the Board may request the Environmental Protection Agency to make observations within such period (which period shall not in any case be less than 3 weeks from the date of the request) as may be specified by the Board in relation to the proposed development.

(ii) When making its decision the Board shall have regard to the observations, if any, received from the Agency within the period specified under *subparagraph (i)*.

(d) The Board may, at any time after the expiration of the period specified by the Board under *paragraph (c)(i)* for making observations, make its decision on the application.

(e) The making of observations by the Agency under this *section* shall not prejudice any other function of the Agency under [the *Environmental Protection Agency Act, 1992*].

(11)

(a) The Minister may make regulations to provide for such matters of procedure and administration as appear to the Minister to be necessary or expedient in respect of applications for approval under this *section*.

(b) Without prejudice to the generality of *paragraph (a)*, regulations under this *subsection* may make provision for—

(i) enabling a local authority to request the Board to give a written opinion on the information to be contained in an environmental impact statement,

(ii) matters of procedure relating to the making of observations by the Environmental Protection Agency under this *section* and matters connected therewith,

(iii) the notification of another Member State of the European Communities or other parties to the *Transboundary Convention* in relation to proposed development, receiving observations and submissions from the State or party and entering into consultations with them, and

(iv) requiring the Board to give information in respect of its decision regarding the proposed development for which approval is sought.

(12) In considering under *subsection (6)* information furnished relating to the likely consequences for proper planning and sustainable development of a proposed development in the area in which it is proposed to situate such development, the Board shall have regard to—

(a) the provisions of the development plan for the area,

(b) the provisions of any special amenity area order relating to the area,

(c) if the area or part of the area is a European site or an area prescribed for the purposes of *section 10(2)(c)*, that fact,

(d) where relevant, the policies of the Government, the Minister or any other Minister of the Government, and

(e) the provisions of this *Act* and regulations under this *Act* where relevant.

(13) A person who contravenes a condition imposed by the Board under this *section* shall be guilty of an offence.

(14) This *section* shall not apply to proposed road development within the meaning of the *Roads Act, 1993,* by or on behalf of a road authority.

AMENDMENT HISTORY

Subsection (4) Clauses (III) and (IV) inserted by reg.6(1) of the European Communities (Environmental Impact Assessment)(Amendment) Regulations 2006 (S.I. No. 659 of 2006).

Subsections (5) and (6) substituted by s.34 of the Planning and Development (Strategic Infrastructure) Act 2006 (No. 27 of 2006).

Subsection (9) substituted by s.34 of the Planning and Development (Strategic Infrastructure) Act 2006 (No. 27 of 2006).

Subsection (8) para.(b) substituted by reg.6(2) of the European Communities (Environmental Impact Assessment)(Amendment) Regulations 2006 (S.I. No. 659 of 2006).

Subsection (9A) was inserted by s. 34 of the Planning and Development (Strategic Infrastructure) Act 2006 (No. 27 of 2006).

Subsection (10) was inserted by s.247 of the Local Government Act 2001 (No. 37 of 2001), which, by the Local Government Act 2001 (Commencement) Order 2001 (S.I. No. 458 of 2001), came into effect on October 9, 2001.

NOTE

This section concerns development carried out by a local authority (or a person in agreement with the local authority) of a type which requires an EIS under s.176. The local authority is obliged to prepare an EIS where the proposed development falls into a category of development which requires an EIS. The local authority must submit the proposed development with the EIS for approval by An Bord Pleanála before it can carry out the proposed development. Subsection (14) provides that the section does not apply to a proposed road development under the Roads Act 1993, by or on behalf of the road authority. Sections 50 and 51 of the Roads Acts 1993 as amended set out a separate procedure for the submission of an EIS and the carrying out of an EIA in respect of certain road developments. Subsection (2) provides that the proposed local authority development cannot be carried unless the Board approves the development with or without modifications. Subsection (3) means that the EIS must be prepared prior to the local authority applying to the Board. Article 118 of the 2001 Regulations sets out the matters which must accompany such application to the Board. Article 120 provides that where a local authority proposes to carry out a sub-threshold development, and where it considers that the development would be likely to have significant effects on the environment in accordance with Sch.7 to the 2001 Regulations, it shall prepare, or cause to be prepared, an EIS in respect thereof. Article 120(3)(a) states that the Board shall, where it considers that sub-threshold development proposed to be carried out by a local authority would be likely to have significant effects on the environment, require the local authority to prepare, or cause to be prepared, an EIS in respect thereof.

However, subs.(4) provides that before submitting the application to the Board, the local authority must publish a notice in a local newspaper specifying, inter alia, that such a submission is being made to the Board, that the EIS may be inspected at a specified place and time (for not less than six weeks), and inviting submissions to the Board concerning the proper planning and development of the development and any likely effect on the environment. The application and EIS must also be sent to the prescribed authorities along with a notice inviting submissions. Article 121 of the 2001 Regulations as amended by the 2006 Regulations, sets out the prescribed authorities, which will depend on the nature of the development. The notice must also state, where appropriate that it is notifying another

Member State or other party to the Transboundary Convention, of its opinion that it is likely to have significant effects on the environment of that State. The notice must also say that the Board may give approval with or without conditions or may refuse the application.

Subsection (5)(a) provides that the Board may request the local authority to furnish further information in relation to the application where it is considered necessary. The 2006 Act made certain amendments to the subs.(5) which concerns requests for further information or alterations to the proposed development. The changes include the addition of s.5(a)(i)(II) under which the Board may request the local authority to furnish information regarding the consequences for proper planning and sustainable development in the area where the proposed development is to be situated. Also added is subs.(5)(a)(ii) which allows the Board to inform the local authority that it is provisionally of the view that it would grant approval if certain alterations are made and so invite the local authority to submit further information regarding these alterations and a revised EIS, if necessary. The notice must state that such information/alteration or revised EIS have been received; that such matter is available for inspection and that submissions can be made within a period of not less than three weeks. A notice must also be sent to each prescribed authority together with a copy of the information, inviting submissions to be made within a period of not less than three weeks.

Where the Board considers that the response to the request for information includes significant additional information concerning the likely effects on the environment or proper planning and sustainable development of the area, the local authority must publish a notice in the local newspaper in relation to such further information, stating that such information may be inspected and invite submissions in relation thereto (allowing not less than three weeks). In *Kinsella v Dundalk Town Council*, unreported, High Court, Kelly J., December 3, 2004, it was said that:

"The task of assessing whether 'significant additional data' is contained in a response involves the exercise of planning expertise and judgment which this Court does not have and is precisely the kind of question which falls within the competence of an expert decision-maker. This Court can only interfere with such a decision within the strict limitations of its judicial review jurisdiction".

See also *Klohn v An Bord Pleanála*, unreported, High Court, McMahon J., April 23, 2008. A copy must also be sent to the Board and to the prescribed authorities (who are invited to make submissions). It appears from subs.(5)(c)(ii) that where the local authority has made the alterations to the terms of the proposed development specified in the notice sent to the local authority, the local authority is obliged to publish newspaper notice, irrespective of whether the Board considers such alteration constitutes significant additional data relating to the likely effects on the environment or proper planning and sustainable development of the area.

Subsection (6) sets out the matters which the Board is obliged to consider in making a decision in respect of the proposed development. Subsection (12) provides that in considering the information relating to the likely consequences for proper planning and sustainable development in the area, the Board is obliged to have regard to specified matters, which includes the development plan. The EIA process is however, purely procedural and the EIA legislation does not require an authority to refuse approval for a development solely on the basis that it would have adverse effects on the environment. See *Kildare County Council v An Bord Pleanála*, unreported, High Court, McMenamin J., March 10, 2006.

Under subs.(7), the person conducting the oral hearing is entitled to hear evidence relating to the likely effects on the environment or proper planning and sustainable development of the area. Similar to its power under s.172(3), under subs.(8) the Board has power in exceptional circumstances to grant an exemption from the requirement to make an EIS in relation to a proposed local authority development except where the matter has transboundary implications. Where the Board decides to grant such exemption it must publish notice of such exemption. Subsection (8)(b) provides that in granting an exemption, the Board must consider whether the effects, if any, of the proposed on the environment should be assessed in some other form. The Board must make available to the public information relating to the exemption decision, the reasons for granting the exemption and information obtained under any other form of assessment.

New subss.9 and 9A are inserted. The main changes in subs.(9) are that the Board has a wider range of options in determining whether to approve the development, including that the Board may under (ii) approve the development with specified modifications or under (iii) approve, in part only, of the proposed development with or without specified modifications. In respect of ordinary planning applications under s.34, there is no express power to issue split decisions (although this may be implied), i.e. to both grant and refuse a decision by granting permission for only part of the development. A split decision should only be made in certain circumstances. See the note on s.37G, which allows a split decision on a Sch.7 strategic infrastructure application.

The new subs.(9) provides that in respect of any type of approval, the Board may impose conditions. There is a general power to impose conditions which could relate to the proper planning and sustainable development of the area. However, subs.(9)(b) allows the Board to impose a condition which would amount to a planning gain to the community. A similar condition can be imposed in respect of state authority development under s.181B(7) or in respect of approving a road scheme/road development under s.217C(3). This can consist of two types, namely; the construction of a facility or the provision of a service. The subsection gives no further guidance as to the nature of these matters except that it should be of substantial gain to the community. It appears that the gain must be to the community as a whole rather than a limited section of the community. This is not to say the gain must be of interest to all the community but the gain is open to all the community. It may be a question of fact and of planning judgment as to whether there is a substantial gain to the community. Subsection (9)(c) imposes a limit to the scope of the condition which is that the condition must not require an amount of financial resources as would substantially deprive the person granted approval of the benefits likely to accrue from the approval. This is a mandatory requirement and any condition which would have such effect would be ultra vires. It appears that the assessment of whether of a condition has such effect is not one which involves planning expertise and the court ought not to defer to the opinion of the Board. The assessment of the benefits likely to accrue will depend on the type of permission. This would include the financial benefits which would accrue from any approval which would therefore include the value of the land with the approval attached. However, an applicant may decide not to implement a permission if a condition would substantially deprive an applicant of the benefits of the approval. Although the criteria are vague and difficult to apply, the inbuilt proportionality requirement may mean that it would escape a challenge on the basis constitutional invalidity. The condition may be sought to be justified on the basis that it is in the interests of the common good and that it is proportionate to its objective in accordance with the principle set out in the art.26 reference, *Planning and Development Bill* [2002] 2 I.R. 292, in respect of Pt V of the 2000 Act.

Subsection (9A) requires the Board to direct the local authority concerned to pay the reasonable expenses of the Board with regard to the oral hearing, fees of consultants and remunerations/expenses of Board staff member engaged in respect of an application. The local authority must pay such costs and the Board may sue the local authority in default of payment. In allowing the Board to assess its own expenses to be paid, there is an element of potential bias. However, the reference to "reasonable expenses" imports an objective standard as to the nature of the costs.

Subsection (10) provides that where the proposed development requires an integrated pollution control licence or waste licence, the Board may not impose a condition concerning the development in relation to emissions. The Board may refuse the development on environmental grounds even where such licences have been granted. Before making its determination, the Board may, at its discretion, request observations from the Environmental Protection Agency under art.117 of the Regulation. The Board may approve the development, refuse the development, or approve the development subject to conditions. Under art.122 of the Regulations, the decision must state the main reasons and considerations on which it is based. In making such determination, it must take into account the matters enlisted under subss.6 and 12 (submission, formation concerning the likely effect on the environment, views of another State where appropriate, and of a person conducting an oral hearing, etc.).

Article 123 of the 2001 Regulations, as amended by the 2006 Regulations, provides that the Board shall, as soon as may be following the making of its decision on an application for approval notify the local authority concerned, and any person or body who made a submission or observation in accordance with s.175(4) of the Act, of its decision. Section

100 of the Waste Management Act 2001, as inserted by s.26(2)(d) of the Protection of the Environment Act 2003, provides that in performing their functions under the Planning Acts, in particular under Pt III, ss.175 or 179, planning authorities and An Bord Pleanála shall ensure that such measures as are reasonably necessary are taken to secure the appropriate provisions for the management of waste.

Prescribed classes of development requiring assessment

176.—(1) The Minister may, in connection with the *Council Directive* or **1–206** otherwise, make regulations-
- **(a)** identifying development which may have significant effects on the environment, and
- **(b)** specifying the manner in which the likelihood that such development would have significant effects on the environment is to be determined.

(2) Without prejudice to the generality of *subsection (1),* regulations under that *subsection* may provide for all or any one or more of the following matters:
- **(a)** the establishment of thresholds or criteria for the purpose of determining which classes of development are likely to have significant effects on the environment;
- **(b)** the establishment of different such thresholds or criteria in respect of different classes of areas;
- **(c)** the determination on a case-by-case basis, in conjunction with the use of thresholds or criteria, of the developments which are likely to have significant effects on the environment;
- **(d)** where thresholds or criteria are not established, the determination on a case-by-case basis of the developments which are likely to have significant effects on the environment;
- **(e)** the identification of selection criteria in relation to—
  - **(i)** the establishment of thresholds or criteria for the purpose of determining which classes of development are likely to have significant effects on the environment, or
  - **(ii)** the determination on a case-by-case basis of the developments which are likely to have significant effects on the environment.

(3) Any reference in an enactment to development of a class specified under *Article 24 of the European Communities (Environmental Impact Assessment) Regulations, 1989* (S.I. No. 349 of 1989), shall be deemed to be a reference to a class of development prescribed under this *section.*

NOTE

Regulations for this section have been provided for under art.93 of the 2001 Regulations, which states that the prescribed classes of development for the purposes of s.176 are set out in Sch.5. The Directive distinguishes between projects under which an EIA is mandatory (set out in Annex I) and projects which require an EIA where they are considered in each individual case to have a significant effect on the environment (set out in Annex II). The Directive allows Member States to set out criteria or thresholds in determining whether an Annex II project is deemed to have a significant effect on the environment and so requires an EIA.

Part I of Sch.5 sets out 21 classes, specifying the criteria involved. Part I of Sch.5 includes miscellaneous categories, such as, for example, a crude oil refinery, a thermal power station, smelting of iron and steel, the extraction of asbestos, etc. Part 2 of Sch.5 sets out 13 broader classes, with the relevant criteria. The criteria set out include the size of the project, the nature of the project and also its location. Under the previous Regulations, Ireland was held in breach of the Directive, in *Commission v Ireland*, Case 392/96 [1999] E.C.R. 5901 in confining the threshold regarding peat extraction projects to the size of the projects, and so not taking into account the nature and location of the project. This flaw has, however, been remedied under threshold level set out in the 2001 Regulations. The 13 categories set out in Pt II of Sch.5 include:

- agriculture, silviculture and aquaculture;
- extractive industry;
- energy industry;
- production and processing of metals;
- mineral industry;
- chemical industry;
- food industry;
- textile leather, wood and paper industries;
- rubber industry;
- infrastructure projects;
- other projects;
- tourism and leisure; and
- changes, extensions, development and testing, etc.

Even where the development falls below the threshold requirements of Sch.5, an EIA may also be required for a development which is deemed to be likely to have significant effects on the environment based on the criteria set out in Sch.7 of the 2001 Regulations. Article 92 of the Regulations defines a sub-threshold development as a development of a type set out in Sch.5 which does not exceed the quantity, area or other limit specified in the Schedule. Schedule 7 sets out three criteria in this respect in relation to the characteristics of the proposed development; the location of the proposed development; and the characteristics of potential impacts.

Prescribed information regarding environmental impact statements

1–207   **177.—(1)** The Minister may prescribe the information that is to be contained in an environmental impact statement.

(2) Any reference in an enactment to the information to be contained in an environmental impact statement specified under *Article 25 of the European Communities (Environmental Impact Assessment) Regulations, 1989,* shall be deemed to be a reference to information prescribed under this *section.*

NOTE

By virtue of art.94 of the 2001 Regulations, the EIS must contain the information specified in para.1 of Sch.6. Paragraph 1 of Sch.6 sets out this information as:

- a description of the proposed development, comprising information on the site, design and size of the proposed development;
- a description of the measures envisaged in order to avoid, reduce and, if possible, remedy significant adverse effects;
- the date required to identify and assess the main effects which the proposed development is likely to have on the environment;
- an outline of the main alternatives studied by the developer and an indication of the main reasons for his or her choice, taking into account the effects on the environment.

Also, art.94 provides that the EIS shall contain the information specified in para.2 of Sch.6 to the extent that:

- such information is relevant to a given stage of the consent procedure and to the

specific characteristics of the development or type of development concerned and of the environmental features likely to be affected; and
- the person or persons preparing the EIS may reasonably be required to compile such information having regard, among other things, to current knowledge and methods of assessment.

Article 94 also provides that the EIS shall contain a summary in non-technical language of the information required. In considering whether an EIS fulfils the requirements of information to be contained in an EIS an over-formalistic approach should not be adopted. See *Klohn v An Bord Pleanála*, unreported, High Court, McMahon J., April 23, 2008, where it was said:

"To adopt such an approach would stifle commendable progress and render the planning system unworkable. Bearing in mind that the assessment is a dynamic process which is much more important than the original EIS, which merely sets out the agenda, and that substance is more important than form, the crucial question is: whether the EIS is so deficient as to prevent a subsequent proper assessment by the decision maker or is such as to deprive the relevant parties in the process (or the public where relevant) of a real opportunity to participate".

See *R (Burkett) v London Borough of Hammersmith and Fulham* [2003] All E.R. (D) 203. In *R. (Blewett) v Derbyshire County Council* [2004] J.P.L. 751 O'Sullivan J. said:

"[I]t is an unrealistic counsel of perfection to expect that an applicant's environmental statement will always contain the 'full information' about the environmental impact of a project. The Regulations are not based upon such an unrealistic expectation. They recognise that an environmental statement may well be deficient and make provision through the publicity and consultation processes for any deficiencies to be identified so that the resulting 'environmental information' provides the local planning authority with as full a picture as possible. There will be cases where the document purporting to be an environmental statement is so deficient that it could not reasonably be described as an environmental statement as defined in the Regulations but they are likely to be few and far between".

PART XI

DEVELOPMENT BY LOCAL AND STATE AUTHORITIES, ETC.

Restrictions on development by certain local authorities

178.—(1) The council of a county shall not effect any development in its functional area, exclusive of any borough or urban district, which contravenes materially the development plan.   **1–208**

(2) The corporation of a county or other borough shall not effect any development in the borough which contravenes materially the development plan.

(3) The council of an urban district shall not effect any development in the district which contravenes materially the development plan.

NOTE

This section prohibits local authority development which is in material contravention of the development plan. The phrase "shall not effect" any development means that this prohibition extends to development carried out by the local authority itself or which it causes others to carry out. This constitutes the principal restriction to local authority development, as local authority development is generally exempt under s.4. A similar prohibition was contained in s.39 of the 1963 Act, which was invoked to prohibit certain development. It is well established that any member of the public can seek to restrain local authority development in material contravention of the development plan. See *Attorney-General (McGarry) v Sligo County Council* [1991] 1 I.R. 99. It appears that substantial local authority development must be included in the development plan, otherwise it will be prohibited. It is necessary for a local authority to include all of its objectives in its plan, otherwise it would mean that the local authority could totally override its own plan; see *Keogh v Galway Corporation (No. 2)* [1995] 3 I.R. 457; *Roughan v Clare County Council*, unreported, High Court, Barron J., December 18, 1996 and *Wicklow Heritage Trust Ltd v Wicklow County Council*, unreported, High Court, McGuinness J., February 5, 1998. In order for a development to be a material contravention, there must be a contravention and this contravention must be material. Material in this respect means material in planning terms. In order to amount to a contravention, the provision of the development plan must be of sufficient specificity so as to constitute contravention. Some provisions of a development plan may be of such a broad and general nature, that it is not strictly possible to describe any specific development as being a contravention. Also the plan must be read as a whole; the mere fact that a development is consistent with certain objectives does not mean that it cannot be in contravention of other objectives in the plan. For a more detailed discussion of notion of material contravention see the note on s.10 in relation to development plans.

There are some statutory exceptions to this general prohibition. Thus under s.20 of the Roads Act 1993, a local authority is obliged to follow a direction of the national road authority, though it may materially contravene a development plan by completing a special procedure under that Act. This include publishing a newspaper notice and inviting submissions. Also under s.4 of the Waste Management Acts 1996–2001, the prohibition on material contravention does not apply in respect of the implementation of a waste management plan. However, the manager must publish a newspaper notice and invite submissions. See also the transitional provisions under the Housing (Traveller Accommodation) Act 1998.

Local authority own development

1–209 179.—(1)

(a) The Minister may prescribe a development or a class of development for the purposes of this *section* where he or she is of the opinion that by reason of the likely size, nature or effect on the surroundings of such development or class of development there should, in relation to any such development or development belonging to such class of development, be compliance with the provisions of this *section* and regulations under this *section*.

(b) Where a local authority that is a planning authority proposes to carry out development, or development belonging to a class of development prescribed under *paragraph (a)* (hereafter in this *section* referred to as "proposed development") it shall in relation to the proposed development comply with this *section* and any regulations under this *section*.

(c) [...]

(d) This *section* shall also apply to proposed development which is carried out within the functional area of a local authority which is a planning authority, on behalf of, or in partnership with the local authority, pursuant to a contract with the local authority.

(2) The Minister shall make regulations providing for any or all of the following matters:

(a) the publication by a local authority of any specified notice with respect to proposed development;

(b) requiring local authorities to—

        (i)

            (I) notify prescribed authorities of such proposed development or classes of proposed development as may be prescribed, or

            (II) consult with them in respect thereof,

        and

        (ii) give to them such documents, particulars, plans or other information in respect thereof as may be prescribed;

    (c) the making available for inspection, by members of the public, of any specified documents, particulars, plans or other information with respect to proposed development;

    (d) the making of submissions or observations to a local authority with respect to proposed development.

(3)

    (a) The manager of a local authority shall, after the expiration of the period during which submissions or observations with respect to the proposed development may be made, in accordance with regulations under *subsection (2),* prepare a written report in relation to the proposed development and submit the report to the members of the authority.

    (b) A report prepared in accordance with *paragraph (a)* shall—

        (i) describe the nature and extent of the proposed development and the principal features thereof, and shall include an appropriate plan of the development and appropriate map of the relevant area,

        (ii) evaluate whether or not the proposed development would be consistent with the proper planning and sustainable development of the area to which the development relates, having regard to the provisions of the development plan and giving the reasons and the considerations for the evaluation,

        (iii) list the persons or bodies who made submissions or observations with respect to the proposed development in accordance with the regulations under *subsection (2),*

        (iv) summarise the issues, with respect to the proper planning and sustainable development of the area in which the proposed development would be situated, raised in any such submissions or observations, and give the response of the manager thereto, and

        (v) recommend whether or not the proposed development should be proceeded with as proposed, or as varied or modified as recommended in the report, or should not be proceeded with, as the case may be.

(4)

    (a) The members of a local authority shall, as soon as may be, consider the proposed development and the report of the manager under *subsection (3).*

    (b) Following the consideration of the manager's report under *paragraph (a),* the proposed development may be carried out as recommended in the manager's report, unless the local authority, by resolution, decides to vary or modify the development, otherwise than as recommended in the manager's report, or decides not to proceed with the development.

    (c) A resolution under *paragraph (b)* must be passed not later than 6 weeks after receipt of the manager's report.

(5) [*Sections 138, 139 and 140 of the Local Government Act, 2001,*] shall not apply to development under this *section.*

(6) This *section* shall not apply to proposed development which—

    (a) consists of works of maintenance or repair, other than works which would materially affect the character of a protected structure or proposed protected structure,

    (b) is necessary for dealing urgently with any situation which the manager considers is an emergency situation calling for immediate action,

    (c) consists of works which a local authority is required by or under statute or by order of a court to undertake, or

    (d) is development in respect of which an environmental impact statement is required under *section 175* or under any other enactment.

AMENDMENT HISTORY

Subsection (5) was amended by s.5 of the Local Government Act 2001 (No. 37 of 2001), which, by the Local Government Act 2001 (Commencement) (No. 3) Order 2001 (S.I. No. 588 of 2001), came into effect on January 1, 2002.

Subsection (1)(c) repealed by s.247 of the Local Government Act 2001 (No. 37 of 2001), which, by the Local Government Act 2001 (Commencement) Order 2001 (S.I. No. 458 of 2001), came into effect on October 9, 2001.

NOTE

This section sets out a public consultation procedure which must be followed with respect to certain prescribed local authority development. It also applies to development carried out in partnership with any person or on behalf of the planning authority. The current section allows for regulations to be prescribed, which are contained in Pt 8 of the Planning Regulation 2001. Article 80 declares that the procedure applies to the following classes of development:

    (a) the construction or erection of a house;

    (b) the construction of a new road or the widening or realignment of an existing road, where the length of the new road or of the widened or realigned portion of the existing road, as the case may be, would be:

      i. in the case of a road in an urban area, 100 metres or more; or

      ii. in the case of a road in any other area, 1 kilometre or more;

    (c) the construction of a bridge or tunnel;

    (d) the construction or erection of pumping stations, treatment works, holding tanks or outfall facilities for waste water or storm water;

    (e) the construction or erection of water intake or treatment works, overground aqueducts or dams or other installations designed to hold water or to store it on a long-term basis;

    (f) drilling for water supplies;

    (g) the construction of a swimming pool;

    (h) the use of land, or the construction or erection of any installation or facility, for the disposal of waste, not being:

      i. development which comprises or is for the purposes of an activity in relation to which a waste licence is required; or

    ii. development consisting of the provision of a bring facility which comprises not more than five receptacles;

(i) the use of land as a burial ground;

(j) the construction or erection of a fire station, a library or a public toilet; and

(k) any development other than those specified in paras (a)–(j), the estimated cost of which exceeds €126,000, not being development consisting of the laying underground of sewers, mains, pipes or other apparatus.

Article 145 of the 2001 Regulations provide that local authority development which relates to the provision of, or modification to, a major accident establishment and which could have a significant repercussions on major accident hazards is prescribed for the purposes of s.179 and the provisions therein apply. The procedure does not apply to any development set out in subs.(6). This includes under (d) proposed development for which an EIS is required under s.175. Such classes of development are set out under s.176 and Sch.4 of the 2001 Regulations. In respect of such development, a separate public consultation process applies. The procedure only applies to local authority development outside its functional area in the case of roads, bridges or tunnels. A further exception under (c) is development necessary to deal urgently with a situation which the manager considers an emergency calling for immediate action. The exception is in similar terms to s.138(4) of the Local Government Act 2001 concerning the requirement to inform elected members of certain works which provides:

"Nothing in this section prevents the manager from dealing immediately with any situation which he or she considers is an emergency situation calling for immediate action without regard to subsections."

While the above s.138 is disapplied under subs.(5), it may noted by analogy that in *O'Reilly v O'Sullivan*, unreported, Supreme Court, Feburary 26, 1997, commenting on an earlier repealed provision, Keane J. said:

"It was clear that it was intended to give an artificial and extended meaning to the expression 'emergency' situation calling for immediate action which would otherwise be confined to emergencies in the conventional sense, i.e. situations which arose suddenly and unexpectedly".

It appears that it would be a matter within the discretion of the Manager to decide whether a situation is an emergency to require urgent development. However, in *Byrne v Fingal County Council* [2001] 4 I.R. 565, McKechnie J. suggested, obiter, that the power of the Manager to deal with an emergency situation calling for immediate action could not be invoked to construct a halting site which had not been indicated in the development plan. This also follows from the terms of s.178, where in relation to the prohibition on local authority development in material contravention of the development plan no exception is made for an emergency situation.

The procedure which must be followed is a combination of steps which are set out under the section and under the 2001 Regulations as amended. Article 81 provides that a local authority shall give notice of proposed development in an approved newspaper, and erect or fix a site notice or site notices on the land on which the proposed development would be situated. The mandatory content of the newspaper and site notice are set out in art.81(2). This provides that the site notice must:

(a) indicate the location, townland or postal address of the proposed development (as may be appropriate);

(b) indicate the nature and extent of the proposed development;

(c) where the proposed development consists of or comprises the carrying out of works:

    (i) which would materially affect the character of a protected structure or a proposed protected structure;

    (ii) to the exterior of a structure which is located within an architectural conservation area or an area specified as an architectural conservation area in a draft of a proposed development plan or a proposed variation of a development plan, and the development would materially affect the character of the area concerned, indicate this fact; and

(d) state that:

(i) plans and particulars of the proposed development will be available for inspection or purchase at a fee not exceeding the reasonable cost of making a copy during office hours at the offices of the local authority for a specified period (which shall be not less than six weeks beginning on the day of publication of the notice in a newspaper in accordance with sub-art.(1)(a)), [note the period was extended from four to six weeks under the 2006 Regulations];

(ii) submissions or observations with respect to the proposed development, dealing with the proper planning and sustainable development of the area in which the development would be situated, may be made in writing to the local authority before a specified date (which shall be not less than two weeks after the end of the period for inspection of plans and particulars specified pursuant to sub-paragraph (i)).This includes that plans and particulars must be available for inspection for not less than four weeks and that submissions may be made before a specified date, which is not less than two weeks after the end of the period for inspection.

Article 145 provides that where the development which relates to the provision of, or modification to, a major accident establishment and which could have a significant repercussions on major accident hazards, the site notice must indicate that fact. Article 81(3) prescribes the physical nature of the site notice and art.81(4) states that where the land does not adjoin a public road, it should be erected in a conspicuous position, easily visible by persons outside. Article 81(5) states that the site notice must be erected not later than the publication of the newspaper notice and must be maintained for at least two weeks. Article 82 states that the local authority must send notice of the proposed development to the prescribed bodies set out in art.82(3), as amended by the 2006 Regulations, depending on the nature of the development. In the case of development which relates to the provision of, or modification to, a major accident establishment and which could have a significant repercussions on major accident hazards, art.147 provides that notice must be sent to the Health and Safety Authority. Article 83 as amended, provides that the local authority must make available for inspection or purchase certain documents, particulars, maps and layout plans. Although the public consultation is a public process, it is possible that fair procedures may supplement the general requirements depending on the nature of development and the parties affected. In *Aughey Enterprise Ltd v Monaghan County Council*, unreported, High Court, Sheehan J., June 4, 2008, in the context of a road bypass, project development in carrying out a process under s.179, the applicants were allegedly assured at a meeting that a roundabout would include a fifth arm. However, on the facts, a claim of legitimate expectation was rejected where the court rejected that any such assurance was given.

Subsection (3) provides that at the end of the period for submissions, the manager must prepare a written report, stating the nature and extent of the development, whether it is consistent with proper planning and development, list the persons who made submissions, the issues raised and also recommend whether the development should advance as proposed or whether it should be varied, modified or refused. The requirements of the report which must be prepared by the manager is more extensive than the reports which the manager prepares in respect of submissions received from members of the public in relation to the development plan or a variation of the development plan under ss.11(4), 12(4) or 13(4). In addition to dealing with the submissions, the report must:

- describe the nature and extent of the proposed development and its principal feature;
- include an appropriate plan of the development;
- include an appropriate map of the relevant area;
- evaluate whether or not the proposed development would be consistent with the planning and development of the area having regard to the provisions of the development plan; and
- give the reasons and consideration for the evaluation.

Article 148 of the 2001 Regulations provide that as regards development which relates to the provision of, or modification to, a major accident establishment and which could have a significant repercussions on major accident hazards, the report shall include a copy of any relevant technical advice received from the Health and Safety Authority. As regards the requirement to summarise the submissions, by analogy with the preparation of a report by the Manager in the making or variation of a development, there is no obligation to circulate to each member of the planning authority the entirety of the objections and submissions received, prior to their consideration of the proposal. See *Sandyford Environmental Planning v Dun Laoghaire Rathdown County Council*, unreported, High Court, McKechnie J. June 30, 2004, where the court rejected a claim that that the manager was so influenced by institutional bias that he was incapable of compiling an objective report. In summarising the submissions the manager is not bound to use any formula or follow any specified method.

Under subs.(4), the elected members must consider the proposed development and report of the manager "as soon as may be". The elected members having considered the report, the development may be carried out as recommended unless the local authority passes a resolution within six weeks, deciding to vary, modify or not to proceed. The requirement to pass a resolution within six weeks is mandatory where the Council's wishes to vary the development. However, this does not mean that that the Council cannot change its mind outside the six weeks to cancel a variation. See *Daibhis v South Dublin County Council*, unreported, High Court, Murphy J., December 14,2007, the Council decided by resolution of the December 12, 2005 to modify a proposed development pursuant to s.179(4)(b) to provide for an increase of playing area and alterations to stand facilities to facilitate other sports and uses subject to funding. Where it ascertained funding was not available, on February 13, 2006, it issued another resolution which was outside the six-week period from consideration of the manager's report, resolving to proceeding with the development as originally planned without the modification. It was held in the circumstances, if the time limit were to apply, such time limits were merely directory. The requirements of justice in the substance of the procedure had been observed and there was no prejudice to the applicants.

If the planning authority decides to vary or amend the scheme, there is no requirement to re-advertise the scheme and again allow for objections from the public; see *Duffy v Waterford Corporation*, unreported, High Court, McGuinness J., July 21, 1999. Article 84 provides that the local authority must send notice of its decision to the prescribed bodies notified and any person who made submissions. Where the development which relates to the provision of, or modification to, a major accident establishment and which could have a significant repercussions on major accident hazards, art.149 provides that notice shall also be sent to the Health and Safety Authority. Article 85 concerns transitional arrangements.

Section 36(21) of the Water Services Act 2007 provides that in considering a proposed development under s.179 of the 2000 Act, a local authority shall not decide that the development should not be proceeded with solely on the grounds that the said development is not specifically referred to in the water services strategic plan in force in relation to the functional area of the authority if the authority considers the development will facilitate the achievement of the objectives of that water services strategic plan.

Subsection (5) provides that the provisions under ss.138 to 140 of the Local Government Act 2001 do not apply to development covered by the section. This includes under s.137 the requirement that the manager shall inform the elected council or joint body concerned before any works (other than works of maintenance or repair) of the local authority or joint body concerned are undertaken, or before committing the local authority or joint body concerned to any expenditure in connection with proposed works (other than works of maintenance or repair). Also inapplicable is the general power of the elected members under s.139 of the Local Government Act 2001 to direct that these works will not proceed. Also unavailable is the power of the elected members under s.140, to require any particular act, matter or thing, to be done or effected by the manager. These exclusion therefore significantly limit the power of elected members to interfere with or frustrate the development.

Apart from the general consultation procedure, there is no requirement for a local authority to consult with neighbouring owners before developing its own land; see *Wilkinson v Dublin County Council* [1991] I.L.R.M. 605. Section 100 of the Waste Management Act 2001, as inserted by s.26(2)(d) of the Protection of the Environment Act 2003, provides that in performing their functions under the Planning Acts 2000 to 2002, in particular under Pt III, ss.175 or 179, planning authorities and An Bord Pleanála shall ensure that such measures as are reasonably necessary are taken to secure the appropriate provision for the management of waste.

Taking in charge of estates

1–210   **180.**—**(1)** Where a development for which permission is granted under *section 34* or under *Part IV of the Act of 1963* includes the construction of 2 or more houses and the provision of new roads, open spaces, car parks, sewers, watermains or drains, and the development has been completed to the satisfaction of the planning authority in accordance with the permission and any conditions to which the permission is subject, the authority shall, where requested by the person carrying out the development, or, subject to *subsection (3)*, by the majority of the qualified electors who are owners or occupiers of the houses involved, as soon as may be, initiate the procedures under *section 11 of the Roads Act, 1993*.

(2)

    (a) Notwithstanding *subsection (1)*, where the development has not been completed to the satisfaction of the planning authority and enforcement proceedings have not been commenced by the planning authority within seven years beginning on the expiration, as respects the permission authorising the development, of the appropriate period, within the meaning of *section 40* or the period as extended under *section 42*, as the case may be, the authority shall, where requested by the majority of qualified electors who own or occupy the houses in question, comply with *section 11 of the Roads Act, 1993*, except that *subsection (1)(b)(ii) of that section* shall be disregarded.

    (b) In complying with *paragraph (a)*, the authority may apply any security given under *section 34(4)(g)* for the satisfactory completion of the development in question.

(3)

    (a) The planning authority may hold a plebiscite to ascertain the wishes of the qualified electors.

    (b) The Minister may make or apply any regulations prescribing the procedure to be followed by the planning authority in ascertaining the wishes of the qualified electors.

(4) Where an order is made under *section 11(1) of the Roads Act, 1993*, in compliance with this *section*, the planning authority shall, in addition to the provisions of that *section*, take in charge any open spaces, car parks, sewers, watermains, or drains within the attendant grounds of the development.

(5) Where a planning authority acts in compliance with this *section*, references in *section 11 of the Roads Act, 1993*, to a road authority shall be deemed to include references to a planning authority.

(6) In this *section*, "qualified electors" *means every person who, in relation to the area of the dwelling houses in question, is registered as a local government elector in the register of local government electors for the time being in force.*

NOTE

    This section obliges a local authority to take charge of the roads of housing estates in certain circumstances. For the section to apply there must be development for which permission was granted which involves the construction of two or more houses and the provision of new roads, open spaces, car parks, sewers, watermains or drains. The mechanism by which these matters are taken in charge is by making an order pursuant to s.11 of the Roads Act 1993 which states:

"A road authority may, by order, declare any road over which a public right of way exists to be a public road, and every such road shall be deemed to be a public road and responsibility for its maintenance shall lie on the road authority".

Where such an order is made, subs.(4) declares that the planning authority shall also take in charge open spaces, car parks, sewers, watermains or drains within the attendant grounds of the development. Section 11 of the Roads Act 1993 sets out a procedure to be followed before such a declaration may be made. The precise meaning of "take in charge" is not defined. However, it appears to involve assuming responsibility for the maintenance of the matters taken in charge. It may be noted that a condition of planning permission under s.34(4)(m) may expressly provide for the taking in charge of certain specified matters.

Subsection (1), provides that where the development has been completed to the satisfaction of the planning authority in accordance with the permission and conditions of permission, the local authority is obliged to commence the procedure under s.11 when requested by the person carrying out the development or when requested by a majority of qualified electors who are owners or occupiers of the houses involved. However, the obligation is merely to initiate the procedure under s.11; the section does not say that it is obliged to take in charge the matters. Nonetheless the planning authority has no discretion to decline to initiate such procedure in such circumstances and an order of mandamus could compel the planning authority to do so. The planning authority must initiate such procedure "as soon as may be". As to the meaning of this phrase see See *Harding v Cork County Council*, unreported, Supreme Court, May 2, 2008, where it was said the phrase must be interpreted having regard to the ordinary burdens of administration in any organisation or body. The development must be both complete and fully in accordance with planning permission before this obligation arises. It cannot arise where there is any unauthorised development except in the circumstances set out in subs.(2).

Subsection (2), provides that where the development has not been completed to the satisfaction of the planning authority and enforcement proceedings have not been commenced within seven years from when the period for carrying out the development expired, the planning authority is obliged to initiate the procedure under s.11 of the 1993 Act where a majority of qualified electors who own or occupy houses in the development make such a request. Again this obligation is mandatory and the planning authority can be compelled to take such steps. The significance of the reference to seven years is that this is the time limitation for taking enforcement action in respect of unauthorised development under Pt VIII. Subsection (2) therefore relates to development which is unauthorised development but is immune from enforcement action, although it may be noted there is no time limit for enforcement action to enforce a condition governing the ongoing use of land. In order for subs.(2) to arise, seven years must have elapsed after the life of the planning permission. As the normal life of a planning permission is five years, this means that there must be a minimum of 12 years from the grant of permission. This period can be longer where the life of the permission was varied so as to be more than five years or where the life of the permission was extended. Under subs.(3) a plebiscite may be held to ascertain the wishes of qualified electors. However, the section does not exclude the possibility that a majority of the qualified electors can be identified by other means. For the purposes of subss.1 and 2, the request must be made by the majority of persons who are qualified electors and owners or occupiers of the houses involved. A person who is an owner or occupier will not qualify unless they are also a qualified elector under subs.(6) having being registered as a local government elector in the register of local government electors.

With respect to drains and sewers, there are other statutory means of taking these in charge. Section 43(12) of the Water Services Act 2007 provides that a water services authority (being the local authority) may, at its discretion and subject to such conditions as it may decide, take in charge a connection, which shall thereafter come under the sole control and responsibility of the water services authority. In this respect "connection" is defined as "a drain, a distribution system or a service connection and includes part of such drain, distribution system or service connection". Also s.95 of the 2007 Act provides that the local authority may by agreement take in charge or acquire all or part of waterworks or waste water works or any rights connected to it.

Development by State authorities

1–211   **181.—(1)**

(a) The Minister may, by regulations, provide that, except for this *section* [and *sections 181A to 181C*], the provisions of this *Act* shall not apply to any specified class or classes of development by or on behalf of a State authority where the development is, in the opinion of the Minister, in connection with or for the purposes of public safety or order, the administration of justice or national security or defence and, for so long as the regulations are in force, the provisions of this *Act* shall not apply to the specified class or classes of development.

(b) The Minister may, by regulations, provide for any or all of the following matters in relation to any class or classes of development to which regulations under *paragraph (a)* apply:

(i) the publication by a State authority of any specified notice with respect to development that it proposes to carry out or to have carried out on its behalf;

(ii) the giving by a State authority, to the planning authority for the area in which proposed development is to be carried out, or any other specified person, of any specified notice, documents, particulars, plans or other information with respect to the proposed development;

(iii) the making available for inspection by members of the public of any specified documents, particulars, plans or other information with respect to the proposed development;

(iv) [...]

(v) the making of submissions or observations to a State authority with respect to the proposed development;

(vi) the reference to a specified person of any dispute or disagreement, with respect to the proposed development, between a State authority and the planning authority for the area in which the proposed development is to be carried out;

(vii) requiring a State authority, in deciding whether the proposed development is to be carried out, to have regard to any specified matters or considerations.

(2)

(a) Where development is proposed to be carried out by or on behalf of a Minister of the Government or the Commissioners, the Minister of the Government concerned or, in the case of development proposed to be carried out by or on behalf of the Commissioners, the Minister for Finance, may, if he or she is satisfied that the carrying out of the development is required by reason of an accident or emergency, by order provide that this *Act* or, as may be appropriate, any requirement or requirements of regulations under *subsection (1)(b)* specified in the order, shall not apply to the development, and for so long as such an order is in force this *Act* or the said requirement or requirements, as the case may be, shall not apply to the development.

(b) A Minister of the Government may by order revoke an order made by him or her under *paragraph (a)*.

(c) A Minister of the Government shall cause an order made by him or her under this *subsection* to be published in Iris Oifigiúil and notice of the making of the order to be published in a newspaper circulating in the area of the development concerned.

AMENDMENT HISTORY

Subsection (1) para.(a) amended and para (b)(iv) deleted by s.35 of the Planning and Development (Strategic Infrastructure) Act 2006 (No. 27 of 2006).

NOTE

This section allows for the prescription of certain rules concerning development carried out by state authorities. Unlike local authority development, state authority development is not generally exempted development and so planning permission is required; see *Howard v Commissioner of Public Works* [1994] 1 I.R. 101. Subsection (1) allows for regulations declaring that the requirements under the Act such as to obtain planning permission does not apply to certain developments concerning public safety or order, the administration of justice, or national security or defence. It goes to provide that instead of the planning permission, the Minister may make regulations for a public consultation process in respect of such development. In this respect Pt 9 of the 2001 Regulations sets out the regulations regarding certain state authority development. Article 86 designates the development for the purposes of subs.(1)(a). Among the development listed are:

- garda stations;
- prisons;
- courthouses;
- barracks;
- office relating to the legislature and Ministerial departments;
- extensions to the previously enlisted buildings, where the any of the previous buildings are a protected structure works within the curtilage of such development;
- works within the curtilage of such buildings for reasons of national security;
- development within the curtilage of the residence of certain public officeholders or servants; and
- development within the curtilage of a person in receipt of Garda protection.

Article 87 as amended by the 2006 Regulations, provides for public notice of the proposed development, which includes a newspaper notice and site notice which must, inter alia, invite submissions from the public and which must be within six weeks from the date of publication in the case of a newspaper notice. No period is specified in respect of the site notice. However, excluded from the public notice requirements are:

- development consisting of the construction or erection of such temporary structures for the purposes of or in connection with the operations of the Defence Forces or An Garda Síochána as are urgently required for reasons of national security; or
- development identified as likely to have significant effects on the environment in accordance with s.176 of the Act.

Article 88 requires notice of the proposed development to be given to certain bodies. Article 89 concerns the availability for inspection of plans and particulars, which must be at the locations and times specified during the period of six weeks beginning on the date of the notice of the proposed development (the period was extended from four to six weeks under the 2006 Regulations). Article 90 requires state authorities to have regard to submissions made by any planning authority in deciding whether to carry out the proposed development with or without modification. Article 91 requires notice of the decision to the planning authority in which the development is situated, as well as notice to persons who made submissions. It may be noted that Pt IV of the Prisons Act 2007, now governs the construction and erection of prisons.

Subsection (2) allows that a Minister or the Commissioner may by order disapply the requirements of the regulations where the development is required by reason of an accident or emergency. The order must be published in the official publications and in a newspaper notice. The 2006 Act amended the section to provide that the general provisions of the Act will not apply to state authority development except ss.181, 181A and 181C. Section 181B(12) provides that for a state authority development which requires an EIS, which would otherwise fall within the public consultation procedure, the procedure set out in s.181A to 181C will apply instead of the procedures under Pt 9 of the Regulations.

[Approval of certain State development requiring environmental impact assessment

1–212   **181A.—(1)** Subject to *section 181B(4),* where a State authority proposes to carry out or have carried out development—

  (a) of a class specified in regulations made under *section 181(1)(a),* and

  (b) identified as likely to have significant effects on the environment in accordance with *section 176,* (hereafter referred to in this section and *sections 181B and 181C* as "proposed development"), the authority shall prepare, or cause to be prepared, an application for approval of the development under *section 181B* and an environmental impact statement in respect of the development and shall apply to the Board for such approval accordingly.

(2) Subject to *section 181B(4),* the proposed development shall not be carried out unless the Board has approved it with or without modifications.

(3) Before a State authority makes an application for approval under *subsection (1),* it shall—

  (a) publish in one or more newspapers circulating in the area or areas in which it is proposed to carry out the development a notice indicating the nature and location of the proposed development and—

  (i) stating that—

    (I) it proposes to seek the approval of the Board for the proposed development,

    (II) an environmental impact statement has been prepared in respect of the proposed development,

    (III) where relevant, the proposed development is likely to have significant effects on the environment in another Member State of the European Communities or other party to the Transboundary Convention,

  (ii) specifying the times and places at which, and the period (not being less than 6 weeks) during which, a copy of the application and the environmental impact statement may be inspected free of charge or purchased on payment of a specified fee (which fee shall not exceed the reasonable cost of making such copy),

  (iii) inviting the making, during such period, of submissions and observations to the Board relating to—

    (I) the implications of the proposed development for proper planning and sustainable development in the area or areas concerned, and

    (II) the likely effects on the environment of the proposed development, if carried out, and

(iv) specifying the types of decision the Board may make, under *section 181B,* in relation to the application,

(b) send a copy of the application and the environmental impact statement to the local authority or each local authority in whose functional area the proposed development would be situate and to any prescribed bodies, together with a notice stating that submissions or observations may, during the period referred to in *paragraph (a)(ii),* be made in writing to the Board in relation to—

    (i) the implications of the proposed development for proper planning and sustainable development in the area concerned, and

    (ii) the likely effects on the environment of the proposed development, if carried out, and

(c) where the proposed development is likely to have significant effects on the environment of a Member State of the European Communities or a state which is a party to the Transboundary Convention, send a prescribed number of copies of the application and the environmental impact statement to the prescribed authority of the relevant state or states together with a notice stating that submissions or observations may, during the period referred to in *paragraph (a)(ii),* be made in writing to the Board.

(4) The Board may—

(a) if it considers it necessary to do so, require a State authority that has applied for approval for a proposed development to furnish to the Board such further information in relation to the effects on proper planning and sustainable development or the environment of the proposed development as the Board may specify, or

(b) if it is provisionally of the view that it would be appropriate to approve the proposed development were certain alterations (specified in the notification referred to in this paragraph) to be made to the terms of it, notify the State authority that it is of that view and invite the State authority to make to the terms of the proposed development alterations specified in the notification and, if the State authority makes those alterations, to furnish to it such information (if any) as it may specify in relation to the development, in the terms as so altered, or, where necessary, a revised environmental impact statement in respect of it.

(5) If a State authority makes the alterations to the terms of the proposed development specified in a notification given to it under *subsection (4),* the terms of the development as so altered shall be deemed to be the proposed development for the purposes of this section and *section 181B.*

(6) The Board shall—

(a) where it considers that any further information received pursuant to a requirement made under *subsection (4)(a)* contains significant additional data relating to—

    (i) the likely effects on the environment of the proposed development, and

    (ii) the likely consequences for proper planning and sustainable development in the area or areas in which it is proposed to situate the said development of such development,

or

(b) where the State authority has made the alterations to the terms of the proposed development specified in a notification given to it under *subsection (4)(b),* require the State authority to do the things referred to in *subsection (7).*

(7) The things which a State authority shall be required to do as aforesaid are—

    (a) to publish in one or more newspapers circulating in the area or areas in which the proposed development would be situate a notice stating that, as appropriate—

        (i) further information in relation to the proposed development has been furnished to the Board, or

        (ii) the State authority has, pursuant to an invitation of the Board, made alterations to the terms of the proposed development (and the nature of those alterations shall be indicated) and, if it be the case, that information in relation to the terms of the development as so altered or a revised environmental impact statement in respect of the development has been furnished to the Board, indicating the times at which, the period (which shall not be less than 3 weeks) during which and the place, or places, where a copy of the information or the environmental impact statement referred to in *subparagraph (i) or (ii)* may be inspected free of charge or purchased on payment of a specified fee (which fee shall not exceed the reasonable cost of making such copy) and that submissions or observations in relation to that information or statement may be made to the Board before the expiration of the indicated period, and

    (b) to send to each prescribed authority to which a notice was given pursuant to *subsection (3)(b) or (c)* —

        (i) a notice of the furnishing to the Board of, as appropriate, the further information referred to in *paragraph (a)(i)* or the information or statement referred to in *paragraph (a)(ii),* and

        (ii) a copy of that further information, information or statement, and to indicate to the authority that submissions or observations in relation to

that further information, information or statement may be made to the Board before the expiration of a period (which shall be not less than 3 weeks) beginning on the day on which the notice is sent to the prescribed authority by the State authority.]

AMENDMENT HISTORY

Inserted by s.36 of the Planning and Development (Strategic Infrastructure) Act 2006 (No. 27 of 2006).

NOTE

This section concerns the approval of certain state authority development which requires an EIS. State authority development which is identified in the Regulations as having significant effect on the environment, will require approval by the Board. An application for approval with the EIS must be submitted to the Board. The Board will conduct an EIA on the development which will be principally based on the EIS. For the distinction between an EIA and EIS see *Klohn v An Bord Pleanála*, unreported, High Court, McMahon J., April 23, 2008. Article 214 of the 2001 Regulations (as inserted by the 2006 Regulations) provides that when making an application for strategic infrastructure development, the applicant shall send to the Board:

- 10 copies of the plans and particulars of the proposed development (including any plans, particulars or other information indicated by the Board under art.210(2)) and of the EIS;
- a copy of the published newspaper notice in accordance as may be appropriate;
- a list of the bodies notified of the application, as may be appropriate, and an indication of the date on which notice was sent; and
- a list of any other public notice given or other public consultations conducted by the applicant, including any notice or consultations done on foot of a requirement by the Board under art.210, and an indication of the date or dates of such additional notice or consultations.

Article 214(2) states that where the Board so consents or specifies, any or all of the copies or other information specified in sub-art.(1) shall be given in electronic form.

Under subs.(3), before lodging the application, the state authority must publish a newspaper notice specifying certain mandatory matters. The notice must refer to the proposed application and the EIS and state, where applicable, if the development affects the environment of another Member State and specify the time and place where the matter may be inspected, which must be for a period of not less than six weeks. Article 212 of the 2001 Regulations as amended provides that any notice which an applicant is required to give to the public shall indicate the types of decision the Board can make in relation to the application. The notice must also invite submissions relating to the implications of the development on proper planning and development and the likely effects on the environment, allowing a period of not less than six weeks and must further specify the types of decision the Board may make. Article 217 of the 2001 Regulations as amended prescribes a specific form in which any submissions must be made. The Board shall acknowledge in writing the receipt of any submission or observation as soon as may be following receipt of the submission or observation. Any submissions or observations that do not comply with the prescribed form shall not be considered by the Board. A person who makes submissions or observations to the Board shall not be entitled to elaborate upon the submissions or observations or make further submissions or observations except where the Board before making its decision asks any person to make submissions or observations or elaborate upon submissions or observations in relation to an application. A copy of the application and EIS must be sent to local authorities whose area are affected, to prescribed bodies and where applicable, to the prescribed bodies of other Member States (or Transboundary states) whose environments are likely to be affected—with written submissions being invited from them.

Under subs.(4), the Board may request the state authority to submit further information or if it is of the view that the development should be approved if altered, invite the state authority to alter the proposed development and submit information relating to such alteration, along with a revised EIS, if necessary. Article 218 of the 2001 Regulations as amended allows the Board some further powers whereby the Board may request further submissions either from the applicant, from persons who made submissions or from other persons. It also allows the Board to make information available for inspection, to notify the public, to invite further submissions and to hold meeting (for which a record must be kept). Under subs.(6), the Board will require the state authority to publish a notice where it considers that the further information received contains significant additional information regarding the likely effects on the environment and the likely consequences for the proper planning and sustainable development of the area where the proposed development is situated. In any proceeding to challenge a decision of the Board not to require a notice, the courts will defer to the decision of the Board that such information was not significant unless such decision was irrational. See *Kinsella v Dundalk Town Council,* unreported, High Court, Kelly J., December 3, 2004, and *Dietacaron Ltd v An Bord Pleanála* [2005] 2 I.L.R.M. 32 and *White v Dublin City Council* [2004] 1 I.R. 545. A notice is also required where the Board invites the state authority to alter the terms of the proposed development. In the latter case, there is a requirement to publish a notice irrespective of whether the alteration reflects significant additional information regarding the likely effects on the environment and likely consequences for proper planning and sustainable development. The notice must, inter alia, invite submissions, allowing a period of not less than three weeks. Both a notice and a copy of the further information together with information concerning alterations or revised EIS must be sent to the prescribed bodies, allowing a period of not less than three weeks to make submissions.

[Section 181A: criteria for decision, certain exemptions, etc.

1–213   **181B.—(1)** Before making a decision in respect of a proposed development the subject of an application under *section 181A,* the Board shall consider—

   (a) the environmental impact statement submitted pursuant to *section 181A(1) or (4),* any submissions or observations made in accordance with *section 181A(3) or (7)* and any other information furnished in accordance with *section 181A(4)* relating to—

      (i) the likely consequences for proper planning and sustainable development in the area in which it is proposed to situate the proposed development of such development, and

      (ii) the likely effects on the environment of the proposed development,

   and

   (b) the report and any recommendations of a person conducting any oral hearing relating to the proposed development.

(2) The Board may, where it is satisfied that exceptional circumstances so warrant, grant an exemption in respect of proposed development from a requirement under *section 181A(1)* to prepare an environmental impact statement except that no exemption may be granted in respect of proposed development where another Member State of the European Communities or a state which is a party to the Transboundary Convention has indicated that it wishes to furnish views on the effects on the environment in that Member State or state of the proposed development.

(3) The Board shall, in granting an exemption under *subsection (2),* consider whether—

   (a) the effects, if any, of the proposed development on the environment should be assessed in some other manner, and

   (b) the information arising from such an assessment should be made available to the members of the public, and it may apply such requirements regarding these matters in relation to the application for approval as it considers necessary or appropriate.

(4) The Minister for Defence may, in the case of proposed development in connection with, or for the purposes of, national defence, grant an exemption in respect of the development from a requirement under *section 181A(1)* to apply for approval and prepare an environmental impact statement if he or she is satisfied that the application of *section 181A or 181C* would have adverse effects on those purposes.

(5) Notice of any exemption granted under *subsection (2) or (4),* of the reasons for granting the exemption and, where appropriate, of any requirements applied under *subsection (3)* shall, as soon as may be—

    (a) be published in *Iris Oifigiúil* and in at least one daily newspaper published in the State, and

    (b) be given, together with a copy of the information, if any, made available to the members of the public in accordance with *subsection (3),* to the Commission of the European Communities.

(6) The Board may, in respect of an application under *section 181A* for approval of proposed development—

    (a) approve the proposed development,

    (b) make such modifications to the proposed development as it specifies in the approval and approve the proposed development as so modified,

    (c) approve, in part only, the proposed development (with or without specified modifications of it of the foregoing kind), or

    (d) refuse to approve the proposed development, and may attach to an approval under *paragraph (a), (b) or (c)* such conditions as it considers appropriate.

(7) Without prejudice to the generality of the foregoing power to attach conditions, the Board may attach to an approval under *subsection (6)(a), (b) or (c)* a condition requiring—

    (a) the construction or the financing, in whole or in part, of the construction of a facility, or

    (b) the provision or the financing, in whole or in part, of the provision of a service, in the area in which the proposed development would be situated, being a facility or service that, in the opinion of the Board, would constitute a substantial gain to the community.

(8) A condition attached pursuant to *subsection (7)* shall not require such an amount of financial resources to be committed for the purposes of the condition being complied with as would substantially deprive the person in whose favour the approval under this section operates of the benefits likely to accrue from the grant of the approval.

(9) The Minister may make regulations to provide for such matters of procedure and administration as appear to the Minister to be necessary or expedient in respect of consultations under *section 181C* or applications for approval under *section 181A.*

(10) Without prejudice to the generality of *subsection (9),* regulations under that subsection may make provision for requiring the Board to give information in respect of its decision regarding the proposed development for which approval is sought.

(11) In considering under *subsection (1)* information furnished relating to the likely consequences for proper planning and sustainable development of a proposed development in the area in which it is proposed to situate such development, or on the environment, the Board shall have regard to—

    (a) the provisions of the development plan for the area,

    (b) the provisions of any special amenity area order relating to the area,

(c) if the area or part of the area is a European site or an area prescribed for the purposes of *section 10(2)(c),* that fact,

(d) if the proposed development would have an effect on a European site or an area prescribed for the purposes of *section 10(2)(c),* that fact,

(e) where relevant, the matters referred to in *section 143,* and

(f) the provisions of this Act and regulations under this Act where relevant.

(12) Regulations made under *section 181(1)(b)* shall not apply to any development which is approved under this section.

(13) Nothing in this section or *section 181A or 181C* shall require the disclosure by a State authority or the Board of details of the internal arrangements of a development which might prejudice the internal or external security of the development or facilitate any unauthorised entrance to, or exit from, the development of any person when it is completed.

(14) Without prejudice to the generality of *section 18(a) of the Interpretation Act 2005,* a reference, however expressed, in this section to the area in which the proposed development would be situated includes, if the context admits, a reference to the 2 or more areas in which the proposed development would be situated and cognate references shall be construed accordingly.]

AMENDMENT HISTORY

Inserted by s.36 of the Planning and Development (Strategic Infrastructure) Act 2006 (No. 27 of 2006).

NOTE

This section concerns the determination of the Board on an application for state authority development which requires an EIS. The Board must carry out an EIA of the development based on the information. For the distinction between an EIA and EIS see *Klohn v An Bord Pleanála*, unreported, High Court, McMahon J., April 23, 2008. The matters set out in subs.(1)(a) concern the matters to be considered as part of this assessment, which include the EIS, submissions received and any other information concerning the likely consequences for proper planning and sustainable development and the likely effects on the environment. The Board must also consider the report and recommendation of a person conducting an oral hearing. In making its determination under this section, the Board must have regard to the matters specified in subs.(11).

Subsection (3) allows the Board in respect of certain state authority development, to grant an exemption from the requirement to prepare an EIS. An exemption cannot be granted where another Member State or a State which is a party to the Transboundary Convention has indicated that it wishes to furnish views on the effects on the environment in that Member State or State of the proposed development. The section does not give any clear guidance regarding the exceptional circumstances when the Board may grant an exemption. In granting an exemption, the Board must consider whether the effects, if any, on the environment should be assessed in some other manner, and whether the information arising from such an assessment should be made available to the members of the public. Under subs.(4), the Minister for Defence may grant an exemption for state authority development for national defence, from both the requirement to obtain approval of the Board and the submission of an EIS where this would have an adverse effect on national defence. Notice of any exemption granted by the Board or the Minister for Defence must be published in Iris Oifigúil and in a newspaper notice. Notice (which must include a copy of the newspaper notice) must be sent to the European Commission. Subsection (6) sets out the nature of the determination by the Board. Article 219 of the 2001 Regulations, as amended, provides that the notice of the decision made by the Board shall state that, in making a decision, the Board has had regard to any submissions or observations received in accordance with the Act or the Regulations. Article 220 of the 2001 Regulations as amended states that as soon as may be following the making of its decision the Board shall publish in an approved newspaper notice of its decision, and notify the applicant concerned, the planning authority or authorities in whose area the development would be situated and any person or body who made a submission or observation in respect of the application for approval concerned. The Notice of the decision must include:

- the reference number of the application;
- the development to which the decision relates;
- the nature of the decision;
- the date of the decision;
- the main reasons and considerations on which the decision is based; and
- any conditions attached to a decision, including conditions relating to community gain and the main reasons for the imposition of any such conditions.

The Board may approve the development with or without modifications, approve part of the development or can refuse the development. The Board can issue a split decision, i.e. both granting and refusing permission. See note on s.37G. In respect of any type of approval, the Board may impose conditions.

There is a general power to impose conditions which can relate to the proper planning and sustainable development of the area. However, subs.(7) allows the Board to impose a condition which would amount to a planning gain to the community. A similar condition can be imposed in respect of local authority development under s.175(9) or in respect of approving a road scheme/road development under s.217C(3). This can consist of two types, namely; the construction of a facility or the provision of a service. The subsection gives no further guidance as to the nature of this matter except that it should be of substantial gain to the community. It appears that the gain must be to the community as a whole rather than a limited section of the community. This is not to say the gain must be of interest to all the community but merely than the gain is open to all the community. It may be a question of fact and of planning judgment as to whether there is a substantial gain to the community. Subsection (8) imposes a limit to the scope of the condition, which is that the condition must not require an amount of financial resources to be committed as would substantially deprive the person granted approval of the benefits likely to accrue from the approval. This is a mandatory requirement and any condition which would have such effect would be ultra vires. It appears that the assessment of whether a condition has such effect is not one which involves planning expertise and so the Board ought not to be shown deference in its opinion if being reviewed by a court in any proceedings. The assessment of the benefits likely to accrue will depend on the type of permission. The condition would appear to envisage the financial benefits which would accrue from any approval, which would therefore include the value of the land with the approval attached. Although the criteria are vague and difficult to apply, the inbuilt proportionality requirement may mean that it would escape a challenge on the basis constitutional invalidity. The condition may be sought to be justified on the basis that it is in the interests of the common good and that it is proportionate to its objective in accordance with the principles set out in the Article 26 reference, *Planning and Development Bill* [2002] 2 I.R. 292, in respect of Pt V of the 2000 Act. However, an applicant may decide not to implement a permission if a condition would substantially deprive an applicant of the benefits of the approval. Subsections (9) and (10) allow for making certain regulations, while subs.(12) provides that regulations under s.181 will not apply to state authority development applications made under s.181B. Subsection (13) adds a general protective clause that the state authority or Board will not be required to disclose information concerning the internal arrangements of a development which might prejudice its internal or external security or facilitate any unauthorised entrance to, or exit from, when it is completed. It will depend on the nature of the proposed development as to when this provision could apply. Subsection (14) applies to a situation where the development is situated in the area of more than one planning authority. Section 18(a) of the Interpretation Act 2005 relates to the rule that a word importing the singular shall be read as also importing the plural and vice versa.

[Procedures in advance of Seeking approval under section 181B

1–214   **181C.**—**(1)** A State authority (a "prospective applicant") which proposes to apply for approval under *section 181B* shall, before making the application, enter into consultations with the Board in relation to the proposed development.

(2) In any consultations under *subsection (1),* the Board may give advice to the prospective applicant regarding the proposed application and, in particular, regarding—

(a) the procedures involved in making the application, and

(b) what considerations, related to proper planning and sustainable development or the environment, may, in the opinion of the Board, have a bearing on its decision in relation to the application.

(3) A prospective applicant may request the Board—

(a) to make a determination of whether a development of a class specified in regulations made under *section 181(1)(a)* which it proposes to carry out or have carried out is likely to have significant effects on the environment in accordance with *section 176* (and inform the applicant of the determination), or

(b) to give to the applicant an opinion in writing prepared by the Board on what information will be required to be contained in an environmental impact statement in relation to the proposed development.

(4) On receipt of such a request, the Board shall comply with it as soon as is practicable.

(5) A prospective applicant shall, for the purposes of—

(a) consultations under *subsection (1),* and

(b) the Board's complying with a request under *subsection (3),* supply to the Board sufficient information in relation to the proposed development so as to enable the Board to assess the proposed development.

(6) Neither—

(a) the holding of consultations under *subsection (1),* nor

(b) the provision of an opinion under *subsection (3),*

shall prejudice the performance by the Board of any other of its functions under this Act or regulations under this Act, or any other enactment and cannot be relied upon in the formal planning process or in legal proceedings.

(7) The Board shall keep a record in writing of any consultations under this section in relation to a proposed development, including the names of those who participated in the consultations, and a copy of such record shall be placed and kept with the documents to which any application in respect of the proposed development relates.]

AMENDMENT HISTORY

Inserted by s.36 of the Planning and Development (Strategic Infrastructure) Act 2006 (No. 27 of 2006).

NOTE

This section requires a state authority to enter into pre-planning consultations with the Board prior to submitting an application for approval which requires an EIS under s.181B. This differs from pre-planning consultations for planning applications under s.247 insofar as the requirement for such consultations is mandatory. In such consultations, the Board may give advice regarding the procedures to be followed and also the matters relating to proper planning and sustainable or the environment which may have a bearing on the application. Under subs.(3), the state authority may request the Board to determine whether the proposed development is likely to have significant effects on the environment or what matters are to be contained within an EIS. The state authority must supply the Board with information to perform this function. Article 211(1) of the 2001 Regulations, inserted by the 2006 Regulations, prescribes specified bodies which the Board must consult as:

- the Minister for the Environment, Heritage and Local Government,
- the Environmental Protection Agency,
- the Minister for Communications, Marine and Natural Resources, and
- the relevant planning authority.

Also art.211(2) provides that the Board may invite submissions or observations in relation to the information to be contained in the EIS from the bodies referred to in art.213. The holding of the consultations or the issue of an opinion by the Board cannot prejudice the performance of its functions. Such consultation or opinion cannot create an estoppel or bind the Board and so cannot subsequently be relied upon by the state authority. The Board must keep records of pre-planning consultations and they must be kept with the application file relating to the proposed development.

Cables, wires and pipelines

182.—(1) A local authority may, with the consent of the owner and occupier   **1–215**
of any land not forming part of a public road, place, construct or lay, as may be appropriate, cables, wires or pipelines (including water pipes, sewers or drains) and any ancillary apparatus on, under or over the land, and may, from time to time, inspect, repair, alter, renew or remove any such cables, wires or pipelines.

(2) A local authority may, with the consent of the owner and of the occupier of any structure, attach to the structure any bracket or other fixture required for the carrying or support of any cable, wire or pipeline placed, erected or constructed under this *section.*

(3) A local authority may erect and maintain notices indicating the position of cables, wires or pipelines placed, erected or constructed under this *section* and may, with the consent of the owner and of the occupier of any structure, affix such a notice to the structure.

(4) *Subsections (1) to (3)* shall have effect subject to the proviso that—
- **(a)** a consent for the purposes of any of them shall not be unreasonably withheld,
- **(b)** if the local authority considers that such a consent has been unreasonably withheld, it may appeal to the Board, and
- **(c)** if the Board determines that such a consent was unreasonably withheld, it shall be treated as having been given.

(5) The local authority may permit the use of any cables, wires or pipelines placed, erected or constructed under this *section* and of any apparatus incidental to the cables, wires or pipelines subject to such conditions and charges as it considers appropriate.

NOTE

This section concerns the construction or laying of cables, wires and pipelines over private land. In general, the consent of the owner must be obtained. The local authority can construct or lay any cable or pipeline, attach to the structure any bracket or other fixture for laying the cable or pipeline, and erect and maintain notices indicating the position of the cables or pipeline. However, where the consent is not given by the owner, the local authority can apply to An Bord Pleanála, who may authorise such steps where they consider the consent was unreasonably withheld. Furthermore, under subs.(5), the local authority can permit the use of such cables or pipelines subject to such conditions and charges as it considers appropriate. In imposing such charges, planning authorities must be careful not to fall foul of Irish competition law, in particular the prohibition on the breach of a dominant position under s.6 of the Competition Act 2002. This is because such cables or pipelines may be an essential facility where there are no alternatives open to firms in a particular area; see Case C-7/79 *Bronner v Mediaprint* [1998] E.C.R. I–7791. Section 3(1) of the Competition Act 2002 defines an undertaking as "a person being an individual, a body corporate or an unincorporated body of persons engaged for gain in the production, supply or distribution of goods or the provision of a service". In *Deane v Voluntary Health Insurance Board* [1992] 2 I.R. 319, where the Supreme Court held "gain" meant acquisition and was not limted to pecuniary gain nor to commercial profits. It relates to an activity carried on for a service supplied, in return for a charge or payment. In *Greally v Minister for Education* [1995] I.L.R.M. 481, Costello J. said anybody may be an undertaking in certain circumstances. This contrast with European competition law where in general, planning authorities will not be considered "undertakings" due to their position as part of the State; see *Cali & Figli v SEPG* [1997] E.C.R. I-1547. However they may be considered undertakings where they are deemed to be carrying on economic or commercial activity. In permitting an operator to use cables or pipelines for a charge a planning authority may be deemed to be an undertaking. This will certainly be the case if they permit the use of the cables or pipelines at commercial rates. If this is the case and also if there are no alternatives, a planning authority may be deeded to be in a dominant position as regards the use of such cables or pipelines. Even if they are deemed to be an undertaking in a dominant position, they will only breach competition law where they abuse their dominance. Dominance per se is not prohibited, merely abuse of dominance. In relation to the use of the cables or pipelines, examples of where the planning authority could be held to abuse its position of dominance is, if it applied discriminatory or unfair conditions regarding access to the cables or where it imposed unfair or discriminatory charges. An arrangement to permit use of cables or pipelines, may also possibly constitute a restrictive agreement in breach of s.4 of the Competition Act 2002.

[Electricity transmission lines

1–216   **182A.—(1)** Where a person (hereafter referred to in this section as the "undertaker") intends to carry out development comprising or for the purposes of electricity transmission, (hereafter referred to in this section and *section 182B* as "proposed development"), the undertaker shall prepare, or cause to be prepared, an application for approval of the development under *section 182B* and shall apply to the Board for such approval accordingly.

(2) In the case of development referred to in *subsection (1)* which belongs to a class of development identified for the purposes of *section 176,* the undertaker shall prepare, or cause to be prepared, an environmental impact statement in respect of the development.

(3) The proposed development shall not be carried out unless the Board has approved it with or without modifications.

(4) Before an undertaker makes an application under *subsection (1)* for approval, it shall—

    (a) publish in one or more newspapers circulating in the area or areas in which it is proposed to carry out the development a notice indicating the nature and location of the proposed development and—

        (i) stating that—

       (I) it proposes to seek the approval of the Board for the proposed development,

       (II) in the case of an application referred to in *subsection (1)(a),* an environmental impact statement has been prepared in respect of the proposed development, and

       (III) where relevant, the proposed development is likely to have significant effects on the environment of a Member State of the European Communities or other party to the Transboundary Convention,

    (ii) specifying the times and places at which, and the period (not being less than 6 weeks) during which, a copy of the application and any environmental impact statement may be inspected free of charge or purchased on payment of a specified fee (which fee shall not exceed the reasonable cost of making such copy),

    (iii) inviting the making, during such period, of submissions and observations to the Board relating to—

       (I) the implications of the proposed development for proper planning and sustainable development in the area or areas concerned, and

       (II) the likely effects on the environment of the proposed development, if carried out, and

    (iv) specifying the types of decision the Board may make, under *section 182B,* in relation to the application,

(b) send a copy of the application and any environmental impact statement to the local authority or each local authority in whose functional area the proposed development would be situate and to the prescribed authorities together with a notice stating that submissions or observations may, during the period referred to in *paragraph (a)(ii),* be made in writing to the Board in relation to—

    (i) the implications of the proposed development for proper planning and sustainable development in the area or areas concerned, and

    (ii) the likely effects on the environment of the proposed development, if carried out, and

(c) where the proposed development is likely to have significant effects on the environment of a Member State of the European Communities or a state which is a party to the Transboundary Convention, send a prescribed number of copies of the application and the environmental impact statement to the prescribed authority of the relevant state or states together with a notice stating that submissions or observations may, during the period referred to in *paragraph (a)(ii),* be made in writing to the Board.

(5) The Board may—

(a) if it considers it necessary to do so, require an undertaker that has applied for approval for a proposed development to furnish to the Board such further information in relation to—

    (i) the effects on the environment of the proposed development, or

    (ii) the consequences for proper planning and sustainable development in the area or areas in which it is proposed to situate the said development of such development, as the Board may specify, or

(b) if it is provisionally of the view that it would be appropriate to approve the proposed development were certain alterations (specified in the notification referred to in this paragraph) to be made to the terms of it, notify the statutory undertaker that it is of that view and invite the undertaker to make to the terms of the proposed development alterations specified in the notification and, if the undertaker makes those alterations, to furnish to it such information (if any) as it may specify in relation to the development, in the terms as so altered, or, where necessary, a revised environmental impact statement in respect of it.

(6) If an undertaker makes the alterations to the terms of the proposed development specified in a notification given to it under *subsection (5),* the terms of the development as so altered shall be deemed to be the proposed development for the purposes of this section and *section 182B.*

(7) The Board shall—

(a) where it considers that any further information received pursuant to a requirement made under *subsection (5)(a)* contains significant additional data relating to—

(i) the likely effects on the environment of the proposed development, and

(ii) the likely consequences for proper planning and sustainable development in the area or areas in which it is proposed to situate the said development of such development, or

(b) where the undertaker has made the alterations to the terms of the proposed development specified in a notification given to it under *subsection (5)(b),* require the undertaker to do the things referred to in *subsection (8).*

(8) The things which an undertaker shall be required to do as aforesaid are—

(a) to publish in one or more newspapers circulating in the area or areas in which the proposed development would be situate a notice stating that, as appropriate—

(i) further information in relation to the proposed development has been furnished to the Board, or

(ii) the undertaker has, pursuant to an invitation of the Board, made alterations to the terms of the proposed development (and the nature of those alterations shall be indicated) and, if it be the case, that information in relation to the terms of the development as so altered or a revised environmental impact statement in respect of the development has been furnished to the Board, indicating the times at which, the period (which shall not be less than 3 weeks) during which and the place, or places, where a copy of the information or the environmental impact statement referred to in *subparagraph (i) or (ii)* may be inspected free of charge or purchased on payment of a specified fee (which fee shall not exceed the reasonable cost of making such copy) and that submissions

or observations in relation to that information or statement may be made to the Board before the expiration of the indicated period, and

(b) to send to each prescribed authority to which a notice was given pursuant to *subsection (4)(b) or (c)* —

    (i) a notice of the furnishing to the Board of, as appropriate, the further information referred to in *paragraph (a)(i)* or the information or statement referred to in *paragraph (a)(ii),* and

    (ii) a copy of that further information, information or statement, and to indicate to the authority that submissions or observations in relation to that further information, information or statement may be made to the Board before the expiration of a period (which shall be not less than 3 weeks) beginning on the day on which the notice is sent to the prescribed authority by the undertaker.

(9) In this section "transmission", in relation to electricity, shall be construed in accordance with *section 2(1) of the Electricity Regulation Act 1999* but, for the purposes of this section, the foregoing expression, in relation to electricity, shall also be construed as meaning the transport of electricity by means of—

(a) a high voltage line where the voltage would be 110 kilovolts or more, or

(b) an interconnector, whether ownership of the interconnector will be vested in the undertaker or not.]

AMENDMENT HISTORY

Inserted by s.4 of the Planning and Development (Strategic Infrastructure) Act 2006 (No. 27 of 2006).

NOTE

This section sets out a separate planning approval procedure for developments consisting of electricity and electricity transmission which are to be approved by the Board. The new section is inserted in Pt XI of the 2000 Act which concerns development by Local and State Authorities. The section refers to the applicant for approval as the "undertaker". There is no definition of "undertaker" but it would appear not to be confined to public authorities. The notion of "transmission" incorporates the definition under s.2(1) of the Electricity Regulation Act 1999, which is defined as:

"[T]he transport of electricity by means of a transmission system, that is to say, a system which consists, wholly or mainly, of high voltage lines and electric plant and which is used for conveying electricity from a generating station to a substation, from one generating station to another, from one substation to another or to or from any interconnector or to final customers but shall not include any such lines which the Board may, from time to time, with the approval of the Commission, specify as being part of the distribution system but shall include any interconnector owned by the Board".

In addition, subs.(9), states that the transport of electricity also means a high voltage line where the voltage would be 110 kilovolts or more, or an interconnector, whether ownership of the interconnector will be vested in the undertaker or not. The application for approval must be in the form set out in s.182B and must be accompanied by an EIS if it falls within the classes specified in s.176. Article 214 of the 2001 Regulations (as inserted by the 2006 Regulations) provides that when making an application for strategic infrastructure development, the applicant shall send to the Board:

- 10 copies of the plans and particulars of the proposed development (including any plans, particulars or other information indicated by the Board under art.210(2)) and of the EIS;
- a copy of the published newspaper notice in accordance as may be appropriate;
- a list of the bodies notified of the application, as may be appropriate, and an indication of the date on which notice was sent; and
- a list of any other public notice given or other public consultations conducted by the applicant, including any notice or consultations done on foot of a requirement by the Board under art.210, and an indication of the date or dates of such additional notice or consultations.

Article 214(2) states that where the Board so consents or specifies any or all of the copies or other information specified in sub-art.(1) shall be given in electronic form.

Prior to the application being lodged a newspaper notice must be published setting out the matters specified in subs.(4) including that the application and EIS may be inspected at a specified place for a period of not less than six weeks and that submissions may be made thereon. Article 217 of the 2001 Regulations as amended prescribes a specific form in which the submission must be made. The Board shall acknowledge in writing the receipt of any submission or observation as soon as may be following receipt of the submission or observation. Any submissions or observations that do not comply with the prescribed form shall not be considered by the Board. A person who makes submissions or observations to the Board shall not be entitled to elaborate upon the submissions or observations or make further submissions or observations except where the Board before making its decision asks any person to make submissions or observations or elaborate upon submissions or observations in relation to an application. Article 212 of the 2001 Regulations as amended provides that any notice which an applicant is required to give to the public shall indicate the types of decision the Board can make in relation to the application. A copy of the application and any EIS must be sent to the planning authority for the area. If it affects the environment of another Member State, a copy of the application and any EIS, must be sent to the prescribed authority of any relevant State. Article 213 of the 2001 Regulations sets out the prescribed authorities.

Subsection (5) provides that the Board may request further information where appropriate or may indicate to the applicant that it would provisionally approve permissions subject to certain alterations in the plans. Subsection (6) provides that where the applicant submits such altered plans, permission will be deemed to be granted in those terms. Where the further information includes significant additional information which is likely to both affect the environment and also affect the proper planning and sustainable development of the area, the applicant will be required to publish a newspaper notice setting out the nature of the information/alternations and inviting submissions within a period of not less than three weeks and must also send a notice to the prescribed authorities, inviting submissions within a period of not less than three weeks. It will be a matter within the planning judgment and expertise of the Board as to whether the information includes "significant additional information". See *Dietacaron Ltd v An Bord Pleanála* [2005] 2 I.L.R.M. 32. Article 218 of the 2001 Regulations as amended allows the Board some further powers under which the Board may request further submissions either from the applicant, from persons who made submissions or from other persons. It also allows the Board to make information available for inspection, to notify the public, to invite further submissions and to hold meeting (for which a record must be kept). Also where altered plans have been submitted in response to an invitation by the Board, a newspaper notice must be published along with a notice being sent to the prescribed authorities. This applies in all instances, where altered plans are submitted, regardless of whether the plans include "significant additional information".

[Section 182A: criteria for decision, certain exemptions, etc.

182B.—(1) Before making a decision in respect of a proposed development **1–217** the subject of an application under *section 182A,* the Board shall consider—

    (a) the environmental impact statement submitted pursuant to *section 182A(1) or (5),* any submissions or observations made in accordance with *section 182A(4) or (8)* and any other information furnished in accordance with *section 182A(5)* relating to—

        (i) the likely consequences for proper planning and sustainable development in the area in which it is proposed to situate the proposed development of such development, and

        (ii) the likely effects on the environment of the proposed development,

    and

    (b) the report and any recommendations of a person conducting any oral hearing relating to the proposed development.

(2) The Board may, where it is satisfied that exceptional circumstances so warrant, grant an exemption in respect of a proposed development from a requirement under *section 182A(2)* to prepare an environmental impact statement except that no exemption may be granted in respect of proposed development where another Member State of the European Communities or a state which is a party to the Transboundary Convention has indicated that it wishes to furnish views on the effects on the environment in that Member State or state of the proposed development.

(3) The Board shall, in granting an exemption under *subsection (2),* consider whether—

    (a) the effects, if any, of the proposed development on the environment should be assessed in some other manner, and

    (b) the information arising from such an assessment should be made available to the members of the public, and it may apply such requirements regarding these matters in relation to the application for approval as it considers necessary or appropriate.

(4) Notice of any exemption granted under *subsection (2),* of the reasons for granting the exemption, and of any requirements applied under *subsection (3)* shall, as soon as may be—

    (a) be published in *Iris Oifigiúil* and in at least one daily newspaper published in the State, and

    (b) be given, together with a copy of the information, if any, made available to the members of the public in accordance with *subsection (3)* to the Commission of the European Communities.

(5) The Board may, in respect of an application under *section 182A* for approval of proposed development—

    (a) approve the proposed development,

    (b) make such modifications to the proposed development as it specifies in the approval and approve the proposed development as so modified,

    (c) approve, in part only, the proposed development (with or without specified modifications of it of the foregoing kind), or

     (d) refuse to approve the proposed development, and may attach to an approval under *paragraph (a), (b) or (c)* such conditions as it considers appropriate.

(6) Without prejudice to the generality of the foregoing power to attach conditions, the Board may attach to an approval under *subsection (5)(a), (b) or (c)* a condition requiring—

     (a) the construction or the financing, in whole or in part, of the construction of a facility, or

     (b) the provision or the financing, in whole or in part, of the provision of a service, in the area in which the proposed development would be situated, being a facility or service that, in the opinion of the Board, would constitute a substantial gain to the community.

(7) A condition attached pursuant to *subsection (6)* shall not require such an amount of financial resources to be committed for the purposes of the condition being complied with as would substantially deprive the person in whose favour the approval under this section operates of the benefits likely to accrue from the grant of the approval.

(8) The Minister may make regulations to provide for such matters of procedure and administration as appear to the Minister to be necessary or expedient in respect of applications under *section 182A* for approval.

(9) Without prejudice to the generality of *subsection (8)*, regulations under that subsection may require the Board to give information in respect of its decision regarding the proposed development for which approval is sought.

(10) In considering under *subsection (1)* information furnished relating to the likely consequences for proper planning and sustainable development of a proposed development in the area in which it is proposed to situate such development, the Board shall have regard to—

     (a) the provisions of the development plan for the area,

     (b) the provisions of any special amenity area order relating to the area,

     (c) if the area or part of the area is a European site or an area prescribed for the purposes of *section 10(2)(c)*, that fact,

     (d) if the proposed development would have an effect on a European site or an area prescribed for the purposes of *section 10(2)(c)*, that fact,

     (e) the matters referred to in *section 143*, and

     (f) the provisions of this Act and regulations under this Act where relevant.

(11)

     (a) No permission under *section 34 or 37G* shall be required for any development which is approved under this section.

     (b) *Part VIII* shall apply to any case where development referred to in *section 182A(1)* is carried out otherwise than in compliance with an approval under this section or any condition to which the approval is subject as it applies to any unauthorised development with the modification that a reference in that Part to a permission shall be construed as a reference to an approval under this section.

(12) Without prejudice to the generality of *section 18(a) of the Interpretation*

Act 2005, a reference, however expressed, in this section to the area in which the proposed development would be situated includes, if the context admits, a reference to the 2 or more areas in which the proposed development would be situated and cognate references shall be construed accordingly.]

AMENDMENT HISTORY

Inserted by s.4 of the Planning and Development (Strategic Infrastructure) Act 2006 (No. 27 of 2006).

NOTE

This section comprises three discrete matters: the matters to be considered by the Board in determining an application for electricity or electricity transmission development; a procedure for obtaining exemption from the requirement to carry out an EIS and certain conditions which may attach to the grant of approval which may require some facility or service which would be of substantial gain to the community. Subsection (1) states that the Board is to assess, in particular, the environmental effect of the development and its effect on the proper planning and sustainable of the area. Subsection (10) sets out more general matters to which the Board is to "have regard". On the meaning of "have regard" see *McEvoy v Meath County Council.* The matters to be considered are the same as those stated in ss.37G(2), 146 C(6), 181B(11) and 82D(0).

Under subs.(2), the Board may in exceptional circumstances grant an exemption from the requirement to prepare an EIS. Such exemption cannot be granted where another European Member State or a state party to the Transboundary Convention has indicated that it wishes to furnish views on the effects on the environment in that Member State. There is no guidance as to what may constitute exceptional circumstances. However, the Board must give reasons for granting the exemption which must be stated in a notice published in *Iris Oifigiúil* and in at least one daily newspaper. Such reasons must demonstrate exceptional circumstances. In deciding whether to grant an exemption, the Board must consider whether the effect of the development on the environment should be assessed in some other manner and whether such assessment should be made available for inspection by the public. Subsection (5) provides that the Board can approve the development, with or without modifications, approve part of the development or refuse permission for the development. This explicitly allows the issue of split decisions, i.e. both granting and refusing part of the development. Split decisions should be exercised according to certain principles. In this respect see the note on s.37G. Article 219 of the 2001 Regulations, as amended, provides that the notice of the decision made by the Board shall state that, in making a decision, the Board has had regard to any submissions or observations received in accordance with the Act or the Regulations. Article 220 of the 2001 Regulations as amended states that as soon as may be following the making of its decision the Board shall publish in an approved newspaper, notice of its decision, and notify the applicant concerned, the planning authority or authorities in whose area the development would be situated and any person or body who made a submission or observation in respect of the application for approval concerned. The notice of the decision must include:

- the reference number of the application;
- the development to which the decision relates;
- the nature of the decision;
- the date of the decision;
- the main reasons and considerations on which the decision is based; and
- any conditions attached to a decision, including conditions relating to community gain and the main reasons for the imposition of any such conditions.

Subsection (6) allows for the imposition of a condition requiring a "planning gain" to the community. This is a radical and novel condition which could not be imposed in respect of the development granted under s.34 or 37 of the Act. Any such condition would be ultra vires as not being relevant to the development. The concept of a developer granting a planning gain to the community outside the normal planning process was expressly disapproved of by the Supreme Court in *Ashbourne Holdings v An Bord Pleanála* [2003] 2 I.R. 114. Subsection

(6) affords a statutory status to such planning gain in the context of proposed development under s.182A. Considerable flexibility is afforded as to the nature of the planning gain, which may be either a facility or a service. The only criterion is that the facility or service must be of "substantial gain" to the community. The applicant may be required either to construct the facility or may finance the construction of such facility. Similarly, the applicant may provide or finance the service. Subsection (7) provides that the financial commitment must not be so onerous as to deprive the applicant of the substantial benefit of the grant of approval. There must be a degree of proportionality between the financial burden of the condition and the benefit of the approval. This may prove difficult to assess, in particular, the difficulty in assessing the exact benefit likely to accrue from the approval. Although the criteria is vague and difficult to apply, the inbuilt proportionality requirement may mean that it would escape a challenge on the basis constitutional invalidity. The condition may be sought to be justified on the basis that it is in the interests of the common good and that it is proportionate to its objective in accordance with the principles set out in the Article 26 reference, *Planning and Development Bill* [2002] 2 I.R. 292, in respect of Pt V of the 2000 Act. Subsection (11)(2) makes clear that all the enforcement powers of the planning authority under Pt VIII may be used to ensure that the development is carried out in accordance with the approval and the conditions attached thereto.

Subsection (12) applies to a situation where the development is situated in the area of more than one planning authority. This reflects s.18(a) of the Interpretation Act 2005, which relates to the rule that a word importing the singular shall be read as also importing the plural and vice versa.

[Application for approval of strategic gas infrastructure development

1–218   **182C.—(1)** Where a person (hereafter referred to in this section as the "undertaker") intends to carry out a strategic gas infrastructure development (hereafter referred to in this section and *section 182D* as "proposed development"), the undertaker shall prepare, or cause to be prepared—

(a) an application for approval of the development under *section 182D,* and

(b) an environmental impact statement in respect of the development, and shall apply to the Board for such approval accordingly, indicating in the application whether the application relates to a strategic upstream gas pipeline or a strategic downstream gas pipeline.

(2) An application under *subsection (1)* for approval of a proposed development shall, if it will consist of or include a pipeline, be accompanied by a certificate in relation to the pipeline provided under *section 26 of the Gas Act 1976,* as amended, or *section 20 of the Gas (Amendment) Act 2000* by—

(a) in the case of a strategic upstream gas pipeline, the Minister for Communications, Marine and Natural Resources, or

(b) in the case of a strategic downstream gas pipeline, the Commission.

(3) The proposed development shall not be carried out unless the Board has approved it with or without modifications.

(4) Before an undertaker makes an application for approval under *subsection (1),* it shall—

(a) publish in one or more newspapers circulating in the area or areas in which it is proposed to carry out the development a notice indicating the nature and location of the proposed development and—

(i) stating that—

(I) it proposes to seek the approval of the Board for the proposed development,

(II) an environmental impact statement has been prepared in respect of the proposed development, and

(III) where relevant, the proposed development is likely to have significant effects on the environment of a Member State of the European Communities or other party to the Transboundary Convention,

(ii) specifying the times and places at which, and the period (not being less than 6 weeks) during which, a copy of the application and the environmental impact statement may be inspected free of charge or purchased on payment of a specified fee (which fee shall not exceed the reasonable cost of making such copy),

(iii) inviting the making, during such period, of submissions and observations to the Board relating to—

(I) the implications of the proposed development for proper planning and sustainable development in the area or areas concerned,
and

(II) the likely effects on the environment of the proposed development, if carried out, and

(iv) specifying the types of decision the Board may make, under *section 182D,* in relation to the application,

and

(b) send a copy of the application and the environmental impact statement to—

(i) the local authority or each local authority in whose functional area the proposed development would be situate,

(ii) any prescribed bodies,

(iii) where the proposed development comprises or is for the purposes of a strategic downstream gas pipeline, the Commission, and

(iv) where the proposed development is likely to have significant effects on the environment of a Member State of the European Communities or a state which is a party to the Transboundary Convention, the prescribed body of the relevant state or states, together with a notice stating that submissions or observations may, during the period referred to in *paragraph (a)(ii),* be made in writing to the Board in relation to—

(I) the implications of the proposed development for proper planning and sustainable development in the area concerned, and

(II) the likely effects on the environment of the proposed development, if carried out.

(5) The Board may—

(a) if it considers it necessary to do so, require an undertaker that has applied for approval for a proposed development to furnish to the Board such further information in relation to—

- (i) the effects on the environment of the proposed development, or
- (ii) the consequences for proper planning and sustainable development in the area or areas in which it is proposed to situate the said development of such development, as the Board may specify, or

(b) if it is provisionally of the view that it would be appropriate to approve the proposed development were certain alterations (specified in the notification referred to in this paragraph) to be made to the terms of it, notify the undertaker that it is of that view and invite the undertaker to make to the terms of the proposed development alterations specified in the notification and, if the undertaker makes those alterations, to furnish to it such information (if any) as it may specify in relation to the development, in the terms as so altered, or, where necessary, a revised environmental impact statement in respect of it.

(6) If an undertaker makes the alterations to the terms of the proposed development specified in a notification given to it under *subsection (5),* the terms of the development as so altered shall be deemed to be the proposed development for the purposes of this section and *section 182D*.

(7) The Board shall—

(a) where it considers that any further information received pursuant to a requirement made under *subsection (5)(a)* contains significant additional data relating to—

- (i) the likely effects on the environment of the proposed development, and
- (ii) the likely consequences for proper planning and sustainable development in the area or areas in which it is proposed to situate the said development of such development,

or

(b) where the undertaker has made the alterations to the terms of the proposed development specified in a notification given to it under *subsection (5)(b),* require the undertaker to do the things referred to in *subsection (8)*.

(8) The things which an undertaker shall be required to do as aforesaid are—

(a) to publish in one or more newspapers circulating in the area or areas in which the proposed development would be situate a notice stating that, as appropriate—

- (i) further information in relation to the proposed development has been furnished to the Board, or
- (ii) the undertaker has, pursuant to an invitation of the Board, made alterations to the terms of the proposed development (and the nature of those alterations shall be indicated) and, if it be the case, that information in relation to the terms of the development as so altered or a revised environmental impact statement in respect of the development has been furnished to the Board, indicating the times at which, the period (which

shall not be less than 3 weeks) during which and the place, or places, where a copy of the information or the environmental impact statement referred to in *subparagraph (i) or (ii)* may be inspected free of charge or purchased on payment of a specified fee (which fee shall not exceed the reasonable cost of making such copy) and that submissions or observations in relation to that information or statement may be made to the Board before the expiration of the indicated period, and

(b) to send to each prescribed authority to which a notice was given pursuant to *subsection (4)(b)* —

    (i) a notice of the furnishing to the Board of, as appropriate, the further information referred to in *paragraph (a)(i)* or the information or statement referred to in *paragraph (a)(ii),* and

    (ii) a copy of that further information, information or statement, and to indicate to the authority that submissions or observations in relation to that further information, information or statement may be made to the Board before the expiration of a period (which shall be not less than 3 weeks) beginning on the day on which the notice is sent to the prescribed authority by the undertaker.

(9) In the case of a proposed development comprising or for the purposes of a strategic downstream pipeline, the Board shall request the Commission to make observations within such period (which period shall not be less than 3 weeks from the date of the request) as may be specified by the Board in relation to the proposed development, including observations in relation to any safety or operational matters.

(10) The Minister, after consultation with the Minister for Communications, Marine and Natural Resources, may make regulations to provide for matters of procedure in relation to the making of a request of the Commission under *subsection (9)* and the making of observations by the Commission on foot of such a request.

(11) In this section "Commission" means the Commission for Energy Regulation.]

AMENDMENT HISTORY

Inserted by s.4 of the Planning and Development (Strategic Infrastructure) Act 2006 (No. 27 of 2006).

NOTE

This section sets out the procedure to be followed for approval of a strategic gas infrastructure development. "Strategic gas infrastructure development" is defined under a new definition in s.2 of the Act as:

"[A]ny proposed development comprising or for the purposes of a strategic downstream gas pipeline or a strategic upstream gas pipeline, and associated terminals, buildings and installations, whether above or below ground, including any associated discharge pipe".

The procedure is analogous to the procedure set out in s.182A for electricity or electricity transmission development. The application must state whether it relates to a strategic upstream gas pipeline or a strategic downstream gas pipeline. As regards the certificates to accompany the application subs.(2), s.26(2) of the Gas (Amendment) Act 2000 provides, inter alia, for the grant of a certificate by the Minister that a person has a bona fide intention to apply or give notice of intention to apply for the construction or operation of a pipeline. (Section 26 of the Gas Act 1976 concerns the entry onto land to examine whether it is suitable for acquisition).

The procedure for lodging the application and the manner in which the Board can deal with the application is similar to s.182A in respect of a development for electricity transmission. Thus the application must be in the correct form and must be accompanied by an EIS. Article 214 of the 2001 Regulations (as inserted by the 2006 Regulations) provides that when making an application for strategic infrastructure development, the applicant shall send to the Board:

- 10 copies of the plans and particulars of the proposed development (including any plans, particulars or other information indicated by the Board under art.210(2)) and of the EIS;
- a copy of the published newspaper notice in accordance as may be appropriate;
- a list of the bodies notified of the application, as may be appropriate, and an indication of the date on which notice was sent; and
- a list of any other public notice given or other public consultations conducted by the applicant, including any notice or consultations done on foot of a requirement by the Board under art.210, and an indication of the date or dates of such additional notice or consultations.

Article 214(2) states that where the Board so consents or specifies any or all of the copies or other information specified in sub-art.(1) shall be given in electronic form. Prior to the application being lodged a newspaper notice must be published setting out the matters specified including that the application and EIS may be inspected at a specified place for a period not less than six weeks and that submissions may be made. Article 212 of the 2001 Regulations, as amended, provides that any notice which an applicant is required to give to the public shall indicate the types of decision the Board can make in relation to the application. A copy of the application and any EIS must be sent to the planning authority for the area. If it affects the environment of another Member State, a copy of the application and any EIS must be sent to the prescribed authority of any relevant State. Article 213 of the 2006 Regulations sets out the prescribed authorities. Article 217 of the 2001 Regulations as amended prescribes a specific form in which the submission must be made. The Board shall acknowledge in writing the receipt of any submission or observation as soon as may be following receipt of the submission or observation. Any submissions or observations that do not comply with the prescribed form shall not be considered by the Board. A person who makes submissions or observations to the Board shall not be entitled to elaborate upon the submissions or observations or make further submissions or observations except where the Board before making its decision asks any person to make submissions or observations or elaborate upon submissions or observations in relation to an application. Where the proposed development comprises or is for the purposes of a strategic downstream gas pipeline, the applicant must send a copy to the Commission for Energy Regulation. In such instance, the Board must also under subs.(10) specifically request observations from the Commission, allowing a period of not less than three weeks. A strategic downstream gas pipeline is defined by a new definition in s.2 as "any proposed gas pipeline, other than an upstream gas pipeline, which is designed to operate at 16 bar or greater, and is longer than 20 kilometres in length".

Subsection (5) provides that the Board may request information where appropriate or may indicate to the applicant that it would provisionally approve permissions subject to certain alterations in the plans. Where the applicant submits such altered plans, permission will be deemed to be granted in those terms. Where the further information includes significant additional information which is likely to affect both the environment and the proper planning and sustainable development of the area, the applicant will be required to publish a newspaper notice setting out the nature of the information/alternations and inviting submissions within a period of not less than three weeks and send a notice to the prescribed authorities, inviting submissions within a period of not less than three weeks. Article 218 of the 2001 Regulations as amended allows the Board some further powers whereby the

Board may request further submissions either from the applicant, from persons who made submissions or from other persons. It also allows the Board to make information available for inspection, to notify the public, to invite further submissions and to hold meeting (for which a record must be kept). Also where altered plans have been submitted in response to an invitation by the Board, a newspaper notice must be published along with a notice being sent to the prescribed authorities. This applies in all instances, where altered plans are submitted, regardless of whether the plans include "significant additional information".

[Section 182C: criteria for decision, certain exemptions, etc.

182D.—**(1)** Before making a decision in respect of a proposed development **1–219** the subject of an application under *section 182C,* the Board shall consider—

   (a) the environmental impact statement submitted pursuant to *section 182C(1) or (5),* any submissions or observations made in accordance with *section 182C(4), (8) or (9)* and any other information furnished in accordance with *section 182C(5)* relating to—

      (i) the likely consequences for proper planning and sustainable development in the area in which it is proposed to situate the proposed development of such development, and

      (ii) the likely effects on the environment of the proposed development,

   and

   (b) the report and any recommendations of a person conducting any oral hearing relating to the proposed development.

(2) The Board may where it is satisfied that exceptional circumstances so warrant, grant an exemption in respect of proposed development from a requirement under *section 182C(1)* to prepare an environmental impact statement except that no exemption may be granted in respect of proposed development where another Member State of the European Communities or a state which is a party to the Transboundary Convention has indicated that it wishes to furnish views on the effects on the environment in that Member State or state of the proposed development.

(3) The Board shall, in granting an exemption under *subsection (2),* consider whether—

   (a) the effects, if any, of the proposed development on the environment should be assessed in some other manner, and

   (b) the information arising from such an assessment should be made available to the members of the public, and it may apply such requirements regarding these matters in relation to the application for approval as it considers necessary or appropriate.

(4) Notice of any exemption granted under *subsection (2),* of the reasons for granting the exemption, and of any requirements applied under *subsection (3)* shall, as soon as may be—

   (a) be published in *Iris Oifigiúil* and in at least one daily newspaper published in the State, and

   (b) be given, together with a copy of the information, if any, made available to the members of the public in accordance with *subsection (3),* to the Commission of the European Communities.

(5) The Board may, in respect of an application under *section 182C* for approval of proposed development—

    (a) approve the proposed development,

    (b) make such modifications to the proposed development as it specifies in the approval and approve the proposed development as so modified,

    (c) approve, in part only, the proposed development (with or without specified modifications of it of the foregoing kind), or

    (d) refuse to approve the proposed development, and may attach to an approval under *paragraph (a), (b) or (c)* such conditions as it considers appropriate.

(6) Without prejudice to the generality of the foregoing power to attach conditions, the Board may attach to an approval under *subsection (5)(a), (b) or (c)* a condition requiring—

    (a) the construction or the financing, in whole or in part, of the construction of a facility, or

    (b) the provision or the financing, in whole or in part, of the provision of a service, in the area in which the proposed development would be situated, being a facility or service that, in the opinion of the Board, would constitute a substantial gain to the community.

(7) A condition attached pursuant to *subsection (6)* shall not require such an amount of financial resources to be committed for the purposes of the condition being complied with as would substantially deprive the person in whose favour the approval under this section operates of the benefits likely to accrue from the grant of the approval.

(8) The Minister may, after consultation with the Minister for Communications, Marine and Natural Resources, make regulations to provide for such matters of procedure and administration as appear to the Minister to be necessary or expedient in respect of applications under *section 182C* for approval.

(9) Without prejudice to the generality of *subsection (8),* regulations under that subsection may require the Board to give information in respect of its decision regarding the proposed development for which approval is sought.

(10) In considering under *subsection (1)* information furnished relating to the likely consequences for proper planning and sustainable development of a proposed development in the area in which it is proposed to situate such development, the Board shall have regard to—

    (a) the provisions of the development plan for the area,

    (b) the provisions of any special amenity area order relating to the area,

    (c) if the area or part of the area is a European site or an area prescribed for the purposes of *section 10(2)(c),* that fact,

    (d) if the proposed development would have an effect on a European site or an area prescribed for the purposes of *section 10(2)(c),* that fact,

    (e) the matters referred to in *section 143,* and

    (f) the provisions of this Act and regulations under this Act where relevant.

(11)

    (a) No permission under *section 34 or 37G* shall be required for any development which is approved under this section.

(b) *Part VIII* shall apply to any case where development referred to in *section 182C(1)* is carried out otherwise than in compliance with an approval under this section or any condition to which the approval is subject as it applies to any unauthorised development with the modification that a reference in that Part to a permission shall be construed as a reference to an approval under this section.

(12) Without prejudice to the generality of *section 18(a) of the Interpretation Act 2005,* a reference, however expressed, in this section to the area in which the proposed development would be situated includes, if the context admits, a reference to the 2 or more areas in which the proposed development would be situated and cognate references shall be construed accordingly.]

AMENDMENT HISTORY

Inserted by s.4 of the Planning and Development (Strategic Infrastructure) Act 2006 (No. 27 of 2006).

NOTE

This section comprises the matters to be considered by the Board in determining an application for strategic gas infrastructure development, a procedure for exemption to carry out an EIS and conditions which may attach to its approval. The section is in similar terms to s.182B in relation to electricity or electricity transmission developments. Subsection (1) sets out that the Board is to assess, in particular, the environmental effect of the development and its effect on the proper planning and sustainable of the area. Subsection (10) set out more general matters to which the Board is to "have regard". On the meaning of have regard see *McEvoy v Meath County Council* [2003] 1 I.R. 208.

Under subs.(2), the Board may in exceptional circumstances grant an exemption from the requirement to prepare an EIS. Such exemption cannot be granted where another European Member State or a state party to the Transboundary Convention has indicated that it wishes to furnish views on the effects on the environment in that Member State. There is no guidance as to what may constitute exceptional circumstances. However, the Board must give reasons for granting the exemption which must be stated in a notice published in Iris Oifigiúil and in at least one daily newspaper. Such reasons must demonstrate exceptional circumstances. In deciding whether to grant an exemption, the Board must consider whether the effect of the development on the environment should be assessed in some other manner and whether such assessment should be made available for inspection by the public. Subsection (5) provides that the Board can approve the development, with or without modifications, approve part of the development or refuse permission for the development. This explicitly allows the issue of split decisions, i.e. both granting and refusing part of the development. Split decision should be exercised according to certain principles. In this respect see the note on s.37G. Article 219 of the 2001 Regulations as amended provides that the notice of the decision made by the Board shall state that, in making a decision, the Board has had regard to any submissions or observations received in accordance with the Act or the Regulations. Article 220 of the 2001 Regulations as amended states that as soon as may be following the making of its decision the Board shall publish in an approved newspaper, notice of its decision, and notify the applicant concerned, the planning authority or authorities in whose area the development would be situated and any person or body who made a submission or observation in respect of the application for approval concerned. The notice of the decision must include:

- the reference number of the application;
- the development to which the decision relates;
- the nature of the decision;
- the date of the decision;
- the main reasons and considerations on which the decision is based; and
- any conditions attached to a decision, including conditions relating to community

gain and the main reasons for the imposition of any such conditions.

Subsection (6) allows for the imposition of a condition requiring a "planning gain" to the community. This is a radical and novel condition which could not be imposed in respect of the development granted under s.34 or 37 of the Act. Any such condition would be ultra vires as not being relevant to the development. The concept of a developer granting a planning gain to the community outside the normal planning process was expressly disapproved of by the Supreme Court in *Ashbourne Holdings v An Bord Pleanála* [2003] 2 I.R. 114. Subsection (6) affords a statutory status to such planning gain in the context of proposed development under s.182A. Considerable flexibility is afforded as to the nature of the planning gain which may be either a facility or a service. The only criterion is that the facility or service must be of "substantial gain" to the community. The applicant may be required either to construct the facility or may finance the construction of such facility. Similarly, the applicant may provide or finance the service. Subsection (7) provides that the financial commitment must not be so onerous as to deprive the applicant of the substantial benefit of the grant of approval. There must be a degree of proportionality between the financial burden of the condition with the benefit of the approval. This may prove difficult to assess, in particular, the difficulty in assessing the exact benefit likely to accrue from the approval. Subsection (11)(2) makes clear that all the enforcement powers of the planning authority under Pt VIII may be used to ensure that the development is carried out in accordance with the approval and the conditions attached thereto. Subsection (12) applies to a situation where the development is situated in the area of more than one planning authority. This reflects s.18(a) of the Interpretation Act 2005 which relates to the rule that a word importing the singular shall be read as also importing the plural and vice versa.

[Procedures in advance of seeking approval under section 182B or 182D

1–220   **182E.—(1)** A person (a "prospective applicant") who proposes to apply for approval under *section 182B or 182D* shall, before making the application, enter into consultations with the Board in relation to the proposed development.

(2) In any consultations under *subsection (1),* the Board may give advice to the prospective applicant regarding the proposed application and, in particular, regarding—

(a) the procedures involved in making such an application, and

(b) what considerations, related to proper planning and sustainable development or the environment, may, in the opinion of the Board, have a bearing on its decision in relation to the application.

(3) A prospective applicant may request the Board to give to him or her an opinion in writing prepared by the Board on what information will be required to be contained in an environmental impact statement in relation to the proposed development; on receipt of such a request the Board, after consulting the prospective applicant and such bodies as may be specified by the Minister for the purpose, shall comply with it as soon as is practicable.

(4) A prospective applicant shall, for the purposes of—

(a) consultations under *subsection (1),* and

(b) the Board's complying with a request under *subsection (3),* supply to the Board sufficient information in relation to the proposed development so as to enable the Board to assess the proposed development.

(5) Neither—

(a) the holding of consultations under *subsection (1),* nor

(b) the provision of an opinion under *subsection (3),* shall prejudice the performance by the Board of any other of its functions under this Act or regulations under this Act, or any other enactment and cannot be relied upon in the formal planning process or in legal proceedings.

(6) The Board shall keep a record in writing of any consultations under this section in relation to a proposed development, including the names of those who participated in the consultations, and a copy of such record shall be placed and kept with the documents to which any application in respect of the proposed development relates.

(7) The Board may, at its absolute discretion, consult with any person who may, in the opinion of the Board, have information which is relevant for the purposes of consultations under this section in relation to a proposed development.]

AMENDMENT HISTORY

Inserted by s.4 of the Planning and Development (Strategic Infrastructure) Act 2006 (No. 27 of 2006).

NOTE

This section sets out the procedure to be followed before applying for approval for an electricity transmission development (s.182B) or strategic gas infrastructure development (s.182D). There is a mandatory obligation to engage in consultations with the Board prior to lodging the application. In such consultations, the Board may give advice as to the procedures and considerations relating the proper planning and sustainable development which may be relevant to the application. The conduct of such consultations is set out in the 2001 Regulations (as inserted by the 2006 Regulations). Article 210(1) of the Planning Regulation 2001 provides that on receipt of a request to enter into pre-application consultations, the Board shall notify the relevant planning authority of the request. Article 210(2) states that the Board shall, during the course of a pre-application consultation, indicate to a prospective applicant:

- the plans, particulars or other information which the Board will require for the purposes of consideration of an application;
- the time frames and sequencing to be applied to the application process; and
- any other matters in relation to the application process as the Board considers appropriate.

Article 210(3) prescribes steps where the Board is of the opinion that the proposed development would be likely to have significant effects on the environment in a transboundary State. Article 210(4) provides that the Board may, during the course of a pre-application consultation, require a prospective applicant to give notice to the public or to carry out consultations with the public in advance of an application being submitted, including:

- the erection or fixing of notice or notices on the site in a form to be specified by the Board;
- the provision of a specific place or a specific website to make available the application, EIS and any other relevant documentation for inspection or purchase at a fee not exceeding the reasonable cost of making a copy;
- the use of local or national media; or
- the holding of meetings, with any person or body or for the public.

These requirements are at the discretion of the Board.

Article 210(5) provides that during the course of a pre-application consultation, the Board may indicate to which of the bodies prescribed under art.213 notice should, in the opinion of the Board, be given by the prospective applicant and the prospective applicant shall notify those bodies of the making of the application. Also art.210(6) provides that nothing shall prevent the Board from requiring a prospective applicant for permission to submit further information or from giving further notice to the public or to any person or body. A prospective applicant may request the scoping of any EIS by the Board in respect of the matters to be contained in the EIS. The applicant must supply the Board with sufficient information to carry out this function. Neither the content of the consultations nor the opinion on the EIS can prejudice the Board in subsequently carrying out its functions in processing the application. Any statements made by Board officials at such consultations cannot therefore give rise to an estoppel. Any such statements cannot preclude the Board from reassessing such considerations or taking into account other matters. Furthermore, the fact that the Board has issued an opinion on matters to be contained in an EIS, cannot preclude the Board from subsequently requiring other matters to be included once the application has been lodged. The Board may engage in consultations with other parties it deems fit, although no other party has an entitlement to be consulted. Article 211(1) of the 2001 Regulations, inserted by the 2006 Regulations, prescribes specified bodies which the Board must consult as the Minister for the Environment, Heritage and Local Government, the Environmental Protection Agency, the Minister for Communications, Marine and Natural Resources, and the relevant planning authority. Also art.211(2) provides that the Board may invite submissions or observations in relation to the information to be contained in the EIS from the bodies referred to in art.213.

PART XII

COMPENSATION

CHAPTER I

Compensation generally

Compensation claims: time limits

183.—**(1)** Subject to *subsection (2),* a claim for compensation under this *Part* shall be made not later than 6 months after—

1–221

   (a) in the case of a claim under *section 190,* the date of the decision of the Board,

   (b) in the case of a claim under *section 195,* the date of the decision of the planning authority or the Board, as the case may be,

   (c) in the case of a claim under *section 196,* the removal or alteration of the structure,

   (d) in the case of a claim under *section 197,* the discontinuance or compliance,

   (e) in the case of a claim referred to in *section 198,* the date of the approval of a scheme under *section 85* or the date of complying with a notice under *section 88,* as the case may be,

   (f) in the case of a claim under *section 199,* the date on which the action of the planning authority occurred,

   (g) in the case of a claim under *section 200,* the date on which the order creating the public right of way commences to have effect, and

   (h) in the case of a claim under *section 201,* the date on which the damage is suffered.

(2) The High Court may, where it considers that the interests of justice so require, extend the period within which a claim for compensation under this *Part* may be brought, upon application being made to it in that behalf.

NOTE

This section sets a time limit of six months for the bringing of a claim for compensation in relation to the various enlisted decisions. While the six-month time limit is the same as under the previous Act (s.4 of the 1990 Act), there was previously no provision for extension of this time, which can now be granted by the High Court in the interests of justice. The right to compensation arises from the date of the decision to refuse permission; see *McKone Estates v Dublin County Council* [1995] 2 I.L.R.M. 283. As regards the various enlisted sections, these are:

- s.190 (a decision of appeal from a refusal or grant of planning permission resulting in reduction in value of the land);
- s.195 (where a permission has been revoked or modified under s.44 and the developer has already incurred expenses);
- s.196 (where under s.46, the notice for removal/discontinuance of a structure results in a reduction in value of the structure);
- s.197 (where under s.46, the notice for removal/discontinuance of a structure results in a reduction in value of the land);
- s.198 (where under s.88, a notice has been served relating to a special area of planning control designated under s.85, resulting in a reduction in value of the land);
- s.199 (where under s.182, the local authority has placed or removed cables, pipes, etc. resulting in reduction in value of the land or structures);
- s.200 (where a public right of way has been created);
- s.201 (where an authorised person enters land under s.252 or for enforcement purposes under s.253, resulting in reduction in the value of land).
- s.207 (reducing the value of the land); and

Determination of compensation claim

184.—A claim for compensation under this *Part* shall, in default of **1–222** agreement, be determined by arbitration under the *Acquisition of Land (Assessment of Compensation) Act, 1919,* but subject to—

(a) the *Second Schedule* in respect of a reduction in the value of an interest in land,

(b) the proviso that the arbitrator shall have jurisdiction to make a nil award, and

(c) the application of the *Second Schedule* to a claim for compensation under *Chapter III of this Part* for a reduction in the value of an interest as if a reference to "the relevant decision under *Part III*" or to "the decision" was, in relation to each of the sections in that *Chapter* set out in *column A of the Table to this section,* a reference to the matter set out in *column B of that Table* opposite the reference in *column A to that section.*

TABLE

A	B
Section	
196	the removal or alteration of a structure consequent upon a notice under *section 46*
197	the discontinuance with, or the compliance with conditions on the continuance, of the use of land consequent upon a notice under *section 46*
198	the approval of a scheme under *section 85* or the compliance with a notice under *section 88.*
199	the action by the planning authority under *section 182.*
200	the making by the planning authority of an order under *section 207.*

NOTE

This section provides that in the absence of agreement, compensation is to be assessed by an arbitrator under the Acquisition of Land (Assessment of Compensation) Act 1919. Compensation may be agreed between the parties in which case there will be no need for arbitration. Although there is no mechanism for referral set out, this involves making a request to the reference committee to nominate a property arbitrator.

Section 190 sets out the right to compensation. The compensation will be based on the reduction in value of of the claimant's interest. Subsection (a) provides that the determination of the arbitrator is subject to Sch.2 which sets out rules for the determination of the amount of compensation. By virtue of subs.(b) the arbitrator has jurisdiction to make a determination that no compensation is payable. i.e. a nil award. Subsection (c) provides that insofar as Sch.2 calculates the reduction in value by reference to Pt III (a decision on an application for planning permission), the rules stated therein shall be read as also applying to claims for compensation under the sections sets out in Table A and B.

A party may request the arbitrator to state a case for the High Court. The jurisdiction to state a case is set out in s.6 of the Acquisition of Land (Assessment of Compensation) 1919 which provides:

> "(1) The decision of a property arbitrator upon any question of fact, shall be final and binding on the parties, and the persons claiming under them respectively, but the property arbitrator may, and shall, if the High Court so directs, state at any stage of the proceedings, in the form of a special case for the opinion of the High Court, any question of law arising in the course of the proceedings, and may state his award as to the whole or part thereof in the form of a special case for the opinion of the High Court."

There is also jurisdiction to state a case under s.35 of the Arbitration Act 1954, which provides that:

> "(1) An arbitrator or umpire may, and shall if so directed by the Court, state; (a) any question of law arising in the course of the reference, or (b) any award or any part of an award, in the form of a special case for the decision of the Court. (2) A special case with respect to an interim award or with respect to a question of law arising in the course of a reference may be, stated, or may be ordered by the Court to be stated, notwithstanding that proceedings under the reference are still pending".

The case stated must concern a question of law and so cannot concern a question of fact. It would appear that a question concerning the correct interpretation of any of the Rules or paragraphs of the Schedules including the Sch.2 to Sch.5, will involve a question of law, insofar as it turns on an issue of statutory interpretation. While the interpretation will take place against a particular factual matrix, the question should be drafted in a manner to reflect the legal issue of interpretation in question.

Where an arbitrator declines to state a case, the court may direct an arbitrator to state a case. In *Hogan v St. Kevin's Company and Purcell* [1986] I.R. 80, Murphy J. cited the principles set out by the Court of Appeal decision in *Halfdan Grieg and Co. v Sterling Coal* [1973] Q.B. 843 and noted:

> "[I]f the issues were matters of fact and not of law the arbitrator should refuse to state a case. If, on the other hand, the issue raised points of law, it would depend on the point of law whether or not the arbitrator should exercise his discretion in favour of the application to state the case. Lord Denning then went on to lay down the following three conditions, namely, (1) that the point of law should be real and substantial; (2) that the point of law should be clear-cut and capable of being accurately stated as a point of law; (3) that the point of law should be of such importance that the resolution of it was necessary for the proper determination of the case. The distinguished Master of the Rolls then went on to say that if those three requisites were satisfied then the arbitrator or umpire should state a case."

It may be noted that where the court has refused to compel an arbitrator to state a case such as the above, the rationale for such reluctance is because the parties had voluntarily submitted the dispute to arbitration and the so courts are slow to usurp the function of the chosen tribunal. However, this does not apply in the present case where the arbitrator is a statutory arbitrator and the local authority did not agree to the matter being referred to arbitration. In in *Dublin Corporation v MacGinley and Shackleton*, unreported, High Court, June 22, 1986, Murphy J. stated:

"Whilst I recognise that ordinarily an arbitrator should state a case and the High Court will direct a case to be stated where a point of law arises in the course of an arbitration which is real and substantial and one which is appropriate in its substance and in its form for the decision by the High Court (see the decision in Hogan & Ors, in St. Kevins Company & Anor. delivered on the 22nd day of January 1986) on the other hard both the arbitrator and the Court in the exercise of their respective discretions would properly refuse to state a case or direct the statement of a case on a point of law which was either without substance or adequately covered by authority".

It appears that the determination of an arbitrator is subject to judicial review which is not within the scope of s.50. While private arbitrators are not generally subject to judicial review, it appears that statutory arbitrators are subject to judicial review. The ordinary principles of judicial review will apply as determinations of arbitrators under the 2000 Act. See *Cork County Council v Shackleton*, unreported, High Court, Clarke J., July 17, 2007, where the court quashed the determination of the arbitrator appointed in the context of dispute concerning a planning condition requiring a social and affordable housing agreement under s.96. The court also declined to refuse relief on the basis that that planning authority had failed to request the arbitrator to state a case on the matter. It was noted that it would not necessarily have been a more expeditious or, indeed, more appropriate means of dealing with the issue concerned. It was, therefore a reasonable judgment to take to allow the arbitration to take its course and to permit the property arbitrator to reach his conclusion.

Regulations in relation to compensation

185.—The Minister may make regulations to provide for the following: **1–223**

(a) the form in which claims for compensation are to be made;

(b) the provision by a claimant of evidence in support of his or her claim, and information as to his or her interest in the land to which the claim relates;

(c) a statement by a claimant of the names and addresses of all other persons (so far as they are known to him or her) having an interest in the land to which the claim relates and, unless the claim is withdrawn, the notification by the planning authority or the claimant of every other person (if any) appearing to it or him or her to have an interest in the land.

NOTE

This section enables the Minister to make regulations in respect of making a claim for compensation. This has been provided for under Pt 13 of the Planning Regulations. Article 174 provides that a compensation claim shall be made to the planning authority in writing and shall include:

- the name and address of the claimant and a statement of his or her interest in the land to which the claim relates;
- a statement of the matter in respect of which the claim is made, the provision of the Act under which it is made, the amount of compensation claimed and the basis on which that amount has been calculated; and
- the names and addresses of all other persons (so far as they are known to the claimant) having an interest in the land to which the claim relates, or, where the claimant does not know of any such persons, a statement to that effect claim must be made in writing.

Article 174(2) provides that where a planning authority receives a compensation claim which fails to comply with a requirement, the authority shall, by notice in writing, require the claimant to comply with such requirement and defer consideration of the claim until the claimant has complied with such requirement. In *Abbeydrive Developments Ltd v Kildare*

County Council, unreported, High Court, Macken J., June 17, 2005, it was held that it is not necessary for a claimant to identify in his initial claim, the exact nature of the legal interest under which he holds lands. Under art.175, the planning authority must, within four weeks of receipt of the claim, give notice to such other persons having an interest in the land. Under art.176, the planning authority may require the claimant to provide evidence in support of his claim or his interest in the land.

Prohibition of double compensation

1–224   **186.**—Where a person would, but for this *section,* be entitled to compensation under this *Part* in respect of any matter or thing, and also to compensation under any other enactment in respect of the same matter or thing, he or she shall not be entitled to compensation in respect of the matter or thing both under this *Part* and under the other enactment, and shall not be entitled to any greater amount of compensation under this *Part* in respect of the matter or thing than the amount of the compensation to which he or she would be entitled under the other enactment in respect of the matter or thing.

NOTE

This section prohibits a person from claiming compensation both under this Act and any other Act in respect of the same matter. A person must therefore opt whether to claim under this Act or the 2000 Act, though he cannot claim more compensation under the 2000 Act than he would be entitled to under the other enactment. This section re-enacts s.7 of the 1990 Act.

Recovery of compensation from planning authority

1–225   **187.**—**(1)** All compensation payable under this *Part* by the planning authority shall, when the amount thereof has been determined by agreement or by arbitration in accordance with this *Part,* be recoverable from that authority as a simple contract debt in any court of competent jurisdiction.

(2) All costs and expenses of parties to an arbitration to determine the amount of any compensation shall, in so far as the costs and expenses are payable by the planning authority, be recoverable from that authority as a simple contract debt in any court of competent jurisdiction.

(3) *Sections 69 to 79 of the Lands Clauses Consolidation Act, 1845,* as amended or adapted by or under the *Second Schedule to the Housing of the Working Classes Act, 1890,* or any other *Act,* shall apply in relation to compensation by this *section* made recoverable as a simple contract debt, as if the compensation were a price or compensation under the *Lands Clauses Consolidation Act, 1845,* as so amended or adapted.

(4) Where money is paid into court by the planning authority under *section 69 of the Lands Clauses Consolidation Act, 1845,* as applied by this *section,* no costs shall be payable by that authority to any person in respect of any proceedings for the investment, payment of income, or payment of capital of that money.

NOTE

This section concerns the recovery of compensation and costs from the planning authority, which may be enforced in court as a contract debt. The sections of the Land

Clause Consolidation Act relate to the procedure for the deposit in court of compensation moneys.

Registration of compensation

188.—**(1)** Where, on a claim for compensation under *Chapter II of this Part,* compensation has become payable of an amount exceeding €634.87 [£500], the planning authority shall prepare and retain a statement of that fact, specifying the refusal of permission or grant of permission subject to conditions, or the revocation or modification of permission, the land to which the claim for compensation relates, and the amount of the compensation.　**1–226**

(2)
- **(a)** A planning authority shall enter in the register particulars of a statement prepared by it under this *section.*
- **(b)** Every entry under *paragraph (a)* shall be made within the period of 2 weeks beginning on the day of the preparation of the statement.

NOTE

This section requires the planning authority to keep a record of compensation paid (exceeding €634.87) in a "compensation statement". In addition, particulars of this statement are to be entered in the planning register described under s.7 within two weeks of the preparation of the statement.

Recovery by planning authority of compensation on subsequent development

189.—**(1)** No person shall carry out any development to which this *section* applies, on land in respect of which a statement (a "compensation statement") stands registered (whether under *section 72 of the Act of 1963, section 9 of the Act of 1990* or *section 188 of this Act*) until that amount, as is recoverable under this *section* in respect of the compensation specified in the compensation statement, has been paid or secured to the satisfaction of the planning authority.　**1–227**

(2) This *section* applies to any development (other than exempted development) of a kind specified in *section 192(2),* except that—
- **(a)** this *section* shall not apply to any development by virtue of a permission to develop land under *Part III* referred to in *section 192(5)* where the permission was granted subject to conditions other than conditions of a class or description set out in the *Fifth Schedule,* and
- **(b)** in a case where the compensation specified in the statement became payable in respect of the imposition of conditions on the granting of permission to develop land, this *section* shall not apply to the development for which that permission was granted.

(3) Subject to *subsection (4),* the amount recoverable under this *section* in respect of the compensation specified in a compensation statement—
- **(a)** if the land on which the development is to be carried out (the "development area") is identical with, or includes (with other land) the whole of the land comprised in the compensation statement, shall be the amount of compensation specified in that statement, or

(b) if the development area forms part of the land comprised in the compensation statement, or includes part of that land together with other land not comprised in that statement, shall be so much of the amount of compensation specified in that statement as is attributable to land comprised in that statement and falling within the development area.

(4) The attribution of compensation under *subsection (3)(b)* shall be in accordance with the following—

(a) the planning authority shall (if it appears to it to be practicable to do so) apportion the amount of the compensation between the different parts of the land, according to the way in which those parts appear to it to be differently affected by the refusal of permission or grant of permission subject to conditions;

(b) if no apportionment is made, the amount of the compensation shall be treated as distributed rateably according to area over the land to which the statement relates;

(c) if an apportionment is made, the compensation shall be treated as distributed in accordance with that apportionment, as between the different parts of the land by reference to which the apportionment is made, and so much of the compensation as, in accordance with the apportionment, is attributed to a part of the land shall be treated as distributed rateably according to area over that part of the land;

(d) if any person disputes an apportionment under this *subsection,* the dispute shall be submitted to and decided by a property arbitrator nominated under the *Property Values (Arbitration and Appeals) Act, 1960.*

(5) Where, in connection with the development of any land, an amount becomes recoverable under this *section* in respect of the compensation specified in a compensation statement, then no amount shall be recoverable, in so far as it is attributable to that land, in connection with any subsequent development thereof.

(6) An amount recoverable under this *section* in respect of any compensation shall be payable to the planning authority, and—

(a) shall be so payable, either as a single capital payment or as a series of instalments of capital and interest combined (the interest being determined at the same rate as for a judgment debt), or as a series of other annual or periodical payments, of such amounts, and payable at such times, as the planning authority may direct, after taking into account any representations made by the person by whom the development is to be carried out, and

(b) except where the amount is payable as a single capital payment, shall be secured by that person in such manner (whether by mortgage, covenant or otherwise) as the planning authority may direct.

(7) If any person initiates any development to which this *section* applies in contravention of *subsection (1),* the planning authority may serve a notice upon him or her, specifying the amount appearing to it to be the amount recoverable under this *section* in respect of the compensation in question, and requiring him or her to pay that amount to the planning authority within such period, not being less than 12 weeks after the service of the notice, as may be specified in the notice, and, in default of the amount being paid to the planning authority within the period specified in the notice, it shall be recoverable as a simple contract debt in any court of competent jurisdiction.

NOTE

Where compensation has been awarded in respect of land (for which a compensation statement has been registered), no development can be carried out on such land unless the compensation has been repaid to the planning authority. This applies where the development is of the kind described in s.192(2) as:

"development of a residential, commercial or industrial character, consisting wholly or mainly of the construction of houses, shops or office premises, hotels, garages and petrol filling stations, theatres or structures for the purpose of entertainment, or industrial buildings (including warehouses), or combination thereof".

It does not apply to exempted development or the circumstances specified in s.192(2) concerning development for which compensation was granted subject to certain conditions. If the development covers the full area for which compensation was granted, then all compensation will be recoverable as specified in the compensation statement. However, if it only relates to part of the land, compensation will be repaid only in respect of that part of the land. In such instance, the planning authority can, where practicable, apportion the land for the purpose of calculating the compensation, otherwise the amount of compensation shall be distributed rateably according to area. Where a person disputes an apportionment, it may be referred to an arbitrator. Compensation will not again become repayable for each subsequent development of that same land. Under subs.(6) the planning authority has discretion to decide the manner of repayment, which could be as a single amount or a series of installments or as a series of annual payments. In deciding the manner of repayment they will take account of any representations of the person who carried out the development. Also, except where the repayment is by means of a single capital payment, the person making the repayment must also provide security for repayment as the planning authority may direct.

Subsection (7) provides that where a person commences development without having repaid the compensation in breach of this section, the planning authority may serve a notice requiring payment within a specified period (being not less than 12 weeks). The planning authority may enforce the payment as a contract debt in court. This section largely re-enacts s.10 of the 1990 Act.

CHAPTER II

Compensation in relation to decisions under Part III

Right to compensation

190.—If, on a claim made to the planning authority, it is shown that, as a   **1–228** result of a decision on an appeal under *Part III* involving a refusal of permission to develop land or a grant of permission to develop land subject to conditions, the value of an interest of any person existing in the land to which the decision relates at the time of the decision is reduced, that person shall, subject to the other provisions of this *Chapter,* be entitled to be paid by the planning authority by way of compensation—

  (a) such amount, representing the reduction in value, as may be agreed,

  (b) in the absence of agreement, the amount of such reduction in value, determined in accordance with the *Second Schedule,* and

(c) in the case of the occupier of the land, the damage (if any) to his or her trade, business or profession carried out on the land.

NOTE

This section establishes an entitlement to obtain compensation after a refusal of permission or a grant of permission subject to conditions, which resulted in a reduction in the value of a person's interest in land. This section introduces a new clause as applying only in respect of "a decision on appeal" (i.e. by An Bord Pleanála), compared to s.11 of the 1990 Act, which simply referred to as a result of a decision (which could apply to the planning authority or An Bord Pleanála). This means an appeal must be pursued otherwise a claim cannot be entertained. The claim for compensation is made to the planning authority. The amount of compensation concerns the value by which the interest in land is reduced as a result of the decision. This amount may be determined by agreement or failing so, under the rules for determining the amount of compensation set out in the Second Schedule. In the case of an occupier of the land, the compensation is calculated as being the damage to his trade, business or profession carried out on the land. A person claiming compensation must have an interest in the lands at the time when the decision to refuse or impose conditions was made, although he need not have such interest at the time compensation is assessed; see *Dublin Corporation v Smithwick* [1976–1977] I.L.R.M. 280; *Central Dublin Development Association v Attorney-General* [1975] 109 I.L.T.R. 69; and *Grange Developments v Dublin County Council (No. 2)* [1986] I.R. 246.

The entitlement to compensation must be seen against the constitutional backdrop which underpins the claim for compensation. The compensation provisions are a reflection of the fact that the planning regime is a curtailment of the constitutional property rights of the individual; see *Butler v Dublin Corporation* [1999] 1 I.R. 565 and *In the Matter of Part V of the Planning and Development Bill 1999* [2000] 2 I.R. 321. The institution of private property is protected under art.43 of the Constitution, while art.40.3 protects an individual's exercise of their property rights. The restriction may be justified in the interests of the common good; see *Central Dublin Development Association v Attorney-General* [1975] 109 I.L.T.R. 69. A person's property may also be protected under art.1 of the First Protocol of the European Convention on Human Rights and in the case of a dwelling under art.8. The Long Title to the 2000 Act states that it is "[t]o provide in the interests of the common good, for proper planning and sustainable development". The compensation provisions under Planning Code are therefore payments to compensate persons with property interests from restrictions on their property right in the interests of the common good.

The rules for calculating compensation are set out in the Second Schedule of the 2000 Act, which are identical to the rules under the 1990 Act. The reduction in value will be calculated on the basis of the totality of the lands. Thus where there is a refusal and no undertaking for any other development, a claim for compensation can be based on any development which probably could have been made in accordance with the Planning Acts and which is now prevented; see *Owenbue v Dublin Corporation* [1982] I.L.R.M. 150.

The Second Schedule

The basic principle is that the reduction in value shall be determined by reference to the difference between the antecedent and subsequent values of the land by reference to the relevant decision. In default of agreement, this is determined by an arbitrator under s.184. Paragraph 1 provides that the antecedent value of the land is the amount which the land, if sold on the open market by a willing seller immediately prior to the relevant decision under Pt III (and assuming that the relevant application for permission had not been made), might have been expected to realise, While under (b) the subsequent value of the land is the amount which the land, if sold in the open market by a willing seller immediately after that decision, might be expected to realise. The notion of willing seller and willing buyer means the seller should not be regarded as disinclined to sell, nor should the buyer be regarded as under any urgent necessity to buy. See *Raja Vyricherla Narayana Gajapathiraju v Revenue Divisional Officer, Vizagapatam* [1939] A.C. 302

Paragraph 2(a) sets out matters to which regard shall be had in determining the antecedent value and subsequent value of the land. These are all mandatory considerations, although the precise assessment of their relevance will be a matter within the discretion and expertise of an arbitrator. The application of these criteria will depend on the nature of the relevant decision for which compensation is sought. Under (i) regard must be had to any contribution which a planning authority might have required or might require as a condition precedent to development of the land. Where the relevant decision is refusal of permission, if a planning permission required the payment of contribution under a contribution scheme adopted under ss.48 or 49, this is a payment which the claimant would have had to make after having obtained permission. Also under (ii) regard must be had to any restriction on the development of the land which, without conferring a right to compensation, could have been or could be imposed under any Act or under any order, regulations, rule or bye-law made under any Act. Where restrictions are imposed under the decision, this may reduce the overall subsequent value gain by the person. The nature of such restrictions may well depend both on the nature of the decision and also the nature of the land. In the case of a refusal of permission, the nature of such restrictions would include the type of conditions which could be imposed under s.34(4). Regard must be had to (iii) which concerns the fact that exempted development might have been or may be carried out on the land. This may involve examining what exempted development might still be carried out on the land and also what exempted development might have been carried out. If the land is capable of certain exempted development being carried out, this may effect the subsequent value of the land. Furthermore regard must be had under (iv) to the open market value of comparable land, if any, in the vicinity of the land whose values are being determined. This therefore involves locating a comparator land to that of the claimant. This may be a matter for expert valuation evidence.

Paragraph 2(b) sets out matters to which no account shall be taken in determining their value. In this respect (i) excludes any part of the value of the land attributable to subsidies or grants available from public moneys, or to any tax or rating allowances in respect of development, from which development of the land might benefit. Also excluded under (ii) is the special suitability or adaptability of the land for any purpose if that purpose is a purpose to which it could be applied only in pursuance of statutory powers, or for which there is no market apart from the special needs of a particular purchaser or the requirements of any statutory body as defined. This exclusion is qualified by providing that any bona fide offer for the purchase of the land which may be brought to the notice of the arbitrator shall be taken into consideration. An illustration of special suitability or adaptability is that a house may be worth £750 as a house but £1,000 as an annex to an adjoining nursing home, and so it has a market value of £1,000. See *Inland Revenue Commissioners v Clay* [1914] 3 K.B. 466. The nature of the exclusion means that it is necessary to separate from the market value of land any enhancement in value attributable solely to the presence of the acquiring authority in the market as a purchaser of the land in exercise of its statutory powers. See *Waters v Welsh Development Agency* [2004] 2 P & CR 29. The rationale for the exclusion was explained by Cockburn C.J. in *Stebbing v Metropolitan Board of Works* (1870) LR 6 Q.B. 37, 42, said:

"When Parliament gives compulsory powers, and provides that compensation shall be made to the person from whom property is taken, for the loss that he sustains, it is intended that he shall be compensated to the extent of his loss; and that his loss shall be tested by what was the value of the thing to him, not by what will be its value to the persons acquiring it".

This rationale also explains the qualification to the rule in the case of a bona offer. However, in *Waters v Welsh Development Agency* [2004] 2 P & CR 29, it was held for this exclusion to apply the special suitability must involve something exceptional in character, quality or degree.

No account may be taken of under (iii) any increase in the value of land attributable to the use thereof or of any structure thereon in a manner which could be restrained by any court, or is contrary to law, or detrimental to the health of the inmates of the structure, or to public health or safety, or to the environment. Increase in value as a result of unlawful uses or structures are therefore excluded. However, the exclusion is not confined to uses or structures which are strictly unlawful but also uses or structures which may be restrained by court or are detrimental to the health of the inmates of the structure, or to public health or safety, or to the environment. This is a wide ranging exception. In a planning context it would embrace any unauthorised uses or works. For these purposes it is irrelevant that uses or structures are immune from enforcement action. In *Dublin Corp v Mulligan*, unreported, High Court, May 6, 1980, Finlay P. said:

> "I can see no ground for holding that the restriction imposed … upon the institution of enforcement proceedings … to a period of five years from the unlawful development in any way makes the development lawful".

The rules applies not only to the market value of land, but also its value including compensation for disturbance. See *Hughes v Doncaster M B. Council* [1990] 59 P & CR 365.

Also excluded under (iv) is any depreciation or increase in value attributable to the land, or any land in the vicinity, being reserved for a particular purpose in a development plan. It is recognised that the reservation may increase or depreciate the value of the land. In either case, the value attributable to the reservation is to be excluded. The rationale for this exclusion is that the reservation is for the benefit of the community and so an owner should not suffer or profit from the same. In *Shortt v Dublin County Council* [1982] I.L.R.M. 117, the Supreme Court approved the description of McMahon J. commenting on this rule which was formerly Rule 11 under the 1963 Act, where he said:

> "In the context of Rule 11 the word "reserved" means set apart and "particular purpose" means a purpose distinct from the purpose for which the other land in the area is owned. Rule 11, therefore, refers to land which is set apart from the other land in the area and is zoned for a different purpose and in valuing such land the arbitrator is to disregard the setting apart and value the land at the value it would have had if it had not been so reserved, that is, the value having regard to the purpose for which the land generally in the area is zoned."

In *Monastra Developments Ltd v Dublin Corporation* [1992] 1 I.R. 468, Carroll J. said there must be a point when an area is large enough in its own right not to be considered to be set apart from other adjoining lands. In *Dublin Corporation v McGinley* [1976–77] I.L.R.M. 343, Murphy J. noted that:

> "[T]he reservations themselves are not matters to be taken into account in assessing the value of land under the compensation rules but when such reservations crystalise into or result in the imposition of a specific condition affecting the user of the property of an owner regard must then be had to such as condition".

See also *Holiday Motor Inns v Dublin County Council*, unreported, High Court, McWilliam J., no. 336SS.

Under (v) no account shall be taken of any value attributable to any unauthorised structure or unauthorised use. It would appear irrelevant that the unauthorised structure or use is immune from enforcement action. In *O'Connor v Nenagh UDC*, unreported, High Court, July 16, 1996, Geoghegan J. suggested that the illegal but immune status of an unauthorised development could mean that an owner would not be able to claim compensation if the matter was compulsory acquired by the State. See also *Dublin Corp v Mulligan*, unreported, High Court, May 6, 1980.

Also excluded under (vi) is the existence of proposals for development of the land or any other land by a statutory body and under (vii) the possibility or probability of the land or other land becoming subject to a scheme of development undertaken by a statutory body. In this respect "statutory body" is defined as:

   (a) a Minister of the Government;

   (b) the Commissioners;

   (c) a local authority within the meaning of the Local Government Act 1941;

   (d) a harbour authority within the meaning of the Harbours Act 1946;

   (e) a health board established under the Health Act 1970;

   (f) a vocational education committee within the meaning of the Vocational Education Act 1930;

   (g) a board or other body established by or under statute;

   (h) a company in which all the shares are held by, or on behalf of, or by directors appointed by, a Minister of the Government; or

   (i) a company in which all the shares are held by a board, company, or other body referred to in subpara.(g) or (h).

No value can be taken into account which derives from the scheme; see *Director of Buildings and Land v Shun Fung Ironworks Ltd* [1995] 2 A.C. 111. It may be a question of fact as to whether a particular element forms part of the scheme. Thus in *Re Deansrath Investments* [1974] I.R. 228, the provision of services to the land was not considered to form part of the scheme. Budd J. stated:

> "[T]he words 'if that purpose is a purpose to which it could be applied only in pursuance of statutory power' refer only to such purposes as actually require a particular statutory power to enable a particular purpose to be carried into effect – such as the making of a railway or the like".

However, in *Re Muphy* [1977] I.R. 243, a proposed change to zoning to facilitate the scheme was excluded from consideration. See also *Blandrent Investments Development Ltd v British Gas Corporation* [1979] 252 EG 267.

Paragraph 2(c) provides that all returns and assessments of capital value for taxation made or acquiesced in by the claimant may be considered.

Paragraph 3(1) provides that in assessing the possibilities, if any, for developing the land, for the purposes of determining its antecedent value, regard shall be had only to such reasonable possibilities as, having regard to all material considerations, could be judged to have existed immediately prior to the relevant decision under Pt III. The notion of "possibilities" refers to the hope value of land. Only reasonable possibilities can be taken into account and so remote possibilities are to be disregarded. In determining what were reasonable possibilities all material considerations are to be considered. Paragraph 3(2) then sets out certain matters which are deemed to be material considerations. The matters enlisted are not exhaustive and so there may be other matters which amount to material considerations. These enlisted material considerations are:

(a) the nature and location of the land;
(b) the likelihood or unlikelihood, as the case may be, of obtaining permission or further permission, to develop the land in the light of the provisions of the development plan;
(c) the assumption that, if any permission to develop the land were to be granted, any conditions which might reasonably be imposed in relation to matters referred to in the Fifth Schedule (but no other conditions) would be imposed; and
(d) any permission to develop the land, not being permission for the development of a kind specified in s.192(2), already existing at the time of the relevant decision under Pt III.

Clearly (a) and (b) depend upon the particular facts relating to any land. Also under (c) any assumption can be rebutted on the particular facts of the case. Under (d) any existing permission may give an indication of the type of development which may have been permitted.

Paragragh 4(1) provides that in determining the subsequent value of the land in a case in which there has been a refusal of permission it shall be assumed, subject to subpara.(2), that after the refusal, permission under Pt III would not be granted for any development of a kind specified in s.192(2), and regard shall be had to any conditions in relation to matters referred to in the Fifth Schedule (but no other conditions) which might reasonably be imposed in the grant of permission to develop the land.

Paragraph 4(2) provides that in a case in which there has been a refusal of permission in relation to land in respect of which there is in force an undertaking under Pt VI of the Act of 1963, it shall be assumed in determining the subsequent value of the land that, after the refusal, permission under Pt III of this Act would not be granted for any development other than development to which the undertaking relates.

Restriction of compensation

191.—(1) Compensation under *section 190* shall not be payable in respect **1–229** of the refusal of permission for any development—

(a) of a class or description set out in the *Third Schedule,* or
(b) if the reason or one of the reasons for the refusal is a reason set out in the *Fourth Schedule.*

(2) Compensation under *section 190* shall not be payable in respect of the refusal of permission for any development based on any change of the zoning of any land as a result of the making of a new development plan under *section 12*.

(3) Compensation under *section 190* shall not be payable in respect of the imposition, on the granting of permission to develop land, of any condition of a class or description set out in the *Fifth Schedule*.

(4) Compensation under *section 190* shall not be payable in respect of the refusal of permission, or of the imposition of conditions on the granting of permission, for the retention on land of any unauthorised structures.

NOTE

This section sets out restrictions on the payment of compensation. None of the restrictions apply in the special case of structures substantially replacing structures demolished or destroyed by fire under s.193. The courts have generally stressed that any rule restricting compensation must be interpreted strictly. In *Dublin Corporation v Smithwick* [1976-1977] I.L.R.M. 280, Finlay P. stated that he was satisfied "as to the principle of interpretation of this statute, that I should not put by implication a restriction or condition on a right to compensation unless I am forced to do so". In *Hoburn Homes Limited and Gortalough Holding Limited v An Bord Pleanála* [1993] I.L.R.M. 368, Denham J. stated:

"In coming to this conclusion I am also influenced in construction by the fact that compensation is a statutory right, and it should only be removed in clear precise cases".

It appears however that planning permission cannot be refused on a particular basis merely to exclude compensation as this would be an abuse of power; see *Dublin County Council v Eighty Five Developments Ltd (No. 2)* [1993] 2 I.R. 392.

Under subs.(1)(a) compensation can be excluded in respect of any class or description set out in the Third Schedule. These are eight such classes set out under the Third Schedule (material change of use of a structure; demolition of a habitable house; erection of an advertising structure, etc.). In *Cooper v Cork City Council*, unreported, High Court, Murphy J., November 8, 2006, in a case stated by an arbitrator in a claim for compensation for the imposition of a restrictive planning condition, Murphy J. held that the exclusion of compensation for falling within a condition of a "class or description" (then under the Fourth Schedule to the 1990 Act) was broader than reasons for refusal (then in the Third Schedule). It may be noted that with respect to the 2000 Act, both Sch.3 (refusal of development) and Sch.5 (conditions) use the phrase "class or description".

Also under subs.(1)(b) compensation will not be payable where the reason includes any of the 20 reasons set out in the Fourth Schedule (e.g. premature by reason of lack of facilities or pending a road layout plan; public safety reasons; protecting amenities or development concerning a material change of use). In order to avoid paying compensation, the reasons for refusal should generally follow the wording of the provision of the Fourth Schedule; see *Re XJS Investments* [1996] I.R. 750, and *Grange Developments Ltd v Dublin County Council* [1986] I.R. 246. The strictness of this approach was somewhat tempered in *Dublin County Council v Eighty Five Developments (No. 2)* [1993] 2 I.R. 392, where the Supreme Court indicated that the reasons would not be rejected if they did not come within the exact formula so long as the meaning is otherwise clear. See also *J Wood & Company Ltd v Wicklow County Council* [1995] 1 I.L.R.M. 51 ("visually sensitive location" could not cover the reason of preserving a view or prospect of special amenity value), and *Hoburn Homes Ltd v An Bord Pleanála* [1993] I.L.R.M. 368 (in which it was held that "to slow down the growth in the west harbour" did not indicate a priority for the development of that area). This section re-enacts s.12 of the 1990 Act.

Subsection (2) provides that compensation shall not be payable in respect of a refusal of compensation based on a change of zoning of land, or as a result of the making of a new development plan. Compensation cannot be excluded where the reason for refusal referred to provisons of a draft development plan. See *Ebonwood v Meath County Council* [2004] 3

I.R. 34. Zoning was defined in *O'Connor v Clare County Council*, unreported, High Court, Murphy J., February 11, 1994, as "a wider area where activities or developments having some measure of uniformity may be undertaken by a considerable number of owners or occupiers". However, he went on to say that that there would be:

> "nothing to prevent a planning authority from indicating a specific development objective in relation to a limited area with a view to or as a consequence of formulating a development objective in relation to an adjoining larger area".

The exclusion for zoning reflects s.10(8) which provides that there shall be no presumption in law that any land zoned in a particular development plan shall remained zoned in any subsequent plan. This exclusion is further supported by a separate reason for excluding compensation under para.20 of Sch.4, which provides that compensation is excluded where the development would contravene materially a development objective in the development plan for the zoning of land for the use solely or primarily of particular areas for particular purposes. Under the 1990 Act, compensation remained payable where the proposed development would not have contravened the previous zoning objectives of the land over the previous five years, though it contravenes the current zoning objective. This qualification has not been re-enacted under the 2000 Act. The wording of para.21 of Sch.4 which qualifies para.20 is extremely confusing which provides that that the exclusion of compensation does not apply where the development objective was changed as a result of a variation of the development plan "prior" to the date upon which the relevant application for permission was made to develop the land. This paragraph would appear to only make sense if the word "subsequent" was substituted for "prior". This is supported by the qualification in para.22 which provides that para.21 will not apply where the person acquired his interest in the land after the objective came into operation or after notice concerning the proposed variation or material alteration had been published. Thus the exclusion will not apply to a person who made his planning application prior to the variation being made, if he already had an interest in the land prior to the objective contained in the variation coming into effect and prior to the notice of the variation being published. As the meaning of para.21, is either obscure or on a literal interpretation, absurd, s.5 of the Interpretation Act 2005 would support such a purposive interpretation.

Under subs.(3) compensation will not be payable where the grant of permission is subject to any of the 34 conditions set out in the Sch.5 (e.g. requiring giving of security for completion of the development; requiring a contribution to a public infrastructure benefiting the development, etc.). Much of these conditions relate to matters resulting from the proposed development. In *Cooper v Cork City Council*, unreported, High Court, Murphy J., November 8, 2006, where the reason prohibited development on a particular part of the application site and required the area to be retained in its natural undeveloped state, it was held this condition relation to the "preservation and protection of trees, shrubs, plants and flowers" and so was a condition which excluded compensation.

Subsection (4) excludes compensation in the case of the refusal of a retention permission application.

Notice preventing compensation

192.—(1) Where a claim for compensation is made under *section 190,* the planning authority concerned may, not later than 12 weeks after the claim is received, and having regard to all the circumstances of the case, serve a notice in such form as may be prescribed on the person by whom or on behalf of whom the claim has been made stating that, notwithstanding the refusal of permission to develop land or the grant of permission to develop land subject to conditions, the land in question is in its opinion capable of other development for which permission under *Part III* ought to be granted.

1–230

(2) For the purpose of *subsection (1),* "other development" *means development of a residential, commercial or industrial character, consisting wholly or mainly of the construction of houses, shops or office premises,* *hotels, garages and petrol filling stations, theatres or structures for the purpose of entertainment, or industrial buildings (including warehouses), or any combination thereof.*

(3) A notice under *subsection (1)* shall continue in force for a period of 5 years commencing on the day of service of the notice, unless before the expiration of that period—

  (a) the notice is withdrawn by the planning authority,

  (b) a permission is granted under *Part III* to develop the land to which the notice relates in a manner consistent with the other development specified in the notice, subject to no conditions or to conditions of a class or description set out in the *Fifth Schedule,* or

  (c) the notice is annulled by virtue of *subsection (5)*.

(4) Compensation shall not be payable on a claim made under *section 190* where—

  (a) a notice under *subsection (1)* is in force in relation to that claim,

  (b) a notice under *subsection (1)* was in force in relation to that claim but has ceased to be in force by reason of the expiration of the period referred to in *subsection (3),* and an application for permission under *Part III* to develop the land to which the notice relates, in a manner consistent with the other development specified in the notice, has not been made within that period, or

  (c) a notice under *subsection (1)* was in force in relation to the claim but has ceased to be in force by virtue of *subsection (3)(b)*.

(5) A notice under *subsection (1)* shall be annulled where, upon an application for permission under *Part III* to develop the land to which the notice relates in a manner consistent with the other development specified in the notice, the permission is refused or is granted subject to conditions other than conditions of a class or description set out in the *Fifth Schedule.*

(6) No claim for compensation under *section 190* shall lie in relation to a decision under *Part III* referred to in *subsection (5)*.

NOTE

This section provides that the planning authority may refuse to pay compensation in respect of a refusal of permission or imposition of conditions, where it has served a notice stating its opinion that the land is capable of other development for which compensation ought to be granted.

Under subs.(1) the planning authority must have "regard to all the circumstances of the case", before serving a notice. The planning authority will be afforded a discretion in considering the circumstances of the case. The circumstances of the case will be relevant to whether it is appropriate to the serve a notice expressing its opinion in respect of other development. If the development for which permission was refused or conditions imposed, is radically different to the range of other development defined in s.192(2), that it would not be appropriate to serve such notice. The concept of capable of other development for which permission under Pt III "ought to be granted", sits uneasily with the whole public consultative nature of the planning process. It involves the planning authority expressing an opinion on a planning application that has not been made, the details of which have not been expressed and on which the public have had no input. The provision of such notice was introduced under s.13 of the Local Government (Planning and Development Act 1990, which replaced the previous procedure under the 1963 Act of giving an "undertaking" to grant permission. The reasons given by the Minister for replacing the "undertaking" procedure, was that it involved a quasi-contractual commitment by the executive of the planning authority to grant a particular planning permission. However an undertaking to grant permission was not equated to a grant of permission as noted by Gannon J. in *Byrne v Dublin County Council* [1983] I.L.R.M. 213. In relation to an undertaking to grant permission under the 1963 Act, it was considered appropriate to allow members of the public to make representations. In *Grange Developments Ltd v Dublin County Council* [1986] I.R. 246.

Article 177 of the Planning Regulations 2001 sets out the form of such notice. The notice must:

- indicate the land to which the notice relates;
- state that, notwithstanding the refusal of permission to develop the land or the grant of such permission subject to conditions (as the case may be), the land in question is, in the opinion of the planning authority, capable of other development for which permission under Pt III of the Act ought to be granted, indicate in outline the nature and extent of the other development (being other development within the meaning of s.192 of the Act) of which, in the opinion of the planning authority, the land is capable;
- state that the notice shall continue in force for a period of five years commencing on the day of service of the notice unless, before the expiration of that period:
  — the notice is withdrawn by the planning authority;
  — a permission is granted under Pt III of the Act to develop the land to which the notice relates in a manner consistent with the other development specified in the notice, subject to no conditions or to conditions of a class or description set out in the Fifth Schedule of the Act; or
  — the notice is annulled by virtue of s.192(5) of the Act; and
- state that compensation shall not be payable on the claim in respect of the land in question where:
  — the notice is in force;
  — an application for permission under Pt III of the Act to develop the land to which the notice relates in a manner consistent with the other development specified in the notice has not been made before the expiration of the notice; or
  — permission is granted under Pt III of the Act to develop the land to which the notice relates in a manner consistent with the other development specified in the notice, subject to no conditions or to conditions of a class or description set out in Sch.5 of the Act.

The notice must not be served later than 12 weeks after the claim is received (it was three months under the 1990 Act). The notice must adequately describe the other development. A mere vague assurance that the planning authority concerned would give very favourable consideration to a detailed application is insufficient; see *Grange Development v Dublin County Council (2)* [1989] I.R. 314. The notice will continue in force for five years unless it is withdrawn, annulled or where permission is granted for other development consistent with the development described in the notice. The notice will be annulled where a subsequent application to develop the land consistent with the other development specified in the notice is refused or granted subject to conditions. Where the planning permission is refused, the planning authority will not be able to serve a second notice where the 12 weeks have elapsed. There is no second three-month period of limitation within which a second notice may be served; see *Arthur v Kerry County Council* [2000] 3 I.R. 407. There is no provision for extending the time for service of the notice.

When a valid claim for compensation is received is therefore of considerable importance as time will run from that date. In *Abbeydrive Developments Ltd v Kildare County Council*, unreported, High Court, Macken J., June 17, 2005, Macken J. rejected the argument that the applicant had not properly stated their interest in lands. She held a valid claim had been submitted where the claimant had stated they were the owner holding the land under two identified conveyances, together with a statement that no other person except a bank had any interest in the lands. Macken J. noted that if the exact nature of the precise legal interest under which the claimant, as freeholder, or as leaseholder, charge holder or so forth, holds the land, was an essential regulatory requirement, one would expect to find words in the regulations which would make this clear.

Subsection (2) concerns the other development which must be referred to in the notice. The notice will only be valid where the "other development" falls within this definition.

There are two parts to the definition which is that the development is:
1. of a residential, commercial or industrial character and
2. consisting "wholly or mainly" of the construction of houses, shops or office premises, hotels, garages and petrol filling stations, theatres or structures for the purpose of entertainment, or industrial buildings (including warehouses), or any combination thereof.

Section 10(2)(a) of the 2000 Act describes the zoning of land for particular purposes (whether residential, commercial, industrial, agricultural, recreational, as open space or otherwise, or a mixture of those uses). The notice therefore is not applicable, for example, where the potential other development is agricultural or recreational. As regards the second part of the definition, the use of the phrase "wholly or mainly" means that the primary use must relate to the named structures although it may be used for some other purpose so long as it is subsidiary to the named primary use. In addition to the requirement that development in the notice falls within the definition of "other development", it would also appear necessary that such "other development" be described with a degree of precision. It is certainly advisable for the planning authority to define the other development with a degree of precision which could form the subject matter of a planning application. Where there is ambiguity this may lead to refusal of the application submitted and time for service of another notice may have expired. It is not sufficient merely to state the general formula. Article 177(c) provides that the notice should "indicate in outline the nature and extent of the other development". The planning authority should strictly follow the wording in expressing the opinion that the development "ought" to be granted. This was certainly the case under the case law dealing with the giving of undertakings which may offer some guidance. See *Grange Developments Limited v Dublin County* Council [1986] I.R. 246. A planning authority can specify other development for which compensation ought to be granted, even where such development is a material contravention of the development plan. In *Browne v Cashel UDC*, unreported, High Court, Geoghegan J., March 26, 1993, Geoghegan J. had said that this other development must not be in material conflict with the development plan. However, this was not followed by the Supreme Court in *Ballymac Designer Village Ltd v Clare County Council* [2002] 3 I.R. 247. The Supreme Court noted that a planning authority may by invoking a special procedure, grant planning permission even where the proposed development involves a material contravention of the development plan.

Special provision for structures substantially replacing structures demolished or destroyed by fire

1–231   **193.—(1)** Nothing in *section 191* shall prevent compensation being paid—

(a) in a case in which there has been a refusal of permission for the erection of a new structure substantially replacing a structure (other than an unauthorised structure) which has been demolished or destroyed by fire or otherwise than by an unlawful act of the owner or of the occupier with the agreement of the owner within the 2 years preceding the date of application for permission, or there has been imposed a condition in consequence of which the new structure may not be used for the purpose for which the demolished or destroyed structure was last used, or

(b) in a case in which there has been imposed a condition in consequence of which the new structure referred to in *paragraph (a)* or the front thereof, or the front of an existing structure (other than an unauthorised structure) which has been taken down in order to be re-erected or altered, is set back or forward.

(2) Every dispute and question as to whether a new structure would or does replace substantially within the meaning of *subsection (1)* a demolished or destroyed structure shall be referred to the Board for determination.

This section provides that compensation will be payable where there has been a refusal of permission concerning the erection of a new structure substantially replacing a structure which was demolished or destroyed by fire, or where a condition was imposed whereby the new structure cannot be used for the purpose of the demolished or destroyed structure. However, for this provision to apply the previous structure must have been demolished within the two years preceding the date of application for permission. Furthermore the previous structure must not have been an unauthorised structure. Equally the structure must not have been demolished or destroyed as a result of the unlawful act of the owner or occupier with the agreement of the owner. Compensation may also be payable where as a result of conditions the new structure or front of such structure or the front of an existing structure which had been taken down has been set back or forward. The restrictions on payment of compensation set out in s.191 are inapplicable. The new structure need not be identical to the previous structure as long as it would substantially replace such structure, for the determination of which a referral may be made to An Bord Pleanála. This section re-enacts s.15 of the 1990 Act.

Restriction on assignment of compensation under section 190

194.—A person shall not be entitled to assign to any other person all or any part of any prospective compensation under *section 190,* and every purported assignment or promise, express or implied, to pay any other person any money in respect of any such compensation is void.   1–232

NOTE

This section makes an agreement to assign a right to compensation unenforceable and void. This section re-enacts s.16 of the 1990 Act. In *Dublin Corporation v Smithwick* [1977–78] 1 I.L.R.M. 280, it was held that it was not necessary that the claimant would have to retain their interest in the land up to the date of the assessment of compensation.

Compensation where permission is revoked or modified

195.—(1) Where permission to develop land has been revoked or modified by a decision under *section 44* —   1–233
- **(a)** if, on a claim made to the planning authority, it is shown that any person interested in the land has incurred expenditure or entered into a contract to incur expenditure in respect of works which are rendered abortive by the revocation or modification, the planning authority shall pay to that person compensation in respect of that expenditure or contract,
- **(b)** the provisions of this *Part* shall apply in relation to the decision where it revoked the permission or modified it by the imposition of conditions—
  - **(i)** in case it revoked the permission, as they apply in relation to refusal of permission to develop land, and
  - **(ii)** in case it modified the permission by the imposition of conditions, as they apply in relation to a grant of permission to develop land subject to conditions.

(2) For the purposes of this *section,* any expenditure reasonably incurred in the preparation of plans for the purposes of any works or upon other similar

matters preparatory thereto shall be deemed to be included in the expenditure incurred in carrying out those works but, no compensation shall be paid by virtue of this *section* in respect of any works carried out before the grant of the permission which is revoked or modified, or in respect of any other loss or damage arising out of anything done or omitted to be done before the grant of that permission.

NOTE

This section provides for compensation to be paid where a planning authority has served a notice under s.44 to revoke or modify a planning permission because it is no longer in accordance with the development plan. Compensation will be paid to any person interested in the land for expenditure incurred or a contract entered into in respect of the work rendered useless because of the revocation or modification. For the purposes of compensation, revocation or modification of a permission is treated as the equivalent of a refusal of permission or a grant subject to conditions. Thus the compensation provisions apply to a revocation as if permission was refused and to a modification as if the permission was granted subject to conditions. Compensation will be paid for expenditure reasonably incurred in relation to the preparation of plans for the purposes of any work, though no compensation will be payable for any expenditure or loss incurred on works carried out prior to the grant of permission which has been revoked or modified or any loss or damages as a result of anthing done or omitted before the grant of permission. This provision re-enacts s.17 of the 1990 Act.

CHAPTER III

Compensation in relation to sections 46, 85, 88, 182, 207 and 252

Compensation regarding removal or alteration of structure

1–234   **196.**—If, on a claim made to the planning authority, it is shown that, as a result of the removal or alteration of any structure consequent upon a notice under *section 46,* the value of an interest of any person in the structure existing at the time of the confirmation of the notice is reduced, or that any person having an interest in the structure at that time has suffered damage by being disturbed in his or her enjoyment of the structure, that person shall, subject to the other provisions of this *Part,* be entitled to be paid by the planning authority by way of compensation the amount of the reduction in value or the amount of the damage.

NOTE

This section provides for compensation where a notice for removal or discontinuance under s.46 has been served. Compensation will be paid to a person who has an interest in the structure in respect of a reduction in value of the structure or damage as a result of being disturbed in the enjoyment of the structure. This section re-enacts s.18 of the 1990 Act.

Compensation regarding discontinuance of use

1–235   **197.—(1)** If, on a claim made to the planning authority, it is shown that, as a result of the discontinuance, or the compliance with conditions on the continuance, of any use of land consequent upon a notice under *section 46,* the value of an interest of any person in the land existing at the time of the confirmation of the notice is reduced, or that any person having an interest in the land at that time has suffered damage by being disturbed in his or her enjoyment of the land, that person shall, subject to the other provisions in this *Part,* be entitled to be paid by the planning authority by way of compensation the amount of the reduction in value or the amount of the damage.

(2) Notwithstanding *subsection (1),* no compensation shall be paid under this *section* in relation to reduction in value or damage resulting from the imposition under *section 46* of conditions on the continuance of the use of land, being conditions imposed in order to avoid or reduce serious water pollution or the danger of such pollution.

(3) *Subsection (1)* shall not apply where the use of land is for the exhibition of advertising unless at the time of the discontinuance or compliance, the land has been used for the exhibition of advertising for less than 5 years, whether the use was continuous or intermittent or whether or not, while the land was being so used, advertising was exhibited at the same place on the land.

NOTE

This section provides for compensation where a notice for discontinuance (or continuance subject to conditions) of use of land under s.46 has been served. Compensation will be paid to a person who has an interest in the land in respect of a reduction in value of the land or damage as a result of being disturbed in the enjoyment of the land. Under s.197(1) compensation is not automatic and it must be shown that as a result of the restrictive condition, either the value of an interest of any person in the land existing at the time of the imposition of the condition is reduced, or any person having an interest in the land at that time has suffered damage by being disturbed in his or her enjoyment of the land.

Subsection (2) provides that compensation will not be payable where a condition for continuance is imposed to avoid water pollution or where the use of land is for the exhibition of advertising unless the land had been so used for less than five years. Such exceptions do not apply in the case of compensation under s.196. Apart from the new provision for the non-payment of compensation for conditions to avoid pollution, this section largely re-enacts s.19 of the 1990 Act.

Compensation claim relating to area of special planning control

198.—If, on a claim made to a planning authority, it is shown that—   **1–236**

    (a) the value of an interest of any person in land in an area of special planning control has been reduced, or

    (b) as a result of complying with a notice under *section 88,* the value of an interest of any person in the land existing at the time of the notice has been reduced, or that any person, having an interest in the land at the time, has suffered damage by being disturbed in his or her enjoyment of the structure or other land,

that person shall be paid by the planning authority, by way of compensation, a sum equal to the amount of the reduction in value or a sum in respect of the damage suffered.

NOTE

Under this section compensation is payable in relation to land within an special area of planning control. A special area of planning control scheme may be adopted under s.85. Under s.88, the planning authority may serve a notice in pursuance of the special control scheme requiring an occupier or owner of land to take certain steps (such as restoration, demolition, discontinuance of use, etc.). Compensation may be payable where the value of land has been reduced by the designation of an area as an area of special planning control or, as a result of complying with a s.88 notice, where the value of the land has been reduced or such person has suffered damage by being disturbed in the enjoyment of the land. Under s.88(2)(g), the planning authority is also required to pay any expenses reasonably incurred by the owner/occupier in carrying out the steps specified in the notice, other than relating to unauthorised development carried out within seven years prior to service of the notice. This section is new, having no counterpart in the previous Acts, as the designation of an area of special planning control was newly introduced under the 2000 Act.

Compensation regarding cables, wires and pipelines

1–237   **199.**—If, on a claim made to the local authority, it is shown that, as a result of the action of the authority pursuant to *section 182* in placing, renewing or removing any cable, wire or pipeline, attaching any bracket or fixture or affixing any notice, the value of an interest of any person in the land or structure existing at the time of the action of the planning authority is reduced, or that any person having an interest in the land or structure at that time has suffered damage by being disturbed in his or her enjoyment of the land or structure, that person shall, subject to the other provisions of this *Part,* be entitled to be paid by the local authority by way of compensation the amount of the reduction in value or the amount of the damage.

NOTE

This section provides for compensation where the local authority has used its power under s.182, in placing or removing cables, pipes, etc. or attaching a bracket or fixture, etc. Compensation will be paid to a person who has an interest in the structure/land in respect of reduction in value of the structure/land or damage as a result of being disturbed in the enjoyment of the structure/land. This section re-enacts s.24 of the 1990 Act.

Compensation regarding creation of public rights of way

1–238   **200.**—If, on a claim made to the planning authority, it is shown that the value of an interest of any person in land, being land over which a public right of way has been created by an order under *section 207* made by that authority, is reduced, or that any person having an interest in the land has suffered damage by being disturbed in his or her enjoyment of the land, in consequence of the creation of the public right of way, that person shall, subject to the other provisions of this *Part,* be entitled to be paid by the planning authority by way of compensation the amount of the reduction in value or the amount of the damage.

NOTE

This section provides for compensation where the local authority has used its power under s.207 for the compulsory creation of a public right of way over land. Under s.207, the planning authority can pass a resolution for the creation of a public right of way where they consider there is a need. Compensation will be paid to a person in respect of a reduction in value of the land or damage as a result of being disturbed in the enjoyment of the land. This section re-enacts s.22 of the 1990 Act. However, certain rights of way may be preserved by a development plan without giving rise to a compensation claim.

Compensation regarding entry on land

201.—If, on a claim made to the planning authority, it is shown that, as **1–239**
a result of anything done under *section 252 or 253,* any person has suffered
damage, the person shall, subject to the other provisions of this *Part,* be entitled
to be paid by the planning authority by way of compensation the amount of
the damage.

NOTE

This section provides for compensation for damage as a result of the planning authority
using its power under s.252 for an authorised person to enter or under s.253, any land for
enforcement purposes. Under s.252 an authorised person may enter on any land at all
reasonable times between the hours of 9am and 6pm, or during business hours in respect
of a premises which is normally open outside those hours, for any purpose connected with
the Act. An authorised person may also do all things reasonably necessary for the purposes
of entry, including making plans, taking photographs, levels, making excavations, and
examining the depth and nature of the subsoil. Under s.253, an authorised person may, for
any purpose of enforcement under Pt VIII (at all reasonable times, or at any time if he or
she has reasonable grounds for believing that an unauthorised development been, is being
or likely to be carried out), enter any premises and bring such persons (members of the
Garda Síochána) or equipment necessary for such purpose.

PART XIII

AMENITIES

Area of special amenity

202.—(1) Where, in the opinion of the planning authority, by reason of— **1–240**
   (a) its outstanding natural beauty, or
   (b) its special recreational value,
and having regard to any benefits for nature conservation, an area should
be declared under this *section* to be an area of special amenity, it may, by
resolution, make an order to do so and the order may state the objective of
the planning authority in relation to the preservation or enhancement of the
character or special features of the area, including objectives for the prevention
or limitation of development in the area.
   (2) Where it appears to the Minister that an area should be declared under
this *section* to be an area of special amenity by reason of—
   (a) its outstanding natural beauty, or
   (b) its special recreational value,
and having regard to any benefits for nature conservation, he or she may, if
he or she considers it necessary, direct a planning authority to make an order
under this *section* in relation to an area specified in the direction and may, if he
or she thinks fit, require that objectives specified in the direction be included
by the planning authority in the order in respect of matters and in a manner
so specified, and if the Minister gives a direction under this *subsection* the
planning authority concerned shall comply with the direction.
   (3) An order made pursuant to a direction under *subsection (2)* shall be
revoked or amended only with the consent of the Minister.
   (4) An order under this *section* shall come into operation on being confirmed,

whether with or without modification, under *section 203.*

(5) Where the functional areas of two planning authorities are contiguous, either authority may, with the consent of the other, make an order under this *section* in respect of an area in or partly in the functional area of the other.

(6) Any order under this *section* may be revoked or varied by a subsequent order under this *section.*

(7) Subject to *subsection (3),* a planning authority may, from time to time, review an order made under this *section* (excepting any order merely revoking a previous order), for the purpose of deciding whether it is desirable to revoke or amend the order.

NOTE

This section allows the planning authority to designate an area as an area of special amenity. The criteria for determining whether to make such a designation is that the area is of outstanding natural beauty or has special recreational value, with regard being had to any benefits of nature conservation. This section largely re-enacts s.42 of the 1963 Act. The order may state the objectives in relation to preservation or enhancement of the character or special features of the area, including objectives for the prevention or limitation of development in the area. In addition to designating an area, the order should also include objectives in relation to its preservation and enhancement. This indicates that the objectives may be positive as well negative, i.e. not limited to simply restricting development.

Under subs.(2) the Minister may also direct the local authority to make such an order, setting out the objectives in the directions, which the local authority are obligated to obey. An order made following a direction of the Minister can only be revoked with the consent of the Minister. Where the area is partly in the functional area of two contiguous planning authorities, either authority may make the order with the consent of the other. Subsection (7) states that a planning authority may from time to time review such order.

Where a special amenity order is made this has considerable significance for development with the area of the order. Section 34(2)(a)(ii) provides that, in determining a planning application, regard should be had, inter alia, to the provisions of any special amenity order relating to the area. Section 10(2)(e) requires a development plan to include objectives in relation to, inter alia, the preservation of amenities. The subject of an amenity order may well be reflected in the development plan, in which case it would be a material contravention of the development plan to carry out development in the area which is the subject of the order. Also, art.9(1)(b) of the Planning Regulations 2001 provides that certain classes of development within the area of a special amenity area will not be exempted development. These classes include the construction, erection, lowering, repair or replacement of any fence or wall of brick, stone, blocks with decorative finish, other concrete blocks or mass concrete; certain industrial development; development by statutory undertakers; and certain use of land for the exhibition of certain advertisements. Furthermore, under art.9(1)(b)(iv), the planning authority may state in an order that certain classes of development are not entitled to be exempted. The procedure for making an order of designation involves the elected members passing a resolution, which must be confirmed under the procedure set out in s.203, when the order will then take effect. Article 28 of the 2001 Regulations states there is a requirement to notify An Chomhairle Ealaíon; Fáilte Éireann and An Taisce (the National Trust for Ireland) where there is a planning application within an area of special amenity. Paragraph 6 of Sch.3 provides that compensation is not payable where planning permission is refused in respect of development within a special amenity area. Meanwhile, s.22 of the Roads Act 1993 provides that the National Road Authority must have regard to the provisions of a special amenity area order when performing functions in relation to the construction or maintenance of a national road. The planning authority may review the orders at its discretion, though it can only revoke or amend such orders with the consent of the Minister.

Confirmation of order under section 202

203.—(1) As soon as may be after it has made an order under *section 202,*   **1–241**
a planning authority shall publish in one or more newspapers circulating in
the area to which the order relates a notice—

  (a) stating the fact of the order having been made, and describing the
      area to which it relates,

  (b) naming a place where a copy of the order and of any map referred
      to therein may be seen during office hours,

  (c) specifying the period (not being less than 4 weeks) within which,
      and the manner in which, objections to the order may be made to
      the planning authority, and

  (d) specifying that the order requires confirmation by the Board and
      that, where any objections are duly made to the order and are not
      withdrawn, an oral hearing will be held and the objections will be
      considered before the order is confirmed.

(2) As soon as may be after the period for making objections has expired,
the planning authority may submit the order made under *section 202* to the
Board for confirmation, and, when making any such submission, it shall also
submit to the Board any objections to the order which have been duly made
and have not been withdrawn.

(3)

  (a) If no objection is duly made to the order, or if all objections so made
      are withdrawn, the Board may confirm the order made under *section
      202,* with or without modifications, or refuse to confirm it.

  (b) Where any objections to the order are not withdrawn, the Board
      shall hold an oral hearing and shall consider the objections, and may
      then confirm the order, with or without modifications, or refuse to
      confirm it.

(4) Any reference in this *Act,* or any other enactment, to a special amenity
area order shall be construed as a reference to an order confirmed under this
section.

NOTE

This section sets out the procedure for confirming an order designating an area as an
area of special amenity. Having made the order by resolution, the planning authority must
publish a newspaper notice, stating the fact of the order and describing the area, that the
order and maps can be inspected at a specified place for a period not being less than four
weeks and the manner by which submissions may be made. Unlike in the case of a proposal
for a tree preservation order, there is no express requirement to state the reasons behind
the order, although the reasons may be required to be furnished under the principles of
natural and constitutional justice. Equally there is no requirement to notify occupiers or
owners of land within the area of the order. However, under the principles of natural and
constitutional justice, the planning authority may well be advised to specifically notify
such occupiers or owners. Where the period for submissions has expired, the authority may
submit the order to An Bord Pleanála for confirmation, along with any objections. Where
no objections have been received or they have been withdrawn, the Board may confirm
the order, with or without modification, or may refuse it. It appears that in the case of no
objections, the role of the Board is not simply a formal process of confirmation. The Board
still has a discretion to determine whether to confirm the order. However, where there is an
objection, the Board must hold an oral hearing. Having considered such objections at the

oral hearing, the Board may confirm the order, with or without modification, or may refuse it. The conduct of an oral hearing would be in accordance with s.135.

Landscape conservation areas

1–242

204.—(1) A planning authority may, by order, for the purposes of the preservation of the landscape, designate any area or place within the functional area of the authority as a landscape conservation area.

(2)

    (a) Notwithstanding any exemption granted under *section 4* or under any regulations made under that *section,* the Minister may prescribe development for the purpose of this *section,* which shall not be exempted development.

    (b) Development prescribed under *paragraph (a)* may be subject to any conditions or restrictions that the Minister may prescribe.

(3) An order made by a planning authority under this *section* may specify, in relation to all or any part of the landscape conservation area, that any development prescribed by the Minister under *subsection (2)* shall be considered not to be exempted development in that area.

(4) Where a planning authority proposes to make an order under this *section,* it shall cause notice of the proposed order to be published in one or more newspapers circulating in the area of the proposed landscape conservation area.

(5) A notice under *subsection (4)* shall state that—

    (a) the planning authority proposes to make an order designating a landscape conservation area, indicating the place or places and times at which a map outlining the area may be inspected, and shall give details of the location of the area and any prescribed development which it proposes to specify in the order, and

    (b) submissions or observations regarding the proposed order may be made to the planning authority within a stated period of not less than 6 weeks, and that the submissions or observations will be taken into consideration by the planning authority.

(6) The members of a planning authority, having considered the proposed order and any submissions or observations made in respect of it, may, as they consider appropriate, by resolution, make the order, with or without modifications, or refuse to make the order.

(7) Where a planning authority wishes to amend or revoke an order made under this *section,* the planning authority shall give notice of its intention to amend or revoke the order, as the case may be.

(8) A notice under *subsection (7)* (which shall include particulars of the proposed amendment or revocation of the order) shall be published in one or more newspapers circulating in the landscape conservation area.

(9) A notice under *subsection (7)* shall state that—

    (a) the planning authority proposes to amend or revoke the order, and

    (b) submissions or observations regarding the proposed amendment or revocation of the order may be made to the planning authority within a stated period of not less than 6 weeks, and that the submissions or observations will be taken into consideration by the planning authority.

(10) The planning authority, having considered the proposed amendment or revocation of the order and any submissions or observations made in respect of it, may by resolution, as it considers appropriate, revoke the order or amend the order, with or without modifications, or refuse to make the order, as the case may be.

(11) Before making an order under this *section,* the planning authority shall consult with any State authority where it considers that any order relates to the functions of that State authority.

(12)

(a) A planning authority shall give notice of any order made under this *section* in at least one newspaper circulating in its functional area, and the notice shall give details of any prescribed development which is specified in the order.

(b) Notice under this *subsection* shall also be given to the Board and to any other prescribed body which in the opinion of the planning authority has an interest in such notice.

(13) Where 2 or more planning authorities propose to jointly designate any area or place, which is situated within the combined functional area of the planning authorities concerned, as a landscape conservation area, the functions conferred on a planning authority under this *section* shall be performed jointly by the planning authorities concerned, and any reference to "planning authority" shall be construed accordingly.

(14) Particulars of an order under this *section* shall be entered in the register.

NOTE

This section allows a planning authority to designate an area as a landscape conservation area. The Minister may prescribe certain development within an area as not being exempted development and the order of the planning designating the area as a landscape conservation area may specify that any development prescribed by the Minister will not be exempted development within such area. The Minister has yet to make any such regulations. However, where such regulations are made, the development within an area will only lose the status of exempted development where additionally the order specifies, in relation to all or part of the area, that any development prescribed by the Minister shall not be exempted development.

Prior to making the order of designation, the planning authority must publish a newspaper notice of such proposal, inter alia, inviting submissions from the public within a specified period of not less than six weeks. The notice must indicate the places and times at which a map outlining the area may be inspected and give details of the location of the area and any prescribed development. Subsection (11) provides that before making an order the planning authority must also consult with any State authority where it considers the order relates to any State Authority. The planning authority, having considered any submissions, may by resolution make the order with or without modifications or may refuse to do so. Having made the order, the planning authority must publish a newspaper notice specifying the order and must send a notice to the Board or other prescribed body which has an interest. Unlike the making of a special amenity order under s.203, there is no requirement for confirmation by the Board. Two or more planning authorities may propose to jointly designate any area or place as a landscape conservation area in which case the functions for making the order must be performed jointly.

Where the planning authority proposes to amend or revoke an order, the planning authority must follow the same procedure of publishing a newspaper notice of the proposal inviting submissions. Paragraph 17 of Sch.4 provides that the entitlement to compensation is excluded where a reason for refusal of planning permission is that the development would adversely affect a landscape conservation order. This is further supported by para.8 of Sch.4, where the reason was that the development would interfere, inter alia, with the character of a landscape.

Tree preservation orders

1–243   **205.—(1)** If it appears to the planning authority that it is expedient, in the interests of amenity or the environment, to make provision for the preservation of any tree, trees, group of trees or woodlands, it may, for that purpose and for stated reasons, make an order with respect to any such tree, trees, group of trees or woodlands as may be specified in the order.

(2) Without prejudice to the generality of *subsection (1),* an order under this *section* may—

   (a) prohibit (subject to any conditions or exemptions for which provision may be made by the order) the cutting down, topping, lopping or wilful destruction of trees, and

   (b) require the owner and occupier of the land affected by the order to enter into an agreement with the planning authority to ensure the proper management of any trees, group of trees or woodlands (including the replanting of trees), subject to the planning authority providing assistance, including financial assistance, towards such management as may be agreed.

(3)

   (a) Where a planning authority proposes to make an order under this *section,* it shall—

      (i) serve a notice (which shall include particulars of the proposed order) of its intention to do so on the owner and the occupier of the land affected by the order, and

      (ii) cause notice of the proposed order to be published in one or more newspapers circulating in its functional area.

   (b) A notice under *paragraph (a)(i)* shall be accompanied by a map indicating the tree, trees, group of trees or woodland to be preserved.

(4) A notice under *subsection (3)* shall state that—

   (a) the planning authority proposes to make an order preserving the tree, trees, group of trees or woodlands,

   (b) submissions or observations regarding the proposed order may be made to the planning authority within a stated period of not less than 6 weeks, and that the submissions or observations will be taken into consideration by the planning authority, and

   (c) any person who contravenes an order or, pending the decision of a planning authority, a proposed order under this *section,* shall be guilty of an offence.

(5) The planning authority, having considered the proposal and any submissions or observations made in respect of it, may by resolution, as it considers appropriate, make the order, with or without modifications, or refuse to make the order, and any person on whom notice has been served under *subsection (3)* shall be notified accordingly.

(6) Where a planning authority intends to amend or revoke an order made under this *section,* the planning authority shall give notice of its intention to amend or revoke the order, as the case may be.

(7)
   (a) A notice under *subsection (6)* (which shall include particulars of the proposed order) shall be—
      (i) served on the owner and the occupier of the land affected by the order, and on any other person on whom a notice was served under *subsection (3),* and
      (ii) published in one or more newspapers circulating in the functional area of the planning authority.
   (b) A notice under *subsection (6)* shall be accompanied by a map indicating the tree, trees, group of trees or woodland to be affected by the amendment or revocation of the order.

(8) A notice under *subsection (6)* shall state that—
   (a) the planning authority proposes to amend or revoke the order, and
   (b) submissions or observations regarding the proposal may be made to the planning authority within a stated period of not less than 6 weeks, and that the submissions or observations will be taken into consideration by the planning authority.

(9) The planning authority, having considered the proposal and any submissions or observations made in respect of it, may by resolution, as it considers appropriate, revoke the order or amend the order, with or without modifications, or refuse to make the order, as the case may be, and any person on whom notice has been served under *subsection (7)* shall be notified accordingly.

(10) Any person who contravenes an order or, pending the decision of a planning authority, a proposed order under this *section,* shall be guilty of an offence.

(11) Without prejudice to any other exemption for which provision may be made by an order under this *section,* no such order shall apply to the cutting down, topping or lopping of trees which are dying or dead or have become dangerous, or the cutting down, topping or lopping of any trees in compliance with any obligation imposed by or under any enactment or so far as may be necessary for the prevention or abatement of a nuisance or hazard.

(12) Particulars of an order under this *section* shall be entered in the register.

NOTE

This section enables a planning authority to make a tree preservation order. The planning authority may decide to make such an order "in the interests of amenity or the environment". The order must also be made for stated reasons, which should involve more than reciting the purpose of the interests of amenity or the environment. The order may be prohibitive in nature, prohibiting the cutting down, topping, lopping or wilful destruction of trees, and also require the owner or occupier to enter into an agreement with the planning authority concerning the proper management of the trees. The order is not restricted to these matters as long as it comes within the purpose of a tree preservation order within subs.(1). As is implied by subs.(11), the order may specify some exemption in certain circumstances.

Before making the order, the planning authority must serve a notice on the owner and occupier (together with a map) and also publish a newspaper notice of the proposal. The notice must, inter alia, state that submissions may be made within a specified period of not less than six weeks. The planning authority, having considered any submissions, may by resolution make the order with or without modifications or may refuse to do so. A similar procedure must be undertaken in the case of amendment or revocation of the order. It is a criminal offence to breach an order or proposed order. Subsection (11) provides that an order cannot be made with respect to trees which are dead or dying or which have become dangerous. It is not entirely clear as to the status of an order made in respect of trees which subsequently die or emerge as dying or subsequently become dangerous. In the case of such occurring, it is doubtful whether any owner or occupier can themselves make such a determination without the consent of the planning authority. Under the previous legislation s.45 of the 1963 Act, the prohibition against cutting or lopping trees could be removed with the consent of the planning authority. This does not exist under the present section. An amendment to any order may therefore be necessary. In relation to an obligation under any other enactment to prevent or abate a nuisance, a court order would, for example, supersede the tree preservation order. This section replaces s.45 of the 1963 Act, the most significant change being the abolition of the right of appeal to An Bord Pleanála against the order. There is no provision for the payment of compensation regarding the making of tree preservation orders as existed in certain circumstances under s.45 of the 1990 Act.

Creation of public rights of way pursuant to agreement

1–244   **206.—(1)** A planning authority may enter into an agreement with any person having the necessary power in that behalf for the creation, by dedication by that person, of a public right of way over land.

(2) An agreement made under this *section* shall be on such terms as to payment or otherwise as may be specified in the agreement, and may, if it is so agreed, provide for limitations or conditions affecting the public right of way.

(3) Where an agreement has been made under this *section,* it shall be the duty of the planning authority to take all necessary steps for securing that the creation of the public right of way is effected in accordance with the agreement.

(4) Particulars of an agreement made under this *section* shall be entered in the register.

NOTE

This section allows the planning authority to enter into an agreement with a person concerning the creation of a public right of way over land. The agreement may include conditions limiting the public right of way and may include provision for payment. Where such an agreement is entered into, the planning authority has a duty to take steps to ensure the agreement is given effect. This section restates s.47 of the 1963 Act.

Compulsory powers for creation of public rights of way

1–245   **207.—(1)** If it appears to the planning authority that there is need for a public right of way over any land, the planning authority may, by resolution, make an order creating a public right of way over the land.

(2)
   (a) Where a planning authority proposes to make an order under this *section,* it shall—
      (i) serve a notice (which shall include particulars of the proposed order) of its intention to do so on the owner and the occupier

of the land over which the public right of way is proposed to be created and on any other person who in its opinion will be affected by the creation of the public right of way, and

    (ii) cause notice of the proposed order to be published in one or more newspapers circulating in its functional area.

(b) A notice under *paragraph (a)(i)* shall be accompanied by a map indicating the public right of way to be created.

(3) A notice under *subsection (2)* shall state that—

    (a) the planning authority proposes to make an order creating the public right of way, and

    (b) submissions or observations regarding the proposed order may be made to the planning authority within a stated period of not less than 6 weeks and that the submissions or observations will be taken into consideration by the planning authority.

(4) The planning authority, having considered the proposal and any submissions or observations made in respect of it, may by resolution, as it considers appropriate, make the order, with or without modifications, or refuse to make the order and any person on whom notice has been served under *subsection (2)* shall be notified accordingly.

(5) Any person who has been notified of the making of an order under *subsection (4)* may appeal to the Board against the order within 4 weeks of being notified under that *subsection.*

(6) Where an appeal is brought under this *section* against an order, the Board may confirm the order with or without modifications or annul the order.

(7) An order under this *section* (other than an order which is annulled) shall take effect—

    (a) in case no appeal against it is taken or every appeal against it is withdrawn before the expiration of the period for taking an appeal, on the expiration of the period for taking an appeal, or

    (b) in case an appeal or appeals is or are taken against it and the appeal or appeals is or are not withdrawn during the period for taking an appeal, when every appeal not so withdrawn has been either withdrawn or determined.

(8) Particulars of a right of way created under this *section* shall be entered in the register.

(9) Any public right of way created under an enactment repealed by this *Act* that was in force immediately before the commencement of this *section* shall be deemed to have been made under this *section.*

NOTE

This section grants the planning authority compulsory powers to create a public right of way. Before making the order, the planning authority must serve a notice on the owner, occupier and any other affected person (together with a map), and also publish a newspaper notice of the proposal. The notice must, inter alia, state that submissions may be made within a specified period of not less than six weeks. The planning authority, having considered any submissions, may by resolution make the order, with or without modifications, or may refuse to do so. Every person notified of the proposal must be notified of the decision. There is no requirement to publish a newspaper notice of the decision. A right to appeal the order to An Bord Pleanála within four weeks is granted to persons who had been notified of the proposal. There is no right of appeal in the case of members of the public or even persons who made submissions. In the case of an appeal, the Board may confirm the order with or without modification or may annul the order. Where no appeal is taken (or an appeal is withdrawn), the order will take effect at the expiry of the period for taking the appeal. In the case of appeal, the order will take effect from when the Board determines the matter or from when an appeal is withdrawn before the Board. This section largely restates s.48 of the 1963 Act. Section 200 allows for the payment of compensation where a person's interest in land has been damaged by being disturbed in his enjoyment of the land, in consequence of the creation of a public right of way.

Supplemental provisions with respect to public rights of way

1–246   **208.—(1)** Where a public right of way is created pursuant to this *Act,* or where a provision in a development plan in force on the commencement of this *section* relates to the preservation of a public right of way, the way shall be maintained by the planning authority.

(2)
  (a) Where a right of way is required by this *section* to be maintained by the planning authority, a person shall not damage or obstruct the way, or hinder or interfere with the exercise of the right of way.
  (b) A person who contravenes this *subsection* shall be guilty of an offence.

(3) Where, in the case of a right of way required by this *section* to be maintained by the planning authority, the way is damaged or obstructed by any person, the planning authority maintaining the right of way may repair the damage or remove the obstruction, and the expenses incurred by it in the repair or removal shall be paid to them by that person and, in default of being so paid, shall be recoverable from him or her as a simple contract debt in any court of competent jurisdiction.

NOTE

This section concerns the maintenance of a public right of way by a planning authority. It is a criminal offence for a person to damage or interfere with the public right of way. Also, where the planning authority repairs or removes any such damage or interference, it may recover the expenses incurred by the person who caused them. This section restates s.49 of the 1963 Act.

Repair and tidying of advertisement structures and advertisements

1–247   **209.—(1)** If it appears to a planning authority that, having regard to the interests of public safety or amenity, an advertisement structure or advertisement in its area should be repaired or tidied, the planning authority may serve on the person having control of the structure or advertisement a notice requiring that person to repair or tidy the advertisement structure or advertisement within a specified period.

(2) If it appears to a planning authority that any advertisement structure or advertisement is derelict, the planning authority may serve on the person having control of the structure or advertisement a notice requiring that person to remove the advertisement structure or advertisement within a specified period.

(3) If within the period specified in a notice under this *section,* the advertisement structure or advertisement is not repaired or tidied, or removed, as the case may be, the planning authority may enter on the land on which the structure is situate or the advertisement is exhibited and repair, tidy or remove the structure or advertisement and may recover as a simple contract debt in any court of competent jurisdiction from the person having control of the structure or advertisement any expenses reasonably incurred by it in that behalf.

NOTE

This section allows the planning authority to serve a notice requiring the repair, tidying or removal of an advertisement. The notice is served on the person having control of the structure or advertisement requiring its repair or tidying within a specified period. This section restates s.54 of the 1963 Act, with a new power under subs.(2) where the planning authority considers the advertisement to be derelict, whereby the notice may require removal of the structure or advertisement within a specified period. Where the person fails to comply with the notice within the specified period, the planning authority may enter the land and carry out the steps required, the expenses for which may be recovered against the person served with the notice.

PART XIV

ACQUISITION OF LAND, ETC.

Appropriation of land for local authority purposes

210.—(1) Where—   1–248
    (a) land is vested in a local authority for the purposes of its functions under this or any other enactment, and
    (b) the local authority is satisfied that the land should be made available for the purposes of any of those functions,
the local authority may appropriate the land for those purposes.

(2) Where land is vested in a local authority by means of compulsory acquisition under any enactment, no claim shall be made for compensation or additional compensation and the acquisition shall not be challenged on account of any appropriation of land in accordance with *subsection (1)*.

NOTE

This section allows the local authority to appropriate land vested in it in order to perform any of its functions. This is not limited to its functions as the planning authority but covers any functions of a local authority as set out in the Local Government Act 2001. Where the local authority decides to appropriate land for these purposes, this will not give rise to a claim for compensation. A compensation claim may only arise at the earlier stage of the process following the confirmation of the CPO.

Disposal of land by local authority

211.—(1) Any land acquired for the purposes of or appropriated under this   1–249
Act or any other *Act* or acquired otherwise, by a local authority, may be sold, leased or exchanged, subject to such conditions as it may consider necessary where it no longer requires the land for any of its functions, or in order to secure—
    (a) the best use of that or other land, and any structures or works which

have been, or are to be, constructed, erected, made or carried out on, in or under that or other land, or

(b) the construction, erection, making or carrying out of any structures or works appearing to it to be needed for the proper planning and sustainable development of its functional area.

(2) The consent of the Minister shall, subject to *subsection (3),* be required for any sale, lease or exchange under *subsection (1)* in case the price or rent, or what is obtained by the local authority on the exchange, is not the best reasonably obtainable, but in any other case, shall not be required notwithstanding the provisions of any other enactment.

(3) The Minister may by regulations provide for the disposal of land under *subsection (1)* without the consent of the Minister as required by *subsection (2)* in such circumstances as may be specified in the regulations and subject to compliance with such conditions (including conditions for the giving of public notice) as may be so specified.

(4) Capital money arising from the disposal of land under *subsection (1)* shall be applied for a capital purpose for which capital money may be properly applied [, or for such purposes as may be approved by the Minister whether generally or in relation to specified cases or circumstances].

(5)

(a) Where, as respects any land acquired for the purposes of or appropriated under this or any other *Act* or acquired otherwise by a local authority, the authority considers that it will not require the use of the land for any of its functions for a particular period, the authority may grant a lease of the land for that period or any lesser period and the lease shall be expressed as a lease granted for the purposes of this *subsection.*

(b) The *Landlord and Tenant Acts, 1967* to *1994,* shall not apply in relation to a lease granted under *paragraph (a)* for the purposes of this *subsection.*

AMENDMENT HISTORY

Subsection (4) was amended by s.247 of the Local Government Act 2001 (No. 37 of 2001), which, by the Local Government Act 2001 (Commencement) Order 2001 (S.I. No. 458 of 2001), came into effect on October 9, 2001.

NOTE

This section allows the local authority to sell or lease or exchange land it has acquired or appropriated in certain circumstances. Subsection (1) gives the local authority a wide discretion in the disposing of land which it has acquired. The local authority may dispose of the land where it is no longer necessary for any of its functions. In addition to this the local authority can also dispose of the land in order to secure:

(a) the best use for such land or any structure or works which have carried out on the land; or

(b) for the construction making of any structures or works which are required for the proper planning and development and sustainable development of the area.

For the purposes of the disposal under (a) or (b) it is not necessary for the local authority to consider that it no longer requires the land for any of its functions. The land may be sold, leased or exchanged "subject to such conditions" as the local authority deem necessary. The power of local authority to "exchange" land, means that the consideration for disposal the land to some person may be the transfer of land or other valuable to the local authority. Section 183 of the Local Government Act 2001 sets out the procedure before land can be disposed of by a local authority. In order to dispose of land, the local authority must send notice of its intention to the elected members of the Council. The notice must set out particulars of:

> "(i) the land, (ii) the name of the person from whom such land was acquired, if this can be ascertained by reasonable inquiries, (iii) the person to whom the land is to be disposed of, (iv) the consideration proposed in respect of the disposal, (v) any covenants, conditions or agreements to have effect in connection with the disposal".

Section 183(1)(b) provides that at the first meeting of the local authority held 10 days after the day on which such notices are sent or delivered, the local authority may resolve that the disposal shall not be carried out or that it shall be carried out in accordance with the terms specified in the resolution. If the elected members do not pass a resolution, then the land may be disposed as proposed.

Under subs.(2), the consent of the Minister is required where the price or matter obtained in exchange for the land is not the best reasonably obtainable. The consent is not required in any other circumstance. It appears that a local authority would want to have a special reason for agreeing to an exchange which was not the best reasonably obtainable. Where a disposal has been made by the local authority without the consent of the Minister, it could be subsequently challenged on the basis that the price or rent was not the best reasonably available. Although the term "best reasonably available" connotes an objective standard, there may be some difficulties in proving that there was some better price reasonably available.

Subsection (3) allows for the making of Regulations to allow for the disposal of land without the consent of the Minister even where subs.(2) applies. In this respect regulations have been made comprised in art.206 of the 2001 Regulations. Article 206 provides that the consent of the Minister shall not be required under s.212(2) where a local authority is of the opinion that, "for economic or social reasons", it is reasonable that the disposal of land be carried out in accordance with the terms specified by the authority in a notice. In addition to following the procedure in s.183 set out above, art.206 of the Planning and Development Regulations adds an additional layer of procedure where the local authority seeks to invoke "social and economic reasons" for selling the land without Ministerial consent for a price which is less than that "best reasonably obtainable". These additional procedural steps are as follows:

- the manager shall prepare a report setting out the economic or social reasons which apply in relation to the disposal of land;
- the report shall be incorporated in or accompany the notice sent to the elected member under s.183;
- the notice and the report shall be made available for public inspection at the offices of the local authority during office hours for a period of one year.

The disposal of land shall then be carried out in accordance with the terms of the notice decided by the elected members.

Subsection (5) allows the granting of the lease for land where it is not required for any of its functions for a particular period. The land may not be required for a "particular period" which is in contrast to the general power to lease under subs.(1), where, inter alia, the land is no longer required for any functions of the local authority. The period of lease must not exceed the period for which the land is not required and so this envisages a temporary or fixed term lease. This provision is similar to s.75(4) of the Local Government (Planning and Development) Act 1963. The local authority has a discretion in making such determination. The Landlord and Tenant Acts are excluded in relation to such lease. It may be noted that s.4 of the Landlord and Tenant (Amendment) Act 1980 restricts the application of such Act where premises were or are provided or deemed to be provided by a housing authority.

Development by planning authority, etc.

1–250   212.—(1) A planning authority may develop or secure or facilitate the development of land and, in particular and without prejudice to the generality of the foregoing, may do one or more of the following:

(a) secure, facilitate and control the improvement of the frontage of any public road by widening, opening, enlarging or otherwise improving;

(b) develop any land in the vicinity of any road or public transport facility which it is proposed to improve or construct;

(c) provide areas with roads, infrastructure facilitating public transport and such services and works as may be needed for development;

(d) provide, secure or facilitate the provision of areas of convenient shape and size for development;

(e) secure, facilitate or carry out the development and renewal of areas in need of physical, social or economic regeneration and provide open spaces and other public amenities;

(f) secure the preservation of any view or prospect, any protected structure or other structure, any architectural conservation area or natural physical feature, any trees or woodlands or any site of archaeological, geological, historical, scientific or ecological interest.

(2) A planning authority may provide or arrange for the provision of—

(a) sites for the establishment or relocation of industries, businesses (including hotels, motels and guesthouses), houses, offices, shops, schools, churches, leisure facilities and other community facilities and of such buildings, premises, houses, parks and structures as are referred to in *paragraph (b),*

(b) factory buildings, office premises, shop premises, houses, amusement parks and structures for the purpose of entertainment, caravan parks, buildings for the purpose of providing accommodation, meals and refreshments, buildings for the purpose of providing trade and professional services and advertisement structures,

(c) transport facilities, including public and air transport facilities, and

(d) any services which it considers ancillary to anything which is referred to in *paragraph (a), (b) or (c),*

and may maintain and manage any such site, building, premises, house, park, structure or service and may make any charges which it considers reasonable in relation to the provision, maintenance or management thereof.

(3) A planning authority may, in connection with any of its functions under this *Act,* make and carry out arrangements or enter into agreements with any person or body for the development or management of land, and may incorporate a company for those purposes.

(4) A planning authority may use any of the powers available to it under any enactment, including any powers in relation to the compulsory acquisition of land, in relation to its functions under this *section* and in particular in order to facilitate the assembly of sites for the purposes of the orderly development of land.

This section empowers the local authority to develop land. Subsection (1) grants a general power to the local authority to "develop or secure or facilitate the development of land" and then enlists certain specified development which the local authority can carry out. The power to develop or secure the development of land is broader than the former s.77 of the 1963 Act. The power to "facilitate" the development of lands appears to enable the local authority to take measures which would make land more amenable to development. This differs from the power to "secure" the development of land, where the local authority may cause the land to be developed (though not necessarily carrying out the development itself). The specific purposes set out subs.(1) may be sufficient to constitute a "particular purpose" for the compulsory acquisition of land under s.213(3). See *Clinton v An Bord Pleanála (2)* [2007] 4 I.R. 171, where the purpose of regeneration of O'Connell Street was deemed to fall within (e) (development and renewal of areas, etc.) and this was considered sufficient to constitute a "particular purpose" and it was not necessary to specify a particular type of development or project. The matters enlisted in subs.(1) are largely addressed in wide terms to developing areas or land for some purpose. Subsection (2) is more specific insofar as it enlists specific matters which the local authority may provide or arrange to provide. Many of the matters enlisted in subss.1 and 2 reflect the functions of local authorites set out in Pt 9 of the Local Government Act 2001, in particular in promoting community interests under s.66 of the Local Government Act 2001 and the amenity, recreation and other functions of a local authority under s.67 of the Local Government Act 2001. Subsection (2)(a) concerns the provision of sites for the specific matters, while subs.(2)(b) concerns the acual provision of the specified matters by the local authority. The final paragraph of subs.(2) enables the local authority to make any charge it considers reasonable in relation to the provision, maintenance or management of the matters or services enlisted. Section 2(1) of the Local Government (Financial Provisions) (No. 2) Act 1983 includes a general power of the local authority to charge for the provision of services.

Subsection (3) is new and makes explicit the power of the local authority to enter agreements or arrangements or to incorporate a company for any of the purposes in the section. Subsection (4) allows the local authority to utilise its powers under other enactments including the power to compulsory acquire land for the purposes of any functions under the section. This may include using its power to facilitate the assembly of sites for the orderly development of land. Thus the local authority can uses its power such as compulsory acquisition in order to acquire a number of sites as part of the broader development of the land.

Land acquisition by local authorities

213.—(1) The power conferred on a local authority under any enactment **1–251** to acquire land shall be construed in accordance with this *section.*

(2)

(a) A local authority may, for the purposes of performing any of its functions (whether conferred by or under this *Act,* or any other enactment passed before or after the passing of this *Act*), including giving effect to or facilitating the implementation of its development plan or its housing strategy under *section 94,* do all or any of the following:

    (i) acquire land, permanently or temporarily, by agreement or compulsorily,

    (ii) acquire, permanently or temporarily, by agreement or compulsorily, any easement, way-leave, water-right or other right over or in respect of any land or water or any substratum of land,

    (iii) restrict or otherwise interfere with, permanently or temporarily, by agreement or compulsorily, any easement, way-leave, water-right or other right over or in respect of any land or water or any substratum of land,

and the performance of all or any of the functions referred to in *subparagraphs (i), (ii) and (iii)* are referred to in this *Act* as an "acquisition of land".

(b) A reference in *paragraph (a)* to acquisition by agreement shall include acquisition by way of purchase, lease, exchange or otherwise.

(c) The functions conferred on a local authority by *paragraph (a)* may be performed in relation to—

(i) land, or

(ii) any easement, way-leave, water-right or other right to which that *paragraph* applies,

whether situated or exercisable, as the case may be, inside or outside the functional area of the local authority concerned.

(3)

(a) The acquisition may be effected by agreement or compulsorily in respect of land not immediately required for a particular purpose if, in the opinion of the local authority, the land will be required by the authority for that purpose in the future.

(b) The acquisition may be effected by agreement in respect of any land which, in the opinion of the local authority, it will require in the future for the purposes of any of its functions notwithstanding that the authority has not determined the manner in which or the purpose for which it will use the land.

(c) *Paragraphs (a) and (b)* shall apply and have effect in relation to any power to acquire land conferred on a local authority by virtue of this *Act* or any other enactment whether enacted before or after this *Act*.

(4) A local authority may be authorised by compulsory purchase order to acquire land for any of the purposes referred to in *subsection (2) of this section and section 10* (as amended by *section 86 of the Housing Act, 1966*) of the *Local Government (No. 2) Act, 1960,* shall be construed so as to apply accordingly and the reference to "purposes" in *section 10(1)(a) of that Act* shall be construed as including purposes referred to in *subsection (2) of this section.*

NOTE

This section concerns land acquisition by local authorities, which may be compulsorily acquired or by agreement. Subsection (1) provides that the power of a local authority to acquire land under other enactments is to be construed in accordance with the section. Thus subs.(1) uses the term "local authority" rather than "planning authority", which makes clear that the section applies to a local authority when acting in any of its different capacities such as housing authority, sanitary authority, etc. Subsection (1) embraces the power of local authorities to compulsory acquire lands under any of the enactments listed in s.214(1). The section is not however confined to acquisition by means of compulsory acquisition but also covers acquisition by means of agreement. The local authorities most frequently invoke the power to compulsorily acquire land under s.86 of the Housing Act 1966, as amended.

Subsection (2) is expressed in very broad terms with the final paragraph of the subsection providing an extended definition of "acquisition of land" so as to include not only acquiring land under (i) but also under (ii) acquiring any easement, way-leave, water right, etc. over land and under (iii) restricting or otherwise interfering with any easement, way-leave, water, etc. over land. Subsection (2) empowers the local authority to engage in such "acquisition of land" for performing any of its functions under any legislation (not only under the Planning Acts) whether passed before or after the 2000 Act and this includes giving effect to or implementing the development plan or housing strategy. Subsection (2)(b) provides that the notion of acquisition by agreement shall include acquisition by way of purchase, lease, exchange or otherwise. As long as there is some agreement, it does not matter the means by which land is acquired. It could therefore include acquiring lands in exchange for performining some service or in exchange for other lands. In fact there need not be any consideration supplied by a local authority as in an agreement under seal. Subsection (2)(c) provides that the general scope of the subsection will apply whether the local authority is performing any function inside or outside its functional area. Section 85 of the Local Government Act 2001 allows a local authority to enter into agreement with another local authority for the performance of its function, while s.86 of the Local Government Act 2001 provides for the joint discharge of functions.

Subsection (3) enables a local authority to acquire land which it considers will be required in the future. This allows a broader discretion to a local authority compared to s.77 of the Housing Act 1966, where land can be acquired where the Minister is "of opinion that there is reasonable expectation that the land will be required by the authority in the future". Subsection (3)(a) enables a local authority to acquire land for a "particular purpose" although not immediately required, if the land will be required by authority for such purpose in the future. Such acquisition may be made either by way of agreement or compulsorily. This is in contrast to subs.(3)(b) which enables the local authority to acquire land for the purposes of any of its functions where it has not determined the manner or purpose for which it will use the land. Under (b) the acquisition can only be by way of agreement and cannot be compulsorily acquired.

In order to be a "particular purpose" within (a) it is not necessary that the local authority has a particular project or scheme for which the land is being acquired. In *Clinton v An Bord Pleanála* [2007] 4 I.R. 171, it was argued that the reference to "particular purpose" in (a) meant the Council could not carry out a Compulsory Purchase Order ("CPO") without specifying the precise development which was to be undertaken on the site which was subject to the CPO. It was held that the purpose of regeneration was sufficient purpose and it was not necessary to have a specific plan as to how the regeneration was to be carried out which would have to be specified in the CPO. The subsection had to be read in the light of the purposes set out in s.212. The CPO decision merely mentioned "development purposes" whereas the confirming decision of An Bord Pleanála referred to "facilitating the implementation of the development plan". The Supreme Court said the former was adequate although it expressed a preference for the latter. The court considered it was open to argument that in a different type of compulsory acquisition that a more detailed indication of the purpose might be required. Geoghegan J. said he would leave open to another case whether a stated "statutory purpose", as Finnegan P. held in the High Court, was always a sufficient particular purpose. Geoghegan J. said there was some force in the argument of the appellant that if a mere statutory purpose were a "particular purpose" within the meaning of s.213(3)(a), then subs.(3)(b) might be regarded as otiose.

However, a CPO which had been made for one purpose cannot lawfully be confirmed for another purpose or for a purpose additional to that for which it was made. See *Procter & Gamble Ltd. v Secretary of State for the Environment* [1991] 63 P & CR 317 and *Crosbie v Custom House Dock Development Authority* [1996] 2 I.R. 531. It will be a question of fact as to whether the purposes are the same.

Subsection (4) provides that a CPO can authorise the acquisition of land for any of the broad statement purposes in subs.(2), which includes any functions of the local authority under any enactment, including for giving effect to or facilitating the implementation of the development plan or the housing strategy. While this subsection could arguably be construed as conferring an independent power to compulsory acquire land, the better view is that it merely governs the exercise of such power which otherwise derives from other enactments. See *Clinton v An Bord Pleanála* [2007] 4 I.R. 171, where it was suggested CPO powers under the various enactments derive from s.10 of the Local Government (Ireland) Act 1898. The definition of purposes under s.10(1)(a) of the Local Government Act 1960 Act is essentially negative, being purposes other than under the Housing of the Working Classes Acts. Section 10(1) states:

> "[W]here (a) a local authority intends to acquire compulsorily any land, whether situate within or outside their functional area, for purposes for which they are capable of being authorised by law to acquire land compulsorily, (b) those purposes are purposes other than the purposes of the Housing of the Working Classes Acts, 1890 to 1958, or are purposes some only of which are purposes of those Acts, and (c) the local authority consider that it would be convenient to effect the acquisition under those Acts".

The subsection incorporates within the scheme the CPO powers under s.86 of the Housing Act 1966, as amended.

Transfer of Minister's functions in relation to compulsory acquisition of land to Board

1–252   **214.—(1)** The functions conferred on the Minister in relation to the compulsory acquisition of land by a local authority under the following enactments are hereby transferred to, and vested in, the Board and any reference in any relevant provision of those Acts to the Minister, or construed to be a reference to the Minister, shall be deemed to be a reference to the Board except that any powers under those enactments to make regulations or to prescribe any matter shall remain with the Minister:

> *Public Health (Ireland) Act, 1878;*
> *Local Government (Ireland) Act, 1898;*
> *Local Government Act, 1925;*
> *Water Supplies Act, 1942;*
> *Local Government (No. 2) Act, 1960;*
> *Local Government (Sanitary Services) Act, 1964;*
> *Housing Act, 1966;*
> *Derelict Sites Act, 1990;*
> *Roads Acts, 1993* and *1998;*
> *Dublin Docklands Development Authority Act, 1997.*

(2) For the purposes of the compulsory acquisition of land by a local authority the following constructions shall apply:

(a) the references construed to be references to the Minister in *section 203 of the Public Health (Ireland) Act, 1878,* shall be construed as referring to the Board and any connected references shall be construed accordingly;

(b) the references to the Minister in *section 68* of, and in the *Sixth Schedule to, the Local Government Act, 1925,* shall be construed as referring to the Board and any connected references shall be construed accordingly;

(c) the references to the Minister in *sections 4, 8, 9 and 10* of, and in the *Schedule to, the Water Supplies Act, 1942,* shall be construed as referring to the Board and any connected references shall be construed accordingly;

(d) the references to the Minister, or to the appropriate Minister, in *section 10* (as amended by *section 86 of the Housing Act, 1966*) of the *Local Government (No. 2) Act, 1960,* shall be construed as referring to the Board and any connected references shall be construed accordingly;

(e) the references to the Minister in *sections 7, 8, 9 and 16 of the Local Government (Sanitary Services) Act, 1964,* shall be construed as referring to the Board and any connected references shall be construed accordingly;

(f)

    (i) the references to the Minister, or to the appropriate Minister, in *sections 76, 77, 78* [and *80*] of, and the *Third Schedule to, the Housing Act, 1966,* shall be construed as referring to the Board and any connected references shall be construed accordingly;

    (ii) [...];

(g) the references to the Minister in *sections 16 and 17 of the Derelict Sites Act, 1990,* shall be construed as referring to the Board and any connected references shall be construed accordingly;

(h) the references to the Minister in *section 27(1) of the Dublin Docklands Development Authority Act, 1997,* shall be construed as referring to the Board and any connected references shall be construed accordingly.

(3) The transfer of the Minister's functions to the Board in relation to the compulsory purchase of land in accordance with *subsection (1)* shall include the transfer of all necessary ancillary powers in relation to substrata, easements, rights over land (including public rights of way), rights of access to land, the revocation or modification of planning permissions or other such functions as may be necessary in order to ensure that the Board can fully carry out its functions in relation to the enactments referred to in *subsection (1).*

(4) In this *section and section 216,* "local authority" *includes the Dublin Docklands Development Authority.*

AMENDMENT HISTORY

Subsection (2)(i) was amended and sub-para.(ii) was repealed by s.247 of the Local Government Act 2001 (No. 37 of 2001), which, by the Local Government Act 2001 (Commencement) Order 2001 (S.I. No. 458 of 2001), came into effect on October 9, 2001.

Section 247(j) of the Local Government Act 2001 amended s.214(2)(f):
(i) by the substitution in subpara.(i) of "and 80" for ", 80 and 85", and
(ii) by the deletion of subparagraph [ii] which had provided "(ii) section 85 of the Housing Act, 1966, shall be construed as if subsections (2) and (3) were deleted".

NOTE

This section transfers the functions of the Minister in relation to compulsory acquisition of land under the enactments specified in subs.(1) to the Board. In the case of all this legislation, the main role of the Minister in connection with the compulsory acquisition of land was to confirm the making of a CPO by the local authority, in most cases following the holding of a public or local inquiry. This role is now transferred to An Bord Pleanála. By virtue of s.218(1), An Bord Pleanála will hold an oral hearing as opposed to a public or local inquiry.

A local authority has the power to make a CPO under numerous enactments. However, it appears that such powers derive from s.10 of the Local Government (Ireland) Act 1898.

See *Clinton v An Bord Pleanála* [2007] 4 I.R. 171 where Geoghegan J. noted that:

"At least ever since the unreported judgment of Kenny J. in the High Court *Movie News v Galway County Council* (judgment delivered 30th March 1973) it has been generally understood that all powers of compulsory acquisition by a local authority for any one or more of its many statutory functions derive in the first place from section 10 of the Local Government (Ireland) Act, 1898 but many subsequent sections have either extended the powers under the section or clarified any doubts as to the scope of the section."

With respect to the enactments listed in subs.(1), relevant sections of such legislation relating to compulsory acquisition include the following: s.203 of the Public Health Act 1878, s.68 of the Local Government Act 1925 provides that any provisional order made by the Minister under the provisions of the Public Health (Ireland) Acts 1878–1919; or of s.10 of the Local Government (Ireland) Act 1898. After the holding of such a local inquiry, the making of the CPO must be confirmed by the Minister. Sections 8–10 of the Water Supplies Act 1942 concern an application for a provisional order for a proposal for the taking of a supply of water from a source of water; s.10 of the Local Government (No. 2) Act 1960 has been amended by s.86 of the Housing Act 1966, and affords a general power on a local authority to acquire land compulsorily; under ss.6–11 of the Local Government (Sanitary Services) Act 1964, the local authority acting as sanitary authority may acquire land compulsorily which is in a dangerous place or that has ceased, by reason of the carrying out of works by the authority, to be a dangerous place; s.76 of the Housing Act 1966 concerns compulsory acquisition by the local authority for housing purposes as opposed to general purposes under s.86 (although the s.86 procedure is the same as that concerning s.76); ss.14–19 of the Derelict Sites Acts 1990 concerns the power and procedure for a local authority to acquire a derelict site. Sections 47–52 of the Roads Act 1993, as amended by the 1998 and 2007 Roads Acts, set out the procedure for acquiring the land in connection with the making by the local authority of:

- a motorway scheme;
- a busway scheme;
- a protected road scheme;
- a protected road scheme amending a protected road scheme approved under s.49; or
- certain prescribed road developments such as bridges.

Under s.27(1) of the Dublin Dockland Act 1997, the Dublin Docklands Development Authority may be authorised to acquire compulsorily land situated in the Dublin Docklands Area (other than land to which s.28 applies).

Subsection (2) provides that with respect to the specified provisions of such enactments, the reference to the Minister is construed as referring to the Board.

Subsection (50)(2)(c) provides for judicial review of the making of a CPO by a local authority under any of the enactments enlisted in s.214. This was introduced under the 2006 Act. Section 78(4) of the Housing Act 1966, provides that:

"(4) Subject to the provisions of subsection (2) of this section, a person shall not question a compulsory purchase order by prohibition or certiorari or in any legal proceedings whatsoever".

Section 78(2) allowed a person aggrieved to challenge the confirmation of a CPO by the Minister (the function is now transferred to the Board) by making an application to the court within three weeks on specified grounds. Although not explicitly repealed, s.78(2) appears to be superseded by s.50 of the Planning and Development Act 2000 as amended, which provides that a person may not question the validity of the enlisted acts or decision otherwise than by way application for judicial review under RSC Ord.84.

Transfer of certain Ministerial functions under Roads Acts, 1993 and 1998, to Board

1–253   **215.—(1)** The functions of the Minister in relation to a scheme or proposed road development under *sections 49, 50 and 51 of the Roads Act, 1993,* are hereby transferred to and vested in the Board and relevant references in that

Act to the Minister shall be construed as references to the Board and any connected references shall be construed accordingly, except that any powers under those sections to make regulations or to prescribe any matter shall remain with the Minister.

(2) The references to the Minister in *section 19(7) and paragraphs (a), (c), (e) and (f) of section 20(1) of the Roads Act, 1993,* shall be deemed to be references to the Board.

NOTE

This section concerns the transfer of the ministerial functions under the Roads Acts 1993 and 1998 to An Bord Pleanála (these Acts have been amended by the Roads Act 2007). A separate section is devoted to the Roads Acts, though the transfer of powers from the Minister to An Bord Pleanála could be said to have been accomplished under the general provision of s.214. Section 49 of the Road Act 1993 concerns the approval of a scheme (whether a motorway, busway, protected road scheme, or a protected road scheme amending a protected road scheme approved under s.49) by the Minister after the holding of a public or local inquiry and consideration of any objections. The Minister could approve a scheme with or without modifications or he could refuse to approve the scheme. A newspaper notice of his decision was required to be published. The Minister also had power to direct the local authority to provide for a person who has been deprived of reasonable access to their property in certain circumstances. Under s.50, the Minster could direct a local authority to carry out an EIA in relation to the construction or improvement of a public road, while under s.51 he could approve a proposed road development along with an EIA. All these functions of the Minister are now performed by the Board. It may be noted that the Roads Act 1993 has been amended by Roads Act 2007 which substitutes several subsections of ss.49 to 51. Such substituted subsections expressly refer to An Bord Pleanála.

Section 19(7) of the 1993 Act relates to where the National Roads Authority decides to perform a particular function (which would include acquisition of land) rather than through the local authority. Sections 20(1), (a), (c), (e) and (f) concerns where the NRA itself decides to make a roadway or protected road scheme and submit it the Minister, or make a CPO or prepare an EIA and submit it to the Minister. In such instance the Minister performs the same role as where the local authority had made the submission.

In *Kildare County Council v An Bord Pleanála*, unreported, High Court, McMenamin J., March 10, 2006, it was noted the concept of proper planning and sustainable development is incorporated, by implication into the s.51 consideration process. It was considered the fact that the confirming function both under s.51 and under the CPO procedure, had been transferred from the Minister to the Board indicated that the adjudication must involve consideration of proper planning and sustainable development.

[Transfer of certain Ministerial functions under Gas Act 1976 to Board

215A.—(1) The functions of—   **1–254**
    (a) the Minister for Communications, Marine and Natural Resources,
    (b) any other Minister of the Government, or
    (c) the Commission for Energy Regulation,
under *sections 31 and 32* of, and the Second Schedule to, the *Gas Act 1976,* as amended, in relation to the compulsory acquisition of land in respect of a strategic gas infrastructure development are transferred to, and vested in, the Board, and relevant references in that Act to the Minister for Communications, Marine and Natural Resources, any other Minister of the Government or the Commission for Energy Regulation shall be construed as references to the Board and any connected references shall be construed accordingly.

(2) The transfer of the functions of the Minister for Communications,

Marine and Natural Resources, any other Minister of the Government or the Commission for Energy Regulation to the Board in relation to the compulsory acquisition of land in accordance with *subsection (1)* shall include the transfer of all necessary ancillary powers in relation to deviation limits, substrata of land, easements, rights over land (including wayleaves and public rights of way), rights of access to land, the revocation or modification of planning permissions or other such functions as may be necessary in order to ensure that the Board can fully carry out its functions in relation to the enactments referred to in *subsection (1)*.

(3) *Article 5 of the Second Schedule to the Gas Act 1976* shall not apply in respect of the function of compulsory acquisition transferred to the Board under *subsection (1)*.]

AMENDMENT HISTORY

Inserted by s.37 of the Planning and Development (Strategic Infrastructure) Act 2006 (No. 27 of 2006).

NOTE

This section transfers certain functions to the Board regarding the compulsory acquisition of land in respect of strategic gas infrastructure. These functions which were formerly performed by the Minister for Communications, other Minister or the Commissioner for Energy Regulations under the Gas Act 1976 as amended, are now vested in the Board. Section 31 of the 1976 Act concerns the approval of deviation limits of pipelines, while s.32 of the 1976 Act allows the Board to approve the acquisition of land:
- required by the Gas Board for or in connection with the performance of any function of the Gas Board;
- required in connection with the provision by a person, other than the Gas Board, of a pipeline by means of which it is intended to supply natural gas to the Gas Board; or
- required in connection with the provision by the Gas Board for another person of a pipeline by means of which it is intended to supply natural gas, otherwise than by the Gas Board, only to that person.

The Board may make an acquisition order in respect of such land. Schedule 2 of the 1976 Act prescribes a detailed procedure for applying for an acquisition order. Under subs.(2), the transfer of the function to the Board also includes certain ancillary powers in relation to specified matters, which are necessary to carry out its function. Subsection (3) provides that the former requirement under art.5 of Sch.2 of the Gas Act 1976 to pay a fixed fee to the Minister on every application for an acquisition order does not apply.

The role of approving compulsory acquisition under s.32, which function is now performed by the Board, was described in *Ballyedmond v The Commission for Energy Regulation*, unreported, High Court, Clarke J., June 22, 2006, where Clarke J. said:

"In considering whether or not to approve of the pipeline project as a whole and, in particular, to specify the route of that pipeline by making acquisition orders in relation to rights over properties along that route, the Commission is not carrying out the sort of role which requires it to make specific findings of fact per se. It may well have to come to conclusions as to certain factual matters as part of its overall assessment of the question of whether it should approve of the project and in determining whether the route proposed should be followed. However those matters are not necessary 'proofs' in themselves, in the sense in which that term might be applied to specific factual matters that need to be established in order that a court may come to a conclusion or, indeed, in order that a statutory or administrative body may come to a similar type of conclusion. Questions such as cost, archaeological consequences, engineering difficulty and the like are but a means to an overall end which is to determine whether the project, as proposed, should go ahead".

[Transfer of certain Ministerial functions under Air Navigation Act 1998

215B.—(1) The functions of the Minister for Transport under *section 17* of, and the Second Schedule to, the *Air Navigation and Transport (Amendment) Act 1998,* as amended, in relation to the compulsory acquisition of land for the purposes set out in *section 18* of that Act, are transferred to, and vested in, the Board, and relevant references in that Act to the Minister for Transport shall be construed as references to the Board and any connected references shall be construed accordingly.

(2) The transfer of the functions of the Minister for Transport in relation to the compulsory acquisition of land in accordance with *subsection (1)* shall include the transfer of all necessary ancillary powers in relation to substrata of land, easements, rights over land (including wayleaves and public rights of way), rights over land or water or other such functions as may be necessary in order to ensure that the Board can fully carry out its functions in relation to the enactments referred to in *subsection (1).*]

1–255

AMENDMENT HISTORY

Inserted by s.37 of the Planning and Development (Strategic Infrastructure) Act 2006 (No. 27 of 2006).

NOTE

This section transfers certain functions formerly performed by the Minister for Transport to the Board with respect to the approval of compulsory acquisition of land by Aer Rianta. Section 17 of the Air Transport and Navigation Act 1998 allows Aer Rianta to acquire compulsorily, any land, easement, interest in or other right over land, or any water right for the purposes set out in s.18. Under s.18 these purposes include:
- to extend or develop an airport belonging to Aer Rianta or establish an airport;
- to secure that any land adjacent to any of the State airports shall not be used in such manner as would interfere with or cause danger or damage to aircraft at, approaching or leaving such airport;
- to alter or demolish any building or installation which, in the opinion of Aer Rianta, is likely to obstruct or interfere with the navigation of aircraft using a State airport;
- to develop civil aviation at a State airport; and
- to carry out the principal objects of the Aer Rianta.

Schedule 2 of the 1998 Act prescribes a detailed procedure for applying for an acquisition order. Under subs.(2) the transfer of functions includes the transfer of all necessary ancillary power.

Confirmation of compulsory purchase order where there are no objections

216.—(1) Where a compulsory purchase order is made in respect of the acquisition of land by a local authority in accordance with any of the enactments referred to in *section 214(1)* and-
   (a) no objections are received by the Board or the local authority, as the case may be, within the period provided for making objections,
   (b) any objection received is subsequently withdrawn at any time before the Board makes its decision, or
   (c) the Board is of opinion that any objection received relates exclusively

1–256

to matters which can be dealt with by a property arbitrator,
the Board shall, where appropriate, inform the local authority and the
local authority shall, as soon as may be, confirm the order with or without
modification, or it may refuse to confirm the order.

(2) *Subsection (1)* shall not prejudice any requirement to obtain approval for
a scheme in accordance with *section 49 of the Roads Act, 1993,* or proposed
road development in accordance with *section 51 of the Roads Act, 1993,* or
for proposed development under *section 175 of this Act.*

(3) This *section* shall not apply with respect to a compulsory purchase under
the *Derelict Sites Act, 1990.*

NOTE

This section concerns the confirmation of a CPO where there are no objections lodged.
Subsection (1) provides that where a CPO is made by a local authority and any of the
three specified circumstances exist, the Board must inform the local authority and local
authority will confirm, modify or refuse to confirm its order. The confirmation is by the
local authority itself as opposed to by the Board. The section therefore introduces a more
streamlined procedure to confirm an CPO in the specified circumstances.

The period for lodging objection will be stated in any newspaper notice and in any
notice served on any owner, occupier or lessee of land. With respect to compulsory
acquisition under the Housing Act 1966, prior to submitting the CPO to An Bord Pleanála
for confirmation, the local authority must give notice of the making of the CPO. Paragraph
4 of Sch.3 to the Housing Act 1966 provides that the local authority must publish a notice in
one or more newspapers circulating in their functional area in the prescribed form, stating
the fact of such an order having been made and naming a place where a copy of the order
and map referred to therein may be seen at all reasonable hours. Form 6 of the Housing
Act (Acquisition of Land) Regulations 2000 constitutes the prescribed form for the CPO.
The local authority must also serve on every owner, lessee and occupier (except tenants
for a month or a period less than a month) of any land to which the order relates a notice
in the prescribed form, stating the effect of the order and that it is about to be submitted
to An Bord Pleanála for confirmation. It must also specify the time and manner in which
objections can be made. In relation to a scheme under s.47 of the Roads Act 1993, the
local authority must advertise the scheme to the general public and invite submissions. The
notice must indicate the times and period (which shall not be less than one month) where a
copy of the scheme and the map may be inspected and further state that objections may be
made in writing to An Bord Pleanála before a specified date (which shall be not less than
two weeks after the end of the period for inspection).

The procedure under subs.(1) will not prejudice any requirement to obtain the approval
of scheme or road development under ss.49 and 51 of the Roads Act 1993 as amended. The
section does not apply to a CPO under the Derelict Sites Act 1990.

Certain time limits in respect of compulsory purchase of land, etc.

1–257   **217.—(1)** Where an objection is made to a sanitary authority in accordance
with *section 6 of the Water Supplies Act, 1942,* and not withdrawn, the sanitary
authority shall, within 6 weeks of receiving the objection, apply to the Board
for a provisional order in accordance with *section 8 of that Act.*

(2) Where an objection is made to a sanitary authority in accordance
with *section 8 of the Local Government (Sanitary Services) Act, 1964,* and
not withdrawn, the sanitary authority shall, within 6 weeks of receiving the
objection, apply to the Board for its consent to the compulsory acquisition of
the land in accordance with that *section.*

(3) Subject to *section 216,* where a local authority complies with the notification provisions in relation to a compulsory purchase order under *paragraph 4 of the Third Schedule to the Housing Act, 1966,* it shall, within 6 weeks of complying with those provisions, submit the compulsory purchase order to the Board for confirmation.

(4) Where a road authority complies with the notification provisions in relation to a scheme in accordance with *section 48 of the Roads Act, 1993,* it shall, within 6 weeks of complying with those provisions, submit the scheme to the Board for approval.

(5) A notice of the making of a confirmation order to be published or served, as the case may be, in accordance with *section 78(1) of the Housing Act, 1966,* shall be published or served within 12 weeks of the making of the confirmation order.

(6) Notwithstanding *section 123 of the Lands Clauses Consolidation Act, 1845,* where a compulsory purchase order or provisional order is confirmed by a local authority or the Board and becomes operative and the local authority decides to acquire land to which the order relates, the local authority shall serve any notice required under any enactment to be served in order to treat for the purchase of the several interests in the land (including under *section 79 of the Housing Act, 1966*) within 18 months of the order becoming operative.

(7)

(a) A decision of the Board made in the performance of a function transferred to it under *section 214 or 215* shall become operative 3 weeks from the date on which notice of the decision is first published.

(b) *Subsections (8) and (9) of section 52 of the Roads Act, 1993* (as inserted by *section 5 of the Roads (Amendment) Act, 1998*) and *subsections (2) to (4) of section 78 of the Housing Act, 1966,* shall not apply in relation to decisions of the Board under this *Part.*

NOTE

This section concerns the CPO process after objections have been lodged or notice of the CPO given. Subsections (1) to (4) sets out the time limits for the local authority applying to the Board for confirmation or approval of the CPO. In the case of legislation specified in ss.1 and 2, the application must be made within six weeks of receiving any objection. Section 6 of the Water Supplies Act 1942 concerns objections to a proposal to take a supply of water from a water source, while s.8 of the Local Government (Sanitary Services) Act 1964 relates to objections to a sanitary authority intending to acquire land compulsorily. Subsections (3) and (4) provide that the CPO or road scheme respectively must be submitted to the Board within six weeks of compliance with the notification provisions of such legislation. The notification provisions under para.4 of Sch.3 to the Housing Act 1966, include publishing a notice in one or more newspapers circulating in their functional area in the prescribed form and serving on every owner, lessee and occupier (except tenants for a month or a period less than a month) of any land to which the order relates a notice in the prescribed form. Similar notification requirements are obligated under s.48 of the Roads Act 1993. The Roads (Schemes) (Forms) Regulation 2008 (S.I. No. 49 of 2008) includes prescribed forms for such notices.

Subsection (5) introduces a time limit of 12 weeks within which notice of the confirmation of a CPO must be published or served. The notice of the making of a confirmation order to be published under s.78(1) of the Housing Act 1966 was formerly required to be served "as soon as may be" after the confirmation.

Subsection (6) provides that the local authority must serve a notice to treat within 18 months of the confirmation of the CPO becoming operative. This reduces the time for service which was formerly three years to 18 months. A notice to treat is a request to a party (in this case persons with interest in the property) to negotiate terms of sale. The notice to treat is necessary for the local authority to acquire the land (the confirmation of the CPO simply grants power to the local authority to acquire it). If the local authority fails to serve the notice to treat within the 18-month period, the order confirming the CPO will be spent. The notice to treat fixes the interests for which compensation is to be paid. Under the Housing Act 1966, the notice will require each such person to state within a specified period (not being less than one month from the date of service of the notice to treat) the exact nature of the interest in respect of which compensation is claimed and the details thereof. Compensation may be assessed for property compulsorily acquired under:

- the Acquisition of Land (Assessment of Compensation) Act 1919;
- the Housing Act 1966, s.84, Third Schedule, arts 2(k) and (l) and the Fourth Schedule; or
- the Planning and Development Act 2000.

Subsection (7) provides the where the Board confirms a CPO, such order will become operative three weeks from the date on which the notice of the decision is first published. Therefore the 18-month period to to serve the notice commences at the end of such three weeks.

It may be noted that the making of a CPO by the local authority and its confirmation of the CPO by the Board may be challenged in judicial review proceedings under s.50(2). Prior to the new s.50 being introduced under the 2006 Act, a challenge to the making of a CPO by the local authority did not fall within s.50. Section 50(7) provides that the eight-week period to bring judicial review proceedings commences on the date on which notice of the decision was first sent or depending on the relevant enactment, when notice was first published.

[Transferred functions under this Part: supplemental provisions

1–258 **217A.—(1)** The Board may, in respect of any of the functions transferred under this Part concerning the confirming or otherwise of any compulsory acquisition, at its absolute discretion and at any time before making a decision in respect of the matter—

(a) request submissions or observations from any person who may, in the opinion of the Board, have information which is relevant to its decision concerning the confirming or otherwise of such compulsory acquisition (and may have regard to any submission or observation so made in the making of its decision), or

(b) hold meetings with the local authority, or in the case of *section 215A* the person who applied for the acquisition order, or any other person where it appears to the Board to be necessary or expedient for the purpose of—

  (i) making a decision concerning the confirming or otherwise of such compulsory acquisition, or

  (ii) resolving any issue with the local authority or the applicant, as may be appropriate, or any disagreement between the authority or the applicant, as may be appropriate, and any other person, including resolving any issue or disagreement in advance of an oral hearing.

(2) Where the Board holds a meeting in accordance with *subsection (1)(b)*, it shall keep a written record of the meeting and make that record available for inspection.

(3) The Board, or an employee of the Board duly authorised by the Board, may appoint any person to hold a meeting referred to in *subsection (1)(b)*.]

AMENDMENT HISTORY

Inserted by s.38 of the Planning and Development (Strategic Infrastructure) Act 2006 (No. 27 of 2006).

NOTE

This new section allows the Board certain powers before making a decision on any compulsory acquisition including inviting submissions or holding meetings. The Board cannot be compelled to take any of the specified measures under this section but can decide to do so at its discretion. The Board can exercise such powers at any time prior to making its decision on the compulsory acquisition. Under subsection (1)(a) the Board may invite submissions from any person or under 1(b) may hold meetings with the local authority, applicant or any other person. The Board may hold the meeting to assist it in deciding whether to confirm the compulsory acquisition or to resolve any issue or disagreement between the local authority or applicant or other person. The subsection does not give any clear guidance as to the issue or disagreement to be resolved but is drafted broadly to include any matter which could arise in the context of confirming the compulsory acquisition or otherwise. A record must be kept of any meeting and a Board employee may be appointed to hold such meeting.

[Section 215: supplemental provisions

217B.—(1) The Board may, at its absolute discretion and at any time before **1–259** making a decision on a scheme or proposed road development referred to in section 215—

    (a) request further submissions or observations from any person who made submissions or observations in relation to the scheme or proposed road development, or any other person who may, in the opinion of the Board, have information which is relevant to its decision on the scheme or proposed road development, or

    (b) hold meetings with the road authority or any other person where it appears to the Board to be necessary or expedient for the purpose of—

        (i) making a decision on the scheme or proposed road development, or

        (ii) resolving any issue with the road authority or any disagreement between the authority and any other person, including resolving any issue or disagreement in advance of an oral hearing.

(2) Where the Board holds a meeting in accordance with *subsection (1)(b)*, it shall keep a written record of the meeting and make that record available for inspection.

(3) The Board, or an employee of the Board duly authorised by the Board, may appoint any person to hold a meeting referred to in *subsection (1)(b)*.

(4) The Board may—

    (a) if it considers it necessary to do so, require a road authority that has submitted a scheme under *section 49 of the Roads Act 1993* or made an application for approval under *section 51* of that Act to furnish to the Board such further information in relation to—

        (i) the effects on the environment of the proposed scheme or road development,

or

    (ii) the consequences for proper planning and sustainable development in the area or areas in which it is proposed to situate the said scheme or road development of such scheme or road development, as the Board may specify, or

  (b) if it is provisionally of the view that it would be appropriate to approve the scheme or proposed road development were certain alterations (specified in the notification referred to in this paragraph) to be made to the terms of it, notify the road authority that it is of that view and invite the authority to make to the terms of the scheme or proposed road development alterations specified in the notification and, if the authority makes those alterations, to furnish to it such information (if any) as it may specify in relation to the scheme or road development, in the terms as so altered, or, where necessary, a revised environmental impact statement in respect of it.

(5) If a road authority makes the alterations to the terms of the scheme or proposed road development specified in a notification given to it under *subsection (4),* the terms of the scheme or road development as so altered shall be deemed to be the scheme or proposed road development for the purposes of *sections 49, 50 and 51 of the Roads Act 1993.*

(6) The Board shall—

  (a) where it considers that any further information received pursuant to a requirement made under *subsection (4)(a)* contains significant additional data relating to—

    (i) the likely effects on the environment of the scheme or proposed road development, and

    (ii) the likely consequences for proper planning and sustainable development in the area or areas in which it is proposed to situate the said scheme or road development of such scheme or road development,

or

  (b) where the road authority has made the alterations to the terms of the proposed development specified in a notification given to it under *subsection (4)(b),* require the authority to do the things referred to in *subsection (7).*

(7) The things which a road authority shall be required to do as aforesaid are—

  (a) to publish in one or more newspapers circulating in the area or areas in which the development to which the scheme relates or, as the case may be, the proposed road development would be situate a notice stating that, as appropriate—

    (i) further information in relation to the scheme or proposed road development has been furnished to the Board, or

    (ii) the road authority has, pursuant to an invitation of the Board, made alterations to the terms of the scheme or proposed road development (and the nature of those alterations shall be indicated) and, if it be the case, that information in relation to the terms of the scheme or road development as so altered or a revised environmental impact statement in respect of the scheme or development has been furnished to the Board, indicating the times at which, the period (which shall not be less than 3 weeks) during which and the place, or places, where a copy of the information or the environmental impact statement referred to in *subparagraph (i) or (ii)* may be inspected free of charge or purchased on payment of a specified fee (which fee shall not exceed the reasonable cost of making such copy) and that submissions or observations in relation to that information or statement may be made to the Board before the expiration of the indicated period, and

(b) to send to each body or prescribed authority to which a notice was given pursuant to *section 51(3)(b) or (c) of the Roads Act 1993* —

(i) a notice of the furnishing to the Board of, as appropriate, the further information referred to in *paragraph (a)(i)* or the information or statement referred to in *paragraph (a)(ii),* and

(ii) a copy of that further information, information or statement, and to indicate to the body or authority that submissions or observations in relation to that further information, information or statement may be made to the Board before the expiration of a period (which shall be not less than 3 weeks) beginning on the day on which the notice is sent to the prescribed authority by the road authority.

(8) The Board shall, in making its decision in respect of a scheme or proposed road development, have regard to any information submitted on foot of a notice under *subsection (4),* including any revised environmental impact statement or any submissions or observations made on foot of a request under *subsection (1)* or a notice under *subsection (7).*]

AMENDMENT HISTORY

Inserted by s.38 of the Planning and Development (Strategic Infrastructure) Act 2006 (No. 27 of 2006).

NOTE

This new section allows the Board certain powers in relation to an application for approval of a road scheme or a proposed road development which includes inviting submissions or holding meetings. The phrase "absolute discretion" suggests that the Board cannot be compelled to take any of the specified measures under this section but it can decide to do so at its discretion. However, this must be subject to the requirements of fair procedures which may arise in a particular case. The Board can exercise such powers at any time prior to making its decision on compulsory acquisition. Under subs.(1)(a) the Board may invite submissions from any person or under subs.(1)(b) may hold meetings with the local authority, applicant or any other person. The Board may hold the meeting to assist it in deciding whether to confirm the compulsory acquisition or to resolve any issue or disagreement between the local authority or applicant or other person. The subsection does not give any clear guidance as to the issue or disagreement to be resolved but is drafted broadly to include any matter which could arise in the context of confirming the compulsory acquisition or otherwise. A record must be kept of any meeting and a Board employee may be appointed to hold such meeting.

Under subs.(4), the Board may request the road authority to submit further information or if it is of the view that the development should be approved if altered, invite the road authority to alter the proposed development and submit information relating to such alteration, along with a revised EIS, if necessary.

Under subs.(6), the Board will require the road authority to publish a notice where it considers that the further information received contains significant additional information regarding the likely effects on the environment and the likely consequences for the proper planning and sustainable development of the area where the proposed development is situated. In any proceeding to challenge a decision of the Board not to require a notice, the courts will tend to defer to the decision of the Board that such information was not significant unless such decision was irrational. See *Kinsella v Dundalk Town Council*, unreported, High Court, Kelly J., December 3, 2004, and *Dietacaron Ltd v An Bord Pleanála* [2005] 2 I.L.R.M. 32 and *White v Dublin City Council* [2004] 1 I.R. 545. A notice is also required where the Board invites the state authority to alter the terms of the proposed development. In the latter case, there is a requirement to publish a notice irrespective of whether the alteration reflects significant additional information regarding the likely effects on the environment and proper planning and sustainable development. The notice must, inter alia, invite submissions, allowing a period of not less than three weeks. Both a notice and a copy of the further information or information concerning alterations or a revised EIS must be sent to the prescribed bodies, allowing a period of not less than three weeks to make submissions. The information and submissions received must be taken into account by the Board in making its decision.

[Board's powers to make decisions on transferred functions

1–260   **217C.—(1)** Notwithstanding any provision of any of the enactments referred to in *section 214, 215A or 215B* concerning the confirming or otherwise of any compulsory acquisition, the Board shall, in relation to any of the functions transferred under this Part respecting those matters, have the power to confirm a compulsory acquisition or any part thereof, with or without conditions or modifications, or to annul an acquisition or any part thereof.

(2) Notwithstanding any provision of the *Roads Act 1993* concerning the approval of any scheme or proposed road development, the Board shall, in relation to any of the functions transferred under this Part respecting those matters, have the power to approve the scheme or development or any part thereof, with or without conditions or modifications, or to refuse to approve the scheme or development or any part thereof.

(3) Without prejudice to the generality of the foregoing power to attach conditions, the Board may attach to any approval of a scheme or proposed road development under the *Roads Act 1993* a condition requiring—

    (a) the construction or the financing, in whole or in part, of the construction of a facility, or

    (b) the provision or the financing, in whole or in part, of the provision of a service,

in the area in which the proposed development would be situated, being a facility or service that, in the opinion of the Board, would constitute a substantial gain to the community.

(4) A condition attached pursuant to *subsection (3)* shall not require such an amount of financial resources to be committed for the purposes of the condition being complied with as would substantially deprive the person in whose favour the approval operates of the benefits likely to accrue from the grant of the approval.]

Inserted by s.38 of the Planning and Development (Strategic Infrastructure) Act 2006 (No. 27 of 2006).

NOTE

Under this section the Board has the power to confirm a compulsory acquisition with or without modification or to annul the acquisition or part thereof. The section removes any doubts as to whether the Board had such powers in respect of the functions transferred to the Board exercised under previous enactments. Subsection (2) also removes any doubt that the Board can issue such decision with respect to road schemes. While there is a general power to impose conditions which could relate to the proper planning and sustainable development of the area, subs.(3) allows the Board to impose a condition which would amount to a planning gain to the community in respect of the approval of road scheme or proposed road development. This subsection does not apply to the confirmation of compulsory acquisition under subs.(1) and so there would appear to be no power to impose such a condition in respect of general compulsory acquisition. A similar condition can be imposed in respect of local authority development under s.175(9) or state authority development under s.181B(7). This can consist of two types, namely, the construction of a facility or the provision of a service. The subsection gives no further guidance as to the nature of these matters except that it should be of substantial gain to the community. It appears that the gain must be to the community as a whole rather than a limited section of the community. This is not to say the gain must be of interest to all the community but merely than the gain is open to all the community. It may be a question of fact and of planning judgment as to whether there is a substantial gain to the community. Subsection (8) imposes a limit to the scope of the condition, which is that the condition must not require an amount of financial resources to be committed as would substantially deprive the person granted approval of the benefits likely to accrue from the approval. This clause therefore introduces a proportionality requirement. This requirement is mandatory and any condition which would have such effect would be ultra vires. It appears that the assessment of whether a condition has such effect is a mixed question of fact and law and the better view is that the Board ought not to be shown deference in its opinion if reviewed by a court in any proceedings. The assessment of the benefits likely to accrue will depend on the type of permission. The condition would appear to encompass the financial benefits which would accrue from any approval, which would therefore involve the value of the land with the approval attached.

It may be observed that neither this section nor the entire of Pt XIV, gives any guidance or criteria as to how the Board determines whether to confirm, modify or annul the CPO. It is nonetheless clear that the power of compulsory acquisition must be used in the public interest. This follows from the well established principles that powers of compulsory acquisition are an interference with constitutionally protected property rights. In *Crosbie v Custom House Dock Development Authority* [1996] 2 I.R. 531, Costello P. noted "[t]he making and confirming of an order compulsorily to acquire an objector's property rights results in an interference with the objector's constitutionally protected rights". In *Tormey v Ireland*, unreported, Supeme Court, December 21, 1972, O'Dalaigh C.J. noted that "the acquisition provisions of the Act are an interference with private rights and accordingly the Court will look strictly at the terms of the Act". This was cited with approval in *Blascaod Mor v Commissioner of Public Works (3)*, unreported, High Court, Budd J., February 27, 1998. In *Clinton v An Bord Pleanála* [2007] 4 I.R. 171 it was said that "[i]t is axiomatic that the making and confirming of a compulsory purchase order (CPO) to acquire a person's land entails an invasion of his constitutionally protected property rights". The compulsory acquisition must therefore be justified in the public interest. In *Clinton v An Bord Pleanála* [2007] 4 I.R. 171, Geoghegan J. said "[t]he acquiring authority must be satisfied that the acquisition of the property is clearly justified by the exigencies of the common good". The extent of to which such public interest must be demonstrated may depend on the nature of development. In *Clinton v An Bord Pleanála* [2007] 4 I.R. 171, Geoghehan J. noted:

> "It was at all times perfectly clear that the property was being acquired for regeneration of O'Connell Street. In my view, it was only necessary for the council to demonstrate that a CPO was desirable in the public interest to achieve that purpose.

It was not necessary to prove how exactly it would be carried out".

The onus of proof clearly lies on the acquiring authority. See *Prest v Secretary of State for Wales* [1982] 81 LGR 193. It may appear that the development plan may be a potential source in identifying the public interest where the purpose put forward by the acquiring authority is consistent (or inconsistent) with certain development objectives contained therein. This may particularly be the case where the precise purpose of the CPO is identified in the development plan. However, the mere fact that a matter is contained in a development plan could not be definitive and it will depend on the particular facts of each CPO as to whether it is necessary in the public interest. In judicial review proceedings challenging the confirmation on CPO on the basis that the acquisition was not in the public interest, the Court will apply a heightened level of scrutiny than merely *O'Keeffe* irrationality. In *Clinton v An Bord Pleanála* [2007] 4 I.R. 171, where Geoghegan J. said:

"The power conferred on an administrative body such as a local authority or An Bord Pleanála to compulsorily acquire land must be exercised in accordance with the requirements of the Constitution, including respecting the property rights of the affected landowner (*East Donegal Co-Operative v Attorney General* [1970] I.R. 317). Any decisions of such bodies are subject to judicial review. It would insufficiently protect constitutional rights if the court, hearing the judicial review application, merely had to be satisfied that the decision was not irrational or was not contrary to fundamental reason and common sense".

Oral hearings in relation to compulsory acquisition of land

1–261 **218.**—[(1) Where, as a result of the transfer of functions under *section 214, 215, 215A or 215B,* the Board would otherwise be required to hold a local inquiry, public local inquiry or oral hearing, that requirement shall not apply to the Board but the Board may, at its absolute discretion, hold an oral hearing in relation to the matter, the subject of the function transferred.]

(2) For the avoidance of doubt, it is hereby declared that the provisions of the *Local Government Acts, 1941, 1946, 1955* and *1991,* in relation to public local inquiries shall not apply in relation to oral hearings held by the Board in accordance with *subsection (1).*

(3) For the purposes of this *Part,* the references to local inquiries or public local inquiries in the following provisions shall be deemed to be references to oral hearings under this *section* :

  (a) *section 10 of the Local Government (No. 2) Act, 1960;*

  (b) *section 78 of, and the Third Schedule to, the Housing Act, 1966;*

  (c) *Part IV of the Roads Act, 1993.*

(4) *Sections 135, 143 and 146* shall apply and have effect in relation to the functions transferred to the Board under [*sections 214 to 215B*] and those sections shall be construed accordingly.

AMENDMENT HISTORY

Subsection (1) substituted by s.39 of the Planning and Development (Strategic Infrastructure) Act 2006 (No. 27 of 2006).

NOTE

This section concerns oral hearings by An Bord Pleanála in relation to compulsory acquisition of land. Subsection (1) was substituted under the 2006 Act to provide that the Board is not obliged to hold an oral hearing but may do so at its absolute discretion. The former provision was that the Board was obliged to hold oral hearings where the enactments which transferred the functions to the Board, required the holding of a local inquiry or public local inquiry. The new subsection provides where the Board have been required to hold an oral hearing, this will no longer apply but the Board will have discretion whether to hold such hearing. Notwithstanding that the legislation uses the word "absolute discretion", this must be read subject to the requirements of natural and constitutional justice and rights to fair procedures under art.6 of the European Convention on Human Rights.

The powers of An Bord Pleanála in the conducting of oral hearings are set out in ss.135, 143 and 146 of the 2000 Act and these provisions therefore apply to oral hearings held by the Board in relation to CPOs. In *Kildare County Council v An Bord Pleanála*, unreported, High Court, McMenamin J., March 10, 2006, it was said the fact that the confirming, both under s.51 of the Roads Act 1993 and under the CPO procedure has been transferred from the Minister to the Board indicates that the adjudication must involve consideration of proper planning and sustainable development.

[Power to direct payment of certain costs

219.—**(1)** Where the Board has made a decision in the performance of   **1–262** any functions transferred under *section 214, 215, 215A or 215B,* it may at its absolute discretion direct the payment of such sum as it considers reasonable by the local authority concerned or, in the case of *section 215A or 215B,* the person who applied for the acquisition order (hereafter in this section referred to as the "applicant")—

> **(a)** to the Board towards the costs and expenses incurred by the Board in determining the matter, including—
>
>> **(i)** the costs of holding any oral hearing in relation to the matter,
>>
>> **(ii)** the fees of any consultants or advisers engaged in the matter, and
>>
>> **(iii)** an amount equal to such portion of the remuneration and any allowances for expenses paid to the members and employees of the Board as the Board determines to be attributable to the performance of duties by the members and employees in relation to the matter,
>
> and.
>
> **(b)** to any person appearing at an oral hearing held in relation to the matter as a contribution towards the costs, other than the costs referred to in *section 135,* incurred by that person of appearing at that hearing,

and the local authority or applicant, as appropriate, shall pay the sum.

[(2) The reference in *subsection (1)(b)* to costs shall be construed as a reference to such costs as the Board in its absolute discretion considers to be reasonable costs.

[(3) If a local authority or applicant, as appropriate, fails to pay a sum directed to be paid under *subsection (1),* the Board or any other person concerned, as the case may be, may recover the sum from the authority or applicant, as appropriate, as a simple contract debt in any court of competent jurisdiction.]

Subsections (2) and (3) substituted by s.40 of the Planning and Development (Strategic Infrastructure) Act 2006 (No. 27 of 2006).

NOTE

A new s.219 was substituted under the 2006 which concerns the power of the Board to direct the payment of costs in relation to oral hearings. The main change includes recognition that the applicant for compulsory acquisition may be a person or body other than a local authority and to allow the Board to direct the payment of costs by such person as well as by a local authority. Subsection (1)(a) provides a breakdown of the costs of the Board, while the former section merely referred to costs of the Board. The costs which may be recovered include reasonable costs of the oral hearing, costs of advisors/consultants and costs of employees/members attributable to the matter. The costs which it may order concern costs incurred by the Board in holding the hearing or incurred by any other person appearing at the hearing. It may be noted that under s.145, the Board has a more wide-ranging power to order costs to be paid by the planning authority or the appellant, which may be paid to any party to the appeal or the Board. Despite the reference in s.145 to "planning authority", it appears that s.145 can apply to a CPO oral hearing under this section, irrespective of whether the local authority is acting in its capacity as planning authority or some other capacity.

Certain procedures to run in parallel

1–263   **220.—(1)** The person holding an oral hearing in relation to the compulsory acquisition of land, which relates wholly or in part to proposed development by a local authority which is required to comply with *section 175* or any other statutory provision to comply with procedures for giving effect to the *Council Directive,* shall be entitled to hear evidence in relation to the likely effects on the environment of such development.

(2) Where an application for the approval of a proposed development which is required to comply with *section 175* is made to the Board and a compulsory purchase order or provisional order has been submitted to the Board for confirmation and where the proposed development relates wholly or in part to the same proposed development, the Board shall, where objections have been received in relation to the compulsory purchase order, make a decision on the confirmation of the compulsory purchase order at the same time.

NOTE

This section allows a person conducting an oral hearing in relation to a CPO to hear at the same time evidence concerning the approval of an EIS under s.175 relating to the same development. Where there is both a CPO and a related EIS for approval before the Board concerning the same development, the Board is obliged to arrive at its decision in relation to both at the same time.

Objective of the Board in relation to transferred functions

1–264   **221.—(1)** It shall be the duty of the Board to ensure that any matters submitted in accordance with the functions transferred to it under [*section 214, 215, 215A or 215B*] are disposed of as expeditiously as may be and, for that purpose, to take all such steps as are open to it to ensure that, in so far as is practicable, there are no avoidable delays at any stage in the determination of those matters.

(2) Without prejudice to the generality of *subsection (1)* and subject to *subsections (3), (4), (5) and (6),* it shall be the objective of the Board to ensure that—

    (a) the matter is determined within a period of 18 weeks beginning on the last day for making objections, observations or submissions, as the case may be, in accordance with the relevant enactment referred to in [*section 214, 215, 215A or 215B*], or

(b) the matter is determined within such other period as the Minister may prescribe in relation to *paragraph (a),* either generally or in respect of a particular class or classes of matter.

(3)

(a) Where it appears to the Board that it would not be possible or appropriate, because of the particular circumstances of the matter with which the Board is concerned, to determine the matter within the period prescribed under *subsection (2),* the Board shall, by notice in writing served on any local authority involved and any other person who submitted objections, representations, submissions or observations in relation to the matter before the expiration of that period, inform the authority and those persons of the reasons why it would not be possible or appropriate to determine the matter within that period and shall specify the date before which the Board intends that the matter shall be determined.

(b) Where a notice has been served under *paragraph (a),* the Board shall take all such steps as are open to it to ensure that the matter is determined before the date specified in the notice.

(4) The Minister may by regulations vary the period as specified in *subsection (2)* either generally or in respect of a particular class or classes of matters with which the Board is concerned, in accordance with the transferred functions under this *Part,* where it appears to him or her to be necessary, by virtue of exceptional circumstances, to do so and, for so long as the regulations are in force, this *section* shall be construed and have effect in accordance therewith.

(5) Where the Minister considers it to be necessary or expedient that certain functions of the Board (being functions transferred under [*section 214, 215, 215A or 215B*]) performable in relation to matters of a class or classes that—

(a) are of special strategic, economic or social importance to the State, and

(b) are submitted to the Board for the performance by it of such functions,

be performed as expeditiously as is consistent with proper planning and sustainable development, he or she may give a direction to the Board that in the performance of the functions concerned priority be given to matters of the class or classes concerned, and the Board shall comply with such direction.

(6) *Subsection (2)* shall not apply in relation to the functions under the *Public Health (Ireland) Act, 1878,* the *Local Government Act, 1925,* or the *Water Supplies Act, 1942,* which are transferred to the Board under *section 214.*

(7) For the purposes of meeting its duty under this *section,* the chairperson may, or shall when so directed by the Minister, assign the functions transferred to the Board under [*section 214, 215, 215A or 215B*] to a particular division of the Board in accordance with *section 112.*

(8) The Board shall include in each report made under *section 118* a statement of the number of matters which the Board has determined within

a period referred to in *paragraph (a) or (b) of subsection (2)* and such other information as to the time taken to determine such matters as the Minister may direct.

[(9) The Minister may by regulations provide for such additional, incidental, consequential or supplemental matters as regards procedure in respect of the functions transferred to the Board under *section 214 or 215* as appear to the Minister to be necessary or expedient.]

AMENDMENT HISTORY

Subsections (1), (2) and (7) amended by s.41 of the Planning and Development (Strategic Infrastructure) Act 2006 (No. 27 of 2006).

Subsection (9) was inserted by s.247 of the Local Government Act 2001 (No. 37 of 2001), which, by the Local Government Act 2001 (Commencement) Order 2001 (S.I. No. 458 of 2001), came into effect on October 9, 2001.

NOTE

This section seeks to achieve certain time limits for the Board in completing the oral hearings and other functions in connection with the CPO. It is in similar terms to s.126 of the Act, which applies to all the functions of An Bord Pleanála. There is a duty of the Board to ensure that the matters "are disposed of as expeditiously as may be" and "to take all such steps" as are open to it to ensure that, in so far as is practicable, there are no avoidable delays at any stage in determination of the matters. As already noted, this general duty is also imposed under s.126 of the 2000 Act in relation to all functions carried out by An Bord Pleanála. Subsection (2) provides that it is an objective of the Board to determine the matter within a period of 18 weeks beginning on the last day for making objections, observations or submissions (the Minister may vary this period by regulation.) The Board is not bound to determine the matter within 18 weeks, but merely to strive to attain this as an objective. However, the general duty of expedition is over and above the 18-week period. Thus An Bord Pleanála may be deemed to have not complied with their duty to ensure there are no avoidable delays, even where it has made the determination within the 18-month period. There is no provision for a default decision where the time limit or duty is breached. Subsection (3) provides that where the Board believes it would not be possible or appropriate to determine the matter within the 18-week period, the Board must notify all interested parties including the local authority, stating the reasons why it would not be possible or appropriate and specifying the date before which the Board intends that the matter be determined.

Under subs.(5), the Minister has power to direct the Board to give priority to certain matters of classes of development of particular importance to the State. No such directions have yet to be made. Section 112 of the Act allows the Board to act in divisions, which is expressed as being "for the speedy dispatch of the business of the Board". A division must have no less than three members and will have all the functions of the Board. The reference in subs.(8) to s.118 concerns the Board's Annual Report to the Minister which must be made not later than June 30 in each year.

The 2006 Act amended this section to to take account of other newly inserted provisions.

Amendment of section 10 of Local Government (No. 2) Act, 1960

1–265   **222.**—Section 10 (inserted by section 86 of the Housing Act, 1966) of the Local Government (No. 2) Act, 1960, is hereby amended—
   (*a*) by the deletion of subsection (2), and
   (*b*) in subsection (4), by the substitution for paragraph (*d*) of the following paragraph:

"(*d*) Where—
   (i) an order is made by virtue of this section, and
   (ii) there is a public right of way over the land to which the order relates or any part thereof or over land adjacent to or associated with the land or any part thereof,
the order may authorise the local authority, by order made by them after they have acquired such land or part, to extinguish the right of way.".

NOTE

This section amends s.10 of the Local Government (No. 2) Act 1960. It deletes s.10(2) of the 1960 Act, which provided that:
"Where—(a) a local authority considers that any land, whether situate within or outside their functional area, would, if acquired by them, be suitable for the provision of halls, buildings and offices for the local authority, and (b) the local authority considers that it would be convenient to effect the acquisition under the Housing Act 1966, the local authority may decide so to effect the acquisition".
This provision was unnecessary as s.10(1) granted a general power of acquisition which would cover such matters concerned in this subsection. The new substituted s.10(4)(d) introduces an additional clause into the subsection with, "or over land adjacent to or associated with the land or any part thereof". The effect of this is to broaden the scope of such public rights of way which may be extinguished, to extend to rights which are not strictly on the land which is the subject matter of the acquisition.

References to transferred functions in regulations, etc.

223.—**(1)** A reference in any regulations, prescribed forms or other **1–266** instruments made under the enactments referred to in [*section 214, 215, 215A or 215B* to the Minister, any other Minister of the Government or the Commission for Energy Regulation], and which relate to the functions transferred under those sections, shall be deemed to be references to the Board.

(2) A reference in any regulations, prescribed forms or other instruments made under the enactments referred to in [*section 214, 215, 215A or 215B*] to local inquiries or public local inquiries, and which relate to functions transferred to the Board under those sections, shall be deemed to be references to oral hearings by the Board.

AMENDMENT HISTORY

Subsections (1) and (2) amended by s.42 of the Planning and Development (Strategic Infrastructure) Act 2006 (No. 27 of 2006).

NOTE

This section provides that a reference in any regulation or instrument made under the legislation enlisted in ss.214 or 215, which refers to the Minister, is now deemed to refer to the Board. This follows from the transfer of functions to An Bord Pleanála from the Minister. The 2006 Act makes certain minor amendments to take account of other newly inserted provisions.

PART XV

DEVELOPMENT ON THE FORESHORE

Definition

1–267   **224.**—In this *Part* —

"development" *includes development consisting of the reclamation of any land on the foreshore*;

"foreshore" has the meaning assigned to it by the *Foreshore Act, 1933,* but includes land between the line of high water of ordinary or medium tides and land within the functional area of the planning authority concerned that adjoins the first-mentioned land.

NOTE

Part XV concerns development taking place on the foreshore, introducing a requirement to obtain planning permission. The Foreshore Act 1933 (the "1933 Act") defines the foreshore under s.1 as "the bed and shore, below the line of high water of ordinary or medium tides, of the sea and of every tidal river and tidal estuary and of every channel, creek and bay of the sea or of any such river or estuary". This definition arguably gives rise to some confusion insofar as it refers to "below" the high water mark but does not state any seaward limit to the foreshore. However, the definition has since been amended by the insertion of s.1A under s.60 of the Maritime Safety Act 2005 which provides:

"The outer limit of the foreshore is, and shall be deemed always to have been and to be, coterminous with the seaward limit of the territorial seas of the State as provided, from time to time, by Act of the Oireachtas".

The definition of the foreshore under s.224 is broader than under the 1933 Act insofar as it incorporates the definition but also adds that the foreshore includes "land between the line of high water of ordinary or medium tides and land within the functional area of the planning authority concerned that adjoins the first-mentioned land". The notion of the foreshore is often used interchangeably with the seashore. However, in *Mahoney v Neenan* [1966] I.R. 559, McLoughlin J. distinguished the terms stating "the word 'foreshore' means the bed and shore, below the line of high water of ordinary or medium tides, of the sea and of every tidal river and tidal estuary"; "the word 'seashore' means the foreshore and every beach, bank, and cliff continuous thereto and includes all sands and rocks contiguous to the foreshore." It also defines "beach materials" so as to include, inter alia, "seaweed". The foreshore is generally vested in the State. However, it is permissible for parts of the foreshore to be within private ownership. Development beyond the foreshore, i.e. beyond the line of high water of ordinary or medium tides, is the responsibility of the Department of Marine and Communications.

The foreshore was not a matter covered by the previous planning Acts, while under the Foreshore Acts, planning permission was not required except under a ministerial order. The Foreshore Acts 1933–2003 require that a lease or licence be obtained from the Minister for the Marine and Natural Resources before undertaking any works or placing structures or material on, or for the occupation of or removal of material from, State-owned foreshore. Any foreshore lease, licence or permission given is without prejudice to the powers of the local planning authority whether or not to grant planning permission. An application to the Minister for a lease, a license, approval of development on privately owned foreshore or for the removal of beach material, which involves development falling within Pt I and Pt II of Sch.1 to the European Communities (Environmental Impact Assessment) Regulations, 1989, must be accompanied by an EIS. Any of the types of development set out in Pt I and Pt II of Sch.1 to the European Communities (Environmental Impact Assessment) Regulations, 1989, which takes place on the foreshore will require an EIS. However, even where the development falls short of the thresholds set out in art.24, the Minister may require an EIS to be submitted where he considers the development is likely to have significant effects on the environment. The Minister may also waive the requirement for an EIS in "exceptional circumstances", where a specified procedure is carried out.

Obligation to obtain permission in respect of development on foreshore

225.—(1) Subject to the provisions of this *Act,* permission shall be required **1–268** under *Part III* in respect of development on the foreshore not being exempted development, in circumstances where, were such development carried out, it would adjoin—

    (a) the functional area of a planning authority, or

    (b) any reclaimed land adjoining such functional area,

and accordingly, that part of the foreshore on which it is proposed to carry out the development shall for the purposes of making an application for permission in respect of such development be deemed to be within the functional area of that planning authority.

(2) That part of the foreshore on which a development has been commenced or completed pursuant to permission granted under *Part III* shall, for the purposes of this *Act* or any other enactment, whether passed before or after the passing of this *Act,* be deemed to be within the functional area of the planning authority that granted such permission.

(3) This *section* shall not apply to—

    (a) development to which *section 226* applies, or

    (b) development consisting of underwater cables, wires, pipe-lines or other similar apparatus used for the purpose of—

        (i) transmitting electricity or telecommunications signals, or

        (ii) carrying gas, petroleum, oil or water,

or development connected to land within the functional area of a planning authority solely by means of any such cable, wire, pipeline or apparatus.

(4) This *section* is in addition to and not in substitution for the *Foreshore Acts, 1933* to *1998.*

Note

    This section provides that planning permission is required for development on the foreshore, as defined in s.224, which adjoins the functional area of the planning authority or which adjoins any reclaimed land which adjoins such functional area. Local government areas are defined under s.10 the Local Government Act 2001. The section, while not extending the functional area of the local authority, "deems" the part of the foreshore where the development is proposed to be carried out to be within the functional area of the planning authority. Thus the functional area is extended only to the relevant part of the foreshore and only for the purposes of receiving a planning application. Under subs.(2) where permission is granted for development of the foreshore, that part of the foreshore where development is completed or commenced is deemed to be within the functional area of the planning authority. It follows from this that the planning authority can perform any of its functions under this Act or any other Act, including taking enforcement action under Pt VIII. Prior to the 2000 Act, planning permission was not required as development on the foreshore was not subject to the planning code. However, this did not mean that the foreshore could never arise under the planning code. Thus it has been established that a condition of planning permission may be imposed with respect to the foreshore. See *Arklow Holidays Ltd v An Bord Pleanála*, unreported, High Court, Clarke J., January 18, 2006, where the court rejected the claim that conditions imposed by the Board in respect of the foreshore were invalid as it had no jurisdiction over the foreshore.

    There are two specific categories of exempted development concerning the foreshore.

Class 53 of Pt II of Sch.2 to the 2001 Regulations provides that development pursuant to a foreshore licence granted under the Fisheries (Amendment) Act 1997 is exempted development. This specifically concerns a foreshore licence for aquaculture. Also Class 54 exempts developments comprising reclamation of an area, not exceeding 100 square metres, of foreshore for the purpose of protecting a pier, slipway or other structure on the foreshore. Article 28(1)(t) of the 2001 Regulations provides that where a planning application is received which might impact on the foreshore, the planning authority must send notice to the Minister for Marine.

Subsection (3) excludes certain types of development, including local authority development under s.226, underwater cables, wires, pipelines or other similar apparatus used for the purpose of transmitting electricity or telecommunications signals, or carrying gas, petroleum, oil or water, or development connected to land within the functional area of a planning authority. Applicants seeking permission to lay an outfall or discharge pipe on the foreshore must also apply to the local authority or the Environmental Protection Agency for a licence under the Local Government (Water Pollution) Acts.

Subsection (4) makes clear that the requirement to obtain planning permission is in addition to and not in substitution for the Foreshore Acts 1933–1998. The Foreshore Acts 1933–2003 require that a lease or licence be obtained from the Minister for the Marine and Natural Resources before undertaking any works or placing structures or material on, or for the occupation of or removal of material from, the State-owned foreshore. It also follows that any foreshore lease, licence or permission given is without prejudice to the powers of the local planning authority whether or not to grant planning permission. An application to the Minister for a lease, a license, approval of development on privately owned foreshore or for the removal of beach material, which involves development falling within Pt I and Pt II of Sch.1 to the European Communities (Environmental Impact Assessment) Regulations 1989, must be accompanied by an EIS. Any of the types of development set out in Pt I and Pt II of Sch.1 to the European Communities (Environmental Impact Assessment) Regulations 1989, which take place on the foreshore will require an EIS. However even where the development falls short of the thresholds set out in art.24, the Minister may require an EIS to be submitted where he considers the development is likely to have significant effects on the environment. The Minister may also waive the requirement for an EIS in "exceptional circumstances", where a specified procedure is carried out.

Local authority development on foreshore

1–269   **226.—(1)** Where development is proposed to be carried out wholly or partly on the foreshore—

    (a) by a local authority that is a planning authority, whether in its capacity as a planning authority or otherwise, or

    (b) by some other person on behalf of, or jointly or in partnership with, a local authority that is a planning authority, pursuant to an agreement entered into by that local authority whether in its capacity as a planning authority or otherwise,

(hereafter in this *section* referred to as "proposed development"), the local authority concerned shall apply to the Board for approval of the proposed development.

    [(2)

    (a) The Board may approve, approve subject to conditions, or refuse to approve a proposed development.

    (b) Without prejudice to the generality of *paragraph (a),* the Board may attach to an approval under this section conditions for or in connection with the protection of the marine environment (including the protection of fisheries) or, if the subject of a recommendation by the Minister for Transport to the Board with regard to the exercise of the power under this subsection in the particular case (which recommendation that Minister of the Government may, by virtue of this subsection, make), the safety of navigation.]

(3) *Section 175* shall apply to proposed development belonging to a class of development, identified for the purposes of *section 176,* subject to—

    (a) the modification that the local authority concerned shall not be required to apply for approval under *subsection (3) of the said section 175* in respect of the proposed development,

    (b) the modification that the reference in *subsection (4)* to approval under *subsection (3)* shall be construed as a reference to approval under *subsection (1) of this section,*

    (c) any modifications consequential upon *paragraph (a),* and

    (d) any other necessary modifications.

(4) *Subsections (4), (5), (6), (7), (9), (10), (11)(a), (11)(b)(ii), (11)(b)(iii), (12), (13) and (14) of section 175* shall apply to a proposed development other than one referred to in *subsection (3),* subject to—

    (a) the modification that the reference in *subsection (4) of the said section 175* to approval under *subsection (3)* shall be construed as a reference to approval under *subsection (1) of this section,*

    (b) the modification that—

        (i) references in *subsections (4) and (5) of the said section 175* to environmental impact statement shall be construed as references to such documents, particulars, plans or other information relating to the proposed development as may be prescribed,

        (ii) references to likely effects on the environment shall be disregarded, and

        (iii) the reference in *subsection (11)(a) of the said section 175* to applications for approval under this *section* shall be construed as references to applications for approval under *subsection (1) of this section,* and

    (c) any other necessary modifications.

(5) *Sections 32 and 179* shall not apply to a proposed development.

[(6)

    (a) In the following case:

        (i) the local authority concerned, if it is of the opinion that the development concerned would be likely to have significant effects on the environment, shall refer; or

        (ii) the Minister for Communications, Marine and Natural Resources may refer;

    to the Board for its determination the question of whether the following development would be likely to have significant effects on the environment.

    (b) That case is one of development that is identified for the purposes of *section 176* (other than development falling within a class of development identified for the purposes of that section) and which is proposed to be carried out wholly or partly on the foreshore—

        (i) by a local authority that is a planning authority, whether in its capacity as a planning authority or otherwise, or

   (ii) by some other person on behalf of, or jointly or in partnership with a local authority that is a planning authority, pursuant to an agreement entered into by that authority, whether in its capacity as a planning authority or otherwise.

  (c) Where required by the Board, the local authority or the Minister for Communications, Marine and Natural Resources shall provide to the Board such information as may be specified by the Board in respect of the effects on the environment of the proposed development, the subject of the question referred to it under this subsection.

[(7)

  (a) The Board shall consider and determine the question referred to it under *subsection (6)* and, where it determines that the development concerned would be likely to have significant effects on the environment, it shall—

   (i) notify the local authority concerned (and, where the question has been referred by the Minister for Communications, Marine and Natural Resources, that Minister of the Government) that it has determined that the development would be likely to have those effects, and

   (ii) specify, in that notification, that any application by the local authority concerned for approval under *subsection (1)* in respect of the development shall be accompanied by an environmental impact statement prepared or caused to be prepared by the authority in respect of the development,

and, where that notification so specifies, any such application shall be accompanied by such a statement accordingly.

  (b) In making that determination, the Board shall have regard to the criteria for the purposes of determining which classes of development are likely to have significant effects on the environment set out in any regulations made under *section 176.*

  (c) Notwithstanding any other enactment, the determination of the Board of a question referred to it under *subsection (6)* shall be final.]

[(8) The Minister may make regulations to provide for such matters of procedure and administration as appear to the Minister, after consultation with the Minister for Communications, Marine and Natural Resources, to be necessary or expedient in respect of referring a question under *subsection (6)* or of making a determination under *subsection (7).*]

[(9) This section shall apply to proposed development—

  (a) that, if carried out wholly within the functional area of a local authority that is a planning authority, would be subject to the provisions of *section 175,*

  (b) that a local authority has been notified under *paragraph (a)(i)* of *subsection (7)* is one which the Board has determined under that subsection would be likely to have significant effects on the environment, or

  (c) that is prescribed for the purposes of this section.]

AMENDMENT HISTORY

Subsections (2), (6), (7) and (8) substituted by s.43 of the Planning and Development (Strategic Infrastructure) Act 2006 (No. 27 of 2006).

Subsection (7) inserted by s.43 of the Planning and Development (Strategic Infrastructure) Act 2006 (No. 27 of 2006).

Subsection (9) inserted by s.43 of the Planning and Development (Strategic Infrastructure) Act 2006 (No. 27 of 2006).

NOTE

This section provides that development carried out on the foreshore by the local authority, or by some other person in agreement with the local authority, must be granted approval by An Bord Pleanála. The development may be wholly or partly situated on the foreshore and may be carried out by the local authority or by some other person on behalf of, or jointly or in partnership with a local authority. The provisions concerning local authority development under s.179 or planning permission under s.32 are inapplicable. The Board has a discretion whether to approve with or without modification or to refuse it. Subsection (3) provides that s.175, concerning the requirement of a local authority to prepare an EIS, will apply to development on the foreshore which come within with classes of development set out in s.176. Section 175(3), concerning the approval of an EIS by the local authority, is inapplicable, as this would be a duplication of the referral to An Bord Pleanála under subs.(1). Subsection (4) applies certain provisions of s.175 including:

- s.175(4), concerning the requirement to publish notice in a newspaper stating that approval is sought and to send copies of the application to prescribed bodies (the approval referred to in s.175(4) is taken to refer to s.226(1) rather than s.175(3));
- s.175(5), concerning the Board's request for further information;
- s.175(6), on the matters to be considered by the Board;
- s.175(7), on evidence heard in oral hearing for compulsory purchase of land connected to the development;
- s.175(8), on exemption from the requirement to prepare an EIS;
- s.175(9), concerning the decision of the Board;
- s.175(10), where development also requires an integrated pollution licence or a waste licence;
- s.175(11), allowing for the Minister to make regulations;
- s.175(12), concerning the matters to be considered by the Board relating to proper planning and sustainable development;
- s.175(13), making it an offence to contravene a condition of the Board; and
- s.175(14), rendering the section inapplicable to proposed road development.

The 2006 Act made certain changes to subs.(2) to expressly allow for the imposition of conditions for approval by the Board in connection with the protection of the marine environment (including the protection of fisheries) or in relation to safety navigations where recommended by the Minister for Transport. The former s.227(9), now deleted, allowed the Board to impose conditions regarding the protection of the marine environment although there was no reference to the protection of fisheries.

The procedure for approval of a local authority development by the Board is set out in s.227(5) to 227(7). The Board must send copies of all maps and documents with the application to the Minister for Communications, Marine and Natural Resources and the Minister for Transport. By notice in writing, the Board must invite observations from the Minister on the application within the period specified in the notice, which must not be less than eight weeks. The Board must have regard to any observations received. Section 227(8) provides that the Foreshore Acts 1933 to 2005, shall not apply to any application to the Board under s.226. This subsection is poorly drafted. Its intention appears to be that there is no requirement for a local authority to also obtain a foreshore lease or licence with respect to development which is approved by the Board. However, it does not clearly state this. It could also have referred to the non-application of the Foreshore Acts to the "development" rather than "application"". Subsection (8)(b) goes on to provide that the local authority "may" apply for a foreshore lease or licence in certain circumstances. Insofar as there is no requirement for local authority development to obtain a foreshore lease or licence, this is in contrast to applications for planning permission under s.225, where there is a requirement to obtain both planning permission and a foreshore lease or licence from the Minister. Prior to the 2000 Act, local authority development on the foreshore certainly required a foreshore lease or license.

The 2006 Act also added new subss.6 to 8, which set out a procedure to refer the question of whether certain development on the foreshore requires an EIS to the Board for determination. The local authority or Minister for Communications may make a reference to the Board to determine whether development on the foreshore would be likely to have significant effects on the environment. The Board may request the local authority or the Minister to submit information in respect of the effects on the environment, in order to determine the matter. The Board will apply the criteria set out in Sch.7 of the 2001 Regulations as amended in deciding whether the development has significant effects on the environment. If the Board decides that the development will have significant effects on the environment, it will notify the local authority and the Minister (where he made the referral) and state that an application for such proposed development must also be accompanied by an EIS. While subs.(7)(c) states that the determination of the question by the Board is final, this will not exclude the judicial review of the Board's determination. Subsection (8) allows regulations to be made in respect of this section.

It may also be noted that art.82(3)(p) of the 2001 Regulations provides that where a local authority development might impact on the foreshore, the planning authority must send notice to the Minister for Marine.

Acquisition of land etc. on foreshore

1–270   **227.—(1)** The powers of a local authority to compulsorily acquire land under the enactments specified in *section 214(1)* shall, where the local authority concerned is a planning authority and for the purposes specified in those enactments, extend to that part of the foreshore that adjoins the functional area of the local authority concerned.

(2) The functions of a road authority under *sections 49, 50 and 51 of the Roads Act, 1993,* shall extend to the foreshore adjoining the functional area of the road authority concerned.

(3) The functions transferred to the Board under *section 214* shall be performable by the Board in relation to any compulsory acquisition of land to which *subsection (1)* applies.

(4) The functions transferred to the Board under *section 215* shall be performable in relation to any scheme approved under *section 49 of the Roads Act, 1993,* relating to the foreshore.

(5) Where a local authority—

    (a) applies for approval under *section 226,*

    (b) in relation to land on the foreshore, submits any matter (howsoever described under the enactment concerned) to the Board in relation to which it falls to the Board to perform functions in respect thereof under an enactment specified in *section 214,* or

    (c) submits a scheme under *section 49 of the Roads Act, 1993,*

it shall send copies of all maps, documents (including any environmental impact statement) and other materials sent to the Board in connection with the application or scheme concerned to the [Minister for Communications, Marine and Natural Resources and the Minister for Transport].

(6) The Board shall, before performing any function conferred on it by *section 226* or (in respect of land on the foreshore) under an enactment specified in *section 214(1)* or referred to in *subsection (5),* by notice in writing, invite observations in relation to the application or scheme concerned from the Minister for the Marine and Natural Resources within such period as may be specified in the notice being a period of not less than 8 weeks from the date of receipt of the notice.

(7) The Board shall in the performance of the functions referred to in *subsection (6)* have regard to any observations made pursuant to a notice under that *subsection.*

[(8)

    (a) Subject to *paragraph (b),* the *Foreshore Acts 1933* to *2005* shall not apply in relation to any application to the Board under *section 226,* or matters to which *subsection (5)(b)* applies or a scheme submitted under *section 49 of the Roads Act 1993.*

    (b) In any case where a local authority that is a planning authority applies for an approval for proposed development under *section 226* or has been granted such an approval by the Board, but has not sought the compulsory acquisition of any foreshore on which the proposed development would be carried out under an enactment specified in *section 214,* the authority may apply for a lease or licence under *section 2 or 3 of the Foreshore Act 1933* in respect of that proposed development; in such cases, it shall not, notwithstanding the provisions of any other enactment, be necessary for—

        (i) the local authority to submit an environmental impact statement in connection with its application for such lease or licence, or

        (ii) the Minister for Communications, Marine and Natural Resources to consider the likely effects on the environment of the proposed development.]

(9) [...]

(10) Nothing in the *State Property Act, 1954,* shall operate to prevent a local authority compulsorily acquiring land on the foreshore.

(11) This *section* shall not apply to any application to the Minister for the Marine and Natural Resources for a lease under *section 2 of the Foreshore Act, 1933,* or for a licence under *section 3 of that Act* made before the coming into operation of this *section.*

<small>AMENDMENT HISTORY</small>

    Subsection (5) amended by s.44 of the Planning and Development (Strategic Infrastructure) Act 2006 (No. 27 of 2006).

    Subsection (9) deleted by s.44 of the Planning and Development (Strategic Infrastructure) Act 2006 (No. 27 of 2006).

<small>NOTE</small>

    This section provides that certain powers of the local authority under the 2000 Act and other enactments extend to the foreshore. Subsection (1) provides that the compulsory acquisition powers of the local authority under s.214 extend to the foreshore and the Board on appeal under subs.(3). Under subs.(2), the role of the local authority concerning the submissions of a motorway scheme and preparation of an EIA under ss.49–51 of the Roads Act 1993 also extend to the foreshore. Subsections (3) and (4) provide that the functions performed by the Board in relation to approval of a compulsory acquisition and motorway scheme also extend to the foreshore. Subsection (5) provides in relation to an application for local authority development under s.226, an application for compulsory acquisition under s.214 or the submission of a road scheme, the Board must send copies of all maps and documents with the application to the Minister for Communications, Marine and Natural Resources and to the Minister for Transport. By notice in writing, the Board must invite observations from the Minister on the application within the period specified in the notice, which must not be less than eight weeks. Subsection (8) provides that the Board must have regard to any observations received. Section 227(8) provides that the Foreshore Acts 1933–2005, shall not apply to any application to the Board under s.226. The precise import of this is not entirely clear. However, its intention appears to be that with respect to local authority development under s.226, a compulsory acquisition application under s.214 or a road scheme, there is no additional requirement to also obtain a foreshore lease or licence from the Minister. Such a construction is supported by contrasting it with s.225(4) which provides that s.225 concerning the requirement to obtain planning permission is in addition to the Foreshore Acts 1933 to 1998 (this has not been amended to refer to the 2005 Act). Nonetheless the subsection could have removed any doubt by explicitly stating that there is no requirement to obtain such a foreshore lease or licence. Subsection (8)(b) which was inserted by the 2006 Act goes on to provide that the local authority "may" apply for a foreshore lease or licence in certain circumstances. It provides that where the local authority has applied for or been granted approval for development on the foreshore and it is not seeking the compulsory acquisition of land on which the development is to be carried out, it may apply for a foreshore lease or licence. Where it applies for such lease/license, the local authority will not be required to submit an EIS and the Minister for Communications will not be required to consider the likely effects on the environment of the proposed development. Thus it appears that while there is no obligation on the local authority to apply for a foreshore lease/license in such instance, where it decides to do so it will be exempt from any obligation to submit an EIS. The former subs.(9) is deleted which concerned the imposition of a condition by the Board regarding the protection of the marine environment. This is now covered by s.226(2).

Subsection (10) provides that nothing in the State Property Act 1954 shall operate to prevent a local authority compulsorily acquiring land on the foreshore. As most of the foreshore is owned by the State, this effectively means that a local authority can seek to compulsory acquire state land. This would appear to be an exception to the rule that State land is not subject to compulsory acquisition. See *Murphy v Wicklow County Council*, unreported, High Court, Kearns J., March 19, 1999.

Entering on foreshore for certain purposes

1–271   **228.—(1)** Where a local authority proposes to enter onto the foreshore for the purposes of carrying out site investigations, it shall not later than 4 weeks before the carrying out of such investigations—

(a) publish in at least one newspaper circulating in the area of the proposed site investigations, and

(b) serve on the Minister for the Marine and Natural Resources and to the prescribed bodies,

a notice of its intention to so do, and where any such site investigations would involve excavations, borings or other tests that would be capable of causing disturbance to the marine environment, it shall inform that Minister and those bodies of the details of the proposed investigations.

(2) The Minister for the Marine and Natural Resources may make recommendations to the local authority concerned in relation to investigations referred to in *subsection (1)* and the local authority shall have regard to any such recommendations when carrying out such investigations.

(3) Where there has been compliance with this *section, section 252* shall not apply in relation to entry onto the foreshore for the purposes specified in *subsection (1)*.

(4) Compliance with this *section* shall, in relation to entry onto the foreshore for the said purposes, constitute compliance with any other enactment requiring the giving of notice of entry on land by a local authority.

[(5) No licence shall be required under the *Foreshore Act 1933* in respect of any such entry or any site investigations carried out in accordance with this section.]

AMENDMENT HISTORY

Subsection (5) inserted by s.45 of the Planning and Development (Strategic Infrastructure) Act 2006 (No. 27 of 2006).

NOTE

This section sets out the procedure which must be followed by the local authority before it can enter the foreshore to carry out site investigations. The local authority may wish to do so in connection with an application for planning permission, enforcement action, or concerning its own development. Not later than four weeks before such investigation, the local authority must publish a notice in a newspaper of its proposal and must serve a notice of its intention on the Minister and the prescribed bodies. In addition, where the investigations would involve excavations, borings or other tests capable of causing disturbance to the marine environment, it must inform the Minister of the details. The Minister may then make recommendations regarding the investigation, which must be taken into account. There is no right of the general public to make submissions or representations. Where the procedure in the section is followed, there is no additional requirement that the general procedure for authorised persons of the local authority to enter land under s.252 or under any other enactment must also be followed. The 2006 Act added a new subs.(5) which provides that no foreshore licence is required for the local authority entering the foreshore for the purposes of site investigation.

PART XVI

EVENTS AND FUNFAIRS

Interpretation

229.—In this *Part* —   1–272
    "event" *means*—
        (a) *public performance which takes place wholly or mainly in the open air or in a structure with no roof or a partial, temporary or retractable roof, a tent or similar temporary structure and which is comprised of music, dancing, displays of public entertainment or any activity of a like kind, and*
        (b) *any other event as prescribed by the Minister under section 241;*
    "funfair" has the meaning assigned to it by *section 239;*
    "licence" *means a licence granted by a local authority under section 231*
    "local authority" *means*—

(a) **in** the case of a county, the council of the county, and

(b) **in** the case of a county borough, the corporation of the borough.

NOTE

This Part introduces a licensing system for events and funfairs, taking such matters outside the scope of planning control or the requirement to abtain planning permission under Pt III. Under the previous planning legislation, the issue arose as to whether planning permission was required for transient events, such as for pop concerts. It was eventually decided by the Supreme Court in *Butler v Dublin Corporation* [1999] 1 I.R. 565, in relation to the holding of a pop concert, that a fleeting change of use did not constitute a material change in use so as to require planning permission. Section 240 states that events do not constitute development so as to require planning permission (although it appears to omit funfairs in error). Regulations have been made in relation to events and funfairs under Pt XVI of the Planning Regulations (S.I. No. 600 of 2001), contained in arts 182–199. Part XVI of the 2000 Act, in relation to outdoor events, entered into force on April 17, 2001, by Commencement Order S.I. No. 153 of 2001, together with the Planning and Development (Licensing of Outdoor Events) Regulations 2001 (S.I. No. 154 of 2001), which regulations are now incorporated in the Planning Regulations (S.I. No. 600 of 2001).

Section 229 concerns definitions under Pt XVI. The key definition of "event" above indicates that it does not include private performances nor performances which take place indoors with a non-retractable roof. The activities of an event are widely drawn to include music, dancing, displays of public entertainment or any activity of a like kind. The definition of a funfair in s.239 involves the use of fair equipment, which again must be open to the public. Planning control may still apply to matters not within the definition of an event or a funfair. Article 182(1) of the 2001 Regulations defines "audience" as persons attending the event on any particular day, other than persons working or performing, and shall include persons there by invitation. Where a number of different performances take place on different stages on a particular day, the audience is taken to be the total number attending at all stages.

Article 182(2) provides that the Part applies to an application for a licence for an event to be held on more than one day or an application for a licence for a number of events at a venue in a period not exceeding one year, subject to any necessary modifications.

Obligation to obtain a licence for holding of an event

1–273 **230.—(1)** Subject to *subsection (4),* a licence shall be required in respect of the holding of an event or class of event prescribed for the purpose of this *section.*

(2) When prescribing events or classes of events under *subsection (1),* the Minister shall have regard to the size, location, nature or other attributes of the event or class of event.

(3) Any person who—

   (a) organises, promotes, holds or is otherwise materially involved in the organisation of an event to which this *section* applies, or

   (b) is in control of land on which an event to which this *section* applies is held,

other than under and in accordance with a licence, shall be guilty of an offence.

(4) A licence shall not be required for the holding of an event prescribed in accordance with *subsection (1)* by a local authority.

This section provides that a licence is required for the holding of events prescribed by the Minister. In this respect, art.183 of the Planning Regulations 2001 has prescribed events at which the audience comprises 5,000 or more people. Although subs.(2) states that, in prescribing such, the Minister should have regard to the size, location, nature or other attributes of the event, the only attribute under art.183 is the size. Subsection (3) makes it a criminal offence to hold a prescribed event without a licence. In this respect, the persons liable include persons who control the land as well as any person who organises, promotes, holds or is otherwise materially involved. The penalties for such offence are set out in s.156. A licence is not required under this section in relation to events held by the local authority, which is governed by s.238.

Grant of licence

231.—(1) The Minister may by regulations provide for matters of procedure and administration in relation to applications for and the grant of licences for events. **1–274**

(2) Without prejudice to the generality of *subsection (1)*, regulations under this *section* may make provision for—

    (a) requiring the publication of a notice of intention to make an application for a licence,

    (b) requiring the notification of prescribed persons or bodies,

    (c) the form and content of an application for a licence,

    (d) the plans, documents and information to be submitted with an application for a licence,

    (e) the persons and bodies which must be consulted in relation to a licence,

    (f) enabling persons to make submissions or observations within a prescribed time,

    (g) requiring the applicant to submit any further information with respect to their application, and

    (h) the time within which a decision on an application for a licence must be made.

(3)

    (a) Where an application for a licence is made in accordance with regulations under this *section,* the local authority may decide to grant the licence, grant the licence subject to such conditions as it considers appropriate or refuse the licence.

    (b) in considering an application for a licence under this *section,* the local authority shall have regard to—

        (i) any information relating to the application furnished to it by the applicant in accordance with *subsection (2)(d) or (g),*

        (ii) any consultations under *subsection (2)(e),*

        (iii) any submissions or observations made to it in accordance with *subsection (2)(f),*

        (iv) whether events have previously been held on the land concerned,

        (v) the matters referred to in *subsection (4),* and

        (vi) any guidelines or codes of practice issued by the Minister or by any other Minister of the Government.

(4) Without prejudice to the generality of *subsection (3)(a),* conditions subject to which a licence is granted may relate to all or any of the following—

   (a) compliance with any guidelines or codes of practice issued by the Minister or any other Minister of the Government, or with any provisions of those guidelines or codes of practice;

   (b) securing the safety of persons at the place in connection with the event;

   (c) the provision of adequate facilities for the health and welfare of persons at the place in connection with the event, including the provision of sanitary facilities;

   (d) the protection of the environment in which the event is to be held, including the control of litter;

   (e) the maintenance of public order;

   (f) the avoidance or minimisation of disruption to the neighbourhood in which the event is to take place;

   (g) ensuring the provision of adequate means of transport to and from the place in which the event is to be held;

   (h) the number of events which are permitted at a venue within a specified period not exceeding one year;

   (i) the payment of a financial contribution to the authority of a specified amount or an amount calculated on a specified basis towards the estimated cost to the local authority of measures taken by the authority in connection with the event;

   (j) the payment of a financial contribution to a person or body consulted in accordance with *subsection (2)(e)* of a specified amount or an amount calculated on a specified basis towards the estimated cost to that person or body of measures taken by the person or body in connection with the event;

   (k) maintaining public liability insurance;

   (l) the display of notices for persons attending the event as to their obligations and conduct at the event.

(5) Conditions under *subsection (4)(i) or (j)* requiring the payment of a financial contribution may only relate to an event which is held wholly or mainly for profit.

(6) A person shall not be entitled solely by reason of a licence under this *section* to hold an event.

NOTE

This section concerns the procedure for the grant of a licence, along with the decision whether to grant the licence. The procedure for making an application is set out in arts 184–191 of the Planning Regulations (S.I. No. 600 of 2001). Under art.184, a person who intends to make an application for a licence must enter into a pre-application consultation with the local authority or other prescribed bodies to discuss the application, including the draft plan for the management of the event. The authority or the prescribed bodies may give advice relating to the application, although this cannot prejudice the performance of any of their functions, nor can the consultations be relied upon in the application or in legal proceedings. The prescribed bodies are defined in art.182(1) as the relevant Chief Superintendent of An Garda Síochána, and the relevant Health Board or other local authorities, the area of which may be affected by the event. Under art.185, within two weeks of lodging the application, the applicant must publish a notice of intention to make the application in one local and in one national newspaper. The notice must state the applicant's name, that the applicant is applying for a license, the location, type and date of the proposed event, the name of the local authority and also the anticipated numbers.

The notice must state that the application may be inspected at the local authority's office for a period of five weeks from lodging the application and that submissions or observations may be made to the local authority within the five weeks. The local authority may require a further newspaper notice where it considers the notice is misleading or inadequate. Article 186 provides that an application must be made within 16 weeks prior to the holding of event or where there are several events over the period of one year, within 16 weeks prior to the holding of the first event. This long time limit is intended to ensure that the local authority has adequate time to consult locally and with the state bodies before making a decision on a licence. As soon as may be after receipt of the application, the local authority will consider whether the requirements of the regulations are met and either acknowledge receipt of the application in writing or inform the applicant that the application is invalid, by reason of an inadequate fee or for any other reason, and so cannot be considered by the local authority, stating the requirement of the regulation which has not been met. Article 187, as amended by the 2006 Regulations, sets out the matters which an application must contain, which include many matters set out in the notice. It should also be accompanied by such matters as the consent of the owner, where the applicant is not the owner; a draft plan for the management of the event; the newspaper notice; and a location map of the site. There should also be provision for the reinstatement of the land. Under art.188, the local authority must make the application available for inspection at its office during office hours for a period of five weeks. The documents must also be available for purchase on payment of a fee. Some information relating to events may be sensitive, such as protection of VIPs. Such information should not be included with the application, but should be agreed with the local authority after the licence is granted, which could be laid down as a condition of the licence. Article 189 provides that within one week of receipt of the application, the local authority should consult with the prescribed bodies by sending them a copy and state that submissions may be made within five weeks. The local authority can grant an extension of time to consider the application, at a body's request, where it is necessary to ensure the safety and effective management of the event. The local authority may consult bodies other than prescribed bodies if it deems it appropriate. These bodies could for example include the Harbour authorities or the OPW, where appropriate. Under art.190, any person may make a submission or observation in writing in respect of the application within five weeks of the receipt of the application by the local authority. Under art.191, the local authority can request further information from the applicant or from any person who made a submission, which it deems necessary to make a decision. It may also invite other persons to make a submission. The local authority may take whatever measures it deems necessary, including convening meetings or taking oral submissions, to seek the views of persons regarding the application. These consultations are designed to ensure that the local community is consulted on the details of an event. Under subs.(3), the local authority in making its decision may decide to grant the licence, grant the licence subject to such conditions, or refuse the licence. Article 192 provides that, in making its decision, the local authority must make the decision not earlier than five weeks after receiving the application. Also, having made the decision, the local authority should send a notice to the applicant, the prescribed bodies and to any other person who made submissions or observations. Subsection (4) sets out the conditions according to which a licence can be granted. The local authority has a general discretion to impose whatever conditions it deems appropriate, with the subsection setting out certain examples of conditions. A condition imposing the payment of a financial contribution can only apply where the event is held wholly or mainly for profit. Subsection (6) is similar to s.34(13) concerning planning permission, insofar as a licence will not in itself entitle a person to hold an event. A person holding an event may need the permission of other property owners and also other licences, depending on the event.

Codes of practice in relation to events

1–275   **232.**—**(1)** The Minister or any Minister of the Government may draw up and issue codes of practice for the purpose of providing practice guidance with respect to the requirements of any of the relevant provisions of or under this *Part.*

(2) The Minister or any Minister of the Government, as appropriate, shall, before issuing a code of practice, consult any other Minister of the Government or other person or body that appears to that Minister to be appropriate.

(3) The Minister or any Minister of the Government, as appropriate, may amend or revoke any code of practice, following consultation with any other Minister of the Government or any other person or body that appears to the Minister to be appropriate.

NOTE

This section allows the Minister to draw up codes of practice for the purposes of guidance in relation to events. The Minister must consult other Ministers, or other persons he/she deems appropriate, in making or revoking the code of practice.

Service of notice in relation to events

1–276   **233.**—**(1)** Where a local authority has reason to believe that an event in respect of which a licence under *section 230* is required is occurring or is likely to occur—

(a) without such a licence, or

(b) in contravention of the terms of such a licence,

the authority may serve a notice under this *section.*

(2) A notice may require, as appropriate—

(a) the immediate cessation of any event or the discontinuation or alteration of any preparations which are being made in relation to an event,

(b) the removal of any temporary buildings, structures, plant, machinery or the like from land which the authority believes is intended to be used as the location of an event, and

(c) the restoration of the land to its prior condition.

(3) Any person who fails to comply with the requirements of the notice served under *subsection (1)* shall be guilty of an offence.

NOTE

This section relates to where an event is taking place without a licence or in breach of a licence. Where this is the case, the local authority can serve a notice requiring immediate cessation of the event or the discontinuation or alteration of any preparations in relation to an event, the removal of any temporary buildings or structures from the location of an event, and the restoration of the land to its prior condition. It is a criminal offence to fail to comply with the notice.

General obligations with regard to safety at events

1–277   **234.**—**(1)** A person to whom a licence is granted under *section 231* shall take such care as is reasonable in all the circumstances, having regard to the care which a person attending the event may reasonably be expected to take for his or her own safety and, if the person is at the event in the company of another person, the extent of the supervision and control the latter person may be expected to exercise over the former person's activities, to ensure that persons on the land in connection with the event do not suffer injury or damage by reason of any danger arising out of the licensed event or associated activities.

(2) It shall be the duty of every person, being on land in connection with an event to which this *section* applies, to conduct himself or herself in such a way as to ensure that as far as reasonably practicable any person on the land is not exposed to danger as a consequence of any act or omission of his or hers.

NOTE

This section imposes a duty of care on the licence holder to take reasonable care for the safety of persons on the land in relation to the events to ensure they do not suffer injury. The section elaborates on the standard of care by providing that regard may be had to the care which a person may have for their own safety and the extent of control and supervision a person may exercise over another person in their company. This latter part would therefore cover children accompanied by adults, who may be expected to exercise some care over them. Subsection (2) also qualifies the extent of the duty of care by providing that there is a duty on persons at the event to conduct themselves so as not to expose themselves to danger. The occupier, who may be the licence holder, may also owe a duty of care under the Occupiers Liability Act 1995.

Powers of inspection in connection with events

235.—**(1)** An authorised person (subject to the production by him or her, if so requested, of his or her authority in writing) or a member of the Garda Síochána shall be entitled at all reasonable times to enter and inspect any land or any structure for any purpose connected with this *Part*.   1–278

(2) Without prejudice to the generality of *subsection (1)*, an authorised person or a member of the Garda Síochána shall, in the performance of his or her functions under *subsection (1)*, be entitled to—

(a) require the person in control of the land or structure concerned to—

   (i) inform him or her of any matter which the authorised person or the member of the Garda Síochána considers to be relevant, or

   (ii) provide such plans, documentation or other information as are necessary to establish that the requirements of this *Part* and any regulations made under this *Part* or any licence or any conditions to which the licence is subject are being complied with,

(b) take with him or her on to land such persons and equipment as he or she considers necessary and to carry out such tests or to do such other things which he or she considers necessary for the purposes referred to in *subsection (1)*.

(3) Any person who—

(a) refuses to allow an authorised person or a member of the Garda Síochána to enter any land in exercise of his or her powers under this *section,*

(b) obstructs or impedes an authorised person or a member of the Garda Síochána in exercise of his or her powers under this *section,* or

(c) wilfully or recklessly gives, either to an authorised person or a member of the Garda Síochána, information which is false or misleading in a material respect,

shall be guilty of an offence.

(4) In this *section,* "authorised person" *means a person authorised for the purposes of this Act by a local authority.*

NOTE

This section enables authorised persons of the local authority or a member of the Garda Síochána to inspect the land or structures in connection with an event or funfair. Section 252 sets out the power of authorised persons to enter land. The power to enter is confined to all reasonable times, although there is no definition of what constitutes all reasonable times. While the authorised person or garda has a general power of inspection, they can specifically request the person in control of land to inform them of any matter which they consider relevant and to provide plans, documentation or other information to demonstrate that the conditions and regulations are complied with. The authorised person and garda also have a general power to take other persons or equipment onto the land in order to carry out tests or other activities they consider necessary. It appears that some form of reasonable standard must be read into the power under this section.

Limitation of civil proceedings

1–279   **236.—(1)** No action or other proceeding shall lie or be maintainable against the Minister or a local authority or any other officer or employee of a local authority or any person engaged by a local authority or a member of the Garda Síochána for the recovery of damages in respect of any injury to persons, damage to property or other loss alleged to have been caused or contributed to by a failure to exercise any function conferred or imposed on the local authority by or under this *Part.*

(2) A person shall not be entitled to bring any civil proceedings pursuant to this *Part* by reason only of the contravention of any provision of this *Part,* or of any regulations made thereunder.

NOTE

This section exempts the Minister, the local authority, persons engaged by the local authority and the Garda Síochána from liability for damages for failing to perform any function imposed on the local authority under this Part of the Act. The section does not however completely absolve these parties from any liability for any acts connected with the event. The section merely provides that a breach or failure to perform its functions under the Act will not be actionable in damages.

Subsection (2) makes clear that mere breach of Pt XVI of the Act or Regulations will not give rise to a cause of action.

Consequential provisions for offences

1–280   **237.—(1)** The local authority by whom a licence under *section 231* was granted may revoke it if the person to whom the licence is granted is convicted of an offence under this *Part.*

(2) Proceedings for an offence under this *Part* may be brought by the local authority in whose area the offence is committed.

NOTE

This section enables the local authority to revoke a licence granted where the grantee of the licence was convicted of an offence under Pt XVI. Section 233(3) makes it an offence not to comply with a notice regarding the holding of an event without a licence, or in contravention of the terms of such a licence. Section 235(3) makes it an offence to prevent an authorised person or a member of the Garda Síochána from entering land to carry out an inspection for the event, to exercise any of their powers while there, or to wilfully or recklessly give information which is false or misleading in a material respect. A local authority is permitted to prosecute offences within its area. It therefore differs from offences under Pt VIII, where the offence need not be committed within the authority's functional area.

Holding of event by local authority

238.—(1) An event that is prescribed in accordance with *section 230(1)*   **1–281** and is proposed to be carried out by a local authority (in this *section* referred to as a "proposed event") shall be carried out in accordance with this *section* and any regulations made under *subsection (2)*.

(2) The Minister may make regulations providing for—

   (a) the publication by the local authority of any specified notice with respect to the proposed event,

   (b) the notification or consultation by the local authority of any specified person or persons,

   (c) the making available for inspection, by members of the public, of any specified documents, particulars, plans or other information with respect to the proposed event, and

   (d) the making of submissions or observations to the local authority within a prescribed time with respect to the proposed event.

(3)

   (a) The manager of a local authority shall, after the expiration of the period prescribed under *subsection (2)(d)* for the making of submissions or observations, prepare a written report in relation to the proposed event and submit the report to the members of the local authority.

   (b) A report prepared in accordance with *paragraph (a)* shall—

      (i) specify the proposed event,

      (ii) specify the matters referred to in *section 231(4)* to which the holding of the proposed event will be subject,

      (iii) list the persons or bodies who made submissions or observations with respect to the proposed event in accordance with the regulations made under *subsection (2)*,

      (iv) summarise the issues raised in any such submissions or observations and state the response of the manager to them, and

      (v) recommend whether or not the proposed event should be held.

   (c) the members of the local authority shall, as soon as may be, consider the proposed event and the report of the manager under *paragraph (a)*.

(d) following the consideration of the manager's report under *paragraph (c)*, the proposed event may be carried out as recommended in the manager's report, unless the local authority, by resolution, decides to vary or modify the event, otherwise than as recommended in the manager's report, or decides not to proceed with the event.

(e) resolution under *paragraph (d)* must be passed not later than 6 weeks after receipt of the manager's report.

NOTE

This section concerns the procedure for the holding of an event by the local authority. Article 193 of the 2001 Regulations provides that where a local authority proposes to hold an event, it shall publish a notice in one local and one national newspaper. The contents of such notice should include:

- the name of the local authority;
- that it is being held under Pt XVI of the 2000 Act;
- the venue, type, date and anticipated number at the proposed event;
- that the proposal including draft plan for management, can be inspected during office hours at the offices of the local authority for five weeks from the date of publication; and
- that submissions or observations can be made in respect of the event during this period.

Article 194 provides that the local authority must make the proposal and draft plan, including maps, available for inspection as stated in the notice. The proposal must state the anticipated numbers, the number of tickets to be sold, and the date and duration (including when it will commence and conclude) of the event. A draft plan for management of the event must be prepared in accordance with the codes of practice, which should include the names and responsibilities of the event controller, safety officer and their deputies, and also several draft plans, including for site emergency, traffic management, safety strategy and an environmental monitoring programme before, during and after the event. There must also be provision for removal of structures and carrying out of works for reinstatement. The maps must also be available which must be a specified detail. A copy of the proposal must be available for purchase. Article 195 provides that a local authority must notify the prescribed bodies of the proposed event within one week of publication of the notice. The notice must be accompanied by the proposal and must also state that submissions or observations may be made to the local authority within five weeks. This period may be extended where the prescribed body so requests and where the local authority considers it necessary to ensure the safe and effective management of the proposed event. The local authority also has a discretion to notify or consult any other body or person. Article 196 provides that any person may make a submission in writing to the local authority within five weeks of the publication of the notice.

Subsection (3) sets out the procedure following the expiry of the period for making submissions or observations. This involves the manager preparing a report, which must be submitted to the members of the planning authority. The report must specify the event, the conditions enlisted in s.231(4) to which the event will be subject, list the persons who made submissions, summarise the issues raised by such submissions and finally make a recommendation as to whether to hold the event. Following this, the elected members must consider the report and event. The recommendation in the Manager's report will have effect unless the local authority by resolution decides to vary or modify the event as recommended or refuses to proceed with the event. Such resolution must be passed within six weeks of receipt of the Manager's report. Article 198 of the 2001 Regulations provides that after the local authority makes its decision, it must issue a notice of its decision to the prescribed bodies and any person who made a submission or observation. Article 198 declares that where a large number of submissions or observations are made as part of an organised campaign, or it is not possible to ascertain readily the full names and addresses of persons who made submissions, the local authority need not notify each person, but may take steps it considers reasonable to inform such persons, such as in the case of an organised campaign, by giving notice to the person who organised the campaign.

Control of funfairs

239.—(1) In this *section —*   1–282

"fairground equipment" *includes any fairground ride or any similar equipment which is designed to be in motion for entertainment purposes with members of the public on or inside it, any equipment which is designed to be used by members of the public for entertainment purposes either as a slide or for bouncing upon, and any swings, dodgems and other equipment which is designed to be in motion wholly or partly under the control of, or to be put in motion by, a member of the public or any equipment which may be prescribed, in the interests of public safety, for the purposes of this section;*

"funfair" *means an entertainment where fairground equipment is used.*

(2) The organiser of a funfair and the owner of fairground equipment used at a funfair shall take such care as is reasonable in the circumstances, having regard to the care which a person attending the funfair may reasonably be expected to take for his or her own safety, and, if the person is at the event in the company of another person, the extent of the supervision and control the latter person may be expected to exercise over the former person's activities to ensure that persons on the land in connection with the funfair do not suffer injury or damage by reason of any danger arising out of the funfair or associated activities.

(3) It shall be the duty of every person being on land in connection with a funfair to which this *section* applies to conduct himself or herself in such a way as to ensure that as far as is reasonably practicable any person on the land is not exposed to danger as a consequence of any act or omission of his or hers.

(4)

    (a) An organiser of a funfair or an owner of fairground equipment shall not make available for use by the public any fairground equipment unless such equipment has a valid certificate of safety in accordance with regulations made under *subsection (5).*

    (b) an organiser of a funfair or owner of fairground equipment who makes available for use by the public any fairground equipment otherwise than in accordance with *paragraph (a),* shall be guilty of an offence.

(5) The Minister shall by regulations provide for such matters of procedure, administration and control as appear to the Minister to be necessary or expedient in relation to applications for and the grant of certificates of safety for fairground equipment.

(6) Without prejudice to the generality of *subsection (5),* regulations under that *subsection* may provide for—

    (a) the class or classes of persons who are entitled to grant certificates of safety,

    (b) the matters to be taken into account in determining applications for safety certificates,

   (c) the payment of a prescribed fee for an application for a certificate of safety,

   (d) the period of validity of a certificate of safety, and

   (e) any class of fairground equipment to be exempt from the provisions of this *section.*

[(6A) *Regulations* under this *section* may be made to any extent by reference to a document published by or on behalf of the Minister.]

   (7)

   (a) A person who intends to hold or organise a funfair, other than at a place where the operation of funfair equipment has been authorised by a permission under *Part III of this Act* or *Part IV of the Act of 1963* or is not otherwise an unauthorised use, shall give 2 weeks notice (or such other period of notice as may be prescribed) in writing to the local authority in whose functional area the funfair is to be held.

   (b) The notice referred to in *paragraph (a)* shall be accompanied by a valid certificate of safety for the fairground equipment to be used at the funfair and shall give details of the names of the organiser of the funfair, the owner or owners of the fairground equipment to be used at the funfair and the location and dates on which the funfair is to be held.

   (8)

   (a) Where a local authority has reason to believe that a funfair is taking place, or is likely to take place, which is not in compliance with *subsection (4) or (7),* the authority may serve a notice on any person it believes to be holding, organising or otherwise materially involved in the organisation of the funfair.

   (b) A notice under *paragraph (a)* may require, as appropriate—

     (i) the immediate cessation of any activity or any preparations which are being made in relation to the funfair within a specified time,

     (ii) the immediate cessation of the use of any fairground equipment without a valid certificate of safety,

     (iii) the removal, within a specified time, of any fairground equipment, temporary buildings or structures, plant, machinery or similar equipment which the authority believes is intended to be used in relation to the funfair, and

     (iv) the restoration of the land to its prior condition within a specified time.

   (c) A person who is served with a notice under *paragraph (a)* and who fails to comply with the requirements of the notice shall be guilty of an offence.

   (d) Where a person fails to comply with a notice served on the person under this *section,* the local authority concerned may, through its employees or agents—

     (i) give effect to the terms of the notice, and

     (ii) where necessary for that purpose, enter on the land concerned, and may recover the expenditure reasonably incurred by it in

> so doing from the person as a simple contract debt in any court of competent jurisdiction.

(e) A person who obstructs or impedes the local authority in the performance of its functions under *paragraph (d)* shall be guilty of an offence.

AMENDMENT HISTORY

Subsection (6A) inserted by s.14 of the Planning and Development (Amendment) Act 2002 (No. 32 of 2002) which came into effect on December 24, 2002.

NOTE

This section relates to the control of funfairs. Subsections (2) and (3) concern the duty of care regarding persons at the funfair and are in similar terms to s.234 concerning events. The standard of care owed by organisers is defined by reference to the regard which a person may have for their own safety and the extent of supervision and control a person may be expected to have over persons in their company, which would include children. Every person must conduct themselves to ensure, as far as reasonably practicable, that no person is exposed to danger. This provision covers both organisers and members of the public, in terms of the duty and the persons protected. The duty also applies to their own safety. Fairground equipment open to the public must have been granted a valid certificate of safety, otherwise the organiser will be guilty of a criminal offence. Provision is made for regulations concerning such certificates. A person intending to hold a funfair at a place other than where planning permission has been granted must give the local authority two weeks' notice, accompanied by a valid certificate of safety and details of the funfair. Similar to s.233 concerning events, where there is a funfair without a valid certificate, or for which two weeks' notice has not been given, the local authority can serve a notice requiring immediate cessation of activities, the removal within a specified time of equipment, and the restoration of the land. Failure to comply with a notice is an offence. Also, where there is failure to comply, the local authority may give effect to the terms, including by entering the land, and may recover the expenditure in doing so. It is further an offence to obstruct the local authority in doing so.

Exclusion of events and funfairs from planning control

240.—(1) Subject to *subsection (2),* the holding of an event to which this **1–283** *Part* applies and works directly or solely relating to the holding of such an event shall not be construed as "development" within the meaning of this *Act.*

(2)

(a) Notwithstanding *section 230 or 239,* the provisions of this *Part* shall not affect the validity of any planning permission granted under *Part IV of the Act of 1963* for the holding of an event or events or for a funfair.

(b) Where a planning permission referred to in *paragraph (a)* has been granted for the holding of an event or events in respect of land, a licence under this *Part* shall be required for the holding of any additional event on the land concerned.

NOTE

This section provides that the holding of an event is not development and does not require planning permission. The side note mentions both events and funfairs, however the text refers to only events. While the better view is that side notes or marginal notes form part of the Act, they serve only as a guide to the content of the section. See Bennion,

Statutory Interpretation, 4th edn (London: Butterworths Lexis Nexis, 2002) at p.636. Thus while the side note implies that both events and funfairs do not constitute development, requiring planning permission, s.240(1) states only events do not constitute development and the content of s.240(1) must supersede the side note. On the other hand, it could be said the licensing scheme set out in ss.230 to 239 indicates that funfairs and events are to be treated the same. While a literal interpretation leads to the conclusion that funfairs are not excluded, a purfusive interpretation mandated under s.5 of the Interpretation Act 2005 may support the conclusion that funfairs are excluded from planning control. However a funfair may in any case not constitute development on the basis that it is a transient event. See *Butler v Dublin Corporation* [1999] 1 I.R. 565.

Regulations for event

1–284   **241.**—The Minister may make regulations providing that any activity or class of activity to which the public have access and which takes place wholly or mainly in the open air or in a structure with no roof or a partial, temporary or retractable roof, a tent or other similar temporary structure to be an event for the purposes of this *Part*.

NOTE

This section allows the making of regulations providing that certain activities constitute events.

PART XVII

Financial Provisions

Expenses of administration of Minister

1–285   **242.**—The expenses incurred by the Minister in the administration of this *Act* shall, to such extent as may be sanctioned by the Minister for Finance, be paid out of moneys provided by the Oireachtas.

NOTE

This section provides that the expenses of the Minister for the Environment and Local Government in carrying out his functions are paid out by the Oireachtas. This restates s.12 of the 1963 Act. The Financial Provisions were formerly contained in Pt II of 1963 Act.

Charging of expenses of planning authority that is council of a county

1–286   **243.**—Expenses under this *Act* of a planning authority that is the council of a county shall be charged on the county (exclusive of every borough and urban district therein).

NOTE

This section provides that the expenses of a planning authority which is the county council are to be taken out of the budget of county. This section restates s.13 of the 1963 Act.

Apportionment of joint expenses of planning authorities

1–287   **244.**—(1) Two or more planning authorities may, by resolution, make and carry out an agreement for sharing the cost of performing all or any of their functions under this *Act* and, where an agreement has been made under this *subsection,* the planning authorities concerned may, by resolution, terminate it at any time if they so agree.

(2) Where a planning authority proposes to perform in its functional area a function under this *Act* at the request of or wholly or partially in the interests of the area of another planning authority (being a planning authority whose area is contiguous with the area of the first-mentioned planning authority), the other planning authority shall defray the cost of the performance of the function to such extent as may be agreed upon between the authorities or, in default of agreement, as may be determined by the Minister.

NOTE

This section allows for the sharing or apportioning of expenses between two or more planning authorities. This section may be invoked where two or more planning authorities act jointly or on behalf of another. Examples of such joint action include under s.9(7), whereby two or more planning authorities co-ordinate their development plans. Any arrangement to apportion expenses between the planning authorities must be agreed by means of an individual resolution of each planning authority. This means that the elected members of each planning authority must decide by passing a resolution. It appears that once an agreement is entered into between planning authorities, it cannot unilaterally be terminated by one planning authority but will require the agreement of the other planning authorities.

Subsection (2) provides that where one planning authority carries out a function wholly or partly in the interests of another planning authority, that other planning authority must pay the expenses of the other planning authority, as agreed or in default thereof, as determined by the Minister. This section restates s.16 of the 1963 Act.

Power to set-off

245.—Where a sum is due under this *Act* to any person by a planning   **1–288**
authority and, at the same time, another sum under this *Act* is due by that person to that authority, the former sum may be set-off against the latter either, as may be appropriate, in whole or in part.

NOTE

This section allows money owed or due from a planning authority to be set off against the other. It appears that either the individual or planning authority may avail of this set-off. However, before any set-off can apply, there must not be any dispute as to whether any amount is owed or due. This section restates s.17 of the 1963 Act.

Fees payable to planning authorities

246.—**(1)** The Minister may make regulations providing for—   **1–289**
  (a) the payment to planning authorities of prescribed fees in relation to applications for—
    (i) permission under *Part III,* or
    (ii) extensions or further extensions under *section 42,*
  (b) the payment to planning authorities of prescribed fees in relation to the making of submissions or observations respecting applications for permission referred to in *paragraph (a),*
  (c) the payment to planning authorities of prescribed fees in relation to requests for declarations under *section 5,*

582 Planning and Development Acts 2000–2007

(d) the payment to local authorities of prescribed fees in relation to applications for grants of licences under *section 231* or for certificates of safety under *section 239,* and

(e) the payment to planning authorities of prescribed fees in relation to applications for grants of licences under *section 254,*

and the regulations may provide for the payment of different fees in relation to cases of different classes or descriptions, for exemption from the payment of fees in specified circumstances, for the waiver, remission or refund (in whole or in part) of fees in specified circumstances and for the manner in which fees are to be disposed of.

(2) The Minister may prescribe that the fee payable to the authority for an application for permission under *section 34(12)* shall be an amount which shall be related to the estimated cost of the development, or the unauthorised part thereof, as the case may be.

(3)

(a) Where, under regulations made under this *section,* a fee is payable to a planning authority or local authority by an applicant in respect of an application under *paragraph (a), (d) or (e) of subsection (1)* or by a person making a request for a declaration under *paragraph (c) of subsection (1),* the application shall not be decided, or the declaration issued, unless the authority is in receipt of the fee.

(b) With regard to applications under *paragraph (a) of subsection (1),* notwithstanding anything contained in *section 34(8) or 42(2),* a decision of a planning authority shall not be regarded, pursuant to any of those sections, as having been given on a day which is earlier than that which is 8 weeks after the day on which the authority is in receipt of the fee, and *sections 34(8) and 42(2)* shall be construed subject to and in accordance with the provisions of this *paragraph.*

(4) Where under regulations under this *section* a fee is payable to a planning authority or local authority and the person by whom the fee is payable is not the applicant for a permission, approval or licence, submissions or observations made, as regards the relevant application, appeal or referral by or on behalf of the person by whom the fee is payable, shall not be considered by the planning authority or local authority unless the fee has been received by the authority.

(5) A planning authority shall specify fees for the making of copies under *sections 7, 16(1) and 38(4),* not exceeding the reasonable cost of making such copies.

NOTE

This section allows the Minister to make regulations concerning fees payable to the planning authority in relation to certain applications. These applications include:
- a fee in relation to a planning application (Pt III);
- for an extension of the life of a planning permission (s.42);
- a request for a declaration that a development is or is not exempted development (s.5);
- an application for a licence for an event (s.231);
- for a certificate of safety in relation to a funfair (s.239); and
- for the licensing of appliances and cables on public roads (s.254).

The payment of a fee is an essential element of a valid application; see *Calor Teo v Sligo County Council* [1991] 2 I.R. 267. An application may be deemed to have lapsed if the fee has not been paid; see *Murray v Wicklow County Council* [1996] 2 I.R. 552. A new provision also allows for the charging of a fee for the making of submissions or observations. Schedule 9 of the 2001 Regulations sets out the fees for planning applications. The Schedule sets out a table of fees depending on the class of development, with a greater fee charged in each case where the application is for retention permission.

Part 12 of the 2001 Regulations, comprising arts 156–172, sets out certain rules concerning the payment of fees. Article 157 provides that no fee applies where the development is to be carried out by or on behalf of a voluntary organisation for use by a religious denomination or for persons with disabilities (none of which involve profit or gain). No fee also applies to an application for the provision of houses by an approved body under s.6 of the Housing Act 1992.

Article 160 provides that the amount payable in respect of an application for outline permission is three quarters of the amount indicated in respect of the normal application for planning permission. Article 161 states that one quarter of the normal fee is payable in respect of an application consequent on the grant of planning permission, an application which differs from a previous authorised development only by reason of a change in the type of house or modification in the design or external appearance of the structure, or in the case of an application for permission under s.95(16), before the adoption of a housing strategy.

Article 162 allows for the refunding of three quarters of the fee paid, where a planning application is either withdrawn or determined and a subsequent application is made which relates to development of the same character or description, where certain conditions are satisfied. These conditions are that the fee was paid for the earlier application; the subsequent application is not made more than one year later; the application relates to land substantially consisting of the same site or part of the site; no previous refund was made; and where a reduced fee was not paid under other provisions. The claim for a refund must be made in writing within eight weeks of the decision on the subsequent application. Under art.163, the planning authority has an absolute discretion to refund part of a fee where it would not be just and equitable to pay the full fee, considering the limited extent and cost of the development and fees payable for other developments of a similar character, extent or description. Article 164 provides that where an application involves development in more than one class of development, the fee will be calculated based on the development within each class. This does not apply to a development which includes the provision of roads, car parks, etc. which are incidental to the development. Where an application concerns a building which contains floor space in order to provide common access or services for persons occupying the building, the calculation of the amount of floor space appropriate to each class of development will be the proportion of common floor space coming within the class relative to the gross floor space in the building. Article 165 provides that where a development is capable of multiple uses, the fee payable will be based upon the highest amount payable of such uses. Article 166 states that where a planning application includes proposals for materially different layouts or designs, a fee is payable for each proposal as if they were separate planning applications. Article 167 provides that a site area, for the purposes of calculating a fee, will constitute the area of the land to which the application relates. It further provides for the calculation of the fee where the site area or area of gross floor space is less than or not an exact multiple of the unit of measurement specified in col.1 of s.2 of Sch.9. Article 168 concerns fees to be paid for submissions or observations. No fee will be paid in respect of a local authority, prescribed body notified, state authority, or transboundary state. No fee will be payable in respect of any further submissions or observation in respect of the same application. Article 169 concerns fees for requests for declaration as to whether a development is or is not exempted development under s.5, while art.170 concerns an application to extend the life of a planning permission. Articles 171 and 172 concern certain transitional provisions.

Subsection (3)(a) prohibits the planning authority from making a decision or determination unless the correct fee has been paid. Also under subs.(4), submissions or observations cannot be considered unless the correct fee has been paid. Where a submission or observation must be within a specified period such as five weeks in the case of submissions or observations on a planning application under Art.30 of the Planning Regulations 2001, failure to pay the fee within the five weeks will mean any submission or observation will be invalid.

PART XVIII

MISCELLANEOUS

Consultations in relation to proposed development

1–290   **247.—(1)** A person who has an interest in land and who intends to make a planning application may, with the agreement of the planning authority concerned (which shall not be unreasonably withheld), enter into consultations with the planning authority in order to discuss any proposed development in relation to the land and the planning authority may give advice to that person regarding the proposed application.

(2) In any consultations under *subsection (1),* the planning authority shall advise the person concerned of the procedures involved in considering a planning application, including any requirements of the permission regulations, and shall, as far as possible, indicate the relevant objectives of the development plan which may have a bearing on the decision of the planning authority.

(3) The carrying out of consultations shall not prejudice the performance by a planning authority of any other of its functions under this *Act,* or any regulations made under this *Act* and cannot be relied upon in the formal planning process or in legal proceedings.

(4)

   (a) In order to satisfy the requirements of this *section,* a planning authority may specify that consultations may be held at particular times and at particular locations and the authority shall not be obliged to enter into consultations otherwise than as specified by it.

   (b) Where a planning authority decides to hold consultations in accordance with *paragraph (a)* it shall, at least once in each year, publish notice of the times and locations at which consultations are held in one or more newspapers circulating in the area of the authority.

(5) The planning authority shall keep a record in writing of any consultations under this *section* that relate to a proposed development, including the names of those who participated in the consultations, and a copy of such record shall be placed and kept with the documents to which any planning application in respect of the proposed development relates.

(6) A member or official of a planning authority is guilty of an offence if he or she takes or seeks any favour, benefit or payment, direct or indirect (on his or her own behalf or on behalf of any other person or body), in connection with any consultation entered into or any advice given under this *section.*

NOTE

This section concerns pre-planning consultations. Such consultation were given statutory recognition under the Act, although such consultations may have existed in practice. The informal existence of such pre-planning consultations has been noted by the courts in certain cases, such as *State (Aprile) v Naas UDC*, unreported, High Court, O'Hanlon J., November 22, 1983, where O'Hanlon J. made express reference to the possibility of developers engaging in consultation with officials of planning authorities. See also *Ballintubber Heights Ltd v Cork Corporation*, unreported, High Court, Ó Caoimh J., June 21, 2002. Subsection (1) provides that a person may enter into consultations with the planning authority to discuss a proposed development and for the purpose of advice in relation to a proposed application. It appears that a planning authority can be compelled to enter into such consultation where they unreasonably refuse to consult with a person. The person seeking the consultation must have an interest in the land where the development is proposed. The planning authority may specify that consultations may be held at a particular time and particular places and where they do so, a planning authority cannot be compelled to enter consultations other than at such specified times and places. However, for this to apply, the planning authority must at least once a year publish in one or more newspapers circulating in the area notice of the times and locations at which the consultations are to be held.

Subsection (3) provides that advice given by the planning authority shall include the procedures involved in making a planning application, the requirements of the permission regulations and an indication of any relevant objectives of the development plan which may have a bearing on the decision of the planning authority. It appears however that the advice may include additional matters insofar as comes within the general scope of subs.(1) as "regarding the proposed application". Subsection (4) provides that the consultation is entirely without prejudice to any function performed by the planning authority under the Act or regulations and cannot be relied upon in the formal planning process or legal proceedings. Although the phrase used is the "carrying out of consultations", it appears that the disclaimer is not confined to the fact that such consultation were held but also extends to the content and advice given at such consultation. This means that notwithstanding anything discussed or advice given at the consultation, this can in no way hinder or fetter the planning authority in the manner of dealing with the planning application once lodged. A person at the consultation cannot rely upon any matter discussed or advice given in any legal proceedings. It appears that even if erroneous, albeit bona fide, advice is given at the consultations, this cannot be used to estop the planning authority from taking the proper steps or considerations in its decision. Even without subs.(4), statements made by planning officials at such consultation would be unlikely to bind the planning authority on the basis that such statements may be ultra vires. However, it appears that the statutory disclaimer in subs.(4), ought not to be read as offering a complete immunity from suit for the officials concerned. Thus where the officials were guilty of the tort of misfeasance of public office in the manner in which they conducted the consultation, such officials could not rely upon subs.(4) as providing immunity. Subsection (4) may be read as excluding reliance on any statements regarding the planning merits of the planning application and this does not extend to improper conduct in the manner of processing such planning application. Therefore it is possible that if an official made statements of an improper nature at such consultations regarding the manner in which it would deal with the application and such official subsequently dealt with such application, subs.(4) may not exclude a subsequent allegation of breach of fair procedures. See by analogy *Jerry Beades v Dublin City Council*, unreported, High Court, McKechnie J., September 7, 2005.

Subsection (5) provides that the planning authority is obliged to keep a record of the consultation. Other than stating that the record must be in writing and include the names of the persons who attended, the section does not expand upon the contents of such record. However, in order to constitute a record, it would appear that it should at least include a brief, although not exhaustive, outline of what was discussed at the consultation. The subsection provides that the record shall be "placed and kept" with documents to which the planning application relates. Thus if a subsequent planning application is lodged which relates to the consultation, the record must be maintained with such application. It is not entirely clear whether the requirement that a copy of record is "placed and kept" with the planning application means that copies of the same should be made available to the public as part of the planning file or whether it simply means that a record should be internally kept and placed with the planning application. The record does not fall within the scope of documents which are to be made available to the public under s.38 and so the better view is they are not strictly required to be placed on the planning file, although a planning authority may at their discretion choose to do so in the interests of transparency and informing the public. However, such records should be disclosable under a freedom of information request.

While this section deals with pre-planning consultations, there is no provision in the Act dealing with post-planning consultations where consultations are entered into when the planning application is under consideration. However, it appears that such post-planning meetings are are not per se prohibited. In *Ballintubber Heights Ltd v Cork Corporation*, unreported, High Court, Ó Caoimh J., June 21, 2002, although decided on locus standi grounds, Ó Caoimh J. said:

> "[T]here is no basis upon which the company can complain about the discussions entered into by the developer with the planning authority as the company was not deprived of any right to make full submissions in regard to the planning application including the revised aspects of same".

In *Jerry Beades Construction Ltd v Dublin Corporation*, unreported, High Court, McKechnie J., September 7, 2005, McKechnie J. said in relation to discussions between a planner and an applicant as to the planners opinion on an application, "[i]n my opinion these are the type of matters which can quite properly form the subject matter of discussions (frequently had) between planners and those making applications". In the English case of *Britannia (Cheltenham) Ltd v Secretary of State for the Environment and Tekesbury* [1979] JPL 534, it was recognised that an applicant and planning authority could consult over certain amendments to a proposal. The court said "[t]o take any other view would fly in the face of everyday practice and make the planning machine even more complicated than it was". While it appears to be the case that post-planning consultations are permissible, this is subject to the fact such consultations should not result in the public being prejudiced by being excluded from the process. It may therefore depend on facts of particular case whether this may be the case. Post-planning consultations deal with a response to a request for further information or revised plans may be legitimate. However where the consultation is subsequent to the response, this may be more difficult to justify.

Information to be provided in electronic form

1–291   **248.—(1)** Subject to *subsection (2)*, any document or other information that is required or permitted to be given in writing under this *Act* or any regulations made under this *Act* by the Minister, the planning authority, the Board or any other person, may be given in electronic form.

(2) A document or information referred to in *subsection (1)* may be given in electronic form only—

   (a) if at the time it was given it was reasonable to expect that it would be readily accessible to the planning authority, Board or other person to whom it was directed, for subsequent reference or use.

   (b) where such document or information is required or permitted to be given to a planning authority or the Board and the planning authority or the Board consents to the giving of the information in that form, but requires—

      (i) the information to be given in accordance with particular information technology and procedural requirements, or

      (ii) that a particular action be taken by way of verifying the receipt of the information,

   if the requirements of the planning authority or the Board have been met and those requirements have been made public and are objective, transparent, proportionate and non-discriminatory, and

   (c) where such document or such information is required or permitted to be given to a person who is neither a planning authority nor the Board, if the person to whom the document or other information is required or permitted to be given consents to the information being given in that form.

(3) A document or information that the planning authority or the Board is required or permitted to retain or to produce, whether for a particular period or otherwise, and whether in its original form or otherwise, may be so retained or produced, as the case may be in electronic form.

(4) *Subsections (1), (2) and (3)* are without prejudice to any other law requiring or permitting documents or other information to be given, retained or produced, as the case may be, in accordance with specified procedural requirements or particular information technology.

(5) The Minister may make regulations providing for or requiring the use of particular information technology or other procedural requirements in relation to the giving, retaining or production of a specified class or classes of documents or other information in electronic form.

(6) Without prejudice to the generality of *subsection (5),* the regulations may apply to a particular class or classes of documents or other information, or for a particular period.

(7) This *section* applies to a requirement or permission to give documents or other information whether the word "give", "make", "make available", "submit", "produce" or similar word or expression is used.

(8)

(a) This *section* is without prejudice to the requirements under *section 250* in relation to the service or giving of a notice or copy of an order unless prescribed in regulations made under *paragraph (b).*

(b) The Minister may by regulation extend the application of this *section* to the service or giving of a notice or copy of an order under *section 250,* where the Minister is of the opinion that the public interest would not be prejudiced by so doing and the *section* as so extended shall apply accordingly.

(9) In this *section —*

"documents or other information" *includes but is not limited to—*

(a) *a development plan or any draft or variation of it,*

(b) *an application for permission or any other document specified in section 38(1),*

(c) *any map, plan or other drawing, and*

(d) *written submissions or observations;*

"electronic form" *means information that is generated, communicated, processed, sent, received, recorded, stored or displayed by electronic means and is capable of being used to make a legible copy or reproduction of that communicated information but does not include information communicated in the form of speech and such electronic means includes electrical, digital, magnetic, optical, electromagnetic, biometric, photonic and any other form of related technology.*

NOTE

This section provides that information or documents required or permitted to be given in writing may be provided in electronic form in certain circumstances. It applies to documents or information to be given to a planning authority, the Board or any other person. The latter could therefore include any member of the public. Electronic form is defined as information which is generated, communicated, processed, sent, received, recorded, stored or displayed by electronic means, capable of being used to make a legible copy or reproduction, but does not include that communicated by means of speech. It also applies where the requirement or permission is expressed in terms of a requirement to "give", "make", "make available", "submit", "produce" or similar words or expressions used. Subsection (9) provides that documents which can be provided by such means include a development plan or any draft or variation of it, an application for permission or any other document specified in s.38(1), and any map, plan or other drawing, and written submissions or observations. Subsection (2) sets out three circumstances which must be met before such information or documents may be provided in such form. These circumstances do not appear to be related nor are they cumulative conditions which must be satisfied. The first circumstance is if at the time it was given it was readily accessible to the planning authority, Board or other person to whom it was directed, for subsequent reference or use. This is wide-ranging and imports an objective standard of reasonableness. The second circumstance is where documents or information are to be given to the Board or planning authority. This provides that the planning authority or Board must consent to the giving of information in such form. The planning authority and Board can require the information to be given in accordance with certain information technology and procedural requirements or that particular action be taken to verify receipt of the information. However, before these requirements may be imposed the planning authority or Board must have made them public and such requirements must have the quality of being objective, transparent, proportionate and non-discriminatory. There is no necessity for the Board or planning authority to impose any requirements. The third circumstance is where a document or information is required to be given to a person who is neither the planning authority nor the Board and requires that such person's consents to the information to be given in that form. In the case of the second and third circumstance, it appears that the prior consent must be obtained.

Under subs.(3), a document required to be retained or produced by the planning authority may be so retained or produced in electronic form. Subsection (4) provides that the section is without prejudice to requirements under any other law which could include the Freedom of Information Acts or Data Protection Acts. Subsection (8) provides that electronic form cannot be used in connection with the services of a notice under s.250 of the Act, unless the Minister makes a special regulation. Subsection (8) provides that the section is without prejudice to requirements in s.250 relating to the service or giving of a notice or copy of an order except where the Minister has extended the application of the section to notices or orders, where he is of the opinion that the public interest would not prejudiced.

Additional requirements for public notification

1–292   **249.—(1)** Where any provision of this *Act* requires notice to be given in one or more newspapers circulating in the area of a planning authority, the planning authority may, in addition to the requirements of the particular provision and to the extent they consider appropriate, give the notice or draw the attention of the public to the notice through other forms of media including the broadcast media and the use of electronic forms for the provision of information.

[(2) Where any provision of this *Act,* or of any regulations made thereunder, requires notice to be given to any person who has made representations, submissions or observations to a planning authority or the Board, the planning authority or the Board may dispense with that requirement where—

(a) a large number of representations, submissions or observations are made as part of an organised campaign, or

(b) it is not possible to readily ascertain the full name and address of those persons who made the representations, submissions or observations,

provided that the authority or the Board uses some other means of giving notice to the public that the authority or the Board is satisfied can adequately draw the attention of the public to that notice including, in the case of an organised campaign referred to in *paragraph (a),* giving notice to any person who, in the opinion of the planning authority or the Board, organised the campaign.**]**

AMENDMENT HISTORY

Subsection (2) was substituted by s.247 of the Local Government Act 2001 (No. 37 of 2001), which, by the Local Government Act 2001 (Commencement) Order 2001 (S.I. No. 458 of 2001), came into effect on October 9, 2001.

NOTE

This section provides that where newspaper notice is required to be given under the Act, the planning authority may also provide additional means of notice by other means such as the broadcast media, which would include television or radio, and/or through electronic forms which could include the Internet. It is a matter entirely for the discretion of the planning authority where it deems this appropriate. These means are in addition to and not in substitution of the requirement to provide a newspaper notice. Subsection (1) only applies to the planning and not to the Board. Subsection (2) provides that where there are a large number of representations or observations, or where it is not possible to ascertain with certainty the full names or addresses of persons who made submissions or observations, the planning authority or the Board may dispense with the usual requirement of notice by adequately drawing the attention of the public by other means. In the case of an organised campaign, notice may be given to any person who, in the opinion of the planning authority, organised the campaign.

Service of notices, etc.

250.—(1) Where a notice or copy of an order is required or authorised by this *Act* or any order or regulation made thereunder to be served on or given to a person, it shall be addressed to him or her and shall be served on or given to him or her in one of the following ways—   **1–293**

   (a) where it is addressed to him or her by name, by delivering it to him or her;

   (b) by leaving it at the address at which he or she ordinarily resides or, in a case in which an address for service has been furnished, at that address;

   (c) by sending it by post in a prepaid registered letter addressed to him or her at the address at which he or she ordinarily resides or, in a case in which an address for service has been furnished, at that address;

   (d) where the address at which he or she ordinarily resides cannot be ascertained by reasonable inquiry and the notice or copy is so required or authorised to be given or served in respect of any land or premises, by delivering it to some person over the age of 16 years resident or employed on the land or premises or by affixing it in a conspicuous place on or near the land or premises;

   (e) in addition to the methods of service provided for in *paragraphs (a), (b), (c) and (d),* by delivering it (in the case of an enforcement notice) to some person over the age of 16 years who is employed, or otherwise engaged, in connection with the carrying out of the development to which the notice relates, or by affixing it in a conspicuous place on the land or premises concerned.

   (2) Where a notice or copy of an order is required by this *Act* or any order or regulation made under this *Act* to be served on or given to the owner or to the occupier of any land or premises and the name of the owner or of the occupier cannot be ascertained by reasonable inquiry, it may be addressed to "the owner" or "the occupier", as the case may require, without naming him or her.

(3) For the purposes of this *section,* a company registered under the *Companies Acts, 1963* to *1999,* shall be deemed to be ordinarily resident at its registered office, and every other body corporate and every unincorporated body shall be deemed to be ordinarily resident at its principal office or place of business.

(4) Where a notice or copy of an order is served on or given to a person by affixing it under *subsection (1)(d),* a copy of the notice or order shall, within two weeks thereafter, be published in at least one newspaper circulating in the area in which the person is last known to have resided.

(5) A person who, at any time during the period of 12 weeks after a notice is affixed under *subsection (1)(d),* removes, damages or defaces the notice without lawful authority shall be guilty of an offence.

(6) A person who, without lawful authority, removes, damages or defaces a notice required to be erected at the site of a development under the permission regulations or by the Board under *section 142(4),* shall be guilty of an offence.

(7) Where the Minister or the Board is satisfied that reasonable grounds exist for dispensing with the serving or giving under this *Act* or under any order or regulation made under this *Act* of a notice or copy of an order and that dispensing with the serving or giving of the notice or copy will not cause injury or wrong, the Minister or the Board may dispense with the serving or giving of the notice or copy and every such dispensation shall have effect according to the tenor thereof.

(8) A dispensation under *subsection (7)* may be given either before or after the time when the notice or copy would, but for the dispensation, be required to be served or given and either before or after the doing of any act to which the notice or copy would, but for the dispensation, be a condition precedent.

(9) In this *section,* "notice" *includes a warning letter.*

NOTE

This section concerns the means of service of notices or copies of orders throughout the Act. Subsection (3) sets out several alternative means of service. Notices or orders are not defined except to say a notice includes a warning letter issued under s.152. The better view is that a notice under this section does not include a notice of motion served in relation to judicial review proceedings. This follows from the fact that a motion on notice is not strictly a notice per se and that s.250 merely relates to notices within the context of the Planning Code and not legal proceedings. Furthermore, s.50 also requires service of a statement of grounds and a grounding affidavit, which certainly do not constitute notices or orders and it would appear anomalous that the notice of motion could be served but the statement of grounds and affidavit could not.

The means of service include:

- personal service;
- leaving it at the address where a person ordinarily resides or at an address for service where this has been furnished;
- by sending it by prepaid registered letter to such address.

Section 25 of the Interpretation Act 2005 provides that service by post will be effected by properly addressing, prepaying (where required) and posting a letter containing the document, and in that case the service of the document is deemed, unless the contrary is proved, to have been effected at the time at which the letter would be delivered in the ordinary course of post. See *Freeney v Bray UDC* [1982] I.L.R.M. 29, where O'Hanlon J. noted (under the former s.18 of the Interpretation Act 1937) that the onus is thereby shifted to an applicant who asserts that the notice was not given by the planning authority within the statutory period. Under subs.(1)(d) where the address at which person ordinarily resides cannot be ascertained by reasonable inquiry, and the notice or order is required in respect of any land or premises, it may be delivered to some person over the age of 16 years resident or employed on the land or premises or by affixing it in a conspicuous place on or near the land or premises. This method can only apply where the address cannot be ascertained by reasonable inquiry. Where a notice is so affixed, the planning authority must publish a copy of the order or notice in a newspaper circulating in the area within two weeks. Subsection (5) provides that it is a criminal offence for a person within 12 weeks after the notice is affixed, to remove damage or deface the notice without lawful authority. It is not therefore a criminal offence at least under this section (it may constitute criminal damage to property) to take such steps after a period of 12 months. Subsection (1)(e) sets out two additional methods of service in the case of an enforcement notice whereby it can be served by delivering it to a person over the age of 16 who is employed or otherwise, engaged in connection with the carrying out of the unauthorised development or by affixing it on the land of the premises concerned. It appears that the person must be employed/engaged in the carrying out of the unauthorised development. It is not sufficient for example that they are employed in a business which has some unauthorised development such as an unauthorised sign, the person must be directly employed/engaged in the actual unauthorised development. The methods of service must be strictly followed. In *Molloy v Dublin C.C.* [1990] 1 I.R. 90, the plaintiff applied for permission stating his address to be notified of the decision. The council sought further information in relation to a will and the second plaintiff's sister sent the information. Where notification was sent to the second plaintiff's sister, this was held not to be proper compliance.

Where the name of the owner or occupier of land or premises cannot be identified, the notice may be addressed to "the owner" or "the occupier" without naming such person. It is a criminal offence for a person to remove or damage a notice affixed or a notice required by the Board to be published under s.142(4) in connection with an appeal. Subsection (7) allows the Minister or Board to dispense with the notice requirements (either before or after they arise) where they consider reasonable grounds exist and where it does not cause injury or wrong. The section does not elaborate on what are reasonable grounds. It appears the Minister and Board has a discretion to form such opinion. However, a precondition for dispensing with notice is that it does not cause injury or wrong, which implies if there is any prejudice to the person concerned there is no jurisdiction to dispense with the notice.

Calculation of appropriate period and other time limits over holidays

251.—(1) Where calculating any appropriate period or other time limit **1–294** referred to in this *Act* or in any regulations made under this *Act,* the period between the 24th day of December and the first day of January, both days inclusive, shall be disregarded.

(2) *Subsection (1)* shall not apply to any time period specified in *Part II of this Act.*

NOTE

This section provides that in the calculation of any time period under the Act or Regulations, the period between December 24 and January 1 shall not be taken into account. Subsection (1) is drafted very widely to include any time limit under the Act and also under the regulations. The one exception is under subs.(2) which provides that the exclusion of such time does not apply in the context of Pt II which concerns development plans, local area plans and regional planning guidelines.

Power of authorised person to enter on land

1–295   252.—(1) An authorised person may, subject to the other provisions of this *section,* enter on any land at all reasonable times between the hours of 9 a.m. and 6 p.m., or during business hours in respect of a premises which is normally open outside those hours, for any purpose connected with this *Act.*

(2) An authorised person entering on land under this *section* may do all things reasonably necessary for the purpose for which the entry is made and, in particular, may survey, carry out inspections, make plans, take photographs, take levels, make excavations, and examine the depth and nature of the subsoil.

(3) Before an authorised person enters under this *section* on any land, the appropriate authority shall either obtain the consent (in the case of occupied land) of the occupier or (in the case of unoccupied land) the owner or shall give to the owner or occupier, as the case may be, not less than 14 days' notice in writing of the intention to make the entry.

(4) A person to whom a notice of intention to enter on land has been given under this *section* by the appropriate authority may, not later than 14 days after the giving of the notice, apply, on notice to the authority, to the judge of the District Court having jurisdiction in the district court district in which the land or part of the land is situated for an order prohibiting the entry, and, upon the hearing of the application, the judge may either wholly prohibit the entry or specify conditions to be observed by the person making the entry.

(5) Where a judge of the District Court prohibits under this *section* a proposed entry on land, it shall not be lawful for any person to enter under this *section* on the land, and where a judge of the District Court specifies conditions to be observed by persons entering on land, every person who enters under this *section* on the land shall observe the conditions so specified.

(6)
   (a) Where (in the case of occupied land) the occupier or (in the case of unoccupied land) the owner refuses to permit the exercise of a power conferred by this *section* on an authorised person, the appropriate authority may apply to the District Court to approve of the entry.
   (b) An application under this *subsection* shall be made, on notice to the person who refused to permit the exercise of the power of entry, to the judge of the District Court having jurisdiction in the district court district in which the land or part of the land is situated.

(7) *Subsections (3), (4) and (5)* shall not apply to entry for the purposes of *Part III* and, in a case in which any such entry is proposed, if the occupier (in the case of occupied land) or the owner (in the case of unoccupied land) refuses to permit the entry—
   (a) the entry shall not be effected unless it has been authorised by an order of the judge of the District Court having jurisdiction in the district court district in which the land or part of the land is situate and, in the case of occupied land, until after at least 24 hours' notice of the intended entry, and of the object thereof, has been given to the occupier,
   (b) an application for such an order shall be made on notice (in the case

of occupied land) to the occupier or (in the case of unoccupied land) to the owner.

(8) An authorised person may, in the exercise of any power conferred on him or her by this *Act*, where he or she anticipates any obstruction in the exercise of any other power conferred on him or her by or under this *Act*, request a member of the Garda Síochána to assist him or her in the exercise of such a power and any member of the Garda Síochána of whom he or she makes such a request shall comply therewith.

(9) Every person who, by act or omission, obstructs an authorised person in the lawful exercise of the powers conferred by this *section* shall be guilty of an offence.

(10) Every authorised person shall be furnished with a certificate of his or her appointment and when exercising any power conferred on him or her by or under this *Act*, the authorised person shall, if requested by any person affected, produce the certificate to that person.

(11) In this *section and section 253* —

"appropriate authority" *means—*

(a) *in a case in which the authorised person was appointed by a local authority - that authority,*

(b) *in a case in which the authorised person was appointed by the Minister - the Minister, and*

(c) *in a case in which the authorised person was appointed by the Board - the Board;*

"authorised person" *means a member of the Board or a person who is appointed by a local authority, the Minister or the Board to be an authorised person for the purposes of this section and section 253.*

NOTE

This section specifies the conditions which must apply before an authorised person of the local authority, Board or the Minister can enter land. An authorised person is a person appointed by the relevant authority to act as such and who holds a certificate of appointment, which must be produced when requested. The section therefore has general application throughout the Act in circumstances where an authorised person wishes to enter land for any purpose connected with the Act. Under subs.(1), an authorised person can enter land at all reasonable times between the hours of 9am and 6pm, or during business hours of the premises where they are normally outside these hours. This means that in addition to entering between the limits of these hours, the entry must also be at "reasonable times". It may depend upon the nature of the land and indeed purpose of entry whether the time was reasonable. The purpose must clearly be proved to be connected with the Act. Subsection (2) empowers such authorised person upon entering the land, to do all things reasonably necessary for the purposes of entry, which can include (although this is not exhaustive) surveying, carrying out inspections, making plans, taking photographs, levels, excavations, examining the depth and nature of the subsoil. Again what is "reasonably necessary" will depend upon the purpose of entry.

However, an essential precondition before entering is that the authorised person must obtain the consent of the owner or occupier or must give them not less than 14 days' notice in writing of the intention to enter. Where land is occupied, the consent of the occupier must be obtained and the consent of the owner is not necessary. Where land is unoccupied, the consent of the owner must be obtained. Service of the notice would be effected in accordance with one of the methods set out in s.250. The alternative of giving the owner or occupier 14 days notice in writing of the intention to make the entry implies that it is not necessary to obtain their positive consent. If no response is received, the authorised officer can enter the land. However, within the 14 days, the owner/occupier may apply to the District Court, which may prohibit entry or specify conditions. Subsection (5) provides that the authorised officer must comply with any such determination.

Subsection (6) provides that where the owner or occupier, as appropriate, refuses the authorised person permission to exercise any power under the section (which could include entry or any power under subs.(2), an application can be made on notice to the District Court to approve such entry or exercise of powers.

Subsection (7) provides that the requirements under subss.(3) to (5), involving obtaining consent and notice, do not apply with respect to entry for the purposes of Pt III. Part III concerns control of development, which includes assessment of planning applications. However, these requirements are dispensed with in respect of any functions mentioned in Pt III. It appears that for Pt III purposes, so long as an authorised person falls within the scope of subs.(1), there is no requirement to obtain consent or give any notice. As the requirement to obtain notice does not apply, the restriction under subs.(1) of all reasonable times between the relevant hours, may have more relevance depending on the facts of the case. Subsection (7) further provides that where the occupier or owner as appropriate, refuses to permit entry, an order from the relevant District Court may be obtained. The application to the District Court must be made on notice to the occupier in the case of occupied land and the owner in the case of unoccupied land. There is therefore no requirement to put the owner on the notice in the case of occupied land. Where entry is authorised by the District Court, there is an additional requirement in the case of occupied land to give at least 24 hours notice of the intended entry which must also include notice of the object of such entry.

Where an authorised person anticipates an obstruction in the exercise of their power, they may request a member of the Garda Síochána to assist them and such Garda is obliged to so assist the authorised officer. Subsection (9) makes it a criminal offence for a person to obstruct an authorised person in the lawful exercise of the powers, the penalties for which are specified in s.156. Subsection (11) provides that all members of the Board are authorised officers, as well as other persons appointed for the purposes of this section. All authorised persons must be issued with a certificate of appointment and when exercising any power under Act, must produce the certificate when requested by any person affected. There is no obligation on an authorised officer to produce such certificate except when requested. It appears that if an authorised person is requested to produce such certificate it would not be appropriate for any authorised person to continue to exercise any powers he has under Act until such request is satisfied.

Powers of entry in relation to enforcement

1–296   **253.—(1)** Notwithstanding *section 252,* an authorised person may, for any purpose connected with *Part VIII,* at all reasonable times, or at any time if he or she has reasonable grounds for believing that an unauthorised development has been, is being or is likely to be carried out, enter any premises and bring thereon such other persons (including members of the Garda Síochána) or equipment as he or she may consider necessary for the purpose.

(2) Subject to *subsection (4),* an authorised person shall not, other than with the consent of the occupier, enter into a private house under *subsection (1)* unless he or she has given to the occupier of the house not less than 24 hours' notice in writing of his or her intended entry.

(3) Whenever an authorised person enters any premises pursuant to *subsection (1),* the authorised person may exercise the powers set out in *section 252(2)* and, as appropriate, in addition—

   (a) require from an occupier of the premises or any person employed on the premises or any other person on the premises, such information, or

   (b) require the production of and inspect such records and documents, and take copies of or extracts from, or take away, if it is considered necessary for the purposes of inspection or examination, any such records or documents,

as the authorised person, having regard to all the circumstances, considers necessary for the purposes of exercising any power conferred on him or her by or under this *Act.*

(4)

(a) Where an authorised person in the exercise of his or her powers under *subsection (1)* is prevented from entering any premises or has reason to believe that evidence related to a suspected offence under this *Act* may be present in any premises and that the evidence may be removed therefrom or destroyed or that any particular structure may be damaged or destroyed, the authorised person or the person by whom he or she was appointed may apply to a judge of the District Court for a warrant under this *subsection* authorising the entry by the authorised person in the premises.

(b) If on application being made to him or her under this *subsection,* a judge of the District Court is satisfied, on the sworn information of the applicant, that the authorised person concerned has been prevented from entering a premises or that the authorised person has reasonable grounds for believing the other matters referred to in *paragraph (a),* the judge may issue a warrant under his or her hand authorising that person, accompanied, if the judge considers it appropriate so to provide, by such number of members of the Garda Síochána as may be specified in the warrant, at any time within 4 weeks from the date of the issue of the warrant, on production, if so requested, of the warrant, to enter, if need be by force, the premises concerned and exercise the powers referred to in *subsection (3).*

NOTE

This section concerns special powers of entry onto premises in the case of enforcement which includes enforcement in relation to unauthorised development. The general requirements of s.252 do not apply in relation to entry onto land for the purposes of enforcement. While enforcement under Pt VIII is principally concerned with unauthorised development, it also covers enforcement of other criminal offences under the Act at s.156 and so s.253 also applies to enforcement of any of these offences. The basic principle in the case of all enforcement is that an authorised person (defined under s.252(11)) may enter any premises for any purposes connected with Pt VIII at all reasonable times and bring other person which may include members of the Garda Síochána or equipment as they may consider appropriate. Unlike under s.252, where entry can only be made at all reasonable times which are within specified hours, there is no specific restriction on the potential hours when an authorised person can enter. However, what is "reasonable times" may depend upon the entire facts of the case, including the nature of the premises and the purpose of entry. Subsection (1) refers to entry on any "premises" rather than land. There is no definition of premises so it unclear whether the use of different terminology when compared with s.252 was intended to give a more restrictive scope to s.253. The cross-reference in subs.(2), means that a private house constitutes a "premises". Subsection (1) goes on to say that where an authorised officer has reasonable grounds for believing that unauthorised development, "has been, is being or is likely to be carried out", the authorised person may enter the premise "at any time" and may bring other persons which may include members of the Garda Síochána or equipment as they may consider appropriate.

The reference to "any time" means that it is not necessary to show the entry was at a "reasonable time". However, the notion of "reasonable grounds" implies an objective standard and so the subjective view of the authorised person will not be sufficient if such believe is not objectively justified. However, considering the expertise of an authorised person, their opinion should carry considerable weight. Nonetheless, considering that this section empowers a significant intrusion on private property, the terms and requirements of the section ought to be strictly construed. Subsection (1) may relate to unauthorised development which has been carried out in the past, is being carried out in the present or is likely to be carried out in the future. Subsection (2) qualifes the automatic right of entry in the case of a private house by providing that an authorised person cannot enter a private house except with the consent of the occupier, unless they have given written notice to the occupier not less than 24 hours prior to their entry. This restriction applies to both entry for the purposes of general enforcement and in relation to unauthorised development under subs.(1). The occupier can dispense with the requirement of notice where they give consent. The notion of "private house" is not defined, however in the light of the definition of "house" in s.2, it would appear to constitute a private dwelling.

Subsection (3) provides that where an authorised person enters any premises under the section, they may exercise any powers set out under s.252(2) which can in particular include (although this is not exhaustive) surveying, carrying out inspections, making plans, taking photographs, levels, excavations, examining the depth and nature of the subsoil. In addition, the authorised officer can require from an occupier of the premises or persons employed or person on the premises, any information they necessary consider in all circumstances, for the purposes of exercising their power. The information requested must therefore be related to the purpose of entry. The authorised person may also require the production of records and documents and may inspect the same and take copies or extracts from or take away such record and documents, if it is considered necessary for the purposes of the inspection, where he consider this necessary having regard to all the circumstances, for the purpose of exercising any power. Unlike under (a) concerning information, the requirement to produce does not refer to any particular person. The specific requirements of giving information or producing records and documents, implies there is a duty on such person to comply. However, the subsection does not seek to provide for any specific sanction for non-compliance with such duty.

Subsection (4) deals with three circumstances in which an application may be made to the District Court to issue a warrant to authorise entry for a purpose connected with Pt VIII. These are where:

(a) an authorised person was preventing from entering any premises under his powers;

(b) there is reason to believe that evidence related to a suspected offence under the Act may be present in any premises and that evidence may be removed therefrom or destroyed; or

(c) that any particular structure may be damaged or destroyed.

This subsection applies to enforcement for any purpose and not simply in connection with unauthorised development. Subsection (4)(c) therefore captures situations of urgency where a structure, which would include a protected structure, may be damaged or destroyed and where there is no permission for the same. It appears that the application to the District Court is ex parte and so there is no requirement to give notice to the occupier, which may otherwise defeat the purpose of the application. The application for a warrant may be made by an authorised person or by the person whom appointed him. Where the court is satisfied on the basis of sworn evidence that the relevant circumstance pertains, the court may issue the warrant authorising the applicant to enter the premises, by force if necessary and and exercise their powers. The court may order the applicant is to be accompanied where the judge considers appropriate, by such members of the Garda Síochána as may be specified in the warrant. The warrant will authorise entry at any time within four weeks from the date of issue of the warrant and such warrant must be produced when so requested.

Licensing of appliances and cables, etc., on public roads

254.—**(1)** Subject to *subsection (2),* a person shall not erect, construct, **1–297**
place or maintain—

    (a) a vending machine,

    (b) a town or landscape map for indicating directions or places,

    (c) a hoarding, fence or scaffold,

    (d) an advertisement structure,

    (e) a cable, wire or pipeline,

    [(ee) overground electronic communications infrastructure and any associated physical infrastructure.]

    (f) a telephone kiosk or pedestal, or

    (g) any other appliance, apparatus or structure, which may be prescribed as requiring a licence under this *section,*

on, under, over or along a public road save in accordance with a licence granted by a planning authority under this *section.*

    (2) This *section* shall not apply to the following—

    (a) an appliance, apparatus or structure which is authorised in accordance with a planning permission granted under *Part III;*

    (b) a temporary hoarding, fence or scaffold erected in accordance with a condition of planning permission granted under *Part III;*

    (c) the erection, construction, placing or maintenance under a public road of a cable, wire or pipeline by a statutory undertaker.

    (3) A person applying for a licence under this *section* shall furnish to the planning authority such plans and other information concerning the position, design and capacity of the appliance, apparatus or structure as the authority may require.

    (4) A licence may be granted under this *section* by the planning authority for such period and upon such conditions as the authority may specify, including conditions in relation to location and design, and where in the opinion of the planning authority by reason of the increase or alteration of traffic on the road or of the widening of the road or of any improvement of or relating to the road, the appliance, apparatus or structure causes an obstruction or becomes dangerous, the authority may by notice in writing withdraw the licence and require the licensee to remove the appliance, apparatus or structure at his or her own expense.

    (5) In considering an application for a licence under this *section* a planning authority, or the Board on appeal, shall have regard to—

    (a) the proper planning and sustainable development of the area,

    (b) any relevant provisions of the development plan, or a local area plan,

    (c) the number and location of existing appliances, apparatuses or structures on, under, over or along the public road, and

    (d) the convenience and safety of road users including pedestrians.

    (6)

    (a) Any person may, in relation to the granting, refusing, withdrawing or continuing of a licence under this *section* or to the conditions specified by the planning authority for such a licence, appeal to the

Board.

(b) Where an appeal under this *section* is allowed, the Board shall give such directions with respect to the withdrawing, granting or altering of a licence under this *section* as may be appropriate, and the planning authority shall comply therewith.

(7) Development carried out in accordance with a licence under this *section* shall be exempted development for the purposes of this *Act.*

(8) A person shall not be entitled solely by reason of a licence under this *section* to erect, construct, place or maintain on, under, over or along a public road any appliance, apparatus or structure.

(9) Subject to *subsection (10),* any person who—

(a) erects, constructs, places or maintains an appliance, apparatus or structure referred to in *subsection (1)* on, under, over or along any public road without having a licence under this *section* to do so,

(b) erects, constructs, places or maintains such an appliance, apparatus or structure on, under, over or along any public road otherwise than in accordance with a licence under this *section,* or

(c) contravenes any condition subject to which a licence has been granted to him or her under this *section,*

shall be guilty of an offence.

(10)

(a) A planning authority may, by virtue of this *subsection,* itself erect, construct, place or maintain, on, under, over or along a public road any appliance, apparatus or structure referred to in *subsection (1),* and it shall not be necessary for the planning authority to have a licence under this *section.*

(b) Nothing in this *subsection* shall be construed as empowering a planning authority to hinder the reasonable use of a public road by the public or any person entitled to use it or as empowering a planning authority to create a nuisance to the owner or occupier of premises adjacent to the public road.

(11) Where a planning authority is not the road authority for the purposes of national or regional roads in its area, it shall not grant a licence under this *section* in respect of any appliance, apparatus or structure on, under, over or along a national or regional road or erect, construct or place any appliance, apparatus or structure on, under, over or along a national or regional road except after consultation with the authority which is the road authority for those purposes.

AMENDMENT HISTORY

Paragraph (ee) inserted by s.54 of the Communication Regulation Act 2002 (No. 20 of 2002) which came into effect on April 27, 2002.

NOTE

This section requires a licence to be granted by the planning authority before certain appliances or cables may be erected on, under, over or along a public road. This section was formerly stated in s.89 of the 1963 Act. The section therefore specifically relates to matters on public roads. Section 2 defines "public road" as having the same meaning as in the Roads Act 1993. Section 2 of the Roads Act 1993 defines a public road as "a road over which a public right of way exists and the responsibility for the maintenance of which lies on a road authority". It also defines "road" as

> "(a) [A]ny street, lane, footpath, square, court, alley or passage, (b) any bridge, viaduct, underpass, subway, tunnel, overpass, overbridge, flyover, carriageway (whether single or multiple), pavement or footway, (c) any weighbridge or other facility for the weighing or inspection of vehicles, toll plaza or other facility for the collection of tolls, service area, emergency telephone, first aid post, culvert, arch, gulley, railing, fence, wall, barrier, guardrail, margin, kerb, lay-by, hard shoulder, island, pedestrian refuge, median, central reserve, channelliser, roundabout, gantry, pole, ramp, bollard, pipe, wire, cable, sign, signal or lighting forming part of the road, and (d) any other structure or thing forming part of the road and (i) necessary for the safety, convenience or amenity of road users or for the construction, maintenance, operation or management of the road or for the protection of the environment, or (ii) prescribed by the Minister."

Subsection (7) provides that where a licence is granted for development carried out in accordance with licence, it is exempted development so there is no additional requirement to obtain planning permission.

Among the appliances for which a licence is required include a vending machine, a town or landscape map, a hoarding, fence or scaffold, an advertisement structure, a cable, wire or pipeline, overground electronic communications infrastrucre and asscoiated physical infrastrucre, a telephone kiosk or pedestal, or any other prescribed appliance. Article 201 of the 2001 Regulations prescribes several other appliances for these purposes which include: a case, rack, shelf or other appliance for displaying articles in connection with an adjacent business; tables and chairs outside a hotel, restaurant or public house, where food is sold for consumption on the premises; a coin-operated machine other than vending machine; an advertisement consisting of any text, symbol, emblem, model, device or logo; a pipe or appliance with pipe attachment for dispensing air or water, not being attached to a petrol or oil pump; a weighing machine; bring facility; a cabinet used by a licensed wired broadcast relay service; a lamp-post; a bridge, arch, tunnel, passage or other similar structure not for use by the public; a cellar or other underground structure. Article 202 concerns the fees payable for the licence, which depends upon whether the licence is for one year or less or more than one year. The fees are specified in Sch.12. Article 203 provides that an additional fee is payable in respect of an appliance which is also used for advertising purposes.

Subsection (1) prohibits the erection, construction, placing or maintenance of any of the specified appliances "on, under, over or along" a public road, otherwise than in accordance with the licence.

Subsection (2) concerns exclusions from the requirement to obtain a licence. Thus a licence is not required in respect of an appliance authorised under a planning permission, a temporary hoarding, fence or scaffold under a condition of a planning permission, or concerning a cable, wire or pipeline installed by a statutory undertaker. Section 2 defines "statutory undertaker" as a person, for the time being, authorised by or under any enactment or instrument under an enactment to:

> "(a) [C]onstruct or operate a railway, canal, inland navigation, dock, harbour or airport,
> (b) provide, or carry out works for the provision of, gas, electricity or telecommunications services, or
> (c) provide services connected with, or carry out works for the purposes of the carrying on of the activities of, any public undertaking".

Under subs.(3), an applicant for a license must furnish plans and other information for the position, design and capacity of the appliance, apparatus or structure as the planning authority may require. Under subs.(4), the planning authority has discretion whether to grant a licence subject to conditions which may include in relation to location and design. A specified period for the licence will typically be prescribed. The planning authority can withdraw the licence where it causes an obstruction or becomes dangerous as a result of an increase or alteration of traffic on the road or of the widening of the road or of any improvement of or relating to the road. Subsection (5) sets out the matters to be considered by the planning authority in considering a licence, which includes the proper planning and development of the area, the development plan or local area plan, the number and location of existing appliances, and the convenience and safety of road users. Any person can appeal the decision of the planning authority on the licence to An Bord Pleanála, which will direct the planning authority to comply with its decision. Subsection (8) provides that the grant of the licence will not solely authorise the person to erect, construct, place or maintain the appliance. A similar provision applies in relation to the granting of planning permission under s.34(13). Therefore, a person may still require authorisation under other laws, such as property law, before they can erect or maintain the appliance. Subsection (9) makes it a criminal offence to erect or maintain an appliance without a licence or to so not in accordance with its conditions. The planning authority is exempt from the requirement to obtain a licence, although it cannot hinder the reasonable use of a public road or create a nuisance. In relation to national or regional roads, where the planning authority is not the road authority, it may not grant a licence except in consultation with the relevant road authority.

Performance of functions by planning authorities

1–298   **255.—(1)** A planning authority shall supply the Minister with such information relating to the performance of its functions as he or she may from time to time request.

(2)

(a) A planning authority shall conduct, at such intervals as it thinks fit or the Minister directs, reviews of its organisation and of the systems and procedures used by it in relation to its functions under this *Act.*

(b) Where the Minister gives a direction under this *subsection,* the planning authority shall report to the Minister the results of the review conducted pursuant to the direction and shall comply with any directive which the Minister may, after consultation with the planning authority as regards those results, give in relation to all or any of the matters which were the subject of the review.

(3) The Minister may appoint a person or body, not being the planning authority concerned, to carry out a review in accordance with *subsection (2).*

(4) Without prejudice to the powers of the Minister under the *Local Government Act, 1941,* if the Minister has formed the opinion from information available to him or her that—

(a) a planning authority may not be carrying out its functions in accordance with the requirements of or under this *Act,*

(b) a planning authority is not in compliance with guidelines issued under *section 28,* a directive issued under *section 29,* or a direction issued under *section 31,*

(c) there may be impropriety in the conduct of any of its functions by a planning authority, or

(d) there are serious diseconomies or inefficiencies in the conduct of its functions by a planning authority,

he or she may, where he or she considers it necessary or appropriate, for stated reasons appoint a commissioner to carry out and have full responsibility for all or any one or more of the functions of the planning authority under this *Act* and in doing so may distinguish between reserved functions and other functions.

(5) In considering whether it is necessary or expedient to appoint a commissioner under this *section,* the Minister may have regard to any loss of

public confidence in the carrying out of its functions by the planning authority and the need to restore that confidence.

(6) A commissioner appointed under this *section* shall be appointed in accordance with such terms and conditions and for such period as may be specified by the Minister.

(7) A planning authority may on stated grounds based on the provisions of *subsection (4),* by resolution, request the Minister to appoint a commissioner to carry out all or any of the functions of the authority under this *Act* and the Minister shall have regard to any such request.

(8) It shall be the duty of every member and every official of a planning authority to co-operate with any commissioner appointed under this *section.*

NOTE

This is a new section which concerns a review of the planning authority's performance of its functions under the Act, and the appointment of a commissioner to carry out its functions in certain circumstances. The planning authority is accountable to the Minister in the performance of his functions. The planning authority must supply the Minister with information requested by the Minister or carry out a review of its organisation, system or procedures when directed by the Minister. It may also undertake a review on its own initiative when it considers such appropriate. The Minister may appoint an independent body to carry out the review. Under subs.(4), the Minister has the power to appoint a commissioner to take over the functions or particular function of a planning authority, for stated reasons, where it considers one of four circumstances prevail. These are: where the planning authority has not carried out its functions in accordance with the requirements; where it has not complied with guidelines under s.28; a directive under s.29; or a direction under s.31; also, in the case of impropriety by a planning authority; or serious diseconomies or inefficiencies in the functions of the planning authority. The reference to without prejudice to the powers of the Minister under the Local Government Act 1941 is unclear as much of this has been repealed, although provisions such as for the removal from office of certain members survives. It is clear that a commissioner will only be appointed in the rarest of circumstances. In appointing a commissioner, the Minister may have regard to the loss of public confidence and the need to restore confidence. The planning authority may also, for stated grounds, request the Minister to appoint a commissioner and it must also co-operate with a commissioner appointed.

Amendment of Environmental Protection Agency Act, 1992

256.—*Repealed by s.3 and Schedule of the Protection of the Environment Act 2003 (No. 27 of 2003) with effect from July 1, 2004 (S.I. No. 393 of 2004).*   **1–299**

NOTE

This section which concerned the grant of permission where an intergrated pollution licence is required for the activity has been repealed under Sch.3 to the Protection of the Environment Act 2003. The matter is now governed by s.99F of the Environmental Protection Agency Act 1992, as inserted by s.15 of the 2003 Act which almost identically reproduces the repealed provision except that there are additional provisions concerning a lease granted by the Minister for Communications, Marine and Natural Resources under the Minerals Development Acts 1940 to 1999.

The repealed section amended s.98 of the Environmental Protection Agency Act 1992, by substituting a new s.98(1), in respect of the grant of planning permission in circumstances where an integrated pollution control licence has been granted. Under the former s.98(1), the planning authority or the Board could not refuse a permission or an approval for the reason that the development would cause environmental pollution, or grant such permission subject to conditions which are for the purposes of the prevention, limitation, elimination, abatement or reduction of environmental pollution from the activity. Also the planning authority was precluded from considering any matters relating to the risk of environmental pollution from the activity. In *O'Connell v Environmental Protection Agency* [2003] 1 I.R. 530, the Supreme Court rejected that Ireland had failed to properly implement the EIS Directive, holding that s.98(1) prohibited the planning authorities and the Board from considering the risk of evironmental pollution at the substantive decision stage and not at the earlier stage, when deciding whether to seek an EIS. Also in *Martin v An Bord Pleanála*, unreported, Supreme Court, May 10, 2007, the Supreme Court upheld a similar division of responsibility with respect to waste licences. The Directive did not require that one competent body must carry out a "global assessment" or a "single assessment" of the relevant environmental factors. However, the former restrictions under s.98(1) were abolished under the repealed provision with much narrower restrictions placed on consideration of such matters by the planning authority or the Board. The planning authority was not precluded from refusing permission on such basis or from considering such matters but is prohibited from imposing conditions in relation to control of emissions. The planning authority or Board was also authorised to refuse permission concerning development comprising an activity for which a licence has been granted, where the development was unacceptable on environmental grounds, having regard to the proper planning and sustainable development of the area. Before making such decision, the planning authority or Board must have requested the Environmental Protection Agency to make submissions or observations in relation to the application within a specified period, being not less than three weeks, in respect of which the planning authority or Board must have regard before arriving at their decision.

As noted this section has been repealed but largely reproduced under s.99F of the 1992 Act, which may be set out as follows:

"99F.—(1) Notwithstanding section 34 of the Act of other Acts. 2000, or any other provision of that Act, where a licence or revised licence under this Part has been granted or is or will be required in relation to an activity, a planning authority or An Bord Pleanála shall not, where it decides to grant a permission under section 34 of that Act in respect of any development comprising or for the purposes of the activity, subject the permission to conditions which are for the purposes of—

(*a*) controlling emissions from the operation of the activity, including the prevention, elimination, limitation, abatement, or reduction of those emissions, or

(*b*) controlling emissions related to or following the cessation of the operation of the activity.

(2) Where a licence or revised licence under this Part has been granted or is or will be required in relation to an activity, a planning authority or An Bord Pleanála may, in respect of any development comprising or for the purposes of the activity, decide to refuse a grant of permission under section 34 of the Act of 2000, where the authority or An Bord Pleanála considers that the development, notwithstanding the licensing of the activity under this Part, is unacceptable on environmental grounds, having regard to the proper planning and sustainable development of the area in which the development is or will be situate.

(3)(*a*) Before making a decision in respect of a development comprising or for the purposes of an activity, a planning authority or An Bord Pleanála may request the Agency to make observations within such period (which period shall not in any case be less than 3 weeks from the date of the request) as may be specified by the authority or the Board in relation to the development, including in relation to any environmental impact statement submitted.

(*b*) When making its decision, the authority or An Bord Pleanála, as the case may be, shall have regard to the observations, if any, received from the Agency within the period specified under paragraph (*a*).

(4) The planning authority or An Bord Pleanála may, at any time after the expiry of the period specified by the authority or An Bord Pleanála under subsection (3)(*a*) for making observations, make its decision on the application or appeal.

(5) The Minister may by regulations make such incidental, consequential or

supplementary provision as may appear to him to be necessary or proper to give full effect to any of the provisions of this section.

(6) Without prejudice to the generality of subsection (5), regulations under this section may provide for matters of procedure in relation to the request for or the making of observations from or by the Agency under this section and related matters.

(7) The making of observations by the Agency under this section shall not prejudice any other function of the Agency under this Act.

(8) Notwithstanding the provisions of the Minerals Development Acts 1940 to 1999, where a licence or revised licence under this Part has been granted or is or will be required in relation to an activity, a lease granted by the Minister for Communications, Marine and Natural Resources under the said Acts in respect of the same activity shall not contain conditions which are for the purpose of the prevention, elimination, limitation, abatement or reduction of emissions to the environment from the activity.

(9) Without prejudice to the preceding subsections, where a licence or revised licence under this Part is granted in relation to an activity and—

(a) a permission under section 34 of the Act of 2000, or

(b) a lease under the Minerals Development Acts 1940 to 1999, has been granted in respect of the same activity or in relation to development for the purposes of it, any conditions attached to that permission or contained in that lease, as the case may be, shall, so far as they are for the purposes of the prevention, elimination, limitation, abatement or reduction of emissions to the environment, cease to have effect.

(10) The grant of a permission or lease under any of the Acts of the Oireachtas referred to in this section in relation to any activity shall not prejudice, affect or restrict in any way the application of any provision of this Act to such activity".

Where the EPA forms the view that an IPC licence is not required, the planning authority is entitled to accept such opinion and proceed with the application and is not required to form its own independent view. See *Hickey v An Bord Pleanála*, unreported, High Court, Smyth J., June 10, 2004; and *Harrington v An Bord Pleanála* [2006] 1 I.R. 388. The compromise arrived at whereby the planning authority or Board can refuse permission where the development is unacceptable on environmental grounds but cannot grant permission subject to the specified conditions poses some problem in practice, where a planning application has been made at a stage when the licence has not been granted. The planning authority does not have the benefit of knowing the conditions controlling emissions which have been imposed by EPA. This is offset somewhat by the requirement to request the Agency to make observations on the planning application.

Amendment of Waste Management Act, 1996

257.—The Waste Management Act, 1996, is hereby amended in *section 54*— **1–300**

(a) by the substitution for subsection (3) of the following subsections:
   "(3) Notwithstanding *section 34* of the *Planning and Development Act, 2000*, or any other provision of that Act, where a waste licence has been granted or is or will be required in relation to an activity, a planning authority or An Bord Pleanála shall not, where it decides to grant a permission under *section 34* of that Act in respect of any development comprising the activity or for the purposes of the activity, subject the permission to conditions which are for the purposes of—

   (a) controlling emissions from the operation of the activity, including the prevention, limitation, elimination, abatement or reduction of those emissions, or

(*b*) controlling emissions related to or following the cessation
of the operation of the activity.

(3A) Where a waste licence has been granted under this Part or is or
will be required in relation to an activity, a planning authority or An
Bord Pleanála may, in respect of any development comprising the
activity or for the purposes of the activity, decide to refuse a grant
of permission under *section 34* of the *Planning and Development
Act, 2000*, where the authority or An Bord Pleanála considers that
the development, notwithstanding the licensing of the activity under
this Part, is unacceptable on environmental grounds, having regard
to the proper planning and sustainable development of the area in
which the development is or will be situate.

(3B) (*a*) Before making a decision in respect of a development
comprising or for the purposes of an activity, a planning
authority or An Bord Pleanála may request the Agency to
make observations within such period (which period shall
not in any case be less than 3 weeks from the date of the
request) as may be specified by the authority or the Board
in relation to the development, including in relation to any
environmental impact statement submitted.

(*b*) When making its decision, the authority or An Bord
Pleanála, as the case may be, shall have regard to the
observations, if any, received from the Agency within the
period specified under paragraph (*a*).

(3C) The planning authority or An Bord Pleanála may, at any time
after the expiration of the period specified by the authority or An
Bord Pleanála under subsection (3B)(*a*) for making observations,
make its decision on the application or appeal.

(3D) The Minister may make regulations making such incidental,
consequential, or supplementary provision as may appear to him
or her to be necessary or proper to give full effect to any of the
provisions of this section.

(3E) Without prejudice to the generality of *subsection (3D)*,
regulations made under this section may provide for matters of
procedure in relation to the request for or the making of observations
from or by the Agency under this section and related matters.

(3F) The making of observations by the Agency under this
section shall not prejudice any other function of the Agency under
this Act.

(*b*) in subsection (4), by the substitution for "Part IV of the Act of 1963"
of "*section 34* of the *Planning and Development. Act, 2000* in each
place it occurs, and

(*c*) in subsection (5), by the substitution for "the Local Government
(Planning and Development) Acts, 1963 to 1993, and a condition
attached to a permission granted under Part IV of the Act of 1963" of
"the *Planning and Development Act, 2000*, and a condition attached
to a permission under *section 34* of that Act".

NOTE

This section amends s.54 of the Waste Management Act 1996 in relation to waste licences in similar fashion to the amendment of the Environmental Protection Agency Act 1992 under s.256. Under the former s.54, the planning authority or the Board could not refuse a permission or an approval for the reason that the development would cause environmental pollution, or grant such permission subject to conditions which are for the purposes of the prevention, limitation, elimination, abatement or reduction of environmental pollution from the activity. Also, the planning authority was precluded from considering any matters relating to the risk of environmental pollution from the activity. The Supreme Court addressed these former provisions in *Martin v An Bord Pleanála*, unreported, Supreme Court, May 10, 2007, where it held the division of responsibility between the EPA and the Board in carrying out an EIA was in compliance with Directive 85/337/EEC. The Board in carrying out an EIA for the planning application was precluded from considering any matter relating to "the risk of environmental pollution from the activity", which would be considered by the EPA in granting a waste licence. An EIA in relation to a project may be carried out by more than one competent authority, whose decisions will comprise the "development consent". The Directive does not require that one competent body must carry out a "global assessment" or a "single assessment" of the relevant environmental factors. Planning permission on its own (without the waste licence) does not constitute "development consent". Once the competent authorities have carried out an EIA before development consent is given, there is compliance with the Directive.

However, the restrictions under the former s.54 were abolished under the 2000 Act with much narrower restrictions placed on matters which can be considered by the planning authority or the Board. The planning authority is not precluded from refusing permission on such basis or from considering such matters but it is prohibited from imposing conditions in relation to control of emissions. In *Cosgrove v An Bord Pleanála*, unreported, High Court, Kelly J., May 27, 2004, Kelly J. noted that s.257 invests an environmental pollution jurisdiction in a planning authority and in An Bord Pleanála on appeal.

The new subs.(1A) authorises the planning authority or Board to refuse permission concerning development comprising an activity for which a licence has been granted, where the development is unacceptable on environmental grounds, having regard to the proper planning and sustainable development of the area. Before making such a decision, the planning authority or Board must request the EPA to make submissions or observations in relation to the application within a specified period, being not less than three weeks, in relation to which the planning authority or Board must have regard before arriving at their decision. The compromise arrived at whereby the planning authority or Board can refuse permission where the development is unacceptable on environmental grounds but cannot grant permission subject to the specified conditions poses some problem in practice, where a planning application has been made at a stage when the licence has not been granted. The planning authority does not have the benefit of knowing the conditions controlling emissions which have been imposed by EPA. This is offset somewhat by the requirement to request the Agency to make observations on the planning application. The planning authority or Board can refuse permission on environmental grounds, having regard to the proper planning and sustainable development of the area. The notion of "environmental grounds" is potentially very broad and is not confined to issues of pollution. The general division of responsibility is also reflected in s.34(3)(c) which states that where a planning application:

"[R]elates to development which comprises or is for the purposes of an activity for which an integrated pollution control licence or a waste licence is required, a planning authority shall take into consideration that the control of emissions arising from the activity is a function of the Environmental Protection Agency".

It may also be noted that under s.54(5) of the Waste Management Act 1996, as amended, works consisting of or incidental to the carrying out of development comprised in a licence that were the subject of consultation in accordance with that provision and in respect of which a condition has been attached to a waste licence are exempted development.

The EPA in granting a licence can also refuse where the activity will cause environmental pollution. Section 40 of the Waste Management Act 1996, as amended, expressly provides that the EPA shall not grant a waste licence for an activity unless it is satisfied that the activity, if carried out subject to the conditions attached to the licence, will not cause environmental pollution and will comply with the provisions of the Landfill Directive. In *Power v An Bord Pleanála*, unreported, High Court, Quirke J., January 17, 2006, in a challenge to permission granted by the Board for a waste management the court held the applicant could not sustain her claim that the decision of the Board was invalid for failure to comply with the provisions of the Waste and Landfill Directives as the obligation to comply with the provisions of the Waste and Landfill Directives rests upon the State.

Limitation on connection to sanitary authority sewers

1–301   **258.**—*Repealed under the Water Services Act 2007*

NOTE

This section has been repealed under the Water Services Act 2007. The former section prohibited any person from connecting his or her drains to any sewer of the sanitary authority without the consent of the authority. The section only applied to structures erected on or after June 10, 1990 or which are not connected to a sewer of a sanitary authority. Thus even if erected prior to June 10, 1990, the section applied if such structure was connected to the sewer of the sanitary authority. However, this provision has now been replaced by the Water Services Act 2007 which provides a new comprehensive legal framework for the provision of water services. Under the Act "sanitary authorities" are renamed "water services authorities" (defined in terms of county and city councils) in so far as delivery of water services are concerned. The authority may grant the consent subject to conditions it deems reasonable.

The former subs.(4) made it a criminal offence to connect a drain to a sewer without the consent of the authority or in breach of the conditions. Where a person does so, the authority may close any such connection and also recover any expenses incurred by the authority as a result of such connection. Section 8(1) of the Local Government (Sanitary Services) Act 1962 allows the sanitary authority to serve a notice on the owner of a premises to connect a premises to the public sewerage system, where it considers that the premises are not drained in a satisfactory manner and are capable of being served by the sewerage system by means of a connection not exceeding one hundred feet.

Under the former subs.(7), the grant of a planning permission was deemed to include the consent of the sanitary authority to connect a drain to a sewer. However, s.61 of the Water Services Act 2007 concerns a condition of permission requiring the agreement of the water services authority. Section 61(5) provides that:

"[W]here a water services authority is also the relevant planning authority, the grant of a permission under Part III of the Act of 2000 in relation to a structure to which this section applies may, if it is indicated in the permission, include the agreement of the water services authority to the connection of that structure to its waste water works for the purposes of this section, subject to such conditions as the water services authority may require consistent with its powers under this section".

Section 61(6)(a) states:

"As a condition to the agreement of a water services authority to the connection of a premises to waste water services which are provided, or to be provided, by the water services authority or any person providing water services jointly with it or on its behalf, the water services authority may, at its absolute discretion and for the purposes of this section, require— (i) that the length or overall capacity of the service connection, or such related pipes or accessories as it considers necessary, be increased to such extent beyond technical requirements as it may specify so as to enable adjoining or other premises to be connected to a waste water works, but subject to the water services authority—(I) paying for any consequential increase in the cost of providing and installing the service connection or related pipes or accessories, and (II) taking the service connection or related pipes or accessories into its charge or otherwise entering into an agreement in relation to their future use with the person seeking its agreement to connect the premises to the said waste water services, as if the requirement was a requirement under section 34(4)(m) of the Act of 2000, or

(ii) that the service connection, or such related drainage pipes or accessories as it considers necessary, be opened for inspection or testing, or otherwise inspected or tested, by an authorised person. (b) For the purposes of the application of section 34(4)(m) of the Act of 2000 to this subsection, a reference to a planning authority shall be deemed to include a reference to a water services authority".

Section 61(7) provides that a connection to water services shall not be made until the authorised person is satisfied that first, the service connection or related pipes or accessories are of a proper standard and have been installed correctly, and secondly, a connection to the water services in question may be properly made. Section 61(8) allows an authorised person to issue directions.

It may be noted in relation to water supply, s.55(4) of the Water Services Act 2007 provides that where a water services authority is also the relevant planning authority, the grant of a permission under Pt III of the 2000 Act in relation to a structure, if it is indicated in the permission, includes the agreement of the water services authority to the connection of that structure to its waterworks for the purposes of the section, subject to such conditions as the water services authority may require, consistent with its functions.

Limitation of section 53 of the Waterworks Clauses Act, 1847

259.—*Repealed under the Water Services Act 2007*   1–302

NOTE

This has been repealed under the Water Services Act 2007. The former section restricted s.53 of the Waterworks Clauses Act 1847 and other enactment, in respect of unauthorised development, which otherwise provides that every owner and occupier is entitled to receive a sufficient supply of water for domestic purposes. The section has no effect on the right of the authority to serve a notice requiring a premises to be connected to the public sewerage scheme under s.8(2) of the 1962 Act.

Saving for national monuments

260.—Nothing in this *Act* shall restrict, prejudice, or affect the functions of   1–303
the Minister for Arts, Heritage, Gaeltacht and the Islands under the *National Monuments Acts, 1930* to *1994,* in relation to national monuments as defined by those Acts or any particular monuments.

NOTE

This section provides that none of the provisions of the 2000 Act may restrict the functions of the Minister for Arts, Heritage and the Islands under the National Monuments Acts 1930–1994. Among the provisions of the 2000 Act which could apply to national monuments include the provisions on protected structures. For the recent Carrickmines cases under the National Monuments Acts, see *Mulcreevy v Minister for the Environment* [2004] 1 I.L.R.M. 419 and *Dunne & Lucas v Dun Laoghaire-Rathdown County Council* [2003] 1 I.R. 567.

Control of quarries

261.—**(1)** The owner or operator of a quarry to which this *section* applies   1–304
shall, not later than one year from the coming into operation of this *section,* provide to the planning authority, in whose functional area the quarry is situated, information relating to the operation of the quarry at the commencement of this *section,* and on receipt of such information the planning authority shall, in accordance with *section 7,* enter it in the register.

(2) Without prejudice to the generality of *subsection (1),* information provided under that *subsection* shall specify the following—

    (a) the area of the quarry, including the extracted area delineated on a map,

    (b) the material being extracted and processed (if at all),

    (c) the date when quarrying operations commenced on the land (where known),

    (d) the hours of the day during which the quarry is in operation,

    (e) the traffic generated by the operation of the quarry including the type and frequency of vehicles entering and leaving the quarry,

    (f) the levels of noise and dust generated by the operations in the quarry,

    (g) any material changes in the particulars referred to in *paragraphs (a) to (f)* during the period commencing on the commencement of this *section* and the date on which the information is provided,

    (h) whether—

        (i) planning permission under *Part IV of the Act of 1963* was granted in respect of the quarry and if so, the conditions, if any, to which the permission is subject, or

        (ii) the operation of the quarry commenced before 1 October 1964,

        and

        (iii) such other matters in relation to the operations of the quarry as may be prescribed.

(3) A planning authority may require a person who has submitted information in accordance with this *section* to submit such further information as it may specify, within such period as it may specify, relating to the operation of the quarry concerned and, on receipt thereof, the planning authority shall enter the information in the register.

    (4)

    (a) A planning authority shall, not later than 6 months from the registration of a quarry in accordance with this *section,* publish notice of the registration in one or more newspapers circulating in the area within which the quarry is situated.

    (b) A notice under *paragraph (a)* shall state—

        (i) that the quarry has been registered in accordance with this *section,*

        (ii) where planning permission has been granted in respect of the quarry, that it has been so granted and whether the planning authority is considering restating, modifying or adding to conditions attached to the planning permission in accordance with *subsection (6)(a)(ii),* or

        (iii) where planning permission has not been granted in respect of the quarry, that it has not been so granted and whether the planning authority is considering—

            (I) imposing conditions on the operation of the quarry in accordance with *subsection (6)(a)(i),* or

            (II) requiring the making of a planning application and the preparation of an environmental impact statement in respect of the quarry in accordance with *subsection (7),*

(iv) the place or places and times at which the register may be inspected,

(v) that submissions or observations regarding the operation of the quarry may be made to the planning authority within 4 weeks from the date of publication of the notice.

(c) A notice under this *subsection* may relate to one or more quarries registered in accordance with this *section.*

(5)

(a) Where a planning authority proposes to—

(i) impose, restate, modify or add to conditions on the operation of the quarry under this *section,* or

(ii) require, under *subsection (7),* a planning application to be made and an environmental impact statement to be submitted in respect of the quarry in accordance with this *section,*

it shall, as soon as may be after the expiration of the period for making observations or submissions pursuant to a notice under *subsection (4)(b),* serve notice of its proposals on the owner or operator of the quarry.

(b) A notice referred to in *paragraph (a),* shall state—

(i) the reasons for the proposals, and

(ii) that submissions or observations regarding the proposals may be made by the owner or operator of the quarry to the planning authority within such period as may be specified in the notice, being not less than 6 weeks from the service of the notice.

(c) Submissions or observations made pursuant to a notice under *paragraph (b)* shall be taken into consideration by a planning authority when performing its functions under *subsection (6) or (7).*

(6)

(a) Not later than 2 years from the registration of a quarry under this *section,* a planning authority may, in the interests of proper planning and sustainable development, and having regard to the development plan and submissions or observations (if any) made pursuant to a notice under *subsection (4) or (5) —*

(i) in relation to a quarry which commenced operation before 1 October 1964, impose conditions on the operation of that quarry, or

(ii) in relation to a quarry in respect of which planning permission was granted under *Part IV of the Act of 1963* restate, modify or add to conditions imposed on the operation of that quarry,

and the owner and operator of the quarry concerned shall as soon as may be thereafter be notified in writing thereof.

(b) Where, in relation to a grant of planning permission conditions have been restated, modified or added in accordance with *paragraph (a),* the planning permission shall be deemed, for the purposes of this *Act,* to have been granted under *section 34,* and any condition so restated, modified or added shall have effect as if imposed under *section 34.*

(c) Notwithstanding *paragraph (a),* where an integrated pollution control licence has been granted in relation to a quarry, a planning authority or the Board on appeal shall not restate, modify, add to or impose conditions under this *subsection* relating to—

    (i) the control (including the prevention, limitation, elimination, abatement or reduction) of emissions from the quarry, or

    (ii) the control of emissions related to or following the cessation of the operation of the quarry.

(7)

  (a) Where the continued operation of a quarry—

    (i)

      (I) the extracted area of which is greater than 5 hectares, or

      (II) that is situated on a European site or any other area prescribed for the purpose of *section 10(2)(c),* or land to which an order under *section 15, 16 or 17 of the Wildlife Act, 1976,* applies,

    and

    (ii) that commenced operation before 1 October 1964, would be likely to have significant effects on the environment (having regard to any selection criteria prescribed by the Minister under *section 176(2)(e)*), a planning authority shall not impose conditions on the operation of a quarry under *subsection (6),* but shall, not later than one year after the date of the registration of the quarry, require, by notice in writing, the owner or operator of the quarry to apply for planning permission and to submit an environmental impact statement to the planning authority not later than 6 months from the date of service of the notice, or such other period as may be agreed with the planning authority.

  (b) *Section 172(1)* shall not apply to development to which an application made pursuant to a requirement under *paragraph (a)* applies.

  (c) A planning authority, or the Board on appeal, shall, in considering an application for planning permission made pursuant to a requirement under *paragraph (a),* have regard to the existing use of the land as a quarry.

(8)

  (a) Where, in relation to a quarry for which permission was granted under *Part IV of the Act of 1963,* a planning authority adds or modifies conditions under this *section* that are more restrictive than existing conditions imposed in relation to that permission, the owner or operator of the quarry may claim compensation under *section 197* and references in that *section* to compliance with conditions on the continuance of any use of land consequent upon a notice under *section 46* shall be construed as including references to compliance with conditions so added or modified, save that no such claim may be made in respect of any condition relating to a matter specified in *paragraph (a), (b) or (c) of section 34(4),* or in respect of a condition relating to the prevention, limitation or control of emissions from the quarry, or the reinstatement of land on which the quarry is situated.

   (b) Where, in relation to a quarry to which *subsection (7)* applies, a planning authority, or the Board on appeal, refuses permission for development under *section 34* or grants permission thereunder subject to conditions on the operation of the quarry, the owner or operator of the quarry shall be entitled to claim compensation under *section 197* and for that purpose the reference in *subsection (1) of that section* to a notice under *section 46* shall be construed as a reference to a decision under *section 34* and the reference in *section 197(2) to section 46* shall be construed as a reference to *section 34* save that no such claim may be made in respect of any condition relating to a matter specified in *paragraph (a), (b) or (c) of section 34(4),* or in respect of a condition relating to the prevention, limitation or control of emissions from the quarry, or the reinstatement of land on which the quarry is situated.

(9)

   (a) A person who provides information to a planning authority in accordance with *subsection (1)* or in compliance with a requirement under *subsection (3)* may appeal a decision of the planning authority to impose, restate, add to or modify conditions in accordance with *subsection (6)* to the Board within 4 weeks from the date of receipt of notification by the authority of those conditions.

   (b) The Board may at the determination of an appeal under *paragraph (a)* confirm with or without modifications the decision of the planning authority or annul that decision.

(10)

   (a) A quarry to which this *section* applies in respect of which the owner or operator fails to provide information in relation to the operations of the quarry in accordance with *subsection (1)* or in accordance with a requirement under *subsection (3)* shall be unauthorised development.

   (b) Any quarry in respect of which a notification under *subsection (7)* applies shall, unless a planning application in respect of the quarry is submitted to the planning authority within the period referred to in that *subsection,* be unauthorised development.

(11) This *section* shall apply to—

   (a) a quarry in respect of which planning permission under *Part IV of the Act of 1963* was granted more than 5 years before the coming into operation of this *section,* and

   (b) any other quarry in operation on or after the coming into operation of this *section,* being a quarry in respect of which planning permission was not granted under that *Part.*

(12) The Minister may issue guidelines to planning authorities regarding the performance of their functions under this *section* and a planning authority shall have regard to any such guidelines.

(13) In this *section* —

"emission" *means*—

(a) *an emission into the atmosphere of a pollutant within the meaning of the Air Pollution Act, 1987,*

(b) *a discharge of polluting matter, sewage effluent or trade effluent within the meaning of the Local Government (Water Pollution) Act, 1977, to waters or sewers within the meaning of that Act,*

(c) *the disposal of waste, or*

(d) *noise*;

"operator" *means a person who at all material times is in charge of the carrying on of quarrying activities at a quarry or under whose direction such activities are carried out*;

"quarry" has the meaning assigned to it by *section 3 of the Mines and Quarries Act, 1965.*

NOTE

This is a new provision concerning the control of quarries, requiring registration of quarries and alteration of planning permissions in relation to quarries. This provision was only commenced on April 28, 2004. A quarry is defined under s.3 of the Mines and Quarries Act 1965 as "an excavation or system of excavations made for the purpose of or in connection with the getting of minerals in their natural state or in solution or suspension and or products of minerals, being neither a mine not merely a well or bore hole or a well and bore-hole combined." The scope of the section is stated in subs.(11) where it says it applies to:

(a) a quarry in respect of which planning permission under Part IV of the Act of 1963 was granted more than 5 years before the coming into operation of this section; and

(b) any other quarry in operation on or after the coming into operation of this section, being a quarry in respect of which planning permission was not granted under that Part.

The Department of Local Government and the Environment has published *Guidelines for Planning Authorities on Quarries and Ancillary Activities.*

A quarry in operation prior to October 1, 1964 will be entitled to established use. In *Waterford County Council v John A. Wood Ltd* [1999] 1 I.R. 556, it was held that exclusion for pre-1964 use does not confer on the particular developer a licence to carry on generally the trade or occupation in which he was engaged but merely permits the continuation to completion of the particular works commenced before the appointed day at an identified location. This involves establishing the facts to ascertain what was or might reasonably have been anticipated at the relevant date as having been involved in the works then taking place. However, in *Roadstone v An Bord Pleanála*, unreported, High Court, Finlay Geoghegan J., July 4, 2008, in relation to whether a planned future use amounts to a material change, it was said that the determination must be made following an assessment of all the relevant facts in relation to the use of the lands of the applicant prior to the appointed day and the planned future use. That factual assessment must be made independently of planning considerations. The court must then consider the materiality of such factual change of use. Where after October 1, 1964, the activities of the quarry intensify so to amount to a material change of use, planning permission is required. Considerable case law has arisen regarding whether certain quarries require planning permission, in particular as to whether there is pre-October 1, 1964, use and whether there has been intensification of use; see *Patterson v Murphy* [1978] I.L.R.M. 85; *The State (Stafford and Son) v Roadstone Ltd* [1980] I.L.R.M. 1; *Dublin County Council v Sellwood Quarries Ltd.* [1981] I.L.R.M. 23; *Cork County Council v Artfert Quarries Ltd*, unreported, High Court, Murphy J., December 2, 1982; *Dublin County Council v Tallaght Block Co. Ltd* [1982] I.L.R.M. 534; *Carrick Hall Holdings v Dublin*

Corporation [1983] I.L.R.M. 268; *Monaghan County Council v Brogan* [1987] I.R. 333;
McGrath Limestone Works v Galway County Council [1989] I.L.R.M. 602; *Dublin C.C. v
Macken*, unreported, High Court, O'Hanlon J., May 13, 1994; *Paul Lee and John Flynn v
Michael O'Riordan*, unreported, High Court, O'Hanlon J., February 10, 1995. In *Limerick
County Council v Tobin (No. 2)*, unreported, High Court, Peart J., March 1, 2006, it was noted
that excavation works cannot continue outwards in ever widening circles, like ripples from
a lake, simply because there was evidence that some excavation works had commenced in
a small area prior to October 1, 1964. The use of a quarry will be deemed to be abandoned
where there is a cessation of use for a considerable time, without any evinced intention to
resume the use of the quarry. Where there has been intermittent use, on and off of quarry,
the use may be still held to be abandoned. See *Lee and O'Flynn v O'Riordan and others*,
unreported, High Court, February 10, 1995. In *Kildare County Council v Goode and Others*,
the "haphazard" use of a quarry without any ordered activity, did not prevent the Court
holding that the quarry had been abandoned. In *McGrath Limestone Works v Galway County
Council* [1989] I.L.R.M. 602 the Supreme Court rejected that use of a site for quarrying
had been abandoned when planning permission had been granted for growing mushrooms
in 1983 on five per cent of the site. It was held the permission for growing mushrooms had
not been implemented and had ceased after only two years. See generally the note on s.4.
It appears that any pending imposition of controls under the section, is without prejudice
to the powers of the planning authority to take enforcement action. It should be noted
that the Guidelines states that it is not necessary to defer enforcement proceedings until
after the registration process is completed and that an unauthorised development remains
unauthorised development even after registering with the planning authority.

Subsection (1) imposed an obligation on the owner or operator of a quarry to provide
information to the planning authority on the operation of the quarry within one year of
the commencement of the section. The planning authority was then required to enter the
information in the planning register under s.7. Subsection (2) sets out the content of the
information which was to be provided which includes the area of the quarry, the material
extracted, the date quarrying commenced, the hours of the day in which the quarry operates,
the traffic generated by the quarry, the levels of noise and dust created, any material changes
in the previous particulars since the commencement of the section, whether planning
permission was granted for the quarry, whether the quarry operated before October 1,
1964, and other prescribed matters (October 1, 1964, being the date when the 1963 Act
commenced). Any development or use prior to this date will not require planning permission
so long as such use was not abandoned. The reference in subs.(2)(a) to "including the
extracted area", implies that the area of the quarry is not confined to the extracted area. The
Guidelines for Planning Authorities on Quarries and Ancillary Activities state the object
of the registration system is "to give a snapshot of the current use of land for quarrying". It
is therefore designed to indicate the current factual operation of quarrying activity. Under
subs.(3), the planning authority may request further information. It appears the area of
the quarry should not include areas beyond the extracted area which are not reasonably
anticipated and which would require planning permission. The registration process is not
to confer any benefit on the quarry operator. Nor does registration mean that enforcement
action cannot be taken. Registration is for the purposes of information gathering on the
basis of which the planning authority will take further measures. However, under subs.(10),
where an owner or occupier fails to provide the information, the quarry will be considered
unauthorised development. Thus irrespective of whether the quarry operation was in fact
unauthorised prior to the registration process, the failure to provide the information, means
that its status is unauthorised.

Following registration, subs.(4), provides that the planning authority is obliged to
publish a newspaper notice of the registration of the quarry, not later than six months from
the date of registration (which notice may relate to one or more quarries). The newspaper
notice must state the fact of the registration, whether planning permission has been granted
in respect of the quarry, and whether the planning authority is considering modifying the
conditions. Where planning permission has not been granted, the notice must state whether
the planning authority is considering imposing conditions on the operation of the quarry or
requiring a planning permission application and EIS in respect of the quarry. The notice must
also state the place and time where the register can be inspected and that submissions or

observations may be made within four weeks. It appears that the registration and imposition of conditions constitutes a "development consent" for the purposes of the EIA Directive and so there may be a requirement to carry out an EIA. See *Reg. v North Yorks. C.C., ex p. Brown* [2000] 1 A.C. 397 and *Wells v Secretary of State for Transport, Local Government and the Regions* Case C-201/02 [2004] ECR I-723.

Subsection (5) sets out the procedure for imposing conditions or requiring a planning application in respect of the quarry. It provides that where a planning authority proposes to impose, restate, modify or add conditions to the operation of the quarry, or require a planning application and EIS to be submitted, the planning authority must serve notice of its proposal on the owner or operator. The notice must state the reasons for the proposal and state that submissions or observations may be made regarding the proposal within a specified period, being not less than six weeks.

Under subs.(6), the planning authority may impose conditions in relation to the operation of a quarry commenced before October 1, 1964, or may restate, modify or add to the conditions of a planning permission granted under the 1963 Act in relation to the quarry. In relation to pre-1964 quarries, the planning authority can therefore impose conditions without any planning application as opposed to imposing planning conditions following the submission of a planning application The planning authority must notify in writing the owner and operator of the quarry as soon as may be. In making such decision, the planning decision must have regard to the proper planning and sustainable development of the area, the development plan, and any submissions or observations received. The planning authority has only two years from the date of registration to take such decision. As there may be a gap of nearly two years between the newspaper notice inviting submissions or observations and the actual decision, there is a risk that there could be significant change in relation to quarry. Nevertheless on a strict construction, the planning authority is not obliged to invite further submissions or observations again from the public. The modified conditions of a planning permission will have effect as if imposed under s.34, relating to a decision on a planning permission application. Similar to s.256, where an integrated pollution licence has been granted with respect to the quarry, conditions cannot be imposed in relation to control of emissions. Under subs.(9), a person who supplied the information to the planning authority may appeal the decision to impose or modify the conditions to An Bord Pleanála within four weeks of the receipt of the notice. The Board has a discretion to confirm with or without modification the conditions, or to annul them. Subsection (6)(b) provides that in relation to a grant of permission where the conditions have been restated, modified or added, the planning permission shall be deemed to have been granted under the 2000 Act. It follows from this that in enforcing such conditions, that the planning authority can rely upon its full enforcement powers under Pt VIII of the Act. It may be noted that there are no time limitations in the enforcement of conditions relating to the ongoing use of the development. However, where the conditions are imposed on a quarry in operation before October 1, 1964, the means of enforcement is less clear. A quarry which commenced before October 1, 1964, which does not comply with conditions which are imposed under subs.(6), does not fall within the definition of unauthorised development under s.2(1). Furthermore, there is no provision in the section similar to subs.(10), which would expressly deem such a quarry in non-compliance with the conditions, to be unauthorised development. Also the subsection does not state that conditions are imposed under s.34. In the absence of any mechanism, taking enforcement action under Pt VIII in respect of such condition may be hazardous. Notwithstanding this, considering the scheme of the section and the Act as whole, it is unlikely that the legislature intended that such conditions would not be subject to enforcement action. In this respect s.5 of the Interpretation Act 2005 could be called in aid to adopt a purposive approach on the basis that a literal interpretation of the subsection to the effect that such conditions cannot be subject to the enforcement powers of Pt VIII, would be absurd or more aptly, would fail to reflect the plain intention of the Oireachtas. While s.5(1) excludes such an interpretative approach where a provision relates to the imposition of a penal or other sanction, the better view is that the implication that a condition is subject to enforcement action, does not in itself constitute the imposition of a penal or other sanction within the meaning of the exclusion.

As regards the scope of conditions which may be imposed, subs.(6) does not define what is meant by "conditions" and whether these are the same as conditions which can be imposed under s.34(4) in the context of a planning application. However, subs.(6)

provides such conditions are imposed in "the interests of proper planning and sustainable development" and so is in similar terms to the general power to impose conditions under s.34(4). This is further confirmed by the fact that in the case of conditions which have been restated, modified or added in respect of a planning permission granted under the 1963 Act, the conditions are deemed to have been granted under s.34. Conditions may also be imposed under other provisions of the Act, such as ss.48 and 49 in relation to the payment of development contributions. Although the power to impose such conditions is not entirely clear, insofar as such conditions may be expressly imposed in relation to permissions under s.34, it would also seem to follow that they are not outside the scope of conditions which may be imposed under subs.(6).

Subsection (7) provides that there is a requirement to carry out an EIS in respect of certain quarries. This subsection applies to quarries which commenced before October 1, 1964 where:

- the extracted area is more than five hectares; or
- is on a European site;
- is an area prescribed in the development plan for conservations and protection of the environment (s.10(2)(c));
- is a nature reserve (under ss.15 or 16 of the 1976 Act); or
- is a refuge for fauna (s.17 of the 1976 Act).

Where the continued operation of such quarry would be likely to have significant effects on the environment then the planning authority must, not later than one year after registration, require by notice in writing the owner or occupier to apply for planning permission and submit an EIS, not later than six months from the service of the notice or other agreed period. Where this subsection is invoked then the procedure under subs.(6) for imposing conditions which will not apply. Subsection (7) only applies to pre-1964 quarries and so cannot apply to quarries granted permission under the 1963 Act. It may be noted that under para.2 of Pt II of Sch. 5 to the 2001 Regulations, an EIS is mandatory in respect of a quarry, where the surface area of the quarry site exceeds 25 hectares or in the case of the extraction of stone, gravel sand or clay, where the area of extraction would be greater than 5 hectares. Also under para.13 of Pt 2 of Sch.2, any extension of the quarry which would result in an increase in size greater than 25 per cent or greater than an amount equal to 50 per cent of the appropriate threshold, also requires an EIS.

Section 172 concerning the requirement of an EIS will not apply in the case of such notice. It is not entirely clear as regards the nature of the planning application to be made. It is strictly speaking an application for retention permission insofar as the development has already commenced. Nevertheless, the planning authority is required to have regard to the existing use of the land as a quarry when considering the application. Under subs.(10)(b), unless the planning application is submitted within the required period, the quarry will be deemed unauthorised development. Under the section there is no requirement that the quarry cannot continue operation pending the determination of the planning application. The fact that such quarry may continue is consistent with the fact that such quarry does not constitute unauthorised development within the meaning of s.2(1). It is possible that European law may require that such developments cease pending the EIS assessment. See in particular *Commission v Ireland* Case C-215/06. However, the requirement under the EIS Directive is to carry out an EIS where the project commenced subsequent to July 3, 1988 or where there has been a change or extension of the project which may have significant adverse effects on the environment subsequent to such date. Thus in the case of a pre-1964 quarry, where there has been a change or extension subsequent to July 3, 1988 which may have significant adverse effects on the environment subsequent to that date, European law may require the State to ensure that such quarry does not continue to operate pending the determination of the planning application.

Subsection (8) provides that where a planning authority imposes more restrictive conditions or refuses a planning permission or imposes conditions thereunder in relation to a quarry, the owner or operator may claim compensation for discontinuance of use under s.197 (s.46 concerns a notice for discontinuance of use). There is no entitlement to compensation where conditions are imposed on a pre-1964 quarry under subs.(6). Compensation will not be paid for conditions concerning regulating the use of land which adjoins, abuts or is adjacent to the land and which is controlled by the applicant and which is expedient for the development (s.34(4)(a)); requiring the carrying out of works for the purposes of the authorised development (s.34(4)(b)); reducing or preventing the emission of noise or vibrations; or controlling emissions from the quarry or the reinstatement of land on which the quarry is situated.

The entitlement to compensation for the imposition of restrictive conditions under this subsection only arises where permission has been granted for a quarry under Pt IV of the 1963 Act. There is no entitlement to compensation for the imposition of conditions under s.261(6)(a)(i), where conditions are imposed on the operation of a quarry commenced before October 1, 1964. The power to impose conditions on a pre-1964 quarry is an independent power and is not operated under s.46 concerning conditions on the continuance of use. The right of compensation under s.46 notice does not therefore apply to the imposition of conditions on a quarry under s.261(6)(a)(i).

Regulations generally

1–305   262.—(1) The Minister may make regulations for prescribing any matter referred to in this *Act* as prescribed or to be prescribed, or in relation to any matter referred to in this *Act* as the subject of regulations.

(2) *Regulations* under this *Act* may contain such incidental, supplemental and consequential provisions as appear to the Minister to be necessary or expedient.

(3) Before making any regulations under this *Act,* the Minister shall consult with any relevant State authority where the regulations relate to the functions of that State authority.

(4) Where regulations are proposed to be made under *section 4(2), 19(3), 25(5), 100(1)(b), (c) or (d), 126(4), 176, 179(1), 181(1)[(a)], 221(4), 230(1) or 246,* a draft of the regulations shall be laid before both Houses of the Oireachtas and the regulations shall not be made unless a resolution approving the draft has been passed by each such House.

(5) Every regulation made under this *Act* (other than a regulation referred to in *subsection (4)*) shall be laid before each House of the Oireachtas as soon as may be after it is made and, if a resolution annulling the regulation is passed by either such House within the next 21 days on which that House has sat after the regulation is laid before it, the regulation shall be annulled accordingly but without prejudice to the validity of anything previously done thereunder.

AMENDMENT HISTORY

Subsection (4) amended by s.15 of the Planning and Development (Amendment) Act 2002 (No. 32 of 2002) which came into effect on December 24, 2002.

NOTE

This section applies to any regulations which may be made by the Minister under the provisions of the Act. In addition to any specific prescribed power to make regulations, the Minister may include matters, which are incidental, supplemental and consequential provisions, which he deems necessary. There is a general obligation to consult with state authorities where the regulation relates to its function. Two different procedures are prescribed for the making of regulations, both of which involve laying the draft regulations before both Houses of the Oireachtas. For regulations made in respect of the matters enlisted in subs.(4), the draft regulations will not be adopted unless a specific resolution is passed by both Houses approving the regulation. In respect of all other matters, subs.(5) provides the draft regulations will become law, unless a resolution is passed by either of the Houses within 21 days annulling the draft regulation. The matters covered by subs.(4) are in relation to:

- classes of exempted development (s.4(2));
- preparation of local area plans (s.19(3));
- procedures for making regional planning guidelines (s.25(5));
- governing the determination of income for qualifying for social and affordable housing (s.100(1)(b));
- estimating affordable housing needs or making a scheme for affordable housing (s.100(1)(c));
- setting out terms or conditions of housing supplied under the social and affordable housing provisions (s.100(1)(d));
- varying the period for determination of an appeal or referral by the Board (s.126(4));
- prescribing classes of development which require an EIA (s.176);
- requiring certain development by the local authority to comply with the procedure set out in s.179 (s.179);
- that the procedure under s.181 will not apply to certain development by state authorities;
- varying the period for determination by the Board in relation to motorway schemes and compulsory acquisition (s.221(4));
- the requirement to obtain a license in relation to holding certain events (s.230(1)); and
- in relation to fees payable to the planning authority (s.246).

PART XIX

COMMENCEMENT, REPEALS AND CONTINUANCE

Interpretation

263.—In this *Part,* "repealed enactments" *means the enactments specified*   **1–306** *in column (2) of the Sixth Schedule.*

NOTE

The repealed enactments set out in the Sixth Schedule are:
- Local Government (Planning and Development) Act 1963.
- Local Government (Planning and Development) Act 1976.
- Local Government (Planning and Development) Act 1982, other than s.6.
- Local Government (Planning and Development) Act 1983.
- Local Government (Planning and Development) Act 1990.
- Local Government Act 1991, ss.44 and 45.
- Local Government (Planning and Development) Act 1992.
- Local Government (Planning and Development) Act 1993, other than s.4.
- Roads Act 1993, s.55A (as inserted by s.6 of the Roads (Amendment) Act 1998).
- Local Government (Planning and Development) Act 1998.
- Local Government (Planning and Development) Act 1999.

Repeals

264.—The enactments specified in *column (2) of the Sixth Schedule* are   **1–307** hereby repealed to the extent specified in *column (3) of that Schedule.*

NOTE

In most cases the whole of the Acts are repealed with the exception of s.6 of the Local Government (Planning and Development) Act 1982 Act and s.4 of the Local Government (Planning and Development) Act 1993, while only ss.44 and 45 of the Local Government

Act 1991; Local Government (Planning and Development) Act 1992 and s.55A (as inserted by s.6 of the Roads (Amendment) Act 1998) of the Roads Act 1993 are repealed.

Continuity of repealed enactments

1–308 **265.—(1)**

    (a) Nothing in this *Act* shall affect the validity of anything done under the *Local Government (Planning and Development) Acts, 1963 to 1999,* or under any regulations made under those Acts.

    (b) Any order, regulation or policy directive made, or any other thing done, under the *Local Government (Planning and Development) Acts, 1963 to 1999,* that could have been made or done under a corresponding provision of this *Act,* shall not be invalidated by any repeal effected by this *Act* but shall, if in force immediately before that repeal was effected, have effect as if made or done under the corresponding provision of this *Act,* unless otherwise provided.

  (2) The continuity of the operation of the law relating to the matters provided for in the repealed enactments shall not be affected by the substitution of this *Act* for those enactments, and—

    (a) so much of any enactment or document (including enactments contained in this *Act*) as refers, whether expressly or by implication, to, or to things done or falling to be done under or for the purposes of, any provision of this *Act,* shall, if and so far as the nature of the subject matter of the enactment or document permits, be construed as including, in relation to the times, years or periods, circumstances or purposes in relation to which the corresponding provision in the repealed enactments has or had effect, a reference to, or, as the case may be, to things done or falling to be done under or for the purposes of, that corresponding provision,

    (b) so much of any enactment or document (including repealed enactments and enactments and documents passed or made after the commencement of this *Act*) as refers, whether expressly or by implication, to, or to things done or falling to be done under or for the purposes of, any provision of the repealed enactments shall, if and so far as the nature of the subject matter of the enactment or document permits, be construed as including, in relation to the times, years or periods, circumstances or purposes in relation to which the corresponding provision of this *Act* has effect, a reference to, or, as the case may be, to things done or deemed to be done or falling to be done under or for the purposes of, that corresponding provision.

  (3) *Section 2 of the Acquisition of Land (Assessment of Compensation) Act, 1919,* as amended by *section 69(1) of the Act of 1963* shall, notwithstanding the repeal of *section 69 of the Act of 1963* by the *Act of 1990,* apply to every case, other than a case [under *Part XII*] or the *Act of 1990,* where any compensation assessed will be payable by a planning authority or any other local authority.

  (4) In the case of any application to a planning authority, or any appeal or any other matter with which the Board is concerned which is received by the planning authority or the Board, as the case may be, before the repeal of the relevant provisions or the revocation of any associated regulations, the provisions of the *Local Government (Planning and Development) Acts, 1963* to *1999,* and regulations made thereunder shall continue to apply to the application, appeal or other matter notwithstanding the repeal of any enactment or revocation of any regulation.

AMENDMENT HISTORY

Subsection (3) amended by s.46 of the Planning and Development (Strategic Infrastructure) Act 2006 (No. 27 of 2006).

NOTE

This section provides that the matters or acts under the previous repealed legislation will continue to have force and that the 2000 Act does not have retrospective effect. Subsection (1) provides that the 2000 Act will not affect the validity of acts done under the previous planning Acts. Also, any order, regulation or policy directive made under the previous Acts, will have effect as if done under the 2000 Act, unless otherwise specifically provided. Subsection (2) provides that if any enactment or document refers to things done or failing to be done under the previous planning Acts, they shall be construed if possible, to refer to the corresponding provision of the 2000 Act. However, such a matter will only be construed where the subject matter of the enactment or document permits such construction. This may apply in relation to the times, years or periods, circumstances or purposes, of the corresponding provision. Subsection (3) provides that s.2 of the Acquisition of Land (Assessment of Compensation) Act 1919 applies to all cases of assessment of compensation except under the 2000 Act or under s.69 of the 1990 Act, where the compensation is payable by a planning authority or other local authority. Subsection (4) provides that where an application or appeal is lodged prior to the commencement of the 2000 Act, it will continue to be governed by the previous Acts and Regulations until a decision is made. Article 207(1) of the 2001 Regulations provides that the previous planning acts and regulations will continue to apply to any valid application for planning permission received by the planning authority before March 11, 2002. A planning application received by the planning authority before March 11, 2002, but appealed to the Board, after March 11, 2002, should still be dealt with by the Board unless the previous planning Acts and Regulations. See *Cosgrove v An Bord Pleanála*, unreported, High Court, Kelly J., May 27, 2004. The 2006 Act amended subs.(3) by substituting "the Act" for "Part XIII" which merely concerns amenities, it makes clear the continuity provision applies in respect of all provisions of the Act.

Transitional provisions regarding development plans

266.—(1)   1–309
   (a) Notwithstanding the repeal of any enactment by this *Act,* development plans made under *Part III of the Act of 1963* shall continue in force and shall be deemed to have been made under and in compliance with this *Act.*
   (b) Notwithstanding the repeal of any enactment by this *Act,* where a planning authority has given notice under *section 21 of the Act of 1963* of the preparation of a draft development plan, *Part III of the Act of 1963* shall continue to apply in respect of that draft development plan until the making of such plan.
(2)
   (a) Where, on the commencement of *Part II,* a development plan is in force for longer than 4 years, the planning authority concerned shall, not later than one year after such commencement, initiate the

notification procedures under *section 11.*

(b) Except as is provided for in *paragraph (a) and in subsection (1)(b),* the provisions of *Part II* in relation to the review of development plans and the preparation of new plans shall apply to all existing development plans.

(c) For the purposes of *paragraphs (a) and (b),* the reference to the development plan shall be a reference to the development plan in force for the functional area of the planning authority which covers all, or the greater part of, that functional area and—

   (i) a development plan for a scheduled town, within the meaning of *section 2 of the Act of 1963,* or

   (ii) a development plan covering part only of the functional area of the authority (not being the greater part),

shall be deemed not to be a development plan for the purposes of those paragraphs.

(3) A reference in any enactment or instrument to a development plan shall be deemed to be a reference to a development plan as defined in this *Act.*

NOTE

This section concerns the continuity of development plans under the previous Planning Acts and Regulations. Development plans of a planning authority are construed as the development plan in force for the functional area of the planning authority. A development plan made under the repealed Acts will continue in force as if made under the 2000 Act. Where a planning authority has commenced preparation of a new development plan under the procedure of s.21 of the 1963 Act, that former procedure will continue to apply until the making of the plan. Part II of the 2000 Act commenced on January 1, 2001. Where a development is in force for more than four years since Pt II of the 2000 Act commenced, the planning authority is obliged to initiate the notification procedure for the making of a new plan under the 2000 Act. The procedure in relation to review and preparation of new plans under the 2000 Act will apply to existing plans.

Transitional provisions respecting compulsory acquisition of land

1–310   **267.—(1)** Where, before the transfer of functions to the Board in accordance with *sections 214 and 215,* any matter was to be determined by the Minister under the enactments referred to in those sections, the Board shall, in lieu of the Minister, determine the matter in accordance with those sections.

(2) *Sections 217, 218, 219, 220, 221 and 222* shall not apply to matters referred to in *subsection (1)* to be determined by the Board in accordance with that *subsection.*

NOTE

This section relates to the transferred functions formerly performed by the Minister concerning compulsory acquisition (s.214) or the making of a motorway scheme (s.215), and provides that matters due to be determined by the Minister will now be determined by the Board. In such case, the former procedures rather than the new procedures set out in ss.217–222 will apply to the determination by the Board.

Miscellaneous transitional provisions

268.—**(1)** Notwithstanding the repeal of any enactment by this *Act* — **1–311**

   (a) *subsections (2) to (5) of section 38 of the Act of 1999* continue to apply to a planning authority until the planning authority has made the decisions required by those subsections and served them on the appropriate owners and occupiers,

   (b) a scheme for the granting of pensions, gratuities or other allowances in respect of the chairperson and ordinary members or in respect of wholetime employees of the Board under an *Act* repealed by this *Act* shall continue in force and shall be deemed to be a scheme under *section 119 or 121,* as appropriate,

   (c) a special amenity area order or tree preservation order confirmed or made under an *Act* repealed by this *Act* that is in force immediately before the commencement of this *section* shall be deemed to have been confirmed or made under *section 203 or 205,* as appropriate,

   (d) *paragraph 12 of the Third Schedule to the Act of 1990* shall continue to apply for a period of 3 years from the commencement of this *section,* and

   (e) *section 55A* (inserted by the *Roads (Amendment) Act, 1998*) of the *Roads Act, 1993* (as inserted by *section 6 of the Roads (Amendment) Act, 1998*) shall continue to apply in relation to an order of the Minister under *section 49(3) or 51(6) of that Act.*

(2) Any codes of practice concerning the holding of events issued by the Minister or any other Minister of the Government prior to the coming into force of this *Act* shall be deemed to be codes of practice under *section 232.*

(3)

   (a) Notwithstanding *section 191,* compensation shall be payable under *section 190* where there has been a refusal of permission under *Part III* on the grounds specified in *paragraph 5 of the Fourth Schedule,* and where—

      (i) the development plan contained, prior to the coming into operation of *section 10,* an objective for the zoning of the land to which the application concerned related for use solely or primarily for the purpose for which the application was made, and

      (ii) the application for permission was made not later than 3 years after the coming into operation of this *section.*

   (b) *Paragraph (a)* shall not apply to a refusal of permission if—

      (i) the development is of a class or description set out in the *Third Schedule,* or

      (ii) the refusal was on grounds specified in the *Fourth Schedule* (other than *paragraph (a)*).

NOTE

   This section provides that certain acts done under the repealed enactments are deemed to have been taken under the 2000 Act. Subsections (38)(2)–(5) concern the decision of whether to include a structure in the record of protected structures. Among the matters deemed to be taken under the 2000 Act are: that the grant of pensions, annuities or allowances are deemed to be a scheme for the superannuation of members of the Board (s.119) or of employees of the Board (s.121); a special amenity order or tree preservation order under ss.203 and 205 respectively; para.12 of Sch.3 to the 1990 Act, which provides that the reason for refusal of compensation which excludes compensation stated in para.11 (that it materially contravenes a development plan), will not apply to land where at any time within five years prior to the planning application the development would not have contravened the development plan; and s.55A of the Roads Act 1993, which concerns judicial review of an order of a Minister (now the Board) in relation to a motorway scheme.

Subsection (2) allows Codes of practices in relation to holding events to continue in force, while under subs.(3), compensation will be payable under certain circumstances for refusal of permission even if it falls within para.5 of Sch.4 (which normally excludes compensation), concerning the risk of a major accident or danger to human health or the environment.

Regulations to remove difficulties

1–312   **269.**—If any difficulty arises during the period of 3 years from the commencement of this *Act* in bringing any provision of this *Act* into operation or in relation to the operation of any provision, the Minister may by regulations do anything which appears to the Minister to be necessary or expedient for the purposes of removing the difficulty, bringing that provision into operation, or securing or facilitating its operation.

NOTE

This regulation empowers the Minister to make regulations to remove obstacles in bringing any provisions of the Act into operation.

Commencement

1–313   **270.**—**(1)** This *Act* shall come into operation on such day or days as the Minister may appoint by order or orders either generally or with reference to any particular purpose or provision, and different days may be so fixed for different purposes and provisions.

(2) An order under *subsection (1)* may, in respect of the repeals effected by *section 264* of the enactments mentioned in the *Sixth Schedule,* fix different days for the repeal of different enactments or for the repeal for different purposes of any enactment.

NOTE

See Introductory note for full list of commencement dates for provisions introduced under the 2006 Act. The 2000 Act has been brought into operation as follows:

By the Planning and Development Act 2000 (Commencement) Order 2000 (S.I. No. 349 of 2000):

1. Sections 1, 2 (insofar as it relates to the sections commenced on that date), 13, 28 to 30, 93 to 101, 165 to 171, 262, 266, 269 and 270 came into effect on November 1, 2000.

2. Sections 2 (insofar as it relates to the sections commenced on that date), 9 to 12, 14 to 27, 31 and the First Schedule came into effect on January 1, 2001.

By the Planning and Development Act 2000 (Commencement) (No. 2) Order 2000 (S.I. No. 449 of 2000):

1. Sections 2 (insofar as it relates to the sections commenced on that date), 50 (insofar as it relates to decisions under subs.(2)(b)(iii) of that section), 71 to 78, 182, 210 to 223, 263, 264 (insofar as it relates to the repeal of s.55A of the Roads Act 1993 (as

inserted by s.6 of the Roads (Amendment) Act 1998), 265(3), 267, 268(1) (other than paras (a), (b), (c) and (d) of that subsection), 271 to 277 of the Act came into operation on January 1, 2001.

By the Planning and Development Act 2000 (Commencement) Order 2001 (S.I. No. 153 of 2001):

1. Part XVI (other than s.239), came into effect on April 17, 2001.
2. Sections 156, 157 and 158 insofar as they relate to prosecutions under ss.230, 233 or 235 came into effect on April 17, 2001.
3. Subsections (1) (other than paras.(a), (b), (c) and (e) of that subsection) and (3) (a) of s.246, came into effect on April 17, 2001.
4. Section 268(2) came into effect on April 17, 2001.
5. Section 2, insofar as it relates to the items mentioned in (1) to (4) above, came into effect on April 17, 2001.

By the Planning and Development Act 2000 (Commencement) (No.2) Order 2001 (S.I. No. 335 of 2001)—

1. Section 2, insofar as it relates to Ch.1 of Pt VI, came into effect on July 19, 2001.
2. Section 2 insofar as it relates to the repeals made operational by article 3 of the order (S.I. No. 335 of 2001), came into effect on July 19, 2001.

By the Planning and Development Act 2000 (Commencement) (No.3) Order 2001 (S.I. No. 599 of 2001):

1. Sections 3, 4, 6 and 8, came into effect on January 21, 2002.
2. Part IV, insofar as not previously commenced, came into effect on January 21, 2002.
3. Chapter II of Pt VI, came into effect on January 21, 2002.
4. Part VII, came into effect on January 21, 2002.
5. Sections 156, 157 and 158, insofar as they relate to prosecutions for offences under ss.58, 63, 91, 113, 114, 147, 148, 205 and 208, came into effect on January 21, 2002.
6. Section 180 came into effect on January 21, 2002.
7. Part XIII came into effect on January 21, 2002.
8. Section 264 and the Sixth Schedule insofar as they relate to the repeals specified by art.4 of the Order came into effect on January 21, 2002.
9. Section 268(1)(a), (b) and (c) came into effect on January 21, 2002.
10. Section 2, insofar as it relates to the items mentioned in (1) to (9), above, came into effect on January 21, 2002.
11. The following, insofar as not previously commenced, came into effect on March 11, 2002: ss.2, 5 and 7, Pt III, Ch.III of Pt VI, Pt VIII, Pt X, Pt XI, Pt XII and the Second, Third, Fourth and Fifth Schedules, Pt XV, Pt XVII, Pt XVIII, other than s.261, s.264 and the Sixth Schedule, insofar as they relate to the repeals effected by art.5 of this Order, subss.(265)(1), (2) and (4), and subss.(268)(1) (d) and (3).

By the Planning and Development Act 2000 (Commencement) Order 2003, (S.I. No. 450 of 2003), s.239 came into operation on September 24, 2003.

By the Planning and Development Act 2000 (Commencement) Order 2004, (S.I. No. 152 of 2004), s.261 came into effect on April 28, 2004.

By the Planning and Development (Strategic Infrastructure) Act 2006 (Commencement) Order 2006 (1) (S.I. No. 525 of 2006), ss. 1, 2, 6(a), 7, 8, 9, 10, 11, 13, 21, 24, 26, 28, 31, 43, 44, 45, 46 and 48 of the 2006 Act came into effect on October 17, 2006.

By the Planning and Development (Strategic Infrastructure) Act 2006 (Commencement) (No.2) Order 2006(S.I. No. 553 of 2006) ss.14, 15 and 16 of the Act entered into force on November 14, 2006.

By the Planning and Development (Strategic Infrastructure) Act 2006 (Commencement) (No. 3) Order 2006 (S.I. No. 284 of 2006), ss. 3, 4, 5, 6(b), (c) and (d), 12, 17, 18, 19, 20, 22, 23, 25, 27, 29, 30, 32, 33, 34, 35, 36, 37, 38, 39, 40, 41, 42, 47, 49, 50 and 51 of the Act came into effect on January 31, 2007.

[Exempted developments not affected

1–314   **270A.**—For the avoidance of doubt, any category of exempted development by virtue of *section 4* or regulations thereunder is not affected by the amendments of this Act made by the *Planning and Development (Strategic Infrastructure) Act 2006.*]

AMENDMENT HISTORY

Inserted by s.47 of the Planning and Development (Strategic Infrastructure) Act 2006 (No. 27 of 2006).

NOTE

This new section introduced by the 2006 Act makes clear that categories of exempted development under s.4 of the 2000 Act or the categories of exempted development under the 2001 Regulations are not affected by any amendments made under the 2006 Act.

PART XX

AMENDMENTS OF ROADS ACT, 1993

Amendments of Roads Act, 1993

Amendment of section 57 of Roads Act, 1993

1–315   **271.**—Section 57 of the Roads Act, 1993, is hereby amended—
(*a*) by the substitution of the following for *subsection (l)*:
"(1) A road authority may prepare a scheme for the establishment of a system of tolls in respect of the use of a public road.",
(*b*) in subsection (2), by the substitution for "In making a toll scheme" of "In preparing a scheme under subsection (1)",
(*c*) in subsection (3), by the substitution for "toll scheme" of "scheme prepared under subsection (1)",
(*d*) in subsection (4), by the substitution for "toll scheme" of "scheme under subsection (1)",
(*e*) by the substitution of the following for subsection (5):
"(5) A road authority may prepare a scheme amending a toll scheme adopted by it under *section 58.*",
(*f*) in subsection (6), by the substitution for "toll scheme" of "scheme prepared under subsection (1)", and
(*g*) by the substitution of the following for subsection (7):
"(7)(*a*) The Authority shall, before adopting, under section 58, a scheme prepared under subsection (1) in relation to a national road, send a copy of the scheme to the appropriate road authority under section 13 and serve a notice on the road authority stating—
(i) that a scheme under subsection (1) has been prepared, and
(ii) that representations may be made in writing to the Authority in relation to the scheme before such date as is specified in the notice (being not less than 6

weeks from the date of service of the notice).

(*b*) The Authority shall consider any representations made to it pursuant to a notice under paragraph (a).

(*c*) The making of representations by a road authority under this subsection shall be a reserved function and shall be without prejudice to the right of that authority to make objections to the Authority under section 58.".

NOTE

This section makes certain amendments to s.57 of the Roads Act 1993 in relation to a toll scheme. Section 57(7) of the 1993 Act is altered by removing the requirement to obtain the approval of the Minister before a toll scheme can be adopted by the National Road Authority.

Scheme prepared under section 57 of Roads Act, 1993, to be adopted by road authority

272.—The Roads Act, 1993, is hereby amended by the substitution of the   **1–316** following section for *section 58*:

"58.—(1) A road authority shall publish in one or more news papers circulating in the area where the proposed toll road is located or is to be located a notice—

(*a*) stating that a draft toll scheme has been prepared,

(*b*) indicating the times at which, the period (being a period of not less than one month from the first publication of the notice) during which, and the place at which a copy of the scheme prepared under *section 57*, any map referred to therein and the explanatory statement relating to the scheme may be inspected, and

(*c*) stating that objections to the draft toll scheme may be made in writing to the road authority before such date as is specified in the notice (being not less than 2 weeks from the end of the period for inspection referred to in paragraph (*b*)).

(2)(*a*) Subject to *paragraph (b)*, a road authority may adopt a scheme prepared by it under *subsection (1)*, with or without modifications and, subject to *subsection (3)*, a scheme so adopted is hereafter in this Act referred to as a "toll scheme".

(*b*) If an objection to a draft toll scheme is made to the road authority and the objection is not withdrawn, the road authority shall, before deciding whether to adopt the draft toll scheme or not, cause an oral hearing to be held into the matters to which the objection relates, by a person appointed by the road authority, and shall consider the report of and any recommendation made by the person so appointed.

(3)(*a*) A toll scheme adopted by the road authority under this section shall come into force with the modifications, if any, therein made by the road authority on such day as may be determined by the road authority.

(*b*) Notice of the day on which a toll scheme is to come into force shall be published by the road authority at least one month before such day in one or more newspapers circulating in the area in which the toll road to which the scheme relates is located or will be located.".

NOTE

This section substitutes a new s.58 in the Roads Act 1993. The main effect of the substitution is to remove from the Minister the role of approving the draft toll scheme. Under the new section the decision whether to adopt the toll scheme and the carrying out of the oral hearing to objections is undertaken by the relevant road authority.

Amendment of section 60 of Roads Act, 1993

1–317   **273.**—Section 60 of the Roads Act, 1993, is hereby amended by the substitution of the following for that section:

"60.—(1) A road authority may by order revoke a toll scheme adopted by it under *section 58*.

(2) Where a road authority proposes to make an order under *subsection (1)* it shall, before so making the order, publish in one or more newspapers circulating in the area where the toll road is located a notice—

    (*a*) stating that it proposes to revoke the scheme,

    (*b*) indicating the times at which, the period (being not less than one month from the first publication of the notice) during which, and the place at which, a copy of the proposal may be inspected,

    (*c*) stating that objections or representations may be made in writing to the road authority in relation to the proposal before such date as specified in the notice (being a date that falls not less than 2 weeks from the end of the period for inspection of the proposal).

(3) Before making an order under subsection (1), the road authority shall consider any objections or representations made to it in accordance with a notice under subsection (2).

(4) A road authority may at its discretion cause an oral hearing to be held into any matter to which objections or representations, made in accordance with a notice under subsection (2) and not withdrawn, relate, by a person appointed by the road authority, and where a road authority causes an oral hearing to be so held it shall, before revoking the toll scheme under subsection (3), consider the report of and any recommendation made by that person.

(5) The road authority shall publish in one or more newspapers circulating in the area where the toll road is located notice of the making of any order under subsection (1).

(6) The making of an order under this section in relation to a regional road or a local road shall be a reserved function.".

NOTE

This section substitutes a new s.60 of the Roads Act 1993 concerning the revocation of a toll scheme. The main effect of the change is that the road authority can itself revoke a toll scheme without the need for approval of the Minister. The section further sets out the procedure for revocation, involving a newspaper notice and invitation to make submissions or observations. The road authority has a discretion whether to carry out an oral hearing into any objections, while under the former s.60, the Minster had a discretion whether to carry out a public local inquiry. Also inserted is that the road authority will appoint a person to carry out the oral hearing and that the road authority shall consider the report and recommendation arising therefrom, before revoking the scheme.

Amendment of section 61 of Roads Act, 1993

274.—Section 61 of the Roads Act, 1993, is hereby amended—   **1–318**

    (*a*) by the deletion of subsection (5),

    (*b*) by the substitution of the following subsection for subsection (6):
        "(6) Before making bye-laws, a road authority shall publish in one or more newspapers circulating in the area where the toll road to which the bye-laws relate is located or is to be located a notice—

            (*a*) indicating that it is proposed to make such bye laws and stating the purpose of the bye-laws,

            (*b*) indicating the times at which, the period (being a period of not less than one month from the date of the first publication of the notice) during which, and the place at which, a copy of the draft bye-laws may be inspected,

            (*c*) stating that objections or representations may be made in writing to the road authority in relation to the draft bye-laws before such date as is specified in the notice (being a date that falls not less than 2 weeks from the end of the period for inspection of the draft bye-laws), and

            (*d*) stating that a copy of the draft bye-laws may be purchased on payment of such fee as is specified in the notice not exceeding the reason able cost incurred in the making of such copy.".

    (*c*) by the substitution of the following subsection for subsection (7):
        "(7) Before making bye-laws the road authority shall consider any objections or representations which have been made to it in accordance with a notice under subsection (6) and not withdrawn.".

    (*d*) by the substitution of the following subsection for subsection (8):
        (8) Bye-laws made by a road authority under this section shall come into effect on such date as is specified in those bye-laws.",
        and

    (*e*) in subsection (9), by the substitution for "approved" of "made".

NOTE

    This section amends s.61 of the Roads Act 1993 in relation to making bye-laws for toll scheme. It deletes s.61(5), which provided that bye laws would have no effect unless and until the Minister approved them. The new s.61(6) provides that the newspaper notice must also indicate that it is proposed to make bye-laws and indicate the purpose of the bye-laws. Under the new s.61(7), it is the road authority rather than the Minister which considers the objections or representations. Also, the new s.61(8) removes any mention of the Minister and provides that the bye-laws enter into force on the date specified in the bye-laws.

Amendment of section 63 of Roads Act, 1993

1–319   **275.**—Section 63 of the Roads Act, 1993, is hereby amended—

    (*a*) in subsection (1), by the substitution; for "Where a toll scheme is approved by the Minister, a road authority may, with the consent of the Minister," of "Where a toll scheme is adopted by a road authority, the road authority may," and

    (*b*) in subsection (3), by the deletion of ", with the consent of the Minister,".

NOTE

    This section makes minor changes in the language of s.63 of the Roads Act 1993, such as removing the mention of the consent of the Minister.

Amendment of section 65 of Roads Act, 1993

1–320   **276.**—The Roads Act, 1993, is hereby amended in section 65 by the substitution of "section 57" of "section 58".

NOTE

    This section amends s.65 of the Roads Act 1993 by substituting the reference of "s.58" for "s.57".

Further amendment of Part V of Roads Act, 1993

1–321   **277.**—Part V of the Roads Act, 1993, is hereby amended by the insertion after section 66 of the following sections—

Ministerial policy directives on road tolling

66A.—(1) The Minister may, from time to time, issue policy directives to road authorities regarding the exercise of any of their functions under Part V or any matter connected therewith and road authorities shall comply with any such directives.

    (2) The Minister may revoke or amend a policy directive issued under this section.

    (3) The Minister shall cause a copy of any policy directive issued under this section to be laid before each House of the Oireachtas.

    (4) A road authority shall make available for inspection by members of the public any policy directive issued to it under this section.

    (5) The Minister shall not issue a directive relating to a particular tolling scheme.

Continuance of existing schemes, bye-laws and agreements

66B.—Notwithstanding this Part, every agreement entered into and every toll scheme or bye-law made by a road authority and in force immediately before the commencement of this section shall continue in force as if made or entered into under this Part as amended by the *Planning and Development Act, 2000.*

Transitional provisions regarding toll schemes

66C.—Where, before the commencement of *Part XX* of the *Planning and Development Act, 2000*, any toll scheme, proposal to revoke a toll scheme or bye-law has been submitted to the Minister under Part V and the matter has not been determined by the Minister, the determination of the matter shall continue to rest with the Minister and Part V as amended by P*art XX* of the *Planning and Development Act, 2000*, shall not apply with respect to the matter.".

AMENDMENT

Section 247(m) of the Local Government Act 2001 inserted para.20A.

NOTE

This section inserts a new s.66A, B and C, into Pt V of the Roads Act 1993. Section 66A allows the Minister to issue policy directives to road authorities regarding their functions under Pt V of the 1993 Act, with which the road authorities are obliged to comply. Part V is concerned with the toll roads. It appears that the directives must be of a general nature, with subs.(5) prohibiting the Minister from issuing directives in relation to a particular tolling scheme. The Minister may revoke or amend a policy directive and must also lay a copy of the directive before each House of the Oireachtas. The policy directives must be made available for inspection by the road authority.

Section 66B allows for the continuance in force of agreements, toll scheme or bye-laws made by the road authority as if entered into under Pt V, as amended by the 2000 Act.

Section 66C provides that where a toll scheme, a proposal to revoke a toll scheme or bye law has already been submitted to the Minister, but has yet to be determined, the amendment made under the 2000 Act, whereby the matter is to be determined by the road authority, will not apply and Minister will still determine the matter.

First Schedule 1–322

Purposes for which Objectives may be indicated in Development Plan
Location and Pattern of Development

1. Reserving or allocating any particular land, or all land in any particular area, for development of a specified class or classes, or prohibiting or restricting, either permanently or temporarily, development on any specified land.

2. Promoting sustainable settlement and transportation strategies in urban and rural areas.

3. Preserving the quality and character of urban or rural areas.

4. Regulating, restricting or controlling retail development.

5. Regulating, promoting or controlling tourism development.

6. Regulating, restricting or controlling development in areas at risk of flooding (whether inland or coastal), erosion and other natural hazards.

7. Regulating, restricting and controlling the development of coastal areas and development in the vicinity of inland waterways.

8. Regulating, restricting and controlling development on the foreshore, or any part of the foreshore.

9. Giving effect to the European Spatial Development Perspective towards balanced and sustainable development of the territory of the European Union, adopted by the meeting of Ministers responsible for Regional/Spatial Planning of the European Union at Potsdam, 10 and 11 May, 1999.

10. Regulating, restricting or controlling development in order to reduce

the risk of serious danger to human health or the environment.

11. Regulating, promoting or controlling the exploitation of natural resources.

Control of Areas and Structures

1. Regulating and controlling the layout of areas and structures, including density, spacing, grouping and orientation of structures in relation to roads, open spaces and other structures.

2. Regulating and controlling the design, colour and materials of structures and groups of structures, including streets and townscapes, and structures and groups of structures in rural areas.

3. Promoting design in structures for the purposes of flexible and sustainable use, including conservation of energy and resources.

4. Limiting the number of structures, or the number of structures of a specified class, which may be constructed, erected or made on, in or under any area.

5. Regulating and controlling, either generally or in particular areas, all or any of the following matters:
   (a) the size, height, floor area and character of structures;
   (b) building lines, coverage and the space about houses and other structures;
   (c) the extent of parking places required in, on or under structures of a particular class or size, or services or facilities for the parking, loading, unloading or fuelling of vehicles;
   (d) the objects which may be affixed to structures;
   (e) the purposes for and the manner in which structures may be used or occupied, including, in the case of a house, the letting thereof in separate units.

6. Regulating and controlling, in accordance with the principles of proper planning and sustainable development, the following:
   (a) the disposition or layout of land and structures or structures of any specified class, including the reservation of sufficient open space in relation to the number, class and character of structures in any particular development proposal, road layout, landscaping and planting;
   (b) the provision of water, waste water, waste and public lighting facilities;
   (c) the provision of service roads and the location and design of means of access to transport networks, including public transport;
   (d) the provision of facilities for parking, unloading, loading and fuelling of vehicles on any land.

7. The removal or alteration of structures which are inconsistent with the development plan.

PART III

Community Facilities

1. Facilitating the provision and siting of services and facilities necessary for the community, including the following:
   (a) hospitals and other healthcare facilities;
   (b) centres for the social, economic, recreational, cultural, environmental, or general development of the community;
   (c) facilities for the elderly and for persons with disabilities;
   (d) places of public worship and meeting halls;
   (e) recreational facilities and open spaces, including caravan and camping parks, sports grounds and playgrounds;
   (f) shopping and banking facilities.
2. Ensuring the provision and siting of sanitary services.
3. Reserving of land for burial grounds.

PART IV

Environment and Amenities

1. Protecting and preserving the quality of the environment, including the prevention, limitation, elimination, abatement or reduction of environmental pollution and the protection of waters, groundwater, the seashore and the atmosphere.

2. Securing the reduction or prevention of noise emissions or vibrations.

3. Prohibiting, regulating or controlling the deposit or disposal of waste materials, refuse and litter, the disposal of sewage and the pollution of waters.

4. Protecting features of the landscape which are of major importance for wild fauna and flora.
   (a) Preserving and protecting flora, fauna and ecological diversity.
   (b) Preserving and protecting trees, shrubs, plants and flowers.

5. Protecting and preserving (either in situ or by record) places, caves, sites, features and other objects of archaeological, geological, historical, scientific or ecological interest.

6. Preserving the character of the landscape, including views and prospects, and the amenities of places and features of natural beauty or interest.

7. Preserving any existing public right of way, including, in particular, rights of way which give access to seashore, mountain, lakeshore, riverbank or other place of natural beauty or recreational utility.

8. Reserving land as open spaces, whether public or private (other than open spaces reserved under *Part II of this Schedule*) or as a public park, public garden or public recreation space.

9. Prohibiting, restricting or controlling, either generally or in particular places or within a specified distance of the centre line of all roads or any specified road, the erection of all or any particular forms of advertisement structure or the exhibition of all or any particular forms of advertisement.

10. Preventing, remedying or removing injury to amenities arising from

the ruinous or neglected condition of any structure or from the objectionable or neglected condition of any land.

PART V

Infrastructure and Transport

1. Reserving land for transport networks, including roads, rail, light rail and air and sea transport, for communication networks, for energy generation and for energy networks, including renewable energy, and for other networks, and for ancillary facilities to service those networks.

2. Facilitating the provision of sustainable integrated transport, public transport and road traffic systems and promoting the development of local transport plans.

3. Securing the greater convenience and safety of users of all transport networks and of pedestrians and cyclists.

4. Establishment of public rights of way and extinguishment of public and private rights of way.

5. Construction, alteration, closure or diversion of roads, including cycleways and busways.

6. Establishing—

   (a) the line, width, level and construction of,

   (b) the means of access to and egress from, and

   (c) the general dimensions and character of, roads, including cycleways and busways, and, where appropriate, other transport networks, whether new or existing.

7. Providing for the management and control of traffic, including the provision and control of parking areas.

8. Providing for works incidental to the making, improvement or landscaping of any transport, communication, energy or other network.

1–323

SECOND SCHEDULE

RULES FOR THE DETERMINATION OF THE AMOUNT OF COMPENSATION

1. The reduction in value shall, subject to the other provisions of this *Schedule,* be determined by reference to the difference between the antecedent and subsequent values of the land, where—

   (a) the antecedent value of the land is the amount which the land, if sold in the open market by a willing seller immediately prior to the relevant decision under *Part III* (and assuming that the relevant application for permission had not been made), might have been expected to realise, and

   (b) the subsequent value of the land is the amount which the land, if sold in the open market by a willing seller immediately after that decision, might be expected to realise.

2. In determining the antecedent value and subsequent value of the land for the purposes of *paragraph 1* —

(a) regard shall be had to—
   (i) any contribution which a planning authority might have required or might require as a condition precedent to development of the land,
   (ii) any restriction on the development of the land which, without conferring a right to compensation, could have been or could be imposed under any *Act* or under any order, regulations, rule or bye-law made under any *Act,*
   (iii) the fact that exempted development might have been or may be carried out on the land, and
   (iv) the open market value of comparable land, if any, in the vicinity of the land whose values are being determined;
(b) no account shall be taken of—
   (i) any part of the value of the land attributable to subsidies or grants available from public moneys, or to any tax or rating allowances in respect of development, from which development of the land might benefit,
   (ii) the special suitability or adaptability of the land for any purpose if that purpose is a purpose to which it could be applied only in pursuance of statutory powers, or for which there is no market apart from the special needs of a particular purchaser or the requirements of any statutory body as defined in *paragraph 5*:
      Provided that any bona fide offer for the purchase of the land which may be brought to the notice of the arbitrator shall be taken into consideration,
   (iii) any increase in the value of land attributable to the use thereof or of any structure thereon in a manner which could be restrained by any court, or is contrary to law, or detrimental to the health of the inmates of the structure, or to public health or safety, or to the environment,
   (iv) any depreciation or increase in value attributable to the land, or any land in the vicinity, being reserved for a particular purpose in a development plan,
   (v) any value attributable to any unauthorised structure or unauthorised use,
   (vi) the existence of proposals for development of the land or any other land by a statutory body, or
   (vii) the possibility or probability of the land or other land becoming subject to a scheme of development undertaken by a statutory body; and
(c) all returns and assessments of capital value for taxation made or acquiesced in by the claimant may be considered.

3(1) In assessing the possibilities, if any, for developing the land, for the purposes of determining its antecedent value, regard shall be had only to such reasonable possibilities as, having regard to all material considerations, could be judged to have existed immediately prior to the relevant decision under Part III.

(2) Material considerations for the purposes of subparagraph (1) shall, without prejudice to the generality thereof, include—

    (a) the nature and location of the land,

    (b) the likelihood or unlikelihood, as the case may be, of obtaining permission or further permission, to develop the land in the light of the provisions of the development plan,

    (c) the assumption that, if any permission to develop the land were to be granted, any conditions which might reasonably be imposed in relation to matters referred to in the Fifth Schedule (but no other conditions) would be imposed, and

    (d) any permission to develop the land, not being permission for the development of a kind specified in section 192(2), already existing at the time of the relevant decision under Part III.

4(1) In determining the subsequent value of the land in a case in which there has been a refusal of permission—

    (a) it shall be assumed, subject to subparagraph (2), that, after the refusal, permission under Part III would not be granted for any development of a kind specified in section 192(2),

    (b) regard shall be had to any conditions in relation to matters referred to in the Fifth Schedule (but no other conditions) which might reasonably be imposed in the grant of permission to develop the land.

(2) In a case in which there has been a refusal of permission in relation to land in respect of which there is in force an undertaking under Part VI of the Act of 1963, it shall be assumed in determining the subsequent value of the land that, after the refusal, permission under Part III of this Act would not be granted for any development other than development to which the undertaking relates.

5(1) In paragraph 2, "statutory body" means—

    (a) a Minister of the Government,

    (b) the Commissioners,

    (c) a local authority within the meaning of the Local Government Act, 1941,

    (d) a harbour authority within the meaning of the Harbours Act, 1946,

    (e) a health board established under the Health Act, 1970,

    (f) a vocational education committee within the meaning of the Vocational Education Act, 1930,

    (g) a board or other body established by or under statute,

    (h) a company in which all the shares are held by, or on behalf of, or by directors appointed by, a Minister of the Government, or

    (i) a company in which all the shares are held by a board, company, or other body referred to in subparagraph (g) or (h).

(2) In clauses (h) and (i) of subparagraph (1), "company" means a company within the meaning of section 2 of the Companies Act, 1963.

THIRD SCHEDULE

1–324

DEVELOPMENT IN RESPECT OF WHICH A REFUSAL OF PERMISSION WILL NOT ATTRACT COMPENSATION

1. Any development that consists of or includes the making of any material change in the use of any structures or other land.

2. The demolition of a habitable house.

3. Any development which would materially affect a protected structure or proposed protected structure.

4. The erection of any advertisement structure.

5. The use of land for the exhibition of any advertisement.

6. Development in an area to which a special amenity area order relates.

7. Any development on land with respect to which there is available (notwithstanding the refusal of permission) a grant of permission under *Part III* for any development of a residential, commercial or industrial character, if the development consists wholly or mainly of the construction of houses, shops or office premises, hotels, garages and petrol filling stations, theatres or structures for the purpose of entertainment, or industrial buildings (including warehouses), or any combination thereof, subject to no conditions other than conditions of the kind referred to in the *Fifth Schedule.*

8. Any development on land with respect to which compensation has already been paid under *section 190, section 11 of the Act of 1990* or under *section 55 of the Act of 1963,* by reference to a previous decision under *Part III of this Act* or under *Part IV of the Act of 1963* involving a refusal of permission.

FOURTH SCHEDULE

1–325

REASONS FOR THE REFUSAL OF PERMISSION WHICH EXCLUDE COMPENSATION

1. Development of the kind proposed on the land would be premature by reference to any one or combination of the following constraints and the period within which the constraints involved may reasonably be expected to cease—

   (a) an existing deficiency in the provision of water supplies or sewerage facilities,

   (b) the capacity of existing or prospective water supplies or sewerage facilities being required for prospective development as regards which a grant of a permission under *Part III of this Act,* an undertaking under *Part VI of the Act of 1963* or a notice under *section 13 of the Act of 1990* or *section 192 of this Act* exists,

   (c) the capacity of existing or prospective water supplies or sewerage facilities being required for the prospective development of another part of the functional area of the planning authority, as indicated in the development plan,

   (d) the capacity of existing or prospective water supplies or sewerage facilities being required for any other prospective development or for any development objective, as indicated in the development plan,

(e) any existing deficiency in the road network serving the area of the proposed development, including considerations of capacity, width, alignment, or the surface or structural condition of the pavement, which would render that network, or any part of it, unsuitable to carry the increased road traffic likely to result from the development,

(f) any prospective deficiency (including the considerations specified in *subparagraph (e)*) in the road network serving the area of the proposed development which—

(i) would arise because of the increased road traffic likely to result from that development and from prospective development as regards which a grant of permission under *Part III,* an undertaking under *Part VI of the Act of 1963* or a notice under *section 13 of the Act of 1990* or *section 192* exists, or

(ii) would arise because of the increased road traffic likely to result from that development and from any other prospective development or from any development objective, as indicated in the development plan, and would render that road network, or any part of it, unsuitable to carry the increased road traffic likely to result from the proposed development.

2. Development of the kind proposed would be premature pending the determination by the planning authority or the road authority of a road layout for the area or any part thereof.

3. Development of the kind proposed would be premature by reference to the order of priority, if any, for development indicated in the development plan or pending the adoption of a local area plan in accordance with the development plan.

4. The proposed development would endanger public safety by reason of traffic hazard or obstruction of road users or otherwise.

5. The proposed development—

(a) could, due to the risk of a major accident or if a major accident were to occur, lead to serious danger to human health or the environment, or

(b) is in an area where it is necessary to limit the risk of there being any serious danger to human health or the environment.

6. The proposed development is in an area which is at risk of flooding.

7. The proposed development, by itself or by the precedent which the grant of permission for it would set for other relevant development, would adversely affect the use of a national road or other major road by traffic.

8. The proposed development would interfere with the character of the landscape or with a view or prospect of special amenity value or natural interest or beauty, any of which it is necessary to preserve.

9. The proposed development would cause serious air pollution, water pollution, noise pollution or vibration or pollution connected with the disposal of waste.

10. In the case of development including any structure or any addition to or extension of a structure, the structure, addition or extension would—

(a) infringe an existing building line or, where none exists, a building line determined by the planning authority or by the Board,

(b) be under a public road,

(c) seriously injure the amenities, or depreciate the value, of property in the vicinity,

(d) tend to create any serious traffic congestion,

(e) endanger or interfere with the safety of aircraft or the safe and efficient navigation thereof,

(f) endanger the health or safety of persons occupying or employed in the structure or any adjoining structure, or

(g) be prejudicial to public health.

11. The development would contravene materially a condition attached to an existing permission for development.

12. The proposed development would injure or interfere with a historic monument which stands registered in the Register of Historic Monuments under *section 5 of the National Monuments (Amendment) Act, 1987,* or which is situated in an archaeological area so registered.

13. The proposed development would adversely affect an architectural conservation area.

14. The proposed development would adversely affect the linguistic or cultural heritage of the Gaeltacht.

15. The proposed development would materially contravene an objective indicated in a local area plan for the area.

16. The proposed development would be contrary to any Ministerial guidelines issued to planning authorities under *section 28* or any Ministerial policy directive issued to planning authorities under *section 29.*

17. The proposed development would adversely affect a landscape conservation area.

18. In accordance with *section 35,* the planning authority considers that there is a real and substantial risk that the development in respect of which permission is sought would not be completed in accordance with any permission or any condition to which such a permission would be subject.

19. The proposed development—

(a) would contravene materially a development objective indicated in the development plan for the conservation and preservation of a European site insofar as the proposed development would adversely affect one or more specific—

  (i)

    (I) natural habitat types in *Annex I of the Habitats Directive,* or

    (II) species in *Annex II of the Habitats Directive* which the site hosts, and which have been selected by the Minister for Arts, Heritage, Gaeltacht and the Islands in accordance with *Annex III* (Stage 1) of that *Directive,*

  (ii) species of bird or their habitat or other habitat specified in *Article 4 of the Birds Directive,* which formed the basis of the classification of that site, or

(b) would have a significant adverse effect on any other areas prescribed for the purpose of *section 10(2)(c).*

20. The development would contravene materially a development objective

indicated in the development plan for the zoning of land for the use solely or primarily of particular areas for particular purposes (whether residential, commercial, industrial, agricultural, recreational, as open space or otherwise or a mixture of such uses).

[20A. The proposed development would not be consistent with a planning scheme in force in respect of a strategic development zone.]

[20B. The proposed development would not be consistent with the transport strategy of the DTA.]

21. **(a)** Subject to *paragraph 22, paragraphs 19 and 20* shall not apply in a case where a development objective for the use specified in *paragraph 20* applied to the land at any time during the period of a development plan and the development objective of which was changed as a result of a variation of the plan during such period prior to the date on which the relevant application for permission was made to develop the land, and the development would not have contravened materially that development objective.

(b) *Paragraph 20* shall not apply in a case where, as a result of a direction by the Minister under *section 31(2)* given within one year of the making of a development plan, a planning authority amends or revokes a development objective referred to in *paragraph 19* but without prejudice to any right of compensation which may otherwise arise in respect of any refusal of permission under *Part III* in respect of an application made before such direction was issued by the Minister.

22. *Paragraph 21* shall not apply in a case where a person acquired his or her interest in the land—

(a) after the objective referred to in *paragraph 19 or 20* has come into operation, or

(b) after notice has been published,

   (i) in accordance with *section 12 or 13,* of a proposed new development plan or of proposed variations of a development plan, as the case may be, or

   (ii) in accordance with *section 12,* of a material alteration of the draft concerned, indicating in draft the development objective referred to in *paragraph 19 or 20,* or

(c) in the case of *paragraph 19,* after notice has been published by the Minister for Arts, Heritage, Gaeltacht and the Islands of his or her intention to propose that the land be selected as a European site.

23. For the purposes of *paragraph 22,* the onus shall be on a person to prove all relevant facts relating to his or her interest in the land to the satisfaction of the planning authority.

24. In this *Schedule,* "road authority" and "national road" have the meanings assigned to them in the *Roads Act, 1993.*

AMENDMENT HISTORY

Paragraph 20A inserted by s.247 of the Local Government Act 2001 (No. 37 of 2001), which, by the Local Government Act, 2001 (Commencement) Order 2001 (S.I. No. 458 of 2001), came into effect on October 9, 2001.

Paragraph 20B inserted by s.94 of the Dublin Transport Authority Act 2008, to come into force on such date as the Minister may appoint.

FIFTH SCHEDULE

1–326

CONDITIONS WHICH MAY IMPOSED, ON THE GRANTING OF PERMISSION TO DEVELOP LAND, WITHOUT COMPENSATION

1. A condition, under *paragraphs (g) and (j) of section 34(4)*, requiring the giving of security for satisfactory completion of the proposed development (including maintenance until taken in charge by the local authority concerned of roads, open spaces, carparks, sewers, watermains or drains).

2. A condition, included in a grant of permission pursuant to *section 48 or 49*, requiring the payment of a contribution for public infrastructure benefitting the development.

3. A condition, under *paragraph (n) of section 34(4)*, requiring the removal of an advertisement structure.

4. Any condition under *paragraph (n) of section 34(4)* in a case in which the relevant application for permission relates to a temporary structure.

5. Any condition relating to the reservation or allocation of any particular land, or all land in any particular area, for development of a specified class or classes, or the prohibition or restriction either permanently or temporarily, of development on any specified land.

6. Any condition relating to the preservation of the quality and character of urban or rural areas.

7. Any condition relating to the regulation, restriction and control of development of coastal areas or development in the vicinity of inland waterways.

8. Any provision relating to the protection of the linguistic or cultural heritage of the Gaeltacht.

9. Any condition relating to reducing the risk or limiting the consequences of a major accident, or limiting the risk of there being any serious danger to human health or the environment.

10. Any condition regulating, restricting or controlling development in areas at risk of flooding.

11. Any condition relating to—

    (a) the regulation and control of the layout of areas and structures, including density, spacing, grouping and orientation of structures in relation to roads, open spaces and other structures,

    (b) the regulation and control of the design, colour and materials of structures and groups of structures,

    (c) the promotion of design in structures for the purposes of flexible and sustainable use, including conservation of energy and resources.

12. Any condition limiting the number of structures or the number of structures of a specified class which may be constructed, erected or made on, in or under any area.

13. Any condition regulating and controlling all or any of the following matters—

    (a) the size, height, floor area and character of structures;

    (b) building lines, coverage and the space about houses and other structures;

    (c) the extent of parking places required in, on or under structures of a particular class or size or services or facilities for the parking, loading, unloading or fuelling of vehicles;

    (d) the objects which may be affixed to structures;

    (e) the purposes for and the manner in which structures may be used or occupied, including, in the case of dwellings, the letting thereof in separate units.

14. Any condition relating to the alteration or removal of unauthorised structures.

15. Any condition relating to the provision and siting of sanitary services and waste facilities, recreational facilities and open spaces.

16. Any condition relating to the protection and conservation of the environment including the prevention of environmental pollution and the protection of waters, groundwater, the seashore and the atmosphere.

17. Any condition relating to measures to reduce or prevent the emission or the intrusion of noise or vibration.

18. Any condition prohibiting, regulating or controlling the deposit or disposal of waste materials and refuse, the disposal of sewage and the pollution of rivers, lakes, ponds, gullies and the seashore.

19. Any condition relating to the protection of features of the landscape which are of major importance for wild fauna and flora.

20. Any condition relating to the preservation and protection of trees, shrubs, plants and flowers.

21. Any condition relating to the preservation (either in situ or by record) of places, caves, sites, features or other objects of archaeological, geological, historical, scientific or ecological interest.

22. Any condition relating to the conservation and preservation of—

    (a) one or more specific—

      (i)

        (I) natural habitat types in *Annex I of the Habitats Directive,* or

        (II) species in *Annex II of the Habitats Directive* which the site hosts, contained in a European site selected by the Minister for Arts, Heritage, Gaeltacht and the Islands in accordance with *Annex III* (Stage 1) of that *Directive,*

      (ii) species of bird or their habitat or other habitat contained in a European site specified in *Article 4 of the Birds Directive,* which formed the basis of the classification of that site, or

    (b) any other area prescribed for the purpose of *section 10(2)(c).*

23. Any condition relating to the preservation of the landscape in general, or a landscape conservation order in particular, including views and prospects and amenities of places and features of natural beauty or interest.

24. Any condition for preserving any existing public right of way.

25. Any condition reserving, as a public park, public garden or public recreation space, land normally used as such.

26. Any condition prohibiting, restricting or controlling, either generally or

within a specified distance of the centre line of any specified road, the erection of all or any particular forms of advertisement structure or the exhibition of all or any particular forms of advertisement.

27. Any condition preventing, remedying or removing injury to amenities arising from the ruinous or neglected condition of any structure, or from the objectionable or neglected condition of any land attached to a structure or abutting on a public road or situate in a residential area.

28. Any condition relating to a matter in respect of which a requirement could have been imposed under any other *Act,* or under any order, regulation, rule or bye-law made under any other *Act,* without liability for compensation.

29. Any condition prohibiting the demolition of a habitable house.

30. Any condition relating to the filling of land.

31. Any condition in the interest of ensuring the safety of aircraft or the safe and efficient navigation thereof.

32. Any condition determining the sequence in which works shall be carried out or specifying a period within which works shall be completed.

33. Any condition restricting the occupation of any structure included in a development until the completion of other works included in the development or until any other specified condition is complied with or until the planning authority consents to such occupation.

34. Any conditions relating to the protection of a protected structure or a proposed protected structure.

Sixth Schedule

Enactments Repealed

1–327

Omitted.

Acts referred to

Acquisition of Land (Assessment of Compensation) Act, 1919 (9&10 Geo. c. 5)
Air Pollution Act, 1987 (1987, No. 6)
Capital Acquisitions Tax Act, 1976 (1976, No. 8)
Casual Trading Act, 1995 (1995, No. 19)
City and County Management (Amendment) Act, 1955 (1955, No. 12)
Civil Service Regulation Act, 1956 (1956, No. 46)
Companies Act, 1963 (1963, No. 33)
Companies Act, 1990 (1990, No. 33)
Companies Acts, 1963 to *1999*
County Management Acts, 1940 to *1994*
Derelict Sites Act, 1990 (1990, No. 14)
Dublin Docklands Development Authority Act. 1997 (1997, No. 7)
Environmental Protection Agency Act, 1992 (1992, No. 7)
Ethics in Public Office Act, 1995 (1995, No. 22)
European Communities Act, 1972 (1972, No. 27)
European Parliament Elections Act, 1997 (1997, No. 2)
Foreshore Act, 1933 (1933, No. 12)
Foreshore Acts, 1933 to *1998*
Freedom of Information Act, 1997 (1997, No. 13)
Harbours Act, 1946 (1946, No. 9)
Health Act, 1970 (1970, No. 1)
Holidays (Employees) Act, 1973 (1973, No. 25)

Housing Act, 1966 (1966, No. 21)
Housing Act, 1988 (1988, No. 28)
Housing Acts, 1966 to *1998*
Housing (Miscellaneous Provisions) Act, 1992 (1992, No. 18)
Housing of the Working Classes Act, 1890 (53&54 Vict. c. 70)
Housing (Traveller Accommodation) Act, 1998 (1998, No. 33)
Land Reclamation Act, 1949 (1949, No. 25)
Landlord and Tenant Acts, 1967 to *1994*
Lands Clauses Consolidation Act, 1845 (8 Vict. c. 18)
Local Authorities (Officers and Employees) Act, 1926 (1926, No. 39)
Local Government Act, 1925 (1925, No. 5)
Local Government Act, 1941 (1941, No. 23)
Local Government Act, 1946 (1946, No. 24)
Local Government Act, 1955 (1955, No. 9)
Local Government Act, 1991 (1991, No. 11)
Local Government Act, 1994 (1994, No. 8)
Local Government (Ireland) Act, 1898 (61&62 Vict. c. 37)
Local Government (No. 2) Act, 1960 (1960, No. 40)
Local Government (Planning and Development) Act, 1963 (1963, No. 28)
Local Government (Planning and Development) Act, 1976 (1976, No. 20)
Local Government (Planning and Development) Act, 1982 (1982, No. 21)
Local Government (Planning and Development) Act, 1983 (1983, No. 28)
Local Government (Planning and Development) Act, 1990 (1990, No. 11)
Local Government (Planning and Development) Act, 1992 (1992, No. 14)
Local Government (Planning and Development) Act, 1993 (1993, No. 12)
Local Government (Planning and Development) Act, 1998 (1998, No. 9)
Local Government (Planning and Development) Act, 1999 (1999, No. 17)
Local Government (Planning and Development) Acts, 1963 to *1999*
Local Government (Sanitary Services) Act, 1962 (1962, No. 26)
Local Government (Sanitary Services) Act, 1964 (1964, No. 29)
Local Government (Sanitary Services) Acts, 1878 to *1995*
Local Government (Water Pollution) Act, 1977 (1977, No. 1)
Mines and Quarries Act, 1965 (1965, No. 7)
Ministers and Secretaries (Amendment) Act, 1956 (1956, No. 21)
National Monuments Acts, 1930 to *1994*
National Monuments (Amendment) Act, 1987 (1987, No. 17)
Petty Sessions (Ireland) Act, 1851 (14&15 Vict. c. 93)
Property Values (Arbitration and Appeals) Act, 1960 (1960, No. 45)
Public Health (Ireland) Act, 1878 (41&42 Vict. c. 52)
Registration of Title Act, 1964 (1964, No. 16)
Roads Act, 1993 (1993, No. 14)
Roads Acts, 1993 and *1998*
Roads (Amendment) Act, 1998 (1998, No. 23)
State Property Act, 1954 (1954, No. 25)
Town and Regional Planning Act, 1934 (1934, No. 22)
Urban Renewal Act, 1998 (1998, No. 27)
Vocational Education Act, 1930 (1930, No. 29)
Waste Management Act, 1996 (1996, No. 10)
Water Supplies Act, 1942 (1942, No. 1)
Waterworks Clauses Act, 1847 (10&11 Vict. c. 17)
Wildlife Act, 1976 (1976, No. 39)

Infrastructure Developments for the purposes of sections 37A and 37B

[Section 37A.

Section 1.

Energy Infrastructure

1. Development comprising or for the purposes of any of the following:
   — An installation for the onshore extraction of petroleum or natural gas
   — A crude oil refinery (excluding an undertaking manufacturing only lubricants from crude oil) or an installation for the gasification and liquefaction of 500 tonnes or more of coal or bituminous shale per day.
   — A thermal power station or other combustion installation with a total energy output of 300 megawatts or more.
   — An industrial installation for the production of electricity, steam or hot water with a heat output of 300 megawatts or more.
   — An industrial installation for carrying gas, steam or hot water with a potential heat output of 300 megawatts or more, or transmission of electrical energy by overhead cables, where the voltage would be 220 kilovolts or more, but excluding any proposed development referred to in *section 182A(1)*.
   — An oil pipeline and any associated terminals, buildings and installations, where the length of the pipeline (whether as originally provided or as extended) would exceed 20 kilometres.
   — An installation for surface storage of natural gas, where the storage capacity would exceed 200 tonnes.
   — An installation for underground storage of combustible gases, where the storage capacity would exceed 200 tonnes.
   — An installation for the surface storage of oil or coal, where the storage capacity would exceed 100,000 tonnes.
   — An installation for hydroelectric energy production with an output of 300 megawatts or more, or where the new or extended superficial area of water impounded would be 30 hectares or more, or where there would be a 30 per cent change in the maximum, minimum or mean flows in the main river channel.
   — An installation for the harnessing of wind power for energy production (a wind farm) with more than 50 turbines or having a total output greater than 100 megawatts.
   — An onshore terminal, building or installation, whether above or below ground, associated with a natural gas storage facility, where the storage capacity would exceed 1mscm.
   — An onshore terminal, building or installation, whether above or below ground, associated with an LNG facility and, for the purpose of this provision, "LNG facility" means a terminal which is used for

the liquefaction of natural gas or the importation, offloading and re-gasification of liquefied natural gas, including ancillary services.

Section 2.

Transport Infrastructure

2. Development comprising or for the purposes of any of the following:
   — An intermodal transhipment facility, an intermodal terminal or a passenger or goods facility which, in each case, would exceed 5 hectares in area.
   — A terminal, building or installation associated with a long-distance railway, tramway, surface, elevated or underground railway or railway supported by suspended lines or similar lines of a particular type, used exclusively or mainly for passenger transport, but excluding any proposed railway works referred to in *section 37(3) of the Transport (Railway Infrastructure) Act 2001* (as amended by the *Planning and Development (Strategic Infrastructure) Act 2006*).
   — An airport (with not less than 2 million instances of passenger use per annum) or any runway, taxiway, pier, car park, terminal or other facility or installation related to it (whether as regards passenger traffic or cargo traffic).
   — A harbour or port installation—
      (a) where the area or additional area of water enclosed would be 20 hectares or more, or
      (b) which would involve the reclamation of 5 hectares or more of land, or
      (c) which would involve the construction of one or more quays which or each of which would exceed 100 metres in length, or
      (d) which would enable a vessel of over 1350 tonnes to enter within it.

Section 3.

Environmental Infrastructure

3. Development comprising or for the purposes of any of the following:
   — A waste disposal installation for—
      (a) the incineration, or
      (b) the chemical treatment (within the meaning of Annex IIA to Council Directive 75/442/EEC1 (O.J. No. L194/39 25.7.1975) under heading D9), or
      (c) the landfill,
of hazardous waste to which Council Directive 91/689/EEC (O.J. No. L377/20 31.12.1991) applies (other than an industrial waste disposal installation integrated into a larger industrial facility).
   — A waste disposal installation for—

    (a) the incineration, or

    (b) the chemical treatment (within the meaning of Annex IIA to Council Directive 75/442/EEC1 under heading D9),

of non-hazardous waste with a capacity for an annualintake greater than 100,000 tonnes.

— An installation for the disposal, treatment or recovery of waste with a capacity for an annual intake greater than 100,000 tonnes.

— A groundwater abstraction or artificial groundwater recharge scheme, where the annual volume of water abstracted or recharged is equivalent to or exceeds 2 million cubic metres.

— Any works for the transfer of water resources between river basins, where the annual volume of water abstracted or recharged would exceed 2 million cubic metres.

— A waste water treatment plant with a capacity greater than a population equivalent of 10,000 and, for the purpose of this provision, population equivalent shall be determined in accordance with *Article 2,* point 6, of Council Directive 91/271/EEC3.

— A sludge-deposition site with the capacity for the annual deposition of 50,000 tonnes of sludge (wet).

— Any canalisation or flood relief works where—

    (a) the immediate contributing sub-catchment of the proposed works (namely the difference between the contributing catchments at the upper and lower extent of the works) would exceed 1000 hectares, or

    (b) more than 20 hectares of wetland would be affected, or

    (c) the length of river channel on which works are proposed would be greater than 2 kilometres.

— A dam or other installation designed for the holding back or the permanent or long-term storage of water, where the new or extended area of water impounded would be 30 hectares or more or where a new or additional amount of water held back or stored would exceed 10 million cubic metres.

— An installation of overground aqueducts each of which would have a diameter of 1,000 millimetres or more and a length of 500 metres or more.

— Any coastal works to combat erosion or maritime works capable of altering the coast through the construction, for example, of dikes, moles, jetties and other sea defence works, where in each case the length of coastline on which the works would take place would exceed 1 kilometre, but excluding the maintenance or reconstruction of such works or works required for emergency purposes.

— 3O.J. No. L135/40 30.5.1991

AMENDMENT HISTORY

    Seventh Schedule inserted by s.5 of the Planning and Development (Strategic Infrastructure) Act 2006 (No. 27 of 2006).

NOTE

This Schedule enlists the categories of development to which the special strategic development procedure under ss.37A and 37B applies. The three general categories of development comprise energy infrastructure, environmental infrastructure and transport infrastructure. The development may be carried out by any party including local authorities and state authorities as well as private developers.

PLANNING AND DEVELOPMENT (STRATEGIC INFRASTRUCTURE) ACT 2006
(2006 No.27)

[Amendments which do not form part of the Planning and Development Act 2000 as amended]

PART 4

MISCELLANEOUS

Amendment of Acquisition of Land (Assessment of Compensation) Act 1919

48.—(1) Section 2 of the Acquisition of Land (Assessment of Compensation) Act 1919, as it stands amended in cases where any compensation assessed will be payable by a planning authority or any other local authority, is amended by inserting the following Rule after Rule (16):   **2–00**

"(17) The value of any land lying 10 metres or more below the surface of that land shall be taken to be nil, unless it is shown to be of a greater value by the claimant."

(2) Where the provisions of the Acquisition of Land (Assessment of Compensation) Act 1919 fall to be applied in the assessment of any compensation that a person, other than a planning authority or other local authority, may be liable to pay, a like provision to the Rule inserted by subsection (1) shall be regarded as having effect in relation to the assessment of that compensation.

NOTE

This section amends s.2 of the Acquisition of Land (Assessment of Compensation) Act 1919, which concerns assessment of compensation to be paid by a local authority in case of compulsory acquisition. A new r.17 is added which provides that it will be assumed that the value of land 10 metres or more below the surface will be taken as nil, unless the claimant rebuts any such assumption. This rule also applies where a person other than a local authority may be liable to pay compensation.

Amendment of Transport (Railway Infrastructure) Act 2001

49.—The Transport (Railway Infrastructure) Act 2001 is amended—   **2–01**
    (a) in section 2—
        (i) in the definition of "environmental impact statement", by substituting "section 37(3)(e)" for "section 37(2)(d)",
        (ii) by inserting after the definition of "planning authority" the following definition:
        " 'prescribed', in Part 3, means prescribed by regulations made by the Minister for the Environment, Heritage and Local Government;",
        and
        (iii) in the definition of "railway undertaking", by substituting "section 43(5)" for "section 43(6)",

and

(b) by substituting the following sections for sections 37 to 47 (as amended by the Railway Safety Act 2005):

AMENDMENT HISTORY

This section makes certain minor changes to the definitions section of the Transport (Railway Infrastructure) Act 2001 and inserts new ss.37 to 47 into that Act concerning a railway order. An application for a railway order falls within the definition of an application of "strategic infrastructure development" as now inserted by s.6 of this Act into s.2 of the 2000 Act as amended.

[Application for a railway order

2–02   **37.**—(1) The Agency, CIE, or any other person with the consent of the Agency, may apply to An Bord Pleanála (referred to subsequently in this Act as the "Board") for a railway order.

(2) An application under subsection (1) shall specify if it is as a light rail, a metro or otherwise that the applicant desires the railway concerned be designated by the order.

(3) An application under subsection (1) shall be made in writing in such form as the Minister may specify and shall be accompanied by—

(a) a draft of the proposed order,

(b) a plan of the proposed railway works,

(c) in the case of an application by the Agency or a person with the consent of the Agency, a plan of any proposed commercial development of land adjacent to the proposed railway works,

(d) a book of reference to a plan required under this subsection (indicating the identity of the owners and of the occupiers of the lands described in the plan), and

(e) a statement of the likely effects on the environment (referred to subsequently in this Part as an 'environmental impact statement') of the proposed railway works,

and a draft plan and book of reference shall be in such form as the Minister may specify or in a form to the like effect.

(4) The construction of railway works, the subject of an application for a railway order under this Part, shall not be undertaken unless the Board has granted an order under section 43.

NOTE

The main change in this section is that an application for a railway order is made to An Bord Pleanála rather than the Minister for Transport. Subsection (2) adds a new requirement for an application to state whether the application is for light rail, a metro or otherwise. Article 214 of the 2001 Regulations (as inserted by the 2006 Regulations) provides that when making an application for strategic infrastructure development (which includes an application for a railway order), the applicant shall send to the Board:

- 10 copies of the plans and particulars of the proposed development (including any plans, particulars or other information indicated by the Board under art.210(2) and of the EIS;
- a copy of the published newspaper notice in accordance as may be appropriate;
- a list of the bodies notified of the application, as may be appropriate, and an indication of the date on which notice was sent; and

- a list of any other public notice given or other public consultations conducted by the applicant, including any notice or consultations done on foot of a requirement by the Board under art.210, and an indication of the date or dates of such additional notice or consultations.

Article 214(2) states that where the Board so consents or specifies, any or all of the copies or other information specified in subart.(1) shall be given in electronic form. The former subs.(4) is deleted which provided that the Minister was required to acknowledge receipt of the application within 14 days of receiving the application.

Exempted development

38.—Each of the following shall be exempted development for the purposes   **2–03**
of the Act of 2000:

   (a) development consisting of the carrying out of railway works, including the use of the railway works or any part thereof for the purposes of the operation of a railway, authorised by the Board and specified in a railway order or of any incidental or temporary works connected with such development;

   (b) development consisting of the carrying out of railway works for the maintenance, improvement or repair of a railway that has been built pursuant to a railway order.

NOTE

The only change in this new subsection is to replace the former reference to the Minister with "An Bord Pleanála". The section exempts railway works where authorised by a railway order from the requirement to obtain planning permission under the 2000 Act as amended. "Railways works" is defined in s.2 of the 2001 Act as:

"[A]ny works required for the purposes of a railway or any part of a railway, including works ancillary to the purposes aforesaid such as parking by buses or by persons using vehicles who intend to complete their journey by railway, and relocation of utilities, and in this definition 'works' includes any act or operation of construction, excavation, tunnelling, demolition, extension, alteration, reinstatement, reconstruction, making good, repair or renewal".

Railway works may also be exempted development without the need for a railway order where they fall within any general categories of exempted development under s.4 of the 2000 Act as amended. See *McCabe v CIE*, unreported, High Court, Herbert J., November 10, 2006. Railways works may also be exempted under Classes 22 and 23 of Pt I of Sch.2 to the 2001 Regulations. Where railway works have been authorised under a railway order, subsequent works for its maintenance and improvement will also be exempted development.

Environmental impact statement

39.—(1) An environmental impact statement shall contain the following   **2–04**
information:

   (a) a description of the proposed railway works comprising information on the site, design and size of the proposed railway works;

   (b) a description of the measures envisaged in order to avoid, reduce and, if possible, remedy significant adverse effects;

   (c) the data required to identify and assess the main effects which the proposed railway works are likely to have on the environment;

   (d) an outline of the main alternatives studied by the applicant and an indication of the main reasons for its choice, taking into account the environmental effects; and

(e) a summary in non-technical language of the above information.

(2) An environmental impact statement shall, in addition to and by way of explanation or amplification of the specified information referred to in subsection (1), contain further information on the following matters:

(a)   (i) a description of the physical characteristics of the whole proposed railway works and the land use requirements during the construction and operational phases,

       (ii) an estimate, by type and quantity, of the expected residues and emissions (including water, air and soil pollution, noise, vibration, light, heat and radiation) resulting from the operation of the proposed railway works;

(b) a description of the aspects of the environment likely to be significantly affected by the proposed railway works, including in particular-

       (i) human beings, fauna and flora,

       (ii) soil, water, air, climatic factors and the landscape,

       (iii) material assets, including the architectural and archaeological heritage, and the cultural heritage,

       (iv) the inter-relationship between the matters referred to in this paragraph;

(c) a description of the likely significant effects (including direct, indirect, secondary, cumulative, short, medium and long-term, permanent and temporary, positive and negative) of the proposed railway works on the environment resulting from

       (i) the existence of the proposed railway works,

       (ii) the use of natural resources,

       (iii) the emission of pollutants, the creation of nuisances and the elimination of waste,

and a description of the forecasting methods used to assess the effects on the environment;

(d) an indication of any difficulties (technical deficiencies or lack of know-how) encountered by the applicant in compiling the required information; and

(e) a summary in non-technical language of the above information,

to the extent that such information is relevant to a given stage of the consent procedure and to the specific characteristics of the railway works or type of railway works concerned, and of the environmental features likely to be affected, and the applicant may reasonably be required to compile such information having regard, amongst other things, to current knowledge and methods of assessment.

(3) (a) If a person, before applying to the Board for a railway order, so requests, the Board shall, after consulting the person and such bodies as may be specified by the Minister for the Environment, Heritage and Local Government for that purpose, give a written opinion on the information to be contained in an environmental impact statement.

(b) The giving of a written opinion in accordance with this subsection shall not prejudice the exercise by the Board of its powers pursuant to this Act to require an applicant to furnish further information in relation to the effects on the environment of the proposed railway works.

(4) The European Communities (Environmental Impact Assessment) Regulations 1989 to 2005 and the Act of 2000 and any regulation made thereunder in relation to environmental impact assessment shall not apply to anything done under an order made under this Act.

Note

This section concerns the requirement to submit an EIS with the application for a railway order. The only substantive change from the former s.39 is that the former references to the Minister are replaced with "An Bord Pleanála", as being the decision making authority. As with the former section, subs.(4) provides that the EIA Regulations and the Planning Regulations which contain articles concerning EISs are not applicable to railway orders. The matters to be contained in an EIS for a railway order are more detailed than the contents of an EIS under the Planning Regulations. Nonetheless the contents of an EIS set out in subss.(1) and (2) are similar to Sch.6 to the 2001 Regulations. Where an EIS has been carried out, the court will not enter an investigation as to the quality of the EIS undertaken. See *Kenny v An Bord Pleanála (No. 1)* [2001] 1 I.R. 565, where McKechnie J. said:

"[O]nce the statutory requirements have been satisfied I should not concern myself with the qualitative nature of the EIS or the debate on it had before the Inspector. These are not matters of concern to this Court".

See also *Klohn v An Bord Pleanála,* unreported, High Court, McMahon J., April 23, 2008; *Browne v An Bord Pleanála* [1989] I.L.R.M. 865 and *Waddington v An Bord Pleanála,* unreported, High Court, Butler J., December 21, 2000; *Murphy v Wicklow County Council,* unreported, High Court, Kearns J., March 19, 1999; *Arklow Holidays Ltd v Wicklow County Council,* unreported, High Court, Murphy J., October 15, 2003; *Kildare County Council v An Bord Pleanála,* unreported, High Court, McMenamin J., March 10, 2006.

Publication of notice in relation to application for railway order

40.—(1) Before an application is made for a railway order, the applicant shall— **2–05**

(a) deposit and keep deposited at such place or places, being a place or places which is or are easily accessible to the public, as may be appointed by the Board, a copy of the draft order and all documents which will accompany the application, for not less than 6 weeks following the publication of the notice referred to in paragraph (b),

(b) publish a notice in one or more newspapers circulating in the area to which the order relates-
  (i) indicating that an application will be made for an order,
  (ii) indicating the time and the place or places at which, and the period (which shall be 6 weeks) during which, a copy of the draft order and accompanying documents deposited under this section may be inspected,
  (iii) stating that the Board will consider any submissions in relation to the proposed order or in relation to the likely effects on the environment of the proposed railway works which are submitted in writing to it by any person within the period referred to in subparagraph (ii),

(iv) stating that a copy of or extract from the draft order and accompanying documents may be purchased on payment of a fee not exceeding the reasonable cost of making such copy or extract, and

(v) stating, if it be the case, that the proposed railway works are likely to have significant effects on the environment in Northern Ireland,

(c) serve on the planning authority in whose functional area (or any part thereof) the proposed railway works are proposed to be carried out, on the Minister and on such other persons (if any) as the Board may direct a copy of the draft order and accompanying documents and the notice referred to in paragraph (b),

(d) serve a copy of the notice referred to in paragraph (b) together with relevant extracts from the documents referred to in paragraph (a) on every (if any) occupier and every (if any) owner of a land referred to in the draft order, and

(e) in a case where-

(i) the proposed railway works are likely to have significant effects on the environment in Northern Ireland, or

(ii) the authority referred to subsequently in this paragraph requests that such a copy be so sent to it,

send a copy of the environmental impact statement to the prescribed authority in Northern Ireland, together with a notice, in such form as may be prescribed, stating that an application for approval of the said works has been made and that submissions may be made in writing to the Board (during the period specified in the notice referred to in subsection (1)(b)) in relation to the likely effects on the environment of the said works.

(2) Members of the public may inspect a copy of a draft railway order and accompanying documents deposited under this section free of charge at the times and during the period specified in the notice referred to in subsection (1)(b) and may purchase copies of or extracts from any of the documents aforesaid on payment of a fee to the applicant not exceeding the reasonable cost of making such copies or extracts as may be fixed by the applicant.

(3) A person may, during the period specified in the notice referred to in subsection (1)(h), make submissions in writing to the Board in relation to the proposed railway order or the likely effects on the environment of the proposed railway works.

(4) Where the environmental impact statement and a notice referred to in subsection (1)(e) has been sent to the prescribed authority in Northern Ireland pursuant to that provision, the Agency, CIE, or the Board, in the case of any other applicant, as appropriate, shall enter into consultations with that authority regarding the potential effects on the environment of the proposed railway works and the measures envisaged to reduce or eliminate such effects.

Note

This section concerns the requirement to give notice of the application for a railway order and so makes some changes to the former s.40. The requirement to deposit a copy of the railway order and to publish a newspaper notice must now take place before the application for a railway order is made to the Board. Under the former s.40, these requirements arose after the application for a railway order was lodged and within 14 days of the Minister acknowledging receipt of the application. The documents must be on display for six weeks from the publication of the public notice which increases the period from 28 days under the former s.40. Subsection (2) makes some changes to the content of the public notice. These include that it deletes the former requirement to state that a public inquiry will be held into the application. The minimum period for making submissions is now six weeks. The period for making submissions is the same period during which the documents are available for public inspection. This removes the contradictory references in the former s.40 which provided that submissions may be made within 30 days after the period during which the documents are available for inspection but also said that the Minister must consider submission made within 14 days after the period during which the documents were available for inspection. The notice must state that the Board will consider submissions received by the Board within the relevant period when the documents are available for inspection, while the former subsection provided that the Minister must consider submissions received within 14 days after the period during which the application was available for inspection. Subparagraph 1(b)(v) is new and provides that the notice must state, if it be the case, that the proposed railway works are likely to have significant effects on the environment in Northern Ireland. Subparagraph (c) now provides that the documents must be served on the Minister, which reflects the change that the Board rather than the Minister determines the application. Other changes include new subsections concerning giving notice (and submission of the EIS) to the prescribed authorities in Northern Ireland. Notice must be sent to the prescribed authority in Northern Ireland where it is likely to have significant effects on the environment in Northern Ireland or where such authority requests the documents. The Northern Ireland authority may make such request even where the works are not likely to have significant effects on the environment. Consultations must be entered into with the Northern Ireland authority regarding the potential effects on the environment of the proposed railway works and the measures envisaged to reduce or eliminate such effects.

Further information to Board

41.—(1) Where the Board is of the opinion that an environmental impact   **2–06** statement furnished under section 37 does not comply with the provisions of section 39 or where it otherwise considers it necessary so to do, it shall require the applicant to furnish to it a document containing such further information in relation to the proposed railway works as it may specify and the applicant shall comply with any such requirement within such period as the Board specifies.

   (2) (a) If the document furnished under subsection (1) contains significant data in relation to the likely effects on the environment of the proposed railway works, the Board shall require the applicant

     (i) to deposit and keep deposited at the place or each of the places appointed by the Board, a copy of the aforesaid document,

    (ii) to publish in one or more newspapers circulating in the area to which the proposed railway order relates a notice stating that further information in relation to the likely effects on the environment of the proposed railway works has been furnished to the Board, that copies of the document containing the information will be available for inspection free of charge and for purchase by members of the public, at the place or each of the places appointed by the Board, at specified times during the period of not less than 3 weeks beginning on the day of publication of the notice and that submissions in relation to the further information may be made to the Board before the expiration of the said period, and

   (iii) to serve notice of the furnishing of the further information to the Board, together with relevant extracts from the document aforesaid, on any person on whom notice was served pursuant to section 40(1) and to indicate to the person concerned that submissions in relation to the further information may be made to the Board during the period of not less than 3 weeks beginning on the day on which the notice is sent to the person concerned by the applicant.

  (b) Copies of further information in respect of which notice is published pursuant to a requirement under subsection (2)(a)(ii) shall be made available for purchase by members of the public during the period specified in the notice referred to in that provision for such fee as the applicant may fix not exceeding the reasonable cost of making such copies.

(3) Members of the public may inspect the further information deposited under this section free of charge at the times and during the period specified in the notice referred to in subsection (2)(a)(ii).

(4) A person may, during the period specified in the notice referred to in paragraph (a)(ii) or (iii), as appropriate, of subsection (2), make submissions in writing to the Board in relation to the further information deposited under this section.

NOTE

This section concerns requests for further information by the Board. It makes some minor changes which relate to the substitution of "the Board" for the Minister in making the request and provides that where a newspaper notice is required to be published due to significant additional information being received, the period for inspection and making submissions is not less than three weeks. In any proceeding to challenge a decision of the Board not to require a notice, the courts will tend to defer to the decision of the Board that such information was not significant unless such decision was irrational. See *Kinsella v Dundalk Town Council*, unreported, High Court, Kelly J., December 3, 2004, and *Dietacaron Ltd v An Bord Pleanála* [2005] 2 I.L.R.M. 32 and *White v Dublin City Council* [2004] 1 I.R. 545. Under the former s.41, the period for inspection and making submission was specified as 28 days, while under subs.(2) the period must not be less than 3 weeks.

Oral hearings

2–07   **42.**—(1) The Board may, at its absolute discretion, hold an oral hearing into an application for a railway order.

(2) Sections 135, 143 and 146 of the Act of 2000 (as amended by the Planning and Development (Strategic Infrastructure) Act 2006) shall apply and have effect in relation to an oral hearing referred to in subsection (1) and those sections shall be construed accordingly.

NOTE

This section concerns oral hearings into an application for a railway order and provides that the holding of an oral is a matter for the discretion of the Board. This is a significant change as under the former s.42, there was an obligation on the Minister to hold a public inquiry. However, in a particular case, support may be placed on art.6(1) of the European Convention on Human Rights to justify a right to oral hearing. See *Adlard v Secretary of State* [2002] P & CR 202. The former s.42 also set out detailed provisions governing the conduct of such public inquiry. Subsection (2) provides that the general provisions of the 2006 Act concerning the conduct of oral hearings also applies to an oral hearing into an application for a railway order.

Railway order

43.—(1) Whenever an application is made under section 37, the Board shall, **2–08** before deciding whether to grant the order to which the application relates, consider the following:

(a) the application;

(b) the draft order and documents that accompanied the application;

(c) the report of any oral hearing held under section 42 and the recommendations (if any) contained therein;

(d) any submission duly made to it under section 40(3) or 41(4) and not withdrawn;

(e) any submission duly made to it by an authority referred to in section 40(1)(c) or (e);

(f) any additional information furnished to it under section 41;

(g) the likely consequences for proper planning and sustainable development in the area in which it is proposed to carry out the railway works and for the environment of such works; and (6) the matters referred to in section 143 (inserted by the Planning and Development (Strategic Infrastructure) Act 2006) of the Act of 2000.

(2) If, after such consideration, the Board is of opinion that the application should be granted, it shall make an order authorising the applicant to construct, maintain, improve and, subject to section 11(7) in the case of the Agency, operate the railway or the railway works specified in the order or any part thereof, in such manner and subject to such conditions, modifications, restrictions and requirements (and on such other terms) as the Board thinks proper and specifies in the order and the Board shall furnish the applicant with a copy of the order.

(3) (a) As soon as may be after the making of a railway order, the Board shall—

(i) publish a notice in at least 2 newspapers circulating in the area to which the order relates of the making of the railway order and of the places where, the period during which and the times at which copies thereof and any plan referred to therein may be inspected or purchased at a cost not exceeding the reasonable cost of making such copies, and

(ii) give notice to the prescribed authority in Northern Ireland of its decision in a case where a copy of the environmental statement has been sent to that authority in accordance with section 40(1)(e).

(b) A notice referred to in paragraph (a) shall state

(i) the content and nature of the Board's decision including any conditions attached thereto,

(ii) that, in deciding whether to grant a railway order, the Board has had regard to the matters referred to in subsection (43)(1), and

(iii) a description where necessary of the main measures to avoid any adverse effects of the proposed railway works.

(4) A railway order shall come into operation—

(a) in case an application for leave to apply for judicial review of the order has not been made, upon the expiration of 8 weeks, and

(b) in case such an application has been made and has not been withdrawn, in so far as it has not been declared invalid or quashed pursuant to that review, upon the final determination of the proceedings concerned or such other date as may be determined in those proceedings, and

(c) in case such an application has been made and is withdrawn, upon the date of the withdrawal.

(5) A person who has been granted a railway order may, with the consent of the Minister, make arrangements with another person to construct, maintain, improve or operate the railway or the railway works to which the order relates.

(6) The Board may, if there is a failure or refusal to comply with a condition, restriction or requirement specified in a railway order, revoke the order.

(7) (a) Where the Board proposes to revoke an order under this section, it shall notify the railway undertaking in writing of its proposal and of the reasons for it.

(b) The railway undertaking may, not later than 3 weeks from the date of the sending of the notification, make submissions in writing to the Board and the Board shall—

(i) before deciding the matter, take into consideration any submissions duly made to it under this paragraph in relation to the proposal and not withdrawn, and

(ii) notify the railway undertaking in writing of its decision and of the reasons for it.

(8) A notification of a proposal of the Board under subsection (7) shall include a statement that the railway undertaking may make submissions to the Board not later than 3 weeks from the date of the sending of the notification and a notification of a decision of the Board under subsection (7) shall include a statement that the railway undertaking may appeal to the High Court under subsection (9) against the decision not later than 3 weeks from the date of the sending of the notification.

(9) Notwithstanding section 47(1), the railway undertaking may appeal to the High Court against a decision of the Board under subsection (6) not later than 3 weeks from the date of the sending of the notification of the decision under subsection (7) and that Court may, as it thinks proper, on the hearing of the appeal, confirm the decision of the Board or direct the Board to withdraw its decision and prohibit the making of the proposed order concerned.

NOTE

This section concerns the determination by the Board of the application for a railway order. The matters to be considered by the Board under subs.(1) are similar to the considerations for the Minister under the former s.43, with the addition of subs.(1)(g) which requires the Board to consider the likely consequences for proper planning and sustainable development in the area in which it is proposed to carry out the railway works and for the environment and also the matters set out in s.143. Subsection (2) adds the word "modifications" to the list of "conditions, modifications, restrictions and requirements (and on such other terms)", subject to which the Board may authorise the order. The former subs.(3) is deleted which provided that where the Minister granted an order which involved a substantial material departure from the recommendations contained in the report of the public inquiry, he was required to lay a statement before each House of the Oireachtas. Subsection (3) now concerns the notice of the order (formerly subs.(4)). New elements include a requirement to send notice to the prescribed authority in Northern Ireland in circumstances where a copy of the EIS was sent to it. Subsection (3)(b) also now sets out the content of such notice, the requirements of which are mandatory. Also deleted is the former subs.(7) which allowed the Minister to amend the railway order, including varying the route of the railway. The only changes to the revocation of the order by the Board, is to provide that the applicant is expressed to have 21 days rather than three weeks to make submissions to a proposal to revoke and similarly has 21 days rather than three weeks from the date of notification of the decision, to appeal to the High Court.

Provisions in relation to railway order

44.—(1) A railway order shall contain such provisions as the Board considers   **2–09**
necessary or expedient for the purpose of the order.

(2) Without prejudice to the generality of subsection (1), a railway order
may—

(a) specify any land or any substratum of land, the acquisition of which is, in the opinion of the Board, necessary for giving effect to the order,

(b) specify any rights in, under or over land or water or, subject to the consent of the Minister, in, under or over any public road, the acquisition of which is, in the opinion of the Board, necessary for giving effect to the order,

(c) specify the manner in which the railway or the railway works or any part thereof to which the order relates are to be constructed,

(d) fix the period within which the construction of the railway works is to be completed,

(e) contain provisions as to the manner in which the railway works are to be operated and maintained,

(f) without prejudice to paragraph (g), contain such provisions as the Board thinks proper for the protection of the public generally, of local communities and of any persons affected by the order,

(g) contain provisions requiring

(i) the construction or the financing, in whole or in part, of the construction of a facility, or

(ii) the provision or the financing, in whole or in part, of the provision of a service,

in the area in which the railway works are to be constructed, being a facility or service that, in the opinion of the Board, would constitute a gain to the community,

(h) provide for the determination by arbitration of any specified questions arising thereunder,

(i) contain such provisions ancillary or incidental to any of the matters aforesaid as the Board considers necessary and proper.

(3) A provision of a railway order referred to in subsection (2)(g) shall not require such an amount of financial resources to be committed for the purposes of the provision being complied with as would substantially deprive the person in whose favour the order operates of the benefits likely to accrue from the making of the order.

(4) The Board may, with the consent of the Minister, in a railway order designate the railway to which the order relates as a light railway or as a metro.

AMENDMENT HISTORY

Section 44(2) amended by s.3 of the Local Government (Roads Functions) Act 2007 by substituting a new subs.(2)(b).

NOTE

This section concerns "provisions" which are effectively conditions which the Board may specify in granting the order. There is a general power to do so, with subs.(2) setting out specific matters which may be prescribed. There are some minor changes made to the former subs.(2). These include in subs.(2)(ii) which provides that the consent of the Minister for Transport must be obtained for a national road, while the consent of the Minister for the Environment must be obtained for a public road (the former subsection made no mention of a national road). The only new subparagraph is subpara.(g) which allows for a condition allowing for a planning gain to the community. As noted a similar condition may be imposed with respect to local authority development under s.175, state authority development under s.181B(7) or in respect of approving a road scheme/road development under s.217C(3). Also considerable flexibility is afforded as to the nature of the planning gain, which may be either a facility or a service. The only criterion is that the facility or service must be of "substantial gain" to the community. The applicant may be required either to construct the facility or may finance the construction of such facility. Similarly, the applicant may provide or finance the service. The new subs.(3) provides that the financial commitment must not be so onerous as to deprive the applicant of the substantial benefit of the grant of approval. There must be a degree of proportionality between the financial burden of the condition with the benefit of the approval. This may prove difficult to assess, in particular, the difficulty in assessing the exact benefit likely to accrue from the approval. Although the criteria are vague and difficult to apply, the inbuilt proportionality requirement may mean that it would escape a challenge on grounds of constitutional invalidity. The condition may be sought to be justified on the basis that it is in the interests of the common good and it is proportionate to its objective in accordance with the principles set out in the Article 26 reference, *Re Article 26 and the Planning and Development Bill* [2000] 2 I.R. 321, in respect of Pt V of the 2000 Act. Subsection (4) provides that the railway order may specifically designate that the railway works are for light rail or metro.

Compulsory acquisition of land

2–10   **45.**—(1) Upon the commencement of a railway order, the Agency or CIE shall thereupon be authorised to acquire compulsorily any land or rights in, under or over land or any substratum of land specified in the order and, for that purpose, the railway order shall have effect as if it were a compulsory purchase order referred to in section 10(1) of the Local Government (No. 2) Act 1960 (inserted by section 86 of the Housing Act 1966), which has been duly made and confirmed and, accordingly, that section shall apply and have effect in relation to the order with the modifications that—

    (a) references to the local authority shall be construed as including references to the Agency or CIE as the case may be,

    (b) references to the Minister for the Environment, Heritage and Local Government shall be construed as references to the Board,

    (c) the reference in subsection (4)(a) to section 78 of the Housing Act 1966 shall be construed as including a reference to subsections (1), (4)and (5) of that section, and with any other necessary modifications.

(2) Where the Agency or CIE proposes to acquire land pursuant to subsection (1) and, in the opinion of the Agency or CIE, as the case may be, it is more efficient and economical to acquire,additional adjoining land, the Agency or CIE, as the case may be, may do so with the consent of the Minister and of any person having an interest in or right in, under or over the adjoining land notwithstanding the fact that the adjoining land is not specified in the railway order.

(3) The Agency or CIE shall comply with any directions of the Minister in relation to land acquired by it pursuant to subsection (1).

NOTE

    This section concerns the compulsory acquisition of land specified in the railway order. The changes in the new section are to replace the former references to the Minister with that of An Bord Pleanála. The railway order has effect as if it is a CPO. This is consistent with the Board's function of confirming CPOs made by a local authority under Part IV of the 2000 Act as amended.

Notification of grant of railway

    46.—As soon as may be after the making of a railway order, the railway undertaking shall—   **2–11**

    (a) deposit and keep deposited at the head office of the railway undertaking and at such other place as may be specified by the Board, during the period of 5 years following the opening for traffic of the railway, a copy of the order and the plan referred to therein and the aforesaid order and plan shall, while so deposited, be open to inspection by members of the public free of charge, at all reasonable times, and copies of or extracts from any of the documents aforesaid may be purchased on payment of a fee to the railway undertaking not exceeding the reasonable cost of making such copies or extracts, and

    (b) serve a copy of relevant extracts from the railway order and the plan referred to therein on every planning authority for the area (or any part thereof) to which the order relates and to every (if any) occupier and every (if any) owner of land referred to in the railway order.

NOTE

This section is the same as the former s.46, except the reference to the "Minister" is replaced by "An Bord Pleanála". A copy of the railway order must be available for inspection at the head office of the railway undertaking for a period of five years. In this respect it may be noted that the head office of Iarnród Éireann is at Connolly Station, Dublin 1.

Judicial review of railway order and related acts

2–12   **47.**—(1) A person shall not question the validity of a railway order made or any act done by the Board in the performance or the purported performance of its functions under sections 37 to 46 otherwise than by way of an application for judicial review under Order 84 of the Rules of the Superior Courts (S.I. No. 15 of 1986) (the 'Order').

(2) The Board may, at any time after the bringing of an application for leave to apply for judicial review of any act to which subsection (1) applies and which relates to a matter for the time being before the Board, apply to the High Court to stay the proceedings pending the making of a decision by the Board in relation to the matter concerned.

(3) On the making of such an application the High Court may, where it considers that the matter before the Board is within the jurisdiction of the Board, make an order staying the proceedings concerned on such terms as it thinks fit.

(4) Subject to subsection (5), an application for leave to apply for judicial review under the Order in respect of an order or act to which subsection (1) applies shall be made within the period of 8 weeks beginning on the date on which the order was made or, as the case may be, the date of the doing of the act by the Board.

(5) The High Court may extend the period provided for in subsection (4) within which an application for leave referred to in that subsection may be made but shall only do so if it is satisfied that—

(a) there is good and sufficient reason for doing so, and

(b) the circumstances that resulted in the failure to make the application for leave within the period so provided were outside the control of the applicant for the extension.

(6) References in this section to the Order shall be construed as including references to the Order as amended or replaced (with or without modification) by rules of court.

NOTE

This section concerns judicial challenges to the making of railway orders and makes some alterations to the former s.47. The new s.47 contains general rules concerning the judicial review of a railway order, with the new s.47A dealing specifically with an application for leave for judicial review. Both of these sections are similar to ss.50 and 50A as inserted by s.13 of the 2006 Act, in relation to judicial review of decisions or acts of the planning authority Board in performing planning functions. Reference may therefore be made to the note in respect of such sections. Subsection (1) provides for procedural exclusivity of judicial review as the means of challenging railway orders. One change in this subsection is the addition of the words "or any act done by the Board in the performance", which means not only must the final determination of the Board be challenged under Ord.84 but also any act of the Board leading up to the final determination as part of the railway order application process. A similar change was also made with respect to judicial review of planning decisions or acts of the local authority or Board under s.50. See *Linehan v Cork County Council*, unreported, High Court, Finlay Geoghegan J., February 19, 2008, where it was suggested that such changes may mean an applicant cannot now await the outcome of the decision. Subsections (2) and (3) are new provisions and allows the Board to make an application to stay any judicial review proceeding while the railway application process is still before the Board. Under subs.(3), where the court considers that the matter is properly within the jurisdiction of the Board, it may stay the application for judicial review. However, this will not be the case where the Board has acted in excess of jurisdiction or ultra vires or committed some error of law. It should be noted that pursuant to the inherent jurisdiction of the court, an applicant for judicial review may also make an application to stay the matter before the Board pending the outcome of the judicial review application. See *Harding v Cork County Council*, unreported, High Court, Clarke J., November 30, 2006 and January 31, 2007. As under the former s.47, there is a time limit of eight weeks to commence proceedings and where the challenge relates to an act of the Board, time will run from the date of such act. As regards extending time for instituting proceedings, subs.(5) adds an additional requirement to show good and sufficient reason, by providing that the failure to institute proceedings within the time limit must have been outside the control of the applicant.

Section 47: supplemental provisions

47A.—(1) In this section— **2–13**
  "Court", where used without qualification, means the High Court (but this definition shall not be construed as meaning that subsections (2) to (6) and (9) do not extend to and govern the exercise by the Supreme Court of jurisdiction on any appeal that may be made);
  "Order" shall be construed in accordance with section 47;
  "section 47 leave" means leave to apply for judicial review under the Order in respect of an order or act to which section 47(1) applies.
  (2) An application for section 47 leave shall be made by motion on notice (grounded in the manner specified in the Order in respect of an ex parte motion for leave) to the Board, to the applicant for the railway order, where he or she is not the applicant for leave, and to any other person specified for that purpose by order of the High Court, and the Court shall not grant section 47 leave unless it is satisfied that—
  (a) there are substantial grounds for contending that the order or act concerned is invalid or ought to be quashed, and
  (b) (i) the applicant has a substantial interest in the matter which is the subject of the application, or
      (ii) the applicant—
        (I) is a body or organisation (other than a State authority, a public authority or governmental body or agency) the aims or objectives of which relate to the promotion of environmental protection,
        (II) has, during the period of 12 months preceding the date of the application, pursued those aims or objectives, and
        (III) satisfies such requirements (if any) as a body or organisation, if it were to make an appeal under section 37(4)(c) of the Act of 2000, would have to satisfy by virtue of section 37(4)(d)(iii) of that Act (and, for this purpose, any requirement prescribed under section

37(4)(e)(iv) of that Act shall apply as if the reference in it to the class of matter into which the decision, the subject of the appeal, falls were a reference to the class of matter into which the order or act, the subject of the application for section 47 leave, falls).

(3) A substantial interest for the purposes of subsection (2)(b)(i) is not limited to an interest in land or other financial interest.

(4) Notwithstanding the making of an application for section 47 leave in respect of a railway order, the application shall not affect the validity of the railway order and its operation unless, upon an application to the Court, the Court suspends the operation of the railway order until the application is determined or withdrawn.

(5) If the Court grants section 47 leave, no grounds shall be relied upon in the application for judicial review under the Order other than those determined by the Court to be substantial under subsection (2)(a).

(6) The Court may, as a condition for granting section 47 leave, require the applicant for such leave to give an undertaking as to damages.

(7) The determination of the Court of an application for section 47 leave or of an application for judicial review on foot of such leave shall be final and no appeal shall lie from the decision of the Court to the Supreme Court in either case save with leave of the Court which leave shall only be granted where the Court certifies that its decision involves a point of law of exceptional public importance and that it is desirable in the public interest that an appeal should be taken to the Supreme Court.

(8) Subsection (7) shall not apply to a determination of the Court in so far as it involves a question as to the validity of any law having regard to the provisions of the Constitution.

(9) If an application is made for judicial review under the Order in respect of part only of an order or act to which section 47(1) applies, the Court may, if it thinks fit, declare to be invalid or quash the part concerned or any provision thereof without declaring invalid or quashing the remainder of the order or act or part of the order or act, and if the Court does so, it may make any consequential amendments to the remainder of the order or act or the part thereof that it considers appropriate.

(10) The Court shall, in determining an application for section 47 leave or an application for judicial review on foot of such leave, act as expeditiously as possible consistent with the administration of justice.

(11) On an appeal from a determination of the Court in respect of an application referred to in subsection (10), the Supreme Court shall—

   (a) have jurisdiction to determine only the point of law certified by the Court under subsection (7) (and to make only such order in the proceedings as follows from such determination), and

   (b) in determining the appeal, act as expeditiously as possible consistent with the administration of justice.

(12) Rules of court may make provision for the expeditious hearing of applications for section 47 leave and applications for judicial review on foot of such leave."]

NOTE

This is a new provision dealing specifically with an application for leave to seek judicial review to challenge the railway order or any act done by the Board. This is similar to s.50A of the 2000 Act as inserted by s.13 of the 2006 Act and reference should be made to the note on such section. Among the changes which were formerly contained in s.47, include that subs.(2)(b) introduces an exception to the substantial interest requirement in the case of a body or organisation which promoted environmental protection over the last 12 months. Such body need not demonstrate that it has a substantial interest, where it falls within the qualifying criteria for such body. This relaxation of the substantial interest requirement was made in order to comply with the requirements of the Aahus Convention or more particularly, Directive 2003/35/EC. Subsection (4) makes clear that merely instituting judicial review proceedings will not act as a stay on the railway order unless a court expressly grants a stay. Subsection (5) means that a full hearing of the judicial review proceedings will only be based on the grounds for which leave was granted. Subsection (6) allows the court as a matter of discretion to require an applicant to give an undertaking as to damages as a condition of granting leave. Other new provisions include subs.(10) which requires the court to act as expeditiously as possible and also subs.(11) which provides where a certificate for leave to appeal to the Supreme Court is granted, the Supreme Court which will only have jurisdiction to determine the exact point certified by the High Court. This reverses the position in *Clinton v An Bord Pleanála,* unreported, Supreme Court, Geoghegan J., May 2, 2007, which reaffirmed *Scott v An Bord Pleanála* [1995] 1 I.L.R.M. 424 which held that the Supreme Court was not confined to the exact point certified but could consider all the grounds.

Further amendment of Transport (Railway Infrastructure) Act 2001

50.—The Transport (Railway Infrastructure) Act 2001 is further amended by   **2–14**
inserting the following sections after section 47A (inserted by section 49):

[Discussions with Board before making an application

47B.—(1) The Agency, CIE or any other person who proposes to apply   **2–15**
for a railway order in accordance with section 37(1) shall, before making the application, enter into consultations with the Board in relation to the proposed railway works.

(2) Such a person is referred to subsequently in this section and in section 47C as a "prospective applicant".

(3) In any consultations under subsection (1), the Board may give advice to the prospective applicant regarding the proposed application and, in particular, regarding—
   (a) the procedures involved in making an application under this Part and in considering such an application, and
   (b) what considerations, related to proper planning and sustainable development or the environment, may, in the opinion of the Board, have a bearing on its decision in relation to the application.

NOTE

This is a new section which provides that the applicant for a railway order must enter into pre-application consultations with the Board. This is a mandatory requirement and is not merely at the discretion of the applicant such as with pre-planning consultations under s.247 of the 2000 Act as amended. The requirement for consultation is similar to s.37B which requires a consultation in respect of strategic infrastructure development specified in Sch.7. For the purposes of these consultations, the Board may give advice regarding the procedure and the matters it may take into consideration as bearing on any proposed application.

Section 47B: supplemental provisions

2–16   **47C.**—(1) A prospective applicant shall, for the purposes of consultations under section 47B, supply to the Board sufficient information in relation to the proposed railway works so as to enable the Board to assess those works.

(2) The Board may, at its absolute discretion, consult with any other person who may, in the opinion of the Board, have information which is relevant for the purposes of consultations under section 47B in relation to the proposed railway works.

(3) The holding of consultations under section 47B shall not prejudice the performance by the Board of any other of its functions under this Act or the Planning and Development Act 2000 or regulations under either of those Acts and cannot be relied upon in the formal planning process or in legal proceedings.

(4) The Board shall keep a record in writing of any consultations under section 47B in relation to proposed railway works, including the names of those who participated in the consultations, and a copy of such record shall be placed and kept with the documents to which any application in respect of the proposed railway works relates.

NOTE

This section requires the applicant to supply the Board with sufficient information to allow the Board to assess the proposed works for the purposes of the consultation. The Board may consult with other persons where they believe such persons may have information which is relevant to the consultation. The consultation is entirely without prejudice to the function of the Board in assessing the railway application or any other function. The consultation cannot create an estoppel or be binding on the Board. The Board must maintain a record of the pre-planning consultation which it must include with the file relating to the railway works.

Supplemental powers for the Board

2–17   **47D.**—(1) Before determining an application for a railway order, the Board may, at its absolute discretion and at any time—

   (a) request further submissions or observations from the applicant, any person who made submissions or observations in relation to the application or any other person who may, in the opinion of the Board, have information which is relevant to the determination of the application,

   (b) without prejudice to section 41, make any information relating to the application available for inspection, notify any person or the public that the information is so available and, if it considers appropriate, invite further submissions or observations to be made to it within such period as it may specify, or

   (c) hold meetings with the applicant or any other person where it appears to the Board to be necessary or expedient for the purpose of
       (i) determining the application, or

(ii) resolving any issue with the applicant or any disagreement between the applicant and any other party, including resolving any issue or disagreement in advance of an oral hearing.

(2) Where the Board holds a meeting in accordance with subsection (1)(c), it shall keep a written record of the meeting and make that record available for inspection.

(3) The Board, or an employee of the Board duly authorised by the Board, may appoint any person to hold a meeting referred to in subsection (1)(c).

(4) The Board may, if it is provisionally of the view that it would be appropriate to grant the railway order concerned were certain alterations (specified in the notification referred to in this subsection) to be made to the terms of the application in respect of it or the proposed order, notify the applicant that it is of that view and invite the applicant to make to the terms of the application or the proposed order alterations specified in the notification and, if the applicant makes those alterations, to furnish to it such information (if any) as it may specify in relation to the proposed application or order, in the terms as so altered, or, where necessary, a revised environmental impact statement in respect of it.

(5) If the applicant makes the alterations to the terms of the application or proposed order specified in a notification given to the applicant under subsection (4), the terms of the application or order as so altered shall be deemed to be the application or order for the purposes of this Part.

(6) The Board shall, where the applicant has made the alterations to the terms of the application or proposed order specified in a notification given to the applicant under subsection (4), require the applicant—

(a) to publish in one or more newspapers circulating in the area or areas in which the proposed railway works would be situate a notice stating that the applicant has, pursuant to an invitation of the Board, made alterations to the terms of the application or order (and the nature of those alterations shall be indicated) and, if it be the case, that information in relation to the terms of the application or order as so altered or a revised environmental impact statement in respect of the development has been furnished to the Board, indicating the times at which, the period (which shall not be less than 3 weeks) during which and the place, or places, where a copy of the information or the environmental impact statement may be inspected free of charge or purchased on payment of a specified fee (which fee shall not exceed the reasonable cost of making such copy) and that submissions or observations in relation to that information or statement may be made to the Board before the expiration of the indicated period, and

(b) to send to the planning authority and each person to which a notice was served pursuant to section 40(1)(c) or (e), and to every (if any) occupier and every (if any) owner of land referred to in the order (being, if the terms of it have been so altered, the order as so altered)—

(i) a notice of the furnishing to the Board of the information or statement referred to in paragraph (a), and

(ii) a copy of that information or statement,

and to indicate to that authority or other person that submissions or observations in relation to that information or statement may be made to the Board before the expiration of a period (which shall be not less than 3 weeks) beginning on the day on which the notice is sent to the authority or other person by the applicant.

(7) The Board shall, in deciding whether to grant the railway order to which the application concerned relates, have regard to any information submitted on foot of a notice under subsection (4), including any revised environmental impact statement, or any submissions or observations made on foot of a request under subsection (1) or a notice under subsection (6).

NOTE

This new section allows the Board certain powers which it may exercise before determining an application for a railway order including inviting submissions or holding meetings. It has similar powers which it may exercise when making a decision on a road scheme or road development under s.217B. The Board cannot be compelled to take any of the specified measures under this section but it can decide to do so at its discretion, although this must be read subject to the requirement that the Board must exercise its power in accordance with fair procedures. The Board can exercise such powers at any time prior to making its decision on the railway order, although under subs.(1)(a) the Board may invite submissions from any person or under subs.(1)(b) may hold meetings with the local authority, applicant or any other person. The Board may hold the meetings to assist in deciding whether to confirm the railway order or to resolve any issue or disagreement between the applicant or other person. The subsection does not give any clear guidance as to the issue or disagreement to be resolved but is drafted broadly to include any matter which could arise in the context of confirming the compulsory acquisition or otherwise. A record must be kept of any meeting and a Board employee may be appointed to hold such meeting. Under subs.(4), the Board may request the applicant to submit further information or if it is of the view that the development should be approved if altered, invite the applicant to alter the proposed development and submit information relating to such alteration, along with a revised EIS, if necessary.

Under subs.(6), the Board will require the applicant to publish a notice where it considers that the further information received contains significant additional information regarding the likely effects on the environment and the likely consequences for the proper planning and sustainable development of the area where the proposed development is situated. In any proceeding to challenge a decision of the Board not to require a notice, the courts will tend to defer to the decision of the Board that such information was not significant unless such decision was irrational. See *Kinsella v Dundalk Town Council*, unreported, High Court, Kelly J., December 3, 2004, and *Dietacaron Ltd v An Bord Pleanála* [2005] 2 I.L.R.M. 32 and *White v Dublin City Council* [2004] 1 I.R. 545. A notice is also required where the Board invites the applicant to alter the terms of the proposed development. In the latter case, there is a requirement to publish a notice irrespective of whether the alteration reflects significant additional information regarding the likely effects on the environment and likely consequences for proper planning and sustainable development. The notice must, inter alia, invite submissions, allowing a period of not less than three weeks. Both a notice and a copy of the further information or information concerning alterations or revised EIS as the case may be, must be sent to the prescribed bodies, allowing a period of not less than three weeks to make submissions. The information and submissions received must be taken into account by the Board in making its decision.

Objective of the Board in relation to railway orders

2–18	47E.—(1) It shall be the duty of the Board to ensure that—
	(a) consultations held under section 47B are completed, and

    (b) a decision under section 43 on an application for a railway order is made,

as expeditiously as is consistent with proper planning and sustainable development and, for that purpose, to take all such steps as are open to it to ensure that, in so far as is practicable, there are no avoidable delays at any stage in the holding of those consultations or the making of that decision.

(2) Without prejudice to the generality of subsection (1) and subject to subsections (3) to (6), it shall be the objective of the Board to ensure that a decision under section 43 on an application for a railway order is made—

    (a) within a period of 18 weeks beginning on the last day for making submissions or observations in accordance with the notice referred to in section 40(1)(6), or

    (b) within such other period as the Minister for the Environment, Heritage and Local Government, having consulted with the Minister, may prescribe by regulations either generally or in respect of a particular class or classes of matter.

(3) Where it appears to the Board that it would not be possible or appropriate, because of the particular circumstances of the matter with which the Board is concerned, to determine the matter within the period referred to in paragraph (a) or (b) of subsection (2) as the case may be, the Board shall, by notice in writing served on the applicant, the Minister, any planning authority involved and any other person who submitted submissions or observations in relation to the matter before the expiration of that period, inform the Minister, the authority and those persons of the reasons why it would not be possible or appropriate to determine the matter within that period and shall specify the date before which the Board intends that the matter shall be determined.

(4) Where a notice has been served under subsection (3), the Board shall take all such steps as are open to it to ensure that the matter is determined before the date specified in the notice.

(5) The Minister for the Environment, Heritage and Local Government, having consulted the Minister, may by regulations vary the period referred to in subsection (2)(a) either generally or in respect of a particular class or classes of applications for railway orders, where it appears to him or her to be necessary, by virtue of exceptional circumstances, to do so and, for so long as the regulations are in force, this section shall be construed and have effect in accordance therewith.

(6) Where the Minister for the Environment, Heritage and Local Government, having consulted with the Minister, considers it to be necessary or expedient that a certain class or classes of application for a railway order that are of special strategic, economic or social importance to the State be determined as expeditiously as is consistent with proper planning and sustainable development, he or she may give a direction to the Board that priority be given to the determination of applications of the class or classes concerned, and the Board shall comply with such a direction.

(7) The Board shall include in each report made under section 118 of the Planning and Development Act 2000 a statement of the number of matters which the Board has determined within a period referred to in paragraph (a) or (b) of subsection (2) and such other information as to the time taken to

determine such matters as the Minister for the Environment, Heritage and Local Government may direct.

NOTE

This section concerns the timeframe for the Board to determine the application for the railway order. Under subs.(1) there is a general requirement for the Board to act as expeditiously as possible. Apart from this general obligation, it must be an objective of the Board to determine the application for a railway order within 18 weeks from the expiry of the time for receipt of submissions (unless varied by the Regulations). As this is merely an aspirational objective, this timeframe is not strictly binding on the Board. If the Board fails to meet this time limit, there will be no entitlement to a default approval for a railway order. Where the Board considers that it cannot determine the application within 18 weeks or such other period specified by regulations, it must serve a notice on the specified parties, stating why it would not be possible or appropriate to determine the application within the period and giving a new date when the Board will determine the matter. This notice must be served prior to the expiry of the 18-week period. The reasons given may relate either to the fact that it is not possible to determine the application or even if possible, it would not be appropriate to determine the appeal within the 18-week period. The Minister for the Environment (having consulted with the Minister for Transport) may issue directions to the Board that priority is to given to a certain class or classes of applications for a railway order which the Minister believes are of special strategic, economic or social importance to the State. The Board is obliged to comply with this direction. The Board must include statistics relating to the time to determine railway applications in its annual report.

Construction of certain references and transitional provision

2–19   **47F.**—(1) References to the Minister in a railway order, being an order made before the amendment of this Act by the Planning and Development (Strategic Infrastructure) Act 2006, shall be construed as references to the Board.

(2) Notwithstanding the amendments of this Act made by the Planning and Development (Strategic Infrastructure) Act 2006, any thing commenced under this Part but not completed before the commencement of those amendments may be carried on and completed after the commencement of those amendments as if those amendments had not been made.

(3) The reference in subsection (2) to any thing commenced under this Part includes a reference to—

(a) an application that has been made under section 37 (being that section in the terms as it stood before the commencement of the amendments referred to in that subsection),

(b) an application that has been made under subsection (7) of section 43 (being that section in the terms as it stood before the commencement of those amendments), and

(c) any step (including the holding of a public inquiry) that has been taken in the making of a decision in relation to an application referred to in paragraph (a) or (b) or any step that has been taken on foot of the making of such a decision.

(4) For the avoidance of doubt, any questioning, after the commencement of the amendments referred to in subsection (2), by the procedures of judicial review under the Order (within the meaning of section 47) of the validity of any thing referred to in subsection (2) completed after that commencement, or being carried on after that commencement, shall be done in accordance

with the provisions of this Part as amended by the Planning and Development
(Strategic Infrastructure) Act 2006."]

NOTE

This section concerns transitional measures and allows for the continuity of railway
applications and orders made prior to the entry into force of the 2006 Act. This section
commenced on the January 31, 2007. Under subs.(1), where a railway order was already
made prior to the entry into force of the 2006 Act, the references to the Minister in the
order are to be construed as references to the Board. Subsection (2) provides that where an
application or other matter is commenced prior to the commencement of the 2006 Act, the
former sections under the 2001 Act will continue to apply to such application or matter, even
after the commencement of the 2006 Act. Subsection (3) makes clear the application of the
former sections to certain types of matters. Thus the former law under the 2001 Act will
continue to apply to such matters even after the amendments have commenced. Subsection
(4) provides that judicial review of any matter completed or carried on after commencement
of the relevant sections, will be in accordance with the new s.47 notwithstanding that the
thing commenced prior to the 2006 Act entering into force.

Amendment of Roads Act 1993

51.—(1) In this section "Act of 1993" means the Roads Act 1993.   **2–20**
(2) Section 48 of the Act of 1993 is amended—
  (a) in paragraph (a)(ii), by substituting "(not being less than 6 weeks)"
       for "(which shall not be less than one month)",
  (b) in paragraph (a)(iii), by substituting "during such period" for "before
       a specified date (which shall be not less than two weeks after the
       end of the period for inspection)", and
  (c) in paragraph (b), by substituting the following subparagraph for
       subparagraph (iii):
       "(iii) the period (which shall be that referred to in paragraph (a)(ii))
              within which objections may be made in writing to the Minister
              in relation to the scheme.".
(3) Section 51(3) of the Act of 1993 is amended—
  (a) in paragraph (a)(iii), by substituting "(not being less than 6 weeks)"
       for "(which shall not be less than one month)",
  (b) in paragraph (a)(iv), by deleting "and",
  (c) in paragraph (a)(v), by substituting "during the period referred to in
       paragraph (a)(iii)" for "before a specified date (which shall be not
       less than two weeks after the end of the period for inspection)",
  (d) by inserting the following subparagraphs after subparagraph (v) of
       paragraph (a):
       "(vi) where relevant, stating that the proposed road development
              is likely to have significant effects on the environment in
              Northern Ireland, and
       (vii) specifying the types of decision the Minister may make, under
              section 51(6), in relation to the application;",
       and
  (e) in paragraph (6), by substituting "within a specified period (which
       shall be that referred to in paragraph (a)(iii))" for "before a specified
       date (which shall be not less than two weeks after the end of the
       period for inspection referred to in subsection (3)(a)(iii))".

Section 9(1)(e)(ii) of the Roads Act 2007 amended subs.(3)(a)(vi) by substituting "An Bord Pleanála" for "the Minister".

NOTE

This section contains certain amendments to ss.48 and 51 of the Roads act 1993, which concern the submission of a motorway scheme to the Board for approval (s.48) and the submission of an EIS in connection with that scheme (s.51). Section 215 of the 2000 Act transferred the performance of the functions of the Minister under ss.49 to 51 of the 1993 Act to the Board. Subsection (2) concerns the amendments to s.48 and extends the minimum period during which the roadway scheme can be inspected from not less than one month to not less than six weeks. It also alters the period during which submissions can be made on the scheme from two weeks after the period for inspection to the period during which the scheme is available for inspection, which must be not less than six weeks. Similarly, the period for making submissions by any owner/occupier of land or other person affected by a proposed revocation/modification of a planning permission served with a notice under s.48(b), will be the period during which the scheme is available for inspection, which must not be less than six weeks.

Subsection (3) also makes similar changes with respect to the inspection period and the making of submissions on the EIS submitted to the Board in connection with the road scheme. The period for inspection of the EIS is altered from not less than one month to not less than six weeks, while the period for making submissions on the EIS is altered from not less than two weeks after the inspection period to the period of inspection (which will be not less than six weeks). There are two new subparas (v) and (vi), with (v) providing that the newspaper notice published by the road authority must also state, where applicable, that the proposed road development is likely to have significant effects on the environment in Northern Ireland. Paragraph (vi) provides that the notice must also specify the types of decisions which the Board may make under s.51(6), namely to approve a proposed road development with or without modifications or to refuse to approve such a development. Although the new subpara.(vi) refers to the decision of the Minister, this must be read as the decision of the Board by virtue of s.215 of the 2000 Act.

INDEX

Conditions attached to permissions—
contd
duration
general rules, 1–61
housing strategy, 1–119
Ministerial regulations, 1–64
power to extend, 1–63
power to vary, 1–62
electricity transmission cables,
1–217
exclusion of compensation, 1–325
general powers, 1–44
injunctions against unauthorised use
and development, 1–190
permitted conditions, 1–326
provision of social and affordable
housing, 1–118
quarries, 1–304
revocation or modification, 1–65
State authority developments, 1–213
strategic gas infrastructure, 1–219
use of structures, 1–60
waste management, 1–300
Conflicts of interest. *see* **Disclosure of**
interests
Conservation areas
see also **Nature and wildlife**
acquisition of land by planning
authority, 1–105
exempted development, 1–104
landscaping, 1–242
requirements of development plan,
1–103
Consultation
Board members, 1–149
local area plans, 1–20
planning applications
An Bord Pleanála, 1–50
general requirements, 1–290
pre-application discussions, 1–49
proposed development by local
authorities, 1–209
railway orders, 2–13–2–14
regional planning guidelines, 1–24
social and affordable housing, 1–125
State authority developments, 1–214
strategic gas infrastructure, 1–220
Contribution schemes
general principle, 1–69
supplemental provisions, 1–70
Control of development. *see* **Areas**
of special planning control;
Planning applications

Corporate offences, 1–188
Costs and expenses
appeals and referrals, 1–171
compulsory acquisition, 1–262
contribution schemes, 1–69
enforcement notices, 1–184
injunctions, 1–191
judicial review, 1–72
Ministerial administration, 1–285
planning authorities
apportionment between
authorities, 1–287
county councils, 1–286
set-offs, 1–288
proposed development by local
authorities, 1–205
recovery of compensation, 1–225
warning letters, 1–182
works to protected structures
applications to Court for costs
contributions, 1–89
recovery by planning authority,
1–92
Courts
see also **Criminal offences**
compensation
arbitration by case stated, 1–222
extension of time limits, 1–221
compliance with structures notices,
1–112
determination of exempted
development, 1–05
injunctions against unauthorised use
and development, 1–190
judicial review
general principles, 1–71
procedure, 1–72
protected structures
applications for consent, 1–87
applications for costs
contributions, 1–89
jurisdiction, 1–88
rights of entry
enforcement, 1–296
statutory conditions, 1–295
Criminal offences
areas of special planning control,
1–113
damage to notices, 1–293
disclosure of interests
beneficial interests, 1–178
consent of DPP, 1–179
general requirements, 1–177